I0085160

JEAN (JOHN) GASTON
of
FRANCE

Gaston

Compiled by

Betty Jewell Durbin Carson
DAR Member #832584

HERITAGE BOOKS
2015

HERITAGE BOOKS

AN IMPRINT OF HERITAGE BOOKS, INC.

Books, CDs, and more—Worldwide

For our listing of thousands of titles see our website
at
www.HeritageBooks.com

Published 2015 by
HERITAGE BOOKS, INC.
Publishing Division
5810 Ruatan Street
Berwyn Heights, Md. 20740

Copyright © 2015 Betty Jewell Durbin Carson

Heritage Books by the author:

The Brice Family Who Settled in Fairfield County, South Carolina, about 1785 and Related Families

Durbin and Logsdon Genealogy with Related Families, 1626–1991

The Durbin and Logsdon Genealogy with Related Families, 1626–1991, Volume 2

Durbin and Logsdon Genealogy with Related Families, 1626–1994

Durbin and Logsdon Genealogy with Related Families, 1626–1998

Durbin-Logsdon Genealogy and Related Families from Maryland to Kentucky, Volumes 1–2

CD: The Durbin and Logsdon Genealogy with Related Families, 1626–2000, 3rd Revised Edition

History of Curtis Land, 1635–1683; with Excerpt on Francis Land

Jean (John) Gaston of France

Our Ewing Heritage, with Related Families, Part One and Two, Revised Edition
Betty Jewell Durbin Carson and Doris M. Durbin Wooley

CD: Our Ewing Heritage, with Related Families, Revised Edition
Betty Jewell Durbin Carson and Doris M. Durbin Wooley

Patterson Family History

All rights reserved. No part of this book may be reproduced or transmitted in any form or
by any means, electronic or mechanical, including photocopying, recording or by any
information storage and retrieval system without written permission from the author,
except for the inclusion of brief quotations in a review.

International Standard Book Numbers
Paperbound: 978-0-7884-5625-1
Clothbound: 978-0-7884-6137-8

FOREWORD

This compilation of the GASTON surname is from many sources. Rather than trying to integrate all of the sources into one, I have included several files from major researchers as well as my additions of wills and pictures. Major researchers include Betty J. Carson, Linda Hull, and Robert Brice Land.

William Gaston (born 1642), along with his brothers, John and Alexander, went to County Antrim in Northern Ireland between 1662-1668. He is referred to by genealogists "as the first Irish William Gaston" to distinguish him from brother John's son William and others. He was the father of the Charleston, SC Gastons who emigrated in the 1700's-1770's from County Antrim, Ireland.

William Gaston (born 1680) in Carenleagh, Cloughwater, County Antrim, Ireland was the son of John Gaston (born 1645). He and his brothers, John, Hugh, Joseph, and Alexander arrive in America ca 1720 through the Port of Perth Amboy and settled in New Jersey. He married Olivet Lemon, also known as Mary Lemmon, b. 1688 in Scotland, d. 1752.

Their son, John Gaston, also known as Justice John Gaston (born April 4, 1703) in Ireland, died 1782 in South Carolina, buried in Burnt Meeting House Cemetery, Wylie's Mill, Chester County, SC, resided (settled 1751/52) at Fishing Creek, Chester County, South Carolina, immigrated 1749 to Pennsylvania, occupation farmer, surveyor, Justice in South Carolina. His nine sons served as soldiers in the American Revolution as four of them lost their lives in that war.

Three brothers, Joseph, Robert and Matthew Gaston, said to be the great-grandsons of the first Irish William Gaston, emigrated to South Carolina, with their sister, Jane Gaston Walker, leaving a fourth brother, Alexander, in Ireland, b. about 1750; d. about 1840; of these Joseph Gaston m. Martha Gaston, daughter of Justice John (above). It is from this line that the Town of Gaston, SC is named.

Gaston Coat of Arms / Gaston Family Crest

The surname of GASTON has the associated arms recorded in Sir Bernard Burkes General Armory. Ulster King of Arms in 1884. The name was baptismal 'the son of Gaskin' probably brought to England in the wake of the Norman Conquest of 1066. Early records of the name mention William de Gasconia, 1273, County Buckinghamshire. William Gaston married Sarah Gibbs at St. George's, Hanover Square, London in 1757. Many factors contributed to the establishment of a surname system. For generations after the Norman Conquest of 1066 a very few dynasts and magnates passed on hereditary surnames, but the main of the population, with a wide choice of first-names out of Celtic, Old English, Norman and Latin, avoided ambiguity without the need for a second name. As society became more stabilized, there was property to leave in wills, the towns and villages grew and the labels that had served to distinguish a handful of folk in a friendly village were not adequate for a teeming slum where perhaps most of the householders were engaged in the same monotonous trade, so not even their occupations could distinguish them, and some first names were gaining a tiresome popularity, especially Thomas after 1170. The hereditary principle in surnames gained currency first in the South, and the poorer folk were slower to apply it. By the 14th century however, most of the population had acquired a second name. Gaston Foix (1489-1512) was the French nobleman and soldier, nephew of Louis XII of France. He became Duke of Nemours in 1505. In the Italian wars he displayed such genius and bravery as the earn the title of 'Thunderbolt of Italy'. He twice overthrew the Swiss, at Como and Milan (1511); chased the papal troops from Bolongna; seized Brescia from the Venetians (1512) and defeated the Spaniards at Ravenna, where, however, he was killed. Most of the European surnames were formed in the thirteenth and fourteenth centuries. The process had started somewhat earlier and had continued in some places into the 19th century, but the norm is that in the tenth and eleventh centuries people did not have surnames, whereas by the fifteenth century most of the population had acquired a second name.

Arms - Chequy argent and gules three escallops in bend or

Crest- An owl sable

Motto- GLADIO ET VIRTUTE With sword and valour

Heraldry

Charles Hozier, a functionary under Louis XIV, in 1615, was the judge of armouries in France. He bore the title of King's Counsellor and it was his task to correct arms not conforming to the rules that governed them. He was to judge the significance of Heraldry material and provided to interested parties who requesting confirmation of armouries. This charge had been created by Louis XIII and became a hereditary position of the Hozier family until the Revolution. However, in November 1696, Louis XIV began to search out every means possible to create income for the national coffers and thus created an office of jurisdiction regarding Heraldry materials and the bearers of arms. Everyone, noble or not, both lay communities and religious and all others who could bear arms understood very well that they were legally obligated to pay to register them. The following year, in order to increase receipts until then judged too meagre, many others who were deemed «capable» (financially able) to bear arms were endowed with arms, whether they wanted so or not.

The production of these arms took place in Paris and it was a mass production. The initiative, remarkable in the beginning, sadly becomes the source of many mistakes. Many families had gotten into the habit of bearing the arms register by Hozier's office so that they supplanted the ones more ancient and authentic and those original arms become forgotten.

Nevertheless, this was the only legal registry until the French Revolution and all were obliged to abide by it. This is known as the *Grand Armorial de Charles d'Hozier des familles de France*. It is made up of 70 large books, of which 35 are in colour. Having a coat of arms does not imply nobility. In 1696, of the 116,944 registered persons, 80,000 are commoners. As well, this collection contains the arms of 2171 village, 934 towns, and 28 *généralité* (provincial capitals under the Old Regime)

NAME	COAT OF ARMS	DESCRIPTION	ORIGIN & DATE
Jeannot GASTON		?	Armorial Général de France 1552
Famille GASTON *originaire de l'Artois*	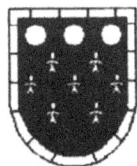	De gueule à trois besants d'argent au chef parti: d'azur semé de fleurs de lis d'or, à la borde componée d'argent et de gueules	

3

Bernard DUGASTON *Languedoc* *Avocat Juge de Salmiech*		D'argent à une cage de sable au chef de même	*Rietstap, Johannes Baptista (1828-1891). Armorial général* *Armorial d'Hozier* *Languedoc 2*
Arnaud GASTON *Jurât de la ville de Bourg*		D'azur semé de billettes d'or avec un lion aussi d'or	Armorial Général de France 1660 Guyenne
Pierre GASTON *de Poudenard*		D'azur à la bande d'or avec trois besants aussi d'or	Armorial Général de France 1660
Michel GASTON *Bourgeois de la ville de Mauriac (Cantal)*		**D'or à un croissant de sable renversé**	Armorial Général de France 1660 Auvergne
Caballero Domingo Gastón *natural de Falces* *hijo de Juan Gastón* *y Autor*		Merced a los servicios prestados por el a la Corona en los estados de Flandes durante 27 años, y de modo especial por recobrar en la expugnación de Amberes, armado de una pica, una pieza de artillería que tenia el enemigo, así como por perder un brazo en otros encuentro y recibir diversas heridas, el Rey Don Felipe le había concedido en 1593 privilegio de hidalguía y escudo de armas, y pidió se asentase en los Libros Reales de la Cámara. Añadió el escudo que pertenecía al Valle de Roncal una pieza de artillería	

Charles de GASTON		D'or à une fleur de lis d'azur	Armorial Général de France 1573
Jean de GASTON *Seigneur Baron de LANDORE, Comtes de VAUVINEUX*		D'Argent, à trois faices degueules, accompagnées en pointe d'une corneille de Sable, au chef d'azur, chargé de trois étoiles d'Argent.	
Jean François GASTON *Capitaine de cavalerie*		D'azur avec un chevron d'or accompagné deux étoiles dominant un lion couronné d'or lampassé de gueule	Armorial Général de France 1660
Jean GASTON		D'Azur au chevron d'or, accompagné en chef de deux étoiles de même, & d'une épie de bled d'or en pointe. L'écu furmonté d'un armet morné, orné de son bourlet & d'un lambrequin aux métail & couleur de l'écu	Nobiliaires Manuscrit
Nicolas GASTON *Bourgmestre de la ville d'Huninghem*		De gueules à un N un G et un D d'or entrelacés sommés et soutenus de deux étoiles de même	?
GASTON *de Cambiac*		D'argent chargé de deux sapins de sinople et d'un lion rampant de gueule, à chef d'azur chargé de trois mulets d'or. D'argent au lion de gueules accosté de deux cyprès arrachés au naturel au chef d'azur ch de trois étoiles d'or	*Rietstap, Johannes Baptista (1828-1891). Armorial général*

5

Miguel Gastón (de la casa solar Iriarte)		Partido en par de alto abajo: en el primer cuartel en campo de oro, seis flores de lis de azur, puestas en dos palos; y en el segundo tres palos de oro en campo de gules,	Armas concedidas en Madrid el 19/6/1721
Gastón (Navarra)		En azur, un árbol de sinople sobre terraza de lo mismo.	Otros, según Cadenas y Vicent
Famille GASTON Valle de Roncal en Navarre Espagnol		En azur, un puente de tres ojos, sobre ondas de azur y plata, superado en el centro del jefe de una cabeza de rey moro coronada de oro y degollada y bajo el arco tres peñas o roca (en otra descripción se menciona "un puente de tres ojos")	Visible en Zúñiga y Lodosa, Navarra
GASTON		En azur, un castillo de oro. Bordura de oro con ocho flores de lis de azur	
GASTON		Otros originarios de Barluenga, radicaron en Zaragoza, Huesca, Sariñena, Almudebar. De sinople, una torre de plata sobre dos mazo o garrotes de su color cruzados, surmontando la torre una caldera de sable a cada lado	Aragón
GASTON de Jaca		1 en oro, cuatro faras de gules, 2 en azur, un castillo con homenaje, al natural	Aragón

6

GASTÓN *Aragonés*		Linaje de infanzones aragoneses, con ramas afincadas en Barluenga y en Santa Eulalia la Mayor; están documentados sus individuos desde 1626. De azur, un castillo de plata y debajo de éste, dos porras en aspa de sinople.	[Enc. G. Carraffa] [Enc. Aragonesa] [Bizén d'O Río].
GASTON of *England, Scotland, Ireland and Wales*		Chequy argent. on gueule. three escallops in bend or. Crest: an owl sable. Motto: Fama semper vivit.	Per Burke's *General Armory of England, Scotland, Ireland and Wales* (Harrison & Sons, 1884),

Château de Foix

The **Château de Foix** is a castle which dominates the town of Foix in the French département of Ariège. An important tourist site, it is known as a centre of the Cathars. It has been listed as a *monument historique* by the French Ministry of Culture.

History

Built on an older 7th century fortification, the castle is known from 987. In 1002, it was mentioned in the will of Roger I, Count of Carcassonne, who bequeathed the fortress to his youngest child, Bernard. In effect, the family ruling over the region were installed here which allowed them to control access to the upper Ariège valley and to keep surveillance from this strategic point over the lower land, protected behind impregnable walls.

In 1034, the castle became capital of the County of Foix and played a decisive role in mediaeval military history. During the two following centuries, the castle was home to Counts with shining personalities who became the soul of the Occitan resistance during the crusade against the Albigensians. The county became a privileged refuge for persecuted Cathars.

Château de Foix

The castle, often besieged (notably by Simon de Montfort in 1211 and 1212), resisted assault and was only taken once, in 1486, thanks to treachery during the war between two branches of the Foix family.

From the 14th century, the Counts of Foix spent less and less time in the uncomfortable castle, preferring the Governors' Palace (*Palais des gouverneurs*). From 1479, the Counts of Foix became Kings of Navarre and the last of them, made Henri IV of France, annexed his Pyrrenean lands to France.

As seat of the Governor of the Foix region from the 15th century, the castle continued to ensure the defence of the area, notably during the Wars of Religion. Alone of all the castles in the region, it was exempted from the destruction orders of Richelieu (1632-1638).

Until the Revolution, the fortress remained a garrison. Its life was brightened with grand receptions for its governors, including the Count of Tréville, captain of musketeers under Louis XIII and Marshal Philippe Henri de Ségur, one of Louis XVI's ministers. The Round Tower, built in the 15th century, is the most recent, the two square towers having been built before the 11th century. They served as a political and civil prison for four centuries until 1862.

Since 1930, the castle has housed the collections of the Ariège départemental museum. Sections on prehistory, Gallo-Roman and mediaeval archaeology tell the history of Ariège from ancient times. Currently, the museum is rearranging exhibits to concentrate on the history of the castle site so as to recreate the life of Foix at the time of the Counts.

Château de Foix seen from the town

Château de Foix

View of the town from Château de Foix

List of counts of Foix

House of Foix

- 1010-1034 : Bernard Roger, count of Couserans, count of Bigorre, lord of Comminges and lord of Foix (second son of Roger I of Carcassonne)

Name	Portrait	Birth	Marriages	Death
Roger I 1034–1064		? second son of Bernard-Roger and Garsenda, Countess of Bigorre	*never married*	c. 1064
Pierre-Bernard 1064–1071		? third son of Bernard-Roger and Garsenda, Countess of Bigorre	Ledgarde two son	c. 1071
Roger II 1071–1124		? eldest son of Pierre-Bernard and Ledgarde	(1) Sicarda 1073 no issues (2) Stephanie of Besalú four children	c. 1124
Roger III 1124–1148		? eldest son of Roger II and Stephanie of Besalú	(1) ? one daughter (2) Jimena of Barcelona bef. 8 July 1130 two children	c. 1148
Roger-Bernard I 1148–1188		c. 1130 only son of Roger III and Jimena of Barcelona	Cecilia of Béziers 11 July 1151 five children	November 1188 aged 57–58
Raymond-Roger 1188–1223		c. 1152 second son of Roger-Bernard I and Cecilia of Béziers	Philippa of Montcada 1189 two children	27 March 1223 Château de Mirepoix aged 70–71
Roger-Bernard II 1223–1241		c. 1195 only son of Raymond-Roger and Philippa of Montcada	(1) Ermesinda, Viscountess of Castelbón 10 January 1203 two children (2) Ermengarde of Narbonne 23 January 1232 one daughter	26 May 1241 aged 45–46
Roger IV 1241–1265		? only son of Roger-Bernard II and Ermesinda, Viscountess of Castelbón	Brunissenda of Cardona 17 February 1231 five children	24 February 1265
Roger-Bernard III 1265–1302		c. 1243 eldest son of Roger IV and Brunissenda of Cardona	Margaret, Viscountess of Béarn 14 October 1252 Tarn-et-Garonne five children	3 March 1302 aged 59

Counts of Foix

The **counts of Foix** ruled the independent County of Foix, in what is now southern France, during the Middle Ages. Later they extended their power to almost the entire Pyrenees mountain range, moving their court to Pau, in Béarn, until eventually the last count of Foix acceded to the French throne as King Henry IV of France.

Coat of arms of the counts of Foix

Gallery of Arms

Arms of the House of Foix

Arms of the House of Foix-Béarn

Arms of the House of Foix-Grailly

Arms of the House of Foix-Grailly-Navarre

Arms of the House of Albret

Arms of the House of Bourbon

House of Foix-Béarn

Name	Portrait	Birth	Marriages	Death
Gaston I 1302–1315		c. 1287 only son of Roger-Bernard III and Margaret, Viscountess of Béarn	Joan of Artois October 1301 Senlis six children	13 December 1315 Maubuisson Abbey, Pontoise aged 27–28
Gaston II 1315–1343		c. 1308 eldest son of Gaston I and Joan of Artois	Eleanor of Comminges 1327 one son	26 September 1343 Seville aged 34–35
Gaston III Phoebus 1343–1391		30 April 1331 Orthez only son of Gaston II and Eleanor of Comminges	Agnes of Navarre Paris 4 August 1349 one son	1 August 1391 L'Hôpital-d'Orion aged 60
Matthew 1391–1398		c. 1363 second son of Roger Bernard IV, Viscount of Castelbon and Gerauda of Navailles	Joanna of Aragon 4 June 1392 Barcelona no issues	August 1398 aged 34–35
Isabella 1398–1428 *with Archambaud (1398–1412) with John I (1412–1428)*		bef. 2 November 1361 only daughter of Roger Bernard IV, Viscount of Castelbon and Gerauda of Navailles	1381 five children	c. 1428 aged 46+
Archambaud de Grailly 1398–1412 *with Isabella*		c. 1329-1330 second son of Pierre II de Grailly and Erembourga de Périgord		c. 1412 aged 81–83

House of Foix-Grailly

Name	Portrait	Birth	Marriages	Death
John I 1412–1436 *with Isabella (1412–1428)*		c. 1382 eldest son of Archambaud and Isabella	(1) Joan of Navarre 12 November 1402 Palacio Real de Olite no issues (2) Jeanne d'Albret 23 May 1422 two sons (3) Joanna of Urgell May 1436 no issues	4 May 1436 Mazères, Ariège aged 53–54

11

Name	Portrait	Birth	Marriages	Death
Gaston IV 1436–1472		27 November 1422 eldest son of John I and Jeanne d'Albret	Eleanor of Navarre 30 July 1436 ten children	25/28 July 1472 Roncevalles aged 49
Francis Phoebus 1472–1483		November/December 1466 only son of Gaston of Foix, Prince of Viana and Magdalena of Valois	*never married*	30 January 1483 Pamplona aged 16
Catherine 1483–1517 *with John II*		1468 only daughter of Gaston of Foix, Prince of Viana and Magdalena of Valois	14 July 1484 Palacio Real de Olite thirteen children	12 February 1517 Mont-de-Marsan aged 48–49
John II 1483–1516 *with Catherine*		1469 second son of Alain I of Albret and Françoise, Countess of Périgord		14 June 1516 Château de Pau aged 46–47

House of Albret

Main article: House of Albret and Albret

Name	Portrait	Birth	Marriages	Death
Henry II 1517–1555		18 April 1503 Sangüesa third son of John II and Catherine	Margaret of Angoulême 24 January 1527 Saint-Germain-en-Laye two children	25 May 1555 Hagetmau aged 52
Joan 1555–1572 *with Anthony*		7 January 1528 Saint-Germain-en-Laye only daughter of Henry I and Margaret of Angoulême	(1) William, Duke of Jülich-Cleves-Berg 14 June 1541 Château de Châtellerault no issues (2) Anthony of Navarre 20 October 1548 Moulins en Bourbonnais, Allier five children	9 June 1572 Paris aged 44
Anthony 1555-1562 *with Joan*		22 April 1518 La Fère, Picardie second son of Charles, Duke of Vendôme and Françoise of Alençon	Joan 20 October 1548 Moulins en Bourbonnais, Allier five children	17 November 1562 Les Andelys, Eure aged 44

House of Bourbon

Name	Portrait	Birth	Marriages	Death
Henry II 1572–1607		13 December 1553 Château de Pau second son of Anthony and Joan	(1) Margaret of Valois 18 August 1572 Notre Dame Cathedral, Paris no issues (2) Marie de' Medici 17 December 1600 Lyon six children	14 May 1610 Paris aged 57

12

DNA Pedigree of Ulster Gastons

DNA markers can help to group members of a lineage into different branches but, like paper documents, markers are not always reliable. Mutations occur more or less randomly from one generation to the next and if we see two or more members with the same mutation this may signal that they inherited it from a common ancestor. However, it is possible that the mutation occurred more than once, which would mean that people with this mutation may not descend from the same individual. This is referred to as a "parallel mutation". (We assume that all our Ulster Gaston members share a common ancestor who lived sometime in the 1600s. Here, we are only considering more recent common ancestors that define branches of this lineage).

The following table attempts to group our Ulster members according to a small number of markers that have mutations shared by two or more people. All of us have been tested for at least 37 and some for 67 or even 111 markers. But only a few of these markers have useful mutations. The randomness of these events explains why we have to test a lot of markers just to find some useful ones for our lineage. Some markers mutate very slowly and others very quickly. Researchers have estimated mutation rates for all markers and this makes it possible to estimate how many we might expect in a group with 25 members sharing a common ancestors about 10 generations ago (these two numbers are somewhat arbitrary and may be wrong, as might be the estimated mutation rates). The expected number of mutations for each marker is shown below the marker name. So, for example, we might expect only 0.2 mutations (1.0 for a group of 250 members) in marker 593 in a group our size in 10 generations. In other words, it is pretty unlikely that there would even be one, but in fact, we see two. However, these two members are brothers, who both inherited the mutation from a relatively recent ancestor. How do we know this? Because nobody else in their branch has this mutation.

Branches of Ulster Gaston lineage

Kit #	Claimed Ancestor	593	Y GATA	389-2	557	460	459	464-d	534	570	CDYa	Markers support paper trail	Comments
	Expected number of mutations	0.2	0.3	0.6	0.9	1	12	14	17	2	8.8		
	Modal value	13	11	29	17	11/12	13	17	14	18	40		
112369	Hugh of Peapack b1685, d. 1772 NJ	13	11	29	17	11/12	13	14	14	18	40	YES	
33824	Hugh of Peapack b1685, d. 1772 NJ	12	11	29	17	12	13	16	14	18	40	YES	
161291	Hugh of Peapack b1685, d. 1772 NJ	12	11	29	17	12	13	17	14	18	40	YES	
206586	Hugh of Peapack b1685, d. 1772 NJ	13	11	29	17	12	13	17	14	18	40	YES	
154444	Samuel bc 1780 Antrim	13	11	29	17	12	13	16	14	18	40		Possible common ancestor, paper trail to c1780 Antrim
967	Alexander b 1714	13	12	29	17	12	13	17	11	18	38		Possible common ancestor but DNA conflicts with other paper trail descendants
155598*	Nathaniel b bef 1840; Rolliana	13	11	29	17	12	13	17	13	19	41		Possible common ancestor but DNA conflicts with other paper trail descendants
112435	Hugh of Peapack b1685, d. 1772 NJ	13	11	29	17	11	13	17	15	18	41		Possible common ancestor but DNA conflicts with other paper trail descendants
110485	Alexander b 1714	13	11	28	17	11	13	17	11	18	39		Possible common ancestor but DNA conflicts
181025	Alexander OH	13	11	29	17	11	13	17	11	18	39		Alexander m. Rachel Perry but conflicting residence - possible St. connection
126891	Alexander OH	13	11	29	17	11	13	17	14	18	42		One of the sons of Dr. Alexander Gaston (d. Belmont county OH 1785)
155400	Alexander 1768, Duncan	13	11	29	17	11	13	17	14	18	40		Possible common ancestor, paper trail to c1785 Antrim
NM274	Rev. Hugh bc 1720	13	11	29	17	11	13	17	14	18	39		Probable descendant of William c1685 Antrim; documented to c1780
148332	Matthew Alexander 1813, TN	13	11	28	16	11	12	17	14	18	42	YES	Probable descendant of William c1685 Antrim
174026	Matthew Alexander 1813, TN	13	11	29	17	11	12	17	14	18	40	YES	Probable descendant of William c1685 Antrim
146508	James W. snr, d 1903 VR	13	11	29	17	12	12	17	14	18	39		
122321	Justice John - son William	13	11	29	16	12	13	17	11	18	40	YES	Descendant of William of Antrim c1685 Antrim
140816	Justice John - son William	13	11	29	16	12	13	17	14	18	41	YES	Descendant of William of Antrim c1685 Antrim
152271	Justice John - son John Jr.	13	11	29	16	11	13	17	11	16	40	YES	Descendant of William of Antrim c1685 Antrim
966	Josiah	13	11	29	16	12	13	17	11	18	41	YES	Probable descendant of William of Antrim, paper trail to c1814
206938	Nathanial Squire b 1833 OH	13	12	29	?	11	13	17	?	18	39		
153564	Benton c 1840 IL	13	11	29	?	12	13	17	?	17	37		
203022	Has not responded to e-mails	13	11	29	?	12	13	17	?	19	41		

Note: "Expected number of mutations" is based on 25 members and the assumption of 10 generations to our common ancestor

*Expected number of mutations" is based on 25 members and the assumption of 10 generations to our common ancestor

At the other extreme, although most of our members have a value of 40 for CDY-a (on the right side of the table), five people have a 39, one has a 38 and 1 has a 37. We cannot be sure but it is very likely that some of these are parallel mutations since we can expect as many as 8 or 9 on this particular marker in a group this size. The two branches for which the markers support members' paper trails – those of Hugh of Peapack and Justice John – are very consistent. All members of these two groups

14

At the other extreme, although most of our members have a value of 40 for **CDY-a** (on the right side of the table), five people have a 39, one has a 38 and 1 has a 37. We cannot be sure but it is very likely that some of these are parallel mutations since we can expect as many as 8 or 9 on this particular marker in a group this size. The two branches for which the markers support members' paper trails – those of Hugh of Peapack and Justice John – are very consistent. All members of these two groups have a 40 in this marker and they probably inherited from a common ancestor. However, several markers, including **CDY-a**, conflict with marker **534** for the three people in the second grouping (below that of Hugh of Peapack). Another possible sub-branch is suggested by the three members who share a 12 in marker **439**. However, one of the members, whose paper trail doesn't go back as early as that of the other two, has different values than them for **460** and **CDY-a**.

These contradictions illustrate the importance of having several members with well documented paper trails in each branch. We can now be fairly confident in the DNA pattern for the Justice John branch (defined by a sixteen in marker 557) and the Hugh of Peapack branch (defined by **460**=12 and **557**=17). This doesn't exclude the possibility that someone with these marker values may turn out to be in a different branch (or the converse), but with four or five members having good paper trails supported by DNA markers, the chances are pretty low.

Another conclusion that can be drawn from this table is that the expected number of mutations is not a very good predictor of the actual number. Marker 460 illustrates this point. Only one mutation is expected but it is clear that there are at least two and possibly more. And if we keep in mind the fact that mutations can go up or down (an ancestor with an 11 may have a descendant with a 12 who, in turn, may have a descendant who is 11 again) then it is really impossible to say precisely how many mutations have occurred since our common ancestor who lived in the 1600s. One can only say that it is less likely that this has happened in a slow marker like **593**, than in a fast one like **CDY-a**.

So, given all this uncertainty is there any point in using DNA for genealogy? Yes, indeed! It is another valuable tool which has to be used with caution. By itself, DNA usually will not provide a conclusive answer, but the same can be said about traditional documentation. With non-paternity events like adoption, confusing naming conventions and gaps in paper trails there is just as much uncertainty when we trace back in time prior to the 1800s. So if you are a male Gaston (or you can sponsor a related male Gaston) and want to be with us in an exciting adventure into the past, please join our project and see how your DNA fits into the big picture.

http://www.familytreedna.com/group-join.aspx?Group=Gaston

JOHN "JEAN" GASTON GENEALOGY

Generation One

1. **Jean (John) Gaston**, b. ca 1600 in Foix, France.[i][1],[ii][2]

   Jean (John) Gaston of France was the first known ancestor of the Gaston family. There has been much speculation regarding his ancestry, ranging from descendancy from the Grand Duke of Tuscany to the possibility that he belonged to the Bourbon family and was a cousin to King Louis XIV of France. Jean Gaston belonged to a Protestant group known as Huguenots. On Apr 13 1598, King Henry IV of France endorsed the Edict of Nantes, which granted rights to the Protestant Huguenots. But the edict was abrogated in 1685 by King Louis XIV, who declared France entirely Catholic again and embarked on a policy of persecuting all Protestants. In the meantime, because of the political and religious climate, at age 40 Jean Gaston had fled with his family to Scotland, and his estate in France was confiscated. His brothers and sisters in France remained Catholics and sent money to him in Scotland until he became established there. Some 25 years later, his three sons fled Scotland for Ireland with their wives, also for religious reasons. Jean died in either Scotland or Ireland. [American Ancestry, Vol V, p. 104]

   "That the Gaston family was a French family there is no doubt. As early as 1445, "two gentlemen" of the name of Gaston, living at or near LaMothe St. Didier, became interested in what were believed to be wonderful cures wrought at the shrine of St. Andrew in that town, especially because one of these Gaston sons was there cured of the disease known as "St. Anthony's Fire." In consequence, they devoted their property to the work, and, seven other persons assisting, built a large hospital. The hospitallers soon founded the "Congregation of Regular Canons of the Order of Anthony," and one of the Gastons was made Grand Master of the Order. (See McClinton and Strong's "Cyclopaedia of Biblical Literature" (1894), Vol. I, p. 252). The name was common in France afterward. Alphonse Daudet, the noted French novelist, used the name "Marie Gaston" as a pseudonym." [Anna Reger Gaston, "Gaston Family Lines of Somerset," published in the "Somerset County Historical Quarterly" in New Jersey]

   There were French Gastons in Scotland as early as the mid-1500s. The Gaston surname (meaning "of Gascony" in SW France) was adopted by many former residents of Gascony after they left their native SW France. John Gaston's family was driven from France and his estate confiscated. The family fled from their home in Foix, Southern France about 1640 to Scotland where John married. Family tradition identifies him as descendant of General Gaston de Foix de Nemours (b. 1489-d 1512 in Revanna, Italy). [Clark Cordell, Pryor, OK]

   His brothers and relatives who remained Catholics in France sent means to Scotland for his living. One anecdote concerning this founder of the Protestant branch of the family was brought by his descendants to America was: Jean Gaston was a devout man and his Calvinistic progency remembered it for over a hundred years. He married in Scotland and had, among other sons, three: John, William, and Alexander. These three sons fled Scotland for Ireland with their wives, also for religious reasons about 1660 to 1680 . Jean died in either Scotland or Ireland. [American Ancestry, Vol V, p. 104]

Of these probably John, whose name appears on Hearth-Money rate list for Ireland in 1669 as of Magheragall, County Antrim, had issue, among others, several sons, some whom remained in Ireland and some emigrated to America, as did also the sons of other brothers.

There are numerous Gaston family crests, or coats of arms, pertaining to Gastons of various origins. Burke's "General Armory of England, Scotland, Ireland and Wales" (Harrison & Sons, 1884) describes the one believed to be of our Gaston lineage as follows: GASTON of England, Scotland, Ireland and Wales. Chequy argent. On gueule. Three escallops in bend or. Crest: an owl sable. Motto: Fama semper vivit.

An excellent resource pertaining to Gaston origins and related information is the website Planet Gaston, found at http://gaston.siteperso.net/. Some Gaston researchers have attempted to show tenuous royal connections and paint a romanticized picture of the family history, and it is therefore likely that some embellishment of the facts has occurred over the years. A highly informative treatment of the facts and myths of the Gaston legend can be found at http://home.mindspring.com/~bgaston2/_images/Gaston_Legend.pdf

This is a genealogy of the descendants of this Jean (John) Gaston, with particular emphasis on those branches of the family tree closest to the principal compilers, Samuel David Gaston and Geneva Gaston Brown. The information presented here was obtained from countless sources over several years of research. Wherever possible, the original source is documented, but the reader can rest assured that even when a source is not specified, the compilers were highly confident of the accuracy of the information before including it in this genealogy. By its very nature, this collection is a work in progress, and additional information regarding the early generations, as well as the current one, will be added as it becomes known. In that vein, the reader is invited to inform the compilers or editor of any errors or additional information for future updates. [Samuel David Gaston & Geneva Gaston Brown (1926-2001), principal compilers; R. L. Brown, editor]

He married in Scotland,[iii][3],[iv][4] **Agnes __**, d. aft 1650 in Melrose, Roxburghshire, Scotland.

Agnes: Some researchers identify Agnes as possibly the daughter of Phillip of Navarre, and it is also said that she was accused of witchcraft in 1650 [per "Surnames of Scotland" by George F. Black]. But other researchers have convincingly refuted those assertions, and have further cast doubt that the wife of Jean Gaston was named Agnes at all. Although we side more with the skeptics, we nonetheless report Jean Gaston's wife as Agnes simply out of tradition.[v][5],[vi][6]

> Children:
> 2. i. WILLIAM GASTON b. ca 1642, d. Ballymena, Ireland.
> 3. ii. JOHN GASTON b. ca 1645, d. Ballymena, Ireland.
>   iii. ALEXANDER GASTON, b. 1648 in Scotland, d. in Ireland, immigrated abt 1660-1668 to County Antrim, Ireland.[3]   Died Ballymena, Ireland.

Alexander Gaston, along with his brothers, John and William, went to County Antrim in Northern Ireland between 1662 and 1668, during the time of the persecution of Protestants in Scotland. Alexander Gaston left many descendants in and around Ballymena, County Antrim, Ireland. One of them was a certain Miss Gaston of Killycowan, who was reportedly the great-grandmother of U.S. President Chester A. Arthur (exact lineage not specified, has never been determined, and the connection is considered tenuous at best).[vii][7]

Generation Two

2.   **William Gaston** (1.Jean[1]), b. ca 1642 in Scotland, d. in Ireland, immigrated abt 1660-1668 to County Antrim, Ireland.[3]

William Gaston (b. 1642), along with his brothers, John and Alexander, went to County Antrim in Northern Ireland between 1662-1668. He is referred to by genealogists as "the first Irish William Gaston" to distinguish him from brother John's son William and others. He was the father of the Charleston, SC Gastons who emigrated in the 1760's-1770's from County Antrim, Ireland.[viii][8],4

He married **Unknown**.
> Children:
> 4.   i.   (MALE) GASTON.

3.   **John Gaston** (1.Jean[1]), b. ca 1645 in Scotland, d. in Mageragall, North Ireland, immigrated abt 1660-1668 to County Antrim, Ireland.[3]

John Gaston (1645) or his father John (1600) was listed on the hearth-money rate list at Magheragall, Upper Massereene Barony, in the extreme south of County Antrim, Ireland, SW of Belfast. The family later moved a few miles north, as John (1645) had a son William ca 1680 at Carenleigh, Cloughwater, near Ballymena. Clough was a few miles north of Ballymena in Kilconway Barony, and held five Gaston households at time of the 1740 Protestant Householders index of County Antrim.[6]

He married **Unknown**.
> Children:
> 5.   i.   WILLIAM GASTON b. 1680.
> 6.   ii.   HUGH GASTON b. ca 1687.
> 7.   iii.   MARY GASTON b. 1695.
> 8.   iv.   JOSEPH GASTON b. ca 1700.
> 9.   v.   JOHN GASTON b. ca 1703.
> 10.   vi.   ALEXANDER GASTON b. 1714.

Ballywallin Presbyterian Church,
Antrim, Ireland

Generation Three

4.   **(Male) Gaston** (2.William[2], 1.Jean[1]). He married in Ireland, **Unknown**.
> Children:
> 11.   i.   ALEXANDER GASTON b. Feb- 5-1702.

5.   **William Gaston** (3.John[2], 1.Jean[1]), b. 1680 in Carenleagh, Cloughwater, County Antrim, Ireland,[ix][9] ["Ohio Valley Genealogies," p. 41, reports birth date as about 1680-90; "Colonial Families of the United States," Vol III, p. 175, reports it as 1685.], d. ca 1770 in Ireland,[3,x[10],xi[11],xii[12]]

William's brothers, John, Hugh, Joseph and Alexander, arrived in America ca 1720 through the Port of Perth Amboy and settled in New Jersey. William himself remained in Ireland, although all his children emigrated to America.[3]

He married[3] **Olivet Lemon**, also known as Mary Lemmon, b. 1688 in Scotland,[12,xiii[13]] d. 1752.[12]

Olivet: Name given as Mary Lemmon (sic) in Colonial Families of the United States, Vol III, p. 175.

Children:
12. i. JOHN GASTON b. Apr- 4-1703.
13. ii. MARY GASTON b. 1712.
14. iii. JANET GASTON b. 1714.
15. iv. MARTHA GASTON b. 1718.
16. v. ROBERT GASTON b. 1720.
17. vi. HUGH GASTON b. 1722.
18. vii. ALEXANDER GASTON b. 1727.
19. viii. ELIZABETH GASTON b. 1727/30.
20. ix. WILLIAM GASTON b. 1735.

6. **Hugh Gaston**, also known as Hugh of Peapack (3.John[2], 1.Jean[1]), b. ca 1687 in County Antrim, Ireland,[xiv][14],[xv][15] d. Dec-23-1772 in Bedminster Twp, Somerset Co, NJ,[14],[xvi][16],[xvii][17] buried in Lamington Presb Church Cem, Somerset Co, NJ.[17],[14]
Hugh, along with his brothers, William, John and Joseph, arrived in America about 1720 through the Port of Perth Amboy and settled in New Jersey. Hugh obtained land in Bucks County, now Northampton County, Pennsylvania, in 1746 and 1751. Later, he lived in Somerset County, New Jersey, where he died.

He married ca 1718,[15] [probably in Ireland], **Jennet Kirkpatrick**, b. ca 1698,[15],[14] d. Aug- 1-1777 in New Jersey,[xviii][18],[15],[14] buried in Lamington Presb Church Cem, Somerset Co, NJ.[17],[14]
Children:
21. i. JOHN GASTON, SR. b. ca 1719.
22. ii. WILLIAM GASTON b. ca 1720.
23. iii. JOSEPH GASTON b. ca 1725.
iv. MARGARET GASTON b. in Ireland.

Probably the daughter of Hugh Gaston (b. 1687), but may have been his granddaughter. She was living in Somerset Co, NJ at the time she was married.
She married[xix][19] Nov- 8-1750 in New Jersey,[xx][20],[14] Thomas Moffat, d. 1770,[19],[15] [Hugh Gaston served as administrator of his estate.], resided in Middlesex Co, NJ.[14],[15]

24. v. HUGH GASTON, JR. b. 1734.
25. vi. ELIZABETH GASTON b. 1737.
vii. REBECCA GASTON b. Dec-12-1739 in Bedminster Twp, Somerset Co, NJ,[15] d. Jun-23-1819.[xxi][21]

Known to be a sister of Hugh Gaston Jr. (b. 1734) and thus the daughter of Hugh Gaston (b. 1687), but he may actually have been their grandfather.

She married[19] William Logan, b. Mar-18-1736,[15] d. Jan- 8-1814,[15] resided in Bedminster Twp, Somerset Co, NJ,[15] resided in Peapack, Somerset Co, NJ,[19] occupation Captain.[19]
viii. JAMES GASTON.

Presumed to be a son of Hugh Gaston (b. 1687), as a James Gaston, probably a brother to John Gaston of New Jersey (b. ca 1719), was listed as a subscriber to the fund for building Allentown Church parsonage, 1758, in connection with that of John Gaston of Upper Freehold. However, that James Gaston may actually have been the one baptized on Mar 28 1742 as the eldest son of John Gaston (b. ca 1719).

The name of James Gaston appears as a member of the congregation of Lamington Church, Bedminster Twp, in the years up to 1766. A James Gaston (probably the James b. ca 1750, son of William b. 1720) also took up land in Mt. Bethel Twp, Northampton Co, Pennsylvania, in 1773. The Name of James Gaston appears on tax lists of Cecil Twp, Washington Co, PA, in 1787 and 1788, and in Rostraver Twp, Westmoreland Co, PA, in 1789.[xxii][22]

        ix.   ALEXANDER GASTON[xxiii][23] b. in Bedminster Twp, Somerset Co, NJ.[23]

7.   **Mary Gaston** (3.John[2], 1.Jean[1]), b. 1695 in Ireland.[xxiv][24] She married in Ireland,[24] **James Cauldwell**, b. 1691 in Ireland.[24] From "Family Records or Genealogies of the First Settlers of the Passaic Valley," p. 68: "James Cauldwell, with his wife Mary, emigrated from Ireland, about the year 1732, when his son William was six years old, and settled on Long Hill, on lot No. 30, addition of the Elizabethtown lots, which it appears he drew. From tradition among the families, it would seem, and I am led to believe, that James Cauldwell's wife was Mary Gaston, sister of the father of Hugh Gaston, of Peapack. Hugh Gaston was brother of Capt. William Logan's wife, and probably also brother of the wife of Thomas Kirkpatrick, at Liberty Corner. His children called him Uncle Hugh Gaston, and Mr. Gaston, Mrs. Logan and the old Kirkpatrick family claimed kin to the Cauldwell family."[xxv][25]

           Children:
    26.   i.   WILLIAM CAULDWELL b. ca 1726.

8.   **Joseph Gaston** (3.John[2], 1.Jean[1]), b. ca 1700 in County Antrim, Ireland,[4,15] d. Apr- -1777 in Bernards Twp, Somerset Co, NJ,[4,15,22] resided aft abt 1720 in Bernards Twp, Somerset Co, NJ,[4] resided until abt 1720 in Ireland,[4,22] occupation farmer.[15]

Joseph, along with his brothers, William, John and Hugh, arrived in America about 1720 through the Port of Perth Amboy and settled in New Jersey. He was a member of Baskingridge Presbyterian Church. He may have been married more than once.[4,8,xxvi[26],15]

He married[22] 1725/28,[15] **Margaret __**, b. ca 1705,[4] d. Aug-31-1795 in Hardwick Twp, Sussex Co, NJ,[4,15] buried in Jellow Frame Presbyterian Church, Frelinghuysen, Sussex Co, NJ.[xxvii][27]

Margaret: Margaret Gaston lived with her son, Joseph, after the death of her husband, Joseph Gaston in 1777.[15]

           Children:
        i.   MARTHA GASTON b. 1726 in Bernards Twp, Somerset Co, NJ.[27] She married[xxviii][28] __ Patterson.
    27.   ii.   MARGARET GASTON b. 1728.
    28.   iii.   JOHN GASTON b. Nov-10-1730.
    29.   iv.   ROBERT GASTON b. Jan-28-1732.
    30.   v.   JOSEPH GASTON b. Nov-10-1738.
        vi.   PRISCILLA GASTON, also known as Purcilla Gaston,[27] also known as Prucilla Gaston, b. in Bernards Twp, Somerset Co, NJ, d. in Hardwick Twp, Sussex Co, NJ,[27] resided 1771 in Somerset Co, NJ.[27] She married Sep-24-1771 in New Jersey,[27,28] Daniel McCain (son of James McCain), resided 1771 in Somerset Co, NJ.[27]
    31.   vii.   ANN GASTON.

9.   **John Gaston** (3.John[2], 1.Jean[1]), b. ca 1703 in County Antrim, Ireland,[7,28] d. Mar-29-1783 in Voluntown, New London Co, CT.[7,28]

John Gaston was born in County Antrim, Ireland, probably near Ballymena (or possibly Ballymoney), in 1703 or 1704. Along with brother Alexander (and possibly a third brother who settled in New Jersey), John arrived in America between 1720-26 through the Port of Perth Amboy, settling at Voluntown, Windham County, Connecticut in 1726 or 1727.

He married ca 1735 in Voluntown, New London Co, CT,[28,6] **Janet Thomson**, b. 1711 in Scotland,[28] (daughter of Alexander Thomson and Mary __), d. Nov- 3-1806 in Killingly, Windham Co, CT.[xxix[29],28]
           Children:
    32.   i.   MARGARET GASTON b. Oct-19-1738.

      ii.   ALEXANDER GASTON b. May- 3-1739 in Voluntown, New London Co, CT,[29] [Birth date of Oct 19 1738 has also been reported, but that appears to be his sister Margaret's.], d. 1760,[7,28] [Died of disease contracted in the French & Indian Wars.], cause of death disease contracted in the French & Indian Wars,[28] occupation Army officer,[7] military French & Indian Wars,[28] never married.

   33.   iii.   JOHN GASTON b. Jan-10-1750.

10. **Alexander Gaston** (3.John[2], 1.Jean[1]), b. 1714 in Ireland,[xxx[30],xxxi[31]] d. Aug-24-1783 in Berkshire Co, MA, buried in Cone Road Cemetery, Richmond, MA,[xxxii[32]] military Officer in French & Indian War.

Emigrated to American with his brother John about 1720-26 and settled at Richmond, Massachusetts. He is thought to have had a third brother who settled in New Jersey. (Mr. Marshall Gaston of Oberlin, Ohio, made before 1892 a nearly complete record of the descendants of the children of this Alexander Gaston, down to his own generation.)[xxxiii[33]]

He married[33] Sep-29-1743,[xxxiv[34]] **Mary "Molly" Wilson**, b. 1716 in Ireland,[xxxv[35],xxxvi[36]] d. Jul-30-1804 in Richmond, Berkshire Co, MA,[34] buried in Cone Road Cemetery, Richmond, MA.[36]

Mary: Emigrated to America in about 1832. Alexander & Mary "Molly" Wilson Gaston may also have had another child, a son/daughter named Ging.[xxxvii[37]]

       Children:
      i.   WILLIAM GASTON b. Aug- 9-1744,[33] d. Aug- 2-1787 in Richmond, Berkshire Co, MA,[xxxviii[38]] buried in Cone Road Cemetery, Richmond, MA,[36] [Headstone carries the title "Captain," presumably from Revolutionary War.]. He married[34] Naomi Tilden, b. Sep- 9-1743,[34] d. May- 6-1822.[34]
   34.   ii.   JOHN GASTON b. Mar- 3-1746.
   35.   iii.   ROBERT GASTON b. Dec-28-1747.
      iv.   MARY GASTON b. Sep-20-1749.[33]
   36.   v.   JANET A. "JENNIE" GASTON b. Dec-27-1750.
      vi.   MARGARET GASTON b. Jan- 5-1753,[33] d. Mar- 8-1807.[34]
   37.   vii.   ALEXANDER GASTON b. Oct-28-1754.
   38.   viii. DAVID GASTON b. Jan-13-1757.
      ix.   THOMAS GASTON b. Mar-16-1759,[33] d. 1823,[26] military Corporal - Revolutionary War.[26] He married[34] Sarah Chatman.
      x.   PHEBE GASTON, also known as Phoebe Gaston, b. Apr-22-1765,[33] d. Dec- 7-1835.[34] She married (1) Jun-11-1788 in Berkshire Co, MA, John Bacon, Jr.. She married[27] (2) Elisha __.

Generation Four

11. **Alexander Gaston** (4.(Male)[3], 2.William[2], 1.Jean[1]), b. Feb- 5-1702 in County Antrim, Ireland,[xxxix[39]] d. in Ireland.

Although other researchers allow that only Alexander Gaston's (b. 1702) four oldest children emigrated to America, at least one, Edward H. Couey of Scotts Mills, OR, contends that all six did so, settling in Chester and York Counties, SC. As he cites specific circumstances for this, we provide that information under this Alexander's son Alexander (b. ca 1750).

He married in Ireland,[6] **Jane Harper**.
       Children:
      i.   ROBERT GASTON b. ca 1733 in Ireland.[6]
   39.   ii.   JOSEPH GASTON b. Oct- 8-1738.
   40.   iii.   JANE GASTON b. 1740.
   41.   iv.   MATTHEW GASTON b. ca 1748.

42. v. ALEXANDER GASTON b. ca 1750.
vi. MARY LOUISA GASTON b. bef 1755 in Ireland.[6]

12. **John Gaston**, also known as Justice John Gaston (5.William[3], 3.John[2], 1.Jean[1]), b. Apr- 4-1703 in Ireland [Headstone has birth date as 1700, while "Gaston of Chester" states ca 1710.], d. 1782 in South Carolina,[17,3,xl[40],xli[41]] buried in Burnt Meeting House Cemetery, Wylie's Mill, Chester Co, SC,[17] resided (settled 1751/52) at Fishing Creek, Chester Co, SC,[3] immigrated 1749 to Pennsylvania,[3,xlii[42]] occupation farmer, surveyor, Justice in South Carolina.[13]

Emigrated first to Pennsylvania in 1749, then to Chester District, South Carolina, in about 1751-52, settling on Fishing Creek. Served as King's Justice before 1776, and as leader of the patriots of his vicinity during the British incursion of 1780-81. He is often referred to by Gaston genealogists as "Justice John." The nine sons of John and Esther Gaston served as soldiers in the American Revolution, and four of them lost their lives in that war.

An account of Justice John Gaston is found in the historical novel "Polly of the Pines," by Adele Eugenia Thompson, published in 1906 by Lothrop, Lee & Shepard Company. Polly was Mary Dunning, a brave girl of the Carolinas, and the events of the story take place in the years 1775-1882. She was an orphan living with her mother's family, who were Scotch Highlanders, and for the most part intensely loyal to the Crown. Polly finds the glamour of royal adherence hard to resist, but her heart turns toward the patriots, and she does much to aid and encourage them. The book is available in reprint and in PDF form online at Google Books.[3,42]

He married[3] in Ireland,[13] **Esther Waugh**, b. 1715 in Ireland,[17,xliii[43],13] d. 1789 in Cedar Shoals, Fishing Creek, Chester Co., SC.,[17,3,43] buried in Burnt Meeting House Cemetery, Wylie's Mill, Chester Co, SC,[17] occupation school teacher.[13]

John Gaston Land Grant in Chester Co., SC: 4th Sept 1759

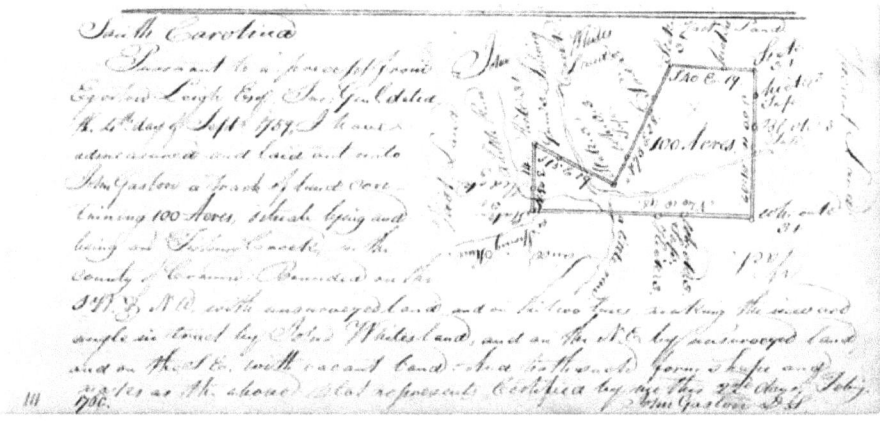

Burnt Meeting House Cemetery
Near Wylie's Mill, Chester Co., SC

Marker of the Home Site of Justice County Historical Society. Shoals on the south side of Fishing Justice of the Peace under both the advanced in years, he was the John Gaston erected 1974 by Chester Inscription: "Two miles south, at Cedar Creek, was the home of John Gaston, Esq., Royal and State governments. Though leading spirit in arousing resistance to the British in this area. All nine of his sons fought for freedom; four died in service." See The Historical Marker Database HMdb.org for more information.

WILL OF
JOHN G STON

IN THE NAME OF GOD AMENt the Eighteenth Day of April one
Thousand Seven Hundred And Eighty Two, I John Gaston of the
State of South Carolina Being Sick of Body But of Good &
Perfect mind & memory Thanks to God, for the mercies, Calling to
mind the uncertainty of This Liff & that it is appointed
for all living once to Die And after Death to come to Judgement
I do Make Constitute Ordain this my Last will And Testament
& Devise that it may be Rec^d. by all as Such. I leave my Soul
to Almighty God my Creator to Jesus Christ my Redeemer & to
the Holy Ghost I Leave my Body to the Eamh to be buried, in
A cristian Decent manner As concerning my worldly Estate
which it HathPPleased God to give me I Devise & Bequeath in the
fooling manner Viz I Leave to my Daughter Esther all that
part of the tract of Land Being on the NorthSide of Fishing Creek
below the Fish Dam Being part of the S Tract Containing One
hundred & Fifty Acred to Her & the Heirs of Her Body begotten
or if not to Revert to the Nix Heirs by Law----------
The Remaining part of Afors^d. Hundred & Fifty Acres of land I
Give And Bequeath to my son James whichlyes in both sides
of thecreek- I give and Bequeath to my Grand Son Samuel Mc
Crary all that Plantation Tract one hundred acres of Land on the
South side of fishing Creek joying old John Nigger Land--
To Him And his Heirs of his BodyBegotten or if he Has non of
His Own / heirs as afors^d. the Said Land is to return to my heirs
I Give and Bequeath to my Grand Daughter Margret McCrary one
Hundred Acres of Land Joying Lands of John Gaston Junr. &
John Bell Likewise Sd Hundred in to return to my heirs if
she the S^d. Margret McCrary Hath no heirs of Her Body Begotten
I bequeathtto my Beloved Wife and my Sons Joseph Gaston all
that Plantatonon which I now Dwel Lying on the South Side of
Fishing Creek and After my Wifes Decease this Plantation or
what of it is un This side theCreek, that is the South Side is
to Bee my son Josephs I leave and Bequeath to my son Ja^s.
Gaston that Part of one Hundred Acres that he now lives un

9

the North Side of Fishing Creek which ought to a having Been
made Over by Deed But for fear of Inconvenience I leave it
to him by will as concerning my moveable affects I dow
Constitute and appoint my Wife to Divide or Dispose off as
she Thinks Proper, Lastly I do hereby appoint my Beloved Wife
my Lawful Executrix of this my Last Will And Testament In
Witness my Hand The Day & year Above Written

John Gaston

Signed Sealed in the presence of
Wm. Willey
James Nealey
John Gaston Jun.

Probated 1782   Recorded Book A Page 88
                       Apt. 21   Pkg.   336

43.　i.　MARGARET GASTON b. Aug-29-1738 in Ireland, d. 1767 in Chester Co., S.C. She married James McCreary.

44.　ii.　MARTHA GASTON b. Jun-11-1741, Pennsylvania, d. 3 Apr 1826 in Chester Co., SC. She married Joseph Gaston 1770 in Chester Co., SC, son of Alexander Gaston, b. 1740 in Ireland, d. 21 Apr 1823; buried in Fishing Creek Presbyterian Cemetery, Chester, SC.

45.　iii.　WILLIAM GASTON b. Jun- 5-1743, Pennsylvania, d. 1814 in Chester Co., S.C. he married Ann Porter; he married second Janet Love abt 1759.

46.　iv.　JOHN GASTON b. Jun-24-1745, Pennsylvania, d. 1816 in Marion Co., IL. He married Jeanette Knox in 1768. She was born abt 1742 in Jefferson Co., IL, and d. 1780 in Chester Co., SC.

Deceased -- Southern Campaign American Revolution Pension Statements

Pension application of John Gaston W30007 Janet fn24SC
Transcribed by Will Graves 9/15/08
State of Illinois, Jefferson County

On this 12th day of September 1836 personally appeared before the Judge of the Court of Probate of the County and State aforesaid Jennet Gaston a resident of Jefferson County and State of Illinois aged 94 years, who, being first duly sworn according to law, doth on her oath, make the following declaration, in order to obtain the benefit of the provision made the act of Congress, passed July 4th, 1836. That she is the widow of John Gaston Deceased late of Chester District State of South Carolina who was a private of the Mounted Militia under the Command of General Sumpter [sic, Thomas Sumter], That previous to General Sumter's organization he the said John Gaston performed 7 tours of duty to suppress the collection of Tories and one tour of 3 months against the Cherokee Indians, Officers not recollected, that Captain McClure was the Captain he served on the first, and after he the said Captain Carr was killed, Captain Steel commanded, previous to the battle of The Rocky Mount he the said John Gaston was taken prisoner and in a few days paroled yet ventured to aid in that Battle of Rocky Mount and that at hanging rock the Sabbath following where he had 2 brothers fall and one wounded, he had another Brother fall at Savannah as Captain of a regular Company -- That the said John Gaston being a quack doctor was employed by General Sumter to dress the wounds he the said General received at Broad River, and was from that time with the person of General Sumter to the best of her recollection as a Surgeon till after the Battle of Eutaw Springs, when he was dismissed. That the said John Gaston was in 5 or 6 battles and skirmishes and was 5 years in the service of his Country without ever receiving a compensation.

She further declares that she was married to the said John Gaston previous to the revolutionary war. That the record of their marriage was lost when the British and Tories robbed them of nearly all their property. But that she recollects their 3rd child was Born the first day of January 1777. That she has no record of the services of her husband the said John Gaston. That he the said John Gaston her husband died some time in January 1808, and that she has remained a widow ever since that period as will more fully appear by reference to the proof hereto annexed. S/ Jannet Gaston, X her mark

Sworn to and subscribed, on the day and year above written before me this 12th day of September 1836
S/ Joel Pace, Judge of Probate

The following questions were put to the above Jennet Gaston while on oath.
What was sure maiden name? Ans: Jannet Knox
By whom were you married? Ans: By Father-in-law John Gaston Senior Esquire
Of what complaint did your husband the aforesaid John Gaston die? Ans: the Influenza.
S/ Jannet Gaston, X her mark
[Zadok Casey and Edward Maxey, a preacher of the gospel, gave the standard supporting affidavit as to the moral character of the claimant and the reputation of her husband as a revolutionary soldier.]
State of Illinois, Marion County
Personally appeared before me a Justice of the Peace

47.   v.   JAMES GASTON b. Apr-15-1747, Pennsylvania, d. abt 1824 in Randolph Co., IL. He married Margaret Harvey.

vi.   ROBERT GASTON b. Mar-11-1749 in Pennsylvania,[xliv][44] d. Aug- 7-1780 in Hanging Rock, SC,[xlv][45],44 [Death date determined by a Judge in Gaston family to be Aug 7 1780, not Aug 6 1780 as reported elsewhere (e.g., Ohio Valley Genealogies, p. 41).].

Killed in Revolutionary War battle at Hanging Rock, South Carolina, along with his two brothers, Ebenezer and David.

48.   vii.   HUGH GASTON b. Mar-12-1751, Pennsylvania or New Jersey, d. 13 Mar 1836 in Wilcox Co., Alabama. He married Hannah Martha McClure, b. abt 1754, d. 21 Dec 1836.

viii.   ALEXANDER GASTON b. Aug-24-1753 in Chester Co., S.C.,[44,45] d. 1781,[45] [Hanna's "Ohio Valley Genealogies," p. 41, reports that Alexander Gaston was killed at the Battle of Hanging Rock, August 1781. But "Heritage History of Chester County, SC," p. 196, states that he contracted smallpox at Wright's Bluff on Black River and died in the home of the McConnell family in 1781.]. Another source gives his death 5 Nov 1785 in Wright's Bluff.

ix.   DAVID GASTON b. Jul- 7-1755,[45,44] d. Aug- 7-1780 in Hanging Rock, SC.[45,44]

Killed in Revolutionary War Battle at Hanging Rock, South Carolina, along with his two brothers, Robert and Ebenezer.[44]

x.   EBENEZER GASTON b. Sep-15-1757,Chester Co., SC, [45,44] d. Aug- 7-1780 in Hanging Rock, SC.[45,44]

Killed in Revolutionary War Battle at Hanging Rock, South Carolina, along with his two brothers, Robert and David.

Schedule of Inhabitants in Chester County, South Carolina 1790 Census, Transcribed by Su Wilson						
Schedule of Inhabitants in Chester County Page 184						
FORENAME	SURNAME	FREE WHITE MALES 16 YEARS UP WARDS AND HEAD OF FAMILIES	FREE WHITE MALES UNDER 16 YEARS	FREE WHITE FEMALES AND HEAD OF FAMILIES	ALL OTHER FREE PERSONS	SLAVES

Samuel	McCOLOUGH	2	2	4	*	*
Hannah	BISHOP	*	*	2	*	*
Hugh	LOCKHART	3	1	4	*	*
John	DUGLAS	2	*	*	*	*
Abram	WRIGHT	2	2	5	*	*
Thomas	MORROSON	1	*	1	*	*
Alexander	ROSBRUGH	4	1	3	*	*
James	ADAMS	1	2	3	*	*
Thomas	SIMPSON	1	2	3	2	*
John	ADAMS	1	2	3	*	*
John	WALKER	1	*	1	*	*
Hugh	GASTON	2	4	2	*	*
Charles	OAR	1	1	2	1	1
Archibald	MARTIN	1	1	1	*	*
Walter	BROWN	2	1	1	*	*
Stephen	TITSHAW	2	1	5	*	*
George	NELSON	2	1	2	*	*
Hugh	BONNER	1	*	4	*	*
George	CLARK	1	1	4	*	*
Hugh	McCORMON	1	2	5	*	*
William	ELIOT	1	2	2	*	*
Ebenezar	ELIOT	1	*	1	*	*
Hugh	STUART	2	*	3	*	*
Thomas	KENNEDY	1	2	4	*	*
John	BRADFORD	2	*	1	*	*
Samuel	LOWRY	1	1	3	*	2
James	BISHOP	1	2	4	*	1
William	SHERROD	1	3	5	2	*
James	NESBIT	1	3	3	*	*
Robert	McCHENNY	3	4	4	*	*
Phillip	WALKER	3	4	1	*	7
Thomas	MORRIS	1	*	1	*	*
Capt. Jacob	COOPER	1	3	6	2	4
William	WYLY	2	1	2	*	*

Totals		55	59	106	7	15
Page 184 Colu mn 2						
Robert	FARGUSON	1	1	5	*	*
James	BLARE	2	1	5	*	*
James	ONAIL	2	1	3	*	*
Edward	McFADDING	2	2	6	*	*
John	WYLY	1	5	4	*	*
Widow	FARGUSON	1	4	2	*	2
Thomas	ADAMS	1	*	1	*	*
George	LEWIS	1	3	4	*	1
Thomas	DUGGINS	1	1	*	3	*
Robert	McFADDING	1	3	1	*	*
John	BANKHEAD	1	1	1	*	1
Jarrel	EDWARDS	1	2	3	*	*
Joseph	GASTON	1	*	1	1	*
James	NEELY	1	*	3	1	*
Thomas	HARDING	1	2	3	*	*
Barbara	McKINY	1	1	1	*	5
John	McKINNY	1	1	1	*	*
Agness	SLEEKER	*	1	3	*	*
Edward	WHITE	2	2	2	*	*
William	McKINNY	1	1	2	1	*
William	CROOK	1	1	2	1	*
William	CROOK, Sen	3	*	*	*	2
Solomon	CROOK	1	*	*	*	*
James	WOODS	2	1	2	*	*
William	REEVES	1	1	7	*	2
Thomas	WALKER	2	3	2	*	2
Alexander	WALKER	1	1	1	*	*
James	GASTON	1	2	3	*	5
Thomas	STEEL	1	2	3	*	*
William	LILES	1	1	3	*	*

14

John	GORDON	2	*	3	*	*
William	McDONALD	1	1	3	*	26
James	KNOX	1	4	4	*	24
William	WALKER	1	2	2	*	10
Benja	BOWEN	1	3	1	*	*
Note: previous transcription has this as ROWAN						
Totals		44	54	88	6	83

49.   xi.   ESTHER GASTON b. Oct-15-1760, d. 1809. She married Alexander Walker 1777, son of Thomas Walker and Esther Jane Gaston.

50.   xii.   JOSEPH GASTON b. Jan-22-1763 in Chester, SC; d. 10 Oct 1836 in Sumpter, SC. He married Janet Brown 20 Apr 1790 in Cedar Shoals, Rocky Mount, SC.

13.   **Mary Gaston** (5.William[3], 3.John[2], 1.Jean[1]), b. 1712 in Ireland,[xlvi][46],[xlvii][47] d. 1802,[46] [DAR Lineage Book (p. 103) states her death date as 1800.], buried in Burnt Meeting House Cemetery, Wylie's Mill, Chester Co, SC,[17] resided (settled) in South Carolina.[44]

Elizabeth F. Ellet's "The Women of the American Revolution" provides a lengthy profile of Mary Gaston McClure, citing her brave and courageous actions during the American Revolution. [Burgess, "The Gaston Genealogy," p. 82] The Lineage Book of the Daughters of the American Revolution, p. 103, states that Mary Gaston McClure "is recorded in history as 'The Cherokee Heroine.'"

Notes for MARY GASTON:
Notes from the Concordance and Collections of Mary Gaston McClure's Ancestry:

"Mary Gaston McClure's husband died just as the Revolutionary War broke out, leaving his widow with a large family of sons and daughters. Her sons were: Matthew, a signer of the (Mecklenburg, North Carolina) Declaration of Independence, Dr. Williams, surgeon in the Revolution, James and Hugh were captains, and Col. John, the brave and gallant hero of the war, who struck the first blow toward rescuing his beloved country, South Carolina, from the British."

She married[41] **James McClure**, occupation Justice.
             Children:
51.   i.   JOHN MCCLURE[44].
52.   ii.   MARTHA MCCLURE b. 1754.
53.   iii.   WILLIAM MCCLURE[44].
        iv.   MARY MCCLURE. She married[44] Samuel Lowry.
        v.   (FEMALE) MCCLURE. She married[44] Edward Martin.
        vi.   MATTHEW MCCLURE.

14. **Janet Gaston**, also known as Jinny Gaston,[41] (5.William[3], 3.John[2], 1.Jean[1]), b. 1714 in Ireland, resided (settled) in South Carolina.[44] She married[41,44] **Charles Strong**.

Notes for JEANETTE GASTON:
This account was taken from the unpublished family history, pp. 225-227, JR Moffatt:
"The following happened at the home of Charles Strong and Jeanette Gaston: On the first incursion of the royal troops (British soldiers of the Revolutionary War) into the remote parts of the State, many outrages were committed upon the helpless families where they passed. On Sunday morning June11, 1780, the troops under Huck arrived at the house of Mr. Strong near Fishing Creek Church. They immediately entered and plundered the house of everything, carrying away also the corn and wheat. Some of the grain being accidently scattered in the yard, a tame pigeon flew down and picked it up.

The brutal captain struck the bird, cutting off its head at a blow with his sword, then turning to Mrs. Strong, said, "Madam, I have cut off the head of the Holy Ghost." She replied, with indignation, "You will never die in your bed, nor will your death be that of the righteous." The prediction thus uttered was in a moment signally fulfilled. Mrs. Strong was a sister of old Justice Gaston. After this insult and blasphemy, some of Huck's men went to the barn where her son, William Strong, had gone shortly before their arrival. He had taken his Bible with him and was engaged in reading the sacred volume. They shot him dead upon the spot, and dragged him out of the barn. The officers then began to cut and hack the dead body with their broadswords, when Mrs. Strong rushed from the house pleading with all a mother's anguish to the officers that they would spare the corpse of her son. They heeded not her agonized entreaties, til she threw herself upon the bleeding and mangled body, resolving to perish as he had done by the cruel hands of her enemies, rather than see her child cut to pieces before her eyes.

Such outrages were of common occurrence, and the example set by officers of the royal army in the slaughter of boys of too tender age to become soldiers, and in the plundering of houses defended only by women or aged men, gave encouragement to the Loyalist, who followed their banner to practice similar cruelties. Robbery, spoilation, and murder were everywhere the order of the day."

Source: Dorothy Wakefield Chance's "Ancestors of Kayleigh Chance Murdoc"
Tombstone inscription retrieved September, 2004 from:
http://ftp.rootsweb.com/pub/usgenweb/sc/fairfield/cemeteries/gladney.txt

Old Gladney Cemetery
Row 6
JENNET GASTON STRONG B.1726 D. 4-28-1801 age 75 yrs w/o Charles Strong

Grave Listing by Family:
Jannet (Jane Strong) Gladney b.1757 d. 1833 age 76 consort/o Richard Gladney III
Jenet Gladney b. 1786 d. 10-5-1786 9 months d/o Richard & Jane Strong Gladney
Charles Gladney b. 7-16-1787 d. 6-13-1828 age 41y s/o Richard & Jane Strong Gladney
Richard Gladney b. 1790 d. 8-24-1793 age 3y s/o Richard & Jane Strong Gladney
William Gladney b. 1781 d. 10-10-1803 age 22 s/o Richard & Jane Strong Gladney
inscription faint

Jennet Gaston Strong b. 1726 d. 4-28-1801 age 75y w/o Charles Strong m/o Jane
Strong Gladney

Old Gladney Cemetery, Winnsboro, Fairfield Co., SC
Bettye Hogue Bond> President Gladneys In America Family Association
The following is submitted with my approval.
Bettye Hogue Bond (4-24-00)
This cemetery is the property of Descendants of Richard & Jane
Wilson Gladney. It is maintained by this family Association.
Any contact may be done through the President:
Bettye Bond --Retteacher@aol.com

USGENWEB NOTICE: In keeping with our policy of providing free information on the Internet,
material may be freely used by non-commercial entities, as long as this message remains on all
copied material, AND permission is obtained from the contributor of the file.

These electronic pages may NOT be reproduced in any format for profit or presentation by other
organizations. Persons or organizations desiring to use this material for non-commercial
purposes, MUST obtain the written consent of the contributor, OR the legal representative of the
submitter, and contact the listed USGenWeb archivist with proof of this consent.

SCGenWeb File Manager: "Victoria Proctor" <vproc@ix.netcom.com>

Contributed to The USGenWeb Archives by: Bettye Hogue Bond
<Retteacher@aol.com> 24 Apr 2000
Cemetery: Old Gladney Cemetery, Fairfield Co., SC[32]

Notes for CHARLES STRONG:
Researching Strong(e)s and Strang(e)s in Britain and Ireland

IRISH AND EMIGRANT PLACES AND LINEAGES

NOTICE: The contents of this WEB SITE are subject to Copyright 1997-1999 by David B. Strong. All rights
are reserved, including the right to reproduce the contents or portions thereof, in any form.
Permission is hereby granted to copy for personal use only limited parts of the written material and
of the attached data files contained herein as text material, provided, that any published reuse of this
material must properly acknowledge and cite the copyright of David B. Strong as the author or
compiler of the information. This material may not be copied except for personal use; and it may not
be duplicated and sold, either separately, or as part of a compilation, either in print, on digitalized
media such as Compact Disks, or electronically, without the express written consent of the author.
Distribution of documents (as opposed to abstracted and reformatted data) downloaded from or
copied from this site, whether in part or in whole, whether in print or via electronic media, is strictly
forbidden, regardless of whether a fee is charged. This copyright applies to all parts of this site as
published on the Internet.

5) Charles Strong, b. ~1713, Ireland, d. ~1783, Kershaw Co. S. Carolina; m. Jeannette Gaston (of Huguenot
descent... parents named in Miss Esther's book), b. ~1726 in Ireland, d. 28 Apr 1801, Fairfield Co. SC;

children, born
in Ireland:

4.1) Jane/Jennet Strong, b. ~1757, Co. Antrim, d. 1833 in S. Carolina; m. M. Richard Gladney, b.~1744, d. 10 Aug.1796 in S.C.

4.2) Christopher Strong, b. 20 Jan 1760, Co. Antrim, d. 22 Nov. 1850, Charlotte, Dickson Co., Tennessee, m.1st on 28 Dec 1782, Frances Elizabeth Dunn, b.~1760, d. 28 Dec 1826; m.2nd 10 Jul 1828 at Chester, S.C., Rosannah McColloch

4.3) William Strong, b. ~1763, Co. Antrim, killed in action, 11 June 1780 in Revolutionary War Battle of Fishing Creek, S.C. 4.4) Letitia Strong, b. 1 Mar 1766, Co. Antrim, d. 27 Nov 1837 in Dickson Co., Tennessee; Note, after the death of her husband, James Strong, in S.C., she moved to the home of her brother, Christopher Strong in Dickson Co.TN, where she died and is buried. Because she m. James Strong, a son of James and Elizabeth Strong, she gives the Charles Strong lineage a Strong descendency, even though her only brother who married, Christopher, had no sons. 4.5) Margaret Strong, b. ~1768, Co. Antrim, d. 11 Mar 1828, in SC;
m. John Simonton, b. 1760 in SC? d. 1841, SC.   Some descendants known.

Retrieved December 26, 2005 from http://216.239.51.104/search?q=cache:-kIkVVE2rMAJ:www.geocities.com/Heartland/Prairie/7530/irplaces.html+McKeown+%2B+chester,+South+Carolina+%2B+genealogy&hl=en

Notes for RICHARD GLADNEY III:
GLADNEY CEMETERY ROSTER

* Original Gladneys from Ireland**
Jane Wilson Gladney b. 1711 Ireland d.10-19-1781 SC. age 70yrs "WIDOW JANE "
Mother of Gladneys

Samuel Gladney b.1737 Ireland d. 10-24-1799 SC age 62y* sp Agnes McCreight Gladney b. 1742 Ireland d.After 1801

Joseph Gladney b. 1747 Ireland d. 7/1776 S.C. age 29yrs first in cem. in SC*

Richard Gladney III b. 1741 Ireland d. 8-10-1793 age 53y *sp Jane Strong Gladney b.1757 d.1833 Ffld.SC age 76y

Thomas Gladney b. 1749 Ireland d. 4-22-1820 SC. age 71y *sp.Agnes Martin Gladney b.? d.1827 Ffld SC.

FAIRFIELD COUNTY, SOUTH CAROLINA - Old GLADNEY Cemetery

RICHARD GLADNEY 111 B. 1741 Ireland D. 8-10-1793 age 52 yrs 9mo 3 days Sp/o Jane Strong Gladney
     RICHARD GLADNEY B. 1790 D.8-24-1793 age 3 yrs (same stone as Richard III)

SCGenWeb File Manager: "Victoria Proctor" <vproc@ix.netcom.com>

Contributed to The USGenWeb Archives by:
Bettye Hogue Bond <Retteacher@aol.com>
24 Apr 2000

Old Gladney Cemetery, Winnsboro, Fairfield Co., SC
  Bettye Hogue Bond> President Gladneys In America Family Association
  The following is submitted with my approval.
  Bettye Hogue Bond (4-24-00)
  This cemetery is the property of Descendants of Richard & Jane
  Wilson Gladney. It is maintained by this family Association.
  Any contact may be done through the President:
  Bettye Bond --Retteacher@aol.com
  ****
  Burial: 03 August 1793, Gladney Cemetery, Fairfield County SC
  Military service: Bet. 1776 - 1783, Revolutionary War, Private, SC Militia, Col. Richard Winn's Reg.,
  Captain Edward Martin's Company
  Source: http://familytreemaker.genealogy.com/users/j/o/h/Timothy-R-Johnson/GENE2-0001.html

****

SOUTH CAROLINA
GEORGE the Third, by the Grace of God, of Great Britain, France, and Ireland, KING, Defender of
the Faith, and fo forth, To all to whom thefe Prefents fhall come, Greeting:
KNOW YE, That We, of our fpecial Grace, certain Knowledge and mere Motion, have given and
granted, and by thefe Prefents for Us, our Heirs and Succeffours, DO GIVE AND GRANT unto
Richard Gladney his Heirs and Affigns, a Plantation or Tract of Land containing One hundred acres
situate in Craven County on the Waters of Jackson Creek bounded North West by land laid out to
Hugh McDaniel the other sides vacant land.
And hath fuch Shape, Form and Marks, as appear by a Plat thereof, hereunto annexed: Together with
all Woods, Underwoods, Timber and Timber-Trees, Lakes, Ponds, Fifhings, Waters, Water-Courfes,
Profits, Commodities, Appurtenances and Hereditaments, whatfoever thereunto belonging, or in
anywise appertaining: Together with Priviledge of Hunting, Hawking and Fowling in and upon the
fame, and all Mines and Minerals whatfoever; Saving and Referving, nevertheless, to Us, Our Heirs
and Succeffours, all white Pine Trees, if any there fhould be found growing theron; and alfo Saving
and Referving, nevertheless, to Us, Our Heirs and Succeffours, One Tenth Part of Mines of Gold and
Silver only: TO HAVE AND TO HOLD, the faid Tract of one hundred Acres of Land, and all and
fingular other the Premifes hereby granted unto the faid Richard Gladney his Heirs and Affigns for
ever, in free and common Soccage. The faid Richard Gladney his Heirs and Affigns yielding and
paying therefor, unto Us, Our Heirs and Succeffours, or to Our Receiver-General for the Time being,
or to his Deputy or Deputies for the Time being. Yearly, that is to fay, on the Twenty-fifth Day on
March, in every Year, at the Rate of Three Shillings Sterling, of Four Shillings Proclamation-Money,
for every Hundred Acres, and fo in Proportion, according to the Number of Acres contained herein;
the fame to commence at the Expiration of Two Years from the date hereof. Provided always, and this
prefent Grant is upon Condition, neverthelefs, that the faid Richard Gladney his Heirs or Affigns, fhall and
do Yearly, and every Year after the Date of thefe Prefents, clear and cultivate at the Rate of Three Acres
for every Hundred Acres of Land, and fo in Proportion, according to the Number of Acres herein

contained, and alfo fhall and do enter a Minute or Docket of thefe Our Letters Patent, in the office of Our Auditor-General for the Time being, in Our faid Province, within Six Months from the Date hereof; And upon Condition, that if the said Rent hereby referved, fhall happen to be in Arrear and unpaid for the fpace of Three Years, from the Time it fhall become due, and no Diftress can be found on the faid Lands, Tenements and Hereditaments hereby granted; or if the faid Richard Gladney his Heirs or Assigns, fhall neglect to clear and cultivate Yearly, and every Year, at the Rate of Three Acres for every Hundred Acres of Land, and fo in Proportion, according to the Number of Acres herein contained; or if a Minute or Docket of thefe Our Letters Patent, fhall not be entered in the Office of Our Auditor-General for the Time being, in Our faid Province, within Six Months from the Date hereof, that then, and in any of thefe Cafes, this prefent Grant fhall ceafe, determine, and be utterly void, and the faid Lands, Tenements and Hereditaments hereby granted, and every Part and Parcel thereof fhall revert to Us, our Heirs and Succeffours, as fully and abfoutely, as if the fame had never been granted. GIVEN UNDER THE GREAT SEAL OF OUR FAID PROVINCE: WITNESS The Honorable William Bull Esqr. Lieut. Governour and Commander in Chief in and over Our faid Province of South Carolina, this twelfth Day of July Anno Dom. 1771 in the Eleventh Year of Our Reign. Wm. (L. M. S.) Bull Signed by his Honor the Lieut. _____ Governour inCouncil, J Woodin P. C. C. And hath thereunto a Plat thereof annexed, reprefenting the fame, certified by John Bremar Dy Surveyour-General. 17th February 1771

Certified to be a true and correct copy as taken from and compared with the records in this office in Royal Grant Book 24, page 16. August 21, 1957 Signed O. Frank Thorton, Secretary of State (Copied exactly from the Certified copy)

Source: http://familytreemaker.genealogy.com/users/j/o/h/Timothy-R-Johnson/GENE2-0001.html

Children of JANNET STRONG and RICHARD GLADNEY are:
   i. WILLIAM[6] GLADNEY[44], b. 1781; d. 10 Oct 1803.

      Notes for WILLIAM GLADNEY:
      FAIRFIELD COUNTY, SOUTH CAROLINA - Old GLADNEY Cemetery

      William Gladney b. 1781 d. 10-10-1803 age 22 s/o Richard & Jane Strong Gladney
      inscription faint

SCGenWeb File Manager: "Victoria Proctor" <vproc@ix.netcom.com>

   Contributed to The USGenWeb Archives by:
   Bettye Hogue Bond <Retteacher@aol.com>
   24 Apr 2000

   Old Gladney Cemetery, Winnsboro, Fairfield Co., SC
   Bettye Hogue Bond> President Gladneys In America Family Association
   The following is submitted with my approval.
   Bettye Hogue Bond (4-24-00)
   This cemetery is the property of Descendants of Richard & Jane
   Wilson Gladney. It is maintained by this family Association.
   Any contact may be done through the President:

Bettye Bond --Retteacher@aol.com

More About WILLIAM GLADNEY:
   Cemetery: Old Gladney Cemetery, Fairfield Co., SC

ii. JENET GLADNEY[44], b. 1786; d. 05 Oct 1786.

Notes for JENET GLADNEY:
   Cemetery Listing:

FAIRFIELD COUNTY, SOUTH CAROLINA - Old GLADNEY Cemetery

Jenet Gladney b. 1786 d. 10-5-1786 9 months d/o Richard & Jane Strong Gladney

iii. CHARLES GLADNEY[44], b. 16 Jul 1787; d. 13 Jun 1828; m. NANCY GLADNEY[44].

   Notes for CHARLES GLADNEY:
      Fairfield County, South Carolina -- Old Gladney Cemetery

Charles Gladney b. 7-16-1787 d. 6-13-1828 age 41y s/o Richard & Jane Strong Gladney

   CHARLES GLADNEY B. 7-16-1787 D. 6-13-1828 age 41 yrs s/oRichard III sp-2 Nancy Gladney d/o
   Thomas

   More About CHARLES GLADNEY:
   Cemetery: Old Gladney Cemetery, Fairfield Co., SC

   iv. RICHARD GLADNEY[44], b. 1790; d. 24 Aug 1793.

      Notes for RICHARD GLADNEY:
         FAIRFIELD COUNTY, SOUTH CAROLINA - Old GLADNEY Cemetery

      Richard Gladney b. 1790 d. 8-24-1793 age 3y s/o Richard & Jane Strong Gladney

      More About RICHARD GLADNEY:
      Cemetery: Old Gladney Cemetery, Fairfield Co., SC

      Children of Janet Gaston and Charles Strong:

i.   WILLIAM STRONG d. ca 1776-83 in Revolutionary War.[44]   KIA Revolutionary War, Battle of Fishing Creek, SC.
ii.   CHRISTOPHER STRONG b. 20 Jan 1760, Antrim, Ireland; d. 22 Nov 1850. Charlotte, Dickson Co., Tennessee. He married (1) Frances Elizabeth Dunn 28 Dec 1782 b. 1760, d. 1826; married (2) Rosannah McColloch, 10 Jul 1828.
iii.   LETITIA STRONG, b. 1 Mar 1766, Antrim, Ireland, d. 27 Nov 1837, d. 27 Nov 1837, Charlotte, Dickson Co., Tennessee; resided in South Carolina. She married[44] James Strong. James and Letitia Strong were cousins.[44]

54.   iv.   MARGARET STRONG[44], b. 1768, Fishing Creek, Chester Co., SC; d. 11 Mar 1828, Fairfield Co., SC.
v.   JANET STRONG, b. 1757 in County Antrim, Ireland and d. Sep 1833 in Winnsboro, Fairfield Co., SC. She married[44] Richard Gladney III, son of Richard and Jane Wilson. He was born 1741 in Kinbally, County Antrim, Ireland and d. 10 Aug 1793 in Winnsboro, Fairfield Co., SC.

15. **Martha Gaston** (5.William[3], 3.John[2], 1.Jean[1]), b. 1718 in Ireland, resided (settled) in Chester Co, SC.[14,41] She married[14,41] **Alexander Rosborough**, also known as Alexander Rosbrough.[14]   Alexander and Martha were members of the Associated Reform Presbyterian Church in Richburg, Chester Co., SC. They furnished supplies for the Colonial Army, Revolutionary War (Claim No. 6599-SC Archives).

Alexander and Martha sailed for America on October 8, 1768 with two children: William Gaston Rosborough and Margaret Rosborough. A new baby named Alexander was born at sea on October 12, 1768. They arrived in Charleston, SC on Feb 24, 1759, and settled near Richburg, Chester Co., SC.
Children:
i.   WILLIAM GASTON ROSBOROUGH occupation minister,[14] never married[14.]
ii.   JOSEPH ROSBOROUGH resided (settled, abt 1800) in Indiana.[14]
55.   iii.   ALEXANDER ROSBOROUGH II[14].
56.   iv.   JOHN ROSBOROUGH[14] b. 1776.
v.   (FEMALE) ROSBOROUGH d. aft 1833, resided (settled) in Tennessee.[14] She married J. Bowman, d. bef 1833, occupation minister.

16. **Robert Gaston** (5.William[3], 3.John[2], 1.Jean[1]), b. 1720 in Caranliegh Cloughwater, County Antrim, Ireland,[xlviii[48],xlix[49],44] d. bef May 9 1787 at Lynch's Creek, Lancaster Co, SC,[49] resided at Lynch's Creek, Lancaster Co, SC.[44]

Resided at Lynch's Creek, Lancaster County, SC. Lived previously in Pennsylvania after his emigration to America. Some of his descendants moved to Illinois. Performed patriotic service during the Revolutionary War by supplying beef and a horse for the American cause. Regarding the children of Robert and Margaret Gaston, Burgess' "The Gaston Genealogy," p. 87, makes no mention of Stephen, and provides Thomas only as an unconfirmed possibility. But other sources, particularly Mary Gaston Gee, provide strong confirmation of Thomas Gaston and also include Stephen. Hanna, without identifying a wife, lists only six children for this Robert Gaston, making no mention of either Thomas or Stephen.[49]

He married[l[50]] 26 Aug 1756 in Lancaster Co, PA, **Margaret Logan**.

Notes for ROBERT GASTON:
From the book, Ancestors of Anzi Williford Gaston, Book II, p.12-13:

"Robert Gaston emigrated to Lancaster Co., Pennsylvania before July 10, 1757.

In 1767, he moved to Lynches Creek, 28 miles north of Camden and 2 miles east of Hanging Rock, in

Lancaster County, South Carolina.

Robert Gaston was a Patriot in the American Revolution. He rendered substantial services as shown by documents on file among records of the Historical Commission of South Carolina in Columbia. One of these documents is a certificate dated April 4, 1782, made by Capt. Hugh McClure, to the effect that Mr. Robert Gaston furnished during the Revolution, "one horse for 70 days in Col. Henry Hampton's Light Dragoons. Certified by me, Hugh McClure, Capt." The other document on record is a similar receipt from S. Mathis of the State Commissary for 280 lbs. of beef furnished during the Revolution and certification for the payment of same under date of August 11, 1785.

Robert Gaston's home was destroyed in the war.

There have been at least two entries into the Daughters of the American Revolution on the records of this Robert Gaston. One of these is to be found in the DAR Lineage Book, Vol. 144, p. 224, Record #143,726. The citation with regard to the Revolution records of Robert Gaston is given as follows: "Robert Gaston was a patriot of S.C., who rendered material aid. He was born in Ireland. Died at Lynches Creek, S.C."

Children:
57.   i.   WILLIAM GASTON[44] b. Jul-10-1757, Lancaster Co. PA; d. 12 Jun 1838 in Marion Co., IL.
58.   ii.   THOMAS GASTON b. Jul-18-1759, Lancaster Co., PA; d. 23 Apr 1832 in Spartanburg, SC; he married Sarah Nickels in 1786.
59.   iii.   JAMES GASTON[44] b. Jul-24-1761, Lancaster Co., PA; d. 7 Mar 1840 in Wayne Co., IL; married Catherine Creighton 20 Mar 1783 in Lancaster Co., PA; she was b. 1764.
       iv.   MARGARET GASTON b. 1764,[12] d. Mar- 6-1816.[12,44] She married[44] John McCreary, b. 1754,[12] (son of James McCreary and Margaret Gaston), d. Nov- 4-1833,[12] occupation Member of Congress,[3] military Revolutionary War.[3] John McCreary and Margaret Gaston were said to be second cousins, but they were actually first cousins once removed, as he was the great-grandson of William Gaston (b. 1680 in Ireland) and she was the granddaughter of the same William Gaston. They had two children.[12]

Notes for JOHN MCCREARY: McCREARY, John, a Representative from South Carolina; born near Fishing Creek, about eighteen miles from Chester, S.C., in 1761; received his schooling from private tutors; became a surveyor; also engaged in agricultural pursuits; served in the Revolutionary War; member of the state house of representatives, 1794-1799 and 1802; sheriff of Chester District (now Chester County); elected as a Republican to the Sixteenth Congress (March 4, 1819-March 3, 1821); resumed agricultural pursuits and surveying; died on his plantation in South Carolina November 4, 1833; interment in the Richardson Church Cemetery, Chester County, S.C. --Biographical Directory of the United States Congress, 1774- present Source: http://bioguide.congress.gov/scripts/biodisplay.pl?index=M000383

       v.   JOHN GASTON b. ca 1766 in Pennsylvania,[12] d. 1836 in Shelby Co, IL,[12] resided formerly in Tennessee, resided originally in South Carolina.
       vi.   JOSEPH GASTON b. ca 1770 in South Carolina,[12] d. Sep- 4-1839 in Greene Co, TN,[12,li[51]] never married[12.]
       vii.   ELIZABETH GASTON[lii[52]] b. ca 1772 in South Carolina,[12] d. ca 1810 in Illinois.[12] She married David Fullerton abt 1796, Chester, SC.

Notes for DAVID FULLERTON:
David and Elizabeth Gaston Fullerton moved from South Carolina to Davidson
County, Tennessee, then to Rutherford County, Tennessee, then to Illinois where they
remained until Elizabeth's death. David then moved to Lincoln County, Tennessee,
where he remained until his death in 1835.

       viii. STEPHEN GASTON[liii][53]
       ix.   MARTHA GASTON b. ca 1774 in South Carolina,[12] d. ca 1851 in Pulaski Co, KY.[12] She
married Alexander Isaac Dye.
   60.   x.   HUGH GASTON[44] b. 1776, d. Indiana.

17. **Hugh Gaston** (5.William[3], 3.John[2], 1.Jean[1]), b. 1722 in Ireland, d. Oct-20-1766 in South Carolina,
buried in Burnt Meeting House Cemetery, Wylie's Mill, Chester Co, SC, immigrated abt 1766,[44]
occupation Presbyterian minister.[44]

Author of a religious book called "Gaston's Concordat." <
http://members.tripod.com/RGaston/Concordance.html > Unlike his siblings, Hugh remained in
Ireland and raised his family there, although some of his children and grandchildren eventually
moved to America. He died at the home of his brother John in South Carolina shortly after landing in
America.[44]

     Hugh Gaston: civil war letters, 1862–1875, 2004
                        Collection Information
                        Biographical Sketch
                 Scope and Content Note
                             Contents
                    Cataloging Information
Processed by
Emily Castle
     18 February 2005
Manuscript and Visual Collections Department
     William Henry Smith Memorial Library
     Indiana Historical Society
     450 West Ohio Street
     Indianapolis, IN 46202-3269
www.indianahistory.org
COLLECTION INFORMATION
VOLUME OF
     COLLECTION:
1 manuscript box, 1 artifact
COLLECTION
     DATES:
September 1862–1875, 2004
PROVENANCE:
Donald W. Janes, Breckenridge, Colorado, 3 November 2004
RESTRICTIONS:
None
COPYRIGHT:
REPRODUCTION
     RIGHTS:
Permission to reproduce or publish material in this collection must be obtained from the Indiana
     Historical Society.
ALTERNATE
     FORMATS:

RELATED
    HOLDINGS:
ACCESSION
    NUMBER:
2005.0036
NOTES:
BIOGRAPHICAL SKETCH
Hugh Gaston was born 10 February 1830 to James and Margaret Gaston, three miles south of Newark,
    Indiana. He was one of eleven children in the family. He married Catharine Steel and they had
    nine children. He was a farmer and a resident of Solsberry, in Greene County, Indiana.
In August 1862 Hugh enlisted in the 97th Indiana Infantry Volunteers as a Corporal. He was mustered
    into Company A on 20 August in Terre Haute. They left the state in late September for Memphis,
    where they were assigned to the 17th Army Corps. They moved towards Vicksburg but returned
    to Moscow, Tennessee after the Holly Springs disaster in December 1862. In April 1863 they
    joined Gen. Sherman's army in the rear of Vicksburg, watching the movements of Gen. Johnston's
    army.
After Vicksburg fell the 97th Indiana took part in the siege of Jackson, then moved to Memphis in
    September. On 13 September they were ordered to join Sherman's army near Chattanooga to
    support Rosecrans' army in stopping an invasion of Tennessee. They were engaged in the battle
    of Chattanooga, and then accompanied the army to the relief of Gen. Burnside who was besieged
    by Gen. Longstreet in eastern Tennessee, and returned to Scottsboro, Ala. where they passed the
    winter.
In May 1864, as a part of the 15th Army Corps, they moved into the Atlanta campaign. From 14 May
    through 2 July the 97th Indiana was involved in five skirmishes: Resaca, Dallas, New Hope
    Church, Big Shanty, and Kennesaw Mountain. On 22 July they participated in the battle of Atlanta.
    The 15th corps formed the extreme right on 28 July against which a fierce assault was made and
    repulsed, the 97th being noticeably engaged. On 29 August the 97th Indiana moved with its corps
    on the flanking march around Atlanta, and was engaged in the battle of Jonesboro. On 1
    September it reached Lovejoy Station, and after the evacuation of Atlanta returned to East Point
    and encamped there.
On 12 November the regiment started with the right wing of Sherman's Army on its march to the sea.
    On the 22nd it participated in a fight at Griswoldville, Georgia, was engaged again on 8 December
    at Little Ogeechee River, and entered Savannah on the 21st. The regiment rested a short time in
    Savannah, and then moved with Sherman's army throughout the Carolinas. They moved on to
    Richmond, and finally to Washington, D.C., where they were mustered out 9 June 1865.
Gaston went back to farming after the war, and died 8 November 1913 in Newark at his daughter
    Lillie's home.
Sources:
Materials in collection.
American Civil War Research Database. Duxbury, MA: Historical Data Systems, Inc., 2005 [cited 23
    February 2005]. Available from World Wide Web: (http://civilwardata.com/)
SCOPE AND CONTENT NOTE
The majority of the collection consists of forty letters written by Hugh Gaston to his wife Catharine
    Steel while he was a soldier fighting in the Civil War. There are also a few letters written by
    William Steel, Catharine's brother, to their parents Joseph A. and Mary Steel, a letter written by
    James Henderson Gaston to his brother Hugh, and letters from J.H. Smith to Jane Steel,
    Catharine's sister. The letters tell of camp life, what Gaston's regiment is doing, and sick and
    wounded soldiers. The letters have been arranged in chronological order from the earliest to the
    latest written.
There are a few items from after the war: a contract and mortgage regarding a tract of land in Greene
    County, Indiana; a piece of cloth that the letters were wrapped in; and the genealogy of the
    Gaston family and provenance of the letters.
CONTENTS
CONTAINER
HG to Catharine and children, re: taking care of the house while he's gone, ca. Sept. 1862

Box 1, Folder 1
HG to Catharine and children, partial letter, ca. autumn 1862
Box 1, Folder 2
J.H. Smith to Jane Steel, at a camp near Louisville, Ky., 21 Sept. 1862
Box 1, Folder 3
HG to Catharine, in Louisville, Ky., 22 Oct. 1862
Box 1, Folder 4
HG to Catharine, in Memphis, Tenn., 24 Nov. 1862
Box 1, Folder 5
William Steel to Joseph A. Steel, in LaGrange, Tenn., 22 Feb. 1863
Box 1, Folder 6
William Steel to Joseph A. and Mary Steel, partial letter, n.d.
Box 1, Folder 7
HG to Catharine and children, in Moscow, Tenn.,
    19 Apr. 1863
Box 1, Folder 8
HG to Catharine, re: Generals and what they are doing, in Moscow, Tenn., 15 May 1863
Box 1, Folder 9
HG to Catharine, camp near LaGrange, Tenn.,
    27 May 1863
Box 1, Folder 10
HG to Catharine, re: what's happening at Vicksburg, in LaGrange, Tenn., 31 May 1863
Box 1, Folder 11
HG to Catharine, re: Vicksburg, in Chickasaw Bluffs, Miss., 12 June 1863
Box 1, Folder 12
HG to Catharine, re: battle fought near Vicksburg, in Mississippi, 28 July 1863
Box 1, Folder 13
HG to Catharine and Jane Steel, re: sick and wounded soldiers, in Mississippi, 9 Aug. 1863
Box 1, Folder 14
HG to Catharine and children, Camp Sherman , Miss., 15 Aug. 1863
Box 1, Folder 15
J.H. Smith to Jane Steel, in Mississippi, 24 Aug. 1863
Box 1, Folder 16
HG to Catharine, Camp Sherman , Miss., 2 Sept. 1863
Box 1, Folder 17
HG to Catharine, in Mississippi, 21 Oct. 1863
Box 1, Folder 18
HG to Catharine, in Winchester, Tenn., 11 Nov. 1863
Box 1, Folder 19
HG to Catharine, re: description of Battle of Chattanooga, in Bridge Port, Ala., 20 Dec. 1863
Box 1, Folder 20
HG to Catharine, in Scottsboro, Ala., 15 Jan. 1864
Box 1, Folder 21
HG to Catharine, re: cooking in camp and clothes, in Scottsboro, Ala., 23 Jan. 1864
Box 1, Folder 22
J.H. Gaston to HG, in Scottsboro, Ala.,
    20 Apr. 1864(?)
Box 1, Folder 23
HG to Catharine, in Nashville, Tenn., 15 May 1864
Box 1, Folder 24
HG to Catharine and parents, n.d.
Box 1, Folder 25
HG to Catharine, in Big Shanty Station, Ga.,
    11 June 1864
Box 1, Folder 26

HG to Catharine and children, re: Siege of Atlanta,
    in Big Shanty Station, Ga., 23 June 1864
Box 1, Folder 27
HG to Catharine, in Scottsboro, Ala., 29 June 1864
Box 1, Folder 28
HG to Catharine, re: working in a hospital and hearing canons in Atlanta, in Marietta, Ga., 27
    July 1864
Box 1, Folder 29
HG to Catharine, re: working in a hospital and prisoners of war, in Marietta, Ga., 7 Aug. 1864
Box 1, Folder 30
HG to Catharine, in Atlanta, Ga. , 16 Oct. 1864
Box 1, Folder 31
HG to Catharine, re: sending money home,
    9 Nov. 1864
Box 1, Folder 32
HG to Catharine, re: when the war will end,
    in Beaufort, S.C., 17 Jan. 1865
Box 1, Folder 33
HG to Catharine, re: activities and path of the regiment, in Fayetteville, N.C., 14 Mar. 1865
Box 1, Folder 34
HG to Catharine, in Goldsboro, N.C., 29 Mar. 1865
Box 1, Folder 35
HG to Catharine, partial letter re: Jane's death and possible up-coming campaign, in
    Goldsboro, N.C.,
    6 Apr. 1865
Box 1, Folder 36
HG to Catharine, re: orders to march in the morning, in Goldsboro, N.C., 9 April 1865
Box 1, Folder 37
HG to Catharine and all the girls, re: end of the war and mustering out, in Alexandria, Va., 22
    May 1865
Box 1, Folder 38
HG to Catharine, re: going home, in Indianapolis, Ind., 15 June 1865
Box 1, Folder 39
HG to Catharine, re: going home once he's paid, in Indiana, 16 June 1865
Box 1, Folder 40
Contract and mortgage between Stephen D. McIntire and William Steel for tract of land in
    Green County, 1875
Box 1, Folder 41
Gaston genealogy and succession of provenance of letters, Oct. 2004
Box 1, Folder 42
Cloth which letters were wrapped in, n.d.
Artifacts: R2262

He married[41] **Mary Thomson** (daughter of James Thomson).
        Children:
        i.   WILLIAM GASTON b. Feb- 6-1749 in Ireland, d. bef 1833 [A surgeon on a Guinea
merchant ship, he died on the coast of Africa.], occupation physician.[44]
        ii.   ALECIA GASTON b. Feb-16-1750 in Ireland,[44] d. ca 1825.[44] She married[44] no children
from this marriage, __ Nelson.
61.   iii. MARTHA GASTON b. Jun-11-1752.
        iv.   JAMES GASTON b. Oct- 6-1754 in Ireland,[44] d. bef 1833. Had eight children.[44]
        v.   MARY GASTON b. Dec- 7-1756 in Ireland,[44] d. young.[44]
62.   vi.   ELIZABETH GASTON b. Jun-16-1759.
63.   vii. THOMAS GASTON.

viii. MARY GASTON b. Apr- 4-1763 in Ireland,[44] never married[44.]
ix. HUGH GASTON b. Apr-27-1765 in Ireland.[44]

18. **Alexander Gaston** (5.William[3], 3.John[2], 1.Jean[1]), b. 1727 in Ballymena, County Antrim, Ireland,[liv[54]] d. Aug-20-1781 in New Bern, Craven Co, NC,[14,lv[55]] occupation physician.[41,44]

Received his medical degree from the University of Edinburgh, then joined the Royal British Navy as a surgeon. He was with the fleet in 1762 when Havana was taken by the British in the Seven Years' War between England and France. He was stricken with dysentery and left the navy for the American colonies to regain his health. He settled in New Bern, NC, sometime before May 1764. He was shot to death by Tory Captain John Cox in full view of his wife. He was a Captain in the North Carolina Militia.[lvi[56]]

He married May- -1775,[56,lvii[57]] **Margaret Sharpe**, b. 1755 in Cumberland County, England,[56] (daughter of ___ Sharpe), d. 1811,[lviii[58]] [late in the year], buried in Cedar Grove Cemetery, New Bern, NC.[58]

Margaret: Educated at a Roman Catholic convent in Calais, France. After witnessing her husband's shooting death in 1781, she raised her two young children alone. In 1784, in recognition of her husband's services, the state granted her a tract of land. She never ceased to mourn her husband, wearing black until her death in 1811. A strict mother, she forbid her daughter to look into a mirror or to let her shoulders touch the back of a chair in her mother's presence. Margaret nursed indigent sailors, but never missed her teatime daily at 4pm.
http://www.americanrevolution.org/women45.html

Children:
i. (MALE) GASTON b. bef 1778, d. in infancy.
64. ii. WILLIAM JOSEPH GASTON b. Sep-19-1778.

William J. Gaston (1778-1844)
Born September 19, 1778, in New Bern, to Alexander and Margaret Sharpe Gaston, William J. Gaston later became a lawyer, politician, and jurist.

Gaston was educated first at New Bern Academy, second at Georgetown College (the first student to enroll), and later at the College of New Jersey (also known as Princeton), where he graduated first in his class. He studied law under New Bern attorney François Xavier Martin (1762-1846), and in 1798 passed the bar. He thereafter took over the practice of John Louis Taylor (1769-1829), his brother-in-law, and gained renown in property and criminal law.

A member of the Federalist Party, Gaston advocated a strong federal government. In 1800, he was elected to the North Carolina Senate. He was later elected to the N.C. House and served three terms, one as speaker from 1808 to 1809. In 1812, he was elected again to the Senate. In 1813, he was elected to the U.S. Congress and served there from 1813 to 1817. As a Congressman, he served on the Ways and Means Committee, opposed the War of 1812, and obtained a Congressional charter for Georgetown University.

Gaston returned to practicing law in New Bern, but constituents called him back to the N.C. Senate from 1818 to 1819; in this post, he also served as chairman of the Judiciary Committee. A supporter of President John Quincy Adams (1767-1848), he went against the popular tide in the Tar Heel State and opposed Andrew Jackson (1767-1845) in 1828.

Gaston joined the generally conservative and pro-business Whig Party—which supported banks and internal improvements—when it was formed in the mid-1830s. As president of the Bank of New Bern, Gaston also supported the formation of the Bank of the United States. He likewise authored an address for the North Carolina Internal Improvements Convention of 1833. In his

28

address, he called attention to his state's dearth of colleges, railroads, hospitals, and appropriate care for the handicapped.

In 1833, Gaston was elected by the legislature to the North Carolina Supreme Court. Although a slaveholder, Gaston surprisingly supported abolition efforts. In the case of State v. Negro Will (1834), the Tar Heel jurist ruled that a slave had a right to defend himself if his master attacked him without justification. In the State v. William Manuel (1838), Gaston ruled that free blacks were North Carolina citizens and thereby protected by the state constitution; in 1857, U.S. Supreme Court Justice Benjamin R. Curtis (1809-1874) cited this case in his dissent of the Dred Scott decision.

At the Constitutional Convention of 1835, Gaston called for continuation of free black suffrage and for basing representation in the N.C. House on the federal census. Article Thirty-Two of the old state constitution, however, drew most of his attention. The section stated that North Carolina's elected officials and civil servants be Protestants; a devout Roman Catholic, Gaston persuaded the delegates to change the requirement to Christian. Gaston's prominence and past political service were evidence that the Protestant provision was ignored in practice.

In the 1830s, few Catholics lived in North Carolina, and as a result, not one Catholic cathedral existed in the state. Bishop John England (1786-1842) of Charleston, South Carolina, selected Gaston as one of five Catholics permitted to conduct services at Gaston's home. Gaston and his Catholic neighbors eventually raised enough money in 1841 to construct St. Paul's Church of New Bern, the oldest Roman Catholic Church in the state.

Gaston is perhaps best known today as the author of the state song "The Old North State." In late 1830s, he composed the song to counter the charge that North Carolina was the "Rip Van Winkle State"—backward and unchanging. This motivation is evidenced in the following line: "Tho' the scorner may sneer at and witlings defame her, Still our hearts swell with gladness whenever we name her." In 1927, the state officially adopted Gaston's song.

Many North Carolinians, and Americans from elsewhere, respected, if not adored, Gaston. John Marshall (1755-1835) once said that he would retire if he knew Gaston would replace him as U.S. Supreme Court Justice. In 1840, the state legislative leaders proposed Gaston as U.S. Senator, but he declined the honor. He likewise turned down an offer to be attorney general for President William Henry Harrison (1773-1841). Later generations also thought highly of Gaston. For example, many North Carolina places are named for him: Gaston County, the city of Gastonia, and Lake Gaston, to name three.

Gaston was married three times and fathered one son and four daughters. He died in his Raleigh office on January 23, 1844. Initially buried in Raleigh, his remains were moved to Cedar Grove Cemetery in New Bern. These were his last words: "We must believe there is a God—All wise and All mighty."

Law Office, Bern, NC

Sources:

Charles H. Bowman, Jr., "William Joseph Gaston," *Dictionary of North Carolina Biography* (Chapel Hill, 1986), v. 2; R. D. W. Connor, *William Gaston: A Southern Federalist of the Old School and His Yankee Friends, 1778-1844* (Worcester, 1934); "William Gaston, 1778-1844: Extended Bibliography" *Biographical Directory of the United States Congress* http://bioguide.congress.gov/scripts/%20bibdisplay.pl?index=G000096 (accessed February 28, 2006); Calvin Jarrett, "Judge William Gaston: Catholic Crusader," *Liberty* (May-June 1968); John L. Sanders, *William Gaston as a Public Man* (Chapel Hill, 1997); J. H. Schauinger, *William Gaston: Carolinian* (Milwaukee, 1949); Robert Strange, *Life and Character of Hon. Wm. Gaston* (Fayetteville, 1844).

By Ronnie W. Faulkner, Campbell University

See Also:
Family of Randall & Patricia Vickers, Ancestry.com, 2007.
Audley D. Gaston (David Gaston), Ancestry.com, 2003.
Related Categories: Political History, Political Documents
  Related Encyclopedia Entries: North Carolina Railroad, Thomas H. Hall (1773-1853), John W. Ellis (1820-1862), Morehead City, Naval Stores, Aaron McDuffie Moore (1863-1923), Charles Manly (1795-1871), David Settle Reid (1813-1891), James Iredell, Jr. (1788-1853), Tyrrell County (1729), Ratification Debates, David Lowry Swain (1801-1868)
  Related Commentary: Nathaniel Macon: American Patriot and Defender of Liberty

  Timeline: 1776-1835 , 1836-1865
  Region: Statewide , Coastal Plain
A member of the Federalist Party, William Gaston advocated a strong federal government and served in the North Carolina House and Senate. Image courtesy of the North Carolina Office of Archives and History, Raleigh, NC.

In the early 1800s, Gaston practiced law in New Bern. His law office, circa 1820, still stands. Image courtesy of Richard Carney.

With other famous North Carolinians, William Gaston is buried at the Cedar Grove Cemetary in New Bern. Image courtesy of Richard Carney.

© 2011 John Locke Foundation | 200 West Morgan St., Raleigh, NC 27601, Voice: (919) 828-3876
  Website design & development by DesignHammer Media Group, LLC. Building Smarter Websites.

     65.   iii.   JANE GASTON b. ca 1780.

19. **Elizabeth Gaston** (5.William[3], 3.John[2], 1.Jean[1]), b. 1727/30 in Ireland,[44] resided in Chester Co, SC.[41,14] She married[44] **John Knox**.
            Children:
          i.   WILLIAM KNOX occupation minister.[44]
     66.   ii.   JAMES KNOX[44].

           iii.   JOHN KNOX.

   67.   iv.   HUGH KNOX[44].

           v.   SARAH KNOX d. aft 1833. She married[44] John Johnston.

20. **William Gaston** (5.William[3], 3.John[2], 1.Jean[1]), b. 1735 in Ireland,[lix[59]] d. 1790 in Kell's Ford, Chester Co, SC,[44,41] cause of death drowned.[44]

Served as captain of a volunteer company, 1775, between Broad and Catawba rivers in South Carolina.[lx[60]]

He married[41] aft 1775,[44] **Jane Harbison**.

Jane: Sister of James Harbison.

           Children:

   68.   i.   HUGH GASTON[44].

   69.   ii.   WILLIAM GASTON[44].

21. **John Gaston, Sr.** (6.Hugh[3], 3.John[2], 1.Jean[1]), b. ca 1719,[lxi[61]] d. aft 1793,[15] resided (settled) in Monmouth Co, NJ, occupation gristmill owner.[lxii[62]]

Settled in Upper Freehold (now Millstone) Twp, Monmouth Co, NJ, about 1741, where in 1758 he was owner of a grist and fulling mill and a member of Dr. William Tennent's Freehold Presbyterian congregation. He was a subscriber in 1758 to the fund for a parsonage for Allentown Church. He deeded a tract of land to his son Hugh in 1793.[19,15]

He married[lxiii[63]] ca 1738,[lxiv[64]] **Jane Hannah Robbins**,[64,23] b. ca 1718 in Bedminster Twp, Somerset Co, NJ.[64]

           Children:

           i.   MARY GASTON b. 1739, baptized Dec- 9-1739 in Old Tennent Church, Monmouth Co, NJ,[lxv[65],19,15] d. in infancy.[15]

   70.   ii.   JAMES GASTON b. 1742.

           iii.   HUGH GASTON b. 1744, baptized Jul-15-1744 in Old Tennent Church, Monmouth Co, NJ,[65,19] d. aft 1801, resided until aft 1801 in Millstone Twp, Monmouth Co, NJ.[15,19]

           iv.   MARY (TWIN) GASTON b. 1747 in New Jersey, baptized Mar- 8-1747 in Old Tennent Church, Monmouth Co, NJ.[65,19,15] She married William Johnson.

           v.   ELIZABETH (TWIN) GASTON b. 1747, baptized Mar- 8-1747 in Old Tennent Church, Monmouth Co, NJ.[65,19,15]

   71.   vi.   DANIEL GASTON b. Jan- 9-1748.

           vii.   CATHARINE GASTON b. 1751, baptized Jun- 2-1751 in Old Tennent Church, Monmouth Co, NJ.[65,22]

   72.   viii. JOHN GASTON, JR. b. Sep-16-1752.

           ix.   WILLIAM GASTON b. 1756 in New Jersey, baptized Jul-18-1756 in Old Tennent Church, Monmouth Co, NJ,[65,22] occupation Soldier in Revolution.

   73.   x.   JANE GASTON b. Dec-11-1758.

22. **William Gaston** (6.Hugh[3], 3.John[2], 1.Jean[1]), b. ca 1720,[61] d. Dec- -1755 in Pennsylvania.[14,15]

Took up land in (Upper) Mount Bethel Township, Bucks (now Northampton) Co, PA, on February 20, 1751. He was killed by Indians in December 1755.[14,15]

He married **Unknown**, d. bef Sep 1762.[14,15]

Unknown: Identified by one researcher (Sharon Wassom, Rt 1, Box 87, Alexandria, NE 68303) as Elizabeth Simanton.

Children:
74.   i.   JOHN GASTON, JR. b. May- -1740.
75.   ii.   WILLIAM GASTON b. ca 1742.
       iii.   HUGH GASTON b. ca 1745,[15] d. Feb- -1812 in Shenango Twp, Beaver (now Lawrence) Co, PA,[12] resided 1795 in Allegheny Co, PA,[lxvi[66],15] resided formerly in Mt. Bethel Twp, Northampton Co, PA,[15] military 1st Lt, 3rd Co, 6th Bn, Northampton Co (PA) Militia (Revolutionary War).[15] He married[lxvii[67]] Jane __.
       iv.   JENNET GASTON, also known as Jane Gaston, b. ca 1748.[15] She married[15,66] Moses Phenix, d. bef 1830 in Beaver Co, PA.[67]
76.   v.   JAMES GASTON b. ca 1750.

23.   **Joseph Gaston** (6.Hugh[3], 3.John[2], 1.Jean[1]), b. ca 1725,[67] d. 1775 in Mt. Bethel Twp, Northampton Co, PA.[66]

Took up land in Mt. Bethel Twp, Northampton Co, PA, in Jan 1765. Served as a King's Justice from 1766 to 1775. Listed in "The DAR Patriot Index" as having performed patriotic service in the time leading up to the War of Independence.[15,66]

He married **Isabel Simonton**, d. aft 1792.

Isabel: Some doubt exists about Isabel's maiden name. She was probably a sister of Robert Simonton, who settled in Bedminster Twp, Somerset Co, NJ, before 1754, whose land at that date adjoined the land of Hugh Gaston, and who moved to Pennsylvania and died in Mount Bethel Twp, Northampton Co, in 1786, leaving children James, Ephraim, Robert, Peter, Benjamin, Margaret Nelson, Jean Britton, and Esther Ross, of whom James & Peter settled in Washington Co, PA. One research team (Gene & Norma Harrington Maas at http://www.genemaas.net/Gaston_roots.htm) report her name as Isabel Simonton Galbraith.[lxviii[68]]

       Children:
77.   i.   HUGH GASTON[66] b. Jan-18-1764.
       ii.   ELIZABETH GASTON.
78.   iii.   JAMES GASTON[66] b. ca 1767.
       iv.   JOHN GASTON resided (settled) in Indiana,[lxix[69]] [probably].
79.   v.   ALEXANDER GASTON[66] b. Jul-22-1769.

24.   **Hugh Gaston, Jr.** (6.Hugh[3], 3.John[2], 1.Jean[1]), b. 1734,[lxx[70],lxxi[71],19] d. Jun-25-1808 in New Jersey,[17,15,19] buried in Lamington Presb Church Cem, Somerset Co, NJ,[17] resided in Peapack, Somerset Co, NJ,[15] resided in Bedminster Twp, Somerset Co, NJ,[19] occupation farmer & lay judge (appointed 1782).[15]

By some accounts, Hugh Gaston Jr. was the grandson of Hugh Gaston (b. 1687), but he was probably his son. Of Hugh Gaston Jr.'s four children, two were borne by his first wife (Mary Sloan), none by his second wife (Mary Adams), and two by his third wife (Mary Kirkpatrick).[15,19]

He married (1) **Mary Sloan**, b. 1742,[19,lxxii[72]] (daughter of William Sloan and Mary Shields), d. Aug-14-1766 in New Jersey,[17] [Anna Reger Gaston reports death date as April 14 1766, rather than August.], buried in Lamington Presb Church Cem, Somerset Co, NJ.[17]

He married[19] (2) **Mary Adams**, b. 1741,[19] (daughter of John Adams and Agnes __), d. Feb-16-1795 in New Jersey,[17] [The listing in the History of the Old Tennent Church gives year of death as 1793, and Hanna's "Ohio Valley Genealogies," p. 45, also states 1793. But date on headstone clearly reads Feb 16 1795.], buried in Lamington Presb Church Cem, Somerset Co, NJ.[17]

He married[19] (3) **Mary "Polly" Kirkpatrick**, also known as Polly Kirkpatrick,[lxxiii][73] b. Nov-23-1761 in Bedminster Twp, Somerset Co, NJ,[19,15] (daughter of David Kirkpatrick and Mary McEowen), d. Jul-1-1842,[19,15] resided in Peapack, Somerset Co, NJ.[73]

> Children by Mary Sloan:
> i. WILLIAM GASTON b. Apr- 2-1763,[15,lxxiv][74] [Hanna, p. 45, reports birth date as Apr 12 1763, but age on headstone calculates to a birth date of Apr 2 1763.], d. Dec-15-1763 in New Jersey,[15,19] buried in Lamington Presb Church Cem, Somerset Co, NJ.[lxxv][75]
> ii. JOSEPH GASTON b. Dec-18-1765,[15,19] d. Aug-14-1777 in New Jersey,[15,19] buried in Lamington Presb Church Cem, Somerset Co, NJ.[lxxvi][76]
> Children by Mary "Polly" Kirkpatrick:
> 80. iii. SAMUEL KIRKPATRICK GASTON b. 1795.
> iv. JOHN GASTON b. Jul- 4-1796,[lxxvii][77] d. Feb-17-1800 in New Jersey,[17,19] buried in Lamington Presb Church Cem, Somerset Co, NJ.[lxxviii][78]

25. **Elizabeth Gaston** (6.Hugh[3], 3.John[2], 1.Jean[1]), b. 1737.[19,15]

Known to be a sister of Hugh Gaston Jr. (b. 1734) and would therefore have been the daughter of Hugh Gaston (b. 1687), although there is a possibility that Hugh Gaston (b. 1687) was their grandfather. One source lists her date of birth as 1730.

She married[19,15] **Thomas Kirkpatrick**, resided (settled) in Bernards Twp, Somerset Co, NJ,[19,15] [near Liberty Corners].

Thomas: Connection, if any, between the families of David Kirkpatrick and Thomas Kirkpatrick, both of Somerset County NJ, is not known.[lxxix][79]

> Children:
> 81. i. JOHN KIRKPATRICK[19].
> ii. JANE KIRKPATRICK d. aged abt 60,[19,15,lxxx][80] never married[19,15,80].

26. **William Cauldwell** (7.Mary[3], 3.John[2], 1.Jean[1]), b. ca 1726 in Ireland,[24] d. 1799 in New Jersey,[lxxxi][81] immigrated 1732.[25]

William and Elizabeth Thompson Cauldwell had a total of ten children.

He married in New Jersey,[24] **Elizabeth Thompson**, d. Mar-20-1794.[24]
> Children:
> i. JOHN CAULDWELL. He married[24] Hannah Rutan (daughter of Abrahm Rutan).

27. **Margaret Gaston** (8.Joseph[3], 3.John[2], 1.Jean[1]), b. 1728 in Bernards Twp, Somerset Co, NJ,[27] resided (settled) in Fayette Co, PA.[22]

Moved with husband from Somerset Co, NJ, to Redstone, Fayette Co, PA.

She married[22] **Andrew Kirkpatrick** (son of Alexander Kirkpatrick and Elizabeth __), resided (settled) in Fayette Co, PA,[22] resided formerly in Bernards Twp, Somerset Co, NJ.[22]

Andrew: Came to America in 1736. Settled in Bernard Township, Somerset County, NJ. Moved to Redstone, Fayette Co. Pa. in 1758.

> Children:
> i. ALEXANDER KIRKPATRICK.
> ii. JENNET KIRKPATRICK. She married[15,22] Abner Johnson (son of Samuel Johnson).

        iii.   ELIZABETH KIRKPATRICK d. Jun-24-1803.[15] She married[15,22] Hugh Bartley, also known as Hugh Barclay,[22] resided in Bedminster Twp, Somerset Co, NJ,[15] occupation farmer.[15]

        iv.   MARGARET KIRKPATRICK. She married[15,22] Joseph McMartin.

82.   v.   MARY KIRKPATRICK[22] b. ca 1755.

83.   vi.   SARAH KIRKPATRICK[22].

        vii. ANNE KIRKPATRICK.

        viii. HANNAH KIRKPATRICK.

28. **John Gaston** (8.Joseph[3], 3.John[2], 1.Jean[1]), b. Nov-10-1730 in Bernards Twp, Somerset Co, NJ,[22,15] d. Oct- 3-1776 in Lamington, Somerset Co, NJ,[22,15] buried in Lamington Presb Church Cem, Somerset Co, NJ,[17] occupation farmer & merchant.

Provided non-military patriotic support during the American Revolutionary War. Was a farmer and active merchant in Somerset County, and was also active in building bridges in his area. From 1772 to 1776, John Gaston was the Clerk of the Board of Freeholders. He was also a member of the Lamington Presbyterian Church.[lxxxii[82]]

He married (1) Jun-27-1758,[22,15] **Elizabeth Ker** (daughter of William Ker and Catherine __), baptized Mar-19-1738 in Old Tennent Church, Monmouth Co, NJ,[lxxxiii[83]] [Hanna and Anna Reger Gaston report this as the date of birth, rather than baptism.], d. May- 6-1765 in New Jersey,[22,15] buried in Lamington Presb Church Cem, Somerset Co, NJ.[17] He married[22] (2) **Sarah Ogden** (daughter of Stephen Ogden and Elizabeth Whitaker).

        Children by Elizabeth Ker:

        i.   CATHERINE GASTON b. May-12-1759,[22] d. Apr-14-1762.[22]

84.   ii.   WILLIAM GASTON[22] b. Jan-13-1761.

85.   iii. JOSEPH GASTON[22] b. May- 2-1763.

        Children by Sarah Ogden:

        iv.   JOHN GASTON resided (settled) in Lansingburg (Troy), Rensselaer Co, NY.[22] He married[22] __ Lansing.

86.   v.   STEPHEN GASTON[22] b. Jul-20-1769.

        vi.   ELIZABETH GASTON d. Sep- 5-1851, resided (settled) in Hamilton Co, OH,[22] [Colerain]. She married[22] Elias Hedges.

87.   vii. ISAAC GASTON[22] b. Mar-25-1773.

88.   viii. MARGARET GASTON[22].

29. **Robert Gaston** (8.Joseph[3], 3.John[2], 1.Jean[1]), b. Jan-28-1732 in Bernards Twp, Somerset Co, NJ,[lxxxiv[84]] [Jan 23 1732 has also been reported.], d. Sep- 2-1793 in Torbet Twp, Northumberland Co, PA,[28] buried in Warrior Run Church Cem, Delaware Twp, Northumberland Co, PA,[28] military Captain, Revolutionary War.

Robert and Rosanna Cooper Gaston resided in Bernard Township, Somerset County, NJ, until about 1770, then in Pequannock Twp, Morris Co, from before 1771 to 1777, returning then to Bedminster Twp, Somerset Co, and then moving to Northumberland Co in about May 1792. He served in the American Revolution as Captain and Lieutenant Colonel of the New Jersey Militia, and as Captain in the Continental Line. He also served as a member of the Committee of Safety for Morris Co, NJ.[28]

He married May-15-1762 in Bedminster Twp, Somerset Co, NJ,[28] **Rosanna Cooper**, b. Mar-23-1742,[84] (daughter of Daniel Cooper and Grace Runyon), d. Jan-14-1817.[84]

        Children:

89.   i.   GRACE GASTON[69] b. Nov-25-1764.

90.   ii.   JOSEPH GASTON[28] b. Nov-19-1766.

91.   iii. MARGARET GASTON[28] b. Dec-17-1768.

        iv.   MARY GASTON b. Feb-12-1770.[28]

        v.   DANIEL GASTON b. Apr- 5-1773.[28]

vi.   ANNE GASTON b. Mar-25-1774.[28]
vii. GEORGE WASHINGTON GASTON b. Apr- 2-1777.[28]
viii. JOHN GASTON b. Feb- 8-1780.[28]

30. **Joseph Gaston** (8.Joseph[3], 3.John[2], 1.Jean[1]), b. Nov-10-1738 in Bernards Twp, Somerset Co, NJ,[27] d. Oct-24-1804 in Hardwick Twp, Sussex Co, NJ,[lxxxv][85] occupation farmer, grist mill owner.

During Revolutionary War, served as Paymaster of the NJ Militia from Somerset and Sussex Counties of New Jersey. He settled in Hardwick Township of Sussex County in about 1783, and had a family. He lived in the village of Huntsville where he owned a grist mill and farm that was five miles from the mill. After Joseph's death, his son-in-law, Dr. Elijah Everitt owned the mill property, and his other son-in-law, Rev. John Boyd, owned the Gaston homestead farm. From 1798-1800, Joseph was an elected member of the General Assembly of the NJ Legislature from Sussex County.

He married[28] Nov- 2-1772 in Somerset Co, NJ,[27] **Margaret Linn**, b. 1751,[lxxxvi][86] (daughter of Joseph Linn and Martha Kirkpatrick), d. Sep-19-1822.
Children:
92.   i.   MARTHA GASTON b. 1774.
        ii.   MARGARET GASTON[27] b. 1776.[27] She married Apr-10-1806,[27] John Boyd, b. in Pennsylvania,[lxxxvii][87] (son of William Boyd and Catherine __), occupation minister. Possibly had one daughter, Margaret Boyd.[15]

31. **Ann Gaston**[27] (8.Joseph[3], 3.John[2], 1.Jean[1]), b. in Bernards Twp, Somerset Co, NJ, d. bef 1777.[15] She married[28] **David Chambers**.
Children:
        i.   JOSEPH CHAMBERS.
        ii.   WILLIAM CHAMBERS.
        iii. JOHN CHAMBERS.

32. **Margaret Gaston** (9.John[3], 3.John[2], 1.Jean[1]), b. Oct-19-1738 in Voluntown, New London Co, CT,[29] [Hanna (p. 47) reports birth on unspecified date in 1734.], d. Feb- 5-1811 in Middlefield, Hampshire Co, MA,[8] [But "Colonial Families of the United States," Vol III, p. 175, reports death on unspecified date in 1810.]. She married[28] **James Dickson**, b. 1728,[28] d. 1815.[28]

James: Name appears as "Dixon" in Colonial Families of the United States, Vol III, p. 175.

Children:
        i.   JAMES DICKSON.
        ii.   JOHN DICKSON.
        iii. ALEXANDER DICKSON.
        iv.   JOSEPH DICKSON.
        v.   NANCY DICKSON. She married[28] William Church.
93.   vi.   PHEBE DICKSON[28].

33. **John Gaston** (9.John[3], 3.John[2], 1.Jean[1]), b. Jan-10-1750 in Voluntown, New London Co, CT,[27] d. Oct-26-1805 in Voluntown, New London Co, CT,[28] [Place of death given as Sterling, Connecticut, in "Colonial Families of the United States," Vol III, p. 175.], occupation Connecticut Legislature.[28,lxxxviii][88] He married Dec-20-1770,[27,28] **Ruth Miller**, b. Nov-16-1750 in Plainfield, Windham Co, CT,[27,28] (daughter of Alexander Miller and Esther Knight), d. May-10-1825 in Killingly, Windham Co, CT.[28,7]
Children:
94.   i.   ALEXANDER GASTON b. Aug- 2-1772.
        ii.   MARGARET GASTON b. Dec-13-1781 in Voluntown, New London Co, CT,[27,33] d. Jul-22-1785 in Sterling, Windham Co, CT.[27]

34. **John Gaston** (10.Alexander[3], 3.John[2], 1.Jean[1]), b. Mar- 3-1746,[33] d. Sep- 6-1834 in Stockbridge, Berkshire Co, MA,[33] [But Jane Farrell Burgess, in "The Gaston Genealogy", p. 46, reports his death as Sep 9 1834 in Richmond, Mass.].

Hanna's "Ohio Valley Genealogies," p. 48, contains an apparent misprint, in that it shows a John Gaston (b. 1746) as a son of Alexander (b. 1754), with that John in turn having a son John (b. 1786). Since this is an absolute impossibility, we conclude that the John (b. 1746) was actually meant to be a son of Alexander (b. 1714), which Hanna also shows. Burgess' "The Gaston Genealogy," p. 44, shows a John Gaston born 1/8/1786 to a John Gaston. Taking all this into account, we believe the lineage is correct as we present it. Burgess also shows other children born to a John Gaston in Berkshire Co, MA, in the same general time frame, but there is insufficient evidence to conclude (particularly since we don't know his wife's name) that that was the same John Gaston (b. 1746). Those children and their parents as listed were: Mary, b. 10/20/1774, dau of John & Miriam Gaston (prob the same as Mary, baptized 2/27/1786, dau of John Ghaston); Eunice, b. 11/16/1777, dau of John & Miriam Gaston (prob the same as Eunice, baptized 12/1/1785, dau of John Ghaston); Elizabeth, baptized 12/1/1785, dau of John Ghaston (poss the same as Elizabeth Gaston, b. 4/10/1784, parents not listed); Rachel, baptized 12/1/1785, dau of John Ghaston (poss the same as Rachel Gaston, b. 5/23/1780, parents not listed); Achsah, baptized 12/1/1785, dau of John Ghaston (poss the same as Achsa Gaston, b. 4/6/1782, parents not listed) (another entry shows Achsah Gaston, granddaughter of Dea. John Gaston, adopted by him and his wife and baptized on 7/21/1811); Harvey, b. 1/4/1788, son of John Ghaston; Joseph, b. 11/15/1789, son of John Ghaston; Harriot, b. 7/15/1792, dau of John Ghaston; and Abi, b. 10/16/1794, dau of John Ghaston.[lxxxix[89],33]

He married 1773,[36] **Miriam Northup**.
> Children:
> i. JOHN GASTON b. Jan- 8-1786 in Berkshire Co, MA,[xc[90]] d. Mar- -1873 in Massachusetts.[33]

35. **Robert Gaston** (10.Alexander[3], 3.John[2], 1.Jean[1]), b. Dec-28-1747,[33] d. Mar- 6-1829.[34] He married[34] **Rozanna (Rhoda) Tilden**, b. Jan-28-1732,[34] d. Sep- 2-1793.[34]
> Children:
> 95. i. ELIJAH L. GASTON b. Jun- 9-1793.

36. **Janet A. "Jennie" Gaston** (10.Alexander[3], 3.John[2], 1.Jean[1]), b. Dec-27-1750.[33]

Identified by Hanna in "Ohio Valley Genealogies" as Janet A. Gaston, daughter of Alexander Gaston & Mary "Molly" Wilson, but by George M. Kasson in "Genealogy of a Part of the Kasson Family in the United States and Ireland" as Jennie Gaston, parents not identified.

She married[33,xci[91]] **Robert Kasson**, b. 1741,[91] (son of William Kasson and Elizabeth McKay), d. Sep-25-1826, resided in Broadalbin, Fulton Co, NY,[91] occupation wheelwright.[91]

Robert: Robert Kasson was a soldier in the French and Revolutionary wars. But in the latter war, he objected to the calling in of French aid, because they were Roman Catholics. He ultimately left the service, for which he was court-martialed, but later reprieved.[91]

> Children:
> 96. i. ROBERT KASSON, JR. b. Apr-10-1773.
> 97. ii. WILLIAM KASSON b. 1775.
> 98. iii. HARVEY KASSON b. Dec- 4-1781.
> iv. ANNA KASSON. She married[xcii[92]] Jeremiah Ferguson.
> v. PHEBE KASSON. She married[92] Henry Ferguson.
> vi. OLIVE KASSON. She married[92] Deacon Brown.
> vii. POLLY KASSON. She married[92] __ Bailey, resided in Adams, Jefferson Co, NY.[92]
> 99. viii. ALEXANDER KASSON b. Apr- -1792.

37. **Alexander Gaston** (10.Alexander[3], 3.John[2], 1.Jean[1]), b. Oct-28-1754 in Richmond, Berkshire Co, MA,[8,36] d. Jul-12-1823 in Richmond, Berkshire Co, MA,[xciii][93] buried in Cone Road Cemetery, Richmond, MA.[36]

Although identified by some sources as a "Captain," one source in particular (Bob Gaston, Longview, WA, in "Gaston Crier" of Nov 1997) specifies that this Alexander Gaston enlisted as a Private in Capt Aaron Rowley's company in John Brown's detachment of the Berkshire County militia on June 30 1777, and that he was discharged 27 days later. // In addition to the ten children given by other sources, Robert "Bob" Gaston of Longview WA, a direct descendant, also identifies an eleventh, Albert Gaston. Since this is Bob Gaston's direct line, we include it here.

He married Feb-12-1782,[xciv][94] **Huldah Norton**, b. Jun- 9-1765,[xcv][95] d. Apr-26-1832.[95]
        Children:
100. i.   ALEXANDER GASTON b. Oct-14-1783.
      ii.   ELCY (ELSIE) GASTON b. Jan-22-1785 in Richmond, Berkshire Co, MA,[90] d. Nov-29-1810.[36]

        The same date, Nov 29 1810, is given by Jane Farrell Burgess for Elcy Gaston's marriage, and by Bob Gaston of Longview WA for her death. Both citations appear credible in their context and are presumed correct.

        She married Nov-29-1810 in Richmond, Berkshire Co, MA,[xcvi][96] Jacob Chamberlain.
101. iii. HEMAN GASTON b. Sep-13-1786.
      iv. AMOS GASTON b. Oct- 6-1788 in Richmond, Berkshire Co, MA,[90] d. Aug-24-1806.[36]
      v.   SARAH GASTON b. Dec- 1-1790 in Richmond, Berkshire Co, MA.[89]
      vi. CATHERINE "CATY" GASTON b. Apr- 5-1798 in Richmond, Berkshire Co, MA,[90] baptized Jun-17-1804 in Richmond, Berkshire Co, MA.[90]
      vii. SAMUEL NORTON GASTON b. Feb- 4-1800 in Richmond, Berkshire Co, MA,[89] baptized Jun-17-1804 in Richmond, Berkshire Co, MA,[89] d. Aug-14-1823.[36]
      viii. HENRY GASTON b. Mar-21-1802 in Richmond, Berkshire Co, MA,[89] baptized Jun-17-1804 in Richmond, Berkshire Co, MA.[89] He married Nov- 9-1824 in Richmond, Berkshire Co, MA,[xcvii][97] Mercy Stevens.
      ix. MARIA GASTON b. Apr- 5-1804 in Richmond, Berkshire Co, MA,[89] d. Aug-18-1839.[36] She married[36] __ Worden.
      x.   ALBERT GASTON b. Dec- 5-1805 in Berkshire Co, MA.[36]
      xi. GROVE NELSON GASTON b. Feb- 3-1811 in Berkshire Co, MA,[36] baptized May-26-1811 in Richmond, Berkshire Co, MA,[89] d. Apr- 1-1855 in Berkshire Co, MA,[36] buried in Richmond, Berkshire Co, MA.[36] He married (1) Jun- 3-1840 in Richmond, Berkshire Co, MA,[xcviii][98] Emeline M. Salmon (daughter of Luther Salmon and Unknown), d. Jun-28-1853.[36] He married[36] (2) Jane Salmon (daughter of Luther Salmon and Unknown), d. Jul- 3-1863.[36]

38. **David Gaston** (10.Alexander[3], 3.John[2], 1.Jean[1]), b. Jan-13-1757 in Voluntown, New London Co, CT,[8] [But direct descendants Audley DeForest Gaston & sister Judy Gaston Woodard report birth as Feb 13 1757 in Voluntown CT.], d. Aug-29-1830 in New York.[xcix][99] He married[34] **Eunice Loomis**, b. Oct-23-1761 in Aurelius, NY,[99] d. Jul-22-1813 in Richmond, Berkshire Co, MA.[99]
        Children:
102. i.   EBENEZER GASTON b. Apr- 6-1782.
      ii.   MARGARETT GASTON b. Sep- 2-1783,[34] d. Mar- 8-1807.[34]
      iii. DAVID GASTON, JR. b. Jun-19-1785, d. Oct- 4-1786.[34]
      iv. JAMES GASTON b. Aug-14-1787.[34]
      v.   NANCY GASTON b. Mar-26-1792.[34]
      vi. WILLIAM GASTON b. Mar- 8-1794.[34]
      vii. IRA GASTON b. Oct- 3-1796.[34]
      viii. LYDIA GASTON b. Jan-22-1802.[34]

ix.   EUNICE GASTON b. Jul- 2-1805,[34] d. Jul- 9-1805.[34]
x.   MARGARET GASTON b. 1807,[34] d. Mar- 3-1807.[34]

Generation Five

39. **Joseph Gaston** (11.Alexander[4], 4.(Male)[3], 2.William[2], 1.Jean[1]), b. Oct- 8-1738 in Ireland,[c[100]] d. Apr-21-1823,[45,ci[101]] buried in Fishing Creek Presb Church Cem, Chester Co, SC,[17,cii[102],ciii[103],45].

Joseph Gaston emigrated to South Carolina with two brothers, Robert and Matthew, and a sister, Jane Gaston Walker, leaving a brother Alexander in Ireland. Joseph Gaston and Martha Gaston were third cousins, as both were great-great-grandchildren of the first John (Jean) Gaston (b. ca 1600 in France).

Notes for JOSEPH GASTON:
JOSEPH5 GASTON (ALEXANDER4, ALEXANDER3, WILLIAM2, JEAN BAPTISTE1)1,2,3,4,5
was born 1739 in County Antrim, Ireland, and died Apr 21, 1823 in Fishing Creek, Chester County, South Carolina. He married MARTHA GASTON6, 7 Abt. 1762 in Chester County, South Carolina, daughter of JOHN GASTON and ESTHER WAUGH.
She was born Jun 11, 1741 in Ireland or South Carolina or Lancaster County, Pennsylvania, and died Mar 04, 1826 in Chester County, South Carolina.

Notes for JOSEPH GASTON:
Joseph is his wife's second cousin once removed. He suffered all the horrors of a famine on board ship while crossing the Atlantic. Three brothers, Joseph, Robert and Matthew Gaston, said to be great grandsons of the first Irish William, emigrated to South Carolina with their sister, Jane Gaston Walker, leaving a fourth brother, Alexander, in Ireland, who was born about 1750 and died about 1840. Of these, Joseph married Martha Gaston, daughter of Justice John Gaston, above.

He was a member of the Fishing Creek Presbyterian Church of Chester County, South Carolina. Joseph and Martha were visited by their pastor, Reverend John Simpson in 1775 or 1776.

A slave owner.
Burial: 1823, Fishing Creek Presbyterian Church Cemetery, Chester County, South Carolina Census 1: 1790, Chester County, South Carolina Census 2: 1800, Chester County, South Carolina Census 3: 1810, Chester County, South Carolina
Religion: Member of the Fishing Creek Presbyterian Church of Chester County, South Carolina

State of South Carolina
Chester District

In the name of God Amen

I John Gaston Senr being of sound mind and disposing memory: Calling to mind the uncertainty of life and the certainty of death: do make and ordain this my last will and testament in manner and form following Viz

1st My will and desire is that my body be decently interred according to the directions of my Executors herein after mentioned

14th I give and bequeath unto my daughter _____ Gaston and to my sons John David Robert & Samuel S Gaston All my Household and Kitchen Furniture and all my stock of every kind all my corn fodder wheat oats Bacon Farming utensils waggon & harness and all my interest in a Blacksmith Shop for their own special use and purposes after my debts are paid — share and share alike

15th I wish it to be understood that my sons John David Robert & Samuel S Gaston is to have an interest in the Gin House Gin head Thrasher Fan and Screw as long as they may last. Lastly I nominate and appoint Joseph A Gaston Robert B Gaston & John H Gaston Executors of this my last will and Testament. Whereof I do hereby set my hand and affix my seal publish the same this the 21st day of August in the year of our Lord One Thousand Eight hundred & Forty four

Signed Sealed published and declared by the testator as for his last will and testament in the presence of us who at his request and in the presence of each other have subscribed our names as witnesses

Wm H Burns
Roy Lumpkin
J D Burns

He married[3] 1770 in Chester Co, SC,[102] **Martha Gaston**, b. Jun-11-1741 in Pennsylvania,[3] (daughter of John Gaston and Esther Waugh), d. Mar- 4-1826, buried in Fishing Creek Presb Church Cem, Chester Co, SC.[17,103,45]

Martha: Birthdate may be Nov 6, 1741. Death date may be Apr 3, 1826.

Children:
103.   i.   ESTHER JANE GASTON b. 1770.
        ii.   ALEXANDER GASTON. He married[3] Mary Blair.
104.   iii.   JOHN GASTON b. Apr- 2-1772.
        iv.   MARTHA GASTON.
        v.   MARGARET GASTON.

Sources:
Perry, Max The American Descendants of John "Jean" Gaston, Pages 10 and 3.
Heritage History of Chester County, South Carolina.
Holcomb, Brent H. and Parker, Elmer O., Early Records of Fishing Creek Presbyterian
        Church, Chester County, South Carolina, 132.
Letter written in response to one received from R. J. McQuiston, Dec. 11, 1916.
Gibb, Gary G ggibb@myfamilyinc.com, page 496.
Heritage History of Chester County, South Carolina, 198.
The American Descendants of John "Jean" Gaston.
Early Records of Fishing Creek Presbyterian Church, Chester County, South Carolina,
        Page 144.

Source: Connie Received via email from R.leaman@comcast.net via SCCHEST2-L@rootsweb.com .
    SCCHEST2-D Digest V06 #45

40. **Esther Jane Gaston** (11.Alexander[4], 4.(Male)[3], 2.William[2], 1.Jean[1]), b. 1740 - 1749 in Ireland.[6] She
     married **Thomas Walker**.
                Children:
     105.   i.   ALEXANDER WALKER b. 1763.

41. **Matthew Gaston** (11.Alexander[4], 4.(Male)[3], 2.William[2], 1.Jean[1]), b. ca 1748 in Ireland,[6] d. Dec- 9-
     1799 in Greene Co, GA,[102] buried in Macedonia Cemetery, Butts Co, GA.[102]

     Received a land grant in present-day Chester Co, SC, but moved soon thereafter to Rowan Co, NC,
     where he married his cousin, Ann Simonton. Her mother, Margaret Gaston, had lived and been
     married in Lancaster Co, PA, moving to North Carolina about 1755. [Per Edward H. Couey, Scotts
     Mills, OR] (Note: Margaret Gaston's presumed connection to other Gastons in this genealogy is not
     known. Ann Simonton's parentage and other personalia as enumerated here is from the Reid
     Genealogy and is considered more reliable than other conflicting info.)

     He married (1) Aug-12-1768 in Lancaster Co, PA,[102] **Ann Simonton**, b. 1746 in Pennsylvania,[civ][104]
     (daughter of Robert Simonton and Margaret Benton), d. Dec-13-1793 in Greene Co, GA.[102] He
     married (2) Dec-12-1793,[102] **Rebeckah Hardin**.

     Rebeckah: A widow at time of marriage; maiden name unknown.[102]

                Children by Ann Simonton:
     106.   i.   ROBERT GASTON b. 1774.
     107.   ii.   JANE GASTON b. Jan- 8-1777.
     108.   iii.   ALEXANDER GASTON b. 1780.
     109.   iv.   MATTHEW GASTON, JR. b. 1785.

42. **Alexander Gaston** (11.Alexander[4], 4.(Male)[3], 2.William[2], 1.Jean[1]), b. ca 1750 in Ireland,[14] d. ca 1840.[14]

Hanna's "Ohio Valley Genealogies," p. 42, states that Alexander Gaston (1750-1840), a great-grandson of the first Irish William, remained in Ireland when his four siblings Joseph (who married Martha Gaston), Robert, Matthew and Jane (who married a Walker) emigrated to America and settled in South Carolina.

But it has been reported by Edward H. Couey, a descendant of this Alexander, that he left Ireland in late 1772 with Reverend William Martin's five shiploads of Scottish Presbyterian Covenanters; was granted land on Jan 6, 1773 in present- day York Co, SC; moved to present-day Madison Co, KY by 1787, back to old Abbeville Co, SC by 1797, back to Kentucky after 1800 where he sold his property in 1808, and moved by 1815 to Randolph Co, IL, where he shortly died. Original sources for this information are not known.[6]

He married **Unknown**.
        Children:
    110.   i.   JOHN GASTON.

43. **Margaret Gaston** (12.John[4], 5.William[3], 3.John[2], 1.Jean[1]), b. Aug-29-1738 in Ireland,[45,cv[105]] [Hanna, p. 40 reports birth date as Aug 29 1739.], d. 1767 in Chester Co, SC.[45,cvi[106]] She married[3] **James McCreary**.
        Children:
        i.   JOHN MCCREARY b. 1754,[12] d. Nov- 4-1833,[12] occupation Member of Congress,[3] military Revolutionary War.[3] He married[44] Margaret Gaston, b. 1764,[12] (daughter of Robert Gaston and Margaret Logan), d. Mar- 6-1816.[12,44] John McCreary and Margaret Gaston were said to be second cousins, but they were actually first cousins once removed, as he was the great-grandson of William Gaston (b. 1680 in Ireland) and she was the granddaughter of the same William Gaston. They had two children.[12]
        ii.   SAMUEL MCCREARY occupation Baptist minister,[3] military Revolutionary War.[3]

Perry, Max The American Descendants of John "Jean" Gaston, Pages 10 and 3.
Heritage History of Chester County, South Carolina.
Holcomb, Brent H. and Parker, Elmer O., Early Records of Fishing Creek Presbyterian
        Church, Chester County, South Carolina, 132.
Letter written in response to one received from R. J. McQuiston, Dec. 11, 1916.
Gibb, Gary G ggibb@myfamilyinc.com, page 496.
Heritage History of Chester County, South Carolina, 198.
The American Descendants of John "Jean" Gaston.
Early Records of Fishing Creek Presbyterian Church, Chester County, South Carolina,
        Page 144.

Source: Connie Received via email from R.leaman@comcast.net via SCCHEST2-L@rootsweb.com .
    SCCHEST2-D Digest V06 #45

Kell and Margaret Ann Gaston, b. 27 Mar 1802 in Chester District, SC; d. 17 Jun 1873 in Marion Co., IL. In Marion Co., IL. He married Jane Kell 1820 in Chester Co, SC, daughter of Thomas

44. **Martha Gaston** (12.John[4], 5.William[3], 3.John[2], 1.Jean[1]) (See marriage to number 39.)

45. **William Gaston** (12.John[4], 5.William[3], 3.John[2], 1.Jean[1]), b. Jun- 5-1743 in Pennsylvania,[3] d. 1814.[45]

Unclear which of his two wives (as listed in military records) was the mother of his children. Hanna, though stating that William had sons William and James, makes no mention of a wife. He served as a Captain from South Carolina in the Revolutionary War, and was also a Chester District (SC) Judge and Civil Magistrate.[3]

He married[45] (1) **Jenet Love**, b. ca 1746. He married[45] (2) **Ann Porter**, b. ca 1747.[cvii][107]

Children by Jenet Love:

i. WILLIAM GASTON.
ii. JAMES GASTON.
iii. KESIAH GASTON.
iv. ANN GASTON.
v. SUSANNA GASTON.
vi. MARTHA GASTON.
vii. ELIZABETH GASTON.
viii. ESTHER GASTON. She married __ Akin.
ix. MARGARET GASTON. She married __ Hoskins.
x. JANE GASTON. She married __ Davis.

GASTON-SC-Jan 17, 1814

Will of WM. GASTON (Long Version)

Taken from the original on file in the office of Probate Judge, Chester County, S.C. in Apt. No 22, Pkg. No. 314, recorded in Will book E at page 312

[I have edited the will format into paragraphs for ease of reference. All other spelling and punctuation is as in the original]

In the nam of God Amen I William Gaston of Chester District in the State of South Carolina being sick & weak in body but of sound mind and memory thanks be to God for the same, and calling to mind the mortality of my body and knowing that it is appointed for all men once to Die do make & ordain this my last will and testament Viz principally & first of all I recomend my soul to the hand of God who gave it, and my body to the Earth to be buried in a desent manner at the Descretion of my Executors, nothing doubting but that I shall receive the same again at the general resurection by the mighty power of God and as touching such worldly goods wherewith it has pleased God to bless me in this life, I give devise and dispose of the same in the following manner. Imprimus I desire that all my just debts and funeral charges be paid & sattisfyed.

... I give and bequeath to my well beloved wife Ann Gaston all that tract of land adjoing John McKelveys land and also all my personal property of every kind (Except as hereafter Excepted) to her own proper use & behoof, and to her heirs and assigns for ever.

... I further give bequeath to my loving wife aforsaid all that plantation on which I now live with all my lands adjoining thereto bound on James Lewis lands and on lands belonging to James Gaston and James Feemster, John Boyd Love and on the Back on the deviding ground between turky Creek and Susey Boles branch for & during the time of her natural life, and after her death to go to my son William Gaston & to his heirs and assigns forever.

... I also give and bequeath to my said son William Gaston all that tract of land on big creek of Saluda, which was originally granted to Robert Gaston, and my negro man Norman & my survey Instruments to him and his heirs and assigns forever-----and my will is that my other lands Viss - my plantation on Susey Booles branch and lands ajacent thereto & one other tract on Wilsons branch, and one other tract adjoining the tract last aforsaid be sold sold when my Executors shall find it conveniant and the money arising from such sale to be

42

Eaqualey devided between my five daughters Kesiah, Ann, Susannah, Martha and Elisabeth - -

... I give and bequeath to my son James Gaston and my three daughters Easter Akin Margret Hoskins and Jane Davis Eight dollars to each of them, to be raised out of my estate - -

... I give & bequeath to my daughter Anna my negro girl Lette dureing the life of sd Anne, and after her death the said negro girl & her increase if any, to go to such Children as the said Anne may leave.

... I give & bequeath to my daughter Martha my negro boy Harry, dureing the life of the said Martha and at her death to go to such Children as she may leave.

... I give and bequeath to my daughter Susannah during her life my negro girl Dorcus and after the death of the said Susannah the said negro girl & her increase if any, to go to such Children as the said Susannah may leave- - -

... I give & bequeath to my daughter Elisabeth dureing her life my negro boy Danil and after her death to go to such Children as she may leave.

... I give and bequeath to my daughter Kisiah the first Child that my negro woman may hereafter have, during the life of the said Kisiah and after her death to go to such Children as she may leave I also bequeath to my daughter Kisiah a certain mare which is now in her possession in order to make up any deficancy supposed to be in the value of the negro willed to mher, & to make her Eaqual with her sisters and

... I do herby ordain dupute & constitute my Loving wife Anne Gaston to be Executrix and my son Willliam Gaston and my friend John McCrary to be Executors of this my last will and testament hereby revoking and disannuling all former wills testaments and biqusts by me heretofore made and declaring this and no other to be my last will and testament In Witness Whereof I have hereunto set my hand and seal this seventeenth day of January in the year of our Lord one thousand Eight hundred & fourteen and in the thirty Eighth year of American independence

[Interlined before assignd in first page & fourth line from bottom (the words Norman curveying instruments & in the second line the words and land adjacent thereto and on second page sixth line the words and Jane Davis]

N B the Legacies Left to James Gaston Ester Akin Margret Hoskins & Jane Davis to be raised from the sale of the lands ordered to be sold

    /s/ Wm. Gaston (LS)

Signed and acknowledg by the said William Gaston as his last will & testament
In presence of us
/s/ Richard Love
/s/ Jas. McCluer
   her
Jane X McCluer
   mark

Contributed by: "Carolyn Carter Johnson" rhunterg@ix.netcom.com
By way of: Mfournier@hankins.com (Mickey Fournier)

46. **John Gaston** (12.John[4], 5.William[3], 3.John[2], 1.Jean[1]), b. Jun-24-1745 in Pennsylvania,[3] d. Jan- -1808,[45] [Hanna reports death date as about 1806.].

Was a Private in General Sumter's Mounted South Carolina Militia. Following his death, his family moved from South Carolina to Illinois.[44]

He married 1768,[45,cviii[108]] **Jannett Knox**,[108] also known as Jannet or Janette Knox, b. ca 1742 in Glasgow, Scotland,[108] (daughter of James Knox, Sr. and Elizabeth Craig), d. Aug- 1-1839 in Jefferson Co, IL,[108,45] resided aft Jan 1808 in Logan Co, KY,[108] resided previously in South Carolina.
        Children:
    111. i.   JAMES GASTON b. 1777.
          ii.   WILLIAM GASTON b. 1779 in South Carolina,[cix[109]] d. 1804,[108] resided (settled) in Illinois.[44]
          iii. ELIZABETH GASTON resided (settled abt 1800) in Logan Co, KY,[108] resided originally in South Carolina. She married[108] Jonathan Ferguson.
    112. iv.   ESTHER WAUGH GASTON.

47. **James Gaston** (12.John[4], 5.William[3], 3.John[2], 1.Jean[1]), b. Apr-15-1747,[44,45] d. bef 1833, resided (settled) in Ohio,[44] resided previously in South Carolina.

Hanna, in "Ohio Valley Genealogies," p. 41, states that this James Gaston, b. Apr 15 1747, had a son Stephen and several daughters, and that they moved to Ohio in about 1801-02. Burgess, in "Gaston Genealogy," p. 119, reports the same children as Hanna. Neither makes mention of James' wife. "Chester County Heritage History," p. 196, states that this James Gaston married Margaret, that they had a son Stephen and a number of daughters, and that they moved first to Tennessee and later to Indiana Territory. Subsequent research by others, as reported on the LDS familysearch.org website, has revealed the family information found here.

He married[45,cx[110]] **Margaret Harvey**, b. ca 1751,[12] d. bef 1820.[12]
        Children:
    113. i.   STEPHEN GASTON[44,45] b. 1774.
          ii.   ROBERT GASTON b. 1776,[12] d. 1817 in Illinois.[12]
          iii. ANN GASTON b. Dec-16-1785,[12] d. 1843 in Illinois.[12]
          iv.   MARGARET GASTON b. May-30-1790 in Kentucky,[12] d. Jan-15-1852 in Illinois.[12] She married[cxi[111]] John H. Pillars, b. Jul-27-1786,[12] d. Jan-11-1852.[12] Eleven children.[12]

          v.   MARY GASTON b. Apr-25-1799 in South Carolina,[12] d. Mar-30-1833 in Illinois.[12] She married John Crain, b. May- 9-1791,[12] d. Jun-22-1850.[12] Ten children.[12]

48. **Hugh Gaston** (12.John[4], 5.William[3], 3.John[2], 1.Jean[1]), b. Mar-12-1751,[26,45] d. Jun-13-1836,[26,45] buried in Shell Creek Cemetery, Wilcox Co, AL,[45] resided (settled) in Mississippi,[44] resided (moved 1826) to Wilcox Co, AL,[44] resided originally in South Carolina.[44] He married[26] **Hannah Martha McClure**, also known as Martha McLure,[44] b. 1754,[45] (daughter of James McClure and Mary Gaston), d. Dec-21-1836,[45] buried in Shell Creek Cemetery, Wilcox Co, AL,[45] resided in Alabama.
        Children:
          i.   JOHN GASTON married Mary Kirkpatrick.
          ii.   EBENEZER GASTON.
          iii. JAMES GASTON.
          iv.   WILLIAM GASTON married Sallig Kee.
          v.   HUGH GASTON.
          vi.   MARY GASTON married David Boyd.
          vii. MARTHA GASTON married Samuel Gamble.
          viii. ESTHER GASTON.
          ix.   MARGARET GASTON married Charles Weir.

Childen:
Hugh Gaston Wier
Ebenezer Weir
Martha Weir
Margaret Weir

49. **Esther Gaston** (12.John[4], 5.William[3], 3.John[2], 1.Jean[1]), b. Oct- -1760,[45,44] [Birth date reported in "Heritage History of Chester County, SC," p. 196, as Oct 15 1760, but Hanna's "Ohio Valley Genealogies," p. 41states Oct 18 1760, while the DAR lineage book shows it as 1761.], d. 1809.[45]

Before her marriage to Alexander Walker, Esther Gaston was cited for her heroic deeds during the American Revolution. During the Battle of Rocky Mount, when she saw three men fleeing, she asked to take their arms and fight in the battle herself. This prompted the men to return to the fighting. With patriotic spirits and kind hearts, she and her sister-in-law aided the wounded and dying during the Battles of Rocky Mount and Hanging Rock, dressing the wounds and quenching the thirsts of the seriously injured.[cxii[112]]

She married **Alexander Walker**, b. 1763,[cxiii[113]] (son of Thomas Walker and Jane Gaston). Alexander Walker was the g-g-g-grandson of Jean Gaston (b. ca 1600 in France), while his wife Esther Gaston was the g-g-grand-daughter of the same Jean Gaston. They were thus third cousins once removed.

Children:
114. i. JOHN GASTON WALKER[44].

50. **Joseph Gaston** (12.John[4], 5.William[3], 3.John[2], 1.Jean[1]), b. Jan-22-1763 in Chester Co, SC,[44,45,cxiv[114]] [Jane Farrell Burgess, in "The Gaston Genealogy," p. 85, states that age 73y 8m 18d in death record would put birth exactly one month earlier, at Jan 22 1763.], d. Oct-10-1836 in Chester Co, SC,[114] buried in Fishing Creek Presb Church Cem, Chester Co, SC.[cxv[115],45]

Joseph Gaston (1763-1836) served at the battles of Hanging Rock and at Buford's defeat. He received a pension as a private in Chester county, where he was born and where he died.[cxvi[116]] Wounded with a shot that hit under his eye in the Battle of Hanging Rock, SC, in the Revolutionary War. He later became a Magistrate for over forty years, and was also an elder of the Presbyterian Church. In 1830, he was elected to the South Carolina Legislature, and shortly before his death he published an article describing his Revolutionary War experiences.[115]

He married[116,8] Apr-20-1790, **Jane Brown**, b. Apr-10-1768,[cxvii[117]] (daughter of Walter Brown and Margaret __), d. Jun-27-1858,[45] buried in Fishing Creek Presb Church Cem, Chester Co, SC.[112,45]
Children:
115. i. JOHN BROWN GASTON b. Jan-23-1791.
116. ii. NARCISSA GASTON b. Nov-17-1792.
      iii. ELIZA GASTON b. Sep-20-1794,[44] d. Jun- 7-1845. She married[44] __ Neely.
      iv. ESTHER GASTON b. Dec- 4-1795,[cxviii[118]] d. May-25-1856. She married[44] D. G. Stinson.

       D.: Probably Daniel G. Stinson, b. ca 1794, resident of South Carolina. [Based on letter from Louisa Beecher Gaston of Boston to H. B. Gaston, Dec 5 1883.]

      v. MARGARET GASTON b. Apr-29-1797,[cxix[119]] d. Oct- 1-1802.[106]
      vi. JANE GASTON b. Aug-17-1800,[44] d. Oct- 4-1880.[106] She married[44] __ Crawford.
      vii. JAMES A. H. GASTON b. Oct-17-1801,[44] d. Jul-26-1859,[106] buried in Fishing Creek Presb Church Cem, Chester Co, SC.[112]
      viii. ROBERT GASTON b. Jan- 1-1808,[44] d. Jun-27-1810.[106]

51. **John McClure** (13.Mary[4], 5.William[3], 3.John[2], 1.Jean[1]), d. Aug- 6-1780 at Hanging Rock, SC,[44] military Captain in Revolutionary War.

John McClure was one of the master spirits of the Revolution. He was mortally wounded at Hanging Rock, 1780, while bravely leading his volunteer company against the British regulars. He died in Liberty Hall, where the Mecklenburg Declaration was written. He had three brothers who served in the army, and his mother is recorded in history as "The Cherokee Heroine."[cxx[120]]

He married[cxxi[121]] **Mary Porter**.
        Children:
    117.   i.   HUGH MCCLURE.

52. **Martha McClure**, also known as Martha McLure,[44] (13.Mary[4], 5.William[3], 3.John[2], 1.Jean[1]) (See marriage to number 48.)

53. **William McClure** (13.Mary[4], 5.William[3], 3.John[2], 1.Jean[1]), occupation military physician, rank of General.[cxxii[122],44] He married[122] **Sarah Davis**.
        Children:
    118.   i.   HANNAH MCCLURE b. ca 1786.

54. **Margaret Strong** (14.Janet[4], 5.William[3], 3.John[2], 1.Jean[1]). She married[44] **John Simonton**. She was born 1768 in Fishing Creek, Chester County, South Carolina[46], and died 11 Mar 1828 in Fairfield County, South Carolina[46]. She married JOHN SIMONTON[47] 01 Jul 1785 in Fishing Creek, Chester County, South Carolina, son of MAJOR SIMONTON and MARY ROSS?. He was born 1760 in Rowan County, North Carolina[48], and died 31 Jan 1841 in Fairfield County, South Carolina[48].

More About MARGARET STRONG:
    Cemetery: New Hope A.R.P. Cemetery, Fairfield Co., SC

Notes for JOHN SIMONTON:
    He was living in that part of the state of South Carolina known as Craven, now known as Chester County during the Revolution and took part as militiaman in the military operations in the Carolina.
    He was wounded and confined in the home of Charles Strong and was nursed by his daughter, Margaret, whom John married afterwards.

(Office of Sec. of State, Columbia, SC, Stub Book "L" #415, issued Oct. 28, 1784, to John Simonton. Military duty, 1178-1791)

He inherited several tracts of land in York and Chester Counties from his father (Maj. Robt.), and in addition we find him buying other lands about the time of his marriage to Margaret Strong. He lived in that section until 1798 when he moved down into Fairfield County. A portion of his York County land was sold to Andrew Tipping in 1799, the last conveyance of this land was to Robert Caughran, May 26, 1824. The County records of Fairfield show that John Simonton both purchased and sold land from the year 1790 to the time of his death in 1840.

His tombstone remarks: "He was an elder in the Presbyterian Church for 50 years."

Source: Dorothy Wakefield Chance's "Ancestors of Kayleigh Chance Murdoc".

More About JOHN SIMONTON:
Cemetery: New Hope A.R.P. Cemetery, Fairfield Co., SC

Children of MARGARET STRONG and JOHN SIMONTON are:

  i.   ROBERT ROMAINE SIMONTON SR., b. 19 Jul 1786; d. 12 Nov 1862, Tipton County,
       Tennessee; m. MARGARET MCQUISTON; b. 29 Sep 1794; d. 01 Feb 1884.
  ii. CHARLES S. SIMONTON, b. 02 Mar 1788; m. ELIZABETH ROSS[48].
  iii. WILLIAM SIMONTON, b. 03 Feb 1791; d. 1844, Salem, Tipton County, Tennessee; m.
       (1) MARGARET GALLOWAY; m. (2) MARY MCDILL; m. (3) KATHERINE FERGUSON.

     More About MARGARET GALLOWAY:
       Cemetery: New Hope A.R.P. Cemetery, Fairfield Co., SC

  iv. CHRISTOPHER SIMONTON, b. 27 Oct 1792, South Carolina; d. 27 Oct 1792, South
       Carolina.
  v.   SARAH SIMONTON, b. 06 May 1795; d. 29 Jun 1861; m. DAVID WILSON.

  vi. JOHN SIMONTON[6] JR. *(MARGARET[5] STRONG, JEANETTE[4] GASTON, WILLIAM[3], JOHN[2],*
JOHN "JEAN"[1])[69] was born 08 Nov 1797 in South Carolina[70], and died 13 May 1880[70]. He married (1)
NANCY BRICE, daughter of JAMES BRICE and JANE WILSON. She was born 1802 in Fairfield County,
South Carolina, and died 28 Jun 1864. He married (2) ELLEN KIRKPATRICK[71].

More About NANCY BRICE:
    Cemetery: New Hope A.R.P. Cemetery, Fairfield Co., SC

Children of JOHN JR. and NANCY BRICE are:
    a. W. B.[7] SIMONTON[71].

       Notes for W. B. SIMONTON:
           From "The Brice Family" by L. S. Brice:
           W. B. Simonton was a son of Nancy Brice and John Simonton. He was in Co. H, 12th SCV
           and lost a leg at the Battle of Sharpsburg, Sept. 17, 1862.

    b. MARY E. SIMONTON, b. 07 Oct 1835; d. 01 Sep 1885, Fairfield County, South Carolina.
    c. SAMUEL ROBERT SIMONTON, b. 1847; d. 27 Oct 1889.

vii. JEANETTE[6] SIMONTON *(MARGARET[5] STRONG, JEANETTE[4] GASTON, WILLIAM[3], JOHN[2], JOHN*
     "JEAN"[1])[72] was born 08 Sep 1799[73], and died 03 Jan 1873 in Fairfield County, South Carolina[74]. She
     married ALEXANDER DOUGLASS[75] 1826. He was born 14 Oct 1799, and died 18 Jul 1863.

Notes for JEANETTE SIMONTON:
    Obituary take from Lois Rebecca Brice's scrapbook:

Died, of consumption, at the residence of her son, John A. Douglas, Esq., Fairfield County, S. C., on the 3d inst., Mrs. Jane Douglas, in the 73d year of her age.

Mrs. D. was the daughter of the late John Simonton, Sr., and sister of John Simonton, of Little River, of the same county. Her father, being a man of distinguished intelligence and piety, and for many years Ruling Elder in New Hope church, like Abraham "commanded his children and household after him." At an early age, Mrs. D. made a profession of her faith, and connected herself with the church at New Hope, at that time under the pastoral care of Rev. Dr. John Hemphill, and adorned that profession till the day of her death. She, with her husband, reared a family of seven children, and she lived to see all her children make a profession of religion, and each of her sons Ruling Elders. Having had several severe attacks of pneumonia, her lungs became permanently affected, and culminated in consumption. During her long confinement, she illustrated the christian graces of patience and submission to the Divine will, and when death came, she was entirely willing to go, reposing in the unfailing promises of her Saviour. Thus has passed away from our church an aged saint, as we think, leaving to her friends and family the heritage of a bright christian example. May they and we "be followers of those who thro' faith and patience are now inheriting the promises." L. McD.

Notes for ALEXANDER DOUGLASS:
Known as a planter, an intellectual, and a good historian, he owned large tracts of land and slaves succeeding well in business. He built the homeplace, Albion about 1840.

"Albion is significant as an unusually intact, although altered, example of a nineteenth-century Fairfield County plantation house with classical design elements which display an awareness of high-
    style design. Alexander Douglas, who is reported to have built Albion ca. 1840, was a wealthy
    planter whose estate was valued in 1860 at $76,750. Albion is a two-story, L-shaped,
    weatherboarded frame residence with a side gabled roof and rear additions. The façade has a two-
    tiered veranda with Ionic columns, plain balustrade, and a simple entablature with triglyphs above
    the first story veranda. The
    second story veranda columns are cropped, indicating possible later alterations. Columns with both
    plain and fluted shafts are paired at the ends of the veranda and in the center. The windows are
    shuttered and have fluted surrounds with corner blocks. Both central entrances have a traceried
    elliptical fanlight and sidelights. An unusual parapeted dormer pierces the front center roof, perhaps
    another alteration. Pedimented end gables are ornamented with block modillions and lunettes
    which
    flank the chimneys. Listed in the National Register December 6, 1984."

Retrieved October 10, 2006, by Linda Hull from South Carolina Department of Archives and History
    records of the National Register Properties in South Carolina, Albion, Fairfield County (S.C. Sec. Rd.
    22, Douglass vicinity) at http://www.nationalregister.sc.gov/fairfield/S10817720001/index.htm

More About ALEXANDER DOUGLASS:
    Cemetery: New Hope A.R.P. Cemetery, Fairfield Co., SC

Children of JEANETTE SIMONTON and ALEXANDER DOUGLASS are:
    a.   MARTHA S.[7] DOUGLASS, b. 02 Jan 1826.
    b.   JOHN A. DOUGLASS, b. 15 May 1828.
    c.   ALEXANDER S. DOUGLASS, b. 25 Dec 1833; d. 05 Jan 1914.

     d.   MARGARET S. DOUGLASS, b. 24 Nov 1836.

     e.   JANE G. DOUGLASS, b. 25 Jun 1839.

     f.   MARY EMERLINE DOUGLASS, b. 26 Oct 1839, Fairfield County, South Carolina; d. 10 Dec 1920, Fairfield County, South Carolina.

     g.   SARAH E. DOUGLASS, b. 10 Sep 1843.

viii. MARGARET[6] SIMONTON *(MARGARET[5] STRONG, JEANETTE[4] GASTON, WILLIAM[3], JOHN[2], JOHN "JEAN"[1])*[75] was born 20 Jun 1801 in Fairfield County, South Carolina[76], and died 13 Feb 1843 in Little River, Fairfield County, South Carolina[76]. She married ROBERT BRICE[77] 25 Dec 1817 in Fairfield County, South Carolina, son of JAMES BRICE and JANE WILSON. He was born 08 Oct 1791 in Fairfield County, South Carolina[78], and died 02 Apr 1871 in Fairfield County, South Carolina.

Notes for MARGARET SIMONTON: Obituary: ("The Christian Magazine of the South" Vol. 1, p.32, January, 43, edited by Rev. James Boyce, DD, published by Morgan's Press, Columbian, S.C. The bound copies of "The Magazine of the South" for four years, in the possession of JR Moffatt, given to the Foundation at Montreat for safekeeping.)

"Departed this life on Little River Fairfield District, S.C. on the morning of Friday, the 13th, instant, Mrs. Margaret Brice in the 42nd year of her age. The deceased had been an exemplary member of the Associate Reformed Church from early life. We believe she was of the true Israel of God. She was pious, prudent and sensible, and remarkably intelligent in the Scriptures. Having enjoyed the advantages of an early religious education herself, and having tested the sweets of religion, she was quite assiduous in her attention to her children (of whom she had many), that they might be brought up in the nurture and admonition of the Lord. She excelled in family discipline, possessing a tact in the management of that department of household affairs which pertains to the mother and wife, which few of her sex possess, and yet all was mildness and gentleness in the absence of everything like austerity or rigidness. During her last illness, which was of seven weeks duration, she was not known to murmur under her afflictions. She expressed herself as not being afraid of the last enemy. She has left a husband and a large family of children. Their loss is sensible felt."

Associate Reformed Presbyterian Death & Marriage Notices, 1843-1863 Associate Reformed Presbyterian Death & Marriage Notices from The Christian Magazine of the South, The Erskine Miscellany, and The Due West Telescope, 1843-1863
The Christian Magazine of the South
I (January, 1843), 32.
page 306
Associate Reformed Presbyterian Death & Marriage Notices, 1843-1863, p.1
Departed this life on Little River, Fairfield District, on the morning of Friday, the 13th instant, Mrs. Margaret Brice, wife of Robert Brice, in the 42nd year of her age.... She left a husband and a large family of children.

Notes for ROBERT BRICE:
"Old Homes of Fairfield: from The News and Herald, Winnsboro, S.C., Sept. 8, 1938:

"No section of Fairfield Co. is richer in history and historic homes than that surrounding New Hope ARP Church. Homes of Revolutionary days have all been burned or replaced by other dwellings, but the names of these pioneers still cling to the land they settled. Most of these early settlers were true patriots. The oldest homes in the community date back more than a hundred years.

The T.S. Brice home is the oldest. The land on which this home stands was given by grant of King George to Robert Wilson. It is known positively that Jane Brice, granddaughter of Robert Brice and his wife, Margaret Simonton Brice (or possibly partly by his father, James Brice) by or before 1817. All twelve children were born here.

It was inherited by their youngest son, Thomas Scott Brice, who married Frances Eliza Adams and brought his bride here...

The grant made by King George III in 1775 is still kept by the family. The land was surveyed February 16, 1778 and was in what was then called Craven County."

From "I Had A Real Good Time" by James Moffatt Brice (1862-1926):

"I do not know much about my grandfather Robert Brice. His picture, since destroyed in a fire, revealed a broad-shouldered, square-jawed man with a somewhat stern and severe countenance. He married a Miss Simonton, from whom many of their descendants inherited a slight, and some a considerable, abdominal rotundity.

I remember my Aunt Amanda saying that sometimes Robert Brice would return home and, on being asked where he had been, would reply, "Just buying another 'wee track' (tract) of land." He acquired a considerable estate in land and slaves, being able, without in any measure detracting from corpus of the estate, to give each child on the occasion of his or her marriage $5000, or its equivalent. He lived to the age of 84.

There was a large family: Jane, who never married; John A.; Anna, who married a photographer named Lee; Robert, and Associate Reformed Presbyterian minister; James Simonton, my father, Christopher; Charles, a lawyer; Walter, a physician; Thomas; Mary, who married my mother's brother, Israel P. Moffatt; and Amanda, who married Major A.B. Enloe, a lawyer.

Some of the Brice boys attended college, notably Robert, Charles and Walter. The others worked on the farm, except for my father, who seems to have looked after a small store on the farm."
Robert was the ruling elder of New Hope ARP Presbyterian church for 50 years.
Excerpt from Ella Lee Boyd's account:

"Educated in private schools, he became a planter and a man of wealth and an uplifting influence in his community," said a local historian of Robert's day. He was ordained an elder in the New Hope Church in 1821.

More About ROBERT BRICE:
    Cemetery: New Hope A.R.P. Cemetary, Fairfield Co., SC[79]

Children of MARGARET SIMONTON and ROBERT BRICE were:

a.   JANE WILSON[7] BRICE, b. 15 Oct 1818, Fairfield County, South Carolina; d. 1887, Fairfield County, South Carolina.
b.   MARGARET STRONG BRICE, b. 29 Jul 1820, Fairfield County, South Carolina; d. 29 Jan 1842, Fairfield County, South Carolina.
c.   JOHN ALEXANDER BRICE, b. 08 Nov 1822, Fairfield County, South Carolina; d. 09 Nov 1890, Woodward, South Carolina.
d.   JAMES SIMONTON BRICE, b. 16 Sep 1824, Fairfield County, South Carolina; d. Jun 1877, Longview, Gregg County, Texas.
e.   REV. ROBERT WILSON BRICE, b. 02 Jul 1826, Fairfield County, South Carolina; d. 14 Mar 1878, Hopewell Church, Chester County, South Carolina.
f.   CHRISTOPHER SIMONTON BRICE, b. 25 Apr 1828, Fairfield County, South Carolina; d. 04 Mar 1900.
g.   DR. WALTER BRICE, b. 07 Feb 1830, Fairfield County, South Carolina; d. 09 Nov 1895, Troy, Obion County, Tennessee.
h.   CHARLES STRONG BRICE, b. 19 Oct 1831, Longview, Gregg County, Texas; d. 1878.
i.   MARTHA BRICE, b. 25 Aug 1833, Fairfield County, South Carolina; d. 30 Oct 1922, Tuscaloosa, Alabama.
j.   SARAH AMANDA BRICE, b. 15 Sep 1835, Fairfield County, South Carolina; d. 07 Nov 1894, Troy, Obion County, Tennessee.
k.   MARY ELIZABETH BRICE, b. 18 May 1838, Fairfield County, South Carolina; d. 12 Jul 1905, Troy, Obion County, Tennessee.
l.   THOMAS SCOTT BRICE, b. 16 Sep 1840, Avon, Fairfield County, South Carolina; d. 05 Mar 1913, Shelby, North Carolina.

ix.   MARY[6] SIMONTON *(MARGARET[5] STRONG, JEANETTE[4] GASTON, WILLIAM[3], JOHN[2], JOHN "JEAN"[1])*[80] was born 16 Dec 1809[81], and died 20 Jun 1890 in Fairfield County, South Carolina[81]. She married WILLIAM BRICE 06 Oct 1829[81], son of JAMES BRICE and JANE WILSON. He was born 1793 in Fairfield County, South Carolina, and died 09 Mar 1872 in Fairfield County, South Carolina.

More About MARY SIMONTON:
Cemetery: New Hope A.R.P. Cemetary, Fairfield Co., SC[82]

Notes for WILLIAM RICE:
From:

Ancestry.com. Slave Narratives. [database onliuine] Orem, UT: Ancestry, Inc., 2000. Original source: Works Project Administration. Federal Writers
Project. Slave Narratives: A Folk History of Slavery in the United States from Interviews with Former Slaves. Washington, D. E.: n.p.

Anne Broome, EX-SLAVE 87 YEARS OLD.

"Does you recollect de Galloway place just dis side of White Oak? Well dere's where I was born. When? Can't name de 'zact year but my ma say, no stork bird never fetch me but the fust railroad train dat come up de railroad track, when they built de line, fetched me. She say I was a baby, settin' on the cow-ketcher, and she see me and say to pa: 'Reubin, run out dere and get our baby befo' her falls off and gets hurt under them wheels! Do you know I believed dat tale 'til I was a big girl? Sure did, 'til white folks laugh me out of it!

"My ma was name Louisa. My marster was Billie Brice, but 'spect God done write sumpin' else on he forehead by dis time. He was a cruel marster; he whip me just for runnin' to de gate for to see de train run by. My missus was a pretty woman, flaxen hair, blue eyes, name Mary Simonton, 'til she marry.

"Us live in a two-room plank house. Pleaty to eat and enough to wear 'cept de boys run 'round in their shirt tails and de ghirls just a on'piece homespun slip on in de summer time. Dat was not a hardship then. Us didn't know and didn't care nothin' 'bout a 'spectable 'pearance in those days. Dats de truth, us didn't.

"Gran'pa name Obe; gran'ma, name Rachel. Shoes? A child never have a shoe. Slaves wore wooden bottom shoes.

"My white folks went to New Hope Church. Deir chillun was mighty good to us all. Dere was Miss Martha, her marry doctor Madden, right here at Winnsboro. Miss Mary marry Marster John Vinson, a little polite smilin' man, nice man, though. Then Miss Jane marry Marster John Young. He passed out, leavin' two lovely chiillun, Kitty and Maggie. Both of them marry Caldwells. Dere was Marster Calvin, he marry Congressman Wallace's daughter, Ellen. There dere was Marster Jim and Marster William, de last went to Florida.

"It was a big place. I tell you, and heaps and heaps of slaves. Some times they git too many and sell them off. My old mistress cry 'bout dat but tears didn't count wid old marster, as long as de money come runnin' in and de rations stayed in de smoke house.

"Us had a fine carriage. Sam was de driver. Us go to Concord one Sunday and New Hope de next. Had quality fair neighbors. Dere was de Cocerells, Piscopalians, dat 'ten St. John in Winnsboro, de Adgers, big buckra, went to Sion in Winnsboro, Marster Burr Cockerell was de sheriff. 'Members he had to hang a man once, right in de open jailyard. Then dere was a oor buckra family name Marshell. Our white folks was good to them, 'cause they say his pappy was close kin to de biggest Jedge of our country, John Marshall.

"When de slaves got bad off sick, marster send for Dr. Walter Brice, his kin folks. Some times he might send for Dr. Madden, him's son-in-law, as how he was.

"When de Yankees come, all de young marsters was off in de 'Federate side. I see them now, gallopin' to the house, canteen boxes on their hips and de bayonets rattlin' by deir sides. De fust thing they ask,
was: 'You got any wine?' They search de house; make us sing: 'Good Old Time Ligion'; put us to runnin' after de chickens and a cookin'. When they leave they burnt de gin house and everything in dere. They burn de smoke-house and wind up wid burnin' de big house.

"You through wid me now, boss? I sho' is glad of dat. Help all you kin to git me dat pension befo' I die and de Lord will bless you, honey. De Lord not gwine to hold His hand any longer 'ginst us. Us cleared de forests, built de railroads, cleaned up de swamps, and nursed de white folks. Now in our old ages, I hopes they lets de old slaves like me see de shine from de hand of de Lord. Good mornin'

and God bless you, will be my prayer alwaysl Has you got a dime to give dis old nigger, boss?"
(Project # -1655, Mrs. Genevieve W. Chandler, Murrells Inlet, S. C.,
Georgetown County, FOLKLORE)
http://www.ancestry.com/search/rectype/biohist/slavnarr/main.htm
William Brice was the ruling elder at New Hope ARP Church for 40 years.

More About WILLIAM BRICE:
    Cemetery: New Hope A.R.P. Cemetary, Fairfield Co., SC[82]

Marriage Notes for MARY SIMONTON and WILLIAM BRICE:
    Ceremony was performed by Rev. John Hemphill.

Children of MARY SIMONTON and WILLIAM BRICE are:
    a.   MARGARET BRICE, b. 18 Dec 1831; d. 1868.
    b.   CALVIN BRICE, b. 05 Oct 1832; d. 20 May 1905.
    c.   ROBERT R. BRICE, b. 13 Sep 1834, Fairfield County, South Carolina; d. 25 Apr 1861, Fairfield County, South Carolina.
    d.   JANE W. BRICE, b. 18 Mar 1836.
    e.   JOHN PRESSLY BRICE, b. 27 Dec 1837, Fairfield County, South Carolina; d. 24 Jul 1862, Fairfield County, South Carolina.

    Notes for JOHN PRESSLY BRICE: Associate Reformed Presbyterian Death & Marriage Notices From the Christian Magazine of the South, the Erskine Miscellany, and the Due West Telescope, 18431863 page 163:

    "Departed this life on the 24th July. John Pressly Brice, aged 24 years and 7 months...He graduated in Erskine college about the year 1856, studied law, and settled in Washington, Ark., where he pursued his profession. He joined the army in March last, and served in the Artillery Department as 2nd Lieutenant in Fort Pillow. After a time he was ordered to Corinth, but falling sick, he returned to his father, William Brice, Fairfield District on the 4th June where he died on the 24th of July, of an affection ot the lungs."
    More About JOHN PRESSLY BRICE:
    Cemetery: New Hope A.R.P. Cemetary, Fairfield Co., SC[82]

    f.   JAMES A. BRICE, b. 22 Nov 1839; d. 1909.
    g.   MARTHA SIMONTON BRICE, b. 12 Nov 1841; d. 1878.
    h.   MARY E. BRICE, b. 30 Nov 1843; d. 1895; m. JOHN VINSON, 04 Sep 1867.
    i.   WILLIAM W. BRICE, b. 04 Mar 1846, Fairfield County, South Carolina.
    j.   SALLIE AGNES BRICE, b. 07 Jun 1848.
    k.   WALTER HENRY BRICE[82], b. 21 Dec 1850, Fairfield County, South Carolina; d. 16 Nov 1855, Fairfield County, South Carolina.

    More About WALTER HENRY BRICE:
    Cemetery: New Hope A.R.P. Cemetary, Fairfield Co., SC[82]

l.   INFANT BRICE, b. 18 Feb 1853, Fairfield County, South Carolina[82]; d. 19 Feb 1853, Fairfield County, South Carolina[82].

        More About INFANT BRICE:
            Cemetery: New Hope A.R.P. Cemetery, Fairfield Co., SC[82]

    m.   FRANCES EMELINE BRICE[82], b. 13 Dec 1854, Fairfield County, South Carolina; d. 29 Jul 1855, Fairfield County, South Carolina.

        More About FRANCES EMELINE BRICE:
            Cemetery: New Hope A.R.P. Cemetery, Fairfield Co., SC[82]

x.   JEANETTE SIMONTON, b. 08 Sep 1799; d. 03 Jan 1873, Fairfield County, South Carolina.
xi.   JAMES STRONG SIMONTON, b. 22 May 1800.
x.   MARGARET SIMONTON, b. 20 Jun 1801, Fairfield County, South Carolina; d. 13 Feb
        1843, Little River, Fairfield County, South Carolina.
xi.   MARTHA SIMONTON[62], b. 08 Sep 1805[63]; d. 10 Sep 1824, Fairfield County, South Carolina[64].

        More About MARTHA SIMONTON:
            Cemetery: New Hopewell ARP Cemetery

xii.   ALEXANDER GASTON SIMONTON[65], b. 12 Dec 1807[66]; d. 01 Feb 1816, Fairfield County, South Carolina[67].

        More About ALEXANDER GASTON SIMONTON:
            Cemetery: New Hopewell ARP Cemetery

xiii.   MARY SIMONTON, b. 16 Dec 1809; d. 20 Jun 1890, Fairfield County, South Carolina.

55.   **Alexander Rosborough II** (15.Martha[4], 5.William[3], 3.John[2], 1.Jean[1]), b. in at sea [The 1900 Census of sons David and Joseph indicated that their father was born at sea, and their mother in South Carolina.], occupation physician.[14]

His first two children, Mary Martha and William Andrew, were by his first wife, Mary Hemphill. Hanna states that Alexander Rosborough II had a total of six sons and two daughters by his second wife, Janet Porter, but identifies only the five children listed here.[14]

He married[14] (1) **Mary Hemphill**. He married[14] (2) **Janet Porter**, b. in South Carolina.
            Children by Mary Hemphill:
        i.   MARY MARTHA ROSBOROUGH.
        ii.   WILLIAM ANDREW ROSBOROUGH.
            Children by Janet Porter:
119.   iii. DAVID D. ROSBOROUGH b. Sep- -1815.
120.   iv.   ALEXANDER M. ROSBOROUGH[14] b. ca 1817.
        v.   JOSEPH BROWN ROSBOROUGH b. Dec- -1821 in South Carolina,[cxxiii][123] census 1900 in Belton, Bell Co, TX, resided (settled) in Salt Lake City, Salt Lake Co, UT,[14] resided (moved in 1848) to California.[14]

            Moved to California in 1848, then to Salt Lake City, Utah.

       vi.   JOHN ROSBOROUGH resided (settled) in Tennessee.
      vii. MACLIN ROSBOROUGH resided (settled) in Tennessee.

56. **John Rosborough**, census name John Rosboro (15.Martha[4], 5.William[3], 3.John[2], 1.Jean[1]), b. 1776,[14] d. 1854,[14] occupation Clerk of the Court, Chester Co, SC. He married[14] **Eleanor Key**. Had a total of four sons and six daughters.[14]

          Children:
       i.   JOHN ROSBOROUGH d. Civil War.[14]
      ii. WILLIAM ROSBOROUGH resided (settled) in Sardis, Panola Co, MS.[14]

57. **William Gaston** (16.Robert[4], 5.William[3], 3.John[2], 1.Jean[1]), b. Jul-10-1757 in Lancaster Co, PA,[44,cxxiv[124]] [Hanna's "Ohio Valley Genealogies," p. 41" reports birth date as Jul 23 1755. Jane Farrell Burgess, in "The Gaston Genealogy," pp. 87 & 96, provides conflicting birth dates of 1755 and Jul 10 1757. Bill Gaston, http://home.mindspring.com/~bgaston2/, reports birth date as Jan 13 1761. William Gaston's birth date accepted by the DAR is 10 July 1757.], d. Jan-12-1838 in Marion Co, IL,[cxxv[125],12] [Death date of Jan 14 1838 reported by Mary Gaston Gee, p. 13.], buried in Old Covenanter Cem, Walnut Hill, Marion Co, IL,[cxxvi[126]] resided in Walnut Hill, Marion Co, IL,[44,124] resided 1808 - ca 1829 in Christian Co, KY,[126,44,124] military Revolutionary War.[44,124]

The following is from a handwritten letter by Frank DeForest Gaston (1853-1920) of Meadville, PA: "A reunion of the Gaston family was recently held at Centralia, Ill at which over 1,000 persons were present, the entire connection numbering over 1300. All were descendants of Wm Gaston who came to Ill in 1827..." "Wm Gaston was born in North Carolina..." (But DAR Lineage Book has birth in Lancaster Co, PA.)

He married[cxxvii[127]] ca 1781,[126] **Mary McClure**, b. 1758 in Chester Co, SC,[126] d. ca 1829 in Christian Co, KY.[126]

Mary: Possibly the daughter of Samuel McClure and Sarah Rankin.[126]
          Another sources gives her as the daughter of John McClure and Mary Porter.

Notes for WILLIAM GASTON:
   Taken from a record written in August 1877:

"William Gaston served in the Revolutionary War under and with General Washington. He moved
     from South Carolina to Kentucky, date unknown. After the death of his wife, he emigrated to Illinois
     with the family of Matthew Rainey in 1829.

His religion was that of Reformed Presbyterian. Politically he was an Old Line Whig. He was a very
quiet unassuming, unpretentious kind of man, a man of integrity, firm in his opinions,
uncompromising when he was contending for the right."

He served in the following battles in the Revolutionary War: Rocky Mountain King's Mountain Houch's
     Defeat Hanging Rock

In 1829, he came to Illinois with his son-in-law, Matthew Rainey and his daughter, Ann Gaston
     Rainey.

He died in 1838, and is buried in the old Covenanter Cemetery near Walnut Hill, Illinois, in Marion
     County.

Pension application of William Gaston S32265 fn67SC
Transcribed by Will Graves rev'd 7/4/10
[Methodology: Spelling, punctuation and/or grammar have been corrected in some instances for
   ease of reading and to facilitate searches of the database. Also, the handwriting of the original
   scribes often lends itself to varying interpretations. Users of this database are urged to view
   the original and to make their own decision as to how to decipher what the original scribe
   actually wrote. Blanks appearing in the transcripts reflect blanks in the original. Folks are
   free to make non-commercial use this transcript in any manner they may see fit, but please
   extend the courtesy of acknowledging the transcriber—besides, if it turns out the transcript
   contains mistakes, the resulting embarrassment will fall on the transcriber. I use speech
   recognition software to make all my transcriptions. Such software misinterprets my
   southern accent with unfortunate regularity and my poor proofreading fails to catch all
   misinterpretations. I welcome and encourage folks to call those and any other errors to my
   attention.]
State of Illinois, County of Marion
On this 24th day of September 1832 personally appeared in open court before the Judge of Circuit
   Court now sitting William Gaston a resident of the County of Marion and State of Illinois aged
   Seventy-five years being first duly sworn according to law doth on his oath make the
   following declaration in order to obtain the benefit of the Act of Congress passed June 7th,
   1832.
That he entered the service of the United States first as a drafted militia in the State of South
   Carolina and County of Chester in the year 1775 first tour of Broad River under Captain
   Marshall to rout some Tories who were encamped 50 or 60 miles from where I lived. The
   second tour drafted militia under the same Captain to Charleston about 150 miles. In 1776,
   in a third tour in the same year under the same Captain to Purysburg on Savannah River.
   Field officers not recollected. In all a service of six or seven months.

After Charlestown fell into the hands of the British in 1780, he entered the service as a mounted
   volunteer under Captain John McClure, Colonel Lacy [sic, Edward Lacey], & General Sumpter
   [sic, Thomas Sumter] field officers. After several skirmishes he fought at the Battles of Rocky
   Mountain, Hanging Rock, Hook's defeat [sic, Huck's defeat or Williamson's Plantation or the
   Battle of Brattonsville], and King's Mountain (when General Sumter was surprised near
   McDonald's Ford on Catawba River he is this applicant's horse fell into the hand of the
   Enemy for which he never was compensated). Afterwards several Scouting parties
   terminated his service of nearly two years as a mounted volunteer when he was dismissed
   by Captain Steel who was his Captain from the time Captain McClure fell at Hanging Rock –
   and also that his discharge if he ever had one is lost. That he has no documentary evidence
   and that he knows of no person whose testimony he can procure who can testify to his
   service except Mrs. Jane Gaston relic of John Gaston deceased aged about 87 years whose
   testimony to a part of his services follows below in her separate affidavit.

I hereby relinquish every claim to a pension or annuity except the present, and declare that my
   name is not on the pension roll of the agency of any State.
Subscribed & sworn to on the year aforesaid. S/ Wm Gaston, ~ his mark

The affidavit of Jane Gaston, who being duly sworn deposes & says that in the year 1780,
   according to the best of her recollection, she with her late husband John Gaston, was living in
   Chester County S. C. and that William Gaston who has subscribed & sworn to the foregoing
   Declaration, was then a single man, & living with this affiant & her said husband John Gaston,
   being a cousin of the said John; and that she recollects distinctly when the said William
   Gaston volunteered under General Sumter to fight the British & Tories – and that he
   remained absent in the service for about two years, except when he would return home a few

days on furlough. She states her age to do be about 87 years. Sworn to and subscribed the
day & year aforesaid S/ Jane Gaston, X her mark
S/ R. Ricker, Clerk in open Court
[fn p. 58: Thomas Rice, a merchant residing in Jefferson County Illinois, and Matthew Rainey of
Marion County Illinois gave the standard supporting affidavit.]
Amended Declaration of William Gaston for a pension under the Act of Congress of June 7th, 1832

Personally appeared in open court before Thomas C. Brown one of the Justices of the Supreme
Court of Illinois & by law assigned to hold Circuit Court in the County of Marion & State of
Illinois William Gaston, who being duly sworn, deposeth and saith by reason of old age & the
consequent loss of memory, he cannot swear positively as to the precise length of his Service,
but according to the best of his recollection he served not less than the periods mentioned
below and in the following grades:

For two months I served as a private under Captain Marshall in the year 1775. For one month &
14 days I served as a private under Captain Marshall in the year 1776. For two months I
served as a private under Captain Marshall in the year 1776. For one year I served as a
private under Captain John McClure in the year 1780 & 1781. For one year I served as a
private under Captain _ Steel in the years 1781 & 1782 and for such service I claim a
pension. And he further states that he did not know that it was necessary to have a
clergyman nor could he learn better, as his declaration was written out by one of his
neighbors who he supposes knew no better himself, if he had known it, he could have
procured one. He further states that he had a record of his age made in his own Bible, & that
he gave the Bible to his son John who lives on Shoal Creek Bond County in this State but he
does not know what has become of it.
Query: Where & in what year were you born?
Ans: I was born in Lancaster County Pennsylvania on the 10th day of July 1757.
Query: Have you any record of your age, if so where is it? Answered above.
Query: Where were you living when called into service, where have you lived since the The
revolution, and where do you now live?
Ans: In Chester S. C. where I lived a while after the Revolution, then I moved to Kentucky & thence
to Illinois: and now live in Marion County. The other interrogatories are already answered in
the best of my recollection.
Subscribed percent sworn in open Court this 23rd day of September A.D. 1833.
S/ Rufus Ricker, Clk S/ William Gaston, ~ his mark
[Daniel Williams, a clergyman, and Donald R. Chance, a clergyman, state that they believe the
applicant to be about 75 years of age and that he is reputed in the neighborhood to have
been a revolutionary war soldier and that they concur in that opinion.]
[Applicant died in Marion County, Ill. on January 12, 1838.]
[fn p. 8: On February 28, 1860, in Marion County Illinois, William Gaston, Junior and Ann Raney
[could be "Ann Rainey"], filed an affidavit stating that they are the heirs of William Gaston
being his son and daughter; that their father died January 12, 1838 in Marion County Illinois;
that they are making this claim to obtain the pension due their father under the act of
Congress of 1818.]
[Veteran was pensioned at the rate of $80 per annum commencing March 4th, 1831, for 2 years
service in the South Carolina militia as a private.]

Children:
MARGARET ANN GASTON b. Feb-15-1783 in Chester Co, SC,[126] d. Aug-18-1831 in Jefferson Co, IL,[126]
resided (settled in 1822) in Marion Co, IL,[44] buried in Old Covenanter Cem, Walnut Hill, Marion
Co, IL.[126] She married[44] ca 1799 in Chester Co, SC,[126] Thomas Kell.
Jane Kell, b. 27 Mar 1802 in Chester District, SC; d. 17 Jun 1873 in Marion Co., IL. She married James
Telford 1820 in Chester Co., SC, son of Samuel Telford and Margaret McCreary. He was b. 2 Feb
1800 in Chester Co., SC; d. 23 Mar 1857 in Marion Co., IL.

  ii. ANN GASTON b. May- 9-1784 in Chester Co, SC,[126] d. May-17-1867 in Marion Co, IL.[126] She married[cxxviii[128]] ca 1804 in Chester Co, SC,[126] Matthew Rainey, also known as Matthew Raney.[128]

  121. iii. WILLIAM GASTON, JR. b. Jan- 1-1786 in Chester Co., SC, d. 21 Sep 1869 in Jefferson Co., IL. He married Jane McMillan abt. 1813 in SC.

  122. iv. SAMUEL GASTON[44] b. Oct-16-1787 d. 1 Mar 1826 I Jefferson Co., IL.

  v. JOHN R. GASTON b. ca 1790 in Chester Co, SC,[126] d. in Bond Co, IL,[126] resided (settled, by 1833) in Bond Co, IL.[44] He married Dec-28-1816 in Christian Co, KY,[126] Elizabeth Carson.

  vi. SARAH MCCLURE GASTON b. Mar-17-1792 in Chester Co, SC,[126] d. Jul- 3-1834 in Marion Co, IL.[126] She married Nov- 5-1812 in Christian Co, KY,[126] Matthew Cunningham.

  vii. ROBERT GASTON b. ca 1794 in Chester Co, SC,[126] d. in Bond Co, IL,[126] resided (settled in 1822) in Bond Co, IL.[44] He married Ann Carson 11 Aug 1814 in Christian Co., KY.

  viii. ELIZABETH GASTON b. 1796 in Chester Co, SC,[126] d. ca 1845 in Barry Co, MO.[126] She married Aug-17-1815 in Christian Co, KY,[126] Andrew Carson.

  ix. MARY ANN GASTON b. in Chester Co, SC,[126] d. 1843 in Jefferson Co, IL.[126] She married Sep-13-1827 in Bond Co, IL,[126] Hugh White.

58. **Thomas Gaston** (16.Robert[4], 5.William[3], 3.John[2], 1.Jean[1]), b. Jul-18-1759 in Lynch's Creek, Lancaster Co, SC,[cxxix[129],cxxx[130]] d. Apr-23-1832,[129] occupation wagon maker,[cxxxi[131]] military Revolutionary War (served as an irregular),[26,cxxxii[132]] [As a wagon maker by trade, in the Revolutionary War he devoted his time to building and repairing wagons for the Continental Army. The same powder horn used by Thomas Gaston in the Revolutionary War was later used by other family member in the War of 1812 and in the Civil War.].

"Thomas Gaston was a devout Presbyterian and was at all times ready to give of his time and money to the advancement of community welfare. He owned a flour and grist mill on Gaston Creek, and later installed one of the first cotton gins for that section of the country."[131]

He married[130] **Sarah Nickels** (daughter of James Nickels), d. Mar-30-1818.[129]
  Children:
  123. i. ROBERT GASTON b. Sep-17-1787.
  124. ii. JAMES NICKELS "JIMMY" GASTON b. Jan-18-1789.
  125. iii. HUGH GASTON b. Sep-29-1790.
  iv. ELIZABETH GASTON b. Feb- 5-1793.[cxxxiii[133]] She married[129] Jesse Wakefield.
  v. WILLIAM GASTON b. Jan- 7-1795,[133] d. Dec-14-1825,[133] never married.[133]
  vi. JOSEPH GASTON b. Jul- 9-1796,[133] d. Jul-13-1847.[133] He married[133] Margaret Caldwell. Had three daughters.[133]
  126. vii. SAMUEL GASTON b. Sep- 4-1798.
  viii. MARGARET LOGAN GASTON b. Jun-13-1800,[133] d. Jul-22-1863.[133]
  127. ix. THOMAS LOGAN GASTON b. Apr- 7-1805.

59. **James Gaston** (16.Robert[4], 5.William[3], 3.John[2], 1.Jean[1]), b. Jul-24-1761,[124,50] d. Mar- 7-1840 in Wayne Co, IL,[12] buried in Bovee Cemetery, Wayne Co, IL,[cxxxiv[134]] resided (settled) in Wayne Co, IL, resided formerly in Christian Co, KY, resided originally in South Carolina.

Hanna, in "Ohio Valley Genealogies," p. 41, and Burgess in "Gaston Genealogy," p. 121, state only that this James Gaston was a son of Robert Gaston, who was a son of William Gaston and Olivet Lemon. More recent researchers have shown that this James Gaston married Catherine Creighton and settled in Wayne Co, IL, raising a family of eight children.

He married[12] Mar-20-1783 in Lancaster Co, SC,[134] **Catherine Creighton**, b. 1764,[12] d. Jan- 5-1848 in Wayne Co, IL,[12] buried in Bovee Cemetery, Wayne Co, IL.[134]
  Children:
  i. MARGARET GASTON b. ca 1784 in South Carolina,[12] d. ca 1806 in South Carolina.[12]

ii. JANE CATHERINE GASTON b. Jul-11-1785 in South Carolina,[12] d. 1865.[12] She married[cxxxv][135] (1) John Murray Massey, also known as Murray Massey,[134] b. ca 1781.[12] One child.[12]

She married[135] (2) John Bovee, b. Sep-11-1788,[12] d. Jan-21-1868.[12] Seven children.[12]

iii. THOMAS CREIGHTON GASTON b. May 4 1790/91 in South Carolina,[12] d. ca 1833 in Illinois.[12] He married[cxxxvi][136] (1) Feb- 1-1814,[12] Elender Clark, b. 1792.[12] He married[136] (2) Feb- 1-1821,[12] Sarah Conner, b. Aug-10-1803.[12]

iv. ROBERT RUTLEDGE GASTON b. Jan-27-1792 in Lancaster Co, SC,[12] d. Nov-12-1837 in Wayne Co, IL.[12] He married[cxxxvii][137] Feb- 4-1812 in Christian Co, KY, Elizabeth "Betsy" Whitney, b. ca 1792,[12] d. Dec-28-1849.[12]

v. ELIHU GASTON b. 1793 in South Carolina,[12] d. 1834 in Illinois.[12] He married[cxxxviii][138] (1) Dec-18-1818,[12] Nancy Wilson, b. 1795.[12] He married[138] (2) Mary Ann Treadway.

vi. JOHN GASTON b. Jan-14-1796 in South Carolina,[12] d. May- 5-1875 in Illinois.[12] He married[cxxxix][139] (1) Dec- 1-1817,[12] Jane Treadway, b. 1781,[12] d. 1834.[12] He married[139] (2) ca 1834,[12] Hannah Bovee, b. Aug-14-1814,[12] d. Nov-25-1856.[12] He married[139] (3) ca 1858,[12] Artimissa M. Perrens, b. ca 1814,[12] d. Sep- 6-1869.[12]

vii. ELIZABETH GASTON b. 1797 in South Carolina.[12] She married[12] Benjamine McGehee.

viii. JAMES CYRUS GASTON b. Aug-28-1798 in South Carolina,[12] d. 1878 in Missouri.[12] He married[cxl][140] Margaret Clark, b. Mar-12-1798.[12]

60. **Hugh Gaston** (16.Robert[4], 5.William[3], 3.John[2], 1.Jean[1]), b. 1776,[12] d. 1830,[12] resided (settled) in Greene Co, IN, resided formerly in Kentucky, resided originally in South Carolina. He married[cxli][141] **Jane __**.

        Children:
128. i. ROBERT GASTON b. 1799.

61. **Martha Gaston** (17.Hugh[4], 5.William[3], 3.John[2], 1.Jean[1]), b. Jun-11-1752 in Ireland.[44] She married **James Ross**.

        Children:
i. JAMES ROSS b. in Ireland.[44]

Emigrated to America, remaining for nine years, but then returned to Ireland and settled at Londonderry. Four children.[44]

He married (Female) Rogan (daughter of __ Rogan and Elizabeth Gaston).
ii. (FEMALE) ROSS b. in Ireland,[44] resided (settled) in Baltimore, MD.[44]

Married and had 10 or 11 children, some of whom settled in Baltimore.[44]

iii. HUGH GASTON ROSS b. in Ireland,[44] d. [Not heard from after 1817.], immigrated[44] military War of 1812.[44]

iv. REBECCA ROSS resided 1833 in New Jersey. She married[44] ca 1818, Stephen Latimer, resided originally in New Jersey.[44]

62. **Elizabeth Gaston** (17.Hugh[4], 5.William[3], 3.John[2], 1.Jean[1]), b. Jun-16-1759 in Ireland.[44] She married[44] **__ Rogan**, b. in Northern Ireland,[44] occupation physician, surgeon.[44] Of their eight children, six were boys, one daughter died unmarried, and the other daughter married Elizabeth's nephew James Ross and moved to Ireland.

        Children:
i. (FEMALE) ROGAN. She married James Ross, b. in Ireland,[44] (son of James Ross and Martha Gaston).

James: Emigrated to America, remaining for nine years, but then returned to Ireland and settled at Londonderry. Four children.[44]

63. **Thomas Gaston** (17.Hugh[4], 5.William[3], 3.John[2], 1.Jean[1]), b. in Ireland,[44] d. bef 1833 in New York, resided (settled) in New York.[44] He married **Unknown**, d. bef 1833.
   Children:
   i. (FEMALE) GASTON resided (settled) in Orange, Essex Co, NJ.[44] She married[44] __ Lindsay.
   ii. (FEMALE) GASTON.

64. **William Joseph Gaston** (18.Alexander[4], 5.William[3], 3.John[2], 1.Jean[1]), b. Sep-19-1778 in New Bern, Craven Co, NC,[cxlii[142],55,14] d. Jan-23-1844 in Raleigh, Wake Co, NC,[cxliii[143],55,14] buried in Cedar Grove Cemetery, New Bern, NC [William Joseph Gaston was initially buried in Raleigh, but his remains were later taken to New Bern for burial by the graves of his parents and daughter.], occupation Congressman & Judge.

William Gaston of North Carolina entered Georgetown on Nov 22 1791 as the first student to enroll. Though health forced his transfer to Princeton, where he was placed in the third year of studies after a year and a half at Georgetown, Gaston remained close to the faculty throughout his life. He served in the U.S. Congress 1813-15, where he introduced the legislation chartering the college, and served as Chief Justice of the North Carolina Supreme Court 1833-44. In 1817, he voluntarily retired from Congress and never again entered national politics, declining in 1840 the offer of the U.S. senatorship and in 1841 the offer of a seat as Attorney General in the cabinet of President Harrison. He wrote the state song of North Carolina, where the city of Gastonia and the county of Gaston are named in his honor.
http://gulib.lausun.georgetown.edu/dept/speccoll/case5.htm

"In 1835, Gaston was an influential delegate to the North Carolina Constitutional Convention, where he fought to have religious qualifications for office holding dropped and where he attempted to protect the voting privileges of free people of color. Gaston also supported federal representation as the basis for representation in the House of Commons and biennial meetings of the state legislature. "Gaston's law practice was very successful and his reputation in legal circles was of national scope. Daniel Webster and John Marshall, among others, consulted with him on legal questions. In 1833, Gaston was elected by the state legislature to a post as an associate justice of the North Carolina Supreme Court, where he served until his death in 1844. Gaston's most famous decision on the bench came in 1834 with the case of State v. Negro Will. Gaston ruled that a slave had the right to defend himself against an unlawful attempt of a master, or an agent of a master, to kill him. In the significant case of State v. William Manuel in 1838, he held that a manumitted slave was a citizen of the state and thus entitled to the guarantees of the constitution. Gaston purchased a library for the state Supreme Court while on a trip to New York City in 1835. "
http://www.lib.unc.edu/mss/inv/g/Gaston,William.html#

Some accounts put his two older children, Alexander and Susan, as being by his first wife, Susan Hay, but according to his biography, "William Gaston, Carolinian," by J. Herman Schauinger (Bruce Publishing Co, Milwaukee, WI, 1949), Susan died just eight months after they were married. Because his second wife, Hannah, died in 1813, it is clear that his first three children were by her, and his last two by his third wife, Eliza Ann Worthington, daughter of the college physician.[cxliv[144]]

He married[14] (1) Sep- 4-1803 in Fayetteville, Cumberland Co, NC,[122] **Susan Hay**, b. ca 1787,[122] (daughter of John Hay and __ Grove), d. Apr-20-1804.[122]

He married[14] (2) Oct- 6-1805 in New Bern, Craven Co, NC,[122] **Hannah McClure**, b. ca 1786,[122] (daughter of William McClure and Sarah Davis), d. Jul-14-1813 in New Bern, Craven Co, NC.

Hannah: Children Alexander and Susan are reported in Hanna's "Ohio Valley Genealogies," p. 42, as being William J. Gaston's children by his first wife. But Hanna also concurs with the 1803 and 1805 dates of William's first two marriages. Several months pregnant, Hannah died of convulsions brought on by news that the British were about to attack her town. Their three children stayed with William's sister Jane in Raleigh for the next three years. William Joseph Gaston and Hannah McClure were first cousins once removed, as he was the grandson of William Gaston (b. 1680 in Ireland) and she was the great-granddaughter of the same William Gaston.

He married (3) Sep- 3-1816 in Georgetown, Washington, DC,[54] **Eliza Ann Worthington** (daughter of Charles Worthington), d. Jan-19-1819 in North Carolina.[122]

        Children by Hannah McClure:
129.   i.   ALEXANDER F. GASTON b. Jan-19-1807.
       ii.   SUSAN JANE GASTON[122] b. Jun- 4-1808 in North Carolina,[122] d. 1866. She married Feb-14-1828 in New Bern, Craven Co, NC,[54] Robert Donaldson.

        Robert: Robert Donaldson was a Scotch merchant from New York City, with financial interests in North Carolina. Robert and Susan were married in the Gaston home by Bishop John England. They lived in Fayetteville, NC during the winter, and in summer at Robert's home in New York on the Hudson River.

130.   iii.   HANNAH MARGARET GASTON b. Mar-18-1811.
        Children by Eliza Ann Worthington:
       iv.   ELIZA ANN GASTON b. Sep-27-1817 in Georgetown, Washington, DC,[122] [Age 30 in 1850 Census and age 50 in 1870 Census would put birth in about 1820. Birthplace given in 1850 Census as Maryland, but in 1870 Census as North Carolina.], d. 1874, census 1850, 1870 in Prince Georges Co, MD. She married Nov-14-1842 in Washington, DC,[54] George W. Graham,[cxlv[145]] b. ca 1813,[cxlvi[146]] (son of John Graham and Susan Hall), resided in Maryland,[145] census 1850 in Prince Georges Co, MD.
       v.   CATHERINE JANE (KATE) GASTON[122] b. Jan- 6-1819 in New Bern, Craven Co, NC,[54,122] d. 1885, never married[14.]

65. **Jane Gaston** (18.Alexander[4], 5.William[3], 3.John[2], 1.Jean[1]), b. ca 1780.[cxlvii[147]] She married ca 1797, **John Louis Taylor**, b. Mar- 1-1769 in London, England,[54,cxlviii[148]] d. Jan-29-1829 near Raleigh, Wake Co, NC,[148] buried Oakwood Cemetery in Raleigh, Wake Co, NC,[148] immigrated ca 1781,[148] occupation lawyer & judge,[148] education William & Mary College.[148]

John: Born in London of Irish parents, John Louis Taylor came to America at the age of twelve. He was licensed to the bar in 1788, and in 1792 he entered politics as a Federalist to represent the town of Fayetteville in the NC House of Commons. In 1798 he was elected a judge of the NC Superior Court, and in 1811 was named the first Chief Justice of North Carolina.

        Children:
       i.   (FEMALE) TAYLOR.

        John Louis Taylor and wife Jane Gaston had an adopted daughter, name unknown, who was widowed by former Attorney General James F. Taylor. This (Female) Taylor may or may not be the same person.[cxlix[149]]

        She married David E. Sumner, resided in Gates Co, TN.[14]
       ii.   WILLIAM TAYLOR occupation Congress/NC Chief Justice.

66. **James Knox** (19.Elizabeth[4], 5.William[3], 3.John[2], 1.Jean[1]), occupation physician.[44]
        Children:
       i.   JANE KNOX.

Possibly the same Jane Knox who married Samuel Polk, Mecklenburg Co, NC.[44]

67. **Hugh Knox** (19.Elizabeth[4], 5.William[3], 3.John[2], 1.Jean[1]). He married[cl[150]] **Jane Nesbit**, also known as Jennet or Jenny.[150]
>
> Children:
> 131. i. NANCY GASTON KNOX b. ca 1797.

68. **Hugh Gaston** (20.William[4], 5.William[3], 3.John[2], 1.Jean[1]). He married **Unknown**.
>
> Children:
> i. WILLIAM GASTON.

69. **William Gaston** (20.William[4], 5.William[3], 3.John[2], 1.Jean[1]), resided in Memphis, Shelby Co, TN,[cli[151],44] resided formerly in Corinth, Alcorn Co, MS.[151,44] He married[151] **Priscilla Buford**,[151] also known as Priscilla Beaufort,[44] [Hanna (p. 41) reports William Gaston's wife as __ Beaufort, while the DAR Lineage Book (p. 322) gives it as Priscilla Buford. The latter is considered the more reliable.].
>
> Children:
> i. LEROY GASTON occupation Presbyterian Minister.[14]
> 132. ii. FRANCES GASTON.

70. **James Gaston** (21.John[4], 6.Hugh[3], 3.John[2], 1.Jean[1]), b. 1742, baptized Mar-28-1742 in Old Tennent Church, Monmouth Co, NJ,[65,19,15] d. bef 1779 [Wife Lydia re-married in 1779.]. He married Apr-20-1773 in Monmouth Co, NJ,[19,15,20] **Lydia Tapscott**, b. 1755, d. 1791.

Lydia: Widowed, Lydia Tapscott Gaston, married Capt. David Baird in 1779. Name may have been Mary Lydia Tapscott.

> Children:
> 133. i. WILLIAM GASTON b. Feb-18-1776.

71. **Daniel Gaston** (21.John[4], 6.Hugh[3], 3.John[2], 1.Jean[1]), b. Jan- 9-1748, baptized Apr- 3-1749 in Old Tennent Church, Monmouth Co, NJ,[65,19,15] d. Jun-20-1838 in Northumberland Co, PA.

Served as soldier in Samuel Forman's Regiment of the New Jersey Militia during American Revolution. Later moved to Northumberland Co, PA, and applied for an American Revolutionary War Pension. Lived in Millstone Twp, Monmouth Co, NJ, during the Revolution. Children identified by Anna Reger Gaston as John, Catherine, John, William and Jane, all baptized at Tennent Church.

He married Nov-10-1774, **Nancy Ann __**, b. Dec-18-1752, d. aft Jan-30-1839.
> Children:
> i. JOHN GASTON baptized Apr-14-1776 in Old Tennent Church, Monmouth Co, NJ.[65,19]
> ii. SARY GASTON b. Sep- -1777.
> iii. JAMES GASTON b. Oct-13-1779.
> iv. STEPHEN GASTON b. Dec-16-1781.
> v. WILLIAM GASTON b. Jul-16-1784.
> vi. ELLEN GASTON b. Jan-23-1787, baptized Jun-24-1787 in Old Tennent Church, Monmouth Co, NJ.[clii[152]]
> vii. JANE GASTON b. Jul- 3-1789.

72. **John Gaston, Jr.** (21.John[4], 6.Hugh[3], 3.John[2], 1.Jean[1]), b. Sep-16-1752 in Monmouth Co, NJ,[74] baptized Jan-20-1754 in Old Tennent Church, Monmouth Co, NJ,[65,22] d. Apr- 6-1829 in Harrison Co, (W)VA,[17] buried in Sinclair Cemetery, Upper Duck Crk Rd, Harrison Co, WV,[cliii[153]] occupation farmer, blacksmith, military Revolutionary War.
John Gaston, Jr. and his wife, Anna Davisson, came to Duck Creek, Harrison County, Virginia (now West Virginia) in 1796. Anna's sister Elizabeth and her husband, Watters Smith, also came to Duck

Creek at the same time and bought land there. John Gaston, Jr. served in the Revolutionary War in Capt. John Covenhoven's (aka Jon Cowenhoven) Company, Col. Samuel Forman's 2nd Regiment, of the Monmouth County NJ Militia. New Jersey Department of Defense records show him as a Sergeant as of Jul-1-1780.

He married 1785 [probably Monmouth Co, NJ], **Anna Davisson**, b. Feb-20-1765 in Tennent, Monmouth Co, NJ,[clv154],[clv155] (daughter of Andrew Davison and Sarah Smith), d. Aug- 8-1854 in Duck Creek, Harrison Co, WV,[clvi156] buried in Sinclair Cemetery, Upper Duck Crk Rd, Harrison Co, WV,[17] [Headstone reads: Anna, wife of John Gaston Sr., died Aug 8 1854, aged 89y 5m 17d.].

Anna: Anna Davisson was known also as Ann and Anne, and also as Davison. The newer spelling has two "ss" and seems to have been adopted by the clerk of the court in Harrison County.

        Children:
134.	i.	ANDREW GASTON b. ca 1782.
135.	ii.	MARY E. "POLLY" GASTON b. May- 4-1785.
136.	iii.	HUGH GASTON b. Jun- 5-1788.
137.	iv.	SARAH GASTON b. Dec-29-1790.
138.	v.	MARGARET GASTON b. Apr-13-1793.
139.	vi.	JOHN GASTON b. May-24-1796.
140.	vii.	DEBORAH GASTON b. Aug- 9-1798.
141.	viii.	JANE GASTON b. Nov-14-1802.
142.	ix.	JAMES GASTON b. 1804.
143.	x.	WILLIAM G. GASTON b. Feb- 1-1806.

73. **Jane Gaston** (21.John[4], 6.Hugh[3], 3.John[2], 1.Jean[1]), b. Dec-11-1758 in New Jersey, baptized Mar-25-1759 in Old Tennent Church, Monmouth Co, NJ,[65,22] d. Jan- 7-1808, buried in Old Tennent Church Cem, Monmouth Co, NJ.

Always resided in the Freehold, New Jersey area. [Names and birth dates of second husband and their children obtained from "This Old Monmouth of Ours," by William S. Horner, p. 114. Names and birthdates of first husband and their children obtained from records at the Old Tennent Church, Monmouth Co, NJ.]

She married (1) 1774, **James Mount**, b. Mar-27-1752 in Upper Freehold, Monmouth Co, NJ, d. Dec-27-1786, buried in Yellow Meeting House Cem, Freehold, NJ. She married (2) Jul- 2-1788,[23] **Lewis Anderson**, b. Jan-22-1757, d. Mar-29-1838, buried in Old Tennent Church Cem, Monmouth Co, NJ.
        Children by James Mount:
    144. i.   JOHN GASTON MOUNT b. Jul-28-1775.
        ii.   EZEKIEL I. MOUNT b. Aug-17-1777 in New Jersey, d. 1865, census 1850, 1860 in Millstone Twp, Monmouth Co, NJ.

        1850 Census, Monmouth Co, New Jersey (Millstone Twp), enumerated on Jul 25
1850:
        Ezekiel I. Mount, 72, farmer; Margaret, 60; Elenor, 46; Rebecca, 35; John G, 31; Margaret, 31; Mary Matilda, 3; Margaret Ann, 1; William Stillwell, 19, laborer. All born in New Jersey.

        1860 Census, Monmouth Co, New Jersey (Millstone Twp), enumerated on Jul 23
1860:
        Ezekle I. Mount, 83, farmer; Margaret, 70; Elliner, 40. All born in Monmouth.

        He married (1) Leah ___. He married (2) Margaret Gaston, b. 1790 in New Jersey, d. 1874, census 1850, 1860 in Millstone Twp, Monmouth Co, NJ.

Margaret: It is not known what relationship, if any, this Margaret Gaston had with any of the other Gastons in this genealogy. Given the times and locations, however, it is likely that there was some connection.

    iii.   SEXTON MOUNT b. Jul-24-1781. He married Jun- 4-1808, Margaret Mount.

Margaret: Unknown what blood relationship, if any, Margaret Mount was to husband Sexton.

    iv.   CATHERINE MOUNT b. 1784, d. Apr- 2-1819. She married Peter Perrine, Jr., b. Mar-3-1768, d. Sep- 6-1846.
    v.   REBECCA MOUNT b. 1786.
    Children by Lewis Anderson:
    vi.   ANNA LLOYD ANDERSON b. Nov-26-1789 in New Jersey.
    vii.   KENNETH ANDERSON b. in New Jersey.
    viii. HANNAH ANDERSON b. May-30-1793 in New Jersey.
    ix.   JAMES ANDERSON b. Feb-15-1795 in New Jersey.
    x.   WILLIAM ANDERSON b. Feb-15-1797 in New Jersey.
    xi.   THOMAS ANDERSON b. Dec-12-1799 in New Jersey.

74. **John Gaston, Jr.** (22.William[4], 6.Hugh[3], 3.John[2], 1.Jean[1]), b. May- -1740 in Monmouth Co, NJ,[17,19,clvii[157],15] d. Sep-10-1823 in Washington Co, PA,[17,157] buried in Mingo Creek Presb Cem, Union Twp, Washington Co, PA,[17,14,15] [Headstone inscription reads "In Memory of John Gaston, who departed this life September 10th A.D. 1823, aged 83 years & 4 months." A separate metal marker staked into the ground adjacent to the headstone reads "Revolutionary Soldier, 1775 - 1883, Placed by the Monongahela Valley Chapter D.A.R."], military Major, Revolutionary War.[15]

Resided in Upper Freehold Township, Monmouth County NJ, from before 1760 until after 1767, moving then to Mt Bethel Twp, Northampton Co, PA, where he took up 275 acres of land in Feb 1772. Served as a Major in the Revolutionary War. Around 1780-82, moved to Rostraver Twp, Westmoreland Co, PA, and in about 1790 to Peters (now Union) Township, Washington Co, PA, his wife's sister Elizabeth accompanying them. He purchased a large tract of land there known as Belmont, after which the area became known as Gastonville. The "Gaston House" there was built in 1908 and occupied by Gastons until 1964.

From a listing of baptisms in "History of the Old Tennent Church," p. 210: "John Gaston Jr., whose Father was Murthered by the Indians; had bap. William, Sep. 6, 1761; Joseph, July 17, 1763; John, Apr. 14, 1765; Samuel & James, Twin Children, Apr. 12, 1767."[clviii[158],clix[159]]

He married Feb-4-1760 in Monmouth Co, NJ,[14] **Charity Cheeseman**, also known as Charety,[17] b. Mar-13-1734 in New Jersey,[14,17] (daughter of Joseph Cheeseman and Lydia Parent), d. Feb-15-1821,[14,17] buried in Mingo Creek Presb Cem, Union Twp, Washington Co, PA.[14,clx[160],15].
    Children:
145. i.   WILLIAM GASTON b. Jul-15-1761.
146. ii.   JOSEPH GASTON b. Apr-25-1763.
    iii.   JOHN GASTON b. Jan- 7-1765,[66] baptized Apr-14-1765 in Old Tennent Church, Monmouth Co, NJ.[159]
    iv.   SAMUEL (TWIN) GASTON b. Feb-18-1767,[66] baptized Apr-12-1767,[159] d. in infancy.[66]
147. v.   JAMES (TWIN) GASTON b. Feb-18-1767.
148. vi.   SAMUEL GASTON, SR. b. Oct-10-1772.
149. vii. MARGARET GASTON b. ca 1776.
    viii. ELIZABETH GASTON b. May- 8-1778,[66] d. Feb-28-1858 in Washington Co, PA,[66,67] buried in Mingo Creek Presb Cem, Union Twp, Washington Co, PA,[67] never married[67.]

The birth/death dates of May 8 1778 & Feb 28 1858 are from Hanna, p. 43. Death and burial locations are from Peter & Jane Topoly, original source not stated. A headstone for this Elizabeth Gaston conforming to those dates could not be found at the Mingo Creek Presbyterian Cemetery. However, there was a headstone there for Elizabeth Gaston, who died Apr 25 1858, age 80. If this is the same person, which is likely, the reason for the discrepancy in the death date is not known.

75. **William Gaston** (22.William[4], 6.Hugh[3], 3.John[2], 1.Jean[1]), b. ca 1742 in Somerset Co, NJ,[15] [Probably. Hanna, p. 43, gives birth date as 1742-48.], d. ca Apr 1801 in Upper Mt. Bethel Twp, Northampton Co, PA.[15,66] He married[15,66] **Elizabeth __**.

Elizabeth: Possibly the sister of Ann Simonton (dau of Robert Simonton), who married Matthew Gaston.[15]

          Children:
        i.   ALEXANDER GASTON resided until aft 1811 in Lower Mt. Bethel Twp, Northampton Co, PA,[66] [Richmond]. He married[66] Huldah __.
        ii.   WILLIAM GASTON.
150.   iii. CHARLES W. GASTON[15,66] b. 1781.
        iv. MARGARET GASTON. She married bef 1806, Elisha Everitt.
        v.   ELIZABETH GASTON. She married 1806-07, Simeon Hart.

76. **James Gaston** (22.William[4], 6.Hugh[3], 3.John[2], 1.Jean[1]), b. ca 1750,[15] d. 1824 in Beaver Co, PA,[67] resided 1773 in Northampton Co, PA.

There is some speculation that this may be the James Gaston who was a Justice of the Peace of Somerset County in 1781 and was appointed a lay Judge in 1783, as further information regarding him is lacking.[15]

He married[67] **Elizabeth Lyle**, b. 1760 in Northampton Co, PA,[67] (daughter of Robert Lyle and Mary Gilleland).
          Children:
        i.   WILLIAM GASTON.
151.   ii.   ROBERT GASTON.
        iii. MARGARET GASTON. She married[67] __ Selby.
        iv. ELEANOR JANE GASTON. She married[67] __ Miller.
152.   v.   MARY "POLLY" GASTON b. Oct-10-1787.

77. **Hugh Gaston** (23.Joseph[4], 6.Hugh[3], 3.John[2], 1.Jean[1]), b. Jan-18-1764 in Somerset Co, NJ,[15,69] d. Jun-24-1839 in East Liverpool, Columbiana Co, OH,[15,clxi[161],69] ["History of the Upper Ohio Valley" (p. 146) reports death date as about 1837.], buried in Columbiana Co, OH.

Birth place appears in "History of the Upper Ohio Valley" (p. 146) as Ireland, which is considered incorrect, as grandfather Hugh Gaston emigrated from there in about 1720. Anna Reger Gaston reports it unequivocally as Somerset Co, NJ. Hugh Gaston resided in Bedminster Twp, Somerset Co, NJ in 1787. According to Hanna's "Ohio Valley Genealogies," p. 44, in about 1795-1799, Hugh moved to Washington County & Lycoming County, and then to western Pennsylvania & Ohio. But the date of his departure from New Jersey is considered suspect, since the birthplace of his older children, born before 1795, is shown in census records not as New Jersey, but as Pennsylvania. Hugh Gaston and Grace Gaston were second cousins, as both were great-grandchildren of John Gaston (b. 1645 in Scotland).[69]

He married Mar-14-1789 in Somerset Co, NJ,[67,15,69] **Grace Gaston**, b. Nov-25-1764,[15,69] (daughter of Robert Gaston and Rosanna Cooper), d. Mar-14-1838.[15,69]

Children:
153. i.   JOSEPH GASTON b. Dec-24-1789.
154. ii.   JAMES WILLIAM GASTON b. Jan-20-1793.
      iii.   ROBERT GASTON b. Feb-23-1794,[15,69] d. Jun- 4-1801.[15,69]
      iv.   ELIZABETH GASTON b. Sep- 7-1797,[15,69] d. Jan-14-1816.[15,69]
155. v.   HUGH GASTON b. Apr- 9-1804.

78. **James Gaston** (23.Joseph[4], 6.Hugh[3], 3.John[2], 1.Jean[1]), b. ca 1767 in Somerset Co, NJ,[15,clxii[162]] d. May-Ju-1813 in Smith Twp, Washington Co, PA,[69] resided (settled abt 1788) in Smith Twp, Washington Co, PA.[69]

In about 1788, moved from Lower Mount Bethel Township, Northampton County, PA, settling in Smith Township, Washington County, PA. One account (Ohio Valley Genealogies) lists 7 children as: William, Mary, Jane, Eleanor (who married a Moore), James W., John, and an unnamed female who also married a Moore. Another account (The Gaston Genealogy by Jane Farrell Burgess) lists 7 children as Mary, William, Joseph, Hugh, Isabella, John, & James W. Yet another account (Anna Reger Gaston's "Gaston Family Lines of Somerset") lists only William, Mary, Jane and John. We list here a combination of the accounts.

He married[15] **Jane __**.
      Children:
      i.   MARY GASTON. She married[69] __ Anderson.
      ii.   WILLIAM GASTON d. 1830 in Brooke Co, (W)VA,[69] never married[69.]
      iii.   JOSEPH GASTON.
      iv.   HUGH GASTON.
      v.   ISABELLA GASTON.
      vi.   JOHN GASTON.
156. vii.   JANE GASTON[69] b. Oct- 2-1792.
157. viii.   JAMES W. GASTON[69] b. Aug-29-1808.
      ix.   ELEANOR GASTON. She married[69] __ Moore.
158. x.   (FEMALE) GASTON[69].

79. **Alexander Gaston** title: Dr. (23.Joseph[4], 6.Hugh[3], 3.John[2], 1.Jean[1]), b. Jul-22-1769 in Northampton Co, PA,[clxiii[163],15,69,clxiv[164]] d. Jul- 9-1825 in Morristown, Belmont Co, OH,[clxv[165],clxvi[166],15,69,164] buried in First Cemetery, Union Twp, Morristown, OH, occupation physician.[15]

Dr. Alexander Gaston settled with his mother in Canton Twp, Washington Co, PA about 1792. He later moved to Brooke Co, (W)VA, and from there, in about 1800, to near St. Clairsville, Belmont Co, OH, and from there, in about 1811, to Morristown, Belmont Co, OH. Upon his move in 1800, he "was accompanied by two men, who helped him cut the timber and build a cabin on his land. They camped out two weeks under the cover of their wagons, and were often awakened from the howling of wolves which infested the forests. His family consisted of a wife and three children. For several years after their settlement, they went all the way to Washington, Pa., to purchase groceries. At the time that Dr. Gaston's mother settled in Washington, the place contained but four houses. He followed blacksmithing for a couple of years. Read medicine and began practice of the same in 1809. In 1811 he removed to Morristown, where he died in 1825. He had an extensive practice which took in Woodsfield, Middletown and Freeport."[69,165]
(Note: Hanna, after presenting Alexander's family and lineage as we have it here, describes another account of this Alexander Gaston which states that he was the son of Ephraim Gaston, who was the son of Ebenezer Gaston, who migrated from Ireland with his brother Matthew (died unmarried); that Alexander had a brother Joseph, who settled in southern Indiana, and another brother who settled in West Virginia. Hanna points out that this account probably assumes Joseph, son of John, who married in South Carolina and settled in Butler County, Ohio, to have been the brother of Alexander.)[19]

He married[15,69] **Rachel Perry**, b. Sep- 1-1773,[69,164] (daughter of John Perry and Jane McMillan), d. Sep-14-1833,[69,164] buried in First Cemetery, Union Twp, Morristown, OH.[67]

Children:

    i.   JOHN PERRY GASTON b. Apr-24-1793 in Washington Co, PA,[69,clxvii[167]] buried in Harrison Co, OH. He married Sep-14-1829 in Belmont Co, OH,[67] Ruth McPherson.

    ii.   JANE GASTON b. Apr-10-1795 in Washington Co, PA,[69,167] d. Nov- 4-1796.[69]

    iii.   ROBERT GASTON b. Jan-17-1797 in Washington Co, PA,[69,167] d. Sep-27-1834.[69] He married[69] Jun- 1-1819 in Belmont Co, OH,[67] Martha McClure.

159.   iv.   EPHRAIM GASTON b. Jun-26-1799.

    v.   MARY GASTON b. May-20-1801 in Belmont Co, OH,[69,167] d. Dec-20-1846,[69] resided (settled) in McConnelsville, Morgan Co, OH.[69] She married Feb-10-1825 in Belmont Co, OH,[67] Andrew Tracy.

160.   vi.   CHARITY GASTON b. Jul-27-1803.

    vii.   JOSEPH GASTON b. May-14-1805 in Belmont Co, OH,[69,167] d. Jul- 9-1833,[69] buried in First Cemetery, Union Twp, Morristown, OH. He married[69] Apr-11-1830 in Belmont Co, OH,[67] Nancy Fowler.

    viii.   ALEXANDER GASTON b. Aug- 4-1807 in Belmont Co, OH.[167]

161.   ix.   MATTHEW GASTON b. Jul- 9-1809.

    x.   ISAAC GASTON b. Sep-16-1811 in Belmont Co, OH,[69,clxviii[168]] d. Apr-30-1881 in Colonna, Iowa.[69]

    xi.   JAMES GASTON b. Nov- 1-1813.[19]

80. **Samuel Kirkpatrick Gaston** (24.Hugh[4], 6.Hugh[3], 3.John[2], 1.Jean[1]), b. 1795,[clxix[169]] d. 1835,[169] resided 1816, 1817 in Bedminster Twp, Somerset Co, NJ,[15] occupation physician.[19,15]

Thought to have moved west after Oct 1817, as there is no trace of him in New Jersey after that date.[15]

He married[19,15,73] 1816,[169] **Nancy T. Cooper**, b. 1794,[169] (daughter of Henry Cooper, Jr. and Rachael Thompson), d. 1866.[169]

Children:

    i.   HENRIETTA GASTON.

162.   ii.   WILLIAM GASTON b. 1833.

81. **John Kirkpatrick** (25.Elizabeth[4], 6.Hugh[3], 3.John[2], 1.Jean[1]). He married[19] **Anne Coriell** (daughter of Elias Coriell).

Children:

163.   i.   SARAH "SALLY" KIRKPATRICK b. ca 1802.

164.   ii.   THOMAS KIRKPATRICK b. ca 1806.

165.   iii.   ELIZABETH KIRKPATRICK b. ca 1808.

166.   iv.   ELIAS KIRKPATRICK b. ca 1808.

167.   v.   JAMES KIRKPATRICK b. ca 1810.

168.   vi.   LYDIA KIRKPATRICK.

169.   vii.   JANE KIRKPATRICK b. ca 1814.

170.   viii.   MARY KIRKPATRICK b. 1816.

    ix.   JOHN KIRKPATRICK d. age abt 30 in Newark, Essex Co, NJ,[clxx[170],19] never married[19,15,170.]

171.   x.   ANN KIRKPATRICK b. ca 1820.

172.   xi.   HUGH KIRKPATRICK b. ca 1822.

82. **Mary Kirkpatrick** (27.Margaret[4], 8.Joseph[3], 3.John[2], 1.Jean[1]), b. ca 1755 in Somerset Co, NJ,[64] d. aft 1794 in Orange Co, NC.[clxxi[171]] He married 1775, **Henry Gomer**, b. ca 1750,[64] d. 1782 in Somerset Co, NJ.[64]

Children:

173.   i.   ELIZABETH "BETSY" GOMER b. ca 1775.

83. **Sarah Kirkpatrick** (27.Margaret[4], 8.Joseph[3], 3.John[2], 1.Jean[1]). She married **Daniel Johnston** (son of James Johnston and Jeannette (Jane) Gaston).

           Children:
- i.   ANDREW JOHNSTON b.[clxxii][172]
- ii.   JANE JOHNSTON b.[172.]
- 174. iii. JAMES THOMPSON JOHNSTON.
- iv. ELIZABETH JOHNSTON b.[172.]
- v.   LAVINIA JOHNSTON b.[172.]
- vi. SARAH ANN JOHNSTON.
- vii. DANIEL JOHNSTON b.[172.]
- viii. CAROLINE JOHNSTON b.[172.]

84. **William Gaston** (28.John[4], 8.Joseph[3], 3.John[2], 1.Jean[1]), b. Jan-13-1761,[clxxiii][173] d. Feb-13-1809,[22] [WILL: Mar-1-1809 William Gaston of Bedminster, Somerset Co, NJ. Int. inventory $464.97; made by William McEowen & Christian Eoff. Lists girting, parcel of livery lace, brass buckles for chair harness, 15 saddle trees, etc. Notes against Thomas Bangham, Jr & "an order" from David Melick. Sworn to by Naomi Gaston, Adm'x. Apr-22-1810 (File 1423 R)], buried in Lamington Presb Church Cem, Somerset Co, NJ,[17] occupation harness maker.[15] He married Dec-10-1782,[22] **Naomi Teeple**, b. Jul-20-1760,[17,27] (daughter of John Teeple and Margaret Castner), d. Jun-20-1818,[17,27] buried in Lamington Presb Church Cem, Somerset Co, NJ,[17] resided in Pluckemin, Somerset Co, NJ.

           Children:
- 175. i.   JOHN W. GASTON b. Sep-26-1783.
- ii.   WALTER GASTON b. Oct-10-1787, d. Nov- 8-1787 in Somerset Co, NJ.
- iii. WILLIAM GASTON b. Sep-26-1787 in Somerset Co, NJ,[22] d. Sep-12-1837 in New York City, NY,[22] resided in Savannah, Chatham Co, GA.[22]
- iv. MARGARET GASTON b. Oct-30-1789 in Somerset Co, NJ,[22] d. Nov- 3-1827,[clxxiv][174],[22] buried in Lamington Presb Church Cem, Somerset Co, NJ.[17] She married[22] Mar-30-1819, John Mehelm McCowen, b. 1788 (son of William McCowen and Martha Mehelm), d. Nov- 7-1820, buried in Lamington Presb Church Cem, Somerset Co, NJ.[17]

       John: Last name sometimes reported as McEowen, but headstone of wife Margaret has it as McCowen.

- v.   JOSEPH GASTON b. Feb-13-1792 in Somerset Co, NJ,[22] d. Apr- 5-1814,[22] buried in Lamington Presb Church Cem, Somerset Co, NJ.[17]
- 176. vi. JAMES (TWIN) GASTON b. Jan- 8-1795.
- vii. OLIVER B. (TWIN) GASTON b. Jan- 8-1795,[22,17] d. Jun-10-1821,[17] ["Ohio Valley Genealogies," p. 46, reports death date as Jan 21 1823, the same date he reports for Oliver's brother Abraham. But Oliver's headstone shows date as Jun 10 1821.], buried in Lamington Presb Church Cem, Somerset Co, NJ.[17]
- viii. ABRAHAM GASTON b. Apr-25-1797,[22] d. Jan-21-1823 in Somerset Co, NJ.[22]
- ix. HUGH GASTON b. Aug-27-1800,[22] d. Mar-30-1821 in Somerset Co, NJ.[22]

85. **Joseph Gaston** (28.John[4], 8.Joseph[3], 3.John[2], 1.Jean[1]), b. May- 2-1763,[22] d. Oct-16-1796.[22] He married Mar-1-1781,[22] **Ida Van Arsdale**, b. Apr-28-1762 (daughter of Philip Van Arsdale and Margaret Stryker).

Ida: Parentage unclear. Daughter of Philip (1734-1776) & Margaret Stryker (1741-1819) Van Arsdale, per "Ohio Valley Genealogies," p. 46. But father identified as Capt. Isaac Van Arsdale by researchers Max Perry (p. 151) and Anna Reger Gaston, with mother not identified. At age 14, Ida Van Arsdale gained glory in 1776 by following the British who had made a raid at Pluckemin and taken her favorite colt, and she recaptured it. [Anna Reger Gaston, citing Snell's "Hunterdon and Somerset," p. 701]

Children:
i.   ELIZABETH GASTON b. Nov-17-1782 in Pluckemin, Somerset Co, NJ,[22] d. Nov-11-1857,[22] census 1850 in Bedminster Twp, Somerset Co, NJ. She married (1) __ Annin. She married (2) John Collyer, census name John Colyer,[146] b. ca 1782 in New Jersey,[146] d. Jan- 5-1865, census 1850, 1860 in Bedminster Twp, Somerset Co, NJ.

1850 Census, Somerset Co, New Jersey (Bedminster Twp), enumerated on Aug 26 1850:
John Colyer, 68, farmer; Elizabeth Colyer, 68; Andrew J. Gulick, 24, merchant; Eliza C. Gulick, 21; Anna V. Gulick, 6 months. All born in New Jersey.

ii.   ISAAC VAN ARSDALE GASTON b. Sep- 9-1784 in Pluckemin, Somerset Co, NJ,[22] d. Feb-11-1811 in Bedminster Twp, Somerset Co, NJ.[22]

Mormon Genealogy, Washington, D.C.--WILLS--Feb. 29, 1812. Isaac Gaston of Bedminister, Somerset Co. Int. Inventory $1,419.20; made by Samuel Baylan & Elias Brown. Includes saddler's tools, leather and unfinished work in shop. Sworn to by Abraham Van Arsdale & Philip H. Van Arsdale, Adm'rs Apr. 22,1812. File 1507R.

He married Mar-15-1810, Jane Van Arsdale.
177.   iii.   JOHN I. GASTON b. Feb-14-1787.
iv.   MARGARET B. GASTON b. Feb-21-1789,[22] d. Jul- 9-1804.[22]
178.   v.   WILLIAM B. GASTON b. Aug- 9-1791.
vi.   SARAH E. GASTON b. Dec- 9-1793,[22] d. 1885,[22] resided at Basking Ridge, Bernard Twp, Somerset Co, NJ, census 1880 in Pluckemin, Somerset Co, NJ, census 1860 in Bedminster Twp, Somerset Co, NJ. She married Garrett Conover, b. ca 1810 in New Jersey, resided at Basking Ridge, Bernard Twp, Somerset Co, NJ, census 1880 in Pluckemin, Somerset Co, NJ, census 1860 in Bedminster Twp, Somerset Co, NJ.

1860 Census, Somerset Co, New Jersey (Bedminster Twp), enumerated on Sep 26 1860:
Garret Conover, 50, b. NJ, shoe maker; Sarah Conover, 65, b. NJ; Elvira B. Annin, 56, b. NJ, seamstress.

1880 Census, Somerset Co, New Jersey (Pluckamin Twp), enumerated on Jun 23 1880:
Garrett Conover, 70, b. NJ, boot & shoemaker; wife Sarah, 86, b. NJ.

vii.   LYDIA GASTON b. 1795,[22] d. 1800.[22]

86.   **Stephen Gaston** (28.John[4], 8.Joseph[3], 3.John[2], 1.Jean[1]), b. Jul-20-1769, d. in Troy, Rensselaer Co, NY. He married in Troy, Rensselaer Co, NY,[15] **Hannah Wright**, b. 1783 in Massachusetts,[15] d. in Troy, Rensselaer Co, NY.
Children:
i.   ELIZABETH GASTON b. Oct- 1-1808.
ii.   SARAH GASTON b. Jan-24-1810.
iii.   MINERVA GASTON b. Feb-14-1812.
iv.   JULIA GASTON b. Feb-26-1815.
179.   v.   OGDEN GASTON b. Mar- 5-1821.

87.   **Isaac Gaston** (28.John[4], 8.Joseph[3], 3.John[2], 1.Jean[1]), b. Mar-25-1773 in New Jersey,[22] resided (settled) near Morristown, Morris Co, NJ. He married Mar-17-1803,[15] **Anna Hedges**.
Children:
i.   AUGUSTUS L. GASTON b. May-15-1806,[22] d. 1841,[22] resided (settled, 1828) in Reily (Oxford), Butler Co, OH.[22]

180. ii.   ELIAS HEDGES GASTON[22] b. ca 1819.

88. **Margaret Gaston** (28.John[4], 8.Joseph[3], 3.John[2], 1.Jean[1]). She married **Smith Scudder** (son of Ephraim Scudder and Martha Spinning), resided originally in New Jersey.
          Children:
    181. i.   WILLIAM MANSFIELD SCUDDER[22] b. ca 1811.
          ii.   ISAAC WILLIAMSON SCUDDER b. Nov-24-1816 in Elizabeth, Union Co, NJ,[64] d. Sep-10-1881 in Jersey City, Hudson Co, NJ,[64] buried St John Episc Church in Elizabeth, Union Co, NJ.[64]

89. **Grace Gaston** (29.Robert[4], 8.Joseph[3], 3.John[2], 1.Jean[1]) (See marriage to number 77.)

90. **Joseph Gaston** (29.Robert[4], 8.Joseph[3], 3.John[2], 1.Jean[1]), b. Nov-19-1766,[17,28] d. Apr-18-1834,[17] ["Ohio Valley Genealogies," p. 47, reports death date as Apr 18 1831. But headstone shows it as Apr 18 1834.], buried in Warrior Run Church Cem, Delaware Twp, Northumberland Co, PA,[clxxv[175]] occupation County Commissioner, military Revolutionary War.[clxxvi[176]]

Moved from New Jersey to Northumberland County, PA, where he was an active member of his Presbyterian Church and served as a County Commissioner.

He married[28] Mar-12-1787,[15,clxxvii[177]] [Marriage date of 1789 reported in Hanna's "Ohio Valley Genealogies," p. 47.], **Margaret Melick**, b. Dec-22-1767,[28,46] (daughter of Aaron Moelich and Catherine Miller), d. Feb- 5-1838,[28,46] buried in Warrior Run Church Cem, Delaware Twp, Northumberland Co, PA.[17]
          Children:
    182. i.   ROBERT GASTON b. Mar-30-1790.
          ii.   CHARLOTTE GASTON b. Sep-22-1792,[clxxviii[178]] d. Aug-13-1824,[28] buried in Warrior Run Church Cem, Delaware Twp, Northumberland Co, PA.[175] She married[28] James Durham, b. 1785,[46] d. 1871,[46] buried in Warrior Run Church Cem, Delaware Twp, Northumberland Co, PA.[175]
          iii.   ROSANNA GASTON b. Jun- 7-1795,[28] d. Nov-19-1845.[28]
    183. iv.   AARON GASTON b. Apr-25-1799.
          v.   DANIEL GASTON b. Jul-26-1801,[28] d. Apr-28-1860 in Philadelphia, PA,[28] [Place of death according to Max Perry, p. 145, who reports death date as April 16, 1865.], census 1850 in Philadelphia, PA, resided (settled) in Philadelphia, PA,[28] occupation Presbyterian minister.[28] He married 1839,[28] Rosanna Morris, also known as Rosa Morris,[28] b. 1803 in Pennsylvania,[28,146] d. 1873,[28] census 1850 in Philadelphia, PA.

                1850 Census, Philadelphia, Pennsylvania (Kensington Ward), enumerated on Aug 17
      1850:

                Daniel Gaston, 48, b. Pa, clergyman; Rosanna Gaston, 45, b. Pa; Ann Morris, 74, b. NJ.

          vi.   MARY GASTON b. May-14-1804,[28,46] d. Jul-11-1880,[28,46] buried in Warrior Run Church Cem, Delaware Twp, Northumberland Co, PA.[175]
          vii.   ANNE GASTON b. Dec-20-1808. She married[28] William Sample.

91. **Margaret Gaston** (29.Robert[4], 8.Joseph[3], 3.John[2], 1.Jean[1]), b. Dec-17-1768,[28] d. Sep-10-1807.[28] She married 1785,[28] **Daniel Melick**, b. Oct-29-1763,[27] (son of Aaron Moelich and Catherine Miller), d. Jul-9-1815 in Bedminster Twp, Somerset Co, NJ,[27] occupation tanner, farmer.[15]
          Children:
          i.   AARON MELICK b. Apr- -1786 in Monmouth Co, NJ,[clxxix[179]] never married.
          ii.   ELIZABETH MELICK. She married Dennis Van Duyon.
          iii.   CHARLOTTE MELICK, census name Charlotta Melick, b. ca 1790 in New Jersey,[146] census 1850 in Bedminster Twp, Somerset Co, NJ, never married.
    184. iv.   ROSANNA MELICK[28] b. ca 1793.
    185. v.   JOHN MELICK[28] b. ca 1794.
          vi.   MARY MELICK. She married Peter Sutphen.

vii.   DAVID MELICK b. ca 1798 in New Jersey,[146] census 1850 in Bedminster Twp, Somerset Co, NJ, occupation farmer,[146] never married.
186.   viii.   WILLIAM MELICK[28] b. ca 1800.
ix.   DANIEL MELICK b. ca 1802 in New Jersey,[146] census 1850 in Bedminster Twp, Somerset Co, NJ, never married.
x.   CATHERINE MELICK. She married John Allen.

92.   **Martha Gaston** (30.Joseph[4], 8.Joseph[3], 3.John[2], 1.Jean[1]), b. 1774,[27] d. Jan-11-1850 in New Jersey.[27] She married[28] Jan- -1800, **Elijah Everett**, b. 1770/80 in Kingwood Township, Hunterdon Co, NJ,[28] (son of Samuel Everett and Nancy Thatcher), d. Jan-11-1850,[28] resided (settled) in Sparta Twp, Sussex Co, NJ,[28] occupation doctor.[28]

Elijah: Spelling of name may have been Everitt.

Children:
i.   JOSEPH G. EVERETT[15.]
ii.   MARGARET G. EVERETT[15.]

93.   **Phebe Dickson** (32.Margaret[4], 9.John[3], 3.John[2], 1.Jean[1]). She married[28] **Uriah Church**.
Children:
187.   i.   ANDREW DICKSON[28.]
ii.   GASTON CHURCH.
iii.   JOHN CHURCH.
iv.   VESTA CHURCH.
v.   NELSON CHURCH.
vi.   DIODATA CHURCH.

94.   **Alexander Gaston** (33.John[4], 9.John[3], 3.John[2], 1.Jean[1]), b. Aug- 2-1772 in Voluntown, New London Co, CT,[7,33] d. Feb-11-1856 in Roxbury, Suffolk Co, MA,[11,33] resided (settled 1838) in Roxbury, Suffolk Co, MA,[33] occupation merchant & Connecticut Legislature.[88]

Was captain of Company 6, 21st Connecticut Regiment, in 1797. Was member of Connecticut Legislature 1810-1812 and 1833-1835. Settled in Roxbury, Mass., in 1838. [American Ancestry, Vol V, p. 104]

He married (1) Apr-1 1803,[33] **Olive Dunlap**, b. Jun- 5-1769 in Plainfield, Windham Co, CT,[27] (daughter of Joshua Dunlap), d. Sep- 7-1814 in Killingly, Windham Co, CT.[7,11,33] He married (2) Apr-2-1816,[27] **Kezia Arnold**, b. Nov-10-1779 in Burrillville, Providence Co, RI,[clxxx[180],33] (daughter of Aaron Arnold and Rhoda Hunt), d. Jan-30-1856 in Roxbury, Suffolk Co, MA.[7,33]

Kezia: Alexander Gaston's second wife, Kezia Arnold, was a descendant of Thomas Arnold (b. 1599), a brother of William Arnold, who accompanied Roger Williams to Rhode Island and was one of the 54 original proprietors of the colony, with Thomas joining them in 1654.[clxxxi[181]]

Children by Olive Dunlap:
i.   ESTHER GASTON b. Jul-17-1804 in Killingly, Windham Co, CT,[27] d. Jun- 3-1860 in Roxbury, Suffolk Co, MA.[27]

Had five children, none of whom had any children of their own.[clxxxii[182]]

She married William K. Potter, b. Aug- 7-1803,[182] d. Sep-10-18__.[182]
ii.   JOHN GASTON b. Aug-30-1806 in Killingly, Windham Co, CT,[182] d. May-29-1824 in Plainfield, Windham Co, CT.[27,clxxxiii[183]]

Had no children.[182]

Children by Kezia Arnold:
188.   iii.   WILLIAM GASTON b. Oct- 3-1820.

95.   **Elijah L. Gaston** (35.Robert[4], 10.Alexander[3], 3.John[2], 1.Jean[1]), b. Jun- 9-1793.[clxxxiv[184]] He married[184] **Eunice Bennett**.
Children:
   i.   LAWRENCE T. GASTON b. Mar- 9-1826 in Ohio.[184]

96.   **Robert Kasson, Jr.** (36.Janet[4], 10.Alexander[3], 3.John[2], 1.Jean[1]), b. Apr-10-1773,[clxxxv[185]] d. Sep- -1846 in Broadalbin, Fulton Co, NY.[185]
Children:
189.   i.   THOMPSON KASSON b. Oct- 2-1795.
   ii.   LOVINA KASSON b. Mar-11-1797.[91]
190.   iii.   JAMES KASSON b. Dec-28-1798.
   iv.   NANCY KASSON b. Jun-23-1801.[91] She married[185] (1) __ Harback. She married[185] (2) __ Tuller.
191.   v.   CHARLES B. KASSON b. Feb-23-1803.
192.   vi.   MASON G. KASSON b. May-12-1804.
   vii.   ELIZABETH KASSON b. May-26-1806.[91]
   viii.   MARGARET KASSON b. Feb-10-1808.[91]
193.   ix.   EPHRAIM KASSON b. Apr- 1-1810.
   x.   NATHAN B. KASSON b. May-12-1814.[91]

97.   **William Kasson** (36.Janet[4], 10.Alexander[3], 3.John[2], 1.Jean[1]), b. 1775,[185] d. 1813,[185] occupation wheelwright.[185] He married 1792,[185] **Sally Richards**, b. 1776,[185] d. 1840.[185]
Children:
194.   i.   ARCHIBALD KASSON b. Jan- 7-1793.
   ii.   JOSEPH KASSON b. 1799,[185] d. 1833.[clxxxvi[186]] He married 1812,[186] Patience A. Sanders.
   iii.   HIRAM KASSON b. 1801,[186] d. 1833.[186]
195.   iv.   NELSON KASSON b. 1803.

98.   **Harvey Kasson** (36.Janet[4], 10.Alexander[3], 3.John[2], 1.Jean[1]), b. Dec- 4-1781,[186] d. Aug-26-1836 in Broadalbin, Fulton Co, NY.[186] He married Oct-11-1803,[186] **Wealthy Burt**, b. Apr-14-1788.[186]
Children:
   i.   JAMES KASSON b. Apr-16-1805.[186]
   ii.   ALVIN KASSON b. Dec- 2-1806,[186] occupation farmer.[186]
   iii.   SMIRA KASSON b. Feb- 1-1809.[186] She married __ Green.
   iv.   DONEY KASSON b. Mar- 9-1811.[186]
196.   v.   CHAUNCEY C. KASSON b. Dec-15-1812.
   vi.   AUSTIN KASSON b. Feb-22-1815.[186]
   vii.   SALLY ANN KASSON b. Feb-23-1817,[186] d. Jul-13-1852.[186]
197.   viii.   AMASA C. KASSON b. Jan-21-1819.
198.   ix.   GEORGE B. KASSON b. Apr-17-1822.
   x.   LYDIA KASSON b. May-29-1824.[186]
   xi.   HARVEY Z. KASSON b. Jun-26-1827,[186] resided in Gloversville, Fulton Co, NY,[186] occupation manufacturer of gloves and mittens.[186]
   xii.   ALEXANDER J. KASSON b. Apr- 5-1829,[186] occupation manufacturer of gloves, etc.[186]

99.   **Alexander Kasson** (36.Janet[4], 10.Alexander[3], 3.John[2], 1.Jean[1]), b. Apr- -1792.[clxxxvii[187]] He married Apr- -1812,[186] **Susan Briggs**, b. Jul- 3-1792.[186]
Children:

          i.   SAMANTHA M. KASSON b. Jan-21-1814.[186]

199.   ii.   MARVIN KASSON b. Nov-24-1815.

         iii.   WATSON KASSON b. Dec- 3-1817,[186] occupation farmer.[186]

         iv.   JANE M. KASSON b. Jan- 3-1820.[186]

         v.   JOSEPH KASSON b. Sep- 5-1822.[186]

         vi.   SUSAN N. KASSON b. Nov-18-1825,[186] d. Oct-25-1853.[clxxxviii[188]] She married[186] __ Sunderland.

         vii.   MELVINA KASSON b. Feb-23-1827.[188]

100. **Alexander Gaston** (37.Alexander[4], 10.Alexander[3], 3.John[2], 1.Jean[1]), b. Oct-14-1783 in Richmond, Berkshire Co, MA,[90] d. Jun-23-1865 in Lorain Co, OH,[36] buried in Pioneer Cemetery, Lorain Co, OH.[36]

Went to Danby, NY as a young man, took up government land and developed a farm, which he sold in 1834 when his family moved near Oberlin, OH. He was a militia captain in New York and active in the Congregational Church.[clxxxix[189]]

He married (1) Sep-21-1807,[36] **Lydia Belcher** (daughter of Joseph Belcher and Lucy Hall), buried in Pioneer Cemetery, Lorain Co, OH,[36] b. Aug- 2-1786. He married (2) 1849,[36] **Harriet Pearse**.

         Children by Lydia Belcher:

         i.   ANDREW GASTON b. Feb- 4-1810,[36] d. Dec-23-1831 in Danby, Tompkins Co, NY.[36]

         ii.   LUCETTA GASTON b. Jul-15-1811,[36] d. Jul-11-1813 in Danby, Tompkins Co, NY.[36]

200.   iii.   LUCY MARIAH GASTON b. Jan-19-1813.

201.   iv.   GEORGE BELCHER GASTON b. Nov- 8-1814.

202.   v.   MARIA GASTON b. Oct-14-1816.

         vi.   ELVIRA GASTON b. Jul-15-1818 in Danby, Tompkins Co, NY,[36] d. Jan-25-1914 in Oberlin, Lorain Co, OH,[cxc[190],36] buried in Tabor, Fremont Co, IA.[190,36]

        Elvira Gaston and her husband, Lester Ward Platt, worked as missionaries with the Pawnee Indians in Nebraska for years. There is much written about her because, as one descendant observed, "she made history." [Bob Gaston, Longview, WA]

        "Elvira Gaston Platt was born in Danby, New York, on July 16, 1818. Her family moved to Ohio in 1834 and she became a student at Oberlin College the following year. She later taught at a rural school in Russia Township, Ohio. In 1841 she married Lester Ward Platt and moved with him to Nebraska to teach the Pawnee Indians. Both were devoted to the causes of abolishing slavery and whiskey. After her husband died in 1875, Elvira Gaston Platt taught in the Industrial School for Indians in Carlisle, Pennsylvania, and served as matron in a school for Indians in Gcoa, Nebraska. She died on January 24, 1914."
[http://www.oberlin.edu/archive/holdings/finding/RG30/SG199/biography.html]

        "Elvira Gaston Platt, teacher and abolitionist and underground railroad worker, was born in Danby, Thompkins County, New York, on July 15, 1818. She studied at Oberlin College in Ohio in 1835 and 1836 and began teaching in area rural schools. In 1841 Elvira Gaston married Lester Ward Platt and in 1842 they began teaching Pawnee Indians in the western territory, in what is now Nebraska. In 1847 they moved to Fremont County, Iowa, turned to farming, and began assisting fleeing slaves on the underground railroad.

        In 1861 Elvira Platt returned to teaching Pawnee children, which she continued until 1872 with a few interruptions for Civil War work. Lester Platt died in 1875 and Elvira Platt joined the staff of the Industrial School for Indians in Carlisle, Pennsylvania, in 1880. Three years later she became matron of a new school for Native Americans in Genoa, Nebraska, where she worked until she retired in 1887. She lived in Tabor, Iowa, until 1897, when she moved to Oberlin, Ohio. She died there on January 25, 1914." [http://sdrc.lib.uiowa.edu/iwa/findingaids/html/PlattElvira.htm]

        HER OBITUARY:

"Elvira Gaston Platt, aged 95 years, died at Oberlin, Ohio, Sunday, January 25, of pneumonia, where a funeral service was read. The body was then brought to Tabor for interment in the Gaston lot where her husband and other relatives lie. Services were held here on Wednesday, January 28, conducted by Rev. C. F. Fisher.

Elvira Gaston Platt was a sister of George B. Gaston, one of the founders of Tabor College, and an aunt of Ed Rossiter, Loren Hume and Harry Gilbert of Tabor. Coming from her native state, New York, she and her father were pioneers of the Oberlin colony, where she was married in 1841, to Lester W. Platt, with whom she soon afterward moved to Nebraska. Here at different intervals, in the Pawnee Indian Nation school she taught and also in the Carlyle school in Pennsylvania, all her life being spent in educational work.

At Percival (then known as Civil Bend) she lived, her home a "shrine" to young and old.

She served in the Sanitary Commission during the civil war, and was later matron of the Soldiers' Orphan Home at Cedar Falls.

Mrs. Platt made her home in Tabor for many years and made her life felt here for uplift. For the last seventeen years she has lived at Oberlin. In the 95 years of her life, Mrs. Platt has combined manifold experiences, and has seen and helped in the upbuilding of our western country.

She was known throughout many states as a woman of great power. A memorial service will be given in her honor here at Tabor."

[http://iagenweb.org/fremont/obits/platt_elvira-hiatt_elizabeth1914.htm]

She married[36] 1841 in Oberlin, Lorain Co, OH,[cxci][191] Lester Ward Platt, d. 1875, buried in Tabor, Fremont Co, IA.[191]

 203. vii. EMALA FAIRCHILD GASTON b. Jun- 5-1820.

    viii. ALONZO GASTON b. Dec-22-1821 in Danby, Tompkins Co, NY,[36] d. Jan- 4-1892 in Oberlin, Lorain Co, OH,[36] buried in Pioneer Cemetery, Lorain Co, OH.[36] He married Oct-13-1844,[36] Amanda E. Stratton.

 204. ix. CELIA H. GASTON b. Jan-16-1824.

    x. EDWARD P. BRADSTREET GASTON[36] (adopted) b. Jun- 6-1830, occupation attorney.[36]

Edward Bradstreet Gaston was adopted by Alexander & Lydia Belcher Gaston when he was about age 8, after his mother died. Edward wrote a letter at age 95 telling of his life with the Gastons. He practiced law in Cincinnati, OH until age 90.[36]

101. Heman Gaston (37.Alexander[4], 10.Alexander[3], 3.John[2], 1.Jean[1]), b. Sep-13-1786 in Richmond, Berkshire Co, MA,[89] d. Aug-10-1855 in Lorain Co, OH.[36,cxcii[192]]

Spelling "Heman" is correct.

He married Jan- 1-1812,[192,cxciii[193]] **Mary Wheeler**, b. Aug-29-1793 in New York,[192,36] (daughter of Elizur Wheeler and Olive Kasson), d. Oct-16-1838.[192,36]

   Children:

   i. CAROLINE S. GASTON b. Oct-19-1812,[192] d. Feb- 8-1817 in Richmond, Berkshire Co, MA.[cxciv[194],192]

   ii. WILLIAM WHEELER GASTON b. Sep-22-1814,[192] d. Dec- 1-1845.[192] He married[192] Mary Sinnott.

   iii. NANCY GASTON b. Jul-24-1816,[192] d. Dec- -1816 in Richmond, Berkshire Co, MA.[cxcv[195]]

   iv. GEORGE RODNEY GASTON b. Nov- 7-1817.[192] He married Dec-29-1840,[192] Louisa Bissell.

   v. MARY AMANDA GASTON b. Aug-17-1819,[192] baptized Mar- 5-1820 in Richmond, Berkshire Co, MA,[cxcvi[196]] d. Jan- -1838 in Richmond, Berkshire Co, MA.[cxcvii[197]]

   vi. BEVEL HULL GASTON b. Sep-30-1821,[192] d. Feb- 1-1823.[192]

 205. vii. HENRY ALEXANDER GASTON b. Aug- 9-1823.

          viii. ANN ELIZA GASTON b. Nov-11-1825,[192] d. Sep-21-1839.[192]

          ix. EMILY CAROLINE GASTON b. Feb- 7-1828,[192] d. Jan-12-1856.[192] She married[192] ___

Smith.

          x. EDGAR KASSON GASTON b. May-10-1830,[192] d. Oct-19-1872.[192]

206.   xi. JAMES KASSON GASTON b. Apr-17-1832.

          xii. ELLEN FRANCES GASTON b. Nov- 8-1834,[cxcviii[198]] d. Aug- 1-1846.[198]

102. **Ebenezer Gaston** (38.David[4], 10.Alexander[3], 3.John[2], 1.Jean[1]), b. Apr- 6-1782 in Old Stockbridge, Berkshire Co, MA,[99] d. Jan-27-1863.[99] He married[34] **Hannah Hammond**, b. Jul-14-1790,[99] d. Oct-11-1853.[99]

          Children:

207.   i. EDMUND WAITE GASTON b. Aug-16-1809.

          ii. NELSON GASTON b. Mar-21-1816,[34] d. Sep-13-1846.[34]

          iii. MARIETTA GASTON b. Jul- 2-1818,[34] d. Jun-28-1861.[34]

          iv. SUSANNA GASTON b. Sep- 5-1821,[34] d. Oct-21-1859.[34]

          v. GRACE GASTON b. Jun-14-1824.[34]

          vi. LUTHER S. GASTON b. Feb-14-1828.[34]

          vii. SCHUYLER MOSES GASTON b. Feb-14-1828,[34] d. Apr-13-1906.[34]

Generation Six

103. **Esther Jane Gaston** (39.Joseph[5], 11.Alexander[4], 4.(Male)[3], 2.William[2], 1.Jean[1]), b. 1770,[cxcix[199]] d. 1814.[199]

Moved with her husband in 1806 to Israel Twp, Preble Co, OH, presumably because they were opposed to slavery. They helped to found the Hopewell Associate Reformed Presbyterian Church in Israel Twp that the Rev. Alexander Porter later pastored. Esther Gaston and Ebenezer Elliott had eight children, and Ebenezer had two more wives, Margaret Mitchell and Nancy Henry.[199]

She married ca 1794 in Fishing Creek, Chester Co, SC,[cc[200]] **Ebenezer Elliott**.

"The first to settle in the congregation, we believe, was William Ramsey, Jr., who was afterwards connected with and became a leading member in the Covenanter church. This was in 1805. During the year 1806 he was joined by Wm. McCreary, Wm. Ramsey, Sr., Jas. Ochiltree, and Ebenezer Elliott; in 1807 Richard Sloan, Robert Martin, John and James Allen, David McDill, Hugh McQuiston, Andrew McQuiston, Robert Boyce, John Patterson, James Brown, and perhaps a few others; in 1808 John and Hugh Ramsey, James Boyce, and Robert Douglass. The Magaws came about the year 1811. In 1814 quite a number came with or followed Rev. A. Porter, such as the Weeks, Bucks, Stewarts, Pinkertons, and Fosters. About the year 1817 the Gilmores and Paxtons came and other families of Ochiltrees and Ramseys. The Grahams, Wilsons, and McKees came from Kentucky about the year 1829. About the year 1807 Mr. Risk gave them one day's preaching, the first sermon ever preached in Preble county by a Presbyterian minister. In 1808 Rev. Mr. Craig preached in the home of David McDill (grandfather of this writer), and organized the congregation which took the name Hopewell."

Many, if not most, came from Chester District.

I am not aware that any of Ebenezer's siblings themselves also traveled to Preble County, Ohio, but I believe the surviving spouse of William Elliott (he died in 1796), Jane Gaston, and her children did move with Ebenezer.

Again, from EEE:

"After his (William's) death in 1796 his brother, Ebenezer, and his wife, Jane, were appointed administrators of his estate, but as the children were all minors the final settlement did not take place until some years after the removal of all parties concerned to Ohio. There were four children (I have a possible 6, but they are not proven), whose careers are outlined in the sketches to follow. Previous to the migration from South Carolina, the widow re-married, her husband being Edward Sutton, by whom she later had at least three children. A controversy arose between the heirs of William Elliott and the Suttons regarding the use of the Elliott estate for the maintenance of the Sutton children, which was settled by an amicable suit but was not satisfactory to all concerned and caused some breach in the family relationships. It is understood that much of the original estate had been dissipated by land speculations of the stepfather in the state of Kentucky."

The 8 children of my Daniel Elliott are:

William, Margaret, Benjamin, Francis, Daniel, Jane, Ebenezer & James. I have absolutely nothing about some of them.

Connie ----- Original Message ----From: <WhitePaul@aol.com> To: <scchest2@rootsweb.com> Sent: Monday, February 12, 2007 6:35 AM Subject: [SCCHEST2] Early Elliotts in Chester

> > Connie, > I understand that Daniel Elliott's descendants supposedly went to Prebble > Co., Ohio, but about when had they all left Chester County, SC. I have > seen a > census for an Ebenezer Elliott in TN and would this be the same person as > Daniel's son who supposedly went to Ohio? > For a long time I have been trying to unwind the three Fishing Creek > families, Daniel, Archibald, and William Elliott there without much luck. > I have > really been concentrating on the William Elliott who presented an infant > named > Jacob for Baptizing in the the Fishing Creek Presbyterian Church in 1818 > (see > church minutes). I have no proof but I believe that this William was > probably > of Archibald Elliott's line. Didn't Daniel's family (or part of) switch > to
> an ARP Church congregation in the area?
> Paul R. White
>
Retrieved by Linda Hull, 2/13/2007

Notes for EBENEZER ELLIOTT:
    Message: 3
    Date: Wed, 14 Feb 2007 09:10:12 -0800
    From: "Connie" <R.leaman@comcast.net>
    Subject: Re: [SCCHEST2] Ebenezer Elliott & Ohio
    To: <WhitePaul@aol.com>, <scchest2@rootsweb.com>
    Message-ID: <000a01c7505c$62dcf690$77ae1318@yourxhtr8hvc4p>
    Content-Type: text/plain; charset="iso-8859-1"
    Interesting, but I don't think my Ebenezer was ever in Tennessee. He died of cholera
    Aug 26 1849 in Israel Township, Preble County, Ohio, and is buried in Hopewell

Church cemetery.

More from his grandson Edwin Ebenezer Elliott:
>From DANIEL ELLIOTT, PATRIOT And a Record of His Descendants 1769 to
1930 page 176 by his grandson, Edwin Ebenezer Elliott.

   "The family record will have much say about Ebenezer Elliott and his descendants.
This is readily understood. In the first place he was the founder of that branch of the
family to which this writer belongs. I was named for him; my own father was born on
the homestead he settled, which he later owned and which also belonged to me for
many years. From boyhood to manhood stories of his life, activities and character were
related to me.

   "I was born in the brick house he had built with his own hands and his marble slab in
old Hopewell cemetery, with its quaint inscription had always a fascination for me.
Brief as this sketch may be it is intended as a tribute to his memory. If his biography is
more extensive or includes greater detail it is due to the fact that more information
about him was available.

"Ebenezer Elliott was the fifth son of Daniel Elliott, Senior, and Elizabeth Ferguson Elliott, if our record is
correct. He was born in 1771 in Chester County, South Carolina, probably very soon after the family settled
on the homestead on Fishing Creek.

   "Just two incidents of his boyhood have come down to us and they both are connected with the
same events. He was a boy of nine or ten when his father was shot down by the Tories, and fearing
for his life, he ran and hid from them. The other story was told me by Mr. W. Julian Elliott of
Columbia, South Carolina, who wrote that, when a boy, he had seen a piece of a British soldier's red
coat which it was said that Ebenezer had worn when he rode into the British lines and recovered a
horse that had been stolen by the marauders who had killed his father. The red coat was doubtless
worn to throw off suspicion and had afterward been cut into pieces and distributed as souvenirs of
that adventure among members of the family.

   "Ebenezer was married to the daughter of Joseph Gaston, whose farm adjoined that of Daniel Elliott.
Her name, Esther Gaston, is one that will be found repeated many times in later generations. She was
a grand-daughter of John Gaston, better known as Justice John, and his wife Esther Waugh. Her
mother was Martha, the second child of the thirteen children in Justice John's family.

   "Justice John Gaston was a noted patriot, who had renounced his allegiance to the crown and
devoted his fortune to the cause of the American Colonies. It is a well established fact that seven of
his sons, all of whom were more than six feet tall, served in the patriot ranks and four of them were
killed and another wounded at the battle of Hanging Rock. The tradition as been handed down
through the years that Martha, their sister, was equally tall, as was her daughter Esther, who
married Ebenezer Elliott and another daughter, Margaret who married Hugh McQuiston. Martha
married her kinsman, Joseph Gaston, whose father was a near relative of Justice John, but not his
brother, as has been supposed.

"His name was Alexander, if our records are correct. Joseph was born in 1732, most likely in Ireland. He had taken up land in Chester County previous to the homesteading of Daniel Elliott and their farms adjoined.

"Joseph and Martha Gaston had at least five children, of which Esther was the fourth. There is a legend that she had red or auburn hair, and this is easy to believe since more than half of her own children were so distinguished and this color of hair still persists in later generations. Her husband had coal black hair, even to the day of his death.

"Ebenezer and Esther Gaston were married September 25, 1794, doubtless in Chester County, South Carolina. She was a year older than her husband and somewhat taller in stature for it is well known that he was a man of moderate size and height. They may have lived on a farm which the records of the county show that he owned at the time of his marriage, although he had probably remained on the home farm for some years during his minority. This homestead passed out of the possession of the family, probably when t he estate was settled. The deed was a sheriff's transfer or court order which would have indicated that the probate proceedings had been carried into court for final settlement.

"Before he was thirty years old Ebenezer had become a man of some influence in his neighborhood. He was a justice of the peace and had been elected to the eldership in Union Associate Reformed Presbyterian Church. In Dr. Lathan's history of Union Church he mentions among others the name of one Ebenezer Elliott as a member of the session but goes on to state that his identity could not be traced and nothing was known of what had become of him. If the good Doctor had followed up the removals of members from old Union in the early part of the last century he would have found that Ebenezer had transferred his membership to old Hopewell Church in Preble County which he helped to found and was a member of the session there to the day when he was laid to rest in its cemetery.

"When the troubles with the Indians had been settled by the victory of General Wayne and made it possible for the settlers to enter lands north of the Ohio River, a migration poured into these new and fertile regions for the purpose of establishing homes. Among these came many, who, because of the attraction of the new country, coupled with their dislike for the institution of slavery, had determined to leave South Carolina. Ebenezer came over the Wilderness trail and through the Cumberland Gap in the Appalachian Range in the later fall of 1806. There were others in the caravan, traveling together for safety's sake. We have practically no facts regarding the journey which took several weeks. The distance, judged by modern standards was not great, probably a little over 400 miles. There is now a good highway over practically the same route and it can by covered by auto in less than two days time. Preparations had been made for the journey by selling out lands and property, retaining only such belongings as could be easily transported. Recently I learned of a copy of Flavius' writings still in existence which has the name of Ebenezer Elliott on the blank page and was one piece of property sold at this dispersal sale.

"It was late in the year when the northward journey began. Preceding the start Ebenezer secured from his friends and neighbors a certificate of character, signed by nineteen prominent persons of the community, most of them holding some military title or civic position. This certificate is too interesting to be omitted.

(Quoting Edwin Ebenezer Elliott)

"State of South Carolina)
Chester District) We, whose names are hereunto
subscribed, do certify that we have long been acquainted with the Bearer, Ebenezer Elliott, that he has

resided in this district since Infancy and has always supported a good moral character & shewen himself a friend to Religion & Virtue, & and enemy to Vice and has for several years acted in the Office of Justice of the Peace in which he has acquitted himself with honour & integrity; and, being about to remove from this Country, we Recommend him as a man of that Character to all good Men wherever Providence may cast his lot.

Given under our hands this 8th day of October, 1806.

Hezekiah Donal, J. P. Jno. M Creary C.O't

Geo. Gill J. P. J. Roseborough - Capt.

Leonard Strait Capt. John Cherry

Alex'r Roseborough M. D.

James Crawford C-p Jno McKown Major

Leach Thompson Capt. Andrew Wherry, Capt.

John Culp. Lt Clement a. Thompson L. Pleasent Furguson Joseph Gaston, J.P. Wm.Chesnut Robert Robinson Jas. Harbison, J.P. John B. Davis, V.D.M.

"This certificate, with its quaint phraseology and spelling was cherished by "the Bearor" through all the years and probably was put to good use more than once. It is significant because of the military and other titles it carries and shows the great importance attached to these in the days following the Revolution.

"The family of our pioneer at this time consisted of himself, wife and six children; the oldest not more than ten. There may have been more than one wagon and several saddle horses and other livestock. A story is told of the break in the journey with each weekend and the camp over the Sabbath. Not all the company with which they traveled were so conscientious, and, as the winter was approaching they pushed on without stopping. Before the journey ended it was demonstrated that Sabbath-keeping paid, as those who had refused to stop for the day were overtaken by those who had.

"The promised land was reached early in December and their neighbor, William McCreary, who had come the preceding spring, gave them a welcome and assisted in locating the tract of land later filed on. While the survey had been established previously the lines were not completely run out and Ebenezer at first settled just over his own north line on an adjoining section. Here they erected a pole shack with one end open but across which was stretched the wagon covers. In this temporary shelter the first winter was passed and to those accustomed to the mild winters of the south it must have been a season of distress and privation.

"In the early spring a log cabin, located almost exactly in the center of the quarter section, had been erected and occupied. A piece of land had been cleared and later planted and the tremendous task of clearing away the dense forest was under way. The extent of these primitive woods can hardly be realized at this late day but the whole of this part of Ohio was covered with a vast expanse of hardwood timber, interspersed with giant tulip trees, better known as yellow poplars, hundreds of years old. They were too large for any sawmill to handle but they were split into rails for fencing and supplied the shakes for roofing the log buildings. The old log cabin stood for many years on its original site but was later removed to another part of the farm and still later it was again moved and rebuilt on a hillside not far from the town of Morning Sun. Another pioneer log cabin, the original home of the James Brown family was also moved and the two cabins joined together with a passsageway between. These cabins are still standing and occupied. It has always been a mystery to me how so large and stirring a family could have been accommodated in so small a building.   "It was only twenty or twenty-five feet square."

Somehow I doubt the buildings still stand in 2007. I wish I had that certificate of character or a facsimile.

Connie ----- Original Message ----From: WhitePaul@aol.com To: R.leaman@comcast.net ; scchest2@rootsweb.com Sent: Wednesday, February 14, 2007 6:43 AM Subject: Re: Ebenezer Elliott & Ohio

Deed Book "DD" 1833-1834
Page 4 - 4 May 1831. Joseph T. Elliott of Morgan Co., Illinois to the rest of the heirs of EBENEZER Elliott, deceased, late of Bedford Co., Tennessee. Ebenezer Elliott paid $200.00 to Joseph T. Elliott, in his lifetime and Joseph T. Elliott acknowledged same. Joseph Elliott sold to the heirs of Ebenezer Elliott, deceased, all the undivided share or interest that Joseph T. Elliott has in the estate of Ebenezer Elliott, deceased, his father, land in Maury and Bedford Counties, Tennessee (2 tracts). Reg: 16 March 1833.

Children:
i.   JOSEPH GASTON ELLIOTT b. 1795,[199] d. 1834.[199]
ii.   JAMES ELLIOTT b. 1797,[199] d. 1883.[199] He married[199] Sarah Boyd, b. 1800,[199] d. 1880.[199]
iii.   JANET ELLIOTT b. 1800,[199] d. 1881.[199] She married[199] (1) Ebenezer Elliott Douglas, Sr., b. 1794,[199] d. 1837.[199] She married[199] (2) William Hood, d. 1850.[199]
iv.   WILLIAM ELLIOTT b. 1801,[199] d. 1854.[199] He married[199] Sarah Hearn, b. 1815,[199] d. 1871.[199]
v.   JOHN ELLIOTT b. 1803,[199] d. 1875.[199] He married[199] (1) Mary Latta, b. 1796,[199] d. 1837.[199] He married[199] (2) Margaret McMillen, b. 1813,[199] d. 1858.[199]
vi.   EBENEZER NEWTON ELLIOTT b. 1805,[199] d. 1892.[199] He married[199] Ann J. Willis, d. 1892.[199]
vii.   HUGH ELLIOTT b. 1808,[199] d. 1894.[199] He married[199] (1) Henrietta Brower, b. 1816,[199] d. 1850.[199] He married[199] (2) Elizabeth Avaline Robertson, b. 1826,[199] d. 1909.[199]
viii.   ISAIAH ELLIOTT b. 1810,[199] d. 1897.[199] He married[199] Isabella Davidson, b. 1807,[199] d. 1886.[199]

104. **John Gaston** (39.Joseph[5], 11.Alexander[4], 4.(Male)[3], 2.William[2], 1.Jean[1]), b. Apr- 2-1772 in Chester Co, SC,[107] d. Jul- 6-1847.[107] He married[107,103] **Anne Porter**, b. Jul- 7-1782,[107] (daughter of John Porter and Mary Brownfield), d. bef 1844.[107]
    Children:
    i.   JOSEPH ALEXANDER GASTON b. Mar- 4-1810 in Chester Co, SC,[107,17] d. Feb-11-1868 in South Carolina,[107,17] buried in Fishing Creek Presb Church Cem, Chester Co, SC.[17,103] He married[107,103] Elizabeth Wylie, b. Oct- 2-1810,[17] d. Oct-11-1850,[17] buried in Fishing Creek Presb Church Cem, Chester Co, SC.[17,103]

105. **Alexander Walker** (40.Jane[5], 11.Alexander[4], 4.(Male)[3], 2.William[2], 1.Jean[1]) (See marriage to number 49.)

106. **Robert Gaston** (41.Matthew[5], 11.Alexander[4], 4.(Male)[3], 2.William[2], 1.Jean[1]), b. 1774 in Greene Co, GA,[102] [But researcher Dallin S. Nielsen, a direct descendant, reports birth in Rowan Co, NC.], d. Apr-6-1829 in Autauga Co, AL.[102] He married in Morgan Co, AL,[102] [But researcher Dallin Nielsen, a direct descendant, reports marriage in 1799 in Greene Co, GA.], **Abalena __**.
    Children:
    208. i.   HUDSON GASTON b. 1813.

107. **Jane Gaston** (41.Matthew[5], 11.Alexander[4], 4.(Male)[3], 2.William[2], 1.Jean[1]), b. Jan- 8-1777 in Greene Co, GA,[102] [Birthplace also reported as Lancaster Co, PA. (http://www.couchgenweb.com/family/reid.htm)], d. 1860.[cci][201] She married[ccii][202],201 **George Reid II**, b. 1774 in Rowan Co, NC,[201] (son of George Reid), d. 1853.[201]

George: Served in the Georgia House of Representatives from Jackson Co, GA as of Jan 12 1801; was Justice of the Inferior Court of Gwinnett Co, GA from Feb 2 1819 to 1821; and was Senator from Gwinnett Co GA 1819-1821 and in Extra Session of 1821. He was among the first settlers in Carroll Co, GA upon its organization in 1826. [The Reid Family, by L. D. McPherson, a Reid descendant, 1938; cited at http://www.couchgenweb.com/family/reid.htm][201]

Children:
- i. JACK REID[202.]
- ii. JOSEPH REID[201.]
- 209. iii. RHESA REID b. 1797.
- 210. iv. ASA REID b. 1799.
- v. ANN REID[202] b. 1800 in Greene Co, GA,[201] d. 1850.[201] She married[201] John McMullen.
- vi. CATHERINE "KATIE" REID[202] b. 1803 in Jackson Co, GA.[202,201] She married[201] (1) Elisha Earnest. She married[201] (2) Isaac Wigginton.
- 211. vii. GEORGE W. REID b. 1803.
- 212. viii. JANE "JENNIE" REID b. 1805.
- ix. MATTHEW GASTON REID[201] b. 1806,[202,201] d. 1876.[201] He married[201] (1) Martha J. __. He married[201] (2) Frances Ann Nix.
- x. MARGARET ANNIE REID[202] b. Feb-29-1809,[202] d. 1862.[201] She married[201] John Lewis Hamilton, d. 1874.[201]
- xi. JOHN S. REID b. 1810.[201]
- xii. ROBERT ALEXANDER REID b. Apr- 3-1811,[202] d. 1885.[201] He married[201] Nancy K. Adrian.
- xiii. ELIZABETH REID[202] b. 1814.[201] She married[201] Wilson Brown.
- 213. xiv. THOMAS HENRY REID b. 1816.

108. **Alexander Gaston** (41.Matthew[5], 11.Alexander[4], 4.(Male)[3], 2.William[2], 1.Jean[1]), b. 1780 in Rowan Co, NC,[cciii][203] [Reid Family Genealogy, on file at Daughters of the American Revolution Library, Washington, DC, gives birthplace as Greene Co, GA.], d. 1837 in Greene Co, GA.[102,203] He married Dec-9-1802 in Greene Co, GA,[203] **Sallie Garner**, b. 1774.[203]
Children:
- i. JOHN GARNER GASTON b. 1803 in Greene Co, GA.[203]
- 214. ii. MATTHEW GASTON b. 1805.
- iii. WILLIAM T. GASTON b. 1814 in Greene Co, GA.[203]

109. **Matthew Gaston, Jr.** (41.Matthew[5], 11.Alexander[4], 4.(Male)[3], 2.William[2], 1.Jean[1]), b. 1785,[102] d. in Jackson, Butts Co, GA.[102] He married[102] **Mary __**.
Children:
- i. MARY ELIZABETH GASTON.
- ii. SARAH JANE GASTON.
- 215. iii. JOHNNIE MATTHEW GASTON.

110. **John Gaston** (42.Alexander[5], 11.Alexander[4], 4.(Male)[3], 2.William[2], 1.Jean[1]), d. 1806 in Abbeville Co, SC.[6] He married **Unknown**.
Children:
- i. ALEXANDER GASTON.

Moved to the Butler/Wilcox County area of Alabama ca 1822/1823.[6]

        ii.   DAVID GASTON.

        Moved to the Butler/Wilcox County area of Alabama ca 1822/1823.[6]

111. **James Gaston** (46.John[5], 12.John[4], 5.William[3], 3.John[2], 1.Jean[1]), b. 1777 in South Carolina,[cciv[204]] d. 1802,[ccv[205]] resided (settled, abt 1800) in Logan Co, KY.[108] He married[108] **Isabella Bigham** (daughter of James Bigham and Nancy "Jane" McFadden).
           Children:
    216. i.   JAMES GASTON b. 1800.

112. **Esther Waugh Gaston**[126] (46.John[5], 12.John[4], 5.William[3], 3.John[2], 1.Jean[1]). She married ca 1806 in South Carolina,[126] **Samuel Gaston**, b. Oct-16-1787 in Chester Co, SC,[126] (son of William Gaston and Mary McClure), d. Mar- 1-1826 in Jefferson Co, IL,[126,44,124] resided (settled, in 1819) in Marion Co, IL.[44,124] Samuel Gaston's wife is identified in the DAR Lineage Book only as Esther Gaston, her parentage not stated. Other sources show her to be his second cousin, as both were great-grandchildren of William Gaston and Olivet Lemon.

           Children:
    217. i.   WILLIAM GASTON.

113. **Stephen Gaston** (47.James[5], 12.John[4], 5.William[3], 3.John[2], 1.Jean[1]), b. 1774,[12] d. 1837.[12]

Probably moved to Ohio with his sisters about 1801 or 1802, and from there to Tennessee and Illinois.[8,45]

He married[ccvi[206]] **Mary Davidson**, b. 1778,[12] d. 1858.[12]
           Children:
        i.   ESTHER GASTON b. Nov-12-1802 in South Carolina,[12] d. Mar-27-1853 in California.[12] She married William Wesley Maddux, b. Dec-28-1803,[12] d. Feb- 8-1885.[12] Eight children.[12]

        ii.   MARGARET GASTON b. ca 1804 in Tennessee.[12]
    218. iii. WILLIAM DAVIDSON GASTON b. Feb-22-1808.
        iv. AGNES GASTON b. ca 1814 in Illinois.[12] She married[12] Thomas S. Dennis, b. 1814,[12] d. 1860.[12] Three children.[12]

    219. v.   STEPHEN HARVEY GASTON b. Nov-30-1818.
        vi. ELIZABETH GASTON b. ca 1820 in Illinois.[12]
        vii. SAMUEL GASTON b. ca 1821 in Illinois.[12]

114. **John Gaston Walker** (49.Esther[5], 12.John[4], 5.William[3], 3.John[2], 1.Jean[1]). He married 1798,[113] **Jane McCain**.
           Children:
    220. i.   WILLIAM WALKER.

115. **John Brown Gaston** title: Dr. (50.Joseph[5], 12.John[4], 5.William[3], 3.John[2], 1.Jean[1]), b. Jan-23-1791,[44] d. Jan-24-1864. He married[44] **Mary Buford "Polly" McFadden**, also known as Polly Buford,[116] also known as Mary Beaufort McFadden,[44] b. 1805,[ccvii[207]] d. 1886.[207]
           Children:
    221. i.   JAMES MCFADDEN GASTON b. 1824.
    222. ii. JOSEPH LUCIUS GASTON.
    223. iii. JOHN BROWN GASTON, JR. b. Jan- 4-1834.

224.   iv.   T. CHALMERS GASTON b. 1847.

116. **Narcissa Gaston** (50.Joseph[5], 12.John[4], 5.William[3], 3.John[2], 1.Jean[1]), b. Nov-17-1792,[44] d. Aug-22-1871, buried in Fishing Creek Presb Church Cem, Chester Co, SC. She married[44] Nov- 2-1819, **Samuel Lewis**. Narcissa Gaston was the second wife of Samuel Lewis.[ccviii[208]]

       Children:
225.   i.   MARGARET ELIZA LEWIS.

117. **Hugh McClure**[121] (51.John[5], 13.Mary[4], 5.William[3], 3.John[2], 1.Jean[1]). He married[121] **Margaret Crane**.
       Children:
226.   i.   ELIZA JANE MCCLURE.

118. **Hannah McClure** (53.William[5], 13.Mary[4], 5.William[3], 3.John[2], 1.Jean[1]) (See marriage to number 64.)

119. **David D. Rosborough** (55.Alexander[5], 15.Martha[4], 5.William[3], 3.John[2], 1.Jean[1]), b. Sep- -1815 in South Carolina,[123] census 1900 in Belton, Bell Co, TX, resided (settled) in Texas.[14]
       Children:
227.   i.   EDWARD E. ROSBOROUGH b. Jul- -1847.

120. **Alexander M. Rosborough** (55.Alexander[5], 15.Martha[4], 5.William[3], 3.John[2], 1.Jean[1]), b. ca 1817 in South Carolina,[146] census 1880 in Oakland, Alameda Co, CA, census 1870 in Yreka, Siskiyou Co, CA, census 1850 in El Dorado Co, CA, resided (settled, in 1848) in Eureka, Humboldt Co, CA,[14] occupation lawyer, judge,[14,ccix[209],ccx[210]] He married **Ellen N. __**, b. ca 1842 in Maine,[209] census 1880, 1910, 1920 in Oakland, Alameda Co, CA, census 1870 in Yreka, Siskiyou Co, CA.

1870 Census, Siskiyou County, California (City of Yreka), enumerated on Sep 3 1870:
Alex M. Rosborough, 54, b. South Carolina, occupation District Judge; Ellen N, 28, b. Maine; Alex J, 5. b. California; Fanny J, 1, b. California.

1880 Census, Alameda Co, California (City of Oakland), enumerated on Jun 8 1880:
A. M. Roxborough, 65, b. SC, lawyer; wife Ellen P, 37, b. Maine; son Alexander J, 14, b. California; dau Fannie J, 11, b. California; son Joseph J, 4, b. California.

1910 Census, Alameda Co, California (Brooklyn Twp, City of Oakland), enumerated on Apr 30 1910 at 1769 (or 1767) Nineteenth Ave:
Head of household Alexander J. Rosborough, 44, single, secretary at power & light company; mother Ellen N, 65, widowed, mother of 6 children (2 still living); brother Joseph J, 34, single, real estate broker; nephew Robert R. Gardiner, 16, b. Calif; nephew Alexander R. Gardiner, 15, b. Calif; help Lee Lim, 13, b. China, kitchen helper.

1920 Census, Alameda Co, California (Brooklyn Twp, City of Oakland), enumerated on Jan 7 1920 at 2531 19th Ave:
Ellen N. Rosborough, 77, b. Maine, widowed; son Alic J. Rosborough, 54, b. Calif, single, manager at power company; grandson Alexander Gardiner, 24, b. Calif, single; sister-in-law Fannie Raynes, 84, b. Maine, widowed.

       Children:
       i.   ALEXANDER J. ROSBOROUGH, census name Alic J. Rosborough, b. ca 1865 in California,[209] census 1880, 1910, 1920 in Oakland, Alameda Co, CA, census 1870 in Yreka, Siskiyou Co, CA, occupation 1910 secretary at power & light company.[ccxi[211]]
       ii.   FANNY J. ROSBOROUGH b. ca 1869 in California,[209] d. bef Apr 1910,[211] census 1880 in Oakland, Alameda Co, CA, census 1870 in Yreka, Siskiyou Co, CA.

iii. JOSEPH J. ROSBOROUGH b. ca 1876 in California,[210] census 1880, 1910 in Oakland, Alameda Co, CA, occupation 1910 real estate broker.[211]

121. **William Gaston, Jr.** (57.William[5], 16.Robert[4], 5.William[3], 3.John[2], 1.Jean[1]), b. Jan- 1-1786 in Chester Co, SC,[126] d. Sep-21-1869 in Jefferson Co, IL,[126] military War of 1812.[44] He married[ccxii[212]] ca 1813 in South Carolina,[126] **Jane "Jennet" McMillan**.
>
> Children:
> 228. i. SAMUEL GASTON.

122. **Samuel Gaston** (57.William[5], 16.Robert[4], 5.William[3], 3.John[2], 1.Jean[1]) (See marriage to number 112.)

123. **Robert Gaston** (58.Thomas[5], 16.Robert[4], 5.William[3], 3.John[2], 1.Jean[1]), b. Sep-17-1787,[129] d. Jul-13-1848.[129] He married[129] **Ann Wakefield**, b. ca 1792 in South Carolina,[209] census 1870 in Reidville, Spartanburg Co, SC, resided originally in Reidville, Spartanburg Co, SC.[129]
>
> Children:
> i. ELIZABETH GASTON.
> ii. SARAH "SALLIE" GASTON. She married[129] Andrew Cowan.
> iii. ROSA GASTON. She married[129] William Pearson.
> 229. iv. WILLIAM ROSBOROUGH GASTON b. Dec-25-1827.

124. **James Nickels "Jimmy" Gaston** (58.Thomas[5], 16.Robert[4], 5.William[3], 3.John[2], 1.Jean[1]), b. Jan-18-1789 in Lancaster Co, SC,[ccxiii[213]] d. Jul-31-1876,[213] buried in Nazareth Presbyterian Church Cemetery, Moore, Spartanburg Co, SC,[213] resided since 1800 in Spartanburg, Spartanburg Co, SC,[213] military War of 1812.[213]

"James Nickels Gaston donated much land around Reidville for the erection and establishment of the Reidville Male and Female colleges. He was a public-spirited and generous hearted citizen with high standing in the community."[213]

He married[129] **Mary Powers**, b. 1789,[213] d. 1860,[213] [Death date either Apr or Aug 28 1860.].
>
> Children:
> 230. i. HAMILTON ROSBOROUGH GASTON b. Feb-10-1811.
> 231. ii. AMZI WILLIFORD GASTON b. Apr-16-1813.
> 232. iii. THOMAS PINKNEY GASTON b. Apr-29-1815.
> 233. iv. SARAH ADELINE GASTON b. 1817.
> v. JAMES A. GASTON d. young,[ccxiv[214]] cause of death killed by a tree.[214]
> vi. WILLIAM POWERS GASTON[214.]
> vii. JOSEPH JAMES GASTON[214.]

125. **Hugh Gaston** (58.Thomas[5], 16.Robert[4], 5.William[3], 3.John[2], 1.Jean[1]), b. Sep-29-1790.[129] He married[129] **__ McElrath**.
>
> Children:
> 234. i. HARVEY GASTON.
> 235. ii. EMILY GASTON.
> iii. MARY JANE GASTON.
>
> Married an Italian. Had no children.[133]

126. **Samuel Gaston** (58.Thomas[5], 16.Robert[4], 5.William[3], 3.John[2], 1.Jean[1]), b. Sep- 4-1798,[133] d. Sep-12-1857.[133] He married[133] **Sarah Wakefield**.
>
> Children:
> i. TOM LARKIN GASTON. He married[133] no children from this marriage,[133] Mary Gillespie.

236. ii. MARGARET GASTON.

127. **Thomas Logan Gaston** (58.Thomas[5], 16.Robert[4], 5.William[3], 3.John[2], 1.Jean[1]), b. Apr- 7-1805,[133] d. Mar-24-1854 in Asheville, Buncombe Co, NC,[133] buried in Nazareth Presbyterian Church Cemetery, Moore, Spartanburg Co, SC,[133] [No grave marker except the engraved initials "T. G." on a field stone, located next to the grave of James A. Gaston.], resided in Asheville, Buncombe Co, NC.[133] He married[133] (1) Apr-16-1829,[ccxv[215]] **Prudence Doolen**, b. Feb- 4-1809,[133] d. Oct- -1837.[133] He married[133] (2) Jul-12-1842,[215] no children from this marriage,[133] **Margaret E. Walker**,[215] resided in Spartanburg District, SC.[133]

Margaret: Identified as "Mrs. Margaret Walker," so Walker was probably her name from a previous marriage.[133]

Children by Prudence Doolen:
i. HARRIET KESIAH GASTON b. Mar-19-1830,[133] d. Aug- -1832.[133]
ii. JOSIAH PERRY GASTON b. Apr-30-1832,[133] d. May- 5-1890.[215] He married Aug-23-1855,[133] Martha Jones.
237. iii. PARLEY CLENNEY GASTON b. Jul-30-1835.

128. **Robert Gaston** (60.Hugh[5], 16.Robert[4], 5.William[3], 3.John[2], 1.Jean[1]), b. 1799.[12] He married[12] **Sarah Bullock**, b. 1803.[12]
Children:
238. i. JAMES BULLOCK GASTON b. 1822.

129. **Alexander F. Gaston**[122] (64.William[5], 18.Alexander[4], 5.William[3], 3.John[2], 1.Jean[1]), b. Jan-19-1807 in North Carolina,[54,122] d. 1848.

In addition to the three children listed here, Alexander F. Gaston may also have had another daughter, Eliza W. Gaston, b. Jul 15 1841, who on Apr 22 1861 married Samuel Simpson Kirkland.[ccxvi[216]]

He married (1) Mar-14-1831 in Christ Episcopal Church, New Bern, NC,[54,122] **Eliza W. Jones**,[122] b. ca 1808,[54] (daughter of Hugh Jones), d. Apr- -1837.[54] He married (2) ca 1839,[54] **Sarah Lauretta Murphy**.
Children by Eliza W. Jones:
i. HUGH JOSEPH GASTON education (as of 1850) Georgetown College, Washington, DC.[122]
ii. WILLIAM F. GASTON[122] education (as of 1850) Georgetown College, Washington, DC.[122]
iii. SUSAN GASTON.

130. **Hannah Margaret Gaston** (64.William[5], 18.Alexander[4], 5.William[3], 3.John[2], 1.Jean[1]), b. Mar-18-1811 in North Carolina,[54,122] d. Mar-16-1835 in North Carolina,[ccxvii[217]] education private school in Baltimore MD.[ccxviii[218]] She married Feb-16-1832 in New Bern, Craven Co, NC,[218] **Mathias Evans Manly**, b. 1801,[148] d. 1881,[148] occupation lawyer and judge,[218] [After William Joseph Gaston's death, Mathias Manly served on the bench of the North Carolina State Supreme Court.].
Children:
i. JANE MANLY.
ii. HANNAH MANLY.

131. **Nancy Gaston Knox**[150] (67.Hugh[5], 19.Elizabeth[4], 5.William[3], 3.John[2], 1.Jean[1]), b. ca 1797 in South Carolina,[146] census 1850 in York Co, SC. She married ca 1820,[150] **Ephraim Moss**, b. ca 1796 in South Carolina,[146] resided in Georgia,[150] census 1850 in York Co, SC, resided originally in York Co, SC,[150] occupation farmer.[146]

Ephraim: 1850 Census, York Co, South Carolina (enumerated on Oct 19 1850:
Ephraim Moss, 54, farmer; Nancy, 53; Mary, 24; Elizabeth A, 18; James, 17; Ephraim, 14. All born in
South Carolina.
In the adjacent household. living alone, was William Moss, 28. farmer, b. SC.

> Children:
> i.   WILLIAM MOSS b. ca 1822 in South Carolina.
> ii. MARY MOSS b. ca 1826 in South Carolina,[146] census 1850 in York Co, SC.
> iii. ELIZABETH A. MOSS b. ca 1832 in South Carolina.[146]
> iv. JAMES MOSS b. ca 1833 in South Carolina,[146] census 1850 in York Co, SC.
> v.   EPHRAIM MOSS b. ca 1836 in South Carolina.

132. **Frances Gaston**[151] (69.William[5], 20.William[4], 5.William[3], 3.John[2], 1.Jean[1]). She married[151] **Robert White**.
> Children:
> 239.   i.   MARY WHITE.

133. **William Gaston** (70.James[5], 21.John[4], 6.Hugh[3], 3.John[2], 1.Jean[1]), b. Feb-18-1776, d. Feb-16-1853,[17] buried in Old Tennent Church Cem, Monmouth Co, NJ,[ccxix[219],ccxx[220]] military Revolutionary War.[15,19]

Data on the children of William Gaston & Catharine Johnson, other than Gertrude & William, is from the baptismal records of Cranbury Church, NJ. Other data on this family was obtained from "History of Old Tennent Church," page 449. As a young man, William Gaston served in the Revolutionary War.

He married[19] Mar-14-1804,[ccxxi[221],ccxxii[222]] **Catharine English**,[17] b. Mar-13-1778,[222] (daughter of James English), d. Aug-22-1843,[ccxxiii[223],ccxxiv[224]] buried in Old Tennent Church Cem, Monmouth Co, NJ.[17,224]
> Children:
> i.   LYDIA TAPSCOTT GASTON b. Dec- 4-1804,[221,222,19] baptized in Cranbury Church, NJ, d. Feb-20-1900. She married[19] Aaron Allen.
> ii. JOHN BAIRD GASTON b. May-25-1806,[221,222,19] baptized in Cranbury Church, NJ.
> iii. MARY ANN P. GASTON, also known as Ann P. Gaston,[221] b. Mar-20-1810,[19,221] baptized in Cranbury Church, NJ, d. Mar-28-1845, buried in Old Tennent Church Cem, Monmouth Co, NJ.[17] She married[19] John Perrine, Jr..
> iv. LETITIA J. GASTON b. Sep- 3-1811,[221,222] d. Feb-20-1900.[221,222] She married (1) Feb-7-1837,[221] Elisha W. Thompson. She married (2) Mar- -1860,[221] Denis Thompson.
> v.   GERTRUDE GASTON b. Sep-17-1813,[221,222] d. Jul-16-1816,[222] buried in Old Tennent Church Cem, Monmouth Co, NJ.
> vi. WILLIAM C. GASTON b. Jan-26-1816,[221,222] d. Sep-13-1821,[221,222] buried in Old Tennent Church Cem, Monmouth Co, NJ.
> vii. HANNAH E. GASTON b. Jan-26-1818,[221,222] d. Feb- 4-1904.[222,221] She married[222,221] ___ Conover.

134. **Andrew Gaston** (72.John[5], 21.John[4], 6.Hugh[3], 3.John[2], 1.Jean[1]), b. ca 1782 in New Jersey,[ccxxv[225]] d. Dec- 6-1866 in Harrison Co, WV, buried unmarked grave in Broad Run Bapt Ch Cem, Jane Lew, Lewis Co, WV, census 1850, 1860 in Harrison Co, (W)VA.

1830 Census, Harrison County, Virginia (now West Virginia):
Household of Andrew Gaston:
1 male, age 40-50
1 male, age 20-30
1 female, age 30-40
1 female, age 20-30
1 female, age 15-20

He married (1) Nov-11-1806 in Harrison Co, (W)VA,[ccxxvi[226],ccxxvii[227]] **Sarah Romine** (daughter of Samuel Romine). He married (2) Sep-27-1821 in Harrison Co, (W)VA,[227] **Dorcas Stephens**, b. ca 1800 in Harrison Co, (W)VA,[225] d. aft 1866,[ccxxviii[228]] census 1850, 1860 in Harrison Co, (W)VA.

        Children by Sarah Romine:
- 240.   i.   ANNA GASTON b. 1814.
- 241.   ii.   MATILDA "TILLIE" GASTON b. ca 1818.
-       iii.   JOHN GASTON.

135. **Mary E. "Polly" Gaston** (72.John[5], 21.John[4], 6.Hugh[3], 3.John[2], 1.Jean[1]), b. May- 4-1785 in Monmouth Co, NJ,[ccxxix[229]] christened in Harrison Co, (W)VA, d. Oct-11-1865 in Harrison Co, WV,[229,17] buried in Sinclair Cemetery, Upper Duck Crk Rd, Harrison Co, WV.[229,ccxxx[230]] She married Jan-4-1803 in Harrison Co, (W)VA,[ccxxxi[231]] **Job West**, b. ca 1774 in Harford Co, MD,[231] (son of John West and Frances Howard), baptized Aug-10-1799 in Smithfield, Fayette Co, PA,[231] d. ca 1823 in Chillicothe, Ross Co, OH,[231] buried unmarked grave in Oldtown Cemetery, Chillicothe, OH,[ccxxxii[232]] census 1810 in Harrison Co, (W)VA,[231] occupation farmer.[231]

        Children:
- 242.   i.   FRANCES WEST b. ca 1803.
- 243.   ii.   RUANNA WEST b. Oct-22-1806.
- 244.   iii.   ELIZABETH "BETSY" WEST b. Oct-13-1809.
-       iv.   SARAH "SALLY" WEST[229] b. Jan-14-1811 in Harrison Co, (W)VA,[229,17] d. Aug-29-1883,[229,17] buried in Sinclair Cemetery, Upper Duck Crk Rd, Harrison Co, WV.[ccxxxiii[233],229]

        Records show that Sarah West was married, but her headstone gives her maiden name. There may have been a divorce and she took back the name of West. Some sources (e.g., Donnelly, p. 411) state that she was not married at all.

        She married Jul-15-1832, Christopher Broherd.
- 245.   v.   ELI R. WEST b. Apr- 5-1813.
-       vi.   PHOEBE WEST b. Dec- 7-1816 in Harrison Co, (W)VA,[229] d. Sep- 8-1898 in Harrison Co, WV,[229] buried in Sinclair Cemetery, Upper Duck Crk Rd, Harrison Co, WV.[229]
-       vii.   JOHN WALDO WEST b. Jun-28-1817 in Harrison Co, (W)VA,[229,17] d. May-18-1829 in Harrison Co, (W)VA,[229,17] buried in Sinclair Cemetery, Upper Duck Crk Rd, Harrison Co, WV,[17,229,230].

        Named for the Reverend John Waldo, an early minister of the Broad Run Baptist Church.[ccxxxiv[234]]

-       viii.   DEBORAH WEST b. Aug-21-1821,[17,ccxxxv[235]] d. Mar-19-1909 in Harrison Co, WV,[229,17] buried in Sinclair Cemetery, Upper Duck Crk Rd, Harrison Co, WV,[17,229,230] census 1900 in Grant District, Harrison Co, WV,[229] never married.

136. **Hugh Gaston**, also known as Hughy Gaston (72.John[5], 21.John[4], 6.Hugh[3], 3.John[2], 1.Jean[1]), b. Jun- 5-1788 in New Jersey,[ccxxxvi[236]] [Birth date calculated from age at death, 100y 1m 21d, stated in death record. This varies by one day from the age stated in his obituary, 100y 1m 20d.], d. Jul-26-1888 in Lewis Co, WV,[ccxxxvii[237]] buried in Gaston-Henry Cemetery, Sassafras Run, Camden, Lewis Co WV,[17] census 1870, 1880 in Lewis Co, WV, census 1840, 50, 60 in Lewis Co, (W)VA, census 1830 in Harrison Co, (W)VA.

Newspaper notice stated "HUGHY GASTON One of our centenarians, aged 100 years, 1 month and 20 days, died at 7 p.m. Wednesday at the residence of his son-in-law, John S. Butcher. By request he was interred on his farm." [Rep. Sat. 7/28/1888]

1830 Census, Harrison County, Virginia (now West Virginia):
Household of Hugh Gaston:

1 male, age 40-50 (this would be Hugh)
1 male, age 15-20 (probably Daniel)
1 male, age 10-15 (probably Eli)
1 male, age 5-10
1 female, age 40-50 (this would be Susannah)
1 female, age 15-20 (probably Anna)

1840 Census, Lewis County, Virginia (now West Virginia):
Household of Hugh Gasting (sic):
1 male, age 50-60
1 female, age 30-40
1 female, age 10-15
1 female, under age 5

1850 Census, Lewis County, Virginia (now West Virginia), enumerated on Oct 3 1850:
Hugh Gaston, 62, farmer, b. New Jersey; Elizabeth Gaston, 48, b. Virginia; Henry H. Gaston, 9, b. Virginia; Credilla Gaston, 11, b. Virginia; Amanda Washburn, 24, b. Virginia.

1860 Census, Lewis County, Virginia (now West Virginia):
Hugh Gaston, 72, farmer, b. New Jersey; Elizabeth Gaston, 58, b. Virginia; Henry H. Gaston, 18, b. Virginia; Amanda S. Washburn, 34, b. Virginia; Marion H. Gaston, 8.

1870 Census, Lewis County, WV:
Hugh Gaston, 81, farmer, b. New Jersey; Elizabeth Gaston, 67, b. Virginia; Marion Gaston, 17, farm laborer, b. Virginia; Amanda Washburn, 43, b. Ohio, cannot write.

1880 Census, Lewis County, WV (Freeman's Creek), enumerated on Jun 2 1880:
Hugh Gaston, 91, farmer, b. New Jersey, both parents b. New Jersey; wife Elizabeth Gaston, 77, b. Virginia, both parents b. Virginia; step-daughter A. Washburn, 53, b. Ohio, both parents b. Virginia.

He married (1) Dec-7-1811 in Harrison Co, (W)VA,[ccxxxviii][238] **Susana Jett**, b. btwn 1780 - 1790,[ccxxxix][239] d. May- 1-184_,[ccxl][240] census 1830 in Harrison Co, (W)VA.

Susana: No record of the parentage or other information of Susana Jett has been found.

In Book 2, p. 388, of Harrison County Marriage Bonds is a record of a bond of $150 being paid by Hugh Gaston and James Coberly (spelling may be Cubberly) in connection with the marriage of Hugh Gaston and "Susana Jett of full age." It is unknown what relationship existed between James Coberly and Susana Jett; we have found only that a James Coberly (b. 1779) and wife Letitia "Tisha" Jett (b. 1783) were residents of Harrison/Gilmer Co in that time period.

A W. Guy Tetrick family information survey completed by great-grandson Ira Dow Gaston in 1931stated that his grandparents were Hugh Gaston, born 1788, died July 5 1888, and Susana Jett, born "unknown," daughter of "unknown," they were married in 1811, and she died May 1 1849. The reported death date is considered suspect,, since husband Hugh Gaston is known to have remarried on June 1 1848.

He married (2) Jun-1-1848 in Lewis Co, WV,[ccxli][241],[ccxlii][242] **Elizabeth King**, b. 1801,[46,ccxliii][243] [Although her death record gives her birth place as Kentucky, the censuses of 1860, 1870 and 1880 all show it as Virginia.], d. Sep-16-1885 in Lewis Co, WV,[ccxliv][244] buried in Gaston-Henry Cemetery, Sassafras Run, Camden, Lewis Co WV,[17] census 1860, 70, 80 in Lewis Co, (W)VA,[ccxlv][245],[ccxlvi][246],[ccxlvii][247] resided 1835 in Ross Co, OH.

Elizabeth: Elizabeth King's first husband was Isaac Washburn, who she married in Kentucky in about 1819. In the 1880 Census of Lewis County, the household of Elizabeth and second husband

Hugh Gaston includes Elizabeth's daughter Amanda Washburn. Amanda is also buried in the Gaston-Henry cemetery, sharing a common headstone with her mother and stepfather. Her name appears on the headstone as Amanda S. Washburn, dates 1825-1901.[234]

Children by Susana Jett:
246.   i.   JOHN HUGH GASTON b. Jul-17-1812.
       ii.   JAMES GASTON[240] b. Jul-17-1812 in Harrison Co, (W)VA.[ccxlviii][248]
      iii.   ANNA M. GASTON b. Jan- 3-1814, d. Jul-30-1892 in Doddridge Co, WV,[ccxlix][249] buried in Gaston Family Cemetery, Upper Run, Summers, Doddridge Co WV, never married.

     Resided with her brother Daniel and his family, according to the censuses of 1850, 1860 and 1880.

247.   iv.   DANIEL H. GASTON b. Jun-27-1816.
248.   v.   ELI MORRIS GASTON b. Aug- 3-1822.
      vi.   WILLIAM GASTON[ccl][250]
     vii.   GRANVILLE GASTON[250.]
249.   viii.   CORDELIA GASTON b. Dec-29-1838.
250.   ix.   HENRY LEE GASTON b. 1841.
      Children by Elizabeth King:
251.   x.   MARION GASTON b. Jun- 7-1852.

137. **Sarah Gaston** (72.John[5], 21.John[4], 6.Hugh[3], 3.John[2], 1.Jean[1]), b. Dec-29-1790 in Monmouth Co, NJ,[ccli][251] [Some researchers (e.g., Edward Couey) have birthdate as Dec 22 1790.], d. May-13-1873 in Harrison Co, WV,[17] buried in Sinclair Cemetery, Upper Duck Crk Rd, Harrison Co, WV.[17,230] She married Dec-26-1811 in Harrison Co, (W)VA,[cclii][252],[ccliii][253] [Marriage date of Dec 26 1811 reported by Hurley in "Maddox: A Southern Maryland Family," p. 105.], **William Maddox**, b. Apr-10-1785 near Sandy Hook (Huntly), Culpeper (now Rappahannock) Co, VA,[251,ccliv][254] [W. N. Hurley Jr., in "Maddox: A Southern Maryland Family," incorrectly identifies William Maddox's birthplace as St. Marys Co, MD. The correct birthplace, "near Sandy Hook in Culpepper Co VA, probably in what is now Rappahannock Co VA," was provided by Raymond A. Mann <dermann@earthlink.net>, a direct descendant, based on his grandmother's notes and other reliable information.] (son of Matthew Maddox and Rachel (twin) Bonnifield), d. Apr-28-1869 in Harrison Co, WV,[251] ["Cemeteries of Grant District," p. 39, reports death date on headstone as Apr 30 1869.], buried in Sinclair Cemetery, Upper Duck Crk Rd, Harrison Co, WV.[17,230] 1860 Census, Harrison County, Virginia (now West Virginia): William Maddox, 75, farmer, b. Virginia; Sarah, 69, b. New Jersey; Matthew, 48, b. Va; Mary E, 49, b. Ohio; Arnold, 31, b. Va; Mary F. Ward, 9, b. Va.

Children:
252.   i.   MATTHEW MADDOX b. Oct- 4-1812.
253.   ii.   JOHN G. MADDOX b. Jul-20-1814.
      iii.   MANSFIELD MADDOX b. Jul- 6-1816 in Harrison Co, (W)VA,[253] d. Aug- 4-1816 in Harrison Co, (W)VA.[253]
254.   iv.   MARGARET MADDOX b. Aug-15-1817.
255.   v.   THOMAS MADDOX b. Jan- 2-1820.
256.   vi.   WILLIAM D. MADDOX, JR. b. Jan-17-1822.
257.   vii.   JAMES GASTON MADDOX b. Nov-11-1823.
     viii.   DORCAS MADDOX b. Nov-12-1825 in Harrison Co, (W)VA.[253] She married Henry Lyons.
      ix.   OLIVER MADDOX b. Jan-25-1828 in Harrison Co, (W)VA,[253] d. Jan-28-1828 in Harrison Co, (W)VA.[253]
258.   x.   ARNOLD M. MADDOX b. Apr- 8-1829.
259.   xi.   ANNA MADDOX b. Sep-19-1831.
260.   xii.   RUHAMA MADDOX b. Aug-26-1833.

138. **Margaret Gaston** (72.John[5], 21.John[4], 6.Hugh[3], 3.John[2], 1.Jean[1]), b. Apr-13-1793 in Pennsylvania, d. Apr-16-1885 in Tazewell Co, IL,[cclv[255]] buried in Tazewell Co, IL.

Lived in Butler County, OH, and in Indiana, and in 1836 moved with her husband to Spring Lake Twp, Tazewell Co, Illinois.

She married Jul-24-1812 in Xenia, Greene Co, OH, **Maxson Clayton**, also known as Maxon Clayton, b. Nov- 2-1785 in Monmouth Co, NJ,[255] (son of Thomas Clayton and Elizabeth "Rosa" Brand), d. Aug-17-1839 in Tazewell Co, IL,[255] buried in Tazewell Co, IL.

Maxson: Maxson Clayton's father, Thomas Claton, bought 250 acres on the Middle Fork of Ten Mile Creek in Harrison Co on Jan 20 1794 from Daniel Davisson. He sold the same to William Tate on Dec 23 1806, giving his residence as Warren Co, OH. [Family data from Berenice Clayton and Alda Vitz, per Susie Davis Nicholson, p. 18]

       Children:
261.   i.   ANNA CLAYTON b. 1813.
      ii.   ELIZABETH CLAYTON b. 1815. She married Jun-29-1837, Thomas Huddleston.
262.   iii.   DEBORAH CLAYTON b. 1817.
      iv.   THOMAS CLAYTON b. 1818, d. 1830.
263.   v.   JOHN CLAYTON b. Jan-15-1820.
      vi.   (INFANT) CLAYTON b. 1823, d. in infancy.
      vii.   (INFANT) CLAYTON b. 1826, d. in infancy.
      viii.   ELLEN CLAYTON b. 1829.
      ix.   SARAH JANE CLAYTON b. Jan- 4-1834, d. Mar-29-1851.
      x.   PAULINE CLAYTON b. 1835.

139. **John Gaston** (72.John[5], 21.John[4], 6.Hugh[3], 3.John[2], 1.Jean[1]), b. May-24-1796 in Harrison Co, (W)VA, d. Oct- 4-1884 in Harrison Co, WV,[cclvi[256]] buried in Duck Creek Missn Chrch Cem, near West Milford, Harrison Co, WV,[cclvii[257]] census 1850 in Harrison Co, (W)VA, occupation farmer.[cclviii[258]] He married Nov-14-1820 in Harrison Co, (W)VA, **Elizabeth Morris**, b. Nov- 8-1797 in New Jersey,[17,225] ["Cemeteries of Grant District, Harrison County, WV," p. 28, reports birth date on headstone as May 8 1797.] (daughter of Samuel Morris and Rebecca Smith), d. Jul-11-1882 in Harrison Co, WV,[17] buried in Duck Creek Missn Chrch Cem, near West Milford, Harrison Co, WV,[17] census 1850 in Harrison Co, (W)VA.

1880 Census, Harrison Co, WV (Grant District), enumerated on Jun 7 1880:
John Gaston, 83, farmer; wife Elizabeth Gaston, 82; granddau Caroline Law, 30, widow, domestic servant; Asby S. Law, 10.
(Note: Relationship of Caroline (aka Mary C.) would more accurately be termed granddaughter-in-law, as she was the widow of their grandson John W. Law. Relationship of Asby was left blank; he was a great-grandson.)

       Children:
      i.   REBECCA ANN GASTON b. Aug- 6-1821 [Birth date calculated from age at death 18y 2m 26d.], d. Nov- 1-1839.
264.   ii.   MARY JANE GASTON b. Jun-23-1823.
265.   iii.   SAMUEL MORRIS GASTON b. Feb-25-1825.
266.   iv.   DEBORAH GASTON b. May-17-1827.
267.   v.   SUSAN GASTON b. 1829.
268.   vi.   JOHN SMITH GASTON b. Dec-12-1830.
269.   vii.   ELIZABETH GASTON b. Aug- 9-1832.
      viii.   ANDREW DAVISSON GASTON b. ca 1836 in Harrison Co, (W)VA,[cclix[259],225] d. 186_ in Civil War, census 1850 in Harrison Co, (W)VA. He married Feb- 5-1859 in Lewis Co,

WV,[cclx[260],cclxi[261]] Sarah Ann Swisher, b. ca 1834 in Lewis Co, WV,[cclxii[262]] (daughter of Lewis D. Swisher and Martha Margaretta Smith).
    270.   ix.   SARAH GASTON b. ca 1837.
    271.   x.   JAMES WILLIAM GASTON b. Oct- -1838.

140. **Deborah Gaston**, also known as Debbie Gaston (72.John[5], 21.John[4], 6.Hugh[3], 3.John[2], 1.Jean[1]), b. Aug- 9-1798 in Harrison Co, (W)VA, d. Nov-10-1885 in Taylor Co, WV,[cclxiii[263],cclxiv[264]] buried in Middleville Baptist Church Cemetery, Taylor Co, WV.[17] She married Feb-11-1822 in Harrison Co, (W)VA,[cclxv[265]] **Joseph Taylor**, b. 1793,[cclxvi[266],cclxvii[267]] d. Sep- 2-1868,[17,234] [Death date for Joseph Taylor reported as Sep 12 1869 by researcher Linn Baiker, Virginia Beach, VA <lb0530@cox.net>, citing Harrison County Heritage 1784-1995. But Joseph Taylor's headstone clearly reads Sep 2 1868.], buried in Middleville Baptist Church Cemetery, Taylor Co, WV.[17]

Joseph: Joseph Taylor probably moved from Orange County Virginia to present-day West Virginia. Nothing of his ancestry is unknown.[234]
Joseph and Deborah Gaston Taylor are buried in the Middleville Cemetery, Taylor Co WV, with five of their children, Nancy Ann Taylor Corbin, Margaret Taylor Carr, William Davidson, Andrew Allen and Josiah Taylor. Nancy, Andrew and Josiah all died in 1856, with Nancy known to have died of typhoid; her brothers are suspected to have suffered the same fate.[234]

          Children:
    272.   i.   JOHN TAYLOR b. Jan-18-1823.
    273.   ii.   NANCY ANN TAYLOR b. Sep-29-1824.
    274.   iii.   ELIZABETH JANE TAYLOR b. Aug-21-1826.
    275.   iv.   MARGARET TAYLOR b. Sep-24-1828.
    276.   v.   JAMES GASTON TAYLOR b. Jan-12-1831.
          vi.   MARY TAYLOR b. Mar- 9-1833, d. Sep-24-1886. She married (1) Dec-8-1864, Francis Findley, b. 1815. She married (2) Jul-3-1884, James Davis, b. 1817.
    277.   vii.   WILLIAM DAVIDSON TAYLOR b. Sep-29-1835.
          viii.   ANDREW ALLEN TAYLOR b. Sep- 2-1837, d. Jun-24-1856, buried in Middleville Baptist Church Cemetery, Taylor Co, WV, cause of death typhoid fever.
          ix.   JOSIAH TAYLOR b. Nov-12-1838, d. Aug- 7-1856, buried in Middleville Baptist Church Cemetery, Taylor Co, WV, cause of death typhoid fever.
    278.   x.   SARAH "SALLY" TAYLOR b. Nov-24-1840.
    279.   xi.   HENRIETTA TAYLOR b. Jun-18-1845.

141. **Jane Gaston** (72.John[5], 21.John[4], 6.Hugh[3], 3.John[2], 1.Jean[1]), b. Nov-14-1802 in Duck Creek, Harrison Co, (W)VA,[cclxviii[268]] d. May- 9-1876 in Hackers Creek, Lewis Co, (W)VA,[268] census 1870 in Lewis Co, WV [in household of son James L. Swisher]. She married Oct-20-1829 in Lewis Co, (W)VA,[cclxix[269],242] **Isaac R. Swisher**, also known as Isaac Switzen,[242] b. Oct-27-1805 in Hackers Creek, Lewis Co, (W)VA,[268] (son of Peter S. Swisher III and Susannah Rinehart), d. Oct-20-1839 in Hackers Creek, Lewis Co, (W)VA.[268]

Isaac: There is some disagreement among researchers as to Isaac R. Swisher's name. Variations offered are Isaac Lewis Swisher, Lewis Isaac Swisher, and Isaac R. Swisher. Based on information in the death records of his son & grandson, we conclude it was Isaac R. Swisher. Researcher E. Murray Taylor is in agreement with this, theorizing that the commonly found variation Lewis Isaac Swisher originated in the hand-written marriage record of Isaac Swisher being married in Lewis County. Nearly all information listed here pertaining to the descendants of Lewis Isaac Swisher and Jane Gaston, unless otherwise noted, is courtesy of the research efforts of E. Murray Taylor, Jr., of Fairmont, WV, much of which centered on an existing Swisher family genealogy and the William A. Marsh 1880 Census of Lewis County, WV.

          Children:

280.   i.   PETER GASTON SWISHER b. Oct-28-1830.
281.   ii.   JAMES LEE SWISHER b. Jul-23-1832.
282.   iii.   SARAH JANE SWISHER b. May- -1834.
283.   iv.   ANNA MARIAH SWISHER b. 1838.
284.   v.   ISAAC RINEHART SWISHER b. Dec-23-1838.

142. **James Gaston** (72.John[5], 21.John[4], 6.Hugh[3], 3.John[2], 1.Jean[1]), b. 1804 in Duck Creek, Harrison Co, (W)VA,[268,225] d. bef Sep 1870,[cclxx[270]] census 1850, 1860 in Harrison Co, (W)VA,[225,cclxxi[271]] occupation farmer.[225] He married Apr-26-1829 in Lewis Co, (W)VA,[cclxxii[272],242] **Charlotte "Lottie" Swisher**, also known as Charlotte Switzen,[242] b. Jun-10-1807 in Hackers Creek, Lewis Co, (W)VA,[17,268] (daughter of Peter S. Swisher III and Susannah Rinehart), d. Aug-31-1875,[cclxxiii[273]] buried in Duck Creek Missn Chrch Cem, near West Milford, Harrison Co, WV,[17] census 1870 in Lewis Co, WV,[270] census 1850, 1860 in Harrison Co, (W)VA.[225,271]

Charlotte: Spoke fluent German.[cclxxiv[274]]
1850 Census, Harrison County, Virginia (now West Virginia), District 22, enumerated Aug 1850: James Gaston, age 46, farmer; Charlotte Gaston, 43; Elizabeth, 20; Mary, 18; Isaac, 14; Margaret, 12; Rebecca, 10; Thomas, 8; Olive, 6; John, 3; Sarah, 9 months; William Law, 15; Susannah Swisher, 70.

1860 Census, Harrison County, Virginia (now West Virginia):
James Gaston, 56, farmer; Charlotte, 53; Margaret D, 22; Thomas M, 17; Oliver (sic) J, 15 (female); John L. M., 13.

1870 Census, Lewis County, WV (Lincoln Twp), enumerated on Sep 21 1870:
Thomas M. Gaston, 27, miller; Helon Gaston, 19; Albert, 2; Charlotte, 63; John M, 23, shoemaker.

         Children:
285.   i.   ELIZABETH ANN GASTON b. May-16-1830.
286.   ii.   MARY CATHERINE GASTON b. Jan-19-1833.
         iii.   WILLIAM GRANVILLE GASTON b. Mar- 4-1834,[cclxxv[275]] d. Oct-12-1839,[17] buried in Sinclair Cemetery, Upper Duck Crk Rd, Harrison Co, WV.[17]
287.   iv.   ISAAC M. GASTON b. Apr- 1-1836.
288.   v.   MARGARET DRUSILLA GASTON b. Feb-19-1838.
289.   vi.   REBECCA ALCINDA GASTON b. May-25-1840.
290.   vii.   THOMAS M. GASTON b. Oct- -1842.
291.   viii. OLIVE JANE GASTON b. Jan-12-1845.
292.   ix.   JOHN M. "LANK" GASTON b. Jun-27-1847.
         x.   SARAH PALESTINE GASTON b. Nov-15-1849 in Duck Creek, Harrison Co, (W)VA,[154] d. Jan- 7-1857 at Duck Creek, Harrison Co, (W)VA,[cclxxvi[276]] [Some researchers (e.g., Lauri Buell Boaz) report death date as Jun 7 1857, but cemetery directory gives death date as Jan 7 1857, and Harrison County Death Records show that S. P. Gaston, dau of James & C., died on Jun 1 1857 at the age of 7y1m23d. Thus, the exact birth and/or death dates are still in question.], buried in Duck Creek Missn Chrch Cem, near West Milford, Harrison Co, WV,[230] cause of death scarlet fever.[276]

143. **William G. Gaston** (72.John[5], 21.John[4], 6.Hugh[3], 3.John[2], 1.Jean[1]), b. Feb- 1-1806 in Harrison Co, (W)VA,[cclxxvii[277],17] d. May-21-1894 in Harrison Co, WV,[cclxxviii[278],17] buried in Duck Creek Missn Chrch Cem, near West Milford, Harrison Co, WV,[17] census 1880 in Grant District, Harrison Co, WV, census 1850 in Harrison Co, (W)VA, occupation farmer.[225] He married May-5-1829 in Harrison Co, (W)VA,[227] **Mary Post**, b. Oct-31-1809 in Harrison Co, (W)VA,[278] (daughter of George Post and Elizabeth Peterson), d. Dec- 4-1887 in Harrison Co, WV,[278] [Cemetery directory gives death date as Dec 24 1887.], buried in Duck Creek Missn Chrch Cem, near West Milford, Harrison Co, WV,[17,230] census 1880 in Grant District, Harrison Co, WV.
         Children:
293.   i.   ABRAHAM GASTON b. Feb- 7-1830.
294.   ii.   GEORGE GASTON b. Sep-23-1831.

295.   iii.   ELIZABETH GASTON b. Jul-29-1835.
296.   iv.   JOHN WILLIAM GASTON b. Dec-26-1838.
297.   v.   ENOCH GASTON b. Aug-16-1841.
298.   vi.   MARY BIRD GASTON b. Jan-12-1853.

144. **John Gaston Mount** (73.Jane[5], 21.John[4], 6.Hugh[3], 3.John[2], 1.Jean[1]), b. Jul-28-1775 in Monmouth Co, NJ, d. Jan-25-1850 in Brighton, Jefferson Co, Iowa, buried in Hillcrest Cem, Jefferson Co, Iowa. He married Jul- 4-1799 in Monmouth Co, NJ,[23] **Ann Emley**, b. May-27-1779, d. Oct-21-1853 in Brighton, Jefferson Co, Iowa, buried in Hillcrest Cem, Jefferson Co, Iowa.
   Children:
   i.   ELIZABETH T. MOUNT b. Aug-11-1800 in Monmouth Co, NJ, d. Sep-25-1866 in Washington Co, IA.
   ii.   JAMES MOUNT b. May-25-1802 in Monmouth Co, NJ, d. Feb- 8-1860 in Warren Co, Iowa.
   iii.   CHARLES MOUNT b. May-21-1804 in Monmouth Co, NJ, d. aft 1861 in Van Wert Co, Ohio.
   iv.   SEXTON EMLEY MOUNT b. Feb-10-1811 in Monmouth Co, NJ, d. Jan-28-1885 in Brighton, Jefferson Co, Iowa. He married Jul- 6-1854 in Big Creek, IL, Tabitha Musgrove, b. Apr-27-1832 in Clark Co, OH, d. Jan-24-1881 in Brighton, Jefferson Co, Iowa.

145. **William Gaston** (74.John[5], 22.William[4], 6.Hugh[3], 3.John[2], 1.Jean[1]), b. Jul-15-1761,[66] baptized Sep- 6-1761 in Old Tennent Church, Monmouth Co, NJ,[159] resided in Ohio.[66,15] He married[157] **Jane __**.
   Children:
299.   i.   SAMUEL GASTON b. 1800.

146. **Joseph Gaston** (74.John[5], 22.William[4], 6.Hugh[3], 3.John[2], 1.Jean[1]), b. Apr-25-1763,[66] baptized Jul-17-1763 in Old Tennent Church, Monmouth Co, NJ,[159] d. Nov-21-1821 in Butler Co, OH,[66] resided (settled abt 1807) in Butler Co, OH,[66] resided in Abbeville Co, SC,[66] military Capt & Major, Savannah Regt, Revolutionary War, 1782.[66] He married[66] **Martha Hutton**.
   Children:
   i.   REBECCA GASTON b. Feb-20-1784.[66] She married[66] John Kerr.
   ii.   ANN GASTON b. Dec-16-1785.[66]
   iii.   MARGARET GASTON b. Mar-17-1788.[66] She married Ezekiel McConnell.
   iv.   JOHN GASTON b. Jun-17-1790.[66]
   v.   MARY GASTON b. Sep-23-1792.[66]
   vi.   WILLIAM GASTON b. Apr-20-1795 in Butler Co, OH,[66] d. aft 1860 in Bartholomew Co, IN.
   vii.   JOSEPH GASTON b. Oct- 9-1796.[66]
   viii.   MATTA ANN GASTON b. Feb- 6-1799.[66] She married William Hayden.
   ix.   LYDIA GASTON b. Jul-22-1801.[66] She married[66] Ebenezer Wilson.
   x.   LUCINDA GASTON b. May- 9-1804.[66] She married[66] Daniel Symmes.
   xi.   ELIZA GASTON b. Feb-16-1807.[66] She married[66] Benjamin R. Symmes.

147. **James (twin) Gaston** (74.John[5], 22.William[4], 6.Hugh[3], 3.John[2], 1.Jean[1]), b. Feb-18-1767,[66] baptized Apr-12-1767 in Old Tennent Church, Monmouth Co, NJ,[159] d. Apr-13-1813,[66] resided (settled) in Hamilton Co, OH.[66]

In 1812, James Gaston sold his property in Washington Co, PA to his brother Samuel (b. 1772). Although reared in Pennsylvania, most of James' and Mary's children later moved west.

He married[66] **Mary Estep**, b. Oct-10-1773,[66] (daughter of Robert Estep and Dorcas Estep), d. Dec- 1-1857.[cclxxix[279]]
   Children:
   i.   NANCY GASTON b. Mar-25-1794.[66] She married[66] __ Spencer.

ii.   DORCAS GASTON b. Aug-19-1796,[66] resided (settled) in Scott Co, IA.[66] She married[66] David Figley.

iii.   CHARITY GASTON b. Dec- 1-1798 in Pennsylvania,[66] d. 1825 in Clark Co, OH, resided (settled) in Clark Co, OH.[66] She married[66] ca 1816, Enoch King, b. ca 1796 in New Jersey,[cclxxx][280] d. 1865 in Clark Co, OH. Enoch King and Charity Gaston had at least two children. The year after Charity's death, Enoch married her sister Martha.

1850 Census, Clark Co, Ohio (Harmony Twp), enumerated on Sep 30 1850:
Enoch King, 52, b. NJ, farmer; Martha, 46, b. Pa; Cyrus, 28, b. Ohio, farmer; Joseph, 24, b. Ohio, farmer; Nancy J, 18, b. Ohio.

1860 Census, Clark Co, Ohio (Harmony Twp), enumerated on Jul 23 1860:
Enoch King, 64, b. NJ, farmer; Martha, 55, b. Pa; Maria, 25, b. Ohio; Daniel, 23, b. Ohio; Thomas, 22, b. Ohio; Enoch, 20, b. Ohio; Daniel, 18, b. Ohio; John, 16, b. Ohio; Martha, 14, b. Ohio; Helen, 10, b. Ohio.

1870 Census, Clark Co, Ohio (Harmony Twp), enumerated on Jun 22 1870:
Martha King, 65, b. Pa; Mariah, 35, b. Ohio; Enock, 29, b. Ohio, farmer; David, 28, b. Ohio, auctioneer; Martha, 24, b. Ohio.

1880 Census, Clark Co, Ohio (Harmony Twp), enumerated on Jun 19 1880:
Martha King, 75, b. Pa, both parents b. in France; dau Martha A. King, 33, b. Ohio, father b. NJ, mother b. Pa, single, school teacher; granddau Lilla M. King, 11, b. Illinois, both parents b. Ohio; granddau Nina King, 28, b. Illinois, both parents b. Ohio, single, school teacher.

iv.   JOSEPH H. GASTON b. Mar-25-1801 in Washington Co, PA,[66] d. Dec- 6-1834 in Steubenville, Jefferson Co, OH,[66] resided (settled) in Carroll Co, OH,[66] occupation minister.[66]
v.   MARIA GASTON b. Apr- 6-1803 in Pennsylvania,[66] d. Oct-20-1803.[66]
300.   vi.   MARTHA GASTON b. Jan-20-1805.
301.   vii.   RACHEL GASTON b. Mar-18-1807.
302.   viii.   JAMES ESTEP GASTON b. Apr-14-1809.
303.   ix.   ROBERT GASTON b. Jul-25-1811.

148. **Samuel Gaston, Sr.** (74.John[5], 22.William[4], 6.Hugh[3], 3.John[2], 1.Jean[1]), b. Oct-10-1772,[66] d. Feb-21-1853 in Washington Co, PA,[67,66,17] buried in Mingo Creek Presb Cem, Union Twp, Washington Co, PA.[cclxxxi][281],67

Some children placed with his first wife Margaret Penny may actually be the children of his second wife Tephanes. Circumstances unclear, but while his second wife Tephanes was mentioned in his will of 1851, his first wife was not.

He married[66] (1) **Margaret Penny**, b. 1776 in Allegheny Co, PA,[66,cclxxxii][282] d. Aug-14-1841,[66,17] buried in Mingo Creek Presb Cem, Union Twp, Washington Co, PA.[cclxxxiii][283],67 He married (2)[17] **Tephanes** __, also known as Tephenes __, b. ca 1796 in Pennsylvania,[146,74] d. Dec-24-1883,[cclxxxiv][284] buried in Mingo Creek Presb Cem, Union Twp, Washington Co, PA,[17] census 1850, 1860 in Union Twp, Washington Co, PA.

Tephanes: Apparently born in Ireland. [1880 Census, Union Twp, Washington Co, PA]

Children by Margaret Penny:
i.   CHARITY GASTON b. ca 1796 in Pennsylvania,[146] [Birth date reported in "Ohio Valley Genealogies," p. 43, as 1802. But age 54 in 1850 Census puts it in about 1796.], census 1850, 1870 in Snowden Twp, Allegheny Co, PA. She married[66] Robert Donaldson, b. ca 1793 in Pennsylvania,[146] census 1850 in Snowden Twp, Allegheny Co, PA.[146]

1850 Census, Allegheny Co, Pennsylvania (Snowden Twp), enumerated on Sep 13 1850:

Robert Donaldson, 57, farmer; Charity Donaldson, 54; Archibald McMurry, 26, farmer; Caroline McMurry, 22; Joseph Standford, 18. All born in Pennsylvania.

ii. NANCY GASTON b. ca 1798 in Pennsylvania,[146] [Birth date given in "Ohio Valley Genealogies," p. 43, as 1805. But age 52 in 1850 Census puts it in about 1798.], census 1850 in Salt Creek Twp, Wayne Co, OH, resided (settled, ca 1837) in Ohio.[66] She married[66] William Peppard, b. ca 1793 in Pennsylvania,[146] census 1850 in Salt Creek Twp, Wayne Co, OH, occupation plasterer.[146]

1850 Census, Wayne Co, Ohio (Salt Creek Twp), enumerated on Aug 31 1850:
William Peppard, 57, b. Pa, occupation plasterer; Nancy, 52, b. Pa; Margaret, 24, b. Ohio; William, 22, b. Ohio.
In the adjoining household, living alone, was Nancy Peppart, 74, b. Pa.

iii. JOHN GASTON b. 1800,[17,66] d. 1868,[17] buried in Mingo Creek Presb Cem, Union Twp, Washington Co, PA.[17,67] He married[66,17] Patience Morrison, b. 1796,[17] (daughter of Henry Morrison and Patience Sayers), d. 1854,[17] buried in Mingo Creek Presb Cem, Union Twp, Washington Co, PA.[67]

iv. MARGARET GASTON b. Jul-25-1802 in Washington Co, PA,[cclxxxv[285]] resided (settled, 1844) near Burlington, Des Moines Co, IA.[66] She married[66] Thomas Jefferson Rice Perry.

304. v. SARAH JANE GASTON b. ca 1805.

305. vi. WILLIAM GASTON b. 1807.

306. vii. ELIZA GASTON b. ca 1809.

307. viii. JOSEPH SMITH GASTON b. Apr- 1-1811.

ix. SAMUEL GASTON, JR. b. ca 1816,[74] d. Sep-13-1841,[17,67] buried in Mingo Creek Presb Cem, Union Twp, Washington Co, PA,[17,67] [Headstone inscription reads "Samuel, son of Samuel Gaston Sen., died Sept 13 1841, in the 25 year of his age." Hanna, p. 43, incorrectly gives birth/death dates as 1814 - 1839. The death date on the headstone clearly reads Sept 13 1841, and the age 25, though not as clear, cannot be anything else.], never married[66.]

Samuel Gaston Jr. studied for the ministry at Washington College, Washington, PA, class of 1841.[67]

149. **Margaret Gaston** (74.John[5], 22.William[4], 6.Hugh[3], 3.John[2], 1.Jean[1]), b. ca 1776,[67] resided (settled) in Nottingham Twp, Washington Co, PA.[66,15] She married **Samuel McClain**, d. ca Mar 1820 in Nottingham Twp, Washington Co, PA,[67] resided originally in New Jersey.[66,15] Had no children, according to Charles Hanna in "Ohio Valley Genealogies," p. 43. But research by Peter J. Topoly and Jane Carson Topoly revealed the two children given here.

Children:
i. CHARITY MCCLAIN[67.]
ii. CHARLES MCCLAIN[67.]

Mentioned in his father's will as being under ten years of age.[67]

150. **Charles W. Gaston** (75.William[5], 22.William[4], 6.Hugh[3], 3.John[2], 1.Jean[1]), b. 1781 in Upper Mt. Bethel Twp, Northampton Co, PA,[cclxxxvi[286]] d. Dec-12-1843/45 in Van Buren Co, Iowa.[286] He married 1805,[286] **Joanna Winters**, b. ca 1787 in New Jersey,[146] d. Feb-20-1870 in Van Buren Co, Iowa,[286,cclxxxvii[287]] resided 1856 in Van Buren Co, Iowa,[cclxxxviii[288]] census 1850 in Van Buren Co, Iowa [Listed in household with son William and his family for both the 1850 Federal Census and the 1856

Iowa State Census. She was not found in the 1860 Census.], resided from abt 1839 in Iowa.[288] Charles and Joanna Winters Gaston had ten children.[286]

Children:
308. i. WILLIAM GASTON b. ca 1820.
309. ii. MARGARET GASTON b. Apr-21-1823.

151. **Robert Gaston** (76.James[5], 22.William[4], 6.Hugh[3], 3.John[2], 1.Jean[1]). He married **Unknown**.
Children:
      i. JAMES GASTON[67.]

152. **Mary "Polly" Gaston** (76.James[5], 22.William[4], 6.Hugh[3], 3.John[2], 1.Jean[1]), b. Oct-10-1787 in Washington Co, PA.[cclxxxix[289]] She married[67] **James Warnock**, b. Mar-30-1783 in Ireland.[289]
Children:
      i. JOHN WARNOCK[67.]
      ii. WILLIAM GASTON WARNOCK[67] b. Apr-29-1825.

153. **Joseph Gaston** (77.Hugh[5], 23.Joseph[4], 6.Hugh[3], 3.John[2], 1.Jean[1]), b. Dec-24-1789 in Pennsylvania,[15,69,146,280] census 1850, 1860 in Columbiana Co, OH, occupation farmer.[146]

1850 Census, Columbiana Co, Ohio (St. Clair Twp), enumerated on Sep 3 1850:
Jos (Jas ?) Gaston, 62, b. Pa, farmer; Mariah, 47, b. Pa; Catherine, 27, b. Ohio; Saml, 25, b. Ohio; Hamilton, 22, b. Ohio; Jacob, 18, b. Ohio; Hugh, 17, b. Ohio; Martin, 20, b. Ohio, school teacher. (Note: Joseph's birthplace has been incorrectly reported elsewhere as New Jersey. The seven children listed by Hanna, p. 44, for Joseph Gaston & Elizabeth Conkle include a son Watson and a daughter Elizabeth, but not a daughter Catherine. It is not clear whether or not Elizabeth and Catherine refer to the same child. Similarly,is unclear whether Mariah is Joseph's second wife or another name for his wife Elizabeth.)

1860 Census, Columbiana Co, Ohio (St. Clair Twp), enumerated in June 1860:
Joseph Gaston, 74, b. Pa, farmer; Mariah, 58, b. Pa; Adelaide A, 19, b. Ohio.
In the adjacent household:
Samuel Gaston, 38, b. Ohio, farm laborer; Mariah, 34, b. Ohio.

He married[69] **Elizabeth Conkle**. Name may be Conkie.

Children:
      i. ELIZABETH GASTON.
      ii. SAMUEL GASTON b. ca 1825 in Ohio,[146] census 1850, 1860 in Columbiana Co, OH. He married Dec- 5-1850 in Columbiana Co, OH,[67] Mariah L. Hamilton, b. ca 1826 in Ohio,[280] census 1860 in Columbiana Co, OH.
310. iii. HAMILTON GASTON[15,69] b. ca 1828.
311. iv. MARTIN GASTON[15,69] b. ca 1830.
      v. JACOB GASTON b. ca 1832 in Ohio,[146] census 1850 in Columbiana Co, OH.
312. vi. HUGH GASTON[15,69] b. ca 1833.
      vii. WATSON GASTON.

154. **James William Gaston**, census name William Gaston (77.Hugh[5], 23.Joseph[4], 6.Hugh[3], 3.John[2], 1.Jean[1]), b. Jan-20-1793,[69,15,146] d. Mar-13-1872,[69,15,12] census 1850 in Columbiana Co, OH. He married[69] **Elizabeth Kilgore**, b. Oct-11-1798,[12] (daughter of __ Kilgore), d. Sep-26-1854,[12] census 1850 in Columbiana Co, OH, resided originally in Cadiz, Harrison Co, OH.[69,15]

1850 Census, Columbiana Co, Ohio (Middleton Twp), enumerated in Aug 1850:

Wm. Gaston, 57, b. Pa, farmer; Elizabeth, 51, b. Pa; Wm, 29, b. Ohio, student at law; Mary, 25, b. Ohio; Filander, 22, b. Ohio; Narcis, 20, b. Ohio; Oliver, 18, b. Ohio; Jane, 16, b. Ohio; John, 14, b. Ohio;

Children:
i.   WILLIAM KILGORE GASTON b. Dec- 6-1820 in Columbiana Co, OH,[67] d. Jun-24-1905 in East Liverpool, Columbiana Co, OH,[67] census 1850 in Columbiana Co, OH, occupation attorney in New Lisbon, OH (1849-1859) and St. Paul, MN (1859),[67] education Washington College, Washington, PA (law degree, class of 1846).[67] He married[69] (1) Jan- 7-1857 in Columbiana Co, OH,[67] Martha Graham. He married[69] (2) 1865,[67] Andora Waage.

ii. HUGH F. GASTON b. Aug-16-1822.[67] He married[69] Mar-11-1851 in Wellsville, Columbiana Co, OH,[67] Elizabeth Stokes.

iii. ELIZABETH GASTON b. ca 1823.[67] She married[69] Joseph Lyons.

iv. MARY GASTON b. ca 1825.[67]

James W. Gaston and Mary Gaston were double cousins, in that they were both first cousins once removed (he was the grandson and she was the great- granddaughter of Joseph Gaston (b. in Ireland, d. 1775)) and also third cousins once removed (he was the great-great-grandson and she was the great- great-great-granddaughter of John Gaston (b. 1645 in Scotland)). Mary's grandparents, Hugh & Grace Gaston, were also cousins.

She married[69] May-__-1846,[67] James W. Gaston, b. Aug-29-1808 in Washington Co, PA,[67] (son of James Gaston and Jane ___), d. Mar-29-1884.[67]

313. v.   NANCY GASTON[69] b. ca 1825.
314. vi. PHILANDER GASTON[69] b. Aug- 1-1828.
315. vii. NARCISSA GASTON[69] b. ca 1830.
      viii. DANIEL OLIVER GASTON[67] census name Oliver Gaston, b. ca 1832 in Ohio,[146,67] census 1850 in Columbiana Co, OH. He married Oct-21-1856 in Coles, IL,[67] [According to Hanna, "Ohio Valley Genealogies," p. 44, Daniel O. Gaston died unmarried. Marriage information given here was provided by Peter J. Topoly and Jane Carson Topoly, citing highly reliable sources.], Elizabeth Taylor.
      ix. ELEANOR JANE GASTON, census name Jane Gaston, b. ca 1834 in Ohio,[146,67] census 1850 in Columbiana Co, OH. She married[69] John Geeting.
      x.   JOHN GASTON b. ca 1836 in Ohio,[146,67] census 1850 in Columbiana Co, OH, never married[69.]

According to Hanna's "Ohio Valley Genealogies," p. 44, this John Gaston died unmarried. Researchers Peter J. Topoly and Jane Carson Topoly have reported that he married Sarah Jane Moore on Oct 1 1862 in Smith Ferry, Beaver Co, PA, but they also report a death date for him of Jul 22 1862 in Dubuque, Iowa, with burial in Linwild Cemetery in Dubuque. Pending further clarification, we leave it as reported by Hanna.

155. **Hugh Gaston** (77.Hugh[5], 23.Joseph[4], 6.Hugh[3], 3.John[2], 1.Jean[1]), b. Apr- 9-1804 in Columbiana Co, OH,[ccxc[290],15] [Birthplace given in 1850 Census as Pennsylvania. "History of the Upper Ohio Valley" [p. 146] reports birth date as 1805.], d. Mar-23-1857,[290,15] [A death date of Mar 27 1854 has been reported by other researchers.], resided in Knox Twp, Jefferson Co, OH,[290] occupation teacher & farmer.[290]

1850 Census, Columbiana Co, OH (Middleton Twp), enumerated in Aug 1850:
Hugh Gaston, 46, b. Pa, farmer; Jane, 43, b. Pa; Hamilton, 25, b. Ohio; Mary, 16, b. Ohio; James, 18 (?), b. Ohio.

"He was a prominent man in public and church affairs, and held several official positions in which he was a faithful servant of the public." Had total of five children.[290]

He married ca 1824,[290] **Jane Mason**, b. ca 1807 in Pennsylvania,[146] d. Jan- -1888,[290] resided in Knox Twp, Jefferson Co, OH.[290]

   Children:
 316. i. HAMILTON D. GASTON[69] b. Dec-26-1825.
   ii. MARTHA GASTON.
   iii. ELIZABETH GASTON.
   iv. MARY GASTON.

156. **Jane Gaston** (78.James[5], 23.Joseph[4], 6.Hugh[3], 3.John[2], 1.Jean[1]), b. Oct- 2-1792 in Washington Co, PA,[67,ccxci[291]] d. 1879 in Moon Twp, Allegheny Co, PA.[67,291] She married[69] Nov-30-1813,[161] **Nathaniel P. Gordon**, b. Jul- 1-1793 in Moon Twp, Allegheny Co, PA,[161,291] (son of William Gordon and Prudence Hays), d. 1850 in Moon Twp, Allegheny Co, PA,[161,291] occupation Capt in Pennsylvania Navy.

Nathaniel: Nathaniel P. Gordon was elected and installed as an elder of the Sharon Presbyterian Church at Moon Township, Allegheny County, PA, at its inception in 1817.[161]

   Children:
   i. (MALE) GORDON b. ca 1815 in Moon Twp, Allegheny Co, PA.
   ii. (FEMALE) GORDON b. ca 1818 in Moon Twp, Allegheny Co, PA.
   iii. ELIZABETH J. GORDON b. Jan- -1819 in Moon Twp, Allegheny Co, PA, never married.
   iv. (FEMALE) GORDON b. ca 1823 in Moon Twp, Allegheny Co, PA.
   v. (FEMALE) GORDON b. ca 1824 in Moon Twp, Allegheny Co, PA.
   vi. LUCINDA GORDON b. ca 1826 in Moon Twp, Allegheny Co, PA.
 317. vii. GILBERT GASTON GORDON b. Jan-10-1832.
   viii. EMALINE GORDON b. ca 1834 in Moon Twp, Allegheny Co, PA.
   ix. MARIA L. GORDON b. ca 1837 in Moon Twp, Allegheny Co, PA.

157. **James W. Gaston** (78.James[5], 23.Joseph[4], 6.Hugh[3], 3.John[2], 1.Jean[1]), b. Aug-29-1808 in Washington Co, PA,[67] d. Mar-29-1884.[67] He married[69] (1) May-_-1846,[67] **Mary Gaston**, b. ca 1825,[67] (daughter of James William Gaston and Elizabeth Kilgore).

Mary: James W. Gaston and Mary Gaston were double cousins, in that they were both first cousins once removed (he was the grandson and she was the great- granddaughter of Joseph Gaston (b. in Ireland, d. 1775)) and also third cousins once removed (he was the great-great-grandson and she was the great- great-great-granddaughter of John Gaston (b. 1645 in Scotland)). Mary's grandparents, Hugh & Grace Gaston, were also cousins.

He married[67] (2) **Rebecca Conkle**, b. ca 1809 in Clarkson, Columbiana Co, OH,[67] d. Nov-11-1875 in East Liverpool, Columbiana Co, OH.[67]

   Children by Rebecca Conkle:
   i. MARY GASTON[67.]
   ii. WILLIAM GASTON b. Apr-19-1835 near Clarkson, Columbiana Co, OH,[67,ccxcii[292]] resided from 1866 in Bellaire, Belmont Co, OH,[292] resided as youth in East Liverpool, Columbiana Co, OH,[292] occupation minister, education Washington College (1858) and Western Theological Seminary in Allegheny Co PA (1861).[292] He married[67] (1) 1865,[292] Julia M. Cunningham (daughter of Samuel Cunningham). He married[67] (2) Jennie L. Wise (daughter of Leroy Wise).

158. **(Female) Gaston** (78.James[5], 23.Joseph[4], 6.Hugh[3], 3.John[2], 1.Jean[1]). She married __ **Moore**.
   Children:
   i. WILLIAM MOORE.

159. **Ephraim Gaston** (79.Alexander[5], 23.Joseph[4], 6.Hugh[3], 3.John[2], 1.Jean[1]), b. Jun-26-1799 in Virginia,[69,ccxciii[293],146] d. May- -1868, buried in Morristown Union Cemetery, Belmont Co, OH,[67] census 1850, 1860 in Morristown, Belmont Co, OH, occupation physician,[ccxciv[294],69,146.]

From "History of the Upper Ohio Valley," p. 635: Dr. Ephraim Gaston "was one of the most distinguished physicians of his time." Also served one term in the legislature, but then returned to medicine until "compelled to abandon it on account of cataract of the eyes, dying about two years afterward."

He married (1) Nov- 7-1826 in Belmont Co, OH,[67] **Mary Wilson**, b. 1805,[67] d. 1847,[67] buried in Morristown Union Cemetery, Belmont Co, OH.[67] He married (2) May-31-1849 in Belmont Co, OH,[ccxcv[295]] **Agnes Vance**, b. ca 1805 in Maryland,[280] [Age was given as 40 in 1850 Census, but as 55 in 1860 Census. Birthplace "Md" (Maryland) in both cases.], d. 1875,[67] buried in Morristown Union Cemetery, Belmont Co, OH,[67] census 1850, 1860 in Morristown, Belmont Co, OH.
   Children by Mary Wilson:
    i. WILLIAM GASTON b. ca 1829 in Ohio,[146] census 1850 in Morristown, Belmont Co, OH, occupation lawyer.[146]
   318. ii. SAMUEL W. GASTON b. 1831.

160. **Charity Gaston** (79.Alexander[5], 23.Joseph[4], 6.Hugh[3], 3.John[2], 1.Jean[1]), b. Jul-27-1803 near St. Clairsville, Belmont Co, OH,[69,165,164] d. Sep-28-1888 in Morristown, Belmont Co, OH,[164] census 1850, 60, 70, 80 in Morristown, Belmont Co, OH. She married[69] Sep-11-1823,[67,165] **John Lippincott**, b. Sep-3-1801 in Westmoreland Co, PA,[67,165] d. Sep- 3-1886 in Morristown, Belmont Co, OH,[164] census 1850, 60, 70, 80 in Morristown, Belmont Co, OH, resided from 1815 in Belmont Co, OH,[165] occupation 1870 debt collector,[209] occupation 1860 hotel keeper,[280] occupation 1850 tavern keeper.[146]

John: In 1815, John Lippincott's parents migrated from Westmoreland Co, PA to Belmont Co, OH. "They came down the Ohio River on a flatboat and landed on Wheeling Island, where they camped out two days and nights before a team could be procured to carry them to Morristown. On the 21st of April, that year, they reached their destination and settled on the lot where William Handy now lives, where his father engaged in the hotel business and continued until 1827, when our subject succeeded him. ... The subject of this sketch has seen the following distinguished gentlemen: James Monroe in 1819; General Jackson in 1824; met Henry Clay frequently; Daniel Webster and son breakfasted at his house in 1830; saw Almonte and Santa Anna, the Mexican statesman and generals in 1853, as they were carried prisoners from their homes to Washington City. He and his wife have been members of the Presbyterian Church for over 50 years. He has served as an elder for 20 years. He has entertained in his hotel persons who traveled on horseback all the way from New Orleans. In early days there were no banks west, and merchants would travel in companies of 18 to 20 persons together, carrying leather bags containing about $2,000 in Spanish eagles. This aged and respected couple are living near the spot where they spent their childhood days."[165]

   Children:
    i. WILSON LIPPINCOTT b. ca 1825,[67] d. 1831,[67] buried in First Cemetery, Union Twp, Morristown, OH.[67]
   319. ii. JOHN WOODROW LIPPINCOTT b. Feb-15-1835.
    iii. MARGARETT LIPPINCOTT b. ca 1836 in Ohio,[146] census 1850 in Morristown, Belmont Co, OH.
   320. iv. MARTHA LIPPINCOTT b. ca 1840.
    v. ALBERT LIPPINCOTT b. 1850 in Ohio,[146] census 1850, 1860 in Morristown, Belmont Co, OH.

161. **Matthew Gaston** (79.Alexander[5], 23.Joseph[4], 6.Hugh[3], 3.John[2], 1.Jean[1]), b. Jul- 9-1809 in Belmont Co, OH,[69,161] d. Mar-17-1878 in Plattsmouth, Cass Co, NE,[69,161] resided (settled) in Plattsmouth, Cass Co, NE,[69] census 1850, 1860, 1870 in Cambridge, Guernsey Co, OH, occupation lawyer.[146] He married[69] **Drusilla Bute**, b. ca 1817 in Pennsylvania,[146] census 1850 in Cambridge, Guernsey Co, OH.

1850 Census, Guernsey Co, OH (Cambridge), enumerated on Sep 28 1850:
Matthew Gaston, 41, lawyer; Druzella, 33; Mary (I or J), 12; Eleanor, 10; Burtha A, 8; Henrietta, 6.

1860 Census, Guernsey Co, OH (Cambridge), enumerated on Jul 12 1860:
Matthew Gaston, 51, lawyer; Louisa, 35; Mary J, 20; Elma, 18; Amelia, 16; Henrietta, 14; Ann, 4; Adora, 1.

The 1870 Census found Matthew Gaston living in a hotel in Cambridge, with no other family members.

In 1877, the Nebraska State Census shows Matthew Gaston residing in the home of his daughter Henrietta and her husband Eli Plummer and their children.

> Children:
> i. MARY J. GASTON b. ca 1838 in Ohio,[146] census 1850, 1860 in Cambridge, Guernsey Co, OH [Middle initial either I or J.].
> ii. ELEANOR "ELMA" GASTON, census name Elma Gaston, b. ca 1840 in Ohio,[146] census 1850, 1860 in Cambridge, Guernsey Co, OH.
> iii. BERTHA AMELIA GASTON, census name Amelia Gaston, b. ca 1842 in Ohio,[146] census 1850, 1860 in Cambridge, Guernsey Co, OH.
> 321. iv. HENRIETTA GASTON b. ca 1844.

162. **William Gaston** (80.Samuel[5], 24.Hugh[4], 6.Hugh[3], 3.John[2], 1.Jean[1]), b. 1833,[169] d. 1864.[169] He married 1856,[169] **Elizabeth Donnelly**, b. 1831,[169] d. 1904.[169]
> Children:
> i. CORDELIA GASTON b. in Jersey Co, IL.[169] She married[169] John Christy.

163. **Sarah "Sally" Kirkpatrick** (81.John[5], 25.Elizabeth[4], 6.Hugh[3], 3.John[2], 1.Jean[1]), b. ca 1802 in New Jersey,[146] census 1850 in Plainfield District, Exxex Co, NJ, resided (settled) in Plainfield, Union Co, NJ.[19,15,80] She married[19,15] **John Layton**, b. ca 1798 in New Jersey,[146] census 1850 in Plainfield District, Exxex Co, NJ, occupation 1850 packing boxes.[146]
> Children:
> i. JOSIAH LAYTON.
> ii. JOHN LAYTON. He married[80] Deborah Melissa Bedell.
> iii. JAMES FINLEY LAYTON b. ca 1832 in New Jersey,[146] census 1850 in Plainfield District, Exxex Co, NJ, occupation 1850 cabinet maker.[146]
> iv. THOMAS LAYTON b. ca 1834 in New Jersey,[146] census 1850 in Plainfield District, Exxex Co, NJ, occupation 1850 box maker.[146]
> v. MARY ANNE LAYTON b. ca 1841 in New Jersey,[146] census 1850 in Plainfield District, Exxex Co, NJ.

164. **Thomas Kirkpatrick** (81.John[5], 25.Elizabeth[4], 6.Hugh[3], 3.John[2], 1.Jean[1]), b. ca 1806 in New Jersey,[146] census 1850 in Newark, Essex Co, NJ, occupation carpenter.[146] He married[19,15] **Maria Hurd**, also known as Mariah Hurd,[80] b. ca 1809 in New Jersey,[146] census 1850 in Newark, Essex Co, NJ.
> Children:
> i. ANNE ELIZA KIRKPATRICK d. age 3.[80]
> ii. JACOB HURD KIRKPATRICK b. ca 1831 in New Jersey,[146] census 1850 in Newark, Essex Co, NJ.
> iii. MANNING RUTAN KIRKPATRICK b. ca 1834 in New Jersey,[146] census 1850 in Newark, Essex Co, NJ.
> iv. ANDREW EUGENE KIRKPATRICK, also known as Eugene Kirkpatrick,[80] b. ca 1835 in New Jersey,[146] census 1850 in Newark, Essex Co, NJ.
> v. AMANDA BAUSABIN KIRKPATRICK, census name Amanda E. Kirkpatrick, b. ca 1840 in New Jersey,[146] census 1850 in Newark, Essex Co, NJ.

165. **Elizabeth Kirkpatrick** (81.John[5], 25.Elizabeth[4], 6.Hugh[3], 3.John[2], 1.Jean[1]), b. ca 1808 in New Jersey, census 1850 in Bernards Twp, Somerset Co, NJ. She married[19,15] **John King**, b. ca 1800 in New Jersey,[146] (son of John King), resided in Bernards Twp, Somerset Co, NJ,[19,15] [Liberty Corners], census 1850 in Bernards Twp, Somerset Co, NJ, occupation farmer.[146]

Children:
   i.   JAMES KING b. ca 1827 in New Jersey,[146] census 1850 in Bernards Twp, Somerset Co, NJ.
   ii.   ELIAS KING b. [Not in 1850 Census.].
   iii. MARY ANNE KING, census name Mary Ann King, b. ca 1830 in New Jersey,[146] census 1850 in Bernards Twp, Somerset Co, NJ.
   iv.   DAVID KING b. ca 1834 in New Jersey,[146] census 1850 in Bernards Twp, Somerset Co, NJ.
   v.   JANE ELIZABETH KING b. ca 1838 in New Jersey,[146] census 1850 in Bernards Twp, Somerset Co, NJ.

166. **Elias Kirkpatrick** (81.John[5], 25.Elizabeth[4], 6.Hugh[3], 3.John[2], 1.Jean[1]), b. ca 1808,[146] resided (settled) in Plainfield, Union Co, NJ,[19,15,80] census 1850 in Plainfield District, Exxex Co, NJ, occupation justice of the peace,[80] occupation 1850 stationer,[146] [In Colonial times, a stationer was a bookseller, or someone who sold paper, quills, ink stands, pencils, and other writing items. Source: http://homepages.rootsweb.ancestry.com/~sam/occupation.html]. He married[19,ccxcvi[296]] **Jane Squier**, b. ca 1809,[146] (daughter of Ludlow Squier and Anna Runyon), census 1850 in Plainfield District, Exxex Co, NJ.

Children:
   i.   ANNE AMELIA KIRKPATRICK, census name Annet Kirkpatrick, b. ca 1833,[146] census 1850 in Plainfield District, Exxex Co, NJ.
   ii.   WILLIAM KIRKPATRICK b. ca 1835,[146] census 1850 in Plainfield District, Exxex Co, NJ.
   iii. EMILY KIRKPATRICK b. ca 1838,[146] census 1850 in Plainfield District, Exxex Co, NJ.
   iv.   ABBY KIRKPATRICK b. [Not in 1850 Census.].
   v.   WALTER KIRKPATRICK b. ca 1846,[146] census 1850 in Plainfield District, Exxex Co, NJ.

167. **James Kirkpatrick** (81.John[5], 25.Elizabeth[4], 6.Hugh[3], 3.John[2], 1.Jean[1]), b. ca 1810 in New Jersey,[146] census 1850 in New York City, NY. He married[19,15,80] (1) **Aletta Van Arsdale** (daughter of Philip Van Arsdale). He married[19,15,80] (2) **Mary Stout**, b. ca 1823 in New Jersey,[146] census 1850 in New York City, NY.

Children by Aletta Van Arsdale:
   i.   ANNA KIRKPATRICK.
   ii.   FREDERICK KIRKPATRICK.
Children by Mary Stout:
   iii. JAMES HARRIS KIRKPATRICK b. ca 1844 in New York,[146] census 1850 in New York City, NY.
   iv.   JOSIAH LAYTON KIRKPATRICK b. ca 1848 in New York,[146] census 1850 in New York City, NY.
   v.   HUGH KIRKPATRICK b. 1850 in New York,[146] census 1850 in New York City, NY.

168. **Lydia Kirkpatrick** (81.John[5], 25.Elizabeth[4], 6.Hugh[3], 3.John[2], 1.Jean[1]), resided (settled) in Chicago, IL.[19,15] She married[19,15,80] **Stephen Woodard** (son of Samuel Woodard).
Children:
   i.   PHEBE ANNE WOODARD.
   ii.   WILLIAM WOODARD.
   iii. JOHN WOODARD.
   iv.   BENJAMIN FRANKLIN WOODARD.

169. **Jane Kirkpatrick** (81.John[5], 25.Elizabeth[4], 6.Hugh[3], 3.John[2], 1.Jean[1]), b. ca 1814 in New Jersey,[146] census 1850 in Tewksbury Twp, Hunterdon Co, NJ. She married[19,15,170] **David Kline**, b. ca 1813 in New Jersey,[146] census 1850 in Tewksbury Twp, Hunterdon Co, NJ.
    Children:
        i.   ANNE ELIZA KLINE, census name Anna E. Kline, b. ca 1835 in New Jersey,[146] census 1850 in Tewksbury Twp, Hunterdon Co, NJ.
        ii.   PHOEBE KLINE b. ca 1837 in New Jersey,[146] census 1850 in Tewksbury Twp, Hunterdon Co, NJ.
        iii.   PETER R. FISHER KLINE, census name Peter R. F. Kline, b. ca 1838 in New Jersey,[146] census 1850 in Tewksbury Twp, Hunterdon Co, NJ.
        iv.   JOHN CASSEDY KLINE b. ca 1840 in New Jersey,[146] census 1850 in Tewksbury Twp, Hunterdon Co, NJ.
        v.   JACOB KLINE b. ca 1842 in New Jersey,[146] census 1850 in Tewksbury Twp, Hunterdon Co, NJ.
        vi.   FRANKLIN MILLER KLINE, census name Frances M. Kline [Listed as a daughter.], b. ca 1844 in New Jersey,[146] census 1850 in Tewksbury Twp, Hunterdon Co, NJ.
        vii.   ELLEN TAYLOR KLINE b. ca 1845 in New Jersey,[146] census 1850 in Tewksbury Twp, Hunterdon Co, NJ.
        viii.   MARY MALVINA POHLMAN KLINE, census name Mary M. P. Kline, b. ca 1847 in New Jersey,[146] census 1850 in Tewksbury Twp, Hunterdon Co, NJ.
        ix.   WILLIAM H. KLINE b. ca 1849 in New Jersey,[146] census 1850 in Tewksbury Twp, Hunterdon Co, NJ.

170. **Mary Kirkpatrick** (81.John[5], 25.Elizabeth[4], 6.Hugh[3], 3.John[2], 1.Jean[1]), b. 1816 in New Jersey,[ccxcvii[297],146] census 1850, 1860, 1870 in Bernards Twp, Somerset Co, NJ. She married[19,15,297] **Tunis Van Nest**, census name Tunis Vanness, also known as Tunis Vannest,[170] b. 1809 in New Jersey,[297,146] (son of John Van Nest), census 1850, 1860, 1870 in Bernards Twp, Somerset Co, NJ, occupation farmer,[146,280,209.]
    Children:
        i.   JOHN VAN NEST d. young.[170]
        ii.   ANNA MARIA VAN NEST b. ca 1839 in New Jersey,[146] census 1850 in Bernards Twp, Somerset Co, NJ.
        iii.   WILLIAM C. A. VAN NEST b. ca 1841 in New Jersey,[146] census 1850, 1860, 1870 in New Jersey.
        iv.   JOHN VAN NEST II b. ca 1845 in New Jersey,[146] census 1850, 1860 in Bernards Twp, Somerset Co, NJ.
        v.   SARAH ELIZABETH VAN NEST b. ca 1847 in New Jersey,[146] census 1850, 1860, 1870 in Bernards Twp, Somerset Co, NJ.
        vi.   MARY JANE VAN NEST b. ca 1849,[146] census 1850, 1860, 1870 in Bernards Twp, Somerset Co, NJ.
        vii.   PHEBE ELLEN VAN NEST, also known as Phebe A. VanNest,[209] b. ca 1853 in New Jersey,[280] census 1860, 1870 in Bernards Twp, Somerset Co, NJ.

171. **Ann Kirkpatrick**, also known as Anne Kirkpatrick,[170] (81.John[5], 25.Elizabeth[4], 6.Hugh[3], 3.John[2], 1.Jean[1]), b. ca 1820 in New Jersey,[146] census 1850 in Bedminster Twp, Somerset Co, NJ. She married[19,15] **Philip Van Arsdale**, b. ca 1816 in New Jersey,[146] (son of Peter Van Arsdale), census 1850 in Bedminster Twp, Somerset Co, NJ.
    Children:
        i.   PETER VAN ARSDALE.
        ii.   JOHN VAN ARSDALE b. ca 1845 in New Jersey,[146] census 1850 in Bedminster Twp, Somerset Co, NJ.
        iii.   ELIZABETH VAN ARSDALE b. ca 1847 in New Jersey,[146] census 1850 in Bedminster Twp, Somerset Co, NJ.

172. **Hugh Kirkpatrick** (81.John[5], 25.Elizabeth[4], 6.Hugh[3], 3.John[2], 1.Jean[1]), b. ca 1822 in New Jersey,[146] census 1850 in Newark, Essex Co, NJ, occupation carpenter.[146] He married[19,170] **Elizabeth King**, b. ca 1825 in New Jersey,[146] census 1850 in Newark, Essex Co, NJ, resided originally in Belleville, Essex Co, NJ.[19,15,170]

> Children:
> i.   JOHN FRANKLIN KIRKPATRICK b. 1849 in New Jersey,[146] census 1850 in Newark, Essex Co, NJ.

173. **Elizabeth "Betsy" Gomer** (82.Mary[5], 27.Margaret[4], 8.Joseph[3], 3.John[2], 1.Jean[1]), b. ca 1775 in New Jersey,[64] census 1850 in White Co, IL [In household with son Alfred Pearce.]. She married Apr- 7- 1794 in Orange Co, NC,[64] **James Pearce**, b. Dec- -1773 in Orange Co, NC,[64] d. Oct-31-1836 in White Co, IL,[64] buried Old Village Cemetery in White Co, IL,[64] resided until 1817 in Orange Co, NC,[64] resided (settled 1817) in White Co, IL,[64] resided 1795 - 1817 in Montgomery Co, TN.[64] Moved from North Carolina to Montgomery County, Tennessee in 1795, and then to White County, Illinois in 1817.[64]

> Children:
> 322. i.   HOSEA PEARCE b. Apr-16-1798.

174. **James Thompson Johnston** (83.Sarah[5], 27.Margaret[4], 8.Joseph[3], 3.John[2], 1.Jean[1]), b.[172] He married[172] **Mary Whetstone Haines**.

> Children:
> 323. i.   DEWITT CLINTON JOHNSTON.
> ii.   WILLIAM WIRT JOHNSTON b.[172]
> iii. JOHN HERRING JOHNSTON b.[172]

175. **John W. Gaston** (84.William[5], 28.John[4], 8.Joseph[3], 3.John[2], 1.Jean[1]), b. Sep-26-1783 in Somerset Co, NJ,[22,27] d. Jun-19-1859.[22] He married 1805,[ccxcviii[298]] **Sarah Castner**, b. Oct-20-1782,[27] (daughter of David Castner and Mary Thompson), d. Apr- 8-1859.[27]

> Children:
> 324. i.   WILLIAM KER GASTON b. Jul-23-1806.
> 325. ii.   DANIEL CASTNER GASTON b. Oct-14-1807.
> 326. iii. SAMUEL BRANT GASTON b. Dec-14-1809.
> 327. iv.   MARGARET GASTON b. Nov-29-1811.
> v.   ROBERT GASTON b. Dec-15-1813,[27] d. Feb-17-1890.[27] He married Feb- 4- 1839,[ccxcix[299]] Martha Jane Lane, b. Nov-28-1813,[299] (daughter of Job Lane and Susanna Nevires), d. Aug-10-1878,[299] resided in Pluckemin, Somerset Co, NJ.
> vi.   JOSEPH GASTON b. Apr-12-1816,[27] d. Dec- 3-1888,[27] never married.
> 328. vii. JOHN GASTON b. Aug-31-1818.
> 329. viii. OLIVER BERTON (TWIN) GASTON b. Jan-14-1821.
> 330. ix.   NAOMI (TWIN) GASTON b. Jan-14-1821.
> 331. x.   HUGH GASTON b. Apr-23-1823.
> 332. xi.   ISAAC GASTON b. Jul-23-1825.

176. **James (twin) Gaston** (84.William[5], 28.John[4], 8.Joseph[3], 3.John[2], 1.Jean[1]), b. Jan- 8-1795 in New Jersey,[22] d. 1860 ["Ohio Valley Genealogies," p. 46, reports death date as March 1820. But 1860 has been reported elsewhere, and he does appear in the 1850 and 1860 censuses. He is not found in the 1870 or later census. The March 1820 date cited by Hanna is presumed to be a marriage date.], census 1860 in New Hope, Madison Co, AL, census 1850 in Huntsville, Madison Co, AL, occupation 1850 town constable.[146] He married Mar- -1820, **Mary __**, b. ca 1802 in Georgia,[146] census 1860 in New Hope, Madison Co, AL, census 1850 in Huntsville, Madison Co, AL.

> Children:
> i.   OLIVER B. GASTON b. ca 1829 in Alabama, census 1850 in Huntsville, Madison Co, AL.[146]

ii. JAMES GASTON b. ca 1832 in Alabama,[280] census 1870 in Madison Co, AL, census 1860 in New Hope, Madison Co, AL, census 1850 in Huntsville, Madison Co, AL.

177. **John I. Gaston** (85.Joseph[5], 28.John[4], 8.Joseph[3], 3.John[2], 1.Jean[1]), b. Feb-14-1787 in New Jersey,[22] d. Mar-23-1846.[22] He married (1) **Catherine Annin**, b. Jan-22-1787,[12] [Name has also appeared as Katherine Annan.], d. Aug-30-1834.[12] He married (2) May-14-1835, **Elizabeth Van Veghten**, d. 1867.

Elizabeth: Elizabeth Van Veghten had been married and was a widow when she and John I. Gaston were married, so Van Veghten was probably not her maiden name.

Children by Catherine Annin:
333. i. JOSEPH ANNIN GASTON b. Jul-14-1807.
ii. IDA MARIE GASTON b. Mar-19-1810, d. Sep- 7-1887.
334. iii. SARAH ELIZABETH GASTON b. Jul- 5-1814.
335. iv. JOANNA GASTON b. May-30-1815.
v. WILLIAM GASTON b. Oct- 4-1817, d. Jan-18-1847.
vi. EVELINA BELMONT LINN GASTON b. Dec-15-1820, d. Jun-23-1838. She married Sep-25-1834, John Reynolds.
336. vii. SAMUEL SWAN GASTON b. Aug- 2-1823.
337. viii. ALETTA SWAN GASTON b. Jul- 3-1825.
338. ix. ISAAC GASTON b. Sep-14-1828.
x. CATHERINE GASTON b. Feb- 1-1831, d. Apr-20-1865.

After Catherine's death, her husband, George Wright Zahniser, married her niece, Elizabeth Sergeant (b. 1835).

She married Jun- 2-1864, George Wright Zahniser, b. Mar-19-1823, d. Jun-12-1889, occupation minister.

178. **William B. Gaston** (85.Joseph[5], 28.John[4], 8.Joseph[3], 3.John[2], 1.Jean[1]), b. Aug- 9-1791 in New Jersey,[22] d. Mar- 9-1859. He married (1) **Elizabeth Kirkpatrick**, b. Sep-21-1789 (daughter of Alexander Kirkpatrick and Sarah "Sally" Carle), d. Jan-28-1837. He married (2) **Martha Demun**, b. Jul-19-1805, d. Oct-19-1863.
Children by Elizabeth Kirkpatrick:
339. i. ALEXANDER KIRKPATRICK GASTON b. Jan-25-1814.
340. ii. JOSEPH GASTON b. Nov- 6-1816.
341. iii. HUGH M. GASTON b. Nov-29-1818.
iv. FREDERICK GASTON b. Jan- 5-1821, d. Feb- 2-1847.
342. v. JOHN GASTON b. Nov-12-1825.
343. vi. WILLIAM GASTON b. Sep-14-1828.

179. **Ogden Gaston** (86.Stephen[5], 28.John[4], 8.Joseph[3], 3.John[2], 1.Jean[1]), b. Mar- 5-1821 in New York, d. bef Jun 1900,[123] census 1870, 1880 in Detroit, MI, census 1860 in Springfield, Oakland Co, MI, census 1850 in Troy, Rensselaer Co, NY, occupation 1870, 1880 laborer.[210] He married **Elizabeth Ann Simpson**, b. Dec- -1825 in New York,[123] (daughter of John Simpson), census 1870, 1880, 1900 in Detroit, MI, census 1860 in Springfield, Oakland Co, MI, census 1850 in Troy, Rensselaer Co, NY.
Children:
344. i. CHARLES HENRY GASTON b. May-15-1850.
ii. MARIETTA GASTON, census name Maryetta Gaston, census name Margaretta Gaston, b. Sep-24-1854 in Michigan,[280] census 1870 in Detroit, MI, census 1860 in Springfield, Oakland Co, MI.
iii. FREMONT GASTON b. Oct-31-1857 in Michigan,[280] d. 1876, census 1870 in Detroit, MI, census 1860 in Springfield, Oakland Co, MI.
345. iv. THEODORE WILLIAM GASTON b. Mar- 7-1860.

v.   ORRA MARIA GASTON, census name Maria Gaston, b. Nov-16-1862 in Michigan, census 1870, 1880 in Detroit, MI.

346.   vi.   GEORGE TIFFANY GASTON b. Mar-28-1867.

180. **Elias Hedges Gaston** (87.Isaac[5], 28.John[4], 8.Joseph[3], 3.John[2], 1.Jean[1]), b. ca 1819 in New Jersey,[280] d. 1875 in Hamilton, Butler Co, OH,[64] resided (settled) in Reily (Oxford), Butler Co, OH,[22] census 1860 in St. Clair Twp, Butler Co, OH, occupation 1860 county treasurer.[280] He married[64] **Martha G. Decker**, b. Mar- 4-1831 in Union Co, OH,[64] d. Jan- 1-1915 in Canton, Stark Co, OH,[64] census 1880 in Reily (Oxford), Butler Co, OH, census 1860 in St. Clair Twp, Butler Co, OH.

Children:

i.   MARTHA GASTON b. ca 1854 in Ohio,[280] census 1860 in St. Clair Twp, Butler Co, OH.

ii.   ELIZABETH GASTON b. ca 1855 in Ohio,[280] census 1860 in St. Clair Twp, Butler Co, OH.

iii.   ELIZA GASTON b. ca 1858 in Ohio,[280] census 1860 in St. Clair Twp, Butler Co, OH.

iv.   STEPHEN GASTON b. 1860 in Ohio,[280] census 1860 in St. Clair Twp, Butler Co, OH.

v.   AUGUSTA GASTON b. ca 1863 in Ohio,[210] census 1880 in Reily (Oxford), Butler Co, OH.

vi.   HAMER E. GASTON, census name E. Hamer Gaston, b. Nov- -1865 in Ohio,[123] census 1900 in Mt. Pleasant Twp, Delaware Co, IN [Listed as a servant and day laborer, 34, single, in the household of Silas A. Klepfer and family.], census 1880 in Reily (Oxford), Butler Co, OH.

vii.   H. JULIA GASTON b. ca 1868 in Ohio,[210] census 1880 in Reily (Oxford), Butler Co, OH.

viii.   ANNIE GASTON b. ca 1870 in Ohio.

181. **William Mansfield Scudder**, also known as Mansfield Scudder,[22] (88.Margaret[5], 28.John[4], 8.Joseph[3], 3.John[2], 1.Jean[1]), b. ca 1811 in New Jersey,[64] d. Jul-22-1850 in Newark, Essex Co, NJ.[64] He married Feb- 1-1840 in Essex Co, NJ,[64] **Charlotte Meeker**, b. ca 1819,[64] d. Apr-23-1870 in Chicago, IL.[64]

Children:

347.   i.   WILLIAM MANSFIELD SCUDDER b. Feb- 2-1843.

ii.   MARY SCUDDER b. ca 1845,[64] d. Jan-11-1915 in Chicago, IL.[64]

182. **Robert Gaston** (90.Joseph[5], 29.Robert[4], 8.Joseph[3], 3.John[2], 1.Jean[1]), b. Mar-30-1790,[28,46] d. Sep-22-1854,[28,46] buried in Warrior Run Church Cem, Delaware Twp, Northumberland Co, PA,[175] military War of 1812.[176] He married Apr-8-1824,[28] **Eleanor Shannon**, b. 1795,[28,46] d. Oct-12-1867,[28,46] buried in Warrior Run Church Cem, Delaware Twp, Northumberland Co, PA.[175]

Children:

i.   MARTHA J. GASTON b. Jun- -1826,[123] [Birth date on headstone reported as 1827, but 1900 Census shows it as June 1826.], d. 1901,[46] buried in Warrior Run Church Cem, Delaware Twp, Northumberland Co, PA,[17] census in Lewis Twp, Northumberland Co, PA, never married[123.]

ii.   MARGARET M. GASTON b. 1828,[46] d. 1857,[46] buried in Warrior Run Church Cem, Delaware Twp, Northumberland Co, PA.[175]

iii.   SOLOMON P. GASTON b. Dec-16-1829 in Pennsylvania,[123,46] d. 1911,[46] buried in Warrior Run Church Cem, Delaware Twp, Northumberland Co, PA,[17] [Name on headstone: S. P. Gaston.], census 1900 in Lewis Twp, Northumberland Co, PA,[123] occupation farmer.[123] He married Nov- 5-1861,[123] Lydia Matchin, b. Jun- -1828 in Pennsylvania,[123] census 1900 in Lewis Twp, Northumberland Co, PA.

1900 Census, Northumberland Co, Pennsylvania (Lewis Twp), enumerated on Jun 18 1900:

Solomon P. Gaston, 70, b. Dec 1829, farmer, married 39 yrs; wife Lydia Gaston, 71, b. Jun 1828, mother of 6 children (3 still living); son Robert Gaston, 36, b. Oct 1863, farmer, single; sister Martha J. Gaston, 74, b. Jun 1826, single; sister Charlotte Gaston, 65, b. Apr 1835, single. All born in Pennsylvania.

iv.   MARY E. GASTON b. ca 1834.

v. CHARLOTTE A. GASTON b. Apr--1835 in Pennsylvania,[123] census 1900 in Lewis Twp, Northumberland Co, PA, never married[123.]
vi. SARAH ANN GASTON b. ca 1841.
vii. SARAH GASTON.

183. **Aaron Gaston** (90.Joseph[5], 29.Robert[4], 8.Joseph[3], 3.John[2], 1.Jean[1]), b. Apr-25-1799,[28,46] d. Oct-24-1868,[28,46] buried in Warrior Run Church Cem, Delaware Twp, Northumberland Co, PA.[175] He married[28] (1) **Sarah Ann Clarke**, b. 1814,[46] d. 1841,[46] buried in Warrior Run Church Cem, Delaware Twp, Northumberland Co, PA.[175] He married[28] (2) **Rosanna Camp**.
Children by Sarah Ann Clarke:
i. CLARK GASTON b. 1841,[46] d. 1842.[46]
Children by Rosanna Camp:
ii. JOHN W. GASTON.
iii. ANNA ROSA GASTON.

184. **Rosanna Melick** (91.Margaret[5], 29.Robert[4], 8.Joseph[3], 3.John[2], 1.Jean[1]), b. ca 1793 in New Jersey,[146] buried in Peapack, Somerset Co, NJ,[ccc[300]] census 1850 in Bedminster Twp, Somerset Co, NJ. She married **William J. Todd**, b. ca 1793 in New Jersey,[146] buried in Peapack, Somerset Co, NJ,[300] census 1850 in Bedminster Twp, Somerset Co, NJ, occupation farmer.[146]
Children:
i. DAVID M. TODD b. ca 1827 in New Jersey, census 1850 in Bedminster Twp, Somerset Co, NJ.
ii. WILLIAM H. TODD b. ca 1830 in New Jersey,[146] census 1850 in Bedminster Twp, Somerset Co, NJ.

185. **John Melick** (91.Margaret[5], 29.Robert[4], 8.Joseph[3], 3.John[2], 1.Jean[1]), b. ca 1794 in New Jersey,[146] census 1850 in Bedminster Twp, Somerset Co, NJ. He married **Ann Nevius**, b. ca 1800 in New Jersey,[146] census 1850 in Bedminster Twp, Somerset Co, NJ.

1850 Census, Somerset Co, New Jersey (Bedminster Twp), enumerated on Aug 21 1850:
John Melick, 56, farmer; Ann Melick, 50; Elizabeth Melick, 24; Elizabeth Ann VanDoren, 8. All born in New Jersey.

The adjacent household included three of John Melick's siblings:
David Melick, 52, farmer; Charlotta Melick, 60; Daniel Melick, 48, no occupation; William Sutphen, 18, laborer; Nicholas Melick, 22, laborer. All born in New Jersey.

Children:
i. ELIZABETH MELICK b. ca 1826 in New Jersey.[146]

186. **William Melick** (91.Margaret[5], 29.Robert[4], 8.Joseph[3], 3.John[2], 1.Jean[1]), b. ca 1800 in New Jersey,[146] census 1850 in Cotton Twp, Switzerland Co, Ind., occupation farmer.[146] He married **Maria Suydam**, b. ca 1801 in New Jersey,[146] census 1850 in Cotton Twp, Switzerland Co, Ind.
Children:
348. i. DANIEL MELICK b. ca 1827.
ii. NICHOLAS A. MELICK b. ca 1828 in New Jersey,[146] census 1850 in Cotton Twp, Switzerland Co, Ind.
iii. JOSEPH G. MELICK b. ca 1832 in New Jersey,[146] census 1850 in Cotton Twp, Switzerland Co, Ind.
iv. EMELINE F. MELICK b. ca 1834 in New Jersey,[146] census 1850 in Cotton Twp, Switzerland Co, Ind.
v. CHARLOTTE M. MELICK b. ca 1836 in New Jersey,[146] census 1850 in Cotton Twp, Switzerland Co, Ind.
vi. WILLIAM H. MELICK b. ca 1839 in Iowa,[146] census 1850 in Cotton Twp, Switzerland Co, Ind.

vii. ELIZABETH MELICK b. ca 1842 in Iowa,[146] census 1850 in Cotton Twp, Switzerland Co, Ind.

187. **Andrew Dickson** (93.Phebe[5], 32.Margaret[4], 9.John[3], 3.John[2], 1.Jean[1]), d. ca 1836.[ccci[301]]

Hanna's "Ohio Valley Genealogies," p. 47, states that Phebe Dickson, daughter of James Dickson & Margaret Gaston, married Uriah Church and had a son Andrew who married Ruth Hall, and they in turn had a daughter Clara who married Horace White and was the mother of Andrew Dickson White. The implication is that Clara's and her father's surname was Church. But that is contradicted by biographical accounts of Andrew Dickson White, which identify his grandfather as Andrew Dickson and his mother as Clara Dickson. Given our limited knowledge of the circumstances, we invite a better informed reader to confirm or refute our speculation that Andrew Dickson was born prior to his mother's marriage to Uriah Church.

In "The Autobiography of Andrew Dickson White," the author states that his mother's "father prospered as a man of business, was known as 'Colonel,' and also as 'Squire' Dickson, and represented his county in the State legislature. He died when I was about three years old, and I vaguely remember being brought to him as he lay upon his death-bed. On one account, above all others, I have long looked back to him with pride. For the first public care of the early settlers had been a church, and the second a school. This school had been speedily developed into Cortland Academy, which soon became famous throughout all that region, and, as a boy of five or six years of age, I was very proud to read on the cornerstone of the Academy building my grandfather's name among those of the original founders. ... I was born into a politically divided family. My grandfather, on my mother's side, whose name I was destined to bear, was an ardent Democrat; had, as such, represented his district in the State legislature, and other public bodies; took his political creed from Thomas Jefferson, and adored Andrew Jackson. My father, on the other hand, was in all his antecedents and his personal convictions, a devoted Whig, taking his creed from Alexander Hamilton, and worshiping Henry Clay."[cccii[302],ccciii[303]]

He married[28] **Ruth Hall**, b. ca 1790 in Connecticut,[280] census 1850, 1860 in Syracuse, Onondaga Co, NY [In household with daughter & son-in-law Clara & Horace Church and their family. In 1850, listed as Ruth Dickison, 60, b. NY. In 1860, listed as Ruth Dickson, 70, b. Connecticut. The latter entry would appear more credible.].
        Children:
    349.   i.   CLARA DICKSON[28] b. ca 1811.

188. **William Gaston** (94.Alexander[5], 33.John[4], 9.John[3], 3.John[2], 1.Jean[1]), b. Oct- 3-1820 in Killingly, Windham Co, CT,[11,33] d. Jan-19-1894 in Boston, MA,[27,33] resided until 1838 in Killingly, Windham Co, CT,[11] resided starting 1838 in Roxbury, Suffolk Co, MA,[11] occupation Governor of Massachusetts.[ccciv[304],33]

Served as a member of the Massachusetts Legislature, as Mayor of Boston from 1871-72, and 1875-76 as Governor of Massachusetts. He also had a private law practice in which his son William Alexander Gaston became a partner. ["The Gaston Genealogy," p. 40] Earned a B.A. & M.A. from Brown University in 1840 and 1843, and a law degree from Brown & Harvard in 1875. [American Ancestry, Vol V, p. 103] "William Gaston had established a successful legal practice in the City of Roxbury before entering politics. He served as a Representative in the State Legislature (1853-1854), as Roxbury's City Solicitor (1856-60), and as its Mayor (1861 and 1862). He resumed his private practice of law until 1868, when he served the Massachusetts Senate for a year. The City of Boston annexed Roxbury in 1868, and in 1871, Gaston was voted Mayor of Boston. Running for Governor as a Democrat, Gaston defeated incumbent Thomas Talbot who had supported the continuance of statewide prohibition by his veto. Gaston promoted a law repealing the Commonwealth's prohibition law, leaving such restrictions to the determination of localities. Governor Gaston was defeated in his reelection bid by Alexander Rice. Mr. Gaston returned to his extremely successful legal practice, gaining renown as a trial attorney."

<http://www.mass.gov/statehouse/massgovs/wgaston.htm>
<http://www.gutenberg.org/dirs/1/4/1/3/14132/14132.txt>

He married May-27-1852,[304,11,33] **Louisa Augusta Beecher**, b. Dec-27-1830 in Boston, MA,[33,11] (daughter of Laban Smith Beecher and Frances Amelia Lines), d. Mar-24-1903 in Boston, MA.[27]
   Children:
   i. SARAH HOWARD GASTON b. Apr-23-1853 in Roxbury, Suffolk Co, MA.[27,33]
 350. ii. WILLIAM ALEXANDER GASTON[11] b. May- 1-1859.
   iii. THEODORE BEECHER GASTON b. Feb- 8-1861 in Roxbury, Suffolk Co, MA,[27,11,33] d.
Jul-16-1869.[304,11,33].

189. **Thompson Kasson** (96.Robert[5], 36.Janet[4], 10.Alexander[3], 3.John[2], 1.Jean[1]), b. Oct- 2-1795 in Broadalbin, Fulton Co, NY,[185] d. Jan-13-1848.[ccv[305]] He married (1) Sep-29-1816,[ccvi[306]] **Mary Warner**, b. Sep- 5-1795,[305] d. Nov-23-1833,[305] resided in Wethersfield, Hartford Co, CT.[306] He married[305] (2) **Unknown**.
   Children by Mary Warner:
   i. SOPHRONIA KASSON b. Aug-29-1817,[305] d. Mar- 9-1848.[305]
   ii. ORANGE H. KASSON b. Feb- 6-1819.[305]
   iii. EMMA JANE KASSON b. Oct-28-1821,[305] d. 1838.[305]
 351. iv. MARY KASSON b. Oct-21-1823.
   v. JAMES W. KASSON b. Jan- 9-1825.[305]
   vi. WILLIAM EARLE KASSON b. Mar- 9-1827,[305] d. Mar-10-1828.[305]
 352. vii. WILLIAM ALEXANDER KASSON b. Mar-10-1829.
   viii. MASON T. KASSON b. Jan-19-1831,[305] d. Oct- 5-1832.[305]
   ix. BERNARD R. KASSON b. Oct-15-1833,[305] twin[305] d. Nov-22-1833.[305]
   x. BURRELL W. KASSON b. Oct-15-1833,[305] d. Apr-20-1834.[305]
   Children by Unknown:
   xi. ROBERT KASSON.
   xii. JANE KASSON.

190. **James Kasson** (96.Robert[5], 36.Janet[4], 10.Alexander[3], 3.John[2], 1.Jean[1]), b. Dec-28-1798.[185] He married Jan-30-1828,[305] **Sarah Sunderland**.
   Children:
   i. CORDELIA R. KASSON b. Jan-11-1830,[305] d. Jan- 7-1862.[305] She married[305] __
Humphrey.
 353. ii. LUCY S. KASSON b. Aug-19-1835.

191. **Charles B. Kasson** (96.Robert[5], 36.Janet[4], 10.Alexander[3], 3.John[2], 1.Jean[1]), b. Feb-23-1803.[185] He married Feb- 9-1835 in Middle Grove, Saratoga Co, NY,[305] **Sarah M. __**.
   Children:
   i. OPHELIA KASSON b. Jan-22-1838.[305]
   ii. ALBERT H. KASSON b. Jan-29-1842.[305]
   iii. ROBERT N. KASSON b. Aug-12-1843.[305]
   iv. DAY H. KASSON b. Jun-17-1845.[305]

192. **Mason G. Kasson** (96.Robert[5], 36.Janet[4], 10.Alexander[3], 3.John[2], 1.Jean[1]), b. May-12-1804,[ccvii[307]] resided 1873 near Topeka, Shawnee Co, KS.[305] He married 1832,[305] __ **Lowell**.
   Children:
   i. MORTIMER BRICKNAL KASSON b. ca 1834,[ccviii[308]] d. 1865 in Vicksburg, Warren Co,
MS,[308] military Civil War (killed).[308]
 354. ii. ARCHIBALD KASSON.
   iii. ELLEN C. KASSON. She married[308] W. Colustin, resided in Macon Co, IL.[308]
   iv. MARY MARILLA KASSON b. May- -1854.[308]

193. **Ephraim Kasson** (96.Robert[5], 36.Janet[4], 10.Alexander[3], 3.John[2], 1.Jean[1]), b. Apr- 1-1810.[185] He married[305] **Maria Nooman**.

Children:
- i. DEXTER N. KASSON b. Feb- 8-1840.[305]
- ii. EMMA JANE KASSON b. Jun-24-1844.[305]
- iii. CLARA E. KASSON b. May-25-1857.[305]

194. **Archibald Kasson** (97.William[5], 36.Janet[4], 10.Alexander[3], 3.John[2], 1.Jean[1]), b. Jan- 7-1793,[185] resided 1861 in South Butler, Wayne Co, NY.[308] He married Jan- -1815,[308] **Polly Dunham**.

Children:
- 355. i. JEREMIAH WILLIAM KASSON b. Dec-16-1815.
- 356. ii. ORSON V. KASSON b. May- 8-1818.
- 357. iii. ACHASH A. KASSON b. May-18-1821.
- 358. iv. SARAH A. KASSON b. Aug-27-1825.
-      v. OLIVE M. KASSON b. Aug-25-1830,[308] d. 1847.[308]
-      vi. LEWIS H. KASSON b. Oct-21-1831.[308]
-      vii. ALEXANDER KASSON b. 1837.[308]

195. **Nelson Kasson** (97.William[5], 36.Janet[4], 10.Alexander[3], 3.John[2], 1.Jean[1]), b. 1803,[186] d. 1837.[308] He married Apr-28-1829,[308] **Sally Hazard**.

Sally: Spelling appears as both Hazard and Hasard in Kasson genealogy.

Children:
- i. HARRIET KASSON d. young in Granby (Fulton), Oswego Co, NY.[308]
- ii. JULIUS KASSON b. 1832.[308]
- iii. HARRIET KASSON b. 1834.[308]
- iv. JAMES KASSON b. 1836.[308]

196. **Chauncey C. Kasson** (98.Harvey[5], 36.Janet[4], 10.Alexander[3], 3.John[2], 1.Jean[1]), b. Dec-15-1812,[186] occupation carpenter.[cccix[309]] He married Jan-31-1838,[309] **Sarah Capron**.

Children:
- 359. i. EARLE C. KASSON b. Jul- 5-1840.
-      ii. SARAH ANTONETTE KASSON b. Apr- 4-1844,[309] d. Aug-14-1849.[309]
-      iii. HARVEY A. KASSON b. Feb- 3-1846,[309] occupation glove maker.[309]
-      iv. JAMES S. KASSON b. Oct-23-1848,[309] d. Aug-21-1849.[309]
-      v. ORRIN N. KASSON b. Dec- 4-1851.[309]
-      vi. MARTIN KASSON b. Feb-16-1854,[309] twin[309].
-      vii. MORTIMER KASSON b. Feb-16-1854,[309] twin[309].

197. **Amasa C. Kasson** (98.Harvey[5], 36.Janet[4], 10.Alexander[3], 3.John[2], 1.Jean[1]), b. Jan-21-1819.[186] He married Jan- 8-1844,[309] **Elizabeth Van Nostram**.

Children:
- i. LOIS CORNELIA KASSON b. Nov- 2-1846.[309]
- ii. SARAH LUELLA KASSON b. Mar- 4-1848.[cccx[310]]

198. **George B. Kasson** (98.Harvey[5], 36.Janet[4], 10.Alexander[3], 3.John[2], 1.Jean[1]), b. Apr-17-1822,[186] occupation carpenter.[186] He married[310] **Jane Gray**.

Children:
- i. GEORGE H. KASSON b. Feb-13-1847,[310] d. Jun-20-1850 in Broadalbin, Fulton Co, NY.[310]
- ii. EDGAR A. KASSON b. Feb- 2-1850.[310]
- iii. GIBSON KASSON b. Jan- 2-1853.[310]
- iv. HELEN J. KASSON b. Oct- 7-1854.[310]
- v. FRANK KASSON b. Sep-22-1856.[310]

vi.   FLORENCE KASSON b. Apr- 7-1859.[310]
vii.   LURA M. KASSON b. Mar-31-1862.[310]
viii.   ANNETTE S. KASSON b. May-15-1864.[310]

199. **Marvin Kasson** (99.Alexander[5], 36.Janet[4], 10.Alexander[3], 3.John[2], 1.Jean[1]), b. Nov-24-1815,[186] d. Jul-11-1861 in Broadalbin, Fulton Co, NY,[186] occupation farmer.[186] He married May-16-1858,[310] **Marian Stone**.
>   Children:
>   i.   SUSAN E. KASSON b. Apr-23-1859.[310]

200. **Lucy Mariah Gaston** (100.Alexander[5], 37.Alexander[4], 10.Alexander[3], 3.John[2], 1.Jean[1]), b. Jan-19-1813 in Danby, Tompkins Co, NY,[36] d. Sep-20-1850 in Jonesville, Hillsdale Co, MI,[36] buried in Sunset View Cemetery, Jonesville, Hillsdale Co, MI.[36]

Lucy Gaston Hickok had four children. The youngest, Fred, "burned to death at Aunt Elvira's" according to notes of Etta Gaston. In 1915, Loren Hume, who visited Elvira's as a child, wrote that Fred died after being scalded when a kettle of hot water fell on him.[36]

She married Aug-28-1834 in Danby, Tompkins Co, NY,[64,36] **Stephen Camp Hickok**, b. 1809 in New Canaan, Fairfield Co, CT,[64] d. Oct- 7-1850 in Hillsdale, Hillsdale Co, MI.[64]
>   Children:
>   i.   FRED HICKOK[36.]

201. **George Belcher Gaston** (100.Alexander[5], 37.Alexander[4], 10.Alexander[3], 3.John[2], 1.Jean[1]), b. Nov- 8-1814 in Danby, Tompkins Co, NY,[36] d. May- 1-1873 in Tabor, Fremont Co, IA,[36,cccxi[311]] buried in Tabor, Fremont Co, IA,[36] resided in Tabor, Fremont Co, IA,[311] resided formerly in Oberlin, Lorain Co, OH.[311]

George Belcher Gaston founded the town of Tabor, Iowa in 1852 and Tabor College. He was "first identified as a young farmer with a missionary spirit. He lived near Oberlin, Ohio. So intense became his mission zeal that he obtained a commission under the American Board of Missions to work among the Pawnee Indians in a territory that later became Nance County in Nebraska. He worked among the Pawnees four years.... When his wife was taken ill, they returned to Ohio, and he became more closely acquainted with Oberlin's history. He conceived the plan of developing a similar community with its colony patterned after Oberlin College. His idea led to its reality...." Enlisting the aid of Deacon Samuel H. Adams and Rev. John Todd (who left a ministry in Clarksfield, Ohio), they and their families took out claims for the town in April 1852. The terrain led them to name the town "Tabor," after the Biblical name of Mount Tabor, a mountain near Nazareth. George B. Gaston's plan for a college was soon put into motion, and Tabor College's first incarnation, Tabor Literary Institute, opened on Nov 3 1857. Meanwhile, the area had come to the attention of John Brown, the famous abolitionist. Born in Connecticut in 1800, Brown moved to New York in 1849 to promote his abolitionist ideas. In 1857, he moved to Kansas, where five of his sons had moved the year before. Continuing his abolitionist mission, Brown became involved in kidnapping and smuggling slaves across the border into Nebraska and Iowa. "With his 'underground railroad' functioning, Brown left Kansas. Brown became aware that the settlers of Tabor were sympathetic to his cause. He also viewed Tabor's location as close-by to set up a station from which smuggled slaves could be relayed to Canada.... John Brown, often accompanied by his four sons, frequently came to Tabor. There were some occasions in which he would remain in town weeks at a time." The home of George B. Gaston was among those in Tabor where John Brown was entertained and that Brown and his associates used for slave hideaways.[311,36]
When George's sister Emala and her husband Julius Hume died at early ages, George and his wife Maria took in Emala's young son Loren and raised him as their son.[36]

He married Feb-22-1837 in South Amherst, Lorain Co, OH,[36] **Maria Cummings**, b. Sep-17-1815 in Thetford, Orange Co, VT.[34]

Children:
360. i. ALEXANDER CUMMINGS GASTON b. Feb-16-1838.
ii. ALONZO MARCELLUS GASTON b. Jul-16-1840 in Bellevue, Sarpy Co, NE.
iii. EUPHELIA MINERVA GASTON b. Dec- 6-1842 in Plum Creek, Loop Fork, NE.

202. **Maria Gaston** (100.Alexander[5], 37.Alexander[4], 10.Alexander[3], 3.John[2], 1.Jean[1]), b. Oct-14-1816 in Danby, Tompkins Co, NY,[36] d. Jun-23-1897 in Fremont Co, IA,[36] buried in Tabor, Fremont Co, IA.[36] She married Feb-28-1835,[36] **Samuel Rossiter**.
Children:
i. ED ROSSITER.

203. **Emala Fairchild Gaston** (100.Alexander[5], 37.Alexander[4], 10.Alexander[3], 3.John[2], 1.Jean[1]), b. Jun- 5-1820 in Danby, Tompkins Co, NY,[36] d. Mar-17-1851 in Wayne, Wayne Co, MI,[36] buried in Wayne, Wayne Co, MI.[36] She married Sep-26-1849,[36] **Julius W. Hume**, d. Oct- -1852,[36] occupation physician.[36]
Children:
i. LOREN CLARK HUME[36].

After the early deaths of his parents, Loren Clark Hume was raised in the home of his mother's brother and his wife, George Belcher Gaston and Maria Cummings.[36]

204. **Celia H. Gaston** (100.Alexander[5], 37.Alexander[4], 10.Alexander[3], 3.John[2], 1.Jean[1]), b. Jan-16-1824 in Danby, Tompkins Co, NY,[36] d. May-28-1858 in Coldwater, Branch Co, MI,[36] buried in Oakgrove Cemetery, Coldwater, MI.[36] She married Nov-26-1846,[36] **James W. Gilbert**, occupation lawyer.[36]
Children:
i. HENRY GILBERT[36].

205. **Henry Alexander Gaston** (101.Heman[5], 37.Alexander[4], 10.Alexander[3], 3.John[2], 1.Jean[1]), b. Aug- 9-1823 in Richmond, Berkshire Co, MA,[cccxii[312]] resided 1875 in San Jose, Santa Clara Co, CA,[312] occupation lawyer and mining business.[312] He married Jul- -1848,[312] **Josephine Ballou**.
Children:
i. ANDREW A. GASTON b. 1849,[312] resided in San Jose, Santa Clara Co, CA,[312] occupation dentist.[312]
ii. NELLIE C. GASTON b. 1851.[312]
iii. WILLIE GASTON[312].

206. **James Kasson Gaston** (101.Heman[5], 37.Alexander[4], 10.Alexander[3], 3.John[2], 1.Jean[1]), b. Apr-17-1832 in Richmond, Berkshire Co, MA,[193,cccxiii[313],198] baptized Sep-16-1832 in Richmond, Berkshire Co, MA,[196] d. Feb-14-1891 in Tabor, Fremont Co, IA,[193,313] resided in Mills Co, IA.[193]

"James K. Gaston, farmer and stock-raiser, was born in Richmond, Berkshire Co, Mass., April 17 1832. He moved with his parents to Lorain Co Ohio at age six, where he remained until he grew to manhood, working on a farm. He received his education chiefly in common schools, but attended Oberlin College several terms. He arrived in Iowa Nov 27 1853, and worked as a farm laborer for some time. In summer 1853, he taught school at Pleasant Grove, near Sidney, in Fremont Co. He was married in Tabor, Fremont Co. Iowa, Nov 23 1857, to Miss Sarah J. Cummings, who was born in Lorain Co, Ohio September 12, 1839. They are the parents of nine children, eight of whom are now living: Emily C., Ellen M., Willard E., Burton C., Vernon L., Lillie J., Lucy May and George R. He has been a member of the Congregational church since 1854, and has always been identified with the work of temperance. He has filled various township offices with credit to himself, and has been school treasurer since 1873. He owns a fine farm of 280 acres, which is well improved especially adapted to stock raising, in which business he is extensively engaged. He has a very fine building upon his farm, which is a model of neatness and convenience." (From "History of Mills County, Iowa," published 1881 in Des Moines by State Historical Company, pp. 608-609)[313]

He married Nov-23-1857 in Tabor, Fremont Co, IA,[cccxiv[314],313] **Sarah Jane Cummings**, b. Sep-12-1839 in Oberlin, Lorain Co, OH,[193,cccxv[315]] (daughter of Oregin Cummings and Hannah Townsend), d. Aug-19-1906 in Tabor, Fremont Co, IA,[193,315] buried in Tabor, Fremont Co, IA.[315]
      Children:
      i.   EMILY CORNELIA GASTON b. Nov-15-1858 in Tabor, Fremont Co, IA,[313] d. Oct-22-1922 in Glenwood, Mills Co, IA,[313] buried in Glenwood, Mills Co, IA,[313] occupation teacher.[313] She married Sep-15-1897 in Tabor, Fremont Co, IA,[313] no children from this marriage, William Cecil Vinton, b. Jan-29-1850 in Marietta, Washington Co, OH.[313]
      ii. ELLEN G. MARIE GASTON b. Apr-19-1860 in Tabor, Fremont Co, IA,[313] d. Oct- 7-1950 in Tabor, Fremont Co, IA.[313]

          Residing in Big Horn, Wyoming, as of 1914.[313]

          She married Dec-23-1896 in Tabor, Fremont Co, IA,[313] Robert W. Hurlbutt.
361. iii. WILLARD EDGAR GASTON b. Jan-25-1862.
362. iv. BURTON CUMMINGS GASTON b. 1864.
363. v. VERNON LINCOLN GASTON b. Feb- 9-1866.
      vi. LILLIE J. GASTON b. 1869 in Tabor, Fremont Co, IA,[313] d. Jun-19-1916 in Los Angeles, CA,[313] buried in Los Angeles, CA.[313] She married Nov-29-1893 in Tabor, Fremont Co, IA,[313] Joseph H. Robbins.
364. vii. LUCY MAY GASTON b. Mar- 6-1872.
365. viii. GEORGE RUTHERFORD GASTON b. Aug-22-1876.
      ix. LEONARD ORIGEN GASTON b. Feb- -1883 in Tabor, Fremont Co, IA,[313] d. Feb- 7-1968 in Corydon, Wayne Co, IA,[313] buried in Corydon, Wayne Co, IA.[313] He married Dec-20-1910 in Bosworth, Carroll Co, MO,[313] Nettie Metcalf.

207. **Edmund Waite Gaston** (102.Ebenezer[5], 38.David[4], 10.Alexander[3], 3.John[2], 1.Jean[1]), b. Aug-16-1809 in Flemming, Allegany Co, NY,[99] d. Jan- 5-1881 in Sadbury Twp, Crawford Co, PA.[99] He married Jan-26-1834,[34] **Phylinda Bristol**, b. Oct-24-1807,[99] d. Apr-22-1878.[99]
      Children:
      i.   WILLIAM GROVER GASTON b. Jun-18-1835,[34] d. Sep-10-1901.[34]
      ii. ATHELSTON GASTON b. Apr-24-1838 in Castile, Wyoming Co, NY,[34] d. Sep-23-1907.[34]

          "GASTON, Athelston, representative, was born in Castile, N.Y., April 24, 1838; son of Edmund W. and Phylinda (Bristol) Gaston; grandson of Ebenezer Gaston; great-grandson of David Gaston, both born at old Stockbridge, Mass., and a descendant of Dr. Alexander Gaston who was born in Ireland in 1714. The family originally emigrated from France to Ireland during the Huguenot persecutions. At the age of sixteen he removed to Pennsylvania, where he received a common school education and then engaged in farming until 1873, when he became a manufacturer and dealer in lumber. He was mayor of Meadville, Pa., in 1891, and again in 1892-95. He was president of the Cassadaga Lake Free association at Lily Dale, N.Y., 1888-99. He was a Democratic representative from the 26th Pennsylvania district in the 56th congress, 1899-1901, having also the endorsement of the People's party." [The Twentieth Century Biographical Dictionary of Notable Americans: Volume IV] <http://www.historicpa.net/bios/2a/athelston-gaston.html>[cccxvi[316]]

          He married Thankful C. Hammond.[cccxvii[317]]
      iii. EPHRIAM HAMMOND GASTON b. May-21-1840,[34] d. Mar- 6-1867.[34]
      iv. (UNNAMED) GASTON b. Mar- -1842,[34] d. Mar- -1842.[34]
      v. ARTHUR B. GASTON b. Dec- 7-1843,[34] d. Nov-28-1923.[34] He married[317] Hannah Jane McMaster.
366. vi. EUNICE LUCINDA GASTON b. Nov-21-1845.
      vii. AZELTHA ARABELLE GASTON b. Nov-24-1849,[34] d. Dec-31-1849.[34]

367.   viii.   FRANK DEFOREST GASTON b. Jan-26-1853.

Generation Seven

208. **Hudson Gaston** (106.Robert[6], 41.Matthew[5], 11.Alexander[4], 4.(Male)[3], 2.William[2], 1.Jean[1]), b. 1813 in Greene Co, GA,[cccxviii[318]] d. Oct- 4-1854 in Washington, Washington Co, TX,[318] buried in Gaston-White Cemetery, Fort Bend, TX.[318] He married Nov- 7-1845 in Brazoria Co, TX,[318] **Caroline Austin**, b. 1828 in New York Co, NY,[318] (daughter of William Tennant Austin and Johanna Stayner).
            Children:
    368.   i.   ANN GASTON b. Sep-21-1850.

209. **Rhesa Reid** (107.Jane[6], 41.Matthew[5], 11.Alexander[4], 4.(Male)[3], 2.William[2], 1.Jean[1]), b. 1797 in Greene Co, GA,[cccxix[319]] [Birth date reported as ca 1799 in "Reid, Gaston and Simonton, Related Families" by Elizabeth Weir McPherson], d. 1870.[201] He married[201] **Mary Kidd**.
            Children:
            i.   MARY ANN REID b. 1822.[201]
            ii.   ELIZABETH REID b. 1822.[201]
            iii.   ASA BARTON REID b. 1825.[201]
            iv.   ADALINE ANNA REID b. 1827.[201]
            v.   MARTHA A. REID b. 1830.[201]
            vi.   NANCY R. M. REID b. 1834.[201]
            vii.   M. LENORA REID b. 1840.[201]
            viii. GEORGIANA REID b. 1842.[201]

210. **Asa Reid** (107.Jane[6], 41.Matthew[5], 11.Alexander[4], 4.(Male)[3], 2.William[2], 1.Jean[1]), b. 1799 in Jackson Co, GA,[cccxx[320]] [Birth date reported as ca 1801 in "Reid, Gaston and Simonton, Related Families" by Elizabeth Weir McPherson], d. 1850.[201] He married[201] **Winny Castleberry**, b. 1805 in Georgia,[201] d. 1880.[201]
            Children:
            i.   SARAH REID b. 1819.[201]
            ii.   JANE REID b. 1821 in Gwinnett Co, GA.[201] She married[201] James Arnold.
    369.   iii.   MATHEW GASTON REID b. 1825.
    370.   iv.   RHESA REID b. 1827.
            v.   MARTHA REID b. 1829.[201]
            vi.   DAVID REID b. 1833.[201]
    371.   vii.   HENRY REID b. 1836.
            viii. FRANCIS M. REID b. 1839 in Benton Co, AL.[201] He married[201] Sarah Jane Teter.
    372.   ix.   GEORGE W. REID b. 1845.

211. **George W. Reid**[202] (107.Jane[6], 41.Matthew[5], 11.Alexander[4], 4.(Male)[3], 2.William[2], 1.Jean[1]), b. 1803 in Greene Co, GA,[201] d. 1881.[201] He married[201] **Nancy Ward Ezzard**, b. 1805,[201] (daughter of John L. Ezzard and Margaret Ward), d. 1875.[201]
            Children:
            i.   JOHN L. REID b. 1822.[201]
            ii.   ROBERT A. REID b. 1827.[201]
            iii.   GEORGE W. REID b. 1834.[201]
            iv.   ASA M. REID b. 1835.[201]
            v.   WESLEY H. REID b. 1838.[201]
            vi.   MARY S. REID b. 1840.[201]
            vii.   MARTHA M. REID b. 1842.[201]
            viii. ISAAC S. REID b. 1845.[201]
            ix.   SARAH O. REID b. 1846.[201]
            x.   CHARLES O. REID b. 1849.[201]

212. **Jane "Jennie" Reid**[202] (107.Jane[6], 41.Matthew[5], 11.Alexander[4], 4.(Male)[3], 2.William[2], 1.Jean[1]), b. 1805 in Jackson Co, GA,[201,202] d. 1875.[201] She married[201] **Charles Norman**.

Children:

    373.   i.   ROBERT LAFAYETTE NORMAN b. 1828.

213. **Thomas Henry Reid**[202,202] also known as Henry Thomas Reid,[201] (107.Jane[6], 41.Matthew[5], 11.Alexander[4], 4.(Male)[3], 2.William[2], 1.Jean[1]), b. 1816,[201] d. 1902.[201] He married[201] **Narcissa Armstrong**, d. 1898.[201]

Children:

        i.   THOMAS REID[201.]
        ii.   WILLIAM H. REID b. 1842.[201]
        iii.   JAMES REID b. 1843.[201]
        iv.   MARY E. REID b. 1844.[201]
        v.   RACHEL REID b. 1848.[201]
        vi.   ROBERT C. REID b. 1848.[201]
        vii.   GEORGE W. REID b. 1850,[201] d. 1916.[201] He married[201] Abbue Sarah __.
        viii.   MARGARET A. REID b. 1852.[201]
        ix.   NANCY J. REID b. 1853.[201]
        x.   JOHN M. REID b. 1854.[201]

214. **Matthew Gaston** (108.Alexander[6], 41.Matthew[5], 11.Alexander[4], 4.(Male)[3], 2.William[2], 1.Jean[1]), b. 1805 in Greene Co, GA,[203] d. 1836 in Greene Co, GA.[203] He married Apr-11-1827 in Greene Co, GA,[203] **Pheriba Jane Brown**, b. 1810 in Greene Co, GA.[203]

Children:

        i.   SARAH JANE GASTON b. 1829 in Greene Co, GA.[203]
        ii.   MARY ELIZABETH GASTON b. 1831 in Greene Co, GA.[203]
    374.   iii.   MATTHEW ALEXANDER GASTON b. Nov- 1-1832.

215. **Johnnie Matthew Gaston** (109.Matthew[6], 41.Matthew[5], 11.Alexander[4], 4.(Male)[3], 2.William[2], 1.Jean[1]).

Children:

        i.   J. AVON GASTON resided in Jackson, Butts Co, GA.[102]

216. **James Gaston** (111.James[6], 46.John[5], 12.John[4], 5.William[3], 3.John[2], 1.Jean[1]), b. 1800,[108] d. 1865.[108] He married 1820 in Monroe Co, TN,[108] **Mary Sheets**, b. 1794,[108] (daughter of Jacob Sheets and Margaret Rule), resided originally in Sullivan Co, TN.[108]

Children:

    375.   i.   DAVID GASTON[108].

217. **William Gaston**[cccxxi][321] (112.Esther[6], 46.John[5], 12.John[4], 5.William[3], 3.John[2], 1.Jean[1]). He married[321] **Rachel Huff**.

Children:

    376.   i.   CAROLINE GASTON.

218. **William Davidson Gaston** (113.Stephen[6], 47.James[5], 12.John[4], 5.William[3], 3.John[2], 1.Jean[1]), b. Feb-22-1808 in Illinois,[12] d. Aug-26-1854 in Illinois.[12] He married[cccxxii][322] **Lucinda White**, b. Oct- 3-1807,[12] d. May-25-1884.[12]

Children:

        i.   MARY ANN GASTON b. 1832 in Illinois.[12]
        ii.   JOHN D. GASTON b. 1836 in Illinois,[12] d. 1840.[12]
        iii.   STEPHEN HARVEY GASTON b. Dec- -1837 in Illinois,[12] d. 1912.[12]
        iv.   JOSEPH W. GASTON b. 1839 in Illinois.[12]
        v.   ROBERT W. GASTON b. Apr- -1841 in Illinois,[12] d. 1911.[12]
        vi.   WILLIAM A. GASTON b. 1843 in Illinois,[12] d. 1865.[12]

      vii. MARGARET JANE GASTON b. 1844 in Illinois,[12] d. 1910.[12] She married[12] Adam M. Correll, b. Jun- 3-1848 in Illinois,[12] d. Jun-23-1923 in Illinois.[12] Three children.[12]

      viii. SAMUEL J. GASTON b. 1846 in Illinois,[12] d. 1910.[12] He married[12] Margaret J. Harvey, b. ca 1850.[12]

      ix. MARTHA GASTON b. 1847 in Illinois,[12] d. 1874.[12]

      x. SARAH B. GASTON b. Jun- -1849 in Illinois,[12] d. 1928.[12]

377.   xi. JAMES HENRY GASTON b. Mar- 3-1853.

219. **Stephen Harvey Gaston** (113.Stephen[6], 47.James[5], 12.John[4], 5.William[3], 3.John[2], 1.Jean[1]), b. Nov-30-1818 in Illinois,[12] d. Jul- 7-1851 in Illinois.[12] He married (1) Feb-25-1842,[cccxxiii][323] **Margaret "Peggy" McConnell**, b. Nov- 4-1821,[12] d. Aug-11-1843.[12] He married (2) Mar- 3-1847,[323] **Cynthia E. Casey**.

      Children by Cynthia E. Casey:

      i. SUSAN LAURA GASTON b. 1848 in Illinois.[12]

      ii. MELINTHA E. GASTON b. 1849 in Illinois.[12]

      iii. JULIA ARABELLA GASTON b. ca 1851 in Illinois,[12] d. 1853.[12]

220. **William Walker** (114.John[6], 49.Esther[5], 12.John[4], 5.William[3], 3.John[2], 1.Jean[1]). He married 1819,[113] **Sarah Edwards**.

      Children:

378.   i. JANE GASTON WALKER b. 1820.

221. **James McFadden Gaston** (115.John[6], 50.Joseph[5], 12.John[4], 5.William[3], 3.John[2], 1.Jean[1]), b. 1824 near Chester, Chester Co, SC,[cccxxiv][324],[cccxxv][325] d. 1903,[324] occupation physician, surgeon & teacher,[324,325] military Confederate Army - Civil War.[324]

James McFadden Gaston (1824-1903) was a Confederate surgeon and physician from South Carolina. He organized medical services while serving as Chief Surgeon of South Carolina Forces and later as Divisional Surgeon General of the South Carolina Volunteers during campaigns in Virginia and Pennsylvania, which included the battles of Manassas, Gettysburg and Chickamauga. His brothers were killed at the Battle of Seven Pines. Immediately after the conclusion of the Civil War in 1865, Gaston left the United States and settled his family in Brazil where he practiced medicine in the city of Campinas. After almost two decades, in 1883, Gaston returned with some of his family to Atlanta, Ga., where he successfully re-entered American medical life, teaching at the Southern Medical College, publishing articles, and carrying out research.[324]

He married[324,cccxxvi][326] **Susan Greening Brumby**, b. 1830,[324] (daughter of Richard Trapier Brumby and Mary Martha Isabella Brevard), d. 1904.[324]

      Children:

      i. JAMES MCFADDEN GASTON, JR. b. Mar-30-1868 in Brazil,[324] d. 1946,[324] occupation physician & surgeon.[324]

      Like his father for whom he was named, James McFadden Gaston (1868-1946) was also a physician and surgeon. Little is known about his practice of medicine in the United States beyond the fact that he worked with his father in private practice as well as at the Southern Medical College. From 1908 until 1936, under the aegis of the Southern Baptist Convention's Foreign Mission Board in Richmond, Va., the younger Gaston and his wife, Annie Bunn Gay Gaston, worked as medical missionaries in Laichowfu, China, at the Mayfield-Tyzzer and Kathleen Mallory hospitals. In 1936, he and his wife returned to the United States and retired in Deland, Fla., where he was involved in local church activities, especially the No Liquor League.[324]

      He married[324] Annie Bunn Gay.

      ii. ELOISE GASTON b. in Brazil.[cccxxvii][327] She married[327] Thomas Bolling Gay.

115

222. **Joseph Lucius Gaston**[cccxxviii[328]] (115.John[6], 50.Joseph[5], 12.John[4], 5.William[3], 3.John[2], 1.Jean[1]). He married[328] **Margaret Hemphill**,[328] (daughter of David Hemphill and Jane Brice).

        Children:
        i.   JANIE GASTON b. in Chester, Chester Co, SC.[116] She married[328] George W. Gage.
        ii.   JOSEPH LUCIUS GASTON, JR. b. Nov-11-1860 in Chester, Chester Co, SC,[325] occupation VP, 1st National Bank of Montgomery AL,[325] education Erskine College, SC.[325] He married[325_325] Josepha "Josie" Bell, b. in Fairfield Co, SC,[cccxxix[329]] (daughter of John P. Bell and Isabella Hemphill Caldwell).

223. **John Brown Gaston, Jr.**[cccxxx[330]] (115.John[6], 50.Joseph[5], 12.John[4], 5.William[3], 3.John[2], 1.Jean[1]), b. Jan-4-1834 in Chester, Chester Co, SC.[325] He married[330] Oct-11-1857,[325] **Sarah Torrance**, resided originally in Mecklenburg Co, NC.[325]

        Children:
        i.   MARY GASTON b. in Montgomery, Montgomery Co, AL.[cccxxxi[331]]

        A member (No. 48975) of the Daughters of the American Revolution.

        She married[331] T. Sidney Moise.

224. **T. Chalmers Gaston** (115.John[6], 50.Joseph[5], 12.John[4], 5.William[3], 3.John[2], 1.Jean[1]), b. 1847,[207] d. 1885,[207] occupation attorney.[207] He married **Adelaide Lee**, b. 1854,[207] d. 1895.[207]

        Children:
   379. i.   ARTHUR LEE GASTON b. Aug-14-1876.

225. **Margaret Eliza Lewis**[cccxxxii[332]] (116.Narcissa[6], 50.Joseph[5], 12.John[4], 5.William[3], 3.John[2], 1.Jean[1]). She married[332] **Richard C. McCalla**.

        Children:
   380. i.   CAROLINA MCCALLA.

226. **Eliza Jane McClure**[120] (117.Hugh[6], 51.John[5], 13.Mary[4], 5.William[3], 3.John[2], 1.Jean[1]). She married[121] **Abram H. DeVega**, occupation Dr.

        Children:
   381. i.   JESSIE A. DEVEGA.

227. **Edward E. Rosborough** (119.David[6], 55.Alexander[5], 15.Martha[4], 5.William[3], 3.John[2], 1.Jean[1]), b. Jul--1847 in Tennessee,[123] census 1900 in Belton, Bell Co, TX, occupation lawyer.[123]

        Children:
        i.   GEORGE B. ROXBOROUGH b. Mar- -1879 in Texas,[123] census 1900 in Belton, Bell Co, TX.

228. **Samuel Gaston** (121.William[6], 57.William[5], 16.Robert[4], 5.William[3], 3.John[2], 1.Jean[1]). He married[212] **Nellie Lucinda Henson**.

        Children:
   382. i.   JOHN WILLIAM "BILLY" GASTON b. Dec- 8-1850.

229. **William Rosborough Gaston**, also known as Rosborough Gaston,[cccxxxiii[333]] (123.Robert[6], 58.Thomas[5], 16.Robert[4], 5.William[3], 3.John[2], 1.Jean[1]), b. Dec-25-1827 near Reidville, Spartanburg Co, SC,[129] d. Nov- -1899,[333] census 1870 in Reidville, Spartanburg Co, SC, occupation physician.[129] He married[129] **Lucy C. Bridwell**, census name Lucie, also known as Lucinda C. Bridwell,[129] b. ca 1855 in South Carolina,[cccxxxiv[334]] d. Aug- -1932,[333] census 1910, 1920, 1930 in Reidville, Spartanburg Co, SC.

1870 Census, Spartanburg Co, South Carolina (Reidville Twp), enumerated on Jun 29 1870: Anthony Wakefield, 57, farmer; James Wakefield, 63, merchant; William Gaston, 41, physician; Elizabeth Gaston, 45, house keeper; Ann Gaston, 78. All born in South Carolina.

In another household, enumerated on Jun 13 1870:
Sally Bridwell, 45; Lucy, 16; Margaret, 13; James, 11; Joseph, 8; Martha Sandling, 25; Sarah Sandling, 9; Ann Sandling, 7; Mary Sandling, 4. All born in South Carolina.
Lucy seems to have been enumerated twice in this census, as she also appears in another household, enumerated on Jun 9 1870:
Wiley Marlin, 20, farmer; Margaret Marlin, 18; Frances Marlin (female), 1; Baby Marlin (male), one month; Lucy Bridwell, 16. All born in South Carolina.

1880 Census, Spartanburg Co, SC (Reidville Twp), enumerated on Jun 17 1880:
Sallie Bridwell, 60, widowed; dau Loucy, 25, single; son James, 22, single; son Joe, 20; dau Georgia, 4. All born in South Carolina.

1910 Census, Spartanburg Co, SC (Reidville Twp), enumerated on May 5 1910:
Lucie Gaston, 56, widowed, mother of 5 children (4 still living); son Belton, 26, single; son Thomas, 20, single. All born in South Carolina.

From "Acts and Joint Resolutions of the General Assembly of the State of South Carolina, Passed at the Regular Session of 1892," p. 118:

No. 65. AN ACT To Declare Georgia Anna Gaston, William Belton Gaston And Lula Geneva Gaston Legitimate Children Of William R. Gaston And Lucy Gaston, And To Enable Them To Inherit From Said Parties.
Section 1. Be it enacted by the Senate and House of Representatives of the State of South Carolina, now met and sitting in General Assembly, and by the authority of the same, That whereas Georgia Anna Gaston, William Belton Gaston and Lula Geneva Gaston are children born to William R. Gaston and Lula [sic] Gaston, and subsequently to their birth the said parents were duly and legally married, and are desirous of having their said issue legitimated, the said Georgia Anna Gaston, William Belton Gaston and Lula Gaston are hereby declared legal heirs as children, of the said William R. Gaston and Lucy Gaston, and shall inherit from them in the same manner as if they had been born in wedlock. Approved December 22nd, A. D. 1892.
<
http://books.google.com/books?id=zLA4AAAAIAAJ&pg=PA118&lpg=PA118#v=onepage&q&f=false
>

Children:
303.   i.   GEORGIA ANNA GASTON b. Jul-19-1875.
384.   ii.   WILLIAM BELTON GASTON b. ca 1884.
        iii. LULA GENEVA GASTON, also known as Geneva Gaston.[129]
385.   iv.   THOMAS ROSBOROUGH GASTON b. ca 1890.

230. **Hamilton Rosborough Gaston** (124.James[6], 58.Thomas[5], 16.Robert[4], 5.William[3], 3.John[2], 1.Jean[1]), b. Feb-10-1811 in South Carolina,[213,146] d. Mar- -1891,[213] census 1870, 1880 in Oconee Co, SC, census 1850, 1860 in Pickens Co, SC, occupation tinner.[146] He married **Mary J. __**, b. Dec- -1821 in South Carolina,[123] census 1870, 1880, 1900 in Oconee Co, SC, census 1850, 1860 in Pickens Co, SC.

1850 Census, Western Division of Pickens District, South Carolina, enumerated on Oct 21 1850:
Hamilton R. Gaston, 39, occupation tinner; Mary J, 29; William, 8; Melissa, 6; Joel R, 4; Elizabeth, 1; Lewis Dawson, 22, occupation apprentice. All born in South Carolina.

1860 Census, 2nd Regiment of Pickens District, South Carolina, enumerated on Jun 23 1860:
H. R. Gaston, 49, farmer; Mary J, 39; Wm J, 18; Malissa A, 16; Joel R P, 14; Henrietta M, 10; Elliott T, 7; Lenora E, 4; Luther G, 2. All born in South Carolina.

1870 Census, Oconee Co (Tugaloo Twp), South Carolina, enumerated in Jul 1870:

H. R. Gaston, 59, farmer; Mary J, 49; M. A. (female), 26; Henrietta, 24; Elliot T, 17; Lenora E, 14; Luther T (or L), 12; Walter S, 9; Anna E, 6; Elwood, 3; black female Jane Gaston, 16, farm laborer. All born in South Carolina.

1880 Census, Oconee Co, (Tugaloo Twp), South Carolina, enumerated on Jun 3 1880:
Hamilton Gaston, 69, farmer; wife Mary, 60; dau Malissa, 30; dau Henrietta, 25; son Luther G, 21; son Walter S, 19; dau Anna E, 15; son Elwood F, 13.

1900 Census, Oconee Co, (Tugaloo Twp), South Carolina, enumerated on Jun 8 1900:
Mary J. Gaston, 79, b. Dec 1821, widow, mother of 8 children (7 still living); dau Hennie M, 49, b. Mar 1851, single; son Luther G, 41, b. Aug 1858, single, farm laborer.

Children:
    i.   WILLIAM J. GASTON b. ca 1842 in South Carolina,[146] d. Civil War,[213] census 1850, 1860 in Pickens Co, SC.
    ii.   MALISSA A. GASTON b. ca 1844 in South Carolina,[146] resided in Westminster, Oconee Co, SC,[cccxxxv[335]] census 1870, 1880, 1900 in Oconee Co, SC, census 1850, 1860 in Pickens Co, SC. She married[335,211] __ Cross, d. bef Apr 1910.[211]
    iii.   JOEL R. P. GASTON b. ca 1846 in South Carolina,[146] d. ca 1868,[cccxxxvi[336]] census 1850, 1860 in Pickens Co, SC.
    iv.   ELIZABETH GASTON b. ca 1849 in South Carolina,[146] d. bef Jun 1860,[280] [She did not appear with the rest of her family in the 1860 Census.].
    v.   HENRIETTA M. GASTON b. Mar- -1851 in South Carolina,[123] d. 1933,[335] census 1870, 80, 1900, 10 in Oconee Co, SC, census 1860 in Pickens Co, SC, never married[335].
    vi.   ELLIOTT T. GASTON b. ca 1853 in South Carolina,[280] d. in California,[335] census 1870 in Oconee Co, SC, census 1860 in Pickens Co, SC, never married[335].
    vii.   LENORA E. GASTON[335] also known as Leonora Gaston,[335] b. ca 1856 in South Carolina,[280] census 1870 in Oconee Co, SC, census 1860 in Pickens Co, SC.
    viii.   LUTHER GOODLETT GASTON[335] b. Aug- -1858 in South Carolina,[123] d. Mar- 7-1933 in Cherokee Co, TX,[cccxxxvii[337]] census 1920 in Jefferson, Marion Co, TX, census 1870, 80, 1900, 10 in Oconee Co, SC, census 1860 in Pickens Co, SC.

    1910 Census, Oconee Co, South Carolina (Tugaloo Twp, Town of Westminster), enumerated on Apr 22 1910:
    Luther G. Gaston, 50, farmer, single; sister Henrietta M. Gaston, 56, single; sister Malissa A. Cross, 60, widow.

    1920 Census, Marion Co, Texas (Town of Jefferson), enumerated on Mar 17 1920:
    L. G. Gaston, 61, b. South Carolina, bottling factory worker; wife Bert, 46, b. South Carolina.

    He married[335] __ Steel.

    ix.   WALTER S. GASTON b. ca 1861 in South Carolina,[209] resided near Tampa, Hillsborough Co, FL,[335] census 1870, 1880 in Oconee Co, SC.
    x.   ANNA E. GASTON[335] b. ca 1864 in South Carolina,[209] census 1870, 1880 in Oconee Co, SC. She married[335] __ Hall, resided in Westminster, Oconee Co, SC.[335]
    xi.   ELWOOD FORREST GASTON b. ca 1867 in South Carolina,[209] d. Jan- 2-1945 in Wichita Co, TX,[cccxxxviii[338]] resided in Wichita Falls, Wichita Co, TX,[335] census 1930 in Wichita Falls, Wichita Co, TX, census 1870, 1880 in Oconee Co, SC, occupation 1930 independent investor.[334]

231. Amzi Williford Gaston (124.James[6], 58.Thomas[5], 16.Robert[4], 5.William[3], 3.John[2], 1.Jean[1]), b. Apr-16-1813 in Spartanburg Co, SC,[cccxxxix[339],214] d. May-18-1841 in Spartanburg Co, SC,[339,214] buried in Nazareth Presbyterian Church Cemetery, Moore, Spartanburg Co, SC.[cccxl[340]] He married Jan-24-1839,[214] **Jane A. Peden**, b. Dec-16-1815 in South Carolina,[339] (daughter of Andrew Peden and Jane

McConnell), d. Oct-13-1893 in Spartanburg Co, SC,[339,340] buried in Nazareth Presbyterian Church Cemetery, Moore, Spartanburg Co, SC,[340] census 1870, 1880 in Reidville, Spartanburg Co, SC, resided originally near Woodruff, Spartanburg Co, SC.[214] Amzi Williford Gaston died the day after his second son, Amzi W. Gaston II, was born. "The young widow continued to live in her home near Duncan for eight years, when death struck again, two-fold -- Jamie Died, and also her mother, Jane McConnell Peden. Then she and Amzi II went to her father's home where she led a long and useful life in her family and community."[340]

Children:
     i.   JAMES ANDREW GASTON b. Oct-13-1839 in South Carolina,[339,335] d. Apr-15-1849,[339,335] buried in Nazareth Presbyterian Church Cemetery, Moore, Spartanburg Co, SC.[339]
386.   ii.   AMZI WILLIFORD GASTON II b. May-17-1841.

232. **Thomas Pinkney Gaston** (124.James[6], 58.Thomas[5], 16.Robert[4], 5.William[3], 3.John[2], 1.Jean[1]), b. Apr-29-1815.[335] He married[335] **Janette Minerva Anderson**, d. Sep-23-1868.[335] Mary Gaston Gee identifies Janette Minerva Anderson as Thomas Pinkney Gaston's first wife, and lists their eight children. But there is no mention made of a second wife. Janette died one month after the birth of their eighth child.[335]

Children:
387.   i.   WILLIAM DENNY GASTON b. Oct-13-1840.
388.   ii.   EDWARD BAXTER GASTON b. Jul-23-1842.
389.   iii.   ANDERSON LEWERS GASTON b. Sep- 9-1845.
390.   iv.   MARY ELIZABETH GASTON b. Oct-16-1847.
     v.   JAMES NEWTON GASTON b. Jun- 9-1854,[335] resided in Texas,[335] never married[335].
     vi.   LAURA ADELINE GASTON b. Dec-22-1856,[335] d. Nov-19-1932,[335] buried in Nazareth Presbyterian Church Cemetery, Moore, Spartanburg Co, SC.[335]
     vii.   OLIVER LAWRENCE GASTON b. Mar-15-1859,[335] d. Mar- 7-1938.[335] He married[214] no children from this marriage,[214] Lucy Grant Bishop.
     viii.   JEANETTE ALICE GASTON b. Aug-22-1868,[214] d. Aug-30-1894,[214] resided in Liberty, Pickens Co, SC.[214] She married[214] no children from this marriage,[214] Hampton Boggs.

233. **Sarah Adeline Gaston** (124.James[6], 58.Thomas[5], 16.Robert[4], 5.William[3], 3.John[2], 1.Jean[1]), b. 1817, d. 1897, resided near Gainesville, Cooke Co, TX,[214] resided previously (aft 1848 -) in Georgia.[214] She married 1848,[214] **John Hawkins**, b. 1813, d. 1897.
Children:
     i.   JANE HAWKINS b. 1849.[214]
     ii.   GEORGIE HAWKINS b. 1852.[214]
391.   iii.   DOCIA HAWKINS b. 1856.
     iv.   BUD HAWKINS b. 1859.[214]

234. **Harvey Gaston** (125.Hugh[6], 58.Thomas[5], 16.Robert[4], 5.William[3], 3.John[2], 1.Jean[1]). He married[129] __ **McElrath**.
Children:
     i.   SAMUEL GASTON.
     ii.   JANE GASTON. She married[129] __ Dobbins, occupation doctor.[129]
     iii.   LINA GASTON. She married[129] Thomas Boyter.
     iv.   LAWRENCE GASTON.

235. **Emily Gaston** (125.Hugh[6], 58.Thomas[5], 16.Robert[4], 5.William[3], 3.John[2], 1.Jean[1]). She married[129] **Tom Wood**.
Children:
     i.   SARAH JANE WOOD.
     ii.   WILLIAM WOOD.

      iii.   JAMES WOOD.
      iv.   NAN WOOD never married[129].
      v.   JOHN WOOD.
      vi.   HARRIETT WOOD never married[129].

236. **Margaret Gaston** (126.Samuel[6], 58.Thomas[5], 16.Robert[4], 5.William[3], 3.John[2], 1.Jean[1]). She married[133] **John Bennett**.
      Children:
      i.   ASHMORE BENNETT d. May-18-1936.[133]
      ii.   LUCRETIA BENNETT.

237. **Parley Clenney Gaston** (127.Thomas[6], 58.Thomas[5], 16.Robert[4], 5.William[3], 3.John[2], 1.Jean[1]), b. Jul-30-1835,[133] d. Jun-18-1891.[215] He married[133] Sep-26-1871,[215] **Margaret Adelaide "Addie" Moore**,[215] b. Dec- 5-1842,[215] d. Mar-12-1924.[215]
      Children:
      i.   BERTHA VIRGINIA GASTON b. Feb-18-1874.[215]
      ii.   MARY GASTON b. Feb-23-1876.[215]
  392. iii.   ELIZABETH LOUISE GASTON b. Jun-25-1879.
      iv.   THOMAS LAWRENCE GASTON b. Jan-31-1881,[215] d. Mar- -1920.[215]

238. **James Bullock Gaston** (128.Robert[6], 60.Hugh[5], 16.Robert[4], 5.William[3], 3.John[2], 1.Jean[1]), b. 1822,[12] d. 1896.[12] He married[12] **Lucinda Ada McConnell**, b. 1827,[12] d. 1896.[12]
      Children:
  393. i.   JAMES MONROE GASTON b. 1864.

239. **Mary White**[151] (132.Frances[6], 69.William[5], 20.William[4], 5.William[3], 3.John[2], 1.Jean[1]). She married[151] **Walter Denny**.
      Children:
      i.   EMILY DENNY b. in West Point, Clay Co, MS.[151]

          Member (No. 39877) of Daughters of the American Revolution.

          She married[151] __ Bloomfield.
      ii.   MARY DENNY b. in Moss Point, Jackson Co, MS.[cccxli[341]]

          Member (No. 39881) of Daughters of the American Revolution.

          She married[341] __ Chamberlin.

240. **Anna Gaston**, also known as Annie Gaston (134.Andrew[6], 72.John[5], 21.John[4], 6.Hugh[3], 3.John[2], 1.Jean[1]), b. 1814 in Harrison Co, (W)VA,[17] d. 1904,[17] buried in Duck Creek Missn Chrch Cem, near West Milford, Harrison Co, WV.[17] She married Oct-26-1843 in Harrison Co, (W)VA,[227] **Benjamin Jones**.
      Children:
      i.   SARAH A. JONES b. ca 1850 in Ohio,[227,276] d. Mar-30-1889 in Kincheloe (Jane Lew), Harrison Co, WV,[cccxliii[342]] buried in Old Bethel Church Cem, Good Hope, Harrison Co, WV,[276] resided from abt 1853 in West Virginia.[276] She married Nov-16-1871 in Harrison Co, WV,[cccliii[343]] William L. Perine, b. ca 1851,[227] (son of Isaac Junior Perine and Nancy Lewis).

241. **Matilda "Tillie" Gaston** (134.Andrew[6], 72.John[5], 21.John[4], 6.Hugh[3], 3.John[2], 1.Jean[1]), b. ca 1818 in Harrison Co, (W)VA,[cccxliv[344],cccxlv[345]] d. 1904 in Doddridge Co, WV,[cccxlvi[346]] buried in West Union, Doddridge Co, WV,[cccxlvii[347]] census 1900 in West Union District, Doddridge Co, WV [in household of son Richard]. She married (1) Aug-27-1840 in Harrison Co, (W)VA,[cccxlviii[348],227] **David L. Perine**, b. ca 1818 in Harrison Co, (W)VA,[cccxlix[349],345] (son of Richard Perine and Julia Ann Tingler), d. Nov-12-1875 in Arnolds Creek (West Union), Doddridge Co, WV,[349,cccl[350]] cause of death killed by log rolling

on him.[347,350] She married[274] (2) Oct- 3-1879 in Doddridge Co, WV,[ccli[351],ccclii[352]] **Robert Willis**,[ccliii[353]] b. Oct- -1800 in Harrison Co, (W)VA,[154,cccliv[354]] (son of William Thomas Willis and Nancy Ann Douglass), d. Feb-29-1888 in Doddridge Co, WV,[ccclv[355],ccclvi[356]] [Minnie Kendall Lowther erroneously reports death as 1886, and birth date as 1799. (HRC, 596)], buried in Oxford, Doddridge Co, WV,[ccclvii[357],ccclviii[358]] resided in Oxford, Doddridge Co, WV,[353] occupation farmer.[357]

Robert: Although Minnie Kendall Lowther lists three marriages for Robert Willis, it appears likely that the first two were one and the same, to Mary Vanhorn in 1852. A previous marriage to a Mary Venort is considered to be incorrect. Doddridge County Marriage Records contain two entries for the same marriage to Mary Vanhorn, which may have led to the confusion.

Children by David L. Perine:
i.   SAMUEL N. PERINE b. ca 1842 in Harrison Co, (W)VA,[344] d. Mar-16-1863 in Braxton Co, WV,[344] military Civil War - Co E, 3rd West Virginia Cavalry.[347]
ii.   JULIA A. PERINE b. Jun-24-1842 in Harrison Co, (W)VA,[ccclix[359],46] d. Dec- 8-1931 in West Union, Doddridge Co, WV,[ccclx[360],354,46] buried in Eddy Cemetery, Miletus, Doddridge Co, WV.[17,344] She married Nov-18-1860 in Harrison Co, (W)VA,[ccclxi[361]] Cain Nicholas, b. 1836 in Pendleton Co, (W)VA,[227,344,46] (son of Francis Nicholas and Barbara __), d. 1916 in Salem, WV,[344,46] buried in Eddy Cemetery, Miletus, Doddridge Co, WV,[17,344] resided 1860 in Doddridge Co, (W)VA.[227]
394.   iii.   ROSETTA PERINE b. Apr-14-1844.
395.   iv.   RICHARD "RICHIE" PERINE b. 1847.
396.   v.   SARAH ANN PERINE b. Feb-12-1850.
397.   vi.   COLUMBUS DAVID PERINE b. Apr- 4-1852.

242. **Frances West** (135.Mary[6], 72.John[5], 21.John[4], 6.Hugh[3], 3.John[2], 1.Jean[1]), b. ca 1803 in Harrison Co, (W)VA,[ccclxii[362],17] d. Sep-14-1880 in Harrison Co, WV,[362,17] buried in Sinclair Cemetery, Upper Duck Crk Rd, Harrison Co, WV,[17,362,230] census 1860 in Harrison Co, (W)VA.[362] She married Sep-24-1835 in Harrison Co, (W)VA,[362] **Isaac Davis**, b. Aug-25-1783 in Fayette Co, PA,[362,ccclxiii[363]] (son of Owen Davis and Hannah James), d. Oct-11-1854 in Harrison Co, (W)VA,[ccclxiv[364],362,ccclxv[365]] [Place of death for Isaac Davis given by researcher Sam D. Lawson, Columbus, IN 47203 <lawson@hsonline.net>, as Crawford Co, PA, but William F. Donnelly, "The Wests of Duck Creek," p. 412, gives it as Harrison Co, (W)VA, citing Harrison County Death Records.], buried in Sinclair Cemetery, Upper Duck Crk Rd, Harrison Co, WV,[17,362,230] census 1850 in Harrison Co, (W)VA,[362] occupation potter, farmer.[365,362]

Isaac: The following is a notation in the back of Isaac Davis' Bible: "Susanna Cassaday, daughter of Felix and Susanna Cassaday, born 20 February 1789, the intended wife if Isaac Davis." [per Sam D. Lawson] When Isaac Davis married Frances West, it was his second marriage. In the 1850 Census of Harrison County, Isaac Davis was described as blind and working as a potter. [William F. Donnelly, p. 412][365,362]

Children:
i.   OWEN VANBUREN DAVIS b. Nov-23-1836 in Harrison Co, (W)VA,[365,362] d. ca 1864 in Civil War,[362] census 1860 in Harrison Co, (W)VA,[362] military Confederate Army,[362] never married[365.]
398.   ii.   HANNAH ALMEDA DAVIS b. Jan- 5-1839.

243. **Ruanna West** (135.Mary[6], 72.John[5], 21.John[4], 6.Hugh[3], 3.John[2], 1.Jean[1]), b. Oct-22-1806 in Duck Creek, Harrison Co, WV,[ccclxvi[366],155] [Birthdate for Ruanna West of Oct 22 1806 based headstone inscription giving death date of Dec 4 1890 and age at death as 84y 1m 12d. But William F. Donnelly (Wests of Duck Creek, p. 412) states her birthdate as Oct 18 1806, citing family Bible entry reported in a May 22 1932 Clarksburg Exponent newspaper article entitled "Bibles Reveal Pioneers."], baptized in Lewis Co, WV,[362] d. Dec- 4-1890 in Harrison Co, WV,[362,17,ccclxvii[367]] buried in Broad Run Bapt Ch Cem, Jane Lew, Lewis Co, WV.[17]

Ruanna West and Watters Smith Jr. were double cousins, in that they were both first cousins once removed (he was the grandson and she was the great-granddaughter of Andrew Davison (b. ca 1730 in NJ)) and also second cousins once removed (he was the great-grandson & she the great-great-granddaughter of John Smith (b. 1699)).

She married Nov- 6-1827 in Harrison Co, (W)VA,[362] [Family Bible reportedly gives marriage date for Ruanna West and Watters Smith Jr. as Nov 6 1829, but William F. Donnelly, citing May 22 1932 Clarksburg Exponent-Telegram newspaper article, states it as Nov 6 1827. Differing still, Omar Davison, Stockton, CA, cites Nov 1 1828.], **Watters Smith, Jr.**, b. Sep- 2-1804 in Duck Creek, Harrison Co, WV,[ccclxviii[368],ccclxix[369],362] (son of Watters Smith and Elizabeth Davison), baptized in Lewis Co, WV,[362] d. Feb-19-1880 in Harrison Co, WV,[362,ccclxx[370]] buried in Broad Run Bapt Ch Cem, Jane Lew, Lewis Co, WV,[17] resided in Harrison Co, WV,[362] occupation Farmer.[362]

Watters: The family of Watters Smith Jr. lived on the farm later owned by Albert McWhorter (kin) in 1971 on Duck Creek near the "new" school house. He was a Confederate sympathizer, although this is disputed by some family members. As Union soldiers arresting him took him away from home, he pulled a silver dollar from his pocket and threw it to his son Edward, who vowed to hold it till his father's safe return. As a prisoner, he was sent to Camp Chase, near Columbus, OH, where he became ill with dysentery. Union neighbors signed a petition for his wife and helped her to get to the camp, where she nursed him back to health. When she was able to bring him home, he weighed only 75 pounds. The silver dollar, dated 1799, has been passed down through the years and remains in the family.[155]

Children:

    i.   SARAH ANN SMITH, also known as Sally Ann Smith,[362] b. May-19-1829 in Harrison Co, (W)VA,[ccclxxi[371],362] d. May-29-1889 in Harrison Co, WV,[362] buried in Broad Run Bapt Ch Cem, Jane Lew, Lewis Co, WV.[17]

    ii.   THOMAS SMITH b. Apr-20-1830 in Harrison Co, (W)VA,[362] d. May-20-1830 in Harrison Co, (W)VA.[362]

    iii.   GILBERT SMITH b. Sep-12-1831 in Harrison Co, (W)VA,[362] d. Nov-25-1831 in Harrison Co, (W)VA.[362]

    iv.   JOHN DAVIDSON SMITH b. Mar-10-1833 in Harrison Co, (W)VA,[362] d. Apr-12-1833 in Harrison Co, (W)VA.[362]

    v.   JAMES SMITH b. Sep- 1-1834 in Harrison Co, (W)VA,[362] d. Oct-22-1834 in Harrison Co, (W)VA.[362]

399.   vi.   WILLIAM (TWIN) SMITH b. Aug- 9-1835.

    vii.   WELLINGTON (TWIN) SMITH b. Aug- 9-1835 in Harrison Co, (W)VA,[362] d. Dec- 8-1841 in Harrison Co, (W)VA.[362]

400.   viii.   MARY ELIZABETH SMITH b. Feb- 3-1838.

401.   ix.   ELIZABETH SMITH b. Mar- 2-1840.

402.   x.   ANDREW JACKSON SMITH b. Apr- 5-1842.

403.   xi.   ELIZA SMITH b. Mar-30-1844.

    xii.   WATTERS SMITH III b. Jul- 7-1846 in Harrison Co, (W)VA,[ccclxxii[372]] d. Sep- 2-1846 in Harrison Co, (W)VA.[372]

    xiii.   VIRGINIA SMITH b. Nov- 4-1849 in Harrison Co, (W)VA,[372] d. Jan- 2-1850 in Harrison Co, (W)VA.[372,ccclxxiii[373]]

404.   xiv.   EDWARD NEWTON SMITH b. Sep-17-1851.

244. Elizabeth "Betsy" West[229] (135.Mary[6], 72.John[5], 21.John[4], 6.Hugh[3], 3.John[2], 1.Jean[1]), b. Oct-13-1809 in Harrison Co, (W)VA,[372] d. Mar- -1892 in Gilmer Co, WV,[372] buried in Coberly Cemetery, Gilmer Co, WV,[372] census 1850 in Harrison Co, (W)VA.[372] She married Jan-25-1835 in Harrison Co, (W)VA,[372] **Daniel M. Coberly**, b. Dec-9-1807 in Harrison Co, VA (now Gilmer Co, WV),[17,372] (son of James Coberly and Letitia "Tisha" Jett), d. Jul- 5-1838 in Harrison Co, (W)VA,[17,372] buried in Sinclair Cemetery, Upper Duck Crk Rd, Harrison Co, WV,[17,372,230] occupation furniture maker and subscription school teacher.[372]

Children:

405.　i.　NATHAN GRANVILLE COBERLY b. Jan-23-1837.

　　　ii.　MARY ANN COBERLY b. Nov- 1-1838 in Harrison Co, (W)VA,[17,372] d. Nov- 1-1838 in Harrison Co, (W)VA,[17,372] buried in Sinclair Cemetery, Upper Duck Crk Rd, Harrison Co, WV.[17,372,230.]

245. **Eli R. West** (135.Mary[6], 72.John[5], 21.John[4], 6.Hugh[3], 3.John[2], 1.Jean[1]), b. Apr- 5-1813 in Harrison Co, (W)VA,[17,372] d. May- 6-1858 in Harrison Co, (W)VA,[17,372] buried in Sinclair Cemetery, Upper Duck Crk Rd, Harrison Co, WV,[17,372,230] census 1850 in Harrison Co, (W)VA,[372] occupation farmer.[372] He married Apr-24-1834 in Harrison Co, (W)VA,[372,227] **Belinda King**, also known as Malinda King,[372,ccclxxiv[374]] also known as Belindy,[17] b. Jun-13-1817 in Harrison Co, (W)VA,[17,372] (daughter of Elijah King and Nancy Hurst), d. Apr- 4-1887 in Harrison Co, WV,[17,372] buried in Sinclair Cemetery, Upper Duck Crk Rd, Harrison Co, WV,[ccclxxv[375],372,230] census 1880 in Grant District, Harrison Co, WV.[372]

Belinda: Recorded in 1880 Census as a widow residing with Samuel and Julia West McIntire.[372]

　　　　　Children:
406.　i.　WILLIAM MARSHALL WEST b. Jun- 9-1835.
407.　ii.　JOHN JACKSON WEST b. Dec- 3-1837.
408.　iii.　MARY LOUISE WEST b. Aug-10-1840.
　　　iv.　FLOYD ALBION WEST b. Jun-14-1843 in Harrison Co, (W)VA,[372] d. Aug- 9-1863 in Staunton, VA,[372] military Private, Co B, 17th Virginia Cavalry.[372]

　　　　　Wounded in battle at Boonesboro, Maryland, on Jul 8 1863. Died in a hospital at Staunton, Virginia, on Aug 9 1863.[372]

409.　v.　SARAH ANN WEST b. Sep-23-1845.
　　　vi.　THOMAS JEFFERSON WEST b. Sep-12-1848 in Harrison Co, (W)VA,[372,ccclxxvi[376]] [Birthdate for Thomas Jefferson West previously reported as Aug 17 1848 (source not documented), but Donnelly (p. 413, citing D. R. Davisson papers) states it as Sep 12 1849. Death record, as reported by Patricia B. Hickman, lists age as 12, but headstone gives age at death on Apr 30 1859 as 10y 7m 18d, which would put birthdate on Sep 12 1848.], d. Apr-30-1859 in Harrison Co, WV,[17] buried in Sinclair Cemetery, Upper Duck Crk Rd, Harrison Co, WV.[17,230]
　　　vii.　VIRGINIA DORR WEST, also known as Virginia Dare West,[372] b. Apr-26-1851 in Harrison Co, (W)VA,[377] d. Mar-25-1908,[372] buried in Big Isaac Cemetery, Doddridge Co, WV.[ccclxxvii[377]] She married May-23-1869 in Harrison Co, WV,[377] Elijah VanBuren King (son of Cornelius King and Nancy Ann Straley).
410.　viii.　JULIA AMANDA WEST b. May-16-1854.
411.　ix.　ELIZA JANE WEST b. Sep-22-1857.

246. **John Hugh Gaston** (136.Hugh[6], 72.John[5], 21.John[4], 6.Hugh[3], 3.John[2], 1.Jean[1]), b. Jul-17-1812 in Harrison Co, (W)VA,[ccclxxviii[378],ccclxxix[379],ccclxxx[380]] buried (unmarked) in Oxford Baptist Church Cemetery, Doddridge Co, WV,[ccclxxxi[381]] [Presumed, based on unmarked grave between headstones of his wife & son Hugh.], census 1870, 1880 in Southwest District, Doddridge Co, WV, census 1850 in Doddridge Co, (W)VA, occupation farmer.[146,ccclxxxii[382]] He married[ccclxxxiii[383]] Feb- 2-1848 in Ritchie Co, (W)VA,[ccclxxxiv[384]] **Mary Jane Pritchard**, also known as Jane Pritchard,[17,345,383,374,382,ccclxxxv[385]] b. Mar- 2-1816 in Virginia,[17,146] (daughter of Thomas Pritchard, Jr. and Mary Moody), d. Nov- 3-1900,[17] buried in Oxford Baptist Church Cemetery, Doddridge Co, WV,[17] census 1880, 1900 in Southwest District, Doddridge Co, WV.

1850 Census, Doddridge County, Virginia (now West Virginia), enumerated on Jul 24 1850:
John Gaston, 37; Jane, 34; Mary E, 6 months.

1880 Census, Doddridge Co, WV (Southwest District), enumerated on Jun 1 1880:

John H. Gaston, 68, farmer; wife Jane, 64; son Hugh, 24, farm worker; brother-in-law William Pritchard, 61, physician. The 1880 Census form contains the following question: "Is the person [on the day of the Enumerator's visit] sick or temporarily disabled, so as to be unable to attend to ordinary business or duties? If so, what is the sickness or disability?" For John H. Gaston, that question was answered with the entry "Epileptic Fits."

Children:
412.   i.   MARY MARTHA GASTON b. Nov-20-1849.
413.   ii.   IVAH JANE GASTON b. Aug- 3-1851.
        iii. C. ANNA GASTON b. Feb-21-1854 at Hughes River, Doddridge Co, WV, d. Nov-17-1854 in Hughes River, Doddridge Co, WV,[ccclxxxvi][386] cause of death scarlet fever.[357]
        iv.   HUGH GASTON b. Apr-26-1856,[17] [Legibility of the weather-worn headstone is poor. Birthdate, though appearing to be Apr 26 1856, could possibly be Apr 28 1858. Inscription reads "Hugh, son of J. H. Gaston, born April 26 1856, died Aug 18 1904."], d. Aug-18-1904,[17] buried in Oxford Baptist Church Cemetery, Doddridge Co, WV,[17] census 1870, 1900 in Southwest District, Doddridge Co, WV.

The 1870 and 1880 Censuses listed him as still living at home with his parents, and the 1900 Census listed him and his mother in the same household as well.

247. **Daniel H. Gaston** (136.Hugh[6], 72.John[5], 21.John[4], 6.Hugh[3], 3.John[2], 1.Jean[1]), b. Jun-27-1816 in Harrison Co, WV, d. Apr-14-1905 in Doddridge Co, WV, buried (unmarked) in Gaston-Hart Cemetery, Upper Run, Summers, Doddridge Co, WV, occupation farmer, Justice of the Peace.[382] He married Jan-21-1840 in Harrison Co, WV,[ccclxxxvii][387] **Nancy Davisson**, b. Jun- 3-1818, d. Aug- 8-1891 in Doddridge Co, WV,[ccclxxxviii][388],356 buried (unmarked) in Gaston-Hart Cemetery, Upper Run, Summers, Doddridge Co, WV. Daniel H. Gaston and his wife Nancy Davisson came to Upper Run in present-day Doddridge County WV in 1843, along with his two brothers, John Hugh and Eli Morris, and their sister Anna M. Gaston. Daniel and Nancy are buried at the Gaston-Hart Cemetery in an unmarked grave beside their son Samuel Eli Gaston.

1850 Census, Doddridge County, Virginia (now West Virginia), enumerated on Jul 24 1850:
Daniel Gaston, 33, farmer; Nancy, 21 (?); Margaret, 6; Sarah A, 4; Susanna, 1; Anna Gaston, 36.

Children:
414.   i.   MARY JANE GASTON b. Sep- 9-1843.
415.   ii.   SARAH ANN GASTON b. Apr-24-1846.
        iii. SUSANNAH GASTON b. ca 1849 in Doddridge Co, WV,[ccclxxxix][389] d. bef Jul 1860.

Susannah Gaston was listed with the family of her father Daniel H. Gaston in the 1850 Census, but in no subsequent census. No other record of her has been found.

416.   iv.   RULINA A. GASTON b. ca 1851.
417.   v.   ELIZABETH LAVERNA GASTON b. Nov- 7-1853.
418.   vi.   NANCY MARIA GASTON b. Jul-22-1856.
        vii. HANNAH E. GASTON b. Jun-24-1859 in Doddridge Co, WV,[cccxc][390] d. Jul- 6-1859 in Doddridge Co, WV.[cccxci][391]

Doddridge County records reflect that Hannah's older sister Sarah died on July 6 1859, at age 12 days, but also that Sarah married in 1865 at age 19. Hannah's birth record shows that she was born on June 24 1859, exactly 12 days before the July 6th date. Also, Sarah was listed in the family of their father Daniel H. Gaston in the 1850 and 1860 Census, but Hannah was never listed in any census. No subsequent record of Hannah has been found. It is clear, then, that it was Hannah who died on July 6th at age 12 days, and the entry of her sister's name was a clerical error.

419.   viii. SAMUEL ELI GASTON b. Aug- -1860.
        ix.   JOHN E. GASTON b. 1863,[357] [Based on age 19 reported at time of death.], d. Nov- 6-
1882 in Doddridge Co, WV.[357],[356]

248. **Eli Morris Gaston** (136.Hugh[6], 72.John[5], 21.John[4], 6.Hugh[3], 3.John[2], 1.Jean[1]), b. Aug- 3-1822 in
Harrison Co, (W)VA,[240] d. Jan-27-1909 in Doddridge Co, WV,[356] [A newspaper memoriam in the West
Union Record of Feb 12 1909 indicated his death date as Jan 28 1909, also reported by family
members. But Doddridge County death records indicate Jan 27 1909.], buried in Gaston Family
Cemetery, Upper Run, Summers, Doddridge Co WV, census 1870, 1880 in Southwest District,
Doddridge Co, WV, census 1850, 1860 in Doddridge Co, (W)VA, occupation minister and farmer.

The Methodist Protestant Church was introduced into Doddridge County, WV by Eli Morris Gaston
and his brother Daniel. These two young men came onto the headwaters of Hughes River in 1843
and purchased several thousand acres of wooded land where they established homes. Eli and his
wife Rulina set up housekeeping in a one-room log cabin on Gaston Run in December 1846. Later
they constructed a two-story log home where they spent their entire married lives. This house
burned down in 1910. In 1846 the Gaston brothers succeeded in having a Methodist Protestant
minister come into the new settlement and preach at Eli's home. Arrangements were made for
regular services, and the people built a log house for school and church services. The new house was
named Harmony because of the fine spirit of harmony and cooperation among the people composing
the new settlement. In 1866 the old log house was replaced by a neat frame building which served
the congregation until 1901, when a large modern house of worship was built. The Reverend
Mortimer Ireland (b. 8/8/1835) was pastor at that time. Charter members included Eli Morris
Gaston and Daniel Gaston and their wives, J. E. Strother and his wife, John Hart and wife, S. M. Gaston
and wife, and Samuel Richards. Others who joined later included R. Husk and wife, Isaac Hileman
and wife, John I. Gaston and wife, T. W. Chapman and wife, J. S. Britton and wife, and George Pierce
and wife. This was considered to be the best congregation of its denomination in Doddridge
County.[ccxcii[392]]

He married Nov-29-1846 in Doddridge Co, (W)VA,[ccxciii[393],ccxciv[394],191] **Rulina A. Lowther**, also
known as Rulina Louthers,[ccxcv[395]] also known as Pauline Lowther,[ccxcvi[396]] b. Aug-12-1825 in
Harrison Co, (W)VA,[240] [Family members give birth date as Aug 12 1826. But Doddridge County
Death Records give age at death on Sep 30 1911 at 86y 1m 18d, putting birth at Aug 12 1825. Also,
1900 Census states her age as 74 and her birth date as Aug 1825. The 1860 Census shows her age as
35, while the 1870 Census has it as 44.], d. Sep-30-1911 in Oxford, Doddridge Co, WV,[ccxcvii[397],356,240]
buried in Gaston Family Cemetery, Upper Run, Summers, Doddridge Co WV, census 1870, 80, 1900,
10 in Southwest District, Doddridge Co, WV [In 1910, identified as Rulina A, mother, in household of
her son Jesse Smith Gaston and his family.], census 1850, 1860 in Doddridge Co, (W)VA.

Rulina: No information regarding the parents of Rulina Lowther has been found. A copy of her
obituary was located, but although it specified her birth as Aug 12 1825 in Harrison County, it made
no mention of parents or siblings. Harrison County in 1825 encompassed a much larger area than it
does now, so her birthplace may actually have been in present-day Doddridge County, which was
created in 1845 from parts of Harrison, Tyler, Ritchie and Lewis Counties. A reference in one
printing of her obituary to her and husband Eli having "20 children" was clearly a typographical
error intended to be "10," as another printing stated that they had "ten children."

The obituary of her son Eli Clark Gaston identified her as Rebecca Lowther, the only time that that
name has been noted and is presumably a misprint intended to be Rulina. Similarly, the original
handwritten death record for her son John Morris Gaston on file at the WV State Archives identifies
his mother as Rulina Lowther, while the corresponding typed death record for him on file in
Harrison County identifies her as Pauline Lowther. Since this was the only time that the name
"Pauline" has been noted in original records, it was presumably a misreading by the typist of
"Rulina" on the original handwritten document. With these two exceptions, all other references to

her are as Rulina. The only reference we have found of her middle initial was in the 1910 Census, which clearly identified her as Rulina A.

Family information sheets completed by her son David Dow Gaston and grandson Ira Dow Gaston identified her as Rulina Lowther, born Aug 12 1825 in Harrison Co, died Sep 30 1911. The space for the names of her parents was left blank on the form filled out by David, while Ira's stated that she was the daughter of "Unknown."

The only photograph we have of her was found among other family photographs.

Three of her grandchildren and one niece were named Rulina.

1850 Census, Doddridge County, Virginia (now West Virginia), enumerated on Jul 24 1850:
Eli M. Gaston, 27, farmer; Rulina, 24; Anna M, 2; Susanna, 7 months; all born in Virginia.

1860 Census, Doddridge County, Virginia (now West Virginia), enumerated on Jul 10 1860:
Eli Gaston, 37, farmer; Ralina Gaston, 35; A. M. Gaston (female), 12; D. H. Gaston (male), 8; J. M. Gaston (male), 6; N. J. Gaston (female), 4; Eli Gaston, 2; J. S. Gaston (male), 1.

1870 Census, Doddridge Co, WV (Southwest Twp):
Eli M. Gaston, 47, farmer; Rhulina, 44; Annie M, 22; Daniel H, 18; John M, 16; Eli, 12; Jesse S, 9; Hannah R, 7; David D, 4; Joseph C, 11 months.

1880 Census, Doddridge Co, WV (Southwest Dist), enumerated in June 1880:
Eli M. Gaston, 57, farmer; wife Rolina, 54; dau Anna M, 32; son Daniel H, 29; son Jesse S, 19; dau Hannah R, 16; son David D, 14; son Eli, 21; son's wife Cassa A, 22; son's dau Rulina M, 4 months (b. Jan).

1900 Census, Doddridge Co, WV (Southwest Dist), enumerated on Jun 18 1900:
Eli M. Gaston, 77, b. Aug 1822 in WV, father b. NJ, mother b. Va, farmer; wife Rulina, 74, b. Aug 1825 in WV, both parents b. Va.; dau Anna M, 52, b. Oct 1847, single; son Jesse S, 39, b. Jun 1860, widowed, farmer; gr-dau Rulina M, 20, b. Jan 1880, single; gr-dau Minnie J, 5, b. Oct 1894; gr-dau Rulina C, 11, b. Apr 1889.

Children:
    i.   ANNA M. GASTON, also known as Annie M. Gaston,[190,cccxcviii[398]] b. Oct-31-1847 in Doddridge Co, (W)VA,[190,398,240] d. Feb-26-1924 in Summers, Doddridge Co, WV,[cccxcix[399],190,cd[400]] buried in Gaston Family Cemetery, Upper Run, Summers, Doddridge Co WV,[398] census 1910 in Southwest District, Doddridge Co, WV [In household with brother Jesse and his family.], never married.
    ii.   SUSANNAH GASTON b. Jan- -1849 in Harrison Co, (W)VA, d. Sep- 7-1854 at Hughes River, Doddridge Co, WV,[cdi[401]] buried in Gaston Family Cemetery, Upper Run, Summers, Doddridge Co WV.
    iii.   DANIEL H. GASTON b. ca 1851 in Doddridge Co, (W)VA,[cdii[402],357] d. Jun-20-1880 in Doddridge Co, WV,[cdiii[403]] census 1870, 1880 in Southwest District, Doddridge Co, WV, census 1860 in Doddridge Co, (W)VA.
420.   iv.   JOHN MORRIS GASTON b. Sep- 4-1853.
    v.   NANCY J. GASTON b. Mar-10-1856 in Doddridge Co, (W)VA,[154] d. Oct- 4-1866 in Doddridge Co, WV,[cdiv[404]] buried in Gaston Family Cemetery, Upper Run, Summers, Doddridge Co WV, cause of death diphtheria.[357]
421.   vi.   ELI CLARK GASTON b. Feb- 1-1858.
422.   vii.   JESSE SMITH GASTON b. Jun-12-1860.
423.   viii.   HANNAH R. GASTON b. Feb- 4-1863.
424.   ix.   DAVID DOW GASTON b. Jul-31-1865.

x.   JOSEPH C. GASTON b. Jun-21-1869 in Doddridge Co, WV, d. Feb-28-1875 in Doddridge Co, WV,[356] buried in Gaston Family Cemetery, Upper Run, Summers, Doddridge Co WV.

249. **Cordelia Gaston**[cdv[405]] census name Credilla, Crevilla, Credellia, Credilia, also known as Caroline Gaston,[396] (136.Hugh[6], 72.John[5], 21.John[4], 6.Hugh[3], 3.John[2], 1.Jean[1]), b. Dec-29-1838 in Lewis Co, (W)VA,[cdvi[406]] d. Mar-30-1919 in Lewis Co, WV,[cdvii[407]] buried in Waldeck Cemetery, Lewis Co, WV,[17] census 1880, 1900, 1910 in Freemans Creek, Lewis Co, WV,[cdviii[408]] census 1870 in Willey District, Lewis Co, WV. She married[407] Apr-22-1855 in Lewis Co, (W)VA,[cdix[409]] ["Gilmer County History 1845-1989," p. 54, gives marriage date as Apr 20 1855.], **John Sherman Butcher**, b. Mar-18-1832 in Lewis Co, (W)VA,[407] (son of Jasper Butcher and Barbara Bush), d. Sep-30-1905 in Sassafras, Camden, Lewis Co, WV,[407] buried in Waldeck Cemetery, Lewis Co, WV,[17] census 1900 in Freemans Creek, Lewis Co, WV.[408] 1870 Census, Willey Twp, Lewis County, WV, enumerated in Sep 1870:
John S. Butcher, 38, farmer; Credilla, 31; John H, 12; James A, 10; George D, 8; Judson R (?), 5; Olive, 1.

1880 Census, Freemans Creek, Lewis County, WV, enumerated on Jun 1 1880:
John S. Butcher, 49, farmer; wife Crevilla, 42 (?); son John H, 22, worker at saw mill; son James A, 18; son George D, 17; son Judson E, 14; dau Olive B, 11; son Hugh D, 8; dau Flora A, 7; dau Etta, 3; dau Alda M, 8 months (b. September).

1900 Census, Freemans Creek, Lewis County, WV, enumerated on Jun 29 1900:
John S. Butcher, 65, b. Mar 1832, married 45 yrs; wife Credellia, 62, b. Dec 1837, mother of 9 children (all still living); dau Branch, 31, b. Nov 1868; dau Flora A., 28, b. Dec 1874 (?); dau Etta, 23, b. Sep 1876; dau Alda M., 20, b. Sep 1880; dau Dona, 14, b. Sep 1885.

1910 Census, Freemans Creek, Lewis County, WV, enumerated on May 2 1910:
Credilia Gaston, 71, widowed, mother of 10 children (all still living); dau Blanche O., 40; dau Flora A., 35; dau Alda M., 28; dau Dona, 24.

Children:
i.   JOHN HENRY BUTCHER[cdx[410]] b. Dec-27-1857 in Lewis Co, WV,[cdxi[411]] d. bef Jun 1940,[cdxii[412]] resided in Salisbury, Wicomico Co, MD,[cdxiii[413]] census 1860 in Lewis Co, (W)VA.[245] He married Aug-18-1884 in Lewis Co, WV,[410] Emma Amanda Dean, b. ca 1859,[410] (daughter of George W. Dean and Mary __).
425.   ii.   JAMES ALVIN BUTCHER b. Oct- 5-1860.
iii.   GEORGE DAVIS BUTCHER b. ca 1863, d. Dec- 6-1926 in Alton, Upshur Co, WV,[cdxiv[414],46] buried in Waldeck Cemetery, Lewis Co, WV,[17] [Death record states Polk Creek Cemetery], resided in Buckhannon, Upshur Co, WV,[413] occupation head sawyer.[398] He married Apr-27-1882 in Lewis Co, WV,[cdxv[415]] Mary Agness Turner, b. ca 1864.[410]
426.   iv.   JUDSON E. BUTCHER b. ca 1865.
v.   OLIVE BLANCHE BUTCHER, also known as Blanche Butcher, b. Nov-13-1868,[17,408] d. May- 4-1911,[17] buried in Waldeck Cemetery, Lewis Co, WV,[17] [Name on headstone reads "Olive B. Butcher," so presumably never married.], census 1900 in Freemans Creek, Lewis Co, WV.[408]
427.   vi.   HUGH D. BUTCHER b. Apr- 1-1870.
vii.   FLORA A. BUTCHER[247] also known as Floda or Flodie,[407,cdxvi[416]] b. Dec-12-1873 in Camden, Lewis Co, WV,[416,cdxvii[417]] d. Jun- -1940 in Weston, Lewis Co, WV,[416] buried in Waldeck Cemetery, Lewis Co, WV,[416] resided in Weston, Lewis Co, WV,[416] census 1900 in Freemans Creek, Lewis Co, WV,[408] occupation nurse,[416] never married[416.]
viii.   ETTA BUTCHER, census name Elta Butcher,[cdxviii[418]] b. Sep- -1876,[408] d. bef Jun 1940,[412] resided in Clarksburg, Harrison Co, WV,[413] census 1920 in Clarksburg, Harrison Co, WV, census 1900 in Freemans Creek, Lewis Co, WV.[408]
ix.   ALDA M. BUTCHER, also known as Aldah,[412] b. Sep- -1879 in Lewis Co, WV,[cdxix[419],247] d. Nov- 8-1960 in Kerr Co, TX,[cdxx[420]] resided 1956 in Kerrville, Kerr Co, TX,[cdxxi[421]] resided 1940 in Texas,[412] census 1930 in Kerrville, Kerr Co, TX, resided 1926 in Weston, Lewis Co, WV,[cdxxii[422]] resided in Clarksburg, Harrison Co, WV.[413,cdxxiii[423]]

1920 Census, Harrison Co, WV (Clark District, city of Clarksburg), enumerated on Jan 5 1920:

Alda Butcher, 40, single, boarding house keeper; sister Elta, 43, single; sister Dona (or Dora), 34, single; sister Sallie, 24, single.

1930 Census, Kerr Co, Texas (town of Kerrville), enumerated on Apr 9 1930:

Alda Evans, 51, b. WVa, widowed; niece Dona Butcher, 44, b. WVa, single; Sallie Butcher, 32, b. WVa, single.

(Note: In view of the relationships given in the 1920 Census, the basis for Dona's relationship being given as niece is not clear. It is also not known exactly how Sallie fits into the family.)

She married[cdxxiv][424] Oct-26-1920 in Clarksburg, Harrison Co, WV,[cdxxv][425] John Wesley Evans, b. ca 1860 in Randolph Co, AL,[419] (son of Joshua R. Evans and Martha E. ___), d. bef Apr 1930,[334] resided 1920 in Bandera, Bandera Co, TX.[419]

    x.   DONA BUTCHER b. 1885 in Lewis Co, WV,[190,408] [Birth date given in obituary as Dec 20 1885, but 1900 Census shows it as Sep 1885.], d. Feb-19-1955 in Kerr Co, TX,[420] buried Glen Rest Cemetery in Kerrville, Kerr Co, TX, resided since 1924 in Kerrville, Kerr Co, TX,[190] census 1930 in Kerrville, Kerr Co, TX, census 1900, 1910 in Freemans Creek, Lewis Co, WV, never married.

250. **Henry Lee Gaston** (136.Hugh[6], 72.John[5], 21.John[4], 6.Hugh[3], 3.John[2], 1.Jean[1]), b. 1841 in Lewis Co, (W)VA,[398,cdxxvi][426] d. Dec-14-1923 in Weston, Lewis Co, WV,[398] buried in Sassafras, Camden, Lewis Co, WV,[398] census 1900 in Center District, Gilmer Co, WV, census 1850, 1860 in Lewis Co, (W)VA,[245] occupation farmer.[cdxxvii][427],398]

On June 1, 1880, Henry Lee Gaston purchased at public auction, for the sum of 94 cents in delinquent taxes, the 21 acre farm of Andrew J. Norman located on the left fork of White Oak Camp Run near Normantown, WV. Henry's grandson Harold Gaston lived there many years later.[cdxxviii][428]

He married May-29-1866 in Lewis Co, WV,[cdxxix][429],242] **Mary Jane Furner**, also known as Mary Jane Turner [The surname "Turner" is frequently found in records pertaining to this family, but "Furner" seems to be the more prevalent form.], b. Jan-28-1846 in Virginia (now West Virginia),[398,74] [Based on age 90y 5m 7d shown on headstone.] (daughter of Jackson Furner and Margarett ___), d. Jul- 5-1936 in Hardman, Gilmer Co, WV,[398,17] buried in Norris Cemetery, Gilmer Co, WV,[17,398] census 1900 in Center District, Gilmer Co, WV.

    Children:

    i.   JOHN E. GASTON b. Mar-21-1867 in Lewis Co, WV, d. Oct-31-1872 in Lewis Co, WV, buried in Meadows Cemetery, Normantown, Gilmer Co, WV.[cdxxx][430]

428.   ii.   WILLIAM ROBERT "BOB" GASTON b. Jul- 7-1868.

429.   iii.   JAMES LLOYD (HUSTON) GASTON b. Sep- 7-1870.

    iv.   EMERETTA GASTON, census name Emaretta Gaston,[247] census name Emma R. Gaston,[cdxxxi][431] b. Jun- -1872 in Lewis Co, WV,[431] d. May-20-1920,[cdxxxii][432] cause of death tuberculosis,[432] census 1900 in Center District, Gilmer Co, WV, never married[432.]

    v.   LUCY BELLE GASTON b. Oct-25-1874, d. aft Sep 1910.[228] She married Nov-29-1899 in Gilmer Co, WV,[cdxxxiii][433],cdxxxiv][434] David D. Norman, b. ca 1865,[434] d. Sep- 9-1910 in Gilmer Co, WV,[432] occupation farmer.[432]

    vi.   OLIVE FLORENCE GASTON[434,432] b. Jul-27-1876 in Camden, Lewis Co, WV,[432] d. Feb-20-1939 in Hardman, Gilmer Co, WV,[432] buried in Norris Cemetery, Gilmer Co, WV,[432] resided in Hardman, Gilmer Co, WV.[432] She married Mar-11-1903 in Gilmer Co, WV,[434] Jennings S. Stalnaker, b. Mar- 2-1872,[432,434] (son of Marcellous Stalnaker and Jarusha Vannoy), d. Jul-18-1941 in Hardman, Gilmer Co, WV,[432] buried in Norris Cemetery, Gilmer Co, WV,[432] occupation farmer.[432]

430.   vii.   NETTA GAY GASTON b. Jun- 2-1881.

431.   viii.   EVA DELL GASTON b. May- -1884.

    ix.   ESTELLA B. GASTON, census name Stella B. Gaston,[431] b. Feb- 5-1888 in Gilmer Co, WV, d. Jan- 7-1936 in Glenville, Gilmer Co, WV,[398,432] buried in Meadows Cemetery, Normantown,

Gilmer Co, WV,[432],[398] census 1900 in Center District, Gilmer Co, WV. She married Nov-23-1913 in Gilmer Co, WV,[cdxxxv][435] Robert Carpenter, b. ca 1883 in Webster Co, WV,[434] d. aft Jan 1936,[cdxxxvi][436] resided 1913 in Gilmer Co, WV.[434]

      432.   x.   EARNEST RAY GASTON b. Jul- 4-1890.

251. **Marion Gaston** (136.Hugh[6], 72.John[5], 21.John[4], 6.Hugh[3], 3.John[2], 1.Jean[1]), b. Jun- 7-1852 in Lewis Co, WV,[398] [Age 96y 5m 28d, stated in death record and on headstone, would put birth date at Jun 4 1852. But death certificate specifies birth date as Jun 7 1852. His death certificate also identifies his mother not as his father's second wife Elizabeth, but as Amanda Washburn, Elizabeth's daughter from a previous marriage to Isaac Washburn. This is consistent with the ages of Elizabeth (51) and Amanda (27) at the time of Marion's birth. Amanda never married, so she presumably remained in the Gaston home. The relationships projected to the public are not known, but since Marion's surname was Gaston, it is assumed that he was raised as the son of Hugh and Elizabeth, with his actual biological mother appearing to others as his stepsister. Stated another way, the Elizabeth Washburn who married Hugh Gaston was born Elizabeth King, she was the widow of Isaac Washburn by whom she had a daughter Amanda, and Marion Gaston, though legally and to all appearances the son of Hugh and Elizabeth, was biologically the son of Hugh and Amanda. Informant for Amanda's death record was listed as her son, not identified by name. Amanda shares a common headstone with her mother Elizabeth and stepfather Hugh.], d. Dec- 2-1948 in Weston, Lewis Co, WV,[cdxxxvii][437],[cdxxxviii][438],[17] buried in Gaston-Henry Cemetery, Sassafras Run, Camden, Lewis Co WV,[17] resided in Weston, Lewis Co, WV,[398] census 1880, 1900 in Freemans Creek District, Lewis Co, WV, occupation farmer, postmaster.[398],[cdxxxix][439]

He was postmaster of Post Office in Aspinall, Lewis Co, WV, in 1888. The Aspinall Post Office was closed in 1907, with service then handled by the Confluence (now Orlando) Post Office.

1880 Census, Lewis Co, WV (Freemans Creek), enumerated on Jun 2 1880:
Marion Gaston, 28, farmer; wife Nancy M, 23; dau Myrtil, 3; (son) Simpson, 8 months.
(Note: Basis for wife's name listed as Nancy is unknown, as both her marriage and death records show it to be Angeline.)

1900 Census, Lewis Co, WV (Freemans Creek District), enumerated on Jun 30 1900:
Marion Gaston, 47, b. Jun 1852, farmer, married 24 yrs; wife Angeline M, 45, b. Dec 1854, mother of 3 children (all still living); son Simpon, 20, b. Sep 1879; son Harvey, 14, b. Jun 1886.[cdxl][440]

He married Jan-5-1876 in Gilmer Co, WV,[cdxli][441] **Angeline M. Keller**, also known as Ellen Kelley,[396] census name Nancy M.,[246] b. Dec-17-1856 in Gilmer Co, WV,[398] (daughter of Franklin Keller and Margaret Hiney), d. Nov- 7-1926 in Weston, Lewis Co, WV,[cdxlii][442],[cdxliii][443] buried in Waldeck Cemetery, Lewis Co, WV,[17],[398] census 1900 in Freemans Creek District, Lewis Co, WV.

Angeline: Maiden name has also been reported as Kelley and Kellar. Obituary (Weston Independent) gave burial in Sassafras Cemetery, and parents being from Gilmer Co, WV. Obituary also gave marriage date as June 6 1876, which is at variance with marriage record of Jan 5 1876. Four surviving brothers were given as residents of Kansas.

          Children:
    433.   i.   MYRTLE GASTON b. Jan-18-1877.
         ii.   J. SIMPSON GASTON, census name Simpon Gaston,[408] b. Sep-21-1879 in Lewis Co, WV,[398] [Death record shows birth date as Sep 21 1879, but headstone reads Sep 22 1879.], d. Jan-16-1957 in Weston, Lewis Co, WV,[398],[cdxliv][444] buried in Gaston-Henry Cemetery, Sassafras Run, Camden, Lewis Co WV,[17],[398] resided in Camden, Lewis Co, WV,[398] census 1900 in Freemans Creek District, Lewis Co, WV, occupation farmer, carpenter.[398]
    434.   iii.   HARVEY L. GASTON b. Jun-28-1886.
    435.   iv.   JOHN MARION GASTON b. Mar-15-1895.

252. **Matthew Maddox** (137.Sarah[6], 72.John[5], 21.John[4], 6.Hugh[3], 3.John[2], 1.Jean[1]), b. Oct- 4-1812 in Harrison Co, (W)VA,[253,17] d. Oct- 4-1863 in Camp Chase, Columbus, OH,[17,cdxiv[445]] [Prisoner of War], buried in Sinclair Cemetery, Upper Duck Crk Rd, Harrison Co, WV,[17,445,230] occupation Baptist Minister, census 1860 in Harrison Co, (W)VA. He married Mar-28-1843,[251] **Mary Emerson**, b. Mar-10-1811 in Ohio,[17,271] d. Sep- 9-1862 in Harrison Co, (W)VA,[17] buried in Sinclair Cemetery, Upper Duck Crk Rd, Harrison Co, WV,[17,230] census 1860 in Harrison Co, (W)VA.

      Children:
      i.   REBECCA MADDOX.

253. **John G. Maddox** (137.Sarah[6], 72.John[5], 21.John[4], 6.Hugh[3], 3.John[2], 1.Jean[1]), b. Jul-20-1814 in Harrison Co, (W)VA,[253] d. Mar-23-1896 in Jackson Co, WV,[253] buried in Grasslick Bapt Ch Cem, Pleasant Valley Rd, Kenna, Jackson Co, WV,[253] resided in Ripley, Jackson Co, WV. He married[cdxlvi[446]] ca 1835,[253] **Elizabeth Hill**, also known as Eliza Hill, b. Sep-22-1821 in Tyler Co, WV,[253] d. Dec- 2-1901 in Jackson Co, WV,[cdxlvii[447]] buried in Grasslick Bapt Ch Cem, Pleasant Valley Rd, Kenna, Jackson Co, WV.[253]

      Children:
   436. i.   MARY ELIZABETH MADDOX b. Jan-15-1844.
   437. ii. ARCHIMEDES ADOLPHUS MADDOX b. ca 1848.
        iii. MARGARET L. MADDOX b. 1851.[253]
        iv. HELEN E. MADDOX b. Jan-23-1857,[253] d. Oct- 2-1878.[253]

254. **Margaret Maddox** (137.Sarah[6], 72.John[5], 21.John[4], 6.Hugh[3], 3.John[2], 1.Jean[1]), b. Aug-15-1817 in Harrison Co, (W)VA,[253] resided in Bens Run, Gilmer Co, WV. She married Nov-24-1842,[cdxlviii[448]] **George Washington Ward**, b. 1820.

      Children:
      i.   MARG F. WARD b. ca 1850,[154] d. Jan-26-1861 in Harrison Co, (W)VA,[276] cause of death diphtheria.[276]
   438. ii. FRANKLIN P. WARD b. ca 1852.

255. **Thomas Maddox** (137.Sarah[6], 72.John[5], 21.John[4], 6.Hugh[3], 3.John[2], 1.Jean[1]), b. Jan- 2-1820 in Harrison Co, (W)VA,[253] d. 1901 in West Virginia,[253] buried in Grasslick Bapt Ch Cem, Pleasant Valley Rd, Kenna, Jackson Co, WV,[253] census 1870, 1880 in Jackson Co, WV, occupation farmer.[cdxlix[449]] He married Oct-26-1846,[253] **Martha Ann Goodwin**, b. Jul-19-1826,[253] d. Oct- 7-1916 in Kenna, Jackson Co, WV,[447] buried in Grasslick Bapt Ch Cem, Pleasant Valley Rd, Kenna, Jackson Co, WV,[253] census 1870, 1880 in Jackson Co, WV.

      Children:
      i.   COLUMBIA A. MADDOX b. 1847.[253] She married[253] Amos Riffle.
      ii. JANE MADDOX b. ca 1848 in Jackson Co, (W)VA,[447] d. Jun-10-1868 in Jackson Co, WV.[447]
      iii. LAVERNA J. MADDOX b. 1849 in Lewis Co, (W)VA,[253,cdl[450]] d. 1879,[253] census 1870 in Jackson Co, WV. She married[253] Feb-10-1878 in Jackson Co, WV,[450] Charles A. Jividen, b. ca 1848 in Putnam Co, (W)VA, resided 1878 in Mason Co, WV.[450]
      iv. SARAH C. MADDOX b. 1851,[253] d. 1924.[253] She married[253] Thomas W. Simmons.
   439. v. FLOURNEY MATTHEW MADDOX b. 1855.
   440. vi. WILLIAM RUFUS MADDOX b. 1857.
      vii. MARY E. MADDOX b. 1860.[253] She married[253] John F. Foglesong.
      viii. HIRAM MADDOX b. 1862 in Jackson Co, WV,[253] d. 1912,[253] census 1880 in Jackson Co, WV. He married[253] Louisa Edwards.
   441. ix. GEORGE G. MADDOX b. Aug- -1864.
      x. THOMAS B. MADDOX b. 1867.[253]

256. **William D. Maddox, Jr.** (137.Sarah[6], 72.John[5], 21.John[4], 6.Hugh[3], 3.John[2], 1.Jean[1]), b. Jan-17-1822 in Harrison Co, (W)VA,[253] d. Jun-21-1906 in Jackson Co, WV,[253] buried in Grasslick Bapt Ch Cem, Pleasant Valley Rd, Kenna, Jackson Co, WV,[253] resided in Jackson Co, WV. He married (1) Nov-30-1843 in Lewis Co, (W)VA,[242] **Emily Stalnaker**, b. 1826. He married[253] (2) Aug-24-1884 in Jackson

Co, WV,[cdli][451] **Rebecca Hickman**, b. ca 1833 in Barbour Co, (W)VA,[450] resided 1884 in Jackson Co, WV.[450]

        Children by Emily Stalnaker:

        i.   MARY L. MADDOX b. 1844, d. 1922. She married __ Thomas.

        ii. SARAH VICTORIA MADDOX b. 1847, d. 1905. She married Martin V. Goodwin.

        iii. WILLIAM U. MADDOX.

        iv. MONTGOMERY H. MADDOX[276,253] also known as Horace M. Maddox, b. Feb- 6-1853,[154] d. Feb- 2-1858 in Harrison Co, (W)VA,[cdlii][452] cause of death pneumonia fever.[276]

442. v.   SUSAN ADALINE MADDOX b. May- -1857.

443. vi. CHARLES GREEN MADDOX b. Feb-16-1858.

        vii. ALBERT M. MADDOX.

257. **James Gaston Maddox** (137.Sarah[6], 72.John[5], 21.John[4], 6.Hugh[3], 3.John[2], 1.Jean[1]), b. Nov-11-1823 in Harrison Co, (W)VA,[253] d. Jan- 3-1901 in Jackson Co, WV,[253] buried in Grasslick Bapt Ch Cem, Pleasant Valley Rd, Kenna, Jackson Co, WV,[253] resided in Jackson Co, WV, occupation Baptist Minister. He married[396] **Flora Ann Hill**, b. Nov- 3-1828,[253] d. Mar-10-1911 in Kenna, Jackson Co, WV,[447] buried in Grasslick Bapt Ch Cem, Pleasant Valley Rd, Kenna, Jackson Co, WV.[253]

        Children:

444. i.   WILLIAM HILL MADDOX b. Mar-28-1850.

445. ii. ALONZO T. MADDOX b. Feb-13-1854.

        iii. MANSFIELD MADDOX b. May-28-1857 in Jackson Co, (W)VA,[154] d. Aug- 8-1889 in Jackson Co, WV,[447] cause of death fever.[447] He married Nancy Belle Parsons, b. 1863, d. 1895.

446. iv. LYCURGUS MADDOX b. Dec- 5-1858.

447. v.   IRVING THOMAS MADDOX b. Jun-12-1863.

258. **Arnold M. Maddox** (137.Sarah[6], 72.John[5], 21.John[4], 6.Hugh[3], 3.John[2], 1.Jean[1]), b. Apr- 8-1829 in Harrison Co, (W)VA,[253,254] d. ca 1879.[254]

The Arnold M. Maddox family moved from Harrison Co, (W)VA to Fauquier Co, VA sometime in the 1860s, probably in concert with Mary Mildred's parents, Jeptha & Catherine Kerns Smith, for both families appeared on the 1870 Census for Fauquier County. The family subsequently moved briefly to Calhoun Co, WV, apparently in concert with Mary Mildred's parents, since both families appeared on the 1880 Census of Calhoun County. It also appears that Arnold Maddox died around this time, specifically between early 1878 and mid-1880, because his last child, William Jeptha, was born in Oct 1878 and Mary Mildred appeared as a widow on the 1880 Census. How long they stayed in Calhoun County in uncertain, but they definitely had returned to Fauquier County by lat 1886, as confirmed by the death records there of two of Mary Mildred's children.[254]

He married May- 2-1861 in Harrison Co, (W)VA,[254] **Mary Mildred Smith**, b. Oct-22-1836 in Fauquier Co, VA,[254] [Marilyn Davis Jones gives birthdate for Mary Mildred Smith as 1826, but the 1836 date is more likely.] (daughter of Jeptha Smith and Catherine Kerns), d. btwn 1900-1910.[254]

        Children:

448. i.   JAMES LEWIS MADDOX b. May-12-1862.

        ii. SARAH C. "SALLIE" MADDOX b. Oct- -1863,[254] [Probably born in Fauquier Co, VA, per Raymond A. Mann.], d. aft 1930 [Probably died in Harrison Co, WV, per Raymond A. Mann.], resided 1910 in Leesburg, Loudoun Co, VA.[cdliii][453] She married 1895,[254] Phillip Houser, also known as Phillip Howser,[254] d. btwn 1900-1910.[453]

        iii. MATTHEW ARNOLD MADDOX b. Apr-16-1866 in Fauquier Co, VA,[254] d. Sep-29-1889 in Fauquier Co, VA,[254] cause of death Typhoid fever.[254]

        Records indicate that he was married at the time of his death, but identity of wife has not been determined.[254]

iv. MARTHA ELIZABETH MADDOX b. Jan-14-1868 in Loudoun Co, VA,[254] d. Sep-25-1886 in Fauquier Co, VA,[254] cause of death Typhoid fever,[254] never married[254]

449. v. FANNIE V. MADDOX b. ca 1870.

vi. ELLIE MADDOX d. in infancy.[254]

vii. NANCY "NANNIE" BELL MADDOX b. Oct- -1872,[254] [Place of birth probably Fauquier Co, VA, per Raymond A. Mann], d. aft 1930,[254] [Place of death probably Harrison Co, WV, per Raymond A. Mann], never married[254]

viii. LUCY J. MADDOX b. ca 1875,[254] d. Jul-29-1877 in Fauquier Co, VA,[254] cause of death whooping cough.[254]

ix. HENRY T. MADDOX b. Jul-11-1877 in Fauquier Co, VA,[254] d. Dec- 1-1877 in Fauquier Co, VA.[254]

x. WILLIAM JEPTHA MADDOX b. Oct- -1878,[254] [Place of birth probably Fauquier Co, VA, per Raymond A. Mann.], d. aft 1930 in Harrison Co, WV,[254] never married[254]

259. **Anna Maddox** (137.Sarah[6], 72.John[5], 21.John[4], 6.Hugh[3], 3.John[2], 1.Jean[1]), b. Sep-19-1831 in Harrison Co, (W)VA,[17] d. 1917,[46] buried in Sinclair Cemetery, Upper Duck Crk Rd, Harrison Co, WV.[17] She married **Hiram Thomas Sinclair**, b. 1823,[46] d. Jan-18-1889,[46] buried in Sinclair Cemetery, Upper Duck Crk Rd, Harrison Co, WV.[17]

Children:

i. DIORA B. SINCLAIR b. 1855.[cdliv[454]]

ii. CHARLES PORTER SINCLAIR b. 1857,[454] d. Oct-12-1895.

iii. FANNIE SINCLAIR b. 1860.[454]

iv. CARY A. SINCLAIR b. 1864.[454]

v. JAMES A. SINCLAIR b. 1868,[17] d. 1890,[17] buried in Sinclair Cemetery, Upper Duck Crk Rd, Harrison Co, WV.[17]

vi. GEORGE R. SINCLAIR b. 1873.[454]

260. **Ruhama Maddox** (137.Sarah[6], 72.John[5], 21.John[4], 6.Hugh[3], 3.John[2], 1.Jean[1]), b. Aug-26-1833 at Duck Creek, Harrison Co, (W)VA,[cdlv[455],cdlvi[456],396] d. Jan-26-1909 in Harrison Co, WV,[456] buried in Sheets Mill (Old West) Cemetery, West Milford, Harrison Co, WV,[cdlvii[457]] resided in West Milford, Harrison Co, WV. She married Sep- 5-1850 in Harrison Co, (W)VA,[456] **Jefferson Bowell West**, b. Sep-26-1826 in Smithfield, Fayette Co, PA,[456,396] (son of Nathaniel "Natty" West and Mary Everly), d. Feb-12-1902 in Harrison Co, WV,[456,17] buried in Sheets Mill (Old West) Cemetery, West Milford, Harrison Co, WV,[456] occupation farmer.[457]

1900 Census, Harrison Co, WV (Grant District), enumerated on Jun 16 1900:
Jefferson B. West, 73, b. Sep 1826 in Pennsylvania, farmer, married 49 yrs; wife Ruhama, 66, b. Aug 1833 in WVa, mother of 13 children (12 still living); son James M, 48, b. Jun 1851, house carpenter, single; dau Mary V, 44, b. Sep 1855, single; dau Emma F, 30, b. Mar 1870, dress maker, single; son Arther E, 26, b. Jul 1873, farmer, single; dau Hattie O, 21, b. Feb 1879; grandson Madison W. Manley, 7, b. Jun 1892.
(Note: Grandson Madison Manley was also enumerated in this census with his parents, Richard & Laura West Manley, in Fairmont District of Marion Co, WV.)

1910 Census, Harrison Co, WV (Grant District), enumerated on May 6 1910:
James M. West, 59, carpenter, single; sister Jennie M. West, 54, single; brother Judson L. West, 41, farmer, widowed; brother Arthur E, 36, farm laborer, single; sister Hattie D. (?) West, 31, single; niece Gladys L. West, 3.

1920 Census, Harrison Co, WV (Grant District), enumerated on Jan 2 1920:
Arthur E. West, 46, farmer, single; brother James M. West, 68, farm laborer, single; brother Judson L. West, 51, farm laborer, single; sister Mary V. West, 68, single; sister Hattie O. West, 40, single; niece Gladys L. West, 13.

Children:

i.   JAMES MADISON WEST b. Jun-26-1851 in West Milford, Harrison Co, (W)VA,[398] d. Oct- 6-1927 near Lost Creek, Harrison Co, WV,[398] buried in Sheets Mill (Old West) Cemetery, West Milford, Harrison Co, WV,[456] census 1910, 1920 in Grant District, Harrison Co, WV, occupation carpenter,[398] never married[398].

450.   ii.   WILLIAM JACKSON WEST b. May-10-1853.

iii.   MARY VIRGINIA "JENNIE" WEST, census name Jennie M. West,[cdlviii[458]] b. Aug-13-1855 in West Milford, Harrison Co, (W)VA,[cdlix[459]] d. Sep- 1-1929 in West Milford, Harrison Co, WV,[398,456] buried in Sheets Mill (Old West) Cemetery, West Milford, Harrison Co, WV,[456] never married[398] census 1910, 1920.

iv.   BELL JANE WEST b. Aug-19-1857 in Harrison Co, WV,[456] d. Nov-24-1861 in Harrison Co, WV.[456]

v.   CHARLES HOWARD WEST b. May-14-1859 in Harrison Co, WV,[456,cdlx[460]] d. Oct-16-1937 in Harrison Co, WV,[456] buried in Elkview Masonic Cemetery, Clarksburg, Harrison Co, WV,[cdlxi[461],cdlxii[462]] census 1910, 1920 in Clark District, Harrison Co, WV, census 1900 in Moundsville, Marshall Co, WV, resided 1887 in Marshall Co, WV,[cdlxiii[463]] occupation 1920 bank watchman,[418] occupation 1910 laborer in box factory,[458] occupation 1900 laborer in mill.[460] He married[461] (1) Dec-29-1887 in Moundsville, Marshall Co, WV,[463] no children from this marriage,[460] Diana Linn, b. Jul- -1865 in Marshall Co, WV,[460,463] (daughter of Andrew Linn and Mary __), census 1900 in Moundsville, Marshall Co, WV, resided 1887 in Marshall Co, WV,[463] occupation dress maker.[460] He married (2) Jan-30-1907 in Ohio,[456] Mary E. Shelhammer, b. ca 1865 in Ohio,[458] d. Oct- 1-1954,[462] buried in Elkview Masonic Cemetery, Clarksburg, Harrison Co, WV,[462] census 1910, 1920 in Clark District, Harrison Co, WV.

451.   vi.   AMBROSE JEFFERSON WEST b. Oct-24-1861.
452.   vii.   LAURA ALICE WEST b. Mar-28-1864.
453.   viii.   HIRAM THOMAS WEST b. Mar-15-1866.
454.   ix.   JUDSON LEE WEST b. Jul- 7-1868.

x.   EMMA FRANCES WEST b. Mar-25-1870 in Harrison Co, WV,[cdlxiv[464]] d. Feb-13-1911 in West Milford, Harrison Co, WV,[464] buried in Sheets Mill (Old West) Cemetery, West Milford, Harrison Co, WV,[464] census 1910 in Grant District, Harrison Co, WV. She married[461] Sep- 1-1901 in West Milford, Harrison Co, WV,[cdlxv[465]] James Warner Kerby, also known as James Warner Kirby,[419] b. ca 1875 in Harrison Co, OH,[419] (son of James F. Kerby and Lyda Jeannie __), resided 1914 in Clarksburg, Harrison Co, WV,[419] census 1910 in Grant District, Harrison Co, WV, resided 1901 in Harrison Co, WV,[419] occupation clergyman.[458]

James: Name spelled Kerby in 1901 marriage record and 1910 Census, but Kirby in 1914 marriage record.

xi.   ARTHUR ERNEST WEST b. Jul- 3-1873 in Harrison Co, WV,[cdlxvi[466],cdlxvii[467]] d. May-21-1929 in West Milford, Harrison Co, WV,[398] buried in Sheets Mill (Old West) Cemetery, West Milford, Harrison Co, WV,[464] resided 1927 near Lost Creek, Harrison Co, WV,[422] census 1900, 1910, 1920 in Grant District, Harrison Co, WV, occupation farmer,[398] never married[398].

455.   xii.   IDA MAE WEST b. Feb- 2-1876.

xiii.   HATTIE ODESSA WEST b. Feb- 8-1879 in Harrison Co, WV,[464,454] [Birth date given in death record as Feb 8 1878, but 1900 Census states birth date as Feb 1879.], d. Aug-13-1963 in Clarksburg, Harrison Co, WV,[276,464] buried in Sheets Mill (Old West) Cemetery, West Milford, Harrison Co, WV,[464,276] resided 1936 in West Milford, Harrison Co, WV,[228] never married[276].

261. **Anna Clayton** (138.Margaret[6], 72.John[5], 21.John[4], 6.Hugh[3], 3.John[2], 1.Jean[1]), b. 1813. She married Oct-26-1831, **James Fleming**, b. ca 1811, d. 1850.
        Children:
        i.   MARY FLEMING b. 1834.
456.   ii.   MARGARET FLEMING b. 1841.
        iii.   SARAH FLEMING b. 1843.

262. **Deborah Clayton** (138.Margaret[6], 72.John[5], 21.John[4], 6.Hugh[3], 3.John[2], 1.Jean[1]), b. 1817. She married 1842, **Charles Seiwell**, b. 1810, d. 1872.
    Children:
    i.   FRED R. SEIWELL b. 1841.

          Two sons, one daughter.

          He married 1863, Frances C. Kuhy.
    ii.   MARY A. SEIWELL b. Jan- 2-1844, christened (9 Children). She married Feb-23-1863, Bennett Bailey.

263. **John Clayton** (138.Margaret[6], 72.John[5], 21.John[4], 6.Hugh[3], 3.John[2], 1.Jean[1]), b. Jan-15-1820, d. Nov-3-1867. He married Jun-10-1841, **Elizabeth Ann Hawkins**, b. Aug-13-1817, d. Jun- 7-1894.
    Children:
    i.   SARAH C. CLAYTON b. 1842. She married 1862, John B. Lowry.
    ii.   WILLIAM HENRY CLAYTON b. Jun-25-1844, d. 1907. He married Sarah E. Cline.
    iii. JOHN C. CLAYTON b. Apr-15-1846, d. Aug- 3-1861.
    iv.   MARY E. CLAYTON b. 1848.
    v.   JOSEPHINE CLAYTON b. May-29-1850, d. Jun- 1-1850.
    vi.   THOMAS A. CLAYTON b. Mar-16-1852, d. Aug-19-1852.
    vii. FLORENCE IRENE CLAYTON b. 1853. She married Dec-28-1871, Frank F. Dayo.

264. **Mary Jane Gaston**, also known as Betty,[345] (139.John[6], 72.John[5], 21.John[4], 6.Hugh[3], 3.John[2], 1.Jean[1]), b. Jun-23-1823 in Harrison Co, (W)VA,[cdlxviii[468]] d. Dec-18-1908,[17] buried in Auburn Community Cemetery, Ritchie Co, WV,[cdlxix[469],cdlxx[470]] resided in Bone Creek, near Auburn, Ritchie Co, WV,[468] resided formerly in Harrison Co, (W)VA.[468] She married Dec-17-1840 in Harrison Co, (W)VA,[468,227] **Martin Carr Ward**, b. Aug- 1-1821 in Harrison Co, (W)VA,[468] (son of William Ward and Sarah Shobe), d. Mar- 8-1897,[470] buried in Auburn Community Cemetery, Ritchie Co, WV.[469,470] "[Mary Jane Gaston and husband Martin Ward] came to Bone Creek [about 1842]. Mrs. Ward rode on horseback through the forest, with her babe in her arms, and her ten-year old sister behind her. Mr. Ward cleared three hundred acres in Union District, and marvelous were the changes their hands helped to bring about.... When they came to Bone Creek there was but few families there, and no other pioneers had longer connection or were held in higher esteem."[cdlxxi[471]]

          Children:
    i.   SARAH ELIZABETH WARD b. Dec-10-1841,[470] d. Jan-20-1855,[470] buried in Auburn Community Cemetery, Ritchie Co, WV.[469]
    ii.   JOHN J. "JASPER" WARD, also known as Jasper Ward,[cdlxxii[472]] b. Oct-11-1843.[470] He married Nov- 1-1864 in Ritchie Co, WV,[cdlxxiii[473]] [Minnie Kendall Lowther (p. 316) reports marriage date as Nov 3 1864.], Martha A. Bond, b. Jul- 3-1844 in Ritchie Co, (W)VA,[472,473] (daughter of Richard E. Bond and Emaline Davis), d. 1931,[472] resided originally in Colorado.[470]
    457. iii. ANNA M. WARD b. Dec- 2-1845.
    iv.   WILLIAM W. WARD b. Feb-29-1848,[470] [But age 17y1m23d on headstone would put birthdate at Feb 20 1848.], d. Apr-12-1865 in Harrisville, Ritchie Co, WV,[470] [Killed while on guard duty.], buried in Auburn Community Cemetery, Ritchie Co, WV.[469]
    v.   LEWIS M. WARD b. Mar-17-1850,[469] ["Ritchie County in History and Romance," p. 316, reports dates for Lewis M. Ward as Mar 14 1850 to Jun 25 1855. But "Ritchie County Cemeteries" reports death date on headstone as Jan 28 1855, at age 4y10m11d, which would put birth date at Mar 17 1850.], d. Jan-28-1855,[469] buried in Auburn Community Cemetery, Ritchie Co, WV.[469]
    458. vi. THOMAS FLOYD WARD b. Mar- 4-1852.
    vii. AMANDA VICTORIA WARD b. Dec- 7-1853,[398,470] d. May-25-1938 in Auburn, Ritchie Co, WV,[398] buried in Auburn Community Cemetery, Ritchie Co, WV,[398] resided in Auburn, Ritchie Co, WV.[398] She married Apr- 8-1877 in Ritchie Co, WV,[473,470] John Townsend Hall, also known as John

Town Hall, b. ca 1855,[473] (son of Elisha M. Hall and Tacy Jane Jeffrey), d. bef May 1938,[436] resided in Auburn, Ritchie Co, WV.[470]

    459.   viii. ELIZA J. WARD b. Jan-29-1856.
    460.   ix. CHARLES ALVIN WARD b. 1858.
    461.   x. CALVIN B. WARD b. May-18-1860.
           xi. SMITH A. WARD b. Nov-30-1862,[470] d. Feb-25-1899.[470] He married Nov- 8-1893,[470] Lilly Delle Thomas, d. 1936 in Parkersburg, Wood Co, WV.[470]

        Lilly: After the death of husband Smith Ward, Lilly married Laban Bush and resided at the Ward homestead below Auburn for years.[470]

           xii. ALBERT M. WARD b. Jan-15-1866 in Auburn, Ritchie Co, WV,[470,cdlxxiv[474],398] d. May- 1-1950 in Auburn, Ritchie Co, WV,[474,cdlxxv[475]] buried in Auburn Community Cemetery, Ritchie Co, WV,[398,469] resided in Auburn, Ritchie Co, WV,[398] occupation farmer.[398] He married Apr-18-1895 in Ritchie Co, WV,[470,cdlxxvi[476]] Flora Bell Wade, b. Mar- 2-1877 in Berea, Ritchie Co, WV,[469,cdlxxvii[477],cdlxxviii[478]] (daughter of Andrew Montgomery Wade and Sally Catherine Bee), d. Dec-26-1960 in Ritchie Co, WV,[cdlxxix[479]] buried in Auburn Community Cemetery, Ritchie Co, WV,[469] resided in Auburn, Ritchie Co, WV.[470]

        Flora: She was known for her home-baked ammonia cookies.[cdlxxx[480]]

265. **Samuel Morris Gaston** (139.John[6], 72.John[5], 21.John[4], 6.Hugh[3], 3.John[2], 1.Jean[1]), b. Feb-25-1825 in Lost Creek, Harrison Co, (W)VA,[190,227,345] [Obituary states birth date as Feb 25 1825. But headstone has birth on Feb 18 1825. And obituary gives age at death as 86y 3m 8d, which would put birth at Jan 18 1825.], d. Apr-26-1911 in Oxford, Doddridge Co, WV,[190,17,cdlxxxi[481],191] buried in Gaston-Hart Cemetery, Upper Run, Summers, Doddridge Co, WV,[cdlxxxii[482],cdlxxxiii[483]] census 1900 in Southwest District, Doddridge Co, WV, census 1850 in Doddridge Co, (W)VA.

Samuel Morris Gaston and his brother John Smith Gaston left Harrison Co, WV in early 1847 and moved to Doddridge County. They bought property from their cousins, John Hugh, Eli and Daniel Gaston, who had come to Doddridge a few years before. They cleared land and built their homes on Camp Run, near Oxford.

1850 Census, Doddridge County, Virginia (now West Virginia), enumerated on Jul 24 1850:
Samuel M. Gaston, 25, farmer; Elizabeth, 25; Mary A, 2.

1870 Census, Doddridge Co, WV (Southwest District):
Samuel M. Gaston, 45, farmer; Elizabeth, 45; Sarah J, 17; Susan, 14; Hannah E, 14; Columbia, 9; Morris S, 7; Martha E, 5.

1900 Census, Doddridge Co, WV (Southwest District):
S. M. Gaston, 75, b. Feb 1825, married 16 yrs; wife Rebecca Jane, 60, b. Jan 1840 in Virginia, both parents b. in Maryland, married 16 yrs, no children; grandson James M. Jones, 14, b. Mar 1886; grandson Howard H. Jones, 11, b. Jan 1889; grandson Samuel Boyd Reed, 20, b. Apr 1880.

1910 Census, Doddridge Co, WV (Southwest District), enumerated on Apr 26 1910:
Morrison S. Gaskins (sic), 85, farmer, married 26 yrs (3rd marriage); wife Rebecca J, 70, married 26 yrs (2nd marriage), no children; grandson Ernest E, 22, single.

He married (1) Sep-3-1846 in Harrison Co, (W)VA,[227,cdlxxxiv[484]] **Elizabeth Law**, b. Apr-17-1825 in Bristol, Harrison Co, (W)VA,[17,345] (daughter of William Law and Hannah Sills), d. Feb-27-1882 in Doddridge Co, WV,[17] buried in Gaston-Hart Cemetery, Upper Run, Summers, Doddridge Co,

WV.[cdlxxxv[485]] He married (2) Nov-6-1883 in Harrison Co, WV,[cdlxxxvi[486],227,191] **Rebecca Jane Furner**, b. Jan-22-1840 in Loudoun Co, VA,[190,227,cdlxxxvii[487],17] (daughter of John Furner and Sarah __), d. Nov-21-1922 at Camp Run, Oxford, Doddridge Co, WV,[190,398,17] buried in Gaston-Hart Cemetery, Upper Run, Summers, Doddridge Co, WV.[17,398]

Rebecca: When she was six months of age, her parents (not identified in her obituary) emigrated from Loudoun County, Virginia "to Harrison County, Virginia, now West Virginia, making the entire trip across the mountains to their new home carrying all their earthly possessions on horseback. ... Her early life was spent in instructing the youths of Harrison County, having devoted twenty-five years to teaching." Upon her marriage in 1883, she moved to Camp Run, Doddridge Co, where she lived the remainder of her life. "She had no children of her own, but was a mother to two of her step-grandsons, who she took almost in their infancy and reared to manhood. ... She has been an invalid for a number of years and helpless for he last six months of her life. While stricken with paralysis, suffering continuously, she never complained of her physical situation but was cheerful and expressed herself as sustained and soothed by an unfaltering trust ...."

1920 Census, Doddridge County, WV (Southwest District), enumerated on Jan 16 1920: Head of household: Rebecca J. Gaston, 79, widowed, b. Virginia, both parents b. Maryland; the only other member of the household was listed as a servant, Elizabeth J. Woofter, 64, married, b. W.Va, both parents b. W.Va. (Elizabeth was the niece of Rebecca's late husband.)[190]

                 Children by Elizabeth Law:
         i.   MARY ANN GASTON b. Nov- 6-1847 in Doddridge Co, (W)VA,[cdlxxxviii[488]] d. Mar-22-1855 in Doddridge Co, (W)VA,[cdlxxxix[489],17] cause of death scarlet fever,[357] buried in Gaston-Hart Cemetery, Upper Run, Summers, Doddridge Co, WV.[17]
         ii.   REBECCA GASTON b. Apr-29-1849,[cdxc[490]] d. Apr-29-1849, buried in Gaston-Hart Cemetery, Upper Run, Summers, Doddridge Co, WV.[17]
   462.   iii. ELIZABETH LUCINDA GASTON b. Jun-16-1850.
   463.   iv. SARAH JANE GASTON b. Mar-29-1853.
   464.   v.   SUSAN GASTON b. Jan- 6-1856.
   465.   vi. HANNAH ELIZABETH GASTON b. Jul- 6-1858.
   466.   vii. COLUMBIA GASTON b. Feb-15-1861.
   467.   viii. MORRIS SAMUEL GASTON b. Feb- 9-1863.
         ix.   MARTHA EMALINE GASTON b. Feb-28-1865 in Doddridge Co, WV,[cdxci[491]] d. Feb- 6-1871,[cdxcii[492]] buried in Gaston-Hart Cemetery, Upper Run, Summers, Doddridge Co, WV.[17]

266. **Deborah Gaston** (139.John[6], 72.John[5], 21.John[4], 6.Hugh[3], 3.John[2], 1.Jean[1]), b. May-17-1827 in Duck Creek, Harrison Co, WV,[373] d. Feb-24-1916 in Lawford, Ritchie Co, WV, buried in Lawford Cemetery, Ritchie Co, WV,[469] resided in Ritchie Co, WV,[473] census 1880, 1910 in Union District, Ritchie Co, WV [In household of son Martin Luther Law.]. She married (1) Oct-23-1845 in Harrison Co, (W)VA,[227] **Asby Poole Law**, also known as Ashby Poole Law, b. Apr- 7-1823 (son of William Law and Hannah Sills), d. Feb-20-1868,[cdxciii[493],cdxciv[494]] buried in Lawford Cemetery, Ritchie Co, WV,[469] occupation Methodist Minister. Reports of two additonal children for this family, Caroline and Asby S, are incorrect. They were actually a daughter-in-law and grandson.

1850 Census, Ritchie Co, Virginia (now West Virginia), enumerated on Aug 28 1850: Asby P. Law, 27, farmer; Deborah, 23; John W, 3; Francis M, 1.

1860 Census, Ritchie Co, Virginia (now West Virginia), enumerated on Aug 25 1860: Asby P. Law, 37, farmer; Deborah, 33; John W, 14; Francis M, 12; Hannah, 10; David G, 8; Elizabeth, 5; Martin L, 2; Levi M, 1.

1870 Census, Ritchie Co, WV (Union Twp), enumerated on Jun 16 1870:

Deborah Law, 43; Hannah, 19; David G, 17; Elizabeth, 14; Martin Luther, 12; Levi M, 10; Newton, 8; Willie, 5.

1880 Census, Ritchie Co, WV (Union District), enumerated on Jun 16 1880:
Deborah Law, 53, widow; dau Elisabeth, 24, single; son Levi Morris, 20, single; son Newton, 18, single; son Willie, 15.
(Note: In this census, Deborah's widowed daughter-in-law Caroline and grandson Asby are found living in Harrison County with Deborah's parents John & Elizabeth (Morris) Gaston.)

The 1910 Census of Ritchie County, listing Deborah Bartlette (sic) as a widow in the household of son Martin, indicates that she was the mother of 10 children, 8 of whom were still living at the time of the census.

She married (2) Jan-28-1883 in Ritchie Co, WV,[cdxcv][495] **Phineas W. Bartlett**, b. ca 1818 in Harrison Co, (W)VA,[473] resided 1883 in Barbour Co, WV.[473]

                    Children by Asby Poole Law:

468.	i.	JOHN WILLIAM LAW b. Aug- -1846.
469.	ii.	FRANCIS MARION LAW b. Sep-15-1848.
470.	iii.	HANNAH LAW b. Nov- 9-1850.
471.	iv.	DAVID GUTHRIE LAW b. Apr- 3-1853.
472.	v.	ELIZABETH LAW b. Jul- 6-1855.
473.	vi.	MARTIN LUTHER LAW b. Jan- 2-1858.
474.	vii.	LEVI MORRIS LAW b. Apr-19-1860.
475.	viii.	NEWTON LAW b. Feb- -1862.
476.	ix.	WILLIAM F. E. "WILLY" LAW b. Sep-17-1864.
	x.	THOMAS SHERMAN LAW b. Nov-18-1866 in Ritchie Co, WV,[74] d. May- 7-1868 in

Ritchie Co, WV,[17,cdxcvi][496] buried in Lawford Cemetery, Ritchie Co, WV.[469]

267. **Susan Gaston** (139.John[6], 72.John[5], 21.John[4], 6.Hugh[3], 3.John[2], 1.Jean[1]), b. 1829,[cdxcvii][497] ["Ritchie County in History and Romance," p. 309, reports her birth as 1829, while "Ritchie County Cemeteries," p. 494, reports it as Apr 27 1827. This, however, conflicts with the May 1827 birth date of a sibling. Age 51 in 1880 Census would also put birth in about 1829.], d. Jul-14-1883 in Otterslide, Ritchie Co, WV,[497,469] buried in Auburn Community Cemetery, Ritchie Co, WV,[469] census 1880 in Union District, Ritchie Co, WV, census 1850, 1860 in Ritchie Co, (W)VA. She married[497] Oct-22-1849, **Martin S. Sommerville**, b. 1828,[497] (son of Robert Sommerville and Mary "Polly" Ward), d. bef Jun 1880 in Otterslide, Ritchie Co, WV,[497] [Wife's marital status listed as widowed in 1880 Census.], buried in Auburn Community Cemetery, Ritchie Co, WV,[497] census 1850, 1860 in Ritchie Co, (W)VA.

Martin: In 1834, Martin Sommerville's father, Robert, was the first settler at Bone Creek, near Auburn in Ritchie County. The creek took its name from a bone lick there. Robert's father, James Simmeral, as the name was originally until corrupted through some errors, came from Cork, Ireland, via Delaware and Maryland to Harrison County, Virginia, where Robert was born on May 1, 1800.[497] Martin and Susan Gaston Sommerville "made their pioneer settlement on the Town Hall Farm below Auburn, and after a brief stay there, they removed to Otterslide, where they lived and died on the farm that fell heir to their son, Robert C. Sommerville, and his heirs."

"Ritchie County in History and Romance," p. 309, reports that Martin and Susan had a daughter Elizabeth, who married a Netz (probably intended to be Nitz). But Elizabeth does not appear in any census, and no other record of her has been found.

1850 Census, Ritchie Co, Virginia (now West Virginia), enumerated on Aug 29 1850:
Martin Sommerville, 22, farmer; Susan, 21.
The adjacent household was that of Martin's parents and their remaining children.

1860 Census, Ritchie Co, Virginia (now West Virginia), enumerated on Aug 22 1860:

Martin S. Sommerville, 32, farmer; Susan, 32; John A T, 10; Robert O, 8; Charles I, 6; Mary E, 4; Sarah O, 2.

1870 Census, Ritchie Co, WV (Union District), enumerated on Jun 30 1870:
Martin S. Sommerville, 42, farmer; Susan, 41; John A T, 19; Robert O, 17; Charles I, 15; Mary E, 13; Sarah O, 11; Caroline V, 9; Martha J, 5; Floyd E, 2.

1880 Census, Ritchie Co, WV (Union District), enumerated on Jun 23 1880:
Susan Sommerville, 51, widowed; dau Caroline V, 19; dau Martha J, 14; son Floyd E, 12.
In the adjacent household was the family of Susan's son Robert, his wife Rosanna, and daughter Icy.[497]

Children:
477. i. JOHN ALVIN T. SOMMERVILLE b. Oct- -1850.
478. ii. ROBERT O. SOMMERVILLE b. Sep-16-1852.
iii. CHARLES I. SOMMERVILLE[497] b. ca 1854,[cdxcviii[498]] [Age reported on headstone would put birth date at Nov 14 1860. But age 6 in 1860 puts it in about 1854.], d. Oct- 2-1877,[17] buried in Auburn Community Cemetery, Ritchie Co, WV,[469] census 1870 in Union District, Ritchie Co, WV, census 1860 in Ritchie Co, (W)VA.
iv. MARY E. SOMMERVILLE b. ca 1856 in Ritchie Co, (W)VA,[227] resided 1880 in Harrison Co, WV,[227] census 1870 in Union District, Ritchie Co, WV, census 1860 in Ritchie Co, (W)VA. She married Nov-25-1880 in Harrison Co, WV,[cdxcix[499]] James A. L. Day, b. ca 1855 in Harrison Co, (W)VA,[227] (son of Joseph T. Day and Ingaby T. __).
v. SARAH OLIVE SOMMERVILLE[497] also known as Olive Sommerville,[497] b. ca 1858 in Ritchie Co, (W)VA,[473,498] resided in Berea, Ritchie Co, WV,[497] census 1870 in Union District, Ritchie Co, WV, census 1860 in Ritchie Co, (W)VA. She married[497] Mar-29-1877 in Ritchie Co, WV,[473] John Fillmore Kelley, also known as Fillmore Kelley,[497] b. ca 1857 in Doddridge Co, (W)VA,[473] (son of Ezekiel Kelley and Estella Ann Davis), resided 1877 in Ritchie Co, WV.[d[500]]
vi. CAROLINE V. SOMMERVILLE b. 1860,[di[501]] resided (settled) in Ohio,[497] census 1870, 1880 in Union District, Ritchie Co, WV.

Married and moved to Ohio.[497]

vii. SUSAN M. SOMMERVILLE b. May-19-1863,[74] d. Sep-10-1864,[17] buried in Auburn Community Cemetery, Ritchie Co, WV.[469]
viii. MARTHA J. SOMMERVILLE b. 1865,[501,473] resided in Roane Co, WV,[497] census 1870, 1880 in Union District, Ritchie Co, WV. She married[497] Oct-25-1883 in Ritchie Co, WV,[473] Spencer E. Barrackman, b. ca 1858.[473]
479. ix. FLOYD E. SOMERVILLE b. Feb-21-1868.
x. ELIZABETH SOMMERVILLE[497.] She married[497] __ Nitz, also known as __ Netz.[497]

268. **John Smith Gaston**, also known as Smith Gaston,[dii[502],diii[503]] (139.John[6], 72.John[5], 21.John[4], 6.Hugh[3], 3.John[2], 1.Jean[1]), b. Dec-12-1830 in Duck Creek, Harrison Co, WV,[div[504],dv[505]] d. Nov-12-1893 in Doddridge Co, WV,[356,17] buried in Gaston-Hart Cemetery, Upper Run, Summers, Doddridge Co, WV.[17]

John Smith Gaston built his log house in 1853 on Camp Run, near Summers, Doddridge Co, WV. He was then able to bring his wife Elizabeth (Richards) from Harrison County to Camp Run. The frame part of the house was built in 1890. He had to buy his farm back after going on the bond of a man he thought was his best friend. That took many years of hard work and put a great financial strain on the family.[dvi[506]]

He married (1) Jun-15-1854 in Doddridge Co, (W)VA,[dvii[507]] **Eliza Richards**, also known as Eliza,[17] b. Feb-27-1835,[74] (daughter of James Tolbert Richards and Elizabeth Childers), d. Jul-27-1864 in Camp

Run, Oxford, Doddridge Co, WV,[506],[17] buried in Gaston-Hart Cemetery, Upper Run, Summers, Doddridge Co, WV,[17] census 1850 in Doddridge Co, (W)VA. He married (2) May-24-1865 in Ritchie Co, WV,[dviii[508]],[433] **Catherine Leggett**, also known as Kathrine Leggett,[503] census name Kathleen,[dix[509]] b. Jul-17-1836 in Marion Co, (W)VA,[17],[473] (daughter of Enoch B. Leggett and Sarah Ann Athey), d. Dec- 2-1914 in Doddridge Co, WV,[dx[510]],[356] [Name spelled "Catherine" in death record, but "Catharine" on headstone.], buried in Gaston-Hart Cemetery, Upper Run, Summers, Doddridge Co, WV,[17] census 1900, 1910 in Southwest District, Doddridge Co, WV,[385] [In 1910, listed as Kathleen Gaston, 73, single, in household of son Marion Gaston and his family.].

Catherine: From Leggett's Mill near Harrisville, Ritchie Co, WV.

1900 Census, Doddridge County WV (Southwest District):
Head of household Catherine Gaston, 63, widowed, b. Jul 1836, mother of 6 children, 5 still living; dau Rosa B. Gaston, 23, single, b. Jul 1876; step-dau E. Jane Gaston, 44, single, b. Sep 1855; servant Stephen Prunty, 12, b. May 1888.[dxi[511]]

 Children by Eliza Richards:
    i.   ELIZABETH JANE GASTON, also known as E. Jane Gaston,[354] b. Dec-23-1855 in Doddridge Co, WV [Birth date may be Sep 23], d. May-29-1932 [Headstone gives death in year 1933.], buried in Archbold Cemetery, Smithburg, Doddridge Co, WV,[17] resided 1929 in Smithburg, Doddridge Co, WV.[412]

    1920 Census, Doddridge County, WV (Southwest District), enumerated on Jan 16 1920:
    Head of household: Rebecca J. Gaston, 79, widowed, b. Virginia, both parents b. Maryland; the only other member of the household was listed as a servant, Elizabeth J. Woofter, 64, married, b. W.Va, both parents b. W.Va. (Elizabeth was the niece of Rebecca's late husband.)

    She married Aug-13-1904 in Doddridge Co, WV,[dxii[512]],[dxiii[513]] John Granviel Woofter,[356] b. Jan-26-1848 in Lewis Co, (W)VA,[354] (son of James Woofter and Rebecca Shannon), d. Feb- 8-1929 in Doddridge Co, WV.[356]
480. ii.   MARY ISABEL "BELL" GASTON b. Aug-29-1857.
    iii.   RULINA O. GASTON b. Feb- 3-1859 in Doddridge Co, WV,[dxiv[514]] d. Apr-19-1859 in Doddridge Co, WV,[dxv[515]],[356],[17] buried in Gaston-Hart Cemetery, Upper Run, Summers, Doddridge Co, WV.[17]
481. iv.   JOHN IRVIN GASTON b. Jun- 4-1860.
    v.   SAMUEL J. GASTON b. 1862 in Doddridge Co, (W)VA, d. Mar-29-1879 in Doddridge Co, WV,[357] [Doddridge County death records reflect a death date of Mar 29 1879, with age given as 17. But headstone reads Mar 2 1889, with age at death of 16y 5m 11d.], buried in Gaston-Hart Cemetery, Upper Run, Summers, Doddridge Co, WV,[dxvi[516]] cause of death fever.[357]
    vi.   HENRY T. GASTON[17] b. Jul-16-1864,[17] d. young,[dxvii[517]] [Death date likely to be July 1864, as headstone gives only his birth date.], buried in Gaston-Hart Cemetery, Upper Run, Summers, Doddridge Co, WV.[17]
    Children by Catherine Leggett:
482. vii.   MARION OSCAR GASTON b. Aug-25-1866.
483. viii.   FRANCIS ENOCH GASTON b. Mar-13-1868.
    ix.   SARAH ANNA GASTON b. Feb- 6-1870, d. Dec-21-1921. She married Mar-16-1893 in Doddridge Co, WV,[dxviii[518]],[354] Abram Job Springston,[dxix[519]] b. May-11-1866, occupation minister.
484. x.   ELIZABETH CATHERINE GASTON b. Dec-26-1872.
    xi.   ROSA BIRD GASTON b. Apr-23-1876,[46] d. Jul-29-1959 in Ritchie Co, WV,[477],[46] buried in IOOF Cemetery, Harrisville, Ritchie Co, WV,[469] resided in Harrisville, Ritchie Co, WV.[dxx[520]],[dxxi[521]] She married Feb-6-1903 in Doddridge Co, WV,[dxxii[522]],[354] Henry Martin Rymer, b. Oct-28-1874 in Stouts Mills, Gilmer Co, WV,[398] (son of Henry A. Rymer and Susan M. Stewart), d. Aug-11-1950 in

Harrisville, Ritchie Co, WV,[398] buried in IOOF Cemetery, Harrisville, Ritchie Co, WV,[398] resided in Harrisville, Ritchie Co, WV,[398] occupation farmer.[398]

   xii. IDA MAE GASTON b. May-17-1878 in Doddridge Co, WV,[dxxiii[523]] d. Aug- 8-1880,[17] buried in Gaston-Hart Cemetery, Upper Run, Summers, Doddridge Co, WV.[17]

269. **Elizabeth Gaston** (139.John[6], 72.John[5], 21.John[4], 6.Hugh[3], 3.John[2], 1.Jean[1]), b. Aug- 9-1832,[17] d. Mar-9-1912,[17] buried in Old Bethel Church Cem, Good Hope, Harrison Co, WV,[17,dxxiv[524]] resided 1911 in Good Hope, Harrison Co, WV.[521] She married Oct-30-1851 in Harrison Co, (W)VA,[419] **Jacob Sommerville**, b. Feb- 5-1828,[17] d. Apr-28-1882,[17] buried in Old Bethel Church Cem, Good Hope, Harrison Co, WV,[17,524] occupation farmer.[271] 1860 Census, Harrison County, Virginia (now West Virginia):
Jacob Sommerville, 32, farmer; Elizabeth, 27; John H, 7; William O, 4; Wesley, 2; Robert F. Stutler, 12.

   Children:
485. i. JOHN H. SOMMERVILLE b. ca 1853.
   ii. WILLIAM OSCAR SOMMERVILLE, also known as W. Oscar Sommerville,[17] b. Apr- 3-1855 in Harrison Co, (W)VA,[398,227,271] d. Nov-19-1924 in Good Hope, Harrison Co, WV,[dxxv[525]] buried in Good Hope Masonic Cemetery, Rt. 19 S, Harrison Co, WV.[398,524] He married Oct- 5-1876 in Harrison Co, WV,[227] Malvonia A. Bell, b. Mar-15-1858 in Doddridge Co, (W)VA,[398,227] (daughter of Colvis Bell and Harriet __), d. Aug- 5-1941 in Good Hope, Harrison Co, WV,[398] buried in Good Hope Masonic Cemetery, Rt. 19 S, Harrison Co, WV,[524,398] resided 1876 in Harrison Co, WV.[227]

   Malvonia: Identified in marriage record as Malvonia A. Bell, daughter of Colvis Bell & Hariett; in death record as Malonia A. Sommerville, daughter of Calvin S. Bell & Henrietta Hoff; and on headstone as Malaina A. Sommerville.

486. iii. JAMES WESLEY SOMMERVILLE b. ca 1858.
487. iv. SARAH ADDA SOMMERVILLE b. Feb-11-1861.
   v. LAURA A. SOMMERVILLE b. ca 1866 in Harrison Co, WV,[454,419] d. bef Mar 1889.[dxxvi[526]] She married Sep-24-1884 in Harrison Co, WV,[419] George M. Lynch, b. Apr-27-1861 in Harrison Co, (W)VA,[398] (son of Isaac Lynch and Mary Jane Burnside), d. Oct- 9-1932 in West Milford, Harrison Co, WV,[398] buried in Rose Hill (formerly IOOF) Cemetery, West Milford, Harrison Co, WV,[398] resided in West Milford, Harrison Co, WV,[dxxvii[527],398] occupation farmer, barber.[419,398]
488. vi. ELLA J. SOMMERVILLE b. 1871.
   vii. ETTA B. SOMMERVILLE b. 1874,[454,17] d. 1950,[17] buried in Good Hope Masonic Cemetery, Rt. 19 S, Harrison Co, WV.[17]

270. **Sarah Gaston**, also known as Sarah A. Gaston (139.John[6], 72.John[5], 21.John[4], 6.Hugh[3], 3.John[2], 1.Jean[1]), b. ca 1837,[225] d. 1916,[373] resided 1911 in Cassoday, Butler Co, KS,[521] [The 1911 obituary of brother Samuel Morris Gaston gave the residence of Sarah Gaston Smith as Cassidy, Kansas. No city of that name is found in Kansas, so it is presumed that "Cassoday" was intended.]. She married Sep-20-1855 in Harrison Co, (W)VA,[dxxviii[528]] **Isaac Rinehart Smith**, b. 1828,[519] (son of John Smith and Mary __).
   Children:
   i. MARY E. SMITH b. ca 1858.[454]
   ii. CHARLES A. SMITH b. ca 1860,[454] census 1880 in Harrison Co, WV.
   iii. LYDIA J. SMITH b. Feb-13-1865,[74] d. Nov-22-1870,[17] buried in Duck Creek Missn Chrch Cem, near West Milford, Harrison Co, WV.[230]
   iv. CAROLINE V. SMITH b. ca 1867.[454]
   v. CORA A. SMITH b. ca 1870.[454]
   vi. JOHN E. SMITH b. ca 1873.[454]
   vii. ICY M. SMITH b. ca 1878.[454]

271. **James William Gaston** (139.John[6], 72.John[5], 21.John[4], 6.Hugh[3], 3.John[2], 1.Jean[1]), b. Oct- -1838 in Harrison Co, (W)VA,[467,419,46] d. Feb- 8-1921 in Clarksburg, Harrison Co, WV,[398] buried in Duck Creek

Missn Chrch Cem, near West Milford, Harrison Co, WV,[17,398] census 1880, 1900 in Grant District, Harrison Co, WV, occupation farmer.[398,467] He married Dec-21-1865 in Harrison Co, WV,[227] **Sarah A. Ward**, b. Oct- -1838 in Harrison Co, (W)VA,[467,419,46] (daughter of Solomon Ward and Nancy __), d. 1916,[46] buried in Duck Creek Missn Chrch Cem, near West Milford, Harrison Co, WV,[17] census 1880, 1900 in Grant District, Harrison Co, WV.

   Children:

    i. HENSON DAVISSON GASTON[419] b. Jun-10-1867 in Harrison Co, WV,[46] d. Feb-23-1920 at Duck Creek, Harrison Co, WV,[dxxix[529],46] buried in Duck Creek Missn Chrch Cem, near West Milford, Harrison Co, WV,[17,398] occupation farmer,[398] census 1880, 1900 in Grant District, Harrison Co, WV. He married (1) Jun-15-1893 in Harrison Co, WV,[dxxx[530]] divorced[419] Hattie E. Hall, b. ca 1872 in Harrison Co, WV,[419] (daughter of David L. Hall and Sarah __), census 1900 in Grant District, Harrison Co, WV. He married (2) Apr-12-1916 in Harrison Co, WV,[dxxxi[531]] Ethel Gaston, b. Oct-24-1882 in Harrison Co, WV,[dxxxii[532],46] (daughter of Enoch Gaston and Flora Bond), d. 1954,[46] buried in Duck Creek Missn Chrch Cem, near West Milford, Harrison Co, WV.[dxxxiii[533]] Henson D. Gaston and Ethel Gaston were double cousins, in that they were both second cousins (both were great-grandchildren of John Gaston, Jr. (b. 1752 in NJ)) and also fourth cousins (both were great-great-great-grandchildren of John Smith (b. 1699)).

    ii. GERTRUDE ELMA GASTON b. Nov-16-1876 in Harrison Co, WV,[276] d. Jul-20-1957 in Clarksburg, Harrison Co, WV,[dxxxiv[534]] buried in Elkview Masonic Cemetery, Clarksburg, Harrison Co, WV,[276] resided 1952 in Clarksburg, Harrison Co, WV,[228] census 1880, 1900 in Grant District, Harrison Co, WV. She married Sep-16-1908 in Harrison Co, WV,[dxxxv[535],dxxxvi[536]] Darwin Maxwell Davis, b. Jul-10-1877 in Doddridge Co, WV,[536,dxxxvii[537],398] (son of Charles Grandison Davis and Elizabeth F. Randolph), d. Dec- 1-1952 in Harrison Co, WV,[dxxxviii[538]] buried in Elkview Masonic Cemetery, Clarksburg, Harrison Co, WV,[398] resided in Clarksburg, Harrison Co, WV,[521,398] resided 1938 in Salem, WV,[521] resided 1908 in Harrison Co, WV,[537] occupation real estate broker.[398]

   Darwin: Identified by Susie Davis Nicholson (p. 48) as Darwin Maxwell Davis, but Wes Cochran's "Harrison County WV Marriages" identifies him as Darwin Maxson Davis. Death record has only Darwin M. Davis.[536,537]

272. **John Taylor** (140.Deborah[6], 72.John[5], 21.John[4], 6.Hugh[3], 3.John[2], 1.Jean[1]), b. Jan-18-1823 in Harrison Co, (W)VA,[dxxxix[539],46] d. Jul-31-1888 in Lewis Co, WV,[539,46] buried in Broad Run Bapt Ch Cem, Jane Lew, Lewis Co, WV,[17,539] census 1880 in Freemans Creek, Lewis Co, WV,[539] resided Jun 1856 in Lewis Co, (W)VA,[539] occupation farmer.[539] He married Jul-10-1849 in Harrison Co, (W)VA,[539] **Amanda West**, b. Jul-28-1829 in Harrison Co, (W)VA,[539,46] (daughter of John West and Abigail Clemens), d. Aug-26-1919 in Lewis Co, WV,[539,46] buried in Broad Run Bapt Ch Cem, Jane Lew, Lewis Co, WV,[17,539] census 1910 in Hackers Creek, Lewis Co, WV,[539] census 1880 in Freemans Creek, Lewis Co, WV.[539] In addition to the four children known to have been born to them, it is said that twelve other children died at birth or in infancy, for which there is no record of names or dates of birth or death. John Taylor moved from Taylor Co, WV to the Jane Lew area of Lewis Co, WV, where many of his descendants are still to be found.

1850 Census, Lewis County, Virginia (now West Virginia), enumerated on Jul 1 1850:
John Taylor, 27, farmer; Amanda Taylor, 19; Elizabeth J. Taylor, 22; Josiah Taylor, 12.

1870 Census, Lewis County, WV (Willey Township), enumerated in Sep 1870:
John Taylor, 47, farmer; Amanda, 40; Lucy E, 15; Helen, 4; Willie G, 11 months.

1880 Census, Lewis County, WV (Freemans Creek), enumerated on Jun 25 1880:
John Taylor, 57, farmer; wife Amanda, 50; dau Helen A, 14; son Willie Grant, 10; dau Ella Nora, 6. (Note: Although daughter Helen's middle initial is given in the census as A, her name appears on her headstone as Helen May Taylor.)

Children:
489.   i.   LUCY E. TAYLOR b. Sep- 6-1854.
        ii.   HELEN MAY TAYLOR, census name Helen A. Taylor,[247] b. Jan- 5-1866, d. Jun- 8-1957, buried in Broad Run Bapt Ch Cem, Jane Lew, Lewis Co, WV,[17] census 1880 in Freemans Creek, Lewis Co, WV, never married.
490.   iii.   WILLIAM GRANT TAYLOR b. Jul- 1-1869.
491.   iv.   ELLA NORA TAYLOR b. Jan-28-1874.

273.   **Nancy Ann Taylor** (140.Deborah[6], 72.John[5], 21.John[4], 6.Hugh[3], 3.John[2], 1.Jean[1]), b. Sep-29-1824 in Peddlers Run, Harrison Co VA (now Taylor Co WV), d. Apr- 8-1856, buried in Middleville Baptist Church Cemetery, Taylor Co, WV.

Nancy Ann Taylor Corbin worked as a nurse during an epidemic of typhoid fever. In the spring of 1856 she contracted the disease and died. Her two brothers, Andrew Allen and Josiah, also died in the summer of 1856 of the same disease. After Nancy Ann's death, her husband, Oliver Perry Corbin, remarried Mary Lindsey on Jan 25, 1857, and in 1858 moved his family to Jackson County near Kenna, WV, where he fathered 12 more children.

She married Mar-2-1845,[dxl[540]] **Oliver Perry Corbin**, b. Nov-10-1821 in Harrison Co, VA (now Taylor Co, WV) (son of John W. Corbin and Rebecca Williams), d. Dec-24-1895, buried in Grasslick Bapt Ch Cem, Pleasant Valley Rd, Kenna, Jackson Co, WV.
        Children:
492.   i.   GUSTAVIUS ADOLPHUS CORBIN b. Jul-22-1846.
493.   ii.   REBECCA ANN CORBIN b. Sep-15-1848.
494.   iii.   JOSEPH TAYLOR CORBIN b. Jul- 1-1850.
        iv.   LORENZO DOW CORBIN b. 1852, d. May- 5-1860 in Jackson Co, WV.
495.   v.   MARTHA COLUMBIA (TWIN) CORBIN b. Apr-20-1855.
496.   vi.   MARY VIRGINIA (TWIN) CORBIN b. Apr-20-1855.

274.   **Elizabeth Jane Taylor** (140.Deborah[6], 72.John[5], 21.John[4], 6.Hugh[3], 3.John[2], 1.Jean[1]), b. Aug-21-1826, d. May-12-1884. She married 1852, **John Robinson**.
        Children:
        i.   JAMES ALVIS ROBINSON b. Aug-26-1853 in Taylor Co, WV.

275.   **Margaret Taylor** (140.Deborah[6], 72.John[5], 21.John[4], 6.Hugh[3], 3.John[2], 1.Jean[1]), b. Sep-24-1828,[17] d. Jan- 4-1909,[17] buried in Middleville Baptist Church Cemetery, Taylor Co, WV.[17] She married **Andrew S. Carr**, b. Mar-10-1823,[17] [But Harrison County death records, which state his death date as Aug 12, 1905, give his age at death as 82y 6m 15d, which would make his birth date January 28, 1823.], d. Aug-17-1905 in Harrison Co, WV,[17] [But Harrison County death records state Aug 12, 1905.], buried in Middleville Baptist Church Cemetery, Taylor Co, WV.[17]
        Children:
        i.   ELOM S. CARR[17] b. Apr-14-1851,[17] d. Mar-17-1879,[17] buried in Middleville Baptist Church Cemetery, Taylor Co, WV.[17]
497.   ii.   WILLIAM COLUMBUS "LUM" CARR b. Aug- 5-1853.
        iii.   THEADORE L. CARR[17] b. Oct- 1-1857,[dxli[541]] d. 1911,[17] buried in Middleville Baptist Church Cemetery, Taylor Co, WV,[17] never married.
        iv.   ALLEN T. CARR b. Sep-21-1859, d. Apr-28-1863, buried in Middleville Baptist Church Cemetery, Taylor Co, WV.[17]
498.   v.   MARTHA OLIVE "OLLIE" CARR b. Jul-20-1864.

276.   **James Gaston Taylor** (140.Deborah[6], 72.John[5], 21.John[4], 6.Hugh[3], 3.John[2], 1.Jean[1]), b. Jan-12-1831 in Taylor Co, WV, d. Dec-26-1908, buried presumably in Clermont Cemetery, Eldora, Marion Co, WV. He married Jul-1-1856, **Mary Jane Yates**, b. 1837 [Birth date may be 1831, per Marilynn Davis Jones.], d. Aug-30-1908, buried presumably in Clermont Cemetery, Eldora, Marion Co, WV. A deed was recorded in 1896 at the Marion Co Court House in Fairmont, WV for a cemetery lot of 8 graves at the

142

Clermont Cemetery near Eldora, Marion Co, WV. It is thought that James G. & Mary Jane Taylor and their daughters, Alma and Estella, are buried there in unmarked graves. The only stone on the lot is for Edna Taylor. The cemetery has no records of actual burials, but they do show proof of the existence of the 8-grave lot in the name of James G. Taylor.

Children:
- i. GEORGE L. TAYLOR b. 1859 in Taylor Co, WV.
- ii. EMMA T. TAYLOR b. 1861 in Taylor Co, WV.
- iii. PRUDIE TAYLOR b. 1864 in Taylor Co, WV.
- 499. iv. CLARA CORNELIA TAYLOR b. Mar-20-1866.
- v. ALMA R. TAYLOR b. Aug-25-1868 in Taylor Co, WV, d. Jul-18-1947, buried presumably in Clermont Cemetery, Eldora, Marion Co, WV, never married.
- vi. MARTHA TAYLOR b. 1870 in Taylor Co, WV.
- vii. ESTELLA TAYLOR b. Mar-28-1873 in Taylor Co, WV, d. Jun-20-1898 in Pittsburgh, Allegheny Co, PA, buried presumably in Clermont Cemetery, Eldora, Marion Co, WV, never married.
- 500. viii. JESSIE L. TAYLOR b. 1874.
- ix. GAY TAYLOR b. Jul-12-1875 in Taylor Co, WV.
- x. CHARLES R. TAYLOR b. Sep-23-1878 in Taylor Co, WV.
- xi. EDDY TAYLOR b. Jul- -1881 in Taylor Co, WV.
- xii. EDNA TAYLOR b. 1883 in Taylor Co, WV, d. 1917, buried in Clermont Cemetery, Eldora, Marion Co, WV. She married F. A. Wallen.

277. **William Davidson Taylor** (140.Deborah[6], 72.John[5], 21.John[4], 6.Hugh[3], 3.John[2], 1.Jean[1]), b. Sep-29-1835, d. Dec-20-1890, buried in Middleville Baptist Church Cemetery, Taylor Co, WV.[17] He married Jan-15-1863, **Nancy Bartlett**, b. Oct-12-1843 (daughter of Samuel Bartlett and Mary Fleming), d. Jan-28-1932, buried in Middleville Baptist Church Cemetery, Taylor Co, WV.[17]

Children:
- 501. i. COLONEL HARVEY TAYLOR b. Nov- 6-1863.
- ii. ADDA "ADDIE" WILMONA TAYLOR b. May-13-1865,[17] d. Oct-30-1913,[17] buried in Middleville Baptist Church Cemetery, Taylor Co, WV,[17] never married.
- 502. iii. JOHN FLOYD TAYLOR b. May-11-1867.
- 503. iv. HATTIE NEVADA TAYLOR b. Dec-18-1868.
- 504. v. FRANCES GERTRUDE "GERTIE" TAYLOR b. Aug- 7-1871.
- vi. MARTHA ELLEN TAYLOR b. May-18-1875, d. May-31-1946, buried in Spring Hill Cemetery, Huntington, WV.

Martha's husband, Jefferson Springston, is buried by his first wife, Maria N. Bartlett, who was a half sister to Martha's mother, Nancy Bartlett. Martha is buried in the same cemetery nearby with former residents of the Foster Memorial Home, where she passed away.

She married Jan-25-1919, Jefferson Davis "Jeff" Springston, b. Jul-19-1862, d. Jun-26-1938, buried in Spring Hill Cemetery, Huntington, WV.
- vii. SALLIE BELLE TAYLOR, also known as Sally Belle Taylor, b. Aug-20-1877, d. Apr-14-1878, buried in Middleville Baptist Church Cemetery, Taylor Co, WV.[17]
- 505. viii. EDWARD MURRAY TAYLOR b. Jul-15-1882.

278. **Sarah "Sally" Taylor** (140.Deborah[6], 72.John[5], 21.John[4], 6.Hugh[3], 3.John[2], 1.Jean[1]), b. Nov-24-1840, d. May- 1-1909, buried in Elkview Masonic Cemetery, Clarksburg, Harrison Co, WV. She married Apr-4-1871 in Taylor Co, WV,[433] **Francis Marion "Frank" Brooks**, b. Jan- 8-1826 in Hampshire Co, VA,[154] (son of Mary __), d. May-12-1883 in Harrison Co, WV,[dxlii[542]] buried in Elkview Masonic Cemetery, Clarksburg, Harrison Co, WV.

Children:
- i. IDA MAY BROOKS b. Mar- 3-1872 in Harrison Co, WV,[dxliii[543]] d. Dec-29-1924 in Clarksburg, Harrison Co, WV,[398] buried in Elkview Masonic Cemetery, Clarksburg, Harrison Co,

WV,[398] census 1900 in Taylor Co, WV,[dxliv[544]] census 1880 in Harrison Co, WV,[dxlv[545]] occupation superintendent, glove dept., Parson Souders Co.,[398] never married[398,dxlvi[546]]

      506.   ii.   FRANCIS NEWTON BROOKS b. Dec-14-1873.

            iii. CHARLES E. BROOKS b. Jul- 3-1875 in Harrison Co, WV. He married Laura __, b. 1875.

      507.   iv. WILLIAM TAYLOR BROOKS b. Jun-15-1878.

            v.   ROBERT B. BROOKS b. Jul-25-1880, d. May-22-1957, buried in Woodlawn Cemetery. He married Willa Pearl Scott, b. Mar-22-1880, d. Aug-24-1972, buried in Woodlawn Cemetery.

279. **Henrietta Taylor**, also known as L. E. Gaul,[433] (140.Deborah[6], 72.John[5], 21.John[4], 6.Hugh[3], 3.John[2], 1.Jean[1]), b. Jun-18-1845, d. Dec-11-1924, buried in Mt. Morris Cemetery, Freemansburg, Lewis Co, WV.

Following her 1874 marriage to Lafayette Erastus Gall, moved to Freemansburg, Lewis Co, WV.[234]

She married (1) Apr-28-1870 in Taylor Co, WV,[433] **Anthony Asbury Robinson**, b. 1848, d. Mar-14-1872. She married (2) Jun-14-1874 in Taylor Co, WV,[433] **Lafayette Erastus Gall**, b. Sep-13-1834, d. Mar-26-1912, buried in Mt. Morris Cemetery, Freemansburg, Lewis Co, WV.

            Children by Anthony Asbury Robinson:

      508.   i.   CURTIS NEWTON ROBINSON b. Aug-16-1871.

            Children by Lafayette Erastus Gall:

      509.   ii. CHARLES MUSSER GALL b. Jul- 5-1878.

280. **Peter Gaston Swisher** (141.Jane[6], 72.John[5], 21.John[4], 6.Hugh[3], 3.John[2], 1.Jean[1]), b. Oct-28-1830 in Laurel Lick Run (Berlin), Lewis Co, WV,[268,408] d. Aug- 7-1913,[268] census 1900 in Hackers Creek District, Lewis Co, WV. He married Dec- -1850 in Lewis Co, (W)VA,[dxlvii[547],268,dxlviii[548]] [Lewis County marriage records contain two entries for this marriage, one showing a marriage date of Dec 9 1850, and the other showing a date of Dec 12 1850.], **Margaret Mary Hinzman**, b. Feb-22-1832 in Berlin, Lewis Co, WV,[268,408] (daughter of Abraham Hinzman and Rebecca Means), d. Feb- 2-1902 in Laurel Lick Run (Berlin), Lewis Co, WV,[268] census 1900 in Hackers Creek District, Lewis Co, WV.

            Children:

            i.   HARRIET JANE SWISHER b. May- 4-1853 in Lewis Co, WV,[dxlix[549]] d. 1915. She married Oct-16-1870 in Lewis Co, WV,[242] John F. Hersman,[242] d. 1932.

            ii. AMANDA ELIZABETH SWISHER b. May-31-1855 in Lewis Co, WV.[dl[550]] She married Sep- 3-1899 in Lewis Co, WV,[410] Jacob Stern, b. ca 1841 in Germany,[410] (son of John Stern and Martha __).

      510.   iii. WILLIAM OSCAR SWISHER b. Apr-18-1857.

      511.   iv. GEORGE WASHINGTON SWISHER b. Feb-28-1859.

            v.   ALICE REBECCA SWISHER b. Dec-17-1860 in Lewis Co, WV,[550] d. 1861.

            vi. MARY MARCELIA SWISHER b. ca 1862.[410] She married Mar-24-1886 in Lewis Co, WV,[410] Peter Elihu Allman, b. ca 1854,[410] (son of William Allman and Margaret __). Not to be confused with the Peter T. Allman and Mary Swisher who married in Lewis Co (W)VA on Dec 27 1860.[242]

      512.   vii. JAMES EDWIN SWISHER b. Nov- 6-1864.

            viii. FLORA LEE SWISHER, also known as Flora Lea Swisher, b. ca 1867.[410] She married Dec- 1-1889 in Lewis Co, WV,[410] William T. Lawson, b. ca 1863,[410] (son of Cornelius Lawson and Anne __).

      513.   ix. JOHN ALDEN SWISHER b. Dec-22-1868.

            x.   IZA FLORENCE SWISHER, also known as Inza Florence Swisher, b. 1870,[410] d. 1917. She married Apr-11-1900 in Lewis Co, WV,[dli[551]] Charles William Taylor, b. ca 1860,[410] (son of Sandy H. Taylor and Augusta __).

            xi. SARAH ANN SWISHER b. May-15-1873 in Laurel Lick Run (Berlin), Lewis Co, WV,[dlii[552],408] census 1900 in Hackers Creek District, Lewis Co, WV.

281. **James Lee Swisher** (141.Jane[6], 72.John[5], 21.John[4], 6.Hugh[3], 3.John[2], 1.Jean[1]), b. Jul-23-1832 in Lewis Co, (W)VA,[268,408] d. May-17-1908 in Lewis Co, WV.[268] He married[396] Feb-25-1855 in Lewis Co, (W)VA,[dliii[553],268,dliv[554]] **Mary "Molly" Hinzman**, b. Aug-17-1835 in Lewis Co, (W)VA,[268,408] (daughter of William B. Hinzman and Mary Ann "Polly" Means), d. 1908.[268]

        Children:

    514. i.   ALVIN SWISHER b. Nov-27-1857.

        ii. WILLIAM HENRY SWISHER[268] b. Sep-13-1860 in Lewis Co, (W)VA,[550] d. Jul-31-1932 in Buckhannon, Upshur Co, WV.[268] He married May-26-1892 in Lewis Co, WV,[dlv[555]] May Cookman, b. ca 1866.[410]

    515. iii. ISAAC COLUMBUS "LUM" SWISHER b. Sep- 6-1861.

        iv. ALFRED WASHINGTON "WASH" SWISHER[268] also known as Alford W. Swisher, b. Apr- 4-1863 in Lewis Co, (W)VA,[dlvi[556]] [Jeffrey Wood gives birth date for Alfred Washington Swisher as Apr 4 1862.], d. May- 7-1898 in Lewis Co, WV.[268,556] He married Mar-25-1886 in Lewis Co, WV,[dlvii[557]] Eliza Irene Allman, b. Feb-12-1864 in Lewis Co, WV,[556] (daughter of William Allman and Kittorah __), d. Dec- 5-1936 in Lewis Co, WV.[556]

    516. v.   ROBERT ERVIN SWISHER b. Dec-12-1866.

        vi. ADA BIRD "ADDIE" SWISHER[268] b. Sep- 1-1868 in Lewis Co, WV,[268] d. 1942.[268] She married Mar-14-1889 in Lewis Co, WV,[410] John Columbus Lawson,[410] b. ca 1866,[410] (son of Henry C. Lawson and Ann __).

    517. vii. CHARLES SWISHER b. Aug-22-1870.

        viii. JOHN EMORY SWISHER[410] b. Aug- 6-1872 in Lewis Co, WV,[268] d. Aug-17-1936 in Vienna, Wood Co, WV.[268] He married Jun-24-1896 in Lewis Co, WV,[dlviii[558]] Minnie McKinney, b. Nov-14-1875 in Harrison Co, WV,[dlix[559],410,dlx[560]] (daughter of Jasper N. McKinney and Lydia J. Queen), d. Jan-24-1966 in Parkersburg, Wood Co, WV,[559] buried in Mt. Olivet Cemetery, Parkersburg, WV,[559] resided in Vienna, Wood Co, WV,[559] census 1880 in Elk District, Harrison Co, WV.

    518. ix. JAMES GOODLOE SWISHER b. Feb-20-1879.

282. **Sarah Jane Swisher** (141.Jane[6], 72.John[5], 21.John[4], 6.Hugh[3], 3.John[2], 1.Jean[1]), b. May- -1834 in Lewis Co, (W)VA,[408] d. Jan- 2-1913 in Berlin, Lewis Co, WV,[dlxi[561]] census 1880, 1900 in Hackers Creek District, Lewis Co, WV. She married Nov-28-1850 in Lewis Co, (W)VA,[dlxii[562]] **Perry Green Hinzman**,[268] census name P. G. Hinzman,[247] b. May- -1830 in Lewis Co, (W)VA,[408] (son of Abraham Hinzman and Rebecca Means), d. Mar-26-1907 in Lewis Co, WV,[548,268] census 1880, 1900 in Hackers Creek District, Lewis Co, WV.

        Children:

    519. i.   JAMES LEWIS HINZMAN b. Nov- 1-1852.

        ii. ISAAC NEWTON HINZMAN b. Sep-29-1853 in Lewis Co, WV.[411] He married Apr-26-1886 in Lewis Co, WV,[410] Eliza Life, b. ca 1853,[410] (daughter of Noah Life and Margaret __).

        iii. ABRAM HINZMAN b. Dec-20-1855 in Lewis Co, (W)VA.[dlxiii[563]]

        iv. REBECCA JANE HINZMAN b. Apr-21-1859,[398] d. Mar-19-1951 in Lewis Co, WV,[398] buried in Friendship Cem (Fairview IOOF), Berlin Rd, Co Rt 7, Lewis Co, WV,[398] census 1880, 1900 in Hackers Creek District, Lewis Co, WV, never married[398].

        v.   MARY CATHERINE HINZMAN b. ca 1866,[410] census 1880 in Hackers Creek District, Lewis Co, WV. She married[373] May-16-1886 in Lewis Co, WV,[410] Theophilus Bailey Lawson, b. ca 1864,[410] (son of Joseph S. Lawson and Emaline M. __).

    520. vi. SARAH ANN HINZMAN b. Sep- -1868.

    521. vii. JOHN WILLIAM HINZMAN b. Dec-17-1869.

        viii. SOPHIA L. HINZMAN b. Dec- -1871,[408,410] census 1880, 1900 in Hackers Creek District, Lewis Co, WV. She married Jul- 4-1915 in Lewis Co, WV,[dlxiv[564]] David Thomas Allman, b. Mar- -1865,[408,410] (son of William Allman and Kittorah __), census 1900, 1910, 1920 in Hackers Creek District, Lewis Co, WV.

    522. ix. FLORENCE MAY HINZMAN b. Nov- 6-1874.

283. **Anna Mariah Swisher** (141.Jane[6], 72.John[5], 21.John[4], 6.Hugh[3], 3.John[2], 1.Jean[1]), b. 1838,[268] d. Feb- 2-1911 in Laurel Lick Run (Berlin), Lewis Co, WV,[268] buried in Friendship Cem (Fairview IOOF), Berlin

Rd, Co Rt 7, Lewis Co, WV. She married Oct- 3-1858 in Lewis Co, (W)VA,[242] **John "Jack" Boram**, b. ca 1829 in Fauquier Co, VA,[268] d. Oct-15-1906 in Laurel Lick Run (Berlin), Lewis Co, WV,[268] buried in Friendship Cem (Fairview IOOF), Berlin Rd, Co Rt 7, Lewis Co, WV.

Children:

i. HARRIET MELISSA BORAM (adopted) b. ca 1854,[dlxv[565]] resided 1936,[521] [Gladys Fork].

We originally identified her as Harriet M. Boram, b. ca 1856, natural parents not known, but adoptive parents as John "Jack" Boram and Anna Mariah Swisher. It later surfaced that a Harriet Melissa Boram, b. ca 1854, was the daughter of William Boram and Elizabeth Ann Hinzman. The relationship between John and William Boram has not been determined, but it appears likely that it is the same Harriet M. Boram.

She married Oct- 5-1880 in Lewis Co, WV,[565,242] Jasper L. Fox.

284. **Isaac Rinehart Swisher**[268] (141.Jane[6], 72.John[5], 21.John[4], 6.Hugh[3], 3.John[2], 1.Jean[1]), b. Dec-23-1838 in Lewis Co, (W)VA,[dlxvi[566]] d. May- 6-1875 in Berlin, Lewis Co, WV,[dlxvii[567]] occupation carpenter.[dlxviii[568]] He married Aug-22-1860 in Lewis Co, WV,[410] **Eda A. Lawson**, b. Dec-25-1839 in Berlin, Lewis Co, WV,[268] (daughter of William Lawson and Nancy __), d. Feb- 1-1900 in Berlin, Lewis Co, WV.[268]

Children:

523. i. IRA ERVIN SWISHER b. ca 1868.

ii. ISAAC H. SWISHER b. Jun-20-1870 in Lewis Co, WV,[236] d. Aug- 6-1871 in Lewis Co, WV.[dlxix[569]]

285. **Elizabeth Ann Gaston** (142.James[6], 72.John[5], 21.John[4], 6.Hugh[3], 3.John[2], 1.Jean[1]), b. May-16-1830 in Doddridge Co, (W)VA,[dlxx[570]] d. Apr-25-1905,[570] buried in Auburn Community Cemetery, Ritchie Co, WV.[570,469] She married marriage bond Jun-12-1849 in Harrison Co, (W)VA,[dlxxi[571]] Jun-21-1849,[dlxxii[572]] **John Hoff**, also known as John Huff,[419,345,498] b. Oct- 9-1825 in Harrison Co, (W)VA,[dlxxiii[573]] d. Aug- 3-1903,[570] buried in Auburn Community Cemetery, Ritchie Co, WV.[570,469]

John: John and Elizabeth Ann Gaston Hoff settled at Bone Creek, Ritchie Co, shortly after their marriage and remained there their entire lives. As well as a farmer, John Hoff was a talented and industrious craftsman. The furniture about the home, even to the loom and spinning wheel, were his own handwork. He was also a mill-wright, blacksmith and stockman. He was also a Captain in the Union Army. The inscription on his headstone reads simply "Honesty is the best policy."[dlxxiv[574]]

Children:

524. i. ERI BENSON HOFF b. Mar-23-1850.

ii. HIRAM J. HOFF b. 1852,[570,469] d. 1855,[570,469] buried in Auburn Community Cemetery, Ritchie Co, WV.[469]

iii. SAMUEL HOFF b. Jan-28-1854,[570] resided at Goose Creek, Ritchie Co, WV,[570] never married.[570]

525. iv. GEORGE S. HOFF b. Dec-27-1855.

526. v. CHARLOTTE COLUMBIA HOFF b. Nov-10-1857.

527. vi. REBECCA JANE HOFF b. Jul- 9-1859.

vii. W. A. L. HOFF b. Sep- 2-1861.[570] He married 1892,[570] Emma J. Clarke.

Emma: Resident of Oklahoma. Referred to as Mrs. Emma J. Clarke, so she was apparently previously married and Clarke was not her maiden name.[570]

viii. MARY C. HOFF b. Mar- 6-1863.[570] She married[570] May- 4-1888 in Ritchie Co, WV,[473] Alva Fitz Randolph, b. Apr-20-1867,[dlxxv[575],473] (son of Asa Fitz Randolph and Marvel Maxson), resided in New York.[570]

146

      ix.   SILAS MARION HOFF b. Mar-14-1865,[570] occupation teacher, county superintendant, prosecuting attorney.[570] He married[570] (1) Sep-21-1898 in Ritchie Co, WV,[473] Minnie C. Wilson. He married (2) 1927,[570] Cora A. Jeffreys, resided in Huntington, Cabell Co, WV.[570]

      x.   ROSA BYRD HOFF b. Apr-13-1867,[570,46] d. Nov-19-1908,[570,46] buried in Auburn Community Cemetery, Ritchie Co, WV,[469] never married[570.]

      xi.   MARTHA N. HOFF b. Mar-20-1870.[570]

      xii.   LEWIS R. HOFF b. Apr-14-1871,[570] occupation Minister - Oklahoma.[570] He married Sep- 6-1899,[570] Emma M. Pohl.

      xiii.   LLOYD L. HOFF b. Feb-10-1873.[570] He married Sep- 8-1901 in Ritchie Co, WV,[473] Emma C. Rinehart, b. ca 1873.[473]

      xiv.   EMMA HOFF[570] resided at Goose Creek, Ritchie Co, WV.[570]

286. **Mary Catherine Gaston** (142.James[6], 72.John[5], 21.John[4], 6.Hugh[3], 3.John[2], 1.Jean[1]), b. Jan-19-1833,[17] [Birth date given in 1900 Census as Jan 1834, but headstone shows it as Jan 19 1833.], d. Jun- 9-1908,[17] buried in Duck Creek Missn Chrch Cem, near West Milford, Harrison Co, WV,[17] census 1870, 1880, 1900 in Grant District, Harrison Co, WV. She married Aug-14-1855 in Harrison Co, (W)VA,[dlxxvi[576]] **George Washington Dayton**, b. May-19-1832 in Frederick Co, MD,[17,227] d. Jun-17-1894,[17] buried in Duck Creek Missn Chrch Cem, near West Milford, Harrison Co, WV,[230] census 1880 in Grant District, Harrison Co, WV, occupation carpenter,[dlxxvii[577]] military Civil War.

1870 Census, Harrison Co, WV (Grant District), enumerated on Sep 1 1870:
George W. Dayton, 38, carpenter, b. in Maryland; Mary C, 38; Ida E, 14; James U, 12; Luella, 8; Willey R, 3; Burke, 9 months.

1880 Census, Harrison Co, WV (Grant District), enumerated in Jun 1880:
Geo. W. Dayton, 47, carpenter; wife Mary C, 47; dau Louella, 18; son Willie R, 12; son Geo B, 10.

1900 Census, Harrison Co, WV (Grant District), enumerated on Jun 29 1900:
Listed as head of household and its only member: Mary C. Dayton, 66, b. Jan 1834, widowed.
The adjacent household was that of her daughter Louella and her family:
William Horner, 35, b. Aug 1864, merchant, married 8 yrs; wife Louilla D, 37, b. Mar 1863, mother of one child (still living); dau Genevieve, 7, b. May 1893.

      Children:

      i.   ALBERT C. DAYTON b. Feb-19-1860,[17] d. Jun-20-1867,[17] buried in Duck Creek Missn Chrch Cem, near West Milford, Harrison Co, WV.[17,230]

    528. ii.   LOUELLA D. DAYTON b. Mar-19-1862.

    529. iii.   WILLIAM RUSH DAYTON b. 1867.

      iv.   GEORGE BURKE DAYTON b. Aug-15-1869,[17] d. Jun-12-1891,[17] buried in Duck Creek Missn Chrch Cem, near West Milford, Harrison Co, WV,[17] census 1880 in Grant District, Harrison Co, WV.

      v.   HOY DAYTON b. Mar-16-1871,[17] d. Mar-24-1871,[17] buried in Duck Creek Missn Chrch Cem, near West Milford, Harrison Co, WV.[230]

287. **Isaac M. Gaston** (142.James[6], 72.John[5], 21.John[4], 6.Hugh[3], 3.John[2], 1.Jean[1]), b. Apr- 1-1836,[17] d. Mar-16-1914 in Weston, Lewis Co, WV,[dlxxviii[578],17] buried in Duck Creek Missn Chrch Cem, near West Milford, Harrison Co, WV,[17] occupation miller.[270]

Isaac and his brother, John, were among the Gaston families for whom the community of GASTON in Lewis County, WV was named.

He married 1857, **Caroline M. West**, b. Jan-26-1835,[17] d. Oct-16-1911 in Weston, Lewis Co, WV,[17,dlxxix[579]] buried in Duck Creek Missn Chrch Cem, near West Milford, Harrison Co, WV.[17]

      Children:

      i.   AZALEA GASTON b. Mar- 2-1857,[363] d. Aug-22-1858,[17] ["Cemeteries of Grant District, Harrison County, WV," p. 28, reports death date as Aug 22 1856, age at death 1y 5m 23d.], buried in Duck Creek Missn Chrch Cem, near West Milford, Harrison Co, WV.[dlxxx[580]]

530. ii.   JOHN LEOLIN GASTON b. Sep-14-1860.

531. iii. THOMAS CHARLES GASTON b. Aug- 3-1863.

      iv. HARVEY GASTON b. 1866 in Harrison Co, WV,[17] d. Sep- 1-1869,[dlxxxi[581]] buried in Duck Creek Missn Chrch Cem, near West Milford, Harrison Co, WV.[17]

      v.   LUCY P. GASTON b. Jun- 4-1868,[dlxxxii[582]] d. Jun-11-1887 in Gaston, Lewis Co, WV,[dlxxxiii[583],17] buried in Duck Creek Missn Chrch Cem, near West Milford, Harrison Co, WV.[dlxxxiv[584]]

532. vi. HARLEY ROACH GASTON b. Jul-21-1871.

288. Margaret Drusilla Gaston (142.James[6], 72.John[5], 21.John[4], 6.Hugh[3], 3.John[2], 1.Jean[1]), b. Feb-19-1838,[278] d. Apr-24-1918 in Fairmont, Marion Co, WV,[278] buried in Woodlawn Cemetery, Fairmont, Marion Co, WV. She married Feb-28-1864 in Harrison Co, WV,[dlxxxv[585]] **Nathaniel David Helmick**, b. Jul-12-1837 in Fairmont, Marion Co, WV,[278] (son of Daniel Ryan Helmick and Mary McNemar), d. Apr-20-1923 in Fairmont, Marion Co, WV,[278] buried in Woodlawn Cemetery, Fairmont, Marion Co, WV.

      Children:

      i.   LUCY HELMICK b. Feb-23-1869 in Fairmont, Marion Co, WV,[398] d. Feb- 7-1950 near Bluefield, Mercer Co, WV,[398] buried in Woodlawn Cemetery, Fairmont, Marion Co, WV.[398] She married May-17-1899 in Fairmont, Marion Co, WV,[dlxxxvi[586]] no children from this marriage, John Scott Pierpoint, also known as John Scott Pierpont,[398] also known as John S. Peirpoint,[dlxxxvii[587],dlxxxviii[588]] b. May-20-1846 in Harrisville, Ritchie Co, WV,[398,46,dlxxxix[589]] (son of Zackquill M. Pierpoint and Martha Vandervort), d. Nov-16-1935 in Fairmont, Marion Co, WV,[398,46] buried in IOOF Cemetery, Harrisville, Ritchie Co, WV,[469] resided 1899 in Marion Co, WV,[589] census 1880 in Union District, Ritchie Co, WV.

533. ii.   FREDERICK HELMICK b. Aug-27-1871.

534. iii. ERNEST HELMICK b. Dec- 5-1873.

      iv. CARL HELMICK b. Feb-24-1876, d. Sep-24-1876, buried in Woodlawn Cemetery, Fairmont, Marion Co, WV.

535. v.   CARROLL HELMICK b. Oct-17-1878.

536. vi. LOUIS GASTON HELMICK b. Nov-23-1882.

289. Rebecca Alcinda Gaston (142.James[6], 72.John[5], 21.John[4], 6.Hugh[3], 3.John[2], 1.Jean[1]), b. May-25-1840 in Harrison Co, (W)VA,[398,227] d. Apr-26-1928 in Weston, Lewis Co, WV,[398] buried in Machpelah Cemetery, Weston, Lewis Co, WV,[398] resided in Harrison Co, (W)VA.[227] She married Dec-7-1859 in Harrison Co, (W)VA,[dxc[590]] **John Stewart**, b. 1834 in Louisa Co, VA,[227] (son of Robert Stewart and Eliza __), d. bef Apr 1928,[436] resided 1859 in Upshur Co, (W)VA.[227]

      Children:

537. i.   CHARLES L. STEWART b. Apr- -1862.

      ii.   JAMES T. STEWART b. 1863.

      iii. WILLIAM STEWART b. Dec- -1865.

      iv. JOHN C. STEWART b. Apr- 5-1868, d. Sep-22-1868,[17] buried in Duck Creek Missn Chrch Cem, near West Milford, Harrison Co, WV.[17]

      v.   FRANKLIN STEWART b. Apr- 1-1869, d. Mar-24-1870,[dxci[591]] buried in Duck Creek Missn Chrch Cem, near West Milford, Harrison Co, WV.[17]

538. vi. HITER STEWART b. Mar- -1871.

      vii. MALITAS STEWART b. 1872.

      viii. ARTHUR D. STEWART b. Aug- -1875 in Harrison Co, WV,[410] resided 1900 in Lewis Co, WV.[410] He married Oct-30-1900 in Lewis Co, WV,[410] Philena Bird Matthews, b. ca 1877,[410] (daughter of William J. Matthews and Sarah Ann __).

      ix. EVA DOVE STEWART[410] b. ca 1877 in Harrison Co, WV,[410] resided 1899 in Lewis Co, WV.[410] She married[519] Nov-22-1899 in Lewis Co, WV,[410] Benjamin Franklin "Frank" Matthews, also known as Frank Benjamin Matthews,[410] b. May- -1870 (son of William J. Matthews and Sarah Ann __).

       x.   DENT STEWART b. Oct- -1879.

       xi.   JOSEPHUS STEWART b. Jan- -1881.

       xii. MARY ELIZA STEWART[410], also known as Eliza Stewart,[dxcii][592] b. Dec- 7-1883,[592] d. Jul- -1978,[592] resided in Weston, Lewis Co, WV.[dxciii][593] She married Nov-22-1921 in Lewis Co, WV,[dxciv][594] Alois J. Salzer, b. ca 1874 in Cuyahoga Co, OH,[410] (son of A. F. Salzer and Sadie M. __), resided 1921 in Lewis Co, WV.[410]

       xiii. ETHEL STEWART b. Aug- -1885.

290. **Thomas M. Gaston** (142.James[6], 72.John[5], 21.John[4], 6.Hugh[3], 3.John[2], 1.Jean[1]), b. Oct- -1842 in Harrison Co, (W)VA,[dxcv][595] d. Jun-22-1913 in Fairmont, Marion Co, WV, buried in Woodlawn Cemetery, Fairmont, Marion Co, WV, resided in Gaston, Lewis Co, WV, occupation miller.[270] He married Nov-5-1867 in Marion Co, WV,[dxcvi][596],595 **Helen Summers**, b. May-11-1851 in Preston Co, (W)VA,[dxcvii][597] (daughter of Alp Summers and Margaret __), d. Dec- 8-1929 in Fairmont, Marion Co, WV, buried in Woodlawn Cemetery, Fairmont, Marion Co, WV.

       Children:

539. i.   ALBERT DALTON GASTON b. Jun-11-1868.

540. ii.   HARRY GASTON b. 1872.

541. iii. LELIA GASTON b. Nov-23-1880.

       iv. CLYDE GASTON b. Oct-24-1884 in Lewis Co, WV, d. May-11-1959 in Marion Co, WV, buried in Woodlawn Cemetery, Fairmont, Marion Co, WV. He married Sep-13-1904 in Marion Co, WV,[dxcviii][598] Mary Elizabeth Watkins, b. Dec-12-1883 in Marion Co, WV (daughter of James A. Watkins and Nancy Thomas), d. Dec-13-1972 in Marion Co, WV,[dxcix][599] buried in Woodlawn Cemetery, Fairmont, Marion Co, WV.

291. **Olive Jane Gaston** (142.James[6], 72.John[5], 21.John[4], 6.Hugh[3], 3.John[2], 1.Jean[1]), b. Jan-12-1845 in Harrison Co, (W)VA,[398] d. Oct- 2-1930 in Weston, Lewis Co, WV,[dc][600] buried in McWhorter Cemetery, Harrison Co, WV.[398] She married (1) Jan-7-1868 in Lewis Co, WV,[242] **William Henry Morris**, b. Apr- 4-1841 in Harrison Co, (W)VA,[17,230] d. Oct- 8-1893,[17,230] buried in McWhorter Cemetery, Harrison Co, WV.[17,230] She married (2) Apr- 6-1897 in Lewis Co, WV,[dci][601] **Wellington Vincent Chidester**, b. ca 1826,[410] (son of Phineas W. Chidester and Susannah __), d. bef Oct 1930.[436]

       Children by William Henry Morris:

542. i.   ETTA MAUDE MORRIS b. Feb-14-1869.

543. ii.   JAMES BENJAMIN MORRIS b. Jun- 3-1871.

544. iii. MARY CHARLOTTE MORRIS b. Sep- -1872.

       iv. THOMAS ERVIN MORRIS, also known as Ervin Morris,[577] b. May- 9-1876 in Harrison Co, WV,[398] d. Jan-30-1945 in Parkersburg, Wood Co, WV,[398] buried in Mt. Olivet Cemetery, Parkersburg, WV,[398] military Spanish-American War,[398] resided in Parkersburg, Wood Co, WV,[dcii][602],398 occupation salesman.[398] He married (1) Nov-24-1907,[dciii][603] Laura Gaston, b. Oct-10-1873 in Lewis Co, WV (daughter of George Gaston and Martha Ann Gibson). As great-grandchildren of John Gaston Jr. and Anna Davisson, Laura Gaston and Thomas Ervin Morris were second cousins.[603]

       He married (2) Aug-19-1922 in Parkersburg, Wood Co, WV,[602] Mayme Ballentine, also known as Mary May Ballantine,[602] b. Oct-18-1881 in Lewis Co, WV,[559,602] (daughter of John T. Ballentine and Merceline Peterson), d. Mar-26-1956 in Parkersburg, Wood Co, WV,[559] buried in Mt. Olivet Cemetery, Parkersburg, WV,[559] resided in Parkersburg, Wood Co, WV,[559] resided 1922 in Ripley, Jackson Co, WV.[602]

       v.   LUCY PAULINE MORRIS b. Feb-17-1879,[592,408,410] d. May- -1969,[592] resided in Grafton, Taylor Co, WV,[dciv][604] census 1900 in Skin Creek, Lewis Co, WV, census 1880 in Grant District, Harrison Co, WV. She married[373] Sep- 1-1914 in Lewis Co, WV,[410] Fay Osborne Watkins, b. ca 1875 in Marion Co, WV,[410] (son of E. F. Watkins and Delilah E. __), resided 1914 in Lewis Co, WV.[410]

292. **John M. "Lank" Gaston** (142.James[6], 72.John[5], 21.John[4], 6.Hugh[3], 3.John[2], 1.Jean[1]), b. Jun-27-1847 in Harrison Co, (W)VA,[398] d. Sep- 6-1926 in Gaston, Lewis Co, WV,[398,dcv[605]] buried in Peterson Cemetery, Lewis Co, WV,[398] resided in Gaston, Lewis Co, WV, census 1920 in Skin Creek, Lewis Co,

WV, occupation dry goods merchant,[247,398] occupation 1870 shoemaker.[270] He married Dec-22-1870 in Lewis Co, WV,[242] **Mary Margaret "Mollie" Morris**, b. ca 1843 in Kentucky,[426] (daughter of Thomas S. Morris and Prudence White), d. Jun- 3-1913 in Gaston, Lewis Co, WV,[289] buried in Peterson Cemetery, Lewis Co, WV.

        Children:
545.   i.   MINNIE IRIS GASTON b. Jan-10-1872.
546.   ii.   DAISY DEAN GASTON b. Mar-11-1874.

293. **Abraham Gaston**, also known as Abram Gaston,[245,246,247,396] (143.William[6], 72.John[5], 21.John[4], 6.Hugh[3], 3.John[2], 1.Jean[1]), b. Feb- 7-1830 in Harrison Co, (W)VA, d. Jun-12-1918,[dcvi[606]] buried in Beech Grove Cemetery, Lewis Co, WV, census 1860, 1870, 1880 in Lewis Co, WV, occupation farmer.[245,dcvii[607]]

1860 Census, Lewis County, Virginia (now West Virginia, enumerated on Jul 23 1860:
Abram Gaston, 30; Sarah A, 30; Mary E, 7; Amanda J, 5; Rebecca V, 2; Ida M, 6 months.

1870 Census, Lewis County, WV (Willey Twp), enumerated on Sep 2 1870:
Abram Gaston, 40; Sarah, 40; Mary C, 17; Mandy J, 15; Rebecca V, 12; Ida May, 10; Enoch A, 8; Adaline, 6; Benjamin, 4; William H, 1.

1880 Census, Freemans Creek, Lewis County, WV, enumerated on Jun 24 1880:
Abram Gaston, 50, wife Sarah, 50; dau Mary E, 27; dau Ida May, 20; son Enoch A, 18; dau Eva Bird, 16; son Benjamin L, 14; son Harvey William, 11, son Lloyd Henry, 6.

It is noted that one daughter was identified as Adaline (age 6) in the 1870 Census, but as Eva Bird (age 16) in the 1880 Census. No other reference to her as Eva Bird has been found.

He married Oct-23-1851 in Harrison Co, (W)VA,[dcviii[608],419] **Sarah Ann Morris**, b. Aug-28-1830 [Birth date on headstone: 1829.] (daughter of Benjamin Morris and Mary E. McWhorter), d. Oct-23-1908 in Freemans Creek, Lewis Co, WV, buried in Beech Grove Cemetery, Lewis Co, WV, census 1860 in Lewis Co, (W)VA.

        Children:
547.   i.   MARY E. GASTON b. Sep-18-1852.
      ii.   ADDISON T. GASTON b. Apr-30-1854 in Lewis Co, WV,[17] d. Apr-19-1856 in Lewis Co, WV,[17] buried in Beech Grove Cemetery, Lewis Co, WV.
548.   iii.   AMANDA JANE GASTON b. Mar- 3-1855.
549.   iv.   REBECCA VIRGINIA "JENNIE" GASTON b. Aug- 7-1857.
550.   v.   IDA MAY GASTON b. Jan- 6-1860.
      vi.   ENOCH ARLANDO GASTON b. Mar-28-1862,[17] d. Apr- 8-1935,[17] buried in Broad Run Bapt Ch Cem, Jane Lew, Lewis Co, WV,[17] resided in Ohio, census 1870, 1880 in Lewis Co, WV.[246,247] He married Sep-29-1908 in Lewis Co, WV,[410] Dove Margaret Whitesel, b. Oct-30-1878 (daughter of James Pope Whitesel and Delia Elvira Smith), d. Jul-17-1959, buried in Broad Run Bapt Ch Cem, Jane Lew, Lewis Co, WV.
551.   vii.   ADALINE BELL GASTON b. Dec-12-1864.
      viii.   LOMAN BENJAMIN GASTON, census name Benjamin L. Gaston,[246,247] b. Mar- 8-1866,[17] d. Aug-23-1951,[17] buried in Broad Run Bapt Ch Cem, Jane Lew, Lewis Co, WV,[dcix[609]] census 1870, 1880 in Lewis Co, WV.[246] He married Aug-14-1904 in Lewis Co, WV,[dcx[610]] Maretta D. "Retta" Norris, b. Jul- 4-1871,[dcxi[611],17] (daughter of J. Wilmer Norris and Jane Minter), d. Aug-28-1938 in Lewis Co, WV,[dcxii[612],17] buried in Broad Run Bapt Ch Cem, Jane Lew, Lewis Co, WV.[dcxiii[613]]
552.   ix.   WILLIAM HARVEY GASTON b. Oct-19-1868.
      x.   FLOYD SIMEON GASTON, also known as Simeon Floyd Gaston,[155] b. Aug- 9-1871, d. Aug- 9-1873 in Lewis Co, WV,[dcxiv[614]] buried in Beech Grove Cemetery, Lewis Co, WV.[dcxv[615]]
553.   xi.   LLOYD HENRY GASTON b. Aug- 4-1873.

294. George Gaston (143.William[6], 72.John[5], 21.John[4], 6.Hugh[3], 3.John[2], 1.Jean[1]), b. Sep-23-1831 [Birthdate has also appeared as Sep 23 1832.], d. Feb- 7-1901 in Freemans Creek, Lewis Co, WV,[dcxvi[616]] buried in Mt. Morris Cemetery, Freemansburg, Lewis Co, WV, census 1860 in Lewis Co, (W)VA, occupation farmer.[dcxvii[617]] He married Aug-25-1856 in Lewis Co, (W)VA,[242,dcxviii[618]] [Aug 26 1856 reported by Jim Comstock in "West Virginia Heritage Encyclopedia."], **Martha Ann Gibson**, b. Jul- 7-1838 (daughter of Smith Gibson and Malinda Hall), d. Feb-13-1909 in Freemans Creek, Lewis Co, WV,[dcxix[619]] buried in Mt. Morris Cemetery, Freemansburg, Lewis Co, WV, census 1860 in Lewis Co, (W)VA.

Children:

    i.   ALVIN S. GASTON b. Dec-17-1857 in Lewis Co, WV, d. Jul-31-1858 in Lewis Co, WV, buried in Gibson Farm, McCann's Run, Lewis Co, WV.[dcxx[620]]

554.   ii.   WILLIAM J. GASTON b. May-18-1859.

555.   iii.   EDWIN GASTON b. Aug- -1862.

    iv.   EMMA GASTON b. Nov-14-1864 at Freemansburg, Lewis Co, WV,[398,dcxxi[621]] d. Dec-12-1955 in Clarksburg, Harrison Co, WV,[398] buried in Good Hope Masonic Cemetery, Rt. 19 S, Harrison Co, WV,[dcxxii[622]] resided in Clarksburg, Harrison Co, WV.[398] She married (1) Sep-25-1887 in Lewis Co, WV,[dcxxiii[623]] Frank Harrison Rymer, b. ca 1861,[410] (son of Silas T. Rymer and Sarah C. Halterman). She married (2) Sep- 3-1893 at Two Lick, near Kincheloe, Harrison Co, WV,[dcxxiv[624]] John Marshall Thrash, b. May- 9-1836 in Hampshire Co, (W)VA,[17,621] d. Jul-17-1910 at Good Hope, Harrison Co, WV,[276,17] buried in Good Hope Masonic Cemetery, Rt. 19 S, Harrison Co, WV,[524] resided 1893 in Frontier Co, NE,[621] occupation farmer.[276] She married (3) Jun-29-1916 in Harrison Co, WV,[dcxxv[625]] Newton Jefferson Strader, also known as N. J. Strader,[398] b. ca 1858 in Lewis Co, (W)VA,[419] (son of Valentine Strader and Mary Jackson), d. Jan-11-1921 in Clarksburg, Harrison Co, WV,[398] buried in IOOF Cemetery, Clarksburg (S Chestnut St), Harrison Co, WV,[398] resided 1916 in Clarksburg, Harrison Co, WV,[419] occupation farmer.[398]

    v.   CLARK GASTON b. Oct- 6-1868 in Lewis Co, WV, d. Mar-22-1914 in Mineral, WV,[dcxxvi[626]] buried in Good Hope Masonic Cemetery, Rt. 19 S, Harrison Co, WV.[17,dcxxvii[627]] He married Dec-24-1890 in Lewis Co, WV,[410,dcxxviii[628]] Ida Bird Post, b. Sep- 9-1871 in Lewis Co, WV,[398,46,410] (daughter of William Post and Mary Hall), d. Sep- 1-1933 in Kincheloe (Jane Lew), Harrison Co, WV,[398,46] buried in Good Hope Masonic Cemetery, Rt. 19 S, Harrison Co, WV,[17,398,524] resided in Kincheloe (Jane Lew), Harrison Co, WV.[398]

    vi.   LAURA GASTON b. Oct-10-1873 in Lewis Co, WV. She married Nov-24-1907,[603] Thomas Ervin Morris, also known as Ervin Morris,[577] b. May- 9-1876 in Harrison Co, WV,[398] (son of William Henry Morris and Olive Jane Gaston), d. Jan-30-1945 in Parkersburg, Wood Co, WV,[398] buried in Mt. Olivet Cemetery, Parkersburg, WV,[398] military Spanish-American War,[398] resided in Parkersburg, Wood Co, WV,[602,398] occupation salesman.[398] As great-grandchildren of John Gaston Jr. and Anna Davisson, Laura Gaston and Thomas Ervin Morris were second cousins.[603]

    vii.   IVAN VALENTINE GASTON b. Jan-26-1880 in Lewis Co, WV,[46] d. Nov- 8-1917 in Weston, Lewis Co, WV,[398,46] buried in Machpelah Cemetery, Weston, Lewis Co, WV,[17] occupation agent for Northwestern Life Insurance Co.,[398] never married[398].

295. Elizabeth Gaston (143.William[6], 72.John[5], 21.John[4], 6.Hugh[3], 3.John[2], 1.Jean[1]), b. Jul-29-1835,[17] d. Apr- 3-1916,[17] buried in Duck Creek Missn Chrch Cem, near West Milford, Harrison Co, WV.[17] She married Oct-30-1856,[17] **John Dawson**, b. Feb-14-1835,[17] d. Sep-12-1881,[17] buried in Duck Creek Missn Chrch Cem, near West Milford, Harrison Co, WV.[17]

Children:

556.   i.   WILLIAM E. DAWSON b. Sep- -1859.

    ii.   MARY E. DAWSON b. May- -1862.

    iii.   EDITH M. DAWSON b. 1864.

    iv.   DORA A. DAWSON b. 1866.

557.   v.   HOMER E. DAWSON b. Jan- -1868.

    vi.   OAKEY C. DAWSON b. Sep- -1874.

558.   vii.   LEWIS D. DAWSON b. Nov- 6-1877.

viii.   OCKMAN T. DAWSON b. Aug- -1879.

296. **John William Gaston** (143.William[6], 72.John[5], 21.John[4], 6.Hugh[3], 3.John[2], 1.Jean[1]), b. Dec-26-1838, d. Aug-16-1910, buried in Rose Hill (formerly IOOF) Cemetery, West Milford, Harrison Co, WV,[17] census 1870, 1880 in Grant District, Harrison Co, WV. He married Dec-29-1859 in Harrison Co, (W)VA,[dcxxix[629]] **Mariah Burnside**, b. Jun- -1840 (daughter of James Burnside and Rebecca __), d. Mar- 3-1922, buried in Rose Hill (formerly IOOF) Cemetery, West Milford, Harrison Co, WV,[17] census 1870, 1880 in Grant District, Harrison Co, WV.

        Children:

        i.   LEONNE BIONA GASTON, census name Lionia Gaston,[527] census name Lione Gaston,[577] b. Oct-25-1860 in Harrison Co, (W)VA, census 1870, 1880 in Grant District, Harrison Co, WV. She married Jan-31-1884 in Harrison Co, WV,[dcxxx[630],433] George A. Davis, b. ca 1859,[227] (son of George A. Davis and Sarah __).

559.   ii.   GEORGE L. GASTON b. Jul- 6-1862.
560.   iii.   HIRAM J. GASTON b. Aug-12-1866.
561.   iv.   JAMES BURNSIDE GASTON b. Nov-22-1872.
562.   v.   MARY EFFIE GASTON b. Oct-20-1875.

        vi.   ALDA MAY GASTON, also known as May Gaston, b. Feb- 2-1879 in Harrison Co, WV,[dcxxxi[631],17] d. Jan-15-1928 in West Milford, Harrison Co, WV,[398,17] buried in Rose Hill (formerly IOOF) Cemetery, West Milford, Harrison Co, WV,[17,398] cause of death influenza,[398] census 1880 in Grant District, Harrison Co, WV, never married[398].

297. **Enoch Gaston** (143.William[6], 72.John[5], 21.John[4], 6.Hugh[3], 3.John[2], 1.Jean[1]), b. Aug-16-1841,[dcxxxii[632],467,46] d. Oct-31-1922 in Duck Creek, Harrison Co, WV,[632,46] buried in Duck Creek Missn Chrch Cem, near West Milford, Harrison Co, WV,[17,230] census 1880 in Grant District, Harrison Co, WV.

Enoch Gaston was a brother of George Gaston who married Martha Ann Gibson. Martha Ann Gibson was the aunt of Flora Bond (Enoch's wife) as well as Enoch's sister-in-law.[632]

He married (1) Nov-9-1865 in Harrison Co, WV,[dcxxxiii[633],433] **Laura T. Sheets**, b. Aug-29-1846 (daughter of George H. Sheets and Mary J. __), d. Feb-19-1877 in Harrison Co, WV,[276,dcxxxiv[634]] buried in Duck Creek Missn Chrch Cem, near West Milford, Harrison Co, WV,[17] cause of death consumption.[276] He married (2) Oct-20-1881 in Harrison Co, WV,[dcxxxv[635],433] **Flora Bond**, b. Feb-26-1858 in Harrison Co, VA,[dcxxxvi[636],46] (daughter of Abel P. Bond and Adeline "Addie" Gibson), d. Jul-14-1944,[46] buried in Duck Creek Missn Chrch Cem, near West Milford, Harrison Co, WV.[17,230]

        Children by Laura T. Sheets:

563.   i.   CORA GASTON b. Nov- -1866.

        ii.   WADE GASTON b. Mar- 7-1868 in Duck Creek, Harrison Co, WV,[dcxxxvii[637]] d. Feb-17-1943 in Lost Creek, Harrison Co, WV,[dcxxxviii[638]] buried in Mt. Olivet Cemetery, Parkersburg, WV,[190] [Harrison Co Death Record incorrectly states burial location as Jane Lew. But West Virginia State Death Certificate shows it as Parkersburg, and obituary specifies Mt. Olivet Cemetery in Parkersburg.], resided from 1927 in Lost Creek, Harrison Co, WV,[190] resided previously in Parkersburg, Wood Co, WV,[190,602] census 1880 in Grant District, Harrison Co, WV, occupation physician in Parkersburg (retired in 1927),[dcxxxix[639],190] education Eclectic Medical College of Cincinnati.[190] He married[484] Jun-30-1909 in Parkersburg, Wood Co, WV,[602] Anna Dell Hart, also known as Dell Hart,[484] b. ca 1887 in Wood Co, WV,[602] (daughter of Edmund B. Hart and Mary C. __), d. 1910.[484]

564.   iii.   CLAUDIUS GASTON b. Oct- 3-1869.
565.   iv.   BERTHA GASTON b. Aug-18-1871.

        Children by Flora Bond:

        v.   ETHEL GASTON b. Oct-24-1882 in Harrison Co, WV,[532,46] d. 1954,[46] buried in Duck Creek Missn Chrch Cem, near West Milford, Harrison Co, WV.[533] She married (1) Apr-12-1916 in Harrison Co, WV,[531] Henson Davisson Gaston,[419] b. Jun-10-1867 in Harrison Co, WV,[46] (son of James William Gaston and Sarah A. Ward), d. Feb-23-1920 at Duck Creek, Harrison Co, WV,[529,46] buried in Duck Creek Missn Chrch Cem, near West Milford, Harrison Co, WV,[17,398] occupation farmer,[398] census

1880, 1900 in Grant District, Harrison Co, WV. Henson D. Gaston and Ethel Gaston were double cousins, in that they were both second cousins (both were great-grandchildren of John Gaston, Jr. (b. 1752 in NJ)) and also fourth cousins (both were great-great-great-grandchildren of John Smith (b. 1699)).

She married (2) Sep- 4-1921 in Lost Creek, Harrison Co, WV,[dcxl[640]] Jesse A. Woofter, b. ca 1873 in Lewis Co, WV,[419] (son of Alfred Woofter and Mary Melvina Reed), resided 1921 in Weston, Lewis Co, WV.[419]

      vi.   CLARA GASTON b. Dec- 3-1884 in Harrison Co, WV.
566.   vii.   CHARLES HORNOR GASTON b. Dec- 3-1884.

298. **Mary Bird Gaston**, also known as Mary Byrd Gaston (143.William[6], 72.John[5], 21.John[4], 6.Hugh[3], 3.John[2], 1.Jean[1]), b. Jan-12-1853 in Harrison Co, (W)VA,[dcxli[641],dcxlii[642],46] d. Mar- 9-1936 in Lost Creek, Harrison Co, WV,[642,46] buried in Duck Creek Missn Chrch Cem, near West Milford, Harrison Co, WV.[17,230] She married Nov-13-1873 in Harrison Co, WV,[642] **Edward Newton Smith**, b. Sep-17-1851 in Harrison Co, WV,[276,46] (son of Watters Smith, Jr. and Ruanna West), d. Jul-29-1936 in Lost Creek, Harrison Co, WV,[276,642,46] buried in Duck Creek Missn Chrch Cem, near West Milford, Harrison Co, WV,[17,230] occupation farmer.[276] Mary Bird Gaston and husband Edward Newton Smith were first cousins once removed by virtue of her being the granddaughter, and his being the great- grandson, of John Gaston, Jr. (b. 1752). They were also second cousins by her being the great-granddaughter, and his being the great-grandson, of Andrew Davison (b. ca 1730). And they were third cousins by her being the great-great-granddaughter, and his being the great-great-grandson, of John Smith (b. 1699).

Children:
567.   i.   CECIL BEAUMONT SMITH b. Aug-27-1874.
      ii.   IVY SMITH b. Feb-13-1876 in Harrison Co, WV,[642,155] d. Mar-18-1877 in Harrison Co, WV,[642,17] buried in Duck Creek Missn Chrch Cem, near West Milford, Harrison Co, WV.[230]

Name sometimes listed as June or Juie, but Ivy is correct.

568.   iii.   LAURA SMITH b. Sep- 8-1878.
569.   iv.   ERNEST WELLINGTON "DOC" SMITH b. Aug- 9-1880.
      v.   CLARA SMITH b. Sep- 5-1882 in Harrison Co, WV,[155,642] d. May-17-1971.[155,642] She married[3/3] Sep-16-1908 in Harrison Co, WV,[dcxliii[643]] Lawrence Golding Kincheloe,[537] b. ca 1880,[537] (son of J. T. Kincheloe and Florence ___).
      vi.   EVERETT HORNER SMITH b. Jan- 9-1885 in Harrison Co, WV,[17,642] d. Feb- 7-1885 In Harrison Co, WV,[17,642] buried in Duck Creek Missn Chrch Cem, near West Milford, Harrison Co, WV.[17,230]
      vii.   BOYD ELSTON SMITH b. Jul-12-1886,[dcxliv[644]] [Donnelly (p. 416) reports birthdate as Jul 18 1886.], d. Jan-14-1887 in Harrison Co, WV,[17,642] buried in Duck Creek Missn Chrch Cem, near West Milford, Harrison Co, WV.[17,230]
      viii.   ARLIE SMITH b. May-25-1891 in Harrison Co, WV,[dcxlv[645]] resided 1977 in Salem, WV,[642] census 1900 in Grant District, Harrison Co, WV,[642] occupation Practical Nurse (19 yrs).[642]
570.   ix.   TENSIE SMITH b. Jun-22-1894.

299. **Samuel Gaston** (145.William[6], 74.John[5], 22.William[4], 6.Hugh[3], 3.John[2], 1.Jean[1]), b. 1800,[157] d. 1842.[157] He married[157] **Susannah Bowman**.
Children:
571.   i.   WILLIAM HENRY GASTON b. 1828.

300. **Martha Gaston** (147.James[6], 74.John[5], 22.William[4], 6.Hugh[3], 3.John[2], 1.Jean[1]), b. Jan-20-1805 in Pennsylvania,[66] d. Oct- 5-1883 in Clark Co, OH, resided (settled) in Clark Co, OH.[66]

Had twelve children. Rode on horseback from Pennsylvania to Clark County, Ohio before her marriage to Enoch King.

She married[66] 1826 [Probably Clark County, Ohio.], **Enoch King**, b. ca 1796 in New Jersey,[280] d. 1865 in Clark Co, OH.
>   Children:
> 572.   i.   NANCY JANE KING b. ca 1832.
>   ii. MARTHA A. KING b. ca 1846 in Ohio,[280] census 1860, 1870, 1880 in Clark Co, OH, occupation school teacher.[210]

301. **Rachel Gaston** (147.James[6], 74.John[5], 22.William[4], 6.Hugh[3], 3.John[2], 1.Jean[1]), b. Mar-18-1807 in Pennsylvania,[66,280] d. Oct- 7-1862,[66] census 1860 in Steubenville, Jefferson Co, OH, census 1850 in Columbiana Co, OH, resided (settled) in Steubenville, Jefferson Co, OH.[66] She married[66] **William S. Manfull**, b. ca 1806 in England,[280] census 1860 in Steubenville, Jefferson Co, OH, census 1850 in Columbiana Co, OH, occupation railroad contractor.[280]
>   Children:
>   i.   DORCAS MANFULL b. ca 1833 in Ohio,[146] census 1850 in Columbiana Co, OH.
>   ii. REBECCA MANFULL b. ca 1835 in Ohio,[146] census 1860 in Steubenville, Jefferson Co, OH, census 1850 in Columbiana Co, OH.
>   iii. SALINA MANFULL b. ca 1837 in Ohio,[146] census 1860 in Steubenville, Jefferson Co, OH, census 1850 in Columbiana Co, OH.
>   iv. BERTHINDA MANFULL b. ca 1841 in Ohio,[146] census 1860 in Steubenville, Jefferson Co, OH, census 1850 in Columbiana Co, OH. She married[12] William Henry Gaston, b. ca 1841 in Ohio,[146] (son of James Estep Gaston and Sarah Kirk), census 1850 in Warren, Trumbull Co, OH.[146]
>   v.   JANE MANFULL b. ca 1843 in Ohio,[146] census 1860 in Steubenville, Jefferson Co, OH, census 1850 in Columbiana Co, OH.

302. **James Estep Gaston** (147.James[6], 74.John[5], 22.William[4], 6.Hugh[3], 3.John[2], 1.Jean[1]), b. Apr-14-1809 in Pennsylvania,[66,146] d. 1888 in Des Moines, IA,[dcxlvi[646],dcxlvii[647],dcxlviii[648]] resided (settled) in Des Moines, IA,[66] census 1850 in Warren, Trumbull Co, OH,[146] occupation minister.[66,146]

1850 Census, District 142, Warren, Trumbull County, Ohio, enumerated on Jul 23 1850:
James E. Gaston, 41, b. Pennsylvania, occupation minister; Sarah Gaston, 35, b. Ohio; Thomas K. Gaston, 11, b. Ohio; William H. Gaston, 9, b. Ohio; Joseph J. Gaston, 7, b. Ohio; John R. (or K. ?) Gaston, 1, b. Ohio; Mary Gaston, 18, b. Ohio.
Household members are given here in the same sequence that they appear in the census. Relationships were not indicated.

In about 1850 (after July, per enumeration date of census), James Estep Gaston and family moved from Warren, Trumbull Co, Ohio, to Monmouth, Illinois, and then to Davenport, Iowa, later settling at Des Moines. [Hanna, p. 43] James Estep Gaston became acquainted with Alexander Campbell, founder of the Christian Church, liked his teachings and became a Christian minister, as did brothers Robert and Joseph. James was the first permanent minister of the Central Christian Church in Des Moines and was one of the early supporters of Drake University, a Christian Church school in Des Moines.[66,dcxlix[649]]

He married (1) 1838,[646,649] **Sarah Kirk**, b. 1815 in Ohio,[646,146] d. 1853,[646,649] census 1850 in Warren, Trumbull Co, OH.[146] He married (2) 1854,[648] **Catherine C. Estep**.

Catherine: James Estep Gaston's second wife, Catherine Estep Atkinson, was a widowed cousin who had two daughters of her own.[648]

>   Children by Sarah Kirk:
> 573.   i.   MARY GASTON[66] (foster) b. ca 1833.

154

ii.   THOMAS KIRK GASTON b. ca 1839 in Ohio,[146] census 1850 in Warren, Trumbull Co, OH.[146]

iii.   WILLIAM HENRY GASTON b. ca 1841 in Ohio,[146] census 1850 in Warren, Trumbull Co, OH.[146] He married[12] Berthinda Manfull, b. ca 1841 in Ohio,[146] (daughter of William S. Manfull and Rachel Gaston), census 1860 in Steubenville, Jefferson Co, OH, census 1850 in Columbiana Co, OH.

574.   iv.   JOSEPH JAMES GASTON[66] b. 1842.

v.   JOHN GASTON b. ca 1849 in Ohio,[146] census 1850 in Warren, Trumbull Co, OH.[146]

vi.   SARAH KIRK GASTON.

Children by Catherine C. Estep:

vii. ELLA GASTON b. 1856.[12]

575.   viii. ERNEST BERRY GASTON b. Nov-21-1861.

303. **Robert Gaston** (147.James[6], 74.John[5], 22.William[4], 6.Hugh[3], 3.John[2], 1.Jean[1]), b. Jul-25-1811 near Pittsburgh, Allegheny Co, PA,[dcl[650],66,17] d. Nov-28-1892 in Cranesville, Preston Co, WV,[dcli[651],17] buried in Cranesville Cemetery, Preston Co, WV,[134,dclii[652]] census 1850, 1860 in Mahaska Co, IA, occupation gunsmith, blacksmith.[146,280]

1840 Census, Vinton, Gallia County, Ohio
Household of Robert Gaston
1 Male 20-30
1 Female 15-20
2 Females under 5

This seems to be this Robert Gaston (b. 1811). A nearby household was that of James McGee (age 50-60), a presumed wife (50-60), and others ranging from 5 to 40. This is possibly Robert Gaston's father-in-law.

1850 Census, Mahaska County, Iowa, enumerated in Aug 1850:
Robert Gaston, 39, b. Pennsylvania, occupation gunsmith; Catherine, 26, b. Ohio; Mary, 16, b. Ohio; Emily, 9, b. Ohio; James, 7, b. Ohio; Cyrus, 5, b. Iowa (sic); David, 3, b. Iowa; Joseph, 1, b. Iowa.

1860 Census, Monroe Twp, Mahaska County, Iowa:
Robert Gaston, 50, b. Pennsylvania, occupation blacksmith; Catharine, 30, b. Ohio; Emily, 19, b. Ohio, seamstress; James, 18, b. Ohio, laborer; Cyrus, 15, b. Ohio; David, 13, b. Iowa; Joseph, 12, b. Iowa; George W, 10, b. Iowa; Robert W, 9, b. Iowa; Rosaltha, 2, b. Iowa.

He married (1) May- 3-1832,[12] **Lydia Soule**, b. 1813,[12] d. 1839.[12] He married (2) Mar- -1840,[652,12] **Catherine McGhee**, b. Feb- 2-1824 in Gallipolis, Gallia Co, OH,[652] d. Jul-20-1906 in Glen Elder, Mitchell Co, KS,[652] census 1850, 1860 in Mahaska Co, IA.

Children by Lydia Soule:

576.   i.   MARY GASTON[66] b. ca 1833.

ii.   DORCAS L. GASTON b. Nov-22-1839 in Ohio,[12] d. Sep-13-1932 in Kansas.[12] She married (1) Feb-11-1855,[12] Caleb Lewis Kirk, b. Feb- 2-1832,[12] d. May-12-1862.[12] Two children.[12]

She married (2) Dec-11-1863,[12] George W. Bump, b. 1840,[12] d. Mar-19-1880.[12] Two children.[12]

She married (3) Apr-21-1887,[12] Levi L. McBride, b. 1836,[12] d. Jul- 4-1904.[12]

Levi: Four children.[12]

Children by Catherine McGhee:

iii. EMILY GASTON b. Jan-10-1841 in Ohio,[12] d. Oct- 1-1922 in Nebraska,[12] census 1860 in Mahaska Co, IA, occupation 1860 seamstress.[280] She married[12] Maletus N. Bump, b. 1836.[12]

577. iv. JAMES ESTEP GASTON b. Jul-20-1842.
578. v. CYRUS GASTON b. Mar- 9-1845.
579. vi. DAVID GASTON b. Dec- 8-1846.
580. vii. JOSEPH GASTON b. Dec-10-1849.
581. viii. GEORGE WASHINGTON GASTON b. Aug-18-1851.
     ix. ROBERT W. GASTON b. Jun- 7-1854 in Iowa,[12,280] d. Sep-15-1938,[12] census 1860 in Mahaska Co, IA. He married[12] Ella Doran, b. Jun-23-1863,[12] d. Nov- 6-1888.[12]
     x. JOSIAH GASTON b. Mar-20-1856,[12] d. 1857.[12]
582. xi. ROSEALTHA GASTON b. Mar-19-1858.
583. xii. DORA GASTON b. Aug- -1860.

304. **Sarah Jane Gaston** (148.Samuel[6], 74.John[5], 22.William[4], 6.Hugh[3], 3.John[2], 1.Jean[1]), b. ca 1805 in Pennsylvania,[146,280] [Birth date reported in "Ohio Valley Genealogies," p. 43, as 1808. But age 45 in 1850 Census and age 55 in 1860 Census puts it at about 1805.], d. 1875,[66] census 1860 in Finleyville, Washington Co, PA, census 1850 in Perry Twp, Fayette Co, PA. She married[66] **James Estep**, b. ca 1800 in Pennsylvania,[280] (son of Robert Estep and Dorcas Estep), d. Feb-26-1861,[66] census 1860 in Finleyville, Washington Co, PA, census 1850 in Perry Twp, Fayette Co, PA, occupation physician, later a Baptist minister,[146,280,66]
     Children:
584. i. JOSIAH MORGAN ESTEP b. Feb-19-1829.
585. ii. HARRISON ESTEP b. Jul- -1833.
     iii. RACHEL ESTEP b. ca 1837 in Pennsylvania,[280] census 1860 in Finleyville, Washington Co, PA.[280]
     iv. ROXANNA ESTEP b. ca 1839 in Pennsylvania,[280] census 1860 in Finleyville, Washington Co, PA,[280] census 1850 in Perry Twp, Fayette Co, PA.
     v. CAROLINE ESTEP b. ca 1840 in Pennsylvania,[146,280] census 1860 in Finleyville, Washington Co, PA.[280]
586. vi. JAMES ESTEP b. Oct- -1841.

305. **William Gaston** (148.Samuel[6], 74.John[5], 22.William[4], 6.Hugh[3], 3.John[2], 1.Jean[1]), b. 1807,[66] d. Jan-16-1884,[17] [Hanna, p. 43, gives William Gaston's birth/death dates as 1807-1880, but headstone states "died Jan 16 1884 in his 77th year."], buried in Mingo Creek Presb Cem, Union Twp, Washington Co, PA.[17,67] He married[66] **Susan (Eliza) Morrison**, also known as Eliza Morrison,[66] b. Mar-15-1809,[67] (daughter of Henry Morrison and Patience Sayers), d. Dec-20-1885,[67] buried in Mingo Creek Presb Cem, Union Twp, Washington Co, PA.[67]

Susan: The name of William Gaston's wife is given by Charles A. Hanna in "Ohio Valley Genealogies," p. 43, as Eliza Morrison. However, Peter J. Topoly and Jane Carson Topoly, having done considerable on-site research in Washington Co, PA, identify her as Susan Morrison, daughter of Henry and Patience Sayers Morrison. It was the Topolys who identified the descendants of William and Susan Morrison Gaston as described in this genealogy.
Residing in the same household, according to the 1850 Census of Union Twp, Washington Co, PA, were Ann Lytle, 32, relationship unknown, and Joseph Estep, 21, relationship unknown, a school teacher.

     Children:
587. i. JAMES M. GASTON b. 1830.
     ii. SUSAN C. A. GASTON[17] b. ca 1836 in Union Twp, Washington Co, PA,[67,dcliii[653]] d. Jul-22-1856,[17] buried in Mingo Creek Presb Cem, Union Twp, Washington Co, PA.[17]

306. **Eliza Gaston** (148.Samuel[6], 74.John[5], 22.William[4], 6.Hugh[3], 3.John[2], 1.Jean[1]), b. ca 1809 in Pennsylvania,[dcliv[654],66] [Birth date reported in "Ohio Valley Genealogies," p. 43, as 1810, but age 42 in 1850 puts it at about 1808.], d. bef 1851, census 1850 in Union Twp, Washington Co, PA. She married[66] **Samuel Morgan**, b. ca 1798 in Pennsylvania,[654] census 1850, 1860 in Union Twp, Washington Co, PA, occupation miller.[654,280]

156

Children:
    i.   HUGH MORGAN b. ca 1828,[dclv[655]] d. May- 2-1833,[17] buried in Mingo Creek Presb Cem, Union Twp, Washington Co, PA.[17]
    ii.   MATILDA MORGAN b. ca 1829,[17] d. Sep-11-1841,[17] buried in Mingo Creek Presb Cem, Union Twp, Washington Co, PA.[dclvi[656]]
    iii.   PATIENCE A. MORGAN b. ca 1836 in Pennsylvania,[654] census 1850 in Union Twp, Washington Co, PA.
    iv.   FRANCIS MORGAN, census name Francess Morgan,[654] b. ca 1838 in Pennsylvania,[654] census 1850, 1860 in Union Twp, Washington Co, PA.
    v.   ANN E. MORGAN b. ca 1840 in Pennsylvania,[654] census 1850 in Union Twp, Washington Co, PA.
    vi.   MARY N. MORGAN b. ca 1842 in Pennsylvania,[654] census 1850, 1860 in Union Twp, Washington Co, PA.
    vii.   TEPHANES MORGAN b. ca 1846 in Pennsylvania,[654] census 1850, 1860 in Union Twp, Washington Co, PA.
    viii.   SAMUEL MORGAN b. ca 1851 in Pennsylvania,[280] census 1860 in Union Twp, Washington Co, PA.

307. **Joseph Smith Gaston** (148.Samuel[6], 74.John[5], 22.William[4], 6.Hugh[3], 3.John[2], 1.Jean[1]), b. Apr- 1-1811,[17,67] d. Jan-15-1879,[dclvii[657],dclviii[658]] buried in Mingo Creek Presb Cem, Union Twp, Washington Co, PA,[17,67] census 1850, 1860 in Union Twp, Washington Co, PA, occupation farmer.[654]

Served 45 years as Justice of the Peace and was twice elected County Commissioner, dying during his second term.[67]

He married 1831,[282] **Jane Hindman**, b. ca 1808 in Pennsylvania,[146,74] (daughter of John Hindman and Sarah Patten), d. Aug- 5-1871,[dclix[659],dclx[660]] [DAR Lineage Book, Vol 163, p. 77, states death date as 1868, while Hanna's "Ohio Valley Genealogies," p. 43, reports it as 1879. But headstone clearly shows it as Aug 5 1871 "in the 63 year of her age."], buried in Mingo Creek Presb Cem, Union Twp, Washington Co, PA,[17,67] census 1850, 1860 in Union Twp, Washington Co, PA.
    Children:
588.   i.   SAMUEL GASTON b. Dec- -1831.
589.   ii.   SARAH GASTON b. ca 1834.
590.   iii.   MARGARET GASTON b. ca 1836.
    iv.   MARY JANE GASTON, census name Jane Gaston, b. ca 1838 in Union Twp, Washington Co, PA,[67] d. bef 1910,[67] census 1850, 1860 in Union Twp, Washington Co, PA. She married[67] Alfred Huffman.
591.   v.   JOHN H. GASTON b. Oct- -1839.
592.   vi.   JOSEPH S. GASTON, JR. b. 1843.
    vii.   WILLIAM R. GASTON b. ca 1846 in Union Twp, Washington Co, PA,[67] d. Oct-10-1868,[dclxi[661]] buried in Mingo Creek Presb Cem, Union Twp, Washington Co, PA,[17] census 1850, 1860 in Union Twp, Washington Co, PA.
    viii.   MARTHA E. GASTON b. ca 1849 in Pennsylvania,[146] census 1850, 1860 in Union Twp, Washington Co, PA.

308. **William Gaston** (150.Charles[6], 75.William[5], 22.William[4], 6.Hugh[3], 3.John[2], 1.Jean[1]), b. ca 1820 in Pennsylvania,[146] census 1850, 1860 in Van Buren Co, Iowa, resided 1856 in Van Buren Co, Iowa,[288] resided from abt 1839 in Iowa,[288] occupation carpenter.[146,288] He married **Rachel __**, b. ca 1826 in Indiana,[146,288] census 1850, 1860 in Van Buren Co, Iowa, resided 1856 in Van Buren Co, Iowa,[288] resided from abt 1839 in Iowa.[288]
    Children:
    i.   JAMES GASTON b. ca 1847 in Iowa,[146] census 1850, 1860 in Van Buren Co, Iowa, resided 1856 in Van Buren Co, Iowa,[288] [Middle initial either W or M.].

ii.   GEORGE W. GASTON b. ca 1849 in Iowa,[146] [Age given as 9 in the 1860 Census, but he appeared in the 1850 Census at age one.], census 1850, 1860 in Van Buren Co, Iowa, resided 1856 in Van Buren Co, Iowa.[288]

iii.   JOHN GASTON b. ca 1855,[288] census 1860 in Van Buren Co, Iowa, resided 1856 in Van Buren Co, Iowa.[288]

iv.   ANNA GASTON b. ca 1858 in Iowa,[280] census 1860 in Van Buren Co, Iowa.

309. **Margaret Gaston** (150.Charles[6], 75.William[5], 22.William[4], 6.Hugh[3], 3.John[2], 1.Jean[1]), b. Apr-21-1823 in Columbia, Washington Co, PA,[286] d. Feb-15-1899 in Bloomfield, Davis Co, IA,[286] buried in Runkle Cemetery, Fox River Twp, Davis Co, IA. She married Apr-23-1843,[286] **Moses Minear**, b. Apr-10-1814 in St. George, Tucker Co, WV,[286] d. Apr- 3-1897 in Bloomfield, Davis Co, IA,[286] buried in Runkle Cemetery, Fox River Twp, Davis Co, IA.[286] Moses and Margaret Gaston Minear had nine children.[286]

Children:
593.   i.   JASPER MINEAR b. Jan-14-1852.

310. **Hamilton Gaston** (153.Joseph[6], 77.Hugh[5], 23.Joseph[4], 6.Hugh[3], 3.John[2], 1.Jean[1]), b. ca 1828 in Ohio,[146] [Age 36 and 56 in 1860 and 1880 censuses would put birth in about 1824, but age 22 in 1850 Census puts it in about 1828.], census 1860, 1880 in Petaluma, Sonoma Co, CA, census 1850 in Columbiana Co, OH, occupation farmer.[210] He married **Mary A. __**, b. ca 1839 in Ohio,[280] census 1860, 1880 in Petaluma, Sonoma Co, CA.

1860 Census, Sonoma Co, California (Petaluma Twp), enumerated on Jun 13 1860:
Hamilton Gaston, 36, b. Ohio, farmer; Mary A, 21, b. Ohio; George, 11 months, b. California. (Note: In a nearby household was Hugh Gaston, 27, b. Ohio, farmer.)

1880 Census, Sonoma Co, California (Petaluma Twp), enumerated on Jun 24 1880:
Hamilton Gaston, 56, b. Ohio (father b. Pa, mother b. Ohio), farmer; wife Mary A, 41, b. Ohio; son George W, 20, b. Cal; son William (H or N), 19, b. Cal; dau Elizabeth, 13, b. Cal; dau Mary E, 6, b. Cal; boarder Agnes W. Conlan, 31, b. Mich, teacher.

Children:
i.   GEORGE W. GASTON b. 1859 in California,[280] census 1860, 1880 in Petaluma, Sonoma Co, CA.

ii.   WILLIAM GASTON b. ca 1861 in California,[210] census 1880 in Petaluma, Sonoma Co, CA.

iii.   ELIZABETH GASTON b. ca 1867 in California,[210] census 1880 in Petaluma, Sonoma Co, CA.

iv.   MARY E. GASTON b. ca 1874 in California,[210] census 1880 in Petaluma, Sonoma Co, CA.

311. **Martin Gaston** (153.Joseph[6], 77.Hugh[5], 23.Joseph[4], 6.Hugh[3], 3.John[2], 1.Jean[1]), b. ca 1830 in Ohio,[146] census 1870, 1880 in Petaluma, Sonoma Co, CA, census 1850 in Columbiana Co, OH, occupation 1880 farmer,[210] occupation 1870 dairyman,[209] occupation 1850 school teacher.[146] He married **Melinda __**, b. ca 1838 in Missouri,[209] d. bef Jun 1880,[210] census 1870 in Petaluma, Sonoma Co, CA.
Children:
i.   JOHN W. GASTON b. ca 1859 in California, census 1880 in Petaluma, Sonoma Co, CA.

ii.   DORA E. GASTON b. ca 1863 in California,[210] census 1880 in Petaluma, Sonoma Co, CA.

312. **Hugh Gaston** (153.Joseph[6], 77.Hugh[5], 23.Joseph[4], 6.Hugh[3], 3.John[2], 1.Jean[1]), b. ca 1833 in Ohio, census 1860, 1880 in Petaluma, Sonoma Co, CA, census 1850 in Columbiana Co, OH. He married **Ellen __**, b. ca 1838 in Ohio,[210] census 1880 in Petaluma, Sonoma Co, CA.
Children:

    i.   MARY B. GASTON b. ca 1870 in California.[210]

    ii.   CATHARINE R. GASTON b. ca 1871 in California, census 1880 in Petaluma, Sonoma Co, CA.

    iii.   LULU I. GASTON b. ca 1878 in California,[210] census 1880 in Petaluma, Sonoma Co, CA.

313. **Nancy Gaston** (154.James[6], 77.Hugh[5], 23.Joseph[4], 6.Hugh[3], 3.John[2], 1.Jean[1]), b. ca 1825 in Ohio,[209] census 1870, 1880 in Cadiz, Harrison Co, OH. She married[69] May- 8-1851 in Columbiana Co, OH,[dclxii[662]] **Stuart Beebe Shotwell**, census name Stewart B. Shotwell, b. Nov-22-1819,[84] (son of William Shotwell and Rhoda Beebe), d. Dec- 3-1890,[84] census 1870, 1880 in Cadiz, Harrison Co, OH, occupation lawyer.[210]

1870 Census, Harrison Co, Ohio (town of Cadiz), enumerated on Jun 6 1870:
S B Shotwell (male), 50; Nancy G, 45; Martha B, 15; Walter G, 13; Stewart B, 10; Rhoda, 76. All born in Ohio except for Rhoda, born in Massachusetts.

1880 Census, Harrison Co, Ohio (town of Cadiz), enumerated on Jun 9 1880:
Stewart B Shotwell, 60, b. Ohio (both parents b. Pa), lawyer; wife Nancy, 56, b. Ohio (both parents b. Pa); dau Mattie, 25, b. Ohio; son Walter, 23, law student; son Stewart B Jr, 19, at school, servant Maggie Hatcher, 19, b. Ohio.

    Children:
    i.   MARY SHOTWELL b. 1853,[84] d. in infancy.[84]
    ii.   MARTHA B. SHOTWELL, census name Mattie Shotwell, b. ca 1855 in Ohio,[209] census 1870, 1880 in Cadiz, Harrison Co, OH.
594.   iii.   WALTER GASTON SHOTWELL b. Dec-27-1856.
595.   iv.   STUART BEEBE SHOTWELL, JR. b. Apr- -1861.
    v.   WILLIAM JAMES SHOTWELL d. in infancy.[84]

314. **Philander Gaston**, census name Filander Gaston (154.James[6], 77.Hugh[5], 23.Joseph[4], 6.Hugh[3], 3.John[2], 1.Jean[1]), b. Aug- 1-1828 in Ohio,[12,67] d. Aug-14-1921 in Columbiana Co, OH,[dclxiii[663]] census 1850, 1920 in Columbiana Co, OH.

The 3038-acre Beaver Creek State Park is located at 12021 Echo Dell Road in East Liverpool, OH. The park area was established in 1945 with a gross average of a possible 20,000 acres. The nucleus of this park is Gaston's Mill, a 19th century grist mill. Thomas Whitacre built the mill in about 1837. The next owner was Philander Gaston who operated it longer than any other owner, hence the name. It operates on waterpower, is built almost entirely of wood and utilizes authentic mill stones. On weekends during the summer it grinds corn meal, whole wheat and buckwheat flour, which may be purchased at the mill. Gaston's Mill and the adjacent pioneer village especially come to life during the annual Pioneer Craft Days event held the first weekend in October.
<http://www.bchistory.org/beavercounty/BeaverCountyTopical/parks/StateParks/StateParksMSU 90.html>
<http://www.dnr.state.oh.us/parks/parks/beaverck.htm>
<http://fpw.isoc.net/KREK/Columbiana_Gastons_Mill_Page.htm>

He married[69] (1) **Lucretia (Lucinda) Conkle**.[12] He married[69] (2) Nov-17-1859 in Columbiana Co, OH,[67,12] **Charity Moore**, b. 1832 in Ohio,[12] d. 1908.[12]
    Children by Lucretia (Lucinda) Conkle:
596.   i.   ELIZABETH "LIZZIE" GASTON b. Feb- -1852.
597.   ii.   NANCY GASTON b. ca 1854.
    Children by Charity Moore:
598.   iii.   MARTHA A. "MATTIE" GASTON b. 1862.
599.   iv.   JOHN C. GASTON b. Jun- -1866.
600.   v.   WILLIAM KILGORE GASTON b. Feb- 6-1868.
601.   vi.   JAMES M. GASTON b. 1872.

315. **Narcissa Gaston** (154.James[6], 77.Hugh[5], 23.Joseph[4], 6.Hugh[3], 3.John[2], 1.Jean[1]), b. ca 1830 in Ohio,[146,210] census 1880 in Decatur, Decatur Co, Iowa, census 1850 in Columbiana Co, OH. She married[69] **Albert Brockway**, b. ca 1828 in Ohio,[210] census 1880 in Decatur, Decatur Co, Iowa.
Children:
    i.   AURE V. BROCKWAY b. ca 1866 in Iowa,[210] census 1880 in Decatur, Decatur Co, Iowa.

316. **Hamilton D. Gaston** (155.Hugh[6], 77.Hugh[5], 23.Joseph[4], 6.Hugh[3], 3.John[2], 1.Jean[1]), b. Dec-26-1825 in Columbiana Co, OH,[290] [Birth date given in 1900 Census as Dec 1823.], census 1900 in Toronto, Jefferson Co, OH, census 1870, 1880 in Knox Twp, Jefferson Co, OH, resided as of Apr 1860 in Knox Twp, Jefferson Co, OH,[dclxiv[664]] occupation farmer.[290] He married Apr-20-1852 in Columbiana Co, OH,[290,295] **Jane Davison**, also known as Jane Davidson,[295] b. ca 1833 in Ohio,[209] (daughter of William Davison), census 1900 in Toronto, Jefferson Co, OH, census 1870, 1880 in Knox Twp, Jefferson Co, OH.

1860 Census, Jefferson Co, Ohio (Knox Twp), enumerated on Jul 1 1860:
Hamilton Gaston, 32, b. Ohio, farmer; Mary, 25, b. Ohio; Hugh, 10, b. Ohio; James, 8, b. Ohio.

1870 Census, Jefferson Co, Ohio (Knox Twp), enumerated in July 1870:
Hamilton D. Gaston, 44, b. Ohio, farmer; Jane, 37, b. Ohio; H. Calvin, 16, b. Ohio; Wm. S, 12, b. Ohio; Mary, 6, b. Ohio.

1880 Census, Jefferson Co, Ohio (Knox Twp), enumerated on Jun 24 1880;
Hamilton Gaston, 56, b. Ohio, farmer; wife Jane, 45, b. Ohio; son William, 23, b. Ohio; dau Mary, 15, b. Ohio; servant Thomas (illegible), 13, b. Pa.

1900 Census, Jefferson Co, Ohio (village of Toronto), enumerated on Jun 5 1900:
Hamilton D. Gaston, 76, b. Dec 1823 in Ohio, retired farmer, married 48 yrs; wife Jane, 67, b. May 1833 in Ohio, mother of 4 children (3 still living).

        Children:
    i.   CALVIN H. GASTON, census name H. Calvin Gaston, b. ca 1854 in Ohio,[209] census 1870 in Knox Twp, Jefferson Co, OH.
    ii.   WILLIAM S. GASTON b. ca 1858 in Ohio,[209] census 1870, 1880 in Knox Twp, Jefferson Co, OH.
    iii.   MARY L. GASTON b. ca 1864 in Ohio,[209] census 1870, 1880 in Knox Twp, Jefferson Co, OH.
    iv.   (UNNAMED FEMALE) GASTON d. in infancy.[290]

317. **Gilbert Gaston Gordon**, also known as Gaston Gordon (156.Jane[6], 78.James[5], 23.Joseph[4], 6.Hugh[3], 3.John[2], 1.Jean[1]), b. Jan-10-1832 in Moon Twp, Allegheny Co, PA,[291] d. Jun- 8-1892,[291] buried in Sharon Presbyterian Cemetery.

Died when struck by lightning on his way back from the barn after milking. Following in his father's footsteps, Gaston, as he was called, was installed as an elder at Sharon Presbyterian Church on March 29 1891.

He married May-20-1875,[291] **Julia Ann Beers**, b. Nov-__-1859 in Newport, KY,[291] (daughter of Charles Beers and Sophia Sandels), d. Jul-12-1929 in Moon Twp, Allegheny Co, PA,[291] buried in Sharon Presbyterian Cemetery.[291]
Children:
    i.   WILLIAM F. GORDON b. Jul-27-1876 in Moon Twp, Allegheny Co, PA, d. Feb- 7-1936.

        Never married.

602. ii. LOUIS CLARK GORDON b. May- 8-1878.
603. iii. GILBERT MONTGOMERY "BERTIE" GORDON b. Mar-16-1880.

318. **Samuel W. Gaston** (159.Ephraim[6], 79.Alexander[5], 23.Joseph[4], 6.Hugh[3], 3.John[2], 1.Jean[1]), b. 1831 in Morristown, Belmont Co, OH,[166] d. ca 1862,[166] buried in Morristown Union Cemetery, Belmont Co, OH,[67] census 1850 in Morristown, Belmont Co, OH, occupation teacher.

"In early manhood he taught school at Wheeling, improving his time meanwhile reading the law. He located at St. Clairsville in 1855, and the following year was elected clerk of the courts. He was a fine scholar and a matchless orator. He died at the early age of thirty-one, the most brilliant and promising young man of his time."[dclxv[665]]

He married Jul- 8-1857 in Belmont Co, OH,[dclxvi[666]] **Margaret F. Hazlett**, b. 1837,[67] d. 1910,[67] buried in Morristown Union Cemetery, Belmont Co, OH,[67] resided in Morristown, Belmont Co, OH.[67]
Children:
i. ISAAC HAZLETT GASTON b. Jul- 6-1858 in St. Clairsville, Belmont Co, OH,[166] d. 1932,[67] buried in Union Cemetery, St. Clairsville, Belmont Co, OH,[67] occupation Judge & U.S. Congressman.

Received his early education in the public schools of Morristown, OH. He entered Washington-Jefferson College in 1876, graduating in 1879. He then entered the law office of the Hon. L. Danford. In 1884 he was elected probate judge of Belmont Co, re-elected in 87. When first elected, he was the youngest man ever chosen to that office in that part of Ohio, but its duties were discharged with such dignity and ability that at his second election, his majority was more than doubled.[dclxvii[667]]

He married[67] Ina Tallman, b. 1870,[67] d. 1956,[67] buried in Union Cemetery, St. Clairsville, Belmont Co, OH.[67]

319. **John Woodrow Lippincott** (160.Charity[6], 79.Alexander[5], 23.Joseph[4], 6.Hugh[3], 3.John[2], 1.Jean[1]), b. Feb-15-1835 in Morristown, Belmont Co, OH,[164,146] d. Feb- 1-1907 in Barnesville, Belmont Co, OH,[164] census 1850, 1860, 1870 in Morristown, Belmont Co, OH, occupation merchant.[280,209] He married **Clarissa Gardner**, census name Clara, b. Feb-18-1838 in Morristown, Belmont Co, OH,[164,280] d. Dec-13-1929 in Barnesville, Belmont Co, OH,[164] census 1860, 1870 in Morristown, Belmont Co, OH.
Children:
604. i. MARGRET ORR LIPPINCOTT b. Jun-29-1859.
ii. CHESTER LIPPINCOTT b. ca 1861 in Ohio,[209] census 1870 in Morristown, Belmont Co, OH.
iii. WOODROW LIPPINCOTT b. ca 1863 in Ohio,[209] census 1870, 1880 in Morristown, Belmont Co, OH.
iv. GEORGE LIPPINCOTT b. ca 1865 in Ohio,[209] census 1870 in Morristown, Belmont Co, OH.
v. MARY LIPPINCOTT b. ca 1869 in Ohio,[209] census 1870 in Morristown, Belmont Co, OH.

320. **Martha Lippincott** (160.Charity[6], 79.Alexander[5], 23.Joseph[4], 6.Hugh[3], 3.John[2], 1.Jean[1]), b. ca 1840 in Ohio,[146] census 1850, 1880 in Morristown, Belmont Co, OH. She married **John O. Fisher**, b. ca 1838 in Virginia (now West Virginia),[210] [Father born in Scotland, mother in Maryland.], census 1880 in Morristown, Belmont Co, OH, occupation druggist.[210]
Children:
i. MARY FISHER b. ca 1864 in Ohio,[210] census 1880 in Morristown, Belmont Co, OH.
ii. BELLE FISHER b. ca 1872 in Ohio,[210] census 1880 in Morristown, Belmont Co, OH.

321. **Henrietta Gaston** (161.Matthew[6], 79.Alexander[5], 23.Joseph[4], 6.Hugh[3], 3.John[2], 1.Jean[1]), b. ca 1844 in Ohio,[146] resided 1877 in Plattsmouth, Cass Co, NE, census 1850, 1860 in Cambridge, Guernsey Co, OH. She married **Eli Plummer**, b. ca 1836 in Ohio, resided 1877 in Plattsmouth, Cass Co, NE.

        Children:

        i.   FREDERICK PLUMMER b. ca 1872 in Nebraska, census 1877 in Plattsmouth, Cass Co, NE.

        ii.   RALPH PLUMMER b. ca 1874 in Nebraska, resided 1877 in Plattsmouth, Cass Co, NE.

322. **Hosea Pearce** (173.Elizabeth[6], 82.Mary[5], 27.Margaret[4], 8.Joseph[3], 3.John[2], 1.Jean[1]), b. Apr-16-1798 in Montgomery Co, TN,[64] d. Jul- 8-1874 in White Co, IL,[64] buried Old Prairie Cemetery in White Co, IL.[64]

He came to White County, Illinois in 1817 with his parents. He was a Colonel in the Black Hawk Wars of 1832 and was the Sheriff of White County for six years.

[64]

He married 1818 in White Co, IL,[64] **Nancy O'Neal**, b. 1800 in Smith Co, TN,[64] d. Sep-14-1883 in White Co, IL.[64]

        Children:

605.   i.   BATHANNA PEARCE b. Jan-22-1822.

323. **DeWitt Clinton Johnston** (174.James[6], 83.Sarah[5], 27.Margaret[4], 8.Joseph[3], 3.John[2], 1.Jean[1]), b.[172.] He married[172] **Margretta Bower**.

        Children:

        i.   WILLIAM WIRT JOHNSTON II b.[172.]

        ii.   JAMES BOWER JOHNSTON b.[172.]

606.   iii. HAROLD WHETSTONE JOHNSTON.

324. **William Ker Gaston** (175.John[6], 84.William[5], 28.John[4], 8.Joseph[3], 3.John[2], 1.Jean[1]), b. Jul-23-1806 in New Jersey,[27,209] d. Dec-24-1885,[27] census 1870 in Bridgewater, Somerset Co, NJ, occupation merchant.[209] He married Nov-10-1846, **Aletta Margaret Tunison**, census name Margaret,[209] b. Aug-5-1821 in New Jersey (daughter of Abraham Tunison), d. Dec-12-1890, census 1870 in Bridgewater, Somerset Co, NJ.

        Children:

        i.   ELIZABETH GASTON b. Sep-13-1847, d. Jan-23-1858.

607.   ii.   WALTER GASTON b. ca 1850.

608.   iii. MARY GASTON b. Sep-10-1851.

325. **Daniel Castner Gaston** (175.John[6], 84.William[5], 28.John[4], 8.Joseph[3], 3.John[2], 1.Jean[1]), b. Oct-14-1807,[dclxviii[668]] d. Aug- 2-1888 in Somerset Co, NJ,[dclxix[669]] census 1860 in Bedminster Twp, Somerset Co, NJ. He married Jan-28-1830, **Ida Ann Vliet**, b. Jul- 9-1811 in New Jersey,[27,280] (daughter of William Vliet and Catherine Van Dyke), d. Feb-29-1880, census 1860 in Bedminster Twp, Somerset Co, NJ.

        Children:

609.   i.   MARGARET GASTON b. Nov-16-1830.

610.   ii.   WILLIAM GASTON b. Oct-26-1839.

611.   iii. JOHN D. GASTON b. ca 1842.

326. **Samuel Brant Gaston** (175.John[6], 84.William[5], 28.John[4], 8.Joseph[3], 3.John[2], 1.Jean[1]), b. Dec-14-1809 in New Jersey,[27,280] d. Nov- 1-1870,[27] census 1860 in Trenton, Mercer Co, NJ, occupation merchant, tailor.[280] He married Jun-15-1833,[27] **Jane Maria Van Derveer**, b. Oct- 4-1815 in New Jersey,[27] (daughter of Tunis Van Derveer and Sarah Van Arsdale), d. Jun-28-1891,[27] census 1860 in Trenton, Mercer Co, NJ.

Children:

    i.   SARAH GASTON.

    Died in infancy.

    ii.   SARAH JANE GASTON b. May-11-1835,[27] d. Jun-11-1836.[27]

612. iii. WILLIAM B. GASTON b. Mar-29-1837.

    iv. CORNELIA JANE GASTON b. Mar-10-1841 in New York,[27,280] d. Dec- 4-1891,[27] census 1860 in Trenton, Mercer Co, NJ. She married Owen Huntington Day, occupation Captain.

    v.   EMMA LOUISE GASTON b. ca 1844 in New York,[280] census 1860 in Trenton, Mercer Co, NJ.

    vi. SAMUEL BRANT GASTON, JR. b. Feb-14-1846 in New York,[27,280] d. Nov-11-1906,[27] census 1860 in Trenton, Mercer Co, NJ.

    Married twice (no further information).

    vii. JOHN GASTON b. ca 1848 in New York,[280] census 1860 in Trenton, Mercer Co, NJ.

    viii. SARAH GASTON b. Feb- 2-1851 in New York,[27,280] d. Apr-29-1908,[27] census 1860 in Trenton, Mercer Co, NJ.

    ix. CHARLOTTE GASTON b. ca 1852 in New York,[280] census 1860 in Trenton, Mercer Co, NJ. She married John Chapman, d. 1906.[27]

613. x.   OLIVER GASTON b. ca 1855.

    xi. LIZZIE GASTON b. Jun- 3-1858 in New Jersey,[27] d. Aug- 2-1867, census 1860 in Trenton, Mercer Co, NJ.

327. **Margaret Gaston** (175.John[6], 84.William[5], 28.John[4], 8.Joseph[3], 3.John[2], 1.Jean[1]), b. Nov-29-1811 in New Jersey,[17,27] d. Oct-31-1869 in New Jersey,[27,17] buried in Lamington Presb Church Cem, Somerset Co, NJ,[17] census 1850 in Bedminster Twp, Somerset Co, NJ. She married **Thomas Blackwell**, b. Oct-16-1804 in New Jersey,[17,146] d. Feb-12-1876 in New Jersey,[27,17] buried in Lamington Presb Church Cem, Somerset Co, NJ,[17] census 1850 in Bedminster Twp, Somerset Co, NJ, occupation farmer, doctor.

  1850 Census, Bedminster Twp, Somerset Co, New Jersey, enumerated on Aug 27 1850:
Thomas Blackwell, 45, farmer, b. NJ; Margaret, 38, b. NJ; Sarah, 12, b. NJ; John, 10, b. NJ; Margaret, 6, b. NJ; John Seigler, 20, b. Germany, laborer; James Hayes, 19, b. Ireland, laborer.
(Note: The birth dates of John Blackwell and his sister Sarah have been widely reported as Sep 9 1839 and Apr 26 1841, respectively. In the case of Sarah, that was based on her age inscribed on her headstone. But the 1850 Census contradicts this, showing that Sarah was the older of the two.)

    Children:

    i.   SARAH G. BLACKWELL b. ca 1838 in New Jersey,[146] d. Feb- 4-1853 in New Jersey,[dclxx[670]] buried in Lamington Presb Church Cem, Somerset Co, NJ,[dclxxi[671]] census 1850 in Bedminster Twp, Somerset Co, NJ.

    ii.   JOHN GASTON BLACKWELL[dclxxii[672]] b. Sep- 9-1839, d. Dec-18-1857 in New Jersey, buried in Lamington Presb Church Cem, Somerset Co, NJ,[17] census 1850 in Bedminster Twp, Somerset Co, NJ.

    iii. MARGARET BLACKWELL b. ca 1844 in New Jersey,[146] census 1850 in Bedminster Twp, Somerset Co, NJ.

328. **John Gaston** (175.John[6], 84.William[5], 28.John[4], 8.Joseph[3], 3.John[2], 1.Jean[1]), b. Aug-31-1818 in New Jersey,[27,146] d. Feb- 3-1888,[27] census 1850, 1860 in Bedminster Twp, Somerset Co, NJ. He married Nov-17-1842,[299] **Rebecca Ann Wortman**, b. Oct- 2-1816 in New Jersey,[299,146] (daughter of John Dwyen Wortman and Catherine Van Nest), d. Dec-15-1902,[299] census 1850, 1860 in Bedminster Twp, Somerset Co, NJ.

    Children:

    i.   JOSEPH GASTON d. in infancy.

ii. JAMES (TWIN) GASTON b. ca 1844 in New Jersey,[146] census 1850, 1860 in Bedminster Twp, Somerset Co, NJ, military Civil War.[190]

Not clear who other twin was, unless it was Joseph, who died in infancy.

He married Jan- 1-___ [Max Perry, p. 148, reports marriage date as January 1, 1783, which is obviously incorrect.], Emma Jane Potter (daughter of Samuel Potter and Jane B. LaRue).

iii. JOHN WORTMAN GASTON b. 1845 in New Jersey,[146] census 1850, 1860 in Bedminster Twp, Somerset Co, NJ. He married Anna Reger (daughter of Augustun Reger and Margaret Vosseller), resided in Somerset Co, NJ.

Anna: Anna Reger Gaston was the author of "Gaston Family Lines of Somerset," published in the "Somerset County Historical Quarterly."
http://homepages.rootsweb.ancestry.com/~windmill/html/somersev.html

614. iv. NAOMI GASTON b. Dec-10-1846.
615. v. WILLIAM KER GASTON b. ca 1849.
vi. OLIVER B. GASTON b. Jul-18-1852,[dclxxiii[673]] d. Sep- 1-1853.[673]
616. vii. HUGH GASTON b. ca 1856.

329. **Oliver Berton (twin) Gaston** (175.John[6], 84.William[5], 28.John[4], 8.Joseph[3], 3.John[2], 1.Jean[1]), b. Jan-14-1821 in New Jersey,[27,317,280] d. Jan- 8-1894 in Glen Head, Long Island, NY,[27,317] census 1860 in New Brunswick, Middlesex Co, NJ. He married Oct- 8-1840, **Sarah Alette Wortman**, b. Apr- 5-1821 in New Jersey,[673,280] (daughter of John Dwyen Wortman and Catherine Van Nest), d. Aug-30-1903 in Baltimore, MD,[673] census 1860 in New Brunswick, Middlesex Co, NJ.
Children:
617. i. JANE MARIA GASTON b. Sep-27-1841.
618. ii. CATHERINE VAN NEST GASTON b. Feb- 4-1844.
iii. IDA ANN GASTON b. Apr- -1846, d. Sep-30-1851,[dclxxiv[674]] buried in Old Bedminster Cemetery, Somerset Co, NJ.
iv. JOSEPH GASTON b. Jun- -1848,[674] d. Sep-10-___ in New Jersey.[674]
v. REBECCA W. GASTON b. 1851,[674] d. Feb-10-1852 in New Jersey.[674]
vi. JOSEPH GASTON II b. Mar- 8-1853,[674] d. Jul-14-1853 in New Jersey.[674]
vii. OLIVA B. GASTON b. Apr- 8-1854 in New Jersey,[280] census 1860 in New Brunswick, Middlesex Co, NJ. She married (1) Oct- 5-1882, William S. Chandler. She married (2) Aug- 3-1898, Abraham Irving Martin, occupation minister.
619. viii. SYLVIA BEAVERS GASTON b. Mar- -1857.
620. ix. LIZZIE GASTON b. 1860.

330. **Naomi (twin) Gaston** (175.John[6], 84.William[5], 28.John[4], 8.Joseph[3], 3.John[2], 1.Jean[1]), b. Jan-14-1821, d. Oct-17-1897. She married **Isaac Farley Stephens** (son of Joseph Stephens and Margaret Farley), d. Oct-17-1900 in Canton, Fulton Co, IL.
Children:
i. GEORGE STEPHENS.
ii. AUGUSTIS STEPHENS.
iii. ANNIE STEPHENS.

331. **Hugh Gaston** (175.John[6], 84.William[5], 28.John[4], 8.Joseph[3], 3.John[2], 1.Jean[1]), b. Apr-23-1823 in New Jersey,[27] d. Mar-28-1899,[27] census 1870, 1880 in Branchburg, Somerset Co, NJ, census 1860 in Bedminster Twp, Somerset Co, NJ, occupation farmer.[280] He married Nov- 2-1844, **Jane VanDeveer Garretson**, b. Sep-29-1828 in New Jersey (daughter of Peter Garretson and Catherine Wilson), census 1870, 1880 in Branchburg, Somerset Co, NJ, census 1860 in Bedminster Twp, Somerset Co, NJ.
Children:
i. ROBERT GASTON b. Aug-21-1845, d. Jun-11-1852.

621. ii. CATHERINE GASTON b. ca 1847.
622. iii. SARAH GASTON b. ca 1849.
iv. MARY (TWIN) GASTON b. 1851, d. 1851.
v. MARTHA (TWIN) GASTON b. 1851, d. 1851.
vi. MARGARET GASTON b. ca 1853 in New Jersey,[280] census 1870 in Branchburg, Somerset Co, NJ, census 1860 in Bedminster Twp, Somerset Co, NJ. She married Dec-25-1872, Ira Voorhees, b. 1851 (son of John S. Voorhees and Sarah Vosselle), d. Apr- 6-1913.
vii. CORNELIA GASTON b. ca 1855 in New Jersey,[280] census 1870 in Branchburg, Somerset Co, NJ, census 1860 in Bedminster Twp, Somerset Co, NJ. She married Sep-30-1879, James Henry.
viii. JANE GASTON b. 1857 in New Jersey,[280] census 1870 in Branchburg, Somerset Co, NJ, census 1860 in Bedminster Twp, Somerset Co, NJ. She married Dec- 6-1876, Isaac Newton Dumont.
623. ix. MARIETTA GASTON b. 1860.
624. x. JOHN GARRETSON GASTON b. ca 1862.
xi. HUGH GASTON b. Jun-11-1865, d. Aug-16-1866.
xii. ISAAC GASTON b. Oct- 2-1867, d. Sep- 9-1868.
625. xiii. WILLIAM GARRETSON GASTON b. ca 1869.

332. **Isaac Gaston** (175.John[6], 84.William[5], 28.John[4], 8.Joseph[3], 3.John[2], 1.Jean[1]), b. Jul-23-1825 in New Jersey,[27] d. 1900,[27] census 1870 in Warren Twp, Somerset Co, NJ, census 1850, 1860 in Bedminster Twp, Somerset Co, NJ, occupation farmer, merchant, miller.[146,209]

Isaac Gaston's two wives, both named Catherine Sutphen, were cousins.

1850 Census, Somerset Co, New Jersey (Bedminster Twp), enumerated on Aug 26 1850:
Isaac Gaston, 25, farmer; Catharine C. Gaston, 24; Arthur S. Gaston, 3; Rebecca Hall, black female, 14.

1860 Census, Somerset Co, New Jersey (Bedminster Twp), enumerated on Sep 26 1860:
Isaac Gaston, 35, farmer; Catharine C, 34; Arthur S, 13; Walter, 7; Anna, 3; Ida, 5 months; George Sutphen, black male, 22, farm laborer.

1870 Census, Somerset Co, New Jersey (Warren Twp), enumerated on Jun 18 1870:
Isaac Gaston, 44, merchant miller; Catherine E, 34; John W, 17; Anna S, 12; Ida, 10; Mary, 8; Sarah VanDerveer, black female, 32, domestic servant. All born in New Jersey.

1880 Census, Somerset Co, New Jersey (North Plainfield Twp), enumerated on Jun 14 1880:
Isaac Gaston, 54, retired; wife Catherine E, 47; dau Anna S, 22; dau Ida V, 19; dau Mary, 17; son Isaac E, 6. All born in New Jersey.

He married (1) **Catharine Cornelia Sutphen**, b. ca 1826 in New Jersey,[146] d. 1869 in Plainfield, Union Co, NJ, census 1850, 1860 in Bedminster Twp, Somerset Co, NJ. He married (2) **Catherine E. Sutphen**, b. ca 1836 in New Jersey,[209] [Age 47 in 1880 Census would put birth in about 1833, but age 34 in 1870 puts it in about 1836.], d. Jan- -1915 in Newark, Essex Co, NJ, census 1870 in Warren Twp, Somerset Co, NJ.
Children by Catharine Cornelia Sutphen:
i. ARTHUR SUTPHEN GASTON b. Nov- -1846 in New Jersey,[123] census 1900, 1910 in Dunellen, Middlesex Co, NJ, census 1880 in Bridgewater, Somerset Co, NJ, census 1850, 1860 in Bedminster Twp, Somerset Co, NJ. He married Dec-20-1871, Ella R. Ramsey, b. Jul- -1849 in New Jersey,[123] (daughter of Joseph Ramsey and Euphenia Cramer), census 1900, 1910 in Dunellen, Middlesex Co, NJ.

1880 Census, Somerset Co, New Jersey (Bridgewater Twp), enumerated on Jun 2 1880:

H. Kline Ramsey, 36, hotel keeper; wife Susie L Ramsey, 34; son Harry K Ramsey, 9; brother-in-law Arthur Gaston, 31, married, bartender; servant Carrie Green, black female, 26. All born in New Jersey.

          1900 Census, Middlesex Co, New Jersey (Borough of Dunellen), enumerated on Jun 1 1900:

          Arthur Gaston, 53, b. Nov 1846 in NJ, brakeman on railroad, married 28 yrs; wife Ella R Gaston, 50, b. Jul 1849 in NJ, mother of 2 children (none still living); mother Euphenia Ramsey, 86, b. Oct 1813 in NJ, widowed, mother of 9 children (5 still living).

          (Note: Euphenia Ramsey should have been listed as Arthur's mother-in-law rather than his mother.)

      ii.   JOHN WALTER GASTON, census name Walter Gaston, b. ca 1853 in New Jersey,[209] census 1870 in Warren Twp, Somerset Co, NJ, census 1860 in Bedminster Twp, Somerset Co, NJ.

      iii.   ANNA S. GASTON b. ca 1857 in New Jersey,[280] census 1880 in North Plainfield Twp, Somerset Co, NJ, census 1870 in Warren Twp, Somerset Co, NJ, census 1860 in Bedminster Twp, Somerset Co, NJ.

          Lived in Newark, NJ.

      iv.   IDA V. GASTON b. 1860 in New Jersey,[280] census 1880 in North Plainfield Twp, Somerset Co, NJ, census 1870 in Warren Twp, Somerset Co, NJ, census 1860 in Bedminster Twp, Somerset Co, NJ.

      v.   MARY "MINNIE" GASTON b. ca 1862 in New Jersey,[209] census 1880 in North Plainfield Twp, Somerset Co, NJ, census 1870 in Warren Twp, Somerset Co, NJ.

      vi.   ISAAC E. "EDDIE" GASTON b. ca 1874 in New Jersey,[210] census 1880 in North Plainfield Twp, Somerset Co, NJ.

333. Joseph Annin Gaston (177.John[6], 85.Joseph[5], 28.John[4], 8.Joseph[3], 3.John[2], 1.Jean[1]), b. Jul-14-1807, d. Jun-20-1852. He married Mar- 2-1836, **Mary Collins**, b. 1808, d. Nov- 2-1892.
          Children:
      i.   CAROLINE CUTBERT GASTON b. 1837. She married John R. Philip.

334. Sarah Elizabeth Gaston (177.John[6], 85.Joseph[5], 28.John[4], 8.Joseph[3], 3.John[2], 1.Jean[1]), b. Jul- 5-1814, d. Jul-19-1842. She married May- 3-1831, **Albert Sergeant**, occupation Doctor.
          Children:
  626. i.   ELIZABETH SERGEANT b. May-25-1835.
  627. ii.   WILLIAM GASTON SERGEANT b. Nov-25-1837.

335. Joanna Gaston (177.John[6], 85.Joseph[5], 28.John[4], 8.Joseph[3], 3.John[2], 1.Jean[1]), b. May-30-1815,[12] d. Feb-20-1869.[12] She married Mar-10-1841, **George Houston Brown**, b. Feb-12-1810,[12] (son of Isaac V. Brown and Mary Houston), d. Aug- 1-1865,[12] occupation Judge.
          Children:
      i.   MARY HOUSTON BROWN b. Feb-15-1842, d. Jan-23-1912 in Somerville, Somerset Co, NJ.
      ii.   WILLIAM REZEAN BROWN b. Nov-25-1844, d. Jul-10-1870 in Roselle, Union Co, NJ.
  628. iii.   JOHN GASTON BROWN b. Jul- 2-1846.
      iv.   CHURCHILL HOUSTON BROWN b. Apr-16-1849, d. Jul- 1-1881.
  629. v.   GEORGE HOUSTON BROWN, JR. b. Jul-30-1852.
      vi.   ISAAC HENRY BROWN b. Dec-18-1854, d. Jan- 6-1860.
      vii.   WILLIAM STEWART BROWN b. Aug-13-1857.

          Lived in Dayton, Ohio

          He married Aug-31-1907, Anna Flora Hugo.

630.   viii.   IDA AUGUSTA BROWN b. Nov-23-1859.

336. **Samuel Swan Gaston** (177.John[6], 85.Joseph[5], 28.John[4], 8.Joseph[3], 3.John[2], 1.Jean[1]), b. Aug- 2-1823, d. Feb- 2-1876. He married Nov-19-1846, **Margaret Ellen Whitenock**, b. Nov-18-1826, d. Jan-24-1895.

> Children:
> 631.   i.   JOANNA BROWN GASTON.
>   ii.   SARAH ELIZA GASTON d. Mar- 8-1857.
> 632.   iii. IDA ELMIRA GASTON.

337. **Aletta Swan Gaston** (177.John[6], 85.Joseph[5], 28.John[4], 8.Joseph[3], 3.John[2], 1.Jean[1]), b. Jul- 3-1825 [Spelling of name may be Alletta.], d. Oct-16-1909. She married Sep- 4-1845, **William Stewart**, b. Sep- 9-1810 in Pennsylvania.

> Children:
> 633.   i.   EVELINA REYNOLDS STEWART b. ca 1847.
> 634.   ii.   MARY STEWART b. ca 1849.
> 635.   iii. ROBERT ANNIN STEWART b. ca 1851.
>   iv.   WILLIAM GASTON STEWART b. ca 1853.[dclxxv][675]
>   v.   IDA MARIA STEWART b. ca 1855.[675]
>   vi.   ALETTA YOUNG STEWART b. ca 1857.[675]
>   vii. GEORGE BROWN STEWART b. Feb- 6-1868, d. Jan- -1893.

338. **Isaac Gaston** (177.John[6], 85.Joseph[5], 28.John[4], 8.Joseph[3], 3.John[2], 1.Jean[1]), b. Sep-14-1828 in New Jersey, d. Mar-28-1901, resided in Newark, Essex Co, NJ, census 1860, 1870 in Newark, Essex Co, NJ. He married Sep-24-1851, **Mary E. Burnet**, b. ca 1828 in New Jersey,[280] census 1860 in Newark, Essex Co, NJ.

1860 Census, Essex Co, New Jersey (Ward 11, City of Newark), enumerated on Jul 14 1860 at house number 2136:
Joseph Gennug, 27, bookkeeper; Mary J. Gennug, 28; Mary E. Ward, 6; Isaac Gaston, 32; Mary Gaston, 32; Frederick A Gaston, 6; William Gaston, 5; __ Gaston (male), 2; __ Gaston (female), 15, domestic; __ Gaston (male), 38, b. Massachusetts, custom house; __ Gaston (age/sex not given), b. NY; Alice Gaston (age/sex not given), b. NY; Harriet __, 33, b. NY; Mary H. __ (age/sex not given), b. Ireland, domestic; Anna Leonard, 16, b. Ireland, domestic.
(Note: Type of household and relationships of its occupants are not given. Starting with the first "__ Gaston" above (who is most likely George), the manner of entry implies the surname Gaston but is subject to interpretation. Unless otherwise indicated, all birthplaces indicated as New Jersey.)

1870 Census, Essex Co, New Jersey (city of Newark), enumerated on Aug 27 1870:
Isaac Gaston, 41, b. NJ, cashier; Jennie Gaston, 34, b. NY; Frederick Gaston, 17, b. NJ, clerk in store; William H Gaston, 14, b. NJ; George H Gaston, 12; Kate Gaston, 6, b. NJ; Meta Walling, white female, 10, b. NY; Elizabeth Walling, white female, 7, b. Pa; Samuel Perry, black male, 24, b. District of Columbia, cook; Annie Perry, 23, black female, b. NY, domestic servant.
(Note: Jennie appears not to be the Mary E. Burnet reported as Isaac's wife, but we have no record of his remarriage.)

> Children:
> 636.   i.   JOHN FREDERICK GASTON b. Sep-12-1852.
> 637.   ii.   WILLIAM HENRY GASTON b. Nov-16-1855.
> 638.   iii. GEORGE HOUSTON GASTON b. Apr-11-1858.
>   iv.   KATE ZAHNISER GASTON b. ca 1864 in New Jersey,[209] census 1870 in Newark.

339. **Alexander Kirkpatrick Gaston** (178.William[6], 85.Joseph[5], 28.John[4], 8.Joseph[3], 3.John[2], 1.Jean[1]), b. Jan-25-1814 in New Jersey,[209] d. Dec-22-1882 [Death date may be Jan 22, 1882 or in 1885.], census 1870 in West Brandywine, Chester Co, PA, occupation physician.[209] He married[dclxxvi][676] Jun-23-1836,

Elizabeth Henderson Denny, b. Jan-11-1817 in West Brandywine, Chester Co, PA,[dclxxvii][677] (daughter of David Denny and Martha McClure), d. Apr- 3-1900 in Philadelphia, PA,[190] buried in Brandywine Manor, Chester Co, PA,[190] census 1870 in West Brandywine, Chester Co, PA.

Elizabeth: Daughter of Captain David Denny of Revolutionary War fame, and was a member of the Pennsylvania Society, Daughters of the Revolution, Quaker City Chapter. She is survived by five children, three of whom are physicians.[190]

Children:
    i.   EMMA LOUISE ADELE GASTON b. Aug-29-1841 in Chester Co, PA, d. Oct-27-1929. She married[dclxxviii][678] Howard Evans.
   639. ii.   EUGENE A. GASTON b. Sep- -1847.
    iii. ELIZABETH BLANCH GASTON b. ca 1852 in Pennsylvania,[209] d. Apr-25-1927 in West Brandywine, Chester Co, PA,[dclxxix][679] buried in Brandywine Manor, Chester Co, PA,[190] census 1870 in West Brandywine, Chester Co, PA, never married.
    iv. WILLIAM F. GASTON b. ca 1854 in Pennsylvania,[209] resided in Pomona, Los Angeles Co, CA, census 1870 in West Brandywine, Chester Co, PA, occupation physician.
    v.   IDA E. GASTON b. ca 1856 in Pennsylvania,[209] d. Sep-21-1928 in West Brandywine, Chester Co, PA,[676] census 1870 in West Brandywine, Chester Co, PA, occupation physician,[676] never married.

340. **Joseph Gaston** (178.William[6], 85.Joseph[5], 28.John[4], 8.Joseph[3], 3.John[2], 1.Jean[1]), b. Nov- 6-1816 in Basking Ridge, Bernard Twp, Somerset Co, NJ, d. Jan-25-1885 in Honey Brook, Chester Co, PA,[190] buried in Methodist Cemetery, Honey Brook, Chester Co, PA,[395] census 1860, 1880 in Honey Brook, Chester Co, PA, occupation physician,[280,210,395].

Practiced medicine in Honey Brook (formerly called Waynesburg), Chester Co, PA, for forty years following his graduation from the University of Pennsylvania. He was noted in the educational field, and long before the existence of a superintendent of schools, he was generally selected as one of those who examined applicants for teaching positions in the public schools. He was a fine debater, taking an active part in lyceums and debating societies.[190]

He married Nov-12-1846, **Agnes Greenbank**, b. Feb-17-1828 in Pennsylvania, d. Aug-20-1910, buried in Methodist Cemetery, Honey Brook, Chester Co, PA,[395] census 1860, 1880 in Honey Brook, Chester Co, PA.

Agnes: Maiden name of Greenfield given in husband's obituary.

Children:
    i.   MARY GASTON b. ca 1848 in Pennsylvania,[280] d. bef 1937,[521] census 1860 in Honey Brook, Chester Co, PA. She married __ Bacon.
    ii. FREDERICK GASTON, census name Fred Gaston,[280] b. ca 1852 in Pennsylvania,[280] d. bef 1937,[521] census 1860 in Honey Brook, Chester Co, PA, occupation life insurance company president.[521]
    iii. FANNIE GASTON, also known as Fanny Gaston,[280] b. ca 1854 in Pennsylvania,[280] census 1860, 1880 in Honey Brook, Chester Co, PA.
    iv. JOSEPH A. GASTON b. ca 1856 in Honey Brook, Chester Co, PA,[280,190] d. Mar-31-1937 in Washington, DC,[190] buried in Arlington National Cemetery, VA,[190] census 1860 in Honey Brook, Chester Co, PA.

Attended West Point Military Academy, graduating 16th in his class in 1881. Took part in military battles against the Apache Indians, 1885-86, and against the Sioux Indians, 1890-91. He served in Cuba, 1899-1902, and in the Philippines, 1908-1910. In 1906 he was superintendent of permanent camps in connection with relief work in San Francisco. He was with the punitive expedition in Mexico in 1916-17. From Aug 1917 to Feb 1919, he served with the rank of Brigadier General in the World War. During this period he commanded the Depot Brigade at Camp Travis, San Antonio, TX, and later with the 90th Div, and with the 37th Div at Montgomery, AL, and at Petersburg, VA. Later he was Camp Commander and then Eecutive Officer at Camp Meade, MD, with the 154th Depot Brigade. He was a graduate of the Army War College at Washington, DC, where he resided following retirement in 1920.[190]

He married (1) May Vernou (daughter of Charles A. Vernou), d. Aug-26-1887 in San Antonio, Bexar Co, TX. He married (2) Lavinia Haskin, d. aft 1937.[484]

v.   AGNES GASTON b. ca 1859 in Pennsylvania,[280,210] resided in Philadelphia, PA, census 1860, 1880 in Honey Brook, Chester Co, PA. She married William Lawson.

vi.   CARRIE GASTON b. ca 1863 in Pennsylvania,[210] resided in Philadelphia, PA, census 1880 in Honey Brook, Chester Co, PA. She married Charles E. Barber.

vii.   JOHN GASTON b. ca 1865 in Pennsylvania,[210] d. bef 1937,[521] census 1880 in Honey Brook, Chester Co, PA, occupation civil engineer.[521]

viii.   LILLIAN GASTON, census name Lillie Gaston,[210] b. 1867 in Pennsylvania,[dclxxx[680],210] d. 1958,[680] census 1880 in Honey Brook, Chester Co, PA, occupation doctor.

Wrote a history of her Gaston ancestors from the 1700's. Upon her death, all her family memorabilia were donated to the Philadelphia Historical Society.

ix.   EDWARD GASTON, census name Edger Gaston,[210] b. ca 1870 in Pennsylvania,[210] resided in Harrisburg, Dauphin Co, PA, census 1880 in Honey Brook, Chester Co, PA.

x.   HELEN GASTON b. ca 1873 in Pennsylvania,[210] resided in Washington, DC, census 1880 in Honey Brook, Chester Co, PA. She married H. G. Sydenham.

341. **Hugh M. Gaston** (178.William[6], 85.Joseph[5], 28.John[4], 8.Joseph[3], 3.John[2], 1.Jean[1]), b. Nov-29-1818 in Bernards Twp, Somerset Co, NJ, d. Apr-21-1892. He married May-24-1849, **Frances Mallet Prevast**, b. Jul- 4-1822 (daughter of Louis Prevast), d. May- 3-1914.
Children:
i.   MARY GASTON.
640.   ii.   EVELYN GASTON.
iii.   FRANCES GASTON.
641.   iv.   LOUIS PREVAST GASTON.
v.   HARRIET PREVAST GASTON b. May-25-1850, d. Dec- 2-1856.
vi.   HUGH KIRKPATRICK GASTON b. Aug-10-1858 He married Oct-1888, Sue D. Cammann.
vii.   ELIZABETH GASTON b. Mar-11-1863, d. Aug-30-1878.

342. **John Gaston** (178.William[6], 85.Joseph[5], 28.John[4], 8.Joseph[3], 3.John[2], 1.Jean[1]), b. Nov-12-1825 in Somerville, Somerset Co, NJ, d. Dec- 1-1901, occupation minister (Doctor of Divinity). He married Nov-12-1852, **Anna Terhune**.
Children:
642.   i.   WILLIAM FREDRICK GASTON b. Feb-11-1854.
ii.   MATILDA B. GASTON d. Sep- 7-1890.
iii.   ANNA E. GASTON.

343. **William Gaston** (178.William[6], 85.Joseph[5], 28.John[4], 8.Joseph[3], 3.John[2], 1.Jean[1]), b. Sep-14-1828 in New Jersey [Birth date given as Sep 1827 in 1900 Census.], d. bef Apr 1910,[211] census 1880, 1900 in Newark, Essex Co, NJ [Address in 1900: 257 North 7th Street.], occupation 1900 life insurance,[123] occupation 1880 bookkeeper.[210] He married Jul-23-1856, **Anna E. Conklin**, b. Nov- -1833 in New Jersey,[123] [Age 44 in 1880 Census would put birth in about 1836, but 1900 Census shows it as Nov 1833, age 66.], d. bef Jan 1920 [She was not with her son in the 1920 Census as she had been in all previous ones.], census 1880, 1900, 1910 in Newark, Essex Co, NJ.
Children:

      i.   BENNETT J. GASTON b. Jul- -1870 in New York,[123] census 1880, 1900, 10, 20 in Newark, Essex Co, NJ [Address in 1910: 61 North 7th Street. His wife and mother were the only other residents of the household.], occupation 1920 assistant manager in insurance,[dclxxxi[681]] occupation 1910 bookkeeper for life insurance company,[211] occupation 1900 insurance agent.[123] He married Oct- 7-1896, no children from this marriage,[211] Luella Pereau, b. Oct- -1873 in New York,[123] census 1900, 1910, 1920 in Newark, Essex Co, NJ.

344. **Charles Henry Gaston** (179.Ogden[6], 86.Stephen[5], 28.John[4], 8.Joseph[3], 3.John[2], 1.Jean[1]), b. May-15-1850 in Troy, Rensselaer Co, NY,[123] census 1900 in New York City, NY, census 1870, 1880 in Detroit, MI, census 1860 in Springfield, Oakland Co, MI, census 1850 in Troy, Rensselaer Co, NY, occupation 1870 clerk in boot store.[209] He married Jun-1873,[123] **Mary Beatrice "Minnie" Warren**, b. Jan- -1852 in Michigan,[123] d. Aug- -1903, census 1900 in New York City, NY, census 1880 in Detroit, MI.

    Mary: Daughter of Rev. Square Warren

        Children:
643. i.   CHARLES ROBERT GASTON b. Sep- 6-1874.
      ii.   ALICE ELIZABETH GASTON b. Jun- 6-1876 in Michigan, census 1880 in Detroit, MI.
      iii. HOMER WARREN GASTON b. Aug-11-1879 in Michigan, d. 1895, census 1880 in Detroit, MI.
      iv. JOHN OGDEN GASTON, census name Arthur F. Gaston, b. Jan-10-1879 in Michigan,[123] census 1920, 1930 in Rochester, Oakland Co, MI, census 1900 in New York City, NY, census 1880 in Detroit, MI, occupation medical doctor.[334] He married Frances M. ___, b. ca 1889 in Michigan,[681] census 1920, 1930 in Rochester, Oakland Co, MI.
      v.   MARY BEATRICE GASTON b. Jan- 6-1888 in Michigan,[123] census 1900 in New York City, NY.
      vi. MARGARET GASTON.

345. **Theodore William Gaston** (179.Ogden[6], 86.Stephen[5], 28.John[4], 8.Joseph[3], 3.John[2], 1.Jean[1]), b. Mar-7-1860 in Michigan,[123] census 1870 80, 1900 10 20 in Detroit, MI, census 1860 in Springfield, Oakland Co, MI, occupation 1920 parcel post motor cab,[681] occupation 1910 deputy county sheriff.[211] He married ca 1887,[123] **Mary E.** ___, b. Feb- -1863 in Michigan,[123] census 1900, 1910, 1920 in Detroit, MI, occupation school teacher.[681]
        Children:
      i.   HARRIET J. GASTON b. Oct- -1889 in Michigan,[123] census 1900, 1910, 1920 in Detroit, MI.
      ii.   RUSSELL OLIVER GASTON b. Sep-19-1892 in Michigan,[592,123] d. May- 6-1982 in Farmington Hills, Oakland Co, MI,[dclxxxii[682],592] resided in Farmington Hills, Oakland Co, MI,[dclxxxiii[683]] census 1900, 1910, 1920 in Detroit, MI, occupation bank manager.[681,dclxxxiv[684]]

346. **George Tiffany Gaston** (179.Ogden[6], 86.Stephen[5], 28.John[4], 8.Joseph[3], 3.John[2], 1.Jean[1]), b. Mar-28-1867 in Michigan,[123] census 1870 80, 1900 10 20 in Detroit, MI, occupation 1920 Chief Probation Officer of Police Court,[681] occupation 1910 Wayne County Sheriff,[211] occupation 1900 City Clerk.[123] He married ca 1890,[211] **Lucy Alice** ___, census name Alice, b. Jun- -1868 in Michigan,[123] census 1900, 1910, 1920 in Detroit, MI.
        Children:
644. i.   GEORGE M. GASTON b. Sep- -1890.

347. **William Mansfield Scudder** (181.William[6], 88.Margaret[5], 28.John[4], 8.Joseph[3], 3.John[2], 1.Jean[1]), b. Feb- 2-1843 in Newark, Essex Co, NJ,[64] d. May-14-1876 in Chicago, IL.[64] He married Aug- 3-1871 in Chicago, IL,[64] **Mary Augusta Arnold**, b. Mar-29-1848 in Illinois,[64] d. May-29-1913.[64]
        Children:
      i.   JOHN ARNOLD SCUDDER b. Jun-24-1872 in Chicago, IL,[64] d. Jun- 4-1956.[64]
      ii.   KATHERINE SCUDDER b. Sep-21-1874 in Chicago, IL,[64] d. Aug-17-1926.[64]
      iii. WILLIAM MANSFIELD SCUDDER III b. Jul-19-1876,[64] d. Jan-21-1942.[64]

348. **Daniel Melick** (186.William[6], 91.Margaret[5], 29.Robert[4], 8.Joseph[3], 3.John[2], 1.Jean[1]), b. ca 1827 in New Jersey,[146] census 1850 in Cotton Twp, Switzerland Co, Ind., occupation farmer.[146] He married **Elizabeth ___**, b. ca 1830 in Ohio,[146] census 1850 in Cotton Twp, Switzerland Co, Ind.

      Children:
        i.   WILLIAM MELICK b. ca 1849 in Iowa,[146] census 1850 in Cotton Twp, Switzerland Co, Ind.

349. **Clara Dickson** (187.Andrew[6], 93.Phebe[5], 32.Margaret[4], 9.John[3], 3.John[2], 1.Jean[1]), b. ca 1811 in New York,[146] census 1850, 60, 70, 80 in Syracuse, Onondaga Co, NY. She married 1831,[28] **Horace White**, b. ca 1805 in New York (son of Asa White), d. bef 1870 [He was not with his wife in the 1870 Census.], resided in Syracuse, Onondaga Co, NY,[28,148] census 1850, 1860 in Syracuse, Onondaga Co, NY, occupation merchant, banker,[148,146,280.] From "The Autobiography of Andrew Dickson White": "Hither came, toward the close of the eighteenth century, a body of sturdy New Englanders, and, among them, my grandfathers and grandmothers. Those on my father's side: Asa White and Clara Keep, from Munson, Massachusetts; those on my mother's side, Andrew Dickson, from Middlefield, Massachusetts, and Ruth Hall from Guilford, Connecticut. They were all of ``good stock.'' When I was ten years old I saw my great-grandfather at Middlefield, eighty-two years of age, sturdy and vigorous; he had mowed a broad field the day before, and he walked four miles to church the day after. He had done his duty manfully during the war, had been a member of the ``Great and General Court'' of Massachusetts, and had held various other offices, which showed that he enjoyed the confidence of his fellow-citizens. As to the other side of the house, there was a tradition that we came from Peregrine White of the Mayflower; but I have never had time to find whether my doubts on the subject were well founded or not. Enough for me to know that my yeomen ancestors did their duty in war and peace, were honest, straightforward, God-fearing men and women, who owned their own lands, and never knew what it was to cringe before any human being."

1850 Census, Onondaga Co, New York (city of Syracuse), enumerated on Sep 12 1850:
Horace White, 45, b. NY, cashier, value of real estate owned $43,000; Clara D White, 39, b. NY; Andrew D White, 17, b. NY; Horace R White, 14, b. NY; Ruth Dickison, 60, b. NY; Bridgett Canon, 22, b. Ireland; May McElroy, 15, b. NY; John McElroy, 21, b. Ireland.
(Note: Could Clara's middle initial stand for Dickson?)

1860 Census, Onondaga Co, New York (city of Syracuse), enumerated on Jul 6 1860:
Horace White, 57, b. NY, banker, value of real estate $55,000, value of personal estate $530,000; Clara D White, 48, b. NY; Horace K (or H) White, 22, b. NY, banker; Ruth Dickson, 70, b. Connecticut; Ellen McGrath, 30, b. Ireland, domestic; Mary Fay, 25, b. Ireland, domestic; Patrick McGee, 23, b. Ireland, laborer.

1870 Census, Onondaga Co, New York (city of Syracuse), enumerated on Jul 7 1870:
Clara D White, 60, b. NY; Mrs. Dixon, 48, b. NY; Ann Boyle, 27, b. Ireland, domestic; Maggie O'Neel, 30, b. Ireland, domestic; Michael Ryan, 25, b. Ireland, coachman.

1880 Census, Onondaga Co, New York (city of Syracuse), enumerated on Jun 7 1880:
Clara D White, 64, b. NY, widowed; servant Maggie Stepleton, 25, b. Ireland, single; servant Hanna Wall, 30, b. Ireland, single; coachman Price Owen, 38, b. Wales, single.[302]

      Children:
645. i.   ANDREW DICKSON WHITE b. Nov- 7-1832.
646. ii. HORACE K. WHITE b. Oct- -1837.

350. **William Alexander Gaston** (188.William[6], 94.Alexander[5], 33.John[4], 9.John[3], 3.John[2], 1.Jean[1]), b. May- 1-1859 in Roxbury, Suffolk Co, MA,[27,33] d. Jul-17-1927 in Barre, Worcester Co, MA,[27] occupation lawyer and banker.

Graduated from Harvard College in 1880, admitted to the bar in 1883, and became a member of [his father's law] firm Gaston & Whitney in October 1883. [American Ancestry, Vol V, p. 103] Was Democratic candidate for Governor of Massachusetts in 1902-03, was a Massachusetts delegate-at-large to the National Democratic Convention in 1904, was nominated by the Democrats in 1905 for U.S. Senator, and was a member of the National Democratic Committee. [Colonial Families of the United States, Vol III, p. 174] "Trustee of the Boston Public Library, 1923-1927. Born 1859 in Roxbury and died 1927 in Barre, MA. Lawyer, banker and Democrat. The son of the Honorable William Gaston, former Boston Mayor and former Governor of Massachusetts, William Alexander Gaston graduated from Harvard in 1880 and was a classmate of Theodore Roosevelt and Josiah Quincy. He studied law at Harvard Law School and his father's firm, and later organized his own Boston firm of Gaston, Snow and Saltonstall, from which he practiced corporation law and the management of estates. His success as a corporate lawyer led to his selection as coordinator for the consolidation of the city's various street railway companies into the Boston Elevated Railway Company. In the banking industry, Mr. Gaston was a leading and influential participant in overseeing several financial institutions as well as organizing the National Shawmut Bank of Boston, of which he was president for a number of years before becoming chairman of its board of directors. Following World War I, he was appointed by the U.S. Government as an arbitrator of labor disputes in Hartford, CT, and Bath, ME. Colonel Gaston was a prominent Massachusetts Democrat, serving on the staff of Governor William Eustis Russell where he attained his title, and ran unsuccessfully for the Massachusetts Governorship. Outside his public life, he maintained a famous herd of cows on his Barre farm where he researched problems related to raising livestock and standardizing food production. In addition to his Library trusteeship, he was a member of the Overseers of Harvard University, of the Massachusetts Horticultural Society and of Trinity Church. Colonel Gaston supported many other organizations and causes associated with education and charity with both his time and money." [Boston Public Library website, www.bpl.org/general/trustees/gaston.htm]

He married[33] Apr- 9-1892,[27] **May Davidson Lockwood**, b. Nov-25-1867 in Charlestown, Suffolk Co, MA,[27] (daughter of Hamilton Davidson Lockwood and Anne Louise Eastman).
> Children:
> i.   RUTH GASTON b. Nov- 9-1894 in Roxbury, Suffolk Co, MA, d. Aug-15-1974,[592] resided in Boston, MA.[592] She married Laurence Foster.
> ii.   WILLIAM GASTON b. Nov-12-1896 in Roxbury, Suffolk Co, MA, d. Aug-15-1970,[592] resided in New Canaan, Fairfield Co, CT.[dclxxxv[685]]
> iii. JOHN GASTON b. Dec-10-1898 in Boston, MA,[dclxxxvi[686]] resided in New York City, NY, resided 1923 in Boston, MA.[686]
> iv.   HOPE GASTON b. Jun-23-1901 in Roxbury, Suffolk Co, MA, d. Jun- -1984,[592] resided in North Haven, Knox Co, ME.[592] She married Cornelius Conway Felton, b. Apr-18-1893,[592] d. Aug-__-1974.[592]

351. **Mary Kasson** (189.Thompson[6], 96.Robert[5], 36.Janet[4], 10.Alexander[3], 3.John[2], 1.Jean[1]), b. Oct-21-1823.[305] She married[dclxxxvii[687]] **Edward Martin**.
> Children:
> i.   EDWARD WILLIAM MARTIN b. 1844,[687] resided 1865 in New York City, NY.[687]
> ii.   JAMES ALLEN MARTIN b. 1849,[687] resided 1872 in Greenville, Montcalm Co, MI.[687]
> iii. CHARLES LEANDER MARTIN b. 1853,[687] resided 1879 in Detroit, MI.[687]
> iv.   FREDERICK H. A. MARTIN b. 1861.[687]
> v.   GEORGE B. MCCLELLAN MARTIN b. 1863.[687]

352. **William Alexander Kasson** (189.Thompson[6], 96.Robert[5], 36.Janet[4], 10.Alexander[3], 3.John[2], 1.Jean[1]), b. Mar-10-1829.[305] He married Jan- 8-1857,[308] **Mary Washburne**.
> Children:
> i.   NELLIE KASSON b. Dec-21-1859 in Gloversville, Fulton Co, NY.[308]

353. **Lucy S. Kasson** (190.James[6], 96.Robert[5], 36.Janet[4], 10.Alexander[3], 3.John[2], 1.Jean[1]), b. Aug-19-1835,[305] d. Oct-25-1861.[305] She married[305] __ **Rawson**.

        Children:
        i.   ALICE C. RAWSON b. Sep- 8-1861.[305]

354. **Archibald Kasson** (192.Mason[6], 96.Robert[5], 36.Janet[4], 10.Alexander[3], 3.John[2], 1.Jean[1]), resided 1873 in Jasper Co, MO.[308]

Archibald Kasson may also have had two additional children, Kate and Herbert Mason.[308]

He married Sep-14-1862,[308] **Unknown**.

        Children:
        i.   HARRY KASSON b. 1865.[308]
        ii.   ELIZA KASSON b. 1866.[308]
        iii. EDWARD KASSON.

355. **Jeremiah William Kasson** (194.Archibald[6], 97.William[5], 36.Janet[4], 10.Alexander[3], 3.John[2], 1.Jean[1]), b. Dec-16-1815,[308] [Conflicting birth dates of Dec 16 1815 and Dec 16 1816 reported in Kasson genealogy.], resided 1873 in Camillus, Onondaga Co, NY.[308] He married Dec-31-1836,[308] **Lucinda Wood**, b. Jun- 5-1821.[308]

        Children:
        i.   EMILY JANE KASSON b. Aug-13-1838.[308]
        ii.   MARY F. KASSON b. May-14-1841.[308]
        iii. WILLIAM A. KASSON b. May-15-1846.[308]
        iv. SAMUEL H. KASSON b. Dec-23-1848.[308]

356. **Orson V. Kasson** (194.Archibald[6], 97.William[5], 36.Janet[4], 10.Alexander[3], 3.John[2], 1.Jean[1]), b. May- 8-1818.[308] He married Jul- 1-1857,[dclxxxviii[688]] **Louisa M. French Otisto**, b. Aug- 7-1838.[688]

        Children:
        i.   STELLA LOUISA KASSON b. Sep-27-1858.[688]
        ii.   FRANK V. KASSON b. Nov-25-1859,[688] d. Feb- 9-1860.[688]

357. **Achash A. Kasson** (194.Archibald[6], 97.William[5], 36.Janet[4], 10.Alexander[3], 3.John[2], 1.Jean[1]), b. May-18-1821.[308] She married 1843,[dclxxxix[689]] **Nathaniel Williams**.

        Children:
        i.   LORANIA O. WILLIAMS b. Dec-26-1844.[689]
        ii.   EMMA O. WILLIAMS b. Feb-20-1851.[689]
        iii. HARRIET A. WILLIAMS b. Feb-20-1854.[689]
        iv. FLORENCE L. WILLIAMS b. Apr- 3-1858.[689]

358. **Sarah A. Kasson** (194.Archibald[6], 97.William[5], 36.Janet[4], 10.Alexander[3], 3.John[2], 1.Jean[1]), b. Aug-27-1825.[308] She married 1841,[689] **James Sample**.

        Children:
        i.   MARGARET M. SAMPLE b. Oct-21-1844.[689]
        ii.   GEORGE J. SAMPLE b. Jan-20-1846.[689]

359. **Earle C. Kasson** (196.Chauncey[6], 98.Harvey[5], 36.Janet[4], 10.Alexander[3], 3.John[2], 1.Jean[1]), b. Jul- 5-1840 in Gloversville, Fulton Co, NY.[309] He married[309] **Ann Burdick**.

        Children:
        i.   HATTIE KASSON.
        ii.   HARRY KASSON.
        iii. NETTIE ANN KASSON.

360. **Alexander Cummings Gaston** (201.George[6], 100.Alexander[5], 37.Alexander[4], 10.Alexander[3], 3.John[2], 1.Jean[1]), b. Feb-16-1838 near Oberlin, Lorain Co, OH,[36,34,dcxc[690]] [Son Alonzo's entry in both the 1920 and 1930 Census states his father's birthplace as New York.], d. 1930 in Hanford, Kings Co, CA.[36]

At the time of their 66th wedding anniversary in 1928, Alexander Cummings Gaston and Mary Frances Jones had 6 children, 21 grandchildren, and 19 great-grandchildren.[690]

He married Mar-27-1862 in Tabor, Fremont Co, IA,[317,690] **Mary Frances Jones**, b. Nov- 6-1842 in East Dover, Windham Co, VT,[317,690] d. Nov-27-1928.[690]
>   Children:
>   i.   OZRO CLAIR GASTON b. Feb-10-1863 in Tabor, Fremont Co, IA,[317] d. May- 1-1932 in Seattle, WA. He married Mary Augusta Fetter.
>   ii.   CORA ELLEN GASTON b. 1864 in Tabor, Fremont Co, IA.[317]
>   iii. ETTA MARY GASTON b. 1868 in Tabor, Fremont Co, IA.[317]
>   iv.   ABBIE MARIE GASTON b. 1871 in Tabor, Fremont Co, IA.[317]
>   v.   GEORGE B. GASTON b. 1874 in Tabor, Fremont Co, IA.[317]
>   vi.   ERNEST HERMAN GASTON b. 1876 in Tabor, Fremont Co, IA.[317]
>   vii. MYRON CLINTON GASTON b. Jul-10-1878 in Tabor, Fremont Co, IA,[317] d. Feb-17-1965 in Fresno, Fresno Co, CA.
> 647. viii. ALONZO ALEXANDER GASTON b. 1881.

361. **Willard Edgar Gaston** (206.James[6], 101.Heman[5], 37.Alexander[4], 10.Alexander[3], 3.John[2], 1.Jean[1]), b. Jan-25-1862 in Malvern, Mills Co, IA,[193,313] d. Jan-29-1944 in Omaha, Douglas Co, NE,[313] buried in Glenwood, Mills Co, IA.[313] He married Sep- 1-1886 in Glenwood, Mills Co, IA,[193,313] **Mary Gleason King**, b. Apr-27-1867 in Iowa,[193,313] [Hal Hatcher gives name as Mary A. King.] (daughter of Charles P. King and Ellen Thompson), d. 1951 in Iowa.[313]
>   Children:
>   i.   CHARLES KASSON GASTON b. Jun-28-1887,[193] d. May-24-1902.[193]
> 648. ii.   GLADYS BOND GASTON b. Mar-22-1890.
>   iii. VERNON KING GASTON b. May-30-1892,[193,592] d. Aug- -1970,[592] resided in San Antonio, Bexar Co, TX,[592] resided formerly in Nebraska.[dcxci[691]] He married Oct-21-1915,[193] Elna Green, b. Jan-27-1896,[592] d. Aug- -1980,[592] resided in Omaha, Douglas Co, NE.[691]

362. **Burton Cummings Gaston** (206.James[6], 101.Heman[5], 37.Alexander[4], 10.Alexander[3], 3.John[2], 1.Jean[1]), b. 1864 in Tabor, Fremont Co, IA,[313] d. Nov- -1909 in Redlands, San Bernardino Co, CA,[313] buried in Redlands, San Bernardino Co, CA,[313] cause of death fell from building while doing carpentry work.[dcxcii[692]] He married[313] **Jennie Childs**.
>   Children:
> 649. i.   HAROLD BURTON GASTON b. Sep-27-1897.
>   ii.   RAYMOND GASTON b.[313]
>   iii. LEONARD GASTON b.[313]

363. **Vernon Lincoln Gaston** (206.James[6], 101.Heman[5], 37.Alexander[4], 10.Alexander[3], 3.John[2], 1.Jean[1]), b. Feb- 9-1866 in Tabor, Fremont Co, IA,[313] d. May-30-1927 in Omaha, Douglas Co, NE,[313] buried in Tabor, Fremont Co, IA.[313] He married Apr- 6-1910 in Tabor, Fremont Co, IA,[313] **Julia Russell**, b. Nov-9-1874 in Tabor, Fremont Co, IA,[313] (daughter of Orlonzo Babook Russell and Josephine Hammond), d. Sep-25-1970 in Culver City, CA,[313] buried in Tabor, Fremont Co, IA.[313]
>   Children:
>   i.   THELMA MAE GASTON b.[313]
>   ii.   ROBERTA JOSEPHINE GASTON b. in Tabor, Fremont Co, IA,[313] d. Feb-23-1970 in Harris Co, TX,[dcxciii[693],313] buried in Belton, Cass Co, MO,[313] cause of death traffic accident.[313] She married[313] Caleb H. Lamar, d. Feb-23-1970 in Brazos Co, TX,[693,313] cause of death traffic accident.[313]
>   iii. WILMA CORNELIA GASTON b. Jan-21-1914 in Tabor, Fremont Co, IA,[313] d. Apr- 8-1914 in Tabor, Fremont Co, IA,[313] buried in Tabor, Fremont Co, IA.[313]

364. **Lucy May Gaston** (206.James[6], 101.Heman[5], 37.Alexander[4], 10.Alexander[3], 3.John[2], 1.Jean[1]), b. Mar-6-1872 in Tabor, Fremont Co, IA,[313] d. Feb-13-1914 in San Antonio, Bexar Co, TX,[313] buried in Tabor, Fremont Co, IA.[313] She married Jun-15-1898 in Tabor, Fremont Co, IA,[313] **Fredrick W. Long**, b. Aug-20-1870,[313] d. Sep-21-1946 in Glenwood, Mills Co, IA.[313]

> Children:
>
> i. GEORGE L. LONG b. 1900 in Tabor, Fremont Co, IA,[313] d. Aug-22-1980 in Laguna Hills, Orange Co, CA,[313] buried in Prairie Village, Johnson Co, KS.[313] He married[313] Ruth __.
>
> ii. FREDRICK THEODORE LONG b. Dec- 2-1902 in Redfield, Spink Co, SD,[313] d. Dec-31-1903 in Redfield, Spink Co, SD,[313] buried 1903 in Redfield, Spink Co, SD,[313] buried aft 1903 in Mills Co, IA.[313]
>
> iii. RONALD LONG b.[313.]
>
> iv. MAYFRED LONG. She married[313] __ Dawson.
>
> v. ETHEL WYN LONG. She married[313] __ Baker, b.[313]

365. **George Rutherford Gaston** (206.James[6], 101.Heman[5], 37.Alexander[4], 10.Alexander[3], 3.John[2], 1.Jean[1]), b. Aug-22-1876 in Tabor, Fremont Co, IA,[313] d. Jul-29-1961 in Malvern, Mills Co, IA,[313] buried in Tabor, Fremont Co, IA.[313] He married Mar- 6-1907 in Malvern, Mills Co, IA,[313] **Mary Edith Davis**, b. Sep-29-1878 in Malvern, Mills Co, IA,[313] (daughter of Marion Taylor Davis and Mary Jane Aistrope), d. May- 8-1962 in Council Bluffs, Pottawattamie Co, IA,[313] buried in Tabor, Fremont Co, IA.[313]

> Children:
>
> i. RALPH LEON GASTON b. Jan-22-1908 in Huron, Beadle Co, SD,[313] d. Aug- 8-1945 in Council Bluffs, Pottawattamie Co, IA,[313] buried in Tabor, Fremont Co, IA,[313] never married[313].

366. **Eunice Lucinda Gaston** (207.Edmund[6], 102.Ebenezer[5], 38.David[4], 10.Alexander[3], 3.John[2], 1.Jean[1]), b. Nov-21-1845 in New York,[34,123] d. Apr- 9-1915 in Crawford Co, PA,[317] buried in Cochranton, Crawford Co, PA,[317] census 1910 in Wayne Twp, Crawford Co, PA, census 1880, 1900 in Greene Co, MO. She married May-16-1865,[64,123] **Henry S. Brown**, b. Jan- -1843 in Pennsylvania,[123] d. 1928 in Erie, Erie Co, PA,[64] buried in Cochranton, Crawford Co, PA,[317] census 1910 in Wayne Twp, Crawford Co, PA, census 1880, 1900 in Greene Co, MO.

1880 Census, Greene Co, Missouri (Campbell Twp), enumerated on Jun 8 1880:
H. S. Brown, 37, b. Pa (father b. Pa, mother b. NY), house carpenter; wife E L, 34, b. NY (both parents b. NY); dau Myrla S, 14, b. Illinois; dau Linda G, 10, b. Illinois; son Frank E, 6, b. Ohio; son Arthur A, 1, b. Missouri; Homer Hasetine, 26, b. Missouri, "lives in family," teacher & surveyor; Judsen Webb, 18, b. England, "lives in family," works on farm.

1900 Census, Greene Co, Missouri (North Campbell Twp), enumerated on Jul 5 1900:
Henry S. Brown, 57, b. Jan 1843 in Pa (father b. Pa, mother b. NY), carpenter, married 35 yrs; wife Unice L, 54, b. Nov 1845 in NY (both parents b. NY), mother of 5 children (all still living); son Arther, 21, b. Jun 1878 in Missouri, bank teller; son Harry G, 16, b. Feb 1884 in Missouri.

1910 Census, Crawford Co, Pennsylvania (Wayne Twp), enumerated on May 7 1910:
Henry S. Brown, 67, b. Pa (father b. Pa, mother b. NY), farmer; wife Eunice L, 64, b. NY (both parents b. NY), mother of 4 children (1 still living).

> Children:
>
> 650. i.   MYRLA SHIRLEY "MERTIE" BROWN b. May-13-1866.
> 651. ii. PHYLINDA GASTON BROWN b. Jan-24-1870.
> 652. iii. FRANK EDMUND BROWN b. Mar- 9-1874.
> 653. iv. ARTHUR ATHELSTON BROWN b. Jun-17-1878.
> 654. v.   HARRY GASTON BROWN b. Feb-26-1884.

367. **Frank DeForest Gaston** (207.Edmund[6], 102.Ebenezer[5], 38.David[4], 10.Alexander[3], 3.John[2], 1.Jean[1]), b. Jan-26-1853 in New York,[99,211] d. Aug- -1920 in Meadville, Crawford Co, PA.[99] He married Sep-26-

1875,[99] **Clara Leona Henry**, b. Nov-29-1851 in Atlantic, Crawford Co, PA,[99,211] (daughter of Samuel Henry and Sara Foulke), d. Feb-22-1928 in Meadville, Crawford Co, PA.[99]

          Children:
          i.   EDNA GRACE GASTON b. Apr- 6-1877,[34] d. Dec-11-1955.[34] She married[317] ___ Whitling.
          ii.   ETHEL GERTRUDE GASTON b. Jul- 5-1879,[34] d. Dec- -1955.[34] She married[317] ___ Hawkins.
655. iii. PHYLINDA ELISE GASTON b. Mar-31-1884.
656. iv. AUDLEY DEFOREST GASTON b. Jun-26-1886.
          v.   MARIE ELEANOR GASTON b. Jun- 7-1888.[34]

Generation Eight

368. **Ann Gaston** (208.Hudson^7, 106.Robert^6, 41.Matthew^5, 11.Alexander^4, 4.(Male)^3, 2.William^2, 1.Jean^1), b. Sep-21-1850 in Brazoria Co, TX,[318] d. May- 3-1916 in Bay City, Matahorda Co, TX.[318] She married Dec- 6-1866 in Fort Bend, TX,[318] **John Rutland Castleton**.
          Children:
657. i.   REBECCA IRENE CASTLETON b. Jun-17-1885.

369. **Mathew Gaston Reid**[201] (210.Asa^7, 107.Jane^6, 41.Matthew^5, 11.Alexander^4, 4.(Male)^3, 2.William^2, 1.Jean^1), b. 1825 in Jackson Co, GA,[201] d. 1864.[201] He married[201] **Martha E. Prince**, b. 1832,[201] d. 1875.[201]
          Children:
658. i.   DAVID GORDON REID b. 1855.
659. ii.   RHECA THOMAS REID b. 1858.
660. iii. MARY PRISCILLA ELIZABETH JANE REID b. 1862.
661. iv. AMERICA PEMBROOK REID b. 1864.

370. **Rhesa Reid** (210.Asa^7, 107.Jane^6, 41.Matthew^5, 11.Alexander^4, 4.(Male)^3, 2.William^2, 1.Jean^1), b. 1827 in Georgia,[201] d. 1865.[201] He married[201] **Martha ___**.
          Children:
662. i.   WILLIAM JEFFERSON REID b. 1848.
          ii.   ASA A. REID b. 1849 in Conway Co, AR.[201]
          iii. MARY JANE REID b. 1852 in Conway Co, AR.[201] She married[201] John W. Beavers.
          iv. JAMES M. REID b. 1854 in Conway Co, AR.[201] He married[201] Jane C. Braden, b. 1851 in Georgia.[201]
          v.   SARAH REID b. 1857.[201] She married[201] J. N. Lee.
663. vi. WINNEY EUNICY REID b. 1859.
          vii. HENRY WAKEFIELD REID b. 1863 in Conway Co, AR,[201] d. 1929.[201]
          viii. ROBERT TIMON REID[201] b. 1865 in Conway Co, AR.[201] He married[201] Josephine Prince.

371. **Henry Reid** (210.Asa^7, 107.Jane^6, 41.Matthew^5, 11.Alexander^4, 4.(Male)^3, 2.William^2, 1.Jean^1), b. 1836 in Benton Co, AL,[201] d. 1905.[201] He married[201] (1) **Rutha Ann Prince**.[201] He married[201] (2) **Eliza Ann Meeler**, b. 1852 in Arkansas,[201] d. 1931.[201]
          Children by Rutha Ann Prince:
664. i.   SARAH JANE REID b. 1857.
665. ii.   WILLIAM CARY REID b. 1858.
666. iii. MARTHA ELLEN REID b. 1861.
667. iv. MARY PARLEE REID b. 1866.
668. v.   ARDELA TENNESSEE REID b. 1869.
669. vi. ASA ULYSSES SIDNEY LEVI REID b. 1872.
          Children by Eliza Ann Meeler:
670. vii. ROBERT STEPHENSON REID b. 1875.

671.   viii. JAMES HENRY REID b. Mar-12-1877.
672.   ix.   MATHEW FRANKLIN REID b. 1878.
673.   x.   ANDREW NATHAN REID b. 1881.
       xi.   (INFANT) REID b. 1881,[201] d. 1881.[201]
       xii. ADER EVELYN REID b. 1883 in Cleveland, Conway Co, AR,[201] d. 1909.[201] She married[201] John Bowen.
674.   xiii. MARILAND REID b. Oct-16-1884.
675.   xiv. JOHN ALTUS REID b. 1886.
676.   xv.   JOSEPH ALEX REID b. Jun-28-1888.
677.   xvi. EZRA FIZER REID b. Mar-24-1890.
678.   xvii. HOMER REID b. Oct-31-1892.
679.   xviii. CHARLES JACKSON REID b. 1897.

372. **George W. Reid** (210.Asa[7], 107.Jane[6], 41.Matthew[5], 11.Alexander[4], 4.(Male)[3], 2.William[2], 1.Jean[1]), b. 1845,[201] d. 1914.[201] He married[201] **Margaret Grason**.
       Children:
       i.   MARY ALICE REID b. 1872.[201]
       ii. JOHN WILLIAM REID b. 1877.[201]

373. **Robert Lafayette Norman** (212.Jane[7], 107.Jane[6], 41.Matthew[5], 11.Alexander[4], 4.(Male)[3], 2.William[2], 1.Jean[1]), b. 1828 in Alabama,[201] d. aft 1886.[201] He married[201] **Catherine Meeler**, b. 1837 in Hamilton Co, TN,[201] d. 1916.[201]
       Children:
680.   i.   CHARLES STEPHEN NORMAN b. 1857.

374. **Matthew Alexander Gaston** (214.Matthew[7], 108.Alexander[6], 41.Matthew[5], 11.Alexander[4], 4.(Male)[3], 2.William[2], 1.Jean[1]), b. Nov- 1-1832 in Greene Co, GA,[203] d. Jan- 9-1883 in Alto, Cherokee Co, TX.[203] He married (1) Jan-22-1851 in Hancock Co, GA,[203] **Mary Ware**. He married (2) Dec-21-1859 in Alto, Cherokee Co, TX,[203] **Mary Elizabeth Brown**, b. Dec-22-1843 in Meriwether Co, GA.[203]
       Children by Mary Ware:
       i.   SUSAN ELIZABETH GASTON b. May-16-1855.[203]
       Children by Mary Elizabeth Brown:
681.   ii. MATTHEW ALEXANDER GASTON, JR. b. Oct- 8-1860.
       iii. LUELLA GASTON b. 1865.[203]

375. **David Gaston** (216.James[7], 111.James[6], 46.John[5], 12.John[4], 5.William[3], 3.John[2], 1.Jean[1]).
       Children:
       i.   JAMES TAYLOR GASTON.

376. **Caroline Gaston**[321] (217.William[7], 112.Esther[6], 46.John[5], 12.John[4], 5.William[3], 3.John[2], 1.Jean[1]). She married[321] **Silas Mercer**.
       Children:
       i.   IVA MERCER b. in Marion Co, IL.[321]

       Member (No. 67380) of Daughters of the American Revolution.

       She married[321] George C. Habermeyer.

377. **James Henry Gaston**, also known as Henry Gaston,[211] (218.William[7], 113.Stephen[6], 47.James[5], 12.John[4], 5.William[3], 3.John[2], 1.Jean[1]), b. Mar- 3-1853 in Illinois,[12] d. May- 5-1932 in Illinois,[12] census 1910, 1920 in Jefferson Co, IL, occupation farmer.[211]

       1910 Census, Jefferson County, Illinois (Shiloh Township), enumerated on Apr 21 1910: Henry Gaston, 57, widowed, b. Illinois, occupation farmer; son Will, 26, married, occupation farmer.[211]

He married[dcxciv][694] **Mary Jane Harvey**, b. Feb-21-1853 in Illinois,[12] d. Mar-21-1889.[12]
       Children:
682.   i.   NORMAN OSCAR GASTON b. 1871.
         ii.   CATHERINE HARRIET GASTON b. Dec- 6-1872 in Illinois,[12] d. Dec- 8-1954 in
Illinois.[12] She married[12] Charles Willey, b. Aug-12-1871,[12] d. Jan-16-1949.[12] Five children.[12]

        iii. PLEASANT L. GASTON b. Dec- 5-1874,[12] d. Sep-25-1886.[12]
683.   iv. WILLIAM BELL GASTON b. ca 1884.

378. **Jane Gaston Walker** (220.William[7], 114.John[6], 49.Esther[5], 12.John[4], 5.William[3], 3.John[2], 1.Jean[1]), b. 1820,[113] d. 1889.[113] She married 1853,[113] [Jane Gaston Walker was John Jackson's second wife.], **John Jackson**, b. 1829,[113] d. 1900.[113]
       Children:
684.   i.   SARA IDA JACKSON b. 1858.

379. **Arthur Lee Gaston** (224.T. Chalmers[7], 115.John[6], 50.Joseph[5], 12.John[4], 5.William[3], 3.John[2], 1.Jean[1]), b. Aug-14-1876 in Chester, Chester Co, SC,[207] d. 1951,[207] occupation attorney, judge.[207]

"Gaston, Arthur Lee, attorney: born at Chester, SC August 14, 1876; son of T.C. and Adelaide (Lee) Gaston; attended Davidson College, NC, University of Va., Charlottesville, VA; A.B. degree from Davidson College; lieutenant-colonel Gov., R.I Manning's staff four years; member S.C. House of Representatives six years; delegate to Democratic National Convention at San Francisco, 1920; engaged in active law practice in State and Federal Courts, representing interests in cotton mills, banks and industrial companies; at present director of Baldwin Cotton Mill, Commercial Bank (Chester, SC) and Chester Building and Loan Assn.: first Lieutenant Co. D., 1st S.C. Volunteer Inf., Spanish American War, served as chairman local board and as field chairman of district for Liberty Loan campaigns in State during World War; married Virginia Aiken (deceased), Greenwood, SC; next Elizabeth Byrd Smith, August, GA; member of Kappa Alpha Fraternity, Home is Chester SC."
[Who's Who in South Carolina - A dictionary of Contemporaries containing biographical notices of eminent men of South Carolina - Geddings Hardy Crawford, Editor, 1921]

He married (1) **Virginia Aiken**, b. 1881,[207] d. 1907.[207] He married (2) **Elizabeth Byrd Smith**.
       Children by Virginia Aiken:
685.   i.   DAVID AIKEN GASTON b. Aug-21-1903.

380. **Carolina McCalla** (225.Margaret[7], 116.Narcissa[6], 50.Joseph[5], 12.John[4], 5.William[3], 3.John[2], 1.Jean[1]), b. in Chester Co, SC.[332]

A member (no. 48282) of the Daughters of the American Revolution.

She married[332] **Daniel Webster Speake**, occupation Judge.[332]
       Children:
       i.   ELIZABETH SPEAKE b. in Tuscaloosa, Tuscaloosa Co, AL.[dcxcv][695]

381. **Jessie A. DeVega**[121] (226.Eliza[7], 117.Hugh[6], 51.John[5], 13.Mary[4], 5.William[3], 3.John[2], 1.Jean[1]). She married[121] **Joseph D. Means**.
       Children:
       i.   ETHEL MEANS b. in Chester, Chester Co, SC.[121]

Member (No. 28279) of Daughters of the American Revolution.

She married ___ McFadden.

382. **John William "Billy" Gaston** (228.Samuel[7], 121.William[6], 57.William[5], 16.Robert[4], 5.William[3], 3.John[2], 1.Jean[1]), b. Dec- 8-1850 in Haines Twp, Marion Co, IL,[212,17] d. May-16-1936 in Farrington Twp, Jefferson Co, IL,[212,17] buried in McConnaughhay Cem, Farrington Twp, Jefferson Co, IL.[212,17] He married Mar-12-1871 in Jefferson Co, IL,[212] **Amanda Catherine McConnauhhay**, b. Mar-20-1851,[212,17] d. Sep-20-1914,[212,17] buried in McConnaughhay Cem, Farrington Twp, Jefferson Co, IL.[212,17]

> Children:
>
> i. WILLIAM PORTER GASTON, also known as Porter Gaston,[212] b. Mar-26-1874,[17] d. Nov-18-1928 in LaSalle Co, IL,[17] buried in McConnaughhay Cem, Farrington Twp, Jefferson Co, IL,[17] occupation farmer, never married[212.]
>
> Never married, William Porter Gaston was highly self-educated in math, English and history, and he carried a dictionary with him that he studied as he rode along on his horse. A highly religious man, he studied the Bible during much of his free time. He was missing his two front upper teeth, and the story goes that he lost them when someone dared him to sneak up to a large boar hog and bite its tail. He took the dare, and as the hog jumped, Porter lost his teeth.[212]
>
> ii. CURRELL SAMUEL GASTON, also known as Sam Gaston,[212] b. May-15-1875,[212,17] d. Oct-30-1955,[212,17] buried in McConnaughhay Cem, Farrington Twp, Jefferson Co, IL.[dcxcvi[696]] He married[212] (1) Rosella E. "Lizzie" Meador,[212] b. Mar-30-1880,[17] d. Nov- 2-1931,[17] buried in McConnaughhay Cem, Farrington Twp, Jefferson Co, IL.[17]
>
> Rosella: No children, although Lizzie and Sam Gaston did raise two children, brother and sister Hal and Nadine Harr. They likely moved to St. Louis.[212]
>
> He married[212] (2) Nora Clark.
>
> iii. MARY C. GASTON b. 1876,[212] d. 1876,[212] buried in McConnaughhay Cem, Farrington Twp, Jefferson Co, IL.[212,17]
>
> iv. HUBERT "WILLIAM" GASTON b. 1877,[212] d. 1878,[212] buried in McConnaughhay Cem, Farrington Twp, Jefferson Co, IL.[212]
>
> v. JAMES ALBERT GASTON b. 1878,[212] d. 1880.[212]
>
> 686. vi. CHARLES DELBERT GASTON b. May-14-1880.
>
> 687. vii. EDWARD WESLEY GASTON b. Feb-28-1883.
>
> 688. viii. WALTER ANDREW GASTON b. Sep-30-1885.
>
> 689. ix. JOHN AUGUST GASTON b. Mar- 3-1887.
>
> 690. x. NELLIE JANE GASTON b. Oct-16-1889.
>
> xi. HERBERT M. GASTON d. 1926,[212] buried in McConnaughhay Cem, Farrington Twp, Jefferson Co, IL.[212]

383. **Georgia Anna Gaston**, census name Georgia Bridwell (229.William[7], 123.Robert[6], 58.Thomas[5], 16.Robert[4], 5.William[3], 3.John[2], 1.Jean[1]), b. Jul-19-1875,[333] d. Feb-12-1941 in Travelers Rest, Greenville Co, SC,[339,333] buried in Nazareth Presbyterian Church Cemetery, Moore, Spartanburg Co, SC,[339] census 1880, 1900 in Reidville, Spartanburg Co, SC. She married[129,502] Nov- 8-1899,[333] **Amzi Cason "Case" Gaston**, census name A. Cason Gaston, b. Nov- 4-1874 in Spartanburg Co, SC,[684,333,dcxcvii[697]] (son of Amzi Williford Gaston II and Margaret "Maggie" Holder), d. Apr- 9-1962 in Rutherfordton, Rutherford Co, NC,[697] buried in Nazareth Presbyterian Church Cemetery, Moore, Spartanburg Co, SC,[697] resided 1944 near Reidville, Spartanburg Co, SC,[333] census 1900 in Reidville, Spartanburg Co, SC, occupation farmer,[333,398] education Reidville Male Academy, Reidville, SC.[333]

Amzi: He served one term in the South Carolina House of Representatives.[339]
As direct descendants of Thomas Gaston and Sarah Nickels, Amzi Cason Gaston and Georgia Gaston were second cousins, once removed.

> Children:

691. i.   STOBO ROSBOROUGH GASTON b. Aug-23-1900.
692. ii.   AMZI CECIL GASTON b. Feb- 1-1902.
      iii. GEORGIA LEONA GASTON[339] also known as Leona Gaston,[333] b. Apr- 4-1904,[333] d. Jul-6-1906,[333] buried in Nazareth Presbyterian Church Cemetery, Moore, Spartanburg Co, SC.[339]
      iv.   LELA GASTON b. Jun-21-1905,[333] d. Sep- 4-1905.[333]
693. v.   MARGARET LUCILE GASTON b. Dec-28-1906.
694. vi.   JOHN WILLIAM GASTON b. Nov-14-1912.
      vii. PEARL (TWIN) GASTON b. May- 2-1914,[dcxcviii[698]] d. Sep-26-1914.[698]
      viii. BERLE (TWIN) GASTON b. May- 2-1914,[698] d. May-25-1917.[698]

384. **William Belton Gaston**, census name Belton Gaston (229.William[7], 123.Robert[6], 58.Thomas[5], 16.Robert[4], 5.William[3], 3.John[2], 1.Jean[1]), b. ca 1884 in South Carolina,[211] d. Nov- -1936, buried in Nazareth Presbyterian Church Cemetery, Moore, Spartanburg Co, SC, census 1930 in Spartanburg Co, SC, census 1910, 1920 in Reidville, Spartanburg Co, SC. He married[129,502] **Bessie Mae Pearson**, also known as May Pearson,[129] census name Mae, b. Jun-21-1896 in South Carolina,[592,334] d. Oct- -1981,[592] buried in Nazareth Presbyterian Church Cemetery, Moore, Spartanburg Co, SC, census 1930 in Spartanburg Co, SC, census 1920 in Reidville, Spartanburg Co, SC.

1920 Census, Spartanburg Co, SC (Reidville Twp), enumerated on Jan 21 1920:
Lucy Gaston, 64, widowed; son Belton, 36, farmer; dau-in-law Mae, 23; grandson William, 6; granddau Mary, 3 yr 6 mo; grandson George, 2 yr 5 mo; boarder Mattie Wade, 19. All born in South Carolina.

1930 Census, Spartansburg Co, SC (Beech Springs Twp), enumerated on Apr 24 1930:
Belton Gaston, 44, laborer, age 28 at time of first marriage; wife May, 35, age 18 at first marriage; dau Louellen, 13; dau Georgia, 12; dau Dolly May, 7; dau Myrtle, 6; son John Henry, 4 yr 2 mo; dau Virginia, 2 yr 7 mo.

        Children:
      i.   WILLIAM CRAWFORD GASTON b. ca 1914 in South Carolina,[681] d. bef Jan 2005,[412] census 1920 in Reidville, Spartanburg Co, SC. He married Annie Moore, b. May- 6-1913,[592] d. Mar- -1980,[592] resided in Lyman, Spartanburg Co, SC.[592]
      ii.   MARY LOU GASTON, census name Louellen Gaston, b. ca 1917 in South Carolina,[334] d. bef Jan 2005,[412] census 1930 in Spartanburg Co, SC. She married[424] __ McGinnis.
      iii. GEORGIA LEONA GASTON b. Oct- 3-1918 in South Carolina,[592] d. Nov- -1985,[592] resided in Spartanburg, Spartanburg Co, SC,[592] census 1930 in Spartanburg Co, SC.
695. iv.   DOLLIE MAY GASTON b. Apr-24-1922.
      v.   MYRTLE GENEVA GASTON b. Jan-24-1924 in South Carolina,[592] d. Dec-31-2000,[592] resided in Spartanburg, Spartanburg Co, SC,[592] census 1930 in Spartanburg Co, SC. She married[424] __ Wingo.
      vi.   JOHN HENRY GASTON b. Jan-12-1926 in South Carolina,[592,334] d. Mar- -1984,[592] resided in Spartanburg, Spartanburg Co, SC,[dcxcix[699]] census 1930 in Spartanburg Co, SC.
      vii. VIRGINIA DARE "GINNY" GASTON b. Aug-16-1927 in Spartanburg, Spartanburg Co, SC,[190] d. Jan-18-2011 in Spartanburg, Spartanburg Co, SC,[dcc[700]] buried in Nazareth Presbyterian Church Cemetery, Moore, Spartanburg Co, SC,[190] resided in Spartanburg, Spartanburg Co, SC,[190] census 1930 in Spartanburg Co, SC.
      viii. WHITE ONEAL GASTON d. bef Jan 2005.[412]
696. ix.   RACHEL GASTON b. May- 1-1930.

385. **Thomas Rosborough Gaston** (229.William[7], 123.Robert[6], 58.Thomas[5], 16.Robert[4], 5.William[3], 3.John[2], 1.Jean[1]), b. ca 1890 in South Carolina,[681] census 1910, 1920, 1930 in Reidville, Spartanburg Co, SC, occupation 1920 automobile mechanic,[681] occupation 1930 corn farmer.[334] He married[129] ca 1913,[334] **Rebecca "Rebbie" Alverson**, b. ca 1896 in South Carolina,[681] (daughter of Green Alverson and Sylvia Johnson), resided 1920, 30 in Reidville, Spartanburg Co, SC,[129,681,334.]

1920 Census, Spartanburg Co, South Carolina (Reidville Twp), enumerated on Jan 2 1920: Thomas R. Gaston, 30, automobile mechanic; wife Rebbie, 24; son James, 6. All born in South Carolina.

1930 Census, Spartanburg Co, SC (Reidville Twp), enumerated on Apr 23 1930: Thomas R. Gaston, 40, corn farmer, age 23 at time of first marriage; wife Reba, 34, age 17 at first marriage; son James R, 15; dau Elizabeth A, 6; mother Lucy C, 75, widowed. All born in South Carolina.

Children:
  i. JAMES R. GASTON b. ca 1914 in Spartanburg Co, SC,[681] census 1920 in Reidville, Spartanburg Co, SC.
  ii. ELIZABETH A. GASTON b. ca 1924,[334] census 1930 in Reidville, Spartanburg Co, SC.

386. **Amzi Williford Gaston II** (231.Amzi[7], 124.James[6], 58.Thomas[5], 16.Robert[4], 5.William[3], 3.John[2], 1.Jean[1]), b. May-17-1841 near Duncan, Spartanburg Co, SC,[dcci[701]] d. Sep-16-1911 near Duncan, Spartanburg Co, SC,[dccii[702]] buried in Nazareth Presbyterian Church Cemetery, Moore, Spartanburg Co, SC,[339] census 1880, 1900, 1910 in Reidville, Spartanburg Co, SC, military Jeb Stuart's 2nd South Carolina Cavalry, CSA (Civil War).[339,701] He married Aug-16-1870,[214] **Margaret "Maggie" Holder**, census name Maggie,[210] b. May-17-1847 at Olney, Pickens Co, AL,[214] (daughter of John Anthony Holder and Anna Mary Knox), d. Jul-30-1937 near Duncan, Spartanburg Co, SC,[702] buried in Nazareth Presbyterian Church Cemetery, Moore, Spartanburg Co, SC.[339]
  Children:
 697. i. JOHN WILLIFORD "WILL" GASTON b. Jul- 3-1871.
 698. ii. ROBERT WHITE GASTON b. Aug-18-1873.
 699. iii. AMZI CASON "CASE" GASTON b. Nov- 4-1874.
 700. iv. FITZIE HAMPTON GASTON b. Jan-23-1877.
 701. v. JAMES GORDON GASTON b. Mar- 4-1878.
 702. vi. THOMAS CRAIG GASTON b. Sep-29-1879.
 703. vii. JEB STUART GASTON b. Mar-18-1881.
  viii. MARY ELIZABETH "MAYME" GASTON b. Oct-18-1882 in South Carolina,[339,dcciii[703]] d. Jun-16-1961 in Duncan, Spartanburg Co, SC,[339] buried in Nazareth Presbyterian Church Cemetery, Moore, Spartanburg Co, SC,[339] occupation teacher, Spartanburg Co, SC (6 yrs),[703] education Reidville Female College (1900), Converse College, Univ of Tennessee.[703] She married Sep-19-1906,[703] no children from this marriage,[703] Newton Pierce Anderson, b. Jan-26-1877,[703] (son of James Milligan Anderson and Elizabeth Leonard), d. Nov-28-1944 in Richland Co, SC,[339] buried in Nazareth Presbyterian Church Cemetery, Moore, Spartanburg Co, SC.[339]
  ix. PALMER DEWITTE GASTON b. May-16-1884,[703] d. Mar- 7-1886,[703] buried in Nazareth Presbyterian Church Cemetery, Moore, Spartanburg Co, SC.[703]
  x. BAYARD LAMAR GASTON b. Dec-15-1885,[dcciv[704]] d. May-31-1887,[704] buried in Nazareth Presbyterian Church Cemetery, Moore, Spartanburg Co, SC.[704]
  xi. NORTON REID GASTON b. Aug-20-1887 in Woodruff, Spartanburg Co, SC,[339,704] d. Aug-16-1925 in Spartanburg Co, SC,[dccv[705],704] buried in Nazareth Presbyterian Church Cemetery, Moore, Spartanburg Co, SC,[705,704] education Reidville Male Academy, Presbyterian College at Clinton SC,[704] military U.S. Army (Jun 1918 - Jan 1919).[704] He married Jan-15-1913,[704] no children from this marriage,[704] Elizabeth Teasley, b. Feb- 9-1888,[704] (daughter of John Wiley Teasley and Nora McAlister), d. Jun-29-1913,[704] buried in Nazareth Presbyterian Church Cemetery, Moore, Spartanburg Co, SC.[704]
  xii. DAVID HOLDER GASTON b. Mar-23-1889,[704] d. Jun- 7-1910,[704] buried in Nazareth Presbyterian Church Cemetery, Moore, Spartanburg Co, SC,[704] education University of North Carolina (medical student at time of death).[704]

387. **William Denny Gaston** (232.Thomas[7], 124.James[6], 58.Thomas[5], 16.Robert[4], 5.William[3], 3.John[2], 1.Jean[1]), b. Oct-13-1840.[335] He married[335] **Mary Ann Zimmerman**.
  Children:

704.   i.   VIRGIL R. GASTON b. Mar-16-1869.

388. **Edward Baxter Gaston** (232.Thomas[7], 124.James[6], 58.Thomas[5], 16.Robert[4], 5.William[3], 3.John[2], 1.Jean[1]), b. Jul-23-1842,[335] resided since Dec 1870 near Gainesville, Cooke Co, TX.[335] He married[335] (1) **Amanda Winn**. He married[335] (2) **Abbie Dye**.

          Children by Amanda Winn:
- i.   TOM GASTON[335.]
- ii.   NETTIE GASTON[335.]
- iii.   CORRIE GASTON[335.]
- iv.   ANNA GASTON[335.]
- v.   BESSIE GASTON[335.]
- vi.   NEWTON GASTON[335.]

          Children by Abbie Dye:
- vii. LAWRENCE GASTON[335.]
- viii. MARY GASTON d. age 10,[335] cause of death burned to death.[335]
- ix.   ROY GASTON[335.]
- x.   JOSEPHINE GASTON[335.]

389. **Anderson Lewers Gaston**, census name Louis A. Gaston,[123] (232.Thomas[7], 124.James[6], 58.Thomas[5], 16.Robert[4], 5.William[3], 3.John[2], 1.Jean[1]), b. Sep- 9-1845 in Spartanburg District, SC,[335,130] d. Feb-24-1909 in Cooke Co, TX,[dccvi[706]] resided near Gainesville, Cooke Co, TX,[335] census 1900 in Cooke Co, TX, occupation farmer.[123]

Served on staff of General Longstreet during Civil War. Mary Gaston Gee identifies the children of Anderson Lewers Gaston and Mattie McAllister as "William, Dante, Walter, Elbert, and Lee." The seven children listed here were identified by researcher Larry Charles Slaughter, great-great-grandson of the couple through their daughter Sallie Lee.[dccvii[707]]

He married[335] (1) **Sally Rowe**. He married[335] (2) 1879 in Gainesville, Cooke Co, TX,[130] **Mattie E. McAllister**, b. Aug-31-1851 in Alabama,[123,706] d. Feb-18-1934,[706] census 1900 in Cooke Co, TX.

Mattie: Also went by last name Hackleman. There is some confusion as to her true maiden name and where the other name came from.[706]

          Children by Sally Rowe:
- i.   MAY GASTON.

          Children by Mattie E. McAllister:
- ii.   DAINTY EVELENE GASTON b. Jul- 7-1880,[706] d. Sep-30-1885.[706]
- 705. iii.   WILLIAM "WILL" GASTON b. Jun- -1882.
- iv.   GARLAND GASTON[706.]
- 706. v.   SALLIE LEE GASTON b. Jan-23-1886.
- vi.   (INFANT DAUGHTER) GASTON b. Nov-23-1887.[706]
- vii. WALTER JOHN GASTON, census name John W. Gaston,[123] b. May-13-1889 in Texas,[123,706] d. Mar-25-1910,[706] census 1900 in Cooke Co, TX.
- viii. ELBERT A. GASTON b. Jul- -1891 in Texas,[123] d. 1919, census 1900 in Cooke Co, TX.

390. **Mary Elizabeth Gaston** (232.Thomas[7], 124.James[6], 58.Thomas[5], 16.Robert[4], 5.William[3], 3.John[2], 1.Jean[1]), b. Oct-16-1847,[335] resided near Duncan, Spartanburg Co, SC.[335] She married[335] **Jeff Wood**, resided in Duncan, Spartanburg Co, SC,[335] resided originally in Marietta, Cobb Co, GA.[335]

          Children:
- i.   RAYMOND WOOD[335.]
- ii.   ALMA WOOD[335.]
- iii.   RUEL WOOD[335.]
- iv.   CADDIE WOOD[335.]

v.   LILLIAN WOOD[335.]
vi. LORRAINE WOOD[335.]

391. **Docia Hawkins** (233.Sarah[7], 124.James[6], 58.Thomas[5], 16.Robert[4], 5.William[3], 3.John[2], 1.Jean[1]), b. 1856,[214] resided 1944 in Amarillo, TX.[214] She married 1875,[214] **Horace King Jones**.
         Children:
         i.   MARVIN JONES resided in Amarillo, TX.[214]

         Formerly a U.S. Congressman from Texas, he was later a Federal judge. During World War II, he served at the War Food Administrator.[214]

392. **Elizabeth Louise Gaston** (237.Parley[7], 127.Thomas[6], 58.Thomas[5], 16.Robert[4], 5.William[3], 3.John[2], 1.Jean[1]), b. Jun-25-1879.[215] She married Jun-25-1903,[215] **George Henry Crowell**.
         Children:
         i.   MARY ELIZABETH CROWELL b. Apr-22-1908.[215]
         ii.   ADELAIDE GASTON CROWELL b. Oct- 8-1913.[215]
         iii. GEORGE HENRY CROWELL, JR. b. Nov- 4-1918,[215,592] d. Jun-12-1991,[592] resided in Ponte Vedra Beach, Saint Johns Co, FL,[592] resided formerly in North Carolina.[dccviii[708]]

393. **James Monroe Gaston** (238.James[7], 128.Robert[6], 60.Hugh[5], 16.Robert[4], 5.William[3], 3.John[2], 1.Jean[1]), b. 1864,[12] d. 1915.[12] He married[12] **Luella V. Spriggs**, b. 1865,[12] d. 1939.[12]
         Children:
707.   i.   JARVIS FRANK GASTON b. Oct-23-1901.

394. **Rosetta Perine** (241.Matilda[7], 134.Andrew[6], 72.John[5], 21.John[4], 6.Hugh[3], 3.John[2], 1.Jean[1]), b. Apr-14-1844 in Harrison Co, (W)VA,[398] d. Aug-15-1925 in West Union, Doddridge Co, WV,[398,356] buried in Arnolds Creek (West Union), Doddridge Co, WV,[398] census 1870 in West Union District, Doddridge Co, WV. She married Oct-23-1865 in Doddridge Co, WV,[dccix[709]] **William Henry Elliott**, b. ca 1845 in Ritchie Co, (W)VA,[dccx[710]] (son of Jacob Elliott and Barbara Susana Lowther), d. aft Aug 1925,[436] census 1870 in West Union District, Doddridge Co, WV, resided 1865 in Ritchie Co, WV,[dccxi[711]] census 1850 in Ritchie Co, (W)VA, occupation shoe maker.[710]

1870 Census, Doddridge Co, WV (West Union Twp), enumerated in Jun 1870:
Wm. Ellit (sic), 24, farmer; Rosetta, 23; Saml N, 3; Jasper D, 1.

The 1880 Census lists their children as Samuel, Jasper, W.T., Bird, Cora Lee, and Dollie E.

The 1900 Census states Rosetta had 8 children, with 7 still living as of 1900. Their household in 1900 consisted of William Elliott, Rosetta, sons Willie (based on birth date, this would be Waitman), Eddie, and David J., and daughter-in-law Eva.

         Children:
708.   i.   SAMUEL N. ELLIOTT b. Nov- -1868.
709.   ii.   JASPER DAVID ELLIOTT b. Feb-11-1869.
         iii. WAITMAN T. "WILLIE" ELLIOTT, census name Willie Elliott,[123] b. Oct-18-1871 in Doddridge Co, WV,[dccxii[712]] d. Dec-30-1939 in Doddridge Co, WV,[398,356] buried in Ruley Cemetery, Arnolds Creek, Doddridge Co, WV,[398] resided in Doddridge Co, WV,[398] census 1900, 1930 in Doddridge Co, WV.
710.   iv.   MARY BIRD ELLIOTT b. Feb- 3-1874.
711.   v.   CORA LEE ELLIOTT b. Jul- 8-1876.
712.   vi.   DOLLIE B. ELLIOTT b. Sep- 6-1878.
         vii. EDWARD ELLIOTT, also known as Eddy Elliott,[dccxiii[713]] census name Eddie Elliott, b. Jun-10-1881 in Doddridge Co, WV.[dccxiv[714]]

viii. JAMES ELLIOTT b. Apr- 4-1889 in Doddridge Co, WV,[dccxv][715] d. Sep-23-1889 at Arnolds Creek (West Union), Doddridge Co, WV,[dccxvi][716] buried in Ruley Cemetery, Arnolds Creek, Doddridge Co, WV.[357]

395. **Richard "Richie" Perine** (241.Matilda[7], 134.Andrew[6], 72.John[5], 21.John[4], 6.Hugh[3], 3.John[2], 1.Jean[1]), b. 1847 in Harrison Co, (W)VA,[17,347,344] d. 1935,[17,dccxvii][717] buried in Ruley Cemetery, Arnolds Creek, Doddridge Co, WV.[17] He married Apr-12-1872 in Doddridge Co, WV,[dccxviii][718],354 **Mary Jane Fleming**, also known as Jane,[502] b. Mar-25-1857 in Doddridge Co, WV,[dccxix][719] [The headstone for Mary J. Perine gives dates only as the years 1856 and 1932. That birth year conflicts with the Mar 25 1857 birthdate stated in her birth record. Her birth has also been reported as Mar 25 1855, basis for which is not known and which nonetheless conflicts with her birth record. Some researchers report her middle name spelled Jain, basis not specified. Her birth record identifies her only as Jane Fleming.] (daughter of Eli B. Fleming and Sarah Elmina Kinney), d. Nov-23-1932 at Arnolds Creek (West Union), Doddridge Co, WV,[700,46] buried in Ruley Cemetery, Arnolds Creek, Doddridge Co, WV.[17]
Children:
713. i. WAITMAN T. "WILLIE" PERINE b. Dec-15-1872.
714. ii. DONA ALICE PERINE b. Apr-28-1875.
715. iii. LELIA MYRTLE "LEE" PERINE b. Aug-21-1878.
iv. CHARLES PERINE, also known as Charles Prine,[17] b. Jul- 2-1882,[17] d. Dec-15-1901,[17] buried in Ruley Cemetery, Arnolds Creek, Doddridge Co, WV.[dccxx][720]
716. v. ADA MAY PERINE b. Oct-23-1886.
717. vi. LULA BLANCH PERINE b. Mar-30-1889.

396. **Sarah Ann Perine** (241.Matilda[7], 134.Andrew[6], 72.John[5], 21.John[4], 6.Hugh[3], 3.John[2], 1.Jean[1]), b. Feb-12-1850 in Harrison Co, (W)VA,[347,354] [But headstone shows birth date as 1852.], d. Apr- 9-1926 in Grafton, Taylor Co, WV,[347] buried in IOOF Cemetery (Blockhouse Hill), West Union, WV.[dccxxi][721] She married Jul- 2-1874 in Doddridge Co, WV,[dccxxii][722],349 **Edward Pritchard Southworth**, also known as Edwin Pricherd Southworth,[519] b. Feb- 7-1852 in Harrison Co, (W)VA,[349,354] d. Oct-26-1928 in Grafton, Taylor Co, WV,[344] buried in IOOF Cemetery (Blockhouse Hill), West Union, WV.[721]
Children:
i. MARY A. SOUTHWORTH b. Oct- 3-1875 in Doddridge Co, WV,[721,344] d. Dec-26-1900,[721] buried in IOOF Cemetery (Blockhouse Hill), West Union, WV.[721]

Middle name given by researcher John Mark Perine as "Ann," but by researcher Olin Joseph Hartman as "Alice."

ii. VIRGINIA VIOLA SOUTHWORTH, also known as Viola,[433] b. Mar-16-1878 in Doddridge Co, WV.[344] She married[344] Sep-12-1900 in Taylor Co, WV,[dccxxiii][723] John M. Harkins, b. ca 1878.[344]
iii. OLIVE "OCIE" SOUTHWORTH, also known as Virginia V. Southworth,[721] b. May-24-1880 in Doddridge Co, WV,[344] d. 1955,[721] buried in IOOF Cemetery (Blockhouse Hill), West Union, WV,[721] [Headstone reads: Virginia V. Southworth, 1880-1955.].
718. iv. CORA RANDOLPH SOUTHWORTH b. Jun- 7-1883.
v. EDNA ZANA SOUTHWORTH[519] b. Apr-12-1886 in Bridgeport, Harrison Co, WV,[344] d. 1949,[519] resided 1904, 1919 in Taylor Co, WV.[dccxxiv][724] She married (1) Apr-20-1904 in Taylor Co, WV,[724] Marion C. Madera, b. Feb- 5-1881 in Taylor Co, WV,[398,724] (son of J. Clark Madera and Mary Allender), d. May-12-1917 in Grafton, Taylor Co, WV,[398] baptized in Grafton, Taylor Co, WV.[398] She married[519] (2) Jun-28-1919 in Grafton, Taylor Co, WV,[724] Walter F. Handlin, b. ca 1885 in Pennsylvania,[724] resided 1919 in Pittsburgh, Allegheny Co, PA.[724]
vi. JESSIE CHLOE SOUTHWORTH b. Oct-22-1888 in Reynoldsville, Harrison Co, WV,[344,721] d. Dec-15-1896,[721] buried in Blockhouse Hill Cemetery, West Union, WV.[721]
719. vii. BLANCHE "DOC" SOUTHWORTH b. Feb- 5-1892.

397. **Columbus David Perine** (241.Matilda[7], 134.Andrew[6], 72.John[5], 21.John[4], 6.Hugh[3], 3.John[2], 1.Jean[1]), b. Apr- 4-1852 in Harrison Co, (W)VA,[398,354] [Although headstone gives birth date as Apr 4 1851,

death record states Apr 4 1852, and age 21 at time of 1873 marriage would also put birth date in 1852.], d. Feb-18-1929 in West Union, Doddridge Co, WV,[398,dccxxv[725],356,17] buried in Ruley Cemetery, Arnolds Creek, Doddridge Co, WV,[17,398] resided in West Union, Doddridge Co, WV,[398] occupation farmer.[398] He married (1) Apr- 6-1873 in Doddridge Co, WV,[dccxxvi[726],dccxxvii[727]] **Alcindia G. Cain**, b. Oct-25-1858 in Doddridge Co, WV,[dccxxviii[728]] (daughter of Walter Cain and Lydia __), d. Nov-27-1910 in Doddridge Co, WV,[17,344] buried in Ruley Cemetery, Arnolds Creek, Doddridge Co, WV.[17] He married[519] (2) Nov- 4-1914 in Wood Co, WV,[347] **Caroline Riley**, b. 1864 in Monroe Co, OH,[347,519] d. Jun-16-1927.[347]

Children by Alcindia G. Cain:

720.   i.   CHAPMAN J. PERINE b. Jan-16-1874.
721.   ii.   LILLIE MAY PERINE b. Oct-16-1875.
722.   iii.   WALTER MONROE PERINE b. Jun- 4-1877.
723.   iv.   LAURA PERINE b. Oct-30-1878.
724.   v.   LOUIS PERINE b. Dec-25-1881.
         vi.   MARY ARMATHEA PERINE b. Jun- 6-1882 in Doddridge Co, WV,[dccxxix[729]] d. May- 9-1969 in Clarksburg, Harrison Co, WV,[398,46] buried in Ruley Cemetery, Arnolds Creek, Doddridge Co, WV,[dccxxx[730]] resided in Doddridge Co, WV,[398] never married[398.]
725.   vii.   EMERY GOFF PERINE b. Oct-25-1886.
726.   viii.   LUTHER MARTIN PERINE b. Jul-29-1887.
727.   ix.   IRVIN SCOTT PERINE b. Jan-16-1889.
         x.   JOHN C. PERINE b. Jan-26-1890 in Doddridge Co, WV.[dccxxxi[731]]
728.   xi.   MAUDE GAY PERINE b. Oct- -1891.
729.   xii.   ALICE J. "ALLIE" PERINE b. Jun-29-1896.
730.   xiii.   DON COLUMBUS PERINE b. Aug- 9-1897.
731.   xiv.   DAISY P. PERINE b. Jan-14-1900.
         xv.   MATILDA "TILLIE" PERINE b. aft 1900.[344]

398. **Hannah Almeda Davis** (242.Frances[7], 135.Mary[6], 72.John[5], 21.John[4], 6.Hugh[3], 3.John[2], 1.Jean[1]), b. Jan- 5-1839,[365,17,377] d. Oct-18-1894 in Harrison Co, WV,[377,17] buried in McWhorter Cemetery, Harrison Co, WV.[17,377] She married Jan-26-1860 in Harrison Co, (W)VA,[dccxxxii[732]] **William Marshall West**, also known as Marshall West,[dccxxxiii[733]] b. Jun- 9-1835 in Harrison Co, (W)VA,[17,642] (son of Eli R. West and Belinda King), d. Jan-20-1904 in Harrison Co, WV,[17,732] buried in McWhorter Cemetery, Harrison Co, WV,[17,732] census 1880 in Grant District, Harrison Co, WV,[732] occupation farmer.[732] As grandchildren of Job West and Mary E. Gaston, Hannah Almeda Davis and her husband William W. West were first cousins.

Children:

         i.   (DAUGHTER) WEST b. ca 1859 in Harrison Co, (W)VA,[dccxxxiv[734]] d. Mar- 1-1861 in Harrison Co, (W)VA,[17,732] buried in McWhorter Cemetery, Harrison Co, WV.[17,732]
         ii.   (INFANT MALE) WEST d. Apr- 1-1861 in Harrison Co, WV.[276]
         iii.   ARAMITA L. WEST b. Oct-15-1862 in Harrison Co, (W)VA,[732] baptized in West Milford, Harrison Co, WV,[732] d. May- 1-1942 in Harrison Co, WV,[732] buried in Broad Run Bapt Ch Cem, Jane Lew, Lewis Co, WV,[732] census 1920 in Grant District, Harrison Co, WV,[732] never married[dccxxxv[735]]
         iv.   MARY FRANCES WEST b. Apr-29-1867 in Harrison Co, WV,[732] d. Jul-25-1954 in Harrison Co, WV,[732] census 1920 in Grant District, Harrison Co, WV,[732] buried in Broad Run Bapt Ch Cem, Jane Lew, Lewis Co, WV,[732] never married[735.]
732.   v.   OWEN ALDO WEST b. Apr- 4-1868.
         vi.   OLANDUS WEST b. Nov-28-1871 in Harrison Co, WV,[732] d. Jul-28-1939 in Clarksburg, Harrison Co, WV,[732] buried (mausoleum) at Elkview Masonic Cemetery, Clarksburg, Harrison Co, WV,[732] occupation teacher, businessman in coal, gas, oil & glass industries,[732] education Wesleyan College, Buckhannon WV (later a trustee there).[732] He married Nov-29-1906 in Harrison Co, WV,[dccxxxvi[736]] no children from this marriage,[dccxxxvii[737]] Alma McWhorter, b. Sep- 9-1878 at Lost Creek, Harrison Co, WV,[398,537] (daughter of John M. McWhorter and Mary M. Davisson), d. May-14-

1951 in Clarksburg, Harrison Co, WV,[398] buried (mausoleum) in Elkview Masonic Cemetery, Clarksburg, Harrison Co, WV,[462,398] resided in Clarksburg, Harrison Co, WV.[398]

Alma: As one of the participants, a classic photograh of her was printed in the program of "The Shawnee Trail," an historical pageant presented at Clarksburg, WV on June 13 and 15, 1923.

vii.   ALLIE MAY WEST b. Sep-25-1881 in Harrison Co, WV,[17,732] d. Jul-22-1889 in Harrison Co, WV,[17,732] buried in McWhorter Cemetery, Harrison Co, WV.[17,732]

399. **William (twin) Smith** (243.Ruanna[7], 135.Mary[6], 72.John[5], 21.John[4], 6.Hugh[3], 3.John[2], 1.Jean[1]), b. Aug- 9-1835 in Harrison Co, (W)VA,[377,17] d. May-18-1916 in Harrison Co, WV,[377,17] resided in Harrison Co, WV,[377] buried in Broad Run Bapt Ch Cem, Jane Lew, Lewis Co, WV.[17] He married Feb-24-1858, **Caroline E. Ward**, b. ca 1835.[377]
        Children:
    i.   L. CONLEY (adopted) b. ca 1865 in Virginia,[377] adopted by both[377.]

400. **Mary Elizabeth Smith**, also known as Elizabeth Smith,[17] (243.Ruanna[7], 135.Mary[6], 72.John[5], 21.John[4], 6.Hugh[3], 3.John[2], 1.Jean[1]), b. Feb- 3-1838 in Harrison Co, (W)VA,[377] d. ca 1868 in Harrison Co, WV,[377] buried in Duck Creek Missn Chrch Cem, near West Milford, Harrison Co, WV.[dccxxxviii[738]] She married Jan-27-1861 in Harrison Co, (W)VA,[377] **Hiram T. Edmonds**, b. Dec- 3-1838,[377] d. bef 1880 in Freemansburg, Lewis Co, WV.[377]
        Children:
    i.   RUANNA B. EDMONDS b. 1862.
733. ii. DORA E. EDMONDS b. 1865.
734. iii. HIRAM T. EDMONDS, JR. b. Apr- 9-1868.

401. **Elizabeth Smith** (243.Ruanna[7], 135.Mary[6], 72.John[5], 21.John[4], 6.Hugh[3], 3.John[2], 1.Jean[1]), b. Mar- 2-1840 in Harrison Co, (W)VA,[377] d. May- 4-1905,[377] census 1880 in Union District, Harrison Co, WV,[dccxxxix[739]] census 1900 in Warren District, Upshur Co, WV.[377]

Elizabeth Smith's second husband, Anthony Hess, was the brother of her son-in-law Jacob Hess.[dccxl[740]]

She married (1) Apr-17-1870 in Harrison Co, WV,[433,377] **Henry C. Hinkle**, b. Sep- 4-1842 in Harrison Co, (W)VA,[377] (son of Darius Hinkle and Urzelda "Zelda" West), d. Mar-30-1876 in Harrison Co, WV,[377] buried in West Cemetery, Duck Creek, Harrison Co, WV,[377] occupation farmer,[377] military Private, Co E, 20th Virginia Cavalry - Prisoner of War.[377] Elizabeth Smith and Henry C. Hinkle were second cousins, and also third cousins, by virtue of their common ancestry with John West & Frances Howard, Andrew Davison & Sarah Smith, and John Smith & Hannah Waters.

She married (2) Oct-12-1882 in Harrison Co, WV,[433,740] **Anthony Hess**, b. ca 1855 in Harrison Co, (W)VA,[740] (son of Newton Hess and Carrie ___), d. bef 1900.[740]
        Children by Henry C. Hinkle:
    i.   ICY M. HINKLE b. ca 1871 in Harrison Co, WV.[740] She married Dec-23-1888 in Harrison Co, WV,[740] Jacob Hess (son of Newton Hess and Carrie ___).
    ii.   SARAH HINKLE[373] b. ca 1873 in Harrison Co, WV,[740] d. Nov-10-1878 in Harrison Co, WV,[740] buried in West Cemetery, Duck Creek, Harrison Co, WV.[740]
    iii.   CHARLES P. HINKLE b. ca 1875 in Harrison Co, WV,[740] census 1900 in Richland Twp, Clinton Co, OH,[740] occupation farmer.[740] He married ca 1899,[740] Laura D. ___.
    iv.   EVA HINKLE b. in Harrison Co, WV,[740] d. in Harrison Co, WV,[740] buried in West Cemetery, Duck Creek, Harrison Co, WV.[740]

402. **Andrew Jackson Smith** (243.Ruanna[7], 135.Mary[6], 72.John[5], 21.John[4], 6.Hugh[3], 3.John[2], 1.Jean[1]), b. Apr- 5-1842 in Harrison Co, (W)VA,[740] d. Sep-10-1927 in Harrison Co, WV,[740] buried in Broad Run

Bapt Ch Cem, Jane Lew, Lewis Co, WV,[17,740] occupation farmer.[740] He married (1) 1866,[740] **Celia Wolfe**, b. 1848,[17,373] d. 1876,[17,373] buried in Broad Run Bapt Ch Cem, Jane Lew, Lewis Co, WV.[17]

Celia:. He married (2) 1877, **Lucinda F. Kemper**, b. Aug- -1850,[46,740] d. 1921,[17,740] buried in Broad Run Bapt Ch Cem, Jane Lew, Lewis Co, WV.[17]

   Children by Celia Wolfe:
   i.   PORTER W. SMITH b. Oct-14-1867,[17] d. Apr- 8-1879,[17] buried in Broad Run Bapt Ch Cem, Jane Lew, Lewis Co, WV.[17]
   ii. WILLIAM WIRT SMITH, also known as W. Wirt Smith,[17] b. Apr-25-1869,[46] d. 1916,[17,dccxli[741]] buried in Broad Run Bapt Ch Cem, Jane Lew, Lewis Co, WV,[17] [Headstone is for W. Wirt Smith, 1869-1916, and Celia I. Ferrell, 1904-1976. Relationship not clear.]. He married[741] Bertie Neely, b. 1881,[741] d. 1965.[741]
   iii. CLAUDIUS J. SMITH, also known as Claude J. Smith,[17] b. Aug-23-1870,[17] d. Apr-14-1902,[17] buried in Broad Run Bapt Ch Cem, Jane Lew, Lewis Co, WV.[17]
   iv. GERALD N. SMITH b. Mar- -1873,[46] d. 1953,[46] buried in Broad Run Bapt Ch Cem, Jane Lew, Lewis Co, WV.[17]
   v.   EGBERT BASSELL SMITH b. Oct-23-1874.
   Children by Lucinda F. Kemper:
   vi. ELECTA LUETTA SMITH b. Jun-24-1879,[17] d. Dec-10-1955,[17] buried in Broad Run Bapt Ch Cem, Jane Lew, Lewis Co, WV.[17]

      Spelling Electra has also been reported, but headstone reads Electa.

      She married __ Taylor.
   vii. ARNETTE SMITH b. May-15-1883,[17] d. Dec-24-1901,[17] buried in Broad Run Bapt Ch Cem, Jane Lew, Lewis Co, WV.[17]
   viii. JOHN DAVIDSON SMITH b. Oct- 6-1885.

403. **Eliza Smith** (243.Ruanna[7], 135.Mary[6], 72.John[5], 21.John[4], 6.Hugh[3], 3.John[2], 1.Jean[1]), b. Mar-30-1844 in Harrison Co, (W)VA,[740] d. Jan-20-1926.[740] She married Dec-16-1866 in Harrison Co, WV,[740] **George S. Waggoner**, b. Feb-23-1840 in Lewis Co, (W)VA,[740] (son of Elijah Waggoner and Mary Straley), d. Sep- 7-1917,[740] census 1880 in Lewis Co, WV,[740] occupation Farmer.[740]
   Children:
   i.   ALONZO WAGGONER b. ca 1868.[642]
   ii. HARVEY WELLINGTON WAGGONER[642] b. ca 1869.[410] He married Nov- 6-1901 in Lewis Co, WV,[410] Laura Beulah Life, b. ca 1879,[410] (daughter of B. J. Life and Margaret __).
   iii. GEORGE B. WAGGONER[234] b. Nov- -1881,[234] baptized (3rd child).[234]

404. **Edward Newton Smith** (243.Ruanna[7], 135.Mary[6], 72.John[5], 21.John[4], 6.Hugh[3], 3.John[2], 1.Jean[1]) (See marriage to number 298.)

405. **Nathan Granville Coberly** (244.Elizabeth[7], 135.Mary[6], 72.John[5], 21.John[4], 6.Hugh[3], 3.John[2], 1.Jean[1]), b. Jan-23-1837, d. May-18-1900, buried in Coberly Cemetery, Gilmer Co, WV, resided aft 1875 in Gilmer Co, WV,[642] resided bef 1875 in Duck Creek, Harrison Co, WV,[642] occupation shoemaker and carpenter.[642]

As a result of a childhood illness, he had a crippled foot.[642]

He married Sep- -1867,[dccxlii[742],433] **Isabelle Dawson**, b. Nov-15-1844,[742] (daughter of Edward Dawson and Marian Reed), d. Nov-17-1900, buried in Coberly Cemetery, Gilmer Co, WV.[642]
   Children:
   735. i.   DANIEL LUTHER COBERLY b. Jan- 1-1869.

406. **William Marshall West**, also known as Marshall West,[733] (245.Eli[7], 135.Mary[6], 72.John[5], 21.John[4], 6.Hugh[3], 3.John[2], 1.Jean[1]) (See marriage to number 398.)

407. John Jackson West, also known as John Elisha West,[396] (245.Eli[7], 135.Mary[6], 72.John[5], 21.John[4], 6.Hugh[3], 3.John[2], 1.Jean[1]), b. Dec- 3-1837 in Harrison Co, (W)VA,[732] d. Jan-24-1906 in Doddridge Co, WV,[732,dccxliii[743]] [Headstone gives death date as 1907, at variance with death record 2-176. [Donnelly, p. 417 & 443]], buried in Big Isaac Cemetery, Doddridge Co, WV,[732] resided 1885 in Greenbrier District, Doddridge Co, WV,[732] census 1870 in Upshur Co, WV,[732] occupation farmer, carpenter,[732] military Corporal, Co B, 17th Virginia Cavalry.[732] He married Oct-30-1859 in Harrison Co, (W)VA,[dccxliv[744],dccxlv[745],732] **Mary Elizabeth Cozad**, also known as Elizabeth Cozad,[396] b. Mar-29-1840 in Lewis Co, (W)VA,[732] (daughter of Jacob J. Cozad and Sarah Henry), d. Feb-11-1922 in Big Isaac, Doddridge Co, WV,[dccxlvi[746],732,356] buried in Big Isaac Cemetery, Doddridge Co, WV, census 1910, 1920 in Greenbrier District, Doddridge Co, WV,[732] resided 1859 in Harrison Co, (W)VA.[227]

        Children:

    736.   i.   ELI JACOB WEST b. Jul-24-1860.

           ii.   FIDELIA ARRILLA WEST b. Feb-28-1862 in Harrison Co, (W)VA,[dccxlvii[747]] d. Jul-29-1866 in Harrison Co, WV,[747] buried in Sinclair Cemetery, Upper Duck Crk Rd, Harrison Co, WV.[300,747]

    737.   iii. THOMAS FLOYD WEST b. Aug-22-1869.

    738.   iv. SARAH ELIZABETH WEST b. Dec-26-1869.

           v.   OWEN A. WEST b. May-16-1872 in Upshur Co, WV,[747] d. Jul- 2-1938 in Ashland, Ashland Co, OH,[747] buried in Maple Grove Cemetery, Ashland, OH,[747] census 1900 in Marion Co, WV,[747] occupation coal miner.[747]

        Researchers differ on the sequence of his three wives.[747]

        He married (1) bef 1893,[747] Mary Ernest. He married (2) Mar-10-1894 in Harrison Co, WV,[747] Eva Palmer, b. Sep-17-1877,[74] d. Apr-13-1899,[17] buried in Duck Creek Missn Chrch Cem, near West Milford, Harrison Co, WV.[230] He married (3) Mar- 3-1900 in Marion Co, WV,[747] Ellen Watton.

           vi. ROSA SELBY (adopted) b. Feb- 1-1873 in Upshur Co, WV,[747] d. May-16-1945 in Spencer, Roane Co, WV,[747] adopted by both[747.] She married[747] John Stoneking.

    739.   vii. WILLIAM BURR WEST b. 1874.

          viii. BELINDA ROANA WEST b. Nov-29-1876 in Upshur Co, WV,[747] resided 1931 in California.[747]

           ix. ICY GAY WEST b. Feb-25-1883 in Upshur Co, WV,[747] resided 1939 in Ashland, Ashland Co, OH.[747] She married[747] Ross Moffett.

408. Mary Louise West (245.Eli[7], 135.Mary[6], 72.John[5], 21.John[4], 6.Hugh[3], 3.John[2], 1.Jean[1]), b. Aug-10-1840 in Harrison Co, WV,[747] d. Feb-21-1916 in Harrison Co, WV,[747] census 1900 in Union District, Harrison Co, WV.[747] She married Apr-15-1862 in Harrison Co, (W)VA,[747,227] **Norval Gusman Patton**, also known as Norvell G. Patton,[462] b. Apr- 3-1838 in Duck Creek, Harrison Co, (W)VA,[747,398] (son of Zachariah Patton and Christine Gusman), d. Feb-28-1924 in Clarksburg, Harrison Co, WV,[398,462,747] buried in Elkview Masonic Cemetery, Clarksburg, Harrison Co, WV,[462,398] occupation farmer.[398]

        Children:

           i.   WILLIAM N. PATTON b. ca 1863 in Harrison Co, WV,[419,747] occupation teacher.[419] He married Apr-17-1884 in Harrison Co, WV,[419] Columbia A. Smith, b. ca 1863 in Harrison Co, WV,[419] (daughter of L. H. Smith and C. C. ___).

           ii. ZACHARIAH D. PATTON b. ca 1866 in Harrison Co, WV.[747]

    740.   iii. CHARLES C. PATTON b. ca 1869.

           iv. HELEN VIRGINIA PATTON, also known as Virginia Patton, b. Aug- 8-1871 in Harrison Co, WV,[398,467,419] d. Jul- 8-1957 in Lucretia, Taylor Co, WV,[398] buried in Bluemont Cemetery, Grafton, Taylor Co, WV,[398] resided in Lucretia, Taylor Co, WV,[398] resided 1938 in Valley Falls, Taylor Co, WV,[228] census 1900 in Union District, Harrison Co, WV. She married Nov-26-1899 in Harrison Co, WV,[419] Elijah E. Nutter, also known as Elisha Nutter,[419] b. Jan- 3-1850 in Barbour Co, (W)VA,[398,419,467] (son of Charles C. Nutter and Malinda Reed), d. Oct-28-1938 in Valley Falls, Taylor Co, WV,[398] buried in Bluemont Cemetery, Grafton, Taylor Co, WV,[398] resided in Valley Falls, Taylor Co, WV,[398] census 1900 in Union District, Harrison Co, WV, occupation farmer.[398]

741.   v.   JAMES BERYL PATTON b. Nov- 6-1875.
   vi.   WESLEY GUSMAN PATTON[419] also known as Wesley Germannis Patton, b. ca 1878 in Harrison Co, WV,[419,747] resided 1906 in West Milford, Harrison Co, WV.[419] He married Apr- 1-1906 in Lost Creek, Harrison Co, WV,[419] Nora Nutter, b. May- -1885 in Barbour Co, WV,[467,419] (daughter of Elijah E. Nutter and Ida Knight), resided 1906 in Harrison Co, WV.[419]
   vii.   MARY M. "MOLLIE" PATTON b. ca 1881 in Harrison Co, WV.[747]
   viii.   MELINDA C. PATTON b. ca 1883 in Harrison Co, WV.[747]
   ix.   ANNIE OCIE ELZONA PATTON[419] b. Jul-28-1884 in Harrison Co, WV, resided 1924 at Wolf Summit, Harrison Co, WV.[dccxlviii[748]] She married Jun-16-1904 in Harrison Co, WV,[419] Thornton Allen Scott, b. Dec-18-1880 in Harrison Co, WV,[592,419] (son of Jacob F. Scott and Elizabeth __), d. May- -1971,[592] resided at Wolf Summit, Harrison Co, WV.[419,604]
   x.   ARLINGTON A. PATTON[747] b. in Harrison Co, WV.[747]

409. **Sarah Ann West** (245.Eli[7], 135.Mary[6], 72.John[5], 21.John[4], 6.Hugh[3], 3.John[2], 1.Jean[1]), b. Sep-23-1845 in Harrison Co, (W)VA,[dccxlix[749]] d. Sep- 2-1922 in Harrison Co, WV,[749] buried in McWhorter Cemetery, Harrison Co, WV,[749] census 1900 in Grant District, Harrison Co, WV.[749] She married Aug-27-1865 in Harrison Co, WV,[749] **James F. McIntire**, b. 1846 in Lewis Co, (W)VA,[749] (son of Presley McIntire and Louisa Lyons), d. 1918 in Harrison Co, WV,[749] buried in McWhorter Cemetery, Harrison Co, WV,[749] census 1860 in Harrison Co, (W)VA,[749] occupation coal mine owner, at head of Duck Creek.[749]

Children:
742.   i.   MARCODA MELINDA MCINTIRE b. Mar-20-1867.
   ii.   ELLEN LOUISE MCINTIRE, also known as L. Ellen McIntire,[354] census name Louiza E. McIntire,[467] census name Ella,[dccl[750]] also known as Louisa Ellen McIntyre,[398] b. May-19-1870 in Harrison Co, WV,[398,467,749,354] d. Apr-11-1933 in Big Isaac, Doddridge Co, WV,[398,749] buried in Big Isaac Cemetery, Doddridge Co, WV,[398,749] resided 1914 in Doddridge Co, WV,[dccli[751]] census 1900, 10, 20, 30 in Greenbrier District, Doddridge Co, WV,[458] [In home with sister Marcoda (in 1900) and brother-in-law (and future husband) George A. Hinkle.], occupation millinery, dressmaker.[467] She married[749] Mar- 2-1914 in Doddridge Co, WV,[354] George Allen Hinkle, b. Oct- 5-1867 in Harrison Co, WV,[dcclii[752],354] (son of Abraham Hinkle and Catherine Ciscelia Carder), d. May-18-1942 in Doddridge Co, WV,[752,356] census 1900, 1930 in Greenbrier District, Doddridge Co, WV.
   iii.   THOMAS J. MCINTIRE b. 1873,[749] d. Feb-25-1952 in Harrison Co, WV,[749] buried in McWhorter Cemetery, Harrison Co, WV.[749] He married[749] Heta A. "Fleeta" Conley.[749]
   iv.   FLORA D. MCINTIRE b. 1876 in Harrison Co, WV,[537,749] d. Oct-19-1968,[749] buried in IOOF Cemetery, Salem, Harrison Co, WV.[749] She married[749] Sep-20-1900 in Harrison Co, WV,[dccliii[753]] Wade H. Gulley, b. ca 1876 in Doddridge Co, WV,[537] (son of Joseph Gulley and Sarah __).
   v.   JOHN P. MCINTIRE b. 1877,[749] d. Jul-10-1951 in Harrison Co, WV,[749] buried in McWhorter Cemetery, Harrison Co, WV.[749] He married[749] Grace Snyder.
   vi.   ESTELLA MAY MCINTIRE b. 1879 in Harrison Co, WV,[749] d. 1942,[749] buried in McWhorter Cemetery, Harrison Co, WV.[749] She married (1) Jan-29-1903 in Harrison Co, WV,[749] John Earl Hinkle. She married (2)[749] Thurman G. Scott.
   vii.   BERTHA MCINTIRE b. 1882,[749] d. Jul-21-1962 in Jefferson, Ashtabula Co, OH.[749] She married[749] Albert J. Pettigrew.
743.   viii.   DOLPH C. MCINTIRE b. 1887.

410. **Julia Amanda West** (245.Eli[7], 135.Mary[6], 72.John[5], 21.John[4], 6.Hugh[3], 3.John[2], 1.Jean[1]), b. May-16-1854 in Harrison Co, (W)VA,[377,398] d. Jul-31-1938 in Eaton, Wood Co, WV,[398] buried in Mt. Olive Cemetery, Jarvisville, Harrison Co, WV, resided in Clarksburg, Harrison Co, WV,[398] resided 1889 in Wood Co, WV.[377] She married[396] Dec-21-1879 in Harrison Co, WV,[377,227] **Samuel McIntyre**, b. ca 1854 in Lewis Co, (W)VA,[227] (son of Presley McIntire and Mary Elizabeth McDonald).
Children:
744.   i.   FRED C. MCINTYRE b. Jun-20-1886.

411. **Eliza Jane West** (245.Eli[7], 135.Mary[6], 72.John[5], 21.John[4], 6.Hugh[3], 3.John[2], 1.Jean[1]), b. Sep-22-1857 in Harrison Co, WV,[749] d. Apr- -1921.[749] She married Oct- 5-1876 in Harrison Co, WV,[749,433] **Henry B.**

Cottrill, b. ca 1854 in Harrison Co, WV,[749] (son of Luther L. Cottrill and Elizabeth Dawson), census 1900 in Grant District, Harrison Co, WV,[749] census 1860 in Harrison Co, (W)VA.

Children:
- 745. i. MINNIE OTTO COTTRILL b. Jul-24-1877.
- ii. ALDA V. COTTRILL b. ca 1882.[dccliv[754]]
- iii. LULU S. COTTRILL b. ca 1884.[754]
- iv. ETTA N. B. COTTRILL b. ca 1887.[754]
- v. EARL W. COTTRILL b. ca 1890.[754]
- vi. ARDEN B. COTTRILL b. ca 1896.[754]

412. Mary Martha Gaston (246.John[7], 136.Hugh[6], 72.John[5], 21.John[4], 6.Hugh[3], 3.John[2], 1.Jean[1]), b. Nov-20-1849 in Doddridge Co, WV,[190] d. Aug- 9-1932 in Oxford, Doddridge Co, WV,[dcclv[755],190,354] buried in Oxford Baptist Church Cemetery, Doddridge Co, WV,[17] census 1850 in Doddridge Co, (W)VA.

Identified in obituary as Mary A. Haught, daughter of John H. Gaston and Jane Pritchard Gaston. Basis for middle initial "A" is not known, as her middle name has been determined to be Martha and her headstone clearly identifies her as Mary M. Conversely, the obituary of her son Marvel L. Haught identifies her as Mary Ellen Gaston, and she appears in the 1850 Census as Mary E. Gaston, age 6 months. Her own obituary reads in part: "Mrs. Haught was born and reared and spent her entire long and useful life on the same farm in South West District. She was well known to many of the citizens of Doddridge County and was loved and revered by all who knew her; she was always kind and generous to the poor and was always attentive and helpful to the citizens of her community in times of sickness and distress. She lived a useful life, retaining her memory and optimism of life until a few days before she was called. When her life's work was finished, she fell asleep, assuring her relatives and friends that she was prepared to the change and that all was well with her."

She married Mar-27-1868 in Doddridge Co, WV,[dcclvi[756],354] **Marville Lindsay Haught**, census name Marvel L. Haught,[382] b. May-10-1846 in Greene Co, PA,[357,354,46] (son of Peter B. Haught and Bashaba Musgrave), d. Dec-28-1924 in Summers, Doddridge Co, WV,[dcclvii[757],46,354] buried in Oxford Baptist Church Cemetery, Doddridge Co, WV,[dcclviii[758]] military Jul- -1864 - Jun-10-1865 Cpl, Co C, 6th W. Va. Inf, Civil War.[dcclix[759]]

Children:
- i. (INFANT SON) HAUGHT b. Jan-14-1870,[17] d. Jan-14-1870,[17] buried in Hart Cemetery, Taylor Drain Rd, Oxford, Doddridge Co WV.[17]
- ii. JOHN W. HAUGHT b. Oct-16-1871 in Doddridge Co, WV,[dcclx[760]] [Although birth record reflects a date of Oct 17 1871, headstone shows birth date as Sep 16 1871.], d. Oct- 5-1890, buried in Hart Cemetery, Taylor Drain Rd, Oxford, Doddridge Co WV.[17]
- iii. COLUMBIA J. HAUGHT b. May-16-1873 in Doddridge Co, WV,[dcclxi[761]] d. May-31-1875 in Doddridge Co, WV,[17,354] buried in Hart Cemetery, Taylor Drain Rd, Oxford, Doddridge Co WV.[17]
- 746. iv. WILLIAM C. "WILL" HAUGHT b. Feb-21-1876.
- 747. v. LOVE HAUGHT b. Jan- 1-1878.
- 748. vi. IVAH MAY HAUGHT b. Feb-23-1880.
- 749. vii. AMOS PETER HAUGHT b. Sep-29-1882.
- viii. MARTHA HAUGHT b. Feb-23-1886 in Doddridge Co, WV,[dcclxii[762]] d. Oct-14-1887,[17] buried in Hart Cemetery, Taylor Drain Rd, Oxford, Doddridge Co WV.[17]
- ix. MARVEL LINDSEY HAUGHT b. Aug-22-1888 in Oxford, Doddridge Co, WV,[dcclxiii[763],190] d. Mar- 1-1972 in Oxford, Doddridge Co, WV,[700,17,592] buried in Masonic Memorial Park Cemetery, Crystal Lake (West Union), WV,[17,721] resided in Oxford, Doddridge Co, WV,[412,521] occupation Pittsburgh & West Virginia Gas Co; Director at 1st Natl Bank of West Union.[190]

Much confusion has existed over the years concerning the spelling of his name and that of his father, but his father was Marville (despite being listed as Marvel in his wife's obituary), and he named his son Marvel. Nonetheless, both spellings are often seen for both men, even in official records. Headstone gives name as Marvel L. Haught, and the Social Security Death Index identifies him as Marvel Haught.

He married no children from this marriage, Maude Summers, b. Oct-13-1884 in Doddridge Co, WV,[190,46] (daughter of Elijah W. Summers and Caroline Virginia Brown), d. Feb-27-1968 in Marietta, Washington Co, OH,[dcclxiv[764],46] buried in Masonic Memorial Park Cemetery, Crystal Lake (West Union), WV,[17,190,721] resided in Oxford, Doddridge Co, WV.[dcclxv[765],190]

750.   x.   MARY ELLEN HAUGHT b. Jun-17-1891.

           xi.   DOVENER I. HAUGHT b. Oct- 7-1893,[190] d. May-27-1927,[190] buried in Oxford Baptist Church Cemetery, Doddridge Co, WV,[dcclxvi[766]] never married[190.]

413. **Ivah Jane Gaston**, also known as Ivy Gaston (246.John[7], 136.Hugh[6], 72.John[5], 21.John[4], 6.Hugh[3], 3.John[2], 1.Jean[1]), b. Aug- 3-1851,[17,dcclxvii[767]] d. May-29-1907 in Doddridge Co, WV,[dcclxviii[768]] buried in Cabin Run Cemetery, Doddridge Co, WV.[17] She married Aug- 5-1868 in Doddridge Co, WV,[dcclxix[769]] **Harvey Smith**, b. May-26-1845 in Doddridge Co, (W)VA,[398,17] (son of Samuel Smith and Nancy Ann Fleming), d. May- 5-1929 in West Union, Doddridge Co, WV,[398,dcclxx[770],356,17] buried in Cabin Run Cemetery, Doddridge Co, WV,[398,17] census 1880, 1900 in West Union District, Doddridge Co, WV, census 1870 in Southwest District, Doddridge Co, WV, census 1850, 1860 in Doddridge Co, (W)VA, occupation farmer,[357,398] military W. Va. Volunteer Inf - Civil War (POW).

Harvey: After the death of Ivah Jane Gaston, Harvey married Virginia Elliott (who in turn married Ernest Allman after Harvey's death). Harvey served in Civil War 1862-1865 in Co A, Reg 14, WVa Volunteer Infantry. He was captured at Cloyds Mountain, VA, on May-09-1864, and was imprisoned at Andersonville, GA until paroled on Nov-25-1864.[dcclxxi[771]]

1870 Census, Doddridge Co, WV (Southwest Twp), enumerated on Aug 19 1870:
Harvey Smith, 25, farmer; Iva J, 18; James W, 1; Ann, 64.

1880 Census, Doddridge Co, WV (West Union District), enumerated on Jun 8 1880:
Harvey Smith, 35; wife Iva J, 28; son Jas W, 11; son Sam'l J, 8; son Sanford, 5; dau Nacy J, 4; son C L, 3.

1900 Census, Doddridge Co, WV (West Union District), enumerated on Jun 9 1900:
Harvey (looks more like Hary) Smith, 55, b. May 1845, married 22 yrs; wife Ivah J, 48, b. Aug 1851, mother of 12 children (9 still living); dau Nancy J, 23, b. Nov 1876; son Charley L, 21, b. Sep 1878; son Minor F, 15, b. Nov 1884; son Harvey Jr, 13, b. Apr 1887; dau Mary B, 10, b. Jul 1889; son Willie C, 7, b. Mar 1893.

1910 Census, Doddridge Co, WV (West Union District), enumerated on Apr 15 1910 at Arnolds Creek Road:
Harvey Smith, 64, farmer, widowed; dau Nancy J, 33, single; son Miner F, 25, teacher, single; son Harvey Jr, 22, farm laborer, single; dau Mary B, 20, single; son Willie C, 17, single; granddau Edna, 7.

           Children:
751.   i.   JAMES WESLEY SMITH b. Feb-13-1869.

           ii.   (INFANT MALE) SMITH b. Feb- 1-1872 in Doddridge Co, WV,[dcclxxii[772]] d. Feb-10-1872 in Doddridge Co, WV.[dcclxxiii[773]]

752.   iii.   SANFORD SMITH b. Nov-20-1874.

           iv.   NANCY JANE SMITH b. Nov- 8-1876 in Doddridge Co, WV,[dcclxxiv[774]] d. Feb-27-1943, buried in Cabin Run Cemetery, Doddridge Co, WV,[17] census 1920 in West Union, Doddridge Co, WV.[dcclxxv[775]] She married Dec- 3-1911 in Doddridge Co, WV,[dcclxxvi[776],354] Milton Camdon Hickman,[477] b. ca 1871 in Doddridge Co, WV,[dcclxxvii[777],776,477] (son of Thomas Hickman and Mary J. Adams), d. Apr-29-1960 in Ritchie Co, WV,[477] resided 1957 in Ellenboro, Ritchie Co, WV,[412] resided 1952 in Cleveland, Cuyahoga Co, OH,[521] resided 1935 in Pennsboro, Ritchie Co, WV,[521] resided 1923 in Smithton (now Smithburg), Doddridge Co, WV,[dcclxxviii[778]] census 1920 in West Union, Doddridge Co, WV.[775]

           v.   CHARLES LEWIS SMITH b. Sep-18-1878 in Doddridge Co, WV,[dcclxxix[779]] d. Mar- 8-1931, buried in Cabin Run Cemetery, Doddridge Co, WV, census 1930 in Clarksburg, Harrison Co,

WV [Listed as a lodger in household of brother James, marital status single.], never married. Was in mental asylum at Weston, WV for many years.[771]

      vi.   ELLA SMITH b. Sep-19-1882 in Doddridge Co, WV,[dcclxxx780] d. Jul-31-1898 in Arnolds Creek (West Union), Doddridge Co, WV,[dcclxxxi781],[17] buried in Cabin Run Cemetery, Doddridge Co, WV,[17,781] cause of death typhoid fever.[781]

753.   vii. MINER FRANCIS SMITH b. Nov-25-1884.

      viii. HARVEY SMITH, JR. b. Apr-22-1887,[771] d. Jul-26-1940,[771] census 1900, 1910 in West Union District, Doddridge Co, WV.

            Married Aug-12-1922. No children.[771]

754.   ix.   MARY BIRD SMITH b. Jul- 6-1889.

      x.   GRACIE SMITH b. Dec-16-1891 in Arnolds Creek (West Union), Doddridge Co, WV,[dcclxxxii782],[17] d. Feb-10-1892 in Doddridge Co, WV,[17,dcclxxxiii783] buried in Cabin Run Cemetery, Doddridge Co, WV.[17]

755.   xi.   WILLIAM COLUMBUS SMITH b. Mar- 3-1893.

414. **Mary Jane Gaston** (247.Daniel[7], 136.Hugh[6], 72.John[5], 21.John[4], 6.Hugh[3], 3.John[2], 1.Jean[1]), b. Sep- 9-1843 in Harrison Co, (W)VA,[dcclxxxiv784],[711] d. Dec-15-1915 in Doddridge Co, WV,[dcclxxxv785],[356] census 1870 in Doddridge Co, WV.[382] She married Nov-30-1865 in Doddridge Co, WV,[dcclxxxvi786],[354] **Joseph Stephen Britton**, b. Jan- 1-1842 in Monongalia Co, (W)VA,[711,784] (son of George Wade Britton and Mary J. "Polly" Husk), d. Jun-25-1915 in Summers, Doddridge Co, WV,[dcclxxxvii787],[356] census 1870 in Doddridge Co, WV,[382] census 1850 in Monongalia Co, (W)VA, occupation farmer.[382,dcclxxxviii788]

            Children:

756.   i.   DANIEL WEBSTER BRITTON b. Jun-11-1867.

      ii.   MARTHA A. BRITTON b. Jan-17-1869,[17] d. Sep- 2-1901 in Doddridge Co, WV,[dcclxxxix789],[17] buried in Gaston-Hart Cemetery, Upper Run, Summers, Doddridge Co, WV.[17]

      iii. CHARLES L. BRITTON b. Nov-12-1871,[dccxc790] d. Jan-10-1875 in Doddridge Co, WV,[356,17] buried in Gaston-Hart Cemetery, Upper Run, Summers, Doddridge Co, WV.[dccxci791]

757.   iv.   JOHN FRANK BRITTON b. Apr-30-1873.

      v.   ALEXANDER W. BRITTON b. Feb-21-1875 in Doddridge Co, WV,[dccxcii792] d. Jun-24-1875,[17] buried in Gaston-Hart Cemetery, Upper Run, Summers, Doddridge Co, WV.[791]

      vi.   NANCY O. BRITTON b. May-19-1877 in Doddridge Co, WV,[dccxciii793] d. Nov-16-1910 in Doddridge Co, WV.[356] She married Apr-24-1910 in Doddridge Co, WV,[dccxciv794] Arthur A. Valentine, b. ca 1888.

      vii. MARY JANE BRITTON[385] b. Apr-12-1881 in Doddridge Co, WV,[dccxcv795] d. Sep- 2-1901 in Summers, Doddridge Co, WV,[dccxcvi796],[17] [Death record for Mary J. Britton gives date of death as Sep 2 1901, with report filed Sep 7 1901. Death record gives age as 20. Headstone birth date of Apr 12 1880 is incorrect. Birth record shows birth was on Apr 12 1881, consistent with age 20 at time of death. Both Mary J. Britton and her older sister Martha A. Britton died on the same day, of typhoid fever.], buried in Gaston-Hart Cemetery, Upper Run, Summers, Doddridge Co, WV.[dccxcvii797]

      viii. FRANCIS C. BRITTON b. Nov-17-1882 in Doddridge Co, WV,[dccxcviii798] d. 1886,[dccxcix799] buried in Gaston-Hart Cemetery, Upper Run, Summers, Doddridge Co, WV.[17]

758.   ix.   ELIZA ELLEN BRITTON b. Jul-10-1888.

415. **Sarah Ann Gaston**[711] (247.Daniel[7], 136.Hugh[6], 72.John[5], 21.John[4], 6.Hugh[3], 3.John[2], 1.Jean[1]), b. Apr-24-1846 in Harrison Co, (W)VA,[17,711] d. Feb-15-1922,[dccc800] buried in Gaston-Hart Cemetery, Upper Run, Summers, Doddridge Co, WV,[17] census 1900 in Union District, Ritchie Co, WV, census 1870, 1880 in Southwest District, Doddridge Co, WV. She married Aug- 3-1865 in Doddridge Co, WV,[dccci801],[354] **David Richards**, also known as Daniel Richards, b. Apr-16-1843 in Harrison Co, (W)VA,[17,711] (son of James Tolbert Richards and Elizabeth Childers), d. Feb-28-1894,[17] buried in Gaston-Hart Cemetery, Upper Run, Summers, Doddridge Co, WV,[17] census 1870, 1880 in Southwest District, Doddridge Co, WV, census 1850 in Doddridge Co, (W)VA, occupation farmer. While all available records pertaining to him directly give his name as David Richards, he was listed as Daniel Richards in the death record and obituary of his son Daniel.

1870 Census, Doddridge Co, WV (Southwest Twp), enumerated on Sep 2 1870:

David Richards, 27, farmer; Sarah A, 24; Mary J, 4; Daniel J, 2; Columbus, 22, farm laborer.

1880 Census, Doddridge Co, WV (Southwest District), enumerated on Jun 1 1880:
David Richards, 37, farmer; wife Sarah A, 34; dau Mary J, 14; son Daniel J, 12; dau Nancy E, 9; dau Eliza O, 6; dau Sarah R, 2.

1900 Census, Ritchie Co, WV (Union District), enumerated on Jun 7 1900:
Sarah A. Richards, 52, b. Apr 1848, farmer, widowed, mother of 8 children (all still living); son Daniel J, 32, b. May 1868, farm laborer, single; dau Eliza O, 26, b. May 1874, single; dau Lina, 22, b. Sep 1877, single; son Austin D, 18, b. Jul 1881; son Samuel M, 15, b. Nov 1884; dau Icy M, 8, b. Apr 1892; boarder Boyd Lipscomb, 27, b. Oct 1872, day laborer, single.

Children:
i.   MARY J. RICHARDS b. Feb- 5-1866 in Doddridge Co, WV,[dcccii[802]] census 1870 in Southwest District, Doddridge Co, WV.

ii.   DANIEL J. RICHARDS b. May-14-1868 in Doddridge Co, WV,[dccciii[803]] d. Jan-19-1968 in Doddridge Co, WV,[dccciv[804]] buried in IOOF Cemetery, Harrisville, Ritchie Co, WV,[dcccv[805]] resided in Harrisville, Ritchie Co, WV,[191] census 1900 in Union District, Ritchie Co, WV, census 1870, 1880 in Southwest District, Doddridge Co, WV, occupation merchant, general store.[357] He married[484,191,436] Mary Elizabeth "Molly" Lowther, b. Jul- 6-1882,[190,398] [1900 Census of Gilmer County gives her birth date as July 1883. Birthplace not stated in obituary.] (daughter of James Samson Lowther and Margaret F. Holliday), d. Mar- 7-1954 in Parkersburg, Wood Co, WV,[398,dcccvi[806]] buried in IOOF Cemetery, Harrisville, Ritchie Co, WV,[398] resided 1928-54 in Harrisville, Ritchie Co, WV.[190,398]

iii. NANCY E. RICHARDS b. ca 1871,[402] census 1880 in Southwest District, Doddridge Co, WV.

iv.   ELIZA O. RICHARDS, also known as Louiza Richards,[dcccvii[807]] b. May-28-1874 in Doddridge Co, WV,[dcccviii[808]] d. Jun- 5-1901,[17] buried in Gaston-Hart Cemetery, Upper Run, Summers, Doddridge Co, WV,[17] census 1900 in Union District, Ritchie Co, WV, census 1880 in Southwest District, Doddridge Co, WV.

v.   SARAH R. "LINA" RICHARDS, census name Lina Richards,[dcccix[809]] census name Sarah R. Richards,[402] b. Sep-19-1877 in Doddridge Co, WV,[dcccx[810]] [SSDI reports birth date as Sep 18 1877. Name listed in SSDI as Lina Watson.], d. Feb- -1971,[592] resided in Parkersburg, Wood Co, WV,[521,592] census 1900 in Union District, Ritchie Co, WV, census 1880 in Southwest District, Doddridge Co, WV. She married Dec-19-1902 in Ritchie Co, WV,[473] Ezra C. Watson, b. Feb- -1879,[809,473] (son of David Watson and Alice L. Gray), census 1900 in Union District, Ritchie Co, WV.

vi.   AUSTIN D. RICHARDS[521] b. Jul- -1881,[809] resided 1968 in Gratiot, Licking Co, OH,[521] census 1900 in Union District, Ritchie Co, WV.

vii. SAMUEL M. RICHARDS b. Nov-28-1884,[809,17] d. Nov-27-1912,[17] buried in Gaston-Hart Cemetery, Upper Run, Summers, Doddridge Co, WV,[17] census 1900 in Union District, Ritchie Co, WV.

759. viii. ICY M. RICHARDS b. Apr- 1-1892.

416. **Rulina A. Gaston** (247.Daniel[7], 136.Hugh[6], 72.John[5], 21.John[4], 6.Hugh[3], 3.John[2], 1.Jean[1]), b. ca 1851 in Doddridge Co, WV,[382,dcccxi[811],dcccxii[812]] d. Nov-17-1905 in Summers, Doddridge Co, WV,[dcccxiii[813],356] [Death date of Apr 30 1876 appearing in some sources was actually her marriage date.], buried in Summers, Doddridge Co, WV,[812] census 1880, 1900 in Southwest District, Doddridge Co, WV. She married Apr-30-1876 in Doddridge Co, WV,[dcccxiv[814],354] **Samuel Richards**, b. Jan- 2-1838 in Harrison Co, (W)VA,[dcccxv[815],711] (son of James Tolbert Richards and Elizabeth Childers), d. Oct-22-1909 in Oxford, Doddridge Co, WV,[dcccxvi[816],356] census 1880, 1900 in Southwest District, Doddridge Co, WV, census 1850 in Doddridge Co, (W)VA, occupation farmer.

Children:
760. i.   ANNA ELIZA RICHARDS b. Jan-22-1877.
761. ii.   DANIEL TOLBERT RICHARDS b. Jul-17-1878.
762. iii. NANCY M. RICHARDS b. Jul- 7-1880.
iv.   PERRY SAMUEL RICHARDS b. Jul-30-1883,[17,385] [Age 32y 10m 9d at time of death would put birth at Jun-30-1882. But headstone shows birth date as Jul 30 1883.], d. May- 9-1915 in

Summers, Doddridge Co, WV,[815,356,17] buried in Gaston-Hart Cemetery, Upper Run, Summers, Doddridge Co, WV,[17] cause of death consumption (tuberculosis),[357] occupation rural mail carrier,[357] census 1900 in Southwest District, Doddridge Co, WV.[385]

417. **Elizabeth Laverna Gaston**, also known as Laverna,[502] nickname Vern,[395,396] also known as Eliza L. Gaston,[dcccxvii[817]] (247.Daniel[7], 136.Hugh[6], 72.John[5], 21.John[4], 6.Hugh[3], 3.John[2], 1.Jean[1]), b. Nov- 7-1853 in Doddridge Co, WV,[dcccxviii[818],398,17] d. Feb- 7-1940 at Industrial, Harrison Co, WV,[398,17] buried in IOOF Cemetery, Salem, Harrison Co, WV,[817,398] census 1860 in Doddridge Co, (W)VA. She married Dec-18-1873 in Doddridge Co, WV,[dcccxix[819],dcccxx[820]] **Virgil B. Squires**, b. Dec-21-1851 in Barbour Co, (W)VA,[398,dcccxxi[821],46] (son of James Monroe Squires and Mary Ann Gull), d. Mar-22-1933 in Salem, WV,[398,821,46] [Reports of death date of Mar 1 1938 are incorrect. Death record shows date as Mar 22 1933.], buried in IOOF Cemetery, Salem, Harrison Co, WV,[398,817] occupation stone mason.[821]

 Children:
 763. i. NANCY ANN "NANNIE" SQUIRES b. Nov-16-1874.
 764. ii. DANIEL MONROE "ROE" SQUIRES b. May- 8-1876.
 765. iii. ROSA JANE SQUIRES b. Nov- 7-1877.
 766. iv. MARY ARTIE SQUIRES b. Sep- 6-1879.
 767. v. ANDREW MEAD SQUIRES b. Aug-19-1882.
 768. vi. SAMUEL JACKSON "JACK" SQUIRES b. Jan-27-1884.
 769. vii. IDA OMA SQUIRES b. Apr-25-1887.
  viii. FREEMAN GOFF SQUIRES[821] also known as Goff Squires,[821] b. Jun-12-1890 in Doddridge Co, WV,[439] d. Nov-21-1918 in Brest, France,[821,439] buried in Napoleon Cemetery, Brest, France,[439] census 1910 in Coal District, Harrison Co, WV [Listed as a boarder in household of his sister Rosa and her husband William H. Greathouse.], occupation glass worker.[458]

  Killed in World War I.

  ix. FOREST BOON SQUIRES b. Feb-28-1895 in Doddridge Co, WV,[dcccxxii[822]] d. Mar-19-1895 in Doddridge Co, WV.[dcccxxiii[823]]
 770. x. HOBERT GOLDEN SQUIRES b. Jan-13-1898.

418. **Nancy Maria Gaston**, also known as Amariah,[395] also known as Mariah,[345] (247.Daniel[7], 136.Hugh[6], 72.John[5], 21.John[4], 6.Hugh[3], 3.John[2], 1.Jean[1]), b. Jul-22-1856 in Doddridge Co, (W)VA,[dcccxxiv[824],17] d. Jul-20-1891 in Doddridge Co, WV,[dcccxxv[825],17,356] buried in Gaston-Hart Cemetery, Upper Run, Summers, Doddridge Co, WV.[17] She married Dec- 2-1883 in Doddridge Co, WV,[dcccxxvi[826]] **Hughy James "Jim" Pierce**, also known as James Pierce,[190,191,395] b. May-29-1856 in Oxford, Doddridge Co, WV,[190,824] (son of Jesse H. Pierce and Christena Wilson), d. Dec-13-1938 near Oxford, Doddridge Co, WV,[dcccxxvii[827],700,356] buried in South Fork Bapt Church Cem, Oxford, Doddridge Co, WV,[dcccxxviii[828],190] census 1870, 1920 in Southwest District, Doddridge Co, WV, resided 1893 in Preston Co, WV.[dcccxxix[829]]

 Children:
 771. i. OBIDIAH WAYNE PIERCE b. May-14-1885.
  ii. HETTIE JANE PIERCE b. Apr-27-1887 in Doddridge Co, WV,[dcccxxx[830]] [A birth date for Hettie Jane Pierce is given as Apr 27 1889 in both her death record and obituary, but her birth record states Apr 27 1887, and sister Laura was born Jan 17 1889.], d. Jan-30-1955 at Oxford, Doddridge Co, WV,[dcccxxxi[831],700,356] buried in South Fork Bapt Church Cem, Oxford, Doddridge Co, WV,[dcccxxxii[832]] resided at Oxford, Doddridge Co, WV,[190,765] never married.
 772. iii. LAURA MAUD PIERCE b. Jan-17-1889.
  iv. DORA EDNA M. PIERCE b. Jul-14-1891 in Doddridge Co, WV,[dcccxxxiii[833],dcccxxxiv[834]] [We originally had as the fourth child of Hughy James Pierce & Nancy Maria Gaston a daughter, Edna Pierce, source not documented. We had no info on her other than "died young." A later search of birth/death records turned up nothing for Edna Pierce. But we did find another previously unrecorded child: Dora E. Pierce, b. Jul 14 1891 to Hughy & Nancy, d. Jun 24 1898. The conclusion we reached is that Dora and Edna are one and the same, with the middle initial standing for Edna.], d. Jun-24-1898 in Doddridge Co, WV,[dcccxxxv[835]] cause of death jaundice.[357]

419. **Samuel Eli Gaston** (247.Daniel[7], 136.Hugh[6], 72.John[5], 21.John[4], 6.Hugh[3], 3.John[2], 1.Jean[1]), b. Aug- - 1860,[385,46] d. Nov-20-1918 in Summers, Doddridge Co, WV,[398,46,dcccxxxvi[836]] buried in Gaston-Hart Cemetery, Upper Run, Summers, Doddridge Co, WV,[17] census 1900, 1910 in Southwest District, Doddridge Co, WV,[385] occupation farmer.[398]

1900 Census, Doddridge County WV (Southwest District):
S. E. Gaston, 39, b. Aug 1860; wife Ida E, 37, b. Jul 1862; dau Nannie C, 15, b. Jan 1885; son Daniel W, 11, b. Jun 1888; dau Stella Gay, 8, b. Jan 1892; dau Liza Ellen, 3, b. Mar 1897; father Daniel, 83, widowed, b. Jun 1816; servant John W. Hart, 23, b. Sep 1876.

He married Jan-13-1884 in Doddridge Co, WV,[354,191] **Ida Ellen Leeson**, b. Jul- 7-1862,[17,190] (daughter of Eli B. Leeson and Clarinda L. McIntyre), d. Sep-17-1912 in Doddridge Co, WV,[dcccxxxvii[837],17,190,356] buried in Gaston-Hart Cemetery, Upper Run, Summers, Doddridge Co, WV,[17] resided in Summers, Doddridge Co, WV.[190]

Children:

773.   i.   NANCY CLARE GASTON b. Jan-18-1885.

ii.   DAN WELLINGTON GASTON, also known as Danial W. Gaston,[684] b. Jun- 8-1888 near Harmony, Doddridge Co, WV,[684,592,46] d. Apr- -1944,[dcccxxxviii[838],46] buried in Gaston-Hart Cemetery, Upper Run, Summers, Doddridge Co, WV,[dcccxxxix[839]] resided 1922, 32 in Newkirk, Kay Co, OK,[dcccxl[840]] census 1920, 1930 in Newkirk, Kay Co, OK, resided 1916, 17 in Oxford, Doddridge Co, WV,[602,684] occupation oil driller in Oklahoma,[681,334] occupation 1917 tool dresser, Hope Natural Gas Co.[684]

Resident of Newkirk, Kay Co, Oklahoma, as of October 1922, when the original Daniel Gaston's (b. 1816) Harmony property was conveyed to Nancy Gaston Hart by her three siblings. [Doddridge Co Deed Book 79, p. 10] He was also a resident of Oklahoma at the time of Nancy Gaston's Hart's death in 1932, per her obituary. His name is spelled "Danial" on his headstone, but appears simply as "Dan" in his marriage record, on his WW I Draft Registration, and in the 1920 and 1930 Census.

1920 Census, Kay Co, Oklahoma (City of Newkirk), enumerated on Jan 6 1920:
Dan W. Gaston, 32, driller in oil field; wife Lottie L. Gaston, 34; boarder William Lieber, 33, driller in oil field, single. All born in Virginia (sic).

1930 Census, Kay Co, Oklahoma (City of Newkirk), enumerated on Apr 15 1930:
Dan W. Gaston, 41, driller in oil field; wife Lottic L. Gaston, 46 (?), seamstress; mother-in-law Catherine A. Lieber, 76, widowed. All born in West Virginia.

He married[dcccxli[841],684] Oct-14-1916 in Parkersburg, Wood Co, WV,[602] Lottie Laurentine Lieber, b. Oct- -1883 in Lewis Co, WV,[602] [Age 29 given in 1916 marriage record would put birth in about 1887. But age 34 was given in 1920 Census, age 46 in 1930 Census, and age 16 in the 1900 Census, with birth date of Oct 1883. Name spelled Leiber in marriage record, but Lieber in census records.] (daughter of Rudolph Lieber and Catherine A. __), census 1920, 1930 in Newkirk, Kay Co, OK, resided 1916 in New England, Wood Co, WV,[602] census 1900 in Freemans Creek District, Lewis Co, WV.

774.   iii.   STELLA GAY GASTON b. Jan-31-1892.

iv.   ELIZA EILLENE GASTON b. Mar- 2-1897 in Doddridge Co, WV,[190,17] d. Sep-25-1991 in Clarksburg, Harrison Co, WV,[190,17] buried in Gaston-Hart Cemetery, Upper Run, Summers, Doddridge Co, WV,[17] resided 1932 in California,[412] occupation Registered Nurse.[190] She married aft Oct 10 1922,[841] Ray Cailor, d. 1932.[191]

420. **John Morris Gaston** (248.Eli[7], 136.Hugh[6], 72.John[5], 21.John[4], 6.Hugh[3], 3.John[2], 1.Jean[1]), b. Sep- 4-1853 in Summers, Doddridge Co, WV,[190,dcccxlii[842]] d. Nov-11-1927 in Clarksburg, Harrison Co, WV,[dcccxliii[843],190] ["at the home of his son"], buried in Gaston Family Cemetery, Upper Run, Summers, Doddridge Co WV, resided in Oxford, Doddridge Co, WV,[412] occupation Methodist minister & farmer.

He married Aug-16-1876 in Doddridge Co, WV,[dccxliv[844],354] **Elizabeth Hart**, b. Aug-15-1858 in Lower Run, Doddridge Co, WV,[dcccxlv[845],190] (daughter of John G. Hart and Melinda Ann Nutter), d. Feb-28-1921 in Upper Run, Oxford, Doddridge Co, WV,[dcccxlvi[846]] buried in Gaston Family Cemetery, Upper Run, Summers, Doddridge Co WV,[190] resided in Upper Run, Oxford, Doddridge Co, WV.[190] When John Morris Gaston and Elizabeth Hart were buried in the family cemetery in 1927 and 1921, respectively, no permanent marker was put in place. In the Spring of 2002, through the actions of their grandson Samuel David Gaston, surviving principal family members purchased a permanent stone marker for this couple's grave, as well as one for the unmarked grave of their grandchildren, twins William and Lillian Gaston, stillborn in 1923.

Children:
775. i. RULINA BELLE GASTON b. Jan-23-1878.
776. ii. ELI WILLIS GASTON b. Jun- 8-1880.
777. iii. LURANA OLIVE GASTON b. Jan- 2-1883.
iv. JAMES BLAINE GASTON, also known as Blaine Gaston, b. Sep-29-1885 in Oxford, Doddridge Co, WV,[684,190] d. Aug-27-1981 in Clarksburg, Harrison Co, WV,[dcccxlvii[847]] buried in Greenlawn Masonic Cemetery, Clarksburg, WV,[dcccxlviii[848],190] resided in Clarksburg, Harrison Co, WV,[dcccxlix[849],765,190] resided 1917 in Ashley, Doddridge Co, WV,[684] occupation Hazel-Atlas Glass Co (35 yrs), timber worker for A.J. Riddle in Ashley WV (1917),[190,684] military U.S. Army, World War I.[190]

Had no children, but James Blaine Gaston and his wife Hazel raised a boy who was said to have been left on their doorstep. The boy went by the name Jack Gaston, until his late teens when he changed his name and ran away. The boy died sometime between 1974 and 1978, with the funeral held in Salem, WV. Some family members speculate that the boy was born to the unmarried sister of his foster mother Hazel May Yeater.

He married Jun-26-1917 in Doddridge Co, WV,[354] Hazel May Yeater, b. Oct-29-1900 (daughter of Floyd Yeater and Emma Underwood), d. Jun- -1980 in Clarksburg, Harrison Co, WV, buried in Greenlawn Masonic Cemetery, Clarksburg, WV.[dcccl[850]]
778. v. JOHN SHERIDAN GASTON b. May-27-1888.
779. vi. JESSE MORRIS GASTON b. Jan-22-1891.
vii. ELIZABETH ANN GASTON, also known as Elizabeth Anna Gaston,[289] b. Dec-11-1893 in Doddridge Co, WV,[dcccli[851],289] d. Dec-18-1893 in Doddridge Co, WV, buried in Gaston Family Cemetery, Upper Run, Summers, Doddridge Co WV.
780. viii. IRA DOW GASTON b. Dec-31-1894.
ix. JOSEPH CLARK "LITTLE JOE" GASTON b. Nov- 1-1898 in Oxford, Doddridge Co, WV,[190,dccclii[852],684,592,289,17] d. May- 8-1982 in West Union, Doddridge Co, WV,[190,17] buried in Cabin Run Cemetery, Doddridge Co, WV,[17,190] resided 1918, 27 in Oxford, Doddridge Co, WV,[684,765] occupation 1918 pipelining for Philadelphia Gas Co, Doddridge Co,[684] military Pfc, U.S. Army, World War II,[176] never married[190].

421. **Eli Clark Gaston** (248.Eli[7], 136.Hugh[6], 72.John[5], 21.John[4], 6.Hugh[3], 3.John[2], 1.Jean[1]), b. Feb- 1-1858 in Doddridge Co, (W)VA,[dcccliii[853],240] d. Nov-12-1941 at Exchange, Braxton Co, WV,[398,700,dcccliv[854]] [Although death records at the Upshur County courthouse indicate that he died at Buckhannon in Upshur Co, WV, his death certificate on file at the West Virginia Dept of Health's Division of Vital Statistics show that the place of death was at Exchange in the Otter District of Braxton County. His obituary specifies that he died "at his home on Cedar Creek, near Exchange," in Braxton County.], buried in Mt. Carmel Cemetery, Tallmansville, Upshur Co, WV,[17] resided near Exchange, Braxton Co, WV,[190] [Cedar Creek], resided 1941 in Sutton, Braxton Co, WV,[dccclv[855]] census 1930 in Otter District, Braxton Co, WV [in household with son Arnold Marsh Gaston], resided 1927 in Flatwoods, Braxton Co, WV,[521] resided 1924 in Tallmansville, Upshur Co, WV,[412] resided in Upshur Co, WV,[dccclvi[856]] occupation farmer.[190,398] He married (1) Mar-14-1879 in Doddridge Co, WV,[dccclvii[857]] **Cassa Ann Hart**, b. Mar-25-1856 in Doddridge Co, WV (daughter of John G. Hart and Melinda Ann Nutter), d. Nov-28-1894, buried in Gaston Family Cemetery, Upper Run, Summers, Doddridge Co WV. He married (2) Feb-24-1897 in Upshur Co, WV,[dccclviii[858]] **Dora Grimm**, b. Feb-13-1873,[154] (daughter of

Isaac Grimm and Susan __), d. Feb-19-1914 in Upshur Co, WV,[dccclix[859],484] buried in Bailey Cemetery, Braxton Co, WV.

Children by Cassa Ann Hart:

781.   i.   RULINA MELINDA GASTON b. Jan-13-1880.

      ii.   MINNIE ALICE GASTON b. Mar-23-1882 in Doddridge Co, WV,[dccclx[860]] [But immediate family, in W. Guy Tetrick survey, reports birth date as Mar 22 1882, and age at death (11y 4m 7d) reported in death record would also put birth at Mar 22 1882.], d. Jul-29-1893 near Auburn, Ritchie Co, WV,[dccclxi[861]] buried in Gaston Family Cemetery, Upper Run, Summers, Doddridge Co WV,[dccclxii[862]] cause of death diphtheria.[862]

782.   iii.   ANNA ELIZABETH GASTON b. Mar-23-1884.

      iv.   JESSIE C. GASTON b. Jun-30-1886 in Doddridge Co, WV,[dccclxiii[863]] d. Feb-28-1887 in Doddridge Co, WV,[dccclxiv[864],356] buried in Gaston Family Cemetery, Upper Run, Summers, Doddridge Co WV.

783.   v.   ARNOLD MARSH GASTON b. Feb-21-1888.

784.   vi.   BESSIE MAE GASTON b. Sep-17-1890.

      vii.   MINNIE JANE GASTON b. Oct-24-1894 in Ritchie Co, WV,[711,592,240] [Obituary of Minnie Gaston Leeson states she was born Oct 24 1895 and died Oct 5 1979 at age 83, which is mathematically correct. But both her birth record and SSDI give her birth as Oct 24 1894, as does her marriage record and the Guy Tetrick family information sheet she filled out herself in 1931. Her obituary also incorrectly identifies her parents as Eliza (should be Eli) Gaston and Nancy (should be Cassa) Hart.], d. Oct- 5-1979 in Clarksburg, Harrison Co, WV,[190,592,17] buried in Hart Cemetery, Taylor Drain Rd, Oxford, Doddridge Co WV,[17,190] resided in Oxford, Doddridge Co, WV,[190,412] resided 1941 in Greenwood, Doddridge Co, WV,[765] resided 1915 in Doddridge Co, WV,[711] census 1910 in Southwest District, Doddridge Co, WV [In household with uncle Jesse Smith Gaston and his family.]. She married Nov-1-1915 in Doddridge Co, WV,[dccclxv[865],240] no children from this marriage,[484,191] Charles L. Leeson, b. Dec- 5-1865 in Summers, Doddridge Co, WV,[190,240] (son of John P. Leeson and Sophia McIntyre), d. Jan- 6-1955 in Greenwood, Doddridge Co, WV,[700,356] buried in Hart Cemetery, Taylor Drain Rd, Oxford, Doddridge Co WV,[17,190] resided in Greenwood, Doddridge Co, WV,[190,412,521] census 1870, 1880, 1900 in Southwest District, Doddridge Co, WV.

Charles: The obituary of Charles L. Leeson states: "In 1896 he was married to Miss Nancy Husk, and to this union was born two children. His wife and children preceded him in death many years ago. On November 1 1915, Mr. Leeson was married to Miss Minnie Gaston, who survives with a number of nieces and nephews, and many friends to mourn their loss." He was the last survivor of a family of seven. [West Union Herald, Jan 13 1955]

1900 Census, Doddridge Co, WV (Southwest District):
Charles Leeson (age 34, b. Dec 1865), Nancy V. (wife, age 32, b. Mar 1868), Howard G. (son, age 2, b. Apr 1898), and Minnie Jane (dau, age 7 months, b. Oct 1899).

Children by Dora Grimm:

785.   viii.   ALMA GAY GASTON b. Nov-24-1897.

786.   ix.   GEORGIA RACHAEL GASTON b. Mar- 7-1903.

      x.   FRANCES IRENE GASTON, also known as Irene Gaston,[855,520,765] b. Sep-15-1908 in Tallmansville, Upshur Co, WV,[dccclxvi[866],592] d. Mar- -1987,[592] resided in Mamou, Evangeline Parish, LA,[592] resided formerly in California.[dccclxvii[867]]

In the fall of 1941, Frances Irene Gaston Fontenot traveled to San Diego, California to join her husband who was assigned to the USS Blue Destroyer, based at Pearl Harbor, Hawaii. It was long believed that both of them died when Pearl Harbor was attacked on Dec 7 1941, as they were never found or heard from after that. The obituary of her father, Eli Clark Gaston, in Nov 1941, identified her among his surviving children as "Mrs. Irene Fontnot [sic] of California." The obituary of her half-sister, Bess Mae Gaston Adams, in 1981, listed among her survivors "a half sister, Irene, address unknown." But more recently, a listing of all Pearl Harbor casualties revealed no one named Fontenot or anything similar. More significantly, a listing was found in the Social Security Death

Index for Frances Fontenot, born Sep 15 1908, died March 1987, last residence at Mamou, Evangeline County (Parish), Louisiana, Social Security card issued in California in 1952.

> She married __ Fontenot, military U.S. Navy.
>   xi.   DAVID LAWRENCE GASTON b. Nov- 4-1913 in Upshur Co, WV, d. Dec- -1913 in Upshur Co, WV.

422. **Jesse Smith Gaston**, also known as Jessie Smith Gaston,[398] (248.Eli[7], 136.Hugh[6], 72.John[5], 21.John[4], 6.Hugh[3], 3.John[2], 1.Jean[1]), b. Jun-12-1860 in Summers, Doddridge Co, WV,[17,240] [Birthdate would be May 12 1860 based on age 82y 11m 22d given in death record, but obituary and headstone state June 12 1860, and obituary gives his age at death as 82y 10m 22d. Name spelled "Jessie" on headstone and in obituary and death record, but "Jesse" in marriage record and wife's headstone. Birthplace from death record, but no birth record found for him in Doddridge Co. The family information sheet completed by his brother David as part of the W. Guy Tetrick survey in 1932 identified him as Jesse S. Gaston, born Jun 12 1860 in Doddridge Co.], d. May- 4-1943 in West Union, Doddridge Co, WV,[398,dccclxviii[868],356,17] buried in Gaston Family Cemetery, Upper Run, Summers, Doddridge Co WV,[17] resided 1924 in Oxford, Doddridge Co, WV,[412] census 1910 in Southwest District, Doddridge Co, WV. He married Aug-11-1887 in Doddridge Co, WV,[dccclxix[869],484] **Lucy May Swiger**, b. Jan-15-1868,[17] [Birthplace of Lucy May Swiger given as Harrison County WV in marriage record, but as Greenbrier County VA in birth record of daughter Rulina. This was probably meant to indicate the Greenbrier region of the border separating Doddridge and Harrison Counties. She was erroneously identified in daughter Rulina's obituary as Rulina Swiger.] (daughter of Zachous Swiger and Clementine Boice), d. May- 1-1891 in Doddridge Co, WV,[17] [Doddridge County Death Records, Bk 1, p. 42, show a Lucy Gaston, married, age 25y 2m 12d, died Apr 29 1891 at Holbrook, burial at Holbrook. The stated age at death would put birth at Feb 17 1866. The record contained no other information. No other death record for any Lucy Gaston was found in Doddridge Co. Despite the variances in dates, this is almost certainly the same Lucy May Swiger Gaston. Holbrook is located just over the county line in Ritchie Co, about 3 miles from the Gaston-Hart Cemetery.], buried in Gaston-Hart Cemetery, Upper Run, Summers, Doddridge Co, WV,[17] [A headstone at the Gaston-Hart Cemetery reads "Lucy M., wife of Jesse S. Gaston, born Jan 15 1868, d. May 1 1891." But a double headstone at the nearby Gaston Family Cemetery reads "GASTON - Jessie S., June 12 1860 - May 4 1943 --- Lucy Swiger, Jan 15 1858 - May 1 1891." According to their grandson, Samuel Hileman, Lucy's name was placed on the double headstone, despite the different burial location, simply to identify her as Jesse Smith Gaston's wife. Reasons for the variations in dates and name spelling are not known.].
>   Children:
> 787.   i.   RULINA CLEMMA GASTON b. Apr-15-1889.

423. **Hannah R. Gaston** (248.Eli[7], 136.Hugh[6], 72.John[5], 21.John[4], 6.Hugh[3], 3.John[2], 1.Jean[1]), b. Feb- 4-1863 in Doddridge Co, (W)VA,[240] d. Apr-10-1893 in Lewis Co, WV.[dccclxx[870]] She married May-20-1881 in Doddridge Co, WV,[dccclxxi[871]] **James Edmund Strother**, also known as Ed Strother, b. Apr- -1854 in Harrison Co, (W)VA,[dccclxxii[872]] [Susie Davis Nicholson (p. 69) reports birth date as Apr 3 1855. But Harrison Co Birth Record 1-16 shows birth as April 1854. Age at death in Doddridge Co Death Record, 52y 4m 16d, would put birth on May 2 1855.] (son of Aaron Arden Strother and Lucinda Davis), d. Sep-18-1907 in Doddridge Co, WV.[dccclxxiii[873]]
>   Children:
>   i.   GRANVILLE REUBEN STROTHER b. Jun-23-1882 in Doddridge Co, WV,[dccclxxiv[874],17] d. Jun-23-1882 in Doddridge Co, WV,[17] buried in Gaston-Hart Cemetery, Upper Run, Summers, Doddridge Co, WV.[17]
>   ii.   BLANCHE M. STROTHER b. ca 1884 in Doddridge Co, WV,[711] d. aft Nov 1911.[dccclxxv[875]] She married Nov-28-1908 in Doddridge Co, WV,[dccclxxvi[876],354] no children from this marriage,[dccclxxvii[877]] Addison Franklin "Frank" Richards, census name A. Franklin Richards,[385] b. Jun- -1879 in Ritchie Co, WV,[385,711] (son of Granville B. Richards and Mary Jane Wilson), resided 1959 in West Virginia,[521] census 1880 in Murphy District, Ritchie Co, WV.
>   iii.   ELBERT B. STROTHER b. Jul-16-1886 in Doddridge Co, WV.[dccclxxviii[878]]

        iv.   ELI CLARL STROTHER b. Feb-21-1890 in Doddridge Co, WV.[dccclxxix[879]]
788.   v.   CHARLES R. STROTHER b. Aug- 4-1891.

424. **David Dow Gaston** (248.Eli[7], 136.Hugh[6], 72.John[5], 21.John[4], 6.Hugh[3], 3.John[2], 1.Jean[1]), b. Jul-31-1865 near Oxford, Doddridge Co, WV,[190,dccclxxx[880],240] d. Jan-17-1950 in Brushy Fork, New Milton, Doddridge Co, WV,[190,dccclxxxi[881],356] buried in Hart Cemetery, Taylor Drain Rd, Oxford, Doddridge Co WV,[17,190,398] cause of death cerebral hemorrhage,[190] resided near Oxford, Doddridge Co, WV,[240,190,412] occupation farmer.[190,398] He married Sep-18-1887 at Upper Run, Oxford, Doddridge Co, WV,[dccclxxxii[882]] **Hannah Belle Hart**, b. May- 8-1871 in Doddridge Co, WV,[dccclxxxiii[883],240,17] (daughter of John G. Hart and Melinda Ann Nutter), d. Feb- 9-1933 in Doddridge Co, WV,[17,dccclxxxiv[884],484] buried in Hart Cemetery, Taylor Drain Rd, Oxford, Doddridge Co WV,[17,190] resided 1932 in Oxford, Doddridge Co, WV.[240]

        Children:
789.   i.   SARAH RULINA GASTON b. Jul-12-1888.
790.   ii. ELIZABETH JANE GASTON b. Apr- 9-1890.
        iii. LYDIA GASTON b. Apr- 9-1890 in Summers, Doddridge Co, WV,[dccclxxxv[885]] d. Apr- 9-1890 in Summers, Doddridge Co, WV.[885]
791.   iv. LOVIE MAE GASTON b. Dec-21-1891.
        v.   MARION A. GASTON b. Aug-12-1905,[dccclxxxvi[886]] d. Aug-12-1905.[289]

425. **James Alvin Butcher**, also known as Old Doc Butcher (249.Cordelia[7], 136.Hugh[6], 72.John[5], 21.John[4], 6.Hugh[3], 3.John[2], 1.Jean[1]), b. Oct- 5-1860 in Lewis Co, (W)VA,[407] [But 1880 Census of Lewis Co, WV puts birth in about 1862.], d. Jul-27-1923 in Cedarville, Gilmer Co, WV,[407] buried in Cedarville, Gilmer Co, WV,[dccclxxxvii[887]] resided in Cedarville, Gilmer Co, WV,[413] occupation physician.[407] He married Feb-28-1889 in Lewis Co, WV,[410,407] **Florence Almeda Hinzman**, b. Aug-19-1865,[407] (daughter of Robert R. Hinzman and Martha Jane Bonnett), d. May-21-1930,[407] buried in Cedarville, Gilmer Co, WV,[407] occupation teacher.[407]

        Children:
792.   i.   BURKE BUTCHER b. Dec-10-1890.
        ii. HAZEL BUTCHER b. Jun- 7-1892,[407] d. Jun-25-1896,[407] buried in Cedarville, Gilmer Co, WV.[407]

426. **Judson E. Butcher**[407] (249.Cordelia[7], 136.Hugh[6], 72.John[5], 21.John[4], 6.Hugh[3], 3.John[2], 1.Jean[1]), b. ca 1865 in West Virginia,[246,247] [Ages 5 and 14 given in the 1870 and 1880 Census are considered more reliable than the ages 40 and 50 given in the 1910 and 1920 Census.], resided in Wiggins, Stone Co, MS,[407] census 1920 in Stone Co, MS,[681] census 1910 in Brown Co, OH,[211] census 1870, 1880 in Lewis Co, WV.[247] He married ca 1902,[211] **Mary __**, b. ca 1879 in Ohio,[211] census 1920 in Stone Co, MS, census 1910 in Brown Co, OH.[211]

1910 Census, Brown County, Ohio (Washington Twp), enumerated on Apr 15 & 16 1910: Judson E. Butcher, 40, b. W. Va., both parents b. W. Va., married 8 yrs, occupation engineer on stationary engine; wife Mary E. (or C.), 31, b. Ohio, both parents b. Ohio, mother of 2 children (both still living); son John R., 7, b. Ohio; dau Mary B. (or E. or C. ?), 5, b. Ohio.

1920 Census, Stone County, Mississippi, enumerated on Jan 20 1920: Judson E. Butcher, 50, b. W. Va., both parents b. W. Va., occupation chief engineer; wife Mary C. (?), 40, b. Ohio, both parents b. Ohio; dau Mary C., 15, b. Ohio.

        Children:
        i.   JOHN R. BUTCHER b. ca 1903 in Ohio,[211] census 1910 in Brown Co, OH.[211]
        ii. MARY B. BUTCHER b. ca 1905 in Ohio,[211] census 1910 in Brown Co, OH.[211]

427. **Hugh D. Butcher** (249.Cordelia[7], 136.Hugh[6], 72.John[5], 21.John[4], 6.Hugh[3], 3.John[2], 1.Jean[1]), b. Apr- 1-1870 in Lewis Co, WV,[398,408] d. Aug-24-1958 at Camden, Lewis Co, WV,[398] buried in Weston Masonic Cemetery, Lewis Co, WV,[398] resided at Camden, Lewis Co, WV,[398,412,413] census 1880, 1900 10 20 30

in Freemans Creek District, Lewis Co, WV, occupation farmer,[398] occupation 1910 sawmilling, farmer.[408] He married Feb- 1-1899 in Lewis Co, WV,[410] **Willie J. Ward**, b. Oct- -1875,[408] (daughter of Henry M. Ward and Mary Caroline Jennings), census 1930 in Freemans Creek District, Lewis Co, WV, census 1920 in Weston, Lewis Co, WV, census 1900, 1910 in Freemans Creek District, Lewis Co, WV, census 1880 in Court House District, Lewis Co, WV.

1900 Census, Lewis Co, WV (Freemans Creek District), enumerated on Jun 7 1900:
Hugh Butcher, 30, b. Apr 1870, occupation sawmilling, married 1 yr; wife Willie, 24, b. Oct 1875, mother of 1 child (still living); son Allen W, 2 months.

1910 Census, Lewis Co, WV (Freemans Creek District), enumerated on Apr 21 1910:
Hugh D. Butcher, 39, farmer, married 11 yrs; wife Willie W, 36, mother of 4 children (all still living); son Allen W, 10; son Carl E, 8; dau Rita M, 6; dau Pearl, 3.

1920 Census, Lewis Co, WV (Freemans Creek District), enumerated on Jan 23 1920:
Hugh D. Butcher, 47, married, farmer; son Robert H, 7.
In a separate household in the city of Weston, enumerated on Jan 6 1920 at 255 W. Second Street:
Willie Butcher, 43, married, no occupation; son Allen, 19, laborer at street work, single; son Karl, 17, farm laborer, single; dau Greeta, 15; dau Pearl, 12.

1930 Census, Lewis Co, WV (Freemans Creek District), enumerated on Apr 10 1930:
Hugh D. Butcher, 49, farmer (stock farm); wife Willie J, 54; son Allen, 30, salesman at feed store, single; son Carl, 28, laborer on stock farm, single; son Robert, 17, single.

Children:
    i.   ALLEN W. BUTCHER b. Mar- -1900,[408] census 1930 in Freemans Creek District, Lewis Co, WV, census 1920 in Weston, Lewis Co, WV, census 1900, 1910 in Freemans Creek District, Lewis Co, WV.
    ii. CARL E. BUTCHER, census name Karl Butcher,[dccclxxxviii[888]] b. ca 1902,[dccclxxxix[889]] census 1930 in Freemans Creek District, Lewis Co, WV, census 1920 in Weston, Lewis Co, WV, census 1910 in Freemans Creek District, Lewis Co, WV.
    iii. RITA M. BUTCHER, census name Greeta Butcher,[888] b. ca 1904,[889] census 1920 in Weston, Lewis Co, WV, census 1910 in Freemans Creek District, Lewis Co, WV.
    iv. PEARL BUTCHER b. ca 1907,[889] census 1920 in Weston, Lewis Co, WV, census 1910 in Freemans Creek District, Lewis Co, WV.
    v. ROBERT H. BUTCHER b. ca 1913,[888] resided 1958 in Weston, Lewis Co, WV,[748] census 1920, 1930 in Freemans Creek District, Lewis Co, WV.

428. **William Robert "Bob" Gaston** (250.Henry[7], 136.Hugh[6], 72.John[5], 21.John[4], 6.Hugh[3], 3.John[2], 1.Jean[1]), b. Jul- 7-1868 in Lewis Co, WV,[398] d. Nov- 5-1954 near Davisville, Wood Co, WV,[398] buried in Meadows Cemetery, Normantown, Gilmer Co, WV,[398] resided near Davisville, Wood Co, WV,[398] census 1930 in Center District, Gilmer Co, WV, occupation farmer.[398] He married Nov- 2-1898 in Gilmer Co, WV,[433,434] **Emma May Divers**, also known as May Divers,[345] b. May-22-1882 in Gilmer Co, WV (daughter of Charles Wesley Divers and Merinda Catherine Miller), d. May-24-1964 in Wood Co, WV,[dcccxc[890]] buried in Meadows Cemetery, Normantown, Gilmer Co, WV, census 1930 in Center District, Gilmer Co, WV.
    Children:
   793. i. EVALENA C. GASTON b. Feb- 6-1899.
        ii. FREDERICK GASTON buried in Mollahan Cemetery, Normantown, Gilmer Co, WV.
   794. iii. JAMES EUSTACE GASTON b. Apr- 4-1903.

429. **James Lloyd (Huston) Gaston** (250.Henry[7], 136.Hugh[6], 72.John[5], 21.John[4], 6.Hugh[3], 3.John[2], 1.Jean[1]), b. Sep- 7-1870 in Camden, Lewis Co, WV,[398,46,537,396] [But based on age reported in Lewis County Census, birthdate would be about Sep 7 1871.], d. Apr-10-1959 in Charleston, Kanawha Co, WV,[398,46] buried in Waldeck Cemetery, Lewis Co, WV,[17,398] resided in Charleston, Kanawha Co, WV,[398]

occupation salesman.[398] He married[396] Jun- 4-1906 in Harrison Co, WV,[dccxci][891] **Wella Lohan**, b. Jan-13-1880 in Lewis Co, WV,[dccxcii][892],46,537 (daughter of Michael Lohan), d. Jul-13-1944 in Charleston, Kanawha Co, WV,[dccxciii][893],46 buried in Waldeck Cemetery, Lewis Co, WV,[17] resided in Charleston, Kanawha Co, WV,[892] resided 1906 in Harrison Co, WV.[537]

>Children:
>i. JAMES KENDALL GASTON, also known as J. Kendall Gaston,[17] b. Jan-18-1907 in Parkersburg, Wood Co, WV,[892,46] d. May-13-1937 in Charleston, Kanawha Co, WV,[dccxciv][894] [Death date on headstone is 1936, but death record states May 13 1937.], buried in Waldeck Cemetery, Lewis Co, WV,[17] [death record gives burial location as Polk Creek], resided in Charleston, Kanawha Co, WV,[892] occupation salesman,[892] never married.[892]

430. **Netta Gay Gaston**, also known as Gay Gaston, also known as Nettie Gay Gaston,[434,432] (250.Henry[7], 136.Hugh[6], 72.John[5], 21.John[4], 6.Hugh[3], 3.John[2], 1.Jean[1]), b. Jun- 2-1881 in Lewis Co, WV, d. Mar- 4-1910 at Crooked Run, Gilmer Co, WV,[432] buried in Meadows Cemetery, Normantown, Gilmer Co, WV, cause of death consumption (tuberculosis),[432] resided in Gilmer Co, WV.[434] She married[dccxcv][895] Aug-5-1906 in Gilmer Co, WV,[434] **Cecil G. Davis**, b. Nov- 6-1882 in Berlin, Lewis Co, WV,[592,dccxcvi][896] (son of James Davis and Martha Ellen Beasley), d. Jul-25-1971,[dccxcvii][897],592 resided in Glenville, Gilmer Co, WV,[604] resided 1906 in Gilmer Co, WV,[434] occupation brick mason.[896]

Cecil: *After the death of Netta Gay, Cecil Davis married Ila Kelley and had seven more children: Madeline Jordan (1912), Dunbar; Wayne K. Davis (1913), Melbourne, FL; Kathleen Barker (1915), Weston; Ruby Marsh (1919), St Albans; Cecil Davis Jr. (1922), Weston; Ruth Davis (3/15/1927-4/8/1928); and Jean Schlater (1928), East Lansing, MI. [History of Gilmer Co WV, p. 92]*

1910 Census, Gilmer Co, WV (Center District), enumerated in May 1910:
Cecil G. Davis is listed as a 27-yr-old widower, living alone, occupation stone mason.

>Children:
>i. TERESA DAVIS b. Oct- 9-1908,[dccxcviii][898] resided in Phoenix, Maricopa Co, AZ.[895] She married[dccxcix][899] ___ Manley.

431. **Eva Dell Gaston**, also known as Dell Gaston (250.Henry[7], 136.Hugh[6], 72.John[5], 21.John[4], 6.Hugh[3], 3.John[2], 1.Jean[1]), b. May- -1884 in Normantown, Gilmer Co, WV,[398,cm][900],cmi[901] [Death record states birth date as May 24 1884, but headstone reads May 29 1884.], d. Feb-16-1956 in Beckley, Raleigh Co, WV,[398,17] buried in Broad Run Bapt Ch Cem, Jane Lew, Lewis Co, WV,[17,398] resided in Jane Lew, Lewis Co, WV,[398] census 1930 in Greenbrier District, Doddridge Co, WV.[cmii][902] She married Nov-9-1912 in Clarksburg, Harrison Co, WV,[cmiii][903] **Henry Orrahood**, b. Mar-12-1848 in Doddridge Co, WV,[cmiv][904],17,711 (son of Alexander Orrahood III and Mary Elizabeth "Polly" Feaster), d. Jan-29-1939 in Doddridge Co, WV,[190,356,17] buried in Pleasant Hill Cemetery, New Milton, Doddridge Co, WV, census 1900, 1930 in Greenbrier District, Doddridge Co, WV.[902]

>Children:
>i. ROBERT EARL ORRAHOOD, also known as Earl Orrahood,[765,cmv][905] b. ca 1914,[902] resided 1975 in Phoenix, Maricopa Co, AZ,[905] resided 1939 in Camden, Lewis Co, WV.[765]
>795. ii. PAULINE OLIVE ORRAHOOD b. Apr- 1-1916.
>iii. FRED GASTON ORRAHOOD b. Dec-16-1918,[592] d. Oct-18-1988,[592] resided 1975, 88 in Weston, Lewis Co, WV,[905,592] resided 1939 in Moorefield, Hardy Co, WV.[765]

432. **Earnest Ray Gaston**, census name Ray E. Gaston,[cmvi][906] also known as E. Ray Gaston,[395] (250.Henry[7], 136.Hugh[6], 72.John[5], 21.John[4], 6.Hugh[3], 3.John[2], 1.Jean[1]), b. Jul- 4-1890 in Normantown, Gilmer Co, WV,[684] d. Jun-20-1943 in Normantown, Gilmer Co, WV,[398] buried in Meadows Cemetery, Normantown, Gilmer Co, WV,[398,cmvii][907] resided near Normantown, Gilmer Co, WV,[398] resided 1917 in Hardman, Gilmer Co, WV,[684] occupation farmer.[684] He married Sep-11-1915 in Gilmer Co, WV,[434] **Oadney "Oda" Brannon**, b. Aug-31-1888,[907] (daughter of Thornton Brannon and Rosetta Wilson), d. Apr-18-1931, buried in Meadows Cemetery, Normantown, Gilmer Co, WV.[907]
>Children:

  i. LYLE B. GASTON b. Mar-18-1916 in Normantown, Gilmer Co, WV,[190,592] d. Oct-24-2001 in Pratt, Kanawha Co, WV,[700,592] buried in Kanawha Valley Memorial Gardens, Glasgow, Kanawha Co, WV,[190] resided in Pratt, Kanawha Co, WV,[592,521] resided 1940 in Spencer, Roane Co, WV,[cmviii[908]] census 1930 in Center District, Gilmer Co, WV, occupation owner of Gaston Videos.[190] He married Living.

  ii. HAROLD DEAN "TOOTS" GASTON b. Jan-31-1918 in Hardman, Gilmer Co, WV,[907] d. Feb- 4-1997 in Glenville, Gilmer Co, WV,[190] buried in Meadows Cemetery, Normantown, Gilmer Co, WV,[907] resided in Normantown, Gilmer Co, WV,[521] census 1930 in Center District, Gilmer Co, WV, occupation carpenter, electrician, farmer,[907] military Pfc, U.S. Army, World War II.[cmix[909]] He married May-27-1945, Pearl Turner, b. Aug-11-1922 in Normantown, Gilmer Co, WV,[907] (daughter of Floyd Evert Turner and Rhoda Gay Phillips), resided 1997 in Normantown, Gilmer Co, WV.[484]

  iii. ERNEST DALE GASTON, also known as Dale Gaston,[190] census name Dale E. Gaston,[906] also known as Earnest Dale Gaston, b. Jun-16-1921,[592] d. May- 9-2007,[592] resided in Clinton, Summit Co, OH,[604] resided 1997, 2001 in Akron, Summit Co, OH,[521] census 1930 in Center District, Gilmer Co, WV. He married Jul-17-1942,[907] Frances Eileen Stalnaker, also known as Eileen,[cmx[910]] b. Apr- 8-1923,[592] d. Jun- 1-2004,[592] resided in Barberton, Summit Co, OH,[592] resided formerly in West Virginia.[604]

  iv. ELDIN LEE GASTON b. Jul-11-1924 in Normantown, Gilmer Co, WV,[589,592] d. Oct-23-1988 in Cleveland, Cuyahoga Co, OH,[cmxi[911],693,592] buried in Rittman, Wayne Co, OH,[190] resided 34 years in Rittman, Wayne Co, OH,[190,592,693] resided 1943, 1959 in Normantown, Gilmer Co, WV,[748,589] census 1930 in Center District, Gilmer Co, WV, occupation Interlake Steamship Co in Cleveland (retired),[190] military U.S. Navy, World War II.[190] He married Jan-13-1959 in Meadowdale, Marion Co, WV,[589] Jewel Lockie McCumbers, b. Aug-13-1928 in Rosedale, Braxton Co, WV,[589,693] [SSDI entry shows birth date as Mar 13 1928, but her 1959 marriage record and online death record state Aug 12 1928. Her 1945 marriage record states birth date as Aug 13 1929.] (daughter of Albert McCumbers and Virginia Bell McCumbers), d. Sep-22-1994 in Akron, Summit Co, OH,[693,592] buried in Rittman, Wayne Co, OH,[190] resided in Rittman, Wayne Co, OH,[592,484] resided 1959 in Catawba, Marion Co, WV,[589] resided 1945 in Reedy, Roane Co, WV.[908]

433. **Myrtle Gaston**, also known as Merta Gaston (251.Marion[7], 136.Hugh[6], 72.John[5], 21.John[4], 6.Hugh[3], 3.John[2], 1.Jean[1]), b. Jan-18-1877 in Lewis Co, WV,[cmxii[912]] d. Oct-28-1972 in Lewis Co, WV,[912] buried in Waldeck Cemetery, Lewis Co, WV,[17] resided 1948 in Weston, Lewis Co, WV.[748] She married Apr-5-1899 in Lewis Co, WV,[410] **William Bentley Ellis**, b. Jun- 3-1874,[cmxiii[913]] (son of Tyree M. Ellis and Sarah Columbia Rohrbough), d. Nov-20-1956 in Lewis Co, WV,[913] buried in Waldeck Cemetery, Lewis Co, WV.[17]

   Children:

  i. ARCHIE LAWSON ELLIS b. Apr-28-1901,[592] d. Oct-22-1988 in Salem, WV,[cmxiv[914],592] buried in Waldeck Cemetery, Lewis Co, WV,[914] resided in Weston, Lewis Co, WV,[592] occupation photographer. He married Mar-25-1937 in Lewis Co, WV,[cmxv[915]] no children from this marriage, Phyllis Glenn West, b. Jan-22-1903 in Lewis Co, WV,[190] (daughter of Porter West and Olive G. Glenn), d. Apr- 1-2005,[190] buried in Waldeck Cemetery, Lewis Co, WV,[190] resided in Weston, Lewis Co, WV,[190] occupation Lewis County Dep Recorder.

   Phyllis: She was a 4-H leader for more than 50 years and was inducted into the 4-H Hall of Fame on Oct 9 2004. She had taught school in Lewis County and had worked in the Lewis County Clerk's office for many years. She and her husband were the owners of Ellis Studio. She was "survived by Billy and Farina Row and their children Randi, Eddie, Ben and Kasey Rowe, whom she considered her family; her caregiver Patricia Rager of Weston; one niece, Betty Crawford of Philippi; one nephew, Lowell Lemons of Ohio; two great-nieces; one great-nephew; one brother, Aubrey West."[190]

434. **Harvey L. Gaston** (251.Marion[7], 136.Hugh[6], 72.John[5], 21.John[4], 6.Hugh[3], 3.John[2], 1.Jean[1]), b. Jun-28-1886 in Lewis Co, WV, d. 1933, buried in Waldeck Cemetery, Lewis Co, WV,[17] resided in Parkersburg, Wood Co, WV, census 1920 in West Union District, Doddridge Co, WV, census 1900 in Freemans

Creek District, Lewis Co, WV, occupation minister. He married Jul-20-1910 in Lewis Co, WV,[410] **Love Cinderella Jarvis**, also known as Lovie, b. Jul-16-1889 at Camden, Lewis Co, WV,[621,592] (daughter of Samuel Jarvis and Barbara Elizabeth Fisher), d. Mar- -1986,[592] resided in Pawhuska, Osage Co, OK,[604] resided 1947 in Weston, Lewis Co, WV,[621] census 1920 in Doddridge Co, WV.[775]

       Children:

          i.   IRMA ELEANOR GASTON b. Oct-19-1924 in Lewis Co, WV, d. Mar-27-1929 in Jollytown, Gilmore Twp, Greene Co, PA,[cmxvi[916]] buried in Waldeck Cemetery, Lewis Co, WV.[17]

435. **John Marion Gaston** (251.Marion[7], 136.Hugh[6], 72.John[5], 21.John[4], 6.Hugh[3], 3.John[2], 1.Jean[1]), b. Mar-15-1895 in Lewis Co, WV,[398] d. Jul-26-1955 in Upshur Co, WV,[398,cmxvii[917]] buried in Bailey Cemetery, Braxton Co, WV,[398] resided near Buckhannon, Upshur Co, WV,[398] census 1930 in Union District, Upshur Co, WV, census 1920 in Court House District, Lewis Co, WV, occupation farmer,[398] military World War I.[398] He married (1) Oct-17-1919 in Orlando, Lewis Co, WV,[cmxviii[918]] **Carrie Pearl Posey**, also known as Carry Pearl Posey,[621] b. Apr- 4-1902,[154,621] [Birthplace given as Lewis County in marriage record, but as Braxton County in death record.] (daughter of Isaac Posey and Emma Jane Riffle), d. Oct- 6-1929 in Upshur Co, WV,[cmxix[919]] buried Blake Cemetery. He married[374,228] (2) **Stacie Flo Peters**, b. ca 1913,[cmxx[920],cmxxi[921]] resided 1955 near Buckhannon, Upshur Co, WV.[228]

       Children by Carrie Pearl Posey:

          i.   VELMA L. GASTON b. 1919,[888] census 1930 in Union District, Upshur Co, WV, census 1920 in Court House District, Lewis Co, WV.

          ii.   JOHN FRANKLIN GASTON, census name J. Frank Gaston,[cmxxii[922]] b. ca 1921 in Lewis Co, WV,[921] [Birth date given in death record as Aug 6 1920, with age 44 at time of Jan 1965 death. But age 8 in 1930 Census would put birth in about 1922, while age 24 at time of Aug 1945 marriage puts it in about 1921.], d. Jan-31-1965 in Buckhannon, Upshur Co, WV,[cmxxiii[923]] buried in Big Bend Church Cemetery, Sago, Upshur Co, WV,[917,134] resided 1945 in Buckhannon, Upshur Co, WV,[921] census 1930 in Union District, Upshur Co, WV, occupation coal miner.[917] He married Aug- 6-1945 in Buckhannon, Upshur Co, WV,[921] Lois Lucindia Gould, b. Jul-15-1917 in Upshur Co, WV,[cmxxiv[924],921] (daughter of Gilbert Gould and Ethel Blanche Hamilton), resided 1993 in Buckhannon, Upshur Co, WV,[924] resided 1945 in French Creek, Upshur Co, WV.[921]

          iii. CLEDITH GASTON b. ca 1924,[922] census 1930 in Union District, Upshur Co, WV.

       Children by Stacie Flo Peters:

          iv. LIVING. She married Arthur William Lantz, b. Dec- 4-1927 in Upshur Co, WV,[604,921] (son of George Washington Lantz and Madge Jane Linger), d. May- 8-1990,[604] resided in Buckhannon, Upshur Co, WV.[921,924]

          v.   LIVING. She married Living.

436. **Mary Elizabeth Maddox** (253.John[7], 137.Sarah[6], 72.John[5], 21.John[4], 6.Hugh[3], 3.John[2], 1.Jean[1]), b. Jan-15-1844 in Lewis Co, (W)VA,[398] d. Dec- 4-1921 in Jackson Co, WV,[398] buried in Grasslick Bapt Ch Cem, Pleasant Valley Rd, Kenna, Jackson Co, WV.[134] She married **Samuel Edwin "Ned" Stalnaker**, b. Apr-11-1835 in Lewis Co, (W)VA,[134] (son of Charles Stalnaker and Susannah England), d. Apr- 7-1914 in Jackson Co, WV,[134] buried in Grasslick Bapt Ch Cem, Pleasant Valley Rd, Kenna, Jackson Co, WV,[134] occupation postmaster, Edgar (now Given), W. Va.[134]

       Children:

          i.   EDIE STALNAKER. She married Daniel Frank Hill.

          ii.   ODA STALNAKER. She married J. Mance Casto.

          iii. W. BEACH STALNAKER d. aft Jan 1930,[436] resided 1921 in Given, Jackson Co, WV.[778] He married Flora May Hill, b. Dec-19-1868 in Given, Jackson Co, WV,[447] (daughter of Samuel T. Hill and Mary Jane Garnes), d. Jan- 2-1930 in Given, Jackson Co, WV,[447] buried in Grasslick Bapt Ch Cem, Pleasant Valley Rd, Kenna, Jackson Co, WV.[447]

437. **Archimedes Adolphus Maddox**, census name Andrew A. Maddox,[cmxxv[925]] census name Adolphus Maddox,[449] also known as Arkimidas Adolphus Maddox,[621] (253.John[7], 137.Sarah[6], 72.John[5], 21.John[4], 6.Hugh[3], 3.John[2], 1.Jean[1]), b. ca 1848 in Harrison Co, (W)VA,[621] census 1910 in Charleston, Kanawha Co, WV, census 1880 in Jackson Co, WV, resided 1869 in Lewis Co, WV.[621] He married Sep-15-1869 in Lewis Co, WV,[cmxxvi[926]] **Flavilla Catharine Jewell**, census name Catharine,[449] b. ca 1850

in Lewis Co, (W)VA,[621] (daughter of Abert Jewell and Catharine H. ___), census 1910 in Charleston, Kanawha Co, WV, census 1880 in Jackson Co, WV.

1880 Census, Jackson Co, WV, enumerated on Jun 25 1880:
Adolphus Maddox, 32, farmer; wife Catharine, 30; dau Allice, 8; son Earnest, 6; son Junius, 1; father John, 66, farmer, afflicted with neuralgia; mother Eliza, 56.

1910 Census, Kanawha Co, WV (City of Charleston), enumerated on Apr 15 1910 at Kanawha Street: Andrew A. Maddox, 62, laborer at odd jobs, married 42 yrs; wife Catherine, 60, mother of 4 children (all still living).

> Children:
> i. ALICE MADDOX b. ca 1872,[449] census 1880 in Jackson Co, WV.
> ii. EARNEST MADDOX b. ca 1874,[449] census 1880 in Jackson Co, WV.
> iii. JUNIUS MADDOX b. ca 1879,[449] census 1880 in Jackson Co, WV.

438. **Franklin P. Ward** (254.Margaret[7], 137.Sarah[6], 72.John[5], 21.John[4], 6.Hugh[3], 3.John[2], 1.Jean[1]), b. ca 1852 in Harrison Co, (W)VA,[473] resided 1874 in Gilmer Co, WV.[473] He married Mar-12-1874 in Ritchie Co, WV,[cmxxvii[927]] **Mary J. Holbert**, b. ca 1854 in Gilmer Co, (W)VA,[473] (daughter of Reuben Elijah Holbert and Cinderella Bush), resided 1874 in Ritchie Co, WV.[473]
> Children:
> i. THEODOSIA WARD b. Aug-4-1882,[74] d. May-30-1883,[17] buried in Auburn Community Cemetery, Ritchie Co, WV.[469]

439. **Flourney Matthew Maddox** (255.Thomas[7], 137.Sarah[6], 72.John[5], 21.John[4], 6.Hugh[3], 3.John[2], 1.Jean[1]), b. 1855 in Jackson Co, WV,[253] d. 1900,[253] census 1880 in Jackson Co, WV. He married[253] **Sarah B. Adams**, b. Mar-7-1862,[253] d. 1957,[253] buried in Ravenswood Cemetery, Jackson Co, WV.[253]
> Children:
> i. RENNEA MADDOX b. 1886,[253] d. 1973.[253]
> ii. BESS MADDOX b. 1888,[253] d. 1955.[253]
> iii. LEON MADDOX b. 1890,[253] d. 1919 in Jackson Co, WV.[253]

440. **William Rufus Maddox**, census name Rufus Maddox,[449] (255.Thomas[7], 137.Sarah[6], 72.John[5], 21.John[4], 6.Hugh[3], 3.John[2], 1.Jean[1]), b. 1857 in Jackson Co, WV,[253] d. Mar-12-1909 in Jackson Co, WV,[447] census 1880 in Jackson Co, WV.

1900 Census, Jackson Co, WV (Ripley District), enumerated on Jul 6 1900:
William Maddox (middle initial illegible), 40, b. Jun 1859, farmer, married 17 yrs; wife Rosetta, 38, b. Jul 1861, mother of 8 children (5 still living); son Oley E, 16, b. Apr 1884; son Ofa O, 13, b. Apr 1887; son Harley E, 9, b. Mar 1891; dau Marley M, 3, b. Apr 1897; dau Freddie, 1 month, b. Apr 1900.

He married[253] Mar-16-1882,[450] **Rosetta Casto**, also known as Rosa,[345] b. 1861.[253]
> Children:
> i. M. M. MADDOX b. Jan-12-1883,[154] d. Oct-2-1888 in Jackson Co, WV.[447]
> ii. OLEY E. MADDOX b. Apr--1884,[cmxxviii[928]] census 1900 in Jackson Co, WV.
> iii. OFA O. MADDOX b. Apr--1887,[928] census 1900 in Jackson Co, WV.
> iv. KENNA O. MADDOX[253] also known as O. K. Maddox,[447] b. ca 1889 in Liberty, Putnam Co, WV,[447] d. Sep-15-1898 in Jackson Co, WV,[447] cause of death croup.[447]
> v. HARLEY E. MADDOX b. Mar--1891,[928] census 1900 in Jackson Co, WV.
> vi. MARLEY M. MADDOX b. Apr--1897,[928] census 1900 in Jackson Co, WV.
> vii. FREDDIE MADDOX b. Apr--1900,[928] census 1900 in Jackson Co, WV.

441. **George G. Maddox** (255.Thomas[7], 137.Sarah[6], 72.John[5], 21.John[4], 6.Hugh[3], 3.John[2], 1.Jean[1]), b. Aug--1864,[928] [Age 38y 4m 25d given in death record would but birth date at Jun 7 1867. But 1900 Census states birth date as Aug 1864, and age 3 in 1870 Census also puts birth in about 1864.], d. Nov-1-

1905 in Jackson Co, WV,[447] census 1870, 1880, 1900 in Jackson Co, WV. He married[396] Oct-23-1890 in Jackson Co, WV,[253] **Mary Louise Casto**, b. 1873 in Jackson Co, WV,[253] [Birth date given in 1900 Census as May 1874.], d. 1950 in Jackson Co, WV,[253] buried in Grasslick Bapt Ch Cem, Pleasant Valley Rd, Kenna, Jackson Co, WV.[253]

Children:

i.   RALEIGH F. MADDOX, census name Rollie F. Maddox,[928] b. Nov- 6-1892,[253] [Birth date given in 1900 Census as Nov 1891.], d. Oct-31-1972 in Charleston, Kanawha Co, WV.[253] He married Emma Waugh, b. Mar- 7-1894,[253] d. May-27-1971.[253]

Emma: Five children.

796.   ii.   BRADY CRAIG MADDOX b. Dec-16-1895.
797.   iii. OREN CLAIR MADDOX b. Mar-24-1905.

442. **Susan Adaline Maddox**, census name Adaline Maddox,[449] also known as Susan Adelaide Maddox,[398] (256.William[7], 137.Sarah[6], 72.John[5], 21.John[4], 6.Hugh[3], 3.John[2], 1.Jean[1]), b. May- -1857,[928,46] d. Oct-26-1921 in Charleston, Kanawha Co, WV,[398,46] buried in Grasslick Bapt Ch Cem, Pleasant Valley Rd, Kenna, Jackson Co, WV,[17] census 1900, 1910, 1920 in Jackson Co, WV, resided 1886 in Kenna, Jackson Co, WV,[450] census 1880 in Jackson Co, WV [Listed as a servant in the household of her uncle, Thomas Maddox.]. She married Sep-30-1886 in Kenna, Jackson Co, WV,[450] **James Christopher Bradley**, b. Mar- -1857 in Jackson Co, (W)VA,[928,46,450] (son of Charles Bradley and Nancy Staley), d. Jun-12-1935 in Kanawha Co, WV,[398,46] buried in Grasslick Bapt Ch Cem, Pleasant Valley Rd, Kenna, Jackson Co, WV,[17,398] census 1900, 10, 20, 30 in Jackson Co, WV, resided 1886 in Kenna, Jackson Co, WV,[450] occupation farmer,[928,cmxxix[929],398].

Children:

798.   i.   WILBUR O. BRADLEY b. Sep- 8-1887.

ii.   ORA BELLE BRADLEY b. Jan-17-1889 in Jackson Co, WV,[398,928,450] [Birth date on headstone is 1888, but death record states Jan 17 1889, and 1900 Census also shows birth date as Jan 1889.], d. Feb-26-1922 in Jackson Co, WV,[398] buried in Grasslick Bapt Ch Cem, Pleasant Valley Rd, Kenna, Jackson Co, WV,[17] resided 1918 in Kenna, Jackson Co, WV,[450] census 1900, 1910 in Jackson Co, WV. She married Dec-24-1918 in Jackson Co, WV,[cmxxx[930]] Albert Slatton Wolfe, also known as A. Slatton Wolfe,[398] census name Slatton Wolf,[449] census name Abram S. Wolfe,[928] census name Abraham S. Wolf,[929] census name Albert S. Wolf,[cmxxxi[931]] b. Aug- -1875 in Jackson Co, WV,[928,398,450] (son of Abraham Wolf and Miriam Fisher), d. Jul-18-1922 in Charleston, Kanawha Co, WV,[398] buried in Grasslick Bapt Ch Cem, Pleasant Valley Rd, Kenna, Jackson Co, WV,[398] resided 1918 in Kenna, Jackson Co, WV,[450] census 1880, 1900, 10, 20 in Jackson Co, WV.

1920 Census, Jackson Co, WV (Ripley District, Kenna Precinct), enumerated in Jan 1920:

Albert S. Wolf, 44, farmer; wife Ora B, 30.

iii.   CHARLES EDGAR BRADLEY, also known as Edgar Bradley,[929] b. Mar-16-1890 in Jackson Co, WV,[592,928] d. May- -1972,[592] resided in Princeton, Mercer Co, WV,[604] resided 1939 in Bluefield, Mercer Co, WV,[cmxxxii[932]] resided 1935 in Beckley, Raleigh Co, WV,[748] resided 1916 in Kanawha Co, WV,[cmxxxiii[933]] census 1900, 1910 in Jackson Co, WV, occupation carpenter.[933] He married[cmxxxiv[934]] Dec- 6-1916 in Kanawha Co, WV,[933] Willia Maddox, b. Mar- 1-1894 in Kenna, Jackson Co, WV,[cmxxxv[935]] (daughter of Alonzo T. Maddox and Alice Jane Corbin), d. Oct-25-1964 in Bluefield, Mercer Co, WV,[935] buried in Grasslick Bapt Ch Cem, Pleasant Valley Rd, Kenna, Jackson Co, WV,[935] resided 1916 in Kanawha Co, WV.[933] As great-grandchildren of William Maddox and Sarah Gaston, Charles Edgar Bradley and Willa Maddox were second cousins. They had four children.

iv.   NORMA M. BRADLEY b. Oct-17-1894 in Jackson Co, WV,[592,928,450] d. Mar- -1974,[592] resided in Charleston, Kanawha Co, WV,[592] census 1900, 1910 in Jackson Co, WV. She married Jul- 5-1914 in Jackson Co, WV,[450] Benjamin Whittington, also known as Ben Whittington,[933] b. Nov-13-1892 in Jackson Co, WV,[450,592] d. Mar- -1983,[592] resided in Charleston, Kanawha Co, WV.[604]

v. CHESTER C. BRADLEY b. Sep-17-1897,[592,928] d. Jul- 2-1988,[592] resided in Charleston, Kanawha Co, WV,[cmxxxvi[936]] census 1900, 1910, 1920 in Jackson Co, WV.

443. **Charles Green Maddox** (256.William[7], 137.Sarah[6], 72.John[5], 21.John[4], 6.Hugh[3], 3.John[2], 1.Jean[1]), b. Feb-16-1858,[154] d. Nov-28-1935 in Jackson Co, WV,[447] occupation teacher.[447] He married **Delliah Belle Hill**, census name Belle,[cmxxxvii[937]] b. 1866, d. 1945, census 1930 in Jackson Co, WV.
Children:
  i. MYRTLE INA MADDOX b. 1890.
  ii. PEARLY MAE MADDOX b. 1892, d. 1958. She married Russell Harrison.
  iii. ROME BOYD MADDOX b. 1895, d. 1915.
  iv. LLOYD HERBERT MADDOX, census name Herbert Maddox,[937] b. Jan- 7-1900,[154] d. Jun-18-1941 in Jackson Co, WV,[447] cause of death gunshot wound in head,[447] census 1930 in Jackson Co, WV, occupation farmer.[447] He married ca 1925,[937] Odell __, b. ca 1903,[937] census 1930 in Jackson Co, WV.

444. **William Hill Maddox** (257.James[7], 137.Sarah[6], 72.John[5], 21.John[4], 6.Hugh[3], 3.John[2], 1.Jean[1]), b. Mar-28-1850, d. Mar-14-1918, census 1880 in Jackson Co, WV, occupation Baptist minister. He married Feb-25-1875, **Martha Columbia (twin) Corbin**, b. Apr-20-1855 in Harrison Co, WV (daughter of Oliver Perry Corbin and Nancy Ann Taylor), d. Nov- 2-1938, census 1880 in Jackson Co, WV. William Hill Maddox and Martha Columbia Corbin were second cousins by virtue of both being great-grandchildren of John Gaston Jr (1752-1829) and Anna Davisson.

Children:
  i. OKEY V. MADDOX b. May- 4-1876, d. Jul-17-1898 in Kenna, Jackson Co, WV,[447] never married[447.]

Never married

799. ii. MINDIA A. MADDOX b. Jun- 7-1879.
800. iii. OTTO OLY MADDOX b. Oct-28-1881.
801. iv. LORY DOVE MADDOX b. Oct-24-1887.
802. v. FLAVIUS CLINTON MADDOX b. Dec-14-1896.

445. **Alonzo T. Maddox** (257.James[7], 137.Sarah[6], 72.John[5], 21.John[4], 6.Hugh[3], 3.John[2], 1.Jean[1]), b. Feb-13-1854,[398,934,253] d. Mar-17-1929 in Jackson Co, WV,[398,934,253] buried in Grasslick Bapt Ch Cem, Pleasant Valley Rd, Kenna, Jackson Co, WV,[253,398] cause of death tuberculosis,[398] occupation farmer.[398] He married[436,396] Jun-11-1882,[934] **Alice Jane Corbin**, b. Oct-17-1859 in Jackson Co, (W)VA,[398,934] (daughter of Oliver Perry Corbin and Mary Linsey), d. Mar-24-1939 in Bluefield, Mercer Co, WV,[398] buried in Grasslick Bapt Ch Cem, Pleasant Valley Rd, Kenna, Jackson Co, WV.[398]
Children:
803. i. ORVILLE B. MADDOX b. Mar-22-1883.
  ii. CHESTER BOYD MADDOX b. Apr-22-1885,[934] d. bef Apr 1910.[929]
  iii. HOADLEY F. MADDOX b. Oct- 9-1888,[934] d. Feb-25-1917 in Ripley, Jackson Co, WV,[447] cause of death tuberculosis,[447] census 1910 in Jackson Co, WV, occupation newspaper reporter,[447] occupation 1910 school teacher.[929]
  iv. WILLIA MADDOX b. Mar- 1-1894 in Kenna, Jackson Co, WV,[935] d. Oct-25-1964 in Bluefield, Mercer Co, WV,[935] buried in Grasslick Bapt Ch Cem, Pleasant Valley Rd, Kenna, Jackson Co, WV,[935] resided 1916 in Kanawha Co, WV.[933] She married[934] Dec- 6-1916 in Kanawha Co, WV,[933] Charles Edgar Bradley, also known as Edgar Bradley,[929] b. Mar-16-1890 in Jackson Co, WV,[592,928] (son of James Christopher Bradley and Susan Adaline Maddox), d. May- -1972,[592] resided in Princeton, Mercer Co, WV,[604] resided 1939 in Bluefield, Mercer Co, WV,[932] resided 1935 in Beckley, Raleigh Co, WV,[748] resided 1916 in Kanawha Co, WV,[933] census 1900, 1910 in Jackson Co, WV, occupation carpenter.[933] As great-grandchildren of William Maddox and Sarah Gaston, Charles Edgar Bradley and Willa Maddox were second cousins. They had four children.

446. **Lycurgus Maddox**, census name Licurgis Maddox,[931] (257.James[7], 137.Sarah[6], 72.John[5], 21.John[4], 6.Hugh[3], 3.John[2], 1.Jean[1]), b. Dec- 5-1858,[253] d. 1935, census 1920 in Ripley, Jackson Co, WV. He married[253] Apr-22-1886 in Jackson Co, WV,[433] **Luella Jane Morrison**, b. ca 1867,[931] census 1920 in Ripley, Jackson Co, WV.

Luella: A sister to O. J. Morrison

Children:
i. JAMES BRADFORD MADDOX b. 1887, d. 1888.
ii. LONA LEE MADDOX b. 1888, d. 1921. She married Carroll Deem.
iii. GRANVILLE LOEBE MADDOX, census name Lobe Maddox,[931] b. 1891, d. 1921, census 1920 in Ripley, Jackson Co, WV.
iv. FLORA BELLE MADDOX b. 1896, d. 1904.
v. HARRY RECTOR MADDOX b. Dec-23-1897 in Jackson Co, WV,[592,cmxxxviii[938]] d. Sep- -1974,[592] resided in Morgantown, Monongalia Co, WV,[938,604] census 1920 in Ripley, Jackson Co, WV. He married Jun-30-1934 in Morgantown, Monongalia Co, WV,[938] Kathryn Sneddon, b. ca 1907 in California, Washington Co, PA,[938] (daughter of James Sneddon and Catharine Riley), resided 1934 in Morgantown, Monongalia Co, WV.[938]
804. vi. WARREN HAYDEN MADDOX b. Jun- 3-1900.
vii. VERA GRAY MADDOX b. 1903. She married Bernard G. Murphy.
viii. HERMAN BRUCE MADDOX b. 1905, d. 1968. He married Ruth Atkinson.

447. **Irving Thomas Maddox** (257.James[7], 137.Sarah[6], 72.John[5], 21.John[4], 6.Hugh[3], 3.John[2], 1.Jean[1]), b. Jun-12-1863,[253] d. 1951, census 1880 in Jackson Co, WV. He married **Ida Alice Lee**, b. Feb- 6-1865 in Ohio,[154] (daughter of Charles H. Lee and __ Buck), d. Mar-29-1931 in Jackson Co, WV.[447]
Children:
i. ORLANDO ROSCOE MADDOX, also known as Orla R. Maddox.[253]

Resided in the state of Washington.

ii. ONA A. MADDOX b. Nov-19-1887.[253]
iii. JAMES ROY MADDOX b. 1888, d. 1949.
iv. WADE L. MADDOX b. 1890.[253]
v. CHARLES HESS MADDOX b. 1894, d. 1952. He married Erma Parsons.
vi. ASHFORD DALE MADDOX b. 1899, d. 1957. He married Martha Hall.

448. **James Lewis Maddox** (258.Arnold[7], 137.Sarah[6], 72.John[5], 21.John[4], 6.Hugh[3], 3.John[2], 1.Jean[1]), b. May-12-1862 in Harrison Co, (W)VA,[254] d. Aug-18-1936 in Leesburg, Loudoun Co, VA,[254] buried in Ashburn Presbyterian Church Cem, Loudoun Co, VA.[254] He married Apr-27-1887 near Middleburg, Fauquier Co, VA,[254] **Sarah Catherine Herndon**, b. Mar-31-1866 in Fauquier Co, VA,[254] (daughter of Joel Herndon and Nancy Holder), d. Jan- 7-1938 in Hamilton, Loudoun Co, VA,[254] buried in Ashburn Presbyterian Church Cem, Loudoun Co, VA.[254]
Children:
i. LLOYD ARNOLD MADDOX b. May- 4-1888 in Fauquier Co, VA,[254] d. Nov- -1902 in Loudoun Co, VA.[254]
ii. EFFIE RUHAMAH MADDOX b. Jun-11-1890 in Fauquier Co, VA,[254] d. Jul-19-1964 near Leesburg, Loudoun Co, VA.[254]

Maternal grandmother of genealogist Raymond A. Mann <dermann@earthlink.net>, the source of nearly all the information here on the descendants of Arnold Maddox and Mary Mildred Smith.

iii.   ROBERT MATTHEW MADDOX b. Dec- 5-1892,[254] [Birthplace probably Fauquier Co, VA, per Raymond A. Mann.], d. Jun- -1948 in Loudoun Co, VA.[254] He married[254] no children from this marriage,[254] Dorothy Cooper.
iv.   IDA MAY MADDOX b. Jul-17-1895,[254] [Birthplace probably Fauquier Co, VA, but possibly Loudoun Co, VA, per Raymond A. Mann.], d. Oct-29-1979 in Manassas, VA.[254]

Six children.[254]

She married[254] Alvin Carlos Pierson.
v.   RUBY OLIVE MADDOX b. Sep-23-1898,[254] [Birthplace probably Loudoun Co, VA, per Raymond A. Mann.], d. Jun- 4-1990 in Manassas, VA.[254]

Several (3-5) children.[254]

She married[254] Earl Clyburn.
vi.   JAMES LEWIS MADDOX, JR. b. Jan-14-1904 in Loudoun Co, VA,[254] d. May- 2-1969,[254] [Place of death probably Loudoun Co, VA, per Raymond A. Mann.].

Four children.[254]

He married[254] Dorothy Schulke.
vii.   DORCAS ANN "ANNIE" MADDOX[254] b. Jul-20-1905 in Loudoun Co, VA,[254] d. Jul- 8-1978 in Manassas, VA,[254] cause of death automobile accident,[254] resided in Falls Church, Fairfax Co, VA.[592] She married[592] no children from this marriage,[254] Ralph Aubrey Carter, d. 1978,[254] cause of death automobile accident.[254]
viii.   EDITH JEANETTE MADDOX b. Mar- 5-1908 in Loudoun Co, VA,[254] d. Aug-14-1999 in Manassas, VA.[254]

Two children.[254]

She married[254] Garnie Craven Virts, b. Oct- 1-1903,[592] d. Oct- -1957.[592]
805.   ix.   WEST MANSFIELD MADDOX b. Mar-27-1911.

449. **Fannie V. Maddox**, also known as Fanny,[254] (258.Arnold[7], 137.Sarah[6], 72.John[5], 21.John[4], 6.Hugh[3], 3.John[2], 1.Jean[1]), b. ca 1870,[254] [Place of birth probably Fauquier Co, VA, per Raymond A. Mann]. She married ca 1896,[254] **Harry F. Christman**.
Children:
i.   (INFANT) CHRISTMAN d. in infancy.[254]
ii.   MYRTLE CHRISTMAN.
iii.   GEORGE WASHINGTON CHRISTMAN.

450. **William Jackson West** (260.Ruhama[7], 137.Sarah[6], 72.John[5], 21.John[4], 6.Hugh[3], 3.John[2], 1.Jean[1]), b. May-10-1853 in Harrison Co, (W)VA,[454] d. Aug- 7-1900 in West Milford, Harrison Co, WV,[456] occupation carpenter, farmer.[456] He married Sep- 5-1880 in Harrison Co, WV,[456] **Sarah Louise Mick**, b. Sep-27-1858 in Harrison Co, (W)VA,[cmxxxix[939]] (daughter of Mathias J. Mick and Eliza Queen), d. Sep- 8-1930 in West Milford, Harrison Co, WV,[939] buried in Rose Hill (formerly IOOF) Cemetery, West Milford, Harrison Co, WV,[524,939] occupation dress maker.[939]
Children:
806.   i.   FREDERICK BROOK WEST b. Jul- 4-1881.
807.   ii.   ORA JEFFERSON WEST b. Apr- 2-1884.
808.   iii.   WILLIAM KENNA WEST b. Apr- 9-1887.

451. **Ambrose Jefferson West** (260.Ruhama[7], 137.Sarah[6], 72.John[5], 21.John[4], 6.Hugh[3], 3.John[2], 1.Jean[1]), b. Oct-24-1861 in Harrison Co, WV,[454,456] d. Jan- 4-1936 near West Milford, Harrison Co, WV,[398] buried in Sheets Mill (Old West) Cemetery, West Milford, Harrison Co, WV,[464] resided near West Milford,

Harrison Co, WV,[398] resided 1920 in Uniontown, Fayette Co, PA,[464] occupation farmer,[398] occupation trolley conductor.[464] He married Jul-12-1899,[464] divorced[228] **Florence Lillie Lee**, b. Dec-14-1875 in Volcano, Wood Co, WV,[cmxl[940]] (daughter of James F. Lee and Martha Yoho).

        Children:

        i.   LYLE CECIL WEST b. Apr-14-1900 in Marion Co, WV,[940] d. Aug-29-1903 in Harrison Co, WV,[940] buried in Sheets Mill (Old West) Cemetery, West Milford, Harrison Co, WV.[940]

        ii.   WILLIAM RAYMOND WEST b. Oct-19-1902 in Harrison Co, WV,[940] d. Dec- 8-1902 in Harrison Co, WV,[940] buried in Sheets Mill (Old West) Cemetery, West Milford, Harrison Co, WV.[940]

        iii.   AMBROSE JEFFERSON WEST, JR. b. Jul-17-1905 in Harrison Co, WV,[940] d. Oct- 9-1905 in Harrison Co, WV.[940]

        iv.   PAULINE M. WEST b. Aug- 7-1908 in Clarksburg, Harrison Co, WV,[940] resided 1936 in Uniontown, Fayette Co, PA,[765] census 1920 in Uniontown, Fayette Co, PA. She married[cmxli[941]] __ Romesburg.

452. **Laura Alice West** (260.Ruhama[7], 137.Sarah[6], 72.John[5], 21.John[4], 6.Hugh[3], 3.John[2], 1.Jean[1]), b. Mar-28-1864 in Harrison Co, WV,[398] d. Jan- 1-1936 in Fairmont, Marion Co, WV,[398] [Bell Run], buried in Manley Cemetery, Shaver, Marion Co, WV,[464] census 1900, 1910, 1920 in Marion Co, WV, occupation teacher.[464] She married Mar-26-1890 in Harrison Co, WV,[464] **Richard T. Manley**, also known as T. Richard Manley,[464] census name Richard P. Manley,[cmxlii[942]] b. ca 1864 in Marion Co, WV,[398,942] (son of Harrison Manley and Sarah Righter), d. Jan-21-1945 in Weston, Lewis Co, WV,[398] resided in Fairmont, Marion Co, WV,[398] census 1870, 1900, 10, 20 in Marion Co, WV, occupation dairy farmer.[cmxliii[943]]

1900 Census, Marion Co, WV (Fairmont District), enumerated on Jun 8 1900:
Richard Manley, 37, b. May 1862, dairy man, married 10 yrs; wife Laura A 36, b. Mar 1864, mother of 2 children (both still living); son Madison W, 7, b. Jun 1892; son Harrison Jr, 4, b. Oct 1895; employee Wade Lester, 22, b. Jul 1877, laborer, single.

1910 Census, Marion Co, WV (Fairmont District), enumerated in April 1910:
Richard P. Manley, 46, b. WVa, both parents b. WVa, farmer, married 20 yrs; wife Laura A 46, b. WVa, father b. Pennsylvania, mother b. WVa, mother of 2 children (both still living); son West, 17, b. WVa; son Harrison Jr, 14, b. WVa; hired help Solomon Westfall, 54, b. WVa, both parents b. WVa, farm laborer, widowed.

1920 Census, Marion Co, WV (Fairmont District), enumerated in Jan 1920:
Richard T. Manley, 56, b. WVa, both parents b. WVa, dairy farmer; wife Laura A, 55, b. WVa, father b. Pennsylvania, mother b. WVa; son Harrison Jr, 24, dairy farmer, single.

        Children:

809.   i.   MADISON WEST MANLEY b. Jun- 9-1892.

810.   ii.   HARRISON JEFFERSON MANLEY b. Oct-28-1895.

453. **Hiram Thomas West** (260.Ruhama[7], 137.Sarah[6], 72.John[5], 21.John[4], 6.Hugh[3], 3.John[2], 1.Jean[1]), b. Mar-15-1866 in Harrison Co, WV,[464,454,537,17] [Age 43 in 1920 Census would put birth in about 1877, but all other records support the 1866 birth date.], d. Jan-14-1949 in West Milford, Harrison Co, WV,[464,17] buried in Sheets Mill (Old West) Cemetery, West Milford, Harrison Co, WV,[464] census 1920 in West Milford, Harrison Co, WV, occupation carpenter, farmer.[464] He married[345] Jul-28-1895 in West Milford, Harrison Co, WV,[cmxliv[944],464] **Allie Belle Davis**, census name Annabelle,[418] also known as Alice,[398] b. Oct-31-1873 in Harrison Co, WV,[cmxlv[945]] (daughter of William Davis and Mary Limar), d. Feb- 4-1933,[945] buried in Sheets Mill (Old West) Cemetery, West Milford, Harrison Co, WV,[945] census 1920 in West Milford, Harrison Co, WV.

        Children:

        i.   DALE JENNINGS WEST b. Mar-12-1897 in Harrison Co, WV,[945,276] d. Jun-19-1966 in Clarksburg, Harrison Co, WV,[276,945] buried in Sheets Mill (Old West) Cemetery, West Milford, Harrison Co, WV,[276,945] occupation carpenter, painter,[418,276] never married[276.]

     ii.   MARY R. WEST b. May-18-1898 in Harrison Co, WV,[945,592,46] d. Mar- 9-1989,[592] buried in Morris Chapel Cemetery, Benson, Harrison Co, WV,[945,524] resided in Clarksburg, Harrison Co, WV,[592] census 1920 in West Milford, Harrison Co, WV.

     iii.   ALTA BERYL WEST b. Dec-25-1899 in Harrison Co, WV,[945,236] d. Apr-28-1965 in Weston, Lewis Co, WV,[236] buried in Sheets Mill (Old West) Cemetery, West Milford, Harrison Co, WV,[236] resided in West Milford, Harrison Co, WV,[236] never married[236.]

     iv.   LAURA V. WEST b. Jun- 9-1901 in Harrison Co, WV,[945] d. Aug- 5-1902 in Harrison Co, WV.[945]

     v.   LILLY BELLE WEST b. Sep-26-1903 in Harrison Co, WV,[945] d. Jul- -1904 in Harrison Co, WV.[945]

811.   vi.   PEARL M. WEST b. Nov-22-1905.

     vii.   HAZEL WEST b. Aug-30-1907 in Harrison Co, WV,[945] d. Jul- 7-1908 in Harrison Co, WV.[945]

812.   viii.   JESSIE M. WEST b. Jul-18-1909.

813.   ix.   GRACE WEST b. Mar-12-1911.

814.   x.   THOMAS WOODROW WEST b. Nov-18-1913.

815.   xi.   ALICE BESSIE WEST b. Apr-27-1915.

454. **Judson Lee West** (260.Ruhama[7], 137.Sarah[6], 72.John[5], 21.John[4], 6.Hugh[3], 3.John[2], 1.Jean[1]), b. Jul- 7-1868 in Harrison Co, WV,[464] baptized West Milford Bapt Ch in West Milford, Harrison Co, WV,[945] d. Sep-30-1955 in Clarksburg, Harrison Co, WV,[398] buried in Sheets Mill (Old West) Cemetery, West Milford, Harrison Co, WV,[464] resided in West Milford, Harrison Co, WV,[398] census 1910, 1920 in Grant District, Harrison Co, WV,[cmxlvi[946]] occupation farmer.[398] He married Nov-17-1903 at Lost Creek, Harrison Co, WV,[419,946] **Minnie Otto Cottrill**, b. Jul-24-1877 in Harrison Co, WV,[946] (daughter of Henry B. Cottrill and Eliza Jane West), d. Feb- 1-1909,[946] buried in Sheets Mill (Old West) Cemetery, West Milford, Harrison Co, WV.[946] Judson Lee West & Minnie Otto Cottrill were second cousins, once removed, by virtue of their common ancestry with John West & Frances Howard.

     Children:

     i.   GLADYS LEOLA WEST b. Jul- 3-1906 in Grant District, Harrison Co, WV,[946,592] d. Oct-5-1992,[592,946] buried in Sheets Mill (Old West) Cemetery, West Milford, Harrison Co, WV,[946] resided in West Milford, Harrison Co, WV,[592] census 1910, 1920 in Grant District, Harrison Co, WV,[946] occupation teacher.[946]

     Following her mother's death when she was not yet 3 years old, Gladys was raised by her aunt Mary Virginia "Jennie" West.[946]

     She married[946] no children from this marriage,[946] Cecil C. Casto, b. Sep-22-1912,[592] (son of William Casto and Blanche Hardman), d. Jul-29-2001,[592] resided in West Milford, Harrison Co, WV,[604] census 1930 in Grant District, Harrison Co, WV.

455. **Ida Mae West** (260.Ruhama[7], 137.Sarah[6], 72.John[5], 21.John[4], 6.Hugh[3], 3.John[2], 1.Jean[1]), b. Feb- 2-1876 in Harrison Co, WV,[464,17] d. Aug-19-1964 in Harrison Co, WV,[464,17] buried in Rose Hill (formerly IOOF) Cemetery, West Milford, Harrison Co, WV.[524] She married[446,502] Sep-22-1895 in Harrison Co, WV,[464] **George Lemuel Bartlett**, b. Oct-19-1868 in West Milford, Harrison Co, WV,[cmxlvii[947],17] (son of John Calvin Bartlett and Mary Fleming), d. Mar-12-1959 in Harrison Co, WV,[947,17] buried in Rose Hill (formerly IOOF) Cemetery, West Milford, Harrison Co, WV,[524] occupation farmer.[947]

     Children:

     i.   GUY CALVIN BARTLETT b. Oct- 2-1898 in Waverly, Wood Co, WV,[947,592,17] d. Jul-23-1988,[592,17] buried in Pleasant Hill UM Cemetery, near Kincheloe, Harrison Co, WV,[524] resided in Morris, Tioga Co, PA,[cmxlviii[948]] resided 1964 in Wellsboro, Tioga Co, PA,[856] census 1930 in South Parkersburg, Wood Co, WV, resided 1926 in West Milford, Harrison Co, WV.[cmxlix[949]]

     1930 Census, Wood Co, WV (Tygart District, South Parkersburg), enumerated on Apr 4 1930:

Earnest R. Dunn, 28, truck driver for wholesale grocery, age 24 at time of first marriage; wife Ona, 25, reeler at silk mill, age 21 at first marriage; son Donald, 2y 11m; sister Laura Kerns, 24, housekeeper for private family, married, age 17 at first marriage; roomer Guy Bartlett, 31, machinist, marital status illegible, age 27 at first marriage.

He married (1) Oct-23-1926 in Elkins, Randolph Co, WV,[cml][950] divorced[436] Nora Compton, b. Jun- 1-1904 in Randolph Co, WV,[592,949,cmli][951] (daughter of John Compton and Louvena Murphy), d. Sep-22-1969 in Elkins, Randolph Co, WV,[951,592] buried in Mountain State Memorial Gardens, Elkins, Randolph Co, WV,[951] resided in Montrose, Randolph Co, WV,[949,604] occupation cook.[951] He married (2) Roxie Zona Bell, b. May-21-1904 in Harrison Co, WV,[17,419] (daughter of Marion Bell and Madalena C. Ash), d. Oct- 2-1958,[17] buried in Pleasant Hill UM Cemetery, near Kincheloe, Harrison Co, WV,[524] resided 1926 in Kincheloe (Jane Lew), Harrison Co, WV.[419]

ii. ALLISON CLYDE BARTLETT, also known as Clyde Bartlett,[419] also known as A. Clyde Bartlett,[17] b. May-17-1902 in Harrison Co, WV,[cmlii][952],419,592,46 d. May- -1978,[592,46] buried in Rose Hill (formerly IOOF) Cemetery, West Milford, Harrison Co, WV,[524] resided in Clarksburg, Harrison Co, WV,[856,604] resided 1933 in West Milford, Harrison Co, WV.[419] He married Mar-12-1933 in Salem, WV,[419] Mary Virginia Post, also known as Virginia Post,[947,592,17] b. Aug-16-1907 in Ritchie Co, WV,[419,592] (daughter of Carson Post and Cora Corbin), d. Oct-26-1998,[592] buried in Rose Hill (formerly IOOF) Cemetery, West Milford, Harrison Co, WV,[524] resided in Clarksburg, Harrison Co, WV,[604] resided 1933 in West Milford, Harrison Co, WV.[419]

iii. EXEL JEFFERSON BARTLETT b. Apr-21-1904 in Harrison Co, WV,[419,592,46] d. Jan-10-2000,[592] buried in Rose Hill (formerly IOOF) Cemetery, West Milford, Harrison Co, WV,[524] resided in Bridgeport, Harrison Co, WV,[604] resided 1957, 1964 in Clarksburg, Harrison Co, WV,[436,856] resided 1928 in West Milford, Harrison Co, WV.[419] He married[947] Jul-20-1928 in West Milford, Harrison Co, WV,[419] Velma Burl Carder, b. Jun- 8-1907 in Harrison Co, WV,[419,46] (daughter of C. Albert Carder and Bessie Darnold), d. Jan-15-1957 near Clarksburg, Harrison Co, WV,[398,46] buried in Rose Hill (formerly IOOF) Cemetery, West Milford, Harrison Co, WV,[524,398] resided 1928 in Good Hope, Harrison Co, WV.[419]

816. iv. REVA PEARL BARTLETT b. Jul- 8-1908.

456. **Margaret Fleming** (261.Anna[7], 138.Margaret[6], 72.John[5], 21.John[4], 6.Hugh[3], 3.John[2], 1.Jean[1]), b. 1841. She married Dec-1866, **Jesse Wilson Scott**.
 Children:
 i. WILLIAM EDWIN SCOTT b. Dec- 6-1867.

457. **Anna M. Ward**, also known as Annie,[480] (264.Mary[7], 139.John[6], 72.John[5], 21.John[4], 6.Hugh[3], 3.John[2], 1.Jean[1]), b. Dec- 2-1845,[470] d. Feb-27-1934 in Ritchie Co, WV.[cmliii][953]

Minnie Kendall Lowther, apparently incorrectly, states on p. 316 that Anna V. Ward, a daughter of Martin Carr Ward and Mary Jane Gaston, was born on Dec 2 1845 and that she married M. B. Zinn of Holbrook on July 27 1865. M. B. Zinn was a son of Quilla Manley Zinn and Lucy Ann Wilson. But Ritchie County marriage records show that on that date, July 27 1865, Ann M. Ward, age 20, daughter of Martin C. & Mary J. Ward, married William B. Zinn, age 23, born in Lewis Co, son of John W. & Eliza Zinn. Furthermore, a headstone for Luetta Zinn at the Oxford Baptist Church Cemetery identifies her as the daughter of W. B. & A. M. Zinn. But Ritchie County death records show that Anna Ward Zinn, dau of Martin and Betty Gaston Ward, died on Feb 27 1934 at age 88y2m25d.

She married Jul-27-1865 in Ritchie Co, WV,[cmliv][954] **William Buckner Zinn**,[cmlv][955] also known as Buckner Zinn,[480] b. Jul- 9-1842 in Lewis Co, (W)VA,[473,955] (son of John Wesley Zinn and Elizabeth Hoskins), d. Aug-29-1924 in Ritchie Co, WV.[955]

William: A grand-nephew, Larry Bartlett, tells this story: "During the Civil War, Buckner had served in Company E of the Sixth West Virginia Regiment. Dad remembered him as a frisky old gentleman who was bearded like a prophet. Buckner was a self-taught dentist and inventor, and he was the first farmer in Ritchie County to have electric lights. He built a water-powered generator on the Hughes

River, and offered electrical shocks as a treatment for arthritis. He was also a skilled woodcarver, and he created intricate toys that were powered by a water wheel. Two of Buckner Zinn's sons went west to Wyoming in the early 1900's. One of the boys was an oilman, and the other worked as a big game hunter and guide."[480]

Children:
    i.   LUETTA ZINN b. Nov- 7-1868,[17] d. Mar-26-1886,[17] buried in Oxford Baptist Church Cemetery, Doddridge Co, WV.[cmlvi][956]

458. **Thomas Floyd Ward**[396] (264.Mary[7], 139.John[6], 72.John[5], 21.John[4], 6.Hugh[3], 3.John[2], 1.Jean[1]), b. Mar-4-1852 in Harrison Co, (W)VA,[470,396,46] d. 1929,[480,46] buried in Auburn Community Cemetery, Ritchie Co, WV,[469] resided near Berea, Ritchie Co, WV.[480] He married[480] Apr-18-1875 in Ritchie Co, WV,[473,470] **Frances Virginia Frymier**,[473] b. 1854 in Harrison Co, (W)VA,[473,46] (daughter of John Frymier and Margaret __), d. 1910,[46,480] buried in Auburn Community Cemetery, Ritchie Co, WV,[469] resided in Auburn, Ritchie Co, WV.[470]
    Children:
817.   i.   KENNETH BOYD WARD b. Mar- -1879.
818.   ii.   THEO MAY WARD b. Sep- -1881.
    iii.   CLOVIS L. WARD b. Mar-22-1886,[469] d. Nov-16-1905,[cmlvii][957] buried in Auburn Community Cemetery, Ritchie Co, WV,[469] cause of death typhoid fever,[480] census 1900 in Union District, Ritchie Co, WV.
819.   iv.   NELLIE SNOW WARD b. Jan-22-1888.
    v.   LEDRUE K. WARD[473,398] b. Feb-10-1890 in Auburn, Ritchie Co, WV,[398] d. Aug- 8-1943 in Harrisville, Ritchie Co, WV,[cmlviii][958] buried in Auburn Community Cemetery, Ritchie Co, WV,[398,469] resided in Harrisville, Ritchie Co, WV,[398] census 1900 in Union District, Ritchie Co, WV, occupation oil well rig builder.[398]

A grand-nephew, Larry Bartlett, tells this story: "Dad's aunts and uncles often visited the farm, bringing the latest gossip to Shady Lane. A favorite visitor was his colorful uncle, Ledrue Ward. During the oil boom years, Ledrue made good money as a derrick contractor. He raced around Ritchie County in a Stutz Bearcat, indulging a taste for liquor and shouting his strange oath: 'Son of a gun to Peeroo!' When I was a boy in the 1940's, I was taken to see Ledrue on his deathbed. He gave me a fistful of coins to buy ice cream and candy, saying: 'Son of a gun to Peeroo, boys need to have fun.' Those words seemed to summarize his high-spirited life."[480]

He married[436,228] Dec-29-1911 in Ritchie Co, WV,[473] Essie Mona Hardesty, b. May-20-1888 in Auburn, Ritchie Co, WV,[398] (daughter of James H. Hardesty and Mary A. Stazel), d. Jun-21-1931 in Parkersburg, Wood Co, WV,[cmlix][959] buried in Auburn Community Cemetery, Ritchie Co, WV,[398,469] cause of death typhoid fever.[398]
    vi.   JUNIE A. WARD b. ca 1891,[809] census 1900 in Union District, Ritchie Co, WV.

459. **Eliza J. Ward** (264.Mary[7], 139.John[6], 72.John[5], 21.John[4], 6.Hugh[3], 3.John[2], 1.Jean[1]), b. Jan-29-1856,[470,17] d. Feb-22-1932 in Ritchie Co, WV,[17,470] buried in Chevauxdefrise/Kendall Cemetery, Ritchie Co, WV.[469] She married[470] Sep- 1-1885 in Ritchie Co, WV,[cmlx][960] **James Emery Amos**, b. Jul-11-1859 in Washburn, Ritchie Co, WV,[473,474] ["Ritchie County Cemeteries," p. 500, reports birth date on headstone as July 11 1858. But age in marriage record would put birth in 1859, and death record shows birth date as Jul 11 1859.] (son of Henry H. Amos and Malinda Rex), d. Jul-24-1945 in Ritchie Co, WV,[474,469] buried in Chevauxdefrise/Kendall Cemetery, Ritchie Co, WV,[469] resided near Harrisville, Ritchie Co, WV.[470]
    Children:
    i.   ESTA E. AMOS b. Aug-15-1890,[363] d. Aug-22-1897.[17]

460. **Charles Alvin Ward**[396] (264.Mary[7], 139.John[6], 72.John[5], 21.John[4], 6.Hugh[3], 3.John[2], 1.Jean[1]), b. 1858 in Auburn, Ritchie Co, WV,[470,474,46] [Based on age 85y9m29d given in death record, birthdate would be May 5 1858, but Minnie Kendall Lowther reports March 14 1858.], d. Mar- 5-1944 in Ritchie Co,

WV,[474,46] buried in Auburn Community Cemetery, Ritchie Co, WV.[469] He married Feb-24-1881 in Ritchie Co, WV,[470,473] **Catherine Olive Hall**,[474] also known as Katherine Olive Hall,[396] b. Dec-31-1864 in Auburn, Ritchie Co, WV,[474,46] (daughter of Lawson Hall and Sarah Sinnett), d. Jan-14-1944 in Ritchie Co, WV,[474,46] buried in Auburn Community Cemetery, Ritchie Co, WV.[469]

Children:

    i.   CALVIN RAY WARD b. Aug-18-1884,[469] d. Mar-19-1885,[469] buried in Auburn Community Cemetery, Ritchie Co, WV.[469]

    ii.   LENA M. WARD b. Feb- -1886.[809,473] She married[cmlxi[961]] Apr-18-1908 in Ritchie Co, WV,[473] A. Mood Ehret, also known as Moode Ehret, also known as Moode Ehret,[cmlxii[962]] b. Feb-24-1884,[154,473] (son of John Ehret and Elizabeth A. Law), d. Jun-11-1951 in Ritchie Co, WV.[474]

    iii.   GOLDIE WARD b. Oct- -1887.[809]

820.   iv.   MATTIE WARD b. Sep- -1889.

    v.   TENSY WARD b. Oct- -1891 in Ritchie Co, WV,[809,588] resided 1912 in Auburn, Ritchie Co, WV.[588] She married Aug-30-1912 in Auburn, Ritchie Co, WV,[588] Clarence G. Grose, b. ca 1892 in Ritchie Co, WV,[588] resided 1912 in Berea, Ritchie Co, WV.[588]

    vi.   SARAH WARD b. Sep- -1894.[809]

    vii.   HARRY HAZAL WARD[955] b. Jan-19-1898 in Auburn, Ritchie Co, WV,[955,46] d. Jul-26-1920 in Ritchie Co, WV,[955,46] buried in Auburn Community Cemetery, Ritchie Co, WV.[469]

We previously had this child as a female, Mary H. Ward, b. Jan 1898, with no further info. Source not documented, but entry was made Dec 2 1992. But Ritchie Co death records show Harry Hazal Ward, son of Charles Alvin Ward & Katherine Olive Hall, b. at Auburn in Ritchie Co, d. July 26 1920 at age 22y6m7d. This would put his birthdate at Jan 19 1898.

    viii.   NORMA WARD b. Jul-15-1899,[469] d. Sep-15-1899,[469] buried in Auburn Community Cemetery, Ritchie Co, WV.[469]

461. **Calvin B. Ward** (264.Mary[7], 139.John[6], 72.John[5], 21.John[4], 6.Hugh[3], 3.John[2], 1.Jean[1]), b. May-18-1860 in West Virginia,[470,123,46] d. 1944,[46] buried in Velva Cemetery, McHenry Co, ND,[134] census 1930 in Bjornson (Minot), McHenry Co, ND, census 1920 in Minneapolis, MN, census 1910 in Bjornson (Minot), McHenry Co, ND, census 1900 in Minneapolis, MN, occupation 1910, 1930 farmer,[211] occupation 1920 laborer,[681] occupation 1900 waiter.[123] He married Jun- 4-1891,[470] **Jessie E. Krouth**, b. Aug- -1870 in Germany,[123,46] d. 1949,[46] buried in Velva Cemetery, McHenry Co, ND,[134] census 1930 in Bjornson (Minot), McHenry Co, ND, census 1920 in Minneapolis, MN, census 1910 in Bjornson (Minot), McHenry Co, ND, census 1900 in Minneapolis, MN, immigrated 1872 or 73,[681,211] naturalized 1898.[681]

Children:

821.   i.   RUTH M. WARD b. Feb- -1892.

462. **Elizabeth Lucinda Gaston**, also known as Lucinda Gaston,[cmlxiii[963]] [Identified in father's obituary as Mrs. Elizabeth L. Nutter. Her name has also appeared as Lucinda Elizabeth Gaston, although her own family Bible with husband Josiah Porter Nutter identifies her as Elizabeth Lucinda. (per Lane Bush Nutter, grandson)] (265.Samuel[7], 139.John[6], 72.John[5], 21.John[4], 6.Hugh[3], 3.John[2], 1.Jean[1]), b. Jun-16-1850 in Doddridge Co, (W)VA,[963,cmlxiv[964]] d. Mar-27-1939,[373] resided 1911, 34 in Auburn, Ritchie Co, WV,[765,502] census 1920 in Stone Lick, Auburn, Gilmer Co, WV, census 1870, 1900, 1910 in Troy District, Gilmer Co, WV. She married Jan-30-1868 in Doddridge Co, WV,[cmlxv[965],354] ["Doddridge County Marriages" compiled by Wes Cochran reports marriage date as Jan 27 1868.], **Josiah Porter Nutter**,[cmlxvi[966],966] census name Isaiah Nutter,[cmlxvii[967]] b. ca 1844 in Marion Co, (W)VA,[cmlxviii[968],354] (son of John B. Nutter and Mary Hart), d. Jun- 1-1895,[cmlxix[969]] census 1870 in Troy District, Gilmer Co, WV, census 1850, 1860 in Doddridge Co, (W)VA.

1870 Census, Gilmer Co, WV (Troy District), enumerated on Jul 20 1870:
Josiah Nutter, 26, farmer; Elizabeth L. Nutter, 19; Florence C. Nutter, 6 months; Thomas J. Hart, 12; Phineas R. Thorp, 20, farmer; Sarah Thorp, 20.

(Note: Relationships not given. The Thomas J. Hart in this household may be the one who married Nancy Catherine Hileman in 1879.)

Children:
    i.   FLORENCE CORA NUTTER b. Oct-29-1869,[373] d. Oct-18-1887 in Gilmer Co, WV,[cmlxx[970]] [Horn Creek], census 1870 in Troy District, Gilmer Co, WV.
822.   ii.   PORTER GASTON NUTTER b. Oct- 6-1871.
823.   iii.   MARSHALL FIELD NUTTER b. Apr- 7-1874.
824.   iv.   IRA BRENTON NUTTER b. Aug- 6-1876.
    v.   HARLEY W. NUTTER b. Feb-14-1880,[373] d. Jun-24-1884.[373]
    vi.   BERTIE FORD NUTTER b. Oct- -1883,[154] d. Jun-11-1884 at Horn Creek, Ritchie Co, WV,[cmlxxi[971]] cause of death whooping cough.[432]
825.   vii.   JOSIAH BLAINE NUTTER b. Sep-16-1884.
826.   viii.   MARY ELIZABETH NUTTER b. Sep- 1-1889.

463. **Sarah Jane Gaston** (265.Samuel[7], 139.John[6], 72.John[5], 21.John[4], 6.Hugh[3], 3.John[2], 1.Jean[1]), b. Mar-29-1853 in Summers, Doddridge Co, WV,[cmlxxii[972],17] d. Jun-27-1918,[969,17] buried in Pine Grove Cemetery, Berea (Co Rd 7-26), Ritchie Co, WV.[469]

In August 1910, Sarah Gaston Reed moved with five of her children (Belle, Ota, Ethel, Winna and Harvey) to Fairmont, WV. [per daughter Ota in "Genealogy or Family History of John Gaston, Sr."] Also, Samuel Morris Gaston's obituary in April 1911 listed daughter Sarah J. Reed as residing in Fairmont. All references by Ota Reed Fraker to her mother has spelling as "Sara," while all other references are spelled "Sarah."

She married Oct-15-1874 in Doddridge Co, WV,[cmlxxiii[973]] **David Allen Reed**, also known as Allen Reed,[354,17] b. May-11-1853 in Grove, Doddridge Co, WV,[969,17] d. Nov-29-1909,[17,969] buried in Pine Grove Cemetery, Berea (Co Rd 7-26), Ritchie Co, WV,[469] resided 1874 in Ritchie Co, WV.[354]
Children:
827.   i.   LUCY ELIZABETH REED b. Feb- 7-1877.
    ii.   SUSAN BELLE REED, also known as Belle Reed, b. Sep-21-1878 in Berea, Ritchie Co, WV,[cmlxxiv[974]] d. Dec- 8-1958 in Los Angeles, CA.[373]

A Registered Nurse, she practiced her profession in Fairmont, WV, from 1912 to 1920, when she moved to Los Angeles. She had no children.

She married Apr- 5-1922,[373] Sellers E. Jessups, d. Nov-11-1957.[969]
828.   iii.   SAMUEL BOYD REED b. Apr-17-1880.
829.   iv.   OTA LEE REED b. Feb-28-1882.
830.   v.   CECIL ALEXANDER REED b. May- 6-1884.
831.   vi.   HENRY G. REED b. Mar-30-1887.
    vii.   ETHEL JANE REED b. Mar-11-1889 in Berea, Ritchie Co, WV,[969] resided in Los Angeles, CA,[969] resided formerly in Fairmont, Marion Co, WV,[969] resided until Aug 1910 in Ritchie Co, WV,[969] occupation stenographer,[969] no children from this person[969.] She married Aug-12-1934,[969] Morgan T. Olson.
832.   viii.   WINNA FERN REED b. Mar-21-1892.
833.   ix.   HARVEY ALLEN REED b. Jun-25-1894.

464. **Susan Gaston** (265.Samuel[7], 139.John[6], 72.John[5], 21.John[4], 6.Hugh[3], 3.John[2], 1.Jean[1]), b. Jan- 6-1856 in Doddridge Co, (W)VA,[963,cmlxxv[975],cmlxxvi[976]] d. Dec- 3-1890 in Berea, Ritchie Co, WV,[17] [Inscription does not give birthdate, but states age at death on Dec 3 1890 as 34y 10m 27d. Previous reporting of death date of Dec 31 1890 resulted from a misreading of the headstone.], buried in Gaston-Hart Cemetery, Upper Run, Summers, Doddridge Co, WV.[17] She married May-26-1883 in Doddridge Co, WV,[975] **David Haynes Jones**, b. Nov-14-1853 in Marion Co, WV,[975,373,17] (son of Elias Jones and Sarah

Ann Summers), d. Jul-30-1930 in Berea, Ritchie Co, WV,[17] buried in Pine Grove Cemetery, Berea (Co Rd 7-26), Ritchie Co, WV.[17,469]

Children:

834.   i.   MINNIE ELIZABETH JONES b. Aug- 4-1884.
835.   ii.   ERNEST ELIAS "ERNIE" JONES b. Mar-27-1887.
836.   iii. JAMES MORRIS JONES b. Mar- 5-1888.
837.   iv. HOWARD HARRISON JONES b. Jan-23-1889.
838.   v.   BERT DAVID JONES b. Jul-31-1890.

465. **Hannah Elizabeth Gaston** (265.Samuel[7], 139.John[6], 72.John[5], 21.John[4], 6.Hugh[3], 3.John[2], 1.Jean[1]), b. Jul- 6-1858 in Summers, Doddridge Co, WV,[853,398] [But death record states birth date as Jun 27 1858, at Summers.], d. Sep-17-1938 in Glenville, Gilmer Co, WV,[398] buried in Woodford Cemetery, near Glenville, Gilmer Co, WV,[398] resided in Glenville, Gilmer Co, WV,[398] resided 1911 in Revel, Gilmer Co, WV.[765] She married Apr-14-1877 in Doddridge Co, WV,[cmlxxvii[977],cmlxxviii[978]] **Asberoy Stephen Britton**, also known as Stephen A. Britton,[395,396] b. Apr-27-1850 in Monongalia Co, (W)VA,[354,190] [Obituary states birth date as Apr 27 1850. But reported age at death of 70y 10m 27d would put birth on Apr 25 1850, which is probably incorrect. Age at time of Apr 14 1877 marriage given as 26, which would be correct since his 27th birthday was later in the month. Daughter Winnie's death certificate states his birthplace as Pennsylvania.] (son of Horatio Britton and Elizabeth Husk), d. Mar-24-1921 near Revel, Gilmer Co, WV,[cmlxxix[979]] [presumably near Auburn, Ritchie Co], census 1900 in Gilmer Co, WV,[964] census 1850, 1860 in Monongalia Co, (W)VA,[146] occupation farmer.

Children:

839.   i.   LUTHER SHERMAN BRITTON b. Jan-17-1878.
      ii.   WINNIE ODA BRITTON b. Dec-11-1880 in West Virginia,[cmlxxx[980]] d. Feb-28-1928 in Parkersburg, Wood Co, WV,[398,969] buried in Mt. Olivet Cemetery, Parkersburg, WV,[398] never married[398,969].
840.   iii. CHARLES WESLEY BRITTON b. Jul-19-1882.
841.   iv. ZEBIDEE WARNER BRITTON b. Feb- 9-1887.
      v.   MINNIE ALICE BRITTON, also known as Alice Britton,[778] b. Aug-10-1890,[969] d. Oct-10-1954,[969] resided in Charleston, Kanawha Co, WV, resided 1938 in Glenville, Gilmer Co, WV,[778] occupation Registered Nurse, Gilmer Co Health Dept, never married.
842.   vi. DEWITT TALMADGE BRITTON b. Jun-17-1892.
843.   vii. EVA MAUDE BRITTON b. Aug-27-1897.

466. **Columbia Gaston** (265.Samuel[7], 139.John[6], 72.John[5], 21.John[4], 6.Hugh[3], 3.John[2], 1.Jean[1]), b. Feb-15-1861 in Virginia (now West Virginia),[cmlxxxi[981]] d. Oct-16-1946,[969] buried in Carthage Gap Church Cem, Athens Co, OH,[981] resided 1911 in Spencer, Roane Co, WV,[765] census 1900 in New Milton District, Doddridge Co, WV. She married[cmlxxxii[982]] Nov-29-1882 in Doddridge Co, WV,[cmlxxxiii[983],354] **Floyd Wirt Chapman**, also known as Wirt Chapman, b. Nov-29-1860 in West Virginia,[982] (son of David Maxfield Chapman and Ellen Costilow), d. Mar-30-1955,[982] [But Ota Reed Fraker reports date as Mar 31 1955.], buried in Carthage Gap Church Cem, Athens Co, OH, census 1900 in New Milton District, Doddridge Co, WV, census 1870 in Union District, Ritchie Co, WV.

Floyd: Uncle of Clinton Burdett.[981]

Children:

      i.   LEONA MAE CHAPMAN b. Dec-22-1883, d. May- 6-1967, buried in Carthage Gap Church Cem, Athens Co, OH, never married.
844.   ii.   LAURA ELIZABETH CHAPMAN b. Feb-21-1885.
      iii. BRUCE GASTON CHAPMAN b. Jul-10-1887 in Doddridge Co, WV, d. Apr-21-1966, buried in Carthage Gap Church Cem, Athens Co, OH, no children from this person[982.] He married (1) Aug-18-1918, Anna Belle Wilson, d. Feb- 5-1953, buried in Carthage Gap Church Cem, Athens Co, OH. He married (2) Helen Elsie Gillaghy, b. Mar- 3-1907,[982,592] d. Feb-14-1988,[592] resided in Arroyo Grande, San Luis Obispo Co, CA.[cmlxxxiv[984]]

Helen: Originally from California, where she returned following husband Bruce Chapman's death in 1966.[982]

845. iv. EMMA GRACE CHAPMAN b. May-31-1889.
      v. LESTER MAXFIELD CHAPMAN b. Nov-20-1891, d. Jun-10-1980, no children from this person. He married May-15-1919, Helen Annette McCloud, b. Jul-26-1888, d. Apr-27-1970.

      Helen: Last name may be Cloud.

      vi. FAYE MARIE CHAPMAN, also known as Metta Faye Chapman, b. Aug- 7-1894, d. Feb-5-1949. She married Dec- 3-1933, no children from this marriage, Daniel Wesley Ross, b. Jul- 5-1901, d. Feb-18-1988.
846. vii. PALBIE GALE CHAPMAN b. Aug-10-1896.
847. viii. HARLEY HALL CHAPMAN b. Oct-14-1900.
848. ix. MAJEL ELLEN CHAPMAN b. Feb- 3-1905.

467. **Morris Samuel Gaston** (265.Samuel[7], 139.John[6], 72.John[5], 21.John[4], 6.Hugh[3], 3.John[2], 1.Jean[1]), b. Feb- 9-1863 in Doddridge Co, (W)VA,[190,17,cmlxxxv[985]] d. Jul-31-1951 in Oxford, Doddridge Co, WV,[cmlxxxvi[986],700,356] buried in South Fork Bapt Church Cem, Oxford, Doddridge Co, WV,[17,190,985] resided in Oxford, Doddridge Co, WV.[190] He married Sep-18-1895 in Doddridge Co, WV,[cmlxxxvii[987],354,433,969] [Obituary of Hattie Adams Gaston erroneously states the date of her marriage to Morris Samuel Gaston as 1898. Doddridge County marriage records show that they were married in 1895.], **Hattie Idell Adams**,[190] b. Jul-25-1877 in Summers, Doddridge Co, WV,[190,cmlxxxviii[988],17,cmlxxxix[989]] (daughter of Joshua A. Adams and Sarah Elizabeth Woofter), d. Nov-17-1964 in Weirton, Hancock Co, WV,[17,190,989] buried in South Fork Bapt Church Cem, Oxford, Doddridge Co, WV,[17,989] resided in Weirton, Hancock Co, WV,[190] resided formerly in West Union, Doddridge Co, WV,[190] census 1930 in Southwest District, Doddridge Co, WV. Morris Samuel Gaston and Hattie Adams had no children of their own, but raised from infancy Lenora Squires after the death of her mother Lenora Bird Adams Squires, who was Morris Samuel Gaston's first cousin once removed. The 1930 Census of Doddridge County, Southwest District, shows Lenore Squires, age 12, as a "lodger" in the household of Morris S. Gaston and his wife Hattie, while the 1920 Census there shows Leonore Squires, age 2 yrs 2 mo, as a "2nd cousin."

      Children:
849. i. LENORA SQUIRES GASTON (foster) b. Oct-20-1917.

468. **John William Law** (266.Deborah[7], 139.John[6], 72.John[5], 21.John[4], 6.Hugh[3], 3.John[2], 1.Jean[1]), b. Aug- -1846 in Harrison Co, (W)VA,[496] d. 1873 in Colorado,[496] census 1870 in Union District, Ritchie Co, WV. He married[396] Oct-17-1868 in Ritchie Co, WV,[cmxc[990]] **Mary Caroline Lough**, also known as Carrie Lough,[396] census name Caroline,[577] b. Mar-28-1849 in Ritchie Co, (W)VA,[398,46,473,419] (daughter of Nimrod Lough and Elizabeth Francis Butcher), d. Apr-25-1931 in Clarksburg, Harrison Co, WV,[398,46] buried in Brick Church (7th Day Baptist) Cemetery, Lost Creek, Harrison Co, WV,[230] resided in Clarksburg, Harrison Co, WV,[398] [419 E. Main St.], resided 1882 in Harrison Co, WV,[419] census 1880 in Grant District, Harrison Co, WV, census 1870 in Union District, Ritchie Co, WV.

1870 Census, Ritchie Co, WV (Union District), enumerated on Jun 16 1870:
John W. Law, 23, farmer; Mary C. Law, 21; Asby S. Law, age 9 months (born in August); Lovary I. Lough (female), 8.

      Children:
850. i. ASBY STEELE LAW[494] b. Aug-17-1869.

469. **Francis Marion Law**, also known as Marion F. Law,[345,809] (266.Deborah[7], 139.John[6], 72.John[5], 21.John[4], 6.Hugh[3], 3.John[2], 1.Jean[1]), b. Sep-15-1848 in Ritchie Co, (W)VA,[cmxci[991],809] d. Jul-18-1916,[cmxcii[992],991] buried in Lawford Cemetery, Ritchie Co, WV,[469] [Name on headstone: F. M. Law.], resided in Lawford, Ritchie Co, WV.[992]

He married[484] (1) Sep-19-1869 in Ritchie Co, WV,[cmxciii[993]] **Phebe Rebecca Mitchell**, also known as Rebecca Mitchell,[484,345] b. Feb-17-1850 in Ritchie Co, (W)VA,[469,496] (daughter of Daniel Mitchell and Nancy __), d. Feb-21-1900,[469,484] buried in Lawford Cemetery, Ritchie Co, WV.[469]

He married (2) Mar-31-1901 in Ritchie Co, WV,[cmxciv[994],cmxcv[995]] **Hannah Etta Barr**, also known as Marietta "Eliza" Barr, also known as Etta,[cmxcvi[996]] b. Nov- 3-1860 in Smithville, Ritchie Co, WV,[955,cmxcvii[997],885] (daughter of Alfred Barr and Cynthia Ann Smith), d. Mar-24-1937 in Pullman, Ritchie Co, WV,[955,cmxcviii[998]] buried in Pullman Cemetery, Ritchie Co, WV,[469,992,cmxcix[999],190.]

Children by Phebe Rebecca Mitchell:
851.   i.   OLIVE B. LAW b. ca 1870.
      ii.   ROSE LUELLA LAW, census name Ella Law,[809] b. Oct- -1872,[809,473] resided 1916 in Burnt House, Ritchie Co, WV.[765] She married[941] Oct-22-1911 in Ritchie Co, WV,[m[1000]] Ulysses Grant Bonnett, b. ca 1865 in Lewis Co, WV,[473] resided 1911 in Ritchie Co, WV.[473]
852.   iii. ORA ALICE LAW b. 1873.
853.   iv. ALVA A. LAW b. Jan- -1876.
      v.   HOWARD GASTON LAW b. Aug-30-1880 in Auburn, Ritchie Co, WV,[419,236,46] d. Jun-17-1961 in Weston, Lewis Co, WV,[236,46] buried in Stalnaker Cemetery, Glenville, Gilmer Co, WV,[236,mi[1001]] resided in Clarksburg, Harrison Co, WV,[236] resided 1916, 1946 in Burnt House, Ritchie Co, WV,[765,419] resided 1945 in Glenville, Gilmer Co, WV,[436] census 1920, 1930 in Spruce Creek (Auburn), Ritchie Co, WV,[mii[1002],miii[1003]] occupation school teacher.[236] He married (1) Mar-18-1911 in Gilmer Co, WV,[miv[1004]] Lillie G. Reynolds, b. Jul- 1-1884 in Gilmer Co, WV,[398,46] (daughter of Stephen W. Reynolds and Barbara E. Ward), d. Jan-20-1945 in Glenville, Gilmer Co, WV,[398,46] buried in Stalnaker Cemetery, Glenville, Gilmer Co, WV,[1001] resided in Glenville, Gilmer Co, WV,[398] census 1920, 1930 in Spruce Creek (Auburn), Ritchie Co, WV.[1002,1003]

          1920 Census, Ritchie Co, WV (Murphy District, Spruce Creek), enumerated in Feb 1920:
          Howard G. Law, 39, farmer; wife Lilly G, 35; adopted son Earl, 8.

          1930 Census, Ritchie Co, WV (Murphy District), enumerated on Apr 23 1930:
          Howard G. Law, 49, public school teacher, age 30 at first marriage; wife Lillie G, 45, age 26 at first marriage; adopted son Earl, 18, laborer at County Roads

          He married (2) Apr-11-1946 in Clarksburg, Harrison Co, WV,[mv[1005]] Lillie Gertrude Crites, also known as L. Gertrude Crites,[mvi[1006]] also known as Lillian,[228] also known as Gertie,[592] b. Jun- -1894 in Tanner, Gilmer Co, WV,[419] [Birth date given as Jun 8 1894 in marriage record, but Jun 9 1894 in SSDI entry.] (daughter of Joab Crites and Eunice Hinkle), d. May- -1981,[592] resided in Anmoore, Harrison Co, WV,[592] resided 1946 in Clarksburg, Harrison Co, WV.[419]
      vi. ANNA LAW b. Mar- 1-1887,[592,809,473] d. Jan- -1980,[592] resided in Burnt House, Ritchie Co, WV.[765,592] She married[941] Sep-15-1907 in Ritchie Co, WV,[473] Stephen J. Reynolds, b. ca 1882 in Gilmer Co, WV.[473]

Children by Hannah Etta Barr:
      vii. AUDLEY PALL LAW b. Jan-22-1902 at Spruce Creek (Auburn), Ritchie Co, WV,[mvii[1007],992,469] d. Mar-30-1903,[469] buried in Lawford Cemetery, Ritchie Co, WV.[469]

470. **Hannah Law** (266.Deborah[7], 139.John[6], 72.John[5], 21.John[4], 6.Hugh[3], 3.John[2], 1.Jean[1]), b. Nov- 9-1850 in Ritchie Co, (W)VA,[496] d. Aug- 8-1912,[484,46] buried in Lawford Cemetery, Ritchie Co, WV.[469] She married Oct-31-1872 in Ritchie Co, WV,[473,484,496] **William J. Huff**, b. Jun-14-1844 in Harrison Co,

(W)VA,[mviii[1008],473,46] (son of Benjamin Huff and Matilda __), d. Jun-12-1916,[46] buried in Lawford Cemetery, Ritchie Co, WV,[469,1008] military WPA - G.A.R. (Civil War).[469,1008]

      Children:

        i.   CECIL HUFF[765,765,521,496] d. bef Dec 1974.[521]

        ii.   JENNIE MYRTLE HUFF[521,496] b. ca 1880,[477] d. Aug-12-1967 in Ritchie Co, WV,[477] buried in Elkview Masonic Cemetery, Clarksburg, Harrison Co, WV.[462] She married[961] Lewis F. Ehret,[961] b. Dec-24-1874 in Berea, Ritchie Co, WV,[mix[1009]] (son of John Ehret and Elizabeth A. Law), d. Apr-21-1958,[1009] buried (mausoleum) at Elkview Masonic Cemetery, Clarksburg, Harrison Co, WV.[462,1009]

  854.   iii. DORSEY ELDEN HUFF b. Oct- 4-1882.

471. David Guthrie Law (266.Deborah[7], 139.John[6], 72.John[5], 21.John[4], 6.Hugh[3], 3.John[2], 1.Jean[1]), b. Apr-3-1853 in Ritchie Co, (W)VA,[496,46] d. Aug-19-1921,[496,46] buried in Spruce Creek Baptist Church Cemetery (Co Rd 34), Ritchie Co, WV.[469] He married Apr- 1-1880 in Ritchie Co, WV,[473] **Celia M. Bartlett**, also known as Celia Bartlett, b. Oct-18-1858 in Taylor Co, (W)VA,[398,46] (daughter of James F. Bartlett and Zelda Newlon), d. May-16-1939 at Lawford, Ritchie Co, WV,[398,46] buried in Spruce Creek Baptist Church Cemetery (Co Rd 34), Ritchie Co, WV,[398,469] resided at Lawford, Ritchie Co, WV.[398]

      Children:

  855.   i.   RICHIE D. LAW b. Jun-10-1881.

  856.   ii.   LOUIE DOW LAW b. Apr- 3-1883.

        iii. ERMINE D. LAW b.[496] d. in infancy.[496]

  857.   iv. EVA LORA LAW b. Aug- -1885.

  858.   v.   CARL D. LAW b. Jun-14-1888.

        vi. OMA ZELLA LAW[496] census name Zella O. Law,[809] also known as Oma Grace Law,[588] b. Aug-13-1890 in Ritchie Co, WV,[1007,mx[1010],809,mxi[1011]] d. Jun-17-1990 in Zanesville, Muskingum Co, OH,[1011,1010] resided in Muskingum Co, OH,[1011] resided 1909 at Lawford, Ritchie Co, WV,[588] census 1900 in Union District, Ritchie Co, WV. She married Mar- 6-1909 at Lawford, Ritchie Co, WV,[588] Andrew Jason Goff, b. ca 1885 in Ritchie Co, WV,[588] resided 1909 in Juna, WV.[588]

        vii. ILA PEARL LAW b. Jan-22-1893,[17] d. Jul-27-1896,[17] buried in Spruce Creek Baptist Church Cemetery (Co Rd 34), Ritchie Co, WV.[469]

  859.   viii. SYLVIA MIDA LAW b. Nov-20-1897.

        ix. OCEAN WAVE LAW[496] also known as Wave Law,[862] also known as Ruby Wave Law,[496] b. Jun-17-1902 at Lawford, Ritchie Co, WV,[mxii[1012]] d. Nov- -1904 in Ritchie Co, WV.[mxiii[1013]]

472. Elizabeth Law (266.Deborah[7], 139.John[6], 72.John[5], 21.John[4], 6.Hugh[3], 3.John[2], 1.Jean[1]), b. Jul- 6-1855 in Ritchie Co, (W)VA,[496,mxiv[1014]] d. 1925,[496] census 1900 in DeKalb District, Gilmer Co, WV. She married[496] Nov- 7-1881 in Ritchie Co, WV,[473] **James W. Singleton**, b. May- -1851 in Taylor Co, (W)VA,[1014,473] census 1900 in DeKalb District, Gilmer Co, WV.

      Children:

        i.   BERLIN C. SINGLETON b. Dec- -1883,[1014] census 1900 in DeKalb District, Gilmer Co, WV.

        ii.   EARLIE I. SINGLETON b. Mar- -1887,[1014] census 1900 in DeKalb District, Gilmer Co, WV.

        iii. ASBY F. SINGLETON b. Jul- -1891,[1014] census 1900 in DeKalb District, Gilmer Co, WV.

473. Martin Luther Law (266.Deborah[7], 139.John[6], 72.John[5], 21.John[4], 6.Hugh[3], 3.John[2], 1.Jean[1]), b. Jan-2-1858 at Lawford, Ritchie Co, WV,[398] d. Jan- 5-1944 at Lawford, Ritchie Co, WV,[398] buried in Lawford Cemetery, Ritchie Co, WV,[398] resided at Spruce Creek (Auburn), Ritchie Co, WV,[398] occupation farmer, stockman.[398] He married[228] Dec-24-1882 in Ritchie Co, WV,[473] **Mida McKinley**, b. Nov-26-1861 at Pullman, Ritchie Co, WV,[398,46] (daughter of William H. McKinley and Mary J. Pritchard), d. May-14-1934 in Lawford, Ritchie Co, WV,[398,46] buried in Lawford Cemetery, Ritchie Co, WV.[469]

1900 Census, Ritchie Co, WV (Union District), enumerated on Jun 27 1900:

Martin L. Law, 42, b. Jan 1858, farmer, married 17 yrs; wife Mida, 38, b. Nov 1861, mother of 5 children (4 still living); son Clyde O, 16, b. Oct 1863; dau Lura A, 15, b. Jan 1885; son Verner V, 11, b. Sep 1888; son Russell S, 8, b. Oct 1891; son Glenn G, 4, b. Sep 1895; boarder Bertha C. Bartlett, 22, b. Nov 1877, occup servant; boarder William Braden, 30, b. Oct 1869, occup carpenter; boarder Taylor Glover, 25, b. Nov 1874, occup carpenter; boarder Oden Queen, 23, b. Aug 1876, occup carpenter.

1910 Census, Ritchie Co, WV (Union District), enumerated on May 5 1910:
Martin L. Law, 52, farmer, married 27 yrs; wife Mida, 48, mother of 6 children (5 still living); son Clyde O, 26; son Verner V, 21; son Russel L, 18; dau Velmah M, 9; mother Deborah Bartlette, 82, widowed, mother of 10 children (8 still living).

1920 Census, Ritchie Co, WV (Union District, Auburn Precinct #4), enumerated on Feb 3 1920:
M. L. Law, 62, farmer; wife Mida, 58; dau Velma M, 19; son Herman E, 20.

        Children:
        i.   CLYDE O. LAW b. Oct- -1883 in Ritchie Co, WV,[809,473] resided 1914 in Harrison Co, WV,[473] census 1910 in Clarksburg, Harrison Co, WV, census 1900 in Union District, Ritchie Co, WV, occupation high school teacher.[458] He married Jun-24-1914 in Ritchie Co, WV,[473] Maude Lininger, b. ca 1892 in Ritchie Co, WV.[473]
        ii.   LURA ALMA LAW b. Jan- -1885 in Ritchie Co, WV,[809,473] census 1900 in Union District, Ritchie Co, WV. She married Sep-26-1909 in Ritchie Co, WV,[473] Carl Reger, b. ca 1878 in Upshur Co, WV,[473] resided 1909 in San Diego, San Diego Co, CA.[473]
860.   iii. VERNER VADIS LAW b. Sep-16-1888.
        iv. RUSSELL LAW b. Oct- -1891,[809] census 1900 in Union District, Ritchie Co, WV.

        Identified as Russell S. Law in 1900 Census, but Russel L. Law in 1910 Census.

        v.   GLENN GALE LAW b. Sep-12-1895,[17,809] census 1900 in Union District, Ritchie Co, WV.

        "Ritchie County WV Cemeteries through 1993," p. 585, reports a headstone at Lawford Cemetery for Glenn Gale Law, Sep 12 1895 - Jun 25 1897, son of M. L. & Mida Law. But Glenn G. Law, age 4, b. Sep 1895, is found in the 1900 Census as a member of his parents' household.

        vi. VELMA M. LAW, census name Velmah M. Law,[mxv[1015]] b. ca 1901,[1015] census 1910 in Union District, Ritchie Co, WV.

474. **Levi Morris Law**, also known as Morris Law,[493,992,396] (266.Deborah[7], 139.John[6], 72.John[5], 21.John[4], 6.Hugh[3], 3.John[2], 1.Jean[1]), b. Apr-19-1860 in Ritchie Co, (W)VA,[496] d. Dec-20-1935 in Coxs Mills, Gilmer Co, WV,[496] buried in Lawford Cemetery, Ritchie Co, WV,[469] resided in Newberne, Gilmer Co, WV.[493] He married May-18-1883 in Gilmer Co, WV,[496] **Iris Columbia Woodford**, b. 1865 in Gilmer Co, WV,[46] (daughter of Jackson Woodford and Louisa Ellyson), d. Jan-16-1964 in Ritchie Co, WV,[mxvi[1016],46] buried in Lawford Cemetery, Ritchie Co, WV.[469]
        Children:
        i.   IVA V. LAW b. Feb- -1884 in Ritchie Co, WV,[434] resided 1904 in Gilmer Co, WV.[434] She married Feb-28-1904 in Gilmer Co, WV,[434] F. M. Reed, b. ca 1879.[434]
861.   ii.   ROYSTON D. LAW b. Apr- -1886.
        iii. ORMAN D. LAW b. Jun-27-1887,[469] d. Aug-21-1890,[469] buried in Lawford Cemetery, Ritchie Co, WV.[469]
862.   iv. JACKSON WOODFORD LAW b. Feb-26-1888.
863.   v.   ZORA L. LAW b. Aug- 1-1890.
864.   vi. BURLEIGH AUBREY LAW b. Jan-13-1893.
        vii. AUDREY MAE LAW, also known as Audra, b. Sep- -1897.[496] She married in Glenville, Gilmer Co, WV,[496] John William Phillips.
865.   viii. TRACY FOREST LAW b. May-17-1900.

866.   ix.   ARDEN LESTER LAW b. Apr-25-1904.
         x.   MELVA ROXANNA LAW[434,992] also known as Roxana Law,[992] b. ca 1907.[434] She married[992] Nov- 5-1925 in Gilmer Co, WV,[434] no children from this marriage,[992] Lawrence R. Collins,[992] b. Jun-21-1901,[992] [Birth date reported as Jun 10 1901 in SSDI. Name listed as L. Collins.] (son of John Wesley Collins and Jeannettie G. Bartlett), d. Mar- -1978,[592] buried in Mt. Olive Cemetery (new), Rt 47, Burnt House, Ritchie Co, WV,[469] resided in Burnt House, Ritchie Co, WV,[592] resided in Coxs Mills, Gilmer Co, WV.[992]

475. **Newton Law** (266.Deborah[7], 139.John[6], 72.John[5], 21.John[4], 6.Hugh[3], 3.John[2], 1.Jean[1]), b. Feb- -1862 in Ritchie Co, (W)VA,[mxvii[1017],46] d. Aug-25-1925 in Ritchie Co, WV,[496,46] buried in IOOF (Egypt) Cemetery, Cairo, Ritchie Co, WV,[469] resided in Cairo, Ritchie Co, WV,[493,494] census 1900, 1910, 1920 in Grant District, Ritchie Co, WV.

Elected to West Virginia House of Delegates for the 1911 term.[493]

He married (1) Oct-26-1884 in Gilmer Co, WV,[434] **Deskey V. Allman**,[434] also known as Desra Allman,[396] b. ca 1868 in Lewis Co, WV,[434] (daughter of James Madison Allman and Virginia Louisa Wilson), d. bef Aug 1887.[526] He married (2) Aug- 4-1887 in Ritchie Co, WV,[473] **Serusia Clayton**,[398] also known as Serusha Clayton,[473] b. May-26-1866 at Lawford, Ritchie Co, WV,[398,46] [1900 Census, enumerated on Jun 13 1900, shows age as 35 and birth date as May 1865. But death record states May 26 1866.] (daughter of A. A. Clayton and Loraine Baker), d. Aug- 8-1933 in Parkersburg, Wood Co, WV,[398,46] buried in IOOF (Egypt) Cemetery, Cairo, Ritchie Co, WV,[398] census 1900, 1910, 1920 in Grant District, Ritchie Co, WV.

1900 Census, Ritchie Co, WV (Grant District), enumerated on Jun 13 1900:
Newton Law, 38, b. Feb 1862, farmer, married 13 yrs; wife Serusia, 35, b. May 1865, mother of 6 children (all still living); dau Stella M, 11, b. Nov 1888; son Owen B, 10, b. Nov 1889; dau Della A, 7, b. Jun 1892; dau Tossie D, 5, b. Dec 1894; son Icen D, 2, b. Jul 1897; dau Daltie (or Laltie) L, 2 months, b. Mar 1900; boarder Joseph Cunningham, 17, b. Jun 1882, farm laborer.

1910 Census, Ritchie Co, WV (Grant District), enumerated on May 3 1910 at Big Run:
Newton Law, 48, farmer, married 22 yrs (second marriage), farmer; wife Serusia, 43, married 22 yrs (first marriage), mother of 8 children (all still living); dau Stella, 21; son Owen, 20; dau Della, 18; dau Tossie, 15; son Dennis, 12; dau Letha, 10; son Glen, 8; dau Orpha, 5; boarder Henry Layfield, 24, single, teamster in oil field; boarder Harley Rexroad, 28, divorced, teamster in oil field; servant Mattie Boston, 25, single.

1920 Census, Ritchie Co, WV (Grant District), enumerated on Feb 9 1920:
Newton Law, 57, farmer; wife Serusia, 53; dau Stella, 30; son Dennis Ison, 22; son Glenn C, 16; dau Orphia, 14.

         Children by Deskey V. Allman:
867.   i.   JENNINGS VIRGIL LAW b. Feb-17-1886.
         Children by Serusia Clayton:
         ii.   STELLA M. LAW b. Nov- -1888,[1017,46] d. 1959,[46] buried in IOOF (Egypt) Cemetery, Cairo, Ritchie Co, WV,[469] census 1900, 1910, 1920 in Grant District, Ritchie Co, WV. She married ___ Cain.
         iii.   OWEN B. LAW b. Nov- -1889,[1017] census 1900, 1910 in Grant District, Ritchie Co, WV.
         iv.   DELLA A. LAW b. Jun- -1892,[1017] census 1900, 1910 in Grant District, Ritchie Co, WV.
         v.   TOSSIE DARLIE LAW b. Dec- -1894,[1017] census 1900, 1910 in Grant District, Ritchie Co, WV. She married May-30-1918 in Ritchie Co, WV,[996] Olis Clark Hess, b. ca 1896 in Mercer Co, WV,[996] resided 1918 in Ritchie Co, WV.[996]
         vi.   ICEN DENNIS LAW, census name Dennis Ison Law,[mxviii[1018]] census name Dennis Law,[mxix[1019]] census name Icen D. Law,[1017] b. Jul- -1897,[1017] census 1900, 1910, 1920 in Grant District, Ritchie Co, WV.

vii.   LEATHA LORA LAW, census name Daltie L. Law,[1017] census name Letha Law,[1019] b. Mar- 3-1900,[17,1017,1019] d. Feb-23-1914,[17] buried in IOOF (Egypt) Cemetery, Cairo, Ritchie Co, WV,[469] census 1900, 1910 in Grant District, Ritchie Co, WV.

viii.   GLENN C. LAW b. ca 1902,[1019] census 1910, 1920 in Grant District, Ritchie Co, WV.

ix.   ORPHA LAW, census name Orphia Law,[1018] b. ca 1905,[1019] census 1910, 1920 in Grant District, Ritchie Co, WV.

x.   (INFANT SON) LAW b. May- 6-1910,[17] d. May- 6-1910,[17] buried in IOOF (Egypt) Cemetery, Cairo, Ritchie Co, WV.[469]

476.   **William F. E. "Willy" Law**, also known as Willy (or Willie) Law,[473,955,17,mxx[1020],920] (266.Deborah[7], 139.John[6], 72.John[5], 21.John[4], 6.Hugh[3], 3.John[2], 1.Jean[1]), b. Sep-17-1864 in Ritchie Co, WV,[154,46] d. Jan-13-1932 in Ritchie Co, WV,[mxxi[1021],46] buried in Lawford Cemetery, Ritchie Co, WV,[469] [Name on headstone: Willy Law.], census 1900, 10, 20, 30 in Union District, Ritchie Co, WV. He married Aug- 4-1887 in Ritchie Co, WV,[473] **Ida Mae Goff**, b. Dec- 3-1868 at Goffs, Ritchie Co, WV,[154,46] (daughter of Elijah C. Goff and Priscilla Clarissa Bee), d. Apr-13-1945 in Ritchie Co, WV,[474] buried in Lawford Cemetery, Ritchie Co, WV,[469] census 1900, 10, 20, 30 in Union District, Ritchie Co, WV.

1900 Census, Ritchie Co, WV (Union District), enumerated in Jun 1900:
William Law, 35, b. Sep 1864, farmer, married 13 yrs; wife Ida M, 31, b. Dec 1868, mother of 4 children (3 still living); dau Lona O, 11, b. Jul 1888; dau Alta C, 9, b. Feb 1891; dau Murle, 2, b. Jan 1898.

1910 Census, Ritchie Co, WV (Union District, Auburn Precinct), enumerated on May 2 1910:
Willy Law, 44, farmer, married 22 yrs; wife Ida M, 42, mother of 3 children (all still living); dau Lona O, 21; dau Alta C, 19; dau Merle E, 12.

1920 Census, Ritchie Co, WV (Union District), enumerated on Feb 3 1920:
Willy Law, 54, farmer; wife Ida M, 51; dau E. Murle, 22, single.

1930 Census, Ritchie Co, WV (Union District), enumerated on Apr 17 1930:
Willy Law, 65, farmer; wife Ida M, 61.

Children:
i.   HOWARD W. LAW b. Apr- -1887.
868.   ii.   LONA ORPHA LAW b. Jul-12-1888.
iii.   ALTA C. LAW b. Feb-10-1891 at Lawford, Ritchie Co, WV,[mxxii[1022],809,602,17] d. Jul-21-1967 in Monongalia Co, WV,[mxxiii[1023]] buried in IOOF Cemetery, Harrisville, Ritchie Co, WV,[469] resided 1953 in Belington, Barbour Co, WV,[1022] resided 1941 in Cairo, Ritchie Co, WV,[228] resided 1919 at Lawford, Ritchie Co, WV,[602] census 1900, 1910 in Union District, Ritchie Co, WV. She married (1) Oct-29-1919 in Parkersburg, Wood Co, WV,[602] John Jay Morrison, b. Apr- 4-1891 in Butler Co, PA,[398,602,17] (son of Charles A. Morrison and Mary E. Kelley), d. Dec-17-1941 in Cairo, Ritchie Co, WV,[398,17] resided in Cairo, Ritchie Co, WV,[602,398] occupation dentist,[398] buried in IOOF Cemetery, Harrisville, Ritchie Co, WV.[398,469] She married (2) Sep- 9-1953 in Belington, Barbour Co, WV,[1022] Charles Bee Linger, b. Mar- 9-1877 in Weston, Lewis Co, WV,[1022] (son of Nicholas Fairburn Linger and Lucinda Marsh), d. Sep- 7-1962 in Monongalia Co, WV,[mxxiv[1024]] resided 1953 in Terra Alta, Preston Co, WV.[1022]
iv.   EXCEL L. LAW b. May-31-1893 at Lawford, Ritchie Co, WV.[mxxv[1025]]
v.   MERLE E. LAW, census name Murle Law,[809] census name E. Murle Law,[mxxvi[1026]] b. Jan- -1898,[809] census 1900, 1910, 1920 in Union District, Ritchie Co, WV.

477.   **John Alvin T. Sommerville**[497] (267.Susan[7], 139.John[6], 72.John[5], 21.John[4], 6.Hugh[3], 3.John[2], 1.Jean[1]), b. Oct- -1850 in Ritchie Co, (W)VA,[74,498,1006] d. Aug-23-1876,[17] buried in Auburn Community Cemetery, Ritchie Co, WV,[469] census 1870 in Union District, Harrison Co, WV, census 1860 in Ritchie Co, (W)VA. He married Sep-19-1872 in Gilmer Co, WV,[mxxvii[1027]] **Martha F. Brannon**, also known as Mattie F. Brannon,[345] b. ca 1852 in Gilmer Co, (W)VA.[1006]

Children:
869.   i.   ZETA GAY SOMMERVILLE b. Jul- 3-1873.
870.   ii.   ALLENA "ALLIE" SOMMERVILLE b. Aug-18-1875.

478. **Robert O. Sommerville**[497] (267.Susan[7], 139.John[6], 72.John[5], 21.John[4], 6.Hugh[3], 3.John[2], 1.Jean[1]), b. Sep-16-1852 in Auburn, Ritchie Co, WV,[398,473] d. Mar-21-1934 in Auburn, Ritchie Co, WV,[398] buried in Greenlawn Masonic Cemetery, Clarksburg, WV,[398] resided in Auburn, Ritchie Co, WV,[398] resided 1924 in Clarksburg, Harrison Co, WV,[436] census 1870, 1880 in Union District, Ritchie Co, WV, census 1860 in Ritchie Co, (W)VA. He married Nov-22-1877 in Ritchie Co, WV,[mxxviii[1028]] **Rosanna N. Bee**, b. Dec-11-1855 in Doddridge Co, (W)VA,[398,473] (daughter of Benjamin Wilson Bee and Priscilla Hughes), d. May-12-1924 in North View (Clarksburg), Harrison Co, WV,[398] buried in Greenlawn Masonic Cemetery, Clarksburg, WV,[398] census 1870, 1880 in Union District, Ritchie Co, WV [in household of her uncle, Arthur G. Bee].

1900 Census, Ritchie Co, WV (Union District), enumerated in June 1900:
Robert O. Sommerville, 48, b. Dec 1851, farmer, married 22 yrs; wife Rosana, 44, b. Dec 1855, mother of 3 children (all still living); dau Gertie, 17, b. Oct 1882; son Charles W, 8, b. Jul 1891.

Children:
871.   i.   ISA M. SOMMERVILLE[mxxix[1029]] b. ca 1878.
      ii.   GERTIE SOMMERVILLE b. Oct- -1882,[809] census 1900 in Union District, Ritchie Co, WV.
      iii.   CHARLES W. SOMMERVILLE b. Jul- -1891,[809] census 1900 in Union District, Ritchie Co, WV.

479. **Floyd E. Somerville**[191,497] (267.Susan[7], 139.John[6], 72.John[5], 21.John[4], 6.Hugh[3], 3.John[2], 1.Jean[1]), b. Feb-21-1868 in Berea, Ritchie Co, WV,[154,473,809] d. Nov- 2-1943 at Pullman, Ritchie Co, WV,[862] resided in Holbrook, Ritchie Co, WV,[497] census 1870, 1880 in Union District, Ritchie Co, WV, occupation Hope Gas Company (retired).[862] He married May- 6-1900 in Ritchie Co, WV,[473] **Winifred A. Zinn**, also known as Winnie A. Zinn,[809,473] b. Mar- -1881 at Oxford, Doddridge Co, WV,[809,473,190] (daughter of Henry Clay Zinn and Julia Ann Bee), d. Feb-16-1965,[190] buried in South Fork Bapt Church Cem, Oxford, Doddridge Co, WV,[190] resided in Pullman, Ritchie Co, WV.[190]
Children:
      i.   QUEDAR LYNN SOMMERVILLE[996] b. Nov-15-1901,[592] d. Sep- -1968,[592] resided in Dayton, Montgomery Co, OH,[856,592] resided formerly in West Virginia.[604] He married Jun-18-1924 in Ritchie Co, WV,[996] Ada Nell Drummond, b. ca 1904 in Ritchie Co, WV.[996]

480. **Mary Isabel "Bell" Gaston**[190], also known as Isabel Gaston,[396,395] also known as Bell Gaston,[354,433] census name M. Belle,[385] (268.John[7], 139.John[6], 72.John[5], 21.John[4], 6.Hugh[3], 3.John[2], 1.Jean[1]), b. Aug-29-1857 near Summers, Doddridge Co, WV,[190] d. May- 3-1929 in Smithburg, Doddridge Co, WV,[700,356] buried in Archbold Cemetery, Smithburg, Doddridge Co, WV, resided in Smithburg, Doddridge Co, WV,[190] census 1920 in Southwest District, Doddridge Co, WV. She married Nov-26-1874 in Doddridge Co, WV,[mxxx[1030],433] [Obituary of wife erroneously states marriage date as Nov 26 1875.], **Alexander Adams**, also known as Alex Adams,[396] b. May- -1854,[385] d. bef 1929,[191] census 1900, 1920 in Southwest District, Doddridge Co, WV, occupation farmer.[405]
Children:
      i.   ELIZA ALICE ADAMS, also known as Lizzie,[17] census name E. Alice Adams,[385] b. Nov- -1875 in Doddridge Co, WV,[385,mxxxi[1031]] d. bef May 1929,[856] resided 1917 in Oxford, Doddridge Co, WV.[412] She married Jun- 8-1910 in Doddridge Co, WV,[mxxxii[1032]] Marshall Franklin Gray, b. Sep-28-1877 in Oxford, Doddridge Co, WV,[mxxxiii[1033],920,17] (son of John M. Gray and Dora M. Bode), d. Aug-16-1918 in Oxford, Doddridge Co, WV,[mxxxiv[1034],17,356] buried in Oxford Baptist Church Cemetery, Doddridge Co, WV.[17]
872.   ii.   EMMA FRANCES ADAMS b. Dec-27-1877.
873.   iii.   LENORA BIRD ADAMS b. Aug- 7-1880.
874.   iv.   IRA CLINTON ADAMS, SR. b. Jun- 7-1887.

875.   v.   WORTHY EUGENE ADAMS b. Aug-24-1889.

876.   vi.   ETTA O'DELL "ADDIE" ADAMS b. Nov-15-1891.

877.   vii.   ALVA WILMER ADAMS b. Apr-17-1898.

481. **John Irvin Gaston** (268.John[7], 139.John[6], 72.John[5], 21.John[4], 6.Hugh[3], 3.John[2], 1.Jean[1]), b. Jun- 4-1860 in Doddridge Co, WV, resided 1929, 36 in Guysville, Athens Co, OH,[412,mxxxv[1035]] census 1900 in Greenbrier District, Doddridge Co, WV.

Notice in the West Union Herald, Mar 5 1936: "Farms for Sale. Some good farms for sale cheap near Guysville, Ohio, on U.S. Route 50. Come and see them or write J. I. GASTON, Guysville, OH."

He married[191] Nov-30-1882 in Doddridge Co, WV,[mxxxvi[1036]] [Wife's obituary gives marriage date as Nov 30 1883, an apparent error. Online marriage records (identifying him as John O. Gaston) indicate marriage on Nov 30 1882 in Doddridge County. Wes Cochran's "Doddridge County Marriages" (identifying him as John I. Gaston) also show the Nov 30 1882 date.], **Alice Virginia Chapman**, b. Jul-31-1863 in Grove, Doddridge Co, WV,[190] (daughter of David Maxfield Chapman and Ellen Costilow), d. Nov-26-1941 in Guysville, Athens Co, OH,[190] resided in Guysville, Athens Co, OH,[190] census 1900 in Greenbrier District, Doddridge Co, WV, census 1870 in Union District, Ritchie Co, WV.

Alice: Moved with her family from Doddridge Co, WV to Carthage Twp, Athens Co, OH in 1910.[190]

Children:

878.   i.   MINNIE A. GASTON b. Nov-19-1884.

879.   ii.   JAMES LEE GASTON b. Apr- 7-1885.

       iii.   IDA B. GASTON[856] b. Jan-24-1887 in Doddridge Co, WV,[154] d. Nov-30-1887 in Doddridge Co, WV.[mxxxvii[1037],356]

880.   iv.   ELLA MAY GASTON b. Dec- 8-1891.

       v.   CHARLES D. GASTON b. Mar- 2-1894,[592,mxxxviii[1038]] d. Apr- -1982,[592] resided in Tampa, Hillsborough Co, FL,[1010] resided 1941 in Akron, Summit Co, OH,[856] census 1900 in Greenbrier District, Doddridge Co, WV.

       vi.   OKEY M. GASTON b. Aug- -1896,[1038] d. Mar-11-1965 in Athens Co, OH,[693] resided in Athens Co, OH,[693] resided 1941 in Guysville, Athens Co, OH,[856] census 1900 in Greenbrier District, Doddridge Co, WV, never married[693.]

881.   vii.   IRA CLINTON GASTON, SR. b. Mar- 4-1898.

       viii.   MARY ITHA GASTON, also known as Itha Gaston,[1038,856,592] b. Mar-11-1900,[592] d. Sep- -1983,[592] resided in Coolville, Athens Co, OH,[856,mxxxix[1039]] census 1900 in Greenbrier District, Doddridge Co, WV. She married[mxl[1040]] __ Allen.

       ix.   TIDAL WAVE "JAKE" GASTON[mxli[1041]] b. Oct- 7-1902,[592] d. Sep-13-1974 in Athens, Athens Co, OH,[1011,mxlii[1042]] resided in Athens, Athens Co, OH,[856,592,1011.] He married[mxliii[1043]] Florence __, b. Jul-28-1905,[592] d. Jun- -1984,[592] resided in Athens, Athens Co, OH.[592]

       x.   (UNNAMED FEMALE) GASTON b. Sep-19-1905 in Doddridge Co, WV,[mxliv[1044],mxlv[1045]] d. Sep- -1905.

482. **Marion Oscar Gaston** (268.John[7], 139.John[6], 72.John[5], 21.John[4], 6.Hugh[3], 3.John[2], 1.Jean[1]), b. Aug-25-1866 in Oxford, Doddridge Co, WV,[190] d. Sep-10-1956 in Camp Run, Oxford, Doddridge Co, WV,[190,356] buried in South Fork Bapt Church Cem, Oxford, Doddridge Co, WV,[17] resided in Camp Run, Oxford, Doddridge Co, WV,[412,190] census 1900, 1910, 1930 in Southwest District, Doddridge Co, WV.

He was a teacher in Kansas before returning to Doddridge County to care for his mother, sisters and the family farm following the death of his father in 1893.[mxlvi[1046]]

He married Aug-25-1897 in Doddridge Co, WV,[354,484] **Luella Adams**, also known as Ella Adams,[398,502] birth name Lievetta Adams,[mxlvii[1047]] b. Feb- 1-1872 in Oxford, Doddridge Co, WV,[mxlviii[1048],398] (daughter of Joshua A. Adams and Sarah Elizabeth Woofter), d. Apr-15-1949 in Lewis Co, WV,[mxlix[1049],190] [Obituary of Luella Adams Gaston states that she died at her home in Oxford after an illness of 18 months. No death record found for her in Doddridge County, but Lewis County death records (DR 7-132) show that her death occurred in Lewis County, so obituary was in error.], buried in South Fork Bapt Church Cem, Oxford, Doddridge Co, WV,[17,190] resided in Oxford, Doddridge Co, WV,[398] census 1900, 1910, 1930 in Southwest District, Doddridge Co, WV.

Children:

882.   i.   AMY MAE GASTON b. May-21-1898.

883.   ii.   ALPHA LEE GASTON b. Feb- 3-1900.

884.   iii.   ORLEY CARSON GASTON b. Mar-18-1902.

       iv.   VELMA GASTON b. Jan-19-1904 in Camp Run, Oxford, Doddridge Co, WV,[190,46] d. Feb-27-1994 in Harrisville, Ritchie Co, WV,[700,46] buried in South Fork Bapt Church Cem, Oxford, Doddridge Co, WV,[190] resided in Harrisville, Ritchie Co, WV,[190] resided 1974 in Oxford, Doddridge Co, WV,[412] census 1930 in Southwest District, Doddridge Co, WV. She married Oct-7-1939 in Doddridge Co, WV,[ml[1050],191] no children from this marriage, John Ferrell Gray, also known as Ferrell Gray, b. Jun-12-1899,[46] (son of David Wilson Gray and Martha Ellen Leggett), d. Dec-11-1985,[191,46] buried in South Fork Bapt Church Cem, Oxford, Doddridge Co, WV,[17] resided in Oxford, Doddridge Co, WV.[521]

885.   v.   GAIL ADAMS GASTON b. Oct-30-1905.

483. **Francis Enoch Gaston** (268.John[7], 139.John[6], 72.John[5], 21.John[4], 6.Hugh[3], 3.John[2], 1.Jean[1]), b. Mar-13-1868 in Oxford, Doddridge Co, WV,[398,190,17] [Obituary states birth date as Mar 3 1868, but death record and "History of Ritchie County to 1980" (p. 123) show it as Mar 13 1868.], d. Oct-13-1950 in Doddridge Co, WV,[398,356,17] buried in South Fork Bapt Church Cem, Oxford, Doddridge Co, WV,[17,190,398] resided in Harrisville, Ritchie Co, WV,[mlii[1051],398] census 1930 in Southwest District, Doddridge Co, WV, resided 1929 in Oxford, Doddridge Co, WV,[520] occupation farmer.[398]

Francis Enoch Gaston and family spent most of their life on Camp Run in Doddridge Co, WV, moving to Harrisville, WV in 1916 so their children could better attend school.[1051]

He married Aug-13-1893 in Doddridge Co, WV,[354,484,1051] **Mary Virginia Mason**, b. May- 1-1875 in Toll Gate, Ritchie Co, WV,[190,1051] (daughter of Jacob A. Mason and Jane Wilson), d. Nov-27-1961 in Weston, Lewis Co, WV,[190] buried in South Fork Bapt Church Cem, Oxford, Doddridge Co, WV,[17] resided in Harrisville, Ritchie Co, WV,[190] census 1930 in Southwest District, Doddridge Co, WV.

Children:

       i.   ELFA GASTON b. Jul-29-1894 in Doddridge Co, WV,[357] d. Feb-18-1895 in Doddridge Co, WV,[mlii[1052],17] buried in South Fork Bapt Church Cem, Oxford, Doddridge Co, WV.[17]

       ii.   EDGAR GASTON b. Jan-22-1896 in Doddridge Co, WV, d. Jan-22-1896,[17] buried in South Fork Bapt Church Cem, Oxford, Doddridge Co, WV.[17]

886.   iii.   ADA VONDA GASTON b. Nov-29-1904.

       iv.   LYNDON SMITH GASTON b. Jul-24-1908 in Doddridge Co, WV, d. Nov- -1969,[592] buried in South Fork Bapt Church Cem, Oxford, Doddridge Co, WV,[17] resided 1946-69 in Leavittsburg, Trumbull Co, OH, resided 1930 in Doddridge Co, WV.[mliii[1053]] He married no children from this marriage, Lillian E. Kayser, b. May-18-1906 in Linn, Gilmer Co, WV,[190,592,17] (daughter of Scott Kayser and Hattie Farnsworth), d. May- 7-1981 in Warren, Trumbull Co, OH,[190,592,17] buried in South Fork Bapt Church Cem, Oxford, Doddridge Co, WV,[17] resided in Leavittsburg, Trumbull Co, OH,[190,mliv[1054]] resided 1930 in Doddridge Co, WV.[1053]

       v.   (INFANT SON) GASTON b. Jan- 9-1912 in Doddridge Co, WV, d. Jan- 9-1912,[17] buried in South Fork Bapt Church Cem, Oxford, Doddridge Co, WV.[17]

484. **Elizabeth Catherine Gaston**, also known as Eliza,[521,190,354] (268.John[7], 139.John[6], 72.John[5], 21.John[4], 6.Hugh[3], 3.John[2], 1.Jean[1]), b. Dec-26-1872 in Oxford, Doddridge Co, WV,[190] d. Aug-19-1966 in Glen Morgan, Raleigh Co, WV,[190] buried in South Fork Bapt Church Cem, Oxford, Doddridge Co, WV,[17,190] resided in Oxford, Doddridge Co, WV,[521,190] resided 1929 in Parkersburg, Wood Co, WV.[520] She married Sep-23-1896 in Doddridge Co, WV,[mlv[1055],484,354] **Marion Homer Wilson**, also known as Homer Wilson,[191,506] b. Jul-23-1873 in Oxford, Doddridge Co, WV,[190,46] (son of James Kelly Wilson and

Amelia Virginia Griffin), d. Dec- 7-1959 in Parkersburg, Wood Co, WV,[mlvi[1056],46] buried in South Fork Bapt Church Cem, Oxford, Doddridge Co, WV,[17,190] resided in Summers, Doddridge Co, WV,[mlvii[1057]] occupation farmer & carpenter.[1057]

Children:
887. i.   WHEELER SHIRLEY WILSON b. Nov-15-1897.
888. ii. LOUIE ENID WILSON b. May-14-1901.
      iii. AVIS MILDRED WILSON, also known as Mildred,[856,506,412,1057] b. Dec-10-1905 in Doddridge Co, WV, d. Oct- 9-1996 in Parkersburg, Wood Co, WV, buried in Blue Ridge Cemetery, Beckley, WV, resided in Glen Morgan, Raleigh Co, WV,[856] resided 1979 in Beckley, Raleigh Co, WV,[1057] census 1920 in Southwest District, Doddridge Co, WV, occupation music teacher. She married May-24-1947 in Lewisburg, Greenbrier Co, WV,[mlviii[1058]] no children from this marriage,[1057] Clarence Sherman Rule, b. 1898 in Ansted, Fayette Co, WV,[1058] d. May-30-1977.[mlix[1059]]
889. iv. EULA EDITH WILSON b. Oct-12-1910.

485. **John H. Sommerville** (269.Elizabeth[7], 139.John[6], 72.John[5], 21.John[4], 6.Hugh[3], 3.John[2], 1.Jean[1]), b. ca 1853 in Harrison Co, (W)VA.[419,271] He married Sep-10-1874 in Harrison Co, WV,[227] **Elizabeth C. Osborne**, b. ca 1851 in Lewis Co, (W)VA,[227] (daughter of Joseph Osborne and Harriet __), resided 1874 in Harrison Co, WV.[227]

Children:
      i.   FLORA MAY SOMMERVILLE b. Aug-22-1875 in Harrison Co, WV,[398,227,46] d. Jun-30-1957 in Clarksburg, Harrison Co, WV,[398,46] buried in Good Hope Masonic Cemetery, Rt. 19 S, Harrison Co, WV,[398,524] resided in Good Hope, Harrison Co, WV.[398] She married Nov- 3-1892 in Harrison Co, WV,[mlx[1060]] William Sherman Burnside, also known as W. Sherman Burnside,[17] b. 1866 in Harrison Co, WV,[46,227] (son of Isaac N. Burnside and Mary Ann __), d. 1932,[46] buried in Good Hope Masonic Cemetery, Rt. 19 S, Harrison Co, WV.[524]
      ii. ICIE GAY SOMMERVILLE b. Apr- 8-1877 in Harrison Co, WV,[17,537] d. Jan-23-1956,[17] buried in Good Hope Masonic Cemetery, Rt. 19 S, Harrison Co, WV.[524] She married Aug-22-1897 in Harrison Co, WV,[537] Wesley E. Post, b. Jul-11-1874 in Harrison Co, WV,[17,537] (son of Jacob P. Post and Frances __), d. Nov- 4-1967,[17] buried in Good Hope Masonic Cemetery, Rt. 19 S, Harrison Co, WV.[524]

486. **James Wesley Sommerville**, also known as J. Wesley Sommerville,[537] census name Wesley Sommerville,[271] (269.Elizabeth[7], 139.John[6], 72.John[5], 21.John[4], 6.Hugh[3], 3.John[2], 1.Jean[1]), b. ca 1858 in Harrison Co, (W)VA,[227] census 1860 in Harrison Co, (W)VA. He married (1) Feb-19-1880 in Harrison Co, WV,[mlxi[1061]] **Lillie M. Burnside**, also known as Lilly Burnside,[276] b. Mar-22-1864,[17] (daughter of Isaac N. Burnside and Mary Ann __), d. Dec-31-1880 in Harrison Co, WV,[276,mlxii[1062]] cause of death scarlet fever,[276] buried in Old Bethel Church Cem, Good Hope, Harrison Co, WV.[17] He married (2) Dec-24-1882 in Harrison Co, WV,[mlxiii[1063]] **Frances E. McConkey**, b. Nov-24-1864 in Lewis Co, WV,[17,227] (daughter of Jacob McConkey and Mary J. __), d. Aug-24-1897,[17] buried in Old Bethel Church Cem, Good Hope, Harrison Co, WV.[17] He married (3) Dec-25-1898 in Harrison Co, WV,[mlxiv[1064]] **Cora Burnside**, b. ca 1869 in Harrison Co, WV,[537] (daughter of William Burnside and Ruhama Lynch).

Children by Lillie M. Burnside:
      i.   (STILLBORN DAUGHTER) SOMMERVILLE b. Dec-24-1880,[17] d. Dec-24-1880,[17] buried in Old Bethel Church Cem, Good Hope, Harrison Co, WV.[17]
Children by Frances E. McConkey:
      ii. CLARENCE DOYLE SOMMERVILLE b. Jul-10-1884 in Harrison Co, WV,[592,537] d. Dec- -1962.[604] He married Oct-22-1911 in Harrison Co, WV,[537] Zella Williams, b. ca 1885 in Harrison Co, WV,[537] (daughter of G. W. Williams and Della __).
      iii. JAMES BRENNIE SOMMERVILLE b. Dec-28-1890,[17] d. Dec-29-1891,[mlxv[1065]] buried in Old Bethel Church Cem, Good Hope, Harrison Co, WV.[524]

487. **Sarah Adda Sommerville**, also known as Adda Sommerville,[396,17] also known as Addie Sommerville,[398] (269.Elizabeth[7], 139.John[6], 72.John[5], 21.John[4], 6.Hugh[3], 3.John[2], 1.Jean[1]), b. Feb-11-1861 in Harrison Co, (W)VA,[398,964,227] d. Aug-31-1930 in Lost Creek, Harrison Co, WV,[398] buried in Good Hope Masonic Cemetery, Rt. 19 S, Harrison Co, WV,[398,524] census 1930 in Lost Creek, Harrison

Co, WV, census 1900 in Troy District, Gilmer Co, WV. She married Nov- 6-1879 in Harrison Co, WV,[mlxvi][1066] **Lewis A. Law**, census name Louis F. Law,[964] b. May-23-1861 in Harrison Co, (W)VA,[398,964,46,227] (son of James S. Law and Susanna McConkey), d. Jan-19-1924 in Lost Creek, Harrison Co, WV,[398,46] buried in Good Hope Masonic Cemetery, Rt. 19 S, Harrison Co, WV,[524,398] census 1900 in Troy District, Gilmer Co, WV, occupation farmer.[398]

Children:

  i. NORA I. LAW b. Oct- -1880,[964] census 1900 in Troy District, Gilmer Co, WV.

 890. ii. JAMES WESLEY LAW b. May-17-1882.

  iii. OSA E. LAW b. Jan- -1884,[964] census 1900 in Troy District, Gilmer Co, WV.

  iv. IVY GAE LAW, also known as Gay Law,[721] b. Jul-13-1887 in Gilmer Co, WV,[17,964,1006] d. Jul-24-1961,[17] buried in Masonic Memorial Park Cemetery, Crystal Lake (West Union), WV,[721] census 1900 in Troy District, Gilmer Co, WV. She married Jul-12-1911 in Gilmer Co, WV,[mlxvii][1067] William Ivan Rymer, census name Ivan Rymer,[964] b. May- 5-1886 in Gilmer Co, WV,[17,1006] (son of William W. Rymer and Phoebe J. Patton), d. Jul-19-1965,[17] buried in Masonic Memorial Park Cemetery, Crystal Lake (West Union), WV.[721]

  v. ORLA F. LAW b. Mar- -1890,[964] census 1900 in Troy District, Gilmer Co, WV.

  vi. ARGIL G. LAW b. Sep- -1891,[964] census 1900 in Troy District, Gilmer Co, WV.

  vii. AUBREY ELWIN LAW b. May- 4-1896 in Gilmer Co, WV,[592,964,996,46] d. Jan- -1975,[592,46] buried in Good Hope Masonic Cemetery, Rt. 19 S, Harrison Co, WV,[524] resided in Clarksburg, Harrison Co, WV,[604] resided 1931 in Harrison Co, WV,[996] census 1930 in Lost Creek, Harrison Co, WV, census 1900 in Troy District, Gilmer Co, WV. He married May-16-1931 in Ritchie Co, WV,[996] Opal Catherine Watson, b. Feb-23-1898,[592,46,996] d. Jul- -1974,[592,46] buried in Good Hope Masonic Cemetery, Rt. 19 S, Harrison Co, WV,[524] resided in Clarksburg, Harrison Co, WV.

  viii. SELBY G. LAW b. Aug- 9-1898,[592,964] d. Jun-10-1970 in Zanesville, Muskingum Co, OH,[693,592] resided in Zanesville, Muskingum Co, OH,[1010,693] census 1900 in Troy District, Gilmer Co, WV.

488. **Ella J. Sommerville**, census name Elsie J.,[467] (269.Elizabeth[7], 139.John[6], 72.John[5], 21.John[4], 6.Hugh[3], 3.John[2], 1.Jean[1]), b. 1871,[46] d. 1956,[46] buried in Good Hope Masonic Cemetery, Rt. 19 S, Harrison Co, WV.[17,524] She married Aug-19-1894 in Harrison Co, WV,[227] **Claudius Gaston**, also known as Claude Gaston,[17,374,398] b. Oct- 3-1869 in Harrison Co, WV,[mlxviii][1068],398,467 (son of Enoch Gaston and Laura T. Sheets), d. Apr-17-1948 at Lost Creek, Harrison Co, WV,[mlxix][1069],276,17 [Death date of Feb 17 1948 reported elsewhere is incorrect.], buried in Good Hope Masonic Cemetery, Rt. 19 S, Harrison Co, WV,[mlxx][1070] resided at Lost Creek, Harrison Co, WV,[398] census 1880 in Grant District, Harrison Co, WV, occupation farmer.[398] Ella J. Sommerville and Claudius Gaston were double cousins, in that they were both second cousins (both were great-grandchildren of John Gaston, Jr. (b. 1752 in NJ)) and also fourth cousins (both were great-great-great-grandchildren of John Smith (b. 1699)).

Children:

  i. EVA IRENE GASTON b. Sep-13-1897 in Harrison Co, WV,[1068,17] d. Nov- 1-1977,[17] buried in Good Hope Masonic Cemetery, Rt. 19 S, Harrison Co, WV,[17,524] census 1920 in Grant District, Harrison Co, WV. She married Aug-1-1918 in Harrison Co, WV,[419] Ora Lester Law, census name O. Lester Law, b. Aug-24-1896 in Harrison Co, WV,[17,419] (son of William Jesse Law and Lucy Alexander Freeman), d. Oct- 6-1963,[17] buried in Good Hope Masonic Cemetery, Rt. 19 S, Harrison Co, WV,[17,524] census 1920 in Grant District, Harrison Co, WV, military Pvt, U.S. Army, WW I (STU Army Training Corps).[17]

  ii. PARLEY FORD GASTON b. Jan-16-1900,[46] d. May-10-1978 in Wood Co, WV,[mlxxi][1071],46 buried in Good Hope Masonic Cemetery, Rt. 19 S, Harrison Co, WV,[17,524] resided in Belpre, Washington Co, OH.[592] He married Jun-10-1925 in Marion Co, WV,[mlxxii][1072] Mildred Elizabeth Marple, b. Jan- 7-1901,[592,46] (daughter of Theodore Marple and Rosetta Thomas), d. Sep-30-1986 in Wood Co, WV,[mlxxiii][1073],46 buried in Good Hope Masonic Cemetery, Rt. 19 S, Harrison Co, WV,[17,524] resided in Belpre, Washington Co, OH.[592]

  iii. MILDRED ELIZABETH GASTON, also known as Claud Gaston,[374] b. Sep-21-1909 in Harrison Co, WV,[419,592] d. Mar- 7-1989,[592] buried in Good Hope Masonic Cemetery, Rt. 19 S, Harrison Co, WV,[17,524] resided 1948 in Pittsburgh, Allegheny Co, PA,[748] resided 1936 in Good Hope, Harrison

Co, WV.[419] She married Jun-11-1936 in Grafton, Taylor Co, WV,[mlxxiv][1074] Kirk Casto Tallman, b. Nov-1-1907 in Roane Co, WV,[419,17] (son of O. Roy Tallman and Mary Lillian Campbell), d. Nov- 9-1959,[17] buried in Good Hope Masonic Cemetery, Rt. 19 S, Harrison Co, WV,[17,524] resided 1936 in Kincheloe (Jane Lew), Harrison Co, WV.[419]

iv.   FLORA JANE GASTON b. Sep- 4-1913 in Harrison Co, WV, d. Feb- -1992,[592] buried in Good Hope Masonic Cemetery, Rt. 19 S, Harrison Co, WV,[17] resided in Pittsburgh, Allegheny Co, PA.[592] She married Dec-18-1939, John Mason Wolverton, b. Nov-18-1914,[592] d. Nov- -1983,[592] buried in Good Hope Masonic Cemetery, Rt. 19 S, Harrison Co, WV,[17] residence in Clarksburg, Harrison Co, WV.[592]

489. **Lucy E. Taylor** (272.John[7], 140.Deborah[6], 72.John[5], 21.John[4], 6.Hugh[3], 3.John[2], 1.Jean[1]), b. Sep- 6-1854 in Lewis Co, (W)VA,[398,46] d. Oct- 9-1928 near Jane Lew, Lewis Co, WV,[398,46] buried in Broad Run Bapt Ch Cem, Jane Lew, Lewis Co, WV.[17,398] She married Nov- 6-1870, **William R. Neely**, b. Sep-23-1848,[46] d. Feb-11-1921,[46] buried in Broad Run Bapt Ch Cem, Jane Lew, Lewis Co, WV.[17]
Children:
891.   i.   GUINN NEELY b. Sep-20-1871.
892.   ii.   GEORGE W. NEELY b. Nov- 6-1875.
893.   iii. JOHN HOWARD NEELY b. Jul-23-1879.
894.   iv.   ETHEL NEELY b. Feb-26-1887.

490. **William Grant Taylor** (272.John[7], 140.Deborah[6], 72.John[5], 21.John[4], 6.Hugh[3], 3.John[2], 1.Jean[1]), b. Jul-1-1869,[17] d. Apr-23-1944,[17] buried in Broad Run Bapt Ch Cem, Jane Lew, Lewis Co, WV.[17] He married Sep- 9-1890, **Laura Druzilla Davisson**, b. Mar- 5-1866,[17] d. Jan-29-1935,[17] buried in Broad Run Bapt Ch Cem, Jane Lew, Lewis Co, WV.[17]
Children:
i.   BERTIE IVY TAYLOR b. Jun-15-1891, d. Feb-11-1894, buried in Broad Run Bapt Ch Cem, Jane Lew, Lewis Co, WV.
895.   ii.   LULA JESSIE TAYLOR b. Apr-12-1893.
896.   iii. GRACE IRENE TAYLOR b. Jul-11-1895.
iv.   OPAL MERL TAYLOR b. Feb-16-1898, d. Jul-28-1988. She married Nov-24-1960, no children from this marriage, Everett Clayton Zinn, b. Jul-27-1893,[592] d. Feb- 2-1982,[592] buried in Broad Run Bapt Ch Cem, Jane Lew, Lewis Co, WV, resided in Jane Lew, Lewis Co, WV,[592] occupation minister.
897.   v.   RUFUS DAVISSON TAYLOR b. Sep- 1-1900.
898.   vi.   HARLEY GRANT TAYLOR b. Apr-27-1905.

491. **Ella Nora Taylor** (272.John[7], 140.Deborah[6], 72.John[5], 21.John[4], 6.Hugh[3], 3.John[2], 1.Jean[1]), b. Jan-28-1874, d. Mar- 6-1951, buried in Broad Run Bapt Ch Cem, Jane Lew, Lewis Co, WV.[17] She married Apr-29-1896, **Asbury Harper Reed**, b. Sep-18-1871 in Upshur Co, WV,[398] (son of Nelson Reed and Methany Jane Tenney), d. Jul-21-1954 in Weston, Lewis Co, WV,[398] buried in Broad Run Bapt Ch Cem, Jane Lew, Lewis Co, WV,[398] resided in Jane Lew, Lewis Co, WV,[398] occupation farmer.[398]
Children:
899.   i.   MADGE REED b. Apr- 5-1904.
900.   ii.   BERTIE REED b. 1906.

492. **Gustavius Adolphus Corbin** (273.Nancy[7], 140.Deborah[6], 72.John[5], 21.John[4], 6.Hugh[3], 3.John[2], 1.Jean[1]), b. Jul-22-1846, d. Oct-14-1934, buried in Hume, Bates County, Missouri.

Gustavius A. Corbin and Harriett had the misfortune to lose 3 children in infancy. Harriett died soon after. Gustavius remarried and had 5 additional children.

He married (1) Jan-18-1872, **Harriett M. McDonald**, b. 1844. He married (2) **Margaret Lincoln Shockey**, b. 1860, d. Feb-13-1946.
Children by Margaret Lincoln Shockey:
901.   i.   CATHERINE "KATY" CORBIN b. 1884.

ii. (SON) CORBIN d. one month old.
902. iii. OLIVER GUSTAVIUS CORBIN.
903. iv. IVAN SHOCKEY CORBIN.
v. JOHN BYRON CORBIN d. 198_.

493. **Rebecca Ann Corbin** (273.Nancy[7], 140.Deborah[6], 72.John[5], 21.John[4], 6.Hugh[3], 3.John[2], 1.Jean[1]), b. Sep-15-1848 in Charleston, Kanawha Co, WV,[396] d. Aug- 7-1919, buried in Clermont Cemetery, Eldora, Marion Co, WV. She married Dec-18-1871, **Robert L. Janes**, b. Jan-20-1844 in Taylor Co, (W)VA,[363,396] d. Sep-16-1890,[17] buried in Janes Mem Methodist Church Cem, Boothsville, Taylor Co, WV.[17]

Children:
904. i. ZANA B. JANES b. Nov-22-1872.
ii. LOUIS TAYLOR JANES b. Jul-21-1875, d. Sep- 8-1959, buried in Woodlawn Cemetery, Fairmont, Marion Co, WV. He married Dec-22-1897, Ida M. Benson, b. Sep-12-1879, d. Apr-22-1950, buried in Woodlawn Cemetery, Fairmont, Marion Co, WV.
905. iii. HOWARD MARTIN JANES b. Feb-25-1877.

494. **Joseph Taylor Corbin** (273.Nancy[7], 140.Deborah[6], 72.John[5], 21.John[4], 6.Hugh[3], 3.John[2], 1.Jean[1]), b. Jul- 1-1850, d. Dec- 9-1922. He married Mar- 9-1879, **Sabra Ellen McDonald**, b. Sep-10-1856, d. Mar-28-1921.

Children:
906. i. JOHN ELDON CORBIN b. Jan-21-1880.
907. ii. NORA PEARL CORBIN b. Jan-19-1888.

495. **Martha Columbia (twin) Corbin** (273.Nancy[7], 140.Deborah[6], 72.John[5], 21.John[4], 6.Hugh[3], 3.John[2], 1.Jean[1]), b. Apr-20-1855 in Harrison Co, WV, d. Nov- 2-1938, census 1880 in Jackson Co, WV. She married (1) Feb-25-1875, **William Hill Maddox** (See marriage to number 444). William Hill Maddox and Martha Columbia Corbin were second cousins by virtue of both being great-grandchildren of John Gaston Jr (1752-1829) and Anna Davisson.

She married (2) Jan-8-1920, **Columbus Wood**.
Children by William Hill Maddox:
(See marriage to number 444)

496. **Mary Virginia (twin) Corbin** (273.Nancy[7], 140.Deborah[6], 72.John[5], 21.John[4], 6.Hugh[3], 3.John[2], 1.Jean[1]), b. Apr-20-1855 in Harrison Co, WV, d. Jul- 1-1935. She married (1) Sep-24-1874, **John Henry Faber**, b. Jun-18-1847, d. Oct- 6-1921. She married (2) 1928, **James H. Kay**.
Children by John Henry Faber:
908. i. ROBERT HARLAN FABER b. Sep-30-1875.
ii. DENNIS B. FABER b. Nov- 2-1876, d. Nov-17-1878.
909. iii. HIRAM OLIVER FABER b. Mar-20-1878.
910. iv. HUBERT C. FABER b. Mar- 2-1880.
911. v. HEDGEMAN TAYLOR FABER b. Sep-16-1881.
912. vi. ONA BELLE FABER b. Mar- 2-1883.
913. vii. SHELLY OSHEL FABER b. May- 9-1885.
914. viii. GEORGE BENNET FABER b. Feb-27-1887.
915. ix. LINNIE ERIE FABER b. Oct-27-1888.
916. x. HAUNTIE HADEN FABER b. Apr-14-1891.
917. xi. CORBETT LEE FABER b. Feb- 1-1893.
918. xii. DOVENER FABER b. Apr-23-1895.
919. xiii. VELVA FABER b. Sep-14-1900.

497. **William Columbus "Lum" Carr** (275.Margaret[7], 140.Deborah[6], 72.John[5], 21.John[4], 6.Hugh[3], 3.John[2], 1.Jean[1]), b. Aug- 5-1853,[46] d. 1933,[46] buried in Middleville Baptist Church Cemetery, Taylor Co, WV.[17]

The Maple Lake development on US Route 50, about 3 miles east of Bridgeport, WV, was constructed on a part of the "Lum" Carr farm property.

He married (1) Apr-16-1876, **Flora Frances "Fannie" Martin**, b. 1851,[46] d. 1899,[46] buried in Middleville Baptist Church Cemetery, Taylor Co, WV.[mlxxv][1075] He married (2) **Cora M. Cropp**, b. Mar-26-1858 in Harrison Co, WV,[398] (daughter of John R. Cropp and Magdaline Hustead), d. Nov- 9-1940 in Clarksburg, Harrison Co, WV,[398] buried in Bridgeport Cemetery, Harrison Co, WV,[mlxxvi][1076],[398] resided in Clarksburg, Harrison Co, WV.[398]

        Children by Flora Frances "Fannie" Martin:
920.   i.   FRANK CARR b. 1879.
       ii.   LUCY CARR d. at young age.
921.   iii.   MARGARET CARR b. Jul- 7-1882.
922.   iv.   CHARLES HARRY CARR b. Jul- 4-1886.
923.   v.   BERTHA CARR b. 1892.
924.   vi.   FRED CARR.

498. **Martha Olive "Ollie" Carr** (275.Margaret^7, 140.Deborah^6, 72.John^5, 21.John^4, 6.Hugh^3, 3.John^2, 1.Jean^1), b. Jul-20-1864, d. Nov-22-1947, buried in Woodlawn Cemetery, Harrison Co, WV. She married Sep-11-1890, **Othor Jesse Morrow**, b. Jan-20-1856, d. Nov- 9-1934, buried in Woodlawn Cemetery, Harrison Co, WV.

        Children:
925.   i.   HALLIE LOUISE MORROW b. Sep-10-1891.
       ii.   MILDRED MORROW b. Feb-28-1895, d. Aug-22-1908, buried in Woodlawn Cemetery, Fairmont, Marion Co, WV.
926.   iii.   PAULINE E. MORROW b. Jul-29-1906.

499. **Clara Cornelia Taylor** (276.James^7, 140.Deborah^6, 72.John^5, 21.John^4, 6.Hugh^3, 3.John^2, 1.Jean^1), b. Mar-20-1866 in Taylor Co, WV, d. Sep- 3-1934, buried in Clermont Cemetery, Eldora, Marion Co, WV.[17] She married Jul-20-1894, **Arthur Reed**, b. Jan- 8-1861, d. Jul-16-1947, buried in Clermont Cemetery, Eldora, Marion Co, WV.[17]

        Children:
927.   i.   NOLA MARY REED b. Mar-16-1895.
928.   ii.   WALTER SCOTT REED b. Dec- 3-1898.
929.   iii.   HERSCHEL LOWE REED b. Feb-23-1901.
930.   iv.   THOMAS HUGHES (TWIN) REED b. Feb-28-1904.
931.   v.   ARTHUR HARRIS (TWIN) REED b. Feb-28-1904.

500. **Jessie L. Taylor** (276.James^7, 140.Deborah^6, 72.John^5, 21.John^4, 6.Hugh^3, 3.John^2, 1.Jean^1), b. 1874 in Taylor Co, WV. She married Sep-8-1897 in Marion Co, WV, **Archie A. Wolfe**, b. 1872.

        Children:
       i.   MARIAN WOLFE.

501. **Colonel Harvey Taylor**, also known as C. Harvey Taylor,[17] (277.William^7, 140.Deborah^6, 72.John^5, 21.John^4, 6.Hugh^3, 3.John^2, 1.Jean^1), b. Nov- 6-1863, d. Sep-17-1950, buried in Bridgeport Masonic (aka Airport) Cemetery, Harrison Co, WV.[1076] He married Jun-16-1892, **Sarah Savannah "Vannie" Norris**, b. Mar-30-1868 [Birth date on headstone is 1867.], d. Jan-16-1933, buried in Bridgeport Masonic (aka Airport) Cemetery, Harrison Co, WV.[1076]

        Children:
932.   i.   WILLIAM DONLEY TAYLOR b. Apr- 1-1893.
933.   ii.   BARTLEY NORRIS TAYLOR b. Apr- 7-1897.

502. **John Floyd Taylor** (277.William^7, 140.Deborah^6, 72.John^5, 21.John^4, 6.Hugh^3, 3.John^2, 1.Jean^1), b. May-11-1867, d. Feb-17-1947, buried in Middleville Baptist Church Cemetery, Taylor Co, WV.[17] He married Oct-31-1894, **Lillie May Pell**, b. May-12-1868, d. Feb- 3-1956, buried in Middleville Baptist Church Cemetery, Taylor Co, WV.[17]

Children:
934. i. EARL GRAYSON TAYLOR b. Oct-10-1895.
935. ii. BONNIE MARIE TAYLOR b. Sep-26-1897.
936. iii. ARTHUR KELSO TAYLOR b. Feb- 3-1900.

503. **Hattie Nevada Taylor** (277.William[7], 140.Deborah[6], 72.John[5], 21.John[4], 6.Hugh[3], 3.John[2], 1.Jean[1]), b. Dec-18-1868, d. Jul-21-1946, buried in Middleville Baptist Church Cemetery, Taylor Co, WV.[17] She married Nov-15-1906 in Harrison Co, WV, **William Stephen Williams**, b. 1868.
Children:
i. FLORENCE WILLIAMS d. in infancy.

504. **Frances Gertrude "Gertie" Taylor** (277.William[7], 140.Deborah[6], 72.John[5], 21.John[4], 6.Hugh[3], 3.John[2], 1.Jean[1]), b. Aug- 7-1871, d. Sep-15-1931, buried in Benedum Memorial Cemetery, Bridgeport, Harrison Co, WV. She married Apr-27-1892, **Andrew Johnson "Pat" Williams**, b. Apr-25-1867, d. Sep- 5-1941, buried in Benedum Memorial Cemetery, Bridgeport, Harrison Co, WV.
Children:
i. CLARENCE EDWARD WILLIAMS b. Feb-19-1893, d. Jul-17-1970. He married Jul- -1940, Bess Nichols, d. Aug-27-1975.
937. ii. LENA PEARL WILLIAMS b. Feb-28-1897.
iii. MABEL ROXIE WILLIAMS b. Jan-17-1900, d. Jul- 8-1955, buried in Benedum Memorial Cemetery, Bridgeport, Harrison Co, WV. She married Jun-15-1940, no children from this marriage, Hayden Ray Smith, b. Aug-14-1893, d. Dec- 5-1976, buried in Benedum Memorial Cemetery, Bridgeport, Harrison Co, WV.
iv. MADGE BUENA WILLIAMS b. Mar- 9-1903,[592] d. Aug-15-1997,[592] resided in Warwick, Kent Co, RI.[mlxxvii[1077]] She married Apr-30-1932, no children from this marriage, Harold Guy Boggess, b. Sep-28-1908 in Maple Park, Kane Co, IL,[190] (son of John R. Boggess and Edda McCoy), d. Sep- 5-2003 in Kent Co, RI,[190] buried in Bridgeport Cemetery, Harrison Co, WV,[190] resided in Warwick, Kent Co, RI.[190]

Harold: Resided in Clay, Clay Co, WV before moving to Warwick, RI in 1951. He was the owner of Boggess Buick in East Providence, RI from 1951 till his retirement in 1981. From 1927 to 1951, he had been employed with the Elk River Coal & Lumberport Company in Clay, where he served in numerous capacities before leaving the company as its accountant and office manager. He was a member of the Warwick Country Club and a 50-year member of Kent County Masonic Lodge 97.

v. NANCY GENEVIEVE WILLIAMS b. Jan-17-1907,[592] d. Jul-19-1995,[592] resided in Bridgeport, Harrison Co, WV,[592] never married.

505. **Edward Murray Taylor** (277.William[7], 140.Deborah[6], 72.John[5], 21.John[4], 6.Hugh[3], 3.John[2], 1.Jean[1]), b. Jul-15-1882, d. Jul-16-1950, buried in Woodlawn Cemetery, Fairmont, Marion Co, WV. He married Aug-20-1918, **Martha Anderson Hoffman**, b. Jul- 1-1885, d. Nov- 3-1970, buried in Woodlawn Cemetery, Fairmont, Marion Co, WV.
Children:
938. i. BETTIE MARSHALL TAYLOR b. Sep-14-1919.
939. ii. EDWARD MURRAY TAYLOR, JR. b. Aug-28-1921.

506. **Francis Newton Brooks** (278.Sarah[7], 140.Deborah[6], 72.John[5], 21.John[4], 6.Hugh[3], 3.John[2], 1.Jean[1]), b. Dec-14-1873 in Harrison Co, WV,[mlxxviii[1078]] d. Jul-26-1945 in Taylor Co, WV,[398] buried in Bridgeport Masonic (aka Airport) Cemetery, Harrison Co, WV,[1076,134] [Burial location is stated in death record as Elkview Cemetery in Clarksburg. But headstones for him, his wife, and his son Birdsell are found at Bridgeport Masonic (aka Airport, aka Benedum) Cemetery. Entries for them in that cemetery are also found in "Cemeteries of Simpson District, Harrison County, WV," p. 7.], resided in Taylor Co, WV,[398] occupation farmer.[398] He married **Eva Morris**, b. Dec- 1-1880 in West Virginia,[724,46] (daughter

of Ellsworth Morris and Sarah McDonald), d. Feb- 9-1966 in Grafton, Taylor Co, WV,[724,46] buried in Bridgeport Masonic (aka Airport) Cemetery, Harrison Co, WV.[134,1076]

Children:

i.　FRANK M. BROOKS b. Dec-20-1901 in Harrison Co, WV, d. Dec-27-1901, buried in Middleville Baptist Church Cemetery, Taylor Co, WV.

ii.　BIRDSELL LYNN BROOKS b. Dec-18-1903,[46] d. Dec-14-1957,[46] buried in Bridgeport Masonic (aka Airport) Cemetery, Harrison Co, WV.[134,1076] He married Feb- 4-1932 in Marion Co, WV, Hazel Ray Swisher, b. 1911.

507.　**William Taylor Brooks** (278.Sarah[7], 140.Deborah[6], 72.John[5], 21.John[4], 6.Hugh[3], 3.John[2], 1.Jean[1]), b. Jun-15-1878 in Harrison Co, WV, d. Apr-19-1950 in Harrison Co, WV, buried in Elkview Masonic Cemetery, Clarksburg, Harrison Co, WV.[462] He married Aug-22-1900 in Harrison Co, WV, divorced **Ollie Blanche Knight**, b. Apr-17-1881 in Walker Station, Wood Co, WV,[546] (daughter of Edward J. Knight and Mary Linn), d. Apr-21-1941,[546] buried in Sunset Memorial Park Cemetery, Clarksburg, WV.[546]

Children:

i.　HELEN BROOKS b. Apr-17-1899, d. Jan- -1973. She married David Shier.

940.　ii.　LENA A. BROOKS b. 1900.

iii.　WILLIAM E. BROOKS b. Sep- 7-1905, d. May- -1976. He married Apr-11-1945,[546] Donna Ruth Stump.

iv.　(UNNAMED SON) BROOKS b. Jan- 7-1912, d. Jan- 7-1912.

508.　**Curtis Newton Robinson** (279.Henrietta[7], 140.Deborah[6], 72.John[5], 21.John[4], 6.Hugh[3], 3.John[2], 1.Jean[1]), b. Aug-16-1871,[17] d. Apr-21-1949,[17] buried in Mt. Morris Cemetery, Freemansburg, Lewis Co, WV.[17]

Curtis Newton Robinson and Tensie Myrtle Hall were double cousins, in that they were both second cousins once removed (he was the great-grandson and she was the g-g-granddaughter of John Gaston, Jr. (b. 1752 in NJ)) and also fourth cousins once removed (he was the g-g-g-grandson and she was the g-g-g-g-granddaughter of John Smith (b. 1699)).

He married May-6-1900, **Tensie Myrtle Hall**, b. Nov-21-1879,[17] (daughter of Minor James Hall and Amanda Jane Gaston), d. Mar- 6-1957,[17] buried in Mt. Morris Cemetery, Freemansburg, Lewis Co, WV.[17]

Children:

941.　i.　ANTHONY HALL ROBINSON b. Feb 27-1901.

942.　ii.　CHARLES THEODORE "TED" ROBINSON b. Jul-18-1904.

943.　iii.　MINOR HOLLIS "MIKE" ROBINSON b. Apr-11-1908.

944.　iv.　ELMER TRUMAN "PETE" ROBINSON b. Jun-10-1914.

v.　WILMA LOUISE ROBINSON b. May-28-1917,[mlxxix[1079]] d. Feb-11-1920,[1079] buried in Mt. Morris Cemetery, Freemansburg, Lewis Co, WV.[1079]

509.　**Charles Musser Gall** (279.Henrietta[7], 140.Deborah[6], 72.John[5], 21.John[4], 6.Hugh[3], 3.John[2], 1.Jean[1]), b. Jul- 5-1878, d. Feb-16-1960, buried in Mt. Morris Cemetery, Freemansburg, Lewis Co, WV.

Charles Musser Gall and Sarah Della Hall were double cousins, in that they were both second cousins once removed (he was the great-grandson and she was the g-g-granddaughter of John Gaston, Jr. (b. 1752 in NJ)) and also fourth cousins once removed (he was the g-g-g-grandson and she was the g-g-g-g-granddaughter of John Smith (b. 1699)).

He married Sep-20-1905, **Sarah Della Hall**, b. Oct-26-1881 (daughter of Minor James Hall and Amanda Jane Gaston), d. May- 3-1964, buried in Mt. Morris Cemetery, Freemansburg, Lewis Co, WV.

Children:

i.　ROBERT BURL GALL, also known as R. Burl Gall,[592] b. Jul-28-1915,[592] d. Apr-26-1992,[592,191] resided in Weston, Lewis Co, WV.[592] He married Aug-25-1952,[191] no children from this marriage, Norma Lea Jackson, b. Mar-19-1916 in Hundred, Wetzel Co, WV,[190,592] (daughter of P. E. Jackson and Norma Jamison), d. Nov-11-2004 in Elizabethtown, Lancaster Co, PA,[190,592] buried in Mt. Morris Cemetery, Freemansburg, Lewis Co, WV,[190] resided in Silver Spring, Lancaster Co, PA,[592] resided formerly in West Virginia,[mlxxx[1080]] occupation elementary school teacher (Pennsylvania),[190] education California College (Pennsylvania).[190]

510. **William Oscar Swisher** (280.Peter[7], 141.Jane[6], 72.John[5], 21.John[4], 6.Hugh[3], 3.John[2], 1.Jean[1]), b. Apr-18-1857 in Lewis Co, WV.[550] He married Sep-23-1884 in Lewis Co, WV,[410] **Olive Melissa Lawson**, b. ca 1859,[410] (daughter of Cornelius Lawson and Anne __).
>Children:
>i.   MARY ANN SWISHER b. ca 1897 in Lewis Co, WV.[410] She married Sep-25-1915 in Lewis Co, WV,[410] Laco Raymond Hinzman, b. Apr- -1897 in Lewis Co, WV,[410] (son of John William Hinzman and Nancy Burdell Taylor), resided 1915 in Marion Co, WV,[410] census 1900 in Hackers Creek District, Lewis Co, WV. As great-grandchildren of Abraham Hinzman & Rebecca Means, Laco Raymond Hinzman and Mary Ann Swisher were second cousins.

511. **George Washington Swisher** (280.Peter[7], 141.Jane[6], 72.John[5], 21.John[4], 6.Hugh[3], 3.John[2], 1.Jean[1]), b. Feb-28-1859 in Berlin, Lewis Co, WV,[mlxxxi[1081],398,964] d. Feb- 7-1942 in Ripley, Jackson Co, WV,[398] buried in Pine Hill Cemetery, Ripley, Jackson Co, WV,[398] resided in Ripley, Jackson Co, WV,[398] census 1900 in Troy District, Gilmer Co, WV, resided 1897 in Gilmer Co, WV,[410] occupation farmer.[398] He married (1) **Laura Flint**, d. bef Sep 1897.[526] He married (2) Sep-29-1897 in Lewis Co, WV,[410] **Wilma Dondia Ballentine**, b. Apr- -1871,[964,410] (daughter of John T. Ballentine and Merceline Peterson), resided 1942 in Ripley, Jackson Co, WV,[228] census 1900 in Troy District, Gilmer Co, WV.
>Children by Laura Flint:
>i.   FLOSSIE SWISHER b. Jul- 5-1885 in Gilmer Co, WV,[592,410] [Birth date given as Aug 1885 in 1900 Census, but SSDI entry states Jul 5 1885.], d. Jan- -1978,[592] resided in Walker, Wood Co, WV,[592] resided 1908 in Lewis Co, WV,[410] census 1900 in Troy District, Gilmer Co, WV.

>>Middle initial given as L in 1900 Census, but D in marriage record.

>She married Jun-23-1905 in Lewis Co, WV,[410] Harlan Z. Wiseman, b. Jul-13-1884 in Lewis Co, WV,[592,410] (son of John H. Wiseman and Celestia H. __), d. Jul- -1975,[592] resided in Walker, Wood Co, WV.[604]
>Children by Wilma Dondia Ballentine:
>ii.   LACO SWISHER b. Apr- -1899,[964] census 1900 in Troy District, Gilmer Co, WV.

512. **James Edwin Swisher** (280.Peter[7], 141.Jane[6], 72.John[5], 21.John[4], 6.Hugh[3], 3.John[2], 1.Jean[1]), b. Nov-6-1864,[398,410,408] d. Jun-29-1922 in Clarksburg, Harrison Co, WV,[mlxxxii[1082]] buried in Berlin, Lewis Co, WV,[398] resided in Berlin, Lewis Co, WV,[398] occupation farmer,[398] census 1900 in Hackers Creek District, Lewis Co, WV. He married (1) Oct-15-1891 in Lewis Co, WV,[mlxxxiii[1083]] **Annie Gertrude Reger**, b. 1871,[410] (daughter of William Reger and Mary E. __), d. 1911, census 1900 in Hackers Creek District, Lewis Co, WV. He married (2) Oct-25-1913 in Lewis Co, WV,[mlxxxiv[1084],mlxxxv[1085]] **Eva Elizabeth Boram**, b. Jan-24-1874,[1085] (daughter of Francis Marion Boram and Annis Rebecca Marsh), resided 1922, 1936 in Berlin, Lewis Co, WV.[228,765]
>Children by Annie Gertrude Reger:
>i.   GRACE LESLIE SWISHER b. Nov-24-1892,[592] [1900 Census gives birth date as Oct 1892, but SSDI shows it as Nov 24 1892.], d. Jan- -1980,[592] resided in Jane Lew, Lewis Co, WV,[592] census 1900 in Hackers Creek District, Lewis Co, WV. She married Nov-24-1915 in Lewis Co, WV,[410,1085] Nathan Goff Boram, b. Nov-23-1886,[1085,592] (son of Francis Marion Boram and Annis Rebecca Marsh), d. Dec- -1978,[592] resided in Jane Lew, Lewis Co, WV.[592] As great-grandchildren of Abraham Hinzman and Rebecca Means, Grace Leslie Swisher and husband Nathan Goff Boram were second cousins.

ii.   CARL BRENT SWISHER b. Apr-28-1897,[592,408] d. Jun- -1968,[592] resided in Baltimore, MD,[mlxxxvi][1086] census 1900 in Hackers Creek District, Lewis Co, WV. He married Aug-23-1929, Idella Ford Gwatkin, b. Aug-23-1904,[592] d. Jan-18-2001,[592] resided in Baltimore, MD.[mlxxxvii][1087]

iii.   MARGARET ELIZABETH SWISHER b. Dec-11-1898,[592] d. Aug- -1979,[592] resided in Madison, Lake Co, OH,[mlxxxviii][1088] census 1900 in Hackers Creek District, Lewis Co, WV. She married Jan-31-1920 in Lewis Co, WV,[410] Arley Kyle Gould, b. Jan-20-1898,[592] (son of Warren G. Gould and Minnie B. __), d. Mar- -1971,[592] resided in Weston, Lewis Co, WV.[592]

513. **John Alden Swisher** (280.Peter[7], 141.Jane[6], 72.John[5], 21.John[4], 6.Hugh[3], 3.John[2], 1.Jean[1]), b. Dec-22-1868 in Lewis Co, WV,[236,410] d. Aug-24-1961 in Weston, Lewis Co, WV,[236] buried in Friendship Cem (Fairview IOOF), Berlin Rd, Co Rt 7, Lewis Co, WV,[236] occupation farmer.[236] He married Mar- 7-1894 in Lewis Co, WV,[410] **Iza Bush**, b. ca 1873.[410]
          Children:
          i.   FLOE SWISHER b. Jan-13-1905 in Gilmer Co, WV,[592,410] d. May-14-1997,[592] resided in Weston, Lewis Co, WV,[592] resided 1927 in Lewis Co, WV.[410] She married Mar-30-1927 in Lewis Co, WV,[410] Francis Edwin Taylor, b. Mar- 7-1906 in Lewis Co, WV,[592,410] (son of Edward Oliver Taylor and Ardelia Maud Swisher), d. Apr-30-1997,[592] resided in Weston, Lewis Co, WV.[592]

514. **Alvin Swisher** (281.James[7], 141.Jane[6], 72.John[5], 21.John[4], 6.Hugh[3], 3.John[2], 1.Jean[1]), b. Nov-27-1857 in Lewis Co, (W)VA,[17,mlxxxix][1089] d. Jan-18-1906,[17] buried in Hebron Memorial Church Cemetery, Roane Co, WV.[17] He married Sep- 4-1879 in Lewis Co, WV,[410] **Alice Virginia Morrison**,[556] b. Jul-16-1860,[17] d. Mar-15-1943,[17] buried in Hebron Memorial Church Cemetery, Roane Co, WV.[17]
          Children:
          i.   DALE SWISHER b. Nov- 1-1883,[17] d. Jun-21-1914,[17] buried in Hebron Memorial Church Cemetery, Roane Co, WV.[17]

515. **Isaac Columbus "Lum" Swisher**[268] (281.James[7], 141.Jane[6], 72.John[5], 21.John[4], 6.Hugh[3], 3.John[2], 1.Jean[1]), b. Sep- 6-1861 in Lewis Co, (W)VA,[268] d. Mar- 3-1953 in Lewis Co, WV,[268] census 1900 in Hackers Creek District, Lewis Co, WV. He married Mar- 8-1883 in Lewis Co, WV,[410] **Mary Catherine Allman**, b. Dec- -1860,[408,410] (daughter of William Allman and Kittorah __), census 1900 in Hackers Creek District, Lewis Co, WV.
          Children:
          i.   JAMES BLAINE SWISHER b. Jul- 6-1884,[236,410] [1900 Census gives birth date as Aug 1884, but death record states Jul 6 1884. Birthplace given as Lewis County is marriage record, but Doddridge County in death record.], d. Jun-13-1959 in Weston, Lewis Co, WV,[236] buried in Miller Cemetery, Horner, Lewis Co, WV,[236] resided in Weston, Lewis Co, WV,[236] census 1900 in Hackers Creek District, Lewis Co, WV, occupation carpenter for B & O Railroad (retired).[236] He married Nov-16-1913 in Lewis Co, WV,[mxc][1090] Rosa Mildred Kemper, b. ca 1889,[410] (daughter of John W. Kemper and Addie __).
          ii.   RELLA MAY SWISHER b. Apr- -1889,[408,410] census 1900 in Hackers Creek District, Lewis Co, WV. She married Dec-29-1912,[410] E. Dare Darnall, b. ca 1890,[410] (son of R. L. Darnall and Eva __).
          iii.   DORA ETHEL SWISHER b. Sep- -1892,[408,410] census 1900 in Hackers Creek District, Lewis Co, WV. She married Oct- 9-1910 in Lewis Co, WV,[410] Bret Starcher, b. Oct-26-1886,[592,410] (son of William S. Starcher and Rebecca E. Lawson), d. Mar-28-1974 in Ironton, Lawrence Co, OH,[693,592] resided in Wellston, Jackson Co, OH.[592,693]

516. **Robert Ervin Swisher** (281.James[7], 141.Jane[6], 72.John[5], 21.John[4], 6.Hugh[3], 3.John[2], 1.Jean[1]), b. Dec-12-1866 in Berlin, Lewis Co, WV,[268] d. 1958 in Lewis Co, WV,[268] buried in Friendship Cem (Fairview IOOF), Berlin Rd, Co Rt 7, Lewis Co, WV. He married[502] Aug-17-1899 in Lewis Co, WV,[410] **Laura Belle McKinney**, also known as Belle McKinney,[374] b. Oct- -1877,[268] (daughter of William P. McKinney and Caroline M. __), d. 1968, buried in Friendship Cem (Fairview IOOF), Berlin Rd, Co Rt 7, Lewis Co, WV, census 1880 in Elk District, Harrison Co, WV.
          Children:
945. i.   MARY SWISHER b. Mar-26-1901.

ii.   JAMES WILBUR SWISHER b. Sep-17-1903 in Upshur Co, WV,[268,410] d. 1934,[268] buried in Friendship Cem (Fairview IOOF), Berlin Rd, Co Rt 7, Lewis Co, WV, resided 1928 in Lewis Co, WV.[410] He married Mar-14-1928 in Lewis Co, WV,[410] Vivian Daisy Trimble, b. ca 1903 in Barbour Co, WV,[410] (daughter of Hoffman Trimble and Willa __), resided 1928 in Lewis Co, WV.[410]

946.   iii.   BEATRICE SWISHER b. Sep- 2-1906.

iv.   BONNIE IRENE SWISHER b. May-27-1910,[592] d. Nov-28-2002,[592] resided in Weston, Lewis Co, WV.[592] She married Apr-30-1930 in Lewis Co, WV,[410] Ralph Jerome Lough, b. Jul-19-1910,[592,410] (son of Albert J. Lough and Rosa M. __), d. May- -1975,[592] resided in Weston, Lewis Co, WV.[604]

v.   ROBERT ERVIN SWISHER, JR. b. ca 1913,[410] d. bef Oct 2003.[412] He married Sep- 4-1935 in Lewis Co, WV,[410] Alice Victoria Hammer, b. Jul-10-1917,[592,410] (daughter of Grover Cleveland Hammer and Edna Eakin), d. Aug- 5-2002,[592] resided in Weston, Lewis Co, WV.[592]

517. **Charles Swisher** (281.James[7], 141.Jane[6], 72.John[5], 21.John[4], 6.Hugh[3], 3.John[2], 1.Jean[1]), b. Aug-22-1870 in Lewis Co, WV,[268] d. Dec- -1960 in Lewis Co, WV,[268] [Jeffrey Wood reports Charles Swisher's death date as Dec 27 1960, but Tina J. Kutschbach gives it as Dec 29 1960.].

Middle initial is either B or E. It has been reported both ways.

He married Dec-11-1895 in Stone Coal, Lewis Co, WV,[268,410] **Vinnie Bush**, b. Feb-28-1876 in Lewis Co, WV,[268,556] d. Jun-22-1957 in Lewis Co, WV.[268,556]
Children:
i.   MILDRED MAY SWISHER b. Apr-13-1909,[592,410] d. Feb-26-2000,[592] resided in Weston, Lewis Co, WV.[592] She married Nov- 9-1932 in Lewis Co, WV,[410] Virgil Francis Bowman, b. Sep-27-1905 in Jackson Co, OH,[410,592] (son of Frank Bowman and Mamie __), d. Feb- -1972,[592] resided in Weston, Lewis Co, WV.[592]

518. **James Goodloe Swisher** (281.James[7], 141.Jane[6], 72.John[5], 21.John[4], 6.Hugh[3], 3.John[2], 1.Jean[1]), b. Feb-20-1879 in Lewis Co, WV,[398,408] d. Jun-27-1957 in Lewis Co, WV,[mxci[1091]] buried in Friendship Cem (Fairview IOOF), Berlin Rd, Co Rt 7, Lewis Co, WV,[398] resided 1940 in Berlin, Lewis Co, WV,[mxcii[1092]] occupation farmer.[mxciii[1093]] He married Oct-31-1901 in Harrison Co, WV,[mxciv[1094]] **Stella "Ella" Post**, b. Oct-12-1877,[268,556] (daughter of Hiram Post and Statira Cookman), d. Mar-26-1955.[268]
Children:
i.   LENNA M. SWISHER b. ca 1903,[1093] census 1930 in Hackers Creek, Lewis Co, WV.
ii.   VIRGINIA SWISHER b. ca 1907,[1093] census 1930 in Hackers Creek, Lewis Co, WV.
iii.   RUBY J. SWISHER b. Aug-23-1909,[592,410,1093] d. May-12-2003,[592] census 1930 in Hackers Creek, Lewis Co, WV. She married Nov-30-1933 in Lewis Co, WV,[410] Brooks Jennings Queen, b. Aug-17-1909,[592,410] (son of Ira Queen and Floy __), d. Jul- -1973,[592] resided in Weston, Lewis Co, WV.[604]
iv.   JAMES H. SWISHER b. ca 1913,[1093] census 1930 in Hackers Creek, Lewis Co, WV.
v.   ROBERT G. SWISHER b. ca 1917,[1093] census 1930 in Hackers Creek, Lewis Co, WV.
vi.   WILLIAM VAUGHN SWISHER b. ca 1923,[1093] census 1930 in Hackers Creek, Lewis Co, WV. He married May- 6-1940 in Catlettsburg, KY,[mxcv[1095]] Madge Elvira Waldeck, b. Jan-22-1918,[592] (daughter of Early Forrest Waldeck and Willa Jane Lipps), d. Dec- 1-1997,[592] resided in Buckhannon, Upshur Co, WV,[604] census 1930 in Hackers Creek District, Lewis Co, WV.

519. **James Lewis Hinzman** (282.Sarah[7], 141.Jane[6], 72.John[5], 21.John[4], 6.Hugh[3], 3.John[2], 1.Jean[1]), b. Nov-1-1852 in Lewis Co, (W)VA,[398] d. Feb-23-1936 in Ripley, Jackson Co, WV,[398] buried in Weston, Lewis Co, WV,[398] census 1880 in Hackers Creek District, Lewis Co, WV, occupation farmer.[398]

1900 Census, Lewis Co, WV (Hackers Creek Dist), enumerated on Jun 19 1900:
James L. Hinzman, 48, b. Nov 1851, farmer, married 19 yrs; wife Alice B, 43, b. Jul 1856, mother of 2 children (1 still living); dau Effie D, 17, single.

He married (1) Jan-20-1881 in Upshur Co, WV,[mxcvi][1096] **Alice B. Flint**, b. Jul- -1856 in Upshur Co, (W)VA,[408,921] d. Feb- 3-1908 in Ripley, Jackson Co, WV,[447] cause of death apoplexy,[447] census 1900 in Hackers Creek District, Lewis Co, WV. He married[228] (2) Jan-17-1910 in Roane Co, WV,[mxcvii][1097] **Margaret Columbia Morrison**, b. Jul-22-1862,[398] (daughter of Monroe Morrison and Jane Bonnett), d. Apr-18-1947 in Ripley, Jackson Co, WV,[398,447] buried in Friendship Cem (Fairview IOOF), Berlin Rd, Co Rt 7, Lewis Co, WV,[398] resided in Ripley, Jackson Co, WV.[398]

> Children by Alice B. Flint:
>
> i.   EFFIE D. HINZMAN b. Oct- -1882,[408] census 1900 in Hackers Creek District, Lewis Co, WV.

520. **Sarah Ann Hinzman**, also known as Ann Hinzman,[410] census name Anne,[408] (282.Sarah[7], 141.Jane[6], 72.John[5], 21.John[4], 6.Hugh[3], 3.John[2], 1.Jean[1]), b. Sep- -1868,[408,247] d. Aug- 1-1912 in Laurel Lick Run (Berlin), Lewis Co, WV,[mxcviii][1098] cause of death tuberculosis,[236] census 1880, 1900, 1910 in Hackers Creek District, Lewis Co, WV. She married Oct-25-1894 in Lewis Co, WV,[mxcix][1099] **David Thomas Allman**, b. Mar- -1865,[408,410] (son of William Allman and Kittorah __), census 1900, 1910, 1920 in Hackers Creek District, Lewis Co, WV.

> Children:
>
> i.   DARREL ALLMAN, census name Darall Allman,[408] b. Jul- -1895,[408] census 1900, 1910 in Hackers Creek District, Lewis Co, WV.
>
> ii.   NELLIE F. ALLMAN b. Nov- -1897,[408] census 1900, 1910 in Hackers Creek District, Lewis Co, WV.
>
> iii.   CLARENCE DALTON ALLMAN b. Dec-25-1903 in Lewis Co, WV,[592,889] d. Aug- -1987,[592] resided in Baltimore, MD,[604] census 1910 in Lewis Co, WV. He married Aug-30-1926 in Lewis Co, WV,[410] Bonnie Fay Nangle, b. Aug-30-1906 in Doddridge Co, WV,[592,410] (daughter of J. M. Nangle and Elva S. __), d. Feb- 9-1988,[592] resided in Reisterstown, Baltimore Co, MD,[1086] resided 1926 in Lewis Co, WV.[410]

521. **John William Hinzman**, census name John H. Hinzman,[943] (282.Sarah[7], 141.Jane[6], 72.John[5], 21.John[4], 6.Hugh[3], 3.John[2], 1.Jean[1]), b. Dec-17-1869 in Lewis Co, WV,[398,408,410] d. Nov- 5-1950 in Buckhannon, Upshur Co, WV,[398] buried in Miller Cemetery, Horner, Lewis Co, WV,[398] census 1920, 1930 in Fairmont, Marion Co, WV, census 1880, 1900 in Hackers Creek District, Lewis Co, WV, occupation 1930 crude oil salesman,[mc][1100] occupation 1920 oil company sub agent.[943] He married Aug- 3-1893 in Lewis Co, WV,[410] **Nancy Burdell Taylor**, b. Apr- 8-1874,[408,410] [1900 Census gives her age as 27 and birth date as Apr 1873, but death record stated Apr 8 1874, age 61y 9m 25d at time of death.] (daughter of Albert A. Taylor and Caroline Newberger), d. Feb- 3-1936 in Buckhannon, Upshur Co, WV,[917] buried Valley Chapel Cem,[917] census 1920, 1930 in Fairmont, Marion Co, WV, census 1900 in Hackers Creek District, Lewis Co, WV.

> Children:
>
> i.   LACO RAYMOND HINZMAN b. Apr- -1897 in Lewis Co, WV,[410] resided 1915 in Marion Co, WV,[410] census 1900 in Hackers Creek District, Lewis Co, WV. He married Sep-25-1915 in Lewis Co, WV,[410] Mary Ann Swisher, b. ca 1897 in Lewis Co, WV,[410] (daughter of William Oscar Swisher and Olive Melissa Lawson). As great-grandchildren of Abraham Hinzman & Rebecca Means, Laco Raymond Hinzman and Mary Ann Swisher were second cousins.

522. **Florence May Hinzman** (282.Sarah[7], 141.Jane[6], 72.John[5], 21.John[4], 6.Hugh[3], 3.John[2], 1.Jean[1]), b. Nov- 6-1874 in Lewis Co, WV,[398,410] d. Dec-27-1944 in Weston, Lewis Co, WV,[398] buried in Friendship Cem (Fairview IOOF), Berlin Rd, Co Rt 7, Lewis Co, WV,[398] census 1900 in Hackers Creek District, Lewis Co, WV. She married[436] Dec-16-1906 in Lewis Co, WV,[410] **Loman McKinney**, b. ca 1875 in Harrison Co, WV,[410] (son of William P. McKinney and Caroline M. __), resided 1944 in Lewis Co, WV,[436] census 1910 in Hackers Creek District, Lewis Co, WV, census 1880 in Elk District, Harrison Co, WV.

> Children:
>
> i.   RAY MCKINNEY b. ca 1908,[889] census 1910 in Hackers Creek District, Lewis Co, WV.

523. **Ira Ervin Swisher** (284.Isaac[7], 141.Jane[6], 72.John[5], 21.John[4], 6.Hugh[3], 3.John[2], 1.Jean[1]), b. ca 1868.[410] He married[446] Oct- 1-1891 in Lewis Co, WV,[410] **Amrose Kittorah Allman**, b. ca 1873,[410] (daughter of William Allman and Kittorah __).

> Children:
>
> i. HARLAND ALLMAN SWISHER b. ca 1893.[410] He married[mci[1101]] Aug-12-1916 in Lewis Co, WV,[410] Lillie Mabel King, also known as Mabel,[521] b. Nov- 9-1896 in Gilmer Co, WV,[mcii[1102]] (daughter of John Presley King and Sarah Elizabeth West), d. Mar- 4-1964 in Weston, Lewis Co, WV.[1102]
>
> ii. ODBERT SWISHER b. ca 1898.[410] He married Aug-26-1928 in Lewis Co, WV,[410] Mantie May Starcher, b. ca 1904,[410] (daughter of Alvin S. Starcher and Alrose McKinley).
>
> iii. EUGENIA SWISHER b. ca 1906.[410] She married Jun-10-1928 in Lewis Co, WV,[410] Alton B. Oldaker, b. ca 1907 in Ritchie Co, WV,[410] (son of Harrison Oldaker and Lucy __), resided 1928 in Lewis Co, WV.[410]

524. **Eri Benson Hoff**, also known as Eric B. Hoff,[473] census name Eric Hoff,[225] (285.Elizabeth[7], 142.James[6], 72.John[5], 21.John[4], 6.Hugh[3], 3.John[2], 1.Jean[1]), b. Mar-23-1850 in Harrison Co, (W)VA,[570,473] [1870 Census gives birth date as May 1850], resided in Ohio,[570] census 1900 in Wirt Co, WV, census 1850 in Harrison Co, (W)VA, occupation Methodist Episcopal Minister.[570] He married Aug-27-1871 in Ritchie Co, WV,[570,mciii[1103]] **Malinda Ann Hart**, census name Linda A. Hart,[mciv[1104]] b. Apr- -1852,[mcv[1105],473] (daughter of William C. Hart and Sarah Nutter), census 1900 in Wirt Co, WV, census 1870 in Union District, Ritchie Co, WV.

Malinda: Identified by Minnie Kendall Lowther as Malinda B. Hart, but in "Ritchie County WV Marriages" as "Malinda Ann Hoit (?)," age 19, daughter of William C. and Sarah. Some researchers have also reported her name as Martha Melinda Hart, basis for which is not clear.

> Children:
>
> i. ELOSIA M. HOFF b. Jul- -1878,[1105] census 1900 in Wirt Co, WV.
>
> 947. ii. MINNIE MAUD HOFF b. Nov-10-1880.
>
> 948. iii. NEFF CORLISS HOFF b. Apr- 9-1883.
>
> 949. iv. VIRGIL R. HOFF b. Aug-25-1887.
>
> v. VERA M. HOFF b. Feb-16-1890,[592] d. May- -1976,[592] resided in Upper Sandusky, Wyandot Co, OH,[1010] census 1920, 1930 in Harpster, Wyandot Co, OH, occupation 1930 proprietor of beauty shop.[334] She married Apr-21-1910 in Harpster, Wyandot Co, OH,[478] Espie Augustus Wade, b. Jul-21-1881 in Berea, Ritchie Co, WV,[478] (son of Andrew Montgomery Wade and Sally Catherine Bee), d. Jul- -1969,[592] resided in Upper Sandusky, Wyandot Co, OH,[mcvi[1106]] census 1920, 1930 in Harpster, Wyandot Co, OH [No children in either census. With them in 1930 Census was nephew Ucal Hoff, age 17, b. Ohio.], occupation 1920 fireman.[681]
>
> 950. vi. ALICE A. HOFF b. Jun-21-1894.

525. **George S. Hoff** (285.Elizabeth[7], 142.James[6], 72.John[5], 21.John[4], 6.Hugh[3], 3.John[2], 1.Jean[1]), b. Dec-27-1855 in Ritchie Co, (W)VA,[588,570] d. 1904,[570] ["Ritchie County in History and Romance," p. 317, reports death date as Dec 15 1904, but "Ritchie County Cemeteries," p. 490, shows it as Feb 15 1904.], buried in Auburn Community Cemetery, Ritchie Co, WV,[469] census 1900 in Murphy District, Ritchie Co, WV, census 1860 in Ritchie Co, (W)VA. He married Dec-24-1887 in Ritchie Co, WV,[588,570] **Alazan Huldah Amos**,[473] also known as Huldah Amos,[570,473,345] b. Apr- -1863 in Ritchie Co, WV,[mcvii[1107],588] census 1900 in Murphy District, Ritchie Co, WV.

1900 Census, Ritchie Co, WV (Murphy District), enumerated in June 1900: George Hoff, 44, b. Dec 1855, farmer, married 12 yrs; wife Hulda A, 37, b. Apr 1863, mother of 5 children (4 still living); dau Lela P, 11, b. Dec 1888; son Amos, 8, b. Sep 1891; dau Lyda C, 6, b. Nov 1893; son Frank, 1, b. Jul 1898.

> Children:
>
> 951. i. LELA PEARL HOFF b. Dec-31-1888.

    ii.   AMOS LEWIS HOFF b. Sep- 8-1891,[592,1107] d. Oct- 1-1971,[592] buried in Auburn Community Cemetery, Ritchie Co, WV,[469] resided in Harrisville, Ritchie Co, WV,[592] census 1900 in Murphy District, Ritchie Co, WV, military Pvt, 102nd Sp. Sqd., WW I.[469]

    iii.   LYDA C. HOFF b. Nov-30-1893,[17,1107] d. Oct-12-1903,[17] buried in Webb Cemetery, Smithville, Ritchie Co, WV,[469] census 1900 in Murphy District, Ritchie Co, WV.

    iv.   JOHN HOFF b. Jun- 1-1897,[17] d. Jun- 2-1897,[17] buried in Webb Cemetery, Smithville, Ritchie Co, WV.[469]

    v.   FRANK HOFF b. Jul- -1898,[1107] d. Jun-27-1914 in Parkersburg, Wood Co, WV,[398] buried in Auburn Community Cemetery, Ritchie Co, WV,[398,469] census 1900 in Murphy District, Ritchie Co, WV.

    vi.   EDNA A. HOFF b. Dec-11-1900,[17] d. Jan- 3-1901,[17] buried in Webb Cemetery, Smithville, Ritchie Co, WV.[469]

526. **Charlotte Columbia Hoff**, census name Columbia C.,[mcviii[1108]] (285.Elizabeth[7], 142.James[6], 72.John[5], 21.John[4], 6.Hugh[3], 3.John[2], 1.Jean[1]), b. Nov-10-1857,[570,mcix[1109]] d. Aug-20-1941 in Sutton, Braxton Co, WV,[mcx[1110]] census 1880, 1900, 1910 in Webster Co, WV, census 1860 in Ritchie Co, (W)VA. She married Mar-18-1875 in Ritchie Co, WV,[570,473] **William J. Butcher**, b. Jan- -1854,[1109] (son of George W. Butcher and Amy Stansberry), census 1880, 1900, 1910 in Webster Co, WV, census 1860 in Ritchie Co, (W)VA, occupation farmer.[1109]

    Children:

    i.   NORA A. BUTCHER b. May- -1876 in Webster Co, WV,[1109,mcxi[1111]] census 1880, 1900 in Webster Co, WV.

    Middle initial given as A in 1880 Census and in marriage record, but as M in 1900 Census.

    She married Mar- 2-1905 in Webster Co, WV,[1111] Samuel B. Tenny, b. ca 1856 in Upshur Co, (W)VA,[1111] resided 1905 in Upshur Co, WV.[1111]

    ii.   GEORGE W. BUTCHER b. Apr- -1878 in Webster Co, WV,[1109,mcxii[1112]] resided 1905 in Braxton Co, WV,[1112] census 1900 in Webster Co, WV [was not with family in 1880 Census]. He married Mar-12-1905 in Braxton Co, WV,[1112] Albertie Douglas, b. ca 1880 in Lewis Co, WV,[1112] resided 1905 in Braxton Co, WV.[1112]

    iii.   MYRA A. BUTCHER b. Jun- 3-1880 in Webster Co, WV,[592,1109,1111] d. May- -1971,[592] resided in Philadelphia, PA,[592] census 1900 in Webster Co, WV. She married Dec-25-1900 in Webster Co, WV,[1111] Norman L. Harper, b. ca 1877 in Upshur Co, WV,[1111] resided 1900 in Webster Co, WV.[1111]

    iv.   MARY CAROLINE BUTCHER b. Mar- -1882 in Webster Co, WV,[1109,419] resided 1910 in Harrison Co, WV,[419] census 1900 in Webster Co, WV. She married Feb- 9-1910 in Clarksburg, Harrison Co, WV,[419] Truman Guy Robinson, b. ca 1873 in Harrison Co, WV,[419] (son of Rezin R. Robinson and Aultha __), resided 1910 in Custer Co, NE.[419]

    v.   PRESTON RANDOLPH BUTCHER b. Feb-10-1884 in Webster Co, WV,[592,1109,621] d. Jul- - 1963,[592] resided 1909 in Braxton Co, WV,[621] census 1900 in Webster Co, WV. He married Jun-30-1909 near Crawford, Lewis Co, WV,[621] Fernie Oleta McQuain, b. Jul-25-1888 in Lewis Co, WV,[592,621] (daughter of Albert M. McQuain and Esther C. Blagg), d. Apr- -1984,[592] resided in Alloy, Fayette Co, WV,[592] resided 1909 in Lewis Co, WV.[621]

    vi.   ANNA M. BUTCHER, census name Amy M. Butcher,[mcxiii[1113]] b. Apr- -1886,[1109] census 1900, 1910 in Webster Co, WV.

    vii.   ALMA E. BUTCHER b. Dec- -1888,[1109] census 1900, 1910 in Webster Co, WV.

    viii.   JOHN HOFF BUTCHER b. Oct- -1894,[1109] census 1900, 1910 in Webster Co, WV. He married Jun-22-1929 in Webster Springs, Webster Co, WV,[1111] Joda Belcher, b. Nov- 4-1895 in Clay Co, WV,[mcxiv[1114],1111] (daughter of Joseph Belcher and Lydia Summers), d. Feb-18-1961 in Webster Co, WV,[1114] buried in Hacker Valley Cemetery, Webster Co, WV,[1114] resided in Webster Co, WV,[1111] occupation elementary school principal.[1114]

    ix.   DELPHA BLANCH BUTCHER b. Aug- 2-1897 in Webster Co, WV,[1022,mcxv[1115],1109,1111] d. Feb-14-1963 in Philippi, Barbour Co, WV,[1115] buried in Mt. Hebron Cemetery, Barbour Co, WV,[1115] resided 1957 in Rangoon, Barbour Co, WV,[1022] resided 1923 in Hall, Barbour Co, WV,[921] census 1900,

1910 in Webster Co, WV. She married (1) Dec-16-1917 in Webster Co, WV,[1111] Okey Robinson, b. ca 1891 in Braxton Co, WV,[1111] d. bef Aug 1923,[mcxvi][1116] resided 1917 in Webster Co, WV.[1111] She married (2) Aug-25-1923 in Buckhannon, Upshur Co, WV,[921] Arley Cooper George, b. Apr-17-1877 in Barbour Co, WV,[398,921] (son of William Madison George and Elizabeth Ward), d. Feb- 3-1951 in Barbour Co, WV,[398] buried in Mt. Hebron Cemetery, Barbour Co, WV,[398] resided 1923 in Rangoon, Barbour Co, WV,[921] occupation civil engineer.[398] She married (3) Oct-12-1957 in Quiet Dell, Harrison Co, WV,[1022] William Arthur Arms, b. Oct- 3-1889 in Cherokee Co, NC,[1022,592] (son of Charles Henry Arms and Almeta ___), d. Oct- -1982,[592] resided in Glen Dale, Marshall Co, WV,[604] resided 1957 in Volga, Barbour Co, WV.[1022]

        x.   FLORA OGRETTA BUTCHER b. Nov- -1899,[1109] census 1900, 1910 in Webster Co, WV. She married May-11-1918 in Webster Co, WV,[1111] Arnold Alexander Luikart, b. Aug-24-1886 in Webster Co, WV,[592,1111] d. Oct- -1975,[592] resided in Hacker Valley, Webster Co, WV.[592]

527. **Rebecca Jane Hoff**[mcxvii][1117] (285.Elizabeth[7], 142.James[6], 72.John[5], 21.John[4], 6.Hugh[3], 3.John[2], 1.Jean[1]), b. Jul- 9-1859 in Ritchie Co, (W)VA,[570,473,398,46] d. Dec-18-1932 in Wolf Summit, Harrison Co, WV,[mcxviii][1118],[46] buried in IOOF Cemetery, Salem, Harrison Co, WV,[398,817] census 1910 in Berea, Ritchie Co, WV, occupation teacher, census 1860 in Ritchie Co, (W)VA.

From the Notes of Burl L. Hoff (page 16): "Rebecca J. married E. L. Bee and they lived on a farm for several years at Berea in Ritchie County and later moved to Wolf Summit. Aunt Rebecca was a very kind and loving woman. She and Uncle "Sebe" were a very devoted couple and it was always a pleasure for me to visit in their home, because they were so kind, thoughtful and devoted to each other. They raised a large family who all lived at Wolf Summit. I remember only the names of some of their children which were Rose, May, and Owen. Rose married John Anderson."[1117]

She married (1) Nov-12-1879 in Ritchie Co, WV,[433,473] divorced[473] **Lewis W. Butcher**,[433] b. Jan-22-1858 in Ritchie Co, (W)VA,[398,473] (son of George W. Butcher and Amy Stansberry), d. Feb-24-1932 in Exchange, Braxton Co, WV,[398] buried Shaver Cemetery,[398] census 1930 in Otter District, Braxton Co, WV, census 1860 in Ritchie Co, (W)VA, occupation farmer.[398] She married[395,228] (2) Dec- 7-1884 in Ritchie Co, WV,[mcxix][1119],[mcxx][1120] [Minnie Kendall Lowther, in "Ritchie County in History and Romance," p. 317, gives marriage date as Jan 2 1883. But this is contradicted by marriage record.], **Eusebius L. "Sebe" Bee**, also known as E. L. Bee,[570,395] b. Mar- 1-1850 in Doddridge Co, (W)VA,[398,mcxxi][1121],[46] (son of John Nelson Bee and Perdilla Bland), d. Apr-27-1926 at Wolf Summit, Harrison Co, WV,[398,46] buried in IOOF Cemetery, Salem, Harrison Co, WV,[398,817] census 1910 in Berea, Ritchie Co, WV, census 1880 in Union District, Ritchie Co, WV, census 1850 in Doddridge Co, (W)VA, occupation music teacher (Ritchie Co & Salem College) and farmer.

1910 Census, Ritchie Co, WV (Union District, Berea Precinct), enumerated on May 27 1910: Eusebious L. Bee, 61, b. W.Va., father b. Pennsylvania, mother b. W.Va., farmer, married 27 yrs; wife Rebecca J, 50, mother of 7 children (all still living); dau Hertha E, 12; dau Hazel C, 10.

        Children by Eusebius L. "Sebe" Bee:
952. i.   OWEN ULYSSES BEE b. Apr-19-1884.
      ii.   OLENA MAE BEE[398,228] also known as Mae Bee,[419,817] b. Oct-23-1885 in Ritchie Co, WV,[398,419,809] d. Jan-12-1970 in Wolf Summit, Harrison Co, WV,[398] buried in IOOF Cemetery, Salem, Harrison Co, WV,[398,817] resided in Wolf Summit, Harrison Co, WV,[398] census 1900 in Union District, Ritchie Co, WV. She married[1101] Jan-31-1911 in Clarksburg, Harrison Co, WV,[419] Arthur Raymond Davis, b. Jun-15-1880 in Pennsylvania,[398,419] (son of John T. Davis and Melvina Armenia Garvin), d. Nov-23-1940 at Wolf Summit, Harrison Co, WV,[398] buried in IOOF Cemetery, Salem, Harrison Co, WV,[398,817] resided at Wolf Summit, Harrison Co, WV.[398]
      iii. ROSA DALE BEE b. Feb-22-1887 in Berea, Ritchie Co, WV, d. Dec- 9-1955, resided 1950 in Wolf Summit, Harrison Co, WV,[521] census 1910 in Bridgeport, Lawrence Co, IL. She married[1101] Nov- 2-1902 in Harrison Co, WV,[537] no children from this marriage, John Wesley Anderson, b. Apr- 2-1880, d. 1932, census 1910 in Bridgeport, Lawrence Co, IL. 1910 Census, Lawrence County, Illinois (City of Bridgeport), enumerated on Apr 1 1910:

John Anderson, 30, b. W.Va, married 8 yrs; wife Rosa, 23, b. W.Va, no children; brother-in-law Orazs Bee, 19, b. W.Va, single.

    953.   iv.   ORAZS CREED BEE b. Nov-24-1889.
            v.   HEARTHA E. BEE b. ca 1896,[473] resided 1950 in Salem, WV,[521] census 1910 in Berea, Ritchie Co, WV. She married[1101] Mar- 4-1913 in Ritchie Co, WV,[473] Wade H. Mason, b. ca 1892 in Harrison Co, WV.[473]
    954.   vi.   HAZEL C. BEE b. Mar- 1-1900.

528. **Louella D. Dayton** (286.Mary[7], 142.James[6], 72.John[5], 21.John[4], 6.Hugh[3], 3.John[2], 1.Jean[1]), b. Mar-19-1862 at Duck Creek, Harrison Co, (W)VA,[398] d. Dec-26-1943 at Lost Creek, Harrison Co, WV,[398] buried in Brick Church (7th Day Baptist) Cemetery, Lost Creek, Harrison Co, WV,[398,230] census 1880, 1900 in Grant District, Harrison Co, WV. She married Aug-16-1892 in Clarksburg, Harrison Co, WV,[419] **William F. Hornor**, b. Aug-18-1864 at Duck Creek, Harrison Co, WV,[398,419] (son of Thomas M. Hornor and Ann M. Ramage), d. Jan-14-1944 in Clarksburg, Harrison Co, WV,[398] buried in Brick Church (7th Day Baptist) Cemetery, Lost Creek, Harrison Co, WV,[398,230] resided at Lost Creek, Harrison Co, WV,[398] census 1900 in Grant District, Harrison Co, WV.
    Children:
        i.   GENEVIEVE HORNOR b. May- -1893 in Harrison Co, WV,[467,419] d. Apr-15-1951,[1122] resided Jan 1944 in Philadelphia, PA,[748] resided Dec 1943 at Lost Creek, Harrison Co, WV,[778] census 1930 in Parkersburg, Wood Co, WV, census 1920 in Marietta, Washington Co, OH, census 1900 in Grant District, Harrison Co, WV. She married Apr-19-1915 in Clarksburg, Harrison Co, WV,[419] no children from this marriage,[191] Alfred Earle "Greasy" Neale, census name Earle A. Neale,[681] b. Nov- 5-1891 in Wood Co, WV,[592,419,46] (son of William Henry Neale, Jr. and Rena T. Fairfax), d. Nov- 2-1973 in Palm Beach Co, FL,[1123],592,46 buried in Parkersburg Memorial Gardens (aka IOOF Cem, 24th St), Wood Co, WV,[17] resided in West Palm Beach, Palm Beach Co, FL,[948] census 1920, 1930 in Parkersburg, Wood Co, WV [Listed in the household of his parents and siblings. In 1920, his occupation was athletic director, and his marital status was married, but his wife was not accounted for. In 1930, his wife was with him and his occupation was listed as football coach.], census 1920 in Marietta, Washington Co, OH [Listed as on of five "lodgers" (possibly meaning tenants), one of whom was his wife Genevieve. His name was given as Earle A. Neale, and his occupation athletic coach.], resided 1915 in Parkersburg, Wood Co, WV,[419] occupation 1916-1924 baseball player, Cincinnati Reds,[190,148] occupation 1941-1950 head football coach, Philadelphia Eagles.[148,190]

    Alfred: A native of Parkersburg, Earle "Greasy" Neale was one of West Virginia's most gifted athletes, successfully playing football, baseball, basketball and golf. He played football for West Virginia Wesleyan University where, as an end, he caught fourteen consecutive passes in leading his team to their first victory ever over West Virginia University. He went on to play Major League baseball for eight seasons, and was also a highly successful college and professional football coach, taking Washington & Jefferson College to the 1922 Rose Bowl and leading the Philadelphia Eagles to NFL championships in 1948 and 1949. In 1967 he was elected to the College Football Hall of Fame, and in 1969 to the Pro Football Hall of Fame. He was the first coach to be inducted as such into both halls and the only man to play in a World Series, coach in a Rose Bowl and be in enshrined in the Professional Football Hall of Fame.[134]

529. **William Rush Dayton**, census name Willie R. Dayton,[577] (286.Mary[7], 142.James[6], 72.John[5], 21.John[4], 6.Hugh[3], 3.John[2], 1.Jean[1]), b. 1867 in Clarksburg, Harrison Co, WV,[398] d. Nov-13-1946 in Wheeling, Ohio Co, WV,[398] buried in Peninsula Cemetery, Wheeling, Ohio Co, WV,[398] resided in Wheeling, Ohio Co, WV, census 1920 in New Martinsville, Wetzel Co, WV, resided 1907 in New Martinsville, Wetzel Co, WV, census 1880 in Grant District, Harrison Co, WV, occupation weighmaster at Wheeling Steel Corp.,[398] occupation 1920 insurance agent.[1124] He married Aug-24-1907 in New Martinsville, Wetzel Co, WV,[1125] divorced[228] **Elsie M. Dalhoff**, b. ca 1887 in Hardin Co, OH,[1125,1126]

census 1930 in Wheeling, Ohio Co, WV, census 1920 in New Martinsville, Wetzel Co, WV, resided 1907 in New Martinsville, Wetzel Co, WV,[1125] occupation 1930 seamstress.[1126]

1920 Census, Wetzel Co, WV (city of New Martinsville), enumerated on Jan 9 1920 at 420 (?) Ohio Street:
William R. Dayton, 50, insurance agent; wife Elsie M, 31; son Waldo G, 10; dau Helen L, 7.

1930 Census, Ohio Co, WV (city of Wheeling):
Elsie M. Dayton, 43, seamstress, widowed; son George Waldow, 21, machinist, single; dau Helen Waldow, 17, stenographer, single.
(Note: Elsie's marital status as widowed is incorrect and should have been either separated or divorced. Husband William, who died in 1946, was not found in this census. The enumerator also erred by entering son George's middle name as his surname, carrying the error over to his sister Helen. George's marital status is also misleading, since he had married in 1928 and was divorced by the time of his 1934 remarriage.)

Children:
i. GEORGE WALDO DAYTON, census name Waldo G. Dayton,[1124] b. Jan-13-1909 in New Martinsville, Wetzel Co, WV,[592,mcxxvii[1127]] d. Apr- 4-1979,[592] resided in St. Clairsville, Belmont Co, OH,[604] census 1930 in Wheeling, Ohio Co, WV, resided 1928 in Wheeling, Ohio Co, WV,[1127] census 1920 in New Martinsville, Wetzel Co, WV, occupation 1930 machinist.[1126] He married (1) Dec- 1-1928 in Wheeling, Ohio Co, WV,[mcxxviii[1128]] Alice Mowen, b. ca 1908 in Martins Ferry, Belmont Co, OH,[1127] resided 1928 in Wheeling, Ohio Co, WV.[1127] He married (2) Jun- 9-1934 in Wheeling, Ohio Co, WV,[mcxxix[1129]] Anna Virginia Trytko, b. Aug-26-1909 in Maynard, Belmont Co, OH,[1011,592,1127] (daughter of __ Trytko and __ Dlesk), d. Feb-15-1993 in Martins Ferry, Belmont Co, OH,[1011,592] resided in St. Clairsville, Belmont Co, OH,[604] resided 1934 in Bridgeport, Belmont Co, OH.[1127]
ii. HELEN L. DAYTON b. ca 1913 in New Martinsville, Wetzel Co, WV,[1124] census 1930 in Wheeling, Ohio Co, WV, census 1920 in New Martinsville, Wetzel Co, WV, occupation 1930 stenographer.[1126] She married Jul- 2-1930 in Brooke Co, WV,[mcxxx[1130]] Hugh Wilson, b. ca 1908 in Wheeling, Ohio Co, WV,[1130] resided 1930 in Bridgeport, Belmont Co, OH.[1130]

530. **John Leolin Gaston** (287.Isaac[7], 142.James[6], 72.John[5], 21.John[4], 6.Hugh[3], 3.John[2], 1.Jean[1]), b. Sep-14-1860 in Harrison Co, (W)VA, d. Jan-12-1943 in Kanawha Co, WV, census 1930 in Charleston, Kanawha Co, WV, resided 1923 in Clarksburg, Harrison Co, WV,[mcxxxi[1131]] [640 S. 7th St.], census 1900, 1910 in Fairmont, Marion Co, WV, resided 1889 in Lewis Co, WV,[410] occupation 1923, 1930 painter,[1131,mcxxxii[1132]] occupation 1900 insurance agent.[mcxxxiii[1133]] He married Apr-29-1889 in Lewis Co, WV,[410] **Effie Pogue Oliver**, b. Sep- -1864,[1133] (daughter of George P. Oliver and Mary A. __), d. Oct- 7-1939 in Kanawha Co, WV, census 1930 in Charleston, Kanawha Co, WV, census 1900, 1910 in Fairmont, Marion Co, WV. The 1923 City Directory for Clarksburg, WV, lists John L. Gaston, painter, and his wife Effie P. as residents of 640 S. 7th St. Separate entries for Ernest A. Gaston, painter, and Mary Gaston, stenographer, show their residences at that same address. Their relationships are not indicated. The entry for John Leolin Gaston's son George shows his residence as being nearby at 647 S. 7th St.

1900 Census, Marion Co, WV (city of Fairmont), enumerated in June 1900:
John L. Gaston, 39, b. Sep 1860, insurance agent, married 11 yrs; wife Effie, 35, b. Sep 1864, mother of 4 children (3 still living); dau Opal, 9, b. Dec 1890; son Harley, 7, b. Mar 1893; son George, 4, b. Feb 1896; sister-in-law Mary Oliver, 30, b. Jul 1869, single.

1910 Census, Marion Co, WV (city of Fairmont), enumerated on Apr 21 1910:
John L. Gaston, 49, painter, married 21 yrs; wife Effie B, 47, mother of 6 children (5 still living); dau Opal O, 19, stenographer in insurance office; son Harley L, 17, clerk in dry goods store; son George I, 14; dau Mary C, 7; son Earnest A, 5.

1930 Census, Kanawha Co, WV (city of Charleston), enumerated on Apr 14 1930:

John L. Gaston, 69, self-employed painter; wife Effie P, 68; dau Mary C, 26, single, assistant secretary at Chamber of Commerce; son Earnest A, 25, single, painter.

               Children:
- i.   OPAL O. GASTON b. Dec- -1890,[1133] census 1900, 1910 in Fairmont, Marion Co, WV.
- ii.   HARLEY L. GASTON b. Mar- -1893,[1133] census 1900 in Fairmont, Marion Co, WV.
- 955. iii. GEORGE ISAAC GASTON b. Feb-18-1896.
- iv.   JOHN OLIVER GASTON b. Feb-18-1899 in Marion Co, WV,mcxxxiv[1134] [Identified in birth record as his mother's fourth child.], d. Jul-20-1899 in Marion Co, WV.
- v.   MARY C. GASTON b. ca 1903,[942] census 1930 in Charleston, Kanawha Co, WV, census 1910 in Fairmont, Marion Co, WV.
- vi.   EARNEST A. GASTON b. ca 1905,[942] census 1930 in Charleston, Kanawha Co, WV, census 1910 in Fairmont, Marion Co, WV, occupation 1930 painter.[1132]

531. **Thomas Charles Gaston**, also known as Charley Gaston (287.Isaac[7], 142.James[6], 72.John[5], 21.John[4], 6.Hugh[3], 3.John[2], 1.Jean[1]), b. Aug- 3-1863 in Harrison Co, WV,[410] d. May- 4-1945 in Lewis Co, WV,mcxxxv[1135] census 1900 in Weston, Lewis Co, WV, occupation house painter, carpenter.[408,920] He married Sep-16-1884 in Lewis Co, WV,mcxxxvi[1136] **Nona Myrtle Nicoles**, b. May-11-1867 in Lewis Co, WV,mcxxxvii[1137],[410] (daughter of William J. Nicoles and Julia M. Peterson), d. Mar-19-1949 in Weston, Lewis Co, WV,[1137,398] buried in Peterson Cemetery, Lewis Co, WV,[1137,398] census 1900 in Weston, Lewis Co, WV.

               Children:
- i.   STOKES K. GASTON b. Jun- 4-1886 in Lewis Co, WV,mcxxxviii[1138] d. Mar-12-1889 in Lewis Co, WV.mcxxxix[1139]
- 956. ii. GOLDEN "GOLDIE" GASTON b. Nov-28-1887.
- 957. iii. LUCY LACY GASTON b. Apr- 6-1891.
- 958. iv. CHARLES NICOLES GASTON b. Jun- 5-1899.

532. **Harley Roach Gaston** (287.Isaac[7], 142.James[6], 72.John[5], 21.John[4], 6.Hugh[3], 3.John[2], 1.Jean[1]), b. Jul-21-1871 in Lewis Co, WV,mcxl[1140],[236] d. Jun-21-1960 in Weston, Lewis Co, WV,[236] buried in Machpelah Cemetery, Weston, Lewis Co, WV,[236] resided 1910 in Weston, Lewis Co, WV,[419] occupation merchant.[236] He married Nov-15-1910 in Harrison Co, WV,mcxli[1141],[537] **Icie Virginia Norman**, b. Sep-19-1879 in Harrison Co, WV,mcxlii[1142],[398] (daughter of Columbus L. Norman and Sarah Elizabeth Lewis), d. Aug- 5-1955 in Weston, Lewis Co, WV,[398] buried in Machpelah Cemetery, Weston, Lewis Co, WV,[398] resided in Weston, Lewis Co, WV.[398]

               Children:
- 959. i. STOKES NORMAN GASTON b. Sep-27-1911.
- ii.   (INFANT) GASTON b. Aug-24-1912 in Lewis Co, WV, d. Aug-24-1912 in Lewis Co, WV, buried in Machpelah Cemetery, Weston, Lewis Co, WV.

533. **Frederick Helmick** (288.Margaret[7], 142.James[6], 72.John[5], 21.John[4], 6.Hugh[3], 3.John[2], 1.Jean[1]), b. Aug-27-1871 in Palatine (now E. Fairmont), Marion Co, WV,[278] d. Aug-16-1959, buried in Woodlawn Cemetery, Fairmont, Marion Co, WV. He married Jun-29-1898, **Della Mae Brooks**, b. Aug-17-1877 in Webster, Westmoreland Co, PA,[278] (daughter of William Brown "Billy" Brooks and Frances Julia Barbara Spiegel), d. Apr-21-1954, buried in Woodlawn Cemetery, Fairmont, Marion Co, WV.

               Children:
- 960. i. FRANCES VIRGINIA HELMICK b. Mar-20-1900.
- 961. ii. ROBERT J. "JAY" HELMICK b. Jan-12-1906.

534. **Ernest Helmick** (288.Margaret[7], 142.James[6], 72.John[5], 21.John[4], 6.Hugh[3], 3.John[2], 1.Jean[1]), b. Dec- 5-1873, d. Jun-29-1911, buried in Woodlawn Cemetery, Fairmont, Marion Co, WV.

Ernest Helmick's wife Hermione was the stepdaughter of his sister Lucy.

He married **Hermione Pierpoint**, b. Sep- 9-1878 (daughter of John Scott Pierpoint and Isa McCally), d. Dec-14-1951, buried in Woodlawn Cemetery, Fairmont, Marion Co, WV.

Children:
962.   i.   JOHN PIERPONT HELMICK b. Nov-18-1904.

535. **Carroll Helmick** (288.Margaret[7], 142.James[6], 72.John[5], 21.John[4], 6.Hugh[3], 3.John[2], 1.Jean[1]), b. Oct-17-1878, d. Oct-11-1965, buried in Woodlawn Cemetery, Fairmont, Marion Co, WV. He married **Edna Mason**, b. Jun-25-1880, d. Jul-21-1961, buried in Woodlawn Cemetery, Fairmont, Marion Co, WV.

Children:
i.   BESS HELMICK b. Oct-26-1902, d. Oct-29-1902, buried in Woodlawn Cemetery, Fairmont, Marion Co, WV.
ii.   MARY MASON HELMICK b. 1905. She married Samuel Earl Smith, b. 1906, d. 1969, buried in Woodlawn Cemetery, Fairmont, Marion Co, WV.

536. **Louis Gaston Helmick** (288.Margaret[7], 142.James[6], 72.John[5], 21.John[4], 6.Hugh[3], 3.John[2], 1.Jean[1]), b. Nov-23-1882,[592] d. Jul- 5-1973,[592] buried in Woodlawn Cemetery, Fairmont, Marion Co, WV, resided in Fairmont, Marion Co, WV.[592] He married **Harriett Rosendale Smith**, b. Nov- 8-1891, d. Nov-14-1968, buried in Woodlawn Cemetery, Fairmont, Marion Co, WV.

Children:
i.   JANE HELMICK b. Dec-12-1916, d. Dec-16-1916, buried in Woodlawn Cemetery, Fairmont, Marion Co, WV.
ii.   SUSAN HELMICK b. Oct-28-1918, d. Dec-27-1959, buried in Woodlawn Cemetery, Fairmont, Marion Co, WV, never married.
963.   iii.   LOUIS GASTON HELMICK, JR. b. Jul-14-1920.
964.   iv.   HARRIET WRIGHT HELMICK b. May-27-1924.

537. **Charles L. Stewart** (289.Rebecca[7], 142.James[6], 72.John[5], 21.John[4], 6.Hugh[3], 3.John[2], 1.Jean[1]), b. Apr- -1862. He married **Mary A. __**, b. May- -1876.

Children:
i.   KELLY C. STEWART b. Mar- 9-1897,[592] d. Mar- -1975,[592] resided in Beckley, Raleigh Co, WV.[604]
ii.   WANDA MARIE STEWART b. Mar-10-1899 in West Virginia,[592] d. Jun-30-1978 in Fayetteville, Cumberland Co, NC,[592] resided in Fayetteville, Cumberland Co, NC.[604] She married[436] __ Cook.

538. **Hiter Stewart** (289.Rebecca[7], 142.James[6], 72.John[5], 21.John[4], 6.Hugh[3], 3.John[2], 1.Jean[1]), b. Mar- -1871. He married Jul-11-1896 in Lewis Co, WV,[mcxliii[1143]] **Mary Charlotte Morris**, b. Sep- -1872,[mcxliv[1144]] (daughter of William Henry Morris and Olive Jane Gaston). Some researchers report Mary Morris's middle name as Elizabeth. But 1880 Census lists her as Mary C. Morris, and her marriage record identifies her as Mary Charlotte Morris. As grandchildren of James Gaston & Charlotte Swisher, Hiter Stewart and Mary Charlotte Morris were first cousins. His name has also been reported as Hites Stewart.

Children:
i.   EDWIN STEWART b. Mar- -1897.
ii.   MORRIS STEWART b. Aug- 5-1898,[592] d. Dec- -1976,[592] resided in Vienna, Wood Co, WV.[592]
iii.   MARLTON STEWART b. Dec- 6-1899,[592] d. Feb- -1979,[592] resided in Parkersburg, Wood Co, WV.[mcxlv[1145]]

539. **Albert Dalton Gaston**, also known as A. D. "Bert" Gaston (290.Thomas[7], 142.James[6], 72.John[5], 21.John[4], 6.Hugh[3], 3.John[2], 1.Jean[1]), b. Jun-11-1868 in Lewis Co, WV, d. Jun-29-1904 in Weston, Lewis Co, WV,[mcxlvi[1146]] cause of death suicide,[mcxlvii[1147]] occupation railroading.[236] He married Dec-25-1893 in Lewis Co, WV,[410] **Olive Bird Brinkley**, also known as Olive Birdie Brinkley,[410] b. Sep- 7-1873 in

Arnold, Brooke Co, WV,[mcxlviii[1148],410] (daughter of Fleming Brinkley and Margaret Gay), d. Aug-10-1959 in Clarksburg, Harrison Co, WV,[1148] buried in Machpelah Cemetery, Weston, Lewis Co, WV.[1148]

       Children:
965.   i.   BRADY SUMMERS GASTON b. May-21-1897.
966.   ii.   MARGARET HELEN GASTON b. Mar-13-1900.
       iii.   ALBERT DALTON GASTON, JR. d. aft 1972.
       iv.   PAUL BRINKLEY GASTON b. Oct-20-1904 in Weston, Lewis Co, WV,[mcxlix[1149],419] d.

Feb- 6-1958 at Maple Lake (Bridgeport), Harrison Co, WV,[398] buried in Bridgeport Cemetery, Harrison Co, WV,[398] resided 1944 in Clarksburg, Harrison Co, WV,[419] resided at Maple Lake (Bridgeport), Harrison Co, WV,[398] occupation president of foundry.[398] He married Aug-12-1944 in Clarksburg, Harrison Co, WV,[419] Clara Virginia Owens, b. Jun-18-1911 in Clarksburg, Harrison Co, WV,[419,592] (daughter of Roy S. Owens and Ida May Thomas), d. Nov-29-1990,[592] resided 1958 at Maple Lake (Bridgeport), Harrison Co, WV,[228] resided 1944 in Clarksburg, Harrison Co, WV.[419]

540. **Harry Gaston** (290.Thomas[7], 142.James[6], 72.John[5], 21.John[4], 6.Hugh[3], 3.John[2], 1.Jean[1]), b. 1872 in Gaston, Lewis Co, WV,[398] d. Apr-21-1948 in Weston, Lewis Co, WV,[398] buried in Fairmont, Marion Co, WV,[398] resided near Fairmont, Marion Co, WV,[398] resided 1929 in Seattle, WA,[mcl[1150]] occupation machinist, United Airlines.[398]

Identified in father's obituary as Henry Gaston, an apparent error.

He married Oct-18-1900 in Marion Co, WV,[mcli[1151]] **Ota Blanche Dudley**, b. Jul-25-1876,[398] (daughter of Fleming Dudley and Sarah Boggess), d. Jun- 9-1949 in Fairmont, Marion Co, WV,[398] buried in Woodlawn Cemetery, Fairmont, Marion Co, WV,[398] resided in Bentons Ferry (Fairmont), Marion Co, WV.[398]

       Children:
       i.   DOROTHY RUTH GASTON b. Dec-29-1902 in Marion Co, WV.
       ii.   ROBERT DUDLEY GASTON b. Aug-12-1905 in Marion Co, WV,[592] d. Jun-30-1998,[592] resided in Seattle, WA,[592] resided formerly in California.[mclii[1152]]
       iii.   HERBERT LOUIS GASTON b. Feb-28-1907 in Marion Co, WV,[592] d. Jun-23-1991,[592] resided in Washington State.[mcliii[1153]]
       iv.   SARAH HELEN GASTON b. Jul-31-1910 in Marion Co, WV.

541. **Lelia Gaston** (290.Thomas[7], 142.James[6], 72.John[5], 21.John[4], 6.Hugh[3], 3.John[2], 1.Jean[1]), b. Nov-23-1880 in Gaston, Lewis Co, WV,[236] d. Jul-12-1942 in Lewis Co, WV, buried in Weston Masonic Cemetery, Lewis Co, WV.[236] She married Mar-28-1900 in Lewis Co, WV,[410] **Thaddeus Sobisca Stalnaker**,[410] also known as T. S. Stalnaker,[236] b. Sep- 5-1871 in Lewis Co, WV,[410] (son of Sobisca Stalnaker and Christena Waggoner), d. Apr- 5-1944 in Lewis Co, WV,[236] buried in Weston Masonic Cemetery, Lewis Co, WV,[236] occupation farmer.[236]

       Children:
       i.   VESTA PHYLLIS STALNAKER[621] also known as Phyllis Stalnaker,[621,748] b. Feb-14-1901 in Lewis Co, WV,[592,621] d. Sep- -1995,[592] resided in Weston, Lewis Co, WV.[748,604] She married May-15-1920 in Clarksburg, Harrison Co, WV,[mcliv[1154]] Paul Trellan Butcher, b. Apr-25-1900 in Lewis Co, WV,[592,621] (son of Charles Upton Butcher and Mary Genevieve Flesher), d. Dec- -1972,[592] resided in Weston, Lewis Co, WV,[604] occupation stenographer.[621]

542. **Etta Maude Morris**, census name Etta May Morris,[577] (291.Olive[7], 142.James[6], 72.John[5], 21.John[4], 6.Hugh[3], 3.John[2], 1.Jean[1]), b. Feb-14-1869 in Harrison Co, WV,[410,603] d. May-19-1950 near Cimarron, Gray Co, KS,[mclv[1155]] buried in Cimarron Cemetery, Gray Co, KS,[1155] resided from 1903 near Cimarron, Gray Co, KS,[1155] census 1880 in Grant District, Harrison Co, WV. She married Sep- 6-1887 in Lewis Co, WV,[mclvi[1156]] **Jefferson Davis Butcher**, b. Jun- 3-1859,[410] (son of Isaac J. Butcher and Christiana Life), d. Dec-30-1934,[1155] buried in Cimarron Cemetery, Gray Co, KS,[1155] resided from 1903 near Cimarron, Gray Co, KS,[1155] resided until 1903 in Lewis Co, WV.[1155] Following their marriage, J.D. and Etta Maude lived near his parents near Little Skin Creek in Lewis County, WV. The valley where they lived is now covered by Stonewall Jackson Reservoir. J.D. suffered from "brow ague" (sinus trouble)

and needed a drier climate. Also wanting better opportunities for their children, they decided to move west. They bought land near Cimarron, Kansas, and in 1903 moved there with their six children. Traveling by train, J.D. rode in a boxcar with the family belongings, while his wife took the children in the passenger car. They also built a house in town so the children could attend school. They remained in the Cimarron area for the rest of their lives.[1155]

Children:

i.   JENNIE BUTCHER b. Nov-16-1888 in Lewis Co, WV,[1155,592] d. Mar-23-1970 in Bucklin, Ford Co, KS,[1155,592] buried in Cimarron Cemetery, Gray Co, KS,[1155] resided in Bucklin, Ford Co, KS,[592] resided formerly in New York,[mclvii[1157]] occupation teacher (briefly), then bank employee in Cimarron and Oklahoma City,[1155] education Kansas State Teachers College, University of Kansas,[1155] never married[1155].

ii.   CARREL E. BUTCHER b. Jan-23-1890 in Lewis Co, WV,[1155] d. Apr-19-1954 in Dodge City, Ford Co, KS,[1155] buried in Maple Grove Cemetery, Dodge City, KS,[1155] occupation farmer.[1155] He married May-19-1923 in Cimarron, Gray Co, KS,[1155] Florence Smyth, b. May- 4-1902,[1155,592] (daughter of Charles Smith and Katherine Dwyer), d. Mar-17-1997,[1155,592] buried in Maple Grove Cemetery, Dodge City, KS,[1155] resided in Garden City, Finney Co, KS.[mclviii[1158]]

iii.   MAUDE BUTCHER b. Sep- 8-1891 in Lewis Co, WV,[1155,592] d. Jul-22-1981 in Minneola, Clark Co, KS,[1155,592] buried in Fairview Cemetery, near Montezuma, Gray Co, KS,[1155] resided in Medicine Lodge, Barber Co, KS,[592] resided near Ensign, Gray Co, KS,[1155] education Kansas State Teachers College.[1155] She married Aug-16-1916 in Cimarron, Gray Co, KS,[1155] Edwin Denton Jacques, b. Aug-18-1889,[1155] (son of Denton Jacques and Anna Rebecca Clem), d. Mar- 2-1967,[1155] buried in Fairview Cemetery, near Montezuma, Gray Co, KS,[1155] resided near Ensign, Gray Co, KS.[1155] After graduating from 8th grade, Maude took some high school classes then taught school for a time. She attended Kansas State Teachers College in Emporia, then returned to western Kansas and taught until she and Ed Jacques were married. They moved to a farm near Ensign, Kansas, where they raised their family.[1155]

iv.   RUEL V. BUTCHER b. Dec- 2-1893 in Lewis Co, WV,[1155,592] d. Nov-20-1972 in Cimarron, Gray Co, KS,[1155,592] buried in Cimarron Cemetery, Gray Co, KS,[1155] resided in Cimarron, Gray Co, KS,[1158,1155] occupation First National Bank, Cimarron (employee, later president),[1155] education business college, Garden City KS.[1155] He married Jul-26-1924 in New Mexico,[1155] Willa A. Niemeier, b. Nov-14-1904,[1155,592] (daughter of W. H. Niemeier and Alma Edna Simpson), d. Aug- 9-2000,[1155,592] buried in Cimarron Cemetery, Gray Co, KS,[1155] resided in Cimarron, Gray Co, KS.[592,1155]

v.   LULA MAY BUTCHER b. May-19-1896 in Lewis Co, WV,[1155,592] d. May-20-1986 in Dodge City, Ford Co, KS,[1155,592] buried in Cimarron Cemetery, Gray Co, KS,[1155] resided in Cimarron, Gray Co, KS,[1158] occupation teacher,[1155] education Kansas State Teachers College, Emporia KS.[1155] She married Jun-30-1918 in Dodge City, Ford Co, KS,[1155] Ellsworth Victor Bryan, b. Jul-22-1895,[1155] (son of John Bryan), d. Nov-12-1950,[1155] buried in Cimarron Cemetery, Gray Co, KS,[1155] resided in Cimarron, Gray Co, KS,[1155] occupation farmer, president of First National Bank.[1155]

vi.   WINIFRED BUTCHER b. Mar-28-1898 in Lewis Co, WV,[1155,592] d. Nov-26-1986 in Lawrence, Douglas Co, KS,[1155,592] buried Cimarron Cemetery, Gray Co, KS,[1155] resided in Lawrence, Douglas Co, KS,[592,1155] education Kansas University, Kansas State Teachers College in Emporia.[1155] She married Jun- -1924,[1155] William Edwin Hoffman, b. May- 4-1896,[1155,592] d. Sep-12-1989,[1155,592] buried in Cimarron, Gray Co, KS,[1155] resided in Lawrence, Douglas Co, KS,[592,1155] occupation professor, Kansas University.[1155] Winifred and William Edwin Hoffman left the morning after their marriage for China, where he joined the faculty of Lingnan University in Canton. They were both interned during World War II. He was held by the Japanese in Canton, while she was held at Manila, The Philippines, from Pearl Harbor Day until near the end of the war, when the camp was liberated by the 111th Airborne Division. They made their home in later life in Lawrence, Kansas, where he was on the faculty of the Kansas University.[1155]

vii. REVA GLADYS BUTCHER b. Apr-23-1905 in Cimarron, Gray Co, KS,[1155] d. Jan-22-1916,[1155] buried in Cimarron Cemetery, Gray Co, KS,[1155] cause of death scarlet fever.[1155]

viii. VERA JOY BUTCHER b. Apr-23-1905 in Cimarron, Gray Co, KS,[1155,592] d. Jul-12-1990 in Greensburg, Kiowa Co, KS,[1155,592] buried in Fairview Cemetery, Greensburg, Kiowa CO, KS,[1155] education Colorado University.[1155] She married Jun- 2-1934 in Garden City, Finney Co, KS,[1155] George E. Burke, b. Aug-12-1907,[1155,592] (son of James Burke and Caroline Potter), d. May-18-1996,[1155,592] buried in Fairview Cemetery, Greensburg, Kiowa CO, KS,[1155] resided in Greensburg, Kiowa Co, KS.[1158] For many years, Vera and George Burke owned and operated Burke's Cafe, a restaurant in Greensburg, Kansas.[1155]

ix. ALPHA BUTCHER b. Sep-10-1907 in Cimarron, Gray Co, KS,[1155,592] d. Mar-21-2003 in Canon City, Fremont Co, CO,[1155,592] buried in Mountain Vale Memorial Park Cemetery, Canon City, CO,[1155] resided in Canon City, Fremont Co, CO,[592] resided formerly in Kansas,[1158] occupation teacher,[1155] education Kansas State Teachers College (Emporia), Univ of Kansas, Denver Univ.[1155] She married Jul- 1-1931 in Texas,[1155] Robert H. Garrison, b. Jul-18-1909,[1155,592] d. Mar-17-1988,[1155,592] buried in Mountain Vale Memorial Park Cemetery, Canon City, CO,[1155] resided in Canon City, Fremont Co, CO,[592] resided formerly in Kansas,[1158] occupation farmer.[1155]

543. **James Benjamin Morris** (291.Olive[7], 142.James[6], 72.John[5], 21.John[4], 6.Hugh[3], 3.John[2], 1.Jean[1]), b. Jun- 3-1871 in Harrison Co, WV,[398,410,454] d. May-11-1957 in Grafton, Taylor Co, WV,[398] buried in Bluemont Cemetery, Grafton, Taylor Co, WV,[398] resided in Grafton, Taylor Co, WV,[398] census 1930 in Grafton, Taylor Co, WV, census 1920 in Parkersburg, Wood Co, WV, census 1910 in Cumberland, Allegany Co, MD, occupation carpenter.[398,211] He married Sep-27-1894 in Lewis Co, WV,[410] **Addie May Talbott**, b. Nov-26-1873,[603,410] resided 1957 in Grafton, Taylor Co, WV,[228] census 1930 in Grafton, Taylor Co, WV, census 1920 in Parkersburg, Wood Co, WV, census 1910 in Cumberland, Allegany Co, MD.

1910 Census, Allegany Co, Maryland (City of Cumberland), enumerated on Apr 16 1910:
James B. Morris, 38, b. WVa, carpenter on steam railroad, married 15 yrs; wife Addie M, 36, b. WVa, mother of 2 children (both still living); dau Lee D, 14, b. WVa; dau Lillian L, 3, b. WVa; boarder John Kirkpatrick, 24, b. Md, single, telegraph operator on railroad; boarder Earl Hewit, 23, b. Wisc, single, civil engineer.

1920 Census, Wood Co, WV (City of Parkersburg), enumerated in Jan 1920:
J. B. Morris, 48, clerk (?); wife Addie M, 46; dau Lillian L, 13.

1930 Census, Taylor Co, WV (City of Grafton), enumerated on Apr 2 1930:
Carl W. Poe, 36, b. WVa, switchman on steam railroad, widowed; son James E. Poe, 13; dau Geraldine L. Poe, 12; son Carl W. Poe Jr, 10; son Charles Wm. (?) Poe, 9 (8?); father-in-law James B. Morris, 58, grocery clerk; mother-in-law Addie M. Morris, 56; sister-in-law Lillian L. Morris, 23, single.

Children:
967. i. DONA LEIGH MORRIS b. Mar- 6-1896.
ii. LILLIAN L. MORRIS b. ca 1907 in West Virginia,[211] census 1930 in Grafton, Taylor Co, WV, census 1920 in Parkersburg, Wood Co, WV, census 1910 in Cumberland, Allegany Co, MD.

544. **Mary Charlotte Morris** (291.Olive[7], 142.James[6], 72.John[5], 21.John[4], 6.Hugh[3], 3.John[2], 1.Jean[1]) (See marriage to number 538.)

545. **Minnie Iris Gaston** (292.John[7], 142.James[6], 72.John[5], 21.John[4], 6.Hugh[3], 3.John[2], 1.Jean[1]), b. Jan-10-1872 in Lewis Co, WV,[398,410] d. May-22-1946 in Lewis Co, WV,[398] buried in Peterson Cemetery, Lewis Co, WV.[398] She married Oct-7-1896 in Lewis Co, WV,[mclix[1159],410] **John Pence Peterson**, b. Mar-20-1866 in Lewis Co, WV,[398] (son of Jasper Peterson and Martha O. Waggoner), d. Jan-27-1953 in Lewis Co, WV,[398] occupation farmer.[398]

Children:

i. GERTRUDE PETERSON b. Jun-27-1904 in Weston, Lewis Co, WV,[190,621,592] d. Mar-17-1998 in Buckhannon, Upshur Co, WV,[190,592] buried in Peterson Cemetery, Lewis Co, WV,[190] resided in Buckhannon, Upshur Co, WV,[592] resided 1950 near Weston, Lewis Co, WV,[621] occupation teacher,[mclx[1160]] education Washington-Irving HS, Beechwood School (Philadelphia), Salem College WV.[1160] She married[191] Dec-25-1950 near Weston, Lewis Co, WV,[621] no children from this marriage,[mclxi[1161]] Summers R. Hill, b. Jun-22-1886 in Pocahontas Co, WV,[621,592] (son of William B. Hill and Alice Snedegar), d. Feb- -1963,[592] resided 1950 in Buckhannon, Upshur Co, WV.[621]

968.   ii.   HOWARD GASTON PETERSON b. Feb-28-1906.

546. **Daisy Dean Gaston** (292.John[7], 142.James[6], 72.John[5], 21.John[4], 6.Hugh[3], 3.John[2], 1.Jean[1]), b. Mar-11-1874 in Lewis Co, WV,[398] d. Jun-23-1948 at Horner, Lewis Co, WV,[398] buried in Peterson Cemetery, Lewis Co, WV,[398] resided at Horner, Lewis Co, WV.[398] She married Nov-26-1911 in Lewis Co, WV,[410] **Leroy Mifflin "Roy" Lawson**, b. Sep-24-1874 in Upshur Co, WV,[398,410] (son of Elias M. Lawson and Columbia Helen Marple), d. Aug- 6-1954 in Weston, Lewis Co, WV,[398] buried in Peterson Cemetery, Lewis Co, WV,[398] resided in Weston, Lewis Co, WV,[398] census 1920, 1930 in Skin Creek, Lewis Co, WV, occupation farmer,[1093,398] military Spanish-American War.[398]

Children:

i.   MARY ERNESTINE LAWSON, also known as Ernestine Lawson,[1093] b. ca 1916,[888] census 1920, 1930 in Skin Creek, Lewis Co, WV.

547. **Mary E. Gaston** (293.Abraham[7], 143.William[6], 72.John[5], 21.John[4], 6.Hugh[3], 3.John[2], 1.Jean[1]), b. Sep-18-1852 in Lewis Co, WV,[276,234] d. Nov- 2-1937 in Lost Creek, Harrison Co, WV,[398,mclxii[1162]] buried in Beech Grove Cemetery, Lewis Co, WV,[276] resided in Lost Creek, Harrison Co, WV,[398] census 1860, 70, 80 in Lewis Co, WV, never married.

Name given in 1860 Census as Mary E. Gaston, in 1870 Census as Mary C. Gaston, and in 1880 Census as Mary E. Gaston. But Harrison County Death Record and WV State Death Certificate have it has Mary R. Gaston.

Children:

969.   i.   WADE COMPTON GASTON b. Sep-26-1878.

548. **Amanda Jane Gaston**, census name Mandy J. Gaston,[246] (293.Abraham[7], 143.William[6], 72.John[5], 21.John[4], 6.Hugh[3], 3.John[2], 1.Jean[1]), b. Mar- 3-1855 in Lewis Co, WV,[550] d. Aug-28-1937,[17] buried in Beech Grove Cemetery, Lewis Co, WV,[17] census 1860, 1870 in Lewis Co, WV. She married Jan-21-1875 in Lewis Co, WV,[mclxiii[1163],433,mclxiv[1164]] **Minor James Hall**, also known as James Minor Hall,[1164] b. Mar- 9-1853,[17] (son of James Monroe Hall and Nancy Burnside), d. Oct-25-1927,[17,1164] buried in Beech Grove Cemetery, Lewis Co, WV,[17] [Name appears on headstone as Minor J. Hall.].

Children:

i.   WILLIAM HENRY HALL b. Apr-17-1876,[17] d. Jul-20-1878,[17] buried in Beech Grove Cemetery, Lewis Co, WV.

ii.   JAMES CLARK HALL b. Dec-14-1877,[17] d. Sep- 1-1898,[17] buried in Beech Grove Cemetery, Lewis Co, WV.

970.   iii.   TENSIE MYRTLE HALL b. Nov-21-1879.

971.   iv.   SARAH DELLA HALL b. Oct-26-1881.

v.   ENOCH MINOR HALL, also known as Enoch Monroe Hall,[234] b. Nov-12-1883, d. Mar-7-1965.[234] He married Aug-31-1910, Sarah E. Simmons.

vi.   LOMAN EARL HALL b. Jan- 6-1886,[17] d. Feb- 5-1887,[17] buried in Beech Grove Cemetery, Lewis Co, WV.

972.   vii.   BLONDA SCOTT HALL b. Dec- 3-1887.

viii.   LARRY HALL b. Jun- 1-1890,[17] d. Jun- 1-1890,[17] buried in Beech Grove Cemetery, Lewis Co, WV [Spelling of first name on headstone is LARKY.].

973.   ix.   HARVEY ADDISON HALL b. May-30-1891.

       x.   CHARLES ABRAHAM HALL b. Sep-18-1893, d. Oct-18-1918.
      xi.   JOHN HOBERT HALL b. Sep-28-1896,[17] d. Mar-17-1897,[17] buried in Beech Grove Cemetery, Lewis Co, WV.

549. **Rebecca Virginia "Jennie" Gaston** (293.Abraham[7], 143.William[6], 72.John[5], 21.John[4], 6.Hugh[3], 3.John[2], 1.Jean[1]), b. Aug- 7-1857 in Lewis Co, WV,[550,mclxv\[1165\]] d. Jan- 5-1946,[mclxvi\[1166\]] buried in Weston Masonic Cemetery, Lewis Co, WV, census 1860, 1870 in Lewis Co, WV. She married Feb-3-1876 in Lewis Co, WV,[mclxvii\[1167\]] **Richard Harvey Hall**, also known as Harvey Richard Hall, b. May-24-1855,[1165] (son of James Monroe Hall and Nancy Burnside), buried in Weston Masonic Cemetery, Lewis Co, WV.
         Children:
  974. i.   SIMEON ASBURY HALL b. Feb- 2-1877.
      ii.   CLAUDE M. HALL b. Oct- 8-1878,[1165] d. Apr- -1965,[592] buried in Freemansburg Meth Church Cemetery, Lewis Co, WV.[17] He married May- 5-1914 in Lewis Co, WV,[410] Nelle White, b. 1892,[17,410] (daughter of G. L. White and Susan __), d. 1971,[17] buried in Freemansburg Meth Church Cemetery, Lewis Co, WV.

550. **Ida May Gaston** (293.Abraham[7], 143.William[6], 72.John[5], 21.John[4], 6.Hugh[3], 3.John[2], 1.Jean[1]), b. Jan-6-1860 in Lewis Co, WV,[mclxviii\[1168\],398] d. May-10-1941 in Jane Lew, Lewis Co, WV,[398,mclxix\[1169\]] buried in Beech Grove Cemetery, Lewis Co, WV [Death Certificate lists burial at Mt Morris Cemetery, Freemansburg, Lewis Co, WV.], resided in Jane Lew, Lewis Co, WV,[398] census 1920 at Hackers Creek, Lewis Co, WV,[888] census 1860, 70, 80 in Lewis Co, WV, never married[398].
         Children:
      i.   DESSIE BLANCHE GASTON b. Nov-13-1884,[784] d. Nov-11-1961 in Lewis Co, WV,[mclxx\[1170\]] buried in Beech Grove Cemetery, Lewis Co, WV, resided 1941 in Jane Lew, Lewis Co, WV,[778] census 1920 at Hackers Creek, Lewis Co, WV.[888]

551. **Adaline Bell Gaston**[410] (293.Abraham[7], 143.William[6], 72.John[5], 21.John[4], 6.Hugh[3], 3.John[2], 1.Jean[1]), b. Dec-12-1864, d. Mar-22-1896 in Lewis Co, WV,[mclxxi\[1171\]] [Walnut Fork], buried in Freemans Creek, Lewis Co, WV, census 1870 in Lewis Co, WV.

Identified as Adaline (age 6) in the 1870 Census, but as Eva Bird (age 16) in the 1880 Census. No other reference to her as Eva Bird has been found.

She married Apr-10-1881 in Lewis Co, WV,[mclxxii\[1172\]] **Leonidas "Lee" Mundell**, b. ca 1861.[410]
         Children:
      i.   ERNEST G. MUNDELL b. May-10-1881,[592] d. Dec- -1982,[592] resided in West Union, Doddridge Co, WV,[592] buried in Masonic Memorial Park Cemetery, Crystal Lake (West Union), WV.[721] He married Nov- 1-1908, Martha Fling, b. 1878,[721] d. 1959,[721] buried in Masonic Memorial Park Cemetery, Crystal Lake (West Union), WV.[721]
  975. ii.   EDNA E. MUNDELL b. Jun- 4-1883.
      iii. DALE MUNDELL b. May-26-1886, d. Oct- 8-1942. He married Oct- 2-1912, J. P. Young.
      iv. NORA O. MUNDELL b. Apr-20-1889,[592] d. May- -1978,[592] resided in Weston, Lewis Co, WV.[592] She married Oct-16-1919 in Lewis Co, WV,[mclxxiii\[1173\]] Mifflin Blair Norman, b. ca 1881 in Harrison Co, WV,[410] (son of Columbus L. Norman and Sarah Elizabeth Lewis), resided 1919 in Lewis Co, WV.[410]
      v.   OSA D. "OCIE" MUNDELL b. Feb- 8-1892,[592] d. Nov- -1974,[592] resided in Parkersburg, Wood Co, WV,[592] resided formerly in Ohio.[mclxxiv\[1174\]] She married B. M. Andrick.
      vi. GRACE "FRANKIE" MUNDELL b. Jun-17-1895,[592,46] d. Nov- -1976,[592,46] buried in Broad Run Bapt Ch Cem, Jane Lew, Lewis Co, WV,[17] resided in Clarksburg, Harrison Co, WV,[592] census 1900 in Freemans Creek, Lewis Co, WV, never married.

      The 1900 Census listed her as living with her grandparents Abram & Sarah Gaston at Freeman Creek.

552. William Harvey Gaston, also known as Harvey Gaston,[247,374] (293.Abraham[7], 143.William[6], 72.John[5], 21.John[4], 6.Hugh[3], 3.John[2], 1.Jean[1]), b. Oct-19-1868 in Lewis Co, WV,[mclxxv[1175]] d. Apr- 6-1960 in Upshur Co, WV,[mclxxvi[1176]] buried in Heavner Cemetery, Upshur Co, WV,[1176] census 1870, 1880 in Lewis Co, WV.[246,247] He married Aug-31-1893 in Lewis Co, WV,[621] **Ida May Lawson**, also known as May,[396,520] b. Jul-14-1874 in Lewis Co, WV,[398] (daughter of George Lawson and Elizabeth Morrison), d. Apr-27-1947 in Buckhannon, Upshur Co, WV,[398,mclxxvii[1177]] buried in Heavner Cemetery, Upshur Co, WV,[398] resided in Buckhannon, Upshur Co, WV,[520,398] resided 1893 in Lewis Co, WV.[621]

       Children:
976.   i.   GEORGE ELBERT GASTON b. May-23-1894.
       ii.   HOWARD LOMAN GASTON b. Feb- 4-1897 in Lewis Co, WV,[mclxxviii[1178],mclxxix[1179],592] d. Dec-17-1974 in Upshur Co, WV,[1179,592] buried in Heavner Cemetery, Upshur Co, WV,[1179] resided in Buckhannon, Upshur Co, WV.[592,949] He married (1) Dec-8-1925, Lorene Robinson. He married (2) Oct-31-1947 in Elkins, Randolph Co, WV,[949] Nellie Frances Mayo, b. ca 1910 in Upshur Co, WV,[949] (daughter of Edward Mayo and Rebecca Ann Harlan), resided 1947 in Pickens, Randolph Co, WV.[949]
977.   iii. LULA LOREEN GASTON b. Jan-22-1900.
978.   iv. HARVEY JUNIOR GASTON b. Jun- 6-1907.
979.   v.   ABRAM LAWSON GASTON b. Apr- 3-1915.
980.   vi. VIRGINIA MAY "GINNY" GASTON b. Oct-30-1917.

553. Lloyd Henry Gaston (293.Abraham[7], 143.William[6], 72.John[5], 21.John[4], 6.Hugh[3], 3.John[2], 1.Jean[1]), b. Aug- 4-1873 in Lewis Co, WV, d. Oct-24-1918 in Keyser, Mineral Co, WV,[mclxxx[1180]] buried in Keyser, Mineral Co, WV,[mclxxxi[1181]] resided in Keyser, Mineral Co, WV,[mclxxxii[1182],1181] occupation dentist,[398,1182] census 1910 in New Creek, Mineral Co, WV, census 1880 in Lewis Co, WV. He married Jul-11-1904 in Keyser, Mineral Co, WV,[mclxxxiii[1183]] **Edna M. Davis**, b. Jan- 1-1882 in Mineral Co, WV,[1182] (daughter of Samuel Davis and Mary F. __), resided 1918 in Keyser, Mineral Co, WV,[228] census 1910 in New Creek, Mineral Co, WV.

       Children:
981.   i.   LLOYD HENRY GASTON, JR. b. ca 1907.
982.   ii.   GERALDINE GASTON b. Feb-12-1912.
983.   iii. LOUISE GASTON b. Nov-14-1914.

554. William J. Gaston, also known as Willie Gaston,[419] (294.George[7], 143.William[6], 72.John[5], 21.John[4], 6.Hugh[3], 3.John[2], 1.Jean[1]), b. May-18-1859 in Lewis Co, (W)VA,[1162,419] d. Oct-19-1937 in Harrison Co, WV,[1162] buried (mausoleum) in Elkview Masonic Cemetery, Clarksburg, Harrison Co, WV,[462,398] resided 1884 in Lewis Co, WV,[419] occupation physican,[419,398,mclxxxiv[1184]]

Name given as William C. Gaston in 1860 Census of Lewis County, (W)VA, but William J. Gaston elsewhere. He practiced medicine in Good Hope, Harrison Co, WV, from 1884 to 1907, when he joined practice with Dr. Arnett in the Goff Building in Clarksburg, WV.[1184]

He married (1) Sep-11-1884 in Harrison Co, WV,[419,mclxxxv[1185]] **Nellie J. Thrash**, b. Jun-11-1864 in Barbour Co, WV,[mclxxxvi[1186],17] (daughter of Richard Thrash and Louisa Jane __), d. May- 3-1892,[1186,17] buried in Mt. Carmel Bapt Ch Cem, Kincheloe Crk, Harrison Co, WV,[17] resided 1884 in Harrison Co, WV.[419] He married (2) Mar-24-1894 in Harrison Co, WV,[419] **Susan Wolfe**, also known as Sue,[419] b. Jul- -1859 in Harrison Co, (W)VA,[398,419] (daughter of Perry H. Wolfe and Elizabeth A. Bassell), d. Jun- 1-1921 in Clarksburg, Harrison Co, WV,[398,916] buried in Morgantown, Monongalia Co, WV.[398]

       Children by Nellie J. Thrash:
       i.   (DAUGHTER) GASTON b. Jun-16-1891 in Harrison Co, WV,[17] d. Jun-17-1891 in Harrison Co, WV,[17] buried in Mt. Carmel Bapt Ch Cem, Kincheloe Crk, Harrison Co, WV.[17]
       Children by Susan Wolfe:
       ii.   HOWE RUSSELL GASTON b. Jan- 4-1895,[mclxxxvii[1187],1186,592] d. Sep-13-1980 in Bay Pines, Pinellas Co, FL,[1187,592] buried (ashes) in C. E. Prevatt Crematory, Pinellas Park FL,[1187] resided in

St. Petersburg, Pinellas Co, FL,[mclxxxviii][1188] resided 1923, 37, 58 in Clarksburg, Harrison Co, WV,[1131,748,849] [945 W. Pike St., Pt Comfort], occupation sales, Standard Register.[1187]

"Howe Russell Gaston enlisted in the United States Regular Army in 1916, and when the United States became involved in the greatest of all wars was transferred from Troop F, Fourteenth Cavalry, to Company C, Third Division Ammunition Train, and went overseas March 2, 1918, then as corporal, but later became acting first sergeant. He rendered service overseas for eighteen months in the Ammunition Train Division of his unit, and took part in the defensive and offensive at the Marne, was in the St. Mihiel and Argonne campaigns, and later was with the Army of Occupation in Germany. His honorable discharge was dated in April 1920." ["The History of West Virginia, Old and New," published 1923, The American Historical Society, Inc., Chicago and New York, Volume III, pp. 361-362]
http://www.wileygenealogy.com/~usbios/bios/wv/harrison/gastonw.txt[1184]

He married[228] Glada Miller, b. Jan- 1-1898,[592] d. Nov- 9-1985 in Hernando Co, FL,[592,mclxxxix[1189]] resided formerly in West Virginia.[mcxc[1190]]

iii. WILLIAM BRYAN GASTON b. May-20-1897,[1186] d. Dec-12-1932 in Clarksburg, Harrison Co, WV,[mcxci[1191]] buried in Elkview Masonic Cemetery, Clarksburg, Harrison Co, WV,[462,1191] cause of death pneumonia,[1191] occupation physician,[1191] military U.S. Army, World War I, never married[1191].

"William Bryan Gaston volunteered in the service of the United States Army the day after he was twenty-one years of age, at Pittsburgh. He was sent first to Camp Meade, later to Annapolis, still later to Washington, District of Columbia, and in February, 1918 went overseas with the Twenty-third Engineers, an entirely volunteer organization. He rendered service in the truck train for nineteen months in France, and received his honorable discharge in July, 1919." ["The History of West Virginia, Old and New," published 1923, The American Historical Society, Inc., Chicago and New York, Volume III, pp. 361-362]
http://www.wileygenealogy.com/~usbios/bios/wv/harrison/gastonw.txt[1184]

555. **Edwin Gaston** (294.George[7], 143.William[6], 72.John[5], 21.John[4], 6.Hugh[3], 3.John[2], 1.Jean[1]), b. Aug- - 1862,[236,mcxcii[1192]] d. Jan-21-1940 in Lewis Co, WV,[mcxciii[1193],1192] buried in Mt. Morris Cemetery, Freemansburg, Lewis Co, WV,[1192] census 1930 in Freemans Creek District, Lewis Co, WV, occupation farmer.[1093]

Date of birth has been reported as Aug 27 1862 (source not documented), Aug 25 1862 (obituary in Weston Independent, per cited compilation by Betty Mayfield, which also misstates his name as Edward), and Aug 28 1862 (computed from age 77y 4m 24d given in death record).

He married Jun-22-1892 in Lewis Co, WV,[410,1192] **Laura Lillian Lovett**, b. Nov-20-1866,[17,1192] [Birthdate has also been reported as 11/20/1869.] (daughter of Jonas Thomas Lovett and Clarissa Waldeck), d. Nov-12-1939 in Lewis Co, WV,[484,1192] buried in Mt. Morris Cemetery, Freemansburg, Lewis Co, WV, census 1930 in Freemans Creek District, Lewis Co, WV.
Children:
i. NELLE LOVETT GASTON, census name Nellie Gaston,[1093] b. Apr-18-1893 in Lewis Co, WV,[236] d. Aug-21-1964 in Weston, Lewis Co, WV,[236] buried in Broad Run Bapt Ch Cem, Jane Lew, Lewis Co, WV,[236] resided in Weston, Lewis Co, WV,[236] resided 1939, 40 in Lewis Co, WV,[856,765] census 1930 in Freemans Creek District, Lewis Co, WV. She married Dec-20-1941 in Lewis Co, WV, Burl David Yates, b. Dec-15-1891 in Harrison Co, WV,[236] (son of William Marion Yates and Ida Brown), d. Mar- 8-1961 near Jane Lew, Lewis Co, WV,[236] buried in Weston Masonic Cemetery, Lewis Co, WV,[236] cause of death automobile accident,[236] resided at Jane Lew, Lewis Co, WV,[236] occupation construction engineer (retired).[236]

ii.   CLIFFORD GEORGE GASTON title: Dr., b. Oct-14-1897 in Lewis Co, WV, resided 1939, 40 in Shelbyville, Shelby Co, IN.[856,765]

556. **William E. Dawson** (295.Elizabeth[7], 143.William[6], 72.John[5], 21.John[4], 6.Hugh[3], 3.John[2], 1.Jean[1]), b. Sep- -1859. He married **Alice __**, b. Sep- -1860.
Children:
i.   EULA DAWSON b. Jun- -1884.
ii.   GRACE DAWSON b. Feb- -1887.

557. **Homer E. Dawson** (295.Elizabeth[7], 143.William[6], 72.John[5], 21.John[4], 6.Hugh[3], 3.John[2], 1.Jean[1]), b. Jan- -1868,[46] d. 1956,[46] buried in Good Hope Masonic Cemetery, Rt. 19 S, Harrison Co, WV.[17,524] He married Nov-26-1891 in Harrison Co, WV,[227] **Ionia Sommerville**, also known as Iona Sommerville,[227] b. Apr- -1869 in Harrison Co, WV,[46,227] (daughter of James W. Sommerville and Amelia A. McGlaughlin), d. 1912,[46] buried in Good Hope Masonic Cemetery, Rt. 19 S, Harrison Co, WV,[17,524] [Spelling of name is Ionia.].
Children:
i.   JAMES R. DAWSON b. Oct- -1892.
ii.   FRANKLIN E. DAWSON b. Apr- -1894.
iii.   MARTHA A. DAWSON b. Apr- -1896.
iv.   ROSCOE DAWSON b. Mar-20-1900, d. Dec- -1979.[592]
v.   (INFANT) DAWSON b. 1902,[46] d. 1902,[46] buried in Good Hope Masonic Cemetery, Rt. 19 S, Harrison Co, WV.[17,524]
vi.   CHARLES P. DAWSON b. 1911,[46] d. 1912,[46] buried in Good Hope Masonic Cemetery, Rt. 19 S, Harrison Co, WV.[17,524]

558. **Lewis D. Dawson** (295.Elizabeth[7], 143.William[6], 72.John[5], 21.John[4], 6.Hugh[3], 3.John[2], 1.Jean[1]), b. Nov- 6-1877,[592] d. Jan- -1969,[592] resided in Tulsa, OK.[838] He married **Claudia __**, b. Sep- -1877.
Children:
i.   WILLIAM J. DAWSON b. Aug-21-1898,[592] d. Dec- -1975,[592] resided in Belle, Kanawha Co, WV.[604]

559. **George L. Gaston** (296.John[7], 143.William[6], 72.John[5], 21.John[4], 6.Hugh[3], 3.John[2], 1.Jean[1]), b. Jul- 6-1862 in Duck Creek, Harrison Co, WV,[mcxciv[1194]] [But headstone gives birth date as 1863.], d. 1935,[1194,46] buried in Duck Creek Missn Chrch Cem, near West Milford, Harrison Co, WV,[230] census 1880, 1900 in Grant District, Harrison Co, WV. He married[1194,227] Oct-25-1883 in Harrison Co, WV,[mcxcv[1195]] [Linder's "Gibson and Related Families," p. 108, states marriage date as Oct 20 1883, but "Harrison County Marriages" reports Oct 25 1883.], **Rachel Bond**, b. Feb-24-1863 in Harrison Co, (W)VA,[636] [Headstone shows birth date as 1862.] (daughter of Abel P. Bond and Adeline "Addie" Gibson), d. Apr-11-1955,[46] buried in Duck Creek Missn Chrch Cem, near West Milford, Harrison Co, WV,[17] census 1900 in Grant District, Harrison Co, WV.
Children:
984.   i.   OCIE OTA GASTON b. Sep-20-1885.
985.   ii.   NANNIE MAY GASTON b. Mar-20-1889.
986.   iii.   MONNA MARIE GASTON b. May-24-1903.

560. **Hiram J. Gaston** (296.John[7], 143.William[6], 72.John[5], 21.John[4], 6.Hugh[3], 3.John[2], 1.Jean[1]), b. Aug-12-1866 in Harrison Co, WV,[mcxcvi[1196]] d. Apr-30-1934 in Clarksburg, Harrison Co, WV,[276,17] buried in Duck Creek Missn Chrch Cem, near West Milford, Harrison Co, WV,[17,276] resided 1923 in Clarksburg, Harrison Co, WV,[1131] [1630 Gould Ave, North View], census 1920 in Clarksburg, Harrison Co, WV, census 1910 in Coal District, Harrison Co, WV, census 1880, 1900 in Grant District, Harrison Co, WV, occupation miner, farmer.[1131,276] He married[396] Jun- 9-1887 in Harrison Co, WV,[mcxcvii[1197]] **Anna Lee Highland**, also known as Annie E. Highland,[433] also known as Lee A. Highland,[920] b. Dec- 9-1871 in West Virginia,[276] (daughter of James I. Highland and Sarah Eliza Lynch), d. Jun- 3-1934 in Clarksburg, Harrison Co, WV,[276] buried in Duck Creek Missn Chrch Cem, near West Milford, Harrison Co, WV,[276]

census 1920 in Clarksburg, Harrison Co, WV, census 1910 in Coal District, Harrison Co, WV, census 1900 in Grant District, Harrison Co, WV.

1900 Census, Harrison Co, WV (Grant District), enumerated on Jun 21 1900:
Hiram J. Gaston, 33, b. Aug 1866, farm laborer, married 13 yrs; wife Annie L, 28, b. Dec 1871, mother of 6 children (all still living); dau Edna F, 12, b. Jan 1888; dau Alphartta, 10, b. Jan 1889; son (sic) Garnett, 9, b. Jan 1891; dau Dessie W, 6, b. Aug 1893; son Frank, 5, b. May 1895; son Spencer B, 1, b. Sep 1898.

1910 Census, Harrison Co, WV (Coal District), enumerated on Apr 21 1910 on Sycamore Street:
Hiram J. Gaston, 43, laborer at glass house, married 23 yrs; wife Anna L, 39, mother of 7 children (5 still living); son Frank, 14; son Spencer B, 11; son Vance, 5.

1920 Census, Harrison Co, WV (Coal District, City of Clarksburg), enumerated on Jan 24 1920:
Hiram J. Gaston, 53, laborer at public work; wife Annie L, 50; son Spencer, 21; son Vance, 15.

1930 Census, Harrison Co, WV (Coal District, City of Clarksburg), enumerated on Apr 12 1930:
Hiram J. Gaston, 63, laborer in coal mine; wife Anna L, 59.

> Children:
> i. EDNA LILLIE GASTON b. Jan- 7-1888 in Harrison Co, WV,[mcxcviii[1198],mcxcix[1199]] d. Mar-1-1888,[1199,mcc[1200]] buried in Duck Creek Missn Chrch Cem, near West Milford, Harrison Co, WV.[17,230]
> 987. ii. ALPHA LOUISE GASTON b. Jan- 3-1889.
> 988. iii. GARNET HORNOR GASTON b. Jan-24-1891.
> iv. DESSIE W. GASTON b. Aug-11-1892 in Harrison Co, WV,[mcci[1201]] d. Aug-14-1908 at Duck Creek, Harrison Co, WV,[mccii[1202]] buried in Duck Creek Missn Chrch Cem, near West Milford, Harrison Co, WV,[17] cause of death blood poisoning,[1201] census 1900 in Grant District, Harrison Co, WV, occupation sorter at Hazel-Atlas Glass Company.[1201]
> 989. v. FRANK C. GASTON b. May-19-1895.
> 990. vi. SPENCER BRYAN GASTON b. Sep- 1-1898.
> 991. vii. VANCE ORLET GASTON b. Aug-19-1904.

561. **James Burnside Gaston** (296.John[7], 143.William[6], 72.John[5], 21.John[4], 6.Hugh[3], 3.John[2], 1.Jean[1]), b. Nov-22-1872 in Harrison Co, WV,[398,17,684,mcciii[1203]] d. Jun- 1-1953 in Morgantown, Monongalia Co, WV,[398,17,1203] buried in Rose Hill (formerly IOOF) Cemetery, West Milford, Harrison Co, WV,[17,398] resided in Morgantown, Monongalia Co, WV,[398] resided 1918 in West Milford, Harrison Co, WV,[684] census 1880 in Grant District, Harrison Co, WV, occupation oiler.[684] He married (1) Dec-25-1900 in West Milford, Harrison Co, WV,[419,537] **Willa G. Floyd**, census name Willie G. Floyd,[467] b. Sep-16-1885,[17] (daughter of Samuel S. Floyd and Mary E. Myers), d. Mar-15-1905 in West Milford, Harrison Co, WV,[276,17] cause of death tuberculosis,[276] buried in Rose Hill (formerly IOOF) Cemetery, West Milford, Harrison Co, WV,[17] census 1900 in Grant District, Harrison Co, WV. He married (2) Nov-28-1907 in Oakland, Garrett Co, MD,[1203] **Addie Beatrice Moffett**, b. Jul-10-1890 in West Milford, Harrison Co, WV,[mcciv[1204],592] (daughter of George Washington Moffett and Sarah Louise "Sally" West), d. Nov- -1985,[592] buried in Rose Hill (formerly IOOF) Cemetery, West Milford, Harrison Co, WV,[mccv[1205]] resided 1953 in Morgantown, Monongalia Co, WV,[228] resided 1918 in West Milford, Harrison Co, WV.[684]

> Children by Addie Beatrice Moffett:
> i. JAMES HARRY GASTON[938] also known as Harry Gaston,[1203,938] b. Jan-17-1911 in Harrison Co, WV, d. Aug-12-1966 in Marion Co, WV.[mccvi[1206],mccvii[1207]] He married[1203] Jun- 9-1935 in Morgantown, Monongalia Co, WV,[938] Ethel Delia Dorsey, b. ca 1916 in Morgantown, Monongalia Co, WV,[938] (daughter of Alpheus C. Dorsey and Grace Gamble), resided 1935 in Morgantown, Monongalia Co, WV.[938]

562. **Mary Effie Gaston**, census name Mary F. Gaston,[577] (296.John[7], 143.William[6], 72.John[5], 21.John[4], 6.Hugh[3], 3.John[2], 1.Jean[1]), b. Oct-20-1875 in West Milford, Harrison Co, WV,[398,17] d. Mar-21-1939 in

Clarksburg, Harrison Co, WV,[398] buried in Rose Hill (formerly IOOF) Cemetery, West Milford, Harrison Co, WV,[398,524] resided in Clarksburg, Harrison Co, WV.[398] She married Aug-2-1896 in Harrison Co, WV,[537] **Howard B. Post**, b. Jun-23-1874,[17] (son of John B. Post and Mary __), d. Sep-17-1924,[17] buried in Rose Hill (formerly IOOF) Cemetery, West Milford, Harrison Co, WV.[524]

Children:

    i.   J. HAROLD POST, census name Harold Post,[mccviii[1208]] b. ca 1897,[1208] census 1930 in Clarksburg, Harrison Co, WV.

    ii.   BERNARD GASTON POST b. May- 3-1900,[mccix[1209]] d. Mar-13-1904,[1209] buried in Rose Hill (formerly IOOF) Cemetery, West Milford, Harrison Co, WV.[1209,17]

    iii.   RACHEL POST b. ca 1902,[1208] census 1930 in Clarksburg, Harrison Co, WV.

    iv.   MARY CATHARINE POST b. Jan- 5-1905,[154] d. Nov-19-1905 in Clarksburg, Harrison Co, WV,[mccx[1210]] cause of death accidental burns.[276]

    v.   HOWARD POST, JR. b. ca 1913,[1208] census 1930 in Clarksburg, Harrison Co, WV.

563. **Cora Gaston** (297.Enoch[7], 143.William[6], 72.John[5], 21.John[4], 6.Hugh[3], 3.John[2], 1.Jean[1]), b. Nov- -1866,[467,46] d. 1938,[46] buried in McWhorter Cemetery, Harrison Co, WV,[17] census 1880, 1900 in Grant District, Harrison Co, WV. She married Jul-26-1885 in Harrison Co, WV,[433] **Daniel Grant McWhorter**, b. Apr-30-1864,[398,467,46] (son of Walter McWhorter and Ailsey Lawson), d. Jun- 7-1924 at McWhorter, Harrison Co, WV,[398,46] buried in McWhorter Cemetery, Harrison Co, WV,[398,17] census 1870, 1900 in Grant District, Harrison Co, WV, occupation farmer.[467,398]

Children:

    i.   NATHAN G. MCWHORTER b. Jul- 9-1886,[592,467] d. Apr- -1971,[592] resided in McWhorter, Harrison Co, WV,[604,748] census 1900 in Grant District, Harrison Co, WV.

  992. ii.   RALPH MCWHORTER b. Sep- -1890.

564. **Claudius Gaston**, also known as Claude Gaston,[17,374,398] (297.Enoch[7], 143.William[6], 72.John[5], 21.John[4], 6.Hugh[3], 3.John[2], 1.Jean[1]) (See marriage to number 488.)

565. **Bertha Gaston** (297.Enoch[7], 143.William[6], 72.John[5], 21.John[4], 6.Hugh[3], 3.John[2], 1.Jean[1]), b. Aug-18-1871 in Harrison Co, WV,[236] d. Apr- 3-1960 in Jane Lew, Lewis Co, WV,[mccxi[1211]] buried in Good Hope Masonic Cemetery, Rt. 19 S, Harrison Co, WV,[524] resided in Salem, WV,[236] census 1930 in Greenbrier District, Doddridge Co, WV, census 1880 in Grant District, Harrison Co, WV. She married Oct- 7-1903 in Harrison Co, WV,[537] **Lloyd M. Stalnaker**, b. 1873 in Doddridge Co, WV,[46,537] (son of Samuel Marion Stalnaker and Sarah Ann Davisson), d. 1945,[46] buried in Good Hope Masonic Cemetery, Rt. 19 S, Harrison Co, WV,[524] census 1930 in Greenbrier District, Doddridge Co, WV, resided 1925 in Miletus (Salem), Doddridge Co, WV.[778]

Children:

  993. i.   WILLIS E. STALNAKER b. Jun-29-1909.

566. **Charles Hornor Gaston** (297.Enoch[7], 143.William[6], 72.John[5], 21.John[4], 6.Hugh[3], 3.John[2], 1.Jean[1]), b. Dec- 3-1884 in Duck Creek, Harrison Co, WV,[mccxii[1212],46] d. Feb-28-1960 in McWhorter, Harrison Co, WV,[1212,46] buried in Duck Creek Missn Chrch Cem, near West Milford, Harrison Co, WV,[1212,17] occupation painter.[1212] He married Feb-19-1914 in Lewis Co, WV,[mccxiii[1213]] **Nora Melvina Hall**, b. 1886,[46] (daughter of Lot Hall and Elsie Bird "Birdie" Woofter), d. 1967,[46] buried in Duck Creek Missn Chrch Cem, near West Milford, Harrison Co, WV,[17] resided 1960 in McWhorter, Harrison Co, WV.[228]

Children:

    i.   MARY MAXINE GASTON b. Jan-20-1927 in Lewis Co, WV,[17] d. Jan-25-1927,[17] buried in Duck Creek Missn Chrch Cem, near West Milford, Harrison Co, WV.[17]

567. **Cecil Beaumont Smith** (298.Mary[7], 143.William[6], 72.John[5], 21.John[4], 6.Hugh[3], 3.John[2], 1.Jean[1]), b. Aug-27-1874 in Harrison Co, WV,[642,155] d. Oct- 8-1960,[642] resided 1936 in Lost Creek, Harrison Co, WV.[748] He married **Inis M. Watson**, b. Sep-12-1877.[155]

Children:

    i.   RUTH G. SMITH.

    ii.   EARNEST WATSON SMITH b. 1906.[155]

       iii.   HARRY A. SMITH.

       iv.   ESTHER ELIZABETH SMITH b. Mar-28-1908,[17] d. Jul-28-1910,[17] buried in Duck Creek Missn Chrch Cem, near West Milford, Harrison Co, WV.[17,230]

       v.   (SON) SMITH b. 1918,[46] d. 1918,[46] buried in Duck Creek Missn Chrch Cem, near West Milford, Harrison Co, WV.[17,230]

568. **Laura Smith** (298.Mary[7], 143.William[6], 72.John[5], 21.John[4], 6.Hugh[3], 3.John[2], 1.Jean[1]), b. Sep- 8-1878 at Duck Creek, Harrison Co, WV,[276,155,642] d. May- 3-1960 in Clarksburg, Harrison Co, WV,[mccxiv[1214]] buried in McWhorter Cemetery, Harrison Co, WV.[17,276] She married[373] **William Henry McWhorter**, b. 1873,[17] d. 1945,[17] buried in McWhorter Cemetery, Harrison Co, WV.[17]

       Children:

       i.   FRANK W. MCWHORTER b. Aug-28-1905,[17] d. Feb- 4-1906,[17] buried in McWhorter Cemetery, Harrison Co, WV.[17,230]

       ii.   WILLIAM CLAYTON MCWHORTER[64] also known as W. Clayton McWhorter,[17] b. Dec-12-1908,[17] d. Mar-29-1909,[17] buried in McWhorter Cemetery, Harrison Co, WV.[17]

       iii.   HELEN VIRGINIA MCWHORTER b. Jul-28-1915,[mccxv[1215]] d. Jan-31-1916,[64] buried in McWhorter Cemetery, Harrison Co, WV.[17,230]

569. **Ernest Wellington "Doc" Smith** (298.Mary[7], 143.William[6], 72.John[5], 21.John[4], 6.Hugh[3], 3.John[2], 1.Jean[1]), b. Aug- 9-1880 in Lost Creek, Harrison Co, WV,[155] d. Feb- 1-1931 in Washington, DC,[155] buried in Cedar Hill Cemetery, Washington, DC,[155] occupation physician.

Ernest Wellington Smith, his wife Janie Iantha King, and their son Christian Joy Smith were killed in an automobile accident. Some genealogists have incorrectly given his wife's name as Stella, with children other than the ones he had. The "Stella" material is an erroneous reference to the wife of another Ernest Smith, Ernest Hoff Smith (4/29/1880 - 7/21/1928, son of John Smith & Margaret Hoff) of Buckhannon Pike in Nutter Fort, that has been repeated by copyists. Ernest Wellington Smith graduated from George Washington University with an M.D. degree in 1906. Suffering from polio in his youth, he became a doctor of osteopathic medicine and chiropractics.[155]

He married Sep- 6-1905,[155] **Janie Iantha King**, b. Mar- 1-1877 in Goochland Co, VA,[155] (daughter of William King and Iantha Duley Knibb), d. Feb- 1-1931 in Washington, DC,[155] buried in Cedar Hill Cemetery, Washington, DC.[155]

       Children:

994.   i.   E. I. SMITH.

       ii.   CHRISTIAN JOY SMITH b. Feb- 1-1914,[155] d. Feb- 1-1931 in Washington, DC,[155] [Died in an auto accident along with his parents.], buried in Washington, DC.[mccxvi[1216]]

995.   iii.   PAUL HUGH SMITH b. Dec-23-1918.

570. **Tensie Smith** (298.Mary[7], 143.William[6], 72.John[5], 21.John[4], 6.Hugh[3], 3.John[2], 1.Jean[1]), b. Jun-22-1894 in Lost Creek, Harrison Co, WV,[155,642] d. Nov-27-1949 in Clarksburg, Harrison Co, WV,[155,642] buried in IOOF Cemetery, Salem, Harrison Co, WV. She married Nov- 7-1920, **Marshal Jackson Morrison**.

       Children:

       i.   MARSHAL PAUL MORRISON b. Sep- 6-1921, d. Jul-21-1927, buried in IOOF Cemetery, Salem, Harrison Co, WV.

996.   ii.   MARGARET MORRISON b. 1923.

       iii.   LIVING.

       iv.   LIVING.

571. **William Henry Gaston** (299.Samuel[7], 145.William[6], 74.John[5], 22.William[4], 6.Hugh[3], 3.John[2], 1.Jean[1]), b. 1828,[157] d. 1868.[157] He married 1849,[157] **Esther Hogue**, b. 1830.[157]

       Children:

       i.   CHARLOTTE GASTON b. in Bartholomew, IN.[157] She married[157] William D. Pence.

572. **Nancy Jane King** (300.Martha[7], 147.James[6], 74.John[5], 22.William[4], 6.Hugh[3], 3.John[2], 1.Jean[1]), b. ca 1832,[146] census 1850 in Clark Co, OH. She married **Daniel Householder**.
Children:
997.   i.   MILTON HOUSEHOLDER.

573. **Mary Gaston** (302.James[7], 147.James[6], 74.John[5], 22.William[4], 6.Hugh[3], 3.John[2], 1.Jean[1]), b. ca 1833 in Ohio,[146] d. Aug-23-1868, cause of death typhoid fever, buried Oakdale Cemetery in Davenport, Scott Co, IA, census 1860 in Davenport, Scott Co, IA,[280] census July 1850 in Warren, Trumbull Co, OH,[146] census Aug 1850 in Mahaska Co, IA.

In May 1846 in Columbiana County, Ohio, James Estep Gaston became the legal guardian of Mary Gaston. Wording of the guardianship papers implied that she was not an orphan. Her natural parents were not listed in court documents. Analysis of census data indicates the likelihood that Mary's natural parents were James' younger brother Robert and his first wife Lydia Soule.

She married Mar-14-1854 in Davenport, Scott Co, IA, **William P. Egbert**, census name William Eggbert,[280] b. Aug-14-1831 in Pennsylvania,[12,280] d. Jan-19-1903,[12] occupation daguerrean/photographer,[280] census 1860 in Davenport, Scott Co, IA.[280]
Children:
    i.   ELIZABETH EGBERT. She married __ Fitzgerald.

574. **Joseph James Gaston** (302.James[7], 147.James[6], 74.John[5], 22.William[4], 6.Hugh[3], 3.John[2], 1.Jean[1]), b. 1842 in Ohio,[646,146] d. 1929,[646] census 1850 in Warren, Trumbull Co, OH.[146] He married (1) Sep-19-1872,[12,646] **Martha Jane Stanford**, b. 1851,[646] d. 1882.[646] He married (2) Apr-8-1886,[12] **Eleanor E. Hunnington**, b. Apr- -1853.[12]
Children by Martha Jane Stanford:
    i.   BEULAH STANFORD GASTON b. in Winterset, Madison Co, IA.[646]

575. **Ernest Berry Gaston** (302.James[7], 147.James[6], 74.John[5], 22.William[4], 6.Hugh[3], 3.John[2], 1.Jean[1]), b. Nov-21-1861 in Henderson, Knox Co, IL,[649] d. Dec- -1937 in Mobile Co, AL,[693] resided from 1894 in Fairhope, Baldwin Co, AL, resided formerly in Des Moines, IA, education Drake University (1886).[mccxvii[1217]]

Founder of the Fairhope Single Tax Colony in Alabama.

He married Nov-24-1887,[1217] **Clara L. Mershon**, b. Dec- -1862,[12] d. Sep- -1934 in Baldwin Co, AL,[693] resided originally in Jones Co, IA.[1217]
Children:
    i.   FRANCES LILLY GASTON b. Jun- -1889 in Iowa.[12]
998.   ii.   JAMES ERNEST GASTON b. Jun- 2-1890.
999.   iii.   CORNELIUS ALONZO GASTON b. Oct-29-1891.
1000.   iv.   LEAH CATHERINE GASTON b. Nov- -1893.
1001.   v.   ARTHUR F. GASTON b. Aug-16-1896.

576. **Mary Gaston** (302.James[7], 147.James[6], 74.John[5], 22.William[4], 6.Hugh[3], 3.John[2], 1.Jean[1]) (See marriage to number 573.)

577. **James Estep Gaston** (303.Robert[7], 147.James[6], 74.John[5], 22.William[4], 6.Hugh[3], 3.John[2], 1.Jean[1]), b. Jul-20-1842 in Ohio,[12] d. Aug- 8-1874,[12] census 1860 in Mahaska Co, IA. He married[12] **Milda Bridges**.
Children:
    i.   JAMES ESTEP GASTON, JR. b. Jul-27-1874.[12]

578. **Cyrus Gaston** (303.Robert[7], 147.James[6], 74.John[5], 22.William[4], 6.Hugh[3], 3.John[2], 1.Jean[1]), b. Mar- 9-1845 in Carroll Co, OH,[652] d. Jan-19-1940,[652] buried in Rose Valley Cemetery, Glen Elder, KS, census 1900 in Mitchell Co, KS, census 1860 in Mahaska Co, IA, occupation teacher (until 1877).[mccxviii[1218]]

Cyrus Gaston's family moved to Iowa shortly after his birth. He was raised in Oskaloosa, Iowa and attended Oskaloosa College. He enlisted in Co K, 33rd Iowa Volunteer Infantry on Aug 15 1862 and served the next three years in the Civil War. In 1871 he went to Mitchell Co, Kansas, where he taught in a little dugout schoolhouse just south of Glen Elder until 1877, while also developing his homestead. He was also County Superintendent of Schools for several years about that time. [Katie Dailey Gaston & Kenneth E. Forster]

He married Apr-30-1882,[652,123] **Ida Jayne Sharp**, b. Dec-20-1860 in Rest, Vernon Co, WI,[652] (daughter of Henry Sharp and Angeline Jones), d. Jan-12-1939,[652,12] buried in Rose Valley Cemetery, Glen Elder, KS,[652] occupation teacher, census 1900 in Mitchell Co, KS. Two other children died in infancy.[123]

        Children:
     i.   IRL R. GASTON[1218] census name Earl Gaston,[123] b. Nov-11-1885 in Kansas,[592,123] d. Nov- -1975,[592] resided in Chester, Major Co, OK,[948] census 1900 in Mitchell Co, KS.
1002. ii.   AGNES A. GASTON b. Oct- 1-1887.
1003. iii.   RALPH ESTEP GASTON b. Jul-29-1890.
     iv.   CECILE GASTON[1218] b. Aug- -1894 in Kansas,[123] census 1900 in Mitchell Co, KS.[123]
     v.   TRESSA GASTON[1218] b. Mar-21-1897 in Kansas,[123,592] d. Jun- 5-1989,[592] resided in Chester, Randolph Co, IL,[592] census 1900 in Mitchell Co, KS. She married[652,12] Lawrence Earlenbaugh, b. May- 3-1897,[592] d. Oct- -1976,[592] resided in Chester, Randolph Co, IL.[936]
     vi.   J. WAYNE GASTON[1218] b. Aug- -1899 in Kansas,[123] census 1900 in Mitchell Co, KS.[123]
1004. vii. HERBERT BROWNELL GASTON b. Jun-12-1902.

579. **David Gaston** (303.Robert[7], 147.James[6], 74.John[5], 22.William[4], 6.Hugh[3], 3.John[2], 1.Jean[1]), b. Dec- 8-1846 in Iowa,[12,123] d. Jan-18-1929 in Iowa,[12] census 1860, 1900 in Mahaska Co, IA. He married ca 1879,[123] **Matilda Jennie Stout**, census name Jennie,[123] b. Sep-13-1853 in Ohio,[123,12] d. Feb-18-1936,[12] census 1900 in Mahaska Co, IA.
        Children:
1005. i.   ERNEST LEROY GASTON b. Sep- 5-1881.

580. **Joseph Gaston** (303.Robert[7], 147.James[6], 74.John[5], 22.William[4], 6.Hugh[3], 3.John[2], 1.Jean[1]), b. Dec-10-1849 in Iowa,[12] d. Dec-12-1942,[12] census 1860 in Mahaska Co, IA. He married[12] **Victorene (Victoria) Thompson**, b. Jan-13-1866,[12] d. Feb 14-1953.[12]
        Children:
1006. i.   DAVID GASTON b. Apr-13-1887.
     ii.   BENJAMIN H. GASTON b. Apr-26-1888,[592,12] d. Nov- 1-1968,[12,592] resided in Medford, Jackson Co, OR,[592] resided formerly in Kansas.[1158]
1007. iii. LEWIS BURKE "BERT" GASTON b. Apr-24-1889.
     iv.   JULIUS "JUDD" GASTON b. Sep-20-1890,[592,12] d. Oct- 3-1971,[12,592] resided in Beloit, Mitchell Co, KS.[592]
1008. v.   ROBERT "BRUCE" GASTON b. Feb-13-1893.
1009. vi.   ELDRIDGE GASTON b. Oct-24-1894.
     vii. BRYAN W. GASTON b. Oct-26-1896,[592] d. Apr- 3-1971,[12] resided in Denver, CO.[mccxix[1219]]
     viii. RAYBURN J. "RAY" GASTON, also known as Ray Gaston,[592] b. Nov-27-1900,[592,12] d. Jul-15-1990,[592,12] resided in Glen Elder, Mitchell Co, KS.[1158] He married[12] Alberta Booker, b. Mar-23-1901,[592,12] d. May-24-1968,[12,592] resided in Beloit, Mitchell Co, KS.[1158]
     ix.   CLINTON DEWITT GASTON b. May- 2-1902,[592,12] d. Mar-19-1981,[12,592] resided in Ottawa, Franklin Co, KS.[1158] He married[12] Evelyn Bair, b. Aug-17-1901,[592] d. Jul- -1995,[592] resided in Ottawa, Franklin Co, KS.[1158]
     x.   ELSIE A. GASTON b. Oct-21-1907,[592,12] d. Mar-24-1989,[592,12] resided in Beloit, Mitchell Co, KS.[1158]

581. **George Washington Gaston** (303.Robert[7], 147.James[6], 74.John[5], 22.William[4], 6.Hugh[3], 3.John[2], 1.Jean[1]), b. Aug-18-1851 in Iowa,[12] [Birth date given as Aug 1852 in 1900 Census.], d. Sep-11-1935 in Kansas,[12] census 1900 in Mitchell Co, KS, census 1860 in Mahaska Co, IA. He married[12] ca 1877,[123] **Mary E. Ewing**, b. Aug- -1861 in Illinois,[123] d. 1936 in Kansas,[12] census 1900 in Mitchell Co, KS.

1900 Census, Mitchell Co, Kansas (Hayes Twp), enumerated on Jun 11 1900:
George Gaston, 47, b. Aug 1852 in Iowa, father b. Pa, mother b. Ohio, farmer, married 23 yrs; wife Mary, 38, b. Aug 1861 in Illinois, father b. Kentucky, mother b. Tennessee, mother of 4 children (all still living); dau Etta, 19, b. Aug 1880 in Kansas; son Irvin, 17, b. Jun 1882 in Kansas; son Archie, 12, b. Aug 1887 in Kansas.

Children:
i. NELLIE GASTON b. 1880 in Kansas.[12]
ii. ETTA GASTON b. Aug- -1880 in Kansas,[123] census 1900 in Mitchell Co, KS.
iii. IRVIN A. GASTON b. Jun-28-1882 in Kansas,[592,123] d. Aug-15-1971 in Kansas,[592,12] resided in Sabetha, Nemaha Co, KS,[1158] census 1900 in Mitchell Co, KS.
1010. iv. ARCHIE FRANKLIN GASTON b. Aug- -1887.

582. **Rosealtha Gaston**, census name Roseathla,[681] (303.Robert[7], 147.James[6], 74.John[5], 22.William[4], 6.Hugh[3], 3.John[2], 1.Jean[1]), b. Mar-19-1858 in Iowa,[12,123] d. Jul-29-1933,[12] census 1920, 1930 in Holton, Jackson Co, KS, census 1900 in Nemaha Co, KS, census 1880 in Mitchell Co, KS, census 1860 in Mahaska Co, IA. She married[12] ca 1876,[123] **Timothy M. Horton**, b. May- -1845 in Kentucky,[123] census 1920, 1930 in Holton, Jackson Co, KS, census 1900 in Nemaha Co, KS, census 1880 in Mitchell Co, KS, occupation farmer.[123]
Children:
i. IRENE J. HORTON, census name Irena I. Horton,[123] b. Aug- -1877 in Kansas,[123] census 1900 in Nemaha Co, KS, census 1880 in Mitchell Co, KS.
ii. OMER C. HORTON b. Jan- -1879 in Kansas,[123] census 1900 in Nemaha Co, KS, census 1880 in Mitchell Co, KS.
iii. MILLIE M. HORTON b. Dec- -1880 in Kansas,[123] census 1900 in Nemaha Co, KS.
iv. HERSHELL HORTON b. Dec- -1884 in Kansas,[123] census 1900 in Nemaha Co, KS.
v. MARSHALL HORTON b. Aug-21-1887 in Kansas,[592,123] d. Jan- -1971,[592] resided in Lynwood, Los Angeles Co, CA,[1158] census 1900 in Nemaha Co, KS.
vi. ALICE HORTON b. Aug- -1889 in Kansas,[123] census 1900 in Nemaha Co, KS.
vii. EDNA L. HORTON b. May- -1891 in Kansas,[123] census 1900 in Nemaha Co, KS.
viii. LORY HORTON b. Jun- -1893 in Kansas,[123] census 1900 in Nemaha Co, KS.
ix. FRANCIS A. HORTON b. Jun- -1895 in Kansas,[123] census 1900 in Nemaha Co, KS.
x. GEORGIA D. HORTON b. Dec- -1898,[123] census 1900 in Nemaha Co, KS.

583. **Dora Gaston** (303.Robert[7], 147.James[6], 74.John[5], 22.William[4], 6.Hugh[3], 3.John[2], 1.Jean[1]), b. Aug- -1860 in Iowa,[mccxx[1220]] d. 1943,[12] census 1930 in Fayette Co, PA, census 1900, 1920 in Preston Co, WV, census 1880 in Mitchell Co, KS. She married[12] ca 1878,[1220] **Marcellus "Zell" Albright**, census name Zell Albright,[210,mccxxi[1221]] b. Feb- -1843 in Virginia (now West Virginia),[1220] (son of Henry Albright and Elizabeth ___), d. 1914,[12] census 1850, 1860, 1900 in Preston Co, WV, census 1880 in Mitchell Co, KS, census 1870 in Logan Co, IL,[mccxxii[1222]] occupation farmer, grist miller,[1220,1221] military Mar- -1864 - Jun- -1866 Sgt, 6th W.Va. Cav, Civil War.[mccxxiii[1223]]

1880 Census, Mitchell Co, Kansas (Walnut Creek), enumerated on Jun 7 1880:
Zell Albright, 36, b. Va, both parents b. W.Va, farmer; wife Dora, 19, b. Iowa, both parents b. Ohio; dau Alice, 3, b. Kansas; servant Rachel Hunt, 13, b. Michigan; Sylvia Winnie, 16, b. Indiana, single, school teacher.

1900 Census, Preston Co, WV (Portland District), enumerated on Jun 13 1900:

Marcellus Albright, 57, b. Feb 1843 in W.Va., both parents b. W.Va., farmer, married 22 yrs; wife Dora (Dara?) Albright, 39, b. Aug 1860 in Iowa, father b. Pa., mother b. Ohio, mother of 8 children (6 still living); dau Alice M. Albright, 21, b. Oct 1879 in Kansas, single, mother of one child (still living); dau Ada V, 14, b. Aug 1885 in W.Va; dau Susan C, 12, b. Jul 1887 in W.Va; son Archie F, 7, b. May 1893 in W.Va; son Linley L, 1, b. Sep 1898 in W.Va; granddau Olive M. Irvin, 1, b. May 1898 in W.Va.

1910 Census, Preston Co, WV (Portland District), enumerated on May 4 1910:
Zell Albright, 67, b. W.Va, father b. Pa, mother b. W.Va, occupation miller (grist mill), married 31 yrs; wife Dora, 49, b. Iowa, both parents b. Ohio, mother of 8 children (4 still living); son Lloyd L, 11, b. W.Va; son McClure, 9.

1920 Census, Preston Co, WV (Portland District), enumerated in Jan 1920:
Dora Albright, 59, b. Kansas, both parents b. Kansas, widowed; son Lloyd, 21, b. W.Va; son McClure, 19, b. W.Va.

1930 Census, Fayette Co, Pennsylvania (South Union Twp), enumerated on Apr 12 1930:
Joseph M. Albright, 29, married (age 26 at time of first marriage); wife Dorothy, 23 (age 20 at time of first marriage); dau Arleen, 4; son Larry, 1; mother Dora, 69; brother Loyd, 32. (Note: Birthplace of all family members and their parents given as Pennsylvania, except for Dora's father, whose birthplace was given as Iowa. These are clearly incorrect.) [12]

Children:
i. ALICE M. ALBRIGHT b. Oct- -1879 in Kansas,[1220] census 1900 in Preston Co, WV, census 1880 in Mitchell Co, KS.
ii. ADA V. ALBRIGHT b. Aug- -1885 in West Virginia,[1220] census 1900 in Preston Co, WV.
iii. SUSAN C. ALBRIGHT b. Jul- -1887 in West Virginia,[1220] census 1900 in Preston Co, WV.
iv. ARCHIE F. ALBRIGHT b. May- 4-1893 in West Virginia,[mccxxiv[1224],1220] d. Aug- 3-1903 in Terra Alta, Preston Co, WV,[1224] cause of death typhoid,[1224] census 1900 in Preston Co, WV.
v. LLOYD LINLEY ALBRIGHT, census name Linley L. Albright,[1220] b. Sep- -1898,[1220] census 1930 in Fayette Co, PA, census 1900, 1910, 1920 in Preston Co, WV.
1011. vi. JOSEPH MCCLURE ALBRIGHT b. ca 1901.

584. **Josiah Morgan Estep** (304.Sarah[7], 148.Samuel[6], 74.John[5], 22.William[4], 6.Hugh[3], 3.John[2], 1.Jean[1]), b. Feb-19-1829 in Pennsylvania,[66,209] d. May- 5-1888 in Cadiz, Harrison Co, OH,[66] census 1870, 1880 in Cadiz, Harrison Co, OH, occupation lawyer.[709] He married 1857,[66] **Amanda J. Crabb**, b. Sep- -1837 in Ohio,[67,209] (daughter of Jacob Crabb and Jane D. ___), d. Mar-23-1898,[67] census 1870, 1880 in Cadiz, Harrison Co, OH.

1870 Census, Harrison Co, Ohio (City of Cadiz), enumerated on Jun 2 1870:
Josiah M. Estep, 41, b. Pa, lawyer; Amanda, 33, b. Ohio; Charley, 12, b. Ohio; Willie, 10, b. Ohio; Josiah, 5, b. Ohio; Jennie, 2, b. Ohio.

1880 Census, Harrison Co, Ohio (City of Cadiz), enumerated on Jun 9 1880:
Josiah Estep, 51, b. Pa, lawyer; wife Amanda, 42, b. Ohio; son Charles, 21, b. Ohio, law student; son William, 19, b. Ohio; son Josiah, 14, b. Ohio; dau Jennie, 12, b. Ohio; son Junious, 3, b. Ohio; Annie, 7 months, b. Ohio.

Children:
i. CHARLES ESTEP b. ca 1858 in Ohio,[209] census 1870, 1880 in Cadiz, Harrison Co, OH.
ii. WILLIAM ESTEP b. ca 1860 in Ohio,[209] census 1870, 1880 in Cadiz, Harrison Co, OH.
iii. JOSIAH ESTEP b. ca 1865,[209] census 1870, 1880 in Cadiz, Harrison Co, OH.
iv. JENNIE ESTEP b. ca 1868 in Ohio,[209] census 1870, 1880 in Cadiz, Harrison Co, OH.
v. JUNIOUS ESTEP b. ca 1877 in Ohio,[210] census 1880 in Cadiz, Harrison Co, OH.
vi. ANNIE ESTEP b. ca 1879,[210] census 1880 in Cadiz, Harrison Co, OH.

585. **Harrison Estep** (304.Sarah[7], 148.Samuel[6], 74.John[5], 22.William[4], 6.Hugh[3], 3.John[2], 1.Jean[1]), b. Jul- -1833,[123] [Birthplace given in 1850 and 1880 Census as Pennsylvania, but in 1860 and 1900 Census as Ohio.], census 1900 in Marion, Grant Co, IN, resided (settled) in Marion, Grant Co, IN,[66] census 1880 in Pittsburgh, Allegheny Co, PA, census 1860 in Allegheny Co, PA, census 1850 in Perry Twp, Fayette Co, PA, occupation glass blower, glass manufacturer,[146,280,210.] He married ca 1858,[123] **Amanda ___**, b. Aug- -1836 in Pennsylvania,[123] census 1900 in Marion, Grant Co, IN, census 1880 in Pittsburgh, Allegheny Co, PA, census 1860 in Allegheny Co, PA.

1860 Census, Allegheny Co, Pennsylvania (Monongahela Borough, Pittsburgh Post Office), enumerated on Jun 1 1860:
Harison Estep, 27, b. Ohio, master glass blower; Amanda, 24, b. Pa; James Jr, 3 months, b. Pa; James Sr, 19, b. Pa, apprentice to glass blower; Clara Snyder, 17, b. Wertemberg, domestic.

1880 Census, Allegheny Co, Pennsylvania (City of Pittsburgh), enumerated on Jun 1 1880:
Harrison Estep, 45, b. Pa, glass manufacturer; wife Amanda, 43, b. Pa; son James E, 20, glass cutter; dau Marian, 18; son Henry, 17, glass cutter; dau Amanda, 14; son Walter, 12; son Charles, 10; servant Annie Storey, 15.

1900 Census, Grant Co, Indiana (City of Marion), enumerated on Jun 9 1900:
Harrison Estep, 66, b. Jul 1833 in Ohio, glass manufacturer, married 42 yrs; wife Amanda, 63, b. Aug 1836 in Pa, mother of 10 children (6 still living); son Albert S, 33; b. Apr 1867 in Pa, glass cutter, single; son Charles F, 28, b. Apr 1872 in Pa, single.

                    Children:
1012. i.   JAMES EDWARD ESTEP b. Feb- -1860.
       ii.   MARIAN ESTEP b. ca 1862 in Pennsylvania,[210] census 1880 in Pittsburgh, Allegheny Co, PA.
      iii.   HENRY ESTEP b. ca 1863 in Pennsylvania,[210] census 1880 in Pittsburgh, Allegheny Co, PA.
      iv.   AMANDA ESTEP b. ca 1866 in Pennsylvania,[210] census 1880 in Pittsburgh, Allegheny Co, PA.
       v.   WALTER ESTEP b. ca 1868 in Pennsylvania,[210] census 1880 in Pittsburgh, Allegheny Co, PA.
      vi.   CHARLES F. ESTEP b. ca 1870 in Pennsylvania,[210] census 1880 in Pittsburgh, Allegheny Co, PA.

586. **James Estep** (304.Sarah[7], 148.Samuel[6], 74.John[5], 22.William[4], 6.Hugh[3], 3.John[2], 1.Jean[1]), b. Oct- -1841 in Pennsylvania,[123] census 1900 in Marion, Grant Co, IN, resided (settled) in Marion, Grant Co, IN,[66] census 1850 in Perry Twp, Fayette Co, PA, occupation glass blower.[123] He married ca 1875,[123] **Amanda ___**, b. Jul- -1854 in Pennsylvania,[123] census 1900 in Marion, Grant Co, IN.

1900 Census, Grant Co, Indiana (City of Marion), enumerated on Jun 2 1900:
James Estep, 58, b. Oct 1841 in Pa, window glass blower, married 25 yrs; wife Amanda, 45, b. Jul 1854 in Pa, mother of 8 children (7 still living); son Josiah, 22, b. Sep 1877 in Pa, single; son Harry C, 20, b. Oct 1879 in Pa, single; dau Olive, 18, b. Dec 1881 in Pa, single; son Herbert, 15, b. Sep 1884 in Pa; dau Mabel, 11, b. Oct 1888 in Indiana; dau Bessie, 9, b. Feb 1891 in Indiana.

                    Children:
       i.   JOSIAH ESTEP b. Sep- -1877 in Pennsylvania,[123] census 1900 in Marion, Grant Co, IN.
      ii.   HARRY C. ESTEP b. Oct- -1879 in Pennsylvania.
      iii.   OLIVE ESTEP b. Dec- -1881 in Pennsylvania,[123] census 1900 in Marion, Grant Co, IN.
      iv.   HERBERT ESTEP b. Sep- -1884 in Pennsylvania,[123] census 1900 in Marion, Grant Co, IN.
       v.   MABEL ESTEP b. Oct- -1888 in Indiana,[123] census 1900 in Marion, Grant Co, IN.

vi.   BESSIE ESTEP b. Feb- -1891 in Indiana,[123] census 1900 in Marion, Grant Co, IN.

587. **James M. Gaston** (305.William[7], 148.Samuel[6], 74.John[5], 22.William[4], 6.Hugh[3], 3.John[2], 1.Jean[1]), b. 1830 in Union Twp, Washington Co, PA,[67,46] d. 1885,[46,67] buried in Mingo Creek Presb Cem, Union Twp, Washington Co, PA,[17] occupation farmer,[mccxxv[1225]] military Major, 1st Pennsylvania Volunteer Cavalry.[17]

Served 3 years in the 1st Pennsylvania Cavalry, was wounded 3 times, once at Gettysburg.[67]

He married **Matilda Ensell**, b. 1834,[17,67] (daughter of Edward Ensell), d. 1867,[17,67] buried in Mingo Creek Presb Cem, Union Twp, Washington Co, PA.[17]
    Children:
    i.   MARY P. GASTON b. ca 1857.[67]
    ii.   IDA MAY GASTON, also known as Ida S. Gaston, b. 1859,[17,67] d. 1933,[17] buried in Mingo Creek Presb Cem, Union Twp, Washington Co, PA.[17] She married[17,67] John McChain, b. 1846,[17] d. 1927,[17] buried in Mingo Creek Presb Cem, Union Twp, Washington Co, PA.[17]
    iii.   WILLIAM LOUGEAY GASTON b. Apr-15-1861 in Pennsylvania,[398,46] d. Oct- 3-1928 in Monongalia Co, WV,[1024,46] buried in Mingo Creek Presb Cem, Union Twp, Washington Co, PA,[17,67] occupation carpenter.[398] He married Sep-16-1885,[67] Emma Scott, b. 1863 in Pennsylvania,[46] (daughter of Frank P. Scott), d. 1896,[46] buried in Mingo Creek Presb Cem, Union Twp, Washington Co, PA,[17] census 1880 in Washington, Washington Co, PA.
    iv.   HARRIET B. "HATTIE" GASTON b. 1864,[17,67] d. 1942,[17] buried in Mingo Creek Presb Cem, Union Twp, Washington Co, PA.[17] She married[17] William James Estep, b. 1869,[17] d. 1949,[17] buried in Mingo Creek Presb Cem, Union Twp, Washington Co, PA.[17]
    v.   EDWARD GASTON d. in infancy.[67]

588. **Samuel Gaston** (307.Joseph[7], 148.Samuel[6], 74.John[5], 22.William[4], 6.Hugh[3], 3.John[2], 1.Jean[1]), b. Dec- - 1831 in Union Twp, Washington Co, PA,[123,66,67] census 1880, 1900 in Sewickley, Allegheny Co, PA, census 1870 in Columbiana Co, OH, census 1850 in Union Twp, Washington Co, PA, occupation merchant,[209] occupation farmer.[654]

1870 Census, Columbiana Co, Ohio (New Lisbon Twp), enumerated on Jun 1 1870:
Samuel Gaston, 38, merchant; Amanda, 37; Hada, 15; Salley, 13; Sophia, 8; Rebecca, 5; Mallia, 3; Willie, 1; Maggie Neely, 20, domestic servant. All born in Pennsylvania.

1880 Census, Allegheny Co, Pennsylvania (Sewickley Borough), enumerated on Jun 7 1880:
Saml Gaston, 48, general store; wife Amanda, 47; dau Hattie, 25, seamstress; dau Sallie, 23; dau Sophy, 17, clerk in store; dau Rebckie, 13; dau Mallie, 12; son William, 11; son John, 9; dau Mary, 4. All born in Pennsylvania except for John, in Ohio.

1900 Census, Allegheny Co, Pennsylvania (Sewickley Borough), enumerated on Jun 6 1900:
Samuel Gaston, 68, b. Dec 1831, widowed, occupation real estate; dau Sarah E, 43, b. Aug 1856, single; dau Rebecca W, 34, b. Mar 1866, single, sales lady; dau Marian F, 33, b. May 1867, musician; son William R, 31, b. Apr 1869, railroad clerk; servant Ellen Lucas, black female, 21, b. Aug 1878 in Va, cook.

He married[66] (1) **Martha A. McClure**. He married[66] (2) **Amanda M. Way**, b. ca 1833 in Pennsylvania,[209] d. bef Jun 1900,[123] census 1880 in Sewickley, Allegheny Co, PA, census 1870 in Columbiana Co, OH.
    Children by Amanda M. Way:
    i.   JOHN GASTON b. ca 1871 in Ohio,[210] census 1880 in Sewickley, Allegheny Co, PA.
    ii.   MARY GASTON b. ca 1876 in Pennsylvania,[210] census 1880 in Sewickley, Allegheny Co, PA.

589. **Sarah Gaston** (307.Joseph[7], 148.Samuel[6], 74.John[5], 22.William[4], 6.Hugh[3], 3.John[2], 1.Jean[1]), b. ca 1834 in Union Twp, Washington Co, PA,[67,280] d. Nov-29-1868,[67] census 1860 in Washington Co, PA, census 1850 in Union Twp, Washington Co, PA. She married Nov-18-1857,[67] **Ralston Williams**, b. ca 1833 in Pennsylvania,[280] (son of Benjamin Williams and Sarah Ralston), census 1880 in Monongahela, Washington Co, PA, census 1860 in Washington Co, PA, occupation 1880 alderman.[210]

Ralston: 1880 Census, Washington Co, Pennsylvania (city of Monongahela), enumerated in June 1880:
Ralston Williams, 48, widowed, occupation alderman; son Harry, 21, single, clerk in store; dau Maggie, 20, single; dau Jennie, 17; dau Mattie, 16; son Charles, 14; dau Sarah, 11; son Ralston, 6. All born in Pennsylvania.

Children:
   i.   HARVEY H. WILLIAMS[67] census name Harry Williams, b. ca 1859 in Pennsylvania,[280] census 1880 in Monongahela, Washington Co, PA, census 1860 in Washington Co, PA, occupation store clerk.[210]
   ii.   MARGARET L. WILLIAMS[67] census name Maggie Williams, b. ca 1860 in Pennsylvania,[280] census 1880 in Monongahela, Washington Co, PA, census 1860 in Washington Co, PA.
   iii.   JANE M. "JENNIE" WILLIAMS[67] census name Jennie Williams, b. ca 1863 in Pennsylvania,[210] census 1880 in Monongahela, Washington Co, PA.
   iv.   BELLE M. "MATTIE" WILLIAMS[67] census name Mattie Williams, b. ca 1864 in Pennsylvania,[210] census 1880 in Monongahela, Washington Co, PA.
   v.   CHARLES G. WILLIAMS[67] b. ca 1866 in Pennsylvania,[210] occupation minister, Cross Creek Presbyterian,[67] census 1880 in Monongahela, Washington Co, PA.
   vi.   SARAH WILLIAMS[67] b. ca 1869 in Pennsylvania,[210] d. bef 1893,[67] census 1880 in Monongahela, Washington Co, PA.

590. **Margaret Gaston** (307.Joseph[7], 148.Samuel[6], 74.John[5], 22.William[4], 6.Hugh[3], 3.John[2], 1.Jean[1]), b. ca 1836 in Union Twp, Washington Co, PA,[146,67] d. bef 1910,[67] census 1880 in McKeesport, Allegheny Co, PA, census 1870 in Westmoreland Co, PA, census 1850, 1860 in Union Twp, Washington Co, PA. She married[67] **William S. Penny**, b. ca 1839 in Pennsylvania,[209] census 1880 in McKeesport, Allegheny Co, PA, census 1870 in Westmoreland Co, PA.
Children:
   i.   JOHN PENNY b. ca 1867 in Pennsylvania,[209] census 1880 in McKeesport, Allegheny Co, PA, census 1870 in Westmoreland Co, PA.
   ii.   WILLIAM JAMES PENNY, census name James Penny, b. ca 1869 in Pennsylvania,[209] census 1880 in McKeesport, Allegheny Co, PA, census 1870 in Westmoreland Co, PA.
   iii.   MARY J. PENNY, census name Babe Penny, b. 1870 in Pennsylvania,[209] census 1880 in McKeesport, Allegheny Co, PA, census 1870 in Westmoreland Co, PA.
   iv.   RUTH C. PENNY b. ca 1875 in Pennsylvania,[210] census 1880 in McKeesport, Allegheny Co, PA.

591. **John H. Gaston** (307.Joseph[7], 148.Samuel[6], 74.John[5], 22.William[4], 6.Hugh[3], 3.John[2], 1.Jean[1]), b. Oct- - 1839 in Union Twp, Washington Co, PA,[67] census 1850, 1860 in Union Twp, Washington Co, PA.

John H. Gaston served two years in Company I, 1st Pennsylvania Volunteer Cavalry, before being honorably discharged in 1863 due to poor health.[67]

He married 1864,[67] **Sarah A. Frye**, b. May- -1843,[67] (daughter of West Frye).
Children:
   i.   WILHAMENA "MENA" GASTON b. Sep- -1864.[67] She married aft 1900,[67] Samuel Lindsay, resided in Finleyville, Washington Co, PA.[67]
   ii.   WEST F. GASTON d. age 32.[67]
   iii.   SARAH GASTON d. age 6.[67]

592. **Joseph S. Gaston, Jr.** (307.Joseph[7], 148.Samuel[6], 74.John[5], 22.William[4], 6.Hugh[3], 3.John[2], 1.Jean[1]), b. 1843 in Union Twp, Washington Co, PA,[282,67] d. 1887,[282] census 1850, 1860 in Union Twp, Washington Co, PA. He married 1880,[282] **Anna Preisler**, b. 1856.[282]

> Children:
> i.   MILDRED GASTON b. in Gastonville, Washington Co, PA.[282] She married[282] Elliott L. Hibbs.

593. **Jasper Minear** (309.Margaret[7], 150.Charles[6], 75.William[5], 22.William[4], 6.Hugh[3], 3.John[2], 1.Jean[1]), b. Jan-14-1852.[286] He married[286] **Sarah Melissa Moore**.

> Children:
> 1013. i.   WARD MINEAR b. Jul-21-1884.

594. **Walter Gaston Shotwell** (313.Nancy[7], 154.James[6], 77.Hugh[5], 23.Joseph[4], 6.Hugh[3], 3.John[2], 1.Jean[1]), b. Dec-27-1856 in Ohio,[84,123] d. Mar-11-1938 in Cadiz, Harrison Co, OH,[1011,190] cause of death struck by hit-and-run driver,[190] occupation lawyer, judge, author,[123,84] census 1900, 10, 20, 30 in Cadiz, Harrison Co, OH, census 1870, 1880 in Cadiz, Harrison Co, OH, education Yale University, Franklin College.

Attorney and author Walter Gaston Shotwell was born in 1856 in Cadiz, Harrison County, Ohio. He received his bachelor of arts from Yale University in 1878. He returned to Cadiz to study law with his father and Chauncey Dewey. In 1880, Shotwell was admitted to the bar and received his master of arts degree from Franklin College.

Shotwell privately practiced law from 1880 to 1887. In 1887, he was elected prosecuting attorney for Harrison County, Ohio. He served two terms in this office before returning to private practice in 1893. Shotwell sought elected office again when he ran for Common Pleas judge for the Eighth District of Ohio in 1899. He served three terms and retired from the bench in 1913 to pursue his writing career.

Shotwell was exposed to abolitionist sentiments by his parents and professors at Franklin College. As an attorney, he willingly served African-American clients and became known as a "friend to colored people." This background inspired his first book, "The Life and times of Charles Sumner" (1910). His second book, "The Civil War in America" (1923), was notably pro-Union. Shotwell's third published work, "Driftwood: Being Papers on Old-Time American Towns and Some Old People" (1927), is a collection of essays. A fourth work, a biography of writer Washington Irving, was pending publication when Shotwell was killed in a car accident on March 11, 1938.

Source: http://ead.ohiolink.edu/xtf-ead/view?docId=ead/OUN0078.xml;chunk.id=bioghist_1;brand=default

He married Dec-24-1884,[84] **Belle McIlvaine**, b. Dec- -1859 in Ohio,[123] (daughter of George W. McIlvaine and Caroline Rinehart), d. ca 1936,[484] census 1900, 10, 20, 30 in Cadiz, Harrison Co, OH.

> Children:
> i.   MARGARET M. SHOTWELL, census name Margaretta M. Shotwell, b. Mar-28-1886 in Ohio,[592,1123,123] d. Jul-15-1973 in Dade Co, FL,[1123,592] resided in Coshocton, Coshocton Co, OH,[592] resided 1938 in Columbus, Franklin Co, OH,[765] census 1900 in Cadiz, Harrison Co, OH. She married[941] ___ McLaughlin.

595. **Stuart Beebe Shotwell, Jr.**, census name Stewart B. Shotwell (313.Nancy[7], 154.James[6], 77.Hugh[5], 23.Joseph[4], 6.Hugh[3], 3.John[2], 1.Jean[1]), b. Apr- -1861 in Ohio,[123] [Hanna, p. 113, incorrectly reports birth date as 1867.], resided (settled) at St. Paul, Ramsey Co, MN,[84] census 1900 in St. Paul, Ramsey Co, MN, census 1870, 1880 in Cadiz, Harrison Co, OH. He married[84] ca 1891,[123] **Caroline "Carrie" McIlvaine**, census name Carrie, b. Sep- -1864 in Ohio,[123] (daughter of George W. McIlvaine and Caroline Rinehart), census 1900, 1910 in St. Paul, Ramsey Co, MN. Although census records

predominantly identify him, his father and his son as Stewart, other records (e.g., SSDI, draft registration cards, and some censuses) indicated Stuart, as does Hanna's "Ohio Valley Genealogies," p. 113.

1900 Census, Ramsey Co, Minnesota (city of St. Paul), enumerated on Jun 2 1900:
Stewart B. Shotwell, 39, b. Apr 1861 in Ohio, manager of loan company, married 9 yrs; wife Carrie M, 35, b. Sep 1864 in Ohio, mother of one child (still living); son Stewart M, 7, b. Apr 1893 in Minnesota; servant Laura Olson, 28, b. Feb 1872 in Norway, immigrated 1890, single.

1910 Census, Ramsey Co, Minnesota (city of St. Paul), enumerated in Apr 1910:
Stuart B. Shotwell, 49, b. Ohio, broker for copper company; wife Carrie, 45, b. Ohio, mother of one child (still living); son Stewart M, 17, b. Minnesota, single; servant Ida Arneson, 21, b. Minnesota, single.

Children:
1014. i. STUART MCILVAINE SHOTWELL b. Apr-16-1893.

596. **Elizabeth "Lizzie" Gaston**[317] (314.Philander[7], 154.James[6], 77.Hugh[5], 23.Joseph[4], 6.Hugh[3], 3.John[2], 1.Jean[1]), b. Feb- -1852 in Indiana,[12] d. Apr-24-1944 in East Liverpool, Columbiana Co, OH.[mccxxvi[1226]] She married[12] **William H. Crawford**, b. 1851 in Ohio,[12] d. Apr-20-1930 in Columbiana Co, OH.[693,12] Elizabeth Gaston and William H. Crawford had six children.[12]

Children:
1015. i. ELIZA V. CRAWFORD.
1016. ii. MARY JANET CRAWFORD.
      iii. GERTIE CRAWFORD[317.] She married[317] Raymond Pepin.
1017. iv. JEFFERSON CRAWFORD.
1018. v. PHILANDER CRAWFORD.
1019. vi. EDWARD HUGH CRAWFORD.

597. **Nancy Gaston** (314.Philander[7], 154.James[6], 77.Hugh[5], 23.Joseph[4], 6.Hugh[3], 3.John[2], 1.Jean[1]), b. ca 1854 in Ohio.[12] She married[12] **Bazil Rowe**, also known as Bazil Rauch.[12]
Children:
      i. MARY ROWE[317.] She married[317] Harry Lyons.
      ii. WALTER ROWE[317.] He married[317] Lillian Richard.
1020. iii. CHARLES ROWE.
1021. iv. LAURA ROWE.

598. **Martha A. "Mattie" Gaston**[317] (314.Philander[7], 154.James[6], 77.Hugh[5], 23.Joseph[4], 6.Hugh[3], 3.John[2], 1.Jean[1]), b. 1862 in Ohio,[12,211] d. Jul- 7-1930 in Summit Co, OH,[693] census 1910 in East Liverpool, Columbiana Co, OH. She married[12] ca 1881,[211] **Charles Feezel**, b. 1859 in Pennsylvania,[12,211] d. 1934,[12] census 1910 in East Liverpool, Columbiana Co, OH, occupation 1910 salt salesman.[211]
Children:
      i. ETHEL A. FEEZEL[317] b. ca 1883 in Ohio,[211] census 1910 in East Liverpool, Columbiana Co, OH. She married[317] Tom Hurley.
1022. ii. LOLA FEEZEL.
      iii. NILLA A. FEEZEL[693] b. ca 1887 in Ohio,[211] d. Mar-15-1920 in Summit Co, OH,[693,317] census 1910 in East Liverpool, Columbiana Co, OH.
1023. iv. RAYMOND C. FEEZEL b. ca 1890.
1024. v. RILEY L. FEEZEL b. Aug-27-1893.

599. **John C. Gaston** (314.Philander[7], 154.James[6], 77.Hugh[5], 23.Joseph[4], 6.Hugh[3], 3.John[2], 1.Jean[1]), b. Jun- -1866 in Ohio,[123,12] d. 1946 in Ohio,[12] census 1900, 1910, 1920 in Columbiana Co, OH. He married[12] ca 1888,[123] **Esther Hickman**, b. Jun- -1863 in Ohio,[123,12] d. May-28-1932 in Columbiana Co, OH,[693,12]

census 1900, 1910, 1920 in Columbiana Co, OH. Some researchers list four children for John C. Gaston and Esther Hickman: Florence, Emily, Harry and Lee. But this is considered incorrect, based on the following census entries:

1900 Census, Columbiana Co, Ohio (Middleton Twp), enumerated Jun 22 1900:
John Gaston, b. Jun 1866 in Ohio, both parents b. Ohio, occup farmer, married 12 yrs; wife Esther, b. Jun 1863, mother of 3 children, all still living; dau Florence, b. Nov 1889; dau Emily, b. Feb 1891; son Lee H., b. Oct 1893.

1910 Census, Columbiana Co, Ohio (Middleton Twp), enumerated May 4 1910:
John C. Gaston, 43, occup farmer, married 12 yrs; wife Ester, 46, mother of 3 children, all still living; dau Emily, 19; son Henry, 17.

1920 Census, Columbiana Co, Ohio (Middleton Twp), enumerated Jan 27 1920:
John C. Gaston, 53, occup automobile salesman; wife Esther, 54; father Philander, 91.
The adjacent dwelling has the following household members:
Henry Lee Gaston, 27, b. Ohio, occup farmer; wife Florence, 25; dau Thelma M., 1.

> Children:
>   i.   FLORENCE GASTON b. Nov- -1889 in Ohio,[123] census 1900 in Columbiana Co, OH. She married[12] Earl Davis.
> 1025. ii.   EMILY N. GASTON b. Feb- 2-1891.
> 1026. iii. HENRY LEE GASTON b. Oct- -1893.

600. **William Kilgore Gaston** (314.Philander^7, 154.James^6, 77.Hugh^5, 23.Joseph^4, 6.Hugh^3, 3.John^2, 1.Jean^1), b. Feb- 6-1868 in Ohio,[12] d. Jun-24-1905 in Ohio.[12] He married[317] Nov-28-1900,[12] **Nora Edith Culberson**, also known as Edith,[317] b. Feb- 4-1873 in Ohio,[12] d. Mar-22-1962 in Ohio.[12]
> Children:
> 1027. i.   MARTHA ALICE GASTON b. Feb-27-1904.

601. **James M. Gaston** (314.Philander^7, 154.James^6, 77.Hugh^5, 23.Joseph^4, 6.Hugh^3, 3.John^2, 1.Jean^1), b. 1872,[12] d. Jan-13-1947.[12] He married[12] **Ada Dora __**, b. 1878,[12] d. May-19-1961.[12]
> Children:
> 1028. i.   HARRY GASTON.
> 1029. ii.   WALTER GASTON.
>   iii. WILLIAM GASTON[12.]
> 1030. iv. HOWARD GASTON.
> 1031. v.   GLEN GASTON.

602. **Louis Clark Gordon** (317.Gilbert^7, 156.Jane^6, 78.James^5, 23.Joseph^4, 6.Hugh^3, 3.John^2, 1.Jean^1), b. May- 8-1878 in Moon Twp, Allegheny Co, PA, d. Sep-22-1941 in Gary, Lake Co, IN,[161] [Stricken by heart attack while attending church.], buried in Ridgelawn Cemetery, Pittsburgh, PA. He married Sep- 7-1904 in Pittsburgh, Allegheny Co, PA, **Ethel Lucinda Bovard**, b. Jan-11-1881 in Butler Co, PA (daughter of Samuel Finley Bovard and Sarah Emaline Rosenberry), d. Jan-20-1931, buried in Ridgelawn Cemetery, Pittsburgh, PA.
> Children:
> 1032. i.   SARA LOUISE "SALLY" GORDON b. Apr-22-1906.
>   ii.   LOUIS CLARK GORDON b. Jul-17-1909 in Allegheny Co, PA, d. Aug-16-1944 in Saranac Lake, Franklin Co, NY,[mccxxvii[1227]] buried in Ridgelawn Cemetery, Pittsburgh, PA, never married.
> 1033. iii. ALICE JULIA (TWIN) GORDON b. Sep- 9-1912.
> 1034. iv. GILBERT GRIFFITH (TWIN) GORDON b. Sep- 9-1912.

603. **Gilbert Montgomery "Bertie" Gordon** (317.Gilbert^7, 156.Jane^6, 78.James^5, 23.Joseph^4, 6.Hugh^3, 3.John^2, 1.Jean^1), b. Mar-16-1880 in Moon Twp, Allegheny Co, PA, d. Mar- -1971 in Allegheny Co, PA,

buried in Sharon Presbyterian Cemetery. He married Jun-23-1904,[291] **Sarah Jones**, b. ca 1879 in England, d. 1966, buried in Sharon Presbyterian Cemetery.

Children:

i. RUTH M. GORDON b. Jun-23-1905 in Allegheny Co, PA,[592] d. Jun- 8-1989,[592] buried in Sharon Presbyterian Cemetery, resided in Pennsylvania,[mccxxviii[1228]] never married.

ii. ROBERT GASTON GORDON b. Sep-27-1906 in Allegheny Co, PA,[592] d. May- 6-1991.[592]

iii. WILLIAM F. (TWIN) GORDON b. Sep- 2-1911 in Allegheny Co, PA.

iv. (FEMALE) (TWIN) GORDON b. Sep- 2-1911 in Allegheny Co, PA, d. Sep- -1911.

v. DOROTHY GORDON b. Sep-20-1913 in Allegheny Co, PA.

604. **Margret Orr Lippincott** (319.John⁷, 160.Charity⁶, 79.Alexander⁵, 23.Joseph⁴, 6.Hugh³, 3.John², 1.Jean¹), b. Jun-29-1859 in Morristown, Belmont Co, OH,[164,209] [But she was not in 1860 Census.], d. May- 2-1935 in Quaker City, Guernsey Co, OH,[164] census 1870 in Morristown, Belmont Co, OH. She married[164] **Isaac Perego Steele**, b. Jun- 8-1854 in Quaker City, Guernsey Co, OH,[164] d. Dec-10-1926 in Quaker City, Guernsey Co, OH.[164]

Children:

1035. i. DEWEY GEORGE STEELE b. Feb-23-1898.

605. **Bathanna Pearce** (322.Hosea⁷, 173.Elizabeth⁶, 82.Mary⁵, 27.Margaret⁴, 8.Joseph³, 3.John², 1.Jean¹), b. Jan-22-1822 in White Co, IL,[64] d. Feb-13-1905 in White Co, IL.[64] She married (1) Jan-12-1841 in White Co, IL,[64] **William Bryant**, b. Dec- 8-1820, d. Nov-13-1877 in White Co, IL.[64] She married (2) Apr- 4-1896 in White Co, IL,[64] **Simeon N. Hall**, b. 1826.[64]

Children by William Bryant:

1036. i. JULIA ANN BRYANT b. ca 1845.

606. **Harold Whetstone Johnston** (323.DeWitt⁷, 174.James⁶, 83.Sarah⁵, 27.Margaret⁴, 8.Joseph³, 3.John², 1.Jean¹), b.[172] He married[172] **Eugenia Hinricksen**.

Children:

i. MARY JOHNSTON b.[172]

ii. KATHERINE JOHNSTON b.[172]

iii. EUGENE HINRICKSEN JOHNSTON b.[172]

iv. HAROLD BAUER JOHNSTON b.[172]

v. LOUISE JOHNSTON b.[172]

vi. EDWARD SCOTT JOHNSTON b.[172]

vii. ANN WYATT JOHNSTON b.[172]

607. **Walter Gaston** (324.William⁷, 175.John⁶, 84.William⁵, 28.John⁴, 8.Joseph³, 3.John², 1.Jean¹), b. ca 1850 in New Jersey,[209] resided in Buffalo, Erie Co, NY,[27] census 1870 in Bridgewater, Somerset Co, NJ.

It is assumed that Walter Gaston's two children were by his first wife, Gertrude J. Phillips. Walter Gaston and family lived in Buffalo, New York.[27]

He married (1) **Gertrude J. Phillips**, b. Jan- 3-1850,[27] d. Apr- 1-1894.[27] He married (2) **Mary L. __**.

Children by Gertrude J. Phillips:

i. WILLIAM GASTON.

ii. EDWARD GASTON.

608. **Mary Gaston** (324.William⁷, 175.John⁶, 84.William⁵, 28.John⁴, 8.Joseph³, 3.John², 1.Jean¹), b. Sep-10-1851 in New Jersey,[27,209] d. Sep-13-1890, census 1870 in Bridgewater, Somerset Co, NJ. She married **__ Vreeland**.

Children:

i. GERTRUDE VREELAND.

609. **Margaret Gaston** (325.Daniel[7], 175.John[6], 84.William[5], 28.John[4], 8.Joseph[3], 3.John[2], 1.Jean[1]), b. Nov-16-1830,[27] d. Jan-28-___.[27] She married Feb-28-1850,[27] **James English Hedges**, b. 1824,[27] (son of William Woodhull Hedges and Jane English), d. Jan- 7-___.
Children:
1037. i. J. EDWARD HEDGES.

610. **William Gaston** (325.Daniel[7], 175.John[6], 84.William[5], 28.John[4], 8.Joseph[3], 3.John[2], 1.Jean[1]), b. Oct-26-1839 in Somerset Co, NJ,[669] d. Sep-18-1907.[27] He married May-15-1865, **Margaret Ann Keiley** (daughter of Matthew Keiley and Rachael M. Connelly), resided originally in Elizabeth, Union Co, NJ.
Children:
1038. i. FREDERICK KEILEY GASTON b. Jan- 6-1868.
1039. ii. IDA V. GASTON b. Jun- 2-1871.
iii. WILLIAM EDGAR GASTON b. Jul-14-1873,[27] d. Jul-27-1874.[27]
iv. MARY B. GASTON b. Sep- 3-1875.[27] She married Apr-22-1909,[27] James W. Pyle.
1040. v. MARGARET H. GASTON b. Dec-27-1879.

611. **John D. Gaston** (325.Daniel[7], 175.John[6], 84.William[5], 28.John[4], 8.Joseph[3], 3.John[2], 1.Jean[1]), b. ca 1842 in Somerville, Somerset Co, NJ,[27,280] census 1860 in Bedminster Twp, Somerset Co, NJ, military Civil War. He married May-31-1881,[27] **Margaretta G. Brokaw** (daughter of John B. Brokaw and Magdolena Garretson).
Children:
i. LENA MAY GASTON b. Jan-23-1884,[27] d. Feb-12-1884.[27]
ii. JAMES HEDGES GASTON b. Jun-18-1888 in Kansas.[27]

612. **William B. Gaston** (326.Samuel[7], 175.John[6], 84.William[5], 28.John[4], 8.Joseph[3], 3.John[2], 1.Jean[1]), b. Mar-29-1837 in New York,[27,280] d. Mar-23-1902,[27] census 1860 in Trenton, Mercer Co, NJ, occupation 1860 clerk.[280] He married **Sarah Anderson**, d. 1910.[27]
Children:
i. MORRIS GASTON b. 1874,[27] d. 1876.[27]

613. **Oliver Gaston** (326.Samuel[7], 175.John[6], 84.William[5], 28.John[4], 8.Joseph[3], 3.John[2], 1.Jean[1]), b. ca 1855 in New York,[280] census 1860 in Trenton, Mercer Co, NJ. He married **Unknown**.
Children:
i. FRED GASTON.

Went West.

ii. PERCY GASTON resided in Los Angeles, CA, occupation Artist.
iii. ALBERT GASTON resided in Sacramento, Sacramento Co, CA.
iv. OLIVER GASTON, JR..
v. FLORENCE GASTON.
vi. HELEN GASTON.

614. **Naomi Gaston** (328.John[7], 175.John[6], 84.William[5], 28.John[4], 8.Joseph[3], 3.John[2], 1.Jean[1]), b. Dec-10-1846 in New Jersey,[299,209] d. Jun-27-1903,[299] census 1870, 1880 in Branchburg, Somerset Co, NJ, census 1850, 1860 in Bedminster Twp, Somerset Co, NJ. She married Nov-21-1866,[299] **Peter Dumont**, b. ca 1844 in New Jersey,[209] (son of Isaac V. C. Dumont and Maria V. D.), census 1870, 1880 in Branchburg, Somerset Co, NJ, occupation 1870 farmer,[209] occupation 1880 town clerk.[210] Although married to Peter Dumont, Naomi Gaston's three children are listed in Max Perry's Gaston Genealogy with the surname Gaston, and her two sons' children continued to carry the Gaston name. Perry's source for this was not stated, and it was likely the result of incorrect data entry. Census data show that those children and grandchildren in fact carried the Dumont name.

1870 Census, Somerset Co, NJ (Branchburgh Twp), enumerated on Aug 13 1870:

Peter Dumont, 26, farmer; Neomia Dumont, 24; John Dumont, 1; Mariah Dumont, 65. All born in New Jersey.

1880 Census, Somerset Co, NJ (Branchburgh Twp), enumerated on Jun 9 1880:
Peter Dumont, 36, town clerk; wife Naomi Dumont, 34; son John G. Dumont, 10; dau Cora Dumont, 8; son Oliver P. Dumont, 6 months (b. Jan); mother Maria, 74. All born in New Jersey.

    Children:
1041. i.   JOHN G. DUMONT b. ca 1869.
1042. ii. CORA DUMONT b. ca 1872.
1043. iii. OLIVER PILLSBURY DUMONT b. Jan- -1880.

615. **William Ker Gaston** (328.John^7, 175.John^6, 84.William^5, 28.John^4, 8.Joseph^3, 3.John^2, 1.Jean^1), b. ca 1849 in New Jersey,[146] census 1850, 1860 in Bedminster Twp, Somerset Co, NJ. He married Dec- 3-1873,[673] **Eliza Van Arsdale**, b. Jul-18-1846,[673] (daughter of Tunis Van Arsdale and Sarah DeMott), d. May- 4-1916.[673]
    Children:
1044. i.   WILLIAM IRA GASTON b. Jan- 2-1875.
      ii. ANNA REBECCA GASTON.
1045. iii. JAMES HERBERT GASTON.

616. **Hugh Gaston** (328.John^7, 175.John^6, 84.William^5, 28.John^4, 8.Joseph^3, 3.John^2, 1.Jean^1), b. ca 1856 in New Jersey,[280] census 1860 in Bedminster Twp, Somerset Co, NJ. He married Nov-24-1880,[673] **Rachel A. TenEick** (daughter of John S. TenEick and Margaret Hull).
    Children:
1046. i.   ETHEL REBECCA GASTON.

617. **Jane Maria Gaston**[mccxxix[1229]] (329.Oliver^7, 175.John^6, 84.William^5, 28.John^4, 8.Joseph^3, 3.John^2, 1.Jean^1), b. Sep-27-1841 in Jamesburg, Middlesex Co, NJ, d. Nov- 3-1903, census in New Brunswick, Middlesex Co, NJ. She married Nov- 3-1869, **George Henry Smock**, b. Aug-19-1842 (son of Henry Smock and Maria V. Boise), d. Sep-19-1910.
    Children:
      i.   FREDDIE G. SMOCK b. 1872, d. 1880.
1047. ii. CASSIE VAN NEST SMOCK.
1048. iii. GEORGE WILLETS SMOCK b. ca 1887.
      iv. EDNA C. SMOCK.

618. **Catherine Van Nest Gaston**[1229] (329.Oliver^7, 175.John^6, 84.William^5, 28.John^4, 8.Joseph^3, 3.John^2, 1.Jean^1), b. Feb- 4-1844 in New York,[280] d. Jun- 1-1905 in Locust Valley, Nassau Co, NY, census 1860 in New Brunswick, Middlesex Co, NJ. She married Jun-12-1866, **John Henry Smock**, b. Jan-20-1836 in Freehold, Monmouth Co, NJ (son of Henry Smock and Maria V. Boise), d. Jan- 8-1903 in New York, occupation Minister.
    Children:
1049. i.   AUGUSTUS HOBART SMOCK.
      ii. JENNIE ALMA SMOCK d. in infancy.
      iii. CLARENCE MCKAY SMOCK. He married 1900, Eula Whiting.
1050. iv. ETHEL L. SMOCK.

619. **Sylvia Beavers Gaston** (329.Oliver^7, 175.John^6, 84.William^5, 28.John^4, 8.Joseph^3, 3.John^2, 1.Jean^1), b. Mar- -1857 in New Jersey,[123] census 1920 in Woodbury, Gloucester Co, NJ [Listed as Sylvia Willits, 63, b. NJ, widowed, mother-in-law in household of daughter & son-in-law Jessie & Edward Yancy.], census 1910 in Philadelphia, PA, census 1860 in New Brunswick, Middlesex Co, NJ. She married Aug-3-1876, **George Sidney Willits, Jr.**, b. Feb- -1853 in Pennsylvania,[123] (son of George Sidney Willits and Elizabeth Githeus), d. bef Jan 1920,[681] census 1900, 1910 in Philadelphia, PA, military Captain, U.S. Navy,[211] education U.S. Naval Academy, Annapolis (June 1875).[15]

1900 Census, city of Philadelphia, Pennsylvania, enumerated on Jun 1 1900:
Geo S. Willits, 47, b. Feb 1853 in Pennsylvania, Lieutenant in Navy, married 24 yrs; wife Sylvia B, 43, b. Mar 1857 in New Jersey, married 24 yrs, mother of 6 children (5 still living); dau Grace G, 17, b. Oct 1882 in Pa; son Alford, 15, b. Aug 1884 in Pa; dau Jessie A, 12, b. Dec 1887 in Pa; son Oliver G, 8, b. Feb 1892 in Pa.
(Note: There are discrepancies in some birthplaces between this census and the 1910 Census. The latter appears to be more accurate.)

1910 Census, city of Philadelphia, Pennsylvania, enumerated on Apr 15 1910:
George S. Willits, 57, b. Pa, Captain in U.S. Navy, married 32 yrs; wife Sylvia B, 53, b. NJ, married 32 yrs, mother of 6 children (5 still living); dau Grace G, 27, b. Pa; dau Jessie A, 22, b. NJ; son Oliver G, 18, b. NY; servant Mattie Everett, 32, b. NC, married 13 yrs, mother of one child (still living).

                    Children:
        1051. i.   CHARLES C. WILLITS b. ca 1879.
               ii.   ALBERT WILLITS d. age 7 yrs.[15]
        1052. iii. GRACE G. WILLITS b. Oct- -1882.
               iv.   ALFORD WILLITS b. Aug- -1884 in Pennsylvania,[123] census 1900 in Philadelphia, PA.
               v.   JESSIE A. WILLITS b. Dec- -1887 in New Jersey,[123,211] census 1920 in Woodbury,
Gloucester Co, NJ, census 1900, 1910 in Philadelphia, PA. She married Oct-25-1913,[15] Edward B.
Yancy, b. ca 1889 in Virginia,[681] census 1920 in Woodbury, Gloucester Co, NJ.
               vi.   OLIVER G. WILLITS b. Feb-20-1892 in New York,[592,211] d. May- -1971,[592] resided in
Philadelphia, PA,[mccxxx[1230]] census 1900, 1910 in Philadelphia, PA.

620. **Lizzie Gaston** (329.Oliver[7], 175.John[6], 84.William[5], 28.John[4], 8.Joseph[3], 3.John[2], 1.Jean[1]), b. 1860 in New Jersey,[280] census 1910 in Elizabeth, Union Co, NJ, census 1860 in New Brunswick, Middlesex Co, NJ. She married Oct-17-1888, **George Mung Williams**, b. ca 1862 in New Jersey,[211] (son of John R. Williams and Caroline McCormick), census 1910 in Elizabeth, Union Co, NJ.
                    Children:
        1053. i.   CAROLYN GASTON WILLIAMS b. Sep- 5-1889.
               ii.   RALPH SCHUYLER WILLIAMS b. ca 1892 in New York, census 1910 in Elizabeth,
Union Co, NJ, never married.

621. **Catherine Gaston** (331.Hugh[7], 175.John[6], 84.William[5], 28.John[4], 8.Joseph[3], 3.John[2], 1.Jean[1]), b. ca 1847 in New Jersey,[280] census 1860 in Bedminster Twp, Somerset Co, NJ. She married (1) Jan- 1-1869, **Andrew Quick**, d. Nov- -1872 in Virden, Macoupin Co, IL. She married (2) Apr- 4-1894, **Oscar Durham**.
                    Children by Andrew Quick:
        1054. i.   JANE QUICK.

622. **Sarah Gaston** (331.Hugh[7], 175.John[6], 84.William[5], 28.John[4], 8.Joseph[3], 3.John[2], 1.Jean[1]), b. ca 1849 in New Jersey,[280] census 1860 in Bedminster Twp, Somerset Co, NJ. She married Nov- 2-1869, **William Voorhees**, d. Mar-28-1913.
                    Children:
               i.   ELLA RAMSEY VOORHEES resided in Jacksonville, Duval Co, FL.
               ii.   LENA MAY VOORHEES. She married Otto Coultons, resided in Riggston, Scott Co, IL.
               iii. HUGH VOORHEES resided in Woodson, Morgan Co, IL. He married Mar-28-1915,
Harriet Pierson.

623. **Marietta Gaston**, census name Mary Gaston (331.Hugh[7], 175.John[6], 84.William[5], 28.John[4], 8.Joseph[3], 3.John[2], 1.Jean[1]), b. 1860 in New Jersey,[280] census 1870 in Branchburg, Somerset Co, NJ, census 1860 in Bedminster Twp, Somerset Co, NJ. She married Dec-25-1879, **Peter B. Dumont**.
                    Children:

i.   EMMA JANE DUMONT. She married in Somerset Co, NJ, William Perry.
ii.   CORNELIA DUMONT.
iii.   HUGH GASTON DUMONT.
iv.   IRENE DUMONT.
v.   LILLIAN DUMONT.
vi.   MARY DUMONT. She married Jan-22-1913, Clarence Wyckoff.
vii.   HAROLD DUMONT.
viii.   ARTHUR DUMONT.

624. **John Garretson Gaston** (331.Hugh[7], 175.John[6], 84.William[5], 28.John[4], 8.Joseph[3], 3.John[2], 1.Jean[1]), b. ca 1862 in New Jersey,[334] census 1930 in Somerville, Somerset Co, NJ [in household with son George], census 1870 in Branchburg, Somerset Co, NJ. He married Mar-17-1886, **Ella Bergin Smith**, b. in Canada (daughter of Cornelius V. D. Smith and Judith Tunison TenEyck), d. bef Apr 1930.[334]
  Children:
  1055. i.   GEORGE A. GASTON b. ca 1888.

625. **William Garretson Gaston** (331.Hugh[7], 175.John[6], 84.William[5], 28.John[4], 8.Joseph[3], 3.John[2], 1.Jean[1]), b. ca 1869,[209] resided in New York City, NY, census 1870, 1880 in Branchburg, Somerset Co, NJ. He married Oct-12-1897, **Elizabeth Sutphen Craig** (daughter of David Kline Craig and Mary Elizabeth Amermun), resided in New York City, NY.
  Children:
  i.   KATHERINE CRAIG GASTON b. 1903, d. 1903.
  ii.   MARY ELIZABETH GASTON.

626. **Elizabeth Sergeant** (334.Sarah[7], 177.John[6], 85.Joseph[5], 28.John[4], 8.Joseph[3], 3.John[2], 1.Jean[1]), b. May-25-1835 in Somerville, Somerset Co, NJ.

Elizabeth's Sergeant's second husband, George Wright Zahniser, was previously married to her aunt, Catherine Gaston (1831-1865).

She married (1) **Charles McGill**. She married (2) Jul- 5-1866, **George Wright Zahniser**, b. Mar-19-1823, d. Jun-12-1889, occupation minister.
  Children by George Wright Zahniser:
  1056. i.   GEORGE BROWN ZAHNISER.
  ii.   KATHERINE GASTON ZAHNISER.
  1057. iii.   ALBERT WRIGHT ZAHNISER.

627. **William Gaston Sergeant** (334.Sarah[7], 177.John[6], 85.Joseph[5], 28.John[4], 8.Joseph[3], 3.John[2], 1.Jean[1]), b. Nov-25-1837, d. Oct-21-1898. He married 1876 in Waterford, Erie Co, PA, **Jessie Beson**, d. Jun- 2-1910.
  Children:
  i.   WILLIAM GASTON SERGEANT, JR.. He married 1915 in London, England, Mary Jeffrey, b. in New York City, NY.
  ii.   DOROTHY SERGEANT resided in England.

628. **John Gaston Brown** (335.Joanna[7], 177.John[6], 85.Joseph[5], 28.John[4], 8.Joseph[3], 3.John[2], 1.Jean[1]), b. Jul-2-1846, d. Sep-23-1893 in Somerville, Somerset Co, NJ. He married Oct-11-1871, **Jennie B. Bryant**, b. Nov- 3-1852, d. Nov- 9-1889.
  Children:
  1058. i.   REZEAN BLANCHARD BROWN.
  1059. ii.   GEORGE HOUSTON BROWN.
  iii.   ELINOR GARRETSON BROWN.

629. **George Houston Brown, Jr.** (335.Joanna[7], 177.John[6], 85.Joseph[5], 28.John[4], 8.Joseph[3], 3.John[2], 1.Jean[1]), b. Jul-30-1852,[mccxxxi[1231]] d. Mar-25-1908 in Cincinnati, Hamilton Co, OH.[1231] He married (1)

Jun- 6-1883,[1231] **Gertrude Campbell Carmer**, b. Jan- 9-1859 in New York,[1231] (daughter of Charles Whitehead Carmer and Mary Morris Popham), d. Sep-14-1896.[1231] He married (2) Apr-14-1898, **Laura Hasbrouk LeFevre**.

Children by Gertrude Campbell Carmer:
1060. i. MORRIS HOUSTON BROWN b. 1880.
1061. ii. JOAN CHURCHILL BROWN b. Sep-13-1885.
1062. iii. HENRY CARMER BROWN b. Jan-29-1887.
iv. MARY LOONIS BROWN.

630. **Ida Augusta Brown** (335.Joanna[7], 177.John[6], 85.Joseph[5], 28.John[4], 8.Joseph[3], 3.John[2], 1.Jean[1]), b. Nov-23-1859, d. May-29-1883. She married Jul- 1-1880 in Sioux City, Woodbury Co, IA, **Samuel Smiley Mehard, Jr.**.

Children:
i. CHURCHILL BROWN MEHARD. He married Mary Klein, b. in Anniston, Calhoun Co, AL.

631. **Joanna Brown Gaston** (336.Samuel[7], 177.John[6], 85.Joseph[5], 28.John[4], 8.Joseph[3], 3.John[2], 1.Jean[1]), occupation Physican. She married **George Leary**.

Children:
i. LEWIS GASTON LEARY.

Author of several books, including "Andorra: The Hidden Republic. Its Origin and Institutions and a Record of a Journey Thither," published in 1912, and "The Bible When You Want It," a short collection of scriptures keyed to the reader's immediate needs, published in 1932 in West Milford, NJ.

ii. RUSSELL WOODWARD LEARY.
iii. GEORGE DANIEL LEARY.
iv. EVELYN LEARY.

632. **Ida Elmira Gaston** (336.Samuel[7], 177.John[6], 85.Joseph[5], 28.John[4], 8.Joseph[3], 3.John[2], 1.Jean[1]). She married **Ferdinand Adams**.

Children:
i. NELLIE FRANCES ADAMS.
ii. MARGORIE CATHERINE ADAMS.
iii. FLORA ADAMS.
iv. FERDINAND GASTON ADAMS.

633. **Evelina Reynolds Stewart** (337.Aletta[7], 177.John[6], 85.Joseph[5], 28.John[4], 8.Joseph[3], 3.John[2], 1.Jean[1]), b. ca 1847,[675] resided in Seattle, WA. She married **Austin Gillette**.

Children:
i. WILLIAM STEWART GILLETTE b. 1865, d. 1888.
ii. CHARLES AUSTIN GILLETTE. He married Nalilda Freitsche.
iii. ALLETTA MARIA GILLETTE.

634. **Mary Stewart** (337.Aletta[7], 177.John[6], 85.Joseph[5], 28.John[4], 8.Joseph[3], 3.John[2], 1.Jean[1]), b. ca 1849.[675] She married **Daniel T. Gilman**.

Children:
1063. i. SARAH MARSHALL GILMAN.
1064. ii. WILLIAM STEWART GILMAN.

635. **Robert Annin Stewart** (337.Aletta[7], 177.John[6], 85.Joseph[5], 28.John[4], 8.Joseph[3], 3.John[2], 1.Jean[1]), b. ca 1851.[675] He married **Alice Boyle**.

Children:
i. ALETTA STEWART. She married Clinton Brome.

ii. ELIZABETH HUNTER STEWART.

iii. WILLIAM STEWART. He married Ruth Birchard.

636. **John Frederick Gaston**, census name Frederick Gaston (338.Isaac[7], 177.John[6], 85.Joseph[5], 28.John[4], 8.Joseph[3], 3.John[2], 1.Jean[1]), b. Sep-12-1852 in New Jersey, d. Oct- -1892, census 1860, 1870 in Newark, Essex Co, NJ. He married Jun-12-1880, **Rosa A. McNeil**, d. Jan- -1882.
   Children:
   i. ETHELWYN GASTON b. Sep-12-1881, d. Dec- -1972,[592] resided in New York City,
NY.[1157]

637. **William Henry Gaston** (338.Isaac[7], 177.John[6], 85.Joseph[5], 28.John[4], 8.Joseph[3], 3.John[2], 1.Jean[1]), b. Nov-16-1855 in New Jersey, census 1860, 1870 in Newark, Essex Co, NJ. He married Apr- 5-1893, **Suzanna Lauenstein**.
   Children:
   i. MARY ELIZABETH GASTON.
   ii. WILLIAM ISAAC GASTON.

638. **George Houston Gaston** (338.Isaac[7], 177.John[6], 85.Joseph[5], 28.John[4], 8.Joseph[3], 3.John[2], 1.Jean[1]), b. Apr-11-1858 in New Jersey, census 1860, 1870 in Newark, Essex Co, NJ. He married Sep-1885, **Martha Elizabeth Wilson**.
   Children:
   i. HELEN WILSON GASTON d. Sep- 3-1888.
   ii. GEORGE HOUSTON GASTON, JR..
   iii. DOROTHY WILSON GASTON.

639. **Eugene A. Gaston** (339.Alexander[7], 178.William[6], 85.Joseph[5], 28.John[4], 8.Joseph[3], 3.John[2], 1.Jean[1]), b. Sep- -1847 in Pennsylvania,[123] d. Jul-21-1909 in Pratt, Pratt Co, KS, census 1900 in Battle Creek, Calhoun Co, MI, census 1880 in Iroquois Co, IL, occupation physician.[123,190]

Graduate of the Medical Department of the University of Pennsylvania. Began medical practice in Hoopston, IL. In 1881 he went to Kansas and was a prominent physician, much esteemed for his sterling work. He leaves a wife and two sons.[190]

He married ca 1871,[123] **Helen E. __**, b. Apr- -1851 in Illinois,[123] census 1910, 1920, 1930 in Pratt, Pratt Co, KS, census 1900 in Battle Creek, Calhoun Co, MI, census 1880 in Iroquois Co, IL.

1880 Census, Iroquois Co, Illinois, enumerated on Jun 14 1880:
Eugene Gaston, 34, b. Pa, father b. NJ, mother b. Pa, physician old school; wife Helen, 27, b. Ill, father b. NY, mother b. Va; son Paul, 7, b. Ill.

In the 1900 Census, this family was enumerated as the household of son Paul, in Battle Creek, Michigan.

   Children:
   1065. i. PAUL K. GASTON b. Jan- -1873.
   1066. ii. EUGENE A. GASTON b. Aug- -1882.

640. **Evelyn Gaston** (341.Hugh[7], 178.William[6], 85.Joseph[5], 28.John[4], 8.Joseph[3], 3.John[2], 1.Jean[1]). She married Jun-15-1882, **Augustus Van Derveer**.
   Children:
   i. HUGH GASTON VAN DERVEER.
   ii. ELIZABETH K. VAN DERVEER.

641. **Louis Prevast Gaston** (341.Hugh[7], 178.William[6], 85.Joseph[5], 28.John[4], 8.Joseph[3], 3.John[2], 1.Jean[1]). He married Sep- 5-1893, **Maude Safford**.

Children:
  i.   KENNETH S. GASTON.
  ii. MARY GASTON.
  iii. HUGH GASTON.
  iv. BEATRICE GASTON.

642. **William Fredrick Gaston** (342.John[7], 178.William[6], 85.Joseph[5], 28.John[4], 8.Joseph[3], 3.John[2], 1.Jean[1]), b. Feb-11-1854 in Pompton, NJ. He married Oct-11-1876, **Mary Zabriskie** (daughter of Christian A. Zabriskie).
Children:
  i.   JOHN GASTON, JR.[mccxxxii][1232]
  ii. FREDERICK W. GASTON.
  iii. ALICE M. GASTON.

643. **Charles Robert Gaston** (344.Charles[7], 179.Ogden[6], 86.Stephen[5], 28.John[4], 8.Joseph[3], 3.John[2], 1.Jean[1]), b. Sep- 6-1874 in Detroit, MI,[325] census 1930 in Pleasantville, Westchester Co, NY, census 1920 in Queens, New York City, NY, census 1910 in Brooklyn, Kings Co, NY, census 1880 in Detroit, MI, occupation teacher.[325,334]

A Ph.D. and teacher of English at the Richmond Hill High School in New York City. Author of the book "Irving's Oliver Goldsmith: A Biography," published in 1903 by Ginn & Company. Also author of the book "Washington's Farewell Address and Webster's First Bunker Hill Oration," published in 1906 by The Athenaeum Press, Ginn & Company. He and his wife, Edith Fales Gaston, also published in 1927 a collection of biographical readings for high school students, entitled "Modern Lives."

He married Sep-28-1907,[325] **Edith Gertrude Fales**, census name Gertrude F., b. ca 1877 in Michigan,[211] census 1930 in Pleasantville, Westchester Co, NY, census 1920 in Queens, New York City, NY, census 1910 in Brooklyn, Kings Co, NY.
Children:
  i.   EDITH G. GASTON b. ca 1909 in Michigan,[211] census 1920 in Queens, New York City, NY, census 1910 in Brooklyn, Kings Co, NY, census 1930 in Pleasantville, Westchester Co, NY.
  ii. ROBERT S. GASTON b. ca 1911 in New York,[681] census 1930 in Pleasantville, Westchester Co, NY, census 1920 in Queens, New York City, NY.

644. **George M. Gaston** (346.George[7], 179.Ogden[6], 86.Stephen[5], 28.John[4], 8.Joseph[3], 3.John[2], 1.Jean[1]), b. Sep- -1890 in Michigan,[123] census 1900, 1910. 1920 in Detroit, MI, occupation 1930 paper company representative. He married[334] **Mary G. __**, b. ca 1894 in Ohio,[334] census 1930 in Detroit, MI.
Children:
  i.   GEORGE TIFFANY GASTON II b. Jul- 7-1927 in Michigan,[592,334] d. Jan-12-2009,[592] resided in Bloomfield Hills, Oakland Co, MI,[592] census 1930 in Detroit, MI.

645. **Andrew Dickson White** (349.Clara[7], 187.Andrew[6], 93.Phebe[5], 32.Margaret[4], 9.John[3], 3.John[2], 1.Jean[1]), b. Nov- 7-1832 in Homer, NY,[28,302,123] d. Nov- 4-1918 in Ithaca, Tompkins Co, NY,[302] buried Sage Chapel, Cornell in Ithaca, Tompkins Co, NY,[302] census 1870, 1900, 1910 in Ithaca, Tompkins Co, NY, census 1860 in Ann Arbor, Washtenaw Co, MI, census 1850 in Syracuse, Onondaga Co, NY.

A graduate of Yale University, Andrew D. White excelled academically, was renowned for his writing and oratory skills, and competed in the first running of the Harvard-Yale Regatta in 1852. He traveled extensively in Europe following graduation, and in October 1858 accepted a position as a Professor of History and English literature at the University of Michigan, where he remained on faculty until 1863. He then returned to his Syracuse home, was elected to the New York State Senate, and became acquainted with fellow senator Ezra Cornell. Together, in 1865 they founded Cornell University in Ithaca, with Andrew White serving as its first president (1866-1885), as well as a professor of history. His later accomplishments included serving in numerous noted positions: U.S. Ambassador to Germany (1879-1881), first president of the American Historical Association (1884-

1885), Ambassador to Russia (1892-1894), president of the American delegation to The Hague Peace Conference (1899), and again as Ambassador to Germany (1897-1902).

He married (1) Sep-27-1857,[302] **Mary Amanda Outwater**, also known as Amanda Outwater,[302] b. Feb-10-1836,[302] d. Jun- 8-1887,[302] census 1870 in Ithaca, Tompkins Co, NY, census 1860 in Ann Arbor, Washtenaw Co, MI. He married (2) Sep- -1890,[mccxxxiii[1233]] **Helen Magill**, b. Nov-28-1853 in Providence, Providence Co, RI,[1233] [1900 Census states birth as Sep 1853.] (daughter of Edward Hicks Magill), d. Oct-28-1944 in Kittery Point, York Co, ME,[1233] census 1900, 1910 in Ithaca, Tompkins Co, NY.

Helen: A social scientist and educator, she holds the distinction of being the first female Ph.D. recipient in the United States, which she earned from Boston University in 1877. Her father was the second president of Swarthmore College.[1233]
Helen Magill White (b. November 28, 1853, Providence, Rhode Island — d. October 28, 1944, Kittery Point, Maine) was the first woman to earn a Ph.D. in the United States.

Raised in a Quaker family, White always believed that she was deserving of the same education as a man. In 1859, the family moved to Boston, where Helen signed up as the only female student in the Boston Public Latin School, where her father was submaster.[1] Her father was the president of Swarthmore College, which she attended as an undergraduate in 1873. She was a member of the first class to graduate from the university. She continued studies in the classics at Swarthmore and Boston University, where she earned her Ph.D in 1877. After that, up until 1881, she studied at the University of Cambridge, in England, placing third in her tripos (honors examinations) at Newnham College. [2]

After being the principal for a year at a private school in Johnstown, Pennsylvania, she was selected in 1883 to organize Howard Collegiate Institute, in West Bridgewater, Massachusetts. She was the director of Howard until 1887, when she resigned. She taught for a short amount of time at Evelyn College, a women's annex to Princeton University. She then suffered an illness for the next few years, while she taught at a high school.

Helen met Andrew D. White, the retired president of Cornell University, while presenting a paper at the American Social Science Association in 1887, and married him in September 1890. White was also a college classmate of Magill's father, Edward Hicks Magill. She accompanied her husband to his diplomatic posts in St. Petersburg (1892-94) and Berlin (1897-1903). She didn't participate in public or educational affairs after that, except to oppose women's suffrage publicly in 1913. After White died in 1918, she lived abroad and in Ithaca, New York, and then retired to Kittery Point, Maine, where she died in 1944.[3]

http://en.wikipedia.org/wiki/Helen_Magill_White

       Children by Mary Amanda Outwater:
    i.   CLARA D. WHITE b. ca 1858 in New York,[280] d. bef Nov 1918,[302] census 1870 in Ithaca, Tompkins Co, NY, census 1860 in Ann Arbor, Washtenaw Co, MI. She married[302] __ Newbury.
    ii.   FREDERICK DAVIES WHITE b. ca 1859 in Michigan,[280] d. 1901,[302] cause of death suicide,[302] census 1870 in Ithaca, Tompkins Co, NY, census 1860 in Ann Arbor, Washtenaw Co, MI.
    iii.   RUTH WHITE b. Oct- -1866 in New York,[123] census 1870, 1900 in Ithaca, Tompkins Co, NY [Middle initial given as P in 1870 Census, but as M in 1900 Census.]. She married[302] __ Ferry.
       Children by Helen Magill:
    iv.   KARIN A. WHITE, census name Carin A. White, b. Jul- -1893,[123] [Identified as Karin, born in Russia, in the 1900 Census, but as Carin, born in Finland, in the 1910 Census.], census 1900, 1910 in Ithaca, Tompkins Co, NY.

646. **Horace K. White** (349.Clara[7], 187.Andrew[6], 93.Phebe[5], 32.Margaret[4], 9.John[3], 3.John[2], 1.Jean[1]), b. Oct- -1837 in New York, census 1860, 1880, 1900 in Syracuse, Onondaga Co, NY [Middle initial

appears to be R in 1850, but either K or H in 1860. In 1880 he was listed simply as Horace White, 39 (sic), b. NY, banker, widowed, with three sons and several servants. In 1900 he was listed as Horace K White, 62, b. Oct 1937 in NY, banker, widowed. He was not found in the 1870 Census.], census 1850 in Ann Arbor, Washtenaw Co, MI, occupation banker.[280],[210]

Children:

 i. HORACE WHITE, JR. b. Oct- 7-1865 in Buffalo, Erie Co, NY,[mccxxxiv[1234]],[123] d. Nov-27-1943 in New York City, NY,[1234] census 1880, 1900, 20, 30 in Syracuse, Onondaga Co, NY, occupation lawyer, governor of New York (1910),[123],[1234] education Cornell (1887), Columbia Law School (1889).[1234] He married Jane __, b. ca 1866 in New York,[211] census 1920 in Syracuse, Onondaga Co, NY.

 ii. ANDREW WHITE b. ca 1869 in New York,[210] census 1880 in Syracuse, Onondaga Co, NY.

 iii. ERNEST WHITE b. ca 1871 in New York,[210] census 1880 in Syracuse, Onondaga Co, NY.

647. **Alonzo Alexander Gaston** (360.Alexander[7], 201.George[6], 100.Alexander[5], 37.Alexander[4], 10.Alexander[3], 3.John[2], 1.Jean[1]), b. 1881 in Tabor, Fremont Co, IA,[36] d. 1955 in Everett, Snohomish Co, WA,[36] census 1920, 1930 in Everett, Snohomish Co, WA, occupation real estate.[681],[334]

1920 Census, City of Everett, Snohomish Co, Washington, enumerated on Jan 7 1920:
A. A. Gaston, 38, b. Iowa, father b. New York, mother b. Vermont, occup real estate; wife Nathalia, 40, b. Maine, parents b. Sweden; dau Faith, 10, b. California; son Gordon, 6, b. Washington.

1930 Census, City of Everett, Snohomish Co, Washington, enumerated on Apr 5 1930:
Alonzo A. Gaston, 48, b. Iowa, father b. New York, mother b. Vermont, occup realtor, age 27 at first marriage; wife Nathalie L, 50, b. Maine, parents b. Sweden; dau Faith F, 20, b. California; son Gordon B, 16, b. Washington; dau Nathalie L, 9, b. Washington.

He married **Nathalie G. Lundgren**, b. 1878 in Caribou, Aroostook Co, ME,[317] census 1920, 1930 in Everett, Snohomish Co, WA.

Children:

 i. FAITH FRANCES GASTON b. 1909 in Hanford, Kings Co, CA,[317] census 1920, 1930 in Everett, Snohomish Co, WA.

1067. ii. GORDON BROOKS GASTON b. May- 6-1913.

 iii. NATHALIE L. GASTON b. ca 1921 in Washington State,[334] census 1930 in Everett, Snohomish Co, WA.

648. **Gladys Bond Gaston** (361.Willard[7], 206.James[6], 101.Heman[5], 37.Alexander[4], 10.Alexander[3], 3.John[2], 1.Jean[1]), b. Mar-22-1890 in Glenwood, Mills Co, IA,[193],[592] d. Nov- -1986,[592] resided in Riverside, Riverside Co, CA,[592] resided formerly in Iowa.[mccxxxv[1235]] She married[193] **John Sydney Cutter**, b. Apr-3-1889 in Coin, Page Co, IA.[193]

Children:

 i. JOHN SYDNEY CUTTER, JR. b. Jan-11-1912 in Shenandoah, Page Co, IA,[193],[592] d. Jan- -1976,[592] resided in Elyria, Lorain Co, OH,[592] resided formerly in Colorado.[1219]

 ii. CAROLYN LAURABELLE CUTTER b. Jul- 7-1919 in Shenandoah, Page Co, IA.

649. **Harold Burton Gaston** (362.Burton[7], 206.James[6], 101.Heman[5], 37.Alexander[4], 10.Alexander[3], 3.John[2], 1.Jean[1]), b. Sep-27-1897 in California,[313],[592] d. Feb- 6-1989 in Los Angeles Co, CA,[592] resided in Lynwood, Los Angeles Co, CA,[592] census 1930 in Compton, Los Angeles Co, CA. He married[313] **Mary Elizabeth Ryan**, b. Dec-22-1906 in California,[313],[592] (daughter of Harry Edgar Ryan and Myrtle Elizabeth Jones), d. Apr-27-1989 in Los Angeles Co, CA,[313],[592] buried in Los Angeles Co, CA,[313] resided in Lynwood, Los Angeles Co, CA.[mccxxxvi[1236]]

Children:

1068. i. LEONARD HARRY GASTON b. Nov-29-1930.

ii.   DAVID WAYNE GASTON b. Jul- 7-1934,[592] d. Aug-10-2001,[592,313] resided in Tucson, Pima Co, AZ,[592] resided formerly in California.[1152]
iii.   JACK GASTON.

650. **Myrla Shirley "Mertie" Brown** (366.Eunice[7], 207.Edmund[6], 102.Ebenezer[5], 38.David[4], 10.Alexander[3], 3.John[2], 1.Jean[1]), b. May-13-1866 in Illinois,[317,210] d. May- 4-1909 in Chicago, IL,[317] census 1880 in Greene Co, MO. She married[317] **Homer H. Haseltine**, also known as Harry H. Haseltine,[317] b. Jun- -1854 in Wisconsin,[317,211,681] d. Jun-22-1925 in Tampa, Hillsborough Co, FL,[190] buried in Cochranton, Crawford Co, PA,[190] census 1920 in Tampa, Hillsborough Co, FL, census 1910 in Cochranton, Crawford Co, PA, census 1880 in Greene Co, MO [Listed with family of his future in-laws, Henry & Eunice Brown.].
Children:
1069. i.   HUBERT ARTHUR HASELTINE[317] b. Jun-22-1892.

651. **Phylinda Gaston Brown** (366.Eunice[7], 207.Edmund[6], 102.Ebenezer[5], 38.David[4], 10.Alexander[3], 3.John[2], 1.Jean[1]), b. Jan-24-1870 in Illinois,[mccxxxvii[1237],123,210] [Birthplace given as Pennsylvania in 1900 Census, but as Illinois in 1910 Census and in California Death Index.], d. Dec-22-1964 in San Diego Co, CA,[1237] census 1930 in Houston, Harris Co, TX, resided 1918, 1920 in San Francisco, CA,[mccxxxviii[1238]] census 1910 in Cochranton, Crawford Co, PA, census 1900 in Raton, Colfax Co, NM, census 1880 in Greene Co, MO, occupation 1930 secretary for YWCA.[334] She married[317] ca 1889,[123] **William C. Whittaker**, b. May- -1867 in Ohio,[123] d. bef Apr 1910,[211] census 1900 in Raton, Colfax Co, NM, occupation 1900 machinist for railroad.[123]
Children:
1070. i.   CHESTER KIRK WHITTAKER b. Nov-28-1889.
ii.   MERTIE COSETTE WHITTAKER, census name M. Cossett Whitaker, census name Mertie C. Whitaker, b. Jan- -1892,[123] resided 1918 in San Francisco, CA,[1238] census 1910 in Cochranton, Crawford Co, PA, census 1900 in Raton, Colfax Co, NM.

652. **Frank Edmund Brown** (366.Eunice[7], 207.Edmund[6], 102.Ebenezer[5], 38.David[4], 10.Alexander[3], 3.John[2], 1.Jean[1]), b. Mar- 9-1874 in Ohio,[1237,123,210] census 1920, 1930 in Erie, Erie Co, PA, census 1900 in Cochranton, Crawford Co, PA, census 1880 in Greene Co, MO, occupation 1920 salesman (stoves),[681] occupation 1900 clerk (hardware).[123] He married[317] ca 1896,[334] **Belinda Emily "Lynnie" Brittain**, also known as Linnie Brittain,[317,123] also known as Lynnie E. Brittain, b. Dec- -1874 in Ohio,[123] census 1920, 1930 in Erie, Erie Co, PA, census 1900 in Cochranton, Crawford Co, PA.
Children:
1071. i.   ARTHUR EDMON BROWN b. Sep-15-1896.
1072. ii.   LINNIE WINSOME BROWN b. Jun- 2-1898.

653. **Arthur Athelston Brown** (366.Eunice[7], 207.Edmund[6], 102.Ebenezer[5], 38.David[4], 10.Alexander[3], 3.John[2], 1.Jean[1]), b. Jun-17-1878 in Missouri,[317,123,210] census 1880, 1900 in Greene Co, MO. He married 1901 in Springfield, Greene Co, MO,[317] **Florence Etta Silsby**.
Children:
i.   FLORENCE MIRIAM BROWN.
ii.   ARTHUR SILSBY BROWN.
iii.   HARRY SILSBY BROWN.
1073. iv.   ELEANOR ROSE BROWN[317].

654. **Harry Gaston Brown** (366.Eunice[7], 207.Edmund[6], 102.Ebenezer[5], 38.David[4], 10.Alexander[3], 3.John[2], 1.Jean[1]), b. Feb-26-1884 in Missouri,[317,123] [Birth date given in World War I Draft Registration Card as Feb 26 1885. But 1900 Census shows it as Feb 1884.], d. 1952 in Dade Co, FL,[1123] resided 1918 in Pittsburgh, Allegheny Co, PA,[684] census 1900 in Greene Co, MO, occupation real estate developer,[317] occupation 1918 Westinghouse Electric.[684] He married[317] (1) **Eleanor Swann**. He married (2) Dec-10-1910,[317] **Lilly Leora Blair**, also known as Leora Lillie Blair,[mccxxxix[1239]] b. Sep-13-1892 in Sandy Lake, Mercer Co, PA,[317] (daughter of Robert Hawthorne Blair and Martha Maude Shorts), d. Feb-10-1990 in Sylva, Jackson Co, NC,[1239] resided 1918 in Pittsburgh, Allegheny Co, PA.

Children by Lilly Leora Blair:

    i.   ROSEBUD BROWN d. (stillborn).[317]

1074. ii.   DORIS ROWENA BROWN b. Dec- 4-1914.

    iii. HAROLD DURWOOD "BUD" BROWN b. 1916,[317] d. ca 1935,[317] cause of death diabetes.[317]

655. **Phylinda Elise Gaston** (367.Frank[7], 207.Edmund[6], 102.Ebenezer[5], 38.David[4], 10.Alexander[3], 3.John[2], 1.Jean[1]), b. Mar-31-1884 in Pennsylvania,[34] d. Feb- -1965,[34] census 1930 in Manhattan, NY, census 1920 in Yonkers, Westchester Co, NY, census 1910 in Youngstown, Mahoning Co, OH. She married[317] **Arthur Hastings**, b. ca 1884 in Ohio,[211] census 1930 in Manhattan, NY, census 1920 in Yonkers, Westchester Co, NY, census 1910 in Youngstown, Mahoning Co, OH, occupation 1910 civil engineer,[211] occupation 1920 construction engineer,[681] occupation 1930 building contractor.[334]

    Children:

    i.   BEN G. HASTINGS b. ca 1908 in Pennsylvania,[211] census 1930 in Manhattan, NY, census 1920 in Yonkers, Westchester Co, NY, census 1910 in Youngstown, Mahoning Co, OH.

    ii.   HARRIET HASTINGS b. ca 1909 in Pennsylvania,[211] census 1930 in Manhattan, NY, census 1920 in Yonkers, Westchester Co, NY, census 1910 in Youngstown, Mahoning Co, OH.

    iii. ANNE HASTINGS b. ca 1912 in Pennsylvania,[681] census 1930 in Manhattan, NY, census 1920 in Yonkers, Westchester Co, NY.

    iv. PHYLINDA G. HASTINGS b. ca 1914 in Minnesota,[681,334] census 1930 in Manhattan, NY, census 1920 in Yonkers, Westchester Co, NY.

    v.   ARDELE HASTINGS b. ca 1916 in Pennsylvania,[681] census 1930 in Manhattan, NY, census 1920 in Yonkers, Westchester Co, NY.

    vi. BARBARA HASTINGS b. ca 1916 in Pennsylvania,[681] census 1930 in Manhattan, NY, census 1920 in Yonkers, Westchester Co, NY.

    vii. SAMUEL H. HASTINGS b. ca 1918 in New York,[681] census 1920 in Yonkers, Westchester Co, NY, census 1930 in Manhattan, NY.

656. **Audley DeForest Gaston** (367.Frank[7], 207.Edmund[6], 102.Ebenezer[5], 38.David[4], 10.Alexander[3], 3.John[2], 1.Jean[1]), b. Jun-26-1886 in Meadville, Crawford Co, PA,[99] d. Dec-26-1950 in Baytown, Harris Co, TX.[99] He married[99] **Sarah Ellen Nickell**, b. Jan-27-1891 in Limehouse, Ontario, Canada,[99] (daughter of William Nickell and Judith Newton), d. Dec-29-1951 in Baytown, Harris Co, TX.[99]

    Children:

    i.   MARY HANNAH GASTON b. Apr-29-1920 in Sarnia, Ontario, Canada, d. Apr-21-1942.

1075. ii.   LIVING.

1076. iii. LIVING.

Generation Nine

657. **Rebecca Irene Castleton** (368.Ann[8], 208.Hudson[7], 106.Robert[6], 41.Matthew[5], 11.Alexander[4], 4.(Male)[3], 2.William[2], 1.Jean[1]), b. Jun-17-1885 in Sealy, Austin Co, TX,[318] d. May-16-1977 in Fillmore, Millard Co, UT.[318] She married Apr-29-1908 in Sealy, Austin Co, TX,[318] **Julian Bingham McKibbon**.

    Children:

    i.   ANN CATHRYN MCKIBBON b. Sep- 7-1919 in Birmingham, Jefferson Co, AL.[318] She married Nov-26-1943 in New York City, NY,[318] Dallin Spencer Nielsen, b. Oct-23-1912,[592] d. Mar-17-1994,[592] resided in Fillmore, Millard Co, UT.[592]

658. **David Gordon Reid** (369.Mathew[8], 210.Asa[7], 107.Jane[6], 41.Matthew[5], 11.Alexander[4], 4.(Male)[3], 2.William[2], 1.Jean[1]), b. 1855 in Conway Co, AR,[201] d. 1897.[201] He married[201] **Amanda Jane Kelley**, b. 1857 in Alabama,[201] d. 1896.[201]

    Children:

    i.   LILY LENORA REID b. 1881.[201]

    ii.   ANA MAY REID b. 1883.[201]

    iii. DORA ELIZABETH REID b. 1885.[201]

iv.   EMMER ETHEL REID b. 1887.[201]
v.   JOSEPH M. REID b. 1889.[201]
vi.   HESTER FRANCES REID b. 1891.[201]
vii.   RUBEN EARNEST REID b. 1893.[201]
viii.   MARY SUSAN REID b. 1895.[201]

659. **Rheca Thomas Reid**[201] (369.Mathew[8], 210.Asa[7], 107.Jane[6], 41.Matthew[5], 11.Alexander[4], 4.(Male)[3], 2.William[2], 1.Jean[1]), b. 1858 in Conway Co, AR,[201] d. 1943.[201] He married[201] **Martha Lucindacup Sanders**,[201] d. 1907.[201]
    Children:
    i.   PEARLIE REID[201].
    ii.   RENIE REID[201].
    iii.   RICHARD REID[201].
    iv.   WILLIE REID[201].
    v.   NATHAN ANDREW REID b. 1881.[201]
    vi.   WILLIAM DAVID GARFIELD REID b. 1884.[201]
    vii.   MAUDIE JANE REID b. 1888.[201]
    viii.   MARY ELIZABETH REID b. 1889.[201]
    ix.   MATHEW EDWARD REID[201] b. 1891.[201]
    x.   MARTHA LOU REID b. 1893.[201]
    xi.   ADDIE PEMBROOK REID b. 1895.[201]
    xii.   HARMON RUEBEN REID[201] b. 1897.[201]
    xiii.   RHECA ALFORD REID b. 1900.[201]
    xiv.   (INFANT SON) REID b. 1901.[201]
    xv.   GERTRUDE REID b. 1903.[201]
    xvi.   DORA REID b. 1905.[201]
    xvii.   (INFANT SON) REID b. 1907.[201]

660. **Mary Priscilla Elizabeth Jane Reid**[201] (369.Mathew[8], 210.Asa[7], 107.Jane[6], 41.Matthew[5], 11.Alexander[4], 4.(Male)[3], 2.William[2], 1.Jean[1]), b. 1862 in Polk Co, AR,[201] d. 1902.[201] She married[201] **William Johnson Keen**.
    Children:
    i.   MINNIE MAE DELLA KEEN[201].
    ii.   WILLIAM LUTHER KEEN[201].
    iii.   REUBEN ABSELM KEEN[201].
    iv.   THOMAS WAKEFIELD KEEN[201].
    v.   HORACE PORTER KEEN[201].
    vi.   IDA MAE KEEN[201].
    vii.   NORA ANN KEEN[201].

661. **America Pembrook Reid** (369.Mathew[8], 210.Asa[7], 107.Jane[6], 41.Matthew[5], 11.Alexander[4], 4.(Male)[3], 2.William[2], 1.Jean[1]), b. 1864 in Polk Co, AR,[201] d. 1922.[201] She married[201] **Richard Jasper Vinson**.
    Children:
    i.   MARY BELL VINSON b. 1885.[201]
    ii.   NORA ETTA VINSON b. 1885.[201]
    iii.   THOMAS HARRISON VINSON b. Jan-22-1889,[201,592] d. Jul- -1969,[592] resided in Dover, Pope Co, AR.[592]
    iv.   JOHN HENRY VINSON b. 1891.[201]
    v.   (INFANT SON) VINSON b. 1894.[201]
    vi.   MINNIE MAE VINSON b. 1895.[201]
    vii.   STELLA LOU DELLA VINSON[201] b. 1902.[201]

662. **William Jefferson Reid** (370.Rhesa[8], 210.Asa[7], 107.Jane[6], 41.Matthew[5], 11.Alexander[4], 4.(Male)[3], 2.William[2], 1.Jean[1]), b. 1848 in Conway Co, AR,[201] d. 1923.[201] He married[201] **Sarah Ann Prince**.

Children:
i.   HARMON ANDERSON REID b. 1868.[201]
ii. M. ELLEN REID b. 1870.[201]
iii. OLLIE V. REID[201]
iv. WILLIAM H. REID b. 1872.[201]
v. M. A. LON REID b. 1875.[201]
vi. HENRY LEE REID b. 1881.[201]
vii. BEDFORD J. REID b. 1883.[201]

663. **Winney Eunicy Reid**[201] (370.Rhesa[8], 210.Asa[7], 107.Jane[6], 41.Matthew[5], 11.Alexander[4], 4.(Male)[3], 2.William[2], 1.Jean[1]), b. 1859 in Conway Co, AR,[201] d. 1935.[201] She married[201] **Charles Stephen Norman**, b. 1857 in Conway Co, AR,[201] (son of Robert Lafayette Norman and Catherine Meeler), d. 1932.[201] As great-grandchildren of George Reid II and Jane Gaston, Charles Stephen Norman and Winney Eunicy Reid were second cousins.

Children:
i.   EARL NORMAN b. Oct-17-1896 in Conway Co, AR,[592,201] d. May- -1963,[592,201] resided in Texas,[592] resided formerly in Oklahoma.[838] He married[201] Nell Jane Robinson, b. 1895 in Conway Co, AR,[201] d. 1983.[201]
ii. GEORGE W. NORMAN[201]

664. **Sarah Jane Reid** (371.Henry[8], 210.Asa[7], 107.Jane[6], 41.Matthew[5], 11.Alexander[4], 4.(Male)[3], 2.William[2], 1.Jean[1]), b. 1857.[201] She married[201] **Levi Wallis**.
Children:
i.   VIRGIL WALLIS[201]
ii. CORA WALLIS[201]
iii. ORA WALLIS[201]

665. **William Cary Reid** (371.Henry[8], 210.Asa[7], 107.Jane[6], 41.Matthew[5], 11.Alexander[4], 4.(Male)[3], 2.William[2], 1.Jean[1]), b. 1858,[201] d. 1898.[201] He married[201] **Martha Jane Brock**.
Children:
i.   ELMER LEANDER REID b. 1879.[201]
ii. ALONZO CRATIN REID b. 1883.[201]

666. **Martha Ellen Reid** (371.Henry[8], 210.Asa[7], 107.Jane[6], 41.Matthew[5], 11.Alexander[4], 4.(Male)[3], 2.William[2], 1.Jean[1]), b. 1861,[201] d. 1951.[201] She married[201] **Henry G. Brock**.
Children:
i.   SYBIL BROCK[201]
ii. ZORIL BROCK[201]
iii. HARPER BROCK[201]
iv. ORA BROCK[201]
v. JOHN MONROE BROCK[201]
vi. WILLIAM HARPER BROCK[201]

667. **Mary Parlee Reid** (371.Henry[8], 210.Asa[7], 107.Jane[6], 41.Matthew[5], 11.Alexander[4], 4.(Male)[3], 2.William[2], 1.Jean[1]), b. 1866 in Conway Co, AR,[201] d. 1905.[201] She married[201] **James Crayton Reel**, b. 1859,[201] d. 1940.[201]
Children:
i.   JOHN HILLMAN REEL b. 1883.[201]
ii. NORA E. REEL b. 1885.[201]
iii. ETTA A. REEL b. 1888.[201]
iv. ELVIA M. REEL b. 1890.[201]
v. IOLA J. REEL b. 1892.[201]
vi. MARY B. REEL b. 1893.[201]
vii. JAMES M. REEL b. 1895.[201]

viii. GEORGIA REEL b. 1898.[201]

ix. (INFANT FEMALE) REEL b. 1900.[201]

668. **Ardela Tennessee Reid** (371.Henry[8], 210.Asa[7], 107.Jane[6], 41.Matthew[5], 11.Alexander[4], 4.(Male)[3], 2.William[2], 1.Jean[1]), b. 1869,[201] d. 1886.[201] She married[201] **J. A. Smith**.
   Children:
   i. DELBERT SMITH b. 1886.[201]

669. **Asa Ulysses Sidney Levi Reid** (371.Henry[8], 210.Asa[7], 107.Jane[6], 41.Matthew[5], 11.Alexander[4], 4.(Male)[3], 2.William[2], 1.Jean[1]), b. 1872 in Conway Co, AR.[201] He married[201] __ **Cronister**.
   Children:
   i. BYRAN REED[201,201].
   ii. ELLEN REID[201].
   iii. FLOYD REID[201].

670. **Robert Stephenson Reid** (371.Henry[8], 210.Asa[7], 107.Jane[6], 41.Matthew[5], 11.Alexander[4], 4.(Male)[3], 2.William[2], 1.Jean[1]), b. 1875,[201] d. 1963.[201] He married[201] **Minnie Andrews Arnold**, b. 1876,[201] d. 1965.[201]
   Children:
   i. HOMER REID[201].
   ii. HETTIE MAE REID[201].
   iii. ORA M. REID[201].
   iv. BUD REID[201].
   v. TROY LEE REID[201].
   vi. ELMER REID.
   vii. JESSIE REID.

671. **James Henry Reid** (371.Henry[8], 210.Asa[7], 107.Jane[6], 41.Matthew[5], 11.Alexander[4], 4.(Male)[3], 2.William[2], 1.Jean[1]), b. Mar-12-1877 in Cleveland, Conway Co, AR,[201,592] d. Aug- -1964,[592,201] resided in Dos Palos, Merced Co, CA,[592] resided formerly in Arkansas.[ccxl[1240]] He married[201] **Emma Senora Byers**, b. 1879,[201] d. 1964.[201]
   Children:
   i. BULAH REID b. 1899,[201] d. 1900.[201]
   ii. ANDREW JACKSON REID b. Feb- 4-1902,[201,592] d. Jun- -1966,[592,201] resided in Jerusalem, Conway Co, AR.[592] He married[201] Florence Manion, b. Aug- 3-1905,[592] d. Mar- -1975,[592] resided in Jerusalem, Conway Co, AR,[592] resided formerly in California.[1152]
   iii. ROSE ANN REID b. 1904 in Cleveland, Conway Co, AR,[201] d. 1978.[201] She married[201] James William Huffman.
   iv. CHESTER LEE REID b. Apr-23-1906 in Cleveland, Conway Co, AR,[592,201] d. May- - 1985,[592,201] resided in Morrilton, Conway Co, AR,[592] resided formerly in California.[ccxli[1241]] He married[201] Nina Pearl Webb, b. Sep-10-1909,[592,201] d. Apr- 4-1997,[592] resided in Atkins, Pope Co, AR,[592] resided formerly in California.[ccxlii[1242]]
   v. MATTIE OMA REID b. 1908.[201] She married[201] David Childress.
   vi. LESTER JAY REID b. Aug-23-1910 in Arkansas,[592,201,693] d. Jun- 7-1972 in San Joaquin Co, CA,[693,592,201] resided in Stockton, San Joaquin Co, CA,[592] resided formerly in Arkansas.[1240] He married[201] (1) Lydia Chism. He married[201] (2) Georgia Newton.
   vii. TROY KENION REID b. 1912.[201] He married[201] Lela Mae Howard.
   viii. LUTHER EMMETT REID b. 1915.[201] He married[201] Amy Sewell.
   ix. COVA D. REID[201] b. Dec- 7-1917 in Arkansas,[ccxliii[1243],592] d. Jul-23-1970 in Plumas Co, CA,[693,592,201] resided in California.[1152] He married[201] Loavola Mills.[201]
   x. LOIS GERTRUDE REID b. 1918.[201] She married[201] (1) Arlie Campbell. She married[201] (2) Floyd Self. She married[201] (3) William Cozzi.
   xi. ALLIE FAYE REID b. 1922,[201] resided 2006 in Herlong, Lassen Co, CA.[484] She married[201] Gayno Robert Chastain, b. Dec-12-1922 in Quinton, Pittsburg Co, OK,[190,592] d. Mar- 8-2006 in Herlong, Lassen Co, CA,[700,592] buried Diamond Crest Cem in Johnstonville (Susanville), Lassen Co,

CA,[190] resided since May 1951 in Herlong, Lassen Co, CA,[190,592] resided formerly in Oklahoma,[592] occupation Sierra Army Depot (retired 1979),[190] military U.S. Navy, World War II.[190]

Gayno: He worked on the building of Shasta Dam until World War II, when he joined the U.S. Navy, serving on the USS Koiner and the USS Republic. He came to Herlong, Calif., with his wife and children in May 1951. He retired from Sierra Army Depot in 1979. Among others, survived by his grandchildren Dennis Fleming, of Reno, Nev., Brian Eckroat, of Beaverton, Ore., Jennifer Eckroat, of Herlong, Amy Little, of South Boston, Va., and Cortney Stewart, of Copperas Cove, TX; great-grandchildren Joshua and Tasha Fleming, of Reno, Nev., and Savanna and Aubrianna Fisher, of Reno, Nev. Predeceased by his parents, Mae and Dee Chastain, and by a grandson, Steven Fisher.[190]

672. **Mathew Franklin Reid**[201] (371.Henry[8], 210.Asa[7], 107.Jane[6], 41.Matthew[5], 11.Alexander[4], 4.(Male)[3], 2.William[2], 1.Jean[1]), b. 1878 in Cleveland, Conway Co, AR,[201] d. 1960.[201] He married[201] **Mary Margaret Strasner**, b. 1881 in Athens (Umpire), Howard Co, AR,[201] d. 1963.[201]
Children:
i.   ORA CORDELIA REID b. 1899 in Conway Co, AR,[201] d. 1972.[201] She married[201] (1) Robert Bunker, b. 1896,[201] d. 1935.[201] She married[201] (2) L. B. Burns. She married[201] (3) Arthur Hall.
ii.   EDITH E. REID b. Nov-10-1901 in Conway Co, AR,[592,201] d. Nov--1985,[592,201] resided in Stigler, Haskell Co, OK.[592] She married[201] (1) Emanuel Holcomb. She married[201] (2) Harvey Cobb.
iii.   LEE EMILY ANN REID b. Mar-15-1904 in Oklahoma,[592,201] d. Jun--1979,[592,201] resided in Wilburton, Latimer Co, OK.[592] She married[201] John Remel Houston, b. Oct-19-1901,[592,201] d. Apr--1981,[592,201] resided in Wilburton, Latimer Co, OK.[592]
iv.   ZONA MAY REID b. 1906 in Oklahoma,[201] d. 1987.[201] She married[201] (1) Neil Gallagher. She married[201] (2) Vernon Lowder, b. 1902 in Cleveland, Conway Co, AR,[201] d. 1940.[201] She married[201] (3) Marvin Leaman.
v.   BERTHA LOU REID b. 1908 in Weleetka, Okfuskee Co, OK,[201] d. 1930.[201] She married[201] Tracy Slater, b. Feb-28-1907 in Weleetka, Okfuskee Co, OK,[201,592] d. Oct-30-1991,[592,201] resided in Wilburton, Latimer Co, OK,[592] resided formerly in New Mexico.[mccxliv[1244]]
vi.   DORTHA A. REID b. 1911 in Oklahoma,[201] d. 1974.[201] She married[201] Dess Bryan.
vii.   LLOYD HENRY REID b. 1913 in Oklahoma,[201] d. 1989.[201] He married[201] (1) Lena McGee. He married[201] (2) Edith __, d. 1969.[201] He married[201] (3) Ester Steerman.
viii. JAMES OTHEL REID b. Mar-18-1916 in Oklahoma,[592,201] d. Nov-26-1992 in Lubbock, Lubbock Co, TX,[693,592,201] resided in Lubbock, Lubbock Co, TX,[592] resided formerly in Oklahoma.[838] He married[201] (1) Kathleen Scroggins. He married[201] (2) Syble Evelyn Hotubbee,[190,201] b. Jan- 2-1923,[592] d. Feb-19-2004 in Fort Smith, Sebastian Co, AR,[190,592] resided in Tuskahoma, Pushmataha Co, OK.[190,mccxlv[1245]]
ix.   ELBERT JACKSON REID b. Dec- 1-1918 in Oklahoma,[592,201] d. Dec-16-1993,[592,201] resided in Marlow, Stephens Co, OK.[592] He married[201] Floy May Hokit, b. Jul-17-1923,[592] d. Dec- 1-2001,[592] resided in Marlow, Stephens Co, OK,[592] resided formerly in California.[mccxlvi[1246]]
x.   MARION FRANKLIN REID b. 1921 in Oklahoma,[201] d. 1921.[201]
xi.   AUBRA MATHEW "A. M." REID[190] b. Oct- 3-1924 in Oklahoma,[592,201] d. Mar-14-2006,[592] resided in Marlow, Stephens Co, OK,[592] occupation business owner.[190] He married[201] (1) Geraldine Adams. He married[201] (2) Kathryn Thomas.

673. **Andrew Nathan Reid** (371.Henry[8], 210.Asa[7], 107.Jane[6], 41.Matthew[5], 11.Alexander[4], 4.(Male)[3], 2.William[2], 1.Jean[1]), b. 1881 in Cleveland, Conway Co, AR,[201] d. 1932.[201] He married[201] **Margaret Isabella Kennamer**, b. 1884,[201] d. 1952.[201]
Children:
i.   HIRAM LEVI REID b. Jun- 2-1904 in Cleveland, Conway Co, AR,[592,201] d. Dec--1980,[592,201] resided in Cleveland, Conway Co, AR,[592] resided formerly in California.[1152] He married[201] Agnes Eddington.

279

    ii.   CLAUDE HENRY REID b. Jul-10-1906 in Cleveland, Conway Co, AR,[201,693,592] d. Dec-23-1993 in Marion Co, FL,[693,592] resided in Ocala, Marion Co, FL,[592] resided formerly in California.[1152] He married[201] Betty __.

    iii.   LLOYD REID b. 1908 in Clinton, AR,[201] d. 1908 in Clinton, AR.[201]

    iv.   JAMES ROY REID b. Nov- 3-1909 in Clinton, AR,[201,693,592] d. Dec- 9-1996 in Merced Co, CA,[693,592] resided in Dos Palos, Merced Co, CA.[1152] He married[201] Julia Isabel Hunnicutt, b. Apr- -1910 in Arkansas,[693,592] [Birth date reported as Apr 9 1910 in SSDI, but California Death Index reports it as Apr 19 1910.], d. Jul-14-1990 in Merced Co, CA,[mccxlvii[1247],592] resided in Los Banos, Merced Co, CA.[mccxlviii[1248]]

    v.   FLOY MILDRED REID b. Oct-17-1912 in Cleveland, Conway Co, AR,[201,592] d. Mar- 8-2004,[592] resided in Dos Palos, Merced Co, CA.[1152] She married[201] Homer Vivan McDaniel,[693] b. Jun-13-1908 in Oklahoma,[693,592] (son of __ McDaniel and __ Blaylock), d. Mar- 4-1984 in Merced Co, CA,[693,592,201] resided in Dos Palos, Merced Co, CA.[mccxlix[1249]]

    vi.   BESSIE FLORENE REID b. Mar-24-1915 in Cleveland, Conway Co, AR,[201,693,592] d. Jun-26-1995 in Merced Co, CA,[693,592] resided in Dos Palos, Merced Co, CA.[1152] She married[201] Harvey Lee Norman, b. Jun- 2-1912 in Texas,[693,592] (son of __ Norman and __ Mays), d. Mar-23-1982 in Fresno Co, CA,[693,592,201] resided in Fresno, Fresno Co, CA.[1152]

    vii.   MARY LEVONA REID b. Aug- 6-1917 in Cleveland, Conway Co, AR,[201,693,592] d. Mar-16-1996 in Merced Co, CA,[mccl[1250],592] resided in Dos Palos, Merced Co, CA.[mccli[1251]] She married[201] Hershel Ambers Buie,[693] b. Apr-23-1912 in Oklahoma,[693,592] d. Feb-27-1979 in Merced Co, CA,[693,592,201] resided in Dos Palos, Merced Co, CA.[1152]

    viii.   SIDNEY ANDREW REID b. 1920 in Cleveland, Conway Co, AR.[201] He married[201] Avis Marie Mitchell.

    ix.   MAUDIA MURIEL REID b. 1923 in Atkins, Pope Co, AR,[201] d. 1924.[201]

    x.   HAROLD FRANCIS REID b. 1928 in Weleetka, Okfuskee Co, OK,[201] d. 1929.[201]

    xi.   LIVING. She married[201] Living.

674. **Mariland Reid**[592,395] also known as Maryland Reid,[201] (371.Henry[8], 210.Asa[7], 107.Jane[6], 41.Matthew[5], 11.Alexander[4], 4.(Male)[3], 2.William[2], 1.Jean[1]), b. Oct-16-1884 in Cleveland, Conway Co, AR,[592,201] d. Mar-15-1972,[592,201] resided in Morrilton, Conway Co, AR.[592] He married[201,395] (1) **Effie Harmon**. He married[201] (2) **Mary Ann Bost**, b. 1886,[201] d. 1962.[201]

    Children by Mary Ann Bost:

    i.   NORA CALDONIA REID b. Jul-25-1906 in Conway Co, AR,[201,592] d. Oct- -1984,[201,592] resided in McGehee, Desha Co, AR.[mcclii[1252]] She married[201] (1) Burl Justice. She married[201] (2) James Nichols, b. Dec-20-1894,[592] d. Oct- -1979,[592] resided in McGehee, Desha Co, AR.[592]

    ii.   WILLIAM ORVILLE REID b. Mar- 7-1908 in Cleveland, Conway Co, AR,[190,592,201] d. Sep-8-2004,[592] buried Robertsville Cem in Jerusalem, Conway Co, AR,[190] resided in Jerusalem, Conway Co, AR.[190] He married[201,484] Eulah M. Byers, b. Jul-31-1911,[592] d. May- 5-2002,[592] resided in Jerusalem, Conway Co, AR.[592]

    iii.   (INFANT SON) REID b. 1910.[201]

    iv.   CORA SARAH REID b. 1911 in Van Buren Co, AR.[201] She married[201] Leo Emmerson Adams.

    v.   ELIZA ORA REID b. 1911 in Van Buren Co, AR.[201] She married[201] Samuel Elmer Blankenship.

675. **John Altus Reid** (371.Henry[8], 210.Asa[7], 107.Jane[6], 41.Matthew[5], 11.Alexander[4], 4.(Male)[3], 2.William[2], 1.Jean[1]), b. 1886 in Cleveland, Conway Co, AR,[201] d. 1977.[201] He married[201] **Francis Carrie Burks**, b. 1886,[201] d. 1968.[201]

    Children:

    i.   JAMES ARLIE REID b. 1907,[201] d. 1953.[201] He married[201] Louise Ross.

    ii.   FRANCES EDNA REID b. 1909,[201] d. 1909.[201]

    iii.   ALMA MARIE REID b. 1910 in Appleton, Pope Co, AR.[201] She married[201] Payton M. Reddick.

    iv.   (INFANT FEMALE) REID b. 1914,[201] d. 1914.[201]

    v.   (INFANT FEMALE) REID b. 1914,[201] d. 1914.[201]

vi.　JOSEPH DOYLE REID b. 1916.[201] He married[201] Sue Norton.

vii.　HENRY DOLEN REID b. Apr-11-1919 in Lanty (Morrilton), Conway Co, AR,[201,592] d. Mar- -1976,[592,201] resided in Oklahoma.[838] He married[201] Mary Francis Earls.

viii.　CARL FREDERICK REID b. Oct-15-1924 in Lanty (Morrilton), Conway Co, AR,[201,592] d. Nov- 3-2000,[592] resided in Hatfield, Polk Co, AR,[592] resided formerly in Texas.[mccliii[1253]] He married[201] (1) Beatrice Allen. He married[201] (2) Joan Rae Von Staden.

ix.　JOHNNIE CLIFFTON REID b. Apr-20-1927 in Weleetka, Okfuskee Co, OK,[592,201] d. Mar-31-2009, resided in Broken Arrow, Tulsa Co, OK.[1152] He married[201] (1) Ruby Irene Johnson. He married[201] (2) Patricia Wood.

676. **Joseph Alex Reid** (371.Henry[8], 210.Asa[7], 107.Jane[6], 41.Matthew[5], 11.Alexander[4], 4.(Male)[3], 2.William[2], 1.Jean[1]), b. Jun-28-1888 in Cleveland, Conway Co, AR,[201,592] d. Apr- -1970,[201,592] resided in Weleetka, Okfuskee Co, OK.[592] He married[201] **Norma M. Halcomb**, b. 1891,[201] d. 1970.[201]

Children:

i.　ILDA MAE REID b. Sep-26-1911 in Pope Co, AR,[201,592] d. Jul- -1992,[592] resided in Weleetka, Okfuskee Co, OK.[592] She married[201] Elza Hall.

ii.　WILLIE L. REID b. 1913 in Pope Co, AR,[201] d. 1984.[201] She married[201] Hal P. Brown.

iii.　ESTELL REID b. 1915 in Pope Co, AR.[201]

iv.　KATHLEEN REID b. 1925 in Weleetka, Okfuskee Co, OK.[201] She married[201] Archie Fuller.

677. **Ezra Fizer Reid** (371.Henry[8], 210.Asa[7], 107.Jane[6], 41.Matthew[5], 11.Alexander[4], 4.(Male)[3], 2.William[2], 1.Jean[1]), b. Mar-24-1890 in Conway Co, AR,[592,201] d. Mar- -1973,[201] resided in Dos Palos, Merced Co, CA,[592] resided formerly in Oklahoma.[838] He married[201] **Alta Lee Noland**, b. Sep- 2-1892 in Arkansas,[398,201,592] d. Apr- 2-1983 in Merced Co, CA,[mccliv[1254],201,592] resided in Dos Palos, Merced Co, CA,[592] resided formerly in Oklahoma.[838]

Children:

i.　LONNY REID b. 1910,[201] d. 1911.[201]

ii.　THELMA ADA REID b. 1912.[201]

iii.　VELMA MARIE REID b. 1914.[201]

iv.　WILLIAM OLEN REID b. 1917.[201]

v.　SYBIL REID b. 1920,[201] d. 1924.[201]

vi.　MILDRED MAY REID b. 1924 in Atkins, Pope Co, AR.[201] She married Charles Carlos Graves, b. 1924 in Iowa.[201]

vii.　LIVING.

viii.　LIVING.

ix.　LIVING.

678. **Homer Reid** (371.Henry[8], 210.Asa[7], 107.Jane[6], 41.Matthew[5], 11.Alexander[4], 4.(Male)[3], 2.William[2], 1.Jean[1]), b. Oct-31-1892 in Cleveland, Conway Co, AR,[592,201] d. Jul- -1969,[592,201] resided in Okmulgee, Okmulgee Co, OK.[592] He married[201] (1) **Selma Boyd Church**, d. 1926.[201] He married[201] (2) **Emma Adeline Gage**, b. 1905,[201] d. 1972.[201]

Children by Selma Boyd Church:

i.　OLEN JACKSON REID b. 1918.[201]

ii.　HAVNER LYLE REID b. 1922.[201]

iii.　(INFANT) REID[201].

iv.　(INFANT) REID[201].

Children by Emma Adeline Gage:

v.　LIVING.

vi.　LIVING.

vii.　LIVING.

viii.　LIVING.

ix.　LIVING.

x.　LIVING.

xi.　LIVING.

xii. LIVING.
xiii. LIVING.

679. **Charles Jackson Reid** (371.Henry[8], 210.Asa[7], 107.Jane[6], 41.Matthew[5], 11.Alexander[4], 4.(Male)[3], 2.William[2], 1.Jean[1]), b. 1897 in Cleveland, Conway Co, AR,[201] d. 1932.[201] He married[201] **Penny Meta Henley**.
        Children:
        i.   TWILA DEAN REID[201].
        ii.   CECIL JACKSON REID[201].
        iii. CHARLES STEELE REID[201].

680. **Charles Stephen Norman** (373.Robert[8], 212.Jane[7], 107.Jane[6], 41.Matthew[5], 11.Alexander[4], 4.(Male)[3], 2.William[2], 1.Jean[1]) (See marriage to number 663.)

681. **Matthew Alexander Gaston, Jr.** (374.Matthew[8], 214.Matthew[7], 108.Alexander[6], 41.Matthew[5], 11.Alexander[4], 4.(Male)[3], 2.William[2], 1.Jean[1]), b. Oct- 8-1860 in Hancock Co, GA,[203] d. Apr-25-1943 in Alto, Cherokee Co, TX.[203] He married Jan-11-1883 in Fort Lack, Cherokee Co, TX,[203] **Susan Anderson**, b. Dec-24-1859 in Nacogdoches Co, TX.[203]
        Children:
        i.   SUDIE GASTON b.[203].
        ii.   MARY ETHEL GASTON b. ca 1885 in Alto, Cherokee Co, TX.[203]
        iii. LINNIE GASTON b. ca 1895 in Alto, Cherokee Co, TX.[203]
        iv. LUDIE GASTON.
        v.   JAMES TEAGUE GASTON b. Jan- 4-1897 in Alto, Cherokee Co, TX.

682. **Norman Oscar Gaston**, also known as Oscar Gaston,[211] (377.James[8], 218.William[7], 113.Stephen[6], 47.James[5], 12.John[4], 5.William[3], 3.John[2], 1.Jean[1]), b. 1871 in Illinois,[211,12] d. 1922,[12] census 1910, 1920 in Jefferson Co, IL. He married ca 1894,[211] **Luna Troutt**, b. 1871 in Illinois,[12,211] d. 1961,[12] census 1910, 1920 in Jefferson Co, IL.

1910 Census, Jefferson Co, Illinois (Shiloh Twp), enumerated on Apr 21 1910:
Oscar Gaston, 38, b. Illinois, both parents b. Illinois, occupation farmer, married 16 yrs; wife Luna, 38, b. Illinois, both parents b. Illinois, mother of 4 children (one still living); dau May, 9.

1920 Census, Jefferson Co, Illinois (Shiloh Twp), enumerated in Jan 1920:
Oscar Gaston, 48, farmer; wife Luna, 48.[211]

        Children:
        i.   IVA GASTON b. in Illinois.[12] She married[12] number of children (family) One,[12] Thomas Hall Smith.
        ii.   DORIS ALINE GASTON.
        iii. MYRTLE MAE GASTON, also known as Mae Gaston,[12] b. May-17-1900,[592,12] d. Oct-15-1972,[mcclv[1255]] resided in Woodlawn, Jefferson Co, IL.[592] She married[12] Hobart Hayse. Three children.[12]

683. **William Bell Gaston** (377.James[8], 218.William[7], 113.Stephen[6], 47.James[5], 12.John[4], 5.William[3], 3.John[2], 1.Jean[1]), b. ca 1884 in Illinois,[211,681] census 1910, 1920 in Jefferson Co, IL, occupation farmer.[681]

1920 Census, Jefferson Co, IL (Shiloh Twp), enumerated in Jan 1920:
William B. Gaston, 36, farmer; wife Bess B, 24; son William H, 3y 3m; son Henry B, 1y 4m; father James H, 66. All born in Illinois.

He married[mcclvi[1256]] **Bess B. Miller**, b. ca 1896 in Illinois,[681] census 1920 in Jefferson Co, IL.
        Children:

      i.   WILLIAM HARVEY GASTON b. Sep-22-1916 in Illinois,[592,12,681] d. Apr-17-1993,[592,12] resided in Flagstaff, Coconino Co, AZ,[936] census 1920 in Jefferson Co, IL. He married[12] Lillian O'Dell. One child.[12]

      ii.   HENRY BELL GASTON b. ca 1918 in Illinois,[681] census 1920 in Jefferson Co, IL. He married[12] Maxine Olin.

      iii.   BOBBY JACK GASTON.

      iv.   ANNA CATHERINE GASTON, also known as Anne Catherine Gaston,[12] b. Mar- 2-1924,[12] d. Sep-25-1982,[mcclvii[1257],12] resided in Sun City West, Maricopa Co, AZ,[592] resided formerly in Illinois.[936] She married[12] Herman Kirkpatrick. One child.[12]

684. **Sara Ida Jackson** (378.Jane[8], 220.William[7], 114.John[6], 49.Esther[5], 12.John[4], 5.William[3], 3.John[2], 1.Jean[1]), b. 1858.[113] She married 1889,[113] **W. R. Ketchen**, b. 1859,[113] d. 1917.[113]
      Children:
      i.   JANE GASTON KETCHEN b. in Richburg, SC.[113]

685. **David Aiken Gaston** (379.Arthur[8], 224.T. Chalmers[7], 115.John[6], 50.Joseph[5], 12.John[4], 5.William[3], 3.John[2], 1.Jean[1]), b. Aug-21-1903,[592,207] d. Sep- -1988,[592] resided in Chester, Chester Co, SC,[592] occupation attorney. He married **Reubie G. Holliday**, b. Jan-14-1908,[592,207] d. Feb-18-1988,[592] resided in Chester, Chester Co, SC.[592]
      Children:
      i.   LIVING.

686. **Charles Delbert Gaston** (382.John[8], 228.Samuel[7], 121.William[6], 57.William[5], 16.Robert[4], 5.William[3], 3.John[2], 1.Jean[1]), b. May-14-1880,[212] d. Feb-16-1950,[212] buried in New Home Cemetery, Jefferson Co, IL,[212] resided in Earlville, La Salle Co, IL.[212] He married bef 1914,[212] **Della Mae Branson**.
      Children:
      i.   DELBERT B. "COTTON" GASTON[212.]
      ii.   ZELPHA LOUISA GASTON[212.]
      iii.   GENEVA BERYL GASTON[212.]
      iv.   MABEL CONSTANCE CLARISE GASTON[212] also known as Connie Gaston.
      v.   ARCHIE DOYLE GASTON[212.]
      vi.   LOVEL BERTHA GASTON[212.]
      vii. NELLIE ETHEL GASTON[212.]
      viii. ANNA MARIE GASTON[212.]
      ix.   WILLIAM JOHN ORAL GASTON[212.]
      x.   DELLA LOUISE GASTON[212.]

687. **Edward Wesley Gaston**, also known as Edd Gaston (382.John[8], 228.Samuel[7], 121.William[6], 57.William[5], 16.Robert[4], 5.William[3], 3.John[2], 1.Jean[1]), b. Feb-28-1883,[212] d. Mar-22-1910 in Huntsville, Walker Co, TX,[212] buried in New Home Cemetery, Jefferson Co, IL,[212] occupation farmer & railroad worker.[212] He married 1908,[212] **Magnolia "Maggie" Duncan**, b. Apr-13-1888,[212] (daughter of John Oliver Duncan and Martha Elizabeth Meador), d. Feb-16-1975 in Marion Co, IL,[212] buried in New Home Cemetery, Jefferson Co, IL.
      Children:
      i.   RUBY MAY GASTON[212.]
      ii.   ARNOLD RAY GASTON[212.]

688. **Walter Andrew Gaston** (382.John[8], 228.Samuel[7], 121.William[6], 57.William[5], 16.Robert[4], 5.William[3], 3.John[2], 1.Jean[1]), b. Sep-30-1885 in Okawville, Washington Co, IL,[212] d. Oct-24-1966 in Rochelle, Ogle Co, IL,[212] buried in Lawnridge Cem, Rochelle, Ogle Co, IL.[212] He married Nov-11-1916 in Jefferson Co, IL,[212] **Susie Caroline Cooper** (daughter of Joseph Cooper and M. Cora Burns), d. age 94 in Illinois,[212] buried in Lawnridge Cem, Rochelle, Ogle Co, IL.[212]
      Children:
      i.   WILLIAM HERMAN GASTON[212.]
      ii.   MARJORIE GASTON[212.]

iii.   CORA MAE GASTON[212.]

689. **John August Gaston** (382.John[8], 228.Samuel[7], 121.William[6], 57.William[5], 16.Robert[4], 5.William[3], 3.John[2], 1.Jean[1]), b. Mar- 3-1887 in Jefferson Co, IL,[212] d. Apr- 4-1969 in Mt. Vernon, Jefferson Co, IL,[212] buried in New Home Cemetery, Jefferson Co, IL,[212] military World War I - France.[212] He married[212,212] **Phoebe Meador**, b. Mar-17-1898,[212] d. Mar-27-1956,[212] buried in New Home Cemetery, Jefferson Co, IL.[212]
Children:
   i.   LOWELL MELVIN GASTON[212] b. Feb-13-1923,[592] d. Sep-23-1983,[592] resided in Illinois.[936]
   ii.   DOVEL CALVIN GASTON[212.]
   iii.   WILLIAM TOLBERT GASTON[212.]
   iv.   REBA LUCILLE GASTON[212.]
   v.   (INFANT SON) GASTON[212] d. Feb-15-1926,[17,212] buried in McConnaughhay Cem, Farrington Twp, Jefferson Co, IL.[17]

690. **Nellie Jane Gaston** (382.John[8], 228.Samuel[7], 121.William[6], 57.William[5], 16.Robert[4], 5.William[3], 3.John[2], 1.Jean[1]), b. Oct-16-1889,[212] d. Feb-19-1966.[212] She married Nov-13-1915,[212] **Everett James Dobbs**.
Children:
   i.   AUDREY NOAMA DOBBS[212.]
   ii.   ALLEN WILLIAM DOBBS[212.]
   iii.   BERNICE ALEEN DOBBS[212.]
   iv.   CLARA ELSIE DOBBS[212.]

691. **Stobo Rosborough Gaston** (383.Georgia[8], 229.William[7], 123.Robert[6], 58.Thomas[5], 16.Robert[4], 5.William[3], 3.John[2], 1.Jean[1]), b. Aug-23-1900 in Reidville, Spartanburg Co, SC,[339,333] d. Apr- 3-1957 in Travelers Rest, Greenville Co, SC,[339] census 1930 in Greenville Co, SC, occupation physician, owner/operator of Gaston Clinic at Travelers Rest, SC,[333,334] education Medical College of South Carolina at Charleston.[333] He married (1) Dec-27-1924,[333] **Hannah Engleberg**, census name Hanna E.,[334] b. ca 1905 in South Carolina,[681,334] (daughter of Louis Engleberg and Sarah __), census 1930 in Greenville Co, SC, census 1920 in Ridgeville, Dorchester Co, SC, census 1910 in Charleston, SC. He married (2) **Corrie Antha Yount**, b. Feb-11-1906,[1239,592] d. Oct- -1987 in Hendersonville, Henderson Co, NC,[1239] [Date of death given as Oct 13 1987 in NC Death Index, but SSDI shows it as Oct 15 1987.], buried Mountain Page Cem in Saluda, Polk Co, NC,[339] resided in Saluda, Polk Co, NC.[592]
Children by Hannah Engleberg:
   i.   LIVING. She married Joseph Clinton Somers, Jr., b. Dec- 4-1927 in Florida,[1123] d. Jan-18-1980 in Duval Co, FL,[1123] census 1930 in Jacksonville, Duval Co, FL.
Children by Corrie Antha Yount:
   ii.   LIVING. She married Living.

692. **Amzi Cecil Gaston**, also known as Cecil Gaston,[339] (383.Georgia[8], 229.William[7], 123.Robert[6], 58.Thomas[5], 16.Robert[4], 5.William[3], 3.John[2], 1.Jean[1]), b. Feb- 1-1902,[592] [Mary Gaston Gee reports birth date as Feb 1 1901, but SSDI shows it as Feb 1 1902.], d. Aug- 1-1957 in Spartanburg Co, SC,[339,592] resided near Reidville, Spartanburg Co, SC,[333] buried in Nazareth Presbyterian Church Cemetery, Moore, Spartanburg Co, SC.[339] He married Jan- 7-1922,[333] **Isabel Leonard**, b. Jul- 3-1903 in Reidville, Spartanburg Co, SC,[339,333,592] (daughter of David H. Leonard and Hattie Dillard), d. Jan- 7-1990,[592] buried in Nazareth Presbyterian Church Cemetery, Moore, Spartanburg Co, SC,[339] resided in Greer, Greenville Co, SC.[592]
Children:
   i.   MARGARET RACHEL GASTON b. Sep- 1-1923.[333] She married Jan-28-1944,[333] James Robert Cox, b. Sep- 7-1922,[333,592] (son of Robert Carey Cox and Mettie Pearson), d. Sep- -1971,[592] resided in South Carolina.[699]
   ii.   CECIL STODDARD GASTON, also known as Stoddard Gaston,[191] b. Aug-10-1925 in Reidville, Spartanburg Co, SC,[339,333,592] d. Nov- -1966 in Greer, Greenville Co, SC.[592] He married[339]

Mildred Elizabeth Edwards, b. Jun-10-1920 in Laurens Co, SC,[592],[190] (daughter of John "Bub" Edwards and Minnie West), d. Jan-19-2008,[mcclviii[1258]],[592] buried Wood Memorial Park,[190] resided in Greer, Greenville Co, SC,[592] occupation Senior Action of Greenville (retired), owner-operator of 101 Truck Stop.[190]

693. **Margaret Lucile Gaston**, also known as Lucile Gaston,[190] (383.Georgia[8], 229.William[7], 123.Robert[6], 58.Thomas[5], 16.Robert[4], 5.William[3], 3.John[2], 1.Jean[1]), b. Dec-28-1906 in Reidville, Spartanburg Co, SC,[333],[592] d. Apr- 1-2001 in Spartanburg, Spartanburg Co, SC,[764],[592] buried in Sunset Memorial Park, Spartanburg, SC,[190] resided in Forest City, Rutherford Co, NC,[698],[592] occupation co-owner, Hughes Jewelry, Forest City NC.[190] She married Sep- 8-1928,[333] **Johnnie White Hughes**, also known as Johnny W. Hughes,[592] b. Sep-20-1905 in Spartanburg Co, SC,[339],[333],[592],[1239] (son of John B. Hughes and Emma White), d. Feb-11-1994 in Rutherfordton, Rutherford Co, NC,[1239],[592] resided in Forest City, Rutherford Co, NC.[592],[1239]
   Children:
  i. LIVING. She married Living.

694. **John William Gaston** (383.Georgia[8], 229.William[7], 123.Robert[6], 58.Thomas[5], 16.Robert[4], 5.William[3], 3.John[2], 1.Jean[1]), b. Nov-14-1912,[698],[592] d. Nov- -1974,[592] resided in Tucson, Pima Co, AZ,[698],[592] resided formerly in South Carolina.[699] He married Nov-27-1929,[698] **Janie Waddell**, b. Feb-27-1911,[698],[592] (daughter of James P. Waddell and Rhoda Pearson), d. Oct- -1993,[592] resided in Tucson, Pima Co, AZ,[698],[592] resided formerly in South Carolina.[mcclix[1259]]
   Children:
  i. LIVING. He married[339] Living.
  ii. HERBERT EUGENE GASTON b. Aug-25-1934,[698],[592] d. Dec- 9-2002,[592] resided in Bloomfield, San Juan Co, NM,[592] resided formerly in Arizona.[mcclx[1260]] He married[339] Barbara Ann Rice.

695. **Dollie May Gaston**, census name Dolly May Gaston (384.William[8], 229.William[7], 123.Robert[6], 58.Thomas[5], 16.Robert[4], 5.William[3], 3.John[2], 1.Jean[1]), b. Apr-24-1922 in Reidville, Spartanburg Co, SC,[592],[190] d. Jan-13-2005 in Shelby, Cleveland Co, NC,[806] buried Frederick Meml Grdns in Gaffney, Cherokee Co, SC,[190] resided in Shelby, Cleveland Co, NC,[699] census 1930 in Spartanburg Co, SC. She married (1) __ Hudgins. She married (2) ca 1953,[191] **Billy Lee Williams**, resided 2005 in Shelby, Cleveland Co, NC.[191]
   Children by __ Hudgins:
  i. PATRICIA AILEEN HUDGINS b. Jul- 6-1942 in South Carolina,[1239],[592] d. Jul- 8-2003 in Cleveland Co, NC,[1239],[592] resided in Kings Mountain, Cleveland Co, NC.[592] She married[856] divorced[436] __ Pearson.
  ii. LIVING.
  iii. LIVING.
  iv. LIVING.

696. **Rachel Gaston** (384.William[8], 229.William[7], 123.Robert[6], 58.Thomas[5], 16.Robert[4], 5.William[3], 3.John[2], 1.Jean[1]), b. May- 1-1930 in Spartanburg, Spartanburg Co, SC,[190] d. Jan-21-2011 in Spartanburg, Spartanburg Co, SC,[806] buried in Nazareth Presbyterian Church Cemetery, Moore, Spartanburg Co, SC,[190] resided in Spartanburg, Spartanburg Co, SC.[190] She married[424] __ **Lankford**.
   Children:
  i. JOEL ROBERT "JOE" LANKFORD b. Jun-11-1966 in Richmond, VA,[190] d. Jan-18-2011 in Spartanburg, Spartanburg Co, SC,[700] buried in Nazareth Presbyterian Church Cemetery, Moore, Spartanburg Co, SC,[190] resided in Spartanburg, Spartanburg Co, SC.[190]

697. **John Williford "Will" Gaston**[702] (386.Amzi[8], 231.Amzi[7], 124.James[6], 58.Thomas[5], 16.Robert[4], 5.William[3], 3.John[2], 1.Jean[1]), b. Jul- 3-1871 in Spartanburg Co, SC,[702],[592] d. Jul-15-1966 in Duncan, Spartanburg Co, SC,[339],[592] buried in Nazareth Presbyterian Church Cemetery, Moore, Spartanburg Co, SC,[339] resided in Duncan, Spartanburg Co, SC,[592] census 1910, 1920 in Reidville, Spartanburg Co, SC, occupation farmer.[702] He married Dec-21-1893,[702] **Nettie Griffin**, b. Oct- 4-1874,[mcclxi[1261]] (daughter

of John Henry Griffin and Sarah Elizabeth Gresham), d. May-29-1965 in Spartanburg Co, SC,[339] buried in Nazareth Presbyterian Church Cemetery, Moore, Spartanburg Co, SC,[339] resided near Duncan, Spartanburg Co, SC.[702]

Nettie: Nettie Griffin was less than a year old when her mother died, after which time she made her home with her Grandmother Gresham, Uncle Kemp, and Aunt Rosa Gresham until her marriage.[mcclxii[1262]]

Children:
  i.   MARGARET ELIZABETH "MARGIE" GASTON[1262] b. Mar-29-1895,[1262,592] d. Oct- -1986,[592] resided in West Columbia, Lexington Co, SC,[592] education Converse College, Spartanburg, SC (1918),[1262] never married[339].
  ii. AMZI WILLIFORD GASTON III b. Jun-27-1897 in Spartanburg Co, SC,[339,1262] d. Jan-26-1915 in Spartanburg Co, SC,[339,1262] buried in Nazareth Presbyterian Church Cemetery, Moore, Spartanburg Co, SC.[339]
  iii. MARY GASTON b. Jul-29-1899,[1262,592] d. May- -1987,[592] resided in Denmark, Bamberg Co, SC,[592] education Converse College, Spartanburg, SC (1920).[1262]

Author of several highly regarded genealogies, including "The Ancestors and Descendants of Amzi Williford Gaston II (1841-1911) of Spartanburg County, South Carolina," published in Charlottesville, VA in 1944.[mcclxiii[1263]]

She married Jun- 7-1921,[1262] Wilson Gee, b. Sep-18-1888,[1262] (son of Reuben Thompson Gee and Gertrude Gist), d. 1961,[339] resided 1944 in Charlottesville, VA,[mcclxiv[1264]] resided formerly in Union, Union Co, SC,[1262] occupation rural economist, author, professor at Univ of Va,[1262] military lab technician, U.S. Army Medical Corps, World War I - France.[1264]
  iv. TOM MOORE GASTON b. Nov-15-1901,[1264] d. Apr- -1964 in Polk Co, FL,[1123] buried in Nazareth Presbyterian Church Cemetery, Moore, Spartanburg Co, SC,[339] resided 1944 in Woodruff, Spartanburg Co, SC,[1264] census 1930 in Reidville, Spartanburg Co, SC, education Hastoc School for Boys (Spartanburg, SC) and Univ of SC.[1264] He married (1) Nov-14-1922,[1264] divorced Virginia Mason, b. Sep-19-1902,[1264,592] (daughter of Palmer Mason and Josephine Rogers), d. Feb-12-1992 in Marion, McDowell Co, NC,[190,708] buried in New Garden Cemetery, Greensboro, Guilford Co, NC,[190] resided in Shelby, Cleveland Co, NC,[190] resided originally in Woodruff, Spartanburg Co, SC.[190] He married (2) Dec- 7-1942,[1264] Julia Kathleen LeMaster (daughter of Robert Edward LeMaster and Mary Ellen Burnett).
  v.   NETTIE ALLENE GASTON b. Feb- 8-1912,[1264] resided 2004 in Orangeburg, Orangeburg Co, SC,[mcclxv[1265]] education Converse College, Spartanburg, SC (1933).[1264] She married Jun-25-1938,[1264] Henry Briggs Salley, b. Nov-16-1899,[1264,592] (son of Beauden McLeod Salley and Lou Belle Tyler), d. Jan- -1971,[592] resided in Salley, Aiken Co, SC,[1264,592] occupation farmer and merchant,[1264] education Clemson College,[1264] military Captain, U.S. Army Reserves.[1264]
  vi. JOHN WILLIFORD GASTON, JR. b. Aug-26-1915 in Spartanburg Co, SC,[339,1264,592] d. May-23-2001,[592] resided in Duncan, Spartanburg Co, SC,[592] occupation farmer,[mcclxvi[1266]] education Clemson College.[1266] He married[1264] Dec-26-1936,[339] Mattie Cora Gramling, b. Dec-26-1909 in Campobello, Spartanburg Co, SC,[339,592] (daughter of Ben Martin Gramling and Cora Turpin), d. Jan-27-1994,[592] resided in Duncan, Spartanburg Co, SC, education Columbia College (1932).[1264]

698. **Robert White Gaston** (386.Amzi[8], 231.Amzi[7], 124.James[6], 58.Thomas[5], 16.Robert[4], 5.William[3], 3.John[2], 1.Jean[1]), b. Aug-18-1873,[1266,592] d. Nov-26-1967 in Columbia, SC,[339,592] buried in Nazareth Presbyterian Church Cemetery, Moore, Spartanburg Co, SC,[339] resided in Columbia, SC,[592] resided in Spartanburg Co, SC,[1266] census 1910, 1930 in Reidville, Spartanburg Co, SC, occupation farmer, formerly a teacher (4 yrs) and merchant (10 yrs),[1266] education Reidville Male Academy, Presbyterian College (Clinton, SC), Rome (GA) Business College (1893).[1266] He married[502] Dec-22-1903,[mcclxvii[1267]] **Belie Etholia Wofford**,[1267] b. Oct- 8-1882,[1267] (daughter of John Thomas Wofford and Nancy Arnold), d. Sep-13-1965 in Reidville, Spartanburg Co, SC,[339] buried in Nazareth

Presbyterian Church Cemetery, Moore, Spartanburg Co, SC,[339] education Reidville School and Reidville Female College.[1267]

Children:

    i.   LAMAR DEWITT GASTON b. Jan- 6-1905,[1267,592] d. Nov-24-1995,[592] resided in Greenville, SC,[592] education Clemson College (B.S., 1927),[1267] military Lt. Col., U.S. Army Signal Corps - World War II.[1267] He married (1) Nov-11-1931 in Newberry, Newberry Co, SC,[339,1267] Benita Boozer, b. May-10-1904 in Newberry, Newberry Co, SC,[339,1267] (daughter of Benjamin S. Boozer and Lelia __), d. Jun-16-1935 in Newberry, Newberry Co, SC.[339,1267] He married (2) Nov- 2-1935,[339] Dagmar Elizabeth Swenson, b. Oct-16-1905 in Minnesota.[339]

    ii.   MILDRED LEE GASTON b. May-25-1906,[1267,592] d. May-14-1991,[592] resided in Atlantic Beach, Duval Co, FL,[592] resided 1944 in Miami Beach, Miami-Dade Co, FL,[1267] education Queens College, Charlotte, NC (1928),[1267] occupation teacher (1928-35) and dietician.[1267] She married Feb-8-1930,[1267] Walter John Parks, Jr., b. Aug-25-1908 in Davidson, Mecklenburg Co, NC,[190,1267,592] (son of Walter John Parks and Lenora Frazier), d. Aug-12-1999 in Jacksonville, Duval Co, FL,[190,592] buried in Nazareth Presbyterian Church Cemetery, Moore, Spartanburg Co, SC,[190] resided in Jacksonville, Duval Co, FL,[592] resided 1944 in Miami Beach, Miami-Dade Co, FL,[1267] occupation engineer,[1267] education Univ of NC (B.S. in Engineering, 1929).[1267,190]

    Walter: He served as superintendent of the city of Asheville's Bee Tree Watershed from 1935 to 1941. From 1941 to the end of World War II, he served with the U.S. Army Corps of Engineers at Camp David near Wilmington, N.C., and later at the Miami Beach Service Base. As a professional engineer, he worked in the field of sanitary engineering for more than 50 years, and for 30 years he operated a private practice as a consulting engineer. For 34 years, he was a resident of Atlantic Beach, Fla., where he served as an engineering consultant and as a city commissioner.[190]

    iii.   WOFFORD PEDEN GASTON, also known as Peden Gaston,[395] b. Nov- 2-1907 in Spartanburg Co, SC,[339,1267,592] d. Oct-15-1994,[592] resided in Woodruff, Spartanburg Co, SC,[592] education Reidville H.S. and Draughtons Business College.[1267] He married[395] Nov-29-1934,[1267] Grace Walden, b. Sep- 9-1913,[mcclxviii[1268],592] (daughter of Andrew Pinckney Walden and Janie Gates), d. Jan-1-1997,[592] resided in Woodruff, Spartanburg Co, SC,[592] resided originally in Gramling, Spartanburg Co, SC,[1267] occupation teacher (7 yrs),[1268] education Winthrop College (A.B., 1934).[1268]

    iv.   KATHLEEN ETOLIA GASTON b. Jul-22-1909,[1268,592] d. Dec-25-1993,[592] resided in Greenville, SC,[592] education Queens College, Charlotte, NC (B.S., 1932),[1268] occupation teacher (1934-40) and home economist (WPA and SC Dept of Educ),[1268] never married[1268,592].

    v.   JANIE BOB GASTON[1260,592] b. Apr- 7- 1911,[1268,592] d. Jul- 7-1995,[592] buried in Nazareth Presbyterian Church Cemetery, Moore, Spartanburg Co, SC,[339] resided in Greenville, SC,[592] education Queens College, Charlotte, NC (3-1/2 yrs).[1268] She married Dec- 1-1931,[1268] Clarence Steele Bowen, b. Nov- 3-1898,[1268,592] (son of Reese Bowen and Martha Steele), d. Oct-13-1993,[592] buried in Nazareth Presbyterian Church Cemetery, Moore, Spartanburg Co, SC,[339] resided in Greenville, SC,[1268,592] occupation attorney,[1268] education University of South Carolina (1924).[1268]

    vi.   MARGARET ETHEL GASTON b. Nov-29-1912,[1268,592] d. Feb- 8-1999,[592] resided in Greenville, SC,[1268,592] occupation teacher at Greenville City Schools,[1268] education Furman University, Greenville, SC (B.S., 1935).[1268] She married Dec-19-1942,[1268] no children from this marriage,[339] Oliver James Youmans, Jr., also known as O. J. Youmans,[592] b. Sep-14-1912 in Fairfax, Allendale Co, SC,[339,1268,592] (son of Oliver James Youmans and Annie Laurie Lewis), d. Feb- 5-1992,[592] resided in Greenville, SC,[1268,592] resided formerly in Washington, DC,[mcclxix[1269]] occupation shipping & stock clerk at Claussen Bakery, Greenville, SC,[1268] education University of South Carolina (2 yrs),[1268] military World War II (6 months).[1268]

    vii.   BELIE LOUISE GASTON, also known as Louise Gaston,[412] b. Dec-14-1914,[1268] resided 2008, 2010 in Greenville, Madison Co, FL,[412] education Winthrop College, Rock Hill, SC (B.S., 1938).[1268]

    Member of the Nathanael Greene chapter of the DAR, Greenville, SC.[339]

She married Jun- 4-1938,[mcclxx][1270] Edgar Frederick Rankin, b. Mar-14-1906,[1270,592] (son of Charles Edgar Rankin and Violet Howell), d. Mar- -1974,[592] resided in Lutherville, Baltimore Co, MD,[592] resided formerly in South Carolina,[699] resided originally in East Orange, Essex Co, NJ,[1270] occupation (1944) Koppers Company, Baltimore, MD,[1270] education St. John's Cathedral, New York, and Los Angeles Polytechnic School,[1270] military U.S. Navy.[1270]

      viii. MARY ELIZABETH (TWIN) GASTON b. Apr- 7-1917 in Reidville, Spartanburg Co, SC,[190,1270] d. Jul- 4-2008, buried in Nazareth Presbyterian Church Cemetery, Moore, Spartanburg Co, SC,[190] resided in Pass Christian, Harrison Co, MS,[190,1086] resided formerly in Charlotte, NC,[190] occupation teacher, Charlotte Mecklenburg Public Schools (37 yrs),[190] education Winthrop College, Erskine College (A.B., 1940).[190,1270]

      She was a member of the Huguenot Society of South Carolina, the Gov. John Archdale Chapter of the Colonial Dames XVII Century, the Stonewall Jackson Chapter of the Daughters of the American Revolution, and the Col. Mark Bird Chapter of the American Colonies.

      She married May-25-1943,[1270] Theodore Edward Thornburg, b. Sep- 3-1912 in Cleveland Co, NC,[339,1270,592] (son of Robert Samuel Thornburg and Sarah Elizabeth Williams), d. Mar-17-1997,[592] resided in Charlotte, NC,[1270,592] education Erskine College (3 yrs),[1270] military U.S. Army, World War II.[1270]

      ix. MARTHA RUTH (TWIN) GASTON b. Apr- 7-1917,[1270] d. Aug-20-2010 in Jacksonville, Duval Co, FL,[190,592] buried in Nazareth Presbyterian Church Cemetery, Moore, Spartanburg Co, SC,[190] resided in Jacksonville, Duval Co, FL,[592,412] resided originally in Reidville, Spartanburg Co, SC,[190] occupation teacher, guidance counselor,[1270,190] education Erskine College (A.B., 1940), Univ of Florida (M.A.).[1270,190] She married[424] Dec-16-1944,[339] Hanson Seabrook Blizzard, b. Oct-20-1906,[592,1123] d. Jul-21-1986 in Duval Co, FL,[1123,592] resided in Jacksonville, Duval Co, FL.[699]

      x. ROBERT WHITE GASTON, JR. b. Apr-10-1919,[1270] d. Nov-24-1923 in Spartanburg Co, SC,[339,1270] buried in Nazareth Presbyterian Church Cemetery, Moore, Spartanburg Co, SC.[339]

      xi. NANCY WILMA GASTON b. Jun-23-1921 in Reidville, Spartanburg Co, SC,[190,1270,592] d. Jun- 2-2000 in Clearwater, Pinellas Co, FL,[806,592] resided in Clearwater, Pinellas Co, FL,[190] occupation teacher (Greenville SC, Winston-Salem NC),[190] education Montreat College, Black Mountain, NC,[190] education Queens College, Charlotte, NC (A.B., 1942).[1270,190] She married Aug-22-1942,[1270] Samuel Tilden Register, Jr., b. Feb-22-1919 in Florida,[1270,592,334] (son of Samuel Tilden Register and Bertha Elizabeth Gould), d. Sep-13-1993 in Pinellas Co, FL,[1123,592] resided in Clearwater, Pinellas Co, FL,[592] resided originally in Tallahassee, Leon Co, FL,[1270,334] education University of Florida (B.S., 1942),[1270] military Capt, U.S. Army.[1270]

      xii. DAVID HOLDER GASTON b. Mar- 9-1924 in Reidville, Spartanburg Co, SC,[1270,592,190] d. Feb-16-2005 in Lancaster, Lancaster Co, PA,[190,592] buried in Parkwood Cemetery, Parkville, Baltimore Co, MD,[190] resided in Willow Street, Lancaster Co, PA,[604,190] resided formerly in Baltimore, MD,[190] occupation U.S. Post Office, Towson, Maryland (35 yrs),[190] education Clemson College (2 yrs),[1270] military U.S. Marine Corps, World War II.[1270] He married[339] (1) Diane Thelma Zepp. He married (2) Aug-22-1977 in Northampton Co, NC,[mcclxxi][1271] Ruth Christena Fewster, b. Aug-24-1917 in Baltimore, MD,[592,190] (daughter of George C. Fewster and Martha L. Thalheim), d. Jan- 6-2009,[592,190] buried in Parkwood Cemetery, Parkville, Baltimore Co, MD,[190] resided in Willow Street, Lancaster Co, PA,[1086,190] occupation florist.[190]

699. **Amzi Cason "Case" Gaston**, census name A. Cason Gaston (386.Amzi[8], 231.Amzi[7], 124.James[6], 58.Thomas[5], 16.Robert[4], 5.William[3], 3.John[2], 1.Jean[1]) (See marriage to number 383.)

700. **Fitzie Hampton Gaston**[698,592] (386.Amzi[8], 231.Amzi[7], 124.James[6], 58.Thomas[5], 16.Robert[4], 5.William[3], 3.John[2], 1.Jean[1]), b. Jan-23-1877,[698,592] d. Jan- -1968,[592] buried in Nazareth Presbyterian Church Cemetery, Moore, Spartanburg Co, SC,[339] resided in Duncan, Spartanburg Co, SC,[698,592] education Reidville Female College.[698] She married Oct-18-1901,[698] **Joseph Silas Nesbitt**, b. Oct- 7-1867,[698] (son of Isaac Nesbitt and Margaret Benson), d. Jun- 2-1958 in Duncan, Spartanburg Co, SC,[339] buried in Nazareth Presbyterian Church Cemetery, Moore, Spartanburg Co, SC,[339] resided near Duncan, Spartanburg Co, SC,[698] occupation farmer.[698]

Children:

i.   JAMES HAMPTON NESBITT b. Jan-15-1903,[mcclxxii[1272],592] d. Aug- -1982,[592] buried in Nazareth Presbyterian Church Cemetery, Moore, Spartanburg Co, SC,[339] resided in Duncan, Spartanburg Co, SC.[1272,592] He married Dec- 5-1925,[1272] Annie Mae Smith, b. Aug-31-1905,[1272,592] (daughter of T. Jeff Smith and Laura Anne Morgan), d. Mar- -1972,[592] buried in Nazareth Presbyterian Church Cemetery, Moore, Spartanburg Co, SC,[339] resided in Duncan, Spartanburg Co, SC.[592]

ii.   MARGARET MYRTLE NESBITT, also known as Myrtle Nesbitt,[592] b. Jul-22-1904,[1272,592] d. Oct- -1984,[592] resided in Spartanburg, Spartanburg Co, SC,[592] occupation home demonstration agent for Chester Co, SC,[1272] education Due West Woman's College (Erskine College) (1926),[1272] never married[1272,592].

iii.   STUART GASTON NESBITT b. Jul-21-1906,[1272] d. Nov-18-1906,[1272] buried in Nazareth Presbyterian Church Cemetery, Moore, Spartanburg Co, SC.[339]

iv.   CARL BENSON NESBITT b. Sep-25-1907,[1272,592] d. Aug- -1970,[592] buried in Nazareth Presbyterian Church Cemetery, Moore, Spartanburg Co, SC,[339] resided in Spartanburg, Spartanburg Co, SC.[1272,592] He married Apr- 5-1936,[1272] Nina Wall, b. Jun-12-1911,[1272,592] (daughter of Albert M. Wall and Sarah Truette), d. Aug-12-2001,[592] resided in Spartanburg, Spartanburg Co, SC.[592]

v.   SAMUEL LELAND NESBITT b. Aug-11-1909,[1272,592] d. Nov- -1982,[592] resided in Duncan, Spartanburg Co, SC,[592] resided 1944 in Spartanburg, Spartanburg Co, SC.[1272] He married Oct-19-1936,[1272] Edna Taylor, b. Dec-25-1912 in Greenville, SC,[190,1272] (daughter of Walter Taylor and Jessie Satterwhite), d. Feb-27-2008,[190] buried in Nazareth Presbyterian Church Cemetery, Moore, Spartanburg Co, SC,[190] resided in Watkinsville, Oconee Co, GA,[190] resided 1944 in Spartanburg, Spartanburg Co, SC,[1272] resided formerly in Duncan, Spartanburg Co, SC,[190] occupation Registered Nurse (40 yrs),[190] education Parker H.S. in Greenville, Spartanburg Hosp School of Nursing.[190]

vi.   DAVID BERRY NESBITT b. Mar-25-1912 in Spartanburg Co, SC,[1272,592,190] d. Mar-17-1999,[592] buried in Nazareth Presbyterian Church Cemetery, Moore, Spartanburg Co, SC,[190] resided in Spartanburg, Spartanburg Co, SC,[592] occupation farmer.[190]

As of 1944, he was living at the home place and managing his father's farm.[1272]

He married[484] Mary Lew Adams, b. Apr-25-1922,[592] d. Mar-22-1989,[592] resided in Moore, Spartanburg Co, SC.[592]

vii.   MARY ELIZABETH "BESS" NESBITT, also known as Elizabeth Nesbitt,[190,mcclxxiii[1273],592] b. Dec- 6-1913,[1272,592] d. Mar-19-2010 in Dalton, Whitfield Co, GA,[806,592] buried in Nazareth Presbyterian Church Cemetery, Moore, Spartanburg Co, SC,[190] resided in Dalton, Whitfield Co, GA,[699,1273] resided formerly in Spartanburg, Spartanburg Co, SC,[190] education Winthrop College in Rock Hill SC.[190] She married Jun-13-1936,[1272] Everett Ozell Posey, Jr., b. Nov-19-1906,[1272,592] (son of Everett Ozell Posey and Annie Barksdale Parks), d. May- -1976,[592] resided in Decatur, Dekalb Co, GA,[592] resided formerly in South Carolina,[699] military U.S. Army Infantry officer.[1272,191]

viii.   MABEL NORTON NESBITT b. Jul-13-1915,[1272,592] d. Oct-19-2005,[592] resided in Spartanburg, Spartanburg Co, SC.[592] She married Feb-20-1943,[1272] Beverly Henry Tucker, Jr., b. Sep-16-1914,[1272,592] (son of Beverly Henry Tucker and Fleda Burch), d. Dec- -1966,[592] military Major, U.S. Army Air Corps, World War II.[1272]

701. **James Gordon Gaston** (386.Amzi[8], 231.Amzi[7], 124.James[6], 58.Thomas[5], 16.Robert[4], 5.William[3], 3.John[2], 1.Jean[1]), b. Mar- 4-1878,[mcclxxiv[1274]] d. Sep- 6-1958 in Woodruff, Spartanburg Co, SC,[339] buried in Nazareth Presbyterian Church Cemetery, Moore, Spartanburg Co, SC,[339] occupation farmer.[1274] He married Dec-28-1905,[1274] **Stella Aurelia Wofford**, b. Oct-30-1883,[1274] (daughter of John Thomas Wofford and Nancy Arnold), d. Oct-23-1958 in Woodruff, Spartanburg Co, SC,[339] buried in Nazareth Presbyterian Church Cemetery, Moore, Spartanburg Co, SC.[339]

Children:

i.   JOHN GORDON GASTON b. Oct-10-1906,[1274,592] d. Oct-17-1995,[592] resided in Greenville, SC,[mcclxxv[1275]] occupation traffic manager for Greyhound Bus Lines (St. Louis, Memphis, New Orleans),[1274] education Georgia Tech (1929),[1274] military (1942-43) assistant clerk, U.S. Army Medical Corps (early discharge for physical disability).[1274]

ii.   JAMES ANSEL GASTON b. Jan- 1-1909 in South Carolina,[1274,693,592] d. May- 3-1990 in Alameda, Alameda Co, CA,[1237,mcclxxvi[1276]] education Presbyterian College, Clinton, SC (1929),[1274] military Lt. Col., U.S. Army Armor, World War II (North Africa).[1274] He married Jan-10-1938,[mcclxxvii[1277]] Marian Elizabeth Ross, b. Nov-15-1920,[1277,592] (daughter of James Powell Ross and Alva Cooper), d. Jan-13-1993,[592] resided in Las Vegas, Clark Co, NV,[592] resided formerly in California.[mcclxxviii[1278]]

iii.   MARGARET AURELIA GASTON, also known as Aurelia Gaston,[592] b. Oct-19-1910,[1277,592] d. Jan-19-1988,[592] resided in Columbia, SC.[592] She married Apr- 6-1935,[1277] Harold Kirk Taylor, b. Jan- 6-1907,[1277,699] (son of Fletcher Kirk Taylor and Mary Sue Martin), d. Sep- - 1961.[mcclxxix[1279]]

702. **Thomas Craig Gaston**, also known as Tom C. Gaston,[398] (386.Amzi[8], 231.Amzi[7], 124.James[6], 58.Thomas[5], 16.Robert[4], 5.William[3], 3.John[2], 1.Jean[1]), b. Sep-29-1879 in South Carolina,[705,1277] d. Mar-25-1942 in Enoree, Spartanburg Co, SC,[705] buried in Nazareth Presbyterian Church Cemetery, Moore, Spartanburg Co, SC,[705] resided in Enoree, Spartanburg Co, SC,[1277] resided in Woodruff, Spartanburg Co, SC,[1277] occupation farmer, policeman, mayor of Woodruff.[1277] He married May- 3-1903,[1277] **Minnie Iola Rogers**, b. Sep- 7-1884 near Reidville, Spartanburg Co, SC,[339,1277] (daughter of M. Dean Rogers and Elzie Ann Smith), d. Sep-27-1970 in Woodruff, Spartanburg Co, SC,[339] buried in Nazareth Presbyterian Church Cemetery, Moore, Spartanburg Co, SC,[339] resided 1942 in Enoree, Spartanburg Co, SC.[228]

Children:

i.   MARY ANNA GASTON, also known as Anna Gaston,[339] b. Feb- 7-1904,[1277,592] d. Oct- - 1980,[592] resided in Woodruff, Spartanburg Co, SC.[mcclxxx[1280],592] She married Sep- 3-1924,[1277] Franklin Todd Anderson, also known as Todd Anderson,[339] also known as F. Todd Anderson,[424] b. Apr-24-1899,[1280,592] (son of John Newton Anderson and Ina Gaulden), d. Mar- -1964,[592] resided in Woodruff, Spartanburg Co, SC.[1280]

ii.   AGNES GASTON b. Dec-17-1904,[1280,592,190] d. Jul-23-2000,[592,190] buried in Nazareth Presbyterian Church Cemetery, Moore, Spartanburg Co, SC,[190] resided in Greenville, SC,[592,190] resided formerly near Spartanburg, Spartanburg Co, SC,[1280,190] occupation teacher,[1280,190] education Winthrop College.[1280,190] She married Jul-12-1930,[1280] Earl Wharton Wallace, b. Aug-14-1901,[1280,592] (son of William Wilkerson Wallace and Lizzie May Wharton), d. Dec- 7-1949 in Spartanburg Co, SC,[705,592,191] buried in Nazareth Presbyterian Church Cemetery, Moore, Spartanburg Co, SC,[339] resided near Spartanburg, Spartanburg Co, SC.[1280]

iii.   ISOLA GASTON b. Sep-29-1906,[1280] d. Mar-15-1923 in Spartanburg Co, SC,[339,1280] buried in Nazareth Presbyterian Church Cemetery, Moore, Spartanburg Co, SC.[339]

iv.   GUSSIE DEAN GASTON b. Apr- 3-1908,[1280,592] d. Oct-24-2002,[592] buried in Nazareth Presbyterian Church Cemetery, Moore, Spartanburg Co, SC,[190] resided in Woodruff, Spartanburg Co, SC,[190,708] resided 1947 in Hendersonville, Henderson Co, NC,[228] resided 1944 in Detroit, MI,[1280] occupation nurse.[1280] She married Sep-24-1934,[1280] Roy DeVaughan Metz title: Dr., b. Jul-18-1897 near Hebron, Pleasants Co, WV,[1280,mcclxxxi[1281]] (son of Junius Brutus Metz and Sarah Elenor DeVaughan), d. Mar-21-1947 in Woodruff, Spartanburg Co, SC,[705] buried in Nazareth Presbyterian Church Cemetery, Moore, Spartanburg Co, SC,[705] cause of death chronic myocarditis,[705] resided in Woodruff, Spartanburg Co, SC,[705] resided 1944 in Detroit, MI,[1280] census 1930 in Greenville Co, SC [Listed as a boarder at the Chick Springs Hotel Sanitarium, occupation diagnostician.], census 1910, 1920 in Sardis District, Harrison Co, WV, census 1900 in Mannington District, Marion Co, WV, occupation physician.[705]

v.   THOMAS FELDER GASTON, also known as Tom F. Gaston,[592] b. Mar-12-1911,[1280,592] d. Jan- 1-2005,[592,190] buried Graceland Mausoleum,[190] resided in Greer, Greenville Co, SC,[592] resided 1944 near Duncan, Spartanburg Co, SC.[1280] He married Oct-16-1930,[1280] Kate Evelyn Compton, b. Feb-23-1911,[1280,592] (daughter of James Franklin Compton and Mary Etta Jones), d. May-29-2003,[592,190] buried in Greenville, SC,[190] [Graceland East Memorial Park and Mausoleum], resided in Greer, Greenville Co, SC.[592]

vi.   MINNIE HELEN GASTON, also known as Helen Gaston,[521] b. Jun-17-1913,[1280,592] d. May-13-2009 in Spartanburg Co, SC,[806,592] buried Resthaven Cemetery in Washington, Wilkes Co, GA,[190] resided in Woodruff, Spartanburg Co, SC,[190,699,521] resided 1944 in Washington, Wilkes Co,

GA.[1280] She married Sep- 9-1939,[1280] John Kelly Talkington, b. Sep- 7-1909,[1280] (son of James Monroe Talkington and Mary Elizabeth Pendergrass), d. Feb-16-1965 in Wilkes Co, GA,[mcclxxxii][1282] resided in Wilkes Co, GA,[1282] resided 1944 in Washington, Wilkes Co, GA.[1280]

       vii.   WOODROW WILSON "RED" GASTON, also known as W. Wilson Gaston,[412] b. Jul-19-1917,[1280] d. May-18-1962 in Woodruff, Spartanburg Co, SC,[191,339] resided in Woodruff, Spartanburg Co, SC.[mcclxxxiii][1283] He married Apr- 8-1938,[1280] Grace Elizabeth Schultz, b. Sep-19-1918,[1283,592] (daughter of George Schultz and Jimmy Mae Garrett), d. May- 7-2009 in Lancaster, Lancaster Co, SC,[764,592] buried Greenhaven Mem Gdns,[190] resided in Lancaster, Lancaster Co, SC,[699] resided originally in Fountain Inn, Greenville Co, SC,[190] education Fountain Inn H.S.,[190] occupation Reeves Brothers Mills plant in Woodruff (retired).[190]

       viii.   FRANCES LEE GASTON b. Apr-13-1919,[1283,592] d. Jun- -1985,[592] resided in Enoree, Spartanburg Co, SC,[708] resided formerly in Woodruff, Spartanburg Co, SC.[1283] She married (1) Jan-29-1938,[1283] Asa Joe McClellan (son of John David McClellan and Sarah Lou McClellan), d. Jul- 4-1944.[339] She married[424] (2) Wayverly Haynes Hill, b. Sep-19-1901,[592] d. Nov-11-1994,[592] resided in Enoree, Spartanburg Co, SC.[699]

       ix.   MARGARET ELIZABETH GASTON, also known as Elizabeth Gaston,[190,412] b. Oct- 1-1921,[1283] d. Jan- 4-2003,[190] resided in Cross Hill, Laurens Co, SC.[190,412] She married[424] Sep-13-1947,[339] William Gordon Gray, Jr., b. Jan-30-1913 in Spartanburg Co, SC,[339] d. Feb-18-2002 in Cross Hill, Laurens Co, SC.[339]

       x.   JOSEPH NORTON GASTON b. Sep-17-1925,[1283] resided 2000, 2005, 2008 in Woodruff, Spartanburg Co, SC,[412,521,1265] military U.S. Navy, World War II.[1283] He married Living.

703. **Jeb Stuart Gaston** (386.Amzi[8], 231.Amzi[7], 124.James[6], 58.Thomas[5], 16.Robert[4], 5.William[3], 3.John[2], 1.Jean[1]), b. Mar-18-1881 in South Carolina,[1283] d. Dec- 9-1945 in Walton Co, FL,[1123] resided in Defuniak Springs, Walton Co, FL,[1283,334] occupation Florida Dept of Hwys (20 yrs), law enforcement, construction.[1283] He married Jun-16-1915,[1283] **Mary G. Douglass**, b. Sep-11-1885 in Florida,[1283,211] (daughter of John Campbell Douglass and Jennie Gillis), d. Feb- -1967 in Walton Co, FL,[1123] census 1910, 1930 in Defuniak Springs, Walton Co, FL.

    Children:

       i.   MARGARET DOUGLASS GASTON b. Oct-25-1917,[1283] education Florida State College for Women at Tallahassee,[1283] occupation teacher and secretarial work.[1283] She married[339] Howard F. Gates, b. Jan-18-1916,[592] d. Jul-21-2001,[592] resided in Defuniak Springs, Walton Co, FL.[mcclxxxiv][1284]

       ii.   JEB STUART GASTON, JR. b. Aug-31-1920,[703,592] d. Mar- 3-1992 in Gwinnett Co, GA,[1282] [Georgia Death Index states death date as Mar 2 1992, but SSDI shows it as Mar 3 1992.], resided in Lawrenceville, Gwinnett Co, GA,[mcclxxxv][1285] resided in Denver, CO,[592] resided formerly in Florida,[1285] military U.S. Army Corps of Engineers, World War II (India).[703] He married (1) Apr-30-1949,[339] Marjorie Enockson, b. Feb-21-1917,[592] d. Mar- -1978,[592] resided in Denver, CO.[592] He married (2) May- 2-1987 in Walton Co, FL,[mcclxxxvi][1286] Ilene Joyce Schultz.

704. **Virgil R. Gaston** (387.William[8], 232.Thomas[7], 124.James[6], 58.Thomas[5], 16.Robert[4], 5.William[3], 3.John[2], 1.Jean[1]), b. Mar-16-1869,[335] occupation Presbyterian minister.[335] He married Jun- 2-1897,[335] **Mary Elizabeth McCullum**, resided in Sumter, Sumter Co, SC.[335]

    Children:

       i.   DAVID MCCULLUM b. Oct- 4-1900.[335]

       ii.   ELIZABETH GRACE MCCULLUM b. Mar-17-1905.[335]

       iii.   VIRGINIA MCCULLUM b. 1907.[335]

705. **William "Will" Gaston**[706] census name Willie Gaston,[123] (389.Anderson[8], 232.Thomas[7], 124.James[6], 58.Thomas[5], 16.Robert[4], 5.William[3], 3.John[2], 1.Jean[1]), b. Jun- -1882 in Texas,[123] census 1900 in Cooke Co, TX. He married **Unknown**.

    Children:

       i.   KENDRICK GASTON. He married[706] Marie ___.

       ii.   (DAUGHTER) GASTON. She married[706] Carl Cave.

706. **Sallie Lee Gaston** (389.Anderson[8], 232.Thomas[7], 124.James[6], 58.Thomas[5], 16.Robert[4], 5.William[3], 3.John[2], 1.Jean[1]), b. Jan-23-1886 in Gainesville, Cooke Co, TX,[706,123] d. Dec-19-1965 in Hereford, Deaf Smith Co, TX,[706] buried in Memorial Park Cemetery, Amarillo, TX,[706] census 1900 in Cooke Co, TX. She married Aug- 2-1905 in Gainesville, Cooke Co, TX,[706] **Elmer Oscar Slaughter**.
   Children:
   i.   GORDON T. SLAUGHTER b. Mar-18-1910 in Stephenville, Erath Co, TX.[706] He married[706] Lucille Nation.

707. **Jarvis Frank Gaston**, also known as Frank Gaston,[592] (393.James[8], 238.James[7], 128.Robert[6], 60.Hugh[5], 16.Robert[4], 5.William[3], 3.John[2], 1.Jean[1]), b. Oct-23-1901,[12,592] d. Sep-25-1977,[12,592] resided in Norman, Montgomery Co, AR,[592] resided formerly in Oklahoma.[838] He married[12] Sep- 7-1922 in Denison, Grayson Co, TX,[12] **Myrtle Mae Henson**, also known as Mae,[592] b. Oct-31-1906 in Colbert, Bryan Co, OK,[12,592] d. Apr-28-2002 in Norman, Montgomery Co, AR,[12,592] buried Liberty Cemetery in Montgomery Co, AR,[12] resided in Mt. Ida, Montgomery Co, AR.[592]

Myrtle: Myrtle Mae Henson was the foster child of Luetta Myrtle (McDonald) and Hollan Singletary. When the Singletary's first child, Mildred Singletary, died at birth, Mae was raised as their own since her own mother died giving her birth.[12]

   Children:
   i.   LIVING.

708. **Samuel N. Elliott** (394.Rosetta[8], 241.Matilda[7], 134.Andrew[6], 72.John[5], 21.John[4], 6.Hugh[3], 3.John[2], 1.Jean[1]), b. Nov- -1868 in Harrison Co, WV,[mcclxxxvii[1287],588] d. Oct-11-1921 in Clarksburg, Harrison Co, WV,[398] buried in IOOF Cemetery, Salem, Harrison Co, WV,[817,398] [Name on headstone: S. N. Elliott. No dates.], cause of death typhoid fever,[398] census 1900, 1910 in Central District, Doddridge Co, WV, census 1870 in West Union District, Doddridge Co, WV. He married Mar- 5-1892 in Doddridge Co, WV,[mcclxxxviii[1288]] **Dora Mary Richards**, also known as Mary D. Richards,[588] b. May-16-1872 in Ritchie Co, WV,[398] (daughter of John Richards and Liddie Jones), d. Dec- 7-1945 in Bridgeport, Harrison Co, WV,[398] buried in Benedum Memorial Cemetery, Bridgeport, Harrison Co, WV,[398] resided in Bridgeport, Harrison Co, WV,[398] census 1900, 1910 in Central District, Doddridge Co, WV, resided 1892 in Ritchie Co, WV.[588] 1900 Census, Doddridge Co, WV (Central District):
Samuel Elliott, 31, b. Nov 1868, married 8 yrs; wife Dora M, 28, b. May 1872, mother of 4 children (3 still living); son Lloyd H, 6, b. Dec 1893; dau Lydia, 3, b. Nov 1896; son George G D, 10 months, b. Jul 1899.

1910 Census, Doddridge Co, WV (Central District), enumerated on May 5 1910:
Samuel N. Elliott, 35, laborer at odd jobs, married 19 yrs; wife Dora M, 33, mother of 7 children (6 still living); son Lloyd, 16; dau Isabella, 13; son Drury (Denry ?), 10; son William, 8; son Samuel, 6; son James, 5.

   Children:
   i.   LLOYD H. ELLIOTT b. Dec- -1893,[1287] census 1900, 1910 in Central District, Doddridge Co, WV.
   ii.   LYDIA ISABELLA ELLIOTT, also known as Isabella Elliott,[mcclxxxix[1289],778] b. Nov- -1896,[1287] census 1900, 1910 in Central District, Doddridge Co, WV.
   iii. GEORGE G. DRURY ELLIOTT, census name Drury Elliott,[1289] b. Jul- 8-1899,[604,1287] d. May- -1991,[604] census 1900, 1910 in Central District, Doddridge Co, WV.
   iv.   WILLIAM ELLIOTT b. ca 1902,[1289] census 1910 in Central District, Doddridge Co, WV.
   v.   SAMUEL ELLIOTT b. ca 1904,[1289] census 1910 in Central District, Doddridge Co, WV.
   vi.   JAMES ELLIOTT b. ca 1905,[1289] census 1910 in Central District, Doddridge Co, WV.

709. **Jasper David Elliott**, also known as J. David Elliott,[398] census name David J. Elliott,[123,mccxc[1290],775,mccxci[1291]] (394.Rosetta[8], 241.Matilda[7], 134.Andrew[6], 72.John[5], 21.John[4],

6.Hugh[3], 3.John[2], 1.Jean[1]), b. Feb-11-1869,[mccxcii][1292] d. Oct-24-1952 in Doddridge Co, WV,[356] buried in Ruley Cemetery, Arnolds Creek, Doddridge Co, WV,[398] resided in Doddridge Co, WV,[398,123] census 1870, 1910, 20, 30 in West Union District, Doddridge Co, WV, occupation farmer.[398] He married[502] **Sarah Eveleene "Eva" Wenneson**, census name Eva,[123] census name Evlan,[1290] census name Evaline,[775] census name Evelyn,[1291] b. Aug- -1874,[123] d. bef Oct 1952,[228] census 1910, 1920, 1930 in West Union District, Doddridge Co, WV.

Children:
i.   WAITMAN T. ELLIOTT b. ca 1907,[1290] census 1910, 1920, 1930 in West Union District, Doddridge Co, WV.
ii.   DOLLIE ROSETTA ELLIOTT b. Jan- 3-1909 in Doddridge Co, WV,[190] d. Mar- 3-1986 in Clarksburg, Harrison Co, WV,[847] buried in Ruley Cemetery, Arnolds Creek, Doddridge Co, WV,[190,17] resided in Doddridge Co, WV,[190] census 1930 in Central District, Doddridge Co, WV, census 1910, 1920 in West Union District, Doddridge Co, WV.

Among others, predeceased by one daughter, one son, and two brothers.[190]

She married[191,395] Feb- 5-1929 in Doddridge Co, WV,[mccxciii][1293] Clad Adams,[191,395] also known as Charles Adams,[345] b. Apr-20-1903 in Harrison Co, WV,[592,354] (son of Howard Elanus Adams and Sadie Spencer), d. Jun- -1973,[592] resided in Syracuse, Onondaga Co, NY, census 1930 in Central District, Doddridge Co, WV, resided 1929 in Ritchie Co, WV.[354]

1930 Census, Doddridge Co, WV (Central District, Middle Run Road), enumerated on Apr 7 1930:
Clad Adams, 20, farm laborer, age 18 at time of first marriage; wife Dollie, 19, age 17 at time of first marriage; dau Rosetta, 2 yr 6 mo; son Jimmie, one month; lodger Charlie Rollins, 24, no occupation.
Note: Ten days later, Clad E. Adams, 26, married, was listed as a boarder in the household of Claude D. Gough in Lewis County.

iii. EDWARD ELLIOTT, census name Eddie Elliott,[775] also known as Ed Elliott,[711,412] b. ca 1914 at Arnolds Creek (West Union), Doddridge Co, WV,[775,711] [Age 6 in 1920 Census and age 15 in 1930 Census would put birth in about 1914 or 1915. But marriage record states birth date as Jun 10 1918.], resided 1986 in Parkersburg, Wood Co, WV,[412] census 1920, 1930 in West Union District, Doddridge Co, WV. He married Living.
iv.   DAVID ELLIOTT, JR., census name Dean Elliott,[1291] b. ca 1915,[775] census 1920 in West Union District, Doddridge Co, WV.
v.   VIRGINIA ELLIOTT, census name Jennie Elliott,[775,1291] b. ca 1917,[775] resided 1986 in Doddridge Co, WV,[412] census 1920, 1930 in West Union District, Doddridge Co, WV.

710. **Mary Bird Elliott**, also known as Bird Elliott (394.Rosetta[8], 241.Matilda[7], 134.Andrew[6], 72.John[5], 21.John[4], 6.Hugh[3], 3.John[2], 1.Jean[1]), b. Feb- 3-1874 in Doddridge Co, WV,[mccxciv][1294],711 d. 1937,[350] census 1920 in Salem, WV, census 1910 in Grant District, Doddridge Co, WV, census 1900 in Central District, Doddridge Co, WV. She married (1) Jul- 3-1895 in West Union, Doddridge Co, WV,[mccxcv][1295],354 **J. S. Wilson**, b. ca 1874 in Ritchie Co, WV.[mccxcvi][1296],354 She married[350] (2) Aug-22-1899 in Arnolds Creek (West Union), Doddridge Co, WV,[mccxcvii][1297],354 **Daniel Boone Richards**, b. Jun- -1868 in Ritchie Co, WV,[1287,mccxcviii][1298] d. bef Jan 1920,[418] census 1910 in Grant District, Doddridge Co, WV, census 1900 in Central District, Doddridge Co, WV. 1900 Census, Doddridge Co, WV (Central District):
Daniel B. Richards, 31, b. Jun 1868; wife Mary B, 25, b. Feb 1875, mother of one child (still living); stepdau Gracie M. Wilson, 3, b. Nov 1896.

1910 Census, Doddridge Co, WV (Central District), enumerated on Apr 21 1910:
Daniel B. Richards, 39, laborer on railroad, married 12 yrs; wife Mary B, 37, mother of 5 children (all still living); dau Grace W. (?), 13; dau Jessie Cloe, 9; son Okey C, 7; dau Hazel M, 4; son Daniel B. Jr, 2.

1920 Census, Harrison Co, WV (Tenmile District, Town of Salem), enumerated on Jan 2 1920: Mary Richards, 48, widowed; dau Hazel, 16; son Okey, 17; son Danny, 10; dau Rosetta, 7; dau Nellie, 5; dau Mary V, 1y 4m.

Children by J. S. Wilson:
     i.   GRACE MATILDA WILSON, also known as Gracie Wilson,[711] census name Gracie M. Wilson,[1287] b. Nov-15-1896,[350,1287] census 1910 in Grant District, Doddridge Co, WV, census 1900 in Central District, Doddridge Co, WV. She married Jul-14-1912 at Long Run, Doddridge Co, WV,[711] Willie Davis, b. ca 1889 in Doddridge Co, WV.[711]
          Children by Daniel Boone Richards:
     ii.   JESSIE CLOE RICHARDS b. Sep-21-1900 in Doddridge Co, WV,[mccxcix[1299]] [Age given at time of marriage would put birth date at Sep 22 1899, but death record states birth date as Sep 21 1900.], d. Jan- 4-1968 in Salem, WV,[276] census 1930 in Simpson District, Harrison Co, WV, census 1920 in Adamston (Clarksburg), Harrison Co, WV. She married Mar- 4-1916 in Salem, WV,[mccc[1300]] Ellis George Thompson, b. Jul-26-1898 in Doddridge Co, WV,[mccci[1301]] [Although his marriage record in March 1916 states his age to be 21 as of his last birthday, Jul 26 1915, thus putting his birth date at Jul 26 1894, and his death record states his birth date as Jul 26 1897, his birth record shows his actual birth date to be Jul 26 1898. Inasmuch as his parents were married on Sep 8 1897, it would appear that he inflated his age at the time of his marriage.] (son of Marion Thompson and Joanna Collins), d. Mar-20-1965 in Salem, WV,[276] buried in IOOF Cemetery, Salem, Harrison Co, WV,[276] census 1930 in Simpson District, Harrison Co, WV, census 1920 in Adamston (Clarksburg), Harrison Co, WV, occupation coal miner,[1208,276] occupation 1920 teamster.[418]
     iii.   OKEY CLAIR RICHARDS b. ca 1903,[mcccii[1302]] census 1910 in Grant District, Doddridge Co, WV.
     iv.   HAZEL MAMIE RICHARDS[350] b. ca 1905 in Harrison Co, WV,[419,1302] [Age 4 at 1910 Census would put birth in about 1906, but age 16 given at time of Jun 1920 marriage would put it in about 1904.], resided 1941 in Shinnston, Harrison Co, WV.[228] She married Jun-17-1920 in Salem, WV,[419] Clarence Cecil Johnson, b. Jan-13-1898 in Wood Co, WV,[398,419] (son of Albert E. Johnson and Jennie West), d. Mar-11-1941 in Clarksburg, Harrison Co, WV,[398] cause of death dynamite explosion - homocide,[398] buried in Masonic Cemetery, Shinnston, Harrison Co, WV,[398] resided in Shinnston, Harrison Co, WV,[398] occupation coal miner.[398]
     v.   ROSETTA MAY RICHARDS[350] b. Sep-10-1905 in Harrison Co, WV,[419] resided 1928 in Shinnston, Harrison Co, WV.[419] She married Mar- 7-1928 in Shinnston, Harrison Co, WV,[mccciii[1303]] Harry Clifford Skinner, b. Mar- 7-1902 in Gilmer Co, WV,[419] [SSDI lists birth date as Mar 7 1901.] (son of John W. Skinner and Anna D. Holt), d. Nov- -1973,[592] resided in Shinnston, Harrison Co, WV.[419,592]
     vi.   DANIEL B. RICHARDS, JR. b. ca 1908,[1302] census 1910 in Grant District, Doddridge Co, WV.
     vii.   NELLIE CATHERINE RICHARDS[350] b. ca 1915,[418] census 1920 in Salem, WV.
     viii.   MARY VIRGINIA RICHARDS[350] b. ca 1918,[418] census 1920 in Salem, WV.

711. **Cora Lee Elliott** (394.Rosetta[8], 241.Matilda[7], 134.Andrew[6], 72.John[5], 21.John[4], 6.Hugh[3], 3.John[2], 1.Jean[1]), b. Jul- 8-1876 in Doddridge Co, WV,[276,354] d. Mar- 9-1967 in Clarksburg, Harrison Co, WV,[276] buried in Duckworth (Summit) Cemetery, Greenwood, Doddridge Co, WV,[276] census 1930 in Central District, Doddridge Co, WV, census 1920 in Tenmile District, Harrison Co, WV, census 1900, 1910 in Central District, Doddridge Co, WV. She married[350] Sep-20-1895 at Doe Run (West Union), Doddridge Co, WV,[354] **William Walter Thomas**, also known as Walter W. Thomas,[711,1287,418,mccciv[1304]] b. Jun-16-1873 in Doddridge Co, WV,[398] [Birth date given as June 1874 in 1900 Census, but his age was 8 in 1880 Census, and his death record states birth date as Jun 16 1873.] (son of Isaac W. Thomas and Alvina Rollins), d. May- 6-1956 at Greenwood, Doddridge Co, WV,[398] buried in Duckworth (Summit) Cemetery, Greenwood, Doddridge Co, WV,[398] resided at Greenwood, Doddridge Co, WV,[398] census 1930 in Central District, Doddridge Co, WV, census 1920 in Tenmile District, Harrison Co, WV, census 1880, 1900, 1910 in Central District, Doddridge Co, WV, occupation farmer,[398] occupation 1920 coal miner.[418]
          Children:

    i.   CLARA THOMAS b. Nov- -1897 in Doddridge Co, WV,[1287],[711] census 1920 in Tenmile District, Harrison Co, WV, resided 1914 in Doddridge Co, WV,[711] census 1900 in Central District, Doddridge Co, WV. She married Jul-23-1914 in West Union, Doddridge Co, WV,[711] Samuel Freeman, b. ca 1882 in Doddridge Co, WV,[711] census 1920 in Tenmile District, Harrison Co, WV, resided 1914 in Harrison Co, WV,[711] occupation 1920 coal miner.[418]

    ii.   ORA THOMAS b. Sep- -1899,[1287] census 1920 in Tenmile District, Harrison Co, WV, census 1900, 1910 in Central District, Doddridge Co, WV, occupation 1920 coal miner.[418]

    iii.   HARRY C. THOMAS b. Oct-14-1901 in Doddridge Co, WV,[592] d. Dec-10-1991,[592] resided in Salem, WV,[604] resided 1921 in Bristol, Harrison Co, WV,[419] census 1920, 1930 in Tenmile District, Harrison Co, WV, census 1910 in Central District, Doddridge Co, WV, occupation 1920 coal miner.[418] He married[mcccv[1305]] Dec-22-1921 in Clarksburg, Harrison Co, WV,[419] Lena Arizona Swiger, b. Oct- 3-1892 in Harrison Co, WV,[398],[419] (daughter of Isaiah Swiger and Florence Flanigan), d. Sep-28-1970 in Clarksburg, Harrison Co, WV,[398] buried in Big Isaac Cemetery, Doddridge Co, WV,[398] resided in Salem, WV,[398] census 1930 in Tenmile District, Harrison Co, WV, resided 1921 in Harrison Co, WV.[419]

    iv.   RILEY THOMAS b. ca 1905,[418] census 1920 in Tenmile District, Harrison Co, WV.

    v.   TRUMAN L. THOMAS b. Apr-15-1907 in Doddridge Co, WV,[398],[711] d. Sep-16-1950 in Central Station, Doddridge Co, WV,[mcccvi[1306]],[356] buried in Duckworth (Summit) Cemetery, Greenwood, Doddridge Co, WV,[398] cause of death strychnine poisoning (suicide),[398] resided at Central Station, Doddridge Co, WV,[398] census 1920 in Tenmile District, Harrison Co, WV, census 1910 in Central District, Doddridge Co, WV, occupation B & O Railroad.[398] He married Feb- 6-1935 in West Union, Doddridge Co, WV,[711] Grace Bircher, also known as Gracie Bircher,[711] b. ca 1907 in Doddridge Co, WV.[711]

    vi.   EARL D. THOMAS b. Jan- 1-1909 in Doddridge Co, WV,[592],[mcccvii[1307]] d. Feb-13-1995,[592] resided in Salem, WV,[604] resided 1934 at Greenwood, Doddridge Co, WV,[1307] census 1930 in Central District, Doddridge Co, WV, census 1920 in Tenmile District, Harrison Co, WV. He married Oct- 4-1934 in West Union, Doddridge Co, WV,[1307] divorced Lena Pearl Nicholson, also known as Pearl Nicholson,[190],[374],[mcccviii[1308]] b. Oct-11-1918 at Coldwater (New Milton), Doddridge Co, WV,[mcccix[1309]],[190],[419] (daughter of Phillip Carl Nicholson and Julia B. Gallien), d. Dec-24-2010 in Bridgeport, Harrison Co, WV,[847] buried in Union Mission (Sunrise) Cemetery, New Milton, Doddridge Co, WV,[190] resided at East View (Clarksburg), Harrison Co, WV,[190] occupation Manhattan Restaurant, Clarksburg WV.[190]

    vii.   NELLIE J. THOMAS, census name Nelly Thomas,[418] b. Jul-21-1911 in Doddridge Co, WV,[592],[711] d. Apr-26-2001,[592] resided in Flemington, Taylor Co, WV,[604] census 1930 in Central District, Doddridge Co, WV, census 1920 in Tenmile District, Harrison Co, WV. She married Dec-30-1930 in West Union, Doddridge Co, WV,[711] Ellis Sullivan, b. Apr-22-1911 in Doddridge Co, WV,[592],[711] (son of Albert H. Sullivan and Mary L. ___), d. Jun- -1975,[592] resided in Rosemont, Taylor Co, WV,[604] census 1920 in West Union District, Doddridge Co, WV.

    viii.   LONA THOMAS b. Mar- 9-1915,[592],[46],[721] d. Jun- -1987,[592],[46],[721] buried in Blockhouse Hill Cemetery, West Union, WV,[17],[721] resided in Salem, WV,[592] resided 1951 in West Union, Doddridge Co, WV.[mcccx[1310]] She married[1092],[1310],[228] Nov-26-1928 in Doddridge Co, WV,[354] John Lawrence Haught,[398] also known as Lawrence Haught,[1310],[17] also known as Laurence Haught,[395],[mcccxi[1311]] b. Apr- 3-1907 in Tyler Co, WV,[398],[46] (son of Ira Newton Haught and Rosie Columbia Wright), d. Jun-24-1947 in West Union, Doddridge Co, WV,[46] buried in Blockhouse Hill Cemetery, West Union, WV,[17],[721] [Referred to as Freeman Cemetery in death record.], cause of death killed by cave-in of a ten-foot ditch,[398] occupation laborer.[398]

    ix.   VICTORIA THOMAS b. ca 1918,[418] census 1930 in Central District, Doddridge Co, WV, census 1920 in Tenmile District, Harrison Co, WV.

712.   **Dollie B. Elliott** (394.Rosetta[8], 241.Matilda[7], 134.Andrew[6], 72.John[5], 21.John[4], 6.Hugh[3], 3.John[2], 1.Jean[1]), b. Sep- 6-1878 in Doddridge Co, WV,[767],[711] d. 1907,[721] buried in IOOF Cemetery (Blockhouse Hill), West Union, WV,[721] census 1900 in West Union District, Doddridge Co, WV. She married Aug-8-1897 in Doddridge Co, WV,[mcccxii[1312]],[mcccxiii[1313]] **Sanford Smith**,[374],[mcccxiv[1314]],[502] also known as Santford Smith,[354] also known as Sandford Smith,[mcccxv[1315]] b. Nov-20-1874 in Doddridge Co, WV,[1315] (son of Harvey Smith and Ivah Jane Gaston), d. Dec-31-1907 in Doddridge Co, WV,[mcccxvi[1316]] buried

in IOOF Cemetery (Blockhouse Hill), West Union, WV,[721] cause of death tuberculosis,[1314] census 1900 in West Union District, Doddridge Co, WV, occupation laborer.[1314]

1900 Census, Doddridge Co, WV (West Union District), enumerated on Jun 11 1900: Sanford Smith, 25, b. Nov 1874, farmer, married 2 yrs; wife Dollie B, 21, b. Sep 1878, mother of 2 children (both still living); dau Bessie, age 1, b. Jun 1898; and an unnamed daughter, age under one month, born in May 1900.

As g-g-grandchildren of John Gaston Jr. and Anna Davisson, Sanford Smith and Dollie Elliott were third cousins.

Children:
i.   BESSIE SMITH[771] b. Jun-16-1898 in Doddridge Co, WV,[190] d. Jun- 1-1989 in Parkersburg, Wood Co, WV,mcccxvii[1317] buried in IOOF Cemetery (Blockhouse Hill), West Union, WV,[190,721] census 1900 in West Union District, Doddridge Co, WV. She married Jun-19-1919 in Doddridge Co, WV,mcccxviii[1318] John William Pritt, b. Dec- -1877 in Gilmer Co, WV,[354,721] [Age 34 given at time of June 1919 marriage would put birth at about 1885, but headstone states Dec 19 1877, death record states Dec 17 1877, and his age was given as 64 (rather than the correct 63) in his Aug 1941 obituary.] (son of Abraham Pritt and Betsy Williams), d. Aug-19-1941 in Doe Run (West Union), Doddridge Co, WV,[190,356,191,721] buried in IOOF Cemetery (Blockhouse Hill), West Union, WV,[721,357] resided in Doe Run (West Union), Doddridge Co, WV,[190] resided until abt 1923 in Gilmer Co, WV,[190] occupation P. W. A.[357]

1930 Census, Doddridge County WV (West Union District), enumerated on Apr 3 1930:
John Pritt, 52; wife Bessie, 30; dau Mabel, 5; son Ross, 2.[1291]

ii.   EDNA MAY SMITH[771,412] b. Aug-26-1902 in Summers, Doddridge Co, WV,mcccxix[1319] d. Oct-13-1940 in Harrisville, Ritchie Co, WV,mcccxx[1320],mcccxxi[1321] cause of death pulmonary tuberculosis,[398] buried West Union Cemetery,[398] resided in Pennsboro, Ritchie Co, WV,[398] census 1910, 1930 in Doddridge Co, WV, resided 1921 in Harrison Co, WV,[419] resided 1920 in Mannington, Marion Co, WV.[681] She married Aug- 1-1921 in Clarksburg, Harrison Co, WV,[419] divorced[436,mcccxxii[1322]] James Leftridge Bridwell,[1166] census name Leftrage Bridwell,mcccxxiii[1323] b. Aug-16-1899 in Muddlety, Nicholas Co, WV,[1322,592] [Marriage record states birthplace as Lewis Co, but immediate family (granddaughter Pamela Sue Bridwell Hughes) advises Nicholas Co. He did reside later in Lewis County.] (son of Calvin Early Bridwell and Mary Elizabeth "Lizzie" O'Dell), d. May-23-1981 in Columbus, Franklin Co, OH,[693,592] buried (ashes) at Eastlawn Cemetery, Columbus, OH,mcccxxiv[1324] resided in Columbus, Franklin Co, OH,[592,1322] resided 1921 in Clarksburg, Harrison Co, WV,[419] resided 1920 in Middlesex Co, NJ,[681] resided 1910 in Lewis Co, WV,[211] resided 1900 in Nicholas Co, WV,[123] military entered on Sep 12 1918 in Morgantown WV.[1322]
iii.   BERKELEY SMITH[771] b. ca 1904,[889] d. bef Jun 1989,[412] census 1910 in Court House District, Lewis Co, WV [In household of William A. Fisher, his wife Annie, and their two children. Relationship of Berkley Smith to head of household given as "To Raise."].
iv.   LONA SMITH[771] d. bef Jun 1989.[412]

713. **Waitman T. "Willie" Perine** (395.Richard[8], 241.Matilda[7], 134.Andrew[6], 72.John[5], 21.John[4], 6.Hugh[3], 3.John[2], 1.Jean[1]), b. Dec-15-1872 in Center Point, Doddridge Co, WV,mcccxxv[1325],[190] d. Dec- 3-1951 in Wallace, Harrison Co, WV,mcccxxvi[1326],[398,190] [Place of death: Rock Camp. Death record and obituary have spelling of his and his father's name as "Perrine." But "Perine" is the more usual form for him and his family, and it is the spelling found on his grave marker.], buried in Ruley Cemetery, Arnolds Creek, Doddridge Co, WV,[17,190,398] resided in Wallace, Harrison Co, WV,[190,398] resided 1932, 35 in Harmony, Butler Co, PA,[856,mcccxxvii[1327]] census 1930 in Butler Co, PA,[334] census 1900, 1920 in West Union District, Doddridge Co, WV, occupation farmer.[190,398] He married (1) ca 1894,[767] **Cora Cunningham**, b. Oct-23-1873 in Virginia,[347,344] (daughter of John A. Cunningham and Mary E.

Jackson), d. Sep-27-1901 in Doddridge Co, WV,[347] buried in Ruley Cemetery, Arnolds Creek, Doddridge Co, WV,[344] census 1900 in West Union District, Doddridge Co, WV. He married (2) Sep-13-1903 near Greenwood, Doddridge Co, WV,[711] **Georgia May Garrison**, also known as May Garrison,[354,775] b. May-20-1885 in Greenwood, Doddridge Co, WV,[347] (daughter of George Cottrell and Mary Garrison), d. May- 1-1969 in Columbiana Co, OH,[347] buried in Westmoreland Mem Park, Greensburg, PA,[347] census 1930 in Butler Co, PA,[334] resided 1924 in West Union, Doddridge Co, WV,[345] census 1920 in Doddridge Co, WV.[775]

Georgia: Georgia May Garrison was a year-and-a-half old when her mother died of tuberculosis. Georgia was then raised by her mother's sister, Elizabeth L. M. Garrison Hufford.[347]

Children by Cora Cunningham:

i.   TRILBIA FAYE PERINE[395] also known as Fay Perine,[767,354] b. Mar-24-1895 in Doddridge Co, WV,[mcccxxviii[1328]] d. Mar- -1986,[592] resided in Clarksburg, Harrison Co, WV,[592] resided 1951 in Bridgeport, Harrison Co, WV,[765] census 1900 in West Union District, Doddridge Co, WV. She married Jun-17-1918 in Doddridge Co, WV,[mcccxxix[1329],354] Harry Nelson Richards, b. Jul-16-1896 in Ritchie Co, WV,[592,347] (son of Oliver Perry Richards and Rachel Ina Drummond), d. Dec- -1976 in Clarksburg, Harrison Co, WV,[592,347] resided in Clarksburg, Harrison Co, WV,[592] census 1910 in West Union District, Doddridge Co, WV.

ii.   CLAY H. PERINE b. Aug-27-1897 in Doddridge Co, WV,[mcccxxx[1330]] d. Mar- 1-1913 in Doddridge Co, WV,[mcccxxxi[1331],347] census 1900 in West Union District, Doddridge Co, WV, cause of death appendicitis.[357]

iii. CLYDE L. PERINE b. May-19-1900 in West Union, Doddridge Co, WV,[1292] d. Nov-19-1922 in West Virginia,[1292] census 1900, 1920 in West Union District, Doddridge Co, WV.[775]

Children by Georgia May Garrison:

iv.   RICHARD ROSS "REX" PERINE, census name Rex Perine,[775] b. May-14-1905 in Doddridge Co, WV,[mcccxxxii[1332]] d. May- 2-1930 in Pennsylvania.[347] He married[347] Sarah Stewart, d. Mar- -2001 in Pennsylvania.[347]

v.   ELSIE ELLEN PERINE b. Mar-19-1907 in Doddridge Co, WV,[mcccxxxiii[1333]] d. May-19-1998 in Ellwood City, Lawrence Co, PA,[347] buried in Sylvania Hills Mem Park, Ellwood City PA,[347] resided 1951 in Ellwood City, Lawrence Co, PA,[765] census 1930 in Butler Co, PA.[334] She married[941,347] Charles E. Miller, b. in West Virginia,[347] d. in Ellwood City, Lawrence Co, PA,[347] buried in Sylvania Hills Mem Park, Ellwood City PA.[347]

vi.   CHARLES WAYNE PERINE, also known as Wayne Perine,[775,334,765] b. Mar-27-1910 in Doddridge Co, WV,[mcccxxxiv[1334]] d. Aug- 3-2000 in Ellwood City, Lawrence Co, PA,[347] buried in West Virginia,[347] resided 1951 in New Castle, Lawrence Co, PA,[765] census 1930 in Butler Co, PA,[334] census 1920 in Doddridge Co, WV.[775] He married (1) Mar-13-1938 in Harmony, Butler Co, PA,[mcccxxxv[1335]] Juanita May Watson, nickname Skeeter,[347] census name Waneta Watson,[1304] b. Apr-15-1920 in Cabin Run, Doddridge Co, WV,[190] (daughter of George Robert Watson and Bessie M. Williams), d. Jan-16-1999 in Pittsburgh, Allegheny Co, PA,[190] buried in Auburn Community Cemetery, Ritchie Co, WV,[190] resided in New Castle, Lawrence Co, PA.[765,190] He married[191,344] (2) aft 1980, Martha Jane Perine, b. Mar-15-1918 in Blandville, Doddridge Co, WV,[344,190] (daughter of Luther Martin Perine and Beulah (twin) Hess), d. Apr-29-1996 in Parkersburg, Wood Co, WV,[190,344] resided 1977, 92, 96 in Ellenboro, Ritchie Co, WV,[765,412,190] resided 1968, 95 in Harrisville, Ritchie Co, WV.[856,521] Charles Wayne Perine and Martha Jane Perine were second cousins, by virtue of both being great-grandchildren of David L. Perine & Matilda Gaston.

vii. CORA WINNIE PERINE, also known as Winnie Perine,[519] b. Mar-27-1910 in West Union, Doddridge Co, WV,[347] d. Dec- 2-1918 in West Union, Doddridge Co, WV,[344,519] [Death date 1915 reported by Gaston researcher Georgia Hileman Halloran.].

viii. WAITMAN T. WILLARD "JOE" PERINE, also known as Willard Perine,[713,775,592] b. Oct-22-1911 in Doddridge Co, WV,[mcccxxxvi[1336],592] d. Jun-12-2000 in Midland, Beaver Co, PA,[347,592] buried in Highland Cemetery, Ohioville, PA,[347] resided in Ohioville, Beaver Co, PA,[347] resided in Midland,

Beaver Co, PA.[1010] He married[347] (1) Thelma Ruth Nagel. He married[347] (2) Evelyn V. Popp, b. Sep-13-1920 in Pennsylvania,[592,347] d. Apr-20-2000,[592,347] resided in Midland, Beaver Co, PA.[948]

    ix.   LELIA IRENE PERINE[347] also known as Irene Perine,[519] b. May-18-1915 in Doddridge Co, WV,[mcccxxxvii[1337]] d. [She does not appear with the rest of her family in the 1920 Census.].

    x.   WINONA MAY PERINE b. Mar-27-1918 in Doddridge Co, WV,[mcccxxxviii[1338],592] d. Jun-21-2004,[592] resided in West Sunbury, Butler Co, PA,[765,592] census 1930 in Butler Co, PA,[334] census 1920 in Doddridge Co, WV.[775] She married[347] Clyde Kauf, b. May-23-1913,[592] d. Jul- -1981,[592] resided in West Sunbury, Butler Co, PA.[948]

    xi.   ROSS NEALON PERINE b. Jun-26-1920 in Doddridge Co, WV,[mcccxxxix[1339]] census 1930 in Butler Co, PA.[334]

    xii.   ZONA JEAN PERINE, also known as Zona Gene Perine,[398] b. Mar-10-1922 in West Union, Doddridge Co, WV,[398] d. Jul-30-1924 in West Union, Doddridge Co, WV,[398] buried Arnolds Creek.[398]

    xiii.   JACQUE ARLENE PERINE b. Apr-28-1924 in Doddridge Co, WV,[mcccxl[1340]] d. Feb- 8-1981 in Salem, OH,[mcccxli[1341],347] buried in Westmoreland Mem Park, Greensburg, PA,[347] resided in Salem, OH,[1341] resided 1951 in Irwin, Westmoreland Co, PA,[765] census 1930 in Butler Co, PA.[mcccxlii[1342]] She married Oct-22-1944 in Shaner, Westmoreland Co, PA,[347] Leonard James Hileman, b. Oct-22-1923 in Rilton, Sewickley Twp, PA,[592,347] (son of Laurie F. Hileman and Susan Vargo), d. Nov-10-2004 in Albuquerque, Bernalillo Co, NM,[190,592] buried in Westmoreland Mem Park, Greensburg, PA,[190] resided in Albuquerque, Bernalillo Co, NM,[592] resided formerly in Salem, OH,[190] resided formerly in Wadsworth, Medina Co, OH,[190] resided formerly in Pennsylvania,[948] occupation General Motors, Lordstown, OH (retired),[190] military U.S. Navy, World War II.[190]

714. **Dona Alice Perine**[mcccxliii[1343]] also known as Donna,[484] [Incorrectly identified in obituary of sister Lula as "Donna May Britton"] (395.Richard[8], 241.Matilda[7], 134.Andrew[6], 72.John[5], 21.John[4], 6.Hugh[3], 3.John[2], 1.Jean[1]), b. Apr-28-1875 in Arnolds Creek (West Union), Doddridge Co, WV,[mcccxliv[1344]] d. Dec-21-1958 in Parkersburg, Wood Co, WV,[806,17] buried in Ruley Cemetery, Arnolds Creek, Doddridge Co, WV,[mcccxlv[1345]] resided 1956-58 in Parkersburg, Wood Co, WV,[190] resided 1875-1956 in Arnolds Creek (West Union), Doddridge Co, WV.[190] She married Sep- 8-1902 in Arnolds Creek (West Union), Doddridge Co, WV,[mcccxlvi[1346],354,484] **Porter M. Britton**, b. Mar- 1-1881,[190] (son of George W. Britton, Jr. and Cassa Ann "Cassie" Wagoner), d. Aug-30-1946 in Parkersburg, Wood Co, WV,[190] buried in Ruley Cemetery, Arnolds Creek, Doddridge Co, WV.[17]

    Children:

    i.   RUTH BRITTON[17] b. Jul- -1903 in Doddridge Co, WV,[mcccxlvii[1347],mcccxlviii[1348]] d. Jul-15-1903,[17] buried in Ruley Cemetery, Arnolds Creek, Doddridge Co, WV.[mcccxlix[1349]]

    ii.   JESSIE MARIE BRITTON, also known as Marie Britton,[354,mcccl[1350],765,856] b. Dec-21-1904 in Arnolds Creek (West Union), Doddridge Co, WV,[mcccli[1351],592] d. Jul- -1985,[592] resided in Washington, Wood Co, WV,[592] resided 1946, 58 in Parkersburg, Wood Co, WV.[765,856] She married[941,1040] Apr-22-1923 in Doddridge Co, WV,[354] J. W. Riley, b. ca 1899 in Wood Co, WV.[354]

    iii.   RICHIE NOEL BRITTON[176,190] b. Oct- 1-1906 in Doddridge Co, WV,[mccclii[1352],17,176,347] d. Jun-28-1986 in Clarksburg, Harrison Co, WV,[847,191,17,176] buried in Ruley Cemetery, Arnolds Creek, Doddridge Co, WV,[17,mcccliii[1353],190] resided in Doddridge Co, WV,[190] occupation well tender.[190] He married Apr- 7-1928 in Greenwood, Doddridge Co, WV,[mcccliv[1354],354,191,mccclv[1355]] Pauline Agnes Davis, b. Jul-24-1911 in Doddridge Co, WV,[190,592,17] (daughter of Stephen T. Davis and Etta Mae Holliday), d. Aug-22-1995 in Arnolds Creek (West Union), Doddridge Co, WV,[190,592] buried in Ruley Cemetery, Arnolds Creek, Doddridge Co, WV,[17] resided in Arnolds Creek (West Union), Doddridge Co, WV,[190] census 1920 in West Union District, Doddridge Co, WV.

    Pauline: Name listed in obituary as Pauline Britton, but in SSDI as Agnes P. Britton. Headstone has simply Pauline. But obituary of son Allen identifies her as Pauline Virginia Davis.[592]

    iv.   WANDA MAE BRITTON b. Jan-24-1912 in Arnolds Creek (West Union), Doddridge Co, WV,[ccclvi[1356],592] d. Mar- 1-2002,[592] resided in Parkersburg, Wood Co, WV,[856,521,592.] She married May-

8-1937 in Parkersburg, Wood Co, WV,[mccclvii][1357] Ora Howard Hurst (son of Joseph J. Hurst and Rosa Marie Brown).

715. **Lelia Myrtle "Lee" Perine** (395.Richard[8], 241.Matilda[7], 134.Andrew[6], 72.John[5], 21.John[4], 6.Hugh[3], 3.John[2], 1.Jean[1]), b. Aug-21-1878 in Doddridge Co, WV,[mccclviii][1358] d. Sep-12-1945 in Doddridge Co, WV,[347] buried in Ruley Cemetery, Arnolds Creek, Doddridge Co, WV,[17] census 1930 in West Union District, Doddridge Co, WV. She married Apr- 1-1895 in Oakland, Garrett Co, MD,[347] **Alfred Kenneth Rollins**, b. Jan-10-1873 in Doddridge Co, WV,[347,190] (son of Hiram Rollins and Mary E. Gain), d. Apr-25-1950 in Clarksburg, Harrison Co, WV,[806] buried in Ruley Cemetery, Arnolds Creek, Doddridge Co, WV,[190,347] resided in Salem, WV,[190] census 1930 in West Union District, Doddridge Co, WV. 1900 Census, Doddridge Co, WV (Central District):
Alfred Rollins, 37, b. Jan 1873; wife Lela, 21, b. Aug 1878; son Ardeen, 3, b. Feb 1897; dau Jona, 1, b. Oct 1898; sister-in-law Dona Prine, 24, b. Apr 1876.

1920 Census, Doddridge Co, WV (West Union District):
Alf K. Rollins, 46; wife Lelia 41; son Arden, 24; dau Jona, 21; son Charles, 16; dau Ollie, 14; dau Monnie, 7.

1930 Census, Doddridge Co, WV (West Union District):
Alfred Rollins, 57; wife Lelia, 52; dau Monnie, 17.

Children:
i.   DANIEL ARDEN ROLLINS, also known as Arden Rollins,[1287,1291,765] b. Feb-12-1896 in Ritchie Co, WV,[190] d. Nov- 4-1973 in Clarksburg, Harrison Co, WV,[190] buried in Masonic Memorial Park Cemetery, Crystal Lake (West Union), WV,[190,721] resided in Smithburg, Doddridge Co, WV,[765,190] census 1920 in West Union District, Doddridge Co, WV, military U.S. Army, World War I,[190] occupation farmer, oil & gas worker, WV Road Commission (retired). He married Mar-16-1923,[484] Lena Rivers Chapman, b. 1903,[721] (daughter of Gordon Batell Chapman and Queen Victoria Pierce), d. Jul-21-1961 in Doddridge Co, WV,[356,484] buried in Masonic Memorial Park Cemetery, Crystal Lake (West Union), WV.[721]
ii. ZONA MARY ROLLINS, census name Jona Rollins, also known as Zoni Rollins, b. Oct- - 1898,[1287] [1900 Census gives age as 1 and birthdate as Oct 1898, but death certificated states birthdate as Oct 9 1899.], d. Jul- 2-1920 in Parkersburg, Wood Co, WV,[521] cause of death accidental shooting,[398] census 1920 in West Union District, Doddridge Co, WV, census 1900 in Central District, Doddridge Co, WV, never married[398.]
iii. CHARLIE HIRAM ROLLINS b. Apr- 6-1903 in Doddridge Co, WV,[mccclix][1359],190,592] d. Aug-29-1999 in Parkersburg, Wood Co, WV,[190,347,592] buried in Sunset Memory Gardens, Parkersburg, WV,[190] [Chapel of Peace Mausoleum.], resided in Parkersburg, Wood Co, WV,[765] resided 1934 in West Union, Doddridge Co, WV,[436] census 1920 in West Union District, Doddridge Co, WV.

Retired in 1965 from the City of Parkersburg, where he worked as a heavy equipment operator. In that capacity, he participated in the building of the Wood County Airport and the Parkersburg Flood Wall.[190]

He married[484,347] (1) Donna Lucille Maxwell, b. Oct-20-1908 in Doddridge Co, WV,[154,46] (daughter of Lewis Brent Maxwell and Icie D. Michael), d. Oct-26-1934 in Clarksburg, Harrison Co, WV,[398,46] buried in Michael (aka Oxford) Cemetery, Oxford, Doddridge Co, WV,[17,398] cause of death infection following miscarriage,[398] resided in West Union, Doddridge Co, WV.[398] He married[347] (2) Pearl Mae Masten, b. Aug-14-1916,[592] d. Mar-27-1999.[592]
iv. OLLIE L. ROLLINS b. Nov-12-1905,[592,775] d. Mar- 2-1991,[592] resided in Tucson, Pima Co, AZ,[765,521,mccclx][1360] census 1920 in West Union District, Doddridge Co, WV. She married[1101] ___ Russell.
v.   MONNIE B. ROLLINS[347] b. Nov-21-1912 in Ritchie Co, WV,[398,354] d. Jun-13-1969 in Clarksburg, Harrison Co, WV,[398] buried in K of P Memorial Park Cemetery, Salem, WV,[398] resided in Salem, WV,[765,398] census 1920, 1930 in West Union District, Doddridge Co, WV. She married[941]

Dennis Rex Williams, also known as Rex Williams, b. Jun-15-1912 at Shirley, Tyler Co, WV,[190],[354] (son of Archie D. Williams and Carrie Hutson), d. Dec-26-1968 in Salem, WV,[700] buried in K of P Memorial Park Cemetery, Salem, WV,[190] resided in Salem, WV,[190] occupation Consolidated Gas Co.[190]

716. **Ada May Perine** (395.Richard[8], 241.Matilda[7], 134.Andrew[6], 72.John[5], 21.John[4], 6.Hugh[3], 3.John[2], 1.Jean[1]), b. Oct-23-1886 in Doddridge Co, WV,[mccclxi[1361]] d. Jun- 8-1970 in Doddridge Co, WV,[17],[347] buried in Ruley Cemetery, Arnolds Creek, Doddridge Co, WV,[17] resided 1935, 51, 54, 58 in Charleston, Kanawha Co, WV,[mccclxii[1362]],[521],[484],[412] census 1930 in Charleston, Kanawha Co, WV, census 1910, 1920 in Clark District, Harrison Co, WV. She married Jan- 4-1908 in Doddridge Co, WV,[mccclxiii[1363]],[354] **Jacob C. Netzer**, b. Mar-23-1886 in Doddridge Co, WV,[17],[mccclxiv[1364]] (son of George Washington Netzer and Exelissa Cottrill), d. Oct-25-1954 in Charleston, Kanawha Co, WV,[398],[17] buried in Ruley Cemetery, Arnolds Creek, Doddridge Co, WV,[17] resided in Charleston, Kanawha Co, WV,[398] census 1930 in Charleston, Kanawha Co, WV, census 1910, 1920 in Clark District, Harrison Co, WV, census 1900 in New Milton, Doddridge Co, WV,[1364] occupation 1910 snapper in glass house,[458] occupation 1920 rung man at glass plant,[418] occupation 1930 messenger for State of West Virginia.[1132]

Children:
    i.   HARRY G. NETZER b. Feb- 5-1910,[592] d. Jun- -1977,[592] resided in Charleston, Kanawha Co, WV,[592] census 1930 in Charleston, Kanawha Co, WV, census 1910, 1920 in Clark District, Harrison Co, WV.
    ii.   FREDDIE F. NETZER[347] b. ca 1915,[418] census 1930 in Charleston, Kanawha Co, WV, census 1920 in Clark District, Harrison Co, WV.

717. **Lula Blanch Perine** (395.Richard[8], 241.Matilda[7], 134.Andrew[6], 72.John[5], 21.John[4], 6.Hugh[3], 3.John[2], 1.Jean[1]), b. Mar-30-1889 in Arnolds Creek (West Union), Doddridge Co, WV,[mccclxv[1365]],[190] [Obituary of Lula Perine Sullivan gives her birth date as Mar 21 1889 at Arnolds Creek, Doddridge Co. But her birth record states Mar 30 1889.], d. Apr-21-1957 in Morgantown, Monongalia Co, WV,[190] buried in Ruley Cemetery, Arnolds Creek, Doddridge Co, WV,[190] resided 1951 in Morgantown, Monongalia Co, WV.[521] She married Feb-25-1912 in Doddridge Co, WV,[mccclxvi[1366]],[354] **Christopher Columbus "Dick" Sullivan**, also known as Columbus Sullivan,[767],[354] also known as Dick Sullivan, b. Jun-21-1889 in West Union, Doddridge Co, WV,[190],[mccclxvii[1367]] (son of Smith Sullivan and Savilla Ash), d. Dec- 4-1963 in Morgantown, Monongalia Co, WV,[806] buried in Ruley Cemetery, Arnolds Creek, Doddridge Co, WV,[190] resided in Morgantown, Monongalia Co, WV,[190] resided formerly at Arnolds Creek (West Union), Doddridge Co, WV,[190] census 1900 in West Union District, Doddridge Co, WV [Listed in household of George & Nancy (Greathouse) Cottrill as Columbus Sullivan, age 10, servant.], occupation glass worker.[190]

Christopher: Identified in most references as Columbus Sullivan, commonly known as Dick. But identified as Christopher Sullivan in obituary of son Howard, as C. C. Sullivan in wife's obituary, and as Christopher C. (Dick) Sullivan in his own obituary.

Children:
    i.   AUDRA SULLIVAN[347] resided 1963 in Independence, Preston Co, WV,[765] resided 2001 in Morgantown, Monongalia Co, WV.[521] She married[347] Thomas Clyde Smith, b. Nov-14-1917 in Doddridge Co, WV,[347],[1044] (son of Harvey Smith and Mary Virginia Elliott), d. Nov- 5-2000,[592] resided 1972, 2000 in Independence, Preston Co, WV,[856],[592] resided 1993 in Morgantown, Monongalia Co, WV,[521] resided 1957 in West Union, Doddridge Co, WV.[520]
    ii.   MARY SULLIVAN[347].
    iii.   HOWARD K. SULLIVAN[347] b. Feb- 9-1915 in West Union, Doddridge Co, WV,[190] d. Dec- 2-2001 in Puyallup, Pierce Co, WA,[190] buried in Fort Logan National Cem, Denver, CO,[190] resided 1963 in Denver, CO.[765]

Joined the U.S. Army in 1934. He spent 23 years in both the Army and Air Force, retiring as a Master Sergeant in June 1960. Much of his military service was overseas, including Trinidad, Panama, England and Korea, as well as throughout Europe in World War II. His last retirement was from Jefferson County Schools in 1980. Survivors included two grandchildren, Howard of Tacoma, WA, and Amy of Spanaway, WA; and one great-granddaughter, Katelyn Sullivan of Tacoma, WA.[190]

He married Dec-19-1945,[484] Roberta "Judy" Jett, census name Jean Jett,[1291] b. Aug-15-1927 in West Union, Doddridge Co, WV,[190] (daughter of Joseph Jett and Lucy V. Smith), d. Jan-10-2002 in Spanaway, WA,[190] buried in Fort Logan National Cem, Denver, CO,[190] education Doddridge County H.S. (1945),[190] census 1930 in West Union District, Doddridge Co, WV.

Roberta: Lived most of her life as a homemaker in Denver and Golden, CO, before retiring to the state of Washington.[190]

718. **Cora Randolph Southworth** (396.Sarah[8], 241.Matilda[7], 134.Andrew[6], 72.John[5], 21.John[4], 6.Hugh[3], 3.John[2], 1.Jean[1]), b. Jun- 7-1883 in Doddridge Co, WV,[344] d. 1979,[721] buried in IOOF Cemetery (Blockhouse Hill), West Union, WV,[721] [A nearby marker is for Harold H. Hill, 6/20/1916 - 12/18/1944.]. She married[344] **Jesse Homer Hill**, b. 1884,[721] d. 1956,[721] buried in IOOF Cemetery (Blockhouse Hill), West Union, WV.[721]
> Children:
> i. SARAH CAROLINE HILL[519.] She married[519] Frank Leroy Doyle.
> ii. MARY IRENE HILL[519.] She married[519] Robert B. Powell.
> iii. MILDRED VIOLA HILL[519.] She married[519] Glenn M. Duncan.
> iv. HAROLD HOMER HILL[519.] He married[519] Mary Lou __.
> v. ALICE GARLAND HILL[519] b. Sep-29-1918,[592] d. Aug-30-2001,[592] resided in

Parkersburg, Wood Co, WV.[592] She married[519] Scott Fluharty.

719. **Blanche "Doc" Southworth** (396.Sarah[8], 241.Matilda[7], 134.Andrew[6], 72.John[5], 21.John[4], 6.Hugh[3], 3.John[2], 1.Jean[1]), b. Feb- 5-1892 in Reynoldsville, Harrison Co, WV,[344] d. 1957,[721,519] buried in IOOF Cemetery (Blockhouse Hill), West Union, WV.[721] She married[344] **Olin Orwin Hartman**, b. Nov-13-1884 in Howesville, Preston Co, WV,[344] d. 1959,[721,519] buried in IOOF Cemetery (Blockhouse Hill), West Union, WV.[721]
> Children:
> i. EDWARD MARSHALL HARTMAN b. May-20-1909,[592,519] d. May- -1987,[592,519] resided in Greenwood, Sebastian Co, AR.[1275] He married[519] (1) Virginia Belle Coffman, b. 1911,[519] d. 1973.[519] He married[519] (2) Ellen Vera Stoffers, b. Sep-22-1917,[592] d. Mar-30-1992,[592] resided in Greenwood, Sebastian Co, AR,[592] resided formerly in Utah.[mccclxviii][1368]
> ii. ZANA VIRGINIA HARTMAN b. Sep- 4-1911,[519,592] d. Jul-26-2004,[592] resided in Las Vegas, Clark Co, NV,[592] [Social Security card issued in NC/WV before 1951. Name listed in SSDI as Zana V. Zewe.]. She married[519] (1) Lou Merle Keisling. She married[519] (2) Marcus __. She married[519] (3) Louis Nysewander. She married[519] (4) William Zewe.
> iii. OLIN ORWIN HARTMAN, JR. b. Apr- 1-1914,[592,519] d. Oct- 8-2002,[519] resided in Bridgeport, Harrison Co, WV.[519] He married[519] Dorothy Glaydes Nicholas,[519] b. 1911,[519] (daughter of Jeremiah Jedediah Nicholas and Rosa Geneva McKeown), d. 1998.[519]

720. **Chapman J. Perine** (397.Columbus[8], 241.Matilda[7], 134.Andrew[6], 72.John[5], 21.John[4], 6.Hugh[3], 3.John[2], 1.Jean[1]), b. Jan-16-1874 in West Union, Doddridge Co, WV,[398,344] d. Jan-18-1943 in Clarksburg, Harrison Co, WV,[398,344] buried in Ruley Cemetery, Arnolds Creek, Doddridge Co, WV,[17,398] resided in Doddridge Co, WV.[398] He married Jul-29-1894 in Doddridge Co, WV,[354] **Susannah Fleming**,[395] b. May- -1873 in West Union, Doddridge Co, WV,[344] (daughter of Johnson D. Fleming and Arzanna Adams), d. Aug-10-1943 in Doddridge Co, WV,[356,344] buried in Ruley Cemetery, Arnolds Creek, Doddridge Co, WV.[17]
> Children:
> i. JOHN HIRAM PERINE b. May-22-1895 in Arnolds Creek (West Union), Doddridge Co, WV,[190,17,mccclxix[1369],711] d. Feb- 7-1979 in Arnolds Creek (West Union), Doddridge Co,

WV,[mccclxx[1370],17,592] buried in Ruley Cemetery, Arnolds Creek, Doddridge Co, WV,[mccclxxi[1371],190] occupation Columbia Gas Co (42 yrs).[190]

Despite the double-R spelling of his last name on his headstone, all other records have the spelling as Perine, with just one R. It is surmised that he adopted the double-R spelling at some point, as his children seem generally to have been given that form of the name, although his obituary preserved the single-R form for himself and all others. The double-R spelling was also used in his wife's obituary in Dec 1979.

He married Jun-24-1916 in Doddridge Co, WV,[mccclxxii[1372],354] Olga Britton, b. Jul-31-1897 in Doddridge Co, WV,[mccclxxiii[1373],592,mccclxxiv[1374],354] (daughter of George W. Britton, Jr. and Cassa Ann "Cassie" Wagoner), d. Dec-23-1979 in Clarksburg, Harrison Co, WV,[190,mccclxxv[1375]] buried in Ruley Cemetery, Arnolds Creek, Doddridge Co, WV,[190] resided in Arnolds Creek (West Union), Doddridge Co, WV.[484]

ii. GRACE VIRGINIA PERINE, also known as Virginia Grace Perine,[mccclxxvi[1376]] b. Feb-24-1897 in Doddridge Co, WV,[398,344,mccclxxvii[1377]] d. Dec-30-1937 in Snake Run (New Milton), Doddridge Co, WV,[mccclxxviii[1378]] buried in Childers Cemetery, New Milton, Doddridge Co, WV,[398] resided in New Milton, Doddridge Co, WV.[398] She married Aug-25-1934 in West Union, Doddridge Co, WV,[mccclxxix[1379],354] Edward Lee Cox, also known as Ed L. Cox,[354,mccclxxx[1380]] b. Jun-18-1884 in Doddridge Co, WV,[mccclxxxi[1381],1038,mccclxxxii[1382],1377] (son of John S. Cox and Sarah Goldsmith), resided 1932, 37 in New Milton, Doddridge Co, WV,[412,191,436] occupation Constable for Doddridge County in 1930s & 40s.[855]

iii. THERESA HARRIET "RETHA" PERINE[190] b. Jun-26-1899 in Arnolds Creek (West Union), Doddridge Co, WV,[190,mccclxxxiii[1383]] d. Jan-30-1990,[592] buried in Center Point Christian Church Cemetery, Doddridge Co, WV,[190] resided in Salem, WV,[521,190] resided 1989 in Wallace, Harrison Co, WV,[412] census 1930 in Harrison Co, WV. She married May-22-1921 in Doddridge Co, WV,[354,344,191] Arthur Cain, b. Aug-21-1893 in Wetzel Co, WV,[344] (son of Sylvester F. Cain and Rebecca Swiger), d. Feb- -1972,[592] census 1930 in Harrison Co, WV, occupation 1930 sledger at steel plant.[1208]

iv. AGNES LAURA PERINE b. Sep-28-1901,[344] [Birthplace probably Weston, Lewis Co, WV.], d. Jun- 5-1928 in West Union, Doddridge Co, WV,[356,344] buried in Ruley Cemetery, Arnolds Creek, Doddridge Co, WV.[17]

v. SAMUEL R. PERINE b. Mar- 3-1904 in Doddridge Co, WV,[mccclxxxiv[1384],mccclxxxv[1385],190,592,344] [Obituary has birth date of Mar 4 1904, while other records, including birth record, indicate Mar 3 1904.], d. Apr-25-1994 in East Liverpool, Columbiana Co, OH,[592,mccclxxxvi[1386],190] buried in Riverview Cemetery, East Liverpool, OH,[190] resided in East Liverpool, Columbiana Co, OH,[190,592] resided until early 1970s in Clarksburg, Harrison Co, WV,[190] resided formerly in West Virginia,[604] occupation Meter Dept of Clarksburg Water Board (44 yrs, retiring as superintendent).[190] He married[344] Oct-29-1925,[484] Viola Gay Day, b. Mar-27-1907 in West Virginia,[592,mccclxxxvii[1387]] (daughter of Fred L. Day and Ora Shingleton), d. Dec-22-1995 in Ohio,[592,1387] resided in East Liverpool, Columbiana Co, OH.[592]

vi. ALCINDIA A. PERINE[190,592] also known as Alcinda Perine,[521] also known as Arzanna Alcinda Perine,[519,344] b. Nov- 1-1907 in West Union, Doddridge Co, WV,[190,592,mccclxxxviii[1388]] d. Aug-31-1989,[190,592] resided in Clarksburg, Harrison Co, WV,[190,592] occupation school teacher - 41 yrs in Doddridge & Harrison Counties.[190] She married Jan-22-1941 in Salem, WV,[1388,191] Harlin James Bode, also known as James Bode,[mccclxxxix[1389],1388] census name Harland J. Bode,[mcccxc[1390]] b. Dec-20-1917 in Porto Rico (New Milton), Doddridge Co, WV,[190,592] (son of Alfred A. "Dutch" Bode and Gertrude F. Schulte), d. Aug- 3-1994 in Clarksburg, Harrison Co, WV,[190,592] resided in Clarksburg, Harrison Co, WV,[190] resided 1951 in Blandville, Doddridge Co, WV,[765] occupation skilled laborer, Clarksburg Water Board,[190] military U.S. Army, World War II.[190]

vii. BENJAMIN H. PERINE b. Dec-10-1910 in Doddridge Co, WV,[344,592] d. Sep-24-1980,[344,592] buried in Mt. Olivet Cemetery, Parkersburg, WV,[344] resided in Parkersburg, Wood Co, WV,[592] census 1930 at Arnolds Creek (West Union), Doddridge Co, WV. He married[344,mcccxci[1391]] Rachel Amelia Smith, b. Mar- 8-1916 in Doddridge Co, WV,[mcccxcii[1392]] (daughter of Harvey Smith and Mary Virginia Elliott), resided 1972, 93, 2002, 06 in Parkersburg, Wood Co, WV,[856,521,1391,395] occupation school cook, Jefferson Elementary, Wood Co WV (retired in 1979).[1391]

viii. SUSANNA BLANCHE PERINE[344] also known as Blanche,[521,412] b. Apr-23-1914 at Arnolds Creek (West Union), Doddridge Co, WV,[190,592] d. Oct-21-2002 in Columbus, Franklin Co, OH,[806,592] buried Lee Memorial Park in Lehigh Acres, Lee Co, FL,[190] resided in Columbus, Franklin Co, OH,[521,mccexciii[1393]] resided 1989, 90 in Morgantown, Monongalia Co, WV,[412] resided 1979 in Lehigh Acres, Lee Co, FL,[521] census 1930 at Arnolds Creek (West Union), Doddridge Co, WV,[1291] occupation Methodist minister.[190]

Among others, survived by six grandchildren, Walter Jefferson Cain III, Jerry Allen Cain, Jeanette Cain and Jonathan Cain, all of Urbana, OH, and David Cain and Daniel Cain, both of Morgantown; ten great-grandchildren; and three great-great-children.

She married[1101,424] Walter Jefferson Cain, b. Oct-20-1914,[592] (son of Lloyd W. Cain and Fannie Laverna Swiger), d. Feb-22-1988,[592] resided in Lehigh Acres, Lee Co, FL,[592] resided formerly in West Virginia.[604]

721. **Lillie May Perine**, census name Lily,[mccexciv[1394]] (397.Columbus⁸, 241.Matilda⁷, 134.Andrew⁶, 72.John⁵, 21.John⁴, 6.Hugh³, 3.John², 1.Jean¹), b. Oct-16-1875 in Doddridge Co, WV,[354,398,46] d. Mar-18-1928 in Pine Grove, Wetzel Co, WV,[398,46] buried in Five Oaks Cemetery, Alvy, Tyler Co, WV,[mccexcv[1395]] [Death record states burial location as Stringtown, W.Va. There are three communities by that name in West Virginia, one in Marion County (south of Mannington), one in Barbour County (near Belington), and one Roane County west of Looneyville. But a headstone for her is reported at Five Oaks Cemetery, located about 1/3 mile from Alvy Church of Christ in Tyler County.], census 1900, 1910, 1920 in McElroy District, Tyler Co, WV. She married Jun-26-1898 in Doddridge Co, WV,[354,344] **Rufus Lemasters**, also known as Ruffis LeMasters,[344] b. Dec- -1872 in Tyler Co, WV,[mccexcvi[1396],354] (son of Francis M. Lemasters and Emily J. __), d. Feb-23-1917 in Alvy, Tyler Co, WV,[mccexcvii[1397]] buried in Five Oaks Cemetery, Alvy, Tyler Co, WV,[mccexcviii[1398]] cause of death suicide,[1397] census 1880, 1900, 1910 in McElroy District, Tyler Co, WV, occupation carpenter.[1397]

1910 Census, Tyler Co, WV (McElroy District), enumerated on May 9 1910:
Rufus Lemasters, 37, farmer, married 11 yrs; wife Lily M, 34, mother of 5 children (all still living); son Francis M, 10; dau Ruby J, 7; dau Ruth, 4; son Columbus D, 2; dau Nellie, 6 months.

1920 Census, Tyler Co, WV (McElroy District), enumerated on Jan 17 1920 at Indian Creek Road:
Lillie M. Lemasters, 43, widowed; son Frank, 19; dau Ruby J. Allen, 17, son-in-law Zadith Allen, 19; dau Ruth M, 14; son Columbus D, 12; dau Nellie M, 10; dau Nettie, 7; dau Stella, 4 yr 11 mo; grandson William F. Allen, under one month.

Children:
i. FRANCIS MARION LEMASTERS, census name Frank Lemasters,[mccexcix[1399]] b. ca 1901 in Tyler Co, WV,[1125,1394] resided 1925 in Alvy, Tyler Co, WV,[1125] census 1930 in Hastings, Wetzel Co, WV, census 1910, 1920 in McElroy District, Tyler Co, WV, occupation 1930 stationary engineer at gas plant.[mcd[1400]] He married[446] Jun- 6-1925 in New Martinsville, Wetzel Co, WV,[1125] Alwilda Alice Hayes, also known as Alice Hays,[446] census name Allice E.,[1400] b. ca 1903 in Wetzel Co, WV,[1125] census 1930 in Hastings, Wetzel Co, WV, resided 1925 in Jacksonburg, Wetzel Co, WV.[1125]
ii. RUBY JANE LEMASTERS b. 1902,[46,1394] d. 1940,[46] buried in Five Oaks Cemetery, Alvy, Tyler Co, WV,[1398] census 1930 in Pine Grove, Wetzel Co, WV, census 1910, 1920 in McElroy District, Tyler Co, WV. She married[1399] ca 1919,[1400] Martin Zadith Allen, census name Zadith Allen,[1399] b. 1900,[46] d. 1940,[46] buried in Five Oaks Cemetery, Alvy, Tyler Co, WV,[1398] census 1930 in Pine Grove, Wetzel Co, WV, census 1920 in McElroy District, Tyler Co, WV, occupation 1930 repairman for Hope Gas Co.[1400]
iii. RUTH M. LEMASTERS b. 1905 in Tyler Co, WV,[mcdi[1401],46] d. 1992,[46] buried in Alvy Church of Christ Cemetery, Alvy, Tyler Co, WV,[1398] resided 1926 in Alvy, Tyler Co, WV,[1401] census 1910, 1920, 1930 in McElroy District, Tyler Co, WV. She married Sep-16-1926 in Tyler Co, WV,[1401] Burley Oscar Baker, b. ca 1906 in Tyler Co, WV,[1401] (son of Kinsey R. Baker and Rosetta Ash), d. Jul-23-1962 in Alvy, Tyler Co, WV,[1397] buried in Alvy Church of Christ Cemetery, Alvy, Tyler Co, WV,[1398]

cause of death lung cancer,[1397] census 1930 in McElroy District, Tyler Co, WV, resided 1926 in Alvy, Tyler Co, WV,[1401] occupation Weirton Steel,[1397] occupation 1930 laborer in oil fields.[mcdii[1402]]

iv.   COLUMBUS DAVID LEMASTERS b. Jan- 5-1908,[592,46] d. May- -1980,[592,46] buried in Alvy Church of Christ Cemetery, Alvy, Tyler Co, WV,[1398] census 1910, 1920, 1930 in McElroy District, Tyler Co, WV. He married[191] Apr-20-1929 in Tyler Co, WV,[mcdiii[1403]] Virginia Mae Haught, b. Dec-26-1907 in Tyler Co, WV,[190] (daughter of John Wesley Haught and Rachel Amanda Ashenhart), d. Mar-22-2008 in New Martinsville, Wetzel Co, WV,[190] buried in Alvy Church of Christ Cemetery, Alvy, Tyler Co, WV,[190] resided in New Martinsville, Wetzel Co, WV,[190] resided formerly in Alvy, Tyler Co, WV.[190]

v.   NELLIE M. LEMASTERS b. ca 1909 in Tyler Co, WV,[1394] resided 1929 in Alvy, Tyler Co, WV,[1401] census 1910, 1920 in McElroy District, Tyler Co, WV. She married Jan-15-1929 in Alvy, Tyler Co, WV,[1401] Herbert Stockdale, b. ca 1906 in Tyler Co, WV,[1401] (son of C. E. Stockdale and Nettie McCormick), resided 1929 in Lima, Tyler Co, WV.[1401]

vi.   NETTIE LEMASTERS b. 1912 in Tyler Co, WV,[46,1401] d. 1967,[46] buried in Alvy Church of Christ Cemetery, Alvy, Tyler Co, WV,[1398] resided 1929 in Alvy, Tyler Co, WV,[1401] census 1920 in McElroy District, Tyler Co, WV. She married Mar- 6-1929 in Alvy, Tyler Co, WV,[1401] Ira M. Ash, b. Nov-13-1909 in Tyler Co, WV,[592,46,1401] (son of Thomas F. Ash and Mary McIntyre), d. Jul- -1983,[46,592] buried in Alvy Church of Christ Cemetery, Alvy, Tyler Co, WV,[1398] resided in Weirton, Hancock Co, WV,[604] resided 1929 in Alvy, Tyler Co, WV.[1401]

vii.   STELLA LEMASTERS b. ca 1915,[1399] census 1920 in McElroy District, Tyler Co, WV.

722. **Walter Monroe Perine** (397.Columbus[8], 241.Matilda[7], 134.Andrew[6], 72.John[5], 21.John[4], 6.Hugh[3], 3.John[2], 1.Jean[1]), b. Jun- 4-1877 in West Union, Doddridge Co, WV,[17,347] d. Apr-25-1944 in West Union, Doddridge Co, WV,[17,347] buried in Ruley Cemetery, Arnolds Creek, Doddridge Co, WV,[17] census 1920, 1930 in West Union District, Doddridge Co, WV. He married Dec-10-1902 in West Union, Doddridge Co, WV,[mcdiv[1404],mcdv[1405]] **Mattie Jane Netzer**, b. Jun- -1869 in Greene Co, PA,[767,354] (daughter of Jacob S. Netzer and Nancy Jane Dye), d. Sep- 4-1964 in Parkersburg, Wood Co, WV,[700,17] buried in Ruley Cemetery, Arnolds Creek, Doddridge Co, WV,[17,190] resided in Parkersburg, Wood Co, WV,[190] census 1920, 1930 in West Union District, Doddridge Co, WV, resided 1902 in Doddridge Co, WV.[354]

Children:
i.   HOWARD MCKINLEY PERINE b. Nov-30-1903,[344] census 1910, 1920 in West Union District, Doddridge Co, WV. He married[344] Roberta McDonald.
ii.   FLOSSIE LEE PERINE b. Dec-18-1905 in Doddridge Co, WV,[190,344] d. Oct- 3-1992 in Parkersburg, Wood Co, WV,[190,592] buried in Mt. Harmony Masonic Cemetery, Pennsboro, Ritchie Co, WV,[190,469] resided in West Union, Doddridge Co, WV,[190] resided in Pennsboro, Ritchie Co, WV,[190] census 1910 in West Union District, Doddridge Co, WV. She married[344] 1924,[484] Wheeler Ingram, b. Jun-26-1902 in West Union, Doddridge Co, WV,[989,190] (son of Simon Peter Ingram and Zelphia Britton), d. Jul-11-1955 in West Union, Doddridge Co, WV,[190,989] buried in Ruley Cemetery, Arnolds Creek, Doddridge Co, WV,[190,989] resided in West Union, Doddridge Co, WV,[190] occupation sawmill owner & operator.[190]
iii.   LACY VAUDE PERINE, also known as Vaude Perine,[775,1291] b. Oct-20-1908 in Doddridge Co, WV,[344,592] d. Dec- -1983,[592] resided in Parkersburg, Wood Co, WV,[592] census 1910, 1930 in West Union District, Doddridge Co, WV. She married (1) Feb-20-1926 in Doddridge Co, WV,[354] divorced Raymond Kenneth Rollins, b. Apr-20-1907 in Doddridge Co, WV,[190] (son of Wilmer L. Rollins and Myrtle Emma McGary), d. Oct-24-1964 in Arnolds Creek (West Union), Doddridge Co, WV,[190,356] resided in Baltimore, MD,[765,190] census 1930 in West Union District, Doddridge Co, WV.

Raymond: A resident of Baltimore, he was killed in a tractor accident at his Arnolds Creek farm, where he was visiting for the weekend to do farm work. He was an employee of the Baltimore & Ohio Railroad Company and was vice-chairman of the Federation of Brotherhood of Maintenance & Ways.[190]

She married (2) __ Rowe.
iv.   MATTIE OCAL PERINE, also known as Ocal Perine,[775,1291,354] b. ca 1911 in Doddridge Co, WV,[354,344] d. Jul-18-1964 in Stow, Summit Co, OH,[mcdvi[1406]] resided in Stow, Summit Co, OH,[1406]

census 1920, 1930 in West Union District, Doddridge Co, WV. She married Aug-23-1932 in Doddridge Co, WV,[mcdvii[1407],344] Julius E. Moffatt, b. Feb-24-1910 in Doddridge Co, WV,[354,344,592] (son of Lawrence Moffatt and Zella Knight), d. Feb-21-2003,[592] resided in Cuyahoga Falls, Summit Co, OH,[604] resided 1970 in Stow, Summit Co, OH,[521] census 1930 in West Union District, Doddridge Co, WV.

723. **Laura Perine**, census name Laurie,[775] (397.Columbus[8], 241.Matilda[7], 134.Andrew[6], 72.John[5], 21.John[4], 6.Hugh[3], 3.John[2], 1.Jean[1]), b. Oct-30-1878 in Doddridge Co, WV,[mcdviii[1408]] [Headstone gives birth date as 1879.], d. Jan- 9-1939 in Doddridge Co, WV,[356] [Headstone gives death date as 1938.], buried in Ruley Cemetery, Arnolds Creek, Doddridge Co, WV,[17] census 1920, 1930 in West Union District, Doddridge Co, WV. She married Oct-13-1905 in Doddridge Co, WV,[354,344] **John Wesley Batton**, b. 1871 in Doddridge Co, WV,[46,344] (son of Hezakiah Batton and Emeline Cumberledge), d. Feb-22-1947 in Doddridge Co, WV,[356,46] buried in Ruley Cemetery, Arnolds Creek, Doddridge Co, WV,[17] resided 1905 in Ritchie Co, WV,[354] census 1920, 1930 in West Union District, Doddridge Co, WV.

Children:

i. FRANK CARLISS BATTON[398,356] b. Aug-29-1906 in Ritchie Co, WV,[398,46,354] d. Nov-24-1930 in Doddridge Co, WV,[398,mcdix[1409],356,46] cause of death influenza, pneumonia,[398,1409] buried in Ruley Cemetery, Arnolds Creek, Doddridge Co, WV,[17,398] [Name on headstone: "F. C. Batton"], resided in Jaco Hill, West Union, Doddridge Co, WV,[1409] occupation tool dresser, Murphy Oil Co.[1409] He married[1409] Jan-14-1927 in Doddridge Co, WV,[354] Pearl Childers, b. May- 8-1911,[592] (daughter of Claude Childers and Winnie Yates), d. Mar-17-2008,[592] resided in West Union, Doddridge Co, WV,[412,592] resided 1993 in Sunnyside (West Union), Doddridge Co, WV.[521]

ii. WARDER BRENTON BATTON b. Feb-14-1908 in Doddridge Co, WV,[190] d. Dec- 7-1974 in Morgantown, Monongalia Co, WV,[190] buried in Ruley Cemetery, Arnolds Creek, Doddridge Co, WV,[190,mcdx[1410]] resided in Doe Run (West Union), Doddridge Co, WV,[190] census 1930 in West Union District, Doddridge Co, WV. He married[484] Aug-26-1933 in Doddridge Co, WV,[354] Opal Childers, b. Apr- 4-1913,[17,592] (daughter of Claude Childers and Winnie Yates), d. Aug- 7-1999,[17,592] buried in Ruley Cemetery, Arnolds Creek, Doddridge Co, WV.[17]

iii. BEULAH M. BATTON b. Oct-29-1909,[592] d. Jul- 4-1989,[592] resided in Morgantown, Monongalia Co, WV,[521,592] census 1930 in Central District, Doddridge Co, WV. She married[1101] Sep- 7-1929 in Doddridge Co, WV,[354] Theodore "Ted" McIntyre, b. May-19-1909 in Rosemont, Taylor Co, WV,[398] (son of Oliver McIntyre and Iola Hickman), d. Jun- 8-1956 in Morgantown, Monongalia Co, WV,[398] buried in Ruley Cemetery, Arnolds Creek, Doddridge Co, WV,[398] resided near Morgantown, Monongalia Co, WV,[398] census 1930 in Central District, Doddridge Co, WV, occupation coal miner.[398]

iv. PAULINE IDA BATTON[419,521] b. Nov-24-1911 in Doddridge Co, WV,[190,592] d. Nov-22-2005 in Wallace, Harrison Co, WV,[764,592] buried in Lumberport Lions Cemetery, Harrison Co, WV,[190] resided in Lumberport, Harrison Co, WV,[521,592] resided 1930 in Wallace, Harrison Co, WV,[419] census 1930 in West Union District, Doddridge Co, WV. She married[1101] May- 6-1930 in Clarksburg, Harrison Co, WV,[191,mcdxi[1411]] Ernest Everett Williams, b. Feb-16-1914 in Harrison Co, WV,[592] (son of Samuel Preston Williams and Theresa Maude "Tressie" Pope), d. Apr-23-1974,[191,592] resided in Lumberport, Harrison Co, WV,[765,592] resided 1930 in Wallace, Harrison Co, WV,[419] census 1920 in Grant District, Doddridge Co, WV.

v. LONA BELLE BATTON, census name Lonie Batton,[775] b. Nov-30-1913,[190] d. Jan- 7-2008,[190] buried in Masonic Memorial Park Cemetery, Crystal Lake (West Union), WV,[190] resided in West Union, Doddridge Co, WV,[521,412,190,775] census 1930 in West Union District, Doddridge Co, WV, never married[521,190].

vi. EVERETT ALLEN "DUMP" BATTON[17,191] b. Feb-10-1916 in Doddridge Co, WV,[190,592,46] d. Apr-29-1995 in West Union, Doddridge Co, WV,[700,592,46] buried in Ruley Cemetery, Arnolds Creek, Doddridge Co, WV,[17,190] resided in West Union, Doddridge Co, WV,[521,592,190] census 1930 in West Union District, Doddridge Co, WV.

He was retired from Britton Rest Hom in West Union (Sunnyside), where he had been employed as a caretaker and aide. He had formerly worked as a carpenter in Ohio, and had also worked in the oil and gas fields of West Virginia.[190]

He married Aug- -1947,[484] Wanda E. Baumgard, b. Dec-13-1921 in New Matamoras, Washington Co, OH,[190,592,46] (daughter of Leo Benjamin Baumgard and Lizzie Ella Smith), d. Sep-18-1995 in Burning Springs, Wirt Co, WV,[190,592,46] buried in Ruley Cemetery, Arnolds Creek, Doddridge Co, WV,[17,190] resided in Elizabeth, Wirt Co, WV,[592] resided formerly in West Union, Doddridge Co, WV,[190] occupation Nurse's Aide at Britton Rest Home at Sunnyside in Doddridge Co,[190] education New Matamoras High School.[190]

       vii.   HARVEY SCOTT BATTON, also known as Scott Batton,[190,521,412] b. Mar-12-1920 in Doddridge Co, WV,[190,46] d. Jun-14-1970 in North Ridgeville, Lorain Co, OH,[190,46] buried in Ruley Cemetery, Arnolds Creek, Doddridge Co, WV,[190,17] resided in North Ridgeville, Lorain Co, OH,[190] census 1930 in West Union District, Doddridge Co, WV, occupation employed at a garage in Lakewood OH,[190] military U.S. Army, World War II.[190,17] He married[484] Loraine Cunningham, resided 1970 in North Ridgeville, Lorain Co, OH.[484]

724. **Louis Perine**[713] also known as Lewis Perine,[354,357] (397.Columbus[8], 241.Matilda[7], 134.Andrew[6], 72.John[5], 21.John[4], 6.Hugh[3], 3.John[2], 1.Jean[1]), b. Dec-25-1881 in Doddridge Co, WV,[mcdxii[1412]] d. Jul- 1-1903 in Sugar Camp (New Milton), Doddridge Co, WV,[344,mcdxiii[1413]] buried in Arnolds Creek Christian Church, Doddridge Co, WV.[344] He married May-25-1902 in Doddridge Co, WV,[354] **Myrtle Holliday**, b. ca 1884 in Gilmer Co, WV.[354]
       Children:
       i.   LEWIS C. PERINE b. Jun-27-1903.[344]

725. **Emery Goff Perine**, also known as Goff Perine,[190,767] (397.Columbus[8], 241.Matilda[7], 134.Andrew[6], 72.John[5], 21.John[4], 6.Hugh[3], 3.John[2], 1.Jean[1]), b. Oct-25-1886 in Doddridge Co, WV,[mcdxiv[1414],46] d. Mar-6-1972,[592,46] buried in Ruley Cemetery, Arnolds Creek, Doddridge Co, WV,[mcdxv[1415]] resided in Weirton, Hancock Co, WV,[190] resided formerly in West Union, Doddridge Co, WV,[190,748] occupation farmer.[190] He married Jul- 4-1911 in West Union, Doddridge Co, WV,[mcdxvi[1416],354,191,484] **Maggie Lee Bonnell**, b. Aug-22-1891 in Doddridge Co, WV,[190,46] (daughter of Johnathan Bonnell and Mary Catherine "Kate" Jones), d. Sep-21-1966 in West Union, Doddridge Co, WV,[700,484] buried in Ruley Cemetery, Arnolds Creek, Doddridge Co, WV,[17,190] resided in West Union, Doddridge Co, WV.[190]
       Children:
       i.   LILLIAN MARY PERINE b. Jun- 5-1913 in Doddridge Co, WV,[190,592,344] [John Mark Perine gives birthplace as Blandville, but obituary says West Union.], d. Mar- 3-1991 in Pittsburgh, Allegheny Co, PA,[190,592] buried in Masonic Memorial Park Cemetery, Crystal Lake (West Union), WV,[721] resided 1966, 72, 91 in Weirton, Hancock Co, WV,[856,765,190]. She married (1) Jan-27-1934 in Smithburg, Doddridge Co, WV,[mcdxvii[1417],354,344] James Albert Kimball, b. 1909 in Doddridge Co, WV,[1417,721] (son of Samuel Kenard Kimball and Macy M. Murphy), d. 1951,[721] buried in Masonic Memorial Park Cemetery, Crystal Lake (West Union), WV,[721] census 1920 in West Union District, Doddridge Co, WV. She married (2) Jun-27-1959 in West Union, Doddridge Co, WV,[mcdxviii[1418]] Carson Otto Swiger,[1418] b. Aug- 3-1918 in Doddridge Co, WV,[190,1418,592] (son of John Benton Swiger and Allie Mae Riffee), d. Oct-18-1988 in Weirton, Hancock Co, WV,[190,592] buried in Freeman Cemetery, Piggin Run, West Union, WV,[190] resided in Weirton, Hancock Co, WV,[mcdxix[1419],856,521,190] census 1930 in Central District, Doddridge Co, WV, occupation Weirton Steel, Tin Mill Dept (30 yrs).[190]
       ii.   HARRY GOFF PERINE b. Jun-17-1916 in Market, Doddridge Co, WV,[190,17] d. Apr-19-1994 in Clarksburg, Harrison Co, WV,[190,17] buried in Ruley Cemetery, Arnolds Creek, Doddridge Co, WV,[17] resided in Greenwood, Doddridge Co, WV,[190] resided 1991 in Pennsboro, Ritchie Co, WV,[412] resided 1966 in West Union, Doddridge Co, WV,[856] occupation truck driver - Smith Lumber Co (retired 1977, 24 yrs).[190] He married Jan-14-1939 in Smithburg, Doddridge Co, WV,[191,484,344] Mabel Pauline Elliott, also known as Pauline Elliott,[190,765,502] b. Aug-21-1922 in Doddridge Co, WV,[190,17,344] (daughter of Alfred Raymond Elliott and Tressie M. White), d. May- 9-1977 in Clarksburg, Harrison Co, WV,[190,344,17] buried in Ruley Cemetery, Arnolds Creek, Doddridge Co, WV,[17] resided in Doddridge Co, WV.[765]
       iii.   VONDA LENORA PERINE b. Aug-28-1923 in West Union, Doddridge Co, WV,[344] d. Sep-18-1994,[592] resided in Clarksburg, Harrison Co, WV,[856,765,412,521,592.] She married Dec- 4-1943 in Smithburg, Doddridge Co, WV,[344] Jack Franklin Walls, b. Dec-22-1922,[592] d. Apr-12-2001,[592] resided in Clarksburg, Harrison Co, WV.[592]

iv. EVERETT LEE PERINE b. Jul- 4-1925 in Arnolds Creek (West Union), Doddridge Co, WV,[344,17] d. Apr-11-1997 in Harrison Co, WV,[344,17] buried in Ruley Cemetery, Arnolds Creek, Doddridge Co, WV,[17] resided in West Union, Doddridge Co, WV,[856,412,521.] He married Sep- 4-1954 in Central Station, Doddridge Co, WV,[344] Mary Lee Greathouse, b. Nov-12-1929 in Doddridge Co, WV,[190,mcdxx[1420],344,592] (daughter of Henry George Greathouse and Vallie Gay Jones), d. Feb-15-1993 in Clarksburg, Harrison Co, WV,[190,344,592] buried in Masonic Memorial Park Cemetery, Crystal Lake (West Union), WV,[344] resided in West Union, Doddridge Co, WV.[592]

v. LIVING. She married Forest Leland Williams, census name Forrest L. Williams,[1304] b. ca 1926 in Doddridge Co, WV,[711] (son of Lorin Harold "Lonnie" Williams and Gertrude Leona Hoalcraft), d. bef Jan 2005,[856] resided 1948 in Clarksburg, Harrison Co, WV,[711] census 1930 in Central District, Doddridge Co, WV.

vi. GLADYS ROBERTA "BERTIE" PERINE, also known as Roberta,[856,765] b. Sep-18-1932 in Arnolds Creek (West Union), Doddridge Co, WV,[190,344] d. Feb-15-2000 in Long Run, Salem, Harrison Co, WV,[190,344] buried in Ruley Cemetery, Arnolds Creek, Doddridge Co, WV,[190,344] resided in Long Run, Salem, Harrison Co, WV,[190] occupation Custodian at Salem-Teikyo University.[190] She married Dec- 1-1951 in West Union, Doddridge Co, WV,[711,1357] Lloyd Brooks Bonnell, b. Oct- 8-1927,[344] (son of David Edward Bonnell and Nellie Gay Ford), d. Feb-17-1985,[191,344] buried in Ruley Cemetery, Arnolds Creek, Doddridge Co, WV.[344]

726. **Luther Martin Perine**[344] (397.Columbus[8], 241.Matilda[7], 134.Andrew[6], 72.John[5], 21.John[4], 6.Hugh[3], 3.John[2], 1.Jean[1]), b. Jul-29-1887 in Doddridge Co, WV,[mcdxxi[1421]] d. Sep- 5-1977 in Clarksburg, Harrison Co, WV,[806,mcdxxii[1422]] buried in Ruley Cemetery, Arnolds Creek, Doddridge Co, WV,[17,190] occupation farmer.[190]

Luther Martin Perine and his brother Irvin Scott Perine married twin sisters, Beulah and Ila Hess.

He married Dec-24-1914 in West Union, Doddridge Co, WV,[mcdxxiii[1423],354] [Husband's obituary gives marriage date of Dec 14 1914, but marriage record states Dec 24 1914.], **Beulah (twin) Hess**, b. Sep-15-1888 in Blandville, Doddridge Co, WV,[190,344] (daughter of Peter Hess and Lizar M. Bland), d. Sep- 7-1968 in Clarksburg, Harrison Co, WV,[806,484,344] buried in Ruley Cemetery, Arnolds Creek, Doddridge Co, WV,[730,190] resided in West Union, Doddridge Co, WV.[521]

Children:

i. EDITH PEARL PERINE b. 1910,[344,46] d. Nov- 2-1963 in Doddridge Co, WV,[356,46] buried in Ruley Cemetery, Arnolds Creek, Doddridge Co, WV.[730] She married[344] Robert Lyons.

ii. ALICE OPAL PERINE b. Sep-27-1915 in West Union, Doddridge Co, WV,[190,344,592] d. Jun- 4-1992 in Parkersburg, Wood Co, WV,[190,344,mcdxxiv[1424]] buried in IOOF Cemetery, Harrisville, Ritchie Co, WV,[344] resided 1977 in Hurst, Lewis Co, WV,[765] resided 1968 in Parkersburg, Wood Co, WV.[856] She married[344] (2) John Barnes. She married[344] (3) Edwin Bruce McConnell, b. 1911 in Doddridge Co, WV,[344,519] d. Jun-__-1945 in Doddridge Co, WV.[344,519] She married[1040,941] (4) __ Ward.

iii. MARTHA JANE PERINE b. Mar-15-1918 in Blandville, Doddridge Co, WV,[344,190] d. Apr-29-1996 in Parkersburg, Wood Co, WV,[190,344] resided 1977, 92, 96 in Ellenboro, Ritchie Co, WV,[765,412,190] resided 1968, 95 in Harrisville, Ritchie Co, WV.[856,521] She married[344] (1) Aug- 8-1946 in West Union, Doddridge Co, WV,[mcdxxv[1425]] Arthur Wesley Nelson, b. Oct- 6-1920 in Wheeling, Ohio Co, WV,[1425,17,344] (son of John Nelson and Anna __), d. Aug-25-1970 in Parkersburg, Wood Co, WV,[344,17] buried in Ruley Cemetery, Arnolds Creek, Doddridge Co, WV,[17] military World War II - Purple Heart.[17] She married[191,344] (2) aft 1980, Charles Wayne Perine, also known as Wayne Perine,[775,334,765] b. Mar-27-1910 in Doddridge Co, WV,[1334] (son of Waitman T. "Willie" Perine and Georgia May Garrison), d. Aug- 3-2000 in Ellwood City, Lawrence Co, PA,[347] buried in West Virginia,[347] resided 1951 in New Castle, Lawrence Co, PA,[765] census 1930 in Butler Co, PA,[334] census 1920 in Doddridge Co, WV.[775] Charles Wayne Perine and Martha Jane Perine were second cousins, by virtue of both being great-grandchildren of David L. Perine & Matilda Gaston.

iv. CHARLEY LUTHER PERINE b. Jul- 5-1920 in Arnolds Creek (West Union), Doddridge Co, WV,[190,mcdxxvi[1426],17] d. Jun- 7-1995 in Arnolds Creek (West Union), Doddridge Co, WV,[190,mcdxxvii[1427],17] buried in Mt. Harmony Masonic Cemetery, Pennsboro, Ritchie Co, WV,[1427,17] resided in Arnolds Creek (West Union), Doddridge Co, WV,[190] resided 1968 in Clarksburg, Harrison Co, WV,[856] military U.S. Army, World War II.[190,17]

He was a retired truck driver for Central Supply of Clarksburg, with 22 years of service. He was also employed in the construction trade. His name was always seen as Charley, except in his mother's and father's obituaries, where he was identified as Charles L. Perine. In his own obituary and on his headstone, it was Charley L. Perine.[190]

He married (1) Living. He married (2) Living.

v.   HELEN PEARL PERINE b. May-15-1923 in Doddridge Co, WV,[344] resided 2003, 06, 08 in Arnolds Creek (West Union), Doddridge Co, WV,[mcdxxviii[1428],mcdxxix[1429],521] resided 1968, 77, 92, 95, 96 in West Union, Doddridge Co, WV,[856,765,412,521.] She married[344,519] Jan-30-1943 in West Union, Doddridge Co, WV,[mcdxxx[1430],484] Paul Harvey Smith, b. Jan-18-1922 in West Union, Doddridge Co, WV,[190,mcdxxxi[1431],344] [Numerous name variations are found in official records. Doddridge Co Birth Records identify him as Harry [sic] Paul Smith Jr., son of Harvy [sic] Smith & Virginia Elliott. But all other public records, including his marriage & death records, his grave marker, as well as his obituary and the death record of his son Terry, identify him as Paul H. Smith. Since his older half-brother was named Harvey Smith Jr., it is likely that the birth record entry was in error.] (son of Harvey Smith and Mary Virginia Elliott), d. Nov-23-1993 in Arnolds Creek (West Union), Doddridge Co, WV,[190,mcdxxxii[1432],344] buried in Cabin Run Cemetery, Doddridge Co, WV,[190,357] resided in Arnolds Creek (West Union), Doddridge Co, WV,[190] resided 1957 in West Union, Doddridge Co, WV,[520] military U.S. Army - World War II.[190]

Paul: He was a self-employed sawmill operator and the owner of West Union Taxi and Transfer Company. He was the chief Fire Marshal of Doddridge County from the mid-1950s until his death.[190]

vi.   LIVING. He married Patricia Louise Hardman, b. Mar-25-1928 in Parkersburg, Wood Co, WV,[mcdxxxiii[1433],344,190] (daughter of Charles Roscoe Hardman and Ethel Maude Rexroad), d. Nov- 1-2005 in Parkersburg, Wood Co, WV,[mcdxxxiv[1434]] buried in IOOF Cemetery, Harrisville, Ritchie Co, WV,[190] resided in Harrisville, Ritchie Co, WV,[190] education Harrisville H. S. (1946).[190]

Patricia: She was an active member of the First Apostolic Church in Harrisville, which her husband pastored for 31 years. She served as pianist, organist and Sunday School teacher, and was Ladies Auxiliary President and Secretary/Treasurer. She assisted as a cook at the Youth Camp at Point Pleasant for several years.[190]

vii.   RICHIE COLUMBUS PERINE, also known as Columbus Ritchie Perine,[711] b. Mar-27-1930 at Arnolds Creek (West Union), Doddridge Co, WV,[190,711] d. Dec-29-2008 in Marietta, Washington Co, OH,[190] buried in IOOF Cemetery, Harrisville, Ritchie Co, WV,[190] resided 1968, 77, 2008 in Ellenboro, Ritchie Co, WV,[856,765,190] resided 1996 in Washington, Wood Co, WV,[412] resided 1992, 95 in Parkersburg, Wood Co, WV,[412,521] occupation welder.[190] He married Oct-16-1953 in Industrial, Doddridge Co, WV,[mcdxxxv[1435],344] Winola Ruth "Winnie" Stickel, b. Aug-27-1935 in Long Run, Salem, Harrison Co, WV,[190,mcdxxxvi[1436]] (daughter of Okey Ernest Stickel and Jessie Pearl Forinash), d. Jun-10-2003 in Pennsboro, Ritchie Co, WV,[mcdxxxvii[1437]] buried in Fairmont Ridge Cemetery, Co Rd 8 near Ellenboro, Ritchie Co, WV,[190] resided in Ellenboro, Ritchie Co, WV.[190]

727. **Irvin Scott Perine** (397.Columbus[8], 241.Matilda[7], 134.Andrew[6], 72.John[5], 21.John[4], 6.Hugh[3], 3.John[2], 1.Jean[1]), b. Jan-16-1889 in Doddridge Co, WV,[mcdxxxviii[1438]] [Name entered in birth record as "Irvin Perine," with date of birth Jan 16 1889. But grave marker, of the type provided by a funeral home, has name spelled "Irven," with birth in year 1890. There is no permanent headstone. Obituary of daughter Esther gives his name as "Ervin."], d. Dec-11-1957 in Weston, Lewis Co, WV,[344,191] buried in Ruley Cemetery, Arnolds Creek, Doddridge Co, WV,[176] census 1930 in New Milton, Doddridge Co,

WV.[1380] He married[344] Apr-24-1910 in Doddridge Co, WV,[354] **Ila (twin) Hess**, b. Sep-15-1888 in Blandville, Doddridge Co, WV,[344,190] (daughter of Peter Hess and Lizar M. Bland), d. Nov-29-1978 in Clarksburg, Harrison Co, WV,[806,592] buried in Ruley Cemetery, Arnolds Creek, Doddridge Co, WV,[190] resided in New Milton, Doddridge Co, WV,[521,592,1380] resided 1968 in Leopold, Doddridge Co, WV.[412]

Ila: Predeceased by three sons, two brothers, and three sisters.[190]
1930 Census, Doddridge Co, WV (New Milton District):
Irvin S. Perine, 40; wife Ila, 41; son Birt, 18; dau Ester, 17; dau Edna, 14; son Carl, 14; dau Nellie, 9; dau Waneda, 7 months.

Children:
i. BERT B. PERINE b. Jan- -1910 in Blandville, Doddridge Co, WV,[344] d. Mar-21-1938 in Doddridge Co, WV,[356,344] buried in West Union, Doddridge Co, WV.[344]
ii. ESTHER VIRGINIA PERINE b. Jan- 6-1912 in New Milton, Doddridge Co, WV,[190,mcdxxxix[1439],344] d. Jun-17-2004 in Brandon, Hillsborough Co, FL,[190] buried in Ruley Cemetery, Arnolds Creek, Doddridge Co, WV,[190] resided in New Milton, Doddridge Co, WV,[856,190] resided 1964 in West Union, Doddridge Co, WV.[484] She married (1) George Lindsey Cox, also known as Lindsey Cox,[446] d. bef May 1972.[446] She married (2) Jan-21-1959 in Smithburg, Doddridge Co, WV,[1439] Brooks Coplin, also known as Robert Brooks Coplin,[374] b. Aug-30-1892 in Toms Fork, Porto Rico, Doddridge Co, WV,[1439] (son of David Ai Coplin and Emma Rose Radcliffe), d. Oct-28-1964 in West Union, Doddridge Co, WV,[356,592,190] resided 1958 in West Union, Doddridge Co, WV,[856,412] occupation Hope Natural Gas Co (retired) and former Doddridge Co schoolteacher,[190] education Salem Academy and Fairmont State Teachers College,[190] military World War I.[190]
iii. EDNA KATHERINE PERINE b. Jun- 5-1915,[344] resided 1978, 2004, 09, 11 in Parkersburg, Wood Co, WV,[856,412,521.] She married[1040,424] Mar-13-1937 in Doddridge Co, WV,[354] Willis Shafer, b. ca 1910.[354]
iv. ERNEST CARL PERINE, also known as Carl Perine,[412,1380,374] b. Feb-17-1918 in Doddridge Co, WV,[419,592] d. Aug- -1975,[592] resided 1940 in West Union, Doddridge Co, WV.[419] He married Apr-15-1940 in West Union, Doddridge Co, WV,[419] Vesta Gladiola Barnes, also known as Vista,[374] b. Jan-19-1922 in Harrison Co, WV,[419] (daughter of Guy Barnes and Bessie Collins), resided 1940 in Dawmont, Harrison Co, WV.[419]
v. NELLIE JANE PERINE b. Jul-17-1920 in Doddridge Co, WV,[190,711] d. Jan-20-2011,[190] buried in Oxford Baptist Church Cemetery, Doddridge Co, WV,[190] resided in New Milton, Doddridge Co, WV,[190,856,412,484,521.] She married[484] May-16-1946 in West Union, Doddridge Co, WV,[mcdxl[1440]] Shirley Oliver Jones,[521] also known as Oliver Jones,[856,765,412,521] b. Aug-11-1912 in Oxford, Doddridge Co, WV,[mcdxli[1441]] [Obituary states birth date as Jan 11 1913, as does headstone, but birth record indicates Aug 11 1912.] (son of Creed Hill Jones and Lenora J. "Jennie" Hileman), d. Feb-10-2006 in Salem, WV,[190] buried in Oxford Baptist Church Cemetery, Doddridge Co, WV,[190,mcdxlii[1442]] resided in New Milton, Doddridge Co, WV,[765,521,190] resided 1951 in Glenville, Gilmer Co, WV,[856] occupation farmer.[190]

Shirley: Among others, survived by one brother, three half-sisters and three half-brothers. Predeceased by five brothers and three sisters.[190]

vi. IRVIN PERINE, JR., also known as Junior Perine,[412,344,519,mcdxliii[1443]] b. Jun-22-1923 in Doddridge Co, WV,[344] d. bef Jun 2004.[412]
vii. LIVING. She married[1040,424] Roy Glen Shafer,[592] also known as Glenn Shaffer,[748] also known as Glen Shafer,[521] b. Sep-12-1928 in Doddridge Co, WV,[592,602] (son of James A. Garfield Shafer and Alva Dovie Nicholson), d. Mar-31-2002,[592] resided in Vienna, Wood Co, WV,[592,521,602] census 1930 in Southwest District, Doddridge Co, WV.
viii. EDWARD EUGENE "GENE" PERINE, also known as Gene Perine,[412,190] b. Sep- 8-1933 at Market, Doddridge Co, WV,[mcdxliv[1444],190] d. Jun-20-2009 in Clarksburg, Harrison Co, WV,[190] buried in Ruley Cemetery, Arnolds Creek, Doddridge Co, WV,[190] resided in Clarksburg, Harrison Co, WV,[190] resided formerly in Smithburg, Doddridge Co, WV,[190] resided 2004 in Pennsboro, Ritchie Co, WV,[412]

resided 1978 in Youngstown, Mahoning Co, OH,[856] occupation sawmill worker, Blaney Hardwoods of Hartford OH (25 yrs).[190] He married (1) Living. He married (2) Living.

728. **Maude Gay Perine**[395] (397.Columbus[8], 241.Matilda[7], 134.Andrew[6], 72.John[5], 21.John[4], 6.Hugh[3], 3.John[2], 1.Jean[1]), b. Oct- -1891 in Doddridge Co, WV,[344] d. Mar-19-1960,[344] buried in Masonic Memorial Park Cemetery, Crystal Lake (West Union), WV.[721] She married Dec-25-1911 in Doddridge Co, WV,[354,344] **Oscar Blaine Bonnell**, b. May-28-1888 in Arnolds Creek (West Union), Doddridge Co, WV,[344] (son of Johnathan Bonnell and Mary Catherine "Kate" Jones), d. Feb-15-1962 in Doddridge Co, WV,[356] buried in Masonic Memorial Park Cemetery, Crystal Lake (West Union), WV.[721]

Children:

i. VIOLET FAYE "TOOTS" BONNELL b. Jun- 4-1914 at Arnolds Creek (West Union), Doddridge Co, WV,[190] d. Mar-22-2005,[190] buried in Masonic Memorial Park Cemetery, Crystal Lake (West Union), WV,[190,721] resided in West Union, Doddridge Co, WV.[190] She married Dec- -1937,[484] [Obituary of husband Carl Doak gives marriage date as Dec 23 1937, but newspaper article of wife's 90th birthday gives their marriage as Dec 3 1937.], Carl A. Doak, b. Nov-19-1916,[721] (son of Averal Doak and Dessie Ash), d. Nov- 8-1985 in Clarksburg, Harrison Co, WV,[190] buried in Masonic Memorial Park Cemetery, Crystal Lake (West Union), WV,[190,721] resided in West Union, Doddridge Co, WV,[190] occupation oil & gas field worker and employed at Drane Hardware Store,[190] military U.S. Army - World War II.[190]

ii. EDITH GAY BONNELL b. Feb-28-1917 in West Union, Doddridge Co, WV,[190] d. May- 6-2001 in Parkersburg, Wood Co, WV,[190] buried in Masonic Memorial Park Cemetery, Crystal Lake (West Union), WV.[190,721]

Survivors included five grandchildren, Angela Stewart, Columbus, OH, Mark Griffith, Belpre, OH, Tammi Weigand, Findlay, OH, Scott Millner and Lori Milner, both of Waterford, OH; and three great-grandchildren, Taylor Stewart and Joe Stewart, both of Columbus, and Todd Griffith, Belpre.[190]

She married Nov-14-1936 in Doddridge Co, WV,[354] Francis H. Dotson, nickname Friz,[191] b. Dec- 2-1913,[592,721] d. May- 2-1982,[191,592] [Obituary of wife states May 2 1982, but headstone reads May 3 1982.], resided in Parkersburg, Wood Co, WV.[592]

iii. PAUL "BUB" BONNELL[412,190] b. Sep-13-1919,[190] d. Jan-28-2007,[190] buried in Masonic Memorial Park Cemetery, Crystal Lake (West Union), WV,[190] resided in West Union, Doddridge Co, WV,[412,190] occupation carpenter, Smith Lumber Co.[190]

iv. JONATHAN PAIGE BONNELL[191,521,412] also known as Paige Bonnell,[592,521,412,721,1291] b. Jul-17-1923,[592] d. Dec-29-1978,[592,191] buried in Masonic Memorial Park Cemetery, Crystal Lake (West Union), WV,[721] resided in West Union, Doddridge Co, WV,[592,1291] occupation Doddridge County Board of Education.[mcdxlv][1445] He married[mcdxlvi][1446] Dec-29-1943,[191] Wilmadine Ruth Swisher, b. Aug-17-1928,[190] (daughter of Ezra Guy Swisher and Esther Gay Gum), d. Jan-11-2006 in West Union, Doddridge Co, WV,[700] resided in West Union, Doddridge Co, WV,[1446,190] occupation Myles Manufacturing, West Union, and Laura May Manufacturing, Pennsboro (41 yrs),[190] education Doddridge County H.S. (1946).[190]

v. FOREST OLIN "BOB" BONNELL b. Nov-22-1927 in Doddridge Co, WV,[190] d. May-25-1981 in Clarksburg, Harrison Co, WV,[190] buried in Masonic Memorial Park Cemetery, Crystal Lake (West Union), WV,[721] resided in West Union, Doddridge Co, WV,[190] occupation carpenter,[190] military U.S. Navy, World War II.[190] He married[484] Margaret Romaine Cox,[721] also known as Romaine Cox,[190,765,856,521,484,412] b. Feb-13-1935 in New Milton, Doddridge Co, WV,[190,mcdxlvii][1447] (daughter of Ora Florent Cox and Ruth L. Richards), d. Aug-23-2008, buried in Masonic Memorial Park Cemetery, Crystal Lake (West Union), WV,[190] resided in West Union, Doddridge Co, WV,[765,521,856,412,190] occupation seamstress, Quality Garments, West Union (25 yrs).

729. **Alice J. "Allie" Perine**, also known as Allie,[357,398] (397.Columbus[8], 241.Matilda[7], 134.Andrew[6], 72.John[5], 21.John[4], 6.Hugh[3], 3.John[2], 1.Jean[1]), b. Jun-29-1896 in Doddridge Co, WV,[398,770,46] d. Jun-26-1931 in West Union, Doddridge Co, WV,[398,770,356,46] buried in Ruley Cemetery, Arnolds Creek, Doddridge Co, WV,[17,398] census 1920, 1930 in West Union District, Doddridge Co, WV. She married[344]

Harvey Filmore Stickle, also known as Harvey Stickel,[775] b. Mar- 9-1891 in Doddridge Co, WV,[mcdxlviii[1448]] [Headstone has birth as 1890, but birth record states Mar 9 1891.] (son of James Rufus Stickle and Elizabeth Roberta Nicholson), d. Dec-13-1953 in Clarksburg, Harrison Co, WV,[398,46] buried in Ruley Cemetery, Arnolds Creek, Doddridge Co, WV,[17,398] resided in West Union, Doddridge Co, WV,[436,398,775] census 1930 in West Union District, Doddridge Co, WV, census 1900 in Greenbrier District, Doddridge Co, WV, occupation laborer, teamster, farmer.[398]

Harvey: Name spelled "Stickle" for himself, as seen in birth record, death record, and on headstone, but generally appears as "Stickel" in records pertaining to his children.

Children:
i.   HOWARD COLUMBUS STICKEL b. Jul- 1-1914 in Doddridge Co, WV,[mcdxlix[1449],604] d. Nov- 7-1962 in Cleveland, Cuyahoga Co, OH,[693,604] resided in Canton, Stark Co, OH,[693] census 1930 in West Union District, Doddridge Co, WV. He married Mar- 3-1934 in Doddridge Co, WV,[mcdl[1450]] Cledith G. Yerkey, b. ca 1913,[354,693] d. Mar- 1-1974 in Canton, Stark Co, OH,[693] resided in Stark Co, OH.[693]

ii.   FERN STICKEL[344] b. ca 1916,[775] census 1920, 1930 in West Union District, Doddridge Co, WV.[775]

iii. HARVEY FILMORE STICKEL, JR., also known as Harvey Jr. Stickel,[191] b. Oct-17-1924 in Doddridge Co, WV,[mcdlii[1451]] resided 2006, 07 in West Union, Doddridge Co, WV,[191,1265] census 1930 in West Union District, Doddridge Co, WV. He married Jan- 3-1951 in Smithburg, Doddridge Co, WV,[mcdlii[1452],191] Melva R. Sutton, b. Nov- 1-1914 in Berea, Ritchie Co, WV,[190,mcdliii[1453]] (daughter of Sherl Sutton and Ava Simmons), d. Aug- 2-2006,[190] buried in Masonic Memorial Park Cemetery, Crystal Lake (West Union), WV,[190] resided in West Union, Doddridge Co, WV,[190] occupation seamstress, Myles Manufacturing (50 yrs).[190]

730. **Don Columbus Perine**, also known as Davie Perine,[713] also known as Columbus Don Perine,[mcdliv[1454]] (397.Columbus[8], 241.Matilda[7], 134.Andrew[6], 72.John[5], 21.John[4], 6.Hugh[3], 3.John[2], 1.Jean[1]), b. Aug- 9-1897 in Doddridge Co, WV,[mcdlv[1455],46] d. 1960,[46,519] buried in Robinson Cemetery, PortoRico/MaxwellRidge Rd, Doddridge Co, WV.[17] He married Mar-25-1919 in West Union, Doddridge Co, WV,[mcdlvi[1456],354] **Ethel Maude Robinson**, b. Apr- -1895 in Doddridge Co, WV,[1364,46] (daughter of Albert W. Robinson and Addie V. Willis), d. Dec-24-1941,[344,46] buried in Robinson Cemetery, PortoRico/MaxwellRidge Rd, Doddridge Co, WV,[17,344] census 1900, 1910 in New Milton District, Doddridge Co, WV.
Children:
i,   MARY MAGDALENE PERINE b. Apr- 4-1920 in Doddridge Co, WV,[mcdlvii[1457],190] d. Nov-13-2002,[190] buried in Floral Hills Memorial Gardens, Quiet Dell, Harrison Co, WV,[190] resided in Reynoldsville, Harrison Co, WV,[521,190] occupation Postmistress, Reynoldsville Post Office.[190] She married[395] (1) Jesse Franklin Bell, also known as Jessie Franklin Bell,[395] b. Jan-17-1922 in Clarksburg, Harrison Co, WV,[419,mcdlviii[1458]] (son of Jesse Homer Bell and Bessie VanHorn), resided 1945, 48 in Salem, WV,[419] occupation farmer.[405] She married[344,519] (2) bef Dec 1958,[1305] Millard Russell Dennison, b. ca 1917,[902] (son of William C. Dennison and Oma Herrod), census 1930 in Greenbrier District, Doddridge Co, WV.

ii.   MARIE OCAL PERINE, also known as Ocal Marie Perine,[412] b. Jun-21-1921,[344] resided 1989 in Stratford, Fairfield Co, CT.[521] She married[344] William Price.

iii. CLYDE BLAINE PERINE b. Nov-23-1922 in West Union, Doddridge Co, WV,[mcdlix[1459],190,592] d. May-26-1989 in Clarksburg, Harrison Co, WV,[190] [SSDI reports death date as May 15 1989, but obituary specifies Friday, May 26 1989. Name listed in SSDI as C. B. Perine.], buried in Sunset Memorial Park Cemetery, Clarksburg, WV,[190] resided in Wolf Summit, Harrison Co, WV,[190] resided 1956 in Meadville, Crawford Co, PA,[1459] military disabled veteran of U.S. Army in WW II (South Pacific).[190] He married Living.

iv.   ERNEST HAROLD PERINE b. Jul-11-1924 in Doddridge Co, WV,[344] d. Aug- 6-1924 in West Union, Doddridge Co, WV.[356,344]

v.   CECIL DON PERINE b. Jun-26-1925,[344] resided 1989, 2003, 05, 09 in Liberty Addition (Clarksburg), Harrison Co, WV,[521,1092,mcdlx[1460],1101.] He married Nov-26-1955,[191] Ruth JoAnn Fittro, also known as JoAnn Fittro,[521] b. Oct-30-1933 in Reynoldsville, Harrison Co, WV,[190,592] (daughter of Charles Edward Fittro and Virginia M. __), d. Dec- 7-1984 in Clarksburg, Harrison Co, WV,[190,592] buried in Masonic Memorial Park Cemetery, Crystal Lake (West Union), WV,[190,721] [Name reads "R. Joann Perine"], resided in Clarksburg, Harrison Co, WV,[592] occupation Stone & Thomas Dept Store.[190]

      vi.   LIVING.

731. **Daisy P. Perine** (397.Columbus[8], 241.Matilda[7], 134.Andrew[6], 72.John[5], 21.John[4], 6.Hugh[3], 3.John[2], 1.Jean[1]), b. Jan-14-1900 in Doddridge Co, WV,[693,mcdlxi[1461]] d. Jun-24-1994 in Stark Co, OH,[693] resided in Louisville, Stark Co, OH.[mcdlxii[1462]] She married Jul-26-1920 in West Union, Doddridge Co, WV,[mcdlxiii[1463],354] **William Carl Squires**, also known as Carl Squires,[592,1290] also known as W. C. Squires,[354] census name Willie C. Squires,[767] b. Apr-23-1890 in Doddridge Co, WV,[592,767,711] (son of Andrew Jackson Squires and Jessie Booker Brown), d. Sep- -1972,[592] resided in Atwater, Portage Co, OH,[mcdlxiv[1464]] census 1900, 1910, 1920 in West Union District, Doddridge Co, WV.
      Children:
      i.   CARL JACKSON SQUIRES b. Jan- 6-1921 in Doddridge Co, WV.
      ii.   EDWARD GALE SQUIRES b. Apr-18-1923.
      iii.   HARRY GOFF SQUIRES.
      iv.   ANNIE SQUIRES.
      v.   HELEN SQUIRES.

732. **Owen Aldo West**[732] (398.Hannah[8], 242.Frances[7], 135.Mary[6], 72.John[5], 21.John[4], 6.Hugh[3], 3.John[2], 1.Jean[1]), b. Apr- 4-1868 in Harrison Co, WV,[754] d. Sep- 3-1942 in Harrison Co, WV,[754] buried in Broad Run Bapt Ch Cem, Jane Lew, Lewis Co, WV,[754] census 1920 in Grant District, Harrison Co, WV,[754] resided 1942 in Harrison Co, WV,[754] occupation Farmer.[754]

Owen Aldo West and his brother Olandus West married sisters.[732]

He married Nov-28-1894 in Harrison Co, WV,[754] **Eliza Ann McWhorter**, b. Feb-10-1877 in Harrison Co, WV,[754] (daughter of John M. McWhorter and Mary M. Davisson), d. May-16-1952 in Harrison Co, WV,[754] buried in Broad Run Bapt Ch Cem, Jane Lew, Lewis Co, WV.[754]
      Children:
      i.   MABEL ANN WEST b. Nov- 1-1907 in McWhorter, Harrison Co, WV,[754] baptized Broad Run Baptist Ch in Lewis Co, WV, d. Dec-22-1975 in Clarksburg, Harrison Co, WV,[754] buried in Broad Run Bapt Ch Cem, Jane Lew, Lewis Co, WV,[754] education Mount Holyoke College, and MA from Columbia University,[754] never married[735.]

733. **Dora E. Edmonds** (400.Mary[8], 243.Ruanna[7], 135.Mary[6], 72.John[5], 21.John[4], 6.Hugh[3], 3.John[2], 1.Jean[1]), b. 1865,[754] d. 1954,[754] buried in Brick Church (7th Day Baptist) Cemetery, Lost Creek, Harrison Co, WV.[754] She married[754] **Herman A. Bell**, b. 1866,[754] (son of Alvin I. Bell and Mary E. Steele), d. 1949,[754] buried in Brick Church (7th Day Baptist) Cemetery, Lost Creek, Harrison Co, WV,[754] census 1900 in Grant District, Harrison Co, WV,[754] census 1870 in New Milton District, Doddridge Co, WV, military U.S. Army 80th Div, World War I, in France.[754]
      Children:
      i.   EARL BASIL BELL title: Dr., b. Jan-15-1893 in Harrison Co, WV,[754] d. Mar-24-1979 in Clarksburg, Harrison Co, WV,[754] buried in Broad Run Bapt Ch Cem, Jane Lew, Lewis Co, WV,[754] education Kansas City Medical School and Johns Hopkins Hospital,[754] occupation Medical Doctor & Osteopath, Baltimore, MD.[754]
      ii.   WILLIAM W. BELL b. ca 1895 in Harrison Co, WV.[754]
      iii.   LEWIS BELL b. ca 1897 in Harrison Co, WV.[754]
      iv.   OLLIE D. BELL[1216.]
      v.   ICIE B. BELL b. ca 1899 in Harrison Co, WV.[1216]
      vi.   ALTON BELL b. Mar-26-1905 in Lost Creek, Harrison Co, WV,[1216,592] d. Sep-13-1993 in Clarksburg, Harrison Co, WV,[1216,592] buried in Brick Church (7th Day Baptist) Cemetery, Lost Creek, Harrison Co, WV,[1216] resided in Lost Creek, Harrison Co, WV,[1216,592] occupation teacher (43 yrs) and local historian,[1216] never married[1216.]

734. **Hiram T. Edmonds, Jr.** (400.Mary[8], 243.Ruanna[7], 135.Mary[6], 72.John[5], 21.John[4], 6.Hugh[3], 3.John[2], 1.Jean[1]), b. Apr- 9-1868 in Harrison Co, WV,[1216,17] d. Mar-18-1922 in Harrison Co, WV,[1216,17] buried in Duck Creek Missn Chrch Cem, near West Milford, Harrison Co, WV,[17] census 1900 in Grant District, Harrison Co, WV.[1216] He married **Minnie Myrtle Knight**, also known as Myrtle,[17] b. Sep-30-1878,[1216,17] d. May- 7-1927 in Harrison Co, WV,[1216,17] buried in Duck Creek Missn Chrch Cem, near West Milford, Harrison Co, WV.[17]
Children:
i.   HIRAM EVERETT EDMONDS[1216] also known as Everett Edmonds, b. Sep- 4-1898 in Harrison Co, WV,[592,17,mcdlxv[1465]] d. Jul- 1-1980 in Clarksburg, Harrison Co, WV,[1465,592,17] buried in Duck Creek Missn Chrch Cem, near West Milford, Harrison Co, WV,[17,1465] resided in Lost Creek, Harrison Co, WV,[592] occupation WV State Road Commission.[1465] He married Mar- 9-1921 in Clarksburg, Harrison Co, WV,[1465] Gladys Rose Cottrill,[1465] b. Aug-27-1903 in Lewis Co, WV,[1465,17,592] (daughter of Michael D. Cottrill and Minnie Lillian Jordan), d. Sep-29-1978 in Clarksburg, Harrison Co, WV,[1465,17,592] buried in Duck Creek Missn Chrch Cem, near West Milford, Harrison Co, WV,[17,1465] occupation Practical Nurse.[1465]

735. **Daniel Luther Coberly**, also known as Luther Coberly,[345] (405.Nathan[8], 244.Elizabeth[7], 135.Mary[6], 72.John[5], 21.John[4], 6.Hugh[3], 3.John[2], 1.Jean[1]), b. Jan- 1-1869 in Harrison Co, WV,[1216] baptized Dawson Bapt Church in Gilmer Co, WV, d. Jun- 9-1962 in Gilmer Co, WV,[1216] buried in Coberly Cemetery, Gilmer Co, WV,[1216] occupation farmer.[1216]

A founder of Dawson Baptist Church in Gilmer Co, WV. Served as Gilmer County Commissioner for six years in 1910s.[1216]

He married[345] May- 5-1889,[1216] **Ella Jane Rhoades**, b. Nov-25-1870 in Braxton Co, WV,[1216,345] (daughter of John Rhoades and Susan Goldsmith), baptized in Gilmer Co, WV,[1216] [Dawson Baptist Church], d. Mar-25-1942 in Gilmer Co, WV,[1216] buried in Coberly Cemetery, Gilmer Co, WV.[1216]
Children:
i.   ARNETTA BERTHA COBERLY b. Sep- -1890 in Gilmer Co, WV,[mcdlxvi[1466]] d. Jan-26-1948 in Clarksburg, Harrison Co, WV,[398,1466] buried in Stalnaker Cemetery, Glenville, Gilmer Co, WV,[398] resided in Glenville, Gilmer Co, WV.[398] She married[436] Arch Thomas Brown,[432] b. Nov-26-1888,[432] (son of M. Lee Brown and Luta Belle Walters), d. Nov-24-1959,[432] buried in Stalnaker Cemetery, Glenville, Gilmer Co, WV,[432] resided in Glenville, Gilmer Co, WV,[432] occupation farmer.[432]
ii.   ADELAIDE BEATRICE COBERLY, also known as Adla,[276] b. Jul- 6-1892 in Gilmer Co, WV,[276,1466] d. Mar-21-1960,[276,1466] buried in Stalnaker Cemetery, Glenville, Gilmer Co, WV.[276] She married Homer Furr, b. Jul-23-1889,[592] d. Apr- -1971,[592] resided in Glenville, Gilmer Co, WV.[592]
iii.   ART BERNARD COBERLY b. Jun- 3-1894 in Gilmer Co, WV,[1466,592] d. Jun-13-1988,[592] resided in Dundalk, Baltimore Co, MD,[mcdlxvii[1467]] resided 1920 in Clarksburg, Harrison Co, WV.[396] He married Elva Reaser, b. Jan-14-1894,[592] d. Apr-27-1992,[592] resided in Dundalk, Baltimore Co, MD,[592] resided formerly in Florida.[mcdlxviii[1468]]
iv.   ARAMINTA BELL COBERLY b. May-24-1896 in Gilmer Co, WV,[1466,592,434] d. Oct-30-1994,[592] resided in Glenville, Gilmer Co, WV.[228,592] She married Oct- 3-1915 in Gilmer Co, WV,[434] Guy Cecil Brown, b. May- 3-1892 in West Virginia,[432] (son of M. Lee Brown and Luta Belle Walters), d. Jun- 3-1960 in Glenville, Gilmer Co, WV,[432] buried in Stalnaker Cemetery, Glenville, Gilmer Co, WV,[432] resided in Glenville, Gilmer Co, WV,[432] occupation farmer.[432]
v.   VERA BLANCH COBERLY b. May-11-1899 in Gilmer Co, WV,[592,1466] d. Jul- -1995,[592] resided in Glenville, Gilmer Co, WV.[592]

Name has sometimes been reported as Vera Olive Coberly, basis for which is not known. Donnelly (p. 422) lists her name as Vera Blanch Coberly, and her name is listed in SSDI as Vera B. Ellis.[592,1466]

She married Clark Ellis, b. Nov-18-1894,[592] d. Nov- -1975.[592]

vi.   ALFA RETTA COBERLY b. 1901 in Gilmer Co, WV.[1466] She married (1) James Edward Miles. She married (2) Eldon M. Osborn.

vii.   ALTA EDITH COBERLY b. 1904 in Gilmer Co, WV.[1466]

viii.   ARTHO BUHL COBERLY b. Oct- 8-1906 in Gilmer Co, WV,[1466,592] d. Mar- -1969,[1466,592] resided in Baltimore, MD.[1466,592]

ix.   ISOM OPPOLANCE COBERLY b. Feb-22-1909 in Gilmer Co, WV,[1466,592] d. Nov- -1967,[1466,592] resided 1962 in Glenville, Gilmer Co, WV,[1466] resided formerly in Ohio.[1010] He married[1466] Virginia D. Rutherford, b. Jun- 5-1907,[592] d. Sep- 4-1996,[592] resided in Glenville, Gilmer Co, WV.[592]

x.   CHAMP CLARK COBERLY, also known as Clark C. Coberly,[592] b. Jun-10-1915 in Gilmer Co, WV,[1466,592] d. Jun-30-1997,[592] resided 1962, 97 in Glenville, Gilmer Co, WV.[1466,592]

736. **Eli Jacob West** (407.John[8], 245.Eli[7], 135.Mary[6], 72.John[5], 21.John[4], 6.Hugh[3], 3.John[2], 1.Jean[1]), b. Jul-24-1860 in West Milford, Harrison Co, (W)VA,[398,1466] d. Sep-14-1939 near West Milford, Harrison Co, WV,[mcdlxix[1469],1466] cause of death sandbank cave-in,[398,1466] buried in Rose Hill (formerly IOOF) Cemetery, West Milford, Harrison Co, WV,[398,1466] resided in West Milford, Harrison Co, WV,[398] census 1920 in Union District, Harrison Co, WV,[1466] occupation farmer.[398,1466] He married[228,396] Feb-27-1887 in Harrison Co, WV,[1466] **Verona May Lynch**, also known as Bert or Byrd,[374,446] census name Virona Lynch,[527] b. Jun- 8-1863 in West Milford, Harrison Co, WV,[1466] (daughter of Isaac Lynch and Mary Jane Burnside), d. Jan-10-1939 in Buffalo Creek, near West Milford, Harrison Co, WV,[1466] buried in West Milford, Harrison Co, WV.[1466]

Children:

i.   GAILE WEST b. Jul-28-1888 in Harrison Co, WV,[1466] d. Mar-31-1891.[1466]

ii.   HOY D. WEST b. Apr-23-1895 in Parsons, Tucker Co, WV,[398] [Donnelly's "Wests of Duck Creek" reports birth date as Apr 23 1892, citing Eli J. West Family Bible. But death record states birth date as Apr 23 1895, giving age as 58 at time of death on Jun 29 1953. Marriage record, however, shows that he gave his age as 22 at time of his Dec 1913 marriage.], d. Jun-29-1953 in Huntington, Cabell Co, WV,[398] buried in Ridgelawn Mem Park, Huntington, WV,[398] resided in Huntington, Cabell Co, WV,[398] resided 1950 in Marathon, Monroe Co, FL,[1466] resided 1913 in Clarksburg, Harrison Co, WV,[419] occupation grocer, carpenter.[1466,398]

As of 1923, he was running a restaurant on 3rd Street in Clarksburg, WV. He later operated a grocery store in Huntington, WV in the 1930s, prior to moving to Florida.[1466]

He married (1) Dec-26-1913 in Harrison Co, WV,[1466] no children from this marriage,[1466] Virginia Clegg, b. ca 1888 in Allegheny Co, PA,[419] (daughter of Joseph Clegg), resided 1913 in Harrison Co, WV.[419] He married (2) bef 1940 in Cabell Co, WV,[1466] Myrtle __, resided 1953 in Huntington, Cabell Co, WV.[228]

iii.   CALLA OSCIE WEST, also known as Kelley West,[374] b. Sep- 9-1899 in Harrison Co, WV,[1465,46] d. May-14-1968 in Clarksburg, Harrison Co, WV,[1465,46] buried in Rose Hill (formerly IOOF) Cemetery, West Milford, Harrison Co, WV.[524,1465] She married[1465,mcdlxx[1470]] resided (family) 1952 in Buffalo Creek, near West Milford, Harrison Co, WV, Homer W. McKinley, b. Apr- 9-1896 in Harrison Co, WV,[1465,46] (son of John W. McKinley and Mary E. Stalnaker), d. May- 4-1952 in Harrison Co, WV,[1465,46] buried in Rose Hill (formerly IOOF) Cemetery, West Milford, Harrison Co, WV,[524,1465] cause of death farming accident - overturned tractor,[1465] occupation farmer.[1465]

iv.   LESSIE MAE WEST b. Apr-16-1905 in Harrison Co, WV,[1465] [SSDI reports birth date as Apr 16 1904], d. May- 7-1990 in Albuquerque, Bernalillo Co, NM,[1465] buried in Huntington, Cabell Co, WV,[1465] resided in Huntington, Cabell Co, WV,[1465] census 1920 in Harrison Co, WV, occupation Humphreys Tourist Home, Huntington, WV, 1931-1987.[1465] She married[1465] Jul-14-1922 in Salem, WV,[mcdlxxi[1471]] George Thomas Humphreys, b. Apr- 1-1899 in Moundsville, Marshall Co, WV,[mcdlxxii[1472]] [SSDI reports birth date as Mar 31 1899] (son of John James Humphreys and Matilda Elisabeth Causer), d. Oct-23-1983 in Huntington, Cabell Co, WV,[1472] buried in Spring Hill Cemetery, Huntington, WV,[1472] resided in Huntington, Cabell Co, WV,[604] resided 1910, 22 in Newburg, Preston Co, WV,[211,419] occupation 1922 - 1929 accountant, Island Creek Coal Co, McDowell Co, WV,[1472] occupation 1934 - 1970 operated business equipment company, Huntington, WV.[1472]

v.   ROBERT E. WEST b. Jun-23-1907 in West Milford, Harrison Co, WV,[1472] d. Dec-6-1985 in Clarksburg, Harrison Co, WV,[1472] buried in Rose Hill (formerly IOOF) Cemetery, West Milford, Harrison Co, WV,[524,1472] education Salem College (1954),[1472] occupation industrial arts teacher, Lunenburg Co, Harrisonburg & Manassas, VA (17 yrs).[1472] He married (1) Sep- 6-1931 in Wheeling, Ohio Co, WV,[1472] Forrest Xenia Moore, b. Feb- 2-1909 in Salem, WV,[1472,46] (daughter of William Ellsworth Moore and Mable Duncan), d. Jul-29-1969 in Harrison Co, WV,[1472,46] buried in Rose Hill (formerly IOOF) Cemetery, West Milford, Harrison Co, WV,[524,1472] resided in Manassas, VA.[1472]

Forrest: An orphan, she was raised by relatives in Wheeling and West Milford, WV.[1472]

He married (2) Nov-29-1969 in Wheeling, Ohio Co, WV,[1472] Mildred Loew Coleman, b. May-21-1909 in Wheeling, Ohio Co, WV,[1472,592] d. Oct-29-1999,[592] resided 1995 in Wheeling, Ohio Co, WV,[1472] resided 1999 in Moundsville, Marshall Co, WV.[592]

737. **Thomas Floyd West** (407.John[8], 245.Eli[7], 135.Mary[6], 72.John[5], 21.John[4], 6.Hugh[3], 3.John[2], 1.Jean[1]), b. Aug-22-1869 in Harrison Co, WV,[1466] d. Aug-20-1904 in Big Isaac, Doddridge Co, WV,[1466,356] buried in Big Isaac, Doddridge Co, WV,[1102] occupation Carpenter, cobbler, constable, and ran a planing mill.[1102] He married Jan-23-1889 in Big Isaac, Doddridge Co, WV,[1102] **Henrietta Jane "Etta" Hinkle**,[1102] b. Sep-10-1870,[1102] (daughter of Abraham Hinkle and Catherine Ciscelia Carder), d. Dec-23-1957 in Turlock, Stanislaus Co, CA,[1102] buried in Big Isaac Cemetery, Doddridge Co, WV,[1102] census 1910 in Greenbrier District, Doddridge Co, WV.[1102]
Children:
   i.   ELBERT BOYD WEST b. Apr-28-1891 in Big Isaac, Doddridge Co, WV,[1102] d. Mar- 6-1953.[1102]
   ii.   CLARENCE DOVENER WEST b. Aug-23-1893 in Big Isaac, Doddridge Co, WV,[1472] d. Sep-18-1950 in Clarksburg, Harrison Co, WV,[1472] buried in Big Isaac Cemetery, Doddridge Co, WV,[1472] resided in Romulus, Wayne Co, MI,[1472] occupation builder & carpenter.[1472] He married Feb-20-1913 in Doddridge Co, WV,[1472,354] Vera Romine.
   iii.   ESTA PEARL WEST b. Oct-19-1895 in Big Isaac, Doddridge Co, WV,[1472] d. Sep-19-1993 in Wichita, Sedgwick Co, KS,[1472] buried in White Chapel Memorial Gardens, Wichita, KS,[1472] resided in Wichita, Sedgwick Co, KS,[1472] occupation teacher.[1472] She married Aug-11-1917 in Jarvisville, Harrison Co, WV,[1472] William Kile Jarvis, occupation oil well driller.[1472]
   iv.   GUIRA CISCELIA WEST b. Feb-26-1898 in Big Isaac, Doddridge Co, WV,[1102] d. Oct- -1993 in Wichita, Sedgwick Co, KS,[1102] resided in Wichita, Sedgwick Co, KS.[1102] She married[1102] Oakey B. Green.
   v.   JOHN J. "JACK" WEST, birth name Jesse Abraham Jackson West,[mcdlxxiii[1473]] b. Mar-24-1900 in Big Isaac, Doddridge Co, WV,[1473,592] d. Sep-29-1973 in Howard Co, MD,[1473,592] resided in Ellicott City, Howard Co, MD,[592] occupation 1924 - 1973 tax consultant.[1473] He married Dec-15-1923,[1473] Mildred V. Brooks, b. May-14-1904,[1473] (daughter of __ Brooks), resided 1994 in Catonsville, Baltimore Co, MD.[1473]
   vi.   RUSSELL GOFF WEST b. May- 6-1902 in Big Isaac, Doddridge Co, WV,[1473] d. Jul-18-1991 in Clarksburg, Harrison Co, WV,[1473] buried in Bridgeport Cemetery, Harrison Co, WV,[1473] occupation Post Office, moving & transfer, school janitor.[mcdlxxiv[1474]] He married Jun- 3-1923,[1473] Retta Virginia Myers, b. Jun-19-1903,[1473] d. Mar-30-1992 in Salem, WV,[1473] buried in Bridgeport Cemetery, Harrison Co, WV,[1473] occupation loan officer, Union National Bank (45 yrs).[1473]
   vii.   THOMAS FLOYD WEST II b. May-30-1904 in Big Isaac, Doddridge Co, WV,[1473,592] d. Oct-17-1996,[592] resided in Las Vegas, Clark Co, NV,[1086,1473] occupation aircraft mechanic, Boeing Aircraft, Wichita KS (13 yrs),[1473] military 1922-27 U.S. Marine Corps.[1473] He married (1) va 1926 in Alexandria, VA,[1473] Edith Brooks (daughter of __ Brooks), resided 1994 in Maryland.[1473] He married (2) Sep-22-1947 in Wichita, Sedgwick Co, KS,[1473] Marjorie J. Brandon, b. Mar-23-1918.[1473]

738. **Sarah Elizabeth West** (407.John[8], 245.Eli[7], 135.Mary[6], 72.John[5], 21.John[4], 6.Hugh[3], 3.John[2], 1.Jean[1]), b. Dec-26-1869 in Harrison Co, WV,[1102] baptized Mt. Lebanon Bapt Chu in Doddridge Co, WV, d. Nov-

12-1952 in Jane Lew, Lewis Co, WV,[1102] buried in Weston, Lewis Co, WV,[1102] resided 1939 in Deanville (Weston), Lewis Co, WV.[mcdlxxv[1475]]

As of 1931, Sarah West King was reportedly in possession of the family Bible of Job West and Mary "Polly" Gaston.[1102]

She married Oct- 1-1891 in Doddridge Co, WV,[1102,mcdlxxvi[1476]] resided (family) bef 1915 in Troy, Gilmer Co, WV,[1102] resided (family) aft 1915 in Deanville (Weston), Lewis Co, WV,[1102] **John Presley King**, b. Jan- 4-1868 in Doddridge Co, WV,[1102] (son of George Washington King and Louisa Fletcher), d. Aug-21-1946 in Deanville (Weston), Lewis Co, WV,[1102] buried in Weston, Lewis Co, WV,[1102] occupation farmer.[1102]

        Children:
        i.   GEORGE JACKSON KING b. Jul- 5-1892 in Gilmer Co, WV,[1102] d. Oct- -1951 in Fairmont, Marion Co, WV.[1102]
        ii.   LILLIE MABEL KING, also known as Mabel,[521] b. Nov- 9-1896 in Gilmer Co, WV,[1102] d. Mar- 4-1964 in Weston, Lewis Co, WV.[1102] She married[1101] Aug-12-1916 in Lewis Co, WV,[410] Harland Allman Swisher, b. ca 1893,[410] (son of Ira Ervin Swisher and Amrose Kittorah Allman).
        iii.   IRA ARDEN KING b. Apr- 2-1900 in Gilmer Co, WV,[1102] d. bef May 2004.[521]
        iv.   CARL BROOKS KING, also known as Cralie B. King,[521] b. Apr-15-1905 in Gilmer Co, WV,[1102] d. Oct-14-1989 in Akron, Summit Co, OH.[1102]
        v.   META GAY KING b. Feb- 3-1909 in Troy, Gilmer Co, WV,[1102] d. Jul- 7-1996 in Jane Lew, Lewis Co, WV,[1102] buried in Weston Masonic Cemetery, Lewis Co, WV.[1102] She married Dec-23-1933,[1102] Claude B. Hall.
        vi.   MARY LOUISE KING b. Mar-10-1911 in Doddridge Co, WV,[1102,592] d. Jun- -1981 in St. Cloud, Osceola Co, FL,[1102,592] resided in St. Cloud, Osceola Co, FL,[592] resided formerly in West Virginia.[604] She married[1101] __ Engel.
        vii.   JAMES EDWARD "ED" KING[190] b. Aug-27-1913 in Troy, Gilmer Co, WV,[190,1102] d. May-28-2004 in Clarksburg, Harrison Co, WV,[911] cremated[190] resided in Fairmont, Marion Co, WV,[752,190] military U.S. Army, World War II - Purple Heart.[190]

        Retired from the Owens-Illinois plant in Fairmont with 36 1/2 years of service in the maintenance department. He was a member of the Owens-Illinois National Championship Rifle Team of 1952, shooting 40 perfect 10x bullseyes in the championship round. Prior to his years at Owens, he worked at the Westwood Lumber Company in Weston. He was a gifted carpenter and cabinetmaker., and he loved camping and fishing at this camp near Moorefield.[190]

        He married Sep-16-1939 in Monterey, Highland Co, VA,[752] Verda G. Koon, b. Sep- 9-1919,[592] d. Dec-30-2007,[592] resided in Fairmont, Marion Co, WV.[484,604]

739. **William Burr West**[398] also known as William Burrow West,[752] (407.John[8], 245.Eli[7], 135.Mary[6], 72.John[5], 21.John[4], 6.Hugh[3], 3.John[2], 1.Jean[1]), b. 1874 in Upshur Co, WV,[752] [Upshur County birth record (p. 79) shows birth date as May 16 1874 (per Donnelly's "Wests of Duck Creek, p. 424). But death record reports birth as Sep 17 1874 in Upshur Co, with age at death 74y 3m 22d.], d. Jan- 9-1949 in Doddridge Co, WV,[752,398] buried in Big Isaac Cemetery, Doddridge Co, WV,[752,398] resided in Miletus (Salem), Doddridge Co, WV,[752] occupation farmer and carpenter.[752] He married Jan-30-1902 in Doddridge Co, WV,[752] **Mary Etta Carder**,[752] also known as Marietta Carder,[752] census name Ettie,[750] b. Aug-16-1880 in Union District, Harrison Co, WV,[752] (daughter of William C. Carder and Melinda Fultineer), d. Mar-13-1963 in Coudersport, Potter Co, PA,[752] buried in Big Isaac Cemetery, Doddridge Co, WV.[752]

Mary: Raised by Abraham & Catherine C. Carder Hinkle.[752]

        Children:

     i.   RUPERT W. WEST b. Nov-27-1902 in Miletus (Salem), Doddridge Co, WV,[mcdlxxvii[1477]] d. Dec- 2-1992 in Harrisville, Ritchie Co, WV,[1477] buried in Masonic Memorial Park Cemetery, Crystal Lake (West Union), WV,[1477] resided in Oxford, Doddridge Co, WV,[1477] resided later in Harrisville, Ritchie Co, WV,[1477] occupation WV State Road Commission - 35 yrs.[1477] He married Nov-26-1928 in Oakland, Garrett Co, MD,[1477] Hazel N. Nicholson, b. Mar-31-1910,[1477,592] (daughter of William John Nicholson and Cora Morris), d. Sep-16-1997,[592] resided in Harrisville, Ritchie Co, WV.[1477,592]

    ii.   ANNA VERLE WEST, also known as Verle West,[1477,711] b. Nov- 1-1905 in Miletus (Salem), Doddridge Co, WV,[1477] d. Oct- -1932,[1477] buried in Big Isaac, Doddridge Co, WV,[1477] census 1930 in Greenbrier District, Doddridge Co, WV. She married[1477] Sep-17-1923 in West Union, Doddridge Co, WV,[711] William E. Ash, b. ca 1900 in Doddridge Co, WV,[711] resided in Sedalia, Doddridge Co, WV,[1477] census 1930 in Greenbrier District, Doddridge Co, WV.

    iii.   WILLIAM STANLEY "CASEY" WEST b. Jun-16-1908 in Miletus (Salem), Doddridge Co, WV,[1477,592] d. Jun-15-1995 in Palatka, Putnam Co, FL,[1477,592] resided in Salem, WV,[1477,592] occupation mechanic; worked with father on compressor stations; truck driver.[1477] He married Apr-21-1928 in Clarksburg, Harrison Co, WV,[1477] Blanche Geraldine Nicholson, b. Jul- 3-1908 in Harrison Co, WV,[1477] (daughter of William John Nicholson and Cora Morris), d. Aug-15-1989 in Salem, WV,[1477] buried in Big Isaac Cemetery, Doddridge Co, WV,[1477] resided in Salem, WV.[1477]

    iv.   DORUS JACKSON WEST, census name Doras J. West,[902] b. Feb-26-1911 in Miletus (Salem), Doddridge Co, WV,[mcdlxxviii[1478],396] d. Apr- 1-1980 in Clarksburg, Harrison Co, WV,[1478] buried in Big Isaac Cemetery, Doddridge Co, WV,[1478] resided in Salem, WV,[1478] occupation minister.[1478] He married Jul- 3-1935 in Clarksburg, Harrison Co, WV,[1478] Elizabeth Castoline Freeman, also known as L. Castoline Freeman,[396] b. Feb-10-1917 in Walker Station, Wood Co, WV,[1478,396] (daughter of Ebb Freeman and Laura S. Furbee), d. Oct- 5-1996 in Clarksburg, Harrison Co, WV,[1478] buried in Big Isaac Cemetery, Doddridge Co, WV,[1478] resided in Salem, WV.[521,1478]

    v.   HATTIE VIONE WEST, also known as Vione West,[374] also known as H. Vione West,[190,748] b. Jun-16-1914 in Miletus (Salem), Doddridge Co, WV,[1478,190] d. Oct-24-2005 in Clarksburg, Harrison Co, WV,[764] buried in Bridgeport Cemetery, Harrison Co, WV,[190] resided in Clarksburg, Harrison Co, WV,[1478,190] [Liberty Addition], resided 1949 in Bristol, Harrison Co, WV,[748] occupation Maple View Rest Home, Potter Co, PA.[190] She married in Harrison Co, WV,[1478] Clyde Goldsmith, b. Apr-14-1913,[592] d. Jan- -1969,[592] resided in Clarksburg, Harrison Co, WV,[592] occupation Hope Gas Co.[1478]

    vi.   DEWARD CORWIN WEST, also known as Corwin West,[1478,mcdlxxix[1479]] b. Dec-23-1916 in Miletus (Salem), Doddridge Co, WV,[1478,592] d. Dec- 1-2000,[592] resided in Clarksburg, Harrison Co, WV,[592] resided 1995 in Laurel Valley, Harrison Co, WV,[1478] resided 1950 at Big Isaac, Doddridge Co, WV,[mcdlxxx[1480]] occupation food service supervisor, VA Hospital, Clarksburg, WV - 17 yrs,[1478] military U.S. Army, Europe, World War II - wounded in battle,[1478] education Salem College.[1480] He married Jun- 5-1940 in Doddridge Co, WV,[1478] Jewell Snider, b. May-23-1922 in Miletus (Salem), Doddridge Co, WV,[1478] (daughter of Howard Jahu Snider and Willa Julia Middleton), resided 2006 in Clarksburg, Harrison Co, WV.[1479]

    vii.   HAROLD B. WEST b. Jul- 7-1920 in Miletus (Salem), Doddridge Co, WV,[752] d. Dec-25-1982 in Mount Jewett, McKean Co, PA,[752,191] buried in Bridgeport Cemetery, Harrison Co, WV,[752] census 1930 in Greenbrier District, Doddridge Co, WV, occupation minister.[752,191]

        Licensed to preach at age 17; began at Jarvisville United Brethren Church, Harrison Co, WV.[752]

        He married Feb-18-1945 in Huntington, Cabell Co, WV,[752] no children from this marriage,[191] Martha Virginia Petry, b. Jul-30-1926 in Huntington, Cabell Co, WV,[190] (daughter of James Elmer Petry and Lucy May Lapole), d. Oct-14-2004 in Clarksburg, Harrison Co, WV,[847] buried in Bridgeport Cemetery, Harrison Co, WV,[190] resided in Clarksburg, Harrison Co, WV,[190] occupation hospital volunteer.[190]

740. Charles C. Patton (408.Mary[8], 245.Eli[7], 135.Mary[6], 72.John[5], 21.John[4], 6.Hugh[3], 3.John[2], 1.Jean[1]), b. ca 1869 in Harrison Co, WV,[419] occupation farmer.[419] He married[752] Jul-20-1890 in Harrison Co,

WV,[419] **Nancy C. Morrison**, b. ca 1868 in Harrison Co, WV,[419] (daughter of Daniel Morrison and Sarah A. __).

Children:

i.   ROSCOE PATTON b. Sep- 2-1898 in West Virginia,[1478] d. Dec-12-1951 in Clarksburg, Harrison Co, WV,[1478] buried in Sheets Mill (Old West) Cemetery, West Milford, Harrison Co, WV.[1478] He married[1478] Jessie M. West, b. Jul-18-1909 in Harrison Co, WV,[mcdlxxxi[1481]] (daughter of Hiram Thomas West and Allie Belle Davis), d. Feb- 7-1982 in Fairmont, Marion Co, WV,[1481] buried in Sheets Mill (Old West) Cemetery, West Milford, Harrison Co, WV,[1481] census 1920 in Union District, Harrison Co, WV.[1481] As descendants of John West and Frances Howard, Roscoe Patton and Jessie M. West were third cousins, once removed.

741. **James Beryl Patton**, also known as Beryl Patton, also known as Burl J. Patton,[747] (408.Mary[8], 245.Eli[7], 135.Mary[6], 72.John[5], 21.John[4], 6.Hugh[3], 3.John[2], 1.Jean[1]), b. Nov- 6-1875 in Harrison Co, WV,[276] d. Mar- 2-1964 in Clarksburg, Harrison Co, WV,[276] buried in Sheets Mill (Old West) Cemetery, West Milford, Harrison Co, WV.[276]

He was a veteran of the Spanish-American War, and died in a Veterans hospital. He married Bertha Thompson while stationed at Fort Flagler, Maristone Island, Washington.

He married Sep- 1-1912 in Nordland, Jefferson Co, WA, **Bertha Talita Thompson**, b. Jul-11-1895 in Nordland, Jefferson Co, WA, d. bef Mar 1964.[228]

Children:

i.   MARY FRANCES PATTON b. Nov-25-1913 in Fort Flagler, Nordland, WA,[190,592] d. Aug-22-2007,[592,190] buried Woodbine Cemetery,[190] resided in Puyallup, Pierce Co, WA.[1153,190] She married Jul-13-1932 in Tacoma, Pierce Co, WA, Alfred Martinius Barem, b. Apr-26-1906 in Duluth, St. Louis Co, MN,[592] d. Apr-11-1991 in Puyallup, Pierce Co, WA,[mcdlxxxii[1482],592] resided in Puyallup, Pierce Co, WA.[1153] Mary and Al Barem were berry growers in the Puyallup Valley for 35 years. They owned and operated the Washington Farmers Products Control Board berry processing plant, from which Mary retired in 1977.[191]

ii.   JAMES DAVID PATTON b. Jan- 6-1916,[592] d. Sep-29-1994,[592] resided in Port Hadlock, Jefferson Co, WA.[1153] He married Louise W. Swevelhoffer, b. Sep-11-1917,[592] d. Oct- 8-1998,[592] resided in Port Hadlock, Jefferson Co, WA.[592] Six children.

742. **Marcoda Melinda McIntire** (409.Sarah[8], 245.Eli[7], 135.Mary[6], 72.John[5], 21.John[4], 6.Hugh[3], 3.John[2], 1.Jean[1]), b. Mar-20-1867,[752] d. Mar-17-1906 in Harrison Co, WV,[752] census 1900 in Greenbrier District, Doddridge Co, WV. She married[752] ca 1888,[1038] **George Allen Hinkle**, b. Oct- 5-1867 in Harrison Co, WV,[752,354] (son of Abraham Hinkle and Catherine Ciscelia Carder), d. May-18-1942 in Doddridge Co, WV,[752,356] census 1900, 1930 in Greenbrier District, Doddridge Co, WV.

Children:

i.   ELLA GAY HINKLE b. Nov-25-1888,[592,1038,46] d. Nov-10-1967 in Harrison Co, WV,[1481,592,46] buried in Rose Hill (formerly IOOF) Cemetery, West Milford, Harrison Co, WV,[524] resided in Salem, WV,[592] resided 1933 in Jarvisville, Harrison Co, WV.[1481] She married[1481,446,395] Oct-30-1904 in Doddridge Co, WV,[354] Stephen Earnest Bennett,[395] b. 1883 in Harrison Co, WV,[46,354] d. 1933,[46] buried in Rose Hill (formerly IOOF) Cemetery, West Milford, Harrison Co, WV,[524] census 1920 in Union District, Harrison Co, WV, resided 1904 in Doddridge Co, WV.[354]

ii.   DORSEY DOYLE HINKLE.

iii. ETHEL JULIA HINKLE b. Nov-10-1891,[946] d. Dec-28-1978 in Harrison Co, WV,[946] census 1930 in Clarksburg, Harrison Co, WV, census 1920 in Stealey (Clarksburg), Harrison Co, WV, census 1900 in Greenbrier District, Doddridge Co, WV. She married[946] Jul-16-1911 in Doddridge Co, WV,[354] Hoy C. Ward, b. Oct- -1887,[1038,354] (son of William M. Ward and Sarah __), census 1930 in Clarksburg, Harrison Co, WV, census 1920 in Stealey (Clarksburg), Harrison Co, WV, census 1900 in

Greenbrier District, Doddridge Co, WV, occupation 1920 clerk, Hope Gas Co.,[418] occupation 1930 meter engineer for gas company.[1208]

    iv. WALTER GUY HINKLE, census name Guy W. Hinkle,[418] also known as W. Guy Hinkle,[354] b. Jun- -1893,[1038,354] d. Nov-13-1942 in Harrison Co, WV,[752] census 1920 in Clarksburg, Harrison Co, WV, occupation 1920 truck driver, Hope Gas Co.,[418] occupation 1910 pipeline, oil field. He married Sep-20-1914 in Doddridge Co, WV,[354] Ethel Bell, b. ca 1896 in Ritchie Co, WV,[354] census 1920 in Clarksburg, Harrison Co, WV, resided 1914 in Doddridge Co, WV.[354]

    v. WILLIE BERYL HINKLE, also known as Beryl W. Hinkle,[902] b. May-22-1895 at Big Isaac, Doddridge Co, WV,[398,1038,419] [1900 Census gives birth date as May 1895, and death record specifies May 22 1895. But marriage record shows it as March 22 1895.], d. May- 2-1948 in Bridgeport, Harrison Co, WV,[398,946] buried in Bridgeport Cemetery, Harrison Co, WV,[398] resided in Bridgeport, Harrison Co, WV,[398,419] resided 1914 in Harrison Co, WV,[419] census 1900, 1930 in Greenbrier District, Doddridge Co, WV. She married (1) Aug- 9-1914 in Clarksburg, Harrison Co, WV,[mcdlxxxiii[1483]] Raymond Marshall Floyd, b. Oct-21-1891 in Harrison Co, WV,[398,467,419] (son of Samuel S. Floyd and Mary E. Myers), d. Oct-14-1956 in Bridgeport, Harrison Co, WV,[398] cause of death suicide with firearm,[398] buried in Big Isaac Cemetery, Doddridge Co, WV,[398] resided in Bridgeport, Harrison Co, WV,[398] resided 1914 in West Milford, Harrison Co, WV,[419] census 1900 in Grant District, Harrison Co, WV. She married[946,436] (2) Sep- 2-1944 in Bridgeport, Harrison Co, WV,[mcdlxxxiv[1484]] Robert Stuart Windon, b. Oct-28-1897 in Clarksburg, Harrison Co, WV,[419,592] (son of William Windon and Ingaby Mae Stuart), d. Jan- -1964,[604] resided in Bridgeport, Harrison Co, WV.[419,436]

    vi. OPAL MARIE HINKLE b. Nov-16-1897,[592] d. Nov- 2-1975,[946,592] resided in Salem, WV,[592] occupation clerk, general store.[750] She married[946] Sep-22-1920 in Doddridge Co, WV,[354] Wayne W. Kelley, b. Nov-13-1890 in Harrison Co, WV,[592,354] (son of J. Lee Kelley and Cora B. __), d. Apr- -1979,[592] resided in Salem, WV,[604] census 1930 in Greenbrier District, Doddridge Co, WV, census 1910 in Union District, Harrison Co, WV.

743. **Dolph C. McIntire** (409.Sarah[8], 245.Eli[7], 135.Mary[6], 72.John[5], 21.John[4], 6.Hugh[3], 3.John[2], 1.Jean[1]), b. 1887,[749] d. 1957,[749] buried in McWhorter Cemetery, Harrison Co, WV.[749] He married[749,374] **Jessie Rebecca Wilson**.
    Children:
    i. JAMES WILSON MCINTYRE b. Oct-14-1913 at Duck Creek, Harrison Co, WV,[190] d. Jul-14-2005 at Reynoldsville, Harrison Co, WV,[700] buried in Jarvisville Baptist Cemetery, Harrison Co, WV,[190] resided at Reynoldsville, Harrison Co, WV,[190] occupation heavy equipment operator (Huffman Construction Co),[190] military Staff Sgt, U.S. Army - WW II Europe (Co C, 750th Tank Bn) - Purple Heart.[190]

    The "McIntyre" spelling is found in his marriage record and is used for himself and all family members in his obituary. Among others, survived by five grandchildren, eight great-grandchildren, one step-grandson, and one step-granddaughter.

    He married Living.
    ii. IRENE V. MCINTYRE[521] b. Apr-20-1915,[17,592] d. Mar- 5-1991,[17,592] buried in Coplin Church Cemetery, Jarvisville, Harrison Co, WV,[17,817] resided in West Virginia.[604] She married[1101] John D. Furner, b. Jul- 7-1906,[17,592] d. Jul-16-1976,[17,592] buried in Coplin Church Cemetery, Jarvisville, Harrison Co, WV,[17,817] resided in Mt. Clare, Harrison Co, WV.[592]
    iii. GERALDINE DYER MCINTYRE b. Jul-12-1918 in Lost Creek, Harrison Co, WV,[419,592,46] d. May- -1993,[592,46] buried in Coplin Church Cemetery, Jarvisville, Harrison Co, WV,[17] resided in Wallace, Harrison Co, WV,[604] resided 1966 in Bristol, Harrison Co, WV,[419] resided 1957 in Wolf Summit, Harrison Co, WV.[419] She married[1101] Feb-11-1950 in Clarksburg, Harrison Co, WV,[mcdlxxxv[1485]] divorced Apr-28-1966 in Nutter Fort, Harrison Co, WV,[mcdlxxxvi[1486]] Harold Franklin Shaver, b. Feb-23-1921 in Clarksburg, Harrison Co, WV,[419,46] [Birth date given in two marriage records as Feb 23 1921, in one marriage record as Feb 22 1921, and in another marriage record as Feb 23 1916; but SSDI shows it as Feb 23 1918. Headstone reads simply 1921.] (son of Arthur Cyrus Shaver and Dessie Agnes Wickham), d. Aug- -1986,[592,46] buried in Coplin Church Cemetery, Jarvisville, Harrison Co, WV,[17] resided in Wallace, Harrison Co, WV,[604] resided 1966 in Hepzibah,

Harrison Co, WV,[419] resided 1957 in Wolf Summit, Harrison Co, WV,[419] census 1930 in Clarksburg, Harrison Co, WV.

        iv.   MAXINE JUNE MCINTYRE b. Jul- 2-1926 in Harrison Co, WV,[419,592] d. Nov-13-1996,[592] resided at Bristol, Harrison Co, WV.[592,419] She married[1101] Mar-28-1947 at Bristol, Harrison Co, WV,[419] John Lafayette Meredith, b. Feb-21-1923 at Bristol, Harrison Co, WV,[419] (son of James D. Meredith and Clara Haney).

744. **Fred C. McIntyre**, also known as Frederick C. McIntyre,[446] (410.Julia[8], 245.Eli[7], 135.Mary[6], 72.John[5], 21.John[4], 6.Hugh[3], 3.John[2], 1.Jean[1]), b. Jun-20-1886 in Wood Co, WV,[354,276] d. Aug- 5-1969 in Clarksburg, Harrison Co, WV,[276] buried in Bridgeport Cemetery, Harrison Co, WV,[276] resided in Clarksburg, Harrison Co, WV,[276] occupation oil & gas production.[276] He married[502] Sep- 6-1913 in Doddridge Co, WV,[354] **Bessie A. Corder**, b. Nov-23-1892 in Doddridge Co, WV,[398] (daughter of Michael R. Corder and Margaret V. Howell), d. Jul- 2-1946 in Clarksburg, Harrison Co, WV,[398] buried in Bridgeport Cemetery, Harrison Co, WV,[398] resided in Clarksburg, Harrison Co, WV.[398]
        Children:
        i.   JULIA VIRGINIA MCINTYRE b. Jan-28-1917 in Clarksburg, Harrison Co, WV,[190,592] d. Jul-23-2005 in Akron, Summit Co, OH,[806,592] buried in Bridgeport Cemetery, Harrison Co, WV,[190] resided in Clarksburg, Harrison Co, WV,[748,190,604].

        She had worked as a clerk at the Clarksburg Social Security office, was a display advertising clerk at the Clarksburg Publishing Company, and, from 1955 to 1984, was secretary and treasurer for the West Virginia Memorial Monument Company in Clarksburg. Among others, survived by four granddaughters and spouses, Lisa Ann & Robert Woodford, Celina OH, Carrie Swaim, Baker WV, Janna & Kevin Woodrich, Warrenton VA, and Elizabeth & Tony Kozenko, Canton OH, by one great-granddaughter, Stefanie Woodford; and by one great-great-granddaughter, Joleena Rose.[190]

        She married Feb-16-1938,[191] William J. Swiger, b. Jul- 8-1918,[592] d. Aug-27-1984,[191,592] resided in Clarksburg, Harrison Co, WV.[604]
        ii.   HOWARD LEE MCINTYRE[412] b. Jan-16-1920 in Clarksburg, Harrison Co, WV,[419,592] d. Feb-14-1998,[592] resided in Lancaster, Lancaster Co, PA,[592] resided formerly in West Virginia,[604] resided 1942 at Fort Bragg, NC.[419] He married[mcdlxxxvii[1487]] Jan- 9-1942 in Clarksburg, Harrison Co, WV,[419] Charlotte Virginia Wilson, b. Feb-16-1921 in Quinnimont, Fayette Co, WV,[419] (daughter of Thomas R. Wilson and Ethel Warner), resided 2005 in Lancaster, Lancaster Co, PA,[1487] resided 1942 in Clarksburg, Harrison Co, WV.[419]
        iii.   HAROLD FRANKLIN "KONK" MCINTYRE[412,412] b. Jul-21-1925 in Clarksburg, Harrison Co, WV,[419] d. bef Jul 2005,[412] resided in Clarksburg, Harrison Co, WV.[419] He married Living.

745. **Minnie Otto Cottrill** (411.Eliza[8], 245.Eli[7], 135.Mary[6], 72.John[5], 21.John[4], 6.Hugh[3], 3.John[2], 1.Jean[1]) (See marriage to number 454.)

746. **William C. "Will" Haught**, census name Willie C. Haught,[385] (412.Mary[8], 246.John[7], 136.Hugh[6], 72.John[5], 21.John[4], 6.Hugh[3], 3.John[2], 1.Jean[1]), b. Feb-21-1876 in Doddridge Co, WV,[mcdlxxxviii[1488],190] d. Jan-13-1957 in Oxford, Doddridge Co, WV,[190,17] buried in South Fork Bapt Church Cem, Oxford, Doddridge Co, WV,[17,190] resided in Oxford, Doddridge Co, WV,[412,190] census 1920, 1930 in Southwest District, Doddridge Co, WV, occupation farmer,[405,190,1390.] He married[484] Dec- 7-1902 in Doddridge Co, WV,[354] **Lucy Mae Summers**, b. Sep-28-1873 in Doddridge Co, WV,[mcdlxxxix[1489]] (daughter of Elijah W. Summers and Caroline Virginia Brown), d. May-13-1948 in Oxford, Doddridge Co, WV,[190] buried in South Fork Bapt Church Cem, Oxford, Doddridge Co, WV,[17] resided in Oxford, Doddridge Co, WV,[765] census 1920, 1930 in Southwest District, Doddridge Co, WV.
        Children:
        i.   WALLACE BRADY HAUGHT b. Mar-22-1902 in Doddridge Co, WV,[mcdxc[1490],190] d. Nov-29-1984,[17] buried in South Fork Bapt Church Cem, Oxford, Doddridge Co, WV,[17] resided in Summers, Doddridge Co, WV.[190]

A former employee of Miller Instruction Co, Suffield, Portage Co, OH. Retired employee of the West Virginia Department of Highways. He was a member and trustee of the South Fork Baptist Church and was a member of Doddridge County Republican Party Executive Committee.[190,mcdxci[1491]]

He married Apr-8-1929, Mabel Geneva Ruble,[190] also known as Mabel Genevieve Ruble,[446] b. Apr-21-1908 in Jackson Ridge, OH,[190] (daughter of Albert Lee Ruble and Elizabeth "Lizzie" Potts), d. Jan-13-2004 in Summers, Doddridge Co, WV,[190] buried in South Fork Bapt Church Cem, Oxford, Doddridge Co, WV,[17] resided in Summers, Doddridge Co, WV.[190]

    ii.   FOREST G. HAUGHT b. May-15-1903,[592] d. Jan- 4-1998 in Alliance, Stark Co, OH,[mcdxcii[1492],592] resided in Salem, OH,[521,mcdxciii[1493]] resided 1984 in Fruitland Park, Lake Co, FL,[521] resided 1936, 48, 57 in Akron, Summit Co, OH,[855,856,765] census 1920 in Southwest District, Doddridge Co, WV. He married Hazel Hawkins, b. Jun-22-1906,[592] (daughter of Granville Lee Hawkins and Rosa Lee Hall), d. Jul-29-2001 in Salem, OH.[592,mcdxciv[1494]]

    iii.   HAYWARD E. HAUGHT b. Mar-14-1905 in West Virginia,[1237] d. Jan-16-1961 in San Diego Co, CA,[1237] resided 1957 in California,[765] resided 1948 in Tucson, Pima Co, AZ,[856] resided 1932 in San Pedro, Los Angeles Co, CA,[mcdxcv[1495]] census 1920 in Southwest District, Doddridge Co, WV. He married[mcdxcvi[1496]] Louise Anderson.

    iv.   HARRY WILLIAM HAUGHT b. Jun- 5-1906 in Oxford, Doddridge Co, WV,[mcdxcvii[1497],190] d. Aug-16-1972 in Akron, Summit Co, OH,[806] buried in Greenlawn Memorial Park Cemetery, Akron, Summit Co, OH,[190] resided in Akron, Summit Co, OH,[856,765,190] census 1920, 1930 in Southwest District, Doddridge Co, WV, occupation mechanic,[190] [Employed by Fischback Trucking Co for the last 2-1/2 years, and had formerly worked 22 years as a mechanic for the Ace Freight Co., all in Akron.], military U.S. Army, World War II.[190] He married[mcdxcviii[1498]] Freda Alice Davis, b. Sep- 9-1915,[1498,592] (daughter of Hezekiah Stephen Davis and Eliza Ellen Britton), d. Jul- -1986,[592] resided in Akron, Summit Co, OH,[604,484] census 1920, 1930 in Southwest District, Doddridge Co, WV [In 1920 listed as a lodger in the household of Jacob M. Osborn, and in 1930 as a boarder in the home of Jacob's widow Annetta on Lower Run Road.].

Freda: Identified in obituaries of E. Wilson Osborne and W. Frank Osborne as Mrs. Freda Haught of Akron, a surviving sister. But she was identified in obituary of Frank's sister Rella Osborne Snider as Mrs. Harry (Freda) Haught of Akron, a surviving foster sister, and she was identified in obituary of Annetta "Nettie" Cole Osburn as Mrs. Harry (Freda) Haught of Akron, a surviving foster daughter. It would thus appear that Freda, whose mother died in 1919 when Freda was just 4, was raised in the family of Jacob M. and Annetta "Nettie" Cole Osburn. She was listed in their household as a lodger in the 1920 Census. Relationship between the Davis/Britton and Osborne/Cole families, if any, is not known. Confusingly, the obituary of her foster sister, Mary Osborne Gaston, states that she was predeceased by "three sisters, Rella Snider, Freda Haught and Freda Osborne." No birth record for Freda Davis was found in Doddridge County.

    v.   RALPH MARVEL HAUGHT b. Dec-19-1912 in Porto Rico (New Milton), Doddridge Co, WV,[mcdxcix[1499],190] d. Feb-26-1997 in Coronado, San Diego Co, CA,[190] resided 1953-97 in Coronado, San Diego Co, CA,[190] resided 1948 in Fayetteville, Fayette Co, WV,[856] census 1920 in Southwest District, Doddridge Co, WV, occupation teacher.[190]

He received his degree in mathematics from West Virginia University, where he attended on an athletic scholarship. He volunteered in the U.S. Navy as a Lieutenant Junior Grade during World War II. In the war, he served as shipper of a PT boat that helped liberate prisoners in the Pacific, including survivors of the Bataan Death March. After moving with his family from West Virginia in 1953, he taught math and coached golf at Chula Vista High School for over 20 years, retiring in 1976. He was a charter member of the Coronada Municipal Golf Course.[190]

He married ca 1935,[484] Maudaline Stinespring, b. Sep-13-1913,[592] (daughter of Victor Goff Stinespring and Nellie May Nutter), d. Jun-16-2006,[592] resided in Coronado, San Diego Co, CA,[521,484,592] occupation teacher.[md[1500]]

vi.   SUMMERS BROWN HAUGHT b. Jul-14-1915 in Doddridge Co, WV,[mdi[1501]],592 d. Mar-30-1989,[190,592] buried in Hillcrest Memorial Gardens, resided aft 1988 in Fruitland Park, Lake Co, FL,[604] resided until 1988 in Cuyahoga Falls, Summit Co, OH, resided 1957 in Akron, Summit Co, OH,[765] census 1920, 1930 in Southwest District, Doddridge Co, WV, occupation data processor, General Tire. He married Wilma E. Webber, also known as Wilma Weber, b. Nov-22-1916,[924] resided in Fruitland Park, Lake Co, FL.

747. **Love Haught** (412.Mary[8], 246.John[7], 136.Hugh[6], 72.John[5], 21.John[4], 6.Hugh[3], 3.John[2], 1.Jean[1]), b. Jan-1-1878 in Doddridge Co, WV,[190] d. Jul-24-1964 in Pennsboro, Ritchie Co, WV,[mdii[1502]],190 buried in South Fork Bapt Church Cem, Oxford, Doddridge Co, WV,[190,mdiii[1503]] [Identified in obituary as "Love Haught Maxwell," but name on headstone reads "Love Gaston Maxwell"], resided in Pennsboro, Ritchie Co, WV,[190] resided 1937, 55, 57, 58 in Greenwood, Doddridge Co, WV,[1376,412,521,484] census 1930 in Central District, Doddridge Co, WV, resided 1927 in Clarksburg, Harrison Co, WV,[521] census 1900 in Southwest District, Doddridge Co, WV. She married[mdiv[1504]],484 Sep-13-1899 in Doddridge Co, WV,[mdv[1505]] **Boyd Curtis Maxwell**, b. Mar-19-1871 in Doddridge Co, WV,[mdvi[1506]] [Birth record shows birthdate as Mar 19 1871. But headstone reads 1872, and obituary also states Mar 19 1872, with age being 85 at time of death on Feb 14 1958. 1900 Census also reports his birth date as Mar 1872, and age 27 given at time of Sep 1899 marriage would also put his birth in 1872..] (son of Charles Maxwell and Penelope Chapman), d. Feb-14-1958 in Greenwood, Doddridge Co, WV,[190,17,191,356] buried in South Fork Bapt Church Cem, Oxford, Doddridge Co, WV,[17,190] resided 1929-58 in Greenwood, Doddridge Co, WV,[190] census 1930 in Central District, Doddridge Co, WV, census 1880, 1900 in Southwest District, Doddridge Co, WV, occupation farmer, oil field worker.[1504] The home of Boyd & Love Maxwell burned down on March 5, 1946. They lost everything. [From the Diary of Nancy Clark Dotson 1904-1946, p. 614, http://www.westunion-wv.com/greenwood.htm]

Children:
i.   (INFANT SON) MAXWELL b. Aug-12-1902 in Doddridge Co, WV,[mdvii[1507]] d. Aug-12-1902 in Doddridge Co, WV,[mdviii[1508]] buried in South Fork Bapt Church Cem, Oxford, Doddridge Co, WV.[17]
ii.   CHARLES L. MAXWELL b. Sep-24-1906,[17] d. May- 9-1919,[17] buried in South Fork Bapt Church Cem, Oxford, Doddridge Co, WV.[17]
iii. (INFANT SON) MAXWELL b. Sep-24-1906,[1504] d. Sep-24-1906.[1504]
iv.   MABEL I. MAXWELL b. Aug-12-1908 at Oxford, Doddridge Co, WV,[mdix[1509],46] d. May-12-1909 in Southwest District, Doddridge Co, WV,[mdx[1510],46] buried in South Fork Bapt Church Cem, Oxford, Doddridge Co, WV,[17] cause of death meningitis.[357]
v.   MARY GRACE MAXWELL b. Aug-31-1914 in Summers, Doddridge Co, WV,[1504,46] d. Jul-3-1992,[1504,46] buried in IOOF Cemetery, Harrisville, Ritchie Co, WV,[469] resided 1964 in Pennsboro, Ritchie Co, WV,[856] resided 1958 in Greenwood, Doddridge Co, WV,[765] census 1930 in Central District, Doddridge Co, WV.

Member of Doddridge County Republican Party Executive Committee.[1491]

She married Nov- 5-1932 in Greenwood, Doddridge Co, WV,[mdxi[1511],1504] John Kenneth "Scotty" DeBrular, also known as Kenneth DeBrular,[354,mdxii[1512],396,mdxiii[1513]] b. Jul-16-1909 in Bear Run (Cairo), Ritchie Co, WV,[1504,46] (son of Charles Porter DeBrular and Josephine Mae "Dochie" Gribble), d. Aug-12-1964,[1504,46] buried in IOOF Cemetery, Harrisville, Ritchie Co, WV,[469] census 1930 in Toll Gate, Ritchie Co, WV.[1513]

748. **Ivah May Haught**, also known as Iva May Haught (412.Mary[8], 246.John[7], 136.Hugh[6], 72.John[5], 21.John[4], 6.Hugh[3], 3.John[2], 1.Jean[1]), b. Feb-23-1880 in Summers, Doddridge Co, WV,[190] d. Nov- 6-1955 in Smithburg, Doddridge Co, WV,[357,190] buried in Archbold Cemetery, Smithburg, Doddridge Co, WV,[17] [Name appears as Ivah May Hickman.], resided 1910-55 in Smithburg, Doddridge Co, WV.[190] She married Aug-29-1900 in Doddridge Co, WV,[mdxiv[1514],mdxv[1515],191,354] **James Marshall Hickman**, also known as Marshall Hickman,[17,775,1291] b. Nov-28-1875 in Doddridge Co, WV,[190,46,mdxvi[1516]] (son of Thomas Hickman and Mary J. Adams), d. Aug-15-1952 in Philippi, Barbour Co, WV,[806,191] buried in

Archbold Cemetery, Smithburg, Doddridge Co, WV,[17,190] occupation farmer, carpenter, funeral director,[920,775,190.]

1910 Census, Doddridge Co, WV (New Milton District), enumerated on May 2 1910:
James M. Hickman, 34, house carpenter, married 9 yrs; wife Iva M, 30, mother of 3 children (all still living); dau Ortha M, 8; dau Rella J, 6; son Grant, 4; servant Blanche Law, 19, single.

1920 Census, Doddridge Co, WV (West Union District), enumerated on Jan 24 1920:
Marshall Hickman, 44, carpenter (general carpentry); wife Ivah, 39; dau Rella, 16; son Loren, 14; dau Marjorie, 6.

1930 Census, Doddridge Co, WV (West Union District), enumerated on Apr 10 1930:
Marshall Hickman, 54, funeral home proprietor; wife Ivah, 50; dau Rella, 26; dau Marjorie, 16.

Children:
i.   ORTHA MABEL HICKMAN b. Aug-12-1901 in Doddridge Co, WV,[mdxvii[1517],398] d. Feb-23-1959 in Romney, Hampshire Co, WV,[398] resided in Romney, Hampshire Co, WV,[398] resided 1952, 55 in Smithburg, Doddridge Co, WV,[765,856] census 1930 in Cleveland, Cuyahoga Co, OH, occupation housemother, WV School for the Blind.[398] She married divorced[436] Leslie Moore, b. ca 1902 in West Virginia,[334] census 1930 in Cleveland, Cuyahoga Co, OH.

1930 Census, Cuyahoga Co, Ohio (city of Cleveland), enumerated on Apr 5 1930 on East 200th Street:
Leslie Moore, 28, b. W.Va, occupation trimmer in auto body manufacturing, age 20 at time of first marriage; wife Ortha, 28, b. W.Va, age 20 at first marriage; son John, 7, b. W.Va.

ii.   RELLA J. HICKMAN b. May-28-1903 in Doddridge Co, WV,[mdxviii[1518]] d. Jun- 5-2000,[190] buried in Whitakers, Nash Co, NC,[190] resided in Richmond, VA,[190] resided formerly in Whitakers, Nash Co, NC,[190] resided 1950, 52, 55, 59 in Arlington, Arlington Co, VA,[mdxix[1519],856,mdxx[1520]] occupation teacher, social worker,[190] education Salem College.[190]

Identified in parents' Golden Anniversary announcement in 1950 and in mother's 1955 obituary as "Miss Rella Hickman."[592]

She married[191] Emerson Odell Anderson, b. Jul-18-1903,[592] d. Jul- 2-1989,[592] resided in Richmond, VA.[708]
iii.   LOREN GRANT HICKMAN b. Jan-25-1906 in Summers, Doddridge Co, WV,[mdxxi[1521],46] [Death record states birth date as Jan 2 1906.], d. Jun-28-1923 in Grafton, Taylor Co, WV,[398,46] buried in Archbold Cemetery, Smithburg, Doddridge Co, WV,[17,398] cause of death hit by train,[398] resided in Smithburg, Doddridge Co, WV.[398]
iv.   MARJORIE MAY HICKMAN b. May- 6-1913 in Smithton (now Smithburg), Doddridge Co, WV,[1499] resided 1955 in Hot Springs, Garland Co, AR,[856] resided 1952 in Smithburg, Doddridge Co, WV,[765] resided 1950 in Venezuela.[1519] She married Otis Burdell Townsen, census name Odes D. Townsend,[1364] b. Sep- -1892,[1364] (son of Charles Birdwell "Bert" Townsen and Harriet "Hattie" Leggett), resided 1951 in Venezuela,[521] resided 1947 in South America,[765] census 1900 in New Milton, Doddridge Co, WV.[1364] Article in West Union Herald, Sep 21 1944: "Mr. and Mrs. O. B. Townsen left this week for New York City and Miami Beach, Fla., before returning to South America, after spending some time with their parents, Mr. and Mrs. J. M. Hickman of Smithburg, and Mr. and Mrs. Bert Townsen of Holbrook."

749. **Amos Peter Haught**[mdxxii[1522]] (412.Mary[8], 246.John[7], 136.Hugh[6], 72.John[5], 21.John[4], 6.Hugh[3], 3.John[2], 1.Jean[1]), b. Sep-29-1882,[46] [Birth date calculated from age at death (31y 3m 9d) on death record. Headstone reads only 1882.], d. Jan- 7-1914 in Doddridge Co, WV,[mdxxiii[1523],356,46] buried in Oxford Baptist Church Cemetery, Doddridge Co, WV.[17] He married Apr-12-1908 in Doddridge Co, WV,[354]

Susie A. (twin) Nutter, b. Mar- 3-1883 in Doddridge Co, WV,[190,17,592] (daughter of Eli Marion Nutter and Mary Frances Maxwell), d. Mar-13-1985 in Salem, WV,[190,592] buried in Oxford Baptist Church Cemetery, Doddridge Co, WV,[mdxxiv][1524] [Name on headstone: Susie A. Haught.], resided in Pennsboro, Ritchie Co, WV,[856,521,395,190].

    Children:

    i.   EDWARD MARSHALL HAUGHT b. Jul- 1-1911 in Doddridge Co, WV,[190,17] d. Apr-29-1969 in Arnolds Creek (West Union), Doddridge Co, WV,[190,356,17] buried in South Fork Bapt Church Cem, Oxford, Doddridge Co, WV,[17,190] resided in Pennsboro, Ritchie Co, WV,[190] census 1920 in West Union, Doddridge Co, WV, occupation Carnegie Natural Gas Co., military TEC5, HQ Co, 318th Inf, U.S. Army - WW II.[1410]

    Managed the "Woodlawn" estate in Doddridge Co of his grandparents, Eli Marshall Nutter and Mary Frances Maxwell Nutter, from the time of their deaths in 1937-38 until his own.[mdxxv][1525]

    He married[191] Jun-15-1945 in Ritchie Co, WV,[1433] no children from this marriage, Geneva Dera "Jean" Spiker,[mdxxvi][1526],190 b. May-25-1909 at Oxford, Doddridge Co, WV,[190] (daughter of Jacob Spiker and Missouri Gay Zinn), d. Nov-10-2006 in Marietta, Washington Co, OH,[764] buried in South Fork Bapt Church Cem, Oxford, Doddridge Co, WV,[190] resided in Pennsboro, Ritchie Co, WV,[521,190] occupation teacher (40 yrs, retired in 1974),[mdxxvii][1527],190 education Pullman HS, Glenville State College (1938, Bachelors in Education).[190]

750. **Mary Ellen Haught** (412.Mary[8], 246.John[7], 136.Hugh[6], 72.John[5], 21.John[4], 6.Hugh[3], 3.John[2], 1.Jean[1]), b. Jun-17-1891 in Harmony, Doddridge Co, WV,[190] d. Dec-30-1976 in Clarksburg, Harrison Co, WV,[190,592] buried in Mt. Olivet Cemetery, Parkersburg, WV,[190] resided 1972, 76 in Lumberport, Harrison Co, WV,[521,190] resided 1957, 64 in Parkersburg, Wood Co, WV,[521,412] resided 1955, 64 in Harmony, Doddridge Co, WV.[412] She married Oct-10-1915 in Doddridge Co, WV,[191,354] **Worthy Eugene Adams**, b. Aug-24-1889 in Oxford, Doddridge Co, WV,[190] (son of Alexander Adams and Mary Isabel "Bell" Gaston), d. Oct-21-1957 in Parkersburg, Wood Co, WV,[190,mdxxviii][1528] [Wife's obituary gives Worthy Eugene Adams' death as occurring in 1963, but son Worthy's obituary states his father died in 1957. An undated obituary clipping, stating that he was born Aug 24 1889 and died on Monday at his home in Parkersburg at age 68, was annotated with the date Oct 21 1957. That date was a Monday.], resided 1944 - 57 in Parkersburg, Wood Co, WV,[190] resided 1915 - 44 in Clarksburg, Harrison Co, WV,[190] occupation Pure Ice Cream Co.,[190] occupation 1930 salesman at wallpaper store.[1208] Mary Ellen Haught and Worthy Eugene Adams were double cousins, in that they were third cousins (both were great-great-grandchildren of John Gaston Jr. (b. 1752 in NJ)) and also fifth cousins (both were g-g-g-g-grandchildren of John Smith (b. 1699)).

    Children:

    i.   EUGENE ALEXANDER ADAMS b. Nov-27-1918 in Doddridge Co, WV,[190] d. Oct-24-1971 in Clarksburg, Harrison Co, WV,[806] buried in Freemansburg Meth Church Cemetery, Lewis Co, WV,[190] resided in Weston, Lewis Co, WV,[190] resided 1957 in Hamlin, Lincoln Co, WV,[765] resided 1937 in Clarksburg, Harrison Co, WV,[419] census 1920 in Clarksburg, Harrison Co, WV, occupation warehouseman for Consolidated Gas Co.[190] He married (1) Nov- 3-1937 in Clarksburg, Harrison Co, WV,[419] divorced Lorena Dell Bane, b. Jul-31-1915 in Copley, Doddridge Co, WV,[419,592] (daughter of Andrew Melvin Bane and Mary Elizabeth Skinner), d. Aug-14-2000,[592] resided in Bristol, Harrison Co, WV.[1086] He married (2) Jun-30-1945,[484] no children from this marriage, Evalena Jackson, resided 1971 in Weston, Lewis Co, WV.[484]

    ii.   WORTHY BERNARD ADAMS, also known as Bernard Adams,[521] b. Mar-10-1920 in Clarksburg, Harrison Co, WV,[190] d. Jan- 8-1977 in Clarksburg, Harrison Co, WV,[190] buried in K of P Memorial Park Cemetery, Salem, WV,[190] resided in Salem, WV,[521,856,190].

    He was a veteran of World War II, having served in the Infantry of the Seventh Army in Europe. He was a member of the Harrison County Emergency Squad, to which he was elected secretary, and had been a First Aid instructor. For the last ten years, he was an insurance adjuster for the Shelby Insurance Co of Wheeling.[190]

He married Sep- 5-1941,[484,191] Wilma Pearl Grubb, b. Aug-22-1911 in Jack's Run, Monongalia Co, WV,[190] (daughter of William Merritt Grubb and Carol Marsh), d. Oct-17-2002 in Clarksburg, Harrison Co, WV,[190] buried in K of P Memorial Park Cemetery, Salem, WV,[190] resided in Salem, WV.[190]

Wilma: For several years, was a secretary for Triangle Motor Company. In 1957, she opened an antique shop in Bristol, Harrison Co, WV, relocating in 1965 to Salem, where she operated the shop until 1997.[190]

iii.   FLOYD HAUGHT ADAMS b. Apr-10-1922 in Clarksburg, Harrison Co, WV,[602,190] d. Dec-19-2004 in Fort Worth, Tarrant Co, TX,[190] buried Greenwood Mausoleum in Fort Worth, Tarrant Co, TX,[190] resided in Fort Worth, Tarrant Co, TX,[190,604] resided 1957, 71, 77, 2000 in Huntington, Cabell Co, WV,[765,521,mdxxix[1529]] resided 1976 in Barboursville, Cabell Co, WV,[856] resided 1949 in Parkersburg, Wood Co, WV,[602] occupation State Farm Insurance agent (43 yrs).[190] He married Dec-22-1949 in Parkersburg, Wood Co, WV,[mdxxx[1530]] Frankie Leone Sears, b. Dec-28-1928 in Diana, Webster Co, WV,[602,190] (daughter of Herley M. Sears and Alice J. Cool), d. May- 6-2009, buried Greenwood Mausoleum in Fort Worth, Tarrant Co, TX,[190] resided 2004 in Fort Worth, Tarrant Co, TX,[484] resided 1949 in Parkersburg, Wood Co, WV,[602] education Marshall University,[190] occupation teacher (Cabell Co WV, retired).[190]

iv.   EDWARD NELSON ADAMS, also known as Nelson Adams, b. Feb- 6-1924 in Clarksburg, Harrison Co, WV,[419] d. Sep- -1968,[191] resided 1957 in Marietta, Washington Co, OH,[765] resided 1942 in Clarksburg, Harrison Co, WV,[419] census 1930 in Clarksburg, Harrison Co, WV. He married Oct-22-1942 in Clarksburg, Harrison Co, WV,[419] Ada Ruth Wolfe, b. Jul-30-1923 in Clarksburg, Harrison Co, WV,[190,592] [Birth date given in marriage record as Jul 30 1924, but obituary and SSDI state Jul 30 1923.] (daughter of Rudolph Wolfe and Daisy Merryman), d. May-29-2010 in Charleston, Kanawha Co, WV,[806] cremated[190] resided in Spencer, Roane Co, WV,[190] resided 1942 in Clarksburg, Harrison Co, WV,[419] education Victory H.S.[190]

v.   MARY AGNES ADAMS b. Aug-25-1925 in Clarksburg, Harrison Co, WV,[419,592] d. May-22-1994,[592] resided in Fort Pierce, Saint Lucie Co, FL,[604] resided 1971, 76, 77 in Stamford, Fairfield Co, CT,[521,856] resided 1957 in Parkersburg, Wood Co, WV,[765] resided 1943 in Clarksburg, Harrison Co, WV.[419]

Had three daughters.

She married[1101,1040] Jan-24-1943 in Clarksburg, Harrison Co, WV,[419] Walter Hess Hinkle, b. Apr-27-1923 in Clarksburg, Harrison Co, WV,[419,592] (son of Lloyd Hess Hinkle and Lula Green), d. Jun-24-2003,[592] resided in Fort Pierce, Saint Lucie Co, FL,[604] resided 1943 in Clarksburg, Harrison Co, WV.[419]

751. **James Wesley Smith**, also known as Wesley Smith, also known as James W. Smith, Jr.,[711,458] (413.Ivah[8], 246.John[7], 136.Hugh[6], 72.John[5], 21.John[4], 6.Hugh[3], 3.John[2], 1.Jean[1]), b. Feb-13-1869 in Doddridge Co, WV,[398] [Birth date given in 1900 Census as Feb 1869, but death record states Feb 13 1869. Age in 1870 was one.], d. Jul-19-1951 in Harrisville, Ritchie Co, WV,[398] buried in Center Point Christian Church Cemetery, Doddridge Co, WV,[398] resided at Nutter Fort, Harrison Co, WV,[398] census 1930 in Bridgeport, Harrison Co, WV, census 1910, 1920 in Clarksburg, Harrison Co, WV, census 1900 in West Union, Doddridge Co, WV, census 1870 in Southwest District, Doddridge Co, WV, occupation bookkeeper for insurance company,[398] occupation 1900 salesman.[767] He married (1) Apr-30-1889 at Arnolds Creek (West Union), Doddridge Co, WV,[mdxxxi[1531]] divorced btwn 1920-1930,[1208] **Gertrude Hammond**, also known as Gertie Hammond,[711,767] b. May- 7-1872 in St. Marys, Pleasants Co, WV,[190,276,767,711] (daughter of John William Hammond and Eliza Dora LaRue), d. May- 5-1965 in Clarksburg, Harrison Co, WV,[764,276] buried in Sunset Memorial Park Cemetery, Clarksburg,

WV,[276,190] census 1910, 1920, 1930 in Clarksburg, Harrison Co, WV, census 1900 in West Union, Doddridge Co, WV, census 1880 in West Union District, Doddridge Co, WV.

1900 Census, Doddridge Co, WV (West Union District, Town of West Union), enumerated on Jun 1 1900:
James W. Smith, 32, b. Feb 1868, salesman, married 11 yrs; wife Gertie, 28, b. May 1872, mother of 3 children (all still living); son Avery B, 9, b. Jul 1890; dau Myrtil, 7, b. Apr 1893; dau Ruby, 1, b. Apr 1899.

1910 Census, Harrison Co, WV (Coal District, City of Clarksburg), enumerated on Apr 29 1910 at 307 Fifth Street:
James W. Smith Jr, 42, bookkeeper at grocery, married 21 yrs; wife Gertrude, 38, mother of 3 children (all still living); son Avery B, 19; dau Myrtle R, 17; dau Ruby, 11.

1920 Census, Harrison Co, WV (Coal District, City of Clarksburg), enumerated Jan 13 1920 at 371 Broaddus Avenue:
James W. Smith Jr, 50, bookkeeper for insurance company; wife Gertrude, 47; dau Ruby, 20, single; brother Charles L. Smith, commercial tmstr for groceries, single; lodger Mary Grosscup, 29, stenographer at freight office, single; lodger Grace Chapman, 23, stenographer at carbon plant, single.

1930 Census, Harrison Co, WV (Coal District, City of Clarksburg), enumerated Apr 15 1930 at 371 Broaddus Avenue:
Gertrude Smith, 57, no occupation, divorced; lodger Dwight Davis, 25, secretary at electric company, married; lodger Gail Hildreth (male), 30, electrician at electric company, single; lodger Herbert Hoover, 19, waiter at lunch room, married.

He married[228] (2) ca 1930,[1208] **Flora Asher**, census name Liza F. Asher,[mdxxxii[1532]] b. Nov- 4-1885 at Center Point, Doddridge Co, WV,[398] (daughter of Hiram J. Asher and Rosalee George), d. Jul-24-1955 in Clarksburg, Harrison Co, WV,[398] buried in Center Point Christian Church Cemetery, Doddridge Co, WV,[398] resided at Center Point, Doddridge Co, WV,[398] resided 1951 at Nutter Fort, Harrison Co, WV,[228] census 1930 in Bridgeport, Harrison Co, WV, census 1900 in McClellan District, Doddridge Co, WV.

1930 Census, Harrison Co, WV (Simpson District, Town of Bridgeport), enumerated on Apr 14 1930:
J. W. Smith, 62, bookkeeper for insurance company, age 62 at time of first marriage; wife Flora Smith, 43, age 43 at first marriage; stepson Jeardine Asher, 8; stepson Lily Asher, 7; nephew C. H. Fisher, 26, farmer.
(Note: The children listed as James Smith's stepsons are actually the orphaned nieces of wife Flora; both parents of Geraldine Asher and Lillie Asher died of typhoid fever in 1925.)

Children by Gertrude Hammond:
i.   AVERY BIRCHARD SMITH b. Jul- -1890,[767] d. bef May 1965,[856] resided in Uniontown, Fayette Co, PA,[856] census 1930 in Uniontown, Fayette Co, PA, census 1920 in Wilkinsburg, Allegheny Co, PA, census 1910 in Clarksburg, Harrison Co, WV, census 1900 in West Union, Doddridge Co, WV, occupation 1920 salesman for light company,[681] occupation 1930 electrician, radio work.[334] He married[681] Roberta B. ___, b. ca 1891 in West Virginia,[681] census 1930 in Uniontown, Fayette Co, PA, census 1920 in Wilkinsburg, Allegheny Co, PA.
ii.   MYRTLE ROSE SMITH b. Apr-19-1893 in Doddridge Co, WV,[17,767,419] d. Mar-18-1970,[17] buried in IOOF Cemetery, Clarksburg (S Chestnut St), Harrison Co, WV,[462] resided in Clarksburg, Harrison Co, WV,[228,856] census 1910, 1920, 1930 in Clarksburg, Harrison Co, WV, census 1900 in West Union, Doddridge Co, WV. She married Sep-23-1915 in Clarksburg, Harrison Co, WV,[419] Robert Linn Osborn, b. Jun-29-1876 in Clarksburg, Harrison Co, WV,[398,419] (son of Joseph Freeman Osborn and Vianna "Anna" Frum), d. Apr-13-1943 in Clarksburg, Harrison Co, WV,[398] buried in IOOF Cemetery, Clarksburg (S Chestnut St), Harrison Co, WV,[398,462] resided in Clarksburg, Harrison Co,

WV,[419,398] census 1920, 1930 in Clarksburg, Harrison Co, WV, occupation physician, city health officer.[418,398]

       1920 Census, Harrison Co, WV (Coal District, City of Clarksburg), enumerated on Jan 12 1920 at 664 West Pike Street:
       Robert L. Osborn, 43, medical doctor; wife Myrtle, 26; dau Jane, 2 yr 4 mo; mother Anna, 85, widowed.

       1930 Census, Harrison Co, WV (Coal District, City of Clarksburg), enumerated on Apr 16 1930 at 664 West Pike Street:
       Robert L. Osborn, 53, city manager of Clarksburg; wife Myrtle, 36; dau Jean L, 12.
       (Note: The enumerator's entry of daughter's name as Jean, rather than Jane, is incorrect.)

       iii.   RUBY SMITH b. Apr-22-1899 in Doddridge Co, WV,[767,419] d. Feb-16-1976 in Fairfax, VA, resided 1965 in Arlington, Arlington Co, VA,[856] census 1910, 1920 in Clarksburg, Harrison Co, WV, census 1900 in West Union, Doddridge Co, WV. She married Jul-23-1920 in Clarksburg, Harrison Co, WV,[419] John Edward Payne, also known as J. Edward Payne,[419] census name Edward Payne,[458] b. Jun-28-1898 in Lumberport, Harrison Co, WV,[64,419] (son of John Bosworth Payne and Sallie Florida Corpening), d. Jul-27-1953 in Arlington, Arlington Co, VA,[64] resided 1920 in Clarksburg, Harrison Co, WV,[419] census 1910 in Clarksburg, Harrison Co, WV, occupation physician, education University of Maryland Medical School (1922).

752. **Sanford Smith**[374,1314,502] also known as Santford Smith,[354] also known as Sandford Smith,[1315] (413.Ivah[8], 246.John[7], 136.Hugh[6], 72.John[5], 21.John[4], 6.Hugh[3], 3.John[2], 1.Jean[1]) (See marriage to number 712.)

753. **Miner Francis Smith**, census name Minor F. Smith,[767] (413.Ivah[8], 246.John[7], 136.Hugh[6], 72.John[5], 21.John[4], 6.Hugh[3], 3.John[2], 1.Jean[1]), b. Nov-25-1884 in West Union, Doddridge Co, WV,[771] d. Mar-17-1985 in Zanesville, Muskingum Co, OH,[771] buried in Memorial Park Cemetery, Zanesville, OH,[771] resided 1929, 57, 72 in Zanesville, Muskingum Co, OH,[748,412,mdxxxiii[1533]] census 1910 in West Union District, Doddridge Co, WV, occupation 1910 teacher,[1290] education Marshall College, Huntington, WV (1909).[771] He married Mar-30-1918 in Washington, DC,[771] **Bessie Lillian Shuman**, b. Jun-9-1894 at Rock Run (West Union), Doddridge Co, WV,[mdxxxiv[1534]] [Birth date given as Jun 1895 in 1900 Census, but birth record and SSDI show it to be Jun 9 1894.] (daughter of Calvin Leroy Shuman and Lydia Ellen Freeman), d. Dec-23-1966 in Zanesville, Muskingum Co, OH,[1011] buried in Memorial Park Cemetery, Zanesville, OH,[771] resided since 1923 in Zanesville, Muskingum Co, OH,[190] census 1900 in West Union District, Doddridge Co, WV.
       Children:
       i.   NEAL AUSTIN SMITH b. Feb-10-1919 in Norwich, Muskingum Co, OH,[771] d. Jul-15-1989 in Columbus, Franklin Co, OH.[771]

       No children. Served in US Navy 1944-46. Professor of Electrical Engineering at Ohio State University 1947-1984, retiring as Professor Emeritus.[771]

       He married Jun-7-1942 in Millersburg, Holmes Co, OH,[771] Faye Louise Schlupe, b. Nov-18-1915 in Millersburg, Holmes Co, OH,[771] d. Dec-8-1991 in Columbus, Franklin Co, OH.[771]
       ii.   LIVING. He married Living.

754. **Mary Bird Smith** (413.Ivah[8], 246.John[7], 136.Hugh[6], 72.John[5], 21.John[4], 6.Hugh[3], 3.John[2], 1.Jean[1]), b. Jul-6-1889 in Arnolds Creek (West Union), Doddridge Co, WV,[mdxxxv[1535],190] d. Feb-10-1957,[190,771] buried in Masonic Memorial Park Cemetery, Crystal Lake (West Union), WV,[190,721] resided in Cairo, Ritchie Co, WV.[190] She married Aug-13-1913 in Clarksburg, Harrison Co, WV,[mdxxxvi[1536],191,354,771] [Although this marriage is listed in "Doddridge County WV Marriages," obituary of wife states that they were married in Clarksburg, Harrison County.], **Anthony Smith Freeman**, b. Aug-18-

1890,[771,767] (son of Charles Thomas Freeman and Levary Jane Ash), d. Aug-31-1948,[771] buried in Masonic Memorial Park Cemetery, Crystal Lake (West Union), WV.[721]

Children:

i. NEVA LUCILLE FREEMAN b. Dec-26-1914 in Mannington, Marion Co, WV,[190,592] d. Feb-25-2000 in Parkersburg, Wood Co, WV,[190,592] buried in Masonic Memorial Park Cemetery, Crystal Lake (West Union), WV,[190,721] resided in Cairo, Ritchie Co, WV,[856,592] resided formerly in West Union, Doddridge Co, WV.[856]

A graduate of Mannington High School with the class of 1932, attended Fairmont State College, graduated from West Virginia University in 1936, and taught school in the southern part of West Virginia at Stotebury. A 4-H Club leader in Doddridge and Ritchie Counties. She was the co-owner of the Cairo Supply Company in Ritchie County from 1948 to 1965 and sole owner until 1996.[190]

She married[771] Eugene J. "Gene" Edeburn, b. Dec-31-1914 in Tucker Co, WV,[996,771] (son of Samuel H. Edeburn and Dollie __), d. 1965 in Cairo, Ritchie Co, WV,[721,771] [Death date provided by Virginia Dunn Smith as Oct 11 1960.], buried in Masonic Memorial Park Cemetery, Crystal Lake (West Union), WV,[721] resided 1938 in Upshur Co, WV.[996]

ii. HESTER LORENE FREEMAN b. Jan-20-1917 in West Virginia,[693] d. Sep-26-1982 in San Luis Obispo Co, CA,[693] resided 1957 in Burbank, Los Angeles Co, CA.[856] She married Mar- 3-1948,[771] no children from this marriage,[771] Thomas Palmer.

iii. WILMA OLETA FREEMAN b. Dec- 8-1922,[771] d. bef Jun 2007,[521] resided in Zephyrhills, Pasco Co, FL,[412] resided 1957 in Boston, MA.[856] She married[424,1101] __ Perry.

iv. WILLIS KENT "BUD" FREEMAN b. Aug- 6-1930 in Mannington, Marion Co, WV,[190] d. Jun-26-2007,[190] buried Forest Lawn in Cypress, Orange Co, CA,[190] resided in Carson, Los Angeles Co, CA,[412,190] resided 1957 in Hondo, Medina Co, TX,[856] education Cairo H.S. (1948).[190] He married Living.

755. **William Columbus Smith**, census name Willie C. Smith,[767] (413.Ivah[8], 246.John[7], 136.Hugh[6], 72.John[5], 21.John[4], 6.Hugh[3], 3.John[2], 1.Jean[1]), b. Mar- 3-1893 in Doddridge Co, WV,[mdxxxvii[1537]] d. Apr-8-1960, resided 1957 in Brentwood, Prince Georges Co, MD,[412] census 1930 in Wheeling, Ohio Co, WV, census 1900 in West Union District, Doddridge Co, WV, occupation carpenter.[334] He married (1) Apr-14-1916,[334,771] **Hilda E.** __, b. ca 1897,[123] census 1930 in Wheeling, Ohio Co, WV. He married (2) **Goldie Fleming Wolfe**.

Children by Hilda E. __:

i. GERALD H. SMITH b. Feb-21-1917 in Wheeling, Ohio Co, WV,[592,1130] d. Jul-22-1998,[592,771] resided in Conneaut, Ashtabula Co, OH,[604] resided 1941 in Wheeling, Ohio Co, WV,[1130] census 1930 in Wheeling, Ohio Co, WV. He married Aug- 9-1941 in Wellsburg, Brooke Co, WV,[1130] Leanor Swiger, b. Jul- 7-1917 in Jarvisville, Harrison Co, WV,[592,1130] d. May- -1981,[592] resided in Washington, DC,[604] resided 1941 in Wheeling, Ohio Co, WV.[1130]

756. **Daniel Webster Britton** (414.Mary[8], 247.Daniel[7], 136.Hugh[6], 72.John[5], 21.John[4], 6.Hugh[3], 3.John[2], 1.Jean[1]), b. Jun-11-1867 in Doddridge Co, WV,[mdxxxviii[1538]] d. 1911,[469] buried in IOOF Cemetery, Harrisville, Ritchie Co, WV,[469] occupation teacher.[405,920] He married[mdxxxix[1539],396] (1) Mar-17-1895 in Doddridge Co, WV,[mdxl[1540],354,478,mdxli[1541]] **Charlotte Wade**, b. Feb-13-1872 in Ritchie Co, WV,[mdxlii[1542],17,478] (daughter of Andrew Montgomery Wade and Sudna Jane Watson), d. Jan-30-1896,[17] buried in Gaston-Hart Cemetery, Upper Run, Summers, Doddridge Co, WV.[17] As great-grandchildren of Samuel Husk and Elizabeth, Daniel Webster Britton and Charlotte Wade were second cousins.

He married[1539,345] (2) Sep-13-1899 in Ritchie Co, WV,[473] **Bessie Alma McClaskey**, b. Aug-31-1881 in Ellenboro, Ritchie Co, WV,[398,154,473,469] (daughter of Enos McClaskey and Sarah Elizabeth McCullough), d. Nov-29-1942 in Harrisville, Ritchie Co, WV,[398,474,469] buried in IOOF Cemetery, Harrisville, Ritchie Co, WV,[469,398] resided in Harrisville, Ritchie Co, WV.[398]

Children by Charlotte Wade:

i. CECIL ORR BRITTON[1539] b. Jan-20-1896,[469] d. Oct-11-1918 in World War I,[469,mdxliii[1543]] buried in IOOF Cemetery, Harrisville, Ritchie Co, WV,[469] resided in Harrison Co, WV,[1543] military U.S. Army Sergeant - WW I.[469]

Children by Bessie Alma McClaskey:

ii. WILBUR LAUGHTON BRITTON[1539] b. Jun-23-1900 at Stewarts Run, Ritchie Co, WV,[1007,46,996] d. 1939,[46] buried in IOOF Cemetery, Harrisville, Ritchie Co, WV.[469] He married[1539] Nov-29-1929 in Ritchie Co, WV,[996] Edra Ellen Gluck, b. May- 5-1905,[992] [But SSDI reports birth date as May 7 1905.] (daughter of Howard Gluck and Dora Zinn), d. Aug- -1985,[592] resided in Wood Co, WV.[592,521]

iii. LORA VIRGINIA BRITTON[1539] b. Aug-22-1902 at Stewarts Run, Ritchie Co, WV,[1007,955] d. Oct- 7-1931 in Ritchie Co, WV,[955] buried in IOOF Cemetery, Harrisville, Ritchie Co, WV,[469] never married[469].

iv. HORACE AUDUBON BRITTON[1539] b. Jan- 6-1904 at Stewarts Run, Ritchie Co, WV,[1007,996,46] d. Dec-24-1966 in Ritchie Co, WV,[477,469] buried in IOOF Cemetery, Harrisville, Ritchie Co, WV,[469,191] occupation Ritchie County Sheriff (1948-52).[941,mdxliv[1544]] He married[1539,191] Sep- 2-1925 in Ritchie Co, WV,[996] Stella Fay Hedge, b. Oct-26-1906 in Ritchie Co, WV,[190] [Obituary printed in Clarksburg Exponent-Telegram (Apr 10 2003) gives birth as Oct 6 1906, location not specified, while the one printed in the Pennsboro News (Apr 16 2003) gives it as Oct 26 1906 in Ritchie Co.] (daughter of James R. Hedge and Jennie Mahala Hill), d. Apr- 8-2003 in Columbus, Franklin Co, OH,[190] buried in IOOF Cemetery, Harrisville, Ritchie Co, WV,[190] resided in Harrisville, Ritchie Co, WV.[190]

Stella: Attended Glenville State College and taught at the King Knob, Lamb's Run, Macfarlan and Beechwold schools. A prominent Harrisville businesswoman, she operated the Whitehall Hotel for 34 years and the B&B Rexall Drug Store for 15 years. She was active in the Republican Party in West Virginia, receiving an invitation to the inauguration of President Richard Nixon in 1973. She was a contributor to the society column of the Ritchie Gazette newspaper.[190]

v. OTHA RYLAND BRITTON[1539] b. Mar- 6-1906 in Harrisville, Ritchie Co, WV,[1007,46] d. Sep- 6-1963 in Pullman, Ritchie Co, WV,[862,46] buried in Pine Grove Cemetery, Berea (Co Rd 7-26), Ritchie Co, WV,[469] occupation farmer.[862] He married[1539] Ruby Meredith, b. 1910,[469] (daughter of Fred Meredith and Lura Buzzard), d. Jun-20-1992,[469] buried in Pine Grove Cemetery, Berea (Co Rd 7-26), Ritchie Co, WV.[469]

vi. LENA MABEL BRITTON[1539.] She married[1539] John Mickle Faris.

vii. LEOTA FAY BRITTON[1539] b. May-19-1910,[592,996] d. Jan- 3-1993,[592] resided in Cairo, Ritchie Co, WV.[mdxlv[1545],592]

Secretary of the Ritchie County Republican Party Executive Committee.[1545]

She married[1539] Nov-12-1931 in Ritchie Co, WV,[996] Clyde W. Marshall, b. Jul-12-1904 in Wirt Co, WV,[996,592] d. Nov- -1983,[592] resided in Cairo, Ritchie Co, WV.[592]

757. **John Frank Britton** (414.Mary[8], 247.Daniel[7], 136.Hugh[6], 72.John[5], 21.John[4], 6.Hugh[3], 3.John[2], 1.Jean[1]), b. Apr-30-1873 in Doddridge Co, WV,[mdxlvi[1546]] census 1930 in Gregory Co, SD, resided 1919 in South Dakota,[412] census 1910 in Coal District, Harrison Co, WV, resided 1904 in Doddridge Co, WV.[mdxlvii[1547]] He married[1539] Sep- 1-1904 in St. Marys, Pleasants Co, WV,[1547] **Bertha Irene Scott**, b. ca 1882 in Ritchie Co, WV,[1547] (daughter of Albert Scott and Florence __), census 1930 in Gregory Co, SD, census 1910 in Coal District, Harrison Co, WV, resided 1904 in Pleasants Co, WV.[1547]

Children:

i. BELVA D. BRITTON b. Jul-21-1905 in West Virginia,[592,mdxlviii[1548]] d. Mar-24-2005,[592] resided in Broken Arrow, Tulsa Co, OK,[838] census 1930 in Topeka, Shawnee Co, KS, census 1910 in Coal District, Harrison Co, WV. She married[1539] ca 1928,[334] James Lorenzo Lester, b. Jun- 3-1904 in Kansas,[334] d. Sep- -1986,[592] resided in Broken Arrow, Tulsa Co, OK,[1240] census 1930 in Topeka, Shawnee Co, KS.

ii. ARLINGTON GALE BRITTON, census name Gale A. Britton,[458] also known as A. G. Britton,[592] b. Feb-11-1907 in West Virginia,[592,458] d. Mar-21-1996,[592] resided in Tulsa, OK,[838] census 1910 in Coal District, Harrison Co, WV, occupation Amoco (retired).[190] He married[1539] Louise Hawkins, b. Oct-19-1910,[592] d. Apr-30-2005,[592] resided in Centertown, Cole Co, MO,[592] resided formerly in Oklahoma,[838] occupation bookkeeper.[190]

iii. MONA V. BRITTON, census name Monna D. Britton,[334] b. Feb-28-1908 in West Virginia,[592,458] d. Jan- 7-1996,[592] resided in Lincoln, Lancaster Co, NE,[691] census 1930 in Gregory Co, SD, census 1910 in Coal District, Harrison Co, WV. She married[1539] (1) Claude Overton. She married[1539] (2) George Rybin.

iv. AUBREY GLENN BRITTON[1539] census name Glenn Britton,[334] b. ca 1911 in West Virginia,[334] resided 1939 in Egan, Moody Co, SD, census 1930 in Gregory Co, SD. He married[1539] Sep-30-1939 in Sinai, Brookings Co, SD,[mdxlix[1549]] Dorothy Mary Duncan, b. ca 1916,[1549] resided 1939 in Egan, Moody Co, SD.[1549]

v. GORDON Y. BRITTON[1539] also known as Alvin Gordon Britton,[1539] b. Jun-24-1912 in South Dakota,[592,334] d. Jul- -1986,[592] resided in Aurora, Dearborn Co, IN,[mdl[1550]] resided 1937 in Gregory Co, SD,[1271] census 1930 in Gregory Co, SD. He married[1539] Dec-24-1937 in Tripp Co, SD,[1271] Clara Tysdale, b. ca 1913,[1271] resided 1937 in Gregory Co, SD.[1271]

vi. GASTON BILL BRITTON, also known as Bill Gaston,[592,190] b. Sep-20-1913 in Porcupine, Shannon Co, SD,[592,334] d. Jun-20-2007 in Winner, Tripp Co, SD,[700,592] buried Pleasant Lawn Cem in Geddes, Charles Mix Co, SD,[190] resided since 1948 in Winner, Tripp Co, SD,[190,1550] census 1930 in Gregory Co, SD, education South Dakota State College (1942),[190] military 1942-1946 U.S. Army, World War II (Pacific),[190] occupation farmer, teacher of shop and vocational agriculture.[190] He married[1539] 1947,[190] Marjorie Mary McDaniel, b. Aug-16-1915 in Geddes, Charles Mix Co, SD,[190,592] (daughter of Sam McDaniel and Cynthia Holmes), d. Jun-20-2007 in Winner, Tripp Co, SD,[764,592] buried Pleasant Lawn Cem in Geddes, Charles Mix Co, SD,[190] resided since 1948 in Winner, Tripp Co, SD,[190,1550] education Geddes H.S. (1932), Southern State Normal School (1935),[190] occupation teacher.[190]

vii. FRANKIE PAULINE BRITTON[1539] census name Pauline J. Britton,[334] b. ca 1917 in South Dakota,[334] resided 1943 in St. Charles, Gregory Co, SD,[1549] census 1930 in Gregory Co, SD. She married[1539] May-29-1943 in Mitchell, Davison Co, SD,[1549] Edward Henry Fiala, b. Aug- 4-1918 in South Dakota,[592,334] (son of Frank Fiala and Rose A. __), d. Apr-17-1992,[592] resided in Fulton, Hanson Co, SD,[1158] resided 1943 in Herrick, Gregory Co, SD,[1549] census 1930 in Gregory Co, SD.

viii. MARY MARGARET BRITTON b. ca 1920 in South Dakota,[334] d.[592] census 1930 in Gregory Co, SD. She married[1539] (1) Oswald C. Lillimoe, b. May-30-1915,[592] d. Dec-30-1993,[592] resided in Montevideo, Chippewa Co, MN.[1550] She married[1101] (2) __ Thiel.

ix. FLORENCE BRITTON b. ca 1923 in South Dakota,[334] census 1930 in Gregory Co, SD. She married[1539] George C. Smith.

x. LENNA RUTH BRITTON, also known as Ruth Britton,[484] b. ca 1924 in South Dakota,[334] resided 1989 in Decatur, Macon Co, IL,[484] census 1930 in Gregory Co, SD. She married[1539] 1945 in Wheaton, Traverse Co, MN,[484] Raymond F. Berneking, b. Jul- 4-1921 in Wheaton, Traverse Co, MN,[190,592] (son of Rudolph Berneking and Louise Krenz), d. Jan-13-1989 in Decatur, Macon Co, IL,[806,592] buried Graceland Cemetery,[190] resided in Decatur, Macon Co, IL,[1550,190] resided formerly in Springfield, Sangamon Co, IL,[190] occupation FBI agent.[190]

Raymond: He joined the FBI in 1947, serving in Chicago, Wheeling, W.Va., and Springfield, IL. He served as a senior resident agent in the Decatur resident agency of the Springfield office, since 1957, retiring after 27 1/2 years. After his retirement, he was employed by the state Department of Law Enforcement division of criminal investigation for eight years, receiving commendations from J. Edgar Hoover and Clarence M. Kelly.

758. **Eliza Ellen Britton** (414.Mary[8], 247.Daniel[7], 136.Hugh[6], 72.John[5], 21.John[4], 6.Hugh[3], 3.John[2], 1.Jean[1]), b. Jul-10-1888,[190,1498] d. May- 2-1919 in Clarksburg, Harrison Co, WV,[190,1498] buried in Gaston-Hart Cemetery, Upper Run, Summers, Doddridge Co, WV,[190] [Obituary gives burial in Gaston Cemetery. This is probably intended to mean what is now known as the Gaston-Hart Cemetery,

Upper Run, Doddridge Co.], resided in Clarksburg, Harrison Co, WV.[190] She married[mdli[1551]] Sep-4-1907 in Doddridge Co, WV,[354,191,1498] **Hezekiah Stephen Davis**, also known as Henry Stephen Davis,[1224] census name Henry S. Davis,[334] b. Jul-28-1884 in Clay Co, WV,[354,1551,mdlii[1552]] (son of Isaiah Bee "Zed" Davis and Darinda Alice Sutton), d. Dec- 2-1968 at Terra Alta, Preston Co, WV,[1224,1498] census 1930 in Garrett Co, MD, resided 1921 in Terra Alta, Preston Co, WV.[1552]

Children:

i. CLAUDIUS BROOKS DAVIS b. May- 8-1909,[1498] d. Oct-23-1980 in Marion Co, FL,[1123] census 1930 in Garrett Co, MD. He married[1498] Gladys Belle Lewis.

ii. ORVAL DAVIS b. Jan- 9-1912,[1498] d. Jan-18-1912.[1498]

iii. EDWIN GYLE DAVIS, census name Gyle E. Davis,[334] also known as Gyle Davis,[856] b. Apr- 5-1913,[1498,592] d. Jul- -1983,[592] resided in Oakland, Garrett Co, MD,[1086] census 1930 in Garrett Co, MD. He married[1498] Floretta Mae Phillipi, b. May-30-1912,[592] d. Jan-22-1999,[592] resided in Wellington, Lorain Co, OH,[592] resided formerly in West Virginia.[mdliii[1553]]

iv. FREDA ALICE DAVIS b. Sep- 9-1915,[1498,592] d. Jul- -1986,[592] resided in Akron, Summit Co, OH,[604,484] census 1920, 1930 in Southwest District, Doddridge Co, WV [In 1920 listed as a lodger in the household of Jacob M. Osborn, and in 1930 as a boarder in the home of Jacob's widow Annetta on Lower Run Road.].

Identified in obituaries of E. Wilson Osborne and W. Frank Osborne as Mrs. Freda Haught of Akron, a surviving sister. But she was identified in obituary of Frank's sister Rella Osborne Snider as Mrs. Harry (Freda) Haught of Akron, a surviving foster sister, and she was identified in obituary of Annetta "Nettie" Cole Osburn as Mrs. Harry (Freda) Haught of Akron, a surviving foster daughter. It would thus appear that Freda, whose mother died in 1919 when Freda was just 4, was raised in the family of Jacob M. and Annetta "Nettie" Cole Osburn. She was listed in their household as a lodger in the 1920 Census. Relationship between the Davis/Britton and Osborne/Cole families, if any, is not known. Confusingly, the obituary of her foster sister, Mary Osborne Gaston, states that she was predeceased by "three sisters, Rella Snider, Freda Haught and Freda Osborne." No birth record for Freda Davis was found in Doddridge County.

She married[1498] Harry William Haught, b. Jun- 5-1906 in Oxford, Doddridge Co, WV,[1497,190] (son of William C. "Will" Haught and Lucy Mae Summers), d. Aug-16-1972 in Akron, Summit Co, OH,[806] buried in Greenlawn Memorial Park Cemetery, Akron, Summit Co, OH,[190] resided in Akron, Summit Co, OH,[856,765,190] census 1920, 1930 in Southwest District, Doddridge Co, WV, occupation mechanic,[190] [Employed by Fischback Trucking Co for the last 2-1/2 years, and had formerly worked 22 years as a mechanic for the Ace Freight Co., all in Akron.], military U.S. Army, World War II.[190]

v. WILMA VIVA DAVIS, also known as Wilda,[856] b. Apr-18-1918,[1498] d. Apr-20-1920.[1498]

759. **Icy M. Richards** (415.Sarah[8], 247.Daniel[7], 136.Hugh[6], 72.John[5], 21.John[4], 6.Hugh[3], 3.John[2], 1.Jean[1]), b. Apr- 1-1892 in Ritchie Co, WV,[1007,809] resided 1968 in Vincent, Washington Co, OH,[521] census 1900 in Union District, Ritchie Co, WV. She married[1101,446] **Harmon W. Snider**.

Children:

i. DELMIS C. SNIDER b. Jan- 4-1929 in Ritchie Co, WV,[1433,592] d. May- 1-1996,[592] resided in Kissimmee, Osceola Co, FL.[592] He married[941] Aug- 8-1953 in Holbrook, Ritchie Co, WV,[966,1433] [Walnut Grove Methodist Church], Helen Grace Britton, also known as Grace,[765,521] b. Jun-19-1924 in Ritchie Co, WV,[190,966] (daughter of Robert Elsworth Britton and Mary Jane Sweeney), d. Feb-22-1980 in Parkersburg, Wood Co, WV,[190,966] buried in Masonic Memorial Park Cemetery, Crystal Lake (West Union), WV,[721,966] [Headstone reads: Grace Britton Snider.], resided 1979 in Parkersburg, Wood Co, WV,[856] occupation Bell Telephone Co.[190]

760. **Anna Eliza Richards**[190], also known as Annie,[484] (416.Rulina[8], 247.Daniel[7], 136.Hugh[6], 72.John[5], 21.John[4], 6.Hugh[3], 3.John[2], 1.Jean[1]), b. Jan-22-1877 in Oxford, Doddridge Co, WV,[190,46] d. Jul-17-1964 in Oxford, Doddridge Co, WV,[700,356] buried in Hart Cemetery, Taylor Drain Rd, Oxford, Doddridge Co WV,[17,190] resided in Oxford, Doddridge Co, WV,[412,521,190] census 1880, 1900, 1920 in Southwest District, Doddridge Co, WV. She married Aug-20-1905 in Doddridge Co, WV,[354,484] **Ira Thomas**

Parks, also known as Thomas Parks, b. Feb- 4-1869,[190,46] (son of Joseph Parks and Nancy Jane Fox), d. Mar- 4-1935 in Doddridge Co, WV,[190,356,46] buried in Hart Cemetery, Taylor Drain Rd, Oxford, Doddridge Co WV,[17,190] census 1920 in Southwest District, Doddridge Co, WV.

Children:

i.   ARLEY CURTIS PARKS, also known as Curtis Parks,[765,856] b. ca 1906,[mdliv[1554]] d. Mar-20-1944 in World War II,[mdlv[1555]] census 1920 in Southwest District, Doddridge Co, WV, military Pfc, U.S. Army - WW II (KIA in South Pacific).[1554,856] He married Nov-28-1934 in Doddridge Co, WV,[354] Mona Gay "Monnie" Husk, b. Jul- 8-1912 in Doddridge Co, WV (daughter of George Washington Husk and Sarah Columbia Lowther Reed), d. Sep- 1-1935 in Doddridge Co, WV,[mdlvi[1556]] buried in Hart Cemetery, Taylor Drain Rd, Oxford, Doddridge Co WV,[17] census 1930 in Murphy District, Ritchie Co, WV [In household with sister Bessie Husk Wright and family.].

ii.   RAYMOND RICHARDS PARKS b. Apr-25-1910 in Oxford, Doddridge Co, WV,[mdlvii[1557]] d. Aug-28-1985 in Clarksburg, Harrison Co, WV,[190] buried in Bethel U M Church Cemetery, Pullman, WV,[17] census 1920 in Southwest District, Doddridge Co, WV, occupation Consolidated Natural Gas Co, Tollgate & Salem Districts.[190] He married Feb-28-1950,[191] Gwendolyn Hayes, b. Sep-23-1924 in Ritchie Co, WV,[190] (daughter of Harley Hugh Hayes and Shada Ellen Goff), d. Jan-26-1979 in Parkersburg, Wood Co, WV,[190] buried in Bethel U M Church Cemetery, Pullman, WV,[190] resided in Summers, Doddridge Co, WV,[190] census 1930 in McKean Co, PA.

Gwendolyn: She was a former postmistress at Oxford, Doddridge Co, and at the time of her death was the director of the Ritchie County Community Action.[190]

761. **Daniel Tolbert Richards** (416.Rulina[8], 247.Daniel[7], 136.Hugh[6], 72.John[5], 21.John[4], 6.Hugh[3], 3.John[2], 1.Jean[1]), b. Jul-17-1878 in Oxford, Doddridge Co, WV,[190,963] d. Apr-19-1957 in Doddridge Co, WV,[mdlviii[1558],356,764] buried in Hart Cemetery, Taylor Drain Rd, Oxford, Doddridge Co WV,[17,190,398] resided in Oxford, Doddridge Co, WV,[190,398] census 1880, 1900 in Southwest District, Doddridge Co, WV, occupation carpenter & farmer.[190,398] He married[484] divorced[228] **Gladys Augusta Townsend**, b. Jan- -1882 (daughter of John Arkensas Townsend and Rachel Jane Bee), d. Mar-28-1964 in Akron, Summit Co, OH,[693] buried Mt. Hope Cemetery,[64] resided in Akron, Summit Co, OH,[484,693] census 1900 in Roane Co, WV.

Children:

i.   HENRY CLIVE RICHARDS b. Nov- 3-1901,[64,592] d. Jan- 8-1981 in Mesa, Maricopa Co, AZ,[64,592] resided in Mesa, Maricopa Co, AZ,[1010] resided 1957 in Akron, Summit Co, OH.[765] He married[64] Juna Elfie Meadows, b. Jun- 7-1896 in Calhoun Co, WV,[64] (daughter of John Shannon Meadows and Effie __), d. Jan- 5-1947 in Akron, Summit Co, OH.[64]

ii.   DARLIE FLORENCE RICHARDS b. May- 3-1903,[64] resided 1957 in Akron, Summit Co, OH.[765] She married[941] __ Koontz.

iii.   IRA BURWELL RICHARDS, also known as Burwell Richards,[765] b. Jan-25-1905,[64] d. Dec-10-1971 in Akron, Summit Co, OH,[1011,64] resided in Akron, Summit Co, OH.[765,1011]

iv.   ICA GAY RICHARDS, also known as Gay Richards,[765] b. ca 1907,[1011,64] d. Feb-23-1968 in Massillon, Stark Co, OH,[1011] resided 1957 in Massillon, Stark Co, OH,[765] resided in Youngstown, Mahoning Co, OH.[1011] She married[941] divorced[436] __ Mortimer.

v.   CARLTON RICHARDS b. 1909,[64] d. 1910.[64]

vi.   JOHN SAMUEL RICHARDS b. Mar-13-1911 in Doddridge Co, WV,[963,592] d. Mar-20-1979 in Cleveland, Cuyahoga Co, OH,[1011,592] resided in Akron, Summit Co, OH.[765,948,1011]

vii.   CARSON LAWSON RICHARDS b. May- -1913 in Oxford, Doddridge Co, WV,[64] d. Nov-21-2000 in Akron, Summit Co, OH,[700,1011] buried in Greenlawn Memorial Park Cemetery, Akron, Summit Co, OH,[190] resided since childhood in Akron, Summit Co, OH,[190,765,1011] occupation Goodyear rubber,[190] education University of Akron College of Engineering.[190] He married[484] Grace __, resided 2000 in Akron, Summit Co, OH.

viii.   PERRY GAYLORD RICHARDS b. Apr-23-1915 in Doddridge Co, WV,[64,592] d. Feb-11-1987 in Akron, Summit Co, OH,[1011,592] resided in Akron, Summit Co, OH.[765,1010]

ix.   GEORGE CLIFFORD RICHARDS b. ca 1917,[64] d. Oct- 5-1926 in Summit Co, OH.[1011,64]

x.   FRANCIS JANE "CAROL" RICHARDS, also known as Carol Richards,[765] b. Sep-22-1921 in West Virginia,[64] d. Oct- 7-1989 in Akron, Summit Co, OH,[64] resided 1957 in Akron, Summit Co, OH,[765] census 1930 in Akron, Summit Co, OH. She married[64] __ Uhaull. Three daughters, one son.[64]

        xi.   CLAIR "RICH" RICHARDS, also known as Clare Richards,[765] b. Oct-29-1923,[1010] d. Jul-10-2004,[1010] resided 2000 in Green, Summit Co, OH,[521] resided 1957 in Akron, Summit Co, OH.[765] He married[910,64] Wilma Kocher, resided 2000 in Green, Summit Co, OH.[910] One son, one daughter.

762. **Nancy M. Richards** (416.Rulina[8], 247.Daniel[7], 136.Hugh[6], 72.John[5], 21.John[4], 6.Hugh[3], 3.John[2], 1.Jean[1]), b. Jul- 7-1880 in Oxford, Doddridge Co, WV,[190] d. Oct-20-1961 in Doddridge Co, WV,[764,mdlix[1559],356] buried in Stonewall Park Cemetery, Stonewood, Harrison Co, WV,[462] resided in Doddridge Co, WV,[484,190] resided 1957 in Clarksburg, Harrison Co, WV,[521] census 1910 in New Milton, Doddridge Co, WV, census 1900 in Southwest District, Doddridge Co, WV. She married[484,191] Feb-22-1905 in Doddridge Co, WV,[mdlx[1560]] **Perry F. Greathouse**, b. Sep- 6-1871 in Doddridge Co, WV,[190] (son of Albert Morgan Greathouse and Mary Frances Powell), d. Oct-16-1961 in Doddridge Co, WV,[764,191,356] buried in Stonewall Park Cemetery, Stonewood, Harrison Co, WV,[190] census 1880, 1910 in New Milton, Doddridge Co, WV.

1910 Census, Doddridge County WV (New Milton District), enumerated on Apr 18-20 1910: Perry F. Greathouse, 38, farmer, married 5 yrs; wife Nancy M, 28, married 5 yrs, mother of 2 children, both still living; dau Frankie, 4; dau Nellie F, 1 yr 11 mo.

        Children:
    i.   FRANKIE LUZADA GREATHOUSE b. Jan-13-1906 in Harrison Co, WV,[592,419,mdlxi[1561]] d. Jan- -1973,[592] resided in Youngstown, Mahoning Co, OH,[765,856,592] resided 1923 in Harrison Co, WV,[419] census 1910 in New Milton, Doddridge Co, WV.[1561]

        Middle initial has been widely reported as "A", but her marriage record identifies her as Frankie Luzada Greathouse, and she is identified in marriage records of both daughters as Frankie L. Wyckoff.

        She married[941,1040] Sep-20-1923 in Clarksburg, Harrison Co, WV,[mdlxii[1562]] Samuel Matthew Wyckoff, b. ca 1902 in Harrison Co, WV,[419] (son of E. D. Wyckoff and Laura K. __), resided 1923 in Clarksburg, Harrison Co, WV.[419]
    ii.   NELLIE FRANCIS GREATHOUSE b. Apr-27-1908,[592,1561] d. Jul- -1989,[592] resided in Youngstown, Mahoning Co, OH,[765,856,1010] census 1910 in New Milton, Doddridge Co, WV.[1561] She married[941,1040] Robert B. Mullenax, b. Nov-25-1904,[592] d. Jan- 5-1993,[592] resided in Youngstown, Mahoning Co, OH.[1010]
    iii.   AGNES GREATHOUSE resided 1961 in St. Albans, Kanawha Co, WV.[765,856] She married[941,1040] James Marsh.
    iv.   PERRY LEON GREATHOUSE, also known as Leon Perry Greathouse,[693,592] b. Jun-26-1921 in Clarksburg, Harrison Co, WV,[mdlxiii[1563]] d. Sep- 4-1982 in Pinellas Co, FL,[693,592] resided in Largo, Pinellas Co, FL,[592] resided 1961 in Lexington, Fayette Co, KY,[765,856] resided formerly in Ohio.[1010]

763. **Nancy Ann "Nannie" Squires** (417.Elizabeth[8], 247.Daniel[7], 136.Hugh[6], 72.John[5], 21.John[4], 6.Hugh[3], 3.John[2], 1.Jean[1]), b. Nov-16-1874 in Upper Run, Oxford, Doddridge Co, WV,[439] d. Jul-21-1953 in Akron, Summit Co, OH,[439] resided 1919 in Akron, Summit Co, OH,[412] resided 1902 in Harrison Co, WV.[537] She married Mar-17-1902 in Clarksburg, Harrison Co, WV,[mdlxiv[1564],mdlxv[1565],439] **Robert Meredith Orr**, b. ca 1849 in Doddridge Co, (W)VA,[439] (son of John Poston Orr and Louisa Powell), d. bef Jul 1953,[191] resided 1902 in Harrison Co, WV.[537]
        Children:
    i.   (INFANT DAUGHTER) ORR d. at birth.

764. **Daniel Monroe "Roe" Squires**, also known as Monroe Squires,[1287,mdlxvi[1566]] (417.Elizabeth[8], 247.Daniel[7], 136.Hugh[6], 72.John[5], 21.John[4], 6.Hugh[3], 3.John[2], 1.Jean[1]), b. May- 8-1876 in Summers, Doddridge Co, WV,[190,439] d. Dec-27-1959 in New Milton, Doddridge Co, WV,[190,356,439] buried in Masonic Memorial Park Cemetery, Crystal Lake (West Union), WV,[439,721] resided in New Milton, Doddridge Co, WV,[190,1566] occupation oil & gas field worker.[190] He married Aug-25-1898 in Doddridge Co, WV,[mdlxvii[1567],mdlxviii[1568],439,484,191] **Erma Lucretia "Credie" Dotson**, also known as Lucretia Dotson,[1287,412] b. Dec- 1-1879 at Greenwood, Doddridge Co, WV,[mdlxix[1569],1287] [Although her obituary, death record and headstone show her birth date as Dec 1 1882, her age was given as 18 at the time of her Aug 1898 marriage, the 1900 Census shows her birth date as Dec 1879, the 1920 Census shows her age as 39 (b. 1880 if birth month Dec), and the 1930 Census shows her age as 49 (b. 1880 if birth month Dec). The 1880 Census of Doddridge County, enumerated on Jun 2 1880, identifies her as Lucretia Dotson, age 6 months, a daughter in the household of Joslin & Arasonah Dotson (both age 32), other children Mary E. Dotson (14) and Jenavie Dotson (6).] (daughter of Francis Jereline Dotson and Arzanna Davis), d. Jan- 7-1962 in Sunnyside (West Union), Doddridge Co, WV,[mdlxx[1570],764,721] buried in Masonic Memorial Park Cemetery, Crystal Lake (West Union), WV,[190,721] resided in New Milton, Doddridge Co, WV,[190] resided 1938 in Glenville, Gilmer Co, WV,[412] resided 1936, 37 in Blandville, Doddridge Co, WV.[748,mdlxxi[1571]]

1900 Census, Doddridge Co, WV (Central District):
Monroe Squires, 24, b. May 1876, married 2 yrs; wife Lucretia, 20, b. Dec 1879; son Forest, 3 months, b. Mar 1900.

1920 Census, Doddridge Co, WV (New Milton District):
Monroe Squires, 42; wife Ermie L., 39; son Forest L., 20; son Warder, 12; dau Mary, 9; son Giles, 3yrs 10mo; daughter-in-law Leta, 18.

1930 Census, Doddridge Co, WV (New Milton District):
Monroe Squires, 54; wife Erma L., 49; son Guiles, 14.

   Children:
   i. FOREST LEAMON SQUIRES b. Mar- 6-1900 in Doddridge Co, WV,[mdlxxii[1572]] d. Aug- -1972,[592] resided in Howell, Livingston Co, MI,[856,765,592] census 1920 in New Milton District, Doddridge Co, WV [with his wife, in home of his parents]. He married Mar-19-1916, Leta Good, b. Apr-16-1901,[592] d. Dec- 5-1992,[592] resided in Evart, Osceola Co, MI,[592] census 1920 in New Milton District, Doddridge Co, WV.
   ii. WARDER DENZIL SQUIRES b. Jun-20-1907 in Doddridge Co, WV, d. Jan-12-1970 in Zanesville, Muskingum Co, OH, resided in Zanesville, Muskingum Co, OH,[765] resided 1962 in Salem, WV,[856] census 1930 in Grant District, Doddridge Co, WV, census 1920 in New Milton District, Doddridge Co, WV. He married[502,mdlxxiii[1573]] Dec- 5-1925 in Doddridge Co, WV,[354] Gladys Irene Davis, b. May- 5-1908,[1573] (daughter of Ruley Davis and Lillie Simpson), d. Feb-26-1967 in Zanesville, Muskingum Co, OH,[1573] census 1930 in Grant District, Doddridge Co, WV.
   iii. OMA MAY "SHERRY" SQUIRES, census name Mary Squires,[1566] b. Sep-24-1910 in Doddridge Co, WV,[mdlxxiv[1574],592] d. Nov- -1986,[592] resided in Zanesville, Muskingum Co, OH,[765,856,778,592] census 1920 in New Milton District, Doddridge Co, WV. She married Oct- 4-1925, Stanley Brooks Sherwood, b. Feb- 2-1904 in Avon, Doddridge Co, WV (son of Ulysses Grant Sherwood and Elsie Rebecca Devericks), d. Jan-22-1984 in Zanesville, Muskingum Co, OH.
   iv. LELAND GYLES SQUIRES, also known as Giles Squires,[765,856] also known as Gyles Squires,[354] b. Mar-19-1916 in Doddridge Co, WV,[mdlxxv[1575],592] d. Feb-11-1997,[592] resided in Sugarcreek, Tuscarawas Co, OH,[856,592] resided 1959 in Stone Creek, OH,[765] census 1920 in New Milton District, Doddridge Co, WV. He married Jun- 6-1936 in Doddridge Co, WV,[mdlxxvi[1576]] Hazel Virginia Dillon, b. Apr-24-1912 in Doddridge Co, WV,[190,592] (daughter of Eugene Dillon and Delphia D. Cox), d. Apr- 6-2001 in Dover, Tuscarawas Co, OH,[190,592] buried in Grandview Union Cem, Strasburg, Tuscarawas Co, OH,[190] resided in Strasburg, Tuscarawas Co, OH.[mdlxxvii[1577]]

765. **Rosa Jane Squires**, also known as Jane,[190] (417.Elizabeth[8], 247.Daniel[7], 136.Hugh[6], 72.John[5], 21.John[4], 6.Hugh[3], 3.John[2], 1.Jean[1]), b. Nov- 7-1877 near Harmony, Doddridge Co, WV,[190] d. Oct- 6-1919 in Clarksburg, Harrison Co, WV,[mdlxxviii[1578],190] buried in Greenlawn Masonic Cemetery, Clarksburg, WV,[190] census 1910 in Coal District, Harrison Co, WV. She married Mar-16-1904 in Doddridge Co, WV,[mdlxxix[1579]] **William Henry Greathouse**, b. Nov-24-1876 in Doddridge Co, WV,[1364,mdlxxx[1580],711] [Age 26 at 1904 marriage would put birth ca 1878, while age 45 at 1922 marriage would put it ca 1877. Birth date of Nov 1876 given in 1900 Census, and death record states Nov 24 1876. Although both marriage records give his place of birth as Doddridge Co, no record of his birth is on file in Doddridge.] (son of Albert Morgan Greathouse and Mary Frances Powell), d. Dec-27-1956 in Clarksburg, Harrison Co, WV,[1580,398] buried in Greenlawn Masonic Cemetery, Clarksburg, WV,[17,398,1580] resided in Clarksburg, Harrison Co, WV,[398] census 1910 in Coal District, Harrison Co, WV, census 1880, 1900 in New Milton, Doddridge Co, WV, occupation blacksmith, Pittsburgh Plate Glass.[398,405]

William: 1910 Census, Harrison Co, WV (Coal District), enumerated on Apr 20 1910: William H. Gratehouse, 32, engineer, married 6 yrs; wife Rosa J, 32, mother of 2 children (1 still living); dau Goldie, 1y 6m; boarder Freeman G. Squires, 18, laborer in glass house, single; boarder Harold Morris, 17, laborer in glass house, single.

Children:
i. IVA JEWEL GREATHOUSE d. at birth, buried in Monongalia Co, WV.[856]
ii. WILLIAM GREATHOUSE, JR.[856] d. at 5 days old, buried in Childers Cemetery, New Milton, Doddridge Co, WV.[856]
iii. GOLDIE GENEVIEVE GREATHOUSE, also known as Clarice Greathouse, b. Oct- 4-1908 in North View (Clarksburg), Harrison Co, WV,[1068] residence in Canada,[439] census 1910 in Coal District, Harrison Co, WV.

Goldie Genevieve Greathouse was named Goldie Genevieve by her parents, but she moved to Canada following her divorce and changed her name to Clarice Greathouse.[439]

She married (1) divorced 1936,[439] Harmon F. Bayless, b. May-15-1904 in Newport, Washington Co, OH,[276] (son of Matthew Bayless and Carrie Davis), d. May-10-1945 in Harrison Co, WV,[276] cause of death gunshot wounds (self-inflicted),[276] buried in Benedum Memorial Cemetery, Bridgeport, Harrison Co, WV,[276] occupation Hazel Atlas Glass Co.[276] She married (2) 1956,[439] James Pickford, d. 1956.[439]
iv. W. JASON GORDON GREATHOUSE b. May- 8-1912 in Clarksburg, Harrison Co, WV.
v. (UNNAMED MALE) GREATHOUSE b. Jun-12-1914,[mdlxxxi[1581]] d. Jun-13-1914 in Harrison Co, WV.[1581]

766. **Mary Artie Squires**[385] (417.Elizabeth[8], 247.Daniel[7], 136.Hugh[6], 72.John[5], 21.John[4], 6.Hugh[3], 3.John[2], 1.Jean[1]), b. Sep- 6-1879 in Upper Run, Oxford, Doddridge Co, WV,[mdlxxxii[1582],mdlxxxiii[1583]] [Name listed in birth record as "Mary A. Squires," dau of V.B. & E.L. Squires, but identified in obituary as Mary E. Snider. Middle name has been reported as Artie. Obituary of son Coral gives her name as Marie, an apparent error.], d. Aug-16-1970 in Clarksburg, Harrison Co, WV,[806] ["Squires Genealogy," p. 328, gives Mary Squires Snider's death as Aug 16 1969 in Doddridge County. But obituary states Aug 16 1970 "at St. Mary's Hospital, Clarksburg" at age 90. SSDI also states death in Aug 1970.], buried in Mt. Olive Baptist Cemetery, Salem, WV,[190] resided in Salem, WV,[778,412,521,592.] She married Mar-18-1903 in Doddridge Co, WV,[mdlxxxiv[1584],354] **Fairfield E. Snider**, b. Oct- 6-1880 in New Milton, Doddridge Co, WV,[1583,mdlxxxv[1585]] (son of Arnold C. Snider and Nancy Boyce), d. 1952.[191,1583]
Children:
i. ELVIN SQUIRES SNIDER b. Feb- 8-1905 in New Milton, Doddridge Co, WV,[mdlxxxvi[1586]] [Identified in obituary as Elven Snider, born Sep 2 1905, but birth record shows Elvin Snider, born Feb 2 1905.], d. Dec- 2-1950 in Akron, Summit Co, OH,[190] [Obituary, in the form of an undated newspaper clipping, states that he died on Dec 2, year not specified. Previous indication was that his death had occurred in about 1950.], buried in Mt. Olive Baptist Cemetery, Salem, WV.[190]

ii.   CORAL EDWARD SNIDER b. May- 9-1910 in New Milton, Doddridge Co, WV,[190,mdlxxxvii[1587],419,592] d. Jul-27-1985 in Titusville, Brevard Co, FL,[806,592] resided 1973-85 in Brevard Co, FL,[190] resided 1970 in Weirton, Hancock Co, WV,[856] occupation Weirton Steel (retired).[439] He married[484] Oct- 1-1938 in Salem, WV,[419] Ernestine Virginia Meeks, b. May-23-1909 in Berea, Ritchie Co, WV,[592,419] (daughter of Daniel C. Meeks and Anna M. Flowers), d. Dec- -1982,[592] resided 1938 in Salem, WV,[419] resided 1925 in Pullman, Ritchie Co, WV,[588] census 1920 in Smithville, Ritchie Co, WV,[1002] census 1910 in Grant District, Ritchie Co, WV.

iii.   ROSCO PAUL SNIDER b. Jun-17-1917, d. ca Mar 1918.

767. **Andrew Mead Squires**, also known as Mead Squires (417.Elizabeth[8], 247.Daniel[7], 136.Hugh[6], 72.John[5], 21.John[4], 6.Hugh[3], 3.John[2], 1.Jean[1]), b. Aug-19-1882 in Doddridge Co, WV,[190,439,592,mdlxxxviii[1588]] [Harrison County Death Records states his birth as Aug 19 1881, and headstone shows birth in 1881, but obituary, SSDI, and Joy Gilchrist's Squires Genealogy all give it as Aug 19 1882.], d. Oct- 7-1965 in Clarksburg, Harrison Co, WV,[806,mdlxxxix[1589]] buried in South Fork Bapt Church Cem, Oxford, Doddridge Co, WV,[17,190] resided formerly in Pennsylvania,[948] census 1920 in Southwest District, Doddridge Co, WV, resided 1919 in Summers, Doddridge Co, WV,[412] occupation Murphy Oil & Gas Co.[190] He married (1) Apr-18-1903 in Doddridge Co, WV,[191,484] [Wes Cochran's "Doddridge County WV Marriages" reports marriage date as Apr 19 1904.], **Lenora Bird Adams**, census name Nora Bird Adams,[385] b. Aug- 7-1880,[190,17] (daughter of Alexander Adams and Mary Isabel "Bell" Gaston), d. Oct-21-1917 near Summers, Doddridge Co, WV,[190,484,17,398,356] [Death date of Oct 11 1917 is reported in "Doddridge County Deaths" and in death certificate on file at West Virginia Division of Vital Statistics, cause of death listed as childbirth. But obituary, headstone, and husband's obituary give her death date as Oct 21 1917, and daughter Lenora was born on Oct 20 1917, so the latter date must be correct.], cause of death childbirth,[398] buried in Gaston-Hart Cemetery, Upper Run, Summers, Doddridge Co, WV.[17] Andrew Mead Squires and Lenora Bird Adams were double cousins, in that they were both third cousins (both were great-great-grandchildren of John Gaston, Jr (b. 1752 in NJ)) and also fifth cousins (both were great-great-great-great-grandchildren of John Smith (b. 1699)).

He married[484] (2) Dec-25-1918 in Doddridge Co, WV,[354] **Emma Gertrude Prunty**,[395] census name Emily G. Prunty,[587] b. Jan- 8-1880 in Ritchie Co, WV,[190] (daughter of Elmore Prunty and Mary C. Strahan), d. Nov-20-1955 in Pullman, Ritchie Co, WV,[190,484] buried in South Fork Bapt Church Cem, Oxford, Doddridge Co, WV,[17,190] resided in Pullman, Ritchie Co, WV,[190] census 1920 in Southwest District, Doddridge Co, WV, census 1880 in Union District, Ritchie Co, WV.

1920 Census, Doddridge Co, WV (Southwest District), enumerated on Jan 20 1920:
Andrew M. Squires, 38, farmer; wife Emma G. Squires, 39; stepson Charley L. Grimm, 14; stepdau Ruby E. Grimm, 11; stepson Clarence C. Grimm, 9; stepson Dale W. Grimm, 7.

Children by Lenora Bird Adams:
i.   ILDA LEON SQUIRES[190] b. Jun-16-1906 in Doddridge Co, WV,[190] d. Mar- 2-1969 in Oxford, Doddridge Co, WV,[190,484,356] buried in South Fork Bapt Church Cem, Oxford, Doddridge Co, WV,[17,190] occupation Scott's Variety Store - West Union, WV.[190] She married Apr- 3-1927 in Doddridge Co, WV,[354,191,484] Lester Charley Grimm,[354] census name Charley L. Grimm,[1390] b. Nov- 9-1905 in Ritchie Co, WV,[190,17,592] (son of Clem Maise Grimm and Emma Gertrude Prunty), d. Jan-19-1977 in Clarksburg, Harrison Co, WV,[190,17,592] buried in South Fork Bapt Church Cem, Oxford, Doddridge Co, WV,[17,190] resided in Summers, Doddridge Co, WV,[190] occupation WV Dept of Highways,[190] census 1920 in Southwest District, Doddridge Co, WV.
ii.   LENORA SQUIRES GASTON, also known as Alda Lenora Squires, b. Oct-20-1917,[592] d. Dec- 4-2001,[592] resided 1969 in Weirton, Hancock Co, WV,[412] census 1930 in Southwest District, Doddridge Co, WV.

In the wake of her mother's death shortly after giving birth, Lenora Squires Gaston was raised from infancy by Morris Samuel Gaston and his wife Hattie I. Adams Gaston, and she therefore adopted the Gaston family name. Morris Samuel Gaston was a first cousin of baby Lenora's maternal grandmother, Mary Isabelle Gaston Adams, and a second cousin of her paternal grandmother, Elizabeth Laverna Gaston Squires. There is speculation that Hattie Adams was also a blood relative. The obituary of Morris Samuel Gaston identified as a surviving "foster daughter, Mrs. Cyril Scott of Oxford." Lenora took up residence in Weirton, WV. Her mother's obituary identifies her as Lenore [sic] Scott, her husband's obituary identifies her as Lenore [sic] Squires Gaston Scott, and the Social Security Death Index lists her name as Lenore [sic] Scott.

She married Nov-23-1939,[969] Cyril Alfred Scott, b. Feb-25-1914 in West Union, Doddridge Co, WV,[190] (son of Alfred Oran Scott and Ethel G. Dotson), d. Sep-20-1991 in Weirton, Hancock Co, WV,[190] buried in South Fork Bapt Church Cem, Oxford, Doddridge Co, WV,[190,17] resided in Weirton, Hancock Co, WV,[190] occupation bander at Weirton Steel Corp in strip steel dept.[190]
Children by Emma Gertrude Prunty:
iii. WINIFRED SQUIRES b. Dec- 6-1920 in Doddridge Co, WV, resided 1938, 69, 77 in Elizabeth, Wirt Co, WV,[1357,mdxc[1590],mdxci[1591]] resided 1955 in Daytona Beach, Volusia Co, FL.[856] She married[mdxcii[1592]] Nov-29-1938 in Richwood, Nicholas Co, WV,[mdxciii[1593]] James W. Vogeding, b. Feb-9-1914 in West Union, Doddridge Co, WV,[190] (son of Lewis Edward Vogeding and Beulah Irene Stuck), d. Mar- 4-1999 in Melbourne, Brevard Co, FL,[190] census 1920 in West Union District, Doddridge Co, WV, education Doddridge Co H.S.,[1592] occupation 1938 C&P Telephone Co.[1592]

James: Retired as manager of ABC Store in Elizabeth, WV, and also owned & operated the Elizabeth Theater in Elizabeth, WV. Moved from Vincent, Ohio, to central Florida in 1996, taking up residence in Indialantic, FL.[mdxciv[1594]]

768. **Samuel Jackson "Jack" Squires**, also known as Jack Squires,[588] (417.Elizabeth[8], 247.Daniel[7], 136.Hugh[6], 72.John[5], 21.John[4], 6.Hugh[3], 3.John[2], 1.Jean[1]), b. Jan-27-1884 in Doddridge Co, WV,[190,439] d. Nov-18-1967 in Clarksburg, Harrison Co, WV,[806] buried in Masonic Memorial Park Cemetery, Crystal Lake (West Union), WV,[190,721] resided in West Union, Doddridge Co, WV,[190,1291] resided 1919 in Summers, Doddridge Co, WV.[412]

He formerly operated a farm in Doddridge County, later working in the oil and gas fields. He also served as a car salesman, and for many years was well-known as an auctioneer.[190]

He married Jan-27-1915 in Lawford, Ritchie Co, WV,[mdxcv[1595],473,484,191] **Clemma Wright**, b. Feb-15-1884 in Lawford, Ritchie Co, WV,[190] (daughter of Alexander Wright and Louisa Gregg), d. Aug-21-1968 in Norwood, Hamilton Co, OH,[764] buried in Masonic Memorial Park Cemetery, Crystal Lake (West Union), WV,[721] resided in Leavittsburg, Trumbull Co, OH,[190] resided formerly in Doddridge Co, WV,[190] census 1930 in West Union, Doddridge Co, WV, census 1910 in Union District, Ritchie Co, WV.

1930 Census, Doddridge Co, WV (Town of West Union), enumerated on Apr 7 1930 at #1 Columbia Street:
Samuel J. Squires, 46, occup hotel manager, age 31 at time of first marriage; wife Clemma, 46; dau Jewell L, 13; maid Grace M. Cottrill, 21, single, hotel waitress; maid Bessie M. Richards, 19, single, hotel waitress; boarder Hollie W. Shepler, 22, single, oil & gas station agent.

Children:
i. JEWELL L. SQUIRES, census name Lily J. Squires,[1390] b. Nov- 3-1916 in Doddridge Co, WV,[190] d. Apr- 4-1989 in Deltona, Volusia Co, FL,[190] buried in Masonic Memorial Park Cemetery, Crystal Lake (West Union), WV,[190,721] resided in Deltona, Volusia Co, FL,[190] resided 1967, 68 in Leavittsburg, Trumbull Co, OH,[765,856] resided 1965 in Akron, Summit Co, OH,[855] census 1920 in Southwest District, Doddridge Co, WV, occupation technician, GM-Packard.[190] She married divorced Russell Hale Broadwater (son of Russell Broadwater and Beulah Mae Ramsey).

769. **Ida Oma Squires**, also known as Oma Squires,[354] (417.Elizabeth[8], 247.Daniel[7], 136.Hugh[6], 72.John[5], 21.John[4], 6.Hugh[3], 3.John[2], 1.Jean[1]), b. Apr-25-1887 in Doddridge Co, WV,[354] d. Mar-10-1967 in Newark, Licking Co, OH, resided in Newark, Licking Co, OH,[521] resided 1919 in Toledo, Lucas Co, OH,[412] resided 1905 in Doddridge Co, WV.[354] She married Jun-28-1905 in Doddridge Co, WV,[354] **John Edwin Morris**, b. Oct-27-1880 in Jackson Co, WV,[592,354] [Birth date given in 1900 Census as Oct 1881.] (son of Charles Kester Morris and Eliza Jane Britton), d. Mar- 9-1967, resided in Newark, Licking Co, OH,[1010] resided 1905 in Doddridge Co, WV.[354]

Children:

i.   LAVERNA OPAL MORRIS, also known as Opal,[592] b. Aug-19-1906 in Calhoun Co, WV,[592] d. Mar- 1-1995 in Ohio,[592,mdxcvi[1596]] resided in Newark, Licking Co, OH.[mdxcvii[1597]] She married Feb- 1-1932 in Brownsville, Licking Co, OH, Howard E. Morgan, b. Feb- 6-1910 in Licking Co, OH, d. Aug-11-1992,[592] resided in Newark, Licking Co, OH.[592]

ii.   ALTA ESTEL MORRIS b. Jan- 2-1909 in Calhoun Co, WV,[592] d. Apr-15-1982 in Newark, Licking Co, OH,[592] resided in Newark, Licking Co, OH.[1010] She married Nov-10-1926, James Allen Johnston, b. Oct- 8-1906,[592] d. Jul-18-1971 in Licking Co, OH,[592] buried in Newark, Licking Co, OH.

iii.   ERMA MARIE MORRIS b. Mar- 4-1912,[592] d. Apr-21-1999,[592] resided in Newark, Licking Co, OH.[mdxcviii[1598]] She married (1) Mar- 2-1932 in Newark, Licking Co, OH, Paul Swinehart. She married (2) __ Morton.

770. **Hobert Golden Squires** (417.Elizabeth[8], 247.Daniel[7], 136.Hugh[6], 72.John[5], 21.John[4], 6.Hugh[3], 3.John[2], 1.Jean[1]), b. Jan-13-1898 in Upper Run, Oxford, Doddridge Co, WV,[190,mdxcix[1599],592,mdc[1600]] d. Sep-27-1983 in Salem, WV,[190,mdci[1601],592,191,1600] buried in K of P Memorial Park Cemetery, Salem, WV.[1601]

Resident of Industrial, Salem, WV. Although many records and other source materials give his name as "Hobart," his birth record, his obituary, and his wife's obituary all report his and his son's names as "Hobert," and his SSDI entry also has it spelled "Hobert."

He married Sep- 9-1918,[1600,484] **Nettie Pearl Pierce**, b. Jul-23-1903 in Doddridge Co, WV,[190,mdcii[1602],1600] [Social Security Death Index has birthdate as July 22 1903, with name listed as Nettie P. Squires. Obituary gives birthplace as Snake Run, Doddridge Co, but birth record has it as Avon. Birth record states that she was the mother's second child.] (daughter of Christopher Columbus Marion Pierce and Martha Aldora Robinson), d. Dec-29-1990 in Clarksburg, Harrison Co, WV,[190,592] resided in Industrial, Doddridge Co, WV.[592]

Nettie: "History of Doddridge County," p. 249, gives name as "Nellie," an apparent error.

Children:

i.   EDWARD GOFF SQUIRES b. May-12-1920 in Salem, WV,[190,1600] d. Jan-24-1992 in Salem, WV,[190] buried in K of P Memorial Park Cemetery, Salem, WV,[190] resided in Salem, WV,[190] occupation Pittsburgh Plate Glass - 34 yrs,[190] military 1941-46 U.S. Air Force, WW II in China-India-Burma Theatre.[190] He married Nov- 9-1940,[484,1600] Rosemary Smith, b. Jul-15-1920 in Grafton, Taylor Co, WV,[190] (daughter of Lee Gank and Helen Smith), d. Feb-24-2004,[190] buried in K of P Memorial Park Cemetery, Salem, WV,[190] resided in Salem, WV,[190] occupation Assistant Superintendent, WV Industrial Home for Girls.[190]

Rosemary: Identified in husband's obituary and by Susie Davis Nicholson (p. 511) as Rosemary Smith, but in her own obituary as the daughter of Lee and Helen Smith Gank. In addition to her parents and husband, she was also predeceased by a sister, Emma Jane Langford.

ii.   ELIZA KATHLEEN SQUIRES, also known as Kathleen Squires,[765,521] also known as E. Kathleen Jenkins,[190,592] b. Feb-14-1922 in Industrial, Doddridge Co, WV,[190,mdciii[1603]] d. Oct-31-1985 in Morgantown, Monongalia Co, WV,[190,484,592] resided in Industrial, Harrison Co, WV.[604] She married[1603] Sep- 4-1937 in Oakland, Garrett Co, MD, Lawrence D. Jenkins, b. Nov- 9-1916 in Salem, WV,[190,592] (son of Remmie Jenkins and Halcyone McClain), d. Oct-14-2000,[190,592] buried in K of P Memorial Park

Cemetery, Salem, WV,[190] resided in Industrial, Harrison Co, WV,[592] occupation McBride Glass Factory of Salem, and PPG Industries.[190]

iii. HOBERT JACKSON "JACK" SQUIRES, also known as Hobart J. "Jack" Squires,[190] also known as Jackson Hobart Squires, b. May-29-1925 in Salem, WV,[mdciv[1604]] d. Sep-11-2006 in Columbus, Franklin Co, OH,[806] buried in K of P Memorial Park Cemetery, Salem, WV,[190] resided in Greenfield, Highland Co, OH,[190] occupation teacher, McClain H.S. in Greenfield OH (retired Jan 1 1987),[190] education Salem H.S., Emory Univ, Salem College, West Virginia Univ, Ohio State Univ (Master's in Education),[190] military U.S. Navy, World War II.[190] He married[1603] (1) Gertrude Ellen Gabriel. He married[1603,484] (2) Dec-22-1956,[484] Mary Lou Jeffers, b. May-19-1931 in West Virginia,[693,592] (daughter of __ Jeffers and __ Baker), d. Sep- 8-1999 in Greenfield, Highland Co, OH,[693,592,484] cremated[693] resided in Greenfield, Highland Co, OH,[592] resided formerly in West Virginia.[604]

iv. RICHARD FRANKLIN SQUIRES b. Jun-28-1940 in Industrial, Doddridge Co, WV,[1603] d. Jun-28-1940 in Industrial, Doddridge Co, WV,[1603] buried in IOOF Cemetery, Salem, Harrison Co, WV.[1603]

771. **Obidiah Wayne Pierce**, also known as Wayne Pierce,[190,412,1533] (418.Nancy[8], 247.Daniel[7], 136.Hugh[6], 72.John[5], 21.John[4], 6.Hugh[3], 3.John[2], 1.Jean[1]), b. May-14-1885 in Summers, Doddridge Co, WV,[mdcv[1605],190] d. Jul-20-1981 in Harrisville, Ritchie Co, WV,[mdcvi[1606]] buried in IOOF Cemetery, Harrisville, Ritchie Co, WV,[190,mdcvii[1607]] resided in Harrisville, Ritchie Co, WV,[190,412] resided 1938 in Pennsboro, Ritchie Co, WV,[765] census 1920 in Southwest District, Doddridge Co, WV.

"He was a former Doddridge County school teacher and store keeper, and was formerly employed by Dave Corra, junk dealer in Pennsboro. He was also a farmer and nurseryman."[190]

He married[484] Apr-13-1913 in Doddridge Co, WV,[354] **Hallie C. Garner**, b. Mar-13-1892,[592,1532,46] (daughter of Simon H. Garner and Susan Snider), d. Mar- -1987,[592,46] buried in IOOF Cemetery, Harrisville, Ritchie Co, WV,[469] resided in Harrisville, Ritchie Co, WV,[484,592] census 1920 in Southwest District, Doddridge Co, WV, census 1900, 1910 in McClellan District, Doddridge Co, WV.
Children:
i. DOLLIVER WENDELL PIERCE b. ca 1918 in Doddridge Co, WV,[1390,996] resided 1981 in Baden, Beaver Co, PA,[765] resided 1943 in Ritchie Co, WV,[996] census 1920 in Southwest District, Doddridge Co, WV. He married May- 4-1943 in Ritchie Co, WV,[996] Catherine Georgia Rogers, b. May-27-1923,[592,996] (daughter of Ray Rogers and Commella Kiger), d. Dec-28-2001,[592] resided in Baden, Beaver Co, PA.[604]

772. **Laura Maud Pierce** (418.Nancy[8], 247.Daniel[7], 136.Hugh[6], 72.John[5], 21.John[4], 6.Hugh[3], 3.John[2], 1.Jean[1]), b. Jan-17-1889 in Doddridge Co, WV,[mdcviii[1608]] d. Aug- 7-1966 in East Liverpool, Columbiana Co, OH,[693] resided in East Liverpool, Columbiana Co, OH,[412,1533,693] resided 1938 in Porto Rico (New Milton), Doddridge Co, WV.[765] She married[502,941] ca 1911,[1380] **William G. Cornell**,[502] also known as Willie Cornell,[374,502] b. Apr- -1886,[1380,1364] (son of Ciscero Cornell and Mary E. Douglass), census 1900, 1920, 1930 in New Milton, Doddridge Co, WV.
Children:
i. MAMIE E. CORNELL b. Sep-17-1911 in Red Lick (New Milton), Doddridge Co, WV,[190,592] d. Apr- 2-1986 in East Liverpool, Columbiana Co, OH,[190,592] buried in IOOF Cemetery, Salem, Harrison Co, WV,[190] resided in Wellsville, Columbiana Co, OH,[190,592] resided (formerly, 11 yrs) in New Milton, Doddridge Co, WV,[190,1566] resided 1965 in Salem, WV,[228] occupation glasscutter, McBride glass factory, Salem WV.[190] She married[191] (1) Jimmie Davis,[276,191] also known as Jimmy Davis,[592] b. Feb-12-1894 in West Virginia,[276] (son of Benjamin Franklin Davis and Easter Hutson), d. Apr-24-1965 in Salem, WV,[276,191] buried in IOOF Cemetery, Salem, Harrison Co, WV,[276] resided in Salem, WV,[276] occupation pumper, oil refinery.[276] She married (2) Jul-21-1974,[484] [Obituary of wife says marriage was in 1975, but husband's obituary specifies Jul 21 1974. No record of this marriage found in Doddridge Co.], Albert E. Hinterer, b. Dec-24-1901 in Doddridge Co, WV,[190,592,721] (son of Frank Mathias Hinterer and Christina Fischer), d. Dec-20-1986 in Clarksburg, Harrison Co,

WV,[190,592,721] buried in Masonic Memorial Park Cemetery, Crystal Lake (West Union), WV,[190,721] resided in New Milton, Doddridge Co, WV,[190] occupation timberman, farmer & stockman.[190]

  ii. MABEL CORNELL b. Oct-26-1913,[592] d. Aug- -1987,[592] resided in East Liverpool, Columbiana Co, OH,[604] census 1920 in New Milton, Doddridge Co, WV. She married[424] __ McCartney.

  iii. JAMES CORNELL b. ca 1917,[1380] census 1920, 1930 in New Milton, Doddridge Co, WV.

  iv. HAZEL CORNELL b. ca 1919 in Doddridge Co, WV,[711,1380] resided 1986 in Clarington, Monroe Co, OH,[412] census 1920, 1930 in New Milton, Doddridge Co, WV. She married[424] May-29-1937 in Salem, WV,[711] Andrew Waggoner, b. Mar- 7-1910 in Ritchie Co, WV,[592,711] d. May-31-1993,[592] resided in Clarington, Monroe Co, OH,[604] resided 1937 in Lawford, Ritchie Co, WV.[711]

  v. FRED E. CORNELL b. Nov- 8-1920,[592,1380] d. Jul- 2-2000,[592] resided in East Liverpool, Columbiana Co, OH,[592] resided 1986 in Negley, Columbiana Co, OH,[412] resided formerly in West Virginia,[604] census 1930 in Doddridge Co, WV.[1380]

  vi. EDITH CORNELL b. ca 1923,[1380] resided 1986 in East Liverpool, Columbiana Co, OH.[412] She married[424] __ Dailey.

  vii. MARY BELLE CORNELL b. Aug-31-1925 in Salem, WV, resided 1986 in Wellsville, Columbiana Co, OH,[412] resided 1944 in Salem, WV.[419] She married May-18-1944 in Salem, WV,[419] Alaska Ward Merritt, b. Apr-27-1919 in Salem, WV,[419,592] (son of DeWitt Talmadge "Doc" Merritt and Etta Wanda Hart), d. Aug- -1981,[592] resided in Wellsville, Columbiana Co, OH,[604] resided 1975 in East Liverpool, Columbiana Co, OH,[856] resided 1944 in Salem, WV.[419]

  viii. LIVING.

773. **Nancy Clare Gaston**[920], also known as Nannie Gaston,[765,385] (419.Samuel[8], 247.Daniel[7], 136.Hugh[6], 72.John[5], 21.John[4], 6.Hugh[3], 3.John[2], 1.Jean[1]), b. Jan-18-1885 in Doddridge Co, WV,[398,963,240,711,46] d. Aug-21-1932 at Oxford, Doddridge Co, WV,[398,mdcix[1609],356,46] cause of death pneumonia,[1609] buried in Gaston-Hart Cemetery, Upper Run, Summers, Doddridge Co, WV,[17] resided at Oxford, Doddridge Co, WV.[398] She married Aug-13-1901 in Doddridge Co, WV,[mdcx[1610]] [A family information survey completed by John W. Hart in 1931 reported their marriage date as Aug 8 1901.], **John Washington Hart**, b. Sep-22-1875 in Doddridge Co, WV,[mdcxi[1611]] [But headstone shows birth as 1877. Age 52 given at birth of son John in Aug 1932 would put birth in 1879 or 1880.] (son of Andrew N. Hart and Sarah Emaline Britton), d. 1944,[46] buried in Gaston-Hart Cemetery, Upper Run, Summers, Doddridge Co, WV,[17] resided in Oxford, Doddridge Co, WV,[395] occupation saw miller.[920]

  Children:

  i. RUBY ALMA HART b. Feb- 2-1902 in Summers, Doddridge Co, WV,[mdcxii[1612],276,190,989] d. May-14-1968 in Clarksburg, Harrison Co, WV,[398,806,989] buried in South Fork Bapt Church Cem, Oxford, Doddridge Co, WV,[17,989,190,276] resided 1938 in Oxford, Doddridge Co, WV.[521] She married (1) 1920,[191] Simon Peter Ingram, b. Jan- 9-1880 in Doddridge Co, WV,[mdcxiii[1613]] (son of Lathem Ingram and Frances Moore), d. Nov- 1-1937,[191] buried in Clarksburg, Harrison Co, WV.[mdcxiv[1614]] She married (2) Apr-15-1940 in Oakland, Garrett Co, MD,[mdcxv[1615]] Walter Ray "Shiner" Husk, b. Apr- 2-1900 in Fly, Monroe Co, OH,[190] (son of William Leonard Husk and Virginia Elizabeth "Jennie" McNemar), d. Dec-27-1993 in Summers, Doddridge Co, WV,[190] buried in South Fork Bapt Church Cem, Oxford, Doddridge Co, WV,[190] resided in Summers, Doddridge Co, WV, occupation farmer & carpenter,[190] no children from this person. Walter Ray "Shiner" Husk and Ruby Alma Hart were second cousins, once removed, by virtue of his being the great-grandson of Samuel & Elizabeth Husk, and her being their great-great- granddaughter.

  ii. RONNIE BOSWELL HART[398,190] b. Feb- 3-1903 at Summers, Doddridge Co, WV,[398] d. Dec-30-1938 in Clarksburg, Harrison Co, WV,[398,700] buried in Oxford Baptist Church Cemetery, Doddridge Co, WV,[17] [Obituary incorrectly states burial in "South Fork Baptist cemetery at Oxford."], cause of death pneumonia,[398] resided in Clarksburg, Harrison Co, WV,[190,398] occupation oil field worker.[398] He married[484,228] Juanita M. Nutter, b. Jan- 4-1909 in Oxford, Doddridge Co, WV,[190,mdcxvi[1616],17] (daughter of Andrew J. Nutter and Icy Lee McKinney), d. Feb-28-2002 in Salem, WV,[190,1616,17] buried in Oxford Baptist Church Cemetery, Doddridge Co, WV,[190,1616,17] resided 1959, 65 in West Union, Doddridge Co, WV,[905,521] resided 1938 in Clarksburg, Harrison Co, WV.[484]

Juanita: Survived by 5 grandchildren and 4 great-grandchildren. She was also predeceased by nine half-brothers and one half-sister.

iii. OREN VICTOR "VIC" HART, also known as Victor Hart,[521,412] b. Apr-27-1906 in Harmony, Doddridge Co, WV,[190] d. Mar-30-1990 in Harrison Co, WV,[190] buried in Masonic Memorial Park Cemetery, Crystal Lake (West Union), WV,[190] resided in Fairmont, Marion Co, WV,[190] resided 1968 in Clarksburg, Harrison Co, WV,[412] resided 1938 in Oxford, Doddridge Co, WV,[521] occupation Central Supply.[190] He married Aug-24-1938,[484] Zelma A. Cox, b. ca 1920,[1380] (daughter of Brent Clyde Cox and Margaret Pearl Childers), resided 1991, 97 in Fairmont, Marion Co, WV,[765,412] resided 1951, 77 in Clarksburg, Harrison Co, WV.[856,521]

iv. MACEL CLAIRE HART b. Oct-14-1908 in Summers, Doddridge Co, WV,[190] d. Jun-24-2003 in West Union, Doddridge Co, WV,[190] buried in Masonic Memorial Park Cemetery, Crystal Lake (West Union), WV,[190] resided in West Union, Doddridge Co, WV,[190] resided 1968, 90 in New Milton, Doddridge Co, WV,[412,521] resided 1938 in Oxford, Doddridge Co, WV,[521] census 1930 in Southwest District, Doddridge Co, WV [Listed as a boarder in household of Curtis C. Dille and wife Flora D.]. She married Oct- 9-1939,[484] Denver Willis Cox, b. Apr-14-1907 in New Milton, Doddridge Co, WV,[mdcxvii[1617],190] (son of Jacob Martiney Cox and Emma Blanche Willis), d. Jun-20-1994 in Clarksburg, Harrison Co, WV,[190] buried in Masonic Memorial Park Cemetery, Crystal Lake (West Union), WV, resided in New Milton, Doddridge Co, WV.[905,412,190.]

Denver: Retired in 1972 as a well tender for the George Jackson Drilling Company of Clarksburg with over ten years service. He worked many years in the timber and sawmill industry. Along with his father, he operated the Cox Sawmill in Doddridge County. He also helped in the construction of State Route 18 South in Doddridge County.[190]

v. WILMA IDOLENE HART b. Mar-26-1911 in Oxford, Doddridge Co, WV,[mdcxviii[1618]] d. Jun-22-1993 in Clarksburg, Harrison Co, WV,[190] buried in Masonic Memorial Park Cemetery, Crystal Lake (West Union), WV,[190,721] resided in New Milton, Doddridge Co, WV,[521,412,190] resided 1938 in Market, Doddridge Co, WV.[521] She married Feb-26-1930 in Doddridge Co, WV,[711,191] Paul Robinson, b. Aug- 3-1907 in Doddridge Co, WV,[592,711,721] d. Jun-14-1987,[191,592,721] buried in Masonic Memorial Park Cemetery, Crystal Lake (West Union), WV,[721] resided 1930 in Blandville, Doddridge Co, WV.[711]

vi. IRENE VIRGINIA HART b. Jan-25-1913 in Summers, Doddridge Co, WV,[190] d. Sep-17-2002 in Clarksburg, Harrison Co, WV,[190] buried in K of P Memorial Park Cemetery, Salem, WV,[190] resided in Salem, WV,[412] resided 1938 in Market, Doddridge Co, WV.[521] She married Jan-14-1932 in Doddridge Co, WV,[354,484] Carl Newton Cox,[mdcxix[1619],374] b. Aug-16-1908 in New Milton, Doddridge Co, WV,[mdcxx[1620],190,mdcxxi[1621],592] (son of Jacob Martiney Cox and Emma Blanche Willis), d. Jul- 6-1982 in Clarksburg, Harrison Co, WV,[mdcxxii[1622],592] buried in K of P Memorial Park Cemetery, Salem, WV,[190,817] resided in Salem, WV,[190] occupation farmer and school bus driver (Doddridge Co, retired),[190] military U.S. Navy, World War II.[190]

vii. SAMUEL JAMES "JIM" HART, also known as James Hart,[412,521] b. Feb-14-1916 in Oxford, Doddridge Co, WV,[190] d. May-11-1999 in Clarksburg, Harrison Co, WV,[190] buried in Floral Hills Memorial Gardens, Quiet Dell, Harrison Co, WV, resided in Clarksburg, Harrison Co, WV,[521,412,190] occupation Union Carbide (40 years).[190] He married Jan- -1942,[484] Hazel O. Stevens, b. Dec- 9-1918 in Clarksburg, Harrison Co, WV,[190] (daughter of Ira Stevens and Zora Oldaker), d. Dec-12-2004 in Clarksburg, Harrison Co, WV,[847] resided in Clarksburg, Harrison Co, WV,[190] buried in Floral Hills Memorial Gardens, Quiet Dell, Harrison Co, WV.[190]

viii. ELLEN HART b. Sep-24-1918,[17] d. Sep-24-1918,[17] buried in Gaston-Hart Cemetery, Upper Run, Summers, Doddridge Co, WV.[17]

ix. LOTTIE ETHYLN HART[989] b. Sep-28-1919 in Oxford, Doddridge Co, WV,[190,mdcxxiii[1623]] d. Mar-16-1972 in Salem, WV,[190] buried in Middle Island 7th Day Bapt Ch Cem, Sugar Camp, Doddridge Co WV,[17] resided in Salem, WV,[190] resided 1938 in Oxford, Doddridge Co, WV.[521] She married Apr-22-1942 in Smithburg, Doddridge Co, WV,[1623,191] John Stanley Trent, b. Feb-13-1918 in Blandville, Doddridge Co, WV,[190] (son of Henry Trent and Missouri Gauldin), d. Nov- 6-2001 in

Clarksburg, Harrison Co, WV,[190] buried in Middle Island 7th Day Bapt Ch Cem, Sugar Camp, Doddridge Co WV,[17,190] resided in Miletus (Salem), Doddridge Co, WV.[190]

        John: Retired from B&K Tractor, Salem, WV, following which he operated Trent Repair Service, repairing farm equipment.[190]

        x.   PHAME HART b. Apr- 6-1922 at Oxford, Doddridge Co, WV,[711] resided 1968, 90, 2003, 10 in West Union, Doddridge Co, WV,[412,521] resided 1938 in Oxford, Doddridge Co, WV.[521] She married Oct-12-1941 at Harmony, Doddridge Co, WV,[711,484] William Martin Trent, b. Apr- 8-1916 in Toms Fork, Porto Rico, Doddridge Co, WV,[190,17] (son of Henry Trent and Missouri Gauldin), d. Nov-15-1992 in Morgantown, Monongalia Co, WV,[190,17] buried in Middle Island 7th Day Bapt Ch Cem, Sugar Camp, Doddridge Co WV,[17] resided in West Union, Doddridge Co, WV,[190] resided 1936 in Clarksburg, Harrison Co, WV.[mdcxxiv[1624]]

        William: Retired in 1976 from the VA Hospital in Clarksburg as Chief of Building Management after 30 years of service. He received the Purple Heart for injuries sustained at Battle of Okinawa in World War II. He was an avid coon hunter and fisherman.[190]

        xi.   BERNICE ELIZA HART b. Nov- 9-1924 in Summers, Doddridge Co, WV,[190,592] d. Jul-13-1990 in Maryland,[190,592] buried in Maryland Veterans Cem, Cheltenham, MD,[190] resided in Washington, DC,[412,521] resided 1968 in Maryland,[412] resided 1938 in Oxford, Doddridge Co, WV.[521] She married Robert E. Cator, b. Dec-14-1922,[592] d. Dec- 1-2007,[190] buried in Maryland Veterans Cem, Cheltenham, MD,[190] resided in District Heights, Prince Georges Co, MD,[mdcxxv[1625]] military U.S. Coast Guard, World War II.[190]

        xii.   DOLORES GAY "TOOTS" HART b. Mar- 8-1929 in Doddridge Co, WV, d. Aug-15-1997,[592] resided in Livonia, Wayne Co, MI,[412,592] resided 1968 in Detroit, MI,[412] resided 1938 in Oxford, Doddridge Co, WV.[521] She married Ben Brown.

        xiii.   JOHN W. "CHUCK" HART, JR. b. Aug-13-1932 at Oxford, Doddridge Co, WV,[mdcxxvi[1626],190] d. Apr-13-2010,[190] buried in Big Isaac Cemetery, Doddridge Co, WV,[190] resided in Miletus (Salem), Doddridge Co, WV,[mdcxxvii[1627],190] resided 1978 at Big Isaac, Doddridge Co, WV,[1092] resided 1938 in Oxford, Doddridge Co, WV,[521] occupation well tender, Consolidated Natural Gas (33 yrs),[190] military U.S. Navy, Korean War.[190]

        He was founder and former pastor of the Mission of Faith Church, Big Isaac. He was also a former pastor of the Sawyers Run community Church, the West Milford Community Church, and the Long Run Community Church. In his 44 years of ministry, Rev. Hart preached numerous revivals in West Virginia and surrounding states.[190]

        He married Living.

774. **Stella Gay Gaston**, also known as Gay Gaston,[1402,765] (419.Samuel[8], 247.Daniel[7], 136.Hugh[6], 72.John[5], 21.John[4], 6.Hugh[3], 3.John[2], 1.Jean[1]), b. Jan-31-1892, d. Jan- -1986,[592] buried in Wilbur Cemetery, Tyler Co, WV, resided in Macedonia, Summit Co, OH,[592] resided 1967 in Pratt Run (near Shirley), Tyler Co, WV,[484] resided 1932 in Wilbur, Tyler Co, WV,[412] census 1930 in McElroy District, Tyler Co, WV. She married Oct-30-1916 in Doddridge Co, WV,[mdcxxviii[1628],354] **James Andrew Cumberledge**, b. Jan-19-1885 in Pratt Run (near Shirley), Tyler Co, WV,[190] (son of Samuel D. Cumberledge and Mary Ellen Brown), d. Apr-20-1967 in Pratt Run (near Shirley), Tyler Co, WV,[190] buried in Wilbur Cemetery, Tyler Co, WV,[190] resided in Wilbur, Tyler Co, WV,[396] census 1930 in McElroy District, Tyler Co, WV, occupation merchant.[190,1402]

1920 Census, Tyler Co, WV (McElroy District), enumerated Feb 12 1920:
James A. Cumberledge, 35, retail merchant; wife Stella G, 28; son James L, 12 months.

1930 Census, Tyler County, WV (McElroy District), Apr 1930:
James A. Cumberledge, 45, occupation retail merchant in general store; wife Gay, 38; son James L, 11; dau Ruby I, 8; son Jacob A, 7; son Daniel G, 5.

        Children:

        i.   JAMES LESTER CUMBERLEDGE[521] also known as Lester Cumberledge,[765] b. Jun-14-1918 in Wilbur, Tyler Co, WV,[398] d. Aug- 5-1931 in Wilbur, Tyler Co, WV,[765] buried in Wilbur Cemetery, Tyler Co, WV,[398] cause of death accidental gunshot,[398] census 1930 in McElroy District, Tyler Co, WV.

        ii.   RUBY I. CUMBERLEDGE b. Jun-16-1920,[592] d. Sep-30-2002 in Cleveland, Cuyahoga Co, OH,[592] resided in Macedonia, Summit Co, OH,[765,521,592] census 1930 in McElroy District, Tyler Co, WV. She married[941] __ Kester.

        iii.   JACOB A. "JAKE" CUMBERLEDGE b. Jan-22-1922 in Alma, Tyler Co, WV,[190,592] d. Aug-8-1996 in Alma, Tyler Co, WV,[190,592] buried in Wilbur Cemetery, Tyler Co, WV,[190] resided in Pratt Run (near Shirley), Tyler Co, WV,[765,190] census 1930 in McElroy District, Tyler Co, WV, occupation Union Carbide Corp in Sistersville WV (retired).[190]

        In addition to his four children, he was also survived by a foster son, Roger Smith, of Kitty Hawk, NC.[190]

        He married Living.

        iv.   DANIEL G. CUMBERLEDGE b. Feb-20-1925,[924,1402] resided 1996 in Coraopolis, Allegheny Co, PA,[521] resided 1967 in Pittsburgh, Allegheny Co, PA,[765] census 1930 in McElroy District, Tyler Co, WV.

775. **Rulina Belle Gaston**, also known as Belle Gaston (420.John[8], 248.Eli[7], 136.Hugh[6], 72.John[5], 21.John[4], 6.Hugh[3], 3.John[2], 1.Jean[1]), b. Jan-23-1878,[289] d. Jan- 2-1919, buried in Gaston Family Cemetery, Upper Run, Summers, Doddridge Co WV. She married Jun-25-1897 in Doddridge Co, WV,[354] **Alpheus Seymour Richards**, also known as Seamore Richards,[521] b. Feb-25-1877 in Calhoun Co, WV,[190] (son of Granville B. Richards and Mary Jane Wilson), d. Mar- 7-1964 in Clarksburg, Harrison Co, WV,[806,191] buried in Masonic Memorial Park Cemetery, Crystal Lake (West Union), WV, resided in New Milton, Doddridge Co, WV,[190] resided 1959 in Market, Doddridge Co, WV,[521] census 1930 in Greenbrier District, Doddridge Co, WV, census 1880 in Murphy District, Ritchie Co, WV, occupation carpenter & painter.[190]

Alpheus: Among others, survived by "one step-daughter, Mrs. Oma Sutton of Parkersburg."[190]

        Children:

        i.   GLEN RICHARDS b. Aug- 7-1898 in Doddridge Co, WV, d. Aug- 8-1898 in Doddridge Co, WV, buried in Gaston Family Cemetery, Upper Run, Summers, Doddridge Co WV.

        ii.   EDNA RICHARDS b. Jul-16-1899 in Doddridge Co, WV, d. Dec-19-1961 in Doddridge Co, WV,[mdcxxix[1629],356] buried in IOOF Cemetery, Troy, Gilmer Co, WV.[17] She married Oct-25-1915 in Oakland, Garrett Co, MD,[484] Claude Ellsworth Adams, b. May- 5-1889 in Lawford, Ritchie Co, WV,[190] (son of George Washington Adams and Eva D. Wilson), d. May-28-1959 in Clarksburg, Harrison Co, WV,[806] buried in IOOF Cemetery, Troy, Gilmer Co, WV,[17] resided in West Union, Doddridge Co, WV,[190] resided 1938 in Blandville, Doddridge Co, WV,[748] census 1910 in Union District, Ritchie Co, WV, occupation oil worker & engineer, Hope Natural Gas Co,[190] [Birth record of twin daughters in 1925 gives father's occupation as "oil worker," while birth record of daughter Dorothy in 1932 gives father's occupation as Engineer.].

        iii.   ELVIN RICHARDS b. Oct-30-1905 in Doddridge Co, WV,[190] d. Dec-23-1999 in Ravenswood, Jackson Co, WV,[190] buried in Rockland Cemetery, Belpre, Washington Co, OH,[190] occupation US Govt Technical Supervisor.[190]

        Resident of Newark, OH, and Belpre, OH. Member of the Sons of the American Revolution, and a life member of the National Rifle Association.[190]

He married May-8-1927 in Doddridge Co, WV,[354,484] Icy May Heflin, b. Feb-26-1912 in Amy, Lincoln Co, WV (daughter of William Preston Heflin and Essie May Powell), d. Mar- 5-1993 in Belpre, Washington Co, OH,[190] buried in Rockland Cemetery, Belpre, Washington Co, OH,[190] census 1920 at Horn Creek, Gilmer Co, WV.

      iv.   ARLEY M. RICHARDS[765] b. Jul-22-1918,[mdcxxx[1630]] d. Jul-26-1918 in Doddridge Co, WV.[356]

776. **Eli Willis Gaston** (420.John[8], 248.Eli[7], 136.Hugh[6], 72.John[5], 21.John[4], 6.Hugh[3], 3.John[2], 1.Jean[1]), b. Jun- 8-1880 in Doddridge Co, WV,[684,289] d. Sep-25-1919 in Clarksburg, Harrison Co, WV,[700,mdcxxxi[1631],17] buried in Greenlawn Masonic Cemetery, Clarksburg, WV,[mdcxxxii[1632],398] cause of death Bright's disease,[190] resided in Clarksburg, Harrison Co, WV,[684,190] occupation miner, Consolidated Coal Co..[684,190] He married Jun- 8-1903 in Gilmer Co, WV,[mdcxxxiii[1633]] **Launa Capitola Bowyer**, b. Jul-24-1878,[398,17,190,123] (daughter of George Allen Bowyer and Melissa Launa Stout), d. Dec-17-1937 in Clarksburg, Harrison Co, WV,[398,190] buried in Greenlawn Masonic Cemetery, Clarksburg, WV,[1632,190] resided in Clarksburg, Harrison Co, WV,[mdcxxxiv[1634],398] resided 1900 in Troy, Gilmer Co, WV.[123]

      Children:

      i.   AULDRA ASHTON GASTON b. May-10-1904 in Gilmer Co, WV,[mdcxxxv[1635]] d. Jun- 5-1975 in Warren, Trumbull Co, OH, buried in Warren, Trumbull Co, OH, resided 1937 in Niles, Trumbull Co, OH,[856] resided 1923, 29 in Clarksburg, Harrison Co, WV.[mdcxxxvi[1636],1635]. He married (1) Jul-21-1929 in Clarksburg, Harrison Co, WV,[1635] Alice Louise Smith, b. Apr- 5-1910 in Randolph Co, WV,[1635] (daughter of William Hugh Smith and Jessie E. Wolfe), resided 1929 in Clarksburg, Harrison Co, WV.[1635] He married (2) Carmelena Innamorato, d. 19__.

      ii.   SELDON OBRA GASTON b. Feb-25-1906 in Gilmer Co, WV,[621] d. May-10-1965,[592] [SSDI reports death date as May 1965. Headstone states only 1965. Obituary of wife Florence gives his death date as May 10 1962, presumably correct for month & day, but wrong for the year.], buried in Greenlawn Masonic Cemetery, Clarksburg, WV,[1632] resided 1938 in Harrison Co, WV,[621] resided 1923 in Clarksburg, Harrison Co, WV,[1131] [441 Stealey Ave, Stealey Heights; occupation student]. He married Nov-17-1938 at Churchville, Lewis Co, WV,[621] Florence Jessie Quinn, b. Mar-28-1910 in Smithfield, Wetzel Co, WV,[592,419] (daughter of Virgil Quinn and Louise Vandyne), d. Nov-11-1997 in Salem, WV,[190,592] buried in Lumberport Lions Cemetery, Harrison Co, WV, resided 1938 in Lewis Co, WV,[621] census 1930 in Eagle District, Harrison Co, WV, resided 1924 at Lamberts Run, Harrison Co, WV.[419]

      iii.   MARLIN O. GASTON b. Mar- 3-1907 in Harrison Co, WV, d. Sep-14-1907 in Harrison Co, WV.[1201]

      iv.   BONNIE MEREDITH GASTON, also known as Bonnie Meredeth Gaston,[mdcxxxvii[1637]] b. Sep-10-1908 in Adamston (Clarksburg), Harrison Co, WV,[1637,190] d. Dec-29-1958 in Miami, FL,[806] buried in Bridgeport Cemetery, Harrison Co, WV,[mdcxxxviii[1638]] resided 1954-58 in Miami, FL,[190] occupation until 1954 Maureen Coal Co.[190] She married[191] Feb-11-1939 in Clarksburg, Harrison Co, WV,[1637] [Wife's obituary states marriage date as Feb 6 1939, but marriage record shows it to be Feb 11 1939.], no children from this marriage, Harold Stewart, b. Apr-11-1909 in Wilbur, Tyler Co, WV,[1637,398] (son of Rawley J. Stewart and Dora Wise), d. Sep-11-1947 in Clarksburg, Harrison Co, WV,[398,191] buried in Bridgeport Cemetery, Harrison Co, WV,[398,17] resided in Clarksburg, Harrison Co, WV,[398] resided 1939 in Nutter Fort, Harrison Co, WV,[1637] occupation wholesale grocer (Radix Sales Co.).[398]

777. **Lurana Olive Gaston**, also known as Luly Gaston (420.John[8], 248.Eli[7], 136.Hugh[6], 72.John[5], 21.John[4], 6.Hugh[3], 3.John[2], 1.Jean[1]), b. Jan- 2-1883 in Doddridge Co, WV,[mdcxxxix[1639],989,289] d. Apr- 1-1969 in Harrison Co, WV,[989] buried in South Fork Bapt Church Cem, Oxford, Doddridge Co, WV,[17] census 1930 in Southwest District, Doddridge Co, WV, resided 1927 in Oxford, Doddridge Co, WV.[765] She married Dec-8-1904 in Doddridge Co, WV,[mdcxl[1640]] [Wes Cochran's "Doddridge County WV Marriages" reports marriage date as Dec 18 1904.], **Edghar Hamilton Richards**, census name Edgar H. Richards,[1389] b. Nov- 1-1886 in Ritchie Co, WV (son of Granville B. Richards and Mary Jane Wilson), d. Jul-21-1930 in Doddridge Co, WV,[356] buried in South Fork Bapt Church Cem, Oxford, Doddridge Co, WV,[17] census 1900, 1930 in Southwest District, Doddridge Co, WV.

Children:

 i. JOHN EMITT RICHARDS b. Jul- 3-1906 in Holbrook, Doddridge Co, WV,[190] d. Dec-25-1991 in Greenwood, Doddridge Co, WV,[190,mdcxli[1641]] buried in South Fork Bapt Church Cem, Oxford, Doddridge Co, WV,[190] census 1930 in Southwest District, Doddridge Co, WV, occupation carpenter. He married May-11-1927 in Doddridge Co, WV,[354,191,484,877] Lora Hester Nutter, b. Jan- 1-1903 in Oxford, Doddridge Co, WV,[mdcxlii[1642],190] (daughter of Sylvanus Nutter and Sarah E. Hart), d. Sep- 8-1970 in Greenwood, Doddridge Co, WV,[700,484,mdcxliii[1643]] buried in South Fork Bapt Church Cem, Oxford, Doddridge Co, WV,[17] resided in Greenwood, Doddridge Co, WV,[190] [Long Run section], resided 1966 in Central Station, Doddridge Co, WV,[765] resided 1950 in Oxford, Doddridge Co, WV,[856] census 1930 in Southwest District, Doddridge Co, WV.

 ii. WANDA MAE RICHARDS, also known as Mae Richards, b. Feb-18-1911 in Doddridge Co, WV,[190] d. Apr-13-1985 in Clarksburg, Harrison Co, WV,[190] buried in South Fork Bapt Church Cem, Oxford, Doddridge Co, WV,[190] census 1930 in Southwest District, Doddridge Co, WV. She married Feb-11-1932 in Doddridge Co, WV,[mdcxliv[1644],mdcxlv[1645]] [Obituary of husband gives marriage date as Feb 11 1931, which is incorrect.], Charles Floyd Husk, also known as Floyd C. Husk,[1389] b. Jul-11-1908 in Pocahontas Co, WV,[190] [Marriage record gives his birthplace as Doddridge County, an apparent error, as obituary states Pocahontas County.] (son of William Leonard Husk and Virginia Elizabeth "Jennie" McNemar), d. Aug-15-1978 in Clarksburg, Harrison Co, WV,[190] buried in South Fork Bapt Church Cem, Oxford, Doddridge Co, WV,[17] occupation well tender, Equitable Gas Co.[190]

 iii. MAMIE VIRGINIA RICHARDS b. Sep-10-1920 in Doddridge Co, WV,[190] d. Feb- 8-2001 in Clarksburg, Harrison Co, WV,[190] cremated[190] resided in Clarksburg, Harrison Co, WV,[190] resided 1985 in Portsmouth, VA,[412] census 1930 in Southwest District, Doddridge Co, WV, occupation restaurants & nursing homes.[190]

Name appears in many records, including marriage record with Walter Underwood, as "Mayme."

She married (1) Dec-10-1938 in Salem, WV,[mdcxlvi[1646]] Walter Jackson Underwood, also known as Jackson Walter Underwood, b. Aug-12-1918 in Doddridge Co, WV,[1646,592] (son of Wetzel Underwood and Minnie Smith), d. Sep-28-1968,[mdcxlvii[1647]] buried in City Park Cemetery, Portsmouth, VA, resided in Portsmouth, VA,[592] resided formerly in Pennsylvania.[948]

Walter: Identified in birth record as Jackson Walter Underwood, son of Wetzel Underwood and Minnie Smith, but he was always known as Walter J. Underwood. His SSDI entry identifies him as Walter Underwood, resident of Portsmouth, VA, Social Security card issued in Pennsylvania before 1951.

She married (2) Feb-17-1975 in North Carolina, Robert A. "Blackie" Morton, b. Aug-27-1923 in Norfolk, VA,[190] d. Jun- 3-2001 in Harrison Co, WV,[190] occupation sheet metal worker at Norfolk shipyards.[190]

778. **John Sheridan Gaston** (420.John[8], 248.Eli[7], 136.Hugh[6], 72.John[5], 21.John[4], 6.Hugh[3], 3.John[2], 1.Jean[1]), b. May-27-1888 in Toll Gate, Doddridge Co, WV,[mdcxlviii[1648],17,684] d. Jul-17-1972,[592,17] buried in K of P Memorial Park Cemetery, Salem, WV,[817] resided in Lost Creek, Harrison Co, WV,[191] resided 1917 in Smithton (now Smithburg), Doddridge Co, WV,[684] occupation 1917 common laborer for A.J. Riddle & Son of Smithton.[684] He married Aug-21-1913 in Doddridge Co, WV,[354] **Birdie Arizona Cottrill**, b. Aug-17-1889 in Doddridge Co, WV,[190] [Obituary states birth date as Aug 17 1892, but headstone shows it as 1890, and 1900 Census states Aug 1889.] (daughter of Henry J. Cottrill and Mary Alice "Molly" Dotson), d. Sep- 9-1952 in Lost Creek, Harrison Co, WV,[700,46] buried in IOOF Cemetery, Salem, Harrison Co, WV,[817] resided in Lost Creek, Harrison Co, WV,[856,778,190.]
  Children:
 i. ALFRED GASTON b. Jun-12-1914 in Doddridge Co, WV, d. Jun-28-1918 in Doddridge Co, WV,[510,356] buried in IOOF Cemetery, Salem, Harrison Co, WV.

  ii. MILDRED GASTON b. Jul-30-1918 in Doddridge Co, WV,[46] d. Mar-27-1982 in Harrison Co, WV,[46] buried in K of P Memorial Park Cemetery, Salem, WV.[817] She married divorced Lewis Smith.

  iii. JUNIOR DALE GASTON, census name John Gaston, Jr.,[1208] b. Mar-16-1922 in Doddridge Co, WV, buried in IOOF Cemetery, Salem, Harrison Co, WV, census 1930 in Salem, WV.[1208]

  iv. SARAH J. GASTON b. Dec- 8-1925 in Harrison Co, WV,[1068,398] d. Mar-11-1926 in Salem, WV,[398] cause of death crib death,[398] buried in IOOF Cemetery, Salem, Harrison Co, WV.[398]

  v. LIVING. Partner Living.

  vi. LIVING. She married (1) Arnold Glen Monroe, b. May-10-1901 in Mannington, Marion Co, WV,[419,592] (son of William E. Monroe and Mary Ellen Duncan), d. Mar- -1982,[592] resided in Clarksburg, Harrison Co, WV.[419,604] She married (2) John Edward McCall, b. Aug- 4-1906,[592] d. Jun-19-1974,[592] resided in Weston, Lewis Co, WV,[592] resided formerly in Pennsylvania.[948] She married[424] (3) Living.

  vii. ROSALIE COTTRILL GASTON b. Jul- 2-1933 at Lost Creek, Harrison Co, WV,[190] d. Jun-22-2009 in Clarksburg, Harrison Co, WV,[847] buried in Sunset Memorial Park Cemetery, Clarksburg, WV,[190] resided in Clarksburg, Harrison Co, WV,[190] occupation W. T. Grant department store (formerly).[190] She married Living.

779. **Jesse Morris Gaston** (420.John[8], 248.Eli[7], 136.Hugh[6], 72.John[5], 21.John[4], 6.Hugh[3], 3.John[2], 1.Jean[1]), b. Jan-22-1891 in Oxford, Doddridge Co, WV,[684,190,289] [Death record reports birth date as Feb 22 1891, but obituary states birth date as Jan 22 1891, as does his WWI Draft Registration card and his parents' family Bible.], d. Sep-18-1928 in Oxford, Doddridge Co, WV,[398,356,190,17] cause of death killed in accident while working at a water well site,[398] buried in Gaston Family Cemetery, Upper Run, Summers, Doddridge Co WV,[17,190] resided in Oxford, Doddridge Co, WV,[684,765] occupation farmer,[684,398] military World War I (Pvt, 163rd Inf, 41st Div).[190,17] He married Aug-6-1921 in Doddridge Co, WV,[354] **Sarah Elizabeth Williamson**, b. Apr-16-1902 in Ritchie Co, WV (daughter of Joseph W. Williamson and Ida May Vore), d. Aug-19-1991 in Hagerstown, Washington Co, MD, buried in Dulaney Valley Memorial Gardens, Timonium, MD, resided in Baltimore, MD,[521] census 1920 in Clay District, Ritchie Co, WV, census 1910 in Union District, Ritchie Co, WV.
  Children:

  i. EDWARD ULLMONT GASTON b. May-23-1922 in Doddridge Co, WV, d. Oct- 8-1981, buried in Glen Oak Cemetery, Hillside, IL, resided in DuPage, Addison Co, IL,[592] military U.S. Navy. He married Jun-2-1945 in Chicago, IL, Marion Emma Kressman, b. Apr-14-1924,[592] d. Nov- 3-2005,[592] resided in Roselle, DuPage Co, IL.[936]

  ii. GUY EDMOND GASTON b. Jul-15-1923 in Doddridge Co, WV, residence in Abingdon, Harford Co, MD. He married Feb-6-1944 in Baltimore, MD, Gladys June McCown, b. Jun-19-1924 in Kentucky (daughter of Everett McCown and Ora Smallwood), d. Nov-14-2006 in Bel Air, Harford Co, MD,[806] buried in Dulaney Valley Memorial Gardens, Timonium, MD,[190] resided in Abingdon, Harford Co, MD.[190]

  iii. EDGAR HAMILTON GASTON b. Dec- 3-1926 in Doddridge Co, WV, d. Apr-25-2006 in Maryland,[1166] buried in Parkwood Cemetery, Parkville, Baltimore Co, MD,[190] resided in Mt. Airy, Frederick Co, MD, resided formerly in Baltimore, MD. He married Apr-21-1956 in Towson, Baltimore Co, MD, divorced 1994, Mary Katherine "Cass" Ward, also known as Catherine,[mdcxlix[1649]] b. Jun- 9-1928 in Cockeysville, Baltimore Co, MD, d. May-29-2010,[190] buried in Parkwood Cemetery, Parkville, Baltimore Co, MD,[190] resided in Baltimore, MD.[190]

780. **Ira Dow Gaston** (420.John[8], 248.Eli[7], 136.Hugh[6], 72.John[5], 21.John[4], 6.Hugh[3], 3.John[2], 1.Jean[1]), b. Dec-31-1894 in Oxford, Doddridge Co, WV,[289,1166] d. Jul-26-1973 in Washington Co, OH,[1166] buried in Cabin Run Cemetery, Doddridge Co, WV,[17] [Headstone gives the birthdate of 1895, which is incorrect.], occupation oil and gas company.[1166]

Dow Gaston, as he was known, retired from the Equitable Gas Company in 1949 with 28 years of service. He was a member of the Cabin Run Methodist Church; the Friendship Lodge No. 56 A.F. and A.M., and Order of the Eastern Star Chapter No. 56, both of West Union; the Clarksburg Lodge of Perfection; Clarksburg Chapter of Rose Croix; Wheeling Council of Kadosh; and Wheeling Consistory.

[Obit] He served on the Doddridge County Board of Education. [West Virginia Blue Book, 1948, p. 378 & 495]

The small grocery store located next to the family home on Oxford Road at Cabin Run was built in 1949, largely from wood salvaged from an abandoned one-room school building. The store was operated by Ira Dow Gaston and family until shortly before his death. The store and home then stood vacant until June 1974, when daughter Geneva and her husband Armand Brown moved from Ohio to reside and operate the store. The store was closed for the last time on May 31 1985, and the building was dismantled in July 1993, with much of its original wood salvaged for reuse.

He married Apr-26-1921 in West Union, Doddridge Co, WV,[mdcl[1650]] **Ida Opal Husk**, b. May-28-1904 in Oxford, Doddridge Co, WV,[1166] (daughter of William Leonard Husk and Virginia Elizabeth "Jennie" McNemar), d. Jan-16-1970 in Parkersburg, Wood Co, WV,[1434] buried Jan-19-1970 in Cabin Run Cemetery, Doddridge Co, WV,[17] occupation storekeeper.

Children:
  i.   WILLIAM (TWIN) GASTON b. Dec-16-1923 in Doddridge Co, WV,[17] d. Dec-16-1923 in Doddridge Co, WV,[17] buried in Gaston Family Cemetery, Upper Run, Summers, Doddridge Co WV.[17]
  ii.   LILLIAN (TWIN) GASTON b. Dec-16-1923 in Doddridge Co, WV,[17] d. Dec-16-1923 in Doddridge Co, WV,[17] buried in Gaston Family Cemetery, Upper Run, Summers, Doddridge Co WV.[17]
  iii.   ALFRED RANDOLPH GASTON b. Mar-10-1925 in Camp Run, Oxford, Doddridge Co, WV,[190] d. Jul-24-1991 in Ripley, Jackson Co, WV,[764] buried in Cabin Run Cemetery, Doddridge Co, WV.[17]

He was a former employee of the Akron Rubber Company and had worked several years with the Kroger Company as a meat cutter.[190]

He married (1) Apr-8-1945 in West Union, Doddridge Co, WV,[mdcli[1651]] divorced 1951, Virginia Williams Kidd, birth name Virginia Williams, b. Apr-12-1927 in Copen, Braxton Co, WV [Birth date listed in SSDI as Apr 2 1927, but immediate family advises Apr 12 1927.] (daughter of Otis Scott Williams and Lona M. Pulliam), d. Mar-19-2009 in Farmington Hills, Oakland Co, MI, resided in Farmington Hills, Oakland Co, MI,[395] census 1930 in Clarksburg, Harrison Co, WV.

Virginia: When Virginia Williams' mother Lona died three days after Virginia's birth, Virginia and all her siblings were placed in an orphanage in Braxton County. Virginia was soon adopted by Aldridge C. Kidd and Amie Cunningham Boyce Kidd, who raised her in Harrison County.

He married (2) Living.
  iv.   GENEVA PAULINE GASTON b. Nov-15-1926 at Camp Run, Oxford, Doddridge Co, WV, d. Dec-22-2001 in Clarksburg, Harrison Co, WV, buried Dec-27-2001 in Masonic Memorial Park Cemetery, Crystal Lake (West Union), WV, resided in Doddridge Co, WV, resided 1946 - 1974 in Youngstown, Mahoning Co, OH, education Doddridge Co H.S. (1945), Salem College.

Graduate of Doddridge County High School (1945) and attended Salem College, Salem, WV, 1945-46. Worked for two years in the office of the Ford garage in West Union, WV. Upon her marriage to Armand Brown in 1946, she moved to Youngstown, OH, where Armand's family had moved from West Union while he was overseas during World War II. From 1962 to 1974, she worked as cashier and office worker for A&P food stores in Youngstown, OH and vicinity. In June 1974, with Armand's heart problems preventing him from continuing his job with A&P in Youngstown, they returned to Doddridge County, moving into the house on Oxford Road, at Cabin Run, where Geneva had lived with her family for about five years prior to her marriage. From then until his death in 1985, Armand and Geneva operated what had been her parents' small grocery store adjacent to the family home, changing the name from Gaston's Grocery to Brown's Grocery. With her brother Sam, Geneva was a driving force and principal compiler of this genealogy.

She married Aug-4-1946 in West Union, Doddridge Co, WV,[mdclii][1652] Armand Leon Brown, b. Jan-27-1923 in West Union, Doddridge Co, WV,[mdcliii][1653] (son of Addison Avery Brown and Nancy Lou "Babe" Haught), d. Apr- 9-1985 in Doddridge Co, WV, buried Apr-11-1985 in Masonic Memorial Park Cemetery, Crystal Lake (West Union), WV, resided in Doddridge Co, WV, resided 1945 - 1974 in Youngstown, Mahoning Co, OH, resided until 1945 in West Union, Doddridge Co, WV, occupation A&P Grocery Produce Manager, education Doddridge Co H.S. (1941), military U.S Army, World War II (Europe).

    v.   GILBERT EUGENE "GIB" GASTON b. Feb-18-1929 in Upper Run, Oxford, Doddridge Co, WV, d. Oct-23-1999 in Parkersburg, Wood Co, WV, buried in Sunset Memory Gardens, Parkersburg, WV, military U.S. Army, Korean War.

After graduating from Salem College, Salem, WV, he taught in Wood County, WV, public schools for several years. Frustrated with student behavioral problems, he left teaching and became a police officer in Parkersburg, WV, retiring with 20 years service. Even then, he remained active as a successful real estate agent in Parkersburg. Gib was a man of many talents and great determination. In carpentry and other projects, his ultimate solution when something wouldn't quite fit was to call upon a tool he called "the persuader," known to anyone else as a sledgehammer. That usually did the trick.

He married (1) Oct-28-1950 at Greenwood, Doddridge Co, WV,[mdcliv][1654] divorced[1166] Doris Mae Cross, b. Mar-29-1932 in Ritchie Co, WV,[1654,190] (daughter of Johnnie Thurman Cross and Mary Elizabeth Stull), d. Mar-19-2006 in Parkersburg, Wood Co, WV,[700] buried (ashes) at Cabin Run Cemetery, Doddridge Co, WV,[1166] resided in Parkersburg, Wood Co, WV,[190] resided 2000 in Salem, WV.[856] He married (2) Dec-11-1971 in Parkersburg, Wood Co, WV, Ruth Virginia Pickering, b. Sep-18-1932 in Quantico, VA,[190] (daughter of Raymond Wood Pickering and Effie Viola Rutledge), d. Oct-14-2007 in Washington, Wood Co, WV,[190] buried in Sunset Memory Gardens, Parkersburg, WV,[190] resided in Parkersburg, Wood Co, WV,[190] occupation bookkeeper (United Bank, 50 yrs).[190]

    vi.   LIVING. He married Living.
    vii.   LIVING. He married Living.
    viii.   JAMES MORGAN GASTON b. Jun- 6-1940 in Upper Run, Oxford, Doddridge Co, WV, d. Apr-25-2001 in Marietta, Washington Co, OH, buried in Dale Cemetery, Dale, OH, military 1961-65 U.S. Navy.

Served in US Navy as a Yeoman/Clerk and Nuclear Weapons Inspector, 1961-65. Worked as a Chemical Operator with Borg-Warner (General Electric Plastics), 1965-95. Elected to five consecutive terms as Township Trustee, Palmer Twp, Washington Co, OH, 1972-92. He was highly skilled in HVAC, carpentry, and woodcraft, on numerous occasions hand-crafting wooden cradles and rocking horses for the young children of his extended family.

He married (1) Living. He married (2) Living.
    ix.   LIVING. She married James Edward "Chum" Holtz, b. Jul-13-1940 in West Union, Doddridge Co, WV,[mdclv][1655] (son of Frank Edward Holtz and Nadine Knapp), d. Jun-14-1998 near Lordsburg, NM,[mdclvi][1656] buried in Bristol, Sullivan Co, TN,[1166] occupation salesman and trucker.[1166]

781. **Rulina Melinda Gaston**[190], also known as Lina Gaston,[765,228,240] (421.Eli[8], 248.Eli[7], 136.Hugh[6], 72.John[5], 21.John[4], 6.Hugh[3], 3.John[2], 1.Jean[1]), b. Jan-13-1880 in Doddridge Co, WV,[190,240,46] d. Jan-10-1944 in Greenwood, Doddridge Co, WV,[190,356,46] buried in Hart Cemetery, Taylor Drain Rd, Oxford, Doddridge Co WV,[17] resided 1941 in Grafton, Taylor Co, WV,[765] resided 1900 in Doddridge Co, WV.[385] She married Sep-11-1904 in Doddridge Co, WV,[mdclvii][1657],[mdclviii][1658] **Larmar Martin Collins**, b. Apr-28-1875 in Tyler Co, WV,[398,354] (son of Henry Benton Collins and Emily Laverna McIntyre), d. May-22-1943 in Buckhannon, Upshur Co, WV,[mdclix][1659] buried in Mt. Carmel Cemetery, Tallmansville, Upshur Co, WV,[398] resided near Buckhannon, Upshur Co, WV,[398] census 1900 in Southwest District, Doddridge Co, WV [Listed as a servant, age about 20, in household of Eli B. Leeson, widower of his mother's sister Clarinda.], occupation farmer.[398]

    Children:

i.   OVAL EDISON COLLINS b. May-26-1907 in Doddridge Co, WV,[1617] d. Feb- 1-1964 in Fairmont, Marion Co, WV,[mdclx[1660],806] buried in Woodlawn Cemetery, Fairmont, Marion Co, WV, resided in Monongah, Marion Co, WV,[190] resided 1944 in Oxford, Doddridge Co, WV,[856] occupation Wheeling Transfer Co, Fairmont WV (19 yrs).[190] He married May-18-1924 in Doddridge Co, WV,[354] Dephna Pearl Jones, census name Pearle Jones,[509] b. Feb- 7-1906 in Doddridge Co, WV,[190] (daughter of Robert E. Jones and Icy Mae Hileman), d. Nov-28-1988 in Marion Co, WV,[mdclxi[1661],190] buried in Woodlawn Cemetery, Fairmont, Marion Co, WV, resided in Monongah, Marion Co, WV,[190] resided 1963 in Fairmont, Marion Co, WV,[412] resided 1944 in Oxford, Doddridge Co, WV,[765] census 1910, 1920 in Southwest District, Doddridge Co, WV.

782. **Anna Elizabeth Gaston**, also known as Annie E. Gaston (421.Eli[8], 248.Eli[7], 136.Hugh[6], 72.John[5], 21.John[4], 6.Hugh[3], 3.John[2], 1.Jean[1]), b. Mar-23-1884 in Doddridge Co, WV,[mdclxii[1662]] [Obituary states age as 75, born Mar 23 1887, but she was actually 78, as her birth record shows that she was born on Mar 23 1884, the same date reported for her by sister Minnie in a W. Guy Tetrick family information survey completed in 1931.], d. Feb-27-1963 in Akron, Summit Co, OH,[693] buried in Mt. Carmel Cemetery, Tallmansville, Upshur Co, WV,[17] resided in Akron, Summit Co, OH,[693] resided 1941, 44 in Buckhannon, Upshur Co, WV,[765,412] census 1930 in Upshur Co, WV. She married Dec-7-1902 in Upshur Co, WV,[mdclxiii[1663]] divorced bef Apr 1930,[922] **Frederick Burton Shipman**, also known as Fred Burton Shipman,[191] b. May-16-1883 in Upshur Co, WV (son of John Hollis Shipman and Nellie A. Wilfong), d. Nov- 9-1961 in Weston, Lewis Co, WV,[1166] buried in Mt. Herman Cemetery, Upshur Co, WV.

Children:
i.   LILLIE MAUDE SHIPMAN b. Nov-27-1903 in Upshur Co, WV,[592] d. Oct- -1986,[592] buried in Mt. Carmel Cemetery, Tallmansville, Upshur Co, WV,[17] resided in Buckhannon, Upshur Co, WV,[592] resided 1963 in Akron, Summit Co, OH,[856,mdclxiv[1664]] census 1930 in Upshur Co, WV, resided 1920 in Tallmansville, Upshur Co, WV.[921] She married (1) Mar-17-1920 in Buckhannon, Upshur Co, WV,[921] divorced Clifford R. Smith, b. ca 1899 in Upshur Co, WV,[921] (son of William Smith and Isabelle __), d. in Ohio, census 1930 in Upshur Co, WV, resided 1920 in Tallmansville, Upshur Co, WV,[921] occupation coal miner.[922] She married (2) Duran Paul Gifford,[502] also known as Paul Gifford, b. Jul- 1-1913,[592] d. Aug- 6-1997,[592] resided in Buckhannon, Upshur Co, WV.[592]
ii.   ZEDA MAY SHIPMAN b. 1907, d. 1914 in Upshur Co, WV, buried in Mt. Union Cemetery, Upshur Co, WV.
iii. DEMA BELLE SHIPMAN b. Oct- 3-1910 in Upshur Co, WV,[592] d. May-13-1996,[592] resided in Buckhannon, Upshur Co, WV,[592,856] census 1930 in Upshur Co, WV. She married Jul-6-1937 in Upshur Co, WV, Denver Black, b. Jul- 5-1911 in Upshur Co, WV (son of James Black and Maggie Bryan), d. Mar- 1-1973 in Upshur Co, WV, buried in Mt. Carmel Cemetery, Tallmansville, Upshur Co, WV.[17]
iv.   ARCHIE OLEY SHIPMAN b. Sep- 3-1913 in Upshur Co, WV, d. Feb-17-1986, buried in Mt. Carmel Cemetery, Tallmansville, Upshur Co, WV,[17] resided 1963 in Buckhannon, Upshur Co, WV,[856] census 1930 in Upshur Co, WV. He married (1) Nov-16-1935 in Elkins, Randolph Co, WV,[921] Beulah Modeline Strader, b. May-14-1914 in Upshur Co, WV,[921] (daughter of Quincy Strader and May __), d. Jan-20-1977, buried in Mt. Carmel Cemetery, Tallmansville, Upshur Co, WV,[17] resided 1935 near Buckhannon, Upshur Co, WV.[921] He married (2) Jul-9-1979, Ada L. McClellan Stout, b. Oct- 4-1918 (daughter of William McClellan and Ada Bullock).
v.   HARLEY ARBENDALE SHIPMAN b. Oct-12-1917 in Upshur Co, WV, d. Aug-31-1981, buried in Mt. Herman Cemetery, Upshur Co, WV, resided 1963 in Belington, Barbour Co, WV,[856] census 1930 in Upshur Co, WV. He married (1) Oct-24-1937, Cleo Virginia Dilworth, b. ca 1917,[681] (daughter of Sylvester Floyd Dilworth and Georgia S. Adams). He married (2) Dec- 7-1974, Iva Black.

783. **Arnold Marsh Gaston** (421.Eli[8], 248.Eli[7], 136.Hugh[6], 72.John[5], 21.John[4], 6.Hugh[3], 3.John[2], 1.Jean[1]), b. Feb-21-1888 in Oxford, Doddridge Co, WV,[1648,mdclxv[1665]] d. Jan-24-1973 in Hillsville, Pocahontas Co, WV,[mdclxvi[1666]] buried in Stout Cemetery, Flatwoods, Braxton Co, WV, resided 1932, 41, 44, 63, 73 at Exchange, Braxton Co, WV,[1470,765,412,190] census 1930 in Otter District, Braxton Co, WV, resided 1917 in Flatwoods, Braxton Co, WV,[684] resided 1915 in Upshur Co, WV,[mdclxvii[1667]] occupation farmer.[684] He married May-4-1915 in Braxton Co, WV,[mdclxviii[1668],1667] **Iva Sufronia Butcher**, b. Sep-22-1889 in

Lewis Co, WV (daughter of Lewis W. Butcher and Amanda L. Gumm), d. Nov- 5-1969 in Braxton Co, WV,[mdclxix][1669],484 buried in Stout Cemetery, Flatwoods, Braxton Co, WV, census 1930 in Otter District, Braxton Co, WV.

Children:

i. EDITH GAE GASTON b. Apr- 7-1916 in Gassaway, Braxton Co, WV,[190,592] d. Jul-30-2003 in Pinellas Park, Pinellas Co, FL,[190,592] resided 1954-2003 in Seminole, Pinellas Co, FL,[190,592] resided bef 1954 in Fairmont, Marion Co, WV,[190] occupation teacher (18 yrs at Tyrone Elementary School).[190] She married Jun-23-1944 in Charleston, SC, Argel Eugene Jordan, b. Oct-13-1919 in Webster Co, WV,[592] (son of Charles Wamsley Jordan and Blanch Cutlip), d. Jan-10-1997,[592] resided in Seminole, Pinellas Co, FL,[592] resided formerly in West Virginia.[604]

ii. JESSE LAWRENCE GASTON b. Oct-22-1917 in Scott's Fork, Braxton Co, WV,[190] d. Apr-9-1994 in Braxton Co, WV,[190] buried in Stout Cemetery, Flatwoods, Braxton Co, WV,[190] resided in Exchange, Braxton Co, WV.[765] He married Living.

iii. RHODA RACHEAL GASTON b. Dec- 1-1919 in Braxton Co, WV, resided 2003, 04 in St. Petersburg, Pinellas Co, FL,[412,484] resided 1973 in Bethesda, Montgomery Co, MD.[765] She married Walter D. Sutton, b. Sep-26-1923 in Burma,[190,592] d. Jul-17-2004 in St. Petersburg, Pinellas Co, FL,[700,592] buried in Arlington National Cemetery, VA,[190] resided since 1979 in St. Petersburg, Pinellas Co, FL,[190,592] resided formerly in Maryland,[mdclxx][1670] occupation Central Intelligence Agency (1950-1979),[190] military U.S. Navy, World War II.[190]

Walter: He was the son of missionary parents and grew up in Burma, where he spent his childhood. He and his wife spent nearly every summer in Garrett County, MD for the past 30 years. During World War II, he served as a junior officer in the U.S. Navy aboard the USS Caine. He was an official of the Central Intelligence Agency in Washington, D.C., from 1950 until his retirement in 1979 as the director's press review officer. While at the CIA, he held several senior level positions, including the chief of the Southeast Asia Branch of the Office of Current Intelligence, the director's representative in Singapore, and the principal liaison officer with British Intelligence. [mdclxxi][1671]

iv. LOVIE ELIZABETH "BETTY" GASTON b. Apr- 4-1921 in Braxton Co, WV,[592,693] d. Oct-13-1990 in Florida,[mdclxxii][1672],[mdclxxiii][1673] resided in Lady Lake, Lake Co, FL,[604] resided 1973 in Cedartown, Polk Co, GA,[765] census 1930 in Otter District, Braxton Co, WV. She married (1) Royce Bullock. She married (2) Oct-30-1959, Frank C. Lewis, b. Sep-30-1923.

v. MINNIE ALICE GASTON b. Apr- 9-1923 in Braxton Co, WV, resided 2003 in Phoenix, Maricopa Co, AZ,[412] resided 1973 in Blythe, CA,[765] never married.

vi. MARY ISABEL GASTON b. Mar-22-1925 in Braxton Co, WV, resided 2003 in Lady Lake, Lake Co, FL,[412] resided 1973 in Dallas, TX.[765] She married[941] (1) Paul Robinson, b. Jul-10-1922, d. Mar-16-1987. She married (2) Sep-28-1991, Frank C. Lewis, b. Sep-30-1923.

784. **Bessie Mae Gaston** (421.Eli[8], 248.Eli[7], 136.Hugh[6], 72.John[5], 21.John[4], 6.Hugh[3], 3.John[2], 1.Jean[1]), b. Sep-17-1890 in Doddridge Co, WV,[190] d. Aug-20-1981 in Akron, Summit Co, OH,[806] buried in Heavner Cemetery, Upshur Co, WV,[190] resided 1941-80 in Buckhannon, Upshur Co, WV,[765,412,521,190] census 1930 in Upshur Co, WV.

Resided with son Charles David Adams in Stow, OH from Nov 20 1980 until her death, moving from Buckhannon, Upshur Co, WV. She was predeceased by one son, one daughter, two brothers, three sisters, and two half-sisters.

She married Sep-30-1907 in Upshur Co, WV,[mdclxxiv][1674] **Johnson Dee Adams**, also known as Dee Adams,[374,190,922] b. Nov- 2-1879 in Doddridge Co, WV,[190] (son of David Adams and Laverna Costello), d. 1952 in Buckhannon, Upshur Co, WV,[191,806] buried in Heavner Cemetery, Upshur Co, WV, resided 1941 in Tallmansville, Upshur Co, WV,[mdclxxv][1675] census 1930 in Upshur Co, WV, occupation B. & O. Railroad.[190]

Children:

i.   JAMES ARNOLD ADAMS b. Sep-20-1910 in Upshur Co, WV,[mdclxxvi[1676],190] d. Mar- 6-1975 in Buckhannon, Upshur Co, WV,[190] [Became ill while at work on the B&O Railroad at Pickens, Randolph Co, and was pronounced dead on arrival at St. Joseph Hospital, Buckhannon. [obit]], resided in Buckhannon, Upshur Co, WV,[765,412,190] census 1930 in Upshur Co, WV, occupation trackman for B&O Railroad (49 yrs).[190] He married[484] Margie Virginia Hinkle, resided 1975 in Buckhannon, Upshur Co, WV.[484]

ii.   GASTON GALE ADAMS, also known as Gale Adams,[412,521,856,922] b. Mar-29-1913 in Tallmansville, Upshur Co, WV,[190,592] d. Jul-22-1996,[190,592] resided 1952, 62, 81, 96 in Buckhannon, Upshur Co, WV,[765,412,856,190] census 1930 in Upshur Co, WV.

He worked as a bridge and building foreman for the B & O Railroad, retiring in 1980 with 41 years service. Among other survivors were two grandsons, Christopher Wayne Elbon and Michael Lee Bull, two granddaughters, Nicole Lynn Russell and Heather Lee Adams, and two great-grandsons, Nicholas Todd Russell and Nathaniel Scott Russell, all of Buckhannon.[190]

He married Sep- 9-1944,[484] Esther Delores Teets, b. ca 1922.[405]

iii.   GARLTON GAY ADAMS b. Dec- 4-1915 in Buckhannon, Upshur Co, WV,[mdclxxvii[1677],190] d. Mar-20-1999 in Sandusky, Erie Co, OH,[806,592] resided in Sandusky, Erie Co, OH,[592] resided 1952, 62, 75, 81 in Cleveland, Cuyahoga Co, OH,[765,412,521,856] census 1930 in Upshur Co, WV, occupation self-employed upholsterer,[190] military U.S. Army Military Police, Pacific Theater, WW II.[190] He married[484] Doris J. ___, d. bef Mar 1999.[484]

iv.   ARLTON GLENDALE ADAMS b. Jun-28-1917 in Upshur Co, WV,[mdclxxviii[1678],592] d. Aug- 4-2003,[592] resided 1975, 81 in Buckhannon, Upshur Co, WV,[521,856] resided 1952, 62 in Baltimore, MD,[765,412] census 1930 in Upshur Co, WV.

v.   COSBY MARGARITE ADAMS b. May-22-1919 in Upshur Co, WV,[mdclxxix[1679],190] d. Mar-25-1962 in Lima, Allen Co, OH,[806] census 1930 in Upshur Co, WV.

Identified in father's obituary as "Mrs. Claude Crosby Hellinger of Lima, Ohio."

She married[191] Lawrence W. Hullinger, b. Oct-15-1912,[592] d. Jan-19-1994,[592] resided in Lima, Allen Co, OH.[191,mdclxxx[1680]]

vi.   LAUNA ADAMS, also known as Arah Launa Adams,[921] b. Oct- 2-1921 in Upshur Co, WV,[190,592] d. Aug- 2-2007 in Buckhannon, Upshur Co, WV,[700,592] buried in Heavner Cemetery, Upshur Co, WV,[190] resided in Buckhannon, Upshur Co, WV,[765,412,521,856,604] census 1930 in Upshur Co, WV. She married[446] (1) divorced[1116] Verl Edgell. She married[1040] (2) May-19-1947 in Buckhannon, Upshur Co, WV,[921] William Clarence Reeder, b. ca 1923 in Upshur Co, WV,[921] (son of Clarence H. Reeder and Maude McCauley).

vii.   JOHNSON CARLTON ADAMS, also known as Johnnie Adams,[412] b. ca 1925,[922] resided 2007 in Virginia,[412] resided 1981 in Pennsylvania,[856] resided 1975 in Freedom, Beaver Co, PA,[521] resided 1962 in Ambridge, Beaver Co, PA,[412] resided 1952 in Buckhannon, Upshur Co, WV,[765] census 1930 in Upshur Co, WV. He married Living.

viii.   LIVING. He married Living.

ix.   DENNIS WAYNE ADAMS b. Mar- 2-1934 in Upshur Co, WV,[mdclxxxi[1681],592] d. Mar- 8-1999,[592] resided in Lima, Allen Co, OH,[412,521,856,604] resided 1952 in Buckhannon, Upshur Co, WV.[765]

785. **Alma Gay Gaston** (421.Eli[8], 248.Eli[7], 136.Hugh[6], 72.John[5], 21.John[4], 6.Hugh[3], 3.John[2], 1.Jean[1]), b. Nov-24-1897 in Doddridge Co, WV,[398,410] d. Apr-12-1937 in Orlando, Lewis Co, WV,[398] buried at Orlando Cemetery, Lewis Co, WV.[398]

Lewis County birth records show that an Alma Gaston of Doddridge County gave birth to a daughter, Elenor Lee Gaston, on Aug 21 1921. The space for the father's name contains the entry "Refused to give this information." This is probably the same Alma Gaston.

She married (2) Nov-18-1921 in Lewis Co, WV,[mdclxxxii[1682]] **John E. Fretwell**, b. ca 1885 in Randolph Co, WV,[410] d. aft Apr 1937,[436] resided 1937 at Orlando, Lewis Co, WV.[436]

Children:

i. ELLNER LEE GASTON b. Aug-21-1921 in Lewis Co, WV,[398] d. Aug-22-1921 near Orlando, Lewis Co, WV,[398] buried Skinner Cemetery.[398]

Children by John E. Fretwell:

ii. VIRGINIA BELL FRETWELL b. Aug-20-1922 at Orlando, Lewis Co, WV,[398] d. Nov- 7-1922 at Orlando, Lewis Co, WV,[mdclxxxiii[1683]] [Death certificate records place of death as Orlando in Braxton County. The community of Orlando is actually located in Lewis County on the border with Braxton County.], buried in IOOF Cemetery, Orlando, Lewis Co, WV.[398]

iii. STACIE MAE FRETWELL b. 1924. She married Orville Westfall.

iv. LIVING. She married Brooks Arnold Goldsmith, b. Jan-17-1920 (son of Bert Goldsmith and Nellie Frances Donaldson), d. Jan-30-1992, buried in Peterson Cemetery, Lewis Co, WV.

v. JOHN RICHARD FRETWELL b. Mar-24-1930 in Orlando, Lewis Co, WV,[621] d. Aug-31-1989 in Laurel, Sussex Co, DE, buried in Peterson Cemetery, Lewis Co, WV. He married Living.

vi. LAURA ROSE FRETWELL b. Sep-29-1932 at Orlando, Lewis Co, WV,[398] d. Jul-15-1933 at Orlando, Lewis Co, WV,[398] buried in Orlando Cemetery, Lewis Co, WV.[398]

vii. LIVING. He married Living.

786. **Georgia Rachael Gaston**, also known as Georgie,[1271] (421.Eli[8], 248.Eli[7], 136.Hugh[6], 72.John[5], 21.John[4], 6.Hugh[3], 3.John[2], 1.Jean[1]), b. Mar- 7-1903 in Upshur Co, WV,[mdclxxxiv[1684]] d. Feb- 6-1975, resided 1963 in Belleville, Wood Co, WV,[412] resided 1941 in Orlando, Lewis Co, WV.[765] She married (1) Apr-14-1920 in Upshur Co, WV,[mdclxxxv[1685]] **Clarence Birton Skinner**,[1684] b. Sep-25-1896 in Lewis Co, WV,[604,mdclxxxvi[1686],684,408] (son of Charles F. Skinner and Maggie J. __), d. Sep- 2-1983,[604] resided in Warren, Trumbull Co, OH,[604] resided 1918 in Akron, Summit Co, OH,[684] census 1900 in Collins Settlement District, Lewis Co, WV.[604] She married (2) **Creed Connelly**, d. May- 9-1977.

Children by Clarence Birton Skinner:

i. KATHLEEN LILLIE SKINNER b. Aug-16-1922 in Orlando, Lewis Co, WV,[190] d. Apr-16-2003 in Salem, WV,[190] buried in Floral Hills Memorial Gardens, Quiet Dell, Harrison Co, WV,[190] resided in Clarksburg, Harrison Co, WV,[190] education Weston H.S. (1940).[190]

She had been the owner of the Park View Restaurant in the East View section of Clarksburg. In later years, she worked as a caregiver for the elderly infirm.[190]

She married Oct-22-1943, Boyd Odell Booth, b. Oct- 5-1909,[592] d. May- 9-1983,[592] buried in Floral Hills Memorial Gardens, Quiet Dell, Harrison Co, WV.

ii. AVIS JANE SKINNER b. Mar-26-1926,[592] d. Apr- 2-1999,[592] resided in Bristolville, Trumbull Co, OH,[592] resided formerly in West Virginia.[604] She married May-6-1950, Robert Capak.

iii. CLARENCE SKINNER b. Nov- 7-1927 in Braxton Co, WV, d. Feb- -1987 in Casa Grande, Pinal Co, AZ. He married Living.

iv. SYLVESTER LAWRENCE SKINNER, also known as Lawrence Skinner,[412,592] b. Aug-29-1930 in Braxton Co, WV,[592] d. Apr-21-1983,[592] resided in Victor, Teton Co, ID.[1275] He married Sep-21-1957, Georgia __.

v. LIVING. She married Living.

vi. RALPH ARNOLD SKINNER b. Oct-18-1935 in Orlando, Lewis Co, WV,[592,190] d. Oct-29-2007 in Benton Co, WA,[190,592] resided (since 1983) in Mattawa, Grant Co, WA,[190,1010,412] resided formerly in Mullan, Shoshone Co, ID,[mdclxxxvii[1687]] occupation miner.[190]

Ralph Skinner had one daughter by his first wife and adopted the three children of his second wife Bonnie.

He married (1) Unknown. He married (2) Bonnie __.

vii. LIVING. He married Living.

787. **Rulina Clemma Gaston**, also known as Clemma or Clemmie,[395] (422.Jesse[8], 248.Eli[7], 136.Hugh[6], 72.John[5], 21.John[4], 6.Hugh[3], 3.John[2], 1.Jean[1]), b. Apr-15-1889 in Summers, Doddridge Co,

WV,[mdclxxxviii[1688],190,17] d. Nov-21-1967 in Clarksburg, Harrison Co, WV,[190,17] buried in Hart Cemetery, Taylor Drain Rd, Oxford, Doddridge Co WV,[17,190] resided in Arnolds Creek (West Union), Doddridge Co, WV.[190] She married Jun- 5-1907 in Doddridge Co, WV,[mdclxxxix[1689],484] **Anda Aaron Hileman**, also known as Aaron Hileman,[765,395] b. Dec-27-1885 in Ritchie Co, WV,[190,17,mdcxc[1690],mdcxci[1691]] (son of Isaac Lynch Hileman and Juliet Hart), d. Oct-11-1973 in Doddridge Co, WV,[1690,17,190] buried in Hart Cemetery, Taylor Drain Rd, Oxford, Doddridge Co WV,[17,190] resided 1965 in West Union, Doddridge Co, WV,[521] resided 1935 in Oxford, Doddridge Co, WV,[905] occupation Hope Natural Gas Co.[190]

Children:

i.   HOWARD ANDREW TAFT HILEMAN, also known as Howard Taft Hileman,[190] b. Oct-20-1908 in Oxford, Doddridge Co, WV,[190] d. Mar-16-1982 in Fairmont, Marion Co, WV,[190,mdcxcii[1692]] buried in Mt. Zion Cemetery, Marion Co, WV,[190] resided in Fairmont, Marion Co, WV,[856,521,765] resided 1955 in Clarksburg, Harrison Co, WV,[855] occupation Methodist minister.[190] He married Oct-21-1937 in Marion Co, WV, Marguerite Hall, b. Apr-22-1919 in Marion Co, WV (daughter of William E. Hall and Anna Virginia Morgan), d. Nov- 2-1996 in Marion Co, WV,[190] buried in Mt. Zion Cemetery, Marion Co, WV.

ii.   JULIET LUANNA "MAY" HILEMAN, also known as May Hileman,[711,521] b. Oct-27-1910 in Oxford, Doddridge Co, WV,[190] d. Aug-15-1999 in Clarksburg, Harrison Co, WV,[190] buried in Hart Cemetery, Taylor Drain Rd, Oxford, Doddridge Co WV,[17] resided in West Union, Doddridge Co, WV,[521] resided 1973 in Center Point, Doddridge Co, WV,[765] resided 1962, 67 in New Cumberland, Hancock Co, WV,[mdcxciii[1693],856] resided 1955 in Weirton, Hancock Co, WV.[855] She married Oct-18-1942 in West Union, Doddridge Co, WV,[mdcxciv[1694],484,191] Donald Daniel LeMasters, b. May-22-1913 in Wolf Pen Run, New Milton, Doddridge Co, WV,[190] (son of Mitchell J. LeMasters and Frances C. "Fannie" Wadsworth), d. Dec-12-1987 in Clarksburg, Harrison Co, WV,[190] buried in Hart Cemetery, Taylor Drain Rd, Oxford, Doddridge Co WV.[17]

iii.   CHARLES ALFRED LEWIS HILEMAN[989] also known as Lewis Hileman,[856,765,521] b. Nov-13-1912 in Doddridge Co, WV, d. Nov-18-1981, buried in Evergreen North (aka Arlington) Cemetery, Rt 2 N of Parkersburg, Wood Co, WV, resided in Parkersburg, Wood Co, WV,[856,521,765.] He married Jun-13-1939 in Ritchie Co, WV,[mdcxcv[1695]] Lucy Belle Bee, b. Jul-24-1921,[592,693,1020] (daughter of Walter Ezra Bee and Viola Jane Mitchell), d. Aug-26-1985 in Orange Co, FL,[693,592] resided in Altamonte Springs, Seminole Co, FL,[604] resided 1977 in Parkersburg, Wood Co, WV,[856] census 1930 in Union District, Ritchie Co, WV.

iv.   FLOYD ISAAC SMITH HILEMAN b. Jul-21-1915 in Doddridge Co, WV,[190] d. Nov- 8-1992,[17] buried in Hart Cemetery, Taylor Drain Rd, Oxford, Doddridge Co WV,[17] resided in Wilsonburg, Harrison Co, WV,[190] resided 1955 in Clarksburg, Harrison Co, WV.[855]

He retired from Union Carbide Corporation, and was a retired minister of the Union Mission Conference with 50 years of service.[190]

He married Sep- 2-1944,[191] Virginia Murl Mace, also known as Murl,[mdcxcvi[1696],856] b. May-19-1921 in Webster Co, WV,[190] [Headstone gives birthdate as May 21 1921, but both obituary and SSDI state May 19 1921.] (daughter of Oliver Francis Mace and Myrtle I. Hines), d. Oct-27-1985 in Clarksburg, Harrison Co, WV,[190,17,484] buried in Hart Cemetery, Taylor Drain Rd, Oxford, Doddridge Co WV,[17] resided 1977 in Wilsonburg, Harrison Co, WV.[856]

v.   AARON LAWSON HILEMAN, also known as Lawson Hileman,[521] b. Dec-15-1917 in Doddridge Co, WV,[190] d. Sep-14-1983 in Clarksburg, Harrison Co, WV,[847] buried in Sunset Memorial Park Cemetery, Clarksburg, WV,[190,462] resided in Clarksburg, Harrison Co, WV,[190] occupation West Virginia Dept of Highways (retired),[190] military U.S. Army, WW II (Italy, France, Germany, northern Africa).[190] He married Sep-27-1950,[484,191] Velma V. West, b. Feb-17-1924 in Clarksburg, Harrison Co, WV,[190,592] (daughter of Zachariah R. West and Fannie Gay Boggess), d. Mar-26-1987 in Morgantown, Monongalia Co, WV,[190,592] buried in Sunset Memorial Park Cemetery, Clarksburg, WV,[190,462] resided in Clarksburg, Harrison Co, WV,[412,190] census 1930 in Coal District, Harrison Co, WV, occupation Eagle Convex Glass Co (10 yrs).[190]

vi.   MAUDE ARLENE RUTH HILEMAN b. Sep-27-1920 in Doddridge Co, WV,[17] [Age at death (3m 14d) recorded on death record would put birth date at Sep 29 1920. But brother Samuel Jacob Hileman, citing Family Bible, reports Sep 27 1920, the date placed on her headstone many years later.], d. Jan-12-1921 in Doddridge Co, WV,[mdcxcvii[1697],mdcxcviii[1698]] [Obituary erroneously gives death date as Jan 14 1921, which was actually the funeral date. Headstone, which was placed by her brother Samuel nearly 80 years later, erroneously gives death date as Jan 27 1921.], buried in Gaston Family Cemetery, Upper Run, Summers, Doddridge Co WV.[190]

vii. HENRY CARL HILEMAN, also known as Carl Hileman,[856,521] b. Oct-16-1921 at Oxford, Doddridge Co, WV,[419,190] d. Mar-21-1981 in Barberton, Summit Co, OH,[190] buried in Greenlawn Memorial Park Cemetery, Akron, Summit Co, OH,[190] resided in Norton, Summit Co, OH,[190] resided 1956 in Barberton, Summit Co, OH,[419] resided formerly in Weirton, Hancock Co, WV.

He was a minister and had been employed by the Babcock & Wilcox Company in Barberton, OH, for ten years, retiring in about 1971.[190]

He married Living.

viii. CALVIN DAVID HILEMAN b. Jun- 8-1924 in Harmony, Doddridge Co, WV,[190] d. Oct- 1-2003 in Bunnells Run, Ritchie Co, WV,[190] buried in Masonic Memorial Park Cemetery, Crystal Lake (West Union), WV,[190] resided in Bunnells Run, Ritchie Co, WV,[190] resided in Harrisville, Ritchie Co, WV,[521,190] resided 1967, 73 in St. Marys, Pleasants Co, WV,[856,765] resided 1954 in Pullman, Ritchie Co, WV.[855]

Graduate of Doddridge County High School, Glenville State College, and West Virginia University, where he obtained a master's degree in education. He was involved with education most of his life as a teacher and principal, with employment in Doddridge, Wood, Ritchie and Pleasants counties.[190]

He married Zura E. Leggett, b. Dec-23-1923 in Oxford, Doddridge Co, WV,[190] (daughter of Columbus Newman "Lum" Leggett and Bertha Mae Smith), d. Jun-28-2001 in Parkersburg, Wood Co, WV,[190] buried in Masonic Memorial Park Cemetery, Crystal Lake (West Union), WV,[190] resided 1968 in St. Marys, Pleasants Co, WV,[856] resided later in Harrisville, Ritchie Co, WV,[521,190] occupation grocery stores (40 yrs).[190]

ix. LIVING.

x. SAMUEL JACOB HILEMAN b. Dec- 3-1930 at Summers, Doddridge Co, WV,[190] d. Jul-15-2010 in Clarksburg, Harrison Co, WV,[847] buried in Masonic Memorial Park Cemetery, Crystal Lake (West Union), WV,[190] resided at Arnolds Creek (West Union), Doddridge Co, WV,[856,190] never married.

xi. MAUDE LEE "MANDY" HILEMAN b. Jul-28-1933 in Clarksburg, Harrison Co, WV,[276,17] d. Jul-28-1933 in Clarksburg, Harrison Co, WV,[mdcxcix[1699],17] [Identified on headstone as Mandy Lee Hileman, but in death record as Maude Lee Hileman. The name Mandy was provided by brother Samuel, citing Family Bible.], buried in Gaston Family Cemetery, Upper Run, Summers, Doddridge Co WV.[17]

xii. LIVING. He married Living.

788. **Charles R. Strother** (423.Hannah[8], 248.Eli[7], 136.Hugh[6], 72.John[5], 21.John[4], 6.Hugh[3], 3.John[2], 1.Jean[1]), b. Aug- 4-1891,[mdcc[1700]] d. Oct- 1-1961 in Coldwater, Branch Co, MI,[mdcci[1701]] census 1930 in Highland Park, Wayne Co, MI. He married ca 1927,[334] **Thelma Rebecca Sadler**, b. Aug-18-1908 in Salem, WV,[1701] (daughter of Francis Sadler and Isa Williams), d. Mar-27-2002 in Branch Co, MI,[1701] buried in Lakeview Cemetery, Quincy, Branch Co, MI,[1701] census 1930 in Highland Park, Wayne Co, MI.

Children:

i. GARLAND BLAIR STROTHER b. Dec-16-1929 in Michigan,[334] d. Jun-17-2002 in Michigan, resided in Coldwater, Branch Co, MI, census 1930 in Highland Park, Wayne Co, MI.

Had three children, all daughters.

He married Living.

ii. LIVING.

789. **Sarah Rulina Gaston** (424.David[8], 248.Eli[7], 136.Hugh[6], 72.John[5], 21.John[4], 6.Hugh[3], 3.John[2], 1.Jean[1]), b. Jul-12-1888 in Harmony, Doddridge Co, WV,[963,721,989,240] [Obituary and funeral card state birth as Jul 12 1890 in Doddridge Co, but this would not be possible since her twin sisters were born in Apr 1890. Headstone reads Jul 12 1888, and online death record states birth data as "est. 1888."], d. Nov-11-1969 in Dayton, Montgomery Co, OH,[806,721] buried in Masonic Memorial Park Cemetery, Crystal Lake (West Union), WV,[190,989,721] resided in Dayton, Montgomery Co, OH,[190] resided 1950 in Brushy Fork, New Milton, Doddridge Co, WV,[765] census 1930 in West Union District, Doddridge Co, WV. She married Dec-19-1909 in Doddridge Co, WV,[mdccii[1702],354,191] **Burleigh C. Hickman**, b. Sep- 2-1884 in West Union, Doddridge Co, WV,[mdcciii[1703],989,721] (son of Thomas Beau Hickman and Annie Rhoda Riley), d. Aug- 3-1975 in Dayton, Montgomery Co, OH,[1703,989,721] buried in Masonic Memorial Park Cemetery, Crystal Lake (West Union), WV,[989,721] resided in Dayton, Montgomery Co, OH, resided formerly in Brushy Fork, New Milton, Doddridge Co, WV, census 1900, 1930 in West Union District, Doddridge Co, WV. "Davis - The Settlers of Salem WV," p. 465, reports that Burleigh Hickman (with wife Sarah Rulina Gaston) also had a foster child, Elizabeth Jane Travis, of Dayton, OH, who in turn had a daughter, Tonya R. But members of the immediate family, notably Elizabeth Clarke Lerman (the granddaughter of Sarah's sister Elizabeth Jane Gaston Sharps), correct these inaccuracies by identifying Burleigh and Sarah's foster child as their niece Elizabeth Jane "Betty" Sharps (the daughter of Sarah's sister Elizabeth Jane), and Betty's daughter as Tonda Rae Travis. Betty was raised by them from infancy following the death of her mother.

Children:
i. GILBERT ROBERT HICKMAN b. Feb-17-1911 in West Union, Doddridge Co, WV,[190,1703] d. Jul-26-1982 in West Germany,[806,1703] cremated[190] resided 1969 in Plainview, Long Island, NY,[856] resided 1933 in West Union, Doddridge Co, WV,[711] occupation U.S. Military (retired).

Wedding announcement, West Union Herald, July 5 1951:
"Hickman entered the U.S. Army in 1943 and was sent overseas that year. He was honorably discharged from the service in June 1946. He then accepted a position as manager of the post exchange in Mannheim. In 1947 he was transferred to a store in Heidelberg, and in 1948 he entered the Post Engineers where he is now employed. The couple are spending their honemoon in Switzerland. They plan to come to the United States this fall."

According to his sister-in-law Susie Nutter Hickman, he returned to the U.S. from Germany and lived in Long Island, New York, where he was a senior buyer for Hazeltine Electronics. Upon his retirement in 1978, he and his wife returned to West Germany.

He married (1) Jul-30-1933 in Weston, Lewis Co, WV,[mdcciv[1704]] Marguerite Duckworth, b. ca 1907 in Tucker Co, WV,[711] resided 1933 in Doddridge Co, WV.[711] He married (2) Jun-30-1951,[484,mdccv[1705]] Luise J. "Esa" Borlein, b. Sep-22-1921,[592] d. Dec-22-1995 in Mannheim, Germany.[mdccvi[1706]]

Luise: From Mannheim, West Germany. Daughter of Mr. & Mrs. Friedrich Borlein.

ii. DAVID THOMAS HICKMAN b. Aug-26-1912 in Doddridge Co, WV,[mdccvii[1707]] d. Nov-11-1997 in Baltimore, MD,[190] buried in Holly Hills Memorial Gardens, Middle River, MD,[190] resided in Middle River, Baltimore Co, MD,[190,1703,856]. He married Dec-21-1937 in West Union, Doddridge Co, WV,[1707] Susie Alethea Nutter, census name Susie L. Nutter,[1390] b. Sep- 2-1914 in West Union, Doddridge Co, WV,[1707,592] (daughter of Eli Marshal Nutter and Alpha Mary Leggett), d. Jan-14-2011 in Street, Harford Co, MD,[700,592] buried in Holly Hills Memorial Gardens, Middle River, MD,[190] resided (4 yrs) in Street, Harford Co, MD,[190] resided formerly in Baltimore, MD,[1086,412] resided 1997 in Middle River, Baltimore Co, MD,[484] education Pennsboro High School, Salem College,[1707] occupation Glenn L. Martin, Riverdale Apts (clerical).[190]

Susie: According to herself, Susie Alethea Nutter was her true birth name. The first name is Susie, which is not a nickname. The middle name is Alethea, not Althea. She was a graduate of Pennsboro High School and attended Salem College.

790. **Elizabeth Jane Gaston** (424.David[8], 248.Eli[7], 136.Hugh[6], 72.John[5], 21.John[4], 6.Hugh[3], 3.John[2], 1.Jean[1]), b. Apr- 9-1890 in Summers, Doddridge Co, WV,[240,885] d. Feb-23-1930 in Bremen, Fairfield Co, OH,[mdccviii[1708]] buried in Grandview Cemetery, Bremen, OH.[885]

From her obituary: "Always busy, brave, cheerful, sincere without pretense, she did well the labors of her life and leaves to her husband and children memories and influences which will abide in them as vital forces until the whole household gathers in the heaven of a perfect life."

She married Aug-13-1911 in Oxford, Doddridge Co, WV,[mdccix[1709],354] **Alfred Vance Sharps**, also known as Vance Sharps,[395] b. Jun-16-1889 in Smithville, Ritchie Co, WV,[885,592] (son of Martin Luther Sharps and Hannah Etta Barr), d. Mar- 3-1978 in Dayton, Montgomery Co, OH,[885,592] buried in Grandview Cemetery, Bremen, OH,[885] resided in Bremen, Fairfield Co, OH,[856,1010] occupation oil worker.[1701]

Children:

i.   PAUL EDWIN SHARPS b. Aug- 2-1912 in Porto Rico (New Milton), Doddridge Co, WV,[885] d. Mar-23-2005 in Columbus, Franklin Co, OH,[806] buried in Glen Rest Memorial Estate, Reynoldsburg, OH,[190] resided in Reynoldsburg, Franklin Co, OH,[190] occupation Lazarus Dept Store (retired).[190] He married Sep-23-1939 in Columbus, Franklin Co, OH,[997] Lois Ellen Miller, b. Sep-17-1916 in Bruno, Thornville, Perry Co, OH,[997] (daughter of George Miller and Chloe Binkley), d. Feb-28-2005 in Pickerington, Fairfield Co, OH,[764] buried in Glen Rest Memorial Estate, Reynoldsburg, OH,[190] resided in Reynoldsburg, Franklin Co, OH,[190] occupation Xerox Education (retired).[190]

ii.   PEARL WINONA SHARPS b. Mar-22-1914 in Bremen, Fairfield Co, OH,[885] d. Nov- 6-1985 in Columbus, Franklin Co, OH,[885] buried in Glen Rest Memorial Estate, Reynoldsburg, OH,[885] resided 1952 in Richmond, VA.[mdccx[1710]] She married (1) 1941 in Cleveland, Cuyahoga Co, OH,[997] divorced[992] no children from this marriage, Alex Knish, b. Feb-18-1909,[592] d. Oct- -1983,[592] resided in Cleveland, Cuyahoga Co, OH.[592] She married (2) Oct-11-1969 in Dayton, Montgomery Co, OH,[885] Arthur Otto Quast, b. Jul-30-1913,[885,592] d. Nov- -1991.[592]

iii.   ETTA BELLE SHARPS b. Oct- 6-1915 in Bremen, Fairfield Co, OH,[885] d. Oct-29-2003 in Kalispell, Flathead Co, MT,[190,885] buried in Glacier Memorial Gardens, Kalispell, MT,[190] occupation Registered Nurse.[885]

Resident of Kalispell, MT. Graduated from Bremen High School in Fairfield Co, OH in 1932, and from the Zanesville Ohio Good Samaritan School of Nursing in 1936. She followed her profession in Ohio, Michigan, Seattle, and Hammond General Hospital in Modesto, CA as a civilian nurse. At one time, she belonged to the Kalispell Golf Association, Kalispell Ladies Bowling Association, and the Flathead Quilters Guild.[190]

She married Oct-30-1941 in Reno, Washoe Co, NV,[190,885] no children from this marriage, Eaner Peter Higgins, b. Oct-25-1913 in Little Chicago (Black Eagle), MT,[885,190] (son of Peter Gunnar Higgins and Anna Melina Knutsooter Visnes), d. Apr- 4-2003 in Kalispell, Flathead Co, MT,[190,885] buried (ashes) at Glacier Memorial Gardens, Kalispell, MT,[190] occupation physician.[885]

Eaner: Following early schooling in Montana, attended Modesto Junior College, then the University of California at Berkley, before graduating from Loma Linda University Medical School in 1941. He interned at Edward Sparrow Hospital in Lansing, MI, where he met his wife Etta. He was in practice in Ceres, CA when World War II began, and he served as a medical officer with the U.S. Army until Feb 12 1946. After the war, he first took a residency at Stanislaw County Hospital in Modesto, CA, then moved to Kalispell, MT in Nov 1947, where he had a private practice until 1974 when eye surgery necessitated his retirement. In 1975 he joined the medical staff at Galen State Hospital, Anaconda, MT, and was appointed superintendent in 1976. He served in the same capacity at Warm Springs and was in charge of the physicians at the state prison at times during his tenure at Galen. He retired from Galen in Nov 1980, retiring to his home in Kalispell.[190]

       iv.   JAMES EARL SHARPS b. Nov-23-1918 in Bremen, Fairfield Co, OH,[885] d. Aug-14-1939 in Charleston, Kanawha Co, WV,[885] buried in Grandview Cemetery, Bremen, OH.[885]
       v.   MARY EVELYN SHARPS b. Nov-28-1920 in Bremen, Fairfield Co, OH,[885] d. Sep- 7-1999 in Kettering, Montgomery Co, OH,[885] adopted by father[885] occupation Registered Nurse,[885] military U.S. Army Nurse, WW II, Europe.[885]

       Served in Army Nurse Corps in Europe during WW II. Graduated from University of Dayton in 1956. Retired from VA Medical Center in 1979.[190]

       She married (1) Jan- 6-1944 in Shelbyville, Shelby Co, KY,[885] divorced[885] Payne Jeffery Witter, b. Oct-19-1908 in Flagstaff, Coconino Co, AZ,[885] (son of Sylvanus Payne "Ben" Witter and Margaret Sofie Fredrick), d. May-14-1972 in Modesto, Stanislaus Co, CA,[885] buried in Yuma, Yuma Co, AZ.[mdccxi[1711]] She married (2) Jan-31-1953 in Dayton, Montgomery Co, OH,[885] Ronald Frank Clarke, b. Feb- 8-1917 in Dayton, Montgomery Co, OH,[885] (son of Frank M. Clarke and Mary Angeline Carper), d. Jul- 3-1996 in Dayton, Montgomery Co, OH,[885] buried in David Cemetery, Kettering, OH,[885] occupation Sales & X-Ray Technician.[885]
       vi.   DAVID LEE SHARPS, also known as Lee Sharps,[521] b. Oct-13-1922 in Bremen, Fairfield Co, OH,[885,592] d. Oct-24-1998 in Martinsville, VA,[885,592] buried in Columbus, Franklin Co, OH,[885] resided in Martinsville, VA.[592] He married Dec-26-1950 in Columbus, Franklin Co, OH,[997] Harriet Adelle Ream, b. Mar-21-1926,[885] (daughter of Warren B. Ream), d. Apr- 4-1980 in Martinsville, VA,[885] buried in Columbus, Franklin Co, OH.[885]
       vii.   DOROTHY MAXINE SHARPS b. Nov- 2-1924 in Bremen, Fairfield Co, OH,[885] d. Jan- 5-1925 in Bremen, Fairfield Co, OH,[885] buried in Grandview Cemetery, Bremen, OH.[885]
       viii.   ALFRED RAY SHARPS, also known as Ray Sharps, b. Jan- 5-1927 in Lancaster, Fairfield Co, OH,[mdccxii[1712]] d. Jul- 6-2007 in Virginia Beach, VA,[764] buried (ashes) at Arlington National Cemetery, VA,[1166] resided in Virginia Beach, VA, military U.S. Navy (1944-1974).[190]

       Ray Sharps enlisted in the U.S. Navy in January 1944 and retired as a lieutenant after serving more than 30 years. Subsequent to his retirement from active duty, he became a safety officer for the Navy, serving at NAD St. Julians Creek and NAD Yorktown. He served as chairman of the Federal Safety Council in 1975.[190]

       He married (1) Feb-14-1952 in Union City, Hudson Co, NJ,[885] divorced Mar- -1974, Shirley Lorraine Boyd, b. May-12-1927 in Philadelphia, PA,[885,592] (daughter of James Clinton Boyd and Sally Sherman), d. Apr- -1985 in Norfolk, VA,[592,997] buried in Virginia Beach, VA,[885] resided in Virginia Beach, VA,[592] resided formerly in New York.[1157] He married (2) Aug-16-1974 in Virginia Beach, VA,[885] Doris Marie Cressman, also known as Doris Marie Torr, b. Nov-12-1925 in New Hope, Bucks Co, PA,[885] (daughter of Luther Cressman and Grace Tettemer), resided 2007 in Virginia Beach, VA.[484]
       ix.   ELIZABETH JANE "BETTY" SHARPS b. Feb- 9-1930 in Lancaster, Fairfield Co, OH,[885] d. Jul-15-1999 in Dayton, Montgomery Co, OH, buried (cremated) ashes at Christ Episc Church, Dayton, OH, resided in Dayton, Montgomery Co, OH, census 1930 in West Union District, Doddridge Co, WV [in household with aunt Sarah Gaston Hickman].

       Following death of her mother, was raised from infancy by her aunt & uncle, Sarah Gaston Hickman & Burleigh Hickman, in Doddridge Co, WV. Sarah Gaston Hickman's obituary listed Mrs. Elizabeth Travis as a surviving daughter.[1166]

       She married Nov-17-1953,[997] divorced 1965, Donald G. Travis, b. Nov-30-1923,[885,592] (son of Robert Levi Travis and Ollie Gay Sutton), d. Jun-10-1995 in Lake Havasu City, Mohave Co, AZ,[885,592] resided in Lake Havasu City, Mohave Co, AZ,[856,592] resided formerly in West Virginia.[604]

791. **Lovie Mae Gaston** (424.David[8], 248.Eli[7], 136.Hugh[6], 72.John[5], 21.John[4], 6.Hugh[3], 3.John[2], 1.Jean[1]), b. Dec-21-1891 in Doddridge Co, WV,[mdccxiii[1713],190] d. Jan- 5-1949 in Akron, Summit Co, OH,[806] cause of death cerebral hemorrhage,[190] buried in Masonic Memorial Park Cemetery, Crystal Lake (West Union), WV,[190,721] resided in Akron, Summit Co, OH,[190] resided 1933 in Coxs Mills, Gilmer Co, WV,[856] census 1920 in Troy District, Gilmer Co, WV. She married (1) May-15-1913 in Doddridge Co, WV,[mdccxiv[1714],354,191] **L. Brison Bowyer**, census name Brison L. Bowyer,[mdccxv[1715]] b. Dec- -1891 in Gilmer Co, WV,[123,mdccxvi[1716],721] (son of George Allen Bowyer and Mary Burrows), d. Feb-18-1943,[191] buried in Masonic Memorial Park Cemetery, Crystal Lake (West Union), WV,[mdccxvii[1717]] resided 1937 in Oxford, Doddridge Co, WV,[412] census 1920 in Troy District, Gilmer Co, WV, resided 1913 in Gilmer Co, WV,[1716] occupation farmer.[1715] She married (2) Dec- 8-1948,[191] **John Shatzer**, resided 1949 in Akron, Summit Co, OH.[191]

> Children by L. Brison Bowyer:
>
> i. ZELLA LUCILLE BOWYER b. Dec-24-1914 in Gilmer Co, WV,[mdccxviii[1718],711] d. Jul-14-1996,[592] resided 1994 in Pittsfield, Berkshire Co, MA,[521] resided 1949, 68 in Cincinnati, Hamilton Co, OH,[856,521,1010] resided 1935 near Salem, WV,[711] census 1920 in Troy District, Gilmer Co, WV. She married Sep- 5-1935 at Smithburg, Doddridge Co, WV,[711] Fred C. Bonnett, b. Nov- 6-1909 in Doddridge Co, WV,[711] (son of William Thomas Bonnett and Ove Hardman), d. Nov-24-1974 in Cincinnati, Hamilton Co, OH,[1011] resided in Cincinnati, Hamilton Co, OH,[1011] resided 1935 at Troy, Gilmer Co, WV.[711]
>
> ii. ELDON CLAIR BOWYER b. May-10-1918 in Coxs Mills, Gilmer Co, WV,[190] d. Mar-10-1968 in Akron, Summit Co, OH,[806] buried in Akron, Summit Co, OH,[190] resided 1949, 68 in Akron, Summit Co, OH,[856,190] resided as a youth in Oxford, Doddridge Co, WV,[190] census 1920 in Troy District, Gilmer Co, WV, education Doddridge Co H.S. graduate.[190] He married (1) Mary Katheryn Spencer. He married[484] (2) Edna Mae Forzano, resided 1968 in Akron, Summit Co, OH.[484]
>
> iii. CARL ADRON BOWYER b. Mar- 2-1923 in Coxs Mills, Gilmer Co, WV,[190] d. Apr-13-1994 in Clarksburg, Harrison Co, WV,[190] buried in Masonic Memorial Park Cemetery, Crystal Lake (West Union), WV, resided at Big Flint, Doddridge Co, WV,[190,521] resided 1949 in Clarksburg, Harrison Co, WV,[856] occupation route salesman, Mountain State Laundry. He married Apr-25-1943,[484] Betty June Williams, b. Apr-23-1928 in West Union, Doddridge Co, WV,[190] (daughter of Carsie Delman Williams and Loma Ethel Helmick), d. Jul-15-2011 in Bridgeport, Harrison Co, WV,[847] buried in Masonic Memorial Park Cemetery, Crystal Lake (West Union), WV,[190] resided at Big Flint, Doddridge Co, WV,[190,484] census 1930 in Grant District, Doddridge Co, WV,[mdccxix[1719]] occupation school cook, Carr Elementary (21 yrs).[190]

792. **Burke Butcher** (425.James[8], 249.Cordelia[7], 136.Hugh[6], 72.John[5], 21.John[4], 6.Hugh[3], 3.John[2], 1.Jean[1]), b. Dec-10-1890,[407] d. May-16-1952,[407] buried in Cedarville, Gilmer Co, WV.[407] He married[395] Apr-19-1912 in Gilmer Co, WV,[434] **Ora Lucrecia Snyder**, b. Oct-19-1891,[592,434] d. Oct- -1991,[592] resided in Shepherdstown, Jefferson Co, WV.[592]

> Children:
>
> i. MABEL BUTCHER d. in infancy.[412]
>
> ii. LOUISE BUTCHER d. bef Dec 2004.[412]
>
> iii. ROBERT JACKSON BUTCHER b. Sep-23-1918 in Cedarville, Gilmer Co, WV,[190] d. Nov-3-2005 in Glenville, Gilmer Co, WV,[700] buried in Meadow Lane Cemetery, Glenville, Gilmer Co, WV,[190] resided in Glenville, Gilmer Co, WV,[1006,412,190] occupation teacher, auctioneer, County Sanitarian, County Clerk of Court,[190] education Sand Fork H.S. (1937); Glenville State College (B.A., 1941),[190] military 1942-45 U.S. Navy, World War II.[190]

Upon graduation from college, Robert Jackson Butcher taught in the public schools of Nassau Co, FL. Following 33 months service in the U.S. Navy in World War II, he returned to Gilmer Co, WV, where he was a teacher and coach at Burnsville and Spencer high schools. He established Gilmer County's first taxi cab business, building it to a fleet of five vehicles. He took up cattle farming and then entered politics. In 1950, he ran as a Democrat and was elected Circuit Clerk of Gilmer County, and he ran unopposed for re-election in 1956. He also worked with the West Virginia Department of Health, where he served as Chief Sanitarian for Gilmer and Calhoun counties. He also worked with the West Virginia Department of Welfare in Spencer. In 1952, he graduated from the Reppert School of Auctioneering in Decatur, IL, and subsequently became known as one of West Virginia's leading auctioneers. In 1955, he and John Victor Smith co-founded the Gilmer County Auction Barn near Glenville, which remained in business for over 30 years. Around 1965, he and Harry B. McLaughlin established the Elk Auction in Gassaway, which was operated for over 20 years. Among others, he was survived by five grandchildren, Alexis Butcher, Elizabeth Butcher, Andrew Butcher, Matthew Butcher and Catherine Butcher, all of Glenville.[190]

He married[484] (1) Sep-26-1942 in Glenville, Gilmer Co, WV,[1006] no children from this marriage,[484] Mildred Kathleen Keener, b. Sep-10-1921 in Copen, Braxton Co, WV,[398,1006] (daughter of Lertie T. Keener and Edith James), d. Sep- 1-1944 in Gassaway, Braxton Co, WV,[398] cause of death automobile accident,[398] buried in Sugar Creek Church Cem, Shadyside, Braxton Co, WV,[398] resided in Gassaway, Braxton Co, WV,[398] resided 1942 in Gilmer Co, WV,[1006] occupation grade school teacher.[398] He married (2) Sep- 6-1946 in Dunbar, Kanawha Co, WV,[mdccxx[1720]] Marlene Madge Hayhurst,[484] also known as Madge Hayhurst,[1006,592] b. Mar-26-1921 at Burnt House, Ritchie Co, WV,[1006,592] (daughter of Ethan Hayhurst), d. Mar-21-1993,[592] resided in Glenville, Gilmer Co, WV.[1006,592]

    iv.   TERESA BUTCHER b. Oct- 2-1920 in Cedarville, Gilmer Co, WV,[190,592] d. Dec-14-2004 in Charles Town, Jefferson Co, WV,[806,592] buried in Prudence Chapel Cemetery, Minnora, Calhoun Co, WV,[190] resided in Shepherdstown, Jefferson Co, WV,[190,592] resided formerly in New Mexico,[190] occupation teacher,[190] education Sand Fork H.S. (1937); Glenville State College (1941); New Mexico State Univ (M.A., 1966).[190] She married[1101] G. Jennings Jarvis, b. ca 1920 in Chloe, Calhoun Co, WV,[190] (son of Price Jarvis and Stella Ross), d. Jan-21-1969 in Albuquerque, Bernalillo Co, NM,[190] buried in Prudence Chapel Cemetery, Minnora, Calhoun Co, WV,[190] resided in Las Cruces, Dona Ana Co, NM,[190] resided formerly in Calhoun Co, WV,[190] occupation resource development specialist, Cooperative Extension Services, New Mexico State University,[190] education Calhoun Co H.S., Glenville State College, Iowa State Univ,[190] military World War II.[190]

    v.   ROLAND BUTCHER[412,521] b. Oct-13-1922,[592] d. Mar- -1975,[592] resided in West Virginia.[604]

    vi.   JAMES A. BUTCHER title: Dr., resided 2004, 05 in Shepherdstown, Jefferson Co, WV.[412,521]

    vii.   MARY HAZEL BUTCHER resided 2004, 05 in Duluth, Gwinnett Co, GA.[412,521] She married[1101] __ Lilley.

793. **Evalena C. Gaston** (428.William[8], 250.Henry[7], 136.Hugh[6], 72.John[5], 21.John[4], 6.Hugh[3], 3.John[2], 1.Jean[1]), b. Feb- 6-1899,[398] d. Jul-23-1956 in Weston, Lewis Co, WV,[398] buried in Union Cemetery, near Lockney, Gilmer Co, WV,[17] [aka Turner Cemetery], resided near Lockney, Gilmer Co, WV,[398] census 1920, 1930 in Center District, Gilmer Co, WV. She married **John Edward "Ed" Queen**, census name Edd J. Queen,[906] also known as Ed Queen,[374] b. Jun-14-1881 in Gilmer Co, WV,[398,mdccxxi[1721],1006] (son of Albert Queen and Margaret Harris), d. Apr-22-1949 near Normantown, Gilmer Co, WV,[398,1721] buried in Union Cemetery, near Lockney, Gilmer Co, WV,[17] [aka Turner Cemetery], census 1920, 1930 in Center District, Gilmer Co, WV, occupation farmer.[398]

1920 Census, Gilmer Co, WV (Center District), enumerated in Jan 1920:
John E. Queen, 38, farmer; wife Evalena, 20; dau Dessie, 16; dau Bessie, 14; dau Garnett, 12; dau Gladys, 10; son George, 7; dau Lenora, 2.

1930 Census, Gilmer Co, WV (Center District):
Edd J. Queen, 48, farmer, age 22 at time of first marriage; wife Evalene C, 31, age 17 at first marriage; son George A, 17; dau Lennia E, 12; dau Violet R, 6; dau Vera I (?), 4 yr 3 mo; servant Ella Lewis, 74, single.

    Children:
    i.   LENORA E. QUEEN b. ca 1918 at Lockney, Gilmer Co, WV.[1006] She married May-18-1941 at Lockney, Gilmer Co, WV,[1006] Roy Collins, b. ca 1908 in Lockney, Gilmer Co, WV,[1006] (son of Warder P. Collins and Jane Minnie), resided 1930, 41 in Lockney, Gilmer Co, WV.[1006]

ii. NINA LENNIE QUEEN b. Feb- 1-1921,[17] d. Aug-29-1921,[17] buried in Union Cemetery, near Lockney, Gilmer Co, WV.[17]

iii. VERNA INEZ QUEEN b. Jan- 4-1926,[17] d. Apr-26-1938 at Lockney, Gilmer Co, WV,[398,17] buried in Union Cemetery, near Lockney, Gilmer Co, WV,[17] cause of death scarlet fever, meningitis.[398]

iv. THERESA QUEEN b. Oct-29-1930 in Lockney, Gilmer Co, WV,[190] d. Jan- 5-2003 in Tallahassee, Leon Co, FL,[190] resided in Pendleton, Anderson Co, SC,[190] occupation Air Force Civil Service (retired).[190] She married[191] __ Klawinski.

v. HARVEY QUEEN b.[412] resided 2003 in South Carolina.[412]

vi. LIVING. She married Harry Lee Bryner, b. Jan-12-1932 in Volga, Barbour Co, WV,[419,604] (son of Harry S. Bryner and Bernice E. Sayre), d. Mar- -1990,[604] resided 1955 in Clarksburg, Harrison Co, WV.[419]

vii. HARLEY JOHN QUEEN b. Jun-22-1936,[17,592] d. Sep-30-1980,[17,592] buried in Union Cemetery, near Lockney, Gilmer Co, WV,[17] resided in Akron, Summit Co, OH.[mdccxxii[1722]]

794. **James Eustace Gaston**, also known as Eustace Gaston,[434] (428.William[8], 250.Henry[7], 136.Hugh[6], 72.John[5], 21.John[4], 6.Hugh[3], 3.John[2], 1.Jean[1]), b. Apr- 4-1903 in Gilmer Co, WV,[592,396] d. Nov- 2-1973 in Wood Co, WV,[mdccxxiii[1723],592] buried in Mt. Olivet Cemetery, Parkersburg, WV, resided in Parkersburg, Wood Co, WV,[592] resided 1940 in Davisville, Wood Co, WV.[396] He married Nov-2-1924 in Gilmer Co, WV,[434] **Ruby Chloe Kuhl**, b. Jun- 7-1902 in Withers, Gilmer Co, WV,[mdccxxiv[1724]] (daughter of Phillip Aaron Kuhl and Mary Alice Bennett), d. Mar-23-1977 in Wood Co, WV,[mdccxxv[1725]] buried in Mt. Olivet Cemetery, Parkersburg, WV.

Children:

i. JAMES BERYL GASTON b. Jul- 2-1925 in Gilmer Co, WV,[190] d. Jan-16-1998 in San Antonio, Bexar Co, TX,[190] buried in Mt. Olivet Cemetery, Parkersburg, WV,[909] resided in Houston, Harris Co, TX,[190] occupation Aircraft mechanic for United Airlines (35 yrs),[190] education Parkersburg (WV) High School,[190] military MOMM3, 123rd Naval Construction Bn, World War II.[190,909]

As an aircraft mechanic, he spent ten years in the Panama Canal Zone, maintaining the Boeing 737 of the General of the U.S. Southern Command. He was an avid pilot and flew small planes.[mdccxxvi[1726]]

He married (1) Living. He married[484] (2)[484] Margarita __. Among the survivors listed in James Beryl Gaston's obituary were his wife Margarita, sons James and John, daughter Janice, and stepdaughters Peggy (and husband Arturo), Iraima (and husband John), and Maui (and husband Lorenzo). No mention was made of wife Jeannie Barr.

ii. LIVING. She married Living.

iii. LIVING. She married (1) Harry Lee Carez, b. Jul-19-1924,[592] d. Jan- -1970,[592] resided in Parkersburg, Wood Co, WV.[592] She married (2) Living.

iv. LIVING. She married Living.

v. EDGEL THOURL GASTON b. Jul-18-1932 in Parkersburg, Wood Co, WV,[1166,190] d. Jul-6-2005,[190] buried in Mt. Olivet Cemetery, Parkersburg, WV,[190] resided in Parkersburg, Wood Co, WV,[521,190] resided 1953 in Davisville, Wood Co, WV,[602] occupation design engineer at Quantum Resources (retired),[190] military U.S. Air Force, Korean War.[190] He married Living.

vi. LIVING. He married (1) Living. He married (2) Audra Sue Bennett, b. Jul-18-1941 in Davisville, Wood Co, WV,[602] (daughter of Brady Bennett and Anna Elsie Reynolds), d. Aug-24-2000,[592] resided in San Antonio, Bexar Co, TX.[592]

vii. LIVING. He married Living.

viii. LIVING. She married Living.

ix. JACK URAL GASTON b. May- 3-1940 in Davisville, Wood Co, WV,[398] d. Jun-15-1940 in Parkersburg, Wood Co, WV,[398,mdccxxvii[1727]] cause of death pneumonia,[398] buried in Union Cemetery, near Lockney, Gilmer Co, WV.[398]

x. LIVING. She married (1) Living. She married[1101] (2) Living.

795. **Pauline Olive Orrahood** (431.Eva[8], 250.Henry[7], 136.Hugh[6], 72.John[5], 21.John[4], 6.Hugh[3], 3.John[2], 1.Jean[1]), b. Apr- 1-1916 in Doddridge Co, WV,[592,mdccxxviii[1728],419] d. Feb-10-1997,[592,1728] resided in Clarksburg, Harrison Co, WV,[905,592] resided 1939 in Camden, Lewis Co, WV,[765] resided 1936 in Wolf Summit, Harrison Co, WV.[419] She married[941] Oct-31-1936 in Salem, WV,[419] **William Thomas Duckworth**, b. Apr-25-1910 in Garrett Co, MD,[419,592] (son of William Duckworth and Rosa Lease), d. Apr- -1986,[592] resided in Bridgeport, Harrison Co, WV,[592] resided 1936 in Clarksburg, Harrison Co, WV.[419]

   Children:
   i. RICHARD DUCKWORTH.

796. **Brady Craig Maddox** (441.George[8], 255.Thomas[7], 137.Sarah[6], 72.John[5], 21.John[4], 6.Hugh[3], 3.John[2], 1.Jean[1]), b. Dec-16-1895 in Ripley, Jackson Co, WV,[253] [Birth date given in 1900 Census as Oct 1895.], d. Aug-25-1955 in Rodney, Gallia Co, OH,[253] buried in Rio Grande Cem, Gallia Co, OH,[253] resided 1923 in Kanawha Co, WV,[933] census 1900 in Jackson Co, WV. He married Jul- 7-1923 in Charleston, Kanawha Co, WV,[933] **Alma Nicholes**, b. ca 1902 in Kanawha Co, WV.[933]

   Children:
   i. ELIZABETH JEAN MADDOX b.[253]
   ii. ROY LEON MADDOX b.[253]
   iii. (INFANT) MADDOX b.[253]
   iv. ROBERT DALE MADDOX b.[253]
   v. LARRY DONOVAN MADDOX b.[253]
   vi. JANET SUE MADDOX b.[253]

797. **Oren Clair Maddox** (441.George[8], 255.Thomas[7], 137.Sarah[6], 72.John[5], 21.John[4], 6.Hugh[3], 3.John[2], 1.Jean[1]), b. Mar-24-1905 in Jackson Co, WV,[398] d. Mar-15-1957 in Charleston, Kanawha Co, WV,[398] buried in Grasslick Bapt Ch Cem, Pleasant Valley Rd, Kenna, Jackson Co, WV,[253] resided in Charleston, Kanawha Co, WV.[398] He married[253] **Thelma Freda Crago**, b. Jun-23-1914 in Plymouth, Putnam Co, WV,[592,190] d. Oct- 2-1986 in Akron, Summit Co, OH,[806] buried in Sunset Memorial Park Cemetery, South Charleston, Kanawha Co, WV,[190] resided from 1984 in Tallmadge, Summit Co, OH,[190,604] resided formerly in Dunbar, Kanawha Co, WV,[190] occupation school cook (15 yrs, retired 1966).[190]

   Children:
   i. JAMES OREN MADDOX[748] b. Apr- 7-1935 in Charleston, Kanawha Co, WV,[592,190,933] d. Apr-10-2007,[592] buried in Tallmadge, Summit Co, OH,[190] resided in Cuyahoga Falls, Summit Co, OH,[604] education Stonewall Jackson H.S. (WV), Kent State Univ.[190]

   He was captain of the Kent State Basketball team from 1960-1961. He was the head basketball coach for Tallmadge High School for 22 years, and retired from the Tallmadge School system in 1995 after 32 years of service. In 1980 and 1982, he was the Summit County Coach of the Year, was a member of the Summit County Sports Hall of Fame, Summit County Coaches Association Hall of Fame, and Tallmadge High School Hall of Fame.[190]

   He married (1) Living. He married (2) Living.

798. **Wilbur O. Bradley**, census name Wilber Bradley (442.Susan[8], 256.William[7], 137.Sarah[6], 72.John[5], 21.John[4], 6.Hugh[3], 3.John[2], 1.Jean[1]), b. Sep- 8-1887 in Jackson Co, WV,[592,928,450] d. Feb- -1981,[592] resided in Kenna, Jackson Co, WV,[604] census 1900, 10, 20, 30 in Jackson Co, WV. He married Jan- 3-1915 in Jackson Co, WV,[450] **Martha J. Merritt**, b. May- -1886,[mdccxxix[1729]] (daughter of Martin Merritt and Eskline ___), census 1920, 1930 in Jackson Co, WV, census 1900, 1910 in Wayne Co, WV, resided 1903 in Wayne Co, WV.

   Children:
   i. JAMES RUSSELL BRADLEY, census name Russel Bradley,[937] b. Nov-11-1915,[604] d. Jan-17-1990,[604] census 1920, 1930 in Jackson Co, WV.
   ii. WARREN L. BRADLEY b. Mar- 3-1917 in Jackson Co, WV,[592,933] d. Dec- -1982,[592] resided in Kenna, Jackson Co, WV,[604,933] census 1920, 1930 in Jackson Co, WV. He married Feb-14-

1946 in Charleston, Kanawha Co, WV,[933] Hilda M. Thomas, b. Sep-20-1918 in Fayette Co, WV,[592,933] d. Dec- 7-1998,[592] resided in Kenna, Jackson Co, WV,[592] resided 1946 in Sissonville, Kanawha Co, WV.[933]

    iii.   JENNINGS C. BRADLEY b. Dec- 5-1921,[604] d. Jun-23-1991,[604] census 1930 in Jackson Co, WV.

    iv.   LIVING.

799. **Mindia A. Maddox** (444.William[8], 257.James[7], 137.Sarah[6], 72.John[5], 21.John[4], 6.Hugh[3], 3.John[2], 1.Jean[1]), b. Jun- 7-1879, d. Apr-26-1939. She married Feb- 3-1910, **John G. Moss**, b. Jan-21-1884, d. Mar-25-1927.

    Children:

    i.   CHARLES W. MOSS b. Jan-19-1911, d. Feb-27-1942. He married Wilma Simpson, d. Deceased.

    ii.   ALMA R. MOSS b. May-26-1914,[592] d. Apr-10-2002,[592] resided in Willoughby, Lake Co, OH,[592] resided formerly in West Virginia.[604] She married Jun- 3-1937, Charles Oscar Mayer, b. Apr- 5-1912,[592] d. Jan- -1986,[592] resided in Clarksburg, Harrison Co, WV.[592]

800. **Otto Oly Maddox** (444.William[8], 257.James[7], 137.Sarah[6], 72.John[5], 21.John[4], 6.Hugh[3], 3.John[2], 1.Jean[1]), b. Oct-28-1881, d. May- 1-1947. He married Aug-31-1904, **Charlotte M. Fewell**, b. Apr-14-1886, d. Aug- 6-1965.

    Children:

    i.   JAMES CLIFTON MADDOX b. Oct-25-1905, d. Jul-25-1955. He married Jul-29-1924, Nellie Withrow, b. Apr-15-1906.

    ii.   MAE MADDOX b. Oct-20-1907, d. Apr-17-1982. She married J. L. Patterson, occupation Physician.

    iii.   FRANCIS MADDOX b. Jun- 5-1911, d. Jun-10-1911.

    iv.   MAXWELL MADDOX b. Sep-18-1912, d. Dec- 7-1936. He married May-29-1933, Virginia Smith, b. Mar-17-1910.

    v.   NATHAN KING MADDOX b. Jun-15-1916. He married Dec-19-1934, Lucille Parker, b. Oct- 2-1915,[592] d. May- 6-2002,[592] resided in Charleston, Kanawha Co, WV.[592]

    vi.   OTTO OLY MADDOX, JR. b. May- 4-1926,[592] d. Sep-26-2002,[592] resided in Belle, Kanawha Co, WV.[592] He married Dec-25-1945, Dorothy J. Harmon, b. Jun- 6-1924,[592] d. Jan- 9-2002,[592] resided in Belle, Kanawha Co, WV.[592]

    vii.   LIVING. She married Living.

801. **Lory Dove Maddox** (444.William[8], 257.James[7], 137.Sarah[6], 72.John[5], 21.John[4], 6.Hugh[3], 3.John[2], 1.Jean[1]), b. Oct-24-1887, d. Mar-25-1968. She married (1) **Ralph L. Marshall**, b. 1884, d. Sep- -1941. She married (2) **George Adamson**.

    Children by Ralph L. Marshall:

    i.   NAOMI GREY MARSHALL b. Oct- 2-1905,[592] d. Aug-24-2002,[592] resided in Charleston, Kanawha Co, WV.[592] She married Sep-26-1927, Roy Earl Francis, b. Aug-13-1904,[592] d. Nov- 3-1991,[592] resided in Charleston, Kanawha Co, WV.[592]

    ii.   MARTHA EUGENIA MARSHALL b. Feb-15-1908, d. Aug-19-1954. She married (1) 1927, Paul Markam. She married (2) 1944, Edwin Cobb, b. 1902, d. May-29-1955.

    iii.   HARRY RICHARD MARSHALL b. Mar-22-1913, d. Feb-16-1964. He married Jun-17-1939, Mary Louise Board, b. Jan- 6-1916.

802. **Flavius Clinton Maddox** (444.William[8], 257.James[7], 137.Sarah[6], 72.John[5], 21.John[4], 6.Hugh[3], 3.John[2], 1.Jean[1]), b. Dec-14-1896, d. Aug-13-1949. He married Dec-20-1921, **Nelle Stuckey**, b. Dec- 5-1897,[592] d. Oct- -1986,[592] resided in Plainfield, Union Co, NJ.[mdccxxx[1730]]

    Children:

    i.   ROBERT C. MADDOX b. May-22-1924. He married Living.

803. **Orville B. Maddox** (445.Alonzo[8], 257.James[7], 137.Sarah[6], 72.John[5], 21.John[4], 6.Hugh[3], 3.John[2], 1.Jean[1]), b. Mar-22-1883 in Jackson Co, WV,[mdccxxxi[1731]] d. Dec-12-1964 in Fairmont, Marion Co, WV,[1731] buried in Bridgeport Cemetery, Harrison Co, WV,[1731] census 1920, 1930 in Fairmont, Marion

Co, WV, occupation auditor for railroad,[1731] occupation 1930 clerk for coal company.[1100] He married[934] ca 1908,[1100] **May Show**, b. Mar-11-1880 in Confluence, Somerset Co, PA,[1731] (daughter of Jacob Show and Sarah Catherine Reiber), d. Apr-21-1967 in Fairmont, Marion Co, WV,[1731] buried in Bridgeport Cemetery, Harrison Co, WV,[1731] census 1920, 1930 in Fairmont, Marion Co, WV.
Children:
    i.   JAMES S. MADDOX[934] b. ca 1913,[943] census 1920, 1930 in Fairmont, Marion Co, WV.

804. **Warren Hayden Maddox**, census name Hayden Maddox,[931] also known as W. Hayden Maddox,[446] (446.Lycurgus[8], 257.James[7], 137.Sarah[6], 72.John[5], 21.John[4], 6.Hugh[3], 3.John[2], 1.Jean[1]), b. Jun- 3-1900,[592] d. Dec- -1976,[592] resided in Daytona Beach, Volusia Co, FL,[mdccxxxii[1732]] census 1930 in Monongalia Co, WV, resided 1921 in Ashland, Boyd Co, KY,[450] census 1920 in Ripley, Jackson Co, WV, occupation 1930 department store manager.[mdccxxxiii[1733]] He married Sep-25-1921 in Ripley, Jackson Co, WV,[450] **Theo Carson Staats**, b. Jul-21-1900 in Jackson Co, WV,[592,450] d. Dec- -1983,[592] resided in Winter Park, Orange Co, FL,[mdccxxxiv[1734]] census 1930 in Monongalia Co, WV, resided 1921 in Ripley, Jackson Co, WV.[450]
Children:
    i.   MAX E. MADDOX b. May- 1-1923 in Ashland, Boyd Co, KY,[938,592] d. Feb-18-2001,[592] resided in Morgantown, Monongalia Co, WV,[604,938] census 1930 in Monongalia Co, WV. He married Nov-17-1946 in Morgantown, Monongalia Co, WV,[938] Mattie Virginia Sterling, b. Sep- 4-1921 in Rowlesburg, Preston Co, WV,[938] (daughter of Harry C. Sterling and Agnes McVicker), resided 1946 in Morgantown, Monongalia Co, WV.[938]
    ii.   ROBERT C. MADDOX b. Mar- 1-1926 in Clarksburg, Harrison Co, WV,[938] resided 1946 in Morgantown, Monongalia Co, WV,[938] census 1930 in Monongalia Co, WV. He married Living.

805. **West Mansfield Maddox** (448.James[8], 258.Arnold[7], 137.Sarah[6], 72.John[5], 21.John[4], 6.Hugh[3], 3.John[2], 1.Jean[1]), b. Mar-27-1911 in Loudoun Co, VA,[254,592] d. Sep- -1984 in Loudoun Co, VA.[254,592] He married[254] **Marie Cumor**.
Children:
    i.   ROBERT WEST MADDOX b. Feb- 6-1947,[592,254] d. Sep-14-1997,[592,254] resided in Leesburg, Loudoun Co, VA.[592]

806. **Frederick Brook West**, also known as F. Brook West,[17] (450.William[8], 260.Ruhama[7], 137.Sarah[6], 72.John[5], 21.John[4], 6.Hugh[3], 3.John[2], 1.Jean[1]), b. Jul- 4-1881 in West Milford, Harrison Co, WV,[46,mdccxxxv[1735]] d. Nov-28-1968 in Brook Park, Cuyahoga Co, OH,[1735] buried in Rose Hill (formerly IOOF) Cemetery, West Milford, Harrison Co, WV,[524,1735] census 1920 in Union District, Harrison Co, WV, occupation merchant, barber.[1735] He married[mdccxxxvi[1736]] Dec-31-1903 in West Milford, Harrison Co, WV,[1735] **Atha Ula Highland**, b. Feb-13-1885,[1735,46] (daughter of James I. Highland and Sarah Eliza Lynch), d. May-18-1953 in Harrison Co, WV,[1735,46] buried in Rose Hill (formerly IOOF) Cemetery, West Milford, Harrison Co, WV.[524,1735]
Children:
    i.   LESLIE BROOK WEST b. Feb-13-1906 in West Milford, Harrison Co, WV,[1735] d. Feb- 7-1990 in Cleveland, Cuyahoga Co, OH,[1735] resided 1963 in Elyria, Lorain Co, OH,[1735] occupation glass factory worker.[1735] He married (1) Dec-31-1930,[1735] divorced Sep-25-1937 in Harrison Co, WV,[1735] Jane Holla. He married[1735] (2) Mildred Rigsby. He married[1735] (3) Myrle Gonan.
    ii.   FRANKLIN EARL WEST b. Dec- 2-1908 in Union District, Harrison Co, WV,[592,17,mdccxxxvii[1737]] d. Oct-22-1979 in Cleveland, Cuyahoga Co, OH,[1737,592] buried in Rose Hill (formerly IOOF) Cemetery, West Milford, Harrison Co, WV,[524,1737] resided in Brook Park, Cuyahoga Co, OH,[604] occupation private detective,[1737] military Pvt, U.S. Army, World War II.[524] He married Jessie Elizabeth Berger, b. Aug- 8-1914,[1737] (daughter of Joseph Berger and Druza Dell Carrico), d. Dec-23-1950 in Harrison Co, WV,[1737] buried in Greenlawn Masonic Cemetery, Clarksburg, WV.[1737]
    iii.   SARAH LOUISE WEST b. Feb-24-1911 in West Milford, Harrison Co, WV,[1736] d. Nov-18-1993 in Salem, WV,[1736] buried in K of P Memorial Park Cemetery, Salem, WV,[1736] census 1920 in Union District, Harrison Co, WV.[1736] She married Jun-15-1929,[1736] Lester H. "Booze" Bennett, b. Sep-5-1908 in Big Isaac, Doddridge Co, WV,[1736,46] (son of Stephen Earnest Bennett and Ella Gay Hinkle), d. Aug-11-1959 in Salem, WV,[1736,46] buried in K of P Memorial Park Cemetery, Salem, WV,[817] census

1920 in Greenbrier District, Doddridge Co, WV, occupation car sales, Bennett Brothers Ford, Salem, WV.[1736] As descendants of John West and Frances Howard, Lester H. "Booze" Bennett and Sarah Louise West were fourth cousins, once removed.[1736]

      iv.   HUBERT ORION "MONK" WEST b. Dec- 4-1913 in McWhorter, Harrison Co, WV,[mdccxxxviii[1738]] d. Jul- 3-1963 in Clarksburg, Harrison Co, WV,[276,1738] buried in Rose Hill (formerly IOOF) Cemetery, West Milford, Harrison Co, WV,[524,1738] occupation state roads employee,[276] occupation merchant.[1738] He married Feb-15-1935 in Oakland, Garrett Co, MD,[1738] Susan Elizabeth Smallcheck, b. Jul- 8-1917 in Wendel, Taylor Co, WV,[1738] (daughter of Carl Smallcheck and Susan Roman), resided 1963, 94 in West Milford, Harrison Co, WV.[228,1738]

807. **Ora Jefferson West** (450.William[8], 260.Ruhama[7], 137.Sarah[6], 72.John[5], 21.John[4], 6.Hugh[3], 3.John[2], 1.Jean[1]), b. Apr- 2-1884 in West Milford, Harrison Co, WV,[1735,46] d. Sep-30-1958 in Clarksburg, Harrison Co, WV,[1735,46] buried in Rose Hill (formerly IOOF) Cemetery, West Milford, Harrison Co, WV,[524] occupation barber.[1735] He married Feb-24-1903 in Harrison Co, WV,[1735] **Annie Lucy Romine**, b. Jul-12-1882,[1735,46] (daughter of Jacob Romine), d. Jun- 6-1962 in Baltimore, MD,[1735,46] buried in Rose Hill (formerly IOOF) Cemetery, West Milford, Harrison Co, WV.[524]
      Children:
      i.   LEVA WILMA WEST, also known as Wilma West,[395,592] b. Oct-28-1904 in Clarksburg, Harrison Co, WV,[1738,592] d. Nov- -1995,[592] resided in Holden, Worcester Co, MA.[592] She married Nov-30-1930,[1738] Paul Stephen Clarkson, b. Oct- 2-1905,[1738,592] d. Jun-30-1988,[592] resided in Holden, Worcester Co, MA.[1086]
      ii.   THELMA LOUISE WEST b. Aug-17-1908 in West Milford, Harrison Co, WV,[1735] resided 1958 in Titusville, Brevard Co, FL.[1735] She married (1) Mar-25-1932,[1735] Burl Hartzel Kiger. She married[1738] (2) Thomas Ray Dixon.
      iii.   MARY FRANCES WEST b. May- 8-1918 in West Milford, Harrison Co, WV,[1738,592,1237] d. Nov- 2-1992 in Los Angeles, CA,[1237,592,1738] resided in Simi Valley, Ventura Co, CA.[1086] She married Sep-30-1944,[1738] Richard William Bates.

808. **William Kenna West**, also known as W. Kenna West,[17,419] also known as W. Kenneth West,[374] (450.William[8], 260.Ruhama[7], 137.Sarah[6], 72.John[5], 21.John[4], 6.Hugh[3], 3.John[2], 1.Jean[1]), b. Apr- 9-1887,[398,46] d. Feb-21-1959 in West Milford, Harrison Co, WV,[398,46] buried in Rose Hill (formerly IOOF) Cemetery, West Milford, Harrison Co, WV,[398,524] resided in West Milford, Harrison Co, WV,[398] resided 1906 in Clarksburg, Harrison Co, WV,[419] occupation barber.[398] He married (1) Nov-25-1906 in West Milford, Harrison Co, WV,[419] **Hattie Susan Holmes**, also known as Harriet Susan Holmes,[mdccxxxix[1739]] b. 1889,[46] (daughter of John M. Holmes and E. V. __), d. 1916,[46] buried in Rose Hill (formerly IOOF) Cemetery, West Milford, Harrison Co, WV.[524] He married (2) **Lillie M. Ward**, b. May-25-1900,[592,46] d. Jul-28-1999,[592] resided in Morgantown, Monongalia Co, WV.[592]
      Children by Hattie Susan Holmes:
      i.   WILLIAM HOLMES WEST b. Mar-10-1908 in Harrison Co, WV,[1738,46] d. Mar-12-1983 in Harrison Co, WV,[1738,46] buried in Rose Hill (formerly IOOF) Cemetery, West Milford, Harrison Co, WV,[524] occupation candy salesman,[1738] military S2, U.S. Navy, World War II.[524] He married (1) Feb- -1938 in Boyd Co, KY,[1738] divorced 1947 in Lewis Co, WV,[1738] Charlotte Morrison, b. ca 1916.[1738] He married (2) Feb-19-1951 in Oakland, Garrett Co, MD,[1738] Mary Alice Musgrave, b. Jun- 9-1917 in Clarksburg, Harrison Co, WV,[1738,592,46] (daughter of Herbert D. Musgrave and Grace E. Riddle), d. Jun-1-2001,[592] buried in Rose Hill (formerly IOOF) Cemetery, West Milford, Harrison Co, WV,[524] resided in West Milford, Harrison Co, WV.[mdccxl[1740],604]
      ii.   ROBERT WEST b. ca 1909,[1739] d. ca 1909.[1739]
      iii.   PAUL ELDRED WEST b. Dec- 9-1911 in Clarksburg, Harrison Co, WV,[1740] d. Dec-12-1961 in Salem, WV,[1740] buried in Rose Hill (formerly IOOF) Cemetery, West Milford, Harrison Co, WV,[524] occupation athletic coach.[1740] He married[374] Jun- 1-1943,[1740] Anne Isabelle Hardman, b. Feb-10-1920 in Grantsville, Calhoun Co, WV (daughter of Fred C. Hardman and Bessie J. Stalnaker), d. Feb- -1995 in Summit Co, OH,[1740] education Salem College (1961),[1740] occupation professor.[1740]

iv.   WINIFRED JEAN WEST, also known as Jean West,[228] b. Oct- 9-1913 in West Milford, Harrison Co, WV,[419] resided 1969 in Salem, WV,[228] resided 1931 in Clarksburg, Harrison Co, WV.[419] She married Oct-11-1931 in Wallace, Harrison Co, WV,[419] Harold Theodore Bennett, b. Jun-27-1912 in Union District, Harrison Co, WV,[419,398,46] (son of Stephen Earnest Bennett and Ella Gay Hinkle), d. Oct-28-1969 in Salem, WV,[398,46] buried in K of P Memorial Park Cemetery, Salem, WV,[817,398] resided in Salem, WV,[398] resided 1931 at Big Buffalo, Union District, Harrison Co, WV,[419] census 1920 in Greenbrier District, Doddridge Co, WV, occupation warehouseman for natural gas production.[398]

v.   MAXINE WEST b. Nov- 2-1915 in Harrison Co, WV.[1739]

809. **Madison West Manley**, census name West M. Manley,[1100] (452.Laura[8], 260.Ruhama[7], 137.Sarah[6], 72.John[5], 21.John[4], 6.Hugh[3], 3.John[2], 1.Jean[1]), b. Jun- 9-1892 in Marion Co, WV,[1739,938,592] d. Jul- 5-1981,[592] resided in Washington, DC,[592] census 1930 in Grant District, Marion Co, WV, census 1920 in Monongalia Co, WV, resided 1914 in Fairmont, Marion Co, WV,[938] census 1900, 1910 in Fairmont, Marion Co, WV, census 1900 in Grant District, Harrison Co, WV [Without parents, in household of grandparents Jefferson & Ruhama West. But he was also enumerated with his parents in Fairmont District, Marion Co, WV.)], occupation 1920 hoister in coal mine,[mdccxli[1741]] occupation 1930 farmer.[1100] He married[947] Nov-25-1914 in Morgantown, Monongalia Co, WV,[938] **Sarah Elizabeth Glover**, also known as Sara Elizabeth Glover,[938] census name Sarah L.,[1741] b. Feb-27-1894 in Marion Co, WV,[592,938] (daughter of G. F. Glover and Roberta ___), d. Feb- -1975,[592] resided in Washington, DC,[592] census 1930 in Grant District, Marion Co, WV, census 1920 in Monongalia Co, WV, resided 1914 in Morgantown, Monongalia Co, WV.[938]

Children:

i.   CHARLES GLOVER MANLEY b. Mar- 5-1918 in Morgantown, Monongalia Co, WV,[1741] resided 1945 in Washington, DC,[938] census 1930 in Grant District, Marion Co, WV, census 1920 in Monongalia Co, WV. He married Sep-21-1945 in Riverside, Monongalia Co, WV,[938] Katherine E. Dewey, b. Mar- 6-1922 in Elizabeth City, Pasquotank Co, NC,[938] (daughter of Harrey W. Dewey and Anita Barham), resided 1945 in Washington, DC.[938]

810. **Harrison Jefferson Manley**, census name Harrison Manley, Jr.,[1133,942] (452.Laura[8], 260.Ruhama[7], 137.Sarah[6], 72.John[5], 21.John[4], 6.Hugh[3], 3.John[2], 1.Jean[1]), b. Oct-28-1895 in West Milford, Harrison Co, WV,[1739,589] d. Jul- 2-1983 in Fairmont, Marion Co, WV,[1739] buried in Sheets Mill (Old West) Cemetery, West Milford, Harrison Co, WV,[1739] resided 1937 in Fairmont, Marion Co, WV,[589] census 1900, 1910 in Marion Co, WV, occupation tire recapper.[1739] He married Apr- 3-1937 in Fairmont, Marion Co, WV,[589] **Pearl M. West**, b. Nov-22-1905 in Harrison Co, WV,[1739,589,592] (daughter of Hiram Thomas West and Allie Belle Davis), d. May-12-1996,[592] buried in Sheets Mill (Old West) Cemetery, West Milford, Harrison Co, WV,[1739] resided in Fairmont, Marion Co, WV.[589,592] As grandchildren of Jefferson Bowell West and Ruhama Maddox, Harrison Jefferson Manley and Pearl M. West were first cousins.

Children:

i.   LIVING. He married Living.
ii. LIVING. She married Living.

811. **Pearl M. West** (453.Hiram[8], 260.Ruhama[7], 137.Sarah[6], 72.John[5], 21.John[4], 6.Hugh[3], 3.John[2], 1.Jean[1]) (See marriage to number 810.)

812. **Jessie M. West** (453.Hiram[8], 260.Ruhama[7], 137.Sarah[6], 72.John[5], 21.John[4], 6.Hugh[3], 3.John[2], 1.Jean[1]), b. Jul-18-1909 in Harrison Co, WV,[1481] d. Feb- 7-1982 in Fairmont, Marion Co, WV,[1481] buried in Sheets Mill (Old West) Cemetery, West Milford, Harrison Co, WV,[1481] census 1920 in Union District, Harrison Co, WV.[1481] She married[1478] **Roscoe Patton**, b. Sep- 2-1898 in West Virginia,[1478] (son of Charles C. Patton and Nancy C. Morrison), d. Dec-12-1951 in Clarksburg, Harrison Co, WV,[1478] buried in Sheets Mill (Old West) Cemetery, West Milford, Harrison Co, WV.[1478] As descendants of John West and Frances Howard, Roscoe Patton and Jessie M. West were third cousins, once removed.

Children:

i.   LIVING.

813. **Grace West** (453.Hiram[8], 260.Ruhama[7], 137.Sarah[6], 72.John[5], 21.John[4], 6.Hugh[3], 3.John[2], 1.Jean[1]), b. Mar-12-1911 in Harrison Co, WV,[mdccxlii[1742]] d. Jun-25-1988 in Harrison Co, WV,[1742] buried in Sheets Mill (Old West) Cemetery, West Milford, Harrison Co, WV.[1742] She married[446] Aug-16-1930,[1742] **Kenneth Aubrey Stutler**, b. May- 1-1906 in Doddridge Co, WV,[1742] (son of Benjamin L. Stutler and Bessie Day), d. Mar-15-1987 in Clarksburg, Harrison Co, WV,[1742] buried in Sheets Mill (Old West) Cemetery, West Milford, Harrison Co, WV,[1742] occupation farmer.[1742]
        Children:
        i.   LIVING. He married Living.
        ii.   RICHARD A. STUTLER b. Nov- 5-1932,[1742] d. Feb- 8-1993,[1742] buried in Sheets Mill (Old West) Cemetery, West Milford, Harrison Co, WV.[1742]

814. **Thomas Woodrow West**, also known as Woodrow Thomas West,[374] (453.Hiram[8], 260.Ruhama[7], 137.Sarah[6], 72.John[5], 21.John[4], 6.Hugh[3], 3.John[2], 1.Jean[1]), b. Nov-18-1913 in West Milford, Harrison Co, WV,[1742] d. Dec-22-1977 in Harrison Co, WV,[mdccxliii[1743]] buried in Sheets Mill (Old West) Cemetery, West Milford, Harrison Co, WV.[1742] He married[374] Sep-15-1941 in Oakland, Garrett Co, MD,[1742] **Bertha Drucilla Greaver**, also known as Bertha Druzzilla Greaver,[374] b. Aug- 1-1916 in Marion Co, WV,[1742] d. Dec-22-1977 in Harrison Co, WV,[mdccxliv[1744]] buried in Sheets Mill (Old West) Cemetery, West Milford, Harrison Co, WV.[1742]
        Children:
        i.   LIVING. She married Living.
        ii.   (FEMALE) WEST b. Feb-17-1953 in Harrison Co, WV,[1742] d. Feb-17-1953 in Harrison Co, WV,[1742] buried in Sheets Mill (Old West) Cemetery, West Milford, Harrison Co, WV.[1742]
        iii.   LIVING. She married[1474,484] Rodney Lee Myers, b. Apr-16-1944 at Duck Creek, Harrison Co, WV,[190,419] d. May-27-2011 in Nutter Fort, Harrison Co, WV,[700] cremated[190] resided in Nutter Fort, Harrison Co, WV,[190] resided formerly in Lost Creek, Harrison Co, WV.[1687]

815. **Alice Bessie West** (453.Hiram[8], 260.Ruhama[7], 137.Sarah[6], 72.John[5], 21.John[4], 6.Hugh[3], 3.John[2], 1.Jean[1]), b. Apr-27-1915,[1737,592] d. Nov-10-2000,[592] resided in Uniontown, Fayette Co, PA.[948] She married[1737] **Garland F. Phillips**, b. ca 1918,[418] (son of Jessie Lasure Phillips and Alma Fletcher), census 1920, 1930 in West Milford, Harrison Co, WV.
        Children:
        i.   JO ANN PHILLIPS.
        ii.   GARLAND VERNON PHILLIPS.
        iii.   JERRY PHILLIPS.

816. **Reva Pearl Bartlett** (455.Ida[8], 260.Ruhama[7], 137.Sarah[6], 72.John[5], 21.John[4], 6.Hugh[3], 3.John[2], 1.Jean[1]), b. Jul- 8-1908 in Harrison Co, WV,[947,604] d. Sep-24-2004 in Shelby, Cleveland Co, NC,[700,604] buried in Brick Church (7th Day Baptist) Cemetery, Lost Creek, Harrison Co, WV,[190] resided in Shelby, Cleveland Co, NC,[190] resided formerly in Clarksburg, Harrison Co, WV,[190,604,856] census 1930 in Grant District, Harrison Co, WV. She married Mar-21-1925,[947] **John Loman Kennedy**, b. Mar-26-1904,[592,1208] (son of Dorsey C. Kennedy and Allena "Allie" Sommerville), d. Jan-12-1992,[592] resided in Clarksburg, Harrison Co, WV,[604] census 1910, 1930 in Grant District, Harrison Co, WV.
        Children:
        i.   LIVING. She married Living.
        ii.   JACK W. KENNEDY b. May-25-1928,[398] d. Jun- 8-1928 in West Milford, Harrison Co, WV,[398] buried in Brick Church (7th Day Baptist) Cemetery, Lost Creek, Harrison Co, WV.[398,230]

                Middle name given as Wilkes in death record, but as Willis in obituary of mother.

        iii.   LIVING.
        iv.   LIVING. He married (1) Living. He married[mdccxlv[1745]] (2) Living.
        v.   LIVING. He married Living.
        vi.   LIVING. He married Living.

vii.   LIVING. She married Living.

817. **Kenneth Boyd Ward**[473,480], also known as Boyd Ward,[480] (458.Thomas[8], 264.Mary[7], 139.John[6], 72.John[5], 21.John[4], 6.Hugh[3], 3.John[2], 1.Jean[1]), b. Mar- -1879,[809,46,473] d. 1961,[46] buried in Spruce Creek Baptist Church Cemetery (Co Rd 34), Ritchie Co, WV,[469] [Name on headstone: K. Boyd Ward.], census 1900 in Union District, Ritchie Co, WV. He married Mar- 1-1908 in Ritchie Co, WV,[473] **Daisy Alma Bartlett**, b. Feb-18-1884,[398,473,46] (daughter of Lair Dee Bartlett and Sarah Palestine "Pallie" Smith), d. May-25-1952 in Berea, Ritchie Co, WV,[398,46] buried in Spruce Creek Baptist Church Cemetery (Co Rd 34), Ritchie Co, WV,[398,469] resided in Berea, Ritchie Co, WV.[398]

> Children:
> i.   HAZEL WARD[480,778.]

818. **Theo May Ward** (458.Thomas[8], 264.Mary[7], 139.John[6], 72.John[5], 21.John[4], 6.Hugh[3], 3.John[2], 1.Jean[1]), b. Sep- -1881,[809,46,473] d. 1967,[46] buried in Pine Grove Cemetery, Berea (Co Rd 7-26), Ritchie Co, WV,[469] census 1900 in Union District, Ritchie Co, WV. She married Mar-24-1909 in Ritchie Co, WV,[473] **Roy A. Bee**, b. Nov- -1881 in Ritchie Co, WV,[809,477,469,473] (son of Azariah Bee and Sarah Melvian "Vena" Law), d. Mar-14-1965 in Ritchie Co, WV,[477] buried in Pine Grove Cemetery, Berea (Co Rd 7-26), Ritchie Co, WV,[469] resided 1936 in Pullman, Ritchie Co, WV,[765] census 1900 in Union District, Ritchie Co, WV.

> Children:
> i.   VELT BEE b. Feb- 4-1912,[17] d. Feb-14-1912,[17] buried in Pine Grove Cemetery, Berea (Co Rd 7-26), Ritchie Co, WV.[469]
> ii.   BLAKE BEE b. Jan-16-1916 in Ritchie Co, WV,[592,996] d. Sep-25-2007,[592] resided in Surprise, Maricopa Co, AZ,[592] resided formerly in Ritchie Co, WV.[996,604] He married Nov- 2-1939 in Ritchie Co, WV,[996] Lucy G. Hardman, b. ca 1916 in Gilmer Co, WV,[996] (daughter of French Hardman and Minerva __).

819. **Nellie Snow Ward**[473] also known as Snow Ward,[480,592] (458.Thomas[8], 264.Mary[7], 139.John[6], 72.John[5], 21.John[4], 6.Hugh[3], 3.John[2], 1.Jean[1]), b. Jan-22-1888,[17,592,473] d. Oct-12-1968,[17,592] buried in Spruce Creek Baptist Church Cemetery (Co Rd 34), Ritchie Co, WV,[469] resided in Elizabeth, Wirt Co, WV,[mdccxlvi[1746]] census 1900 in Union District, Ritchie Co, WV. She married[480] Apr-11-1908 in Ritchie Co, WV,[473] **Claude V. Bartlett**, b. Mar- 1-1888,[17,473] (son of Lair Dee Bartlett and Sarah Palestine "Pallie" Smith), d. Aug-21-1910,[17] buried in Spruce Creek Baptist Church Cemetery (Co Rd 34), Ritchie Co, WV,[469] cause of death typhoid fever.[480]

> Children:
> i.   LORAN BARTLETT b. Jul- 4-1909 at Spruce Creek (Auburn), Ritchie Co, WV,[480,592] d. Jan- 7-1991,[592] resided in Boulder, CO,[592,480] resided formerly in Wood Co, WV,[480] resided originally in Ritchie Co, WV.[480] He married[480] Lucy Lamm, b. Sep-17-1911,[592] d. Oct-30-2000,[592] resided in Parkersburg, Wood Co, WV,[592] resided formerly in Boulder, CO.[592]
> ii.   ELEANOR BARTLETT b. 1910.[480]

820. **Mattie Ward** (460.Charles[8], 264.Mary[7], 139.John[6], 72.John[5], 21.John[4], 6.Hugh[3], 3.John[2], 1.Jean[1]), b. Sep- -1889,[473,809] d. 1958,[46] buried in Auburn Community Cemetery, Ritchie Co, WV,[469] census 1910 in Auburn, Ritchie Co, WV. She married Sep-24-1907 in Ritchie Co, WV,[473] **Asa James Sheets**, b. 1886 in Harrison Co, WV,[46,473] d. 1946,[46] buried in Auburn Community Cemetery, Ritchie Co, WV,[469] census 1910 in Auburn, Ritchie Co, WV.

> Children:
> i.   ESTA L. SHEETS b. 1909,[mdccxlvii[1747]] census 1910 in Auburn, Ritchie Co, WV.
> ii.   ALVA SHEETS b. May- 2-1915,[17] d. Aug-14-1915,[17] buried in Auburn Community Cemetery, Ritchie Co, WV.[469]
> iii.   DENLEY UDELL SHEETS b. Nov-23-1916,[592,996] d. Dec-29-1989,[592] resided in Newberne, Gilmer Co, WV.[604] He married[446] Oct- 6-1940 in Ritchie Co, WV,[996] Jessie Czigans, b. Oct-20-1916 in Doddridge Co, WV,[190,592,996] [Mt. Union] (daughter of Lawrence Czigans and Mina Jane Leggett), d. Dec-25-2006,[592,190] buried in Mt. Olive Cemetery (new), Rt 47, Burnt House, Ritchie Co, WV,[190] resided in Smithville, Ritchie Co, WV,[592] resided 1940 in Ritchie Co, WV.[996]

821. **Ruth M. Ward** (461.Calvin[8], 264.Mary[7], 139.John[6], 72.John[5], 21.John[4], 6.Hugh[3], 3.John[2], 1.Jean[1]), b. Feb- -1892 in Minnesota,[123,46] d. 1974,[46] buried in Velva Cemetery, McHenry Co, ND,[134] census 1930 in Bjornson (Minot), McHenry Co, ND, census 1920 in Weld Co, CO, census 1910 in Bjornson (Minot), McHenry Co, ND, census 1900 in Minneapolis, MN. She married ca 1915,[334] **DeWitt Clinton Shattuck**, census name Clinton D. Shattuck, b. 1893 in Colorado,[46,681] d. 1970,[46] buried in Velva Cemetery, McHenry Co, ND,[134] census 1930 in Bjornson (Minot), McHenry Co, ND, census 1920 in Weld Co, CO, occupation farmer.[334]

    Children:

    i. LOIS V. SHATTUCK b. ca 1916 in North Dakota,[681] census 1930 in Bjornson (Minot), McHenry Co, ND, census 1920 in Weld Co, CO.

    ii. JESSIE M. SHATTUCK b. 1918 in Colorado,[46,681] d. 1997,[46] buried in Velva Cemetery, McHenry Co, ND,[134] census 1930 in Bjornson (Minot), McHenry Co, ND, census 1920 in Weld Co, CO.

822. **Porter Gaston Nutter** (462.Elizabeth[8], 265.Samuel[7], 139.John[6], 72.John[5], 21.John[4], 6.Hugh[3], 3.John[2], 1.Jean[1]), b. Oct- 6-1871,[373] d. Oct- 6-1932 in Gilmer Co, WV,[398,373] buried in Trinity Cemetery, Gilmer Co, WV,[190] cause of death acute fallicular tonsilitis,[398] resided in Auburn, Ritchie Co, WV,[521] census 1900 in Troy District, Gilmer Co, WV. He married Oct-12-1895 in Gilmer Co, WV,[434] **Edna Cecil Cooper**, b. Jul-16-1874 in Gilmer Co, WV,[mdccxlviii[1748]] (daughter of Charles S. Cooper and Mary Jane Hall), d. May-22-1948 in Harrisville, Ritchie Co, WV,[190,474] resided in Auburn, Ritchie Co, WV,[190] census 1880, 1900 in Troy District, Gilmer Co, WV.

    Children:

    i. MYRL NUTTER, also known as Myrtle Nutter, b. Jun- 3-1897 in West Virginia,[373,964] d. Oct- 6-1948,[373] resided 1930, 48 in Seat Pleasant, Prince Georges Co, MD,[856] census 1900 in Troy District, Gilmer Co, WV. She married Oct-20-1920,[373] Paul Elbert Patrick, b. Nov- 2-1899 in Ohio,[334] resided 1930 in Seat Pleasant, Prince Georges Co, MD.[334]

    ii. MAPLE NUTTER b. Nov- 6-1905,[373,592] d. Aug-15-1994,[592] resided in Harrisville, Ritchie Co, WV,[856,412,592.] She married[374] Aug- 2-1931 in Ritchie Co, WV,[mdccxlix[1749]] Charles Howard Barnard, also known as Howard Barnard,[374,502] b. Dec-16-1900,[373] d. Mar-12-1963.[969]

    iii. PAUL STRADER NUTTER b. Feb-24-1907 in Gilmer Co, WV,[373] d. Apr-24-1997 in Glenville, Gilmer Co, WV,[190,592] buried in Trinity Cemetery, Gilmer Co, WV,[1166] resided in Coxs Mills, Gilmer Co, WV,[190] occupation (retired 1969) teacher, Gilmer Com, WV & Elyria, Lorain Co, OH,[190] education Glenville State College.[190] He married Nov-25-1937,[969] Letha Lane Starcher, b. Nov- 9-1912,[969,592] (daughter of Alvin S. Starcher and Alrose McKinley), d. Oct-18-1994,[484,592] buried in Trinity Cemetery, Gilmer Co, WV, resided in Coxs Mills, Gilmer Co, WV,[592] resided formerly in Ohio.[mdccl[1750]]

    iv. RUTH NUTTER b. Mar- 5-1909 in Auburn, Ritchie Co, WV,[190,373] d. Feb-16-1980 in Coxs Mills, Gilmer Co, WV,[190,592] buried in Trinity Cemetery, Gilmer Co, WV,[190] resided in Coxs Mills, Gilmer Co, WV,[190] resided 1948 in Auburn, Ritchie Co, WV.[856] She married Sep-30-1937 in West Union, Doddridge Co, WV,[mdccli[1751]] Franklin Greydon Ireland, also known as Frank Ireland,[191] b. Apr-10-1905 in Parsons, Tucker Co, WV,[373,1006] (son of Albert Law Ireland and Minnie Hermine McNeill), d. Jul-15-1969,[191] buried in Trinity Cemetery, Gilmer Co, WV.[1166]

823. **Marshall Field Nutter** (462.Elizabeth[8], 265.Samuel[7], 139.John[6], 72.John[5], 21.John[4], 6.Hugh[3], 3.John[2], 1.Jean[1]), b. Apr- 7-1874,[684,964] d. Feb- 3-1940,[373] buried in Greenmound Cemetery, Kilbourne, Delaware Co, OH, resided in Delaware, Delaware Co, OH,[521] census 1920 in Delaware Co, OH, census 1900, 1910 in Troy District, Gilmer Co, WV, occupation carpenter,[1166] [Worked in the construction of Fort Knox, Kentucky.]. He married Aug-29-1895 in Gilmer Co, WV,[434] **Martha Gay Riddle**, also known as Gay Riddle, also known as Mattie G. Riddle,[434,mdcclii[1752]] census name Gay,[964] b. Feb- -1878 in Doddridge Co, WV,[964,434] d. Oct- 1-1960 in Ohio,[1166] buried in Greenmound Cemetery, Kilbourne, Delaware Co, OH, resided in Columbus, Franklin Co, OH,[1166] census 1920 in Delaware Co, OH, census 1900, 1910 in Troy District, Gilmer Co, WV, buried in green.

1900 Census, Gilmer Co, WV (Troy District), enumerated on Jun 20 1900:

Marshal Nutter, 26, b. Mar 1874, farmer, married 5 yrs; wife Gay, 22, b. Feb 1878, mother of 2 children (both still living); son Glen, 4, b. May 1896; son Lowell, 1, b. Oct 1898.

1910 Census, Gilmer Co, WV (Troy District), enumerated on Apr 22 1910:
Elizabeth L. Nutter, 56, widow, mother of 8 children (5 still living); son Marshal F, 36, occupation commercial traveler (hardware), married 14 yrs; son Blane, 25, single; dau Mary E, 21, single; dau-in-law Mattie G, 31, married 14 yrs, mother of 2 children (both still living); grandson Forest G, 13; grandson Lowell D, 11.

1920 Census, Delaware Co, Ohio (Delaware Twp), enumerated on Jan 23 1920:
Marshal F. Nutter, 45, carpenter; wife Mattie G, 41; son Forest G, 23, single, laborer at roundhouse; son Lowell D, 21, single, carpenter; dau Elma, 9. All born in West Virginia.

       Children:
       i.   FOREST GLENN NUTTER, also known as Glenn Nutter,[592] also known as F. Glenn Nutter,[684] census name Glen Nutter,[964] b. May-29-1896 in West Virginia,[684,592,964] d. Jul-20-1981 in Ross Co, OH,[1011,592] buried in Africa Cemetery, Orange Twp, Delaware Co, OH,[1166] resided in Delaware, Delaware Co, OH,[1011,1010] census 1920 in Delaware Co, OH, census 1900, 1910 in Troy District, Gilmer Co, WV. He married Eddith M. Kindle, b. Dec-14-1905,[592] (daughter of Harmon Kindle and Stella B. __), d. Apr-23-1991 in Delaware, Delaware Co, OH,[1011,592] buried in Africa Cemetery, Orange Twp, Delaware Co, OH,[1166] resided in Delaware, Delaware Co, OH,[592,1011] census 1910 in Orange Twp, Delaware Co, OH.
       ii.   LOWELL DEAN NUTTER b. Oct-28-1898 in West Virginia,[592,964] d. Nov-10-1986 in Delaware Co, OH,[1011,592] buried in Greenmound Cemetery, Kilbourne, Delaware Co, OH, resided in Delaware, Delaware Co, OH,[1010] census 1920, 1930 in Delaware Co, OH, census 1900, 1910 in Troy District, Gilmer Co, WV, occupation carpenter, farmer.[1011] He married[373] ca 1924,[334] Hazel B. Temple, b. Nov-27-1902 in Ohio,[1166,334] d. Aug-29-1959 in Delaware, Delaware Co, OH,[1011] buried in Greenmound Cemetery, Kilbourne, Delaware Co, OH, census 1930 in Delaware Co, OH.
       iii.   CONSTANCE ELMA NUTTER, census name Elma Nutter, also known as Alma Fern Nutter, b. Oct- 5-1910 in West Virginia,[592,681] d. Oct-30-2008,[592] resided in Alpharetta, Fulton Co, GA,[1166,1010] resided formerly in Jacksonville, Duval Co, FL, resided formerly in Columbus, Franklin Co, OH,[1166] resided 1960s in New York City, NY,[1166] census 1920 in Delaware Co, OH, occupation church secretary and organist,[1166] never married[969].
       iv.   EUGENE CARLTON "GENE" NUTTER[969] also known as Carleton Eugene Nutter,[969] b. Jan-12-1923 in Delaware Co, OH,[592,mdccliii[1753],1166] d. Jan-16-2008,[592] resided in Lawrenceville, Gwinnett Co, GA,[1010] resided formerly in Florida, resided 1943 in Delaware Co, OH,[1753] military U.S. Army, World War II,[1753] education PhD in agronomy, Cornell University,[1166] occupation golf course consultant.[1166] He married[969] Rose Hansel, b. Jan-22-1925,[924] residence in Georgia.[924]

824. **Ira Brenton Nutter** (462.Elizabeth[8], 265.Samuel[7], 139.John[6], 72.John[5], 21.John[4], 6.Hugh[3], 3.John[2], 1.Jean[1]), b. Aug- 6-1876 in Auburn, Ritchie Co, WV,[373,964] d. Apr-18-1931 in Washington, DC,[190] buried in Fort Lincoln Cemetery, Brentwood, Prince Georges Co, MD,[190] census 1900 in Troy District, Gilmer Co, WV, education West Virginia University.[190]

A graduate of West Virginia University, he taught school in the Philippines for three years. At time of death, was senior clerk in the classification division of the U.S. Post Office Dept in Washington, DC, where he had worked for 24 years. A civic activist, particularly in the area of education, he was a former president of the Rhode Island Avenue Citizens Associaton in Washington, DC.[mdccliv[1754]]

He married Aug-30-1908,[373] **Martha "Mattie" Chase**.
       Children:
       i.   BRENTON WELLINGTON NUTTER b. Sep-29-1911,[592] d. Feb- -1970,[592] resided in Washington, DC.[1625] He married[395,373] Margaret B. McPheeters, b. Oct-28-1914 in Welch, McDowell Co, WV,[190,592] (daughter of Robert Alexander McPheeters and Minnie Beckner), d. Jan- 1-2005 in Staunton, VA,[190,592] buried Bethel Cemetery in Greenville, Augusta Co, VA,[190] resided in Staunton,

VA,[mdcclv][1755] occupation C&P Telephone Co (Silver Spring MD), office of Staunton Treasurer and Commissioner of Revenue.[190]

    ii.   WILLIAM MORRIS NUTTER. He married[373] Evelyn Richards.

    iii.   ELIZABETH NUTTER never married[373.]

825. **Josiah Blaine Nutter**, also known as Blaine Nutter,[1752,412,502] (462.Elizabeth[8], 265.Samuel[7], 139.John[6], 72.John[5], 21.John[4], 6.Hugh[3], 3.John[2], 1.Jean[1]), b. Sep-16-1884 in Gilmer Co, WV,[966,190,964] d. Oct-16-1965 in Auburn, Ritchie Co, WV,[700,966] buried in IOOF Cemetery, Troy, Gilmer Co, WV, resided in Auburn, Ritchie Co, WV,[190,521,412] census 1920 at Stone Lick, Auburn, Gilmer Co, WV, census 1900, 1910 in Troy District, Gilmer Co, WV, occupation mail carrier & farmer.[190] He married[966] Jan-23-1921 in Gilmer Co, WV,[434] **Tracy Ruhana Bush**, b. Sep-18-1896 in Gilmer Co, WV,[190] (daughter of Thomas Hughes Bush and Mary Krenn), d. May- 2-1990 in Weston, Lewis Co, WV,[190] buried in IOOF Cemetery, Troy, Gilmer Co, WV,[966] census 1910 in Troy District, Gilmer Co, WV.

    Children:

    i.   LANE BUSH NUTTER b. Mar-17-1923 in Stone Lick, Auburn, Gilmer Co, WV, resided 1990, 2011 in Coxs Mills, Gilmer Co, WV.[856,412] He married Mar-17-1994 in Stone Lick, Auburn, Gilmer Co, WV,[mdcclvi][1756] no children from this marriage, Eunice Roe, b. Nov-18-1924 in Olive Hill, KY,[1756] (daughter of John Charles Roe and Norma Counts).

    Eunice: Previous married name: Lockney.

    ii.   LAUREL NUTTER b. Oct- 8-1924 in Gilmer Co, WV,[966] d. May-27-2011 in Parkersburg, Wood Co, WV,[764] buried in South Fork Bapt Church Cem, Oxford, Doddridge Co, WV,[190] education Pullman H.S. (1943), nursing school in Charleston,[mdcclvii][1757],[190] occupation during WW II Westinghouse, Fairmont WV.[190] She married Jun-24-1949 in Clarksburg, Harrison Co, WV,[mdcclviii][1758],[mdcclix][1759] Robert Junior Britton, also known as Junior Britton, b. May-31-1926 in Ritchie Co, WV (son of Robert Elsworth Britton and Mary Jane Sweeney), resided 2005 in West Union, Doddridge Co, WV,[521] occupation mail carrier,[1757] education Pullman H.S.,[1757] military U.S. Navy.[1757]

826. **Mary Elizabeth Nutter** (462.Elizabeth[8], 265.Samuel[7], 139.John[6], 72.John[5], 21.John[4], 6.Hugh[3], 3.John[2], 1.Jean[1]), b. Sep- 1-1889 in Gilmer Co, WV,[373,964,1006] d. Apr- 3-1934 in Alice, Gilmer Co, WV,[190,373] buried in Good Hope Masonic Cemetery, Rt. 19 S, Harrison Co, WV,[17] cause of death pneumonia,[190] resided in Coxs Mills, Gilmer Co, WV,[521] resided in Alice, Gilmer Co, WV,[190] census 1920 at Stone Lick, Auburn, Gilmer Co, WV, census 1900, 1910 in Troy District, Gilmer Co, WV, education Glenville State Normal School (class of 1915).[190] She married[373] Nov-20-1921 in Gilmer Co, WV,[434] **Homer R. Sheets**, b. Sep-25-1879 in Gilmer Co, WV,[190,mdcclx][1760] (son of Edward Sheets and Marilla Washburn), d. Nov- -1964 in Coxs Mills, Gilmer Co, WV,[190,592] buried in Good Hope Masonic Cemetery, Rt. 19 S, Harrison Co, WV,[190,17] resided 1936 at Coxs Mills, Gilmer Co, WV,[588] occupation farmer and stockman.[190]

    Children:

    i.   WENDELL ROSS SHEETS title: Dr., also known as Ross Sheets,[856] b. Jun-10-1923 in Coxs Mills, Gilmer Co, WV,[190,592] d. Apr-13-2010 in Florida,[592] buried Sylvan Abbey Mem Pk in Clearwater, Pinellas Co, FL,[190] resided in St. Petersburg, Pinellas Co, FL, resided since 1965 in Clearwater, Pinellas Co, FL,[190] resided until 1965 in Glen Burnie, Anne Arundel Co, MD,[190] census 1930 in Troy District, Gilmer Co, WV, military U.S. Army Air Force, World War II,[190] education Glenville State College (BA), Univ of Maryland (MA, Dr of Ed),[190] occupation teacher, education administrator.[190]

827. **Lucy Elizabeth Reed** (463.Sarah[8], 265.Samuel[7], 139.John[6], 72.John[5], 21.John[4], 6.Hugh[3], 3.John[2], 1.Jean[1]), b. Feb- 7-1877 in Berea, Ritchie Co, WV,[373] d. Dec-25-1956.[373] She married Mar-29-1902,[373] **William Lewis Drain**, d. Feb-16-1945.[969]

    Children:

    i.   CONNIE PAULINE DRAIN, also known as Conza Pauline Reed, b. 1902 in Gilmer Co, WV,[996,373] d. Aug-31-1960,[969] resided 1927 in Ritchie Co, WV.[996] She married[373] (1) Jul-31-1927 in

Ritchie Co, WV,[mdcclxi[1761]] divorced Pryor Hartman Ayers, b. ca 1894 in Ritchie Co, WV,[996] resided 1927 in Wood Co, WV.[996] She married[373] (2) Herbert Grimm.

    ii.   HUNTER HOLMES DRAIN b. Sep-15-1908 in Auburn, Ritchie Co, WV,[969] d. May-31-1963.[969] He married Jul-17-1936,[969] Elizabeth Dagon.

    iii.   WILMA SARAH DRAIN b. May-11-1911 in Auburn, Ritchie Co, WV.[969] She married[mdcclxii[1762]] Daniel Starr Patton, b. Apr-11-1907 at Indian Creek, Ritchie Co, WV,[190] (son of John G. Patton and Eva G. Starr), d. Dec-26-2007 in Parkersburg, Wood Co, WV,[1056] buried in Sunset Memory Gardens, Parkersburg, WV,[190] resided in Harrisville, Ritchie Co, WV,[521,190] education Harrisville H.S. (1929),[190] occupation Ames Baldwin Co, aka O. Ames, Parkersburg (37 yrs).[190]

    iv.   OMA MAXINE DRAIN b. Aug-31-1914 in Berea, Ritchie Co, WV,[602,592] d. Jan- -1968,[592] resided in Parkersburg, Wood Co, WV.[602,1010] She married[373] (1) divorced[1116] James Parsons, d. bef Sep 1949.[969] She married (2) Sep-19-1949 in Parkersburg, Wood Co, WV,[602] Ivan D. Engelhardt, b. May-15-1916 in Roane Co, WV,[602,592] (son of Albert Engelhardt and Rosa __), d. Mar-24-1990,[592] resided in Winchester, VA,[mdcclxiii[1763]] resided 1949 in Parkersburg, Wood Co, WV.[602]

    v.   HAYWARD H. DRAIN b. Jul-31-1917 in Auburn, Ritchie Co, WV,[969,592] d. Feb- -1983,[592] resided in St. Joseph, Berrien Co, MI,[592] resided formerly in West Virginia,[604] education Pullman High School, Ritchie Co WV (1936).[mdcclxiv[1764]] He married Dec-24-1948,[969] no children from this marriage, Clara Kellison.

828. **Samuel Boyd Reed** (463.Sarah[8], 265.Samuel[7], 139.John[6], 72.John[5], 21.John[4], 6.Hugh[3], 3.John[2], 1.Jean[1]), b. Apr-17-1880 in Berea, Ritchie Co, WV,[969] census 1900 in Southwest District, Doddridge Co, WV [In household of grandfather Samuel Morris Gaston.]. He married May-28-1908,[373] **Alice Grapes**.

    Children:

    i.   BOYD ALLEN REED b. Jun-28-1909 in Clarksburg, Harrison Co, WV,[969,592] d. Oct- -1974,[592] resided in Clarksburg, Harrison Co, WV.[592] He married Apr-21-1935,[969] Goldie Harris, b. Mar-10-1908,[969] d. Aug-15-1961.[969]

    ii.   PAUL GRAPES REED b. May-16-1913 in Clarksburg, Harrison Co, WV.[969] He married[969] Clyde McClellan.

    iii.   HELEN CHRISTINE REED, also known as Christine,[592] b. Sep- 7-1918 in Clarksburg, Harrison Co, WV,[969,592] d. May- -1985,[592] [Name listed in SSDI as Christine Tetrick.], resided in Martinsburg, Berkeley Co, WV.[592] She married[969-484] Harlan Marshall Tetrick, Jr., b. Jul- 1-1922 in Shinnston, Harrison Co, WV,[190] (son of Harlan Marshall Tetrick and Sarah Catherine Ambrose), d. Sep-13-2005 in Orange, Orange Co, CA,[190] buried in Falls Church, Fairfax Co, VA,[190] [National Memorial Park], resided aft about 1996 in Orange Co, CA,[190] resided until about1996 in Martinsburg, Berkeley Co, WV,[190] resided formerly near Washington, DC,[190] military U.S. Army (duty in Virginia during World War II).[190]

    Harlan: Worked for 27 years for the Marriott Corporation in the Washington DC area, specializing in purchasing and materials management, and he served as president of the D.C. chapter of the Purchasing Management Association. After moving to Martinsburg WV, he went to work for GEICO and Hospital Corporation of America, retiring at age 70 as the regional director of the Martinsburg branch of the WV Department of Motor Vehicles. In addition, he held U.S. and Japanese patents for perishable goods management and technology. Among others, survived by grandchildren Carrie, Jasmin and Brian, and by great-grandson Malachi.[190]

    iv.   JAMES LESLIE REED, also known as Leslie Reed, b. Nov-21-1920 in Clarksburg, Harrison Co, WV,[969] d. Aug-31-1944 in France.[969]

    Killed in action in the Battle of Cherbourg, France. He was a Staff Sergeant in Co F, 12th Infantry Regiment, 4th Infantry Division. No children.

    He married[373] Naoma Hanna, b. Jan-19-1922.[969]

Naoma: Last name could be Harris.

v. ALICE REED[969] d. young.[969]

829. **Ota Lee Reed** (463.Sarah[8], 265.Samuel[7], 139.John[6], 72.John[5], 21.John[4], 6.Hugh[3], 3.John[2], 1.Jean[1]), b. Feb-28-1882 in Berea, Ritchie Co, WV,[969] d. Jan- 8-1970 in Fairmont, Marion Co, WV.[373] She married Mar-12-1918,[969] **Joseph E. Fraker**, b. Jan-24-1879 in Steelton, Franklin Co, PA,[969] d. Oct-30-1956.[969]
Children:
i. JOSEPH E. FRAKER, JR. b. Apr-26-1921,[969] education Fairmont H.S. (valedictorian), West Virginia University (1954),[969] military World War II.[969] He married Living.
ii. JOHN REED FRAKER b. Aug-23-1922,[969,592] d. Apr- 7-2002,[592] resided in Colorado Springs, El Paso Co, CO,[592] resided formerly in Nebraska,[969] resided 1949 - 1959 in Texas,[969] resided originally in West Virginia,[604] education Ohio State University (1944).[969]

In 1949, he moved to Bellaire, TX, where he worked with the Junior Chamber of Commerce in Houston, and later with the Houston Chamber of Commerce. In Dec 1959, he took a position as Executive Vice President of the Lincoln Chamber of Commerce, Lincoln, Nebraska.[969]

He married Jun- 1-1946,[969] Jeann Louise Soule, b. Dec-21-1924,[969,592] d. Dec-17-2000,[592] resided in Colorado Springs, El Paso Co, CO,[592] resided formerly in West Virginia.[604]
iii. WILLIAM L. FRAKER b. Feb- 4-1926,[969] education West Virginia University, University of Houston (degree),[969] military U.S. Navy, World War II.[969] He married Living.

830. **Cecil Alexander Reed** (463.Sarah[8], 265.Samuel[7], 139.John[6], 72.John[5], 21.John[4], 6.Hugh[3], 3.John[2], 1.Jean[1]), b. May- 6-1884 in Berea, Ritchie Co, WV,[969] d. Mar-19-1952.[969] He married Jun-15-1916,[969] **Marcie Justis**, b. Jun-11-1885,[969] d. Aug- -1966,[592] resided in Canton, Stark Co, OH.[mdcclxv[1765]]
Children:
i. JULIA FRANCES REED b. Oct-22-1920 in Canton, Stark Co, OH.[969] She married May-17-1944,[969] Paul Studer, b. Dec-24-1922.[969]
ii. ALAN JUSTIS REED b. May-20-1922 in Canton, Stark Co, OH.[969] He married Jun-23-1951,[969] Grace Thomas, b. Feb-26-1924.[969]

831. **Henry G. Reed** (463.Sarah[8], 265.Samuel[7], 139.John[6], 72.John[5], 21.John[4], 6.Hugh[3], 3.John[2], 1.Jean[1]), b. Mar-30-1887 in Berea, Ritchie Co, WV,[969] d. Nov-11-1952.[969] He married[969] **Emma Mitchell**.
Children:
i. DOROTHY VIRGINIA REED[969].

832. **Winna Fern Reed** (463.Sarah[8], 265.Samuel[7], 139.John[6], 72.John[5], 21.John[4], 6.Hugh[3], 3.John[2], 1.Jean[1]), b. Mar-21-1892 in Berea, Ritchie Co, WV.[mdcclxvi[1766]] She married Oct-16-1919,[969] **Herman Brannon**, b. Apr-20-1898.[969]
Children:
i. SARA JANE BRANNON b. Dec-18-1924 in Fairmont, Marion Co, WV,[969] education Fairmont State Teachers College.[969] She married Mar- 5-1946,[969] Frank Meyers.
ii. ROBERT HERMAN BRANNON b. Feb-10-1926 in Fairmont, Marion Co, WV,[969] d. Sep-4-1944 in Washington, DC,[969] buried in Woodlawn Cemetery, Fairmont, Marion Co, WV.[969]

Immediately upon graduation from Fairmont West High School, enlisted in the U.S. Army to serve in World War II. While on maneuvers at Fort Meade, MD, he received severe shrapnel wounds. He was taken to Walter Reed Hospital in Washington, DC, where he died two weeks later.[969]

833. **Harvey Allen Reed** (463.Sarah[8], 265.Samuel[7], 139.John[6], 72.John[5], 21.John[4], 6.Hugh[3], 3.John[2], 1.Jean[1]), b. Jun-25-1894 in Berea, Ritchie Co, WV,[mdcclxvii[1767]] d. in Fairmont, Marion Co, WV, resided since ca 1930 in Huntington, Cabell Co, WV,[969] education Fairmont State College,[969] military Sep 6

1918 to Dec 6 U.S. Army - World War I. He married Sep- 3-1918,[969] **Madeline Maddox**, b. Apr-22-1900.[969]

Children:

i. HARVEY ALLEN REED, JR. b. Oct- -1925 in Fairmont, Marion Co, WV,[969,592] [Ota Reed Fraker reports birth date as Oct 25 1925, but SSDI shows it as Oct 18 1925.], d. Aug- -1994,[592] resided in Barboursville, Cabell Co, WV.[592] He married Nov-15-1947,[969] Geneva Faye Adkins, b. Aug-31-1924 at Holden, Logan Co, WV,[190,592] (daughter of Walter Adkins and Fannie __), d. Aug- 2-2004 in Barboursville, Cabell Co, WV,[700,592] buried in Golzaberry Cemetery, Sias, Lincoln Co, WV,[190] resided in Barboursville, Cabell Co, WV.[592]

834. **Minnie Elizabeth Jones**, also known as Minnie Eliza Jones (464.Susan[8], 265.Samuel[7], 139.John[6], 72.John[5], 21.John[4], 6.Hugh[3], 3.John[2], 1.Jean[1]), b. Aug- 4-1884 in Holbrook, Doddridge Co, WV,[mdcclxviii[1768],190,592] d. Dec-10-1967 in Parkersburg, Wood Co, WV,[190,373,592] buried in Pine Grove Cemetery, Berea (Co Rd 7-26), Ritchie Co, WV,[469] resided in Parkersburg, Wood Co, WV.[521,592] She married Jul-20-1905 in Ritchie Co, WV,[473] **Elva Maxson**, b. Aug-17-1872 in Berea, Ritchie Co, WV,[mdcclxix[1769],809,46] (son of Elisha John Maxson and Margaret Catherine Law), d. Jul-27-1953 in Parkersburg, Wood Co, WV,[398,46] buried in Pine Grove Cemetery, Berea (Co Rd 7-26), Ritchie Co, WV,[469,398,mdcclxx[1770]] census 1880, 1900 in Union District, Ritchie Co, WV.

Children:

i. IRIS AZALIA MAXSON b. Jan- 3-1906 in Berea, Ritchie Co, WV,[373] d. Feb-22-1984 in Parkersburg, Wood Co, WV,[373] buried in Evergreen North (aka Arlington) Cemetery, Rt 2 N of Parkersburg, Wood Co, WV, resided 1967 in Oxford, Doddridge Co, WV.[856] She married Jan- 5-1927, Lincoln Brooks Flesher, also known as Brooks Flesher, b. Aug- 5-1900 in Oxford, Doddridge Co, WV,[373] d. Jan-20-1957 in Evergreen North (aka Arlington) Cemetery, Rt 2 N of Parkersburg, Wood Co, WV.[1770]

ii. CARLTON HERSHEL MAXSON b. Aug- 6-1907 in Berea, Ritchie Co, WV,[373,592] d. Feb-21-1970 in Parkersburg, Wood Co, WV,[373,592] buried in Pine Grove Cemetery, Berea (Co Rd 7-26), Ritchie Co, WV,[469] resided in Parkersburg, Wood Co, WV,[856,592] resided formerly in Pennsylvania,[948] census 1930 at Slab Creek, Ritchie Co, WV. He married Feb-26-1930 in Ritchie Co, WV,[996] Mabel Irene Gribble, b. May-24-1913 in Coxs Mills, Gilmer Co, WV,[373] (daughter of Howard Hull Gribble and Bessie Iona Campbell), d. May-25-1991 in Berea, Ritchie Co, WV,[373] buried in Pine Grove Cemetery, Berea (Co Rd 7-26), Ritchie Co, WV,[469] census 1930 at Slab Creek, Ritchie Co, WV, census 1920 in Troy District, Gilmer Co, WV.

iii. SUSAN JANE GERTRUDE MAXSON, also known as Gertrude Maxson,[856] b. Dec-20-1909 in Berea, Ritchie Co, WV,[373] resided 1967, 96 in Mt. Clare, Harrison Co, WV.[856,905] She married Sep-28-1930,[373] Chester Orval Howell, b. Nov-25-1906,[373] d. Dec-24-1981 in Clarksburg, Harrison Co, WV,[373] buried in Quiet Dell, Harrison Co, WV.

iv. OLIVE JOSETTA MAXSON b. Dec-19-1911 in Berea, Ritchie Co, WV,[17] d. Dec-23-1954,[17] buried in South Fork Bapt Church Cem, Oxford, Doddridge Co, WV.[17] She married Sep-18-1930 in Harrisville, Ritchie Co, WV,[996] Earnest Ralph Straley, also known as Ralph Straley,[1479] b. Mar-4-1908 in Copen, Braxton Co, WV (son of Joseph F. Straley and Icie Elizabeth Stout), d. Aug-24-1991 in Parkersburg, Wood Co, WV, buried in South Fork Bapt Church Cem, Oxford, Doddridge Co, WV.[17]

v. JOHN DAVID MAXSON b. May-23-1914 in Berea, Ritchie Co, WV,[373] d. Feb-26-1983 in Ogden, Wood Co, WV,[1770] buried in Evergreen North (aka Arlington) Cemetery, Rt 2 N of Parkersburg, Wood Co, WV, resided 1967 in Waverly, Wood Co, WV.[856] He married Oct-28-1939 in Boyd Co, KY,[mdcclxxi[1771]] Katheryn Louise Shepard,[190] also known as Louise Shepherd, also known as Katherine Louis Shepard,[1271] b. Jun- 1-1922 in Parkersburg, Wood Co, WV,[190] (daughter of Orel C. Shepard and Oma Congelgon), d. May-30-2004,[mdcclxxii[1772]] buried in Evergreen North (aka Arlington) Cemetery, Rt 2 N of Parkersburg, Wood Co, WV,[190] resided in Waverly, Wood Co, WV.[190]

vi. HANNAH PEARL MAXSON, also known as Pearl Maxson,[856] b. Sep-13-1916 in Berea, Ritchie Co, WV,[602,592] [Headstone shows birth date as 1917, but marriage record and SSDI state Sep 13 1916.], d. Apr-10-1976,[373,592] buried in Pine Grove Cemetery, Berea (Co Rd 7-26), Ritchie Co, WV,[469,1770] resided in West Union, Doddridge Co, WV,[604] resided 1952, 67 in Parkersburg, Wood Co, WV.[602,856] She married Jun-16-1952 in Parkersburg, Wood Co, WV,[602] Carl A. Meeks, also known as Ernest Carl Meeks,[1770] b. Mar-22-1918 in Pleasants Co, WV,[602] (son of Brady Jackson Meeks and Ella

V. Hackathorn), d. in Chester, Hancock Co, WV,[1770] buried in Chester, Hancock Co, WV,[1770] resided 1952 in East Liverpool, Columbiana Co, OH.[602]

   vii. WINIFRED LEIGH MAXSON b. Jan-26-1919 in Berea, Ritchie Co, WV,[17] d. Mar- 7-1994 in Baltimore, MD,[17] buried in Pine Grove Cemetery, Berea (Co Rd 7-26), Ritchie Co, WV,[1770] resided 1967 in Baltimore, MD,[856] never married[969,856].

   viii. MARIAM GRACE MAXSON, also known as Grace Maxson,[905] also known as Marion Maxson,[856] b. Mar- 4-1922 in Berea, Ritchie Co, WV,[373] resided 1967, 96 in Baltimore, MD.[856,905] She married Jan-24-1947, Leroy G. Eckman, d. in Baltimore, MD,[1770] buried in Baltimore, MD.[1770]

   ix. WAYMAN EUGENE MAXSON, also known as Eugene Maxson,[905] b. Jan-25-1926,[373] resided 1996, 2007 in Berea, Ritchie Co, WV,[905,191] resided 1967 in Davis, Tucker Co, WV.[856] He married Jan- 4-1947, Betty V. Cantwell, b. Sep-22-1927 near Cairo, Ritchie Co, WV,[190] (daughter of William Wallace Cantwell and Myrtle Lucille Carder), d. Mar-28-2007 in Berea, Ritchie Co, WV,[700] buried in Pine Grove Cemetery, Berea (Co Rd 7-26), Ritchie Co, WV,[190] resided in Berea, Ritchie Co, WV,[190] resided formerly in Davis, Tucker Co, WV,[190] occupation town recorder (Davis, WV) and bank employee,[190] education Parkersburg H.S. (1946).[190]

   Betty: Predeceased by two brothers and four sisters.

835. **Ernest Elias "Ernie" Jones** (464.Susan[8], 265.Samuel[7], 139.John[6], 72.John[5], 21.John[4], 6.Hugh[3], 3.John[2], 1.Jean[1]), b. Mar-27-1887 in Berea, Ritchie Co, WV,[373] d. Sep-18-1948 in Berea, Ritchie Co, WV,[969] buried in Pine Grove Cemetery, Berea (Co Rd 7-26), Ritchie Co, WV,[469] resided in Berea, Ritchie Co, WV.[521] He married Aug-15-1915 in Ritchie Co, WV,[473] **Ava Zetta Pride**, also known as Eva Pride, b. Dec-19-1894,[17,469] d. Aug-26-1963,[17,469] buried in Pine Grove Cemetery, Berea (Co Rd 7-26), Ritchie Co, WV.[469]

   Children:

   i. HAYWARD DENVER "H.D." JONES b. Aug-11-1916 in Berea, Ritchie Co, WV,[373] d. Mar-11-1985 in Little Rock, AR.[373] He married Oct-12-1944 in Carlisle, Lonoke Co, AR, Lavadia Odell Rochelle, b. Nov- 4-1925 in Carlisle, Lonoke Co, AR,[373] d. Jul- 5-1979 in Little Rock, AR.[373]

   ii. HAYNES O. JONES, also known as Hazel Jones, b. Aug-11-1916 in Berea, Ritchie Co, WV,[17,373] d. Oct- 2-1992 in Little Rock, AR,[17,373] buried in Pine Grove Cemetery, Berea (Co Rd 7-26), Ritchie Co, WV,[469] never married[969,982.]

   iii. ROXANA "ROXIE" JONES b. May-14-1918 in Berea, Ritchie Co, WV.[373] She married Oct-20-1943 in Riverdale, Prince Georges Co, MD, Robert Lester Lantz, b. Jun-12-1922 in Brave, Greene Co, PA,[373] d. Dec- 7-1969 in Greenbelt, Prince Georges Co, MD.[373]

   iv. LIVING. He married (1) Ruth Bridges, b. Dec-27-1925 in South Carolina,[373] d. Oct- 9-1979 in Bedford, Cuyahoga Co, OH.[373] He married (2) Living.

836. **James Morris Jones** (464.Susan[8], 265.Samuel[7], 139.John[6], 72.John[5], 21.John[4], 6.Hugh[3], 3.John[2], 1.Jean[1]), b. Mar- 5-1888 in Berea, Ritchie Co, WV,[398,mdcclxxiii[1773],190,721] d. Apr-19-1954 in Smithburg, Doddridge Co, WV,[190,mdcclxxiv[1774],721,398,mdcclxxv[1775]] [The History of Doddridge County, West Virginia, p. 178, gives death in 1954 in Smithburg. "West Union WV Cemeteries" reports headstone reading of Apr 19 1954, and researcher Marilynn Davis Jones also specifies Apr 19 1954, while Ota Reed Fraker reports Apr 19 1957, clearly incorrect. But Doddridge County Death Record and WV State Death Certificate both state Apr 20 1954 in Smithburg. Obituary specifies day of week as Monday at 11 p.m., which would coincide with Apr 19 1954.], buried in Masonic Memorial Park Cemetery, Crystal Lake (West Union), WV,[190,721,1773,398] resided in Smithburg, Doddridge Co, WV,[190,521,398] military U.S. Navy.[1774]

After the death of their mother when they were aged two and one, respectively, James Morris Jones and his brother Howard were reared in the home of their grandfather, Samuel Morris Gaston, and his second wife Rebecca Jane Furner Gaston. James spent four years in the Navy before getting married. He and family resided in Casterberry, Alabama from 1927 to 1930, then returned to West Virginia. During WW II, he and his wife moved to Baltimore, where he worked in the shipyards and she at an airplane factory. They returned to West Virginia only to have their home washed away by the great flood of 1950.[1774]

He married Nov-11-1917 in Doddridge Co, WV,[1774,354,484] **Stella Pearl Nutter**, b. Aug- 7-1898 in Oxford, Doddridge Co, WV,[190] (daughter of Thomas Boyd Nutter and Mary Frances Fleming), d. Jan-20-1999 in Clarksburg, Harrison Co, WV,[190] buried in Masonic Memorial Park Cemetery, Crystal Lake (West Union), WV,[190] resided 1950 in Smithburg, Doddridge Co, WV,[856] occupation cook.[190]
        Children:
        i.   BOYD HAINES JONES, also known as Haines Jones, b. Nov-16-1918 in Doddridge Co, WV,[721] d. Sep- 1-1944 in California,[190,1554,721] [Obituary stated that "Corporal Boyd Haynes Jones, 24, an aviation gunner who was expected to go overseas for duty, was killed in Muroc, California, in combat training." No town of that name can be found. His father's obituary stated only that he had been killed in plane crash in World War II.], buried in Masonic Memorial Park Cemetery, Crystal Lake (West Union), WV,[721] military Jan 1943 - Sep 1944 Cpl, U.S. Army Air Corps, WW II.[190,1554]
        ii.   FRANCES MARIE JONES b. Aug-24-1923,[17] d. Aug-24-1923,[17] buried in South Fork Bapt Church Cem, Oxford, Doddridge Co, WV.[17]
        iii.   LLOYD JAMES "JIM" JONES b. Jul- 4-1926 in Summers, Doddridge Co, WV,[190] d. Jul-13-1989 in West Union, Doddridge Co, WV,[190] buried in Masonic Memorial Park Cemetery, Crystal Lake (West Union), WV,[190,721] military U.S. Navy, WW II & Korean War.[190]

        Attended Salem College, West Virginia University, and was a graduate of the Wheeling Barber College. Operated a barber shop in Harrisville, WV. Owned and operated Jones Esso Service Station in West Union, WV. Was a US Navy veteran of WW II with service in the Pacific, and served during the Korean War. Retired in 1983 from the Weirton Steel Company, with 31 years service.[190]

        He married (1) Oct- 9-1947, divorced Mary Wanda Rose. He married (2) Living.

837. **Howard Harrison Jones** (464.Susan[8], 265.Samuel[7], 139.John[6], 72.John[5], 21.John[4], 6.Hugh[3], 3.John[2], 1.Jean[1]), b. Jan-23-1889 in Berea, Ritchie Co, WV,[190,721] [Birth date reported as Jan 23 1889 in "History of Doddridge County" (p. 177) and by first cousin Ota Reed Fraker. Obituary and headstone state Jan 27 1889. Death certificate, while not specifying birth date, states age at birth as 59y 6m 29d, which calculates to a birth date of Jan 22 1889. Death certificate states place of birth as Doddridge County, while all other sources indicate Ritchie County.], d. Aug-20-1948 near Hinton, Summers Co, WV,[190,mdcclxxvi[1776],1774] [Suffered a heart attack at Camp Thomas Lightfoot, near Hinton, Summers Co, WV. He was serving as an instructor in the camp, operated by a southern West Virginia coal company for the benefit of its employees' children. (obit)], buried in Masonic Memorial Park Cemetery, Crystal Lake (West Union), WV,[190,721] resided in Smithburg, Doddridge Co, WV,[190,398] occupation educator & State Delegate.

After the death of their mother in 1890, Howard Harrison Jones and his brother James were reared in the home of their grandfather, Samuel Morris Gaston, and his second wife Rebecca Jane Furner Gaston. Howard graduated from Glenville College in 1916, and was principal of Hillsboro Grade School in Pocahontas Co, WV. During the school year he was called into the Army due to World War I and was commissioned a Second Lieutenant in the Army Air Corps. He was discharged in 1918. He became Superintendent of Doddridge County Schools for eight years. He and wife Miriam served as counselors at Camp Lightfoot, near Hinton, attended by some 800 miners' children. [Miriam Hill Jones, in The History of Doddridge County, WV, 1979, p. 178] Elected to West Virginia House of Delegates for the 1935 term. [West Virginia Blue Book]

He married Apr-23-1919, **Miriam Hill**, b. Jul-17-1898 in Hillsboro, Pocahontas Co, WV,[190] (daughter of John Abraham Hill and Mary Elizabeth Campbell), d. Nov-30-1991 in Salem, WV,[190] buried in Masonic Memorial Park Cemetery, Crystal Lake (West Union), WV,[190] occupation grade school teacher.
        Children:

      i.   HOWARD HILL "BUCK" JONES b. Jan-22-1923 in Smithburg, Doddridge Co, WV, resided 2006 in Aurora, Portage Co, OH,[191] occupation Eastern Gas & Fuel Associates, Everett, MA & Pittsburgh, PA,[1774] education West Virginia University (1949, B.S. in Chemical Engineering),[1774] military U.S. Army Air Corps (1944-45).[1774] He married[191] Nov-24-1950,[1774] Melva D. Reeves, b. May-21-1926 in Massachusetts,[592,190] d. Nov-27-2006 in Aurora, Portage Co, OH,[700,592] buried in Masonic Memorial Park Cemetery, Crystal Lake (West Union), WV,[190] resided in Aurora, Portage Co, OH,[592] resided formerly in Pittsburgh, Allegheny Co, PA,[592] resided formerly in Massachusetts.[mdcclxxvii][1777]

838. **Bert David Jones** (464.Susan[8], 265.Samuel[7], 139.John[6], 72.John[5], 21.John[4], 6.Hugh[3], 3.John[2], 1.Jean[1]), b. Jul-31-1890 in Berea, Ritchie Co, WV,[190] d. Dec- 6-1956 in Fairmont, Marion Co, WV,[190] buried in West Virginia [Daughter-in-law Marilynn Davis Jones reports his burial at Beverly Hills Cemetery, Morgantown, WV, while his obituary states that "interment was made in Fairmont."], resided in Fairmont, Marion Co, WV,[521] occupation B&O Railroad Engineer.[373] He married Oct-20-1914 in Webster Springs, Webster Co, WV, **Florence Ardelia Shreve**, b. Jul- 9-1895 in Wetzel Co, WV (daughter of Augustus Shreve and Rebecca Utt), d. Nov-12-1981 in Taylor Co, WV, buried in Beverly Hills Memorial Gardens, Westover, Monongalia Co, WV.

Florence: Last name may be Shrieves.[969]

          Children:
      i.   RUBY FERN JONES b. Aug-29-1915 in Fairmont, Marion Co, WV, d. Nov-22-1992 in Fairmont, Marion Co, WV.

          Ruby Jones Fast, with Dr. Vosher, originated what is now the Fairmont Clinic. She transcribed medical records for Fairmont General Hospital, Fairmont Clinic and St. Joseph's Hospital in Tampa, FL.[373]

          She married Sep-27-1935 in Oakland, Garrett Co, MD, Chester LeRoy Fast, b. Dec-13-1910 in Taylor Co, WV, d. Jun-12-1995 in Marion Co, WV.[373]
      ii.   AUGUSTUS REX JONES, also known as Rex Jones, b. Jul-31-1919 in Fairmont, Marion Co, WV,[373] d. Oct-17-1992 in Fairmont, Marion Co, WV,[373] buried in Beverly Hills Memorial Gardens, Westover, Monongalia Co, WV, occupation railroad coal representative, military U.S. Army, World War II.[373]

          Worked for the State Department in Washington, DC, Caracas, Venezuela, and LaPaz, Bolivia.[373]

          He married May-15-1948 in Fairmont, Marion Co, WV,[373] Marilynn Jean Davis, b. Oct-30-1919 (daughter of Cole Davis and Georgia Lora Wade), occupation Fairmont State College.

          Marilynn: Graduate of Fairmont State College, Masters from West Virginia University. Taught in Marion, Monongalia and Baltimore County schools, and was Associate Professor in English at Fairmont State College for 15 years.

      iii.   DALE WREN JONES b. Dec-24-1927 in Fairmont, Marion Co, WV, d. Nov-10-1996 in Cincinnati, Hamilton Co, OH, military U.S. Navy, World War II.[373]

          Graduate of West Virginia University, and earned PhD from University of Cincinnati. Retired from Cincinnati school system as administrator, then worked for IRS and University of Kentucky.[373]

          He married Jun-17-1950 in Fairmont, Marion Co, WV, Virginia Alkire, b. Feb-10-1923 in Idamay, Marion Co, WV,[1011,592] (daughter of __ Alkire and __ Mallow), d. Dec-26-2002 in Cincinnati, Hamilton Co, OH,[592,1011] resided in Cincinnati, Hamilton Co, OH.[604,1011]

839. **Luther Sherman Britton**, census name Sherman L. Brittin,[1733] (465.Hannah[8], 265.Samuel[7], 139.John[6], 72.John[5], 21.John[4], 6.Hugh[3], 3.John[2], 1.Jean[1]), b. Jan-17-1878 in Doddridge Co, WV,[969,938] d. Nov-16-1945,[969] resided 1940 in Clinton District, Monongalia Co, WV, census 1930 in Clinton District, Monongalia Co, WV, census 1910, 1920 in Morgantown, Monongalia Co, WV, resided 1908, 1921 in Morgantown, Monongalia Co, WV.[938,765] He married Aug-18-1908 in Morgantown, Monongalia Co, WV,[mdcclxxviii[1778]] **Pearl J. Rogers**, b. Oct- 1-1887 in Monongalia Co, WV,[398,938] (daughter of Andrew J. Rogers and Mary McGowan), d. Dec-16-1940 in Halleck, Monongalia Co, WV,[398] buried in Halleck Cemetery, Monongalia Co, WV,[398] census 1930 in Clinton District, Monongalia Co, WV, census 1910, 1920 in Morgantown, Monongalia Co, WV, resided 1908 in Morgantown, Monongalia Co, WV.[938] 1910 Census, Monongalia Co, WV (city of Morgantown): Luther S. Britton, 32, no occupation, married 2 yrs; wife Lena A, 26, occupation nurse at city hospital, no children.
(Note: Basis for wife's name being entered as Lena A is not known. She was identified as Pearl in her death record and as Pearl J in her marriage record and 1920 Census.)

1920 Census, Monongalia Co, WV (city of Morgantown), enumerated on Jan 12 1920:
L. S. Britton, 40, salesman; wife Pearl J, 30; son George W, 5; son Luther S, 4 yr 6 mo; son Harold R, 3 yr 2 mo; son Howard J, 1 yr 7 mo.

1930 Census, Monongalia Co, WV (Clinton District), enumerated on Apr 17 1930:
Sherman L. Brittin, 52, school teacher; wife Pearl, 42; son George W, 16; son Luther S, 14; son Harold R, 13; son Howard J, 11; son Morris H, 9; dau Winnie, 4; dau Maude, 2.

Children:
i. GEORGE WASHINGTON BRITTON b. ca 1914,[1741] census 1930 in Clinton District, Monongalia Co, WV, census 1920 in Morgantown, Monongalia Co, WV. He married[969] Mary Ellen Shockey, also known as Ellen Shockey.
ii. LUTHER SHERMAN BRITTON II b. ca 1915,[1741] census 1930 in Clinton District, Monongalia Co, WV, census 1920 in Morgantown, Monongalia Co, WV. He married[969] Ruth D. Rumble.
iii. HAROLD ROGERS BRITTON b. ca 1916,[1741] census 1930 in Clinton District, Monongalia Co, WV, census 1920 in Morgantown, Monongalia Co, WV. He married[969] Ruth Cottrell.
iv. HOWARD J. BRITTON b. ca 1918,[1741] census 1930 in Clinton District, Monongalia Co, WV, census 1920 in Morgantown, Monongalia Co, WV. He married[969] June ___.
v. MORRIS HARDING BRITTON b. ca 1921,[1733] census 1930 in Clinton District, Monongalia Co, WV. He married[969] Betty Bradford.
vi. WINNIE PEARL BRITTON b. ca 1926,[1733] census 1930 in Clinton District, Monongalia Co, WV. She married[969] William M. Lafferty.
vii. LIVING. She married[969] Living.

840. **Charles Wesley Britton** (465.Hannah[8], 265.Samuel[7], 139.John[6], 72.John[5], 21.John[4], 6.Hugh[3], 3.John[2], 1.Jean[1]), b. Jul-19-1882 in Newberne, Gilmer Co, WV,[398,969] d. Nov-14-1950 in Parkersburg, Wood Co, WV,[398,969] buried in Mt. Olivet Cemetery, Parkersburg, WV,[398] resided in Parkersburg, Wood Co, WV,[398] resided 1921 in Charleston, Kanawha Co, WV,[765] occupation oil & gas production.[398] He married May-25-1914, **Mary Ann Riggs**, resided 1950 in Parkersburg, Wood Co, WV.[228]
Children:
i. CHARLES EDWARD BRITTON. He married[1539] Mary Avis Williams.

841. **Zebidee Warner Britton**, also known as Warner Britton,[765,398] [First name has also appeared as Zebedee and Jebidee.] (465.Hannah[8], 265.Samuel[7], 139.John[6], 72.John[5], 21.John[4], 6.Hugh[3], 3.John[2], 1.Jean[1]), b. Feb- 9-1887 in Newberne, Gilmer Co, WV,[398] d. May-24-1955 in Vienna, Wood Co, WV,[398] buried in Mt. Olivet Cemetery, Parkersburg, WV,[398] resided in Vienna, Wood Co, WV,[398] resided 1921 in Louisa, Lawrence Co, KY,[765] occupation oil field contractor,[398] military World War I.[398] He married Feb-14-1920,[969] **Myrtle Samples**, resided 1955 in Vienna, Wood Co, WV.[228]

Children:

i.   AVA ALICE BRITTON. She married[969] Robert W. Trout.

ii.   ANNA LOUISE BRITTON, also known as Louise Britton, b. Jun- 8-1924,[592] d. Jul- 5-2002,[592] resided in Vienna, Wood Co, WV.[604] She married[969] McHenry Page.

iii.   MARIAN ELIZABETH BRITTON. She married[969] D. Beryl Cooper, also known as Berry Cooper.

iv.   WARNER MAX BRITTON, also known as W. Max Britton,[592,909] b. Jan-11-1927,[592] d. Jan-19-1999,[592] buried in Mt. Olivet Cemetery, Parkersburg, WV,[909] resided in Vienna, Wood Co, WV,[604] military U.S. Navy, World War II.[909] He married[969] Mary Louise Carmichael, also known as Mary Lou Carmichael.

842. **DeWitt Talmadge Britton**, also known as D. Talmadge Britton,[190] (465.Hannah[8], 265.Samuel[7], 139.John[6], 72.John[5], 21.John[4], 6.Hugh[3], 3.John[2], 1.Jean[1]), b. Jun-17-1892 in Gilmer Co, WV,[190,969,996] d. Sep-25-1958 in Clarksburg, Harrison Co, WV,[806,969] resided 1921-58 in Mannington, Marion Co, WV,[765,190] occupation Carnegie Natural Gas Co (35 yrs).[190] He married (1) Jun-14-1916,[969] divorced bef Dec 1931,[996] [Husband's marital status listed as divorced at time of his remarriage to Martha M. Riddle on Dec 30 1931. There was no mention of marriage to Ruby in husband's obituary. Only second wife is mentioned.], **Ruby Haskins**. He married (2) Dec-30-1931 in Ritchie Co, WV,[mdcclxxix[1779]] **Martha Magdalene Riddle**, b. ca 1907,[996] resided 1958 in Mannington, Marion Co, WV.[484]

Children by Ruby Haskins:

i.   (UNNAMED TWIN SONS) BRITTON b. 1919,[969] d. 1919,[969] [at birth].

ii.   (UNNAMED SON) BRITTON b. 1921,[969] d. 1921,[969] [at birth].

843. **Eva Maude Britton**, also known as Maude (465.Hannah[8], 265.Samuel[7], 139.John[6], 72.John[5], 21.John[4], 6.Hugh[3], 3.John[2], 1.Jean[1]), b. Aug-27-1897,[969,592] d. Aug-30-1973 [SSDI reports death date as Sep 1973.], resided in Charleston, Kanawha Co, WV,[765,521,592.] She married Feb-20-1924,[969] **Theodore Jackson Childress**.

Children:

i.   THEODORE JACKSON CHILDRESS, JR.. He married[969] Imogene Samples.

ii.   JOSEPH BRITTON CHILDRESS. He married[969] Clara June Fields.

iii.   JEANETTE CHILDRESS. She married[969] (1) Kenneth E. Holmes. She married[1539] (2) Richard G. Jackson.

844. **Laura Elizabeth Chapman** (466.Columbia[8], 265.Samuel[7], 139.John[6], 72.John[5], 21.John[4], 6.Hugh[3], 3.John[2], 1.Jean[1]), b. Feb-21-1885 in Wolf Pen Run, New Milton, Doddridge Co, WV,[mdcclxxx[1780],1166] d. May-22-1983, buried in Bridgeport Cemetery, Harrison Co, WV. She married Apr- 1-1912, **Otto D. Goodwin**, b. Jun-27-1880 (son of Marshall S. Goodwin and Susan Jane Greene), d. Dec-13-1957.

Children:

i.   ELEANOR RUTH GOODWIN b. Jul-19-1913,[982] d. bef Oct 2007, resided in Point Pleasant, Mason Co, WV, never married.

ii.   JAMES CHAPMAN GOODWIN b. Jun- 5-1915 in Clarksburg, Harrison Co, WV,[190,592] d. Oct-15-2007 in Peterstown, Monroe Co, WV,[764,592] resided in Pearisburg, Giles Co, VA,[190,948] occupation chemical engineer at Celanese plant in Narrows, VA.[190]

He was a member of the Pearisburg Volunteer Fire Department, with 15 years as Chief.

He married Elizabeth Arlene McDowell, also known as Arlene McDowell,[484] b. May- 1-1915, d. bef Oct 2007,[484] resided originally in Morgantown, Monongalia Co, WV.

iii.   FRANCES LUCILLE GOODWIN b. Jul-19-1917,[982] d. May-10-1994,[mdcclxxxi[1781]] resided in Durham, Butte Co, CA,[592] resided formerly in West Virginia.[604] She married Jun-27-1947,[982] Roy Emery Logan, b. May-12-1910,[592] d. Sep- 3-1986,[592] resided in Nelson, Butte Co, CA,[592] resided formerly in Salida, CO,[982] resided formerly in Washington State.[1153]

iv. JANE ALDINE GOODWIN b. Mar-30-1919 in Clarksburg, Harrison Co, WV,[17] d. Jan-28-1995 in Morgantown, Monongalia Co, WV,[17] buried in Smith Cemetery, Uler, Roane Co, WV.[17] She married Jun-26-1945 in Bridgeport, Harrison Co, WV, Lionel Leon Smith, b. Sep- 3-1913 in Uler, Roane Co, WV,[190,592] (son of William Cary Smith and Ida Almira Boggs), d. Feb-28-2008 in Huntington, Cabell Co, WV,[806,592] buried in Smith Cemetery, Uler, Roane Co, WV,[190] resided in Point Pleasant, Mason Co, WV,[592,190] resided originally in Uler, Roane Co, WV, occupation teacher, soil conservation agent (Mason Co WV),[190] education Clay Co HS, Glenville State College, West Va. Univ (BA, MA in agriculture),[190] military U.S. Army, World War II in Africa & Italy (Purple Heart).[190]

v. WALTER BRUCE "JACK" GOODWIN b. Apr-21-1921, resided 2007 in Bridgeport, Harrison Co, WV.[521] He married (1) Dec-12-1947, divorced 1949, Wilma Lee Brown, resided in Clarksburg, Harrison Co, WV. He married[910] (2) Nov- 9-1950 in Clarksburg, Harrison Co, WV, Dorothy Lee McCarty, b. Feb-13-1925 (daughter of Omer C. McCarty), resided 2007 in Bridgeport, Harrison Co, WV.[910]

vi. BETTY LEE GOODWIN b. Jul-14-1923, d. Mar- 6-1985. She married Jan-25-1944, Robert Lewis Looney, b. Apr- 4-1923, d. Mar- 2-1986.

845. **Emma Grace Chapman**, also known as Grace Chapman,[982,592] also known as Grace C. Bortz,[693] (466.Columbia[8], 265.Samuel[7], 139.John[6], 72.John[5], 21.John[4], 6.Hugh[3], 3.John[2], 1.Jean[1]), b. May-31-1889 in West Virginia,[693,592,982] d. Oct-29-1977 in Los Angeles Co, CA,[693,592,982] resided in Yorba Linda, Orange Co, CA.[mdcclxxxii[1782]] She married May-25-1925,[982] **Lewis Arthur Bortz**, b. Apr-15-1882 in Iowa,[693] (son of __ Bortz and __ Larson), d. May- 7-1953 in Orange Co, CA.[693]
Children:
i. ALICE ANN BORTZ b. Mar-20-1926. She married Aug-26-1951, Paul Russell Armstrong.
ii. LIVING. She married Living.
iii. LIVING. He married Living.

846. **Palbie Gale Chapman** (466.Columbia[8], 265.Samuel[7], 139.John[6], 72.John[5], 21.John[4], 6.Hugh[3], 3.John[2], 1.Jean[1]), b. Aug-10-1896, d. Apr-24-1976, buried in Carthage Gap Church Cem, Athens Co, OH.

Name has also appeared as Pallie Gall Chapman.[969]

He married Sep- 2-1919, **Faye Mildred Marshall**, b. Sep- 7-1895, d. Jun-30-1987, buried in Carthage Gap Church Cem, Athens Co, OH.
Children:
i. JOSEPH FLOYD CHAPMAN b. May- 6-1920, d. May-24-1984. He married (1) Aug-13-1950, divorced Vivian Halstern.

Vivian: Last name may be Holstein.[969]

He married (2) Jun- -1969, divorced Marie Erwin. He married (3) Jo Jo Goddard.
ii. ROBERT MARSHALL CHAPMAN b. Jul- 6-1923. He married Jun-29-1947, Janet Palk.
iii. LIVING. She married Living.

Jack: Last name may be Nanse.[969]

847. **Harley Hall Chapman**, also known as Hall Chapman (466.Columbia[8], 265.Samuel[7], 139.John[6], 72.John[5], 21.John[4], 6.Hugh[3], 3.John[2], 1.Jean[1]), b. Oct-14-1900, d. May- 5-1979. He married Jan- 2-1925, **Sarah Helen Falls**, also known as Helen Falls, b. Jul-21-1898, d. Aug-13-1979.
Children:
i. LIVING. She married Living.
ii. LIVING. He married Living.

848. **Majel Ellen Chapman** (466.Columbia[8], 265.Samuel[7], 139.John[6], 72.John[5], 21.John[4], 6.Hugh[3], 3.John[2], 1.Jean[1]), b. Feb- 3-1905, d. Apr-29-1981, resided in Fredericktown, Knox Co, OH.[592] She married Dec-23-1928, **Otis Ray Kiracofe**, b. Mar-29-1901, d. Dec-24-1981, resided in Columbus, Franklin Co, OH.[592]

> Children:
> i. LARRY HAMILTON KIRACOFE b. Nov- 6-1934, d. Nov-15-1995,[592] resided in Warren, Trumbull Co, OH.[592] He married Living.
> ii. LIVING. She married Living.
> iii. LIVING. He married Living.

849. **Lenora Squires Gaston**, also known as Alda Lenora Squires (467.Morris[8], 265.Samuel[7], 139.John[6], 72.John[5], 21.John[4], 6.Hugh[3], 3.John[2], 1.Jean[1]), b. Oct-20-1917,[592] d. Dec- 4-2001,[592] resided 1969 in Weirton, Hancock Co, WV,[412] census 1930 in Southwest District, Doddridge Co, WV.

In the wake of her mother's death shortly after giving birth, Lenora Squires Gaston was raised from infancy by Morris Samuel Gaston and his wife Hattie I. Adams Gaston, and she therefore adopted the Gaston family name. Morris Samuel Gaston was a first cousin of baby Lenora's maternal grandmother, Mary Isabelle Gaston Adams, and a second cousin of her paternal grandmother, Elizabeth Laverna Gaston Squires. There is speculation that Hattie Adams was also a blood relative. The obituary of Morris Samuel Gaston identified as a surviving "foster daughter, Mrs. Cyril Scott of Oxford." Lenora took up residence in Weirton, WV. Her mother's obituary identifies her as Lenore [sic] Scott, her husband's obituary identifies her as Lenore [sic] Squires Gaston Scott, and the Social Security Death Index lists her name as Lenore [sic] Scott.

She married Nov-23-1939,[969] **Cyril Alfred Scott**, b. Feb-25-1914 in West Union, Doddridge Co, WV,[190] (son of Alfred Oran Scott and Ethel G. Dotson), d. Sep-20-1991 in Weirton, Hancock Co, WV,[190] buried in South Fork Bapt Church Cem, Oxford, Doddridge Co, WV,[190,17] resided in Weirton, Hancock Co, WV,[190] occupation bander at Weirton Steel Corp in strip steel dept.[190]

> Children:
> i. (SON) SCOTT b. Oct-30-1940,[17] d. Oct-30-1940,[17] buried in South Fork Bapt Church Cem, Oxford, Doddridge Co, WV.[17]
> ii. LIVING. She married Living.
> iii. LIVING. She married Living.

850. **Asby Steele Law**, census name Steel A. Law,[418] also known as A. Steele Law,[724] also known as Ashby S. Law,[398] also known as Steele Law,[493] also known as A. S. Law,[778] (468.John[8], 266.Deborah[7], 139.John[6], 72.John[5], 21.John[4], 6.Hugh[3], 3.John[2], 1.Jean[1]), b. Aug-17-1869 in Union District, Ritchie Co, WV,[mdcclxxxiii[1783],398,467] d. Mar-15-1935 in Clarksburg, Harrison Co, WV,[398] buried in Elkview Masonic Cemetery, Clarksburg, Harrison Co, WV,[462] resided near Bridgeport in Taylor Co, WV,[398] census 1900, 10, 20, 30 in Clarksburg, Harrison Co, WV, census 1880 in Grant District, Harrison Co, WV [Along with his mother, he was listed in the household of his paternal great-grandparents, John & Elizabeth (Morris) Gaston.], census 1870 in Union District, Ritchie Co, WV, occupation truck farmer,[398] occupation 1910, 1920, 1930 book store merchant/manager.[458,418,1208.] He married[228] Oct- 5-1899 in Pruntytown, Taylor Co, WV,[724] **Launa Gawthrop**, b. Oct- -1877 in Taylor Co, WV,[467,724] d. Nov-17-1964,[462] buried in Elkview Masonic Cemetery, Clarksburg, Harrison Co, WV,[462] resided 1935 in Mannington, Marion Co, WV,[228] census 1900, 10, 20, 30 in Clarksburg, Harrison Co, WV, resided 1899 in Pruntytown, Taylor Co, WV.[724]

1900 Census, Harrison Co, WV (Clark District, city of Clarksburg), enumerated in Jun 1900 at 407 Main Street:
A. S. Law, 30, b. Aug 1869, occupation illegible, married 1 yr; wife Launa, 22, b. Oct 1877, no children.

1910 Census, Harrison Co, WV (Clark District, city of Clarksburg), enumerated on Apr 30 1910 at 215 Webster Street:

Asby S. Law, 41, bookstore merchant, married 11 yrs; wife Launa, 32, mother of 2 children (both still living); son Raymond, 10; dau Marie R, 8; cousin Clyde O. Law, 23, single, high school teacher.

1920 Census, Harrison Co, WV (Clark District, city of Clarksburg), enumerated on Jan 16 1920 at 215 Webster Street:
Steel A. Law, 50, bookstore manager; wife Launa, 42; son Raymon G, 19, single; dau Rosalie M, 18, single

1930 Census, Harrison Co, WV (Clark District, city of Clarksburg), enumerated on Apr 16 1930 at 419 East Main Street:
Asby S. Law, 60, bookstore manager; wife Launa, 52; dau R. Marie, 28, single, public school teacher.

        Children:
        i.   RAYMOND G. LAW b. ca 1901,[418] census 1920, 1920 in Clarksburg, Harrison Co, WV.
        ii.   ROSALIE MARIE LAW, census name Marie R. Law,[458] census name R. Marie Law,[1208] b. ca 1902,[418] census 1910, 1920, 1930 in Clarksburg, Harrison Co, WV.

851. **Olive B. Law** (469.Francis[8], 266.Deborah[7], 139.John[6], 72.John[5], 21.John[4], 6.Hugh[3], 3.John[2], 1.Jean[1]), b. ca 1870,[473] resided 1916, 25 in Lawford, Ritchie Co, WV.[765,228] She married[941] Aug-16-1885 in Ritchie Co, WV,[473] **Lafayette Syrus Goff**,[398] b. Jul-27-1862 at Goffs, Ritchie Co, WV,[398,473] (son of Lafayette S. Goff and Carlina Gough), d. Jul-13-1925 at Lawford, Ritchie Co, WV,[398] buried in Lawford Cemetery, Ritchie Co, WV,[398] occupation farmer.[398]
        Children:
        i.   ELMAS TREVY GOFF b. Dec-14-1888,[154] d. Feb-23-1937 in Ritchie Co, WV.[955]
        ii.   RUBLE DOY GOFF, census name Doy Goff,[1020] b. Mar-18-1898,[17] d. Sep-25-1953,[17] buried in IOOF Cemetery, Harrisville, Ritchie Co, WV,[469] census 1930 in Union District, Ritchie Co, WV, occupation farmer,[1020] military Pvt, TNG Corps, U.S. Army, World War I.[469] He married ca 1920,[1020] Martha W. __, b. Mar-21-1900,[17] d. Apr-28-1966,[17] buried in IOOF Cemetery, Harrisville, Ritchie Co, WV,[469] census 1930 in Union District, Ritchie Co, WV.

        1930 Census, Ritchie Co, WV (Union District), enumerated on Apr 17 1930:
        Doy Goff, 32, farmer, age 22 at time of first marriage; wife Martha W, 30; age 20 at time of first marriage; son Jack E, 8; son Joe W (M ?), 7; son Jimmie L, 2y 11m; son John A, 11 months; mother Olive B, 59, widowed, age 15 at time of first marriage; brother Glen L, 19, widowed.

        iii. GLEN L. GOFF b. ca 1911,[1020] census 1930 in Union District, Ritchie Co, WV.

852. **Ora Alice Law** (469.Francis[8], 266.Deborah[7], 139.John[6], 72.John[5], 21.John[4], 6.Hugh[3], 3.John[2], 1.Jean[1]), b. 1873,[46,473] d. May-17-1962 in Ritchie Co, WV,[477,46] buried in Bethany UM Church Cem (Rt 28 btwn Goffs & Prunty), Ritchie Co WV,[469] resided 1916, 45 in Goffs, Ritchie Co, WV.[765,228] She married[941] Aug-16-1891 in Ritchie Co, WV,[473] **Alfieri Goff**, b. Jul-5-1870 at Goffs, Ritchie Co, WV,[398,473] (son of Elijah C. Goff and Priscilla Clarissa Bee), d. Jul-15-1945 at Washburn, Ritchie Co, WV,[398] buried in Bethany UM Church Cem (Rt 28 btwn Goffs & Prunty), Ritchie Co WV,[398,469] resided in Goffs, Ritchie Co, WV,[398] occupation farmer.[398]
        Children:
        i.   MILDRED GOFF b. Oct-4-1915,[17] d. Sep-24-1916,[17] buried in Bethany UM Church Cem (Rt 28 btwn Goffs & Prunty), Ritchie Co WV.[469]

853. **Alva A. Law** (469.Francis[8], 266.Deborah[7], 139.John[6], 72.John[5], 21.John[4], 6.Hugh[3], 3.John[2], 1.Jean[1]), b. Jan--1876,[809,46,473] d. 1950,[46] buried in Lawford Cemetery, Ritchie Co, WV,[469] resided 1916 in Lawford, Ritchie Co, WV.[765] He married Oct-31-1901 in Ritchie Co, WV,[473] **Bertha C. Bartlett**, b. Nov--1877,[809,46,473] d. 1968,[46] buried in Lawford Cemetery, Ritchie Co, WV,[469] census 1900 in Union District, Ritchie Co, WV.
        Children:

i.   TROY G. LAW b. Oct-24-1902,[592,996] d. Jan- -1977,[592] resided in Madison, Boone Co, WV,[604] census 1910 in Union District, Ritchie Co, WV. He married Dec-19-1927 in Ritchie Co, WV, Gertrude Maude Pettit, b. ca 1906 in Marion Co, WV,[996] resided 1927 in Ritchie Co, WV.[996]

ii.   HOLMES G. LAW b. Oct- 7-1906,[592,1015] d. Nov- -1973,[592] resided in Weirton, Hancock Co, WV,[604] census 1910 in Union District, Ritchie Co, WV.

854. **Dorsey Elden Huff** (470.Hannah[8], 266.Deborah[7], 139.John[6], 72.John[5], 21.John[4], 6.Hugh[3], 3.John[2], 1.Jean[1]), b. Oct- 4-1882 in Lawford, Ritchie Co, WV,[190,496] d. Dec-15-1974 in Parkersburg, Wood Co, WV,[mdcclxxxiv[1784]] buried in Masonic Memorial Park Cemetery, Crystal Lake (West Union), WV,[190,721] census 1920, 1930 in Cove District, Doddridge Co, WV, occupation field worker for South Penn Natural Gas Co.[190] He married[484] Apr-19-1903 in Ritchie Co, WV,[473] [Marriage date of Apr 19 1902 given in husband's obituary, but marriage record indicates Apr 19 1903.], **Vicy L. Stansberry**, census name Love P.,[mdcclxxxv[1785]] b. Jun- 5-1885 in Ritchie Co, WV,[190] (daughter of Moses Franklin "Frank" Stansberry and Evelyn Clayton), d. Oct-24-1977 in Oxford, Doddridge Co, WV,[mdcclxxxvi[1786]] buried in Masonic Memorial Park Cemetery, Crystal Lake (West Union), WV,[190,721] resided at Oxford, Doddridge Co, WV,[190] census 1920, 1930 in Cove District, Doddridge Co, WV. 1930 Census, Doddridge Co, WV (Cove District):
Dorsey E. Huff, 46; wife Love P, 44; dau Iala J, 18; dau Hannah E, 15; son Dorsey E Jr, 13; dau Mary M, 9y 8m; son John W, 3y 10m; boarder Willis J. Rymer, 19; boarder Malcolm Conley, 36.

Children:
i.   FERN HUFF b. Jul- 8-1904 in Ritchie Co, WV,[190] d. Oct- 4-1988 in Parkersburg, Wood Co, WV,[190] resided in Glenville, Gilmer Co, WV,[190,856] buried in Meadow Lane Cemetery, Glenville, Gilmer Co, WV.[190]

Resident of Glenville, Gilmer Co, and Parkersburg, Wood Co, WV. She graduated from Glenville Normal School in 1927 and was a former school teacher. For several years, she was president and a director of the West Virginia State Folk Festival, and was intrumental in its development. She was also active in the founding and development of the Country Store in Glenville, supported by the West Virginia State Folk Festival.[190]

She married[191] E. G. "Rolly" Rollyson,[191] d. bef Oct 1988.[191]

ii.   (INFANT FEMALE) HUFF d. in infancy.[765]

iii.   JUANITA HUFF, census name Iala J. Huff,[mdcclxxxvii[1787]] b. May-14-1911,[592,1123] d. Sep-14-1985 in Saint Lucie Co, FL,[592,1123] resided in Fort Pierce, Saint Lucie Co, FL,[765,856,521,412,592] resided formerly in West Virginia.[604] She married (1) Jun-28-1934 in Doddridge Co, WV,[354] James Foley, b. 1909,[354,721] d. 1935,[721] buried in Masonic Memorial Park Cemetery, Crystal Lake (West Union), WV.[721]

James: Middle initial reported as T in "Doddridge County Marriage Records," but as F in "West Union Cemeteries."

She married[941,424] (2) __ Sewick.

iv.   HANNAH E. HUFF b. May-23-1914 in Doddridge Co, WV,[190] d. May-23-1983 in Orlando, Orange Co, FL.[190]

Resident of Sanford, FL for 23 years, formerly of Doddridge Co, WV. She was employed as a school teacher and librarian at the Lakeview Middle School in Sanford.[190,765,856,521]

She married[191,941] no children from this marriage, James Boyd Smith, b. Feb- 9-1912 in West Union, Doddridge Co, WV,[190] (son of James Alvin Smith and Lula M. Drane), d. Sep-29-1974 in Sanford, Seminole Co, FL,[190] buried in Freeman Cemetery, Piggin Run, West Union, WV,[190] resided in Sanford, Seminole Co, FL,[190] resided formerly in West Union, Doddridge Co, WV,[190] census 1920 in West Union District, Doddridge Co, WV, education West Union H.S., West Virginia University Law School,[190] military Lieutenant Commander, U.S. Navy, World War II.[190]

James: He was a former prosecuting attorney for Doddridge County, was formerly employed in the legal department of the Veterans Administration in Huntington, WV, and was former owner and manager of Western Auto Supply at Romney, Hampshire Co, WV. At the time of his death, he was associated with the Jim Hunt Realty in Sanford, FL.[190]

     v.   DORSEY ELDEN "BUD" HUFF, JR. b. Oct- 5-1916 in Grove, Doddridge Co, WV,[190] d. Nov-12-1979,[190] buried (ashes) in Dallas, TX,[190] resided from 1946 in Kermit, Winkler Co, TX,[190] resided until 1946 in West Union, Doddridge Co, WV,[190] occupation water well driller and contractor,[190] military World War II.[190] He married May- 5-1940 in Catlettsburg, KY,[484] Rosalea Williams, b. Dec-17-1922,[592] (daughter of Lee O. Williams and Jessie Smith), d. Oct-15-1998,[592] resided in Kermit, Winkler Co, TX,[765,592,mdcclxxxviii[1788]] resided formerly in West Virginia.[604]

     vi.   MARY M. HUFF b. Jul- 1-1920 in Grove, Doddridge Co, WV,[190] d. Apr-30-2001 in McConnelsville, Morgan Co, OH,[190] buried in Masonic Memorial Park Cemetery, Crystal Lake (West Union), WV,[190,721] resided 1938 in Marion Co, WV,[589] census 1930 in Cove District, Doddridge Co, WV. She married[191] Mar-15-1938 in Nutter Fort, Harrison Co, WV,[589] Frank Burton Christie, Jr., b. Oct-13-1918 in Smithburg, Doddridge Co, WV,[190,592] (son of Frank Burton Christie and Hattie Virginia Stoneking), d. Jul-24-2002 in Marietta, Washington Co, OH,[190,592] buried in Masonic Memorial Park Cemetery, Crystal Lake (West Union), WV,[190,721] resided in Belpre, Washington Co, OH,[190] resided 1938 in Clarksburg, Harrison Co, WV,[589] occupation foreman at River Gas Co of Belpre (retired),[190] education Doddridge Co H.S., Mountain State Business College (Parkersburg),[190] military U.S. Navy, World War II.[190]

     vii.   JOHN WESLEY HUFF b. Jun-27-1926,[721,592] d. Aug-21-1976 in Shinnston, Harrison Co, WV,[190,592] buried in Masonic Memorial Park Cemetery, Crystal Lake (West Union), WV,[190,721] resided 1974 in Shinnston, Harrison Co, WV,[765] census 1930 in Cove District, Doddridge Co, WV.

855. **Richie D. Law** (471.David[8], 266.Deborah[7], 139.John[6], 72.John[5], 21.John[4], 6.Hugh[3], 3.John[2], 1.Jean[1]), b. Jun-10-1881,[496] d. Oct-14-1971,[496] buried in Lawford Cemetery, Ritchie Co, WV,[469] resided 1939 at Lawford, Ritchie Co, WV,[778] census 1920 in Gilmer Co, WV, census 1900 in Union District, Ritchie Co, WV. He married Apr-15-1905 in Ritchie Co, WV,[473] **Lida Viola Bartlett**, also known as Lydia B. Bartlett,[396] b. 1883,[46,473] [Birthdate given in 1900 Census as Dec 1884. But headstone date is 1883.], d. 1971,[46] buried in Lawford Cemetery, Ritchie Co, WV,[469] census 1920 in Gilmer Co, WV, census 1900 in Union District, Ritchie Co, WV [listed as a boarder in household of Lafayette Zinn].

     Children:

     i.   DAVID KYLE LAW b. Apr-30-1906 in Lawford, Ritchie Co, WV,[398,996,1715] d. Jul-24-1954 in Parkersburg, Wood Co, WV,[398] buried in Evergreen Cemetery, Parkersburg, WV,[398] resided in Parkersburg, Wood Co, WV,[398] resided 1939 in Harrisville, Ritchie Co, WV,[396] census 1920 in Gilmer Co, WV, occupation layout man, Parkersburg Rig & Reel Co.[398] He married Sep- 6-1926 in Ritchie Co, WV,[996] Reba Wright, also known as Rebah Wright,[996] also known as Eva Viva Wright,[396] b. ca 1903 in Lawford, Ritchie Co, WV,[996,396] (daughter of Addison A. I. Wright and Lenora L. "Nora" Wright), resided 1954 in Parkersburg, Wood Co, WV,[228] census 1910 in Union District, Ritchie Co, WV.

     ii.   ELDRIDGE DILE LAW b. Nov-27-1907,[17] d. Jun- 9-1980,[17] buried in Lawford Cemetery, Ritchie Co, WV,[469] census 1920 in Gilmer Co, WV, military Pfc, U.S. Army, World War II.[469] He married[374] Feb- 2-1927 in Ritchie Co, WV,[996] Wanda Lee Prather, b. Sep-22-1906,[17] d. Mar- 5-1989,[17] buried in Lawford Cemetery, Ritchie Co, WV.[469]

     iii.   MONA V. LAW b. Jan- 1-1910,[592,46,1715] d. Mar- -1977,[592,46] buried in Lawford Cemetery, Ritchie Co, WV,[469] resided in Parkersburg, Wood Co, WV,[604] census 1920 in Gilmer Co, WV.

     iv.   MARY MILDRED LAW b. Jul-15-1911 in Lawford, Ritchie Co, WV,[190,592,996] d. Mar-13-2008 in Parkersburg, Wood Co, WV,[1056,592] buried in Evergreen Cemetery (South), Parkersburg, WV,[190] resided in Parkersburg, Wood Co, WV,[228,395,604] census 1930 in Union District, Ritchie Co, WV, census 1920 in Gilmer Co, WV, occupation American Viscose and owned a Sunoco gas station.[190] She married[395] Oct- 8-1928 in Ritchie Co, WV,[996] Clyde James Wright, b. Mar-15-1907,[559,592,996] (son of Addison A. I. Wright and Lenora L. "Nora" Wright), d. Mar-22-1964 in Parkersburg, Wood Co,

WV,[559,592] buried in Evergreen Cemetery, Parkersburg, WV,[559] resided in Parkersburg, Wood Co, WV,[559] census 1910, 1930 in Union District, Ritchie Co, WV, occupation gasoline station owner.[559]

     v.   STARLING DALE LAW, also known as S. Dale Law,[396,592] b. Jul-31-1913 in Doddridge Co, WV,[592,1006] d. Dec-13-1995,[592] resided in Harrisville, Ritchie Co, WV,[604] resided 1934 in Lawford, Ritchie Co, WV,[1006] census 1920 in Gilmer Co, WV. He married Nov- 4-1934 in Harrisville, Ritchie Co, WV,[mdcclxxxix[1789]] Wilma Olene Clevenger, b. Jun-15-1917 in Gilmer Co, WV,[592,1006] (daughter of James Calvin Clevenger), d. Aug-11-1996,[592] resided in Harrisville, Ritchie Co, WV,[604] resided 1934 in Newberne, Gilmer Co, WV.[1006]

     vi.   FORD D. LAW b. Apr- 6-1917,[469] d. Apr-12-1917,[469] buried in Lawford Cemetery, Ritchie Co, WV.[469]

     vii.   RICHIE D. LAW, JR. b. Jul-31-1918 in Ritchie Co, WV,[398,1715] d. Dec- 9-1945 in Parkersburg, Wood Co, WV,[398] cause of death suffocated in fire at Hotel Grand, buried in K of P Cemetery, Elizabeth, Wirt Co, WV,[398] resided in Elizabeth, Wirt Co, WV,[398] census 1920 in Gilmer Co, WV, occupation truck driver.[398] He married[228] Orma __, resided 1945 in Elizabeth, Wirt Co, WV.[228]

     viii.   RUTH CLAIRE LAW b. ca 1922.[996] She married Jan-16-1942 in Ritchie Co, WV,[996] Hartsel Junior Riddle, census name Junior H. Riddle,[1715] b. ca 1919,[996] (son of Hartsel Riddle and Otie D. Rutherford), census 1920 in Troy District, Gilmer Co, WV.

     ix.   JOHN LAW resided 2008 in Parkersburg, Wood Co, WV.[412]

     x.   EDITH DAIRE LAW b. Jan-25-1924 in Lawford, Ritchie Co, WV,[602] resided 2008 in Florida,[412] resided 1944 in Parkersburg, Wood Co, WV.[602] She married[424] Apr- 9-1944 in Parkersburg, Wood Co, WV,[602] divorced Mar- -1966 in Orange Co, FL, Lawrence Amos Crew, b. May-26-1918 in LeRoy, Jackson Co, WV,[602,592] (son of L. L. Crew and Lydia __), d. Feb-13-2003,[592] resided in Altamonte Springs, Seminole Co, FL,[604] resided 1944 in Parkersburg, Wood Co, WV.[602]

856. **Louie Dow Law**, also known as L. D. Law,[602,mdccxc[1790]] (471.David[8], 266.Deborah[7], 139.John[6], 72.John[5], 21.John[4], 6.Hugh[3], 3.John[2], 1.Jean[1]), b. Apr- 3-1883 in Lawford, Ritchie Co, WV,[496,469] d. Jun-15-1942 in Ritchie Co, WV,[496,469] buried in Lawford Cemetery, Ritchie Co, WV,[469] census 1920 in Clay District, Ritchie Co, WV, resided 1911 at Lawford, Ritchie Co, WV,[602] census 1900 in Union District, Ritchie Co, WV, occupation 1920 farm manager.[1790] He married (1) May-30-1911 in Waverly, Wood Co, WV,[602] divorced bef Apr 1930,[334] **Bessie Pearl Bee**, b. Mar- -1893 in Ritchie Co, WV,[809] [Birth date given in 1900 Census as Mar 1893, but SSDI and California Death Index show it as May 10 1892. Birthplace given as Ritchie County in marriage record and as West Virginia in 1920 Census, but as Ohio in 1930 Census.] (daughter of Benjamine Z. Bee and Elizabeth V. "Lizzie" Osbourn), d. Mar-10-1984 in Monterey Co, CA,[1237] resided 1967 in Carmel, Monterey Co, CA,[521] census 1930 in Monterey, Monterey Co, CA, census 1920 in Clay District, Ritchie Co, WV, resided 1911 in Waverly, Wood Co, WV,[602] census 1910 in Williams District, Wood Co, WV.

1920 Census, Ritchie Co, WV (Clay District), enumerated on Feb 5 1920:
L. D. Law, 36, b. W.Va, manager of farm; wife Bessie, 27, b. W.Va; dau Thelma, 5, b. W.Va; son Darwin, 3 yr 1 mo, b. W.Va.

1930 Census, Monterey Co, California (City of Monterey), enumerated on Apr 14 1930:
Bess Law, 38, b. Ohio, seamstress at cleaners, age 19 at time of first marriage, divorced; dau Thelma, 15, b. W.Va; son Darwin, 13, b. Ohio, newspaper carrier.

He married (2) Jan-31-1940 in Ritchie Co, WV,[mdccxci[1791]] **Myrtle Haddox**, b. 1888 in Ritchie Co, WV,[46,473,996] d. 1961,[46] buried in Hazelgreen (Buzzard) Cemetery (btwn Co Rds 19/4 & 19/5), Ritchie Co WV.[469]

     Children by Bessie Pearl Bee:
     i.   THELMA V. LAW b. May-18-1914 in West Virginia,[1237,592] d. Sep- 9-1982 in Monterey Co, CA,[1237,592] resided in Monterey, Monterey Co, CA,[1152] census 1930 in Monterey, Monterey Co, CA, census 1920 in Clay District, Ritchie Co, WV. She married[436] __ Neu.

     ii.   DARWIN LAW b. ca 1917,[1790] census 1930 in Monterey, Monterey Co, CA, census 1920 in Clay District, Ritchie Co, WV.

857. **Eva Lora Law** (471.David[8], 266.Deborah[7], 139.John[6], 72.John[5], 21.John[4], 6.Hugh[3], 3.John[2], 1.Jean[1]), b. Aug- -1885,[809,473] d. May-18-1966 in Ritchie Co, WV,[477] resided 1937 in Harrisville, Ritchie Co, WV,[228,484] census 1900 in Union District, Ritchie Co, WV. She married Nov- 6-1910 in Ritchie Co, WV,[473] **Simon D. Goff**, b. Sep-28-1883 in Gilmer Co, WV,[398,473,46] (son of John A. B. Goff and Nancy Elizabeth Stalnaker), d. Apr- 5-1937 in Parkersburg, Wood Co, WV,[806,398,46] buried in IOOF Cemetery, Harrisville, Ritchie Co, WV,[398,190,469] cause of death spinal meningitis,[190] resided in Harrisville, Ritchie Co, WV,[190] resided formerly in Burnt House, Ritchie Co, WV,[190] occupation teacher, principal, school superintendent.[190]

   Children:

   i. BLONDENA W. GOFF b. Feb-19-1912,[592] d. Mar- 3-1997,[mdccxcii[1792]] resided in Harrisville, Ritchie Co, WV,[592] resided formerly in Pennsylvania,[948] resided 1937 in Burnt House, Ritchie Co, WV.[765] She married[484] Nov- 8-1930 in Ritchie Co, WV,[996] Carlton Haden "Budge" Burns,[412,190,412] b. Dec- 1-1910 at Auburn, Ritchie Co, WV,[190] (son of John Emory Burns and Rosa Florence Lowther), d. Dec-12-2006 in Parkersburg, Wood Co, WV,[190] buried in IOOF Cemetery, Harrisville, Ritchie Co, WV,[190] resided in Harrisville, Ritchie Co, WV,[765,412,190] resided 1930 in Pleasants Co, WV,[996] occupation school bus driver, superintendent of transportation,[190] military U.S. Army Field Artillery, World War II (South Pacific).[190]

   Carlton: "Early in his working career, he had the opportunity to drive the first school bus used at Harrisville High School in 1933 and he was employed by the Ritchie County School System as a school bus driver and rose to the position of superintendent of transportation, where he served for 24 years. He also served as supervisor of the Ritchie County highway system for the West Virginia Department of Highways during Cecil H. Underwood's first term as governor and also worked for the Department of Highways during the administration of Arch Moore. He was later employed by Robinson Motors of Harrisville as a salesman."[190]

   ii. VIRGINIA E. GOFF b. ca 1913,[996] resided 1937 in Harrisville, Ritchie Co, WV.[765] She married Feb-14-1934 in Ritchie Co, WV,[996] Hartzel L. "Hart" Burns, b. Aug-30-1913,[592] (son of John Emory Burns and Rosa Florence Lowther), d. Aug- 4-1998,[mdccxciii[1793]] resided in Newark, Licking Co, OH,[604] resided 1954 in Columbus, Franklin Co, OH,[765] census 1930 in Hackers Creek District, Lewis Co, WV.

   iii. CHARLES GOFF resided 1937 in Harrisville, Ritchie Co, WV.[765]
   iv. PAUL GOFF resided 1937 in Harrisville, Ritchie Co, WV.[765]
   v. KENDALL GOFF resided 1937 in Harrisville, Ritchie Co, WV.[765]

858. **Carl D. Law** (471.David[8], 266.Deborah[7], 139.John[6], 72.John[5], 21.John[4], 6.Hugh[3], 3.John[2], 1.Jean[1]), b. Jun-14-1888,[496,46,809] d. Aug-19-1951 in Ritchie Co, WV,[474,46] buried in IOOF Cemetery, Harrisville, Ritchie Co, WV,[469] census 1930 in Troy District, Gilmer Co, WV, census 1900 in Union District, Ritchie Co, WV. He married[496] Nov-15-1916 in Gilmer Co, WV,[mdccxciv[1794]] **Bonnie Nell Bush**, b. Nov-19-1894 in Newberne, Gilmer Co, WV,[398,474] (daughter of James C. Bush and Mary C. Gordon), d. Dec- 6-1947 in Harrisville, Ritchie Co, WV,[mdccxcv[1795],474] buried in IOOF Cemetery, Harrisville, Ritchie Co, WV,[398,469] resided in Harrisville, Ritchie Co, WV,[398] census 1930 in Troy District, Gilmer Co, WV.

   Children:

   i. CARL D. LAW, JR. b. Mar-22-1918,[17] d. Dec-24-1959 in Ritchie Co, WV,[477,17] buried in IOOF Cemetery, Harrisville, Ritchie Co, WV,[469] census 1930 in Troy District, Gilmer Co, WV, military Pvt, Infantry, World War II.[469]

   ii. CELIA CATHERINE LAW, also known as Catherine Law,[521] census name Catharine C. Law,[906] b. ca 1921,[906] d. 1970,[496] census 1930 in Troy District, Gilmer Co, WV. She married[1101] ___ Smith.

   iii. ROSEMARY NELL LAW b. Nov- 3-1921 in Lewis Co, WV,[398] d. Apr- 2-1923 in Lawford, Ritchie Co, WV,[398] cause of death burns of body,[398] buried in Lawford Cemetery, Ritchie Co, WV.[398]

   iv. ELAINE LAW, census name Mildred E. Law,[906] b. Jun-23-1924 in Ritchie Co, WV,[592,588] d. Nov- -1986,[592] resided in Damascus, Montgomery Co, MD,[604] resided 1942 at Goffs, Ritchie Co, WV,[588] census 1930 in Troy District, Gilmer Co, WV. She married[1101] Aug-27-1942 in Smithville,

Ritchie Co, WV,[588] Philip Ireland Brake, b. Mar-16-1921 in Ritchie Co, WV,[592,588] (son of Wilbur Elisha Brake and Amy Lessie Ireland), d. Apr- 8-2003,[592] resided in Damascus, Montgomery Co, MD,[604] resided 1942 near Cairo, Ritchie Co, WV.[588]

        v.   DENVER GENE "SPIDER" LAW[521] b. Oct-19-1926 in Ritchie Co, WV,[1433,592] d. Dec-29-2001,[592] resided in Canton, Stark Co, OH,[604] resided 1951 in Ritchie Co, WV,[1433] census 1930 in Troy District, Gilmer Co, WV. He married Living.

        vi.   JAMES DAVID LAW[mdccxcvi[1796]] also known as David Law,[190] b. Jun-20-1929 in Newberne, Gilmer Co, WV,[190] d. Aug-30-2003 in Parkersburg, Wood Co, WV,[190] buried in IOOF Cemetery, Harrisville, Ritchie Co, WV,[190] resided in Harrisville, Ritchie Co, WV,[190] census 1930 in Troy District, Gilmer Co, WV, occupation farmer, insurance agent,[190] military U.S. Air Force, Korean War.[190]

        After graduation from Harrisville High School and attendance at college, he taught in a one-room schoolhouse and drove a school bus. He was a life-long farmer doing business as David Law & Sons Polled Herefords, and he also owned and operated an independent insurance agency in Harrisville for 47 years. He was actively involved in fund raising for the American Cancer Society, as well as in 4-H Clubs and youth baseball organizations.[190]

        He married Living.
        vii.   LIVING.

859. **Sylvia Mida Law**, census name Mida S. Law,[809] (471.David[8], 266.Deborah[7], 139.John[6], 72.John[5], 21.John[4], 6.Hugh[3], 3.John[2], 1.Jean[1]), b. Nov-20-1897 in Ritchie Co, WV,[592,809,996] d. Nov- -1988,[592] resided in Harrisville, Ritchie Co, WV.[604] She married Apr-23-1927 in Ritchie Co, WV,[996] **Jennings Dallas Snyder**, b. Apr- 8-1900 in Ritchie Co, WV,[592,996] (son of Joseph P. Snyder and Hester McFadden), d. Jan-22-1965 in Ritchie Co, WV,[592,862] resided 1927 in Wood Co, WV,[996] occupation State Roads employee.[862]
        Children:
        i.   LIVING. She married (1) Anthony Raymond Nutt, also known as A. Raymond Nutt,[190] b. Aug-29-1929 in Washburn, Ritchie Co, WV,[1433,190] (son of Anthony David Nutt and Monna Lenore Washburn), d. May- 1-2011 in Parkersburg, Wood Co, WV,[700] resided in Parkersburg, Wood Co, WV,[190] occupation truck driver (Carolina Freight, retired).[190] She married (2) Living.

860. **Verner Vadis Law** (473.Martin[8], 266.Deborah[7], 139.John[6], 72.John[5], 21.John[4], 6.Hugh[3], 3.John[2], 1.Jean[1]), b. Sep-16-1888 in Ritchie Co, WV,[592,809,419] d. May- -1978,[592] resided in Lewisburg, Greenbrier Co, WV,[604] census 1930 in Union District, Harrison Co, WV [In household with wife's parents on Jackson Mill Road.], resided 1911 in Kincheloe (Jane Lew), Harrison Co, WV,[374] resided 1911 at Lawford, Ritchie Co, WV,[419] census 1900, 1910 in Union District, Ritchie Co, WV, occupation 1930 laborer on dairy farm.[1208] He married Sep-20-1911 at Harrison Co, WV,[419] **Edna Winfield Rhodes**, b. Jan- 6-1890 in Harrison Co, WV,[592,419] (daughter of Arthur N. Rhodes and Mary A. __), d. Jul- 9-1992,[592] census 1930 in Union District, Harrison Co, WV.
        Children:
        i.   HELEN LOUISE LAW b. May- 5-1915 in Harrison Co, WV,[419] resided 1937 in Kincheloe (Jane Lew), Harrison Co, WV,[419] census 1930 in Union District, Harrison Co, WV. She married Jun- 3-1937 in Kincheloe (Jane Lew), Harrison Co, WV,[419] Kenneth Eugene Allman, b. Aug-11-1915 in Lewis Co, WV,[419,592] (son of Worthy Dale Allman and Mary Elizabeth Hitt), d. Jul-14-1996,[592] resided in Radford, VA,[604] resided 1937 in Jane Lew, Lewis Co, WV.[419]
        ii.   ELIZABETH R. LAW b. ca 1921,[1208] census 1930 in Union District, Harrison Co, WV.
        iii.   MARY M. LAW b. ca 1924,[1208] census 1930 in Union District, Harrison Co, WV.

861. **Royston D. Law** (474.Levi[8], 266.Deborah[7], 139.John[6], 72.John[5], 21.John[4], 6.Hugh[3], 3.John[2], 1.Jean[1]), b. Apr- -1886,[469] d. 1961,[469] buried in Lawford Cemetery, Ritchie Co, WV,[469] resided 1959 in Burnt House, Ritchie Co, WV,[521] census 1920, 1930 in Murphy District, Ritchie Co, WV. He married[374] ca 1910,[1003] **Gertie G. Swisher**, census name Gertia,[1003] b. 1888,[46,1003] d. 1977,[46] buried in Lawford Cemetery, Ritchie Co, WV,[469] census 1920, 1930 in Murphy District, Ritchie Co, WV.

Children:

    i.   THEO MAYRIE LAW, also known as Mayrie Law, b. Dec-30-1910 in Ritchie Co, WV,[1433,592] d. Dec- 7-2008 in Cumberland, Guernsey Co, OH,[592,700] buried in Zion Cemetery, Westland Twp, near Claysville, Guernsey Co, OH,[190] resided in Cumberland, Guernsey Co, OH,[604] resided 1956 in Burnt House, Ritchie Co, WV,[1433] occupation elementary school teacher, Ritchie Co WV (retired 1956),[190] occupation formerly Naval Supply Depot, Norfolk, VA,[190] census 1920 in Murphy District, Ritchie Co, WV. She married Aug-25-1956 in Ritchie Co, WV,[mdccxcvii][1797] Albert E. Brissey, b. Dec-13-1908 in Ritchie Co, WV,[1433,592] (son of Albert Brissey and Blanche Ayers), d. Oct- 6-1978,[191,592] resided in Cumberland, Guernsey Co, OH.[1433,604]

    ii.   BONEVA LAW b. Apr-27-1912,[592] d. Apr-10-1988,[592] resided in Weirton, Hancock Co, WV,[592] resided formerly in Louisiana,[1284] census 1920 in Murphytown, Wood Co, WV. She married[424] __ Russell.

    iii.   VERNON SWISHER LAW[412] b. Feb-14-1914 in Ritchie Co, WV,[592,1552] d. Mar- -1980,[592] resided in Mentor, Lake Co, OH,[604] resided 1937 in Hollidays Cove, Hancock Co, WV,[1552] census 1920 in Murphy District, Ritchie Co, WV. He married Jan-29-1937 in Hollidays Cove, Hancock Co, WV,[1552] Jean H. Livingston, b. Apr-13-1917 in Jefferson Co, OH,[592,1011,1552] (daughter of __ Livingston and __ Kerr), d. Apr- 3-1992 in Willoughby, Lake Co, OH,[1011,592] resided in Mentor, Lake Co, OH,[1011] resided 1937 in Hollidays Cove, Hancock Co, WV.[1552]

    iv.   BYRL L. LAW[412] b. Nov- 6-1916,[592] d. Jan- -1982,[592] resided in Williamsburg, VA,[604] census 1920 in Murphy District, Ritchie Co, WV.

    v.   IRENE LAW b. ca 1919,[1002] d. bef Dec 2008,[412] census 1920 in Murphy District, Ritchie Co, WV. She married[424] __ Smith.

    vi.   DARRELL G. LAW b. ca 1922,[1003] resided 2008 in New Martinsville, Wetzel Co, WV,[412] census 1930 in Murphy District, Ritchie Co, WV. He married[1487] Sarah __, resided 2008 in New Martinsville, Wetzel Co, WV.[1487]

    vii.   HERMAN LAW b. ca 1925,[1003] d. bef Dec 2008,[412] census 1930 in Murphy District, Ritchie Co, WV.

    viii.   HARLAN M. LAW[412] b. Dec-12-1927,[592,1003] d. Apr-21-1995,[592] resided in Line Lexington, Bucks Co, PA,[604] census 1930 in Murphy District, Ritchie Co, WV.

862. **Jackson Woodford Law**, also known as Jack Law (474.Levi[8], 266.Deborah[7], 139.John[6], 72.John[5], 21.John[4], 6.Hugh[3], 3.John[2], 1.Jean[1]), b. Feb-26-1888 in Lawford, Ritchie Co, WV,[398,434] d. Oct-31-1945 in Clarksburg, Harrison Co, WV,[398] buried in Newberne Cemetery, Gilmer Co, WV,[398] occupation H&K Service Station employee.[398] He married[395] Feb-20-1910 in Gilmer Co, WV,[434] **Alta Faye Gordon**, b. Jun-24-1891,[592] d. Sep- -1979,[592] resided in Pennsboro, Ritchie Co, WV.[228,592]

Children:

    i.   VERL D. LAW b. Sep-12-1914 in Coxs Mills, Gilmer Co, WV,[190] d. Aug-23-2002,[190] resided in Bridgeport, Harrison Co, WV,[190] resided formerly in Pennsboro, Ritchie Co, WV,[190] occupation auto mechanic.[190] He married[1539-190] Bonneta Virginia Britton,[1539] b. Feb-16-1915,[592] (daughter of Cyrus Poling Britton and Vada Dell Byrd), d. Sep-17-2001,[592] resided in New York City, NY,[592] resided formerly in West Virginia.[mdccxcviii][1798]

    ii.   MELVA GAY LAW b. ca 1919 in Gilmer Co, WV,[996] resided 1941 in Ritchie Co, WV.[996] She married Oct- 7-1941 in Ritchie Co, WV,[996] Frederick Flynn Taylor, b. ca 1915 in Ritchie Co, WV.[996]

863. **Zora L. Law** (474.Levi[8], 266.Deborah[7], 139.John[6], 72.John[5], 21.John[4], 6.Hugh[3], 3.John[2], 1.Jean[1]), b. Aug- 1-1890 in Ritchie Co, WV,[1007,154,46] d. Sep-13-1934 in Ritchie Co, WV,[955,46] buried in IOOF Cemetery, Harrisville, Ritchie Co, WV.[469] She married[374,436] **Oda C. Gordon**, b. Dec-12-1889,[592,46] (son of William Wayne Gordon and Alice Rebecca Hinzman), d. Feb-13-1965 in Newberne, Gilmer Co, WV,[432,604,46] buried in IOOF Cemetery, Harrisville, Ritchie Co, WV,[432,469] resided in Newberne, Gilmer Co, WV,[432] census 1910 in Troy District, Gilmer Co, WV, occupation farmer.[432]

Children:

    i.   WINONA MILDRED GORDON b. Aug-31-1913 in Gilmer Co, WV,[1433,592] d. Sep-16-2003,[592] resided in Charlottesville, VA,[604] resided 1952 in Ritchie Co, WV.[1433] She married Aug-17-

1952 in Ritchie Co, WV,[1433] Charles Marion Canby, b. Jun-24-1911 in Berkeley Co, WV,[1433] (son of Charles Canby and Bertha V. __), resided 1952 in Monongalia Co, WV.[1433]

864. **Burleigh Aubrey Law** (474.Levi[8], 266.Deborah[7], 139.John[6], 72.John[5], 21.John[4], 6.Hugh[3], 3.John[2], 1.Jean[1]), b. Jan-13-1893,[398] [Marriage record in Gilmer County states birthplace as Ritchie County, but death record shows birthplace as Gilmer County.], d. Mar-24-1952 in Weirton, Hancock Co, WV,[398] buried in Chapel Hill Memorial Gardens, Weirton, WV,[398] resided from abt 1925 in Weirton, Hancock Co, WV,[398] resided 1917 in Gilmer Co, WV,[434] occupation millwright foreman, Weirton Steel Co.[398] He married Sep- 1-1917 in Gilmer Co, WV,[434] **Mollie A. Rymer**, b. ca 1895,[434] resided 1952 in Weirton, Hancock Co, WV.[228]

        Children:
           i.   MABEL LAW b. May-27-1918,[17] d. May-27-1918,[17] buried in Bethany UM Church Cem (Rt 28 btwn Goffs & Prunty), Ritchie Co WV.[469]

865. **Tracy Forest Law** (474.Levi[8], 266.Deborah[7], 139.John[6], 72.John[5], 21.John[4], 6.Hugh[3], 3.John[2], 1.Jean[1]), b. May-17-1900 in Ritchie Co, WV,[190,46] d. Dec-30-1959 in Pennsboro, Ritchie Co, WV,[700,46] buried in Mt. Harmony Masonic Cemetery, Pennsboro, Ritchie Co, WV,[469] resided in Pennsboro, Ritchie Co, WV.[190]

Owner of the Tracy Law Motor Company in Pennsboro. He was also a member of the Pennsboro City Council for a number of years, and was Chief of the Pennsboro Volunteer Fire Department for 15 years. With his friend Kenneth K. "Tom" McCullough, he worked on a lake for the Pennsboro City Park, the lake now being known as Tracy Lake.

Among others, survived by "two brothers, Lester Law of Newberne, and Royston Law of Burnt House, and three sisters, Mrs. Audra Boone of Harrisville, Mrs. Lovie Rogers of Weston, and Mrs. Roxana Lang of Morgantown."[190]

She married Oct-10-1921 in Ritchie Co, WV,[996,484] **Retha Leona Burns**,[996] b. May- 4-1901 in Braxton Co, WV,[190,996,592,46] (son of John Emory Burns and Rosa Florence Lowther), d. Mar-10-1999 in Danville, Boyle Co, KY,[806,592] buried in Mt. Harmony Masonic Cemetery, Pennsboro, Ritchie Co, WV,[190] resided in Danville, Boyle Co, KY,[190,592] resided 1954, 1959 in Pennsboro, Ritchie Co, WV.[765,484]

        Children:
           i.   ROSALIE IRIS LAW b. Feb-28-1923 in Ritchie Co, WV,[1433] resided 1959, 99 in St. Marys, Pleasants Co, WV,[765,856] resided 1945 in Ritchie Co, WV.[1433] She married[941,1040] Sep-22-1945 in Ritchie Co, WV,[1433] Denton Carl Worstell, also known as Carl Worstell,[592] b. May- 7-1922 in Ritchie Co, WV,[592,1433] (son of Carl Worstell and Carrie Pifer), d. Feb- -1979,[592] resided in St. Marys, Pleasants Co, WV.[604]
           ii.   LIVING. She married Living.

866. **Arden Lester Law**[996,469] also known as Lester Law,[992,521] (474.Levi[8], 266.Deborah[7], 139.John[6], 72.John[5], 21.John[4], 6.Hugh[3], 3.John[2], 1.Jean[1]), b. Apr-25-1904 in Gilmer Co, WV,[992,996] d. 1988,[469] buried in Pine Grove Cemetery, Berea (Co Rd 7-26), Ritchie Co, WV,[469] resided 1959 in Newberne, Gilmer Co, WV.[521] He married (1) Nov- 5-1925 in Ritchie Co, WV,[996,992] **Susie Pearl Collins**, b. Jan- 4-1902,[992] (daughter of Alfred B. Collins and Laura J. Ehret), d. Nov-16-1952,[992] buried in Pine Grove Cemetery, Berea (Co Rd 7-26), Ritchie Co, WV.[469] He married[469] (2) **Lovie J. Singleton**, b. Sep-23-1905,[469] d. Oct-25-1985,[469] buried in Pine Grove Cemetery, Berea (Co Rd 7-26), Ritchie Co, WV.[469]

        Children by Susie Pearl Collins:
           i.   ARDEN RAY LAW b. Dec-17-1925.[mdccxcix[1799]] He married Apr- 1-1952,[992] Barbara Miller.
           ii.   LIVING.
           iii.   LIVING.
           iv.   LIVING.
           v.   LIVING.
           vi.   LIVING. He married Living.

vii.   RAYMOND DOYLE LAW b. Oct- 8-1939,[992,592] d. Apr-15-2000,[592] resided in Glenville, Gilmer Co, WV.[592]

867. **Jennings Virgil Law** (475.Newton[8], 266.Deborah[7], 139.John[6], 72.John[5], 21.John[4], 6.Hugh[3], 3.John[2], 1.Jean[1]), b. Feb-17-1886 in Ritchie Co, WV,[154,1006] d. Apr-20-1920 in Ritchie Co, WV,[955] census 1900 in Troy District, Gilmer Co, WV [In household of grandparents James & Sophia Allman.]. He married Feb-24-1907 in Gilmer Co, WV,[1006] **Dulcie Post**, b. ca 1889 in Gilmer Co, WV.[1006]
     Children:
     i.   LAYTON BROOKS LAW b. Sep-13-1912 in Gilmer Co, WV,[592,996] d. Nov- -1980,[592] resided in Elyria, Lorain Co, OH,[604] resided 1942 in Ritchie Co, WV.[996] He married Jun- 6-1942 in Ritchie Co, WV,[mdccc[1800]] Norene Bee, b. Jan-23-1906 in Auburn, Ritchie Co, WV,[1007,592,190] (daughter of Zed Bee and Fan Watson), d. Oct-19-2006 in North Ridgeville, Lorain Co, OH,[764,592] buried Resthaven Mem Gdn in Avon, Lorain Co, OH,[190] resided 50 years in Elyria, Lorain Co, OH,[190,592] occupation elementary school teacher (retired 1973).[190]

868. **Lona Orpha Law**, birth name Orpha L. Law,[1007] (476.William[8], 266.Deborah[7], 139.John[6], 72.John[5], 21.John[4], 6.Hugh[3], 3.John[2], 1.Jean[1]), b. Jul-12-1888 in Ritchie Co, WV,[mdccci[1801],473,592,46] d. Oct- -1975,[592,46] buried in Lawford Cemetery, Ritchie Co, WV,[469] resided in Spencer, Roane Co, WV,[592] census 1930 in Grant District, Ritchie Co, WV, census 1920 in Grant District, Ritchie Co, WV, census 1900, 1910 in Union District, Ritchie Co, WV. She married Jun-18-1913 in Ritchie Co, WV,[mdcccii[1802]] **Royden Scott Zinn**, also known as Roy S. Zinn,[473] b. Apr- 9-1881,[592] (son of Cortez Lafeyette Zinn and Allie Drummond), d. Jun-12-1970 in Ritchie Co, WV,[477,592] buried in Lawford Cemetery, Ritchie Co, WV,[469] resided in Newberne, Gilmer Co, WV,[592] census 1930 in Cairo, Ritchie Co, WV, census 1920 in Grant District, Ritchie Co, WV, census 1900 in Union District, Ritchie Co, WV, occupation 1920, 1930 driller in oil fields.[1018,mdccciii[1803]]
     Children:
     i.   EVELYN L. ZINN b. ca 1915,[1018] census 1930 in Cairo, Ritchie Co, WV, census 1920 in Grant District, Ritchie Co, WV.
     ii.   ROYDEN SCOTT ZINN, JR., census name Junior Zinn,[1018] census name Roy S. Zinn Jr.,[1803] b. Sep- 1-1917,[592,469] d. Jun-23-1991,[592,469] buried in Lawford Cemetery, Ritchie Co, WV,[469] census 1930 in Cairo, Ritchie Co, WV, census 1920 in Grant District, Ritchie Co, WV, education Cairo HS, Ritchie Co WV (1936).[mdccciv[1804]] He married[446,1454] Pauline Payne.
     iii.   IDA MAE ZINN b. 1919,[1018] census 1930 in Cairo, Ritchie Co, WV, census 1920 in Grant District, Ritchie Co, WV.
     iv.   RAYMOND DRUMMOND ZINN b. Dec-19-1923 in Cairo, Ritchie Co, WV,[190] d. Feb-11-2011 in Terra Alta, Preston Co, WV,[700] cremated[190] buried (ashes) in WV National Cemetery, Pruntytown, Taylor Co, WV,[190] resided in Terra Alta, Preston Co, WV,[190] resided near Cranesville, Preston Co, WV,[190] census 1930 in Cairo, Ritchie Co, WV, occupation veterinarian,[190] education West Virginia Univ (BS, 1948), Ohio State (1957, DVM),[190] military U.S. Air Force (World War II and Korean War).

     Dr. Raymond D. Zinn was a retired doctor of veterinary medicine, holding licenses in Maryland, Ohio, Virginia and West Virginia. Following his retirement from the U.S. Public Health Service, he made his home near Cranesville, W.Va., in Preston Co, WV.
     Dr. Zinn's education included a 1948 Bachelor Science, Agriculture, West Virginia University and 1957- Doctor Veterinary Medicine, Summa Cum Laude, The Ohio State University. He was a veteran of World War II and the Korean Conflict, serving with the U.S. Air Force as Second Lieutenant, 1943-1945; First Lieutenant, 1951-1953; and Captain, U.S. Public Health Service, 1959-1975.
     His profession experiences included: Commissioned Officer, United States Public Health Service; Epidemic Intelligence Service Officer, National Communicable Disease Center; Staff Officer, National Heart Institute, NIH, responsible for program development and implementation for the network of Regional Primate Research Centers. Also, at NIH, Dr. Zinn was responsible for the development operation of the NIH Research Animal Center at Poolesville, Md. He was subsequently awarded the Meritorious Service Medal for this period of service. This award, the second highest

award that may be given a Public Health Service Office, was given "In Recognition of outstanding service and achievement while on active duty in the Commissioned Corps of the Public Health Service... in recognition of the conception and successful development of NIH's unique Canine Blood Donor Colony, standardized research animals and administration of laboratory auxiliary services for the National Institute of Health"; Director, Appalachian Center for Environmental Health, Morgantown, W.Va.; Professor of Public Health and Preventive Medicine, School of Medicine, West Virginia University; and Member, Interim Compliance Panel, Federal Coal Mine Health and Safety Act of 1969; Public Law 91-173.

Societies and honors included: the Meritorious Service Medal, U.S. Public Health Service; Phi Zeta, Phi Epsilon Phi, Alpha Zeta, Gamma Sign Delta, Borden Scholarship Award in Veterinary Medicine and American Veterinary Medical Association.

190

He married[484] Mary Mann, b. Jan-10-1921 in Renick, Greenbrier Co, WV,[190] (daughter of James Forest Mann and Cline C. Christie), d. Jun-13-2006 in Gaithersburg, Montgomery Co, MD,[764] cremated[190] buried (ashes) in Morningside Cemetery, Renick, Greenbrier Co, WV,[190] occupation grants management clerk, National Institutes of Health (retired).[190]

869. **Zeta Gay Sommerville** (477.John[8], 267.Susan[7], 139.John[6], 72.John[5], 21.John[4], 6.Hugh[3], 3.John[2], 1.Jean[1]), b. Jul- 3-1873 in Ritchie Co, WV,[398] d. Aug- 4-1944 in Clarksburg, Harrison Co, WV,[398] buried in Elkview Masonic Cemetery, Clarksburg, Harrison Co, WV,[398] resided in Clarksburg, Harrison Co, WV,[398] resided 1890 in Harrison Co, WV.[419] She married Sep- 4-1890 in Harrison Co, WV,[419] **Owen T. Davis**, b. Feb- 4-1866 in Harrison Co, WV,[1029,419] (son of Moses Hoffman Davis and Emma V. Swisher).

Children:
i. VEDA IRENE DAVIS b. Dec-16-1891 in Harrison Co, WV,[592,419] d. Jan- -1983,[592] resided in Clarksburg, Harrison Co, WV.[592] She married[mdcccv[1805]] Dec-17-1913 in Salem, WV,[419] Frank Valentine Langfitt, b. Mar-24-1883 in Morgansville, Doddridge Co, WV,[mdcccvi[1806]] (son of Valentine Langfitt and Caroline Louise Davis), d. Dec- 3-1972,[1805] resided in Clarksburg, Harrison Co, WV,[604,521] resided 1913 in Salem, WV,[419] census 1900 in Grant District, Doddridge Co, WV, occupation physician.[1805]

870. **Allena "Allie" Sommerville** (477.John[8], 267.Susan[7], 139.John[6], 72.John[5], 21.John[4], 6.Hugh[3], 3.John[2], 1.Jean[1]), b. Aug-18-1875 in Auburn, Ritchie Co, WV,[398,46] d. Nov-17-1936 in Lost Creek, Harrison Co, WV,[398,46] buried in Brick Church (7th Day Baptist) Cemetery, Lost Creek, Harrison Co, WV,[398,230] census 1910, 1930 in Grant District, Harrison Co, WV. She married[mdcccvii[1807]] ca 1896,[458] **Dorsey C. Kennedy**, b. 1874,[46] d. 1928,[46] buried in Brick Church (7th Day Baptist) Cemetery, Lost Creek, Harrison Co, WV,[230] census 1910 in Grant District, Harrison Co, WV, occupation farm manager.[458]

Children:
i. HARRY W. KENNEDY b. ca 1898,[458] census 1910 in Grant District, Harrison Co, WV.
ii. MATTIE E. KENNEDY b. ca 1901,[458] census 1910 in Grant District, Harrison Co, WV.
iii. JOHN LOMAN KENNEDY (See marriage to number 816.)
iv. DORSEY KENNEDY b. ca 1913,[1208] census 1930 in Grant District, Harrison Co, WV.

871. **Isa M. Sommerville**, also known as Ice Sommerville,[446] census name Icy M. Sommerville,[587] (478.Robert[8], 267.Susan[7], 139.John[6], 72.John[5], 21.John[4], 6.Hugh[3], 3.John[2], 1.Jean[1]), b. ca 1878 in Ritchie Co, WV,[588,587] resided 1910 in Auburn, Ritchie Co, WV,[588,1747] census 1880 in Union District, Ritchie Co, WV. She married[446,374,345,1029] (1) Nov- 7-1897 in Ritchie Co, WV,[473] **Albert Carl Brown**, b. Jan- 7-1867,[17] (son of Edward Marshall Brown and Elcy Caroline Tharp), d. Sep-21-1903,[1029,17] buried in Auburn Community Cemetery, Ritchie Co, WV.[469] She married (2) Feb-22-1910 in Auburn, Ritchie Co, WV,[588] **William Henry Hall**, b. Aug- 2-1848 in Lewis Co, (W)VA,[1164,588] (son of James Monroe Hall and Nancy Burnside), d. May-12-1928,[1164] resided 1910 in Auburn, Ritchie Co, WV,[588,1747] occupation farmer.[1747]

Children by Albert Carl Brown:

i.   HARRY WHITMAN BROWN b. May-17-1898 in Ritchie Co, WV,[592,410] d. Apr- -1981,[592] resided in Weston, Lewis Co, WV,[604] census 1930 in Weston, Lewis Co, WV, resided 1924 in Lewis Co, WV,[410] census 1910 in Auburn, Ritchie Co, WV. He married[1101] Jun- 3-1924 in Lewis Co, WV,[410] Inez Merl Hall,[521,373] b. Jul- 4-1903,[592,410] (daughter of Simeon Asbury Hall and Georgia Estella White), d. Nov- -1995,[592] resided in Weston, Lewis Co, WV,[604] census 1930 in Weston, Lewis Co, WV.

ii.   EDNA RUTH BROWN, also known as Ruth Brown,[1747,1093,398] b. Oct-17-1899 in Ritchie Co, WV,[398,621] d. Nov-18-1959 in Weston, Lewis Co, WV,[398] buried in Weston Masonic Cemetery, Lewis Co, WV,[398] resided in Weston, Lewis Co, WV,[398] census 1930 in Weston, Lewis Co, WV, resided 1926 in Lewis Co, WV,[621] census 1910 in Auburn, Ritchie Co, WV, occupation 1930 bookkeeper at sheriff's office.[1093] She married Sep- 2-1926 in Weston, Lewis Co, WV,[621] Ira McKinley Spurgeon, b. Jul- 7-1897 in Doddridge Co, WV,[592,1123,621] [Birth date given in 1900 Census as Aug 1897, but SSDI and Florida Death Index show it as Jul 7 1897.] (son of Henry G. Spurgeon and Melissa Czigans), d. Dec-21-1975 in Polk Co, FL,[1123,592] resided in Lakeland, Polk Co, FL,[604] resided 1959 in Weston, Lewis Co, WV,[436] census 1930 in Weston, Lewis Co, WV, resided 1926 in Lewis Co, WV,[621] census 1900 in Cove District, Doddridge Co, WV, occupation 1926 tool dresser,[621] occupation 1930 retail grocery merchant.[1093]

iii.   JULIA PAULINE BROWN, also known as Pauline Brown,[621,1093] b. Nov-25-1901 in Ritchie Co, WV,[592,621] d. Feb-27-1991,[592] resided in Weston, Lewis Co, WV,[604] census 1930 in Weston, Lewis Co, WV, resided 1925 in Lewis Co, WV,[621] census 1910 in Auburn, Ritchie Co, WV. She married May-10-1925 in Weston, Lewis Co, WV,[621] Denzil Adrian White, b. Jul- 1-1901 in Doddridge Co, WV,[604,621] (son of Embra D. White and Bertha __), d. Apr- 7-1990,[604] census 1930 in Weston, Lewis Co, WV, resided 1925 in Lewis Co, WV,[621] occupation 1925, 1930 bookkeeper (lumber).[621,1093]

872. **Emma Frances Adams** (480.Mary[8], 268.John[7], 139.John[6], 72.John[5], 21.John[4], 6.Hugh[3], 3.John[2], 1.Jean[1]), b. Dec-27-1877 at Oxford, Doddridge Co, WV,[190,276,240] [Birth date given in 1900 Census as Dec 1878, but obituary states Dec 27 1877.], d. Apr- 6-1957 in Clarksburg, Harrison Co, WV,[276,806] buried in Archbold Cemetery, Smithburg, Doddridge Co, WV,[190,276] resided in Smithburg, Doddridge Co, WV,[412,856,521,190] census 1900 in Cove District, Doddridge Co, WV. She married (1) Aug-11-1895 in Doddridge Co, WV,[mdcccviii[1808]] divorced[276] **Elbert Ervin Moran**, b. Apr-10-1875,[240,190,mdcccix[1809]] (son of William E. Moran and Emily Jane Knight), d. Aug-21-1937 near Marshville, Harrison Co, WV,[mdcccx[1810]] buried in Greenlawn Masonic Cemetery, Clarksburg, WV,[190] resided near Marshville, Harrison Co, WV,[190] [Grass Run], census 1900 in Cove District, Doddridge Co, WV, occupation Hazel Atlas Glass Co (18 yrs) and farmer (8 yrs).[190] 1900 Census, Doddridge Co, WV (Cove District): Elbert E. Moran, 25, b. Apr 1875, married 4 yrs; wife Emma F, 21, b. Dec 1878, mother of 2 children (both still living); dau Lora E, 2, b. Jul 1897; dau Hila O, 1, b. Apr 1899; boarder Okey Greathouse, 23, b. Sep 1876.

She married[424] (2) Jul-27-1913 in Doddridge Co, WV,[mdcccxi[1811]] **Levi Maxwell**, b. Oct-27-1867 in Doddridge Co, WV,[398,46,434,354] (son of Abner M. Maxwell and Lydia Jane Woofter), d. Oct- 3-1929 in Smithburg, Doddridge Co, WV,[398,mdcccxii[1812],46] buried in South Fork Bapt Church Cem, Oxford, Doddridge Co, WV,[17,398] occupation merchant in Smithburg.[191]

Children by Elbert Ervin Moran:
i.   EDNA LORA MORAN, census name Lora E. Moran,[1809] b. Jul-17-1897 in Doddridge Co, WV,[276,240] [Birth date given in death record as Jul 17 1896, but 1900 Census shows it as Jul 1897, age 2.], d. Nov-13-1965 in Clarksburg, Harrison Co, WV,[276] resided in Smithburg, Doddridge Co, WV,[765,856] census 1900 in Cove District, Doddridge Co, WV. She married[941] Dec- 4-1912 in Doddridge Co, WV,[mdcccxiii[1813]] Okey Dilly, also known as Okey Dilley,[354] b. Jun- 5-1887,[276,354] [Birthplace given as Barbour Co in marriage record, but Braxton Co in death record.] (son of William Dilly and Rachel Cutlip), d. Mar-14-1966 in Clarksburg, Harrison Co, WV.[276]

ii.   OPAL MORAN[240], census name Hila O. Moran,[1809] b. Apr-20-1899 in Grove, Doddridge Co, WV,[240] resided 1957 in Smithburg, Doddridge Co, WV,[856] resided 1937 in Bristol, Harrison Co, WV,[765] resided 1933 in Mt. Clare, Harrison Co, WV,[240] census 1920 in Stealey (Clarksburg), Harrison Co, WV, census 1900 in Cove District, Doddridge Co, WV. She married Apr-23-1918 in Harrison Co, WV,[941] Maurice Gordon Cunningham, also known as M. Gordon Cunningham, census name Morris G. Cunningham,[418] b. Mar- 7-1888 in Sardis, Harrison Co, WV,[240,398,592] (son of John F. Cunningham and

Margaret Gain), d. Jan-18-1970 in Clarksburg, Harrison Co, WV,[398,592] buried in Archbold Cemetery, Smithburg, Doddridge Co, WV,[398] resided in Clarksburg, Harrison Co, WV,[604] census 1920 in Stealey (Clarksburg), Harrison Co, WV, occupation painter.[398]

       iii.   OCIE VIRL MORAN[240] b. Oct- 6-1900 in Doddridge Co, WV,[240] d. Sep-15-1964 in Doddridge Co, WV,[356] resided 1957 in Smithburg, Doddridge Co, WV,[856,778] resided 1937 in Oxford, Doddridge Co, WV.[765] She married[941] James Zinn.

873. **Lenora Bird Adams**, census name Nora Bird Adams,[385] (480.Mary[8], 268.John[7], 139.John[6], 72.John[5], 21.John[4], 6.Hugh[3], 3.John[2], 1.Jean[1]) (See marriage to number 767.)

874. **Ira Clinton Adams, Sr.** (480.Mary[8], 268.John[7], 139.John[6], 72.John[5], 21.John[4], 6.Hugh[3], 3.John[2], 1.Jean[1]), b. Jun- 7-1887 in Oxford, Doddridge Co, WV,[398] d. Apr-12-1956 in Clarksburg, Harrison Co, WV,[398,806] buried in Stonewall Park Cemetery, Stonewood, Harrison Co, WV,[398] resided in Bristol, Harrison Co, WV,[190,398] resided 1929 in Quiet Dell, Harrison Co, WV,[856] resided 1917 in Clarksburg, Harrison Co, WV,[412] occupation farmer.[398]

In addition to his two sons by Mary Ellen Baker, his obituary listed seven children, all daughters, "by a previous marriage," but did not identify either of his former wives.

1920 Census, Harrison Co WV (City of Clarksburg), enumerated on Jan 3 1920:
Ira C. Adams, 32; wife Lona, 35; dau Beryl, 12; dau Pearl, 10; dau Meryl, 8; dau Lena, 6; dau Edith, 2 yrs 6 mos; dau Loraine, 3 mos.

1930 Census, Harrison Co WV (Elk District), enumerated May 1 1930:
Ira C. Adams, 43, widowed, first married at age 18; dau Edith, 12; dau Loraine, 10; dau June, age 4 yrs 10 mos; housekeeper Velva B. Ice, 27, married, first married at age 21; boarder Mary Ice, 4.[190]

He married (1) Apr-28-1906 in Doddridge Co, WV,[mdcccxiv[1814]] **Lona Mason**, b. Nov-29-1884 at Toll Gate, Ritchie Co, WV,[398,354] d. Oct-11-1928 in Clarksburg, Harrison Co, WV,[398] buried in Stonewall Park Cemetery, Stonewood, Harrison Co, WV,[398] cause of death breast cancer,[398] resided in Quiet Dell, Harrison Co, WV,[398] census 1920 in Clarksburg, Harrison Co, WV.[418]

He married (2) Apr-29-1934 in Wallace, Harrison Co, WV,[mdcccxv[1815]] **Iona Virginia Bartlett**, b. Mar-29-1886 in Harrison Co, WV,[419] (daughter of Worthy T. Bartlett and Ella Howell).

He married (3) Aug-28-1948, **Mary Ellen "Lena" Baker**, also known as Ellen Baker,[765] b. Nov-24-1924 in Salem, WV (daughter of Emery D. Baker and Ada Mae Merritt), d. Aug-21-1994 in Harrison Co, WV,[190] buried in Union Mission (Sunrise) Cemetery, New Milton, Doddridge Co, WV,[190] resided 1956 in Bristol, Harrison Co, WV,[484] resided 1951 in Washington, DC.[765]

       Children by Lona Mason:
       i.   BERYL VITA ADAMS, also known as Vita Burl Adams,[419] b. Apr-29-1907,[592] d. May- -1975,[592] resided in Clarksburg, Harrison Co, WV,[592] resided 1927, 56 in Mt. Clare, Harrison Co, WV.[419,765] She married[941] Nov-12-1927 in Clarksburg, Harrison Co, WV,[419] Clarence C. Stout, b. Jun-29-1903 in Barbour Co, WV,[419,592] (son of Strother Stout and Ona B. Bartlett), d. Jun- -1969,[592] resided in Mt. Clare, Harrison Co, WV.[604]
       ii.   PEARL ADAMS b. ca 1910,[418] resided 1956 in Nutter Fort, Harrison Co, WV,[765] census 1920 in Clarksburg, Harrison Co, WV.[418] She married __ Freshour.
       iii.   MERYL ADAMS b. ca 1912,[418] resided 1956 in Portsmouth, VA,[765] census 1920 in Clarksburg, Harrison Co, WV.[418] She married __ Snodgrass.
       iv.   LENA VERYL "PAT" ADAMS, also known as Pat Adams,[765] b. Dec- 8-1913 in Harrison Co, WV,[592,mdcccxvi[1816],418] d. Dec- -1985,[592] resided in Clarksburg, Harrison Co, WV,[604] resided 1956 in Gore, Harrison Co, WV,[765] resided 1946 in Richwood, Nicholas Co, WV,[1816] resided 1932 in Clarksburg, Harrison Co, WV.[419] She married (1) Nov-19-1932 in Clarksburg, Harrison Co, WV,[419] Asa Eugene Bailey, b. Feb-27-1911 in Cedarville, Gilmer Co, WV,[419] (son of W. J. Bailey and Murgie Stout),

resided 1932 in East View (Clarksburg), Harrison Co, WV.[419] She married[941] (2) Feb-23-1946 in Summersville, Nicholas Co, WV,[1816] Angelo Anthony Second, b. Nov-28-1914 in Harrison Co, WV,[592,1816] (son of Frank Second and Rose __), d. Oct- -1985,[592] resided in Clarksburg, Harrison Co, WV,[604] resided 1946 in Richwood, Nicholas Co, WV.[1816]

   v. EDITH ADAMS b. ca 1917,[mdcccxvii[1817]] d. Dec- 8-1969 in Cincinnati, Hamilton Co, OH,[1817] resided 1956, 69 in Cincinnati, Hamilton Co, OH.[765,1817] She married[941] __ Wehrum, d. bef Dec 1969.[436]

   vi. LORAINE ADAMS b. Sep-26-1919 in Clarksburg, Harrison Co, WV,[419,592] d. Jan- -1986,[592] resided in Stafford, Stafford Co, VA,[604] resided 1956 in Slate Mills, VA,[765] resided 1937 at Center Branch, Harrison Co, WV.[419] She married (1) Aug-17-1937 at Mt. Clare, Harrison Co, WV,[419] divorced[526] Edward Ancel Kearns, b. Oct-18-1911 in West Union, Doddridge Co, WV,[592,419] (son of Ancel Kearns and Edna M. Kinney), d. Jan-20-1992,[592] resided in Clarksburg, Harrison Co, WV,[604] resided 1964 in Buckhannon, Upshur Co, WV,[856] resided 1948 in Park Branch, Harrison Co, WV,[419] resided 1937 at Mt. Clare, Harrison Co, WV,[419] census 1930 in Elk District, Harrison Co, WV. She married[941] (2) __ Fender.

   vii. JUNE ADAMS b. Jun-24-1925,[592] d. May- -1985,[592] resided in Costa Mesa, Orange Co, CA,[592] resided 1956 in Los Angeles, CA,[765] resided formerly in West Virginia.[604] She married[941] __ McMullen.

   Children by Mary Ellen "Lena" Baker:
   viii. IRA CLINTON ADAMS, JR., also known as Clinton Adams, resided 1956 in Bristol, Harrison Co, WV.[765] He married Bertie Nicholson (daughter of Burlin Floyd "Esau" Nicholson and Living).

   ix. DENNIS D. ADAMS resided 1956 in Bristol, Harrison Co, WV.[765]
   x. HARVEY L. ADAMS resided 1956 in Bristol, Harrison Co, WV.[765]
   xi. FRANCIS B. "ZIP" ADAMS.

875. **Worthy Eugene Adams** (480.Mary[8], 268.John[7], 139.John[6], 72.John[5], 21.John[4], 6.Hugh[3], 3.John[2], 1.Jean[1]) (See marriage to number 750.)

876. **Etta O'Dell "Addie" Adams**, census name Addie O. Adams,[385] (480.Mary[8], 268.John[7], 139.John[6], 72.John[5], 21.John[4], 6.Hugh[3], 3.John[2], 1.Jean[1]), b. Nov-15-1891 in Camp Run, Oxford, Doddridge Co, WV,[190] d. Oct-21-1971 in Clarksburg, Harrison Co, WV,[764] buried in Masonic Memorial Park Cemetery, Crystal Lake (West Union), WV,[190] resided in Smithburg, Doddridge Co, WV,[412,521,190] resided 1929 in West Union, Doddridge Co, WV.[856] She married Nov-4-1911 near Oxford, Doddridge Co, WV,[mdcccxviii[1818],191,484] **George Herman "Mike" Jones**, b. Apr- 7-1886 in Tyler Co, WV,[190,1396] (son of Joseph W. Jones and Mary Virginia Ash), d. May-12-1972 in Clarksburg, Harrison Co, WV,[190] buried in Masonic Memorial Park Cemetery, Crystal Lake (West Union), WV,[190,721] resided in Smithburg, Doddridge Co, WV,[190] census 1900 in McElroy District, Tyler Co, WV, occupation Hope Natural Gas Co..[1818,190]

George: Predeceased by two sons, two sisters, and two brothers.

1920 Census, Doddridge Co, WV (West Union District):
George Jones, 33; wife Addie O, 28; dau Flossie, 6, dau Pauline, 5; dau Virginia, 2y 7m; son John, under one month.

1930 Census, Doddridge Co, WV (Grant District):
George H. Jones, 43; wife Addie, 38; dau Pauline, 15; dau Virginia, 12; son Herman, 10, dau Loanna, 5y 6m.

   Children:
   i. FLOSSIE JONES b. ca 1913,[775] resided 2001 in Florida,[412] resided 1971, 72 in Casselberry, Seminole Co, FL,[856,765] census 1920 in West Union District, Doddridge Co, WV. She married[1040] (1) __ Shamblin. She married[424] (2) __ Burgess.

ii.   PAULINE ETHEL JONES b. Oct- 5-1914,[592] [Birth date given as Oct 30 1914 in marriage record, but SSDI shows it as oct 5 1914.], d. Feb- 4-1997,[592] resided in Santa Rosa, Sonoma Co, CA,[856,765,592] resided formerly in West Virginia.[604] She married[1040] Nov-14-1936 in Clarksburg, Harrison Co, WV,[419] Farrell Wesley Knight, b. Mar-13-1908 in Doddridge Co, WV,[592,419] [Birth date given as Mar 13 1909 in marriage record, but SSDI states Mar 13 1908.] (son of William Henry Knight and Louie Rachel Collins), d. Nov- -1960,[604] resided 1956 in Orange Co, CA,[521] resided 1936 in Clarksburg, Harrison Co, WV.[419]

iii.   MARY VIRGINIA JONES, also known as Virginia Jones,[1719,775,856,765] b. Jun- 3-1917 in Doddridge Co, WV,[592,1547] d. Apr-25-2008,[592] resided in Lakeland, Polk Co, FL,[592] resided 2001 in Florida,[412] resided 1971, 72 in Pittsburgh, Allegheny Co, PA,[856,765] resided 1935 in Salem, WV,[1547] census 1930 in Grant District, Doddridge Co, WV, census 1920 in West Union District, Doddridge Co, WV. She married[1040] Jun- 8-1935 in St. Marys, Pleasants Co, WV,[1547] Gerald Eugene Knisely, b. Oct-18-1912 in Doddridge Co, WV,[592,1547] d. Sep- 6-1992 in Polk Co, FL,[1123,592] resided in Lakeland, Polk Co, FL,[948] resided 1935 in Salem, WV.[1547]

iv.   GEORGE HERMAN JONES, JR., also known as Herman Jones,[1719] census name John Jones,[775] b. Jan- 1-1920,[721] d. Sep-26-1936,[721] buried in Masonic Memorial Park Cemetery, Crystal Lake (West Union), WV,[721] census 1930 in Grant District, Doddridge Co, WV,[1719] census 1920 in West Union District, Doddridge Co, WV.

v.   GERALD NOLAN JONES b. Nov- 2-1922,[721] d. Oct-22-1927,[721,356] buried in Masonic Memorial Park Cemetery, Crystal Lake (West Union), WV.[721]

vi.   LOANNA JONES b. Sep-23-1924,[592] d. Mar- -1980,[484,592] resided 1971, 72, 80 in Clarendon, Warren Co, PA,[856,765,592] census 1930 in Grant District, Doddridge Co, WV.[1719] She married[484] David C. Maxwell, b. Aug-25-1920 in Doddridge Co, WV,[190,592] (son of W. Clay Maxwell and Mattie Orel Coplin), d. Dec-22-1993 in Clarendon, Warren Co, PA,[700] buried in Warren Co, PA,[190] resided in Clarendon, Warren Co, PA,[856,190,592] occupation Columbia Gas Co, Warren, PA.[190]

vii.   JANET WINOADENE JONES b. Jan- 6-1932 in Doddridge Co, WV,[419,592] d. Oct-22-2001,[190] resided in Roanoke, VA,[190,604] resided 1971, 72 in Clarksburg, Harrison Co, WV.[856,765] She married (1) Living. She married[1040] (2) ca 1970,[191] James C. Loser, resided 2001 in Roanoke, VA.[191]

877. **Alva Wilmer Adams**, also known as Wilmer Adams,[412] (480.Mary[8], 268.John[7], 139.John[6], 72.John[5], 21.John[4], 6.Hugh[3], 3.John[2], 1.Jean[1]), b. Apr-17-1898 in Doddridge Co, WV,[mdcccxix[1819]] [Name entered as Alvin in birth record, but appears as Alva in all other records. Death record states birth date as Apr 17 1897, but birth record shows it as Apr 17 1898.], d. Jun- 6-1947 in Clarksburg, Harrison Co, WV,[398] buried in Bridgeport Cemetery, Harrison Co, WV,[398] resided in Clarksburg, Harrison Co, WV,[412,856,398] census 1930 in Clarksburg, Harrison Co, WV, census 1920 in Southwest District, Doddridge Co, WV, occupation Adams Transfer Co,[398] military World War I.[398] He married Oct- 5-1919 in Doddridge Co, WV,[mdcccxx[1820],354] **Margaret E. "Maggie" Snider**, b. May-28-1901 in Market, Doddridge Co, WV,[190] (daughter of William Thomas Snider and Anna Mae Willis), d. Jan-11-1989 in Clarksburg, Harrison Co, WV,[190] buried in Bridgeport Cemetery, Harrison Co, WV,[190] resided in Clarksburg, Harrison Co, WV.[521,1208]

Children:

i.   ANNA BELLE ADAMS, census name Annabelle Adams,[1208] b. ca 1922,[1208] resided 1989, 2001 in Clarksburg, Harrison Co, WV,[856,412] resided 1971 in Orlando, Orange Co, FL,[1419] census 1930 in Clarksburg, Harrison Co, WV. She married[mdcccxxi[1821],1040] Louis White.

ii.   MABEL I. ADAMS b. Jul-15-1922 in Oxford, Doddridge Co, WV,[190,592] d. Jun- 9-2001 in Bridgeport, Harrison Co, WV,[190,592] buried in Bridgeport Cemetery, Harrison Co, WV,[190] resided 2001 in Bridgeport, Harrison Co, WV,[190,592] resided 1989 in Clarksburg, Harrison Co, WV,[856] resided 1971 in Oxford, Calhoun Co, AL,[1419] census 1930 in Clarksburg, Harrison Co, WV. She married Dec-27-1941,[191] James E. "Bud" Hawkins.

iii.   MARY MARGARET "MARKEY" ADAMS b. ca 1925,[334] resided 1971, 89, 2001 in Clarksburg, Harrison Co, WV,[1419,856,412] census 1930 in Clarksburg, Harrison Co, WV. She married[1040] (1) __ Hood. She married (2)[1821] Joseph Conge.

878. **Minnie A. Gaston**[1041] (481.John[8], 268.John[7], 139.John[6], 72.John[5], 21.John[4], 6.Hugh[3], 3.John[2], 1.Jean[1]), b. Nov-19-1884,[592] d. May-15-1969,[592] resided in Guysville, Athens Co, OH,[856,592] census 1900 in

Greenbrier District, Doddridge Co, WV. She married[1041] **John Archer**,[1041] b. Sep-24-1874 in Ohio,[592,334] d. Nov-15-1974,[592] resided in Guysville, Athens Co, OH,[592] census 1930 in Athens Co, OH, occupation farmer.[334]

> Children:
> i.   JOHN RUSSELL ARCHER, also known as Russell Archer,[190,334,412] b. Aug- 1-1917 in Bashan, Meigs Co, OH,[190,592] d. May-17-2004,[190,592] buried in Coolville, Athens Co, OH,[190] cause of death farming accident with tractor,[190] resided in Guysville, Athens Co, OH,[592] census 1930 in Athens Co, OH, occupation farmer, employee of McBee Systems, school bus driver for Federal Hocking Schools,[190] military U.S. Army, World War II.[190] He married ca 1953,[484] Eloise Warner, d. bef May 2004.[484]
> ii.   IRIS V. ARCHER b. Jan- 5-1920 in Ohio,[592,334] d. May- 3-1992,[592] resided in Athens, Athens Co, OH,[592] census 1930 in Athens Co, OH. She married[424,1041] Clarence M. Warner, b. Sep- 4-1919,[592] d. Dec-30-2006,[592] resided in Athens, Athens Co, OH.[1010]
> iii.   MARY NAOMI ARCHER[521] census name Naomi M. Archer,[334] b. Aug-29-1922 in Ohio,[190] d. Jan- 8-2009 in Lancaster, Fairfield Co, OH,[764] buried in Coolville, Athens Co, OH,[190] resided in Guysville, Athens Co, OH,[190] resided 2004 in Carroll, Fairfield Co, OH,[521] census 1930 in Athens Co, OH, education Coolville H.S.,[190] never married.

879. **James Lee Gaston**, also known as Lee Gaston,[mdcccxxii[1822]] (481.John[8], 268.John[7], 139.John[6], 72.John[5], 21.John[4], 6.Hugh[3], 3.John[2], 1.Jean[1]), b. Apr- 7-1885 in Doddridge Co, WV, d. May- 6-1968 in Athens, Athens Co, OH,[1041] buried in Carthage Gap Church Cem, Athens Co, OH,[1041] resided 1941 in Guysville, Athens Co, OH,[856] census 1900 in Greenbrier District, Doddridge Co, WV.

Name appears as Lee Maxfield Gaston in Burdette's "Sotha Hickman and Some of His Descendants," with birth given as ca 1885 in Doddridge Co, WV. Name appears elsewhere as James Lee Gaston, and he is identified in marriage record and in mother's obituary as J. Lee Gaston.

He married[1041] Feb-23-1908 in Doddridge Co, WV,[mdcccxxiii[1823]] **Dessie F. Snider**, b. ca 1888 in Doddridge Co, WV,[354,1041] (daughter of Aaron Criss Snider and Rachel Virginia Gum), d. 1946.[1041]

> Children:
> i.   OMA OLENA GASTON b. 1912,[1041] d. Jul- -1966,[1041] occupation professor - Ohio University,[1041] education Ohio University, Athens OH,[1041] never married[1041].
> ii.   GLENN A. GASTON[1041] b. Jul-20-1917,[592] d. Apr- 5-2003,[592] resided in Athens, Athens Co, OH.[592]

880. **Ella May Gaston**, census name Ellen M. Gaston,[1038] (481.John[8], 268.John[7], 139.John[6], 72.John[5], 21.John[4], 6.Hugh[3], 3.John[2], 1.Jean[1]), b. Dec- 8-1891 in Doddridge Co, WV,[mdcccxxiv[1824]] d. Sep-19-1972,[1041] buried in Parkersburg Memorial Gardens (aka IOOF Cem, 24th St), Wood Co, WV,[1041] resided 1941 in Parkersburg, Wood Co, WV,[856] census 1900 in Greenbrier District, Doddridge Co, WV. She married Mar-15-1915,[1041] **Leaven A. Townsend**, d. 1973 in Guysville, Athens Co, OH.[1041]

> Children:
> i.   BEULAH TOWNSEND[1041].

881. **Ira Clinton Gaston, Sr.** (481.John[8], 268.John[7], 139.John[6], 72.John[5], 21.John[4], 6.Hugh[3], 3.John[2], 1.Jean[1]), b. Mar- 4-1898 in Doddridge Co, WV,[1011,592] d. Mar- 5-1984 in Athens, Athens Co, OH,[1011,592] buried in Alexander Cemetery, Albany, Athens Co, OH,[mdcccxxv[1825]] resided in Athens, Athens Co, OH,[856,1010] census 1900 in Greenbrier District, Doddridge Co, WV. He married **Lydia Adeline "Addie" Dye**, b. Mar-26-1899,[1825] d. Jul-12-1953.[1825]

> Children:
> i.   THELMA MARJORIE GASTON b. Nov-20-1922 in Athens Co, OH.[1825] She married Charles F. Carpenter, b. Feb-29-1922 in Athens Co, OH,[1825] d. Apr-22-1964 in Springfield, Clark Co, OH.[1825,693]
> ii.   IRA CLINTON "BUDDY" GASTON, JR. b. May- 1-1924 in Guysville, Athens Co, OH,[1825] d. Oct-23-1998,[592] resided in Athens, Athens Co, OH.[592] He married (1) Living. He married (2)

divorced 1970, Delores Smith, b. 1937,[1825] d. 1990.[1825] He married (3) Aug-16-1970,[1825] Irma Spadotto, b. May-13-1926,[592] d. May- 6-2005,[592] resided in Athens, Athens Co, OH.[1157]

      iii. BETTY CAROLYN GASTON b. Sep-10-1925 in Guysville, Athens Co, OH.[1825] She married Joseph Ernest Fields, b. Nov-21-1923 in Cannonville, OH,[1825] d. May-15-1966.[1825]

      iv. BERNICE HELENA GASTON b. Apr-22-1927 in New England, OH,[1825,592] d. Sep- - 1994,[592] buried in Men. Gardens, Athens, OH, resided in Athens, Athens Co, OH.[592] She married Living.

      v. LIVING. He married Living.

      vi. THOMAS REID GASTON b. Sep-25-1938 in Athens, Athens Co, OH,[1825,592] d. Jan- 6-1999,[592] resided in California.[mdcccxxvi[1826]] He married Living.

      vii. LIVING. She married Living.

882. **Amy Mae Gaston** (482.Marion[8], 268.John[7], 139.John[6], 72.John[5], 21.John[4], 6.Hugh[3], 3.John[2], 1.Jean[1]), b. May-21-1898 in Doddridge Co, WV,[592] d. Feb-23-1998 in Charleston, Kanawha Co, WV,[190,592] buried in South Fork Bapt Church Cem, Oxford, Doddridge Co, WV, resided in Elkview, Kanawha Co, WV,[190] resided formerly in Conings, Gilmer Co, WV,[190] census 1930 in Cove District, Doddridge Co, WV, census 1900 in Southwest District, Doddridge Co, WV, occupation teacher.

Graduate of Harrisville High School. Attended Salem College and Alderson- Broaddus College. [obit] Author of "Those Days of Long Ago," a memoir of her early years in Doddridge County, published Sep 15 1984, reprinted in June 1999 by Michael Ruppert, Jr., of Los Angeles, with the help of Mike Ruppert, Sr., of Grove, WV and Loudon, TN, a copy of which is on file at the Doddridge County Library.

She married Jun-23-1927 in Doddridge Co, WV,[mdcccxxvii[1827]] **Harry Monroe Smith**, b. Feb- 1-1897 near Grove, Doddridge Co, WV,[190,mdcccxxviii[1828],17,592] (son of George William Smith and Anna Czigans), d. Nov-23-1970 in Clarksburg, Harrison Co, WV,[806,1828,17,592] buried in South Fork Bapt Church Cem, Oxford, Doddridge Co, WV,[17,1828,190] resided (past 29 yrs) in Conings, Gilmer Co, WV,[190] resided in Troy, Gilmer Co, WV,[592,1828] census 1930 in Cove District, Doddridge Co, WV, occupation Pennzoil Co (retired).[190]

      Children:

      i. LIVING. She married[941,1040] Living.

883. **Alpha Lee Gaston** (482.Marion[8], 268.John[7], 139.John[6], 72.John[5], 21.John[4], 6.Hugh[3], 3.John[2], 1.Jean[1]), b. Feb- 3-1900 in Oxford, Doddridge Co, WV,[mdcccxxix[1829],190,46,711] d. Mar-31-1974 in Troy, Gilmer Co, WV,[190,46] buried in Spurgeon (aka Pleasant Valley or Dunkard) Cem, Bear Fork (Co Rd 62/2), Doddridge/Gilmer Co WV,[17] [Obituary gives burial location as Pleasant Valley Cemetery. Headstone is at Spurgeon Cemetery.], resided in Troy, Gilmer Co, WV,[190] resided 1956 in Salem, WV,[765] resided 1949 in Auburn, Ritchie Co, WV,[856] census 1930 in Troy District, Gilmer Co, WV, census 1900 in Southwest District, Doddridge Co, WV. She married Oct-5-1924 in Harrisville, Ritchie Co, WV,[mdcccxxx[1830],354] **Clarence A. Spurgeon**, b. May-24-1894 in Gilmer Co, WV,[592,276,46,711] [Birth date given in 1900 Census as May 1895, but date on headstone is 1894, and SSDI specifies May 24 1894.] (son of George Oliver Spurgeon and Mary Ann Sponaugle), d. Dec-30-1962 in Clarksburg, Harrison Co, WV,[276,46,191,506,mdcccxxxi[1831]] [Date of death is incorrectly given in SSDI as Feb 1963. Date on headstone is 1962, and death record specifies Dec 30 1962.], buried in Spurgeon (aka Pleasant Valley or Dunkard) Cem, Bear Fork (Co Rd 62/2), Doddridge/Gilmer Co WV,[17,276] resided 1924 in Gilmer Co, WV,[mdcccxxxii[1832]] census 1920, 1930 in Troy District, Gilmer Co, WV, occupation storekeeper, operator of Dairy Queen.[1831,276]

      Children:

      i. HAYWARD CLINE SPURGEON b. Oct- 1-1925 in Bear Fork, Gilmer Co, WV,[190,46] d. May- 1-1985 in Bear Fork, Gilmer Co, WV,[190,46] buried in Spurgeon (aka Pleasant Valley or Dunkard) Cem, Bear Fork (Co Rd 62/2), Doddridge/Gilmer Co WV,[17,190] resided in Jane Lew, Lewis Co, WV,[856,190,748] resided 1946 at Auburn, Ritchie Co, WV,[711] census 1930 in Troy District, Gilmer Co, WV.

He was a retired Greyhound bus driver with 33 years of service, and he owned and operated the Triple S Sharpening Shop in Jane Lew.

He married Sep-20-1946 at Troy, Gilmer Co, WV,[711,484] Mildred Rosalee McIntyre, b. Dec- 5-1923 in Harrison Co, WV,[592,46,711] (daughter of Forrest Loran McIntyre and Bertha Thompson), d. Nov-10-1992,[592,46] buried in Spurgeon (aka Pleasant Valley or Dunkard) Cem, Bear Fork (Co Rd 62/2), Doddridge/Gilmer Co WV,[17] resided in Jane Lew, Lewis Co, WV,[604] resided 1946 near Troy, Gilmer Co, WV.[711]

ii.   MARION RAY SPURGEON, also known as Ray Spurgeon, d. bef May 1985.[521]

884. **Orley Carson Gaston**, also known as Carson Gaston,[1389,711,856,765,412] (482.Marion[8], 268.John[7], 139.John[6], 72.John[5], 21.John[4], 6.Hugh[3], 3.John[2], 1.Jean[1]), b. Mar-18-1902 in Doddridge Co, WV,[mdcccxxxiii[1833],190] d. Apr- 7-1973 in Akron, Summit Co, OH,[190] buried in South Fork Bapt Church Cem, Oxford, Doddridge Co, WV,[17,190] resided 1949, 56 in Akron, Summit Co, OH,[856,765] census 1930 in Southwest District, Doddridge Co, WV, occupation carpenter; research technician for Goodyear Aerospace,[1831,190,506.] He married Oct-4-1924 in Clarksburg, Harrison Co, WV,[mdcccxxxiv[1834],354] **Mary L. Osburn**, b. Apr-12-1899 at Oxford, Doddridge Co, WV,[190,mdcccxxxv[1835],1833] [Online edition of Ohio death records, Certificate # 006766, show her maiden name as "Osburn," as does husband's obituary. But marriage record has it as "Osborne," and she was listed as a survivor in the obituary of her brother W. Frank Osborne. No birth record for her was found in Doddridge Co.] (daughter of Jacob Manderville Osburn and Annetta "Nettie" Cole), d. Jan-23-1995 in Copley, Summit Co, OH,[190] buried in South Fork Bapt Church Cem, Oxford, Doddridge Co, WV,[190,17] resided in Akron, Summit Co, OH,[856,mdcccxxxvi[1836]] census 1900, 10, 20, 30 in Southwest District, Doddridge Co, WV.

Children:

i.   MARGARET L. GASTON b. Mar-28-1926 in Doddridge Co, WV,[190,1389] d. Mar- 7-2008,[190] buried in South Fork Bapt Church Cem, Oxford, Doddridge Co, WV,[190] resided in Akron, Summit Co, OH,[765,856,484] census 1930 in Doddridge Co, WV,[1389] education West Virginia Business College, Clarksburg WV (1943).[mdcccxxxvii[1837]] She married[941] ca 1945,[484] Amos Ronald Sheets, also known as Ronald Sheets,[191] b. Sep-21-1921 in Ritchie Co, WV,[190,592] d. Apr-24-2007,[190,592] buried in South Fork Bapt Church Cem, Oxford, Doddridge Co, WV,[190] resided in Akron, Summit Co, OH,[592] resided formerly in West Virginia,[604] occupation Pittsburgh Plate Glass Co. (35 yrs, retired),[190] military U.S. Navy, World War II.[190]

ii.   LIVING. She married[941] Robert Gene Leibold, b. Sep- 9-1928 in Bowling Green, Wood Co, OH,[190] (son of George Walter Leibold and Sylvia Barker), d. Jun-17-2005,[190] buried in Arlington National Cemetery, VA,[190] resided in Monroe, Amherst Co, VA,[190,1253] military Chief Petty Officer, U.S. Navy (retired, Korean War),[190] occupation engineer, IBM Federal Systems (20 yrs, retired).[190]

885. **Gail Adams Gaston** (482.Marion[8], 268.John[7], 139.John[6], 72.John[5], 21.John[4], 6.Hugh[3], 3.John[2], 1.Jean[1]), b. Oct-30-1905 in Oxford, Doddridge Co, WV,[1182] d. Mar-24-1951 in Barbour Co, WV,[mdcccxxxviii[1838]] cause of death leukemia,[mdcccxxxix[1839]] buried in Belington Fraternal Cem, Belington, Barbour Co, WV,[17] resided in Belington, Barbour Co, WV,[856] resided 1939 in Keyser, Mineral Co, WV,[1182] occupation Gaston's Pharmacy, Belington, WV.[1831] He married Jul-16-1939 in Keyser, Mineral Co, WV,[1182] **Virginia Maxine Wood**, b. Mar-31-1911 in Marion, Marion Co, OH,[190,17,592] (daughter of Clarence Wood and Lillian Bosley), d. Aug-12-2001 in Morgantown, Monongalia Co, WV,[806,17,592] buried in Belington Fraternal Cem, Belington, Barbour Co, WV,[17,190] resided in Morgantown, Monongalia Co, WV,[1086] resided formerly in Belington, Barbour Co, WV,[190] resided in Keyser, Mineral Co, WV,[1182] occupation pharmacist for WVU hospitals (11 yrs, retired 1975),[190] education West Virginia University (1956, pharmacy degree).[190]

Virginia: A member of the Daughters of the American Revolution.[190]

Children:

i.   LIVING.

ii.   LIVING. She married Living.

          iii.   LIVING.

886. **Ada Vonda Gaston**, also known as Vonda Gaston (483.Francis[8], 268.John[7], 139.John[6], 72.John[5], 21.John[4], 6.Hugh[3], 3.John[2], 1.Jean[1]), b. Nov-29-1904 in Doddridge Co, WV,[592] d. Jan- -1981,[mdcccxl[1840]] resided 1950, 61 in Weston, Lewis Co, WV.[765,856] She married Sep-11-1927 in Doddridge Co, WV,[mdcccxli[1841]] **Clyde Otis Hatfield**, b. May-24-1900 in Addison Run, Cairo, Ritchie Co, WV,[mdcccxlii[1842],190] (son of Harvey Homer Hatfield and Mary Carson Stull), d. Oct-24-1975 in Parkersburg, Wood Co, WV,[mdcccxliii[1843],190] buried in IOOF Cemetery, Harrisville, Ritchie Co, WV,[190] occupation Hope Natural Gas Company.
                    Children:
          i.   MARY LUCILLE HATFIELD, also known as Lucille Hatfield,[412] b. 1928 in Harrisville, Ritchie Co, WV,[46,1843] d. 1929,[46] buried in South Fork Bapt Church Cem, Oxford, Doddridge Co, WV.[17]
          ii.   LIVING. She married[1843] Living.
          iii.   DELMA JEAN HATFIELD b. Aug-30-1932 in Littleton, Wetzel Co, WV,[190,1843] d. Jul- 4-2010 in Clarksburg, Harrison Co, WV,[847] buried in New Bethel Cemetery, Good Hope, Harrison Co, WV,[190] resided in Kincheloe (Jane Lew), Harrison Co, WV,[1843,190] occupation secretary, Hope Gas Co.[190] She married[1843] James Edward Elmer, resided 2010 in Kincheloe (Jane Lew), Harrison Co, WV.[191]
          iv.   LIVING. He married Living.

887. **Wheeler Shirley Wilson**, also known as Shirley Wilson,[506,412,1057] (484.Elizabeth[8], 268.John[7], 139.John[6], 72.John[5], 21.John[4], 6.Hugh[3], 3.John[2], 1.Jean[1]), b. Nov-15-1897,[385] d. ca 1957,[765] occupation teacher,[506,mdcccxliv[1844]] census 1930 in Vienna, Wood Co, WV, census 1900, 1920 in Southwest District, Doddridge Co, WV. He married[1057] Jul- 1-1922 in Ritchie Co, WV,[996] **Eva Jane Pritchard**, b. May- 6-1901,[592,996] (daughter of Francis Ezra Pritchard and Maude Genevra Clayton), d. Jun- 6-1989,[592] resided in Vienna, Wood Co, WV,[592] census 1930 in Vienna, Wood Co, WV, census 1920 in Ritchie Co, WV.[1026]
                    Children:
          i.   FRANK MARCELL WILSON b. Jul- 8-1923 in Parkersburg, Wood Co, WV,[602,592] d. Mar-1-1998,[592] resided in Salem, Marion Co, OR,[604] resided 1946 in Vienna, Wood Co, WV,[602] census 1930 in Vienna, Wood Co, WV. He married Feb- 2-1946 in Vienna, Wood Co, WV,[602] Mabel Ermalee Mullenix, also known as Ermalee Mullenix, b. Apr-16-1926 in Pullman, Ritchie Co, WV,[602,592] (daughter of Larcey Mullenix and Dessie Wamsley), d. Jun- -1968,[604] resided 1946 in Parkersburg, Wood Co, WV.[602]
          ii.   LARRY EUGENE WILSON b. Nov-12-1936 in Parkersburg, Wood Co, WV,[602,592,46] d. Jul-15-1990,[592,46] buried in Mt. Harmony Masonic Cemetery, Pennsboro, Ritchie Co, WV,[469] resided in Vienna, Wood Co, WV.[602,604] He married May- 3-1968 in Lubeck, Wood Co, WV,[602] divorced[436] Donna Lee Jones, b. Jan-24-1932 in Pennsboro, Ritchie Co, WV,[602,592,46] (daughter of Sherman Cleveland Jones and Lenna D. Jeffries), d. Oct-15-1995 in Columbus, Franklin Co, OH,[1011,592] buried in Mt. Harmony Masonic Cemetery, Pennsboro, Ritchie Co, WV,[469] resided in Williamstown, Wood Co, WV,[604] resided 1968 in Vienna, Wood Co, WV,[602] resided 1948 in Pennsboro, Ritchie Co, WV.[588]

888. **Louie Enid Wilson**, also known as Enid,[856,1057] (484.Elizabeth[8], 268.John[7], 139.John[6], 72.John[5], 21.John[4], 6.Hugh[3], 3.John[2], 1.Jean[1]), b. May-14-1901 in Oxford, Doddridge Co, WV,[190] d. Sep-13-1997 in Parkersburg, Wood Co, WV,[190] buried in South Fork Bapt Church Cem, Oxford, Doddridge Co, WV,[190] resided in Oxford, Doddridge Co, WV,[856,190] occupation teacher.[506]

She was the last surviving charter member of the Mutual Benefit Extension Homemakers Club, which was formed in 1927 with 17 members joining. She was a graduate of Alderson-Broaddus College and taught at Leggett School near Oxford, WV. She was a member of South Fork Baptist Church, where she served as clerk for more than 40 years.[190]

She married[mdcccxlv[1845]] Aug-10-1924 in Doddridge Co, WV,[354] [Wilson-Pepper Genealogy 1595-1989, p. 39, reports marriage date as Aug 7 1924.], **Overy Earl Zinn**, also known as Earl Zinn,[1057,mdcccxlvi[1846]] b. Apr-28-1896 in Ritchie Co, WV,[1059] (son of Wesley Worthington "Wirt" Zinn and Jemima White), d. Jul- 9-1970,[17] buried in South Fork Bapt Church Cem, Oxford, Doddridge Co, WV,[17] census 1900 in Union District, Ritchie Co, WV, military PVT, Co E, 319th Infantry, World War I.[17]

Children:

i. NELSON EARL ZINN b. Apr-19-1925 in Porto Rico (New Milton), Doddridge Co, WV,[mdcccxlvii[1847]] resided 1997 in Wilmington, New Castle Co, DE,[856] resided 1957 in Louisville, Jefferson Co, KY,[1696] occupation DuPont Chemical Co. He married Living.

ii. LIVING. She married David Dale Ball, also known as Dale Ball,[765] b. Nov-29-1924 in Ritchie Co, WV,[190] [Straight Fork] (son of Toy Ball and Sylvia B. Heckert), d. Nov-10-2010 in Clarksburg, Harrison Co, WV,[911] buried in South Fork Bapt Church Cem, Oxford, Doddridge Co, WV,[190] resided at Summers, Doddridge Co, WV,[190] military U.S. Army, World War II (Battle of the Bulge),[190] occupation farmer, school bus driver (1968-1987).[190]

iii. DALE WENDELL ZINN b. Apr- 5-1930 in Oxford, Doddridge Co, WV,[190] d. Sep-23-1998 in Morgantown, Monongalia Co, WV,[190] buried in Rockford Methodist Cemetery, Lost Creek, Harrison Co, WV,[190] resided in Morgantown, Monongalia Co, WV,[190] military 1952-54 Captain, U.S. Air Force.[190]

Earned B.S. & M.S. degrees from West Virginia University, and PhD from the University of Missouri. Among other distinguished academic positions, served as Dean of Agriculture & Forestry at WVU from 1975 to 1984, and as Executive Director of Northeastern Federal Agricultural Experiment Stations from 1984 to 1995.[190]

He married Living.

iv. LIVING. He married Living.

v. LIVING. He married Living.

889. **Eula Edith Wilson**, census name Edith E. Wilson,[1390] (484.Elizabeth[8], 268.John[7], 139.John[6], 72.John[5], 21.John[4], 6.Hugh[3], 3.John[2], 1.Jean[1]), b. Oct-12-1910,[1059] d. Feb-28-2005,[190] buried in South Fork Bapt Church Cem, Oxford, Doddridge Co, WV,[190] resided in Columbus, Franklin Co, OH,[765,856,190,1057] census 1920 in Southwest District, Doddridge Co, WV. She married Oct-16-1942,[17] **Allison Bell "George" Davis**,[17] b. Apr-15-1906 in DeKalb, Gilmer Co, WV,[190,17] (son of Robert E. Davis and Ida Bell), d. Feb-27-1986 in Columbus, Franklin Co, OH,[190,17] buried in South Fork Bapt Church Cem, Oxford, Doddridge Co, WV,[17] military PFC, US Army, World War II.[1410]

Children:

i. BARBARA KAY DAVIS. She married Donald Robison.

ii. NELLIE MARGARET DAVIS. She married Manny De la Cruz.

iii. BEVERLY SUE DAVIS resided 1986 in Doylestown, Bucks Co, PA.[765] She married Jeffery Gerber.

890. **James Wesley Law**, also known as J. Wesley Law,[398,748,418] (487.Sarah[8], 269.Elizabeth[7], 139.John[6], 72.John[5], 21.John[4], 6.Hugh[3], 3.John[2], 1.Jean[1]), b. May-17-1882,[398,964,46] [Birthplace given as Gilmer County in marriage record, but Ritchie County in death record.], d. May-27-1941 in Clarksburg, Harrison Co, WV,[398,46] buried in Good Hope Masonic Cemetery, Rt. 19 S, Harrison Co, WV,[524,398] resided in Clarksburg, Harrison Co, WV,[398,748] census 1920 in Clarksburg, Harrison Co, WV, resided 1911 in Taylor Co, WV,[724] census 1900 in Troy District, Gilmer Co, WV, occupation dairyman, Clarksburg Dairy Co..[398,418] He married Jun- 7-1911 in Grafton, Taylor Co, WV,[724] **Maymie Gay Phillips**, b. 1889 in Taylor Co, WV,[46,724] d. 1984,[46] buried in Good Hope Masonic Cemetery, Rt. 19 S, Harrison Co, WV.[524]

Children:

i. JAMES PHILLIPS LAW b. Nov-27-1914,[17] d. Dec-16-1977,[17] buried in Good Hope Masonic Cemetery, Rt. 19 S, Harrison Co, WV,[524] census 1920 in Clarksburg, Harrison Co, WV. He married[191] ca 1937,[191] Ruth Freeman, b. Jan- 2-1915 in Sutton, Braxton Co, WV,[190] (daughter of Isaac Lawrence Freeman and Bertha Ann Harris), d. Dec- 7-2003 in Morgantown, Monongalia Co, WV,[190] cremated[190] resided in Morgantown, Monongalia Co, WV,[190] resided formerly in Fairmont, Marion

Co, WV,[190] occupation elementary school teacher,[190] education W. Va. Wesleyan (A.B.), W.Va. University (M.A.).[190]

     ii.   PAUL WINFIELD LAW b. 1917,[46] d. 1939,[46] buried in Good Hope Masonic Cemetery, Rt. 19 S, Harrison Co, WV,[524] census 1920 in Clarksburg, Harrison Co, WV.

891. **Guinn Neely** (489.Lucy[8], 272.John[7], 140.Deborah[6], 72.John[5], 21.John[4], 6.Hugh[3], 3.John[2], 1.Jean[1]), b. Sep-20-1871 in West Virginia, d. Jan-30-1938, buried in Terrace Heights Memorial Park, Yakima, WA, resided since 1914 in Yakima, Yakima Co, WA,[395] census 1930 in Yakima Co, WA, census 1910 in Barbour Co, WV, occupation 1910 dry goods salesman,[mdcccxlviii[1848]] occupation 1930 fruit farmer.[334] He married 1893, **Maude A. Rankin**, b. Oct-25-1878 in Pennsylvania, d. Oct-31-1955, buried in Terrace Heights Memorial Park, Yakima, WA, census 1930 in Yakima Co, WA, census 1910 in Barbour Co, WV.

     Children:

     i.   EDWIN R. NEELY b. Aug-18-1895, d. Sep- 4-1982, census 1910 in Barbour Co, WV. He married Lucy Peters, d. 1980.

     ii.   ARNETT R. NEELY b. Mar- 8-1898, d. Jan- 1-1966, census 1930 in Yakima Co, WA, census 1910 in Barbour Co, WV, occupation fruit farmer.[334]

     iii.   LUCY VIRGINIA NEELY b. Aug-15-1901, d. Nov- -1966,[592] resided in Ponca City, Kay Co, OK,[838] census 1910 in Barbour Co, WV. She married Jul-21-1921, George Martin Palmer, b. Jun-21-1899, d. Feb-25-1946, buried in Sunnyside Memorial Cem, Long Beach, CA.

     iv.   WILLIAM R. NEELY b. Oct-30-1908, d. Mar- -1967, census 1910 in Barbour Co, WV. He married Helen Barthel, d. 1984.

     v.   DONALD R. NEELY b. May-13-1912 in Century, Barbour Co, WV,[190,592] d. Sep- 6-2006,[592] buried in Terrace Heights Memorial Park, Yakima, WA,[190] resided in Lake Oswego, Clackamas Co, OR,[1153] resided until 2006 in Yakima, Yakima Co, WA,[190] census 1930 in Yakima Co, WA, occupation fruit grower,[190] education Yakima H.S. (1930), Washington State Univ.[190] He married Nov-11-1934, Gwendolyn Mary Longbottom, b. May-30-1912 in Yakima, Yakima Co, WA,[190] (daughter of Irvine Longbottom and Harriet __), d. Nov-10-2007 in Portland, OR,[190] buried in Terrace Heights Memorial Park, Yakima, WA,[190] resided in Lake Oswego, Clackamas Co, OR,[190] resided until 2006 in Yakima, Yakima Co, WA,[190] education Yakima H.S., Yakima Business College.[190]

892. **George W. Neely** (489.Lucy[8], 272.John[7], 140.Deborah[6], 72.John[5], 21.John[4], 6.Hugh[3], 3.John[2], 1.Jean[1]), b. Nov- 6-1875 in Harrison Co, WV,[17,410] d. Jul-12-1949,[17] buried in Broad Run Bapt Ch Cem, Jane Lew, Lewis Co, WV.[mdcccxlix[1849]] He married Nov-12-1901 in Lewis Co, WV,[410] **M. Grace Carpenter**, b. Jun- 6-1877,[17] (daughter of Edward Carpenter and Rizpah B. __), d. Jan-11-1933 in Lewis Co, WV,[17] buried in Broad Run Bapt Ch Cem, Jane Lew, Lewis Co, WV.

     Children:

     i.   WILLIAM EDWARD NEELY b. ca 1913 in Lewis Co, WV,[190] d. May- 5-2006 in Martinsburg, Berkeley Co, WV,[911] buried in Elmwood Cemetery, Shepherdstown, Jefferson Co, WV,[190] resided since 1979 in Shepherdstown, Jefferson Co, WV,[190] education West Virginia University (1934), WVU College of Law (1940),[190] military Captain, JAG, U.S. Navy (1942-1973).[190]

     As a young man, he distinguished himself as an amateur boxer, both in high school in Weston and at WVU. After graduation from WVU in 1934, he was an educational advisor for the Civilian Conservation Corps (CCC), where he served in Pocahontas and Preston counties. Later, he entered the WVU College of Law, graduating in 1950. He then practiced law briefly in Clarksburg at Stathers, Stathers & Cantrell. In January 1942, in the wake of Pearl Harbor, he enlisted in the U.S. Navy for World War II. He was commissioned as an officer in 1943 and served in the Navy's Armed Guard at sea until the conclusion of the war in 1945. He became a career naval officer at that time. Until his retirement in 1973, he served in many duty stations, including American Samoa, Japan, Washington, Seattle, Memphis, Norfolk and Charlottesville. He retired as a Captain, Judge Advocate General Corps (JAG), and then spent the next few years traveling the globe.[190]

     He married[484] (1) Mary Roe, d. 1966.[484] He married (2) Aug-20-1968, Jean Lois Chapman, resided 2006 in Shepherdstown, Jefferson Co, WV.[484]

893. **John Howard Neely**, census name Howard J. Neely,[1848] also known as J. Howard Neely,[17] (489.Lucy[8], 272.John[7], 140.Deborah[6], 72.John[5], 21.John[4], 6.Hugh[3], 3.John[2], 1.Jean[1]), b. Jul-23-1879 in Harrison Co, WV,[46] d. May-14-1955,[46] buried in Broad Run Bapt Ch Cem, Jane Lew, Lewis Co, WV,[17] census 1910 in Barbour Co, WV [In household with brother Guinn and his family.], occupation 1910 grocery salesman.[1848] He married[395] **Claudia Manley**, also known as Claudie Manley,[17,236,374] census name Claudius H. Manley,[mdcccl[1850]] b. Jul-26-1893,[236] [Birth date on headstone is 1891, but death record shows it as Jul 26 1893.] (daughter of James M. Manley and Rilla A. __), d. Aug- 5-1958 in Weston, Lewis Co, WV,[236,46] buried in Broad Run Bapt Ch Cem, Jane Lew, Lewis Co, WV,[17,236] resided in Jane Lew, Lewis Co, WV,[236] census 1900 in Upshur Co, WV.

> Children:
> i. JOSEPH M. NEELY[17] b. Jan-30-1914,[17,592] d. May-15-1984,[17,592] buried in Broad Run Bapt Ch Cem, Jane Lew, Lewis Co, WV,[17] resided in Jane Lew, Lewis Co, WV.[592] He married Alice __.
> ii. EMILY GWENDOLYN NEELY b. Aug-14-1915 in Harrison Co, WV,[419] d. Feb- 6-1992, buried in Bridgeport Cemetery, Harrison Co, WV. She married May-25-1939 in Bridgeport, Harrison Co, WV,[419] William Thomas Steele, b. Apr- -1913 in Harrison Co, WV,[419,592] [Birth date given in marriage record as Apr 4 1913, but SSDI shows it as Apr 13 1913.] (son of Harrison Steele and Rose Bartlett), d. Oct-14-1992,[592] resided in Clarksburg, Harrison Co, WV.[604]
> iii. LEE ROY NEELY b. Dec-11-1922,[592,1006] [Birthplace given as Harrison County in marriage record, but as Jane Lew (Lewis County) in obituary.], d. May-15-2010 in Jane Lew, Lewis Co, WV,[700,592] buried in Broad Run Bapt Ch Cem, Jane Lew, Lewis Co, WV,[190] resided in Jane Lew, Lewis Co, WV,[604] resided 1943 in Lewis Co, WV,[1006] occupation dozer operator, Consolidated Gas Co (42 yrs),[190] military Pfc, U.S. Army, World War II.[190] He married Jan-16-1943 in Weston, Lewis Co, WV,[1006] Marjorie Allman, b. ca 1921 in Lewis Co, WV,[1006] (daughter of Russell Allman and Ruth Hitt), resided 2010 in Jane Lew, Lewis Co, WV,[484] resided 1943 in Glenville, Gilmer Co, WV.[1006]

894. **Ethel Neely** (489.Lucy[8], 272.John[7], 140.Deborah[6], 72.John[5], 21.John[4], 6.Hugh[3], 3.John[2], 1.Jean[1]), b. Feb-26-1887, d. Mar-14-1929, buried in Broad Run Bapt Ch Cem, Jane Lew, Lewis Co, WV. She married **Thomas Riley Moss**, b. Mar-28-1886, d. Mar- 1-1974, buried in Broad Run Bapt Ch Cem, Jane Lew, Lewis Co, WV.

> Children:
> i. MARJORIE CATHERINE MOSS b. Oct- 2-1914,[592] d. Jul-25-1998,[592] resided in St. Albans, Kanawha Co, WV.[592] She married Mar-19-1938, Lloyd Weaver Smith, b. Sep-28-1913,[592] d. Mar- 8-2000,[592] resided in St. Albans, Kanawha Co, WV.[592]
> ii. WILLIAM NEELY MOSS b. Apr- 3-1919, d. May-22-1986. He married 1942, Martha Jean Hammond, b. Apr-12-1920, d. Sep-16-1985.
> iii. WILMA RUTH MOSS b. Apr-25-1922. She married Aug- 4-1943, Earl Smith Goodwin, b. Dec-18-1920,[592] d. Apr- 3-1976.[592]

895. **Lula Jessie Taylor** (490.William[8], 272.John[7], 140.Deborah[6], 72.John[5], 21.John[4], 6.Hugh[3], 3.John[2], 1.Jean[1]), b. Apr-12-1893,[17] d. Aug- 7-1914,[17] buried in Broad Run Bapt Ch Cem, Jane Lew, Lewis Co, WV.[17] She married Sep-9-1913, **Kenzy Bernard Renner**, b. 1880,[46] d. Jan- 1-1915,[46] buried in Broad Run Bapt Ch Cem, Jane Lew, Lewis Co, WV.[17]

> Children:
> i. JASON BERNARD RENNER b. Aug- 3-1914,[17] d. Jan- 8-1915,[17] buried in Broad Run Bapt Ch Cem, Jane Lew, Lewis Co, WV.[17]

896. **Grace Irene Taylor** (490.William[8], 272.John[7], 140.Deborah[6], 72.John[5], 21.John[4], 6.Hugh[3], 3.John[2], 1.Jean[1]), b. Jul-11-1895,[592] d. Dec- 8-1994,[592] resided in Jane Lew, Lewis Co, WV.[mdcccli[1851]] She married[446] Jun-10-1920, **William Clarence Ballard**, b. Jul- 3-1891, d. Jul-23-1955, buried in Broad Run Bapt Ch Cem, Jane Lew, Lewis Co, WV.

> Children:
> i. GRACE EILEEN BALLARD, also known as Eileen Ballard,[484,521] b. Jun-17-1921, resided 2003, 07, 08 in Weston, Lewis Co, WV,[mdccclii[1852],484,521.] She married Jun-26-1942,[484] George Exel "Eck" Arnold,[190] also known as Exel Arnold,[mdcccliii[1853]] b. Mar-25-1914 in Upshur Co, WV,[190] (son of

A. Damon Arnold and Vida Dell Queen), d. Jan-29-2007 in Weston, Lewis Co, WV,[806] buried in Broad Run Bapt Ch Cem, Jane Lew, Lewis Co, WV,[190] resided in Weston, Lewis Co, WV,[190] military U.S. Navy, World War II (South Pacific).[190]

George: A prominent businessman, he retired from the automobile business in Lewis County and later became involved in oil and gas production. He was one of the founders of Stonewall National Bank of Weston and served on the Board of Directors of CB&T for several years. He served three terms in the West Virginia House of Delegates and served on the Lewis County Democratic Committee. He was a Kentucky Colonel and a graduate of the University of Hard Knocks.[190]

    ii.   WILLIAM LEO BALLARD b. Jan-24-1925 in Lewis Co, WV,[190,592] d. Jun- 2-2008 in Jane Lew, Lewis Co, WV,[764,592] buried in Broad Run Bapt Ch Cem, Jane Lew, Lewis Co, WV,[190] resided in Jane Lew, Lewis Co, WV,[604] education Potomac State, WV Wesleyan (bachelors 1950), WV Univ (masters),[190] military 1943-46 tail gunner, Army Air Corps, World War II (Pacific),[190] occupation teacher, coach, athletic director (Lewis County schools).[190] He married Living.
    iii.   WILBUR EUGENE BALLARD, also known as Webb Ballard,[521] b. Jun-21-1926 in Jane Lew, Lewis Co, WV,[419] resided 1946, 2008 in Jane Lew, Lewis Co, WV.[419,521] He married Mar-19-1946 in Clarksburg, Harrison Co, WV,[419] Patricia Joan Adams, b. Feb-16-1926 in Oxford, Doddridge Co, WV,[419] (daughter of Lawrence Alfred Adams and Lucy Gay Law), resided 1986 in Jane Lew, Lewis Co, WV,[765] resided 1946 in Lost Creek, Harrison Co, WV.[419]

897. **Rufus Davisson Taylor** (490.William[8], 272.John[7], 140.Deborah[6], 72.John[5], 21.John[4], 6.Hugh[3], 3.John[2], 1.Jean[1]), b. Sep- 1-1900,[46] d. May- 4-1982,[46] buried in Broad Run Bapt Ch Cem, Jane Lew, Lewis Co, WV.[17] He married Nov-29-1923 in Lewis Co, WV,[410] **Ednah Beeghley Swisher**, b. Mar- 1-1901,[46] (daughter of Wirt Swisher and Mary Adeline Beeghley), d. Aug- 9-1972,[46] buried in Broad Run Bapt Ch Cem, Jane Lew, Lewis Co, WV,[17] resided 1940 in Shinnston, Harrison Co, WV.[856]
    Children:
    i.   DELORES ELAINE TAYLOR b. Oct-11-1924. She married May-26-1948, Charles Lester Brown, b. Oct-24-1922.

898. **Harley Grant Taylor** (490.William[8], 272.John[7], 140.Deborah[6], 72.John[5], 21.John[4], 6.Hugh[3], 3.John[2], 1.Jean[1]), b. Apr-27-1905,[592] d. Aug-16-1981,[592] buried in Three Springs Cemetery, near Weirton, Hancock Co, WV, resided in Weirton, Hancock Co, WV.[948] He married Feb- -1930, **Agnes Davis**, b. Jun-10-1897,[604] (daughter of William Hedges Davis and Etta Larue Haddox), d. Sep-29-1972,[604] buried in Three Springs Cemetery, near Weirton, Hancock Co, WV, resided in Weirton, Hancock Co, WV.[604]
    Children:
    i.   JEANETTE LOUISE TAYLOR b. Apr-27-1930, d. Apr-20-1981, buried in Three Springs Cemetery, near Weirton, Hancock Co, WV. She married Living.
    ii.   LIVING. She married (1) Living. She married (2) Living.

899. **Madge Reed** (491.Ella[8], 272.John[7], 140.Deborah[6], 72.John[5], 21.John[4], 6.Hugh[3], 3.John[2], 1.Jean[1]), b. Apr- 5-1904,[592] d. Feb-11-1999,[592] resided in Arlington, Arlington Co, VA,[mdccliv[1854]] resided formerly in West Virginia.[604] She married May-10-1927, **Weaver S. Barbe**, b. Oct-19-1902,[592] d. Apr- -1986,[592] [A death date of May 1985 has also been reported, but SSDI has Apr 1986.].
    Children:
    i.   LIVING.

900. **Bertie Reed** (491.Ella[8], 272.John[7], 140.Deborah[6], 72.John[5], 21.John[4], 6.Hugh[3], 3.John[2], 1.Jean[1]), b. 1906,[46] d. 1961,[46] buried in Broad Run Bapt Ch Cem, Jane Lew, Lewis Co, WV.[17] She married Aug- 7-1927, **Ralph R. Fletcher**, b. Apr- 4-1908,[592,46] d. Jan-24-1995,[592,46] buried in Broad Run Bapt Ch Cem, Jane Lew, Lewis Co, WV,[17] resided in Jane Lew, Lewis Co, WV.[592]
    Children:
    i.   LIVING.

901. **Catherine "Katy" Corbin** (492.Gustavius^8, 273.Nancy^7, 140.Deborah^6, 72.John^5, 21.John^4, 6.Hugh^3, 3.John^2, 1.Jean^1), b. 1884, d. 1942. She married Jun- 8-1905, **Earl B. Smith**, b. Jun- -1878, d. Dec-16-1962.

    Children:
    i.   EARL DILLON SMITH.

902. **Oliver Gustavius Corbin** (492.Gustavius^8, 273.Nancy^7, 140.Deborah^6, 72.John^5, 21.John^4, 6.Hugh^3, 3.John^2, 1.Jean^1), d. 1946.

    Children:
    i.   OLIVER GENE CORBIN d. Oct- -1958.

903. **Ivan Shockey Corbin** (492.Gustavius^8, 273.Nancy^7, 140.Deborah^6, 72.John^5, 21.John^4, 6.Hugh^3, 3.John^2, 1.Jean^1), d. Mar- -1953.

    Children:
    i.   IVAN BUSH CORBIN d. World War II.

904. **Zana B. Janes** (493.Rebecca^8, 273.Nancy^7, 140.Deborah^6, 72.John^5, 21.John^4, 6.Hugh^3, 3.John^2, 1.Jean^1), b. Nov-22-1872,[17] d. Sep-15-1913,[17] buried in Clermont Cemetery, Eldora, Marion Co, WV. She married Aug-17-1891 in Taylor Co, WV,[433] **Samuel Ray Holbert**, also known as S. Ray Holbert,[433] b. May-24-1863,[17] d. Jan-23-1931,[17] buried in Clermont Cemetery, Eldora, Marion Co, WV.

    Children:
    i.   NELLIE MILDRED HOLBERT b. 1892, d. Feb- 8-1899.
    ii.   IRENE MARGARET HOLBERT b. Jan-16-1895,[592] d. Feb- -1987,[592] resided in Fairmont, Marion Co, WV.[592] She married Mar- 6-1920 in Marion Co, WV, George Washington Lieving, b. Jun-20-1895,[592] d. Oct-22-1969.[592]
    iii.   HAYWARD JANES HOLBERT b. Feb-11-1900,[592] d. Sep- -1956,[592] resided [Social Security card issued in New York in 1951.], never married.
    iv.   CARROLL NIXON HOLBERT b. Apr-24-1903,[592] d. Sep- -1967,[592] resided in Fairmont, Marion Co, WV.[592] He married Helen Irene Joliffe, b. Aug-31-1903,[592] d. Mar-31-1997,[592] resided in Bridgeport, Harrison Co, WV,[592] [Name listed in SSDI as Helen J. Holbert.].
    v.   EDITH ELIZABETH HOLBERT b. ca 1906 in Marion Co, WV,[589] resided 1927 in Fairmont, Marion Co, WV.[589] She married Sep- 5-1927 in Fairmont, Marion Co, WV,[589] James Howard Ross, b. ca 1905 in Indianapolis, Marion Co, IN,[589] resided 1927 in Fairmont, Marion Co, WV.[589]
    vi.   ROBERT TRASIN HOLBERT b. 1908, d. Aug- 9-1916.

905. **Howard Martin Janes** (493.Rebecca^8, 273.Nancy^7, 140.Deborah^6, 72.John^5, 21.John^4, 6.Hugh^3, 3.John^2, 1.Jean^1), b. Feb-25-1877 in Taylor Co, WV,[398] d. Sep-12-1925 in Fairmont, Marion Co, WV.[398] He married Nov-11-1908, **Ruby V. Meredith**, b. Oct-12-1881,[592] d. Feb- -1972,[592] resided in Silver Spring, Montgomery Co, MD,[592] resided formerly in West Virginia.[mdccclv[1855]]

    Children:
    i.   REBECCA LOUISE JANES b. Apr-24-1912.
    ii.   CARLINE MEREDITH JANES b. Apr- 6-1917 in Marion Co, WV.
    iii.   HOWARD MARTIN JANES, JR. b. Aug-26-1919,[592] d. Jul-10-2008,[592] resided in Satellite Beach, Brevard Co, FL.[604] He married Oct-21-1950, Pauline Carrie Douglass, b. Jan-28-1916,[592] (daughter of Samuel Grover Douglass and Georgia Amanda McClain), d. Jul-20-1997,[592] resided in Fairmont, Marion Co, WV.[604]

906. **John Eldon Corbin** (494.Joseph^8, 273.Nancy^7, 140.Deborah^6, 72.John^5, 21.John^4, 6.Hugh^3, 3.John^2, 1.Jean^1), b. Jan-21-1880, d. Dec-16-1931. He married Jun- 8-1921, **Vevia Elliott**, b. Apr-10-1894, d. Oct-18-1971.

    Children:
    i.   LIVING. She married Living.

907. **Nora Pearl Corbin** (494.Joseph[8], 273.Nancy[7], 140.Deborah[6], 72.John[5], 21.John[4], 6.Hugh[3], 3.John[2], 1.Jean[1]), b. Jan-19-1888,[mdccclvi[1856]] d. Jun-20-1978.[1856] She married May-21-1924,[1856] **Late Bruce Davisson**, b. Oct-22-1887 in Harrison Co, WV,[mdccclvii[1857]] [Other sources have given a birth date of Oct 27 1887.] (son of Austin Homer Davisson and Flora May Pickens), d. Jun- 2-1953,[1856] buried in Elkview Masonic Cemetery, Clarksburg, Harrison Co, WV,[1856] occupation 1937-41 Clarksburg City Manager.[mdccclviii[1858]]

> Children:
> i. CORBIN LATE "BUCK" DAVISSON b. Jun- 7-1925 in Clarksburg, Harrison Co, WV,[190,mdccclix[1859]] d. Jan-24-2011 in Bridgeport, Harrison Co, WV,[847] buried in Floral Hills Memorial Gardens, Quiet Dell, Harrison Co, WV,[190] resided in Clarksburg, Harrison Co, WV,[190,1859,mdccclx[1860],412] education West Virginia University (BS in animal husbandry, 1953),[1859,190] education Washington Irving H.S. (1943),[190] military U.S. Army, World War II,[190] occupation Lease & Rights of Way Dept, Consolidated Gas Supply Co (36 yrs).[190] He married Living.
> ii. ELLEN MAE DAVISSON b. Apr- 8-1927 in Clarksburg, Harrison Co, WV,[592,mdccclxi[1861]] d. Mar-13-2004,[592] resided in Lawrenceville, Gwinnett Co, GA.[604] She married Living.
> iii. HELEN JOAN DAVISSON b. Jun-21-1928 in Clarksburg, Harrison Co, WV,[mdccclxii[1862],190] d. Aug-30-2009 in Atlanta, GA,[806] buried in Elkview Masonic Cemetery, Clarksburg, Harrison Co, WV,[190] resided in Cumming, Forsyth Co, GA,[190] resided from 1985 in Georgia,[190] resided 1957 - 1985 in St. Petersburg, Pinellas Co, FL,[190] occupation physical therapist, child care specialist.[190] She married Aug-20-1949,[1862] divorced Albert Ray Poole, b. Nov-12-1926,[1862] [SSDI reports birth date as Nov 14 1926.], d. Apr-15-1979.[1859,592]

908. **Robert Harlan Faber**, also known as R. Harley Faber,[17] (496.Mary[8], 273.Nancy[7], 140.Deborah[6], 72.John[5], 21.John[4], 6.Hugh[3], 3.John[2], 1.Jean[1]), b. Sep-30-1875,[46] d. Oct-13-1959,[46] buried in Grasslick Bapt Ch Cem, Pleasant Valley Rd, Kenna, Jackson Co, WV.[17] He married Aug- 4-1901, **Laura Myrtle Mahan**, b. Apr- 5-1880,[46] d. May- 5-1970,[46] buried in Grasslick Bapt Ch Cem, Pleasant Valley Rd, Kenna, Jackson Co, WV.[17]

> Children:
> i. FORRIS ERNEST FABER b. Sep-23-1902,[592] d. Mar-22-1978,[592] resided in Akron, Summit Co, OH.[1010] He married (1) Mar-19-1925, Catherine Sausaman, d. Jan-25-1949. He married (2) Apr- 5-1952, Sara Reese, d. Feb-25-1969. He married (3) Sep-28-1975, Marguerite Dawson.
> ii. EDITH DALE FABER b. Apr-24-1905, d. Jan-29-1986. She married (1) Virgil Lambright. She married (2) Homer Gaddis, d. Jun-10-1959. She married (3) Fred Reed, d. Oct- -1965.
> iii. FRANK GLEN FABER b. Jul-17-1907,[592] d. Jan-21-1966,[592] resided in West Virginia.[604] He married Oct- -1927, Opal Faye Miller, b. Jun- 9-1906,[592] d. Nov- 2-1986,[592] resided in Charleston, Kanawha Co, WV.[592]
> iv. LILLIE MAE FABER b. Apr-26-1909, d. Oct-16-1981. She married (1) Dec-21-1929, Donovan Alto Moye, d. 1934. She married (2) Mar-21-1941, James M. Sturgis, b. Nov-14-1908.
> v. JOHN HAMILTON FABER b. Jan- 7-1911,[592,17] d. Aug-15-2002,[592] buried in Grasslick Bapt Ch Cem, Pleasant Valley Rd, Kenna, Jackson Co, WV,[17] resided in Irvine, Estill Co, KY.[604] He married Feb-27-1939, Mary Elizabeth Lanham, b. Sep-17-1915,[592,17] d. Feb- 5-2001,[592,17] buried in Grasslick Bapt Ch Cem, Pleasant Valley Rd, Kenna, Jackson Co, WV,[17] resided in Irvine, Estill Co, KY.[1010]
> vi. ROBERT HOYT FABER b. Jun-12-1913,[592] d. Dec-12-1975.[604] He married Eileen Angel, b. Feb-24-1921,[592] d. Apr- -1968.[604]
> vii. CHARLES LEE FABER b. Mar-12-1915,[592] [SSDI lists birth date as Mar 27 1915, but Mar 12 1915 reported elsewhere.], d. May- -1969,[592] resided in West Virginia.[604] He married (1) Marguerite Cornwell. He married (2) Maxine Richmond, b. Aug-12-1918,[592] d. Dec- -1986,[592] resided in Chesapeake, Lawrence Co, OH,[592] resided formerly in West Virginia.[604]
> viii. ROY WARREN FABER b. Jun-12-1920 in Alliance, Stark Co, OH,[589,592,190] d. Dec-29-2004 in Tempe, Maricopa Co, AZ,[mdccclxiii[1863]] cremated[mdccclxiv[1864]] resided in Roosevelt, Gila Co, AZ,[1010,190] resided since 1967 in Arizona,[190] resided 1945 in Mt. Sterling, Madison Co, OH,[589] occupation aircraft mechanic,[190] military U.S. Army Air Corps.[190] He married Nov-24-1945 in Morgantown, Monongalia Co, WV,[589] Vista Stansberry, b. Dec-17-1915 in Monongalia Co, WV,[589] (daughter of Francis Stansberry and Bertha __), resided 1945 in Catawba, Marion Co, WV.[589]

ix.   HENRY MASON FABER b. Jun-11-1925,[592] d. Jul-12-1995,[592] resided in Martinsburg, Berkeley Co, WV.[1010] He married Aug- 4-1943, Jo Lea Rogers, b. Sep-22-1923,[592] (daughter of Joe C. Rogers and Leona Cox), d. Aug-19-2007,[592] buried in Rosedale Cemetery, Martinsburg, Berkeley Co, WV,[190] resided in Hagerstown, Washington Co, MD,[1010,190] resided formerly in Martinsburg, Berkeley Co, WV,[190] occupation bakery manager at Martins Food Market.[190]

909. **Hiram Oliver Faber** (496.Mary[8], 273.Nancy[7], 140.Deborah[6], 72.John[5], 21.John[4], 6.Hugh[3], 3.John[2], 1.Jean[1]), b. Mar-20-1878,[17] d. Apr-15-1961,[17] buried in Grasslick Bapt Ch Cem, Pleasant Valley Rd, Kenna, Jackson Co, WV.[17] He married Feb-26-1904, **Della Mae Smith**, b. Dec-24-1881,[17] d. Oct-23-1977,[17] buried in Grasslick Bapt Ch Cem, Pleasant Valley Rd, Kenna, Jackson Co, WV.[17]
          Children:
          i.   RAYMOND ROCKFORD FABER b. Feb- 1-1905 in Jackson Co, WV,[398] d. Aug-29-1938 in Huntington, Cabell Co, WV,[398] buried in Kenna, Jackson Co, WV,[398] cause of death fractured skull from fall while working on elevator,[398] resided in Dunbar, Kanawha Co, WV,[398] occupation elevator mechanic.[398] He married Sep-18-1925, Bessie Ellen Whetherholt, b. Sep- 3-1903,[592] d. Oct- 2-2000,[592] resided in Dunbar, Kanawha Co, WV.[592]
          ii.   OLIVER KARR FABER b. Mar-16-1906 in Jackson Co, WV,[592,345] d. Jan- 4-1998,[592] [Name listed in SSDI as "O. K. Faber."], resided in Charleston, Kanawha Co, WV,[592] resided 1936 in South Charleston, Kanawha Co, WV.[345] He married (1) Nov- 5-1931, Nola Gladys Fulks, also known as Gladys,[345,502] b. Jun-29-1911 in Braxton Co, WV,[345] d. Feb-23-1936. He married (2) Feb- 8-1941, Dorothy Mevina Fisher, b. Jul-10-1915 in Kanawha Co, WV,[592,mdccclxv[1865]] (daughter of Elbie Fisher and Barcie ___), d. Mar-13-2002 in Sissonville, Kanawha Co, WV,[592,190] resided 1934 in Liberty, Putnam Co, WV.[1865]
          iii.   JOHN SMITH FABER b. Jul-30-1909,[592,46] d. Dec-10-1995,[592,46] buried in Grasslick Bapt Ch Cem, Pleasant Valley Rd, Kenna, Jackson Co, WV,[17] resided in Charleston, Kanawha Co, WV.[592] He married[191] Dec-23-1934, Elaine Melton, b. Mar- 6-1915 in Charleston, Kanawha Co, WV,[190,592,46] (daughter of Harold C. Melton and Wilda Johnson), d. Jul-13-2006,[592] buried in Grasslick Bapt Ch Cem, Pleasant Valley Rd, Kenna, Jackson Co, WV,[190] resided in Charleston, Kanawha Co, WV,[592] education Sissonville H.S., New River State College, Concord College,[190] occupation teacher.[190]
          iv.   ELIZA VIRGINIA FABER b. Nov- 6-1915,[17] d. Dec- 2-1987,[17] buried in Grasslick Bapt Ch Cem, Pleasant Valley Rd, Kenna, Jackson Co, WV.[17] She married Jun- 9-1939, Bernard Lindsey Miller, b. Jan-29-1915,[592,190] d. Jul- 4-2001,[592,190] buried[190] [There was no funeral service, and Mr. Miller donated his body to the Marshall University Human Gift Registry.], resided in Hurricane, Putnam Co, WV,[592,190] occupation owner of Miller Display Service in Charleston, and was a locally known artist.[190]
          v.   ELIZABETH MAE FABER b. Apr-25-1919. She married Apr-25-1943, Carl Robert Sumpter, b. Aug-19-1920 in West Virginia,[592,693] (son of ___ Sumpter and ___ Crew), d. Jun- 9-1997 in Montgomery, Hamilton Co, OH,[693,592] resided in Loveland, Clermont Co, OH,[592] resided formerly in West Virginia,[604] occupation retail sales,[693] military U.S. Army.[693]

910. **Hubert C. Faber** (496.Mary[8], 273.Nancy[7], 140.Deborah[6], 72.John[5], 21.John[4], 6.Hugh[3], 3.John[2], 1.Jean[1]), b. Mar- 2-1880 in Kenna, Jackson Co, WV,[398] d. Aug-21-1947 in Dunbar, Kanawha Co, WV,[398] buried in Putnam Co, WV,[mdccclxvi[1866]] resided in Ripley, Jackson Co, WV,[398] occupation farmer.[398]

Middle name appears on handwritten death record as Clester, but Custer has also been reported, and Chester is also a possibility.

He married (1) 1903, **Ida L. Fisher**, b. Jun-10-1880, d. May-11-1916. He married (2) Sep-26-1920, **Grace Rankin**. He married (3) 1926, **Molly Lawson**.
          Children by Ida L. Fisher:
          i.   VAUGHN HENRY MERL FABER b. May-21-1905,[592] d. Nov-19-1980,[592] resided in Libertyville, Lake Co, IL,[592] resided formerly in California.[1152] He married (1) Apr-24-1943, divorced Nora Vella Keen, b. Dec-31-1910,[592] d. Apr- -1995,[mdccclxvii[1867]] resided in Mesa, Maricopa Co, AZ,[592] resided formerly in Illinois.[936] He married (2) Aug-25-1951, Helen M. Zintz, b. Aug-23-1915,[592] d. Nov- -1992,[592] resided in Libertyville, Lake Co, IL.[mdccclxviii[1868]]

ii.　　DARRELL DRAPER FABER b. Dec-27-1906, d. Mar-14-1967. He married Oct-27-1927, Eva F. Phillippi, b. Jan-10-1904,[592] d. Feb- -1980,[592] resided in Akron, Summit Co, OH.[1010]
　　　iii.　　MYRON HUBERT FABER b. May- 2-1909, d. Jun-23-1957. He married May-14-1947, Genevieve Pfost, b. May-14-1916,[592] d. Jan-11-1999,[592] resided in Palo Alto, San Mateo Co, CA,[592] resided formerly in West Virginia.[604]
　　　iv.　　HAUNTIE MAE FABER, also known as Mae Faber,[748] b. Feb- 6-1912, d. Nov- 1-1951, never married resided 1947 in Dunbar, Kanawha Co, WV.[748]

911.　**Hedgeman Taylor Faber** (496.Mary[8], 273.Nancy[7], 140.Deborah[6], 72.John[5], 21.John[4], 6.Hugh[3], 3.John[2], 1.Jean[1]), b. Sep-16-1881, d. Apr-16-1962. He married Jul- 5-1903, **Hattie Bailey**, b. Jan-19-1884, d. Jun-24-1967.
　　　Children:
　　　i.　　ZORAH VIRGINIA FABER b. Apr-29-1904, d. Dec-30-1951. She married Nov-25-1927, Rembert L. Curry, b. Apr-21-1907.
　　　ii.　　PROCTOR LEANDER FABER b. May-15-1907, d. Feb-11-1980. He married Sep-25-1930, Maysel Lucille Lupardus, b. Aug-17-1915.

912.　**Ona Belle Faber** (496.Mary[8], 273.Nancy[7], 140.Deborah[6], 72.John[5], 21.John[4], 6.Hugh[3], 3.John[2], 1.Jean[1]), b. Mar- 2-1883,[17] d. Mar- 9-1970,[17] buried in Grasslick Bapt Ch Cem, Pleasant Valley Rd, Kenna, Jackson Co, WV.[17] She married Oct-16-1904, **Henry Slawter**, b. Jun-16-1882,[17,592] d. Aug- 7-1968,[17,592] resided in Kenna, Jackson Co, WV,[592] buried in Grasslick Bapt Ch Cem, Pleasant Valley Rd, Kenna, Jackson Co, WV.[17]
　　　Children:
　　　i.　　LEO SLAWTER b. Aug-19-1905,[592] d. Apr-14-1990,[592] resided in West Virginia.[mdccclxix[1869]] She married Sep- 7-1924, Voyd Rathburn Casto, b. Mar-28-1899, d. Apr-10-1969.
　　　ii.　　HIRAM SLAWTER b. Mar-16-1907,[46] d. Jan-31-1985,[46] buried in Grasslick Bapt Ch Cem, Pleasant Valley Rd, Kenna, Jackson Co, WV.[17] He married Dec- 1-1928, Coda Marie Whetherholt, b. Jul- 3-1910,[46] d. Jul- 1-1977,[46] buried in Grasslick Bapt Ch Cem, Pleasant Valley Rd, Kenna, Jackson Co, WV.[17]

913.　**Shelly Oshel Faber** (496.Mary[8], 273.Nancy[7], 140.Deborah[6], 72.John[5], 21.John[4], 6.Hugh[3], 3.John[2], 1.Jean[1]), b. May- 9-1885 in Kenna, Jackson Co, WV,[398] d. Mar-18-1936 in Rutledge, Kanawha Co, WV,[398] cause of death crushed when a shed fell on him,[398] buried in Grasslick Bapt Ch Cem, Pleasant Valley Rd, Kenna, Jackson Co, WV,[398] resided in Rutledge, Kanawha Co, WV,[398] occupation teacher.[398] He married Feb-20-1909, **Ercell Lea Fisher**, b. Sep-15-1887, d. May-21-1981.
　　　Children:
　　　i.　　JUANITA MAY FABER b. Jan-14-1910, d. Jul-11-1935.

　　　Never married

　　　ii.　　BROOKS HADEN FABER b. Feb- 4-1912. He married Sep- 3-1936, Evelyn Grace Coffey, b. Jun-15-1914.
　　　iii.　　ELSIE LEA FABER b. Apr- 1-1921. She married May-31-1941, Conley Glenn White, Jr., b. Nov- 8-1919,[592] d. Mar-18-2001,[592] resided in Port Saint Joe, Gulf Co, FL.[592]

914.　**George Bennet Faber** (496.Mary[8], 273.Nancy[7], 140.Deborah[6], 72.John[5], 21.John[4], 6.Hugh[3], 3.John[2], 1.Jean[1]), b. Feb-27-1887, d. Nov-14-1949. He married May-28-1921, **Geneva Powers Kirby**, b. Oct- 6-1897, d. Aug-28-1978.
　　　Children:
　　　i.　　JEAN ELIZABETH FABER b. Mar- 5-1922. She married Jan-17-1947, Leonard Chester Gibbs, b. Oct-20-1919,[592] d. May- 6-1991,[592] resided in Lake Havasu City, Mohave Co, AZ,[592] resided formerly in New Mexico.[mdccclxx[1870]]
　　　ii.　　GEORGE EDWIN FABER b. Dec- 3-1924. He married Jan-27-1950, Sherlie M. Pitsenbarger, b. Sep- 1-1925.

915. **Linnie Erie Faber** (496.Mary[8], 273.Nancy[7], 140.Deborah[6], 72.John[5], 21.John[4], 6.Hugh[3], 3.John[2], 1.Jean[1]), b. Oct-27-1888, d. Nov-26-1985. She married Aug-13-1913, **William Henry Vickers**, b. Mar- 3-1889, d. Jun-27-1967.

Children:

i. WILLIAM HENRY VICKERS, JR. b. Jun-14-1914, d. Feb-22-1986. He married May-24-1939, Wilma Eileen Statts, b. Jul-13-1916.

ii. MARY ALICE VICKERS b. Jun-25-1915, d. Jun-25-1915.

iii. JOHN FABER VICKERS b. Mar- 6-1917, d. May-21-1931.

iv. CHARLES WARREN VICKERS b. Nov- 7-1920,[592] d. Jul-16-1995,[592] resided in Amonate, Tazewell Co, VA,[592] resided formerly in West Virginia.[604] He married Living.

v. GERALDINE LENORE VICKERS b. Jun-23-1922. She married Apr-20-1946, Henry Spain Harrison, b. Jun-16-1914.

vi. LIVING. She married James Spicer Guthrie, Jr., b. Apr-13-1925.

vii. LIVING. She married Living.

916. **Hauntie Haden Faber** (496.Mary[8], 273.Nancy[7], 140.Deborah[6], 72.John[5], 21.John[4], 6.Hugh[3], 3.John[2], 1.Jean[1]), b. Apr-14-1891,[17] d. Dec-23-1974,[17] buried in Grasslick Bapt Ch Cem, Pleasant Valley Rd, Kenna, Jackson Co, WV.[17] She married Jun-28-1912, **Robert Lee Bird**, b. Apr-23-1886,[17] d. Mar-18-1982,[17] buried in Grasslick Bapt Ch Cem, Pleasant Valley Rd, Kenna, Jackson Co, WV.[17]

Children:

i. ROBERT LEE BIRD, JR. b. Nov-23-1915,[592] d. Mar-24-1999,[592] resided in Charleston, Kanawha Co, WV.[604] He married Jul-26-1943, Ann Cabell Embleton, b. Jul-15-1921.

917. **Corbett Lee Faber** (496.Mary[8], 273.Nancy[7], 140.Deborah[6], 72.John[5], 21.John[4], 6.Hugh[3], 3.John[2], 1.Jean[1]), b. Feb- 1-1893, d. May-12-1983. He married Sep-21-1917, **Myrtle Evans**, b. Sep-19-1899, d. Mar-23-1970.

Children:

i. SARA JUNE FABER b. Jun-27-1918. She married Feb-28-1941, Gordon William Frederick, b. Jan-26-1915,[592] d. Mar-14-1996,[592] resided in Ooltewah, Hamilton Co, TN,[592] resided formerly in Ohio.[1010]

ii. EDWARD EVANS FABER b. Aug- 4-1920,[592] d. Jun- -1959.[592] He married Doris Evelyn Nuckles, b. Jul-20-1918.

iii. OLIVE FLORENCE FABER b. Feb-27-1922. She married Dec- 6-1942, John Wallace Dowswell, b. Sep-21-1922.

iv. CORBETT LEE FABER, JR. b. May-19-1926, d. Feb-27-1945 in World War II.

v. LIVING. He married Living.

vi. LIVING. She married Living.

918. **Dovener Faber** (496.Mary[8], 273.Nancy[7], 140.Deborah[6], 72.John[5], 21.John[4], 6.Hugh[3], 3.John[2], 1.Jean[1]), b. Apr-23-1895, d. Aug-25-1979. He married Apr-10-1918, **Nellie Bly Chandler**, b. Jan-19-1899, d. Jul- 2-1979.

Children:

i. JAMES DOVENER FABER b. Sep-24-1921. He married Jun- 5-1948, Sarah Elizabeth Daniel, b. Oct-30-1921.

ii. JOHN HENRY FABER b. May- 8-1926. He married Jun- 3-1947, Nova Jean Haynes, b. Jun-25-1926.

919. **Velva Faber** (496.Mary[8], 273.Nancy[7], 140.Deborah[6], 72.John[5], 21.John[4], 6.Hugh[3], 3.John[2], 1.Jean[1]), b. Sep-14-1900, d. Feb- 7-1956. She married Apr- 7-1926, **Thomas Frank Yost**, b. Aug-18-1896, d. Jul-6-1954.

Children:

i. LIVING. She married William Henry Forsbach, b. Sep-29-1927,[592] d. Dec-11-2004,[592] resided in Urbana, Champaign Co, OH.[592]

ii. HENRIETTA MAXINE YOST b. Apr-29-1928,[592] d. Apr- 6-1981,[592] resided in Columbus, Franklin Co, OH,[592] resided formerly in West Virginia.[604] She married (1) Earl Roush. She married (2) Oct-11-1963, John R. Phelan, b. Apr-23-1927,[592] d. Oct-20-1998,[592] resided in Reynoldsburg, Franklin Co, OH.[592]

      iii.   ROBERT MILTON "BUCK" YOST b. Jul- 1-1929,[592] d. Dec- 1-2000,[592] resided in Newport, Monroe Co, MI,[592] resided formerly in West Virginia.[604] He married (1) Living. He married (2) Living.

920. **Frank Carr** (497.William[8], 275.Margaret[7], 140.Deborah[6], 72.John[5], 21.John[4], 6.Hugh[3], 3.John[2], 1.Jean[1]), b. 1879,[mdccclxxi[1871]] d. Jul- 3-1948 in Ohio,[mdccclxxii[1872]] buried in Woodlawn Cemetery, Fairmont, Marion Co, WV.[1871] He married Apr-28-1904,[1871] **Katherine M. "Kate" Levelle**, b. 1883,[1871] d. Jul- 3-1948,[1871] buried in Woodlawn Cemetery, Fairmont, Marion Co, WV.[1871]

      Children:

      i.   DORIS LEE CARR b. Apr-22-1906,[592,17] d. Sep- -1976,[592,17] buried in Woodlawn Cemetery, Fairmont, Marion Co, WV,[17] resided in Fairmont, Marion Co, WV.[1275] She married (1) Richard Ours. She married (2) Charles Hudgins.

      ii.   HARRY CARR b. May-30-1908, d. Jul-20-1908, buried in Maple Grove Cemetery, Marion Co, WV.

      iii.   GEORGE CARR b. Feb-28-1910, d. Jan- 9-1917, buried in Woodlawn Cemetery, Fairmont, Marion Co, WV.

      iv.   JACK EDWARD CARR b. Sep-11-1920 in Fairmont, Marion Co, WV,[190] d. Oct- 5-2001 in Fairmont, Marion Co, WV,[190] buried in Woodlawn Cemetery, Fairmont, Marion Co, WV,[190] military U.S. Army Air Corps - World War II.

      Retired as director of purchasing for G.A. Brown & Son in 1985. He was a well-known carpenter in the Fairmont area and worked for Barr-Thomas Lumber Co. He also had his own businesses, including Carr's Construction Co and Carr's Millwork. He was an avid bowler and bowled with the Senior Citizens League until a month before his death.[190]

      He married Dec-30-1943, Rose Bertha Mae Hawkins, nickname Masie,[484] b. Oct-20-1921 (daughter of Charles E. Hawkins and Eugenia Lee Clark), d. Feb- 8-1980,[484,mdccclxxiii[1873]] buried in Woodlawn Cemetery, Fairmont, Marion Co, WV.[1873]

921. **Margaret Carr** (497.William[8], 275.Margaret[7], 140.Deborah[6], 72.John[5], 21.John[4], 6.Hugh[3], 3.John[2], 1.Jean[1]), b. Jul- 7-1882,[1871] d. Oct- -1972,[592] resided in Bridgeport, Harrison Co, WV.[592] She married **Claude Ryan**.

      Children:

      i.   GLADYS RYAN.

922. **Charles Harry Carr** (497.William[8], 275.Margaret[7], 140.Deborah[6], 72.John[5], 21.John[4], 6.Hugh[3], 3.John[2], 1.Jean[1]), b. Jul- 4-1886,[46] d. Sep- 8-1947,[46] buried in Middleville Baptist Church Cemetery, Taylor Co, WV.[17] He married (1)[1871] **Minnie Watkins**. He married (2) May-18-1916, **Edna Hazel Radabaugh**, also known as Hazel,[17] b. Jan-11-1891,[1871,46] d. Feb- 6-1968,[1871,46] buried in Middleville Baptist Church Cemetery, Taylor Co, WV.[17]

      Children by Minnie Watkins:

      i.   ROBERT JAMES CARR b. Jun-27-1913,[592] d. Apr-30-1988,[1871,592] resided in Clarksburg, Harrison Co, WV.[592] He married[1871] Margaret A. Desist, b. Aug-23-1912,[1871,592] d. Jan-10-2000.[592]

      Children by Edna Hazel Radabaugh:

      ii.   ROSALEA CARR b. Feb-21-1917,[1871] no children from this person[1871.] She married Nov-24-1936,[1871] George Bodie Nicholson, b. Aug-23-1911,[1871] d. Aug-16-1961.[1871]

      iii.   CHARLES WILLIAM CARR b. Jan-15-1919, d. Oct- 5-1978, buried in Bridgeport Cemetery, Harrison Co, WV. He married May- 8-1938,[1871] Elizabeth Lee Seman, b. Mar- 2-1917, d. Dec-15-1987.

      iv.   MARY JANE CARR b. Feb- 5-1920,[1871] d. Oct- -1975,[mdccclxxiv[1874]] resided in Youngstown, Mahoning Co, OH,[592] [Social Security card issued in West Virginia before 1951. Name listed in SSDI as Mary Stilwagner.], resided formerly in West Virginia.[604] She married (1) Oct-15-1942,[1871] William Trippett, b. Jun- 6-1920.[1871] She married (2)[592] ___ Stilwagner.

923. **Bertha Carr** (497.William[8], 275.Margaret[7], 140.Deborah[6], 72.John[5], 21.John[4], 6.Hugh[3], 3.John[2], 1.Jean[1]), b. 1892, d. Feb- -1966. She married Jan-14-1915, **Herschel Earle Bartlett**, b. 1888, d. Feb-23-1950.

> Children:
> i. HOLLIS BARTLETT.

924. **Fred Carr** (497.William[8], 275.Margaret[7], 140.Deborah[6], 72.John[5], 21.John[4], 6.Hugh[3], 3.John[2], 1.Jean[1]).

> Children:
> i. FRED CARR, JR..

925. **Hallie Louise Morrow** (498.Martha[8], 275.Margaret[7], 140.Deborah[6], 72.John[5], 21.John[4], 6.Hugh[3], 3.John[2], 1.Jean[1]), b. Sep-10-1891, d. May- 9-1973, buried in Woodlawn Cemetery, Fairmont, Marion Co, WV. She married Nov-26-1913, **Jesse John Lynch**, b. Mar- 4-1886, d. Apr- 9-1955, buried in Woodlawn Cemetery, Fairmont, Marion Co, WV.

> Children:
> i. MARTHA ALICE LYNCH b. Aug-22-1915. She married Apr-19-1933, Virgil H. Byrd, b. Dec-14-1914,[592] d. Nov-23-1986,[592] buried in Woodlawn Cemetery, Fairmont, Marion Co, WV, resided in Alexandria, VA,[592] resided formerly in West Virginia.[604]
> ii. MARY JANE LYNCH b. Jun- 6-1918, d. Jan-11-1978 in Woodlawn Cemetery, Fairmont, Marion Co, WV.
>
> Never married
>
> iii. MONA LOUISE LYNCH b. Oct-28-1923. She married Feb-18-1948, Oric Earl Rinehart, Jr., b. Apr-27-1921, d. Jul-29-1973.
> iv. LIVING. He married Living.

926. **Pauline E. Morrow** (498.Martha[8], 275.Margaret[7], 140.Deborah[6], 72.John[5], 21.John[4], 6.Hugh[3], 3.John[2], 1.Jean[1]), b. Jul-29-1906, d. Dec-26-1980, buried in Woodlawn Cemetery, Fairmont, Marion Co, WV. She married Jul-24-1931, **Robert Lewis Clayton**, b. May-30-1904, d. Oct-15-1975, buried in Woodlawn Cemetery, Fairmont, Marion Co, WV.

> Children:
> i. PATRICIA ANN CLAYTON b. Dec- 1-1935, d. Apr-23-1989. She married Living.

927. **Nola Mary Reed** (499.Clara[8], 276.James[7], 140.Deborah[6], 72.John[5], 21.John[4], 6.Hugh[3], 3.John[2], 1.Jean[1]), b. Mar-16-1895, d. Oct- 4-1982, buried in Janes Mem Methodist Church Cem, Boothsville, Taylor Co, WV. She married Sep- 6-1920, **Max Welty Wilson**, b. Feb-24-1896, d. Apr-11-1964, buried in Janes Mem Methodist Church Cem, Boothsville, Taylor Co, WV.

> Children:
> i. LIVING.
> ii. LIVING.

928. **Walter Scott Reed** (499.Clara[8], 276.James[7], 140.Deborah[6], 72.John[5], 21.John[4], 6.Hugh[3], 3.John[2], 1.Jean[1]), b. Dec- 3-1898, d. Oct-12-1957, buried in Clermont Cemetery, Eldora, Marion Co, WV. He married Aug-22-1927, **Susan V. "Susie" Smith**, b. Jul-20-1895, d. Oct-14-1958, buried in Clermont Cemetery, Eldora, Marion Co, WV.

> Children:
> i. LIVING. He married Living.

929. **Herschel Lowe Reed** (499.Clara[8], 276.James[7], 140.Deborah[6], 72.John[5], 21.John[4], 6.Hugh[3], 3.John[2], 1.Jean[1]), b. Feb-23-1901, d. Feb-19-1956, buried in Clermont Cemetery, Eldora, Marion Co, WV. He married (1) **Nola Ingram**. He married (2) **Norma ___**.

Children by Nola Ingram:

    i.   KEITH REED.

930. **Thomas Hughes (twin) Reed** (499.Clara[8], 276.James[7], 140.Deborah[6], 72.John[5], 21.John[4], 6.Hugh[3], 3.John[2], 1.Jean[1]), b. Feb-28-1904, d. Jun-16-1956, buried in Penn Yan, Yates Co, NY. He married **Margaret Madson**.
    Children:

    i.   LIVING.
    ii. LIVING.
    iii. LIVING.

931. **Arthur Harris (twin) Reed** (499.Clara[8], 276.James[7], 140.Deborah[6], 72.John[5], 21.John[4], 6.Hugh[3], 3.John[2], 1.Jean[1]), b. Feb-28-1904, d. Mar-27-1962, buried in Janes Mem Methodist Church Cem, Boothsville, Taylor Co, WV. He married Dec-18-1925, **Ella Gladys Curry**, b. Jan-18-1906.
    Children:

    i.   LIVING. She married Living.

932. **William Donley Taylor** (501.Colonel[8], 277.William[7], 140.Deborah[6], 72.John[5], 21.John[4], 6.Hugh[3], 3.John[2], 1.Jean[1]), b. Apr- 1-1893, d. Aug-18-1957, buried in Woodlawn Cemetery, Fairmont, Marion Co, WV. He married Sep- 2-1923, **Hazel Marie Gwynn**, b. May-11-1898, d. May-20-1977, buried in Woodlawn Cemetery, Fairmont, Marion Co, WV.
    Children:

    i.   WILLIAM MARION TAYLOR b. Oct- 9-1924,[592] d. Dec-13-2000,[592] resided in Wallace, Harrison Co, WV.[592] He married Jun- 8-1946, Flora Jane Stewart, b. Mar-18-1925.

933. **Bartley Norris Taylor** (501.Colonel[8], 277.William[7], 140.Deborah[6], 72.John[5], 21.John[4], 6.Hugh[3], 3.John[2], 1.Jean[1]), b. Apr- 7-1897,[592,234] d. Mar- 3-1966,[592,234] buried in Bridgeport Masonic (aka Airport) Cemetery, Harrison Co, WV,[1076] resided in Bridgeport, Harrison Co, WV.[592] He married[234] **Erma Leota Roberts**, b. Nov-24-1909,[592] d. Jan-21-1985,[592] [Name listed in SSDI as Erma Malle.], buried in Tesia Cemetery, Braxton, WV,[234] resided in Clarksburg, Harrison Co, WV.[592]
    Children:

    i.   BETTY JEAN TAYLOR b. Aug-21-1926 in Fairmont, Marion Co, WV,[190] d. Jul- 3-2005 in Clarksburg, Harrison Co, WV,[847] buried in Bridgeport Cemetery, Harrison Co, WV,[190] resided in Clarksburg, Harrison Co, WV,[190] occupation Taylor's Lunch & Trailer Court, Bridgeport WV (owner/operator, 38 yrs).[190] She married[191] John Cropp, b. Dec-23-1920,[592] d. Feb- -1974,[592,191] resided in West Virginia.[604]

    ii. VIRGINIA LEE TAYLOR b. Mar-20-1928 in Fairmont, Marion Co, WV,[419] d. Jun-13-1976 in Ursina, Somerset Co, PA,[64] buried St Paul Lutheran Cem in Somerset Co, PA,[64] resided 1945 in Bridgeport, Harrison Co, WV.[419] She married Sep- -1945,[234] [Marriage license issued on Sep 10 1945, but there was no minister's return or endorsement.], no children from this marriage, George Daniel Bowser, b. Jul- 2-1924 in Somerset Co, PA,[419] (son of Bruce E. Bowser and Esther M. Cramer), resided 1945 in Bridgeport, Harrison Co, WV.

934. **Earl Grayson Taylor**, also known as Grayson Taylor,[395] (502.John[8], 277.William[7], 140.Deborah[6], 72.John[5], 21.John[4], 6.Hugh[3], 3.John[2], 1.Jean[1]), b. Oct-10-1895, d. Mar- 9-1979, buried in Bridgeport Masonic (aka Airport) Cemetery, Harrison Co, WV.[1076] He married[395] (1) Sep-12-1916, **Evelyn Clara McKinney**, b. Sep- 1-1896, d. Sep-22-1954, buried in Bridgeport Masonic (aka Airport) Cemetery, Harrison Co, WV.[1076] He married (2) Nov- 1-1955, **Sibyl Evelyn Schutte Price**, b. Jun- 5-1901,[592] d. Dec-16-1993,[592] resided in Winston-Salem, Forsyth Co, NC,[592] resided formerly in West Virginia.[mdccclxxv[1875]]
    Children by Evelyn Clara McKinney:

    i.   VIRGIL CLAUDIUS TAYLOR b. Jun- 1-1918,[592] d. Jun- 5-1992.[592] He married (1) Mar- -1939, Dortha Lee Kester, b. Jul-28-1920, d. Aug-24-1960, buried in Harmony Grove Cemetery, Taylor Co, WV. He married (2) Nov-17-1961, Eileen Lucricia Bradshaw Ellison, b. Aug- 3-1918.

ii.   MARY MARGARET TAYLOR b. Dec-23-1921, resided 2007 in Bridgeport, Harrison Co, WV.[521] She married Mar- 3-1962, no children from this marriage, George Willard Moses, b. Jun-22-1917,[592] d. May-25-1996,[592] resided in Bridgeport, Harrison Co, WV.[592]

iii.   JAMES ROBERT "BOB" TAYLOR b. Jul-27-1923 in Taylor Co, WV,[190] d. Jul- 6-2007 in Bridgeport, Harrison Co, WV,[700] buried in Bridgeport Cemetery, Harrison Co, WV,[190] resided in Bridgeport, Harrison Co, WV,[190] occupation Hope Gas Co/CNG Transmission Corp (44 yrs),[190] military U.S. Army, World War II.[190] He married Living.

935.   **Bonnie Marie Taylor** (502.John[8], 277.William[7], 140.Deborah[6], 72.John[5], 21.John[4], 6.Hugh[3], 3.John[2], 1.Jean[1]), b. Sep-26-1897, d. Aug-28-1928, buried in Middleville Baptist Church Cemetery, Taylor Co, WV.[17] She married Aug-18-1915, **Arnett Lawson**.
Children:
i.   CHARLES EDWARD LAWSON b. Mar-28-1916, d. Jan-24-1964, buried in Oak Grove Cemetery, Taylor Co, WV. He married Apr-25-1944, Lillian Virginia Davis, b. Jul-29-1917, d. Aug-17-1986, buried in Oak Grove Cemetery, Taylor Co, WV.

936.   **Arthur Kelso Taylor** (502.John[8], 277.William[7], 140.Deborah[6], 72.John[5], 21.John[4], 6.Hugh[3], 3.John[2], 1.Jean[1]), b. Feb- 3-1900, d. Sep-16-1969, buried in Middleville Baptist Church Cemetery, Taylor Co, WV.[17] He married Aug-21-1933, **Monnie Elizabeth Yoak**, b. Feb-28-1906, d. Jan-14-1988, buried in Middleville Baptist Church Cemetery, Taylor Co, WV.[17]
Children:
i.   LIVING. He married Betty Landrum, b. Mar-28-1935, d. Nov- 1-1986.

Betty: Divorced and remarried 9/10/1982

ii.   LIVING. He married Living.
iii.   LIVING. He married Living.
iv.   LIVING. He married (1) Living. He married (2) Living.

937.   **Lena Pearl Williams** (504.Frances[8], 277.William[7], 140.Deborah[6], 72.John[5], 21.John[4], 6.Hugh[3], 3.John[2], 1.Jean[1]), b. Feb-28-1897, d. Dec-20-1939, buried in Benedum Memorial Cemetery, Bridgeport, Harrison Co, WV. She married Jun-21-1922, **Dennis B. "Jack" Ryan**, b. 1897.
Children:
i.   LIVING. She married Living.

938.   **Bettie Marshall Taylor** (505.Edward[8], 277.William[7], 140.Deborah[6], 72.John[5], 21.John[4], 6.Hugh[3], 3.John[2], 1.Jean[1]), b. Sep-14-1919 in Fairmont, Marion Co, WV,[190] d. Nov-20-2005 in Waldorf, Charles Co, MD,[764] buried Cedar Hill Cemetery in Suitland, Prince Georges Co, MD,[190] resided since 2003 in North Beach, Calvert Co, MD,[190] resided 1993-2003 in Frederick, Frederick Co, MD,[190] education Fairmont State College, West Virginia Business College.[190] She married Sep-15-1941,[191] **James Thomas Wakenight**, b. Oct-16-1918,[592] d. Jan-15-1990,[592] resided in Clinton, Prince Georges Co, MD.[1625]
Children:
i.   LIVING. He married Living.
ii.   LIVING. She married Living.

939.   **Edward Murray Taylor, Jr.** (505.Edward[8], 277.William[7], 140.Deborah[6], 72.John[5], 21.John[4], 6.Hugh[3], 3.John[2], 1.Jean[1]), b. Aug-28-1921 in Fairmont, Marion Co, WV,[234,mdccclxxvi[1876]] residence in Lake Mary, Seminole Co, FL,[234] resided formerly in Charlottesville, VA,[234] resided formerly in Marion Co, WV,[234] occupation Monongahela Power Co (37 yrs, retired Jan 1983).[1876] He married Jun-21-1947,[234] **Betty Nell Burrows**, b. Apr-26-1923 in Weston, Lewis Co, WV,[190] (daughter of Willis A. Burrows and Beatrice Wilson), d. Feb-19-2000 in Stanardsville, VA,[190] buried in Woodlawn Cemetery, Fairmont, Marion Co, WV, occupation secretary.[190]

Betty: Valedictorian, Weston High School class of 1941. Graduate of West Virginia Business College, Clarksburg, WV.[190]

Children:
i. LIVING. She married (1) Living. She married (2) Living.
ii. LIVING. He married Living.

940. **Lena A. Brooks** (507.William^8, 278.Sarah^7, 140.Deborah^6, 72.John^5, 21.John^4, 6.Hugh^3, 3.John^2, 1.Jean^1), b. 1900, d. Dec-29-1918 in Harrison Co, WV,[546] cause of death Spanish flu epidemic,[546] buried in Elkview Masonic Cemetery, Clarksburg, Harrison Co, WV.[546] She married Apr-14-1917 in Oakland, Garrett Co, MD,[546] **Carl David Newell**, b. Aug-29-1896 in Marion Co, WV,[546] (son of Charles E. Newell and Minnie Leola Glover), d. Nov-25-1985, buried in Sunset Memorial Park Cemetery, Clarksburg, WV.[546]
Children:
i. CHARLES EDWARD NEWELL b. Jul-30-1918 in Clarksburg, Harrison Co, WV,[546] d. May-11-1970,[546] buried in Stonewall Park Cemetery, Stonewood, Harrison Co, WV.[546] He married Sep- 6-1942 in Oakland, Garrett Co, MD,[546] Bonnie Beatrice Norman, b. Jan-16-1921 in Walker Station, Wood Co, WV,[546] (daughter of Robert A. Norman and Henrietta Miller), residence in Bucks Co, PA.[546]

941. **Anthony Hall Robinson**, also known as A. Hall Robinson, nickname Robby (508.Curtis^8, 279.Henrietta^7, 140.Deborah^6, 72.John^5, 21.John^4, 6.Hugh^3, 3.John^2, 1.Jean^1), b. Feb-27-1901,[234] d. Jun-11-1959. He married Sep- 1-1931,[234] **Marian Keener**, b. Dec-26-1906,[234] d. Oct- 7-1958.[234]
Children:
i. LIVING. She married Living.

942. **Charles Theodore "Ted" Robinson** (508.Curtis^8, 279.Henrietta^7, 140.Deborah^6, 72.John^5, 21.John^4, 6.Hugh^3, 3.John^2, 1.Jean^1), b. Jul-18-1904,[234] d. May-16-1954,[191,234] buried in Restland Memorial Park, Monroeville, Allegheny Co, PA.[234] He married Jan-27-1927,[234,191] **Roxie Elizabeth Smith**, b. Feb-19-1904 in Manor, Westmoreland Co, PA,[190,234,592] (daughter of Edward Smith and Rebecca Greenawalt), d. Mar- 4-2001 in Huntingdon, Huntingdon Co, PA,[764,234,592] buried in Restland Memorial Park, Monroeville, Allegheny Co, PA,[234] resided in State College, Centre Co, PA,[190] occupation service receptionist, Peoples Natural Gas Co, Wilkinsburg (retired 1967).[190]
Children:
i. LIVING. He married (1) Living. He married (2) Living.
ii. LIVING. She married Living.

943. **Minor Hollis "Mike" Robinson**, also known as M. Hollis Robinson (508.Curtis^8, 279.Henrietta^7, 140.Deborah^6, 72.John^5, 21.John^4, 6.Hugh^3, 3.John^2, 1.Jean^1), b. Apr-11-1908,[234] d. Jul-21-1996,[234] buried in Mt. Morris Cemetery, Freemansburg, Lewis Co, WV. He married Jun-14-1935, **Ruth E. Jackson**, buried in Mt. Morris Cemetery, Freemansburg, Lewis Co, WV.
Children:
i. LIVING. He married Living.

944. **Elmer Truman "Pete" Robinson**, also known as E. Truman Robinson (508.Curtis^8, 279.Henrietta^7, 140.Deborah^6, 72.John^5, 21.John^4, 6.Hugh^3, 3.John^2, 1.Jean^1), b. Jun-10-1914, d. Aug-23-1978, buried in Mt. Morris Cemetery, Freemansburg, Lewis Co, WV.[1079] He married Aug- 8-1934,[1079] **Iva Lou Wiant**, b. Mar-23-1918,[1079] d. Nov- 6-1996,[1079] buried in Mt. Morris Cemetery, Freemansburg, Lewis Co, WV.[1079]
Children:
i. LIVING. She married Living.
ii. LIVING.
iii. GARY TRUMAN ROBINSON b. May-31-1944,[1079] d. Dec-16-1999,[1079] buried in Mt. Morris Cemetery, Freemansburg, Lewis Co, WV.[1079] He married Living.

945. **Mary Swisher** (516.Robert[8], 281.James[7], 141.Jane[6], 72.John[5], 21.John[4], 6.Hugh[3], 3.John[2], 1.Jean[1]), b. Mar-26-1901 in Lewis Co, WV,[592,921] d. Jun- 6-1988,[592] resided in Buckhannon, Upshur Co, WV,[592] census 1930 in Upshur Co, WV, resided 1923 in Weston, Lewis Co, WV.[921] She married[424] Sep- 8-1923 in Lorentz, Upshur Co, WV,[921] **Loy R. Reger**, b. Jun-11-1901 in Upshur Co, WV,[592,921] (son of R. S. Reger and Ida __), d. Jan- -1985,[592] resided in Buckhannon, Upshur Co, WV,[604,921] census 1930 in Upshur Co, WV, occupation farmer.[922]

        Children:

    i.   JAMES MARION REGER b. Jul-14-1924 near Weston, Lewis Co, WV,[190,1022,592] d. Jul-16-2006 in Elkins, Randolph Co, WV,[764,592] buried in Friendship Cem (Fairview IOOF), Berlin Rd, Co Rt 7, Lewis Co, WV,[190] resided in Buckhannon, Upshur Co, WV,[604,1022] census 1930 in Upshur Co, WV, occupation coal miner,[190] military U.S. Army, World War II.[190] He married Mar-16-1948 in Philippi, Barbour Co, WV,[1022] Erma Ruth Peters, b. Aug-30-1925 in Buckhannon, Upshur Co, WV,[1022,190] (daughter of Eddie Peters and Erma Post), d. Feb-23-2008 in Elkins, Randolph Co, WV,[764] buried in Friendship Cem (Fairview IOOF), Berlin Rd, Co Rt 7, Lewis Co, WV,[190] resided in Elkins, Randolph Co, WV,[190,484] resided 1948 in Buckhannon, Upshur Co, WV.[1022]

946. **Beatrice Swisher** (516.Robert[8], 281.James[7], 141.Jane[6], 72.John[5], 21.John[4], 6.Hugh[3], 3.John[2], 1.Jean[1]), b. Sep- 2-1906 in Weston, Lewis Co, WV,[190] d. Oct- 2-2003 in Weston, Lewis Co, WV.[190]

Resident of Weston, Lewis Co, WV. She was a 1923 graduate of Weston High School and attended West Virginia Business College. She taught school in Braxton and Lewis counties and was a retired bookkeeper for Swisher Feed.[190]

She married Aug-18-1926 in Lewis Co, WV,[410,191] **Ormand Jerome Bourn**, b. ca 1895 in Braxton Co, WV,[410] (son of Charles R. Bourn and Ida __), d. Dec-27-1959.[191]

        Children:

    i.   ROBERT JEROME BOURN resided 2003 in Rosedale, WV.[856] He married[1745] Joy __.

    ii.   RICHARD L. BOURN resided 2003 in Kingsport, Sullivan Co, TN.[856] He married[1745] Willa Jean __.

    iii.   JOYCE E. BOURN resided 2003 in Dallas, TX.[856] She married[1040] Boxley Boggs.

    iv.   RELLA M. BOURN resided 2003 in West Milford, Harrison Co, WV.[856] She married[1040] Bruce Wright.

    v.   JUDITH A. BOURN resided 2003 in Roanoke, Lewis Co, WV.[856] She married[1040] Gerald Stalnaker.

947. **Minnie Maud Hoff** (524.Eri[8], 285.Elizabeth[7], 142.James[6], 72.John[5], 21.John[4], 6.Hugh[3], 3.John[2], 1.Jean[1]), b. Nov-10-1880 in Newark, Wirt Co, WV,[592,1105,1125] d. Aug- -1975,[592] resided in Dallas, TX,[592] census 1930 in Fort Worth, Tarrant Co, TX, census 1920 in Logan, Hocking Co, OH, census 1910 in Smithfield, Wetzel Co, WV, resided 1903 in Smithfield, Wetzel Co, WV,[1125] census 1900 in Wirt Co, WV. She married May-29-1903 in New Martinsville, Wetzel Co, WV,[1125] **Benjamin F. Zeigler**, census name Frank Zeigler,[681] b. Aug-21-1878 in Harmony, Butler Co, PA,[592,1125] d. Mar- -1973,[592] resided in Dallas, TX,[604] census 1930 in Fort Worth, Tarrant Co, TX, census 1920 in Logan, Hocking Co, OH, census 1910 in Smithfield, Wetzel Co, WV, resided 1903 in Smithfield, Wetzel Co, WV,[1125] occupation 1930 foreman in blacksmith shop.[334]

        Children:

    i.   BENJAMIN F. ZEIGLER, census name Frank Zeigler,[681] b. ca 1904 in West Virginia,[mdccclxxvii[1877]] census 1920 in Logan, Hocking Co, OH, census 1910 in Smithfield, Wetzel Co, WV.

    ii.   EARL E. ZEIGLER b. ca 1908 in West Virginia,[1877] census 1920 in Logan, Hocking Co, OH, census 1910 in Smithfield, Wetzel Co, WV.

    iii.   HELEN MAY ZEIGLER b. ca 1916 in Pennsylvania,[681] census 1930 in Fort Worth, Tarrant Co, TX, census 1920 in Logan, Hocking Co, OH.

948. **Neff Corliss Hoff** (524.Eri[8], 285.Elizabeth[7], 142.James[6], 72.John[5], 21.John[4], 6.Hugh[3], 3.John[2], 1.Jean[1]), b. Apr- 9-1883, d. Jun-25-1961 in Cincinnati, Hamilton Co, OH, census 1920 in Middletown, Butler Co, OH, census 1910 in Steubenville, Jefferson Co, OH, census 1900 in Wirt Co, WV. He married Jun-13-1907 in Ritchie Co, WV,[mdccclxxviii[1878]] **Olive Lorina "Mollie" Bee**, also known as Ola Bee,[473] b. Feb-21-1891, (daughter of Emmaretta Bee), d. Feb- 7-1962 in Cincinnati, Hamilton Co, OH,[693] census 1920 in Middletown, Butler Co, OH, resided in Cincinnati, Hamilton Co, OH.[693]

  Children:
  i.   ADRIAN C. HOFF b. 1908,[693,681] d. Nov-23-1966 in Dayton, Montgomery Co, OH,[693] resided in Dayton, Montgomery Co, OH,[693] census 1920 in Middletown, Butler Co, OH.
  ii.   CLELLAND HOFF b. ca 1910,[681] census 1920 in Middletown, Butler Co, OH.
  iii. CATHELINE HOFF b. ca 1915,[681] census 1920 in Middletown, Butler Co, OH.
  iv.   ELIZABETH HOFF b. ca 1916,[681] census 1920 in Middletown, Butler Co, OH.
  v.   ROBERT HOFF b. ca 1918,[681] census 1920 in Middletown, Butler Co, OH.

949. **Virgil R. Hoff** (524.Eri[8], 285.Elizabeth[7], 142.James[6], 72.John[5], 21.John[4], 6.Hugh[3], 3.John[2], 1.Jean[1]), b. Aug-25-1887 in West Virginia,[592,1105] d. Jan- -1963,[592] resided in Illinois,[936] census 1920, 1930 in Clinton, DeWitt Co, IL, census 1900 in Wirt Co, WV, occupation 1930 restaurant manager.[334] He married ca 1904,[334] **Betty J. ___**, b. ca 1886 in Kentucky,[334] census 1920, 1930 in Clinton, DeWitt Co, IL.

  Children:
  i.   VIRGIL R. HOFF, JR. b. Dec-21-1909,[592,681] d. Jan-14-1990,[936] census 1920 in Clinton, DeWitt Co, IL.

950. **Alice A. Hoff** (524.Eri[8], 285.Elizabeth[7], 142.James[6], 72.John[5], 21.John[4], 6.Hugh[3], 3.John[2], 1.Jean[1]), b. Jun-21-1894 in Newark, Wirt Co, WV,[190] d. ca 1968 in Gassaway, Braxton Co, WV,[190] resided in Shock, Gilmer Co, WV,[190] resided 1917 in Clay Co, WV.[mdccclxxix[1879]] She married[191] Oct-13-1917 in Wallback, Clay Co, WV,[1879] **Ben F. Miller**, also known as B. F. Miller,[1879,191] b. Mar-20-1889 in Braxton Co, WV,[592,1879] (son of George Miller), d. May- -1975,[mdccclxxx[1880]] resided in Shock, Gilmer Co, WV,[191,592] occupation farm laborer.[906]

  Children:
  i.   HUNTER MILLER b. ca 1919, resided 1968 in Vienna, Wood Co, WV,[856] census 1930 in Gilmer Co, WV.
  ii.   VERA MABEL MILLER, census name Vira M. Miller,[906] b. ca 1924 in Pennsylvania,[1006,906] resided 1943, 68 in Shock, Gilmer Co, WV,[1006,856] census 1930 in Gilmer Co, WV. She married[1040] Sep- 4-1943 in Shock, Gilmer Co, WV,[1006] Thomas Glen Brady, b. May-17-1916 in Shock, Gilmer Co, WV,[592,1006] (son of Andrew Brady and Mary Elizabeth ___), d. Oct- -1969,[592] resided in Shock, Gilmer Co, WV.[604]
  iii. LIVING.

951. **Lela Pearl Hoff** (525.George[8], 285.Elizabeth[7], 142.James[6], 72.John[5], 21.John[4], 6.Hugh[3], 3.John[2], 1.Jean[1]), b. Dec-31-1888 in Ritchie Co, WV,[398,46] [Death record states birth date as Dec 31 1888, but then gives age at death as 74y 4d, which would put birth date at Jan 1 1879. Birth date given in 1900 Census as Dec 1888.], d. Jan- 5-1955 at Auburn, Ritchie Co, WV,[398,46] buried in Auburn Baptist (aka Hall) Cemetery, Ritchie Co, WV,[398,469] resided at Auburn, Ritchie Co, WV,[398] census 1900 in Murphy District, Ritchie Co, WV. She married[396] Nov-24-1908 in Ritchie Co, WV,[473] **Hall Evert Sommerville**, b. May-10-1885 in Ritchie Co, WV,[592,473,46] (son of Robert A. Sommerville and Lydia Ellen Bartlett), d. Jul- -1973,[592,46] buried in Auburn Baptist (aka Hall) Cemetery, Ritchie Co, WV,[469] resided in Parkersburg, Wood Co, WV,[604] census 1900 in Union District, Ritchie Co, WV.

  Children:
  i.   ORLA ROBERT SOMMERVILLE b. Apr-28-1910 in Auburn, Ritchie Co, WV,[592,477,46] d. Feb-15-1960 in Ritchie Co, WV,[477,592,46] buried in Auburn Community Cemetery, Ritchie Co, WV.[469] He married[1101,424] Apr- 6-1934 in Ritchie Co, WV,[996] Wanita Lee Hinzman, b. Jan- -1917 at Bone Creek, near Auburn, Ritchie Co, WV,[190] (daughter of Eathen Egbert "Tom" Hinzman and Justina Melrose "Jettie" Goode), d. Jan-11-2011 in Buckhannon, Upshur Co, WV,[764] buried in Auburn Community Cemetery, Ritchie Co, WV,[190] resided in Buckhannon, Upshur Co, WV,[190] resided 1997,

2004, 05 Clarksburg, Harrison Co, WV,[412,1487] census 1920 in Berea, Ritchie Co, WV, occupation United Hospital Center, Clarksburg WV (retired).[190]

    ii.   VIRGINIA W. SOMMERVILLE b. Nov-22-1912 at Auburn, Ritchie Co, WV,[190] d. Mar-18-2004 at Jane Lew, Lewis Co, WV,[190] buried in Auburn Baptist (aka Hall) Cemetery, Ritchie Co, WV,[190] resided in Clarksburg, Harrison Co, WV,[190] resided formerly in Parkersburg, Wood Co, WV,[190] occupation manager, Adkins Fat Boy Restaurant, Parkersburg,[190] education Harrisville H.S. (1930).[190]

952. **Owen Ulysses Bee**, census name Ulissus O. Bee,[809] (527.Rebecca[8], 285.Elizabeth[7], 142.James[6], 72.John[5], 21.John[4], 6.Hugh[3], 3.John[2], 1.Jean[1]), b. Apr-19-1884 in Berea, Ritchie Co, WV,[190,46] d. Aug-23-1950 in Parkersburg, Wood Co, WV,[764,46] buried in IOOF Cemetery, Salem, Harrison Co, WV,[190,817] resided in Morgansville, Doddridge Co, WV,[190] resided 1941 at Wolf Summit, Harrison Co, WV,[436] census 1930 in Tenmile District, Harrison Co, WV, census 1900 in Union District, Ritchie Co, WV. He married Oct-24-1909 in Ritchie Co, WV,[473] **Iva Gay Mitchell**, also known as Gay Mitchell,[473,484] b. Mar-25-1888 in Smithville, Ritchie Co, WV,[398] [Headstone shows birth date as 1891, but death record states Mar 25 1888, with age as 53.] (daughter of Mart Mitchell and Phoebe Smith), d. Jul-15-1941 in Tenmile District, Harrison Co, WV,[398] buried in IOOF Cemetery, Salem, Harrison Co, WV,[398,817] resided at Wolf Summit, Harrison Co, WV.[398]

1930 Census, Harrison Co, WV (Tenmile District), enumerated on Apr 4 1930:
Owen Bee, 46, laborer in boiler shop; wife Iva, 39; son Olas, 12; dau Ethlyn, 2 yr 5 mo; son Guy, 7; son Paul 2 yr 10 mo.
(Note: Children are listed here in the same sequence as on the Census form, with ages as they appear on the form.)[190]

    Children:
    i.   KESTER O. BEE b. Dec- 9-1912,[592,46] d. Jul- -1976,[592,46] buried in IOOF Cemetery, Salem, Harrison Co, WV,[817] resided in Weirton, Hancock Co, WV,[592] resided 1950 in Clarksburg, Harrison Co, WV.[765]
    ii.   OLAS BEE b. Aug-23-1917,[592] d. Aug- -1976,[592] resided 1950 in Sutton, Braxton Co, WV.[765]
    iii.   ETHELYN MAE BEE b. Oct-17-1919,[419] resided 1950 in Morgansville, Doddridge Co, WV,[765] resided 1938 at Wolf Summit, Harrison Co, WV.[419] She married[941] Dec-24-1938 in Morgansville, Doddridge Co, WV,[419] John Ira McMillan, b. Jan- 9-1916 at Morgansville, Doddridge Co, WV,[419,592,17] (son of Clyde S. McMillan and Lura McIntire), d. Aug-28-1998,[592,17] buried in Chestnut Grove Cemetery, Big Flint, Doddridge Co, WV,[17] resided in Weirton, Hancock Co, WV,[604] census 1930 in Grant District, Doddridge Co, WV.
    iv.   GUY BEE b. Mar-14-1923,[592] d. Sep- -1967,[592] resided 1950 in Clarksburg, Harrison Co, WV.[765]
    v.   PAUL BEE b. May- 3-1927 in Harrison Co, WV,[398,17] d. Aug- 5-1947 at Wolf Summit, Harrison Co, WV,[398,17] cause of death struck by train (suicide),[398] buried in IOOF Cemetery, Salem, Harrison Co, WV,[398,817] military World War II.[398,817]
    vi.   JAMES LAWRENCE BEE b. May-22-1934 in West Virginia,[693,592] d. Oct- 3-2001 in Steubenville, Jefferson Co, OH,[592] resided in Wintersville, Jefferson Co, OH,[693] resided 1950 in Clarksburg, Harrison Co, WV,[765] military U.S. Army.[693]

953. **Orazs Creed Bee**[mdccclxxxi[1881]] census name Oris Bee,[418] census name Oras Bee,[1208] (527.Rebecca[8], 285.Elizabeth[7], 142.James[6], 72.John[5], 21.John[4], 6.Hugh[3], 3.John[2], 1.Jean[1]), b. Nov-24-1889 in Berea, Ritchie Co, WV,[1881,46] d. 1961,[46] buried in IOOF Cemetery, Salem, Harrison Co, WV,[817] resided 1954 in Bristol, Harrison Co, WV,[1881] resided 1950 in Salem, WV,[521] resided 1926 at Wolf Summit, Harrison Co, WV,[748] census 1920, 1930 in Tenmile District, Harrison Co, WV, census 1910 in Bridgeport, Lawrence Co, IL [in household with sister Rosa and her husband John Anderson].

1920 Census, Harrison Co, WV (Tenmile District), enumerated on Jan 7 1920:
Oris Bee, 29; wife Bessie, 20; son Robert, 2y 2m; son Hearald, 1y 8m.

1930 Census, Harrison Co, WV (Tenmile District, Town of Wolf Summit), enumerated on Apr 30 1930:
Oras Bee, 40, occupation pumper in oil field; wife Bessie, 33; son Robert, 13; son Harold, 12; dau Irene, 10; son Kenneth, 8; dau Lucile, 5.

He married[374,446,mdccclxxxii[1882]] (1) divorced **Bessie Anna Wanstreet**, b. ca 1900,[418] census 1920, 1930 in Tenmile District, Harrison Co, WV. He married (2) Feb-26-1954 in Clarksburg, Harrison Co, WV,[1881] **Nora Mae Emerson**, b. Apr- 9-1896 in Jane Lew, Lewis Co, WV,[1881,17] (daughter of Joseph Emerson and Viola May Eakle), d. Jul-30-1975,[17] buried in Marshville Cemetery, Harrison Co, WV.[817]
Children by Bessie Anna Wanstreet:
i.   ROBERT LEWIS BEE b. Oct-25-1916 in Harrison Co, WV,[419,592] d. Nov- 1-1997,[592] resided in Clarksburg, Harrison Co, WV,[592,1882] resided 1940 at Wolf Summit, Harrison Co, WV,[419] census 1920, 1930 in Tenmile District, Harrison Co, WV. He married Aug-23-1940 at Wolf Summit, Harrison Co, WV,[419] Wilson Victoria Howell, b. Nov-11-1918 at Dry Branch, Kanawha Co, WV,[419,592] (daughter of David Lenzie Howell and Ella Davisson), d. Jul- 7-1993,[592] resided in Clarksburg, Harrison Co, WV.[419,604]
ii.   HAROLD LEE BEE b. Apr- 7-1918 at Wolf Summit, Harrison Co, WV,[419,592] d. Jun-21-1997,[592] resided in Nutter Fort, Harrison Co, WV,[1882] resided 1940 at Wolf Summit, Harrison Co, WV,[419] census 1920, 1930 in Tenmile District, Harrison Co, WV. He married Jan- 6-1940 in Clarksburg, Harrison Co, WV,[419] Mabel Pauline Dearing, b. Jun-27-1919 in Clarksburg, Harrison Co, WV,[419] (daughter of Edward Newton Dearing and Orena Seckman), resided 2010 in Clarksburg, Harrison Co, WV.[1487]
iii. IRENE BEE b. ca 1920,[1208] resided 2004, 2010 in Salem, WV,[1882,412] census 1930 in Tenmile District, Harrison Co, WV. She married[1882,424] __ Greer.
iv.   KENNETH RAY BEE b. ca 1922,[1208] resided 2004, 2010 in Tampa, Hillsborough Co, FL,[1882,412] census 1930 in Tenmile District, Harrison Co, WV. He married[1487] Patty __, resided 2010 in Tampa, Hillsborough Co, FL.[1487]
v.   LUCILLE REBECCA BEE, census name Lucile Bee,[1208] b. Nov- 5-1924 at Wolf Summit, Harrison Co, WV,[419,1882] d. Feb-26-2010 in Fairmont, Marion Co, WV,[764] buried in Greenlawn Masonic Cemetery, Clarksburg, WV,[190] resided in Fairmont, Marion Co, WV,[1882,764] [nursing home], resided formerly at Wolf Summit, Harrison Co, WV,[190] census 1930 in Tenmile District, Harrison Co, WV, education Bristol H.S., WV Business College.[190]

A 1942 graduate of Bristol High School (Harrison Co, WV) and of West Virginia Business College. She was then employed at the Mutual Insurance Company and the Clarksburg Terminal. An accomplished pianist, she enjoyed playing the piano and organ for the Evangelical Church in Clarksburg. She and her brother Bob appeared on Channel 12 television on Sunday mornings singing together for the Evangelical Church services. They developed an audience who wrote to them and expressed their appreciation for the songs and the dedications made to them. Lucille was also a great boating enthusiast. [from a newspaper announcement of her 80th birthday celebration][1882]

She married[1882] Jun- 6-1948 at Wolf Summit, Harrison Co, WV,[419] Willis Martin Cunningham, b. Nov-21-1915 in Jarvisville, Harrison Co, WV,[419,592] (son of Daniel Martin Cunningham and Maude Matheny), d. Oct-26-1996,[592] resided at Lost Creek, Harrison Co, WV.[604]

954. **Hazel C. Bee** (527.Rebecca[8], 285.Elizabeth[7], 142.James[6], 72.John[5], 21.John[4], 6.Hugh[3], 3.John[2], 1.Jean[1]), b. Mar- 1-1900,[17,1026] d. Dec-21-1991,[17] buried in IOOF Cemetery, Salem, Harrison Co, WV,[817] resided 1950 in Salem, WV,[521] census 1910 in Berea, Ritchie Co, WV. She married (1) Sep- 4-1916 in Ritchie Co, WV,[996] divorced[526] **Lewis Earl Pierce**, census name Earl Pierce,[1015] b. Sep- -1895,[809,996] (son of Jacob I. Pierce and Mary J. __), census 1900, 1910 in Union District, Ritchie Co, WV. She married[1101] (2) **Lance O. "Shorty" Davis**, b. Aug- 5-1897,[17] d. Dec-29-1962,[17] buried in IOOF Cemetery, Salem, Harrison Co, WV.[817]
Children by Lance O. "Shorty" Davis:

        i. ROBERT DAVIS b. 1933,[46] d. 1938,[46] buried in IOOF Cemetery, Salem, Harrison Co, WV.[817]

955. **George Isaac Gaston** (530.John[8], 287.Isaac[7], 142.James[6], 72.John[5], 21.John[4], 6.Hugh[3], 3.John[2], 1.Jean[1]), b. Feb-18-1896 in West Milford, Harrison Co, WV,[684,1191,398] d. Jun- 4-1932 in Harrison Co, WV,[mdccclxxxiii[1883],398] cause of death intestinal obstruction,[1191,398] buried in Sunset Memorial Park Cemetery, Clarksburg, WV,[1191,398] resided 1923 in Clarksburg, Harrison Co, WV,[mdccclxxxiv[1884]] census 1920 in Stealey (Clarksburg), Harrison Co, WV, census 1900, 1910 in Fairmont, Marion Co, WV, occupation manager, Superior Woolen Mills (per 1923 city directory), merchant & tailor (per obit).[1131,398] He married Sep-30-1919, **Lola Josephine "Jo" Queen**, also known as Josephine Queen,[228] b. Feb-28-1896 in Evergreen, Upshur Co, WV,[190] (daughter of Okey Lee Queen and Pearl Alena Russell), d. Nov-11-1997 in Clarksburg, Harrison Co, WV,[190] buried in Sunset Memorial Park Cemetery, Clarksburg, WV,[190] resided in Clarksburg, Harrison Co, WV,[849] census 1920 in Stealey (Clarksburg), Harrison Co, WV, occupation beautician.[190]

Lola: Member of Duff Street United Methodist Church, an honorary member of the Stealey Civic and Garden Club, and was a volunteer for Meals on Wheels for many years. She was also the co-owner of the former El Dora Beauty Shop in Clarksburg.[190]

        Children:
        i. GEORGE IRWIN "BUD" GASTON[190] b. Mar-15-1921 in Clarksburg, Harrison Co, WV,[190,mdccclxxxv[1885]] d. Mar-23-2004 in Clarksburg, Harrison Co, WV,[190] [Obituary stated that there was no visitation and that a private memorial service would be held in Arizona. There was no indication of burial location.], resided in Clarksburg, Harrison Co, WV,[190] resided previously in Scottsdale, AZ,[190] education West Virginia University College of Engineering,[190] military U.S. Army, WW II and Korean War.[190]

        Employed by General Electric, RCA, and was Director of Marketing for Motorola in the Governmnet Electronics Division in Scottsdale, AZ.[190]

        He married (1) Jan-19-1946 in Harrison Co, WV,[mdccclxxxvi[1886]] Mary Patricia Smith, b. 1925, d. bef Mar 2004.[484] He married[484,424] (2) Geraldine Spelsberg, b. Oct-31-1924 in Clarksburg, Harrison Co, WV,[190] (daughter of Charles A. Spelsberg and Kathleen "Peggy" Leonard), d. Aug-23-2004 in Clarksburg, Harrison Co, WV,[700] resided in Clarksburg, Harrison Co, WV,[484,190] occupation Harrison County Board of Education (retired).[190]

        Geraldine: Among others, survived by seven grandchildren, Dean Brown, Joe Bynum, Josh Bynum, Jake Bynum, Zachary Bynum, Alyssa Cline, and Lindsey Jo Cline.[190]

        ii. MARY JO GASTON b. Jan-10-1924 in Clarksburg, Harrison Co, WV,[mdccclxxxvii[1887],419] resided 2007, 09 in Bridgeport, Harrison Co, WV,[1595,484] resided 1942 in Clarksburg, Harrison Co, WV.[419] She married Mar- 1-1942 in Clarksburg, Harrison Co, WV,[mdccclxxxviii[1888],mdccclxxxix[1889]] Gordon Glenwood Brown, also known as G. Glenwood Brown,[1595] b. Sep-18-1917 in Kirby, Hampshire Co, WV,[419,190] (son of William Gordon Brown and Erma Viola Davis), d. Sep- 6-2009 in Bridgeport, Harrison Co, WV,[700] buried (ashes) in Sunset Memorial Park Cemetery, Clarksburg, WV,[190] resided in Bridgeport, Harrison Co, WV,[1595,190] resided 1942 in Clarksburg, Harrison Co, WV,[419] occupation Gen Mgr, James & Law Co,[190] education Romney H.S., Salem College, West Virginia Univ,[190] military 1942 - 1945 U.S. Army Signal Corps, World War II (European-African-Middle Eastern Theatre).[190]

956. **Golden "Goldie" Gaston**, census name Goldie Gaston,[408] (531.Thomas[8], 287.Isaac[7], 142.James[6], 72.John[5], 21.John[4], 6.Hugh[3], 3.John[2], 1.Jean[1]), b. Nov-28-1887 in Lewis Co, WV,[mdcccxc[1890],592] d. Nov- - 1974 in Kanawha Co, WV,[592] buried in Machpelah Cemetery, Weston, Lewis Co, WV, resided in Charleston, Kanawha Co, WV,[592] census 1900 in Weston, Lewis Co, WV. She married Sep-14-1910 in

Lewis Co, WV,[410] **Paul Sumpter Zobrist**, b. Apr-17-1887 in Lewis Co, WV,[mdcccxci[1891]] [Death certificate states birth date as Dec 1 1889, with age at death as 48y9m23d.] (son of Samuel J. Zobrist and Mary Sumpter), d. Sep-24-1938 in Weston, Lewis Co, WV,[398] buried in Broad Run Bapt Ch Cem, Jane Lew, Lewis Co, WV,[398] resided in Weston, Lewis Co, WV,[398] occupation salesman.[398]

Children:

    i.   JEAN GASTON ZOBRIST b. Mar-28-1915 in Weston, Lewis Co, WV,[190,mdcccxci[1892]] d. Apr-19-2004,[190] buried in Machpelah Cemetery, Weston, Lewis Co, WV,[190] resided in Charleston, Kanawha Co, WV.[190]

Jean Gaston Zobrist was an independent, sophisticated and strong woman who enjoyed winning at bridge and poker games, doing crossword puzzles, and keeping company with her cat. Always stylish and proud of being a smart businesswoman, she worked as an executive legal secretary in West Virginia and Washington, DC for companies that included the West Virginia State Attorney General's Office, Jackson-Kelly law firm, and Greyhound Bus Lines. She moved to Charleston after graduating from Weston High School. In her earlier years, she liked to dance. Active in the First Presbyterian Church, she was a longtime member of the exercise group, Doc Struthers Bible Study class, and the Women of the Church.[190]

She married Nov- -1941 in Maryland, Gordon A. Zeller, also known as Gordan A. Zeller,[191,502] b. Feb- 5-1902 in Pennsylvania,[398] (son of Lewis Zeller and Alyce Hanley), d. Jul-29-1946 in South Charleston, Kanawha Co, WV,[398] buried in Blockhouse Hill Cemetery, West Union, WV,[398,721] resided in West Union, Doddridge Co, WV,[419,398] occupation glass cutter,[398] military WW I and WW II.[398] Gordan and Jean were in the process of getting a divorce. The day before the divorce was to be final, Gordan was killed in a plane crash. Jean went back to her maiden name of Zobrist.

    ii.   BETTY LOUISE ZOBRIST b. May-29-1917 in Lewis Co, WV,[mdcccxciii[1893]] d. Feb-10-1987 in Kanawha Co, WV,[mdcccxciv[1894]] buried in Sunset Memorial Park Cemetery, South Charleston, Kanawha Co, WV, resided in Charleston, Kanawha Co, WV. She married Mar-1939, Charles Francis Stuart, b. Mar-15-1905, d. Jun-14-1972 in Kanawha Co, WV,[mdcccxcv[1895]] buried in Sunset Memorial Park Cemetery, South Charleston, Kanawha Co, WV.

    iii.   PAUL SUMPTER ZOBRIST, JR. b. Jun-29-1921 in Lewis Co, WV,[1893] d. Feb-14-1978, buried in Seattle, WA. He married Marie Ramstead, b. ca 1926, resided 2004 in Seattle, WA.[1487]

    iv.   THOMAS CHARLES ZOBRIST b. Oct- 7-1922 in Lewis Co, WV,[1893] d. Mar-11-1923 in Lewis Co, WV,[mdcccxcvi[1896]] buried in Machpelah Cemetery, Weston, Lewis Co, WV.

957. **Lucy Lacy Gaston**, also known as Lacy Lucy Gaston,[410] (531.Thomas[8], 287.Isaac[7], 142.James[6], 72.John[5], 21.John[4], 6.Hugh[3], 3.John[2], 1.Jean[1]), b. Apr- 6-1891 in Lewis Co, WV,[46] d. 1943,[46] buried in McWhorter Cemetery, Harrison Co, WV,[17,230] census 1900, 1920 in Weston, Lewis Co, WV. She married Nov-22-1916 in Lewis Co, WV,[mdcccxcvii[1897]] **Ralph McWhorter**, b. Sep- -1890 in Harrison Co, WV,[467,46,410] (son of Daniel Grant McWhorter and Cora Gaston), d. 1948,[46] buried in McWhorter Cemetery, Harrison Co, WV,[17,230] census 1920 in Weston, Lewis Co, WV, census 1900 in Grant District, Harrison Co, WV, occupation dentist.[888] As great-great-grandchildren of John Gaston Jr. & Anna Davisson, Ralph McWhorter and Lucy Lacy Gaston were third cousins.

Children:

    i.   RALPH MCWHORTER, JR. b. Jun-12-1919,[17] d. Sep-19-1919,[17] buried in McWhorter Cemetery, Harrison Co, WV.[17,230]

958. **Charles Nicoles Gaston**[mdcccxcviii[1898]] (531.Thomas[8], 287.Isaac[7], 142.James[6], 72.John[5], 21.John[4], 6.Hugh[3], 3.John[2], 1.Jean[1]), b. Jun- 5-1899 in Lewis Co, WV,[621,592,1898] d. Jun-19-1967,[1898,592] buried in Baltimore National Cemetery, Baltimore, MD,[1898] resided in Baltimore, MD,[592] resided 1929, 49 in Weston, Lewis Co, WV,[419,621] census 1900 in Weston, Lewis Co, WV, occupation 1918 mail carrier.[684] He married (1) divorced[mdcccxcix[1899],526] **Velma Smith**, b. ca 1906,[1899] (daughter of Robert S. Smith and Tabitha __), census 1930 in Philippi, Barbour Co, WV. He married (2) Jul- 3-1929 in Grafton, Taylor Co, WV,[mcm[1900]] **Henrietta Mae Beckman**, b. May-26-1899 in Preston Co, WV,[419] (daughter of

Henry Beckman and Lillian Thompson), resided 1929 in Shinnston, Harrison Co, WV.[419] He married (3) Apr-15-1949 in Clarksburg, Harrison Co, WV,[mcmi[1901]] **Lena Esta Coffman**, b. Nov-22-1901 in Taylor Co, WV,[621,1898,592] (daughter of Arthur Lee Coffman and Emily Susan McDaniel), d. Jul-29-1982,[1898,592] buried in Baltimore National Cemetery, Baltimore, MD,[1898] resided in Pittsburgh, Allegheny Co, PA,[592] resided 1949 in Lewis Co, WV.[621]

Children by Velma Smith:

i.   MILTON C. GASTON b. Sep-17-1924 in Philippi, Barbour Co, WV,[190,592] d. Dec- 6-2009 in York, York Co, PA,[806,592] buried in Blue Ridge Cemetery, Thurmont, Frederick Co, MD,[190] resided in Gettysburg, Adams Co, PA,[190,604] census 1930 in Philippi, Barbour Co, WV, occupation Continental Can Co of Reading PA (30 yrs),[190] military U.S. Marine Corps & U.S. Navy, World War II.[190] He married[484] (2) ca 1954,[191] Louise A. Valentine, b. Nov-27-1914 in Rocky Ridge, Frederick Co, MD,[190,592] (daughter of Nathan L. Valentine and Cora F. Sharrer), d. May- 1-2007 in Emmitsburg, Frederick Co, MD,[764,592] buried in Blue Ridge Cemetery, Thurmont, Frederick Co, MD,[190] resided in Gettysburg, Adams Co, PA.[1086,190]

959. **Stokes Norman Gaston** (532.Harley[8], 287.Isaac[7], 142.James[6], 72.John[5], 21.John[4], 6.Hugh[3], 3.John[2], 1.Jean[1]), b. Sep-27-1911 in Lewis Co, WV,[mcmii[1902]] d. Sep-28-1947 in Lewis Co, WV,[mcmiii[1903]] buried in Machpelah Cemetery, Weston, Lewis Co, WV. He married[191] **Dorotha Jean Ramsburg**, b. Jan-10-1910 in Weston, Lewis Co, WV,[592,190] (daughter of Arville O. Ramsburg and Dora Coburn), d. Mar-14-2009 in Weston, Lewis Co, WV,[806,592] buried in Machpelah Cemetery, Weston, Lewis Co, WV,[190] resided in Weston, Lewis Co, WV,[592] occupation sales person, Specialty Shop of Weston,[190] education Weston H.S.[190]

Children:

i.   LIVING. He married (1) Patty Jo Flesher, b. May- 1-1932 in Weston, Lewis Co, WV,[190] (daughter of Nay Ercil Flesher and Lorena Edna Cawthorn), d. May-25-2001 in Morgantown, Monongalia Co, WV,[806] resided in Clarksburg, Harrison Co, WV,[190] resided 1962-98 in Las Vegas, Clark Co, NV,[190] education Weston High School.[190]

Patty: Co-owner of Tire Service, Inc., Sand Dollar Lounge, and Fast Break Lounge in Las Vegas, NV, retiring in 1996. She lived in Las Vegas for 36 years before moving back to West Virginia with her daughter in April 1998.[190]

He married (2) Living.

ii.   (STILLBORN FEMALE) (TWIN) GASTON b. Jul-20-1936 in Lewis Co, WV, d. Jul-20-1936 in Lewis Co, WV.[mcmiv[1904]]

iii. LIVING. He married Living.

iv.   GEORGE NORMAN GASTON b. Feb-11-1942 in Lewis Co, WV,[mcmv[1905]] d. Dec- -1994 in Harrison Co, WV,[mcmvi[1906],592] [Lewis County Death Records (Book 12, p. 151) give date of death as Dec 31 1994. But Social Security Death Index reports death date as Dec 15 1994.], buried in Machpelah Cemetery, Weston, Lewis Co, WV.[1906]

960. **Frances Virginia Helmick** (533.Frederick[8], 288.Margaret[7], 142.James[6], 72.John[5], 21.John[4], 6.Hugh[3], 3.John[2], 1.Jean[1]), b. Mar-20-1900 in Fairmont, Marion Co, WV,[mcmvii[1907]] d. Dec- 4-1985 in Worthington, Franklin Co, OH,[1907] buried in Walnut Grove Cemetery, Columbus, OH.[1907] She married Jun-19-1926 in Fairmont, Marion Co, WV,[278] **Harold Hobart Buell**, b. Aug-30-1896 in Marietta, Washington Co, OH,[278] d. 1964 in Worthington, Franklin Co, OH,[278] buried in Walnut Grove Cemetery, Columbus, OH.[278]

Children:

i.   ROBERT GOODE BUELL b. Apr-27-1932 in Worthington, Franklin Co, OH,[1907] d. Feb-16-1995 in Worthington, Franklin Co, OH,[1907] buried in Walnut Grove Cemetery, Columbus, OH.[1907] He married Living.

961. **Robert J. "Jay" Helmick** (533.Frederick[8], 288.Margaret[7], 142.James[6], 72.John[5], 21.John[4], 6.Hugh[3], 3.John[2], 1.Jean[1]), b. Jan-12-1906, d. May-30-1996 in Hilton Head, Beaufort Co, SC.[1907] He married Sep-30-1933, **Jane Louise Kelly**, b. 1911.

Children:

 i. LIVING.

962. John Pierpont Helmick (534.Ernest[8], 288.Margaret[7], 142.James[6], 72.John[5], 21.John[4], 6.Hugh[3], 3.John[2], 1.Jean[1]), b. Nov-18-1904, d. Dec-10-1961, buried in Woodlawn Cemetery, Fairmont, Marion Co, WV, occupation Doctor. He married **Clare Dean Johnson**.

 Children:

 i. LIVING. He married Living.

963. Louis Gaston Helmick, Jr. (536.Louis[8], 288.Margaret[7], 142.James[6], 72.John[5], 21.John[4], 6.Hugh[3], 3.John[2], 1.Jean[1]), b. Jul-14-1920, resided 2008 in Marathon, Monroe Co, FL.[412]

 Children:

 i. LIVING.

964. Harriet Wright Helmick (536.Louis[8], 288.Margaret[7], 142.James[6], 72.John[5], 21.John[4], 6.Hugh[3], 3.John[2], 1.Jean[1]), b. May-27-1924 in Fairmont, Marion Co, WV,[190,592] d. Jan-22-2008,[592] resided in Grand Island, Hall Co, NE,[190,604] resided originally in Fairmont, Marion Co, WV,[190] education Duke University (1946), Carnegie-Mellon (1947).[190] She married Jun-18-1949 in Fairmont, Marion Co, WV,[191] **James Edward Wenger**, b. Dec-16-1922.

 Children:

 i. LIVING.

 ii. LIVING.

 iii. LIVING. She married Living.

965. Brady Summers Gaston[446] also known as Brady Gaston,[1131] (539.Albert[8], 290.Thomas[7], 142.James[6], 72.John[5], 21.John[4], 6.Hugh[3], 3.John[2], 1.Jean[1]), b. May-21-1897 in Lewis Co, WV,[592] d. Jun-18-1975,[592] resided in Clarksburg, Harrison Co, WV,[1131,592] occupation core maker, Hart Bros Machine Co.[1131] He married **Thelma Louella Riggs**, b. Oct-31-1899 in West Virginia,[592,123] (daughter of William A. Riggs and Stella Findley), d. Mar-10-1979,[592] resided in Clarksburg, Harrison Co, WV,[592] census 1920 in Clarksburg, Harrison Co, WV, census 1910 in New Haven, Mason Co, WV [Listed as a granddaughter in the home of Lavina Finley, 63, b. Ohio (father b. W.Va, mother b. Pa.), widowed. They were the only members of the household.], census 1900 in Belmont, Belmont Co, OH.

 Children:

 i. JAMES BRADY GASTON b. Jul-17-1924,[592] d. Nov- 3-1988,[592] resided in Clarksburg, Harrison Co, WV.[592] He married[191] Carole Kibler, b. Feb- 9-1926,[190] (daughter of Charles H. Kibler and Celia Lois Doyle), d. Jul-15-2011 in Bridgeport, Harrison Co, WV,[847] buried in Bridgeport Cemetery, Harrison Co, WV,[190] resided in Clarksburg, Harrison Co, WV,[190] education Ohio University.[190]

 ii. LIVING. He married Living.

966. Margaret Helen Gaston (539.Albert[8], 290.Thomas[7], 142.James[6], 72.John[5], 21.John[4], 6.Hugh[3], 3.John[2], 1.Jean[1]), b. Mar-13-1900, d. Oct-16-1983, resided 1959 in Clarksburg, Harrison Co, WV.[778] She married Dec-2-1919 in Lewis Co, WV,[410] **Archie David Swecker**, b. Oct-12-1894 (son of John E. Swecker and Nettie C. Allman), d. Aug- 8-1955.

 Children:

 i. DAVID GASTON SWECKER b. Dec-16-1920,[592] d. May- 4-1990.[592] He married[374] Aug-10-1946,[191] Anita Mae Alkire, b. Jan-24-1927 in Salem, WV,[190,592] (daughter of Layman O. Alkire and Louia Mae Carder), d. Sep- 9-2004 in Oakdale, Allegheny Co, PA,[806,592] buried in Bridgeport Cemetery, Harrison Co, WV,[190] resided in Maple Lake (Bridgeport), Harrison Co, WV,[190,604] occupation secretary, Harrison Co Board of Educ (16 yrs).[190]

 ii. JO ANN SWECKER b. Sep-12-1927,[592] d. Jun-29-1993,[592] resided in Decatur, Dekalb Co, GA,[592] resided formerly in West Virginia.[mcmviii[1908]] She married[592] ___ Barnes.

967. Dona Leigh Morris, census name Lee D. Morris,[211] (543.James[8], 291.Olive[7], 142.James[6], 72.John[5], 21.John[4], 6.Hugh[3], 3.John[2], 1.Jean[1]), b. Mar- 6-1896 in Lewis Co, WV,[398,724,211] d. Apr- 3-1923 in

Grafton, Taylor Co, WV,[398] buried in Bluemont Cemetery, Grafton, Taylor Co, WV,[398] cause of death pneumonia,[398] resided 1915 in Grafton, Taylor Co, WV,[724] census 1910 in Cumberland, Allegany Co, MD. She married Jul-27-1915 in Grafton, Taylor Co, WV,[mcmix[1909]] **Carl Wayne Poe**, b. ca 1892 in Taylor Co, WV,[724] resided in Grafton, Taylor Co, WV.[724,mcmx[1910]]

> Children:
> i. JAMES E. POE b. ca 1917,[1910] census 1930 in Grafton, Taylor Co, WV.
> ii. GERALDINE L. POE b. ca 1918,[1910] census 1930 in Grafton, Taylor Co, WV.
> iii. CARL W. POE, JR. b. ca 1920,[1910] census 1930 in Taylor Co, WV.
> iv. CHARLES POE b. ca 1922,[1910] census 1930 in Grafton, Taylor Co, WV.

968. **Howard Gaston Peterson** (545.Minnie[8], 292.John[7], 142.James[6], 72.John[5], 21.John[4], 6.Hugh[3], 3.John[2], 1.Jean[1]), b. Feb-28-1906,[1161,592] d. May--1990,[1010] census 1930 at Hackers Creek, Lewis Co, WV. He married[1161] **Virginia Ferrell**.

> Children:
> i. LIVING. She married Living.

969. **Wade Compton Gaston** (547.Mary[8], 293.Abraham[7], 143.William[6], 72.John[5], 21.John[4], 6.Hugh[3], 3.John[2], 1.Jean[1]), b. Sep-26-1878 in Freemans Creek, Lewis Co, WV,[mcmxi[1911]] d. Jul-27-1964 in Clarksburg, Harrison Co, WV,[mcmxii[1912],191] buried in Broad Run Bapt Ch Cem, Jane Lew, Lewis Co, WV,[mcmxiii[1913]] resided 1937 in Lost Creek, Harrison Co, WV,[778] occupation painter.[mcmxiv[1914]] He married[191] Dec-4-1912 in Weston, Lewis Co, WV,[mcmxv[1915]] **Nannie May Gaston**, census name May Gaston,[467] also known as Mae Gaston, b. Mar-20-1889 in Doddridge Co, WV,[mcmxvi[1916]] [Penny Linder, in "The Gibson and Related Families" (p. 108), identifies Nannie May Gaston as "D. Mae Gaston," born on the same date in Doddridge Co, WV. A birth record does exist for her in both counties (see footnote). Based on locations of other events in her family, Harrison County would be considered more likely, but her obituary states that she was born in Doddridge County. The obituary identifies her as "N. May Gaston," while the Social Security Death Index lists her simply as "May Gaston."] (daughter of George L. Gaston and Rachel Bond), d. Jan-13-1976 in Clarksburg, Harrison Co, WV,[mcmxvii[1917],190] buried in Broad Run Bapt Ch Cem, Jane Lew, Lewis Co, WV,[mcmxviii[1918],276,190] resided in Clarksburg, Harrison Co, WV,[190] resided formerly in McWhorter, Harrison Co, WV,[190] census 1900 in Grant District, Harrison Co, WV. Wade Compton Gaston and Nanny May Gaston were second cousins, as both were great-grandchildren of William G. Gaston (1806-1894) and Mary Post (1809-1887). They were also fifth cousins, as they were the fourth-great- grandchildren of John Smith (1699-1748) and Hannah Waters.

> Children:
> i. ROBERT ABRAM GASTON b. Dec-4-1914 in Lewis Co, WV,[17,592] d. May-11-1981,[17,592] buried in Broad Run Bapt Ch Cem, Jane Lew, Lewis Co, WV,[17] resided in Galloway, Franklin Co, OH,[592] resided 1975 in Columbus, Franklin Co, OH.[856] He married Dec-29-1934 in West Milford, Harrison Co, WV,[mcmxix[1919]] Melba Louise Spicer, b. Sep-8-1917 in Harrison Co, WV,[190,592] (daughter of Orville Spicer and Susan Pratt), d. Apr-23-2005 in Marengo, Morrow Co, OH,[764,604] buried in Broad Run Bapt Ch Cem, Jane Lew, Lewis Co, WV,[190,17] resided in Columbus, Franklin Co, OH,[190] occupation Gold Circle Department Stores (retired).[190]

> Melba: Among others, survived by one sister, Norma Popovich, and nine grandchildren, Marsha Simmons, David L. Gaston Jr., Michael Gaston, Susie Gaston, Barbara Dick, Robert (Bobby) Gaston, Timothy Gaston, Kodi Asman, and Eric Gaston; and by 15 great-grandchildren. Predeceased by one sister, Jean Thompson, and one brother, Kenneth LeMasters.[190]

> ii. LUELLA GASTON b. Nov-29-1916 in Lewis Co, WV,[592] d. Sep--1986,[592] resided in Anmoore, Harrison Co, WV,[592] resided 1975 in Clarksburg, Harrison Co, WV.[856] She married Dec-18-1935 in West Milford, Harrison Co, WV,[mcmxx[1920]] Hunter Cooper, b. May-22-1913 in Gilmer Co, WV,[mcmxxi[1921],592] (son of Andrew Cooper and Stella Bond), d. Apr--1980,[592] resided in Clarksburg, Harrison Co, WV.[592]

iii.   GEORGE HAROLD GASTON b. Dec-12-1923 in Harrison Co, WV,[mcmxxii[1922]] d. Jan-19-1993 in Harrison Co, WV,[1922] buried in Broad Run Bapt Ch Cem, Jane Lew, Lewis Co, WV,[190] resided in Clarksburg, Harrison Co, WV,[190] military U.S. Army, World War II.[190]

A disabled veteran, he served with the US Army in World War II, receiving a Purple Heart, a Bronze Star, and a Good Conduct Medal.[190]

He married Loristeen Juanita Swartz, b. Apr- 9-1930 in McWhorter, Harrison Co, WV,[276,17] (daughter of Robert Swartz and Versa Walker), d. Mar-11-1991 in Clarksburg, Harrison Co, WV,[mcmxxiii[1923],17,484] buried (ashes) in Broad Run Bapt Ch Cem, Jane Lew, Lewis Co, WV.[mcmxxiv[1924]]

iv.   MARY RACHEL GASTON b. Mar-20-1930 in Grant District, Harrison Co, WV,[mcmxxv[1925]] d. Apr-13-1930 in Harrison Co, WV.

970. **Tensie Myrtle Hall** (548.Amanda[8], 293.Abraham[7], 143.William[6], 72.John[5], 21.John[4], 6.Hugh[3], 3.John[2], 1.Jean[1]) (See marriage to number 508.)

971. **Sarah Della Hall** (548.Amanda[8], 293.Abraham[7], 143.William[6], 72.John[5], 21.John[4], 6.Hugh[3], 3.John[2], 1.Jean[1]) (See marriage to number 509.)

972. **Blonda Scott Hall**, census name Blonda B. Hall,[1093] (548.Amanda[8], 293.Abraham[7], 143.William[6], 72.John[5], 21.John[4], 6.Hugh[3], 3.John[2], 1.Jean[1]), b. Dec- 3-1887 in Lewis Co, WV,[17,419] d. Mar-30-1981,[17] buried in Beech Grove Cemetery, Lewis Co, WV, resided 1921 in Weston, Lewis Co, WV.[419] He married May-28-1921 in Clarksburg, Harrison Co, WV,[419] **Lucy L. Sapp**, b. Apr- 7-1894,[17] (daughter of Marcus D. Sapp and Mattie Jane Riffle), d. Jun-11-1983,[17] buried in Beech Grove Cemetery, Lewis Co, WV.
Children:
i.   CHARLES ABRAM "BUCKSHOT" HALL[190] b. Feb-23-1922 in Freemansburg, Lewis Co, WV,[190] d. Jul-21-2003 in Weston, Lewis Co, WV,[190] buried in Beech Grove Cemetery, Lewis Co, WV,[190] resided in Weston, Lewis Co, WV,[190] occupation farmer.[190] He married Living.
ii.   LIVING. She married[1101] Living.

973. **Harvey Addison Hall** (548.Amanda[8], 293.Abraham[7], 143.William[6], 72.John[5], 21.John[4], 6.Hugh[3], 3.John[2], 1.Jean[1]), b. May-30-1891,[17] d. Oct-28-1946,[17] buried in Beech Grove Cemetery, Lewis Co, WV. He married Dec-15-1915, **Mabel McGinnis**, b. Sep-22-1891,[17] d. Dec- 4-1979,[17] buried in Beech Grove Cemetery, Lewis Co, WV.
Children:
i.   ROBERTA JEAN HALL b. ca 1920 in Lewis Co, WV,[621] resided 1948 in Weston, Lewis Co, WV.[621] She married Aug- 7-1948 in Weston, Lewis Co, WV,[621] Charles Herbert Stephens, b. ca 1921 in Joppa, Harford Co, MD,[621] (son of Herbert Stephens and Beata Anderson), resided 1948 in Joppa, Harford Co, MD.[621]
ii.   MARJORIE ANN HALL b. Oct-27-1922 in Gilmer Co, WV,[621] resided 1947 in Weston, Lewis Co, WV.[621] She married Jun- 7-1947 in Weston, Lewis Co, WV,[621] Robert Stewart Cosby, Jr., b. Aug-27-1921 in Richmond, VA,[592,621] [Birth date given in marriage record as Aug 27 1922, but SSDI shows it as Aug 27 1921.] (son of Robert Stewart Cosby and Nora Virginia Ramey), d. Nov- -1980,[592] resided in Richmond, VA.[621,mcmxxvi[1926]]
iii.   JAMES HAMLIN HALL b. ca 1925,[1093] census 1930 in Freemans Creek District, Lewis Co, WV.
iv.   MABEL JANE HALL b. ca 1926,[1093] census 1930 in Freemans Creek District, Lewis Co, WV.

974. **Simeon Asbury Hall** (549.Rebecca[8], 293.Abraham[7], 143.William[6], 72.John[5], 21.John[4], 6.Hugh[3], 3.John[2], 1.Jean[1]), b. Feb- 2-1877,[1165] d. Dec- -1973,[592] buried in Weston Masonic Cemetery, Lewis Co, WV,[1166] resided in Weston, Lewis Co, WV,[592] occupation farmer.[621] He married Oct-31-1900 in Lewis Co, WV,[621,410] **Georgia Estella White**, b. ca 1881,[410] (daughter of John A. White and Jane A. ___), buried in Weston Masonic Cemetery, Lewis Co, WV.[1166]

Children:

i. FREDA MAE HALL b. Oct- 3-1901,[592] d. Jun-18-2002,[592] resided in Weston, Lewis Co, WV,[592] no children from this person. She married Oct-26-1921 in Lewis Co, WV,[410] Cecil Loring Kittle, b. Dec-25-1895 (son of M. B. Kittle and Daisy __), d. Dec-14-1966, buried in Weston Masonic Cemetery, Lewis Co, WV.

ii. INEZ MERL HALL[521,373] b. Jul- 4-1903,[592,410] d. Nov- -1995,[592] resided in Weston, Lewis Co, WV,[604] census 1930 in Weston, Lewis Co, WV. She married[1101] Jun- 3-1924 in Lewis Co, WV,[410] Harry Whitman Brown, b. May-17-1898 in Ritchie Co, WV,[592,410] (son of Albert Carl Brown and Isa M. Sommerville), d. Apr- -1981,[592] resided in Weston, Lewis Co, WV,[604] census 1930 in Weston, Lewis Co, WV, resided 1924 in Lewis Co, WV,[410] census 1910 in Auburn, Ritchie Co, WV.

iii. DOYLE A. HALL[373] d. bef Mar 2001.[521]

iv. RUHL RICHARD HALL[410,373] b. Mar-20-1906,[592] d. Jun-10-1990.[592] He married Jun-16-1928 in Lewis Co, WV,[410] Ineva Lillian Sumpter, b. ca 1911 in Gilmer Co, WV,[410] (daughter of O. L. Sumpter and Lenna __), resided 1928 in Lewis Co, WV.[410]

v. GENEVA HALL[373] d. bef Mar 2001.[521] She married[1101] __ Wyant.

vi. SIMEON A. HALL, JR.[373] b. Dec-12-1917 in Freemansburg, Lewis Co, WV,[190,592] d. Mar-21-2001 in Weston, Lewis Co, WV,[806,592] buried in Weston Masonic Cemetery, Lewis Co, WV,[190] resided in Weston, Lewis Co, WV,[190,592] occupation farmer, stockman, owner/operator of Hall's Tractor Sales,[190] education West Virginia University (degree in agriculture).[190] He married[374] Jan- 3-1944,[484] Irene See, resided 2001 in Weston, Lewis Co, WV.[484]

vii. JOHN HARVEY HALL[373] d. bef Mar 2001.[521]

975. **Edna E. Mundell** (551.Adaline[8], 293.Abraham[7], 143.William[6], 72.John[5], 21.John[4], 6.Hugh[3], 3.John[2], 1.Jean[1]), b. Jun- 4-1883,[592] d. Nov-18-1966 in Ritchie Co, WV,[477,592] resided in Parkersburg, Wood Co, WV.[592] She married May-25-1904 in Lewis Co, WV,[mcmxxvii[1927]] **James Thaddeus Alfred**, b. ca 1870,[410] (son of James Alfred and Marcelus __).

Children:

i. DUANE ALFRED[412] b. Mar-21-1905,[592] d. Jul- -1987,[592] resided in Youngstown, Maricopa Co, AZ,[592] resided formerly in West Virginia.[604] He married[1487] Ola H. __, b. ca 1911,[190] d. Jun- 3-2005 in Peoria, Maricopa Co, AZ,[190] resided in Youngstown, Maricopa Co, AZ,[1487,190] resided formerly in Parkersburg, Wood Co, WV,[190] resided formerly in Marietta, Washington Co, OH.[190]

ii. OLGA ALFRED d. bef Mar 2005.[412] She married[424] __ Ott.

iii. JAMES "JACK" ALFRED d. bef Mar 2005.[412]

iv. IMOGENE ALFRED resided 2005 in Parkersburg, Wood Co, WV.[412] She married[424] __ Thomas.

v. EDNA MAXINE ALFRED b. Oct- 4-1920 in Wirt Co, WV,[592,190] d. Mar- 7-2005 in Marietta, Washington Co, OH,[592,764] buried in Pisgah Cemetery, Wirt Co, WV,[190] resided in Reno, Washington Co, OH,[592] resided formerly in Parkersburg, Wood Co, WV,[190] occupation Wood County Board of Education (retired).[190] She married[191] Roy E. Smith, b. Jan-26-1917,[592] d. Mar-20-1985,[191,592] resided in Parkersburg, Wood Co, WV.[592]

976. **George Elbert Gaston**, also known as G. Elbert Gaston, also known as Gilbert E. Gaston,[502] (552.William[8], 293.Abraham[7], 143.William[6], 72.John[5], 21.John[4], 6.Hugh[3], 3.John[2], 1.Jean[1]), b. May-23-1894 in Lewis Co, WV,[mcmxxviii[1928],1179] d. Jan-28-1960 in Upshur Co, WV,[1179] buried in Heavner Cemetery, Upshur Co, WV.[1179] He married Sep-23-1915 in Upshur Co, WV,[mcmxxix[1929]] **Clara Margaret Mader**, b. Oct-16-1893 in Randolph Co, WV (daughter of Henry C. Mader and Augusta Karnowsky), d. Feb- 2-1981 in Upshur Co, WV,[1177] buried in Heavner Cemetery, Upshur Co, WV.

Children:

i. ELIZABETH MADER GASTON b. Jun-28-1916 in Upshur Co, WV,[mcmxxx[1930],398] d. Oct-3-1953 in Philippi, Barbour Co, WV,[398,484] cause of death automobile accident,[398] buried in Mt. Vernon Memorial Cemetery, Philippi, Barbour Co, WV,[398] resided in Philippi, Barbour Co, WV.[398] She married May-21-1934 in Lewis Co, WV,[mcmxxxi[1931],mcmxxxii[1932]] Thomas Knotts "T.K." Wolfe,[190] b. Aug-19-1915 in Akron, Summit Co, OH,[190] (son of Thomas Lincoln Wolfe and Oda Madeline Knotts), d. Feb- 7-2008 in Philippi, Barbour Co, WV,[700] buried in Mt. Vernon Memorial Cemetery, Philippi, Barbour Co, WV,[190] resided in Philippi, Barbour Co, WV,[190] resided formerly in Buckhannon, Upshur

Co, WV,[190] resided (as child) in Ravenswood, Jackson Co, WV,[190] education Buckhannon H.S., Wesleyan College,[190] military U.S. Marine Corps, World War II.[190]

Thomas: A prominent Philippi businessman and councilman, he started his business in Barbour County in 1937, when he opened a feed store in what was known as the Hawkins House. Two years later, he expanded his business and erected a new building, which was later occupied by Smokey Ray's Restaurant. The new business was called Wolfe & Co. and eventually expanded to a Belington location. Five warehouses were utilized to store the wide variety of merchandise sold in the two stores. In addition to the feed, farm supply, warehouse and builders supply business, Mr. Wolfe opened the first discount store in Barbour County in the Crim Building, which he closed when he sold the building to First National Bank. He also dealt extensively in real estate, buying and selling eleven farms and three service stations. At one time, he owned property where the following businesses were located at the time of his death: Hardees of Philippi; Freedom Bank and the parking lots of the the BC Bank; and the Philippi City Building. Mr Wolfe owned the Geneva Motel & Lido Theater in Philippi and St. Dennis Milling Co. in Ravenswood. A Philippi City Councilman for several years, he was instrumental in securing federal funds for the erection of the city building. He was also a sportsman, winning the West Virginia Senior Skeet Championship for three consecutive years, as well as being a licensed pilot.
[190]

ii.   MARGARET GENE GASTON, also known as Gene Gaston,[190] b. Dec-16-1924 in Upshur Co, WV,[mcmxxxiii[1933]] d. Dec-25-2008 in Buckhannon, Upshur Co, WV,[700] buried in Heavner Cemetery, Upshur Co, WV,[190] resided in Buckhannon, Upshur Co, WV,[190] education Buckhannon-Upshur H.S. (valedictorian), West Virginia Univ (biology, magna cum laude),[190] occupation accountant (family business Buckhannon Milling Co.).[190]

Along with husband Steve, opened the first drive-thru car wash in Buckhannon in the 1960s. She was a competitive golfer, winning several country club championships.[190]

She married Jun-14-1946 in Upshur Co, WV,[mcmxxxiv[1934]] Stephen Joseph Smega, b. Sep-18-1925,[592] d. Jun-15-1989,[592] resided in Buckhannon, Upshur Co, WV,[592] resided formerly in New Jersey,[1230] education West Virginia University.[191]

977. **Lula Loreen Gaston**, also known as Loreen Gaston,[228,374] (552.William[8], 293.Abraham[7], 143.William[6], 72.John[5], 21.John[4], 6.Hugh[3], 3.John[2], 1.Jean[1]), b. Jan-22-1900 in Lewis Co, WV,[mcmxxxv[1935],921] resided 1952, 64 in Buckhannon, Upshur Co, WV.[228,921] She married (1) Jan-30-1922 in Upshur Co, WV,[mcmxxxvi[1936]] **Russell Frank Reeder**, b. Oct-11-1897 in West Virginia,[398,1936] (son of Lloyd B. Reeder and Anna Karickhoff), d. Oct-18-1952 in Buckhannon, Upshur Co, WV,[398] buried in Heavner Cemetery, Upshur Co, WV,[398] resided in Buckhannon, Upshur Co, WV,[398] occupation candy salesman.[398] She married (2) Mar-28-1964 in Weirton, Hancock Co, WV,[921] **Edwin McKinley Phillips**, b. Nov-17-1896 in Pennsylvania,[592,921] (son of William Phillips and Peninah Ayers), d. Jun- -1974,[592] resided in Burgettstown, Washington Co, PA.[921,592]
Children by Russell Frank Reeder:
i.   RUTH LOREEN REEDER b. Jun-29-1923 in Upshur Co, WV.[921] She married Aug-23-1947 in Buckhannon, Upshur Co, WV,[921] James Kenneth (John) Myers, b. ca 1922 in Tucker Co, WV,[921] (son of Wade Myers and Luella Blanche Brown), resided 1947 in Buckhannon, Upshur Co, WV.[921]
ii.   ANNA MAY DELORES REEDER b. Nov-29-1927, d. May-27-1929.

978. **Harvey Junior Gaston** (552.William[8], 293.Abraham[7], 143.William[6], 72.John[5], 21.John[4], 6.Hugh[3], 3.John[2], 1.Jean[1]), b. Jun- 6-1907 in Buckhannon, Upshur Co, WV,[mcmxxxvii[1937],mcmxxxviii[1938]] d. Jan-20-1995 in Buckhannon, Upshur Co, WV,[1937,1938,191] buried in Omega Crematory, Morgantown, WV.[1937,1938.] He married Aug-10-1927,[191] **Wilma Frances "Billie" Rollins**,[190] b. Jul-15-1909 in Buckhannon, Upshur Co, WV,[190] (daughter of Alonzo Rollins and Sarah Stansberry), d. May- 4-2006 in Bridgeport, Harrison Co, WV,[764] buried in Heavner Cemetery, Upshur Co, WV.[190]

Children:
    i.   LIVING. He married Living.
    ii. LIVING. He married Living.
    iii. LIVING. She married[1040] Edward William Fellows, b. Oct-24-1931 in Allegheny Co, PA,[921,592] (son of Edward Fellows and Alice Simms), d. Mar-27-1984,[948] resided 1957 in Pittsburgh, Allegheny Co, PA.[921]

979. **Abram Lawson Gaston** (552.William[8], 293.Abraham[7], 143.William[6], 72.John[5], 21.John[4], 6.Hugh[3], 3.John[2], 1.Jean[1]), b. Apr- 3-1915,[mcmxxxix[1939]] d. Jul-15-1994 in Upshur Co, WV,[1939,592] buried in Heavner Cemetery, Upshur Co, WV,[1939] resided in Buckhannon, Upshur Co, WV.[592] He married (1) Apr- 7-1946, **Mary Doris Brooks**, b. Sep-15-1918 (daughter of Richard Thomas Brooks and Landona Curry), d. Dec-31-1985, resided in Buckhannon, Upshur Co, WV.[592] He married (2) May-1991, **Evelyn Bennett**.
    Children by Mary Doris Brooks:
    i.   LIVING.
    ii. LIVING. She married Living.

980. **Virginia May "Ginny" Gaston** (552.William[8], 293.Abraham[7], 143.William[6], 72.John[5], 21.John[4], 6.Hugh[3], 3.John[2], 1.Jean[1]), b. Oct-30-1917 in Upshur Co, WV,[mcmxl[1940]] residence in Buckhannon, Upshur Co, WV. She married **Albert Victor Gemmill, Jr.**, b. Jan-20-1916,[592] d. May-19-1990,[mcmxli[1941]] buried in Round Hill Cemetery, Crossroads, PA.
    Children:
    i.   LIVING. She married Living.
    ii. LIVING. She married Living.

981. **Lloyd Henry Gaston, Jr.** (553.Lloyd[8], 293.Abraham[7], 143.William[6], 72.John[5], 21.John[4], 6.Hugh[3], 3.John[2], 1.Jean[1]), b. ca 1907,[211] census 1910 in New Creek, Mineral Co, WV. He married **Edis Lemely**, b. Jul-31-1906,[592] d. Jan-16-2004,[592] resided in Gulf Breeze, Santa Rosa Co, FL,[592] resided formerly in New York.[592]
    Children:
    i.   LLOYD HENRY GASTON III.
    ii. FAY GASTON.

982. **Geraldine Gaston** (553.Lloyd[8], 293.Abraham[7], 143.William[6], 72.John[5], 21.John[4], 6.Hugh[3], 3.John[2], 1.Jean[1]), b. Feb-12-1912. She married **Robert Mann**.
    Children:
    i.   LIVING.
    ii. LIVING.
    iii. LIVING. She married Living.

983. **Louise Gaston** (553.Lloyd[8], 293.Abraham[7], 143.William[6], 72.John[5], 21.John[4], 6.Hugh[3], 3.John[2], 1.Jean[1]), b. Nov-14-1914,[592] d. Feb-12-1998,[592] resided in Ronceverte, Greenbrier Co, WV,[592] resided in Cumberland, Allegany Co, MD.[1086] She married 1940, **John G. Nicklin**, b. Jul- 1-1914,[592] d. Apr-28-1992,[592] resided in Cumberland, Allegany Co, MD.[1086]
    Children:
    i.   LIVING.
    ii. LIVING. She married Living.

984. **Ocie Ota Gaston** (559.George[8], 296.John[7], 143.William[6], 72.John[5], 21.John[4], 6.Hugh[3], 3.John[2], 1.Jean[1]), b. Sep-20-1885 in Harrison Co, WV,[mcmxlii[1942]] d. bef Jan 1976,[412] census 1900 in Grant District, Harrison Co, WV. She married Sep- 2-1903 in Harrison Co, WV,[mcmxliii[1943],537] **William G. Davisson**, b. Jun-28-1882 in Harrison Co, WV,[mcmxliv[1944]] (son of W. H. Davisson and Mary L. __), resided 1903 in Belington, Barbour Co, WV.
    Children:

    i.   (DAUGHTER) DAVISSON b. Mar- 2-1906, d. Mar- 2-1906, buried in Duck Creek Missn Chrch Cem, near West Milford, Harrison Co, WV.[17]
    ii.   EVELYN DAVISSON b. Mar- 5-1907, d. Jun-29-1907, buried in Duck Creek Missn Chrch Cem, near West Milford, Harrison Co, WV.[17]

985. Nannie May Gaston, census name May Gaston,[467] also known as Mae Gaston (559.George[8], 296.John[7], 143.William[6], 72.John[5], 21.John[4], 6.Hugh[3], 3.John[2], 1.Jean[1]) (See marriage to number 969.)

986. Monna Marie Gaston, also known as Marie Gaston,[711,228,412,592] (559.George[8], 296.John[7], 143.William[6], 72.John[5], 21.John[4], 6.Hugh[3], 3.John[2], 1.Jean[1]), b. May-24-1903 in Harrison Co, WV,[592] d. Oct-31-1991,[592] resided in Taylors, Greenville Co, SC,[mcmxlv[1945]] resided 1976 in St. Petersburg, Pinellas Co, FL,[412] resided 1940 in Cameron, Marshall Co, WV,[228] census 1930 in Cameron, Marshall Co, WV. She married (1) Feb-24-1923 at Duck Creek, Harrison Co, WV,[419] **James Leeman Reed**, b. Jan- 6-1900 in Doddridge Co, WV,[398,385,419,mcmxlvi[1946]] (son of James Reed and Sarah Melissa Smith), d. Jan-21-1940 in Wheeling, Ohio Co, WV,[398] buried in Auburn Community Cemetery, Ritchie Co, WV,[398] resided in Cameron, Marshall Co, WV,[398] census 1930 in Cameron, Marshall Co, WV, resided 1923 in West Union, Doddridge Co, WV,[419] census 1900 in Southwest District, Doddridge Co, WV, occupation oil & gas producer,[398] occupation 1930 bank cashier.[mcmxlvii[1947]] She married (2) bef Jan 1976,[424] ___ **Foose**.
    Children by James Leeman Reed:
    i.   JAMES H. REED b. ca 1924,[1947] census 1930 in Cameron, Marshall Co, WV.
    ii.   CHARLES E. REED b. ca 1925,[1947] census 1930 in Cameron, Marshall Co, WV.

987. Alpha Louise Gaston, also known as Alpharetta Gaston,[374] (560.Hiram[8], 296.John[7], 143.William[6], 72.John[5], 21.John[4], 6.Hugh[3], 3.John[2], 1.Jean[1]), b. Jan- 3-1889 in Harrison Co, WV,[mcmxlviii[1948],419] d. Jan-29-1972,[462] buried in Sunset Memorial Park Cemetery, Clarksburg, WV,[462] census 1920, 1930 in Clarksburg, Harrison Co, WV, census 1900 in Grant District, Harrison Co, WV. She married Dec-25-1912 in Clarksburg, Harrison Co, WV,[mcmxlix[1949]] **Peter John Kowalsky**, b. Jan-12-1886 in Germany,[592,419] (son of Peter Kowalsky and Mary A. Salba), d. Dec-10-1974,[462,592] buried in Sunset Memorial Park Cemetery, Clarksburg, WV,[462] resided in Clarksburg, Harrison Co, WV,[604] census 1920, 1930 in Clarksburg, Harrison Co, WV, resided 1912 in Fairmont, Marion Co, WV,[419] immigrated 1892 or 1898,[1208,418] occupation 1930 mechanic in steel mill.

1920 Census, Harrison Co, WV (Coal District, City of Clarksburg), enumerated on Jan 24 1920: Peter Kowalsky, 34, b. Germany, immigrated 1898, naturalized in 1910, messenger for B&O Railroad; wife Alpha, 31, b. W.Va; dau Francis, 6; dau Genevieve, 6; son Edward, 1y 3m.

1930 Census, Harrison Co, WV (Coal District, City of Clarksburg), enumerated on Apr 10 1930: Peter Kawalsky, 44, b. Germany, immigrated 1892, naturalized, mechanic in steel mill, age 29 at time of first marriage; wife Apha, 41, b. W.Va, age 23 at first marriage; dau Frances, 16; dau Genevieve, 16; son Edward, 11; dau Hellen, 8; dau Anna, 6.

    Children:
    i.   FRANCES KOWALSKY b. Jan- 6-1914 in Harrison Co, WV,[604,418] d. Dec-13-1991,[604] census 1920, 1930 in Clarksburg, Harrison Co, WV. She married Nov-20-1933 in Philippi, Barbour Co, WV,[1022] Ralph Riddle, b. Sep-19-1908 in Harrison Co, WV,[1022] [Birth date given as Sep 19 1908 in marriage record, but SSDI shows it as Sep 18 1908.] (son of Wayne Riddle and Hattie ___), d. Sep- -1985,[592] resided in Clarksburg, Harrison Co, WV,[604] resided 1933 in Salem, WV.[1022]
    ii.   GENEVIEVE KOWALSKY b. Jan- 6-1914 in Harrison Co, WV,[419,592] d. Nov-22-2000,[592] resided in Lebanon, Lebanon Co, PA,[592] resided 1933 in Clarksburg, Harrison Co, WV,[419] census 1920, 1930 in Clarksburg, Harrison Co, WV.[1208] She married Sep-16-1933 in Clarksburg, Harrison Co, WV,[mcml[1950]] Charles Wilbur Duty, b. Apr-16-1915 in Harrison Co, WV,[592,419] (son of Elery Duty and Zela Koon), d. Jul-18-1993,[592] resided in Lancaster, Lancaster Co, PA,[948] resided 1933 in Mt. Joy, Lancaster Co, PA.[419]

iii.   EDWARD KOWALSKY b. ca 1918,[418] census 1920, 1930 in Clarksburg, Harrison Co, WV.

iv.   HELEN KOWALSKY b. ca 1922,[1208] census 1930 in Clarksburg, Harrison Co, WV.

v.   ANNA KOWALSKY b. Aug-29-1923,[462] d. Dec-25-1984,[462] buried in Sunset Memorial Park Cemetery, Clarksburg, WV,[462] census 1930 in Clarksburg, Harrison Co, WV. She married (1) Dec-23-1943 in Clarksburg, Harrison Co, WV,[mcmli[1951]] Melvin Clifford Hardman, Jr., b. Oct- 4-1921 in Clarksburg, Harrison Co, WV,[419,17] (son of Melvin Clifford Hardman and Artie Glee Fittro), d. Oct-28-1962,[17] buried in O'Neal Cemetery, near Wilsonburg, Harrison Co, WV,[mcmlii[1952]] military Pvt, Ohio 1550th Svc Unit, World War II.[1952] She married[462] (2) __ Miklewski.

988.   **Garnet Hornor Gaston** (560.Hiram[8], 296.John[7], 143.William[6], 72.John[5], 21.John[4], 6.Hugh[3], 3.John[2], 1.Jean[1]), b. Jan-24-1891 in Harrison Co, WV,[276] d. Jan-19-1961 in Clarksburg, Harrison Co, WV,[276,462] buried in Elkview Masonic Cemetery, Clarksburg, Harrison Co, WV,[276,462] census 1920, 1930 in Clarksburg, Harrison Co, WV, census 1910 in Coal District, Harrison Co, WV, census 1900 in Grant District, Harrison Co, WV. She married Sep-27-1908 in Clarksburg, Harrison Co, WV,[mcmliii[1953]] **Charles Leonard Gray**, b. Jun-20-1887 in Ritchie Co, WV,[276,419] (son of James Riley Gray and Elizabeth Finch), d. Apr-23-1963 in Clarksburg, Harrison Co, WV,[276] buried in Elkview Masonic Cemetery, Clarksburg, Harrison Co, WV,[276,462] census 1920, 1930 in Clarksburg, Harrison Co, WV, census 1910 in Coal District, Harrison Co, WV, resided 1908 in Harrison Co, WV,[419] occupation repairman & signalman, B&O Railroad,[418,1208,276] occupation 1910 glass factory worker.[458]
Children:

i.   CARL LONIE GRAY b. Jul-15-1909 in Harrison Co, WV,[419,398] d. Aug-21-1960 in Clarksburg, Harrison Co, WV,[398] buried in Greenlawn Masonic Cemetery, Clarksburg, WV,[398] resided (rural) near Clarksburg, Harrison Co, WV,[398] census 1920, 1930 in Clarksburg, Harrison Co, WV, census 1910 in Coal District, Harrison Co, WV, occupation coal miner.[398] He married Mar-26-1931 in Harrison Co, WV,[419] Dorothy Pearl Pribble, b. Mar- 4-1910 in Ritchie Co, WV,[419] (daughter of Frank Pribble and Jessie Elmira Bunner), resided 1960 near Clarksburg, Harrison Co, WV,[228] resided 1931 in Wilsonburg, Harrison Co, WV.[419]

ii.   CHARLES LEONARD GRAY, JR., also known as Leonard Gray,[418,1208,748,604,17] b. Sep-11-1910 in Clarksburg, Harrison Co, WV,[419,592,46] [Birth date in SSDI is Aug 11 1910, but both of his marriage records show it as Sep 11 1910.], d. Jan- -1985,[592] buried in Brick Church (7th Day Baptist) Cemetery, Lost Creek, Harrison Co, WV,[230] resided in Jane Lew, Lewis Co, WV,[604] resided 1947, 1963 in Lost Creek, Harrison Co, WV,[419,748] census 1920, 1930 in Clarksburg, Harrison Co, WV. He married (1) Dec-31-1932 in Clarksburg, Harrison Co, WV,[419] divorced[1116] Beulah Loretta Collins, b. Apr-10-1913 in Clarksburg, Harrison Co, WV,[589,592] (daughter of Grover C. Collins and Mary Etta Harris), d. Aug-22-1979,[592] resided in Clarksburg, Harrison Co, WV,[592,419] resided 1946 in Fairmont, Marion Co, WV.[589] He married (2) Apr-19-1947 in Rockford (Lost Creek), Harrison Co, WV,[419] Vada Christina Wilmoth, b. Jan-28-1917 in Gypsy, Harrison Co, WV,[419,46] (daughter of Alva Wilmoth and Hattie Bowman), d. Mar-14-1970 in Clarksburg, Harrison Co, WV,[398,46] buried in Brick Church (7th Day Baptist) Cemetery, Lost Creek, Harrison Co, WV,[230,398] resided in Jane Lew, Lewis Co, WV,[398] resided 1947 in Gypsy, Harrison Co, WV.[419]

iii.   ARTHUR GRAY b. ca 1914,[418] census 1920, 1930 in Clarksburg, Harrison Co, WV.

iv.   JAMES GRAY b. ca 1919,[418] resided 1961 in Bristol, Harrison Co, WV,[778] census 1920, 1930 in Clarksburg, Harrison Co, WV.

989.   **Frank C. Gaston** (560.Hiram[8], 296.John[7], 143.William[6], 72.John[5], 21.John[4], 6.Hugh[3], 3.John[2], 1.Jean[1]), b. May-19-1895 in Harrison Co, WV,[398,mcmliv[1954],684] d. Apr-21-1944 in Clarksburg, Harrison Co, WV,[398] buried in Stonewall Park Cemetery, Stonewood, Harrison Co, WV,[462] resided in Nutter Fort, Harrison Co, WV,[398] census 1930 in Clarksburg, Harrison Co, WV, resided 1923 in Clarksburg, Harrison Co, WV,[mcmlv[1955],748] census 1910 in Coal District, Harrison Co, WV, census 1900 in Grant District, Harrison Co, WV, occupation machinist, Hazel Atlas Glass Company.[1131,1208] He married May-21-1916 in Clarksburg, Harrison Co, WV,[1954] **Nellie M. Rouse**, b. Jun- 5-1897 in Wood Co, WV,[1954] (daughter of Robert C. Rouse and Anna Leap), d. Sep-16-1971 in Englewood Cliffs, Bergen Co, NJ, resided 1944 in Nutter Fort, Harrison Co, WV.[228]
Children:

     i.   FRANK CARLTON GASTON b. Apr-25-1917 in Harrison Co, WV, d. Oct- -1971.[592]

     ii.   LONNIE DOYLE GASTON b. Feb- 1-1919 in Harrison Co, WV,[592] d. Oct-4-1988,[592] resided in Edgewood, Harford Co, MD.[604] He married[395] (1) Hazel May Fortney, b. ca 1921,[1208] (daughter of Ralph Young Fortney and Marcelia Ellen Zinn), census 1930 in Eagle District, Harrison Co, WV. He married[446] (2) Edna Lee Claypool, b. Dec-23-1912 in Upshur Co, WV,[419,592] (daughter of John E. Claypool and Emma R. Radcliff), d. Jan-14-1996,[592] resided in Wallace, Harrison Co, WV,[604] resided 1933 in Clarksburg, Harrison Co, WV.[419]

     iii.   ROBERT LEE GASTON b. Mar-11-1925 in Harrison Co, WV, d. Mar-26-1926.

     iv.   BETTY JANE GASTON b. Mar- 6-1927 in Harrison Co, WV,[592] d. Feb-27-2005,[592] resided in Carlstadt, Bergen Co, NJ,[683] occupation cook, East Brook School, Paramus NJ (retired 1977).[190] She married[191,1101] __ Camarata.

     v.   HAROLD RANDALL GASTON b. Nov- 4-1929 in Harrison Co, WV,[592] d. Apr- 2-1991,[592] buried Grge Wshngtn Mem Prk in Paramus, Bergen Co, NJ,[190] resided in Rutherford, Bergen Co, NJ,[190] resided formerly in Carlstadt, Bergen Co, NJ,[190] occupation factory worker, Grief Brothers, Teterboro NJ (23 yrs, retired abt 1977).[190] He married[484] Mildred V. Langdon, b. Nov-22-1928,[592] d. Dec- 6-1992,[592] buried Grge Wshngtn Mem Prk in Paramus, Bergen Co, NJ,[190] resided in Rutherford, Bergen Co, NJ,[484,190,1157] resided formerly in Carlstadt, Bergen Co, NJ.[190]

     vi.   LIVING. She married[1101] Living.

     vii.   LIVING.

990. **Spencer Bryan Gaston** (560.Hiram[8], 296.John[7], 143.William[6], 72.John[5], 21.John[4], 6.Hugh[3], 3.John[2], 1.Jean[1]), b. Sep- 1-1898 in Harrison Co, WV,[398] d. May-15-1942 in Clarksburg, Harrison Co, WV,[mcmlvi[1956],398] buried in Sunset Memorial Park Cemetery, Clarksburg, WV,[639,398,462] cause of death homicide, gunshot wound to chest,[398,276] resided in Clarksburg, Harrison Co, WV,[398] [1630 Gaston Ave.], resided 1923 in Clarksburg, Harrison Co, WV,[1131] [1630 Gould Ave, North View; occupation laborer], census 1920 in Clarksburg, Harrison Co, WV, census 1910 in Coal District, Harrison Co, WV, census 1900 in Grant District, Harrison Co, WV, occupation mechanic, West Penn Co.[639] He married[228] **Edna P. Furbee**, b. Apr-23-1910 in Salem, WV,[589,592,462] (daughter of John S. Furbee and Carrie Ford), d. Sep-18-1976,[462,592] buried in Sunset Memorial Park Cemetery, Clarksburg, WV, resided 1944 in Fairmont, Marion Co, WV,[589] resided 1942 in Clarksburg, Harrison Co, WV,[228] census 1920 in Salem, WV.

     Children:

     i.   SPENCER BRYAN GASTON, JR. b. Jan-18-1931 in Harrison Co, WV,[mcmlvii[1957]] d. Feb-11-1991 in Lane Co, OR,[1957] resided in Oregon, military U.S. Coast Guard,[mcmlviii[1958]] [Entered Jan 29 1948 at Mayport, Florida.]. He married Living.

991. **Vance Orlet Gaston**, also known as Orlet Vance Gaston,[446] also known as Orletta Vance Gaston (560.Hiram[8], 296.John[7], 143.William[6], 72.John[5], 21.John[4], 6.Hugh[3], 3.John[2], 1.Jean[1]), b. Aug-19-1904 in Harrison Co, WV, d. Dec- 7-1963, buried in Duck Creek Missn Chrch Cem, near West Milford, Harrison Co, WV,[17] resided in Clarksburg, Harrison Co, WV,[1131,849] [1630 Gould Ave, North View], census 1920, 1930 in Clarksburg, Harrison Co, WV, census 1910 in Coal District, Harrison Co, WV, occupation glass worker, Continental Can Co.[1131,849] He married Jul-30-1923 in Lewis Co, WV,[410] **Reva Lucille Craig**, b. Oct- 3-1904,[592] (daughter of Alva Lawrence Craig and Louesa Mae Weaver), d. Nov-11-1991,[592] buried in Duck Creek Missn Chrch Cem, near West Milford, Harrison Co, WV.[17]

     Children:

     i.   ALVA HIRAM GASTON b. Sep-24-1924 in Clarksburg, Harrison Co, WV,[190,mcmlix[1959]] d. Feb-13-2011 in Bridgeport, Harrison Co, WV,[764] buried in Stonewall Park Cemetery, Stonewood, Harrison Co, WV,[190] resided in Clarksburg, Harrison Co, WV,[190,521] occupation production supervisor, Brockway Glass (40 yrs),[190] occupation 1957-58 glass worker, Continental Can Co,[849] education Victory H.S. (1942),[190] military U.S. Navy, World War II (South Pacific).[190,1958] He married Living.

     ii.   DONALD BRYAN GASTON b. Apr-17-1927 in Clarksburg, Harrison Co, WV,[190,592] d. Dec-14-2005 in Clarksburg, Harrison Co, WV,[847,592] buried in Stonewall Park Cemetery, Stonewood, Harrison Co, WV,[190] resided in North View (Clarksburg), Harrison Co, WV,[190,mcmlx[1960],849,592] occupation Anchor Hocking (41 yrs),[1960,190] education Victory H.S.,[1958] military (entered Apr 12 1945 -) U.S. Navy, World War II.

He was a member and licensed ham radio operator of AARL, with call letters KC8DQT.[190]

He married Living.

      iii.   CHARLES LEE GASTON b. Jun-11-1929 in Harrison Co, WV, d. Nov-15-1986, buried in Duck Creek Missn Chrch Cem, near West Milford, Harrison Co, WV,[17] resided 1958 in Clarksburg, Harrison Co, WV,[849] occupation glass worker, Continental Can Co.[849] He married (1) Living. He married (2) Living.

      iv.   ROBERT VANCE GASTON b. Jul-24-1933 in Clarksburg, Harrison Co, WV,[190] d. Sep-16-1998,[190] buried in Stonewall Park Cemetery, Stonewood, Harrison Co, WV,[190] occupation Anchor-Hocking Tank Operator.[190] He married Living.

992. Ralph McWhorter (563.Cora[8], 297.Enoch[7], 143.William[6], 72.John[5], 21.John[4], 6.Hugh[3], 3.John[2], 1.Jean[1]) (See marriage to number 957.)

993. Willis E. Stalnaker (565.Bertha[8], 297.Enoch[7], 143.William[6], 72.John[5], 21.John[4], 6.Hugh[3], 3.John[2], 1.Jean[1]), b. Jun-29-1909,[592,902] d. Sep- -1982,[592] resided in Salem, WV,[604] census 1930 in Greenbrier District, Doddridge Co, WV. He married Apr-21-1934 in Doddridge Co, WV,[354] **Opal Gallien**, b. Sep-26-1911,[592,354] d. Jan- 6-1995,[592] resided in Grantsville, Calhoun Co, WV.[592]

      Children:

      i.   CHARLES A. STALNAKER b. Feb-11-1936 in Clarksburg, Harrison Co, WV,[190] d. Nov-7-2010, buried in K of P Memorial Park Cemetery, Salem, WV,[190] resided in Weston, Lewis Co, WV,[190] occupation Carnegie Natural Gas Co. (39 yrs).[190] He married Living.

994. E. I. Smith (569.Ernest[8], 298.Mary[7], 143.William[6], 72.John[5], 21.John[4], 6.Hugh[3], 3.John[2], 1.Jean[1]). She married[1216] **G. C. Whittaker**.

      Children:

      i.   LIVING.

      ii.   LIVING.

      iii.   LIVING.

      iv.   LIVING.

      v.   LIVING.

995. Paul Hugh Smith (569.Ernest[8], 298.Mary[7], 143.William[6], 72.John[5], 21.John[4], 6.Hugh[3], 3.John[2], 1.Jean[1]), b. Dec-23-1918 in Washington, DC,[1216,592] d. Mar- 5-2005 in Tucson, Pima Co, AZ,[190,592] resided since 1956 in Tucson, Pima Co, AZ,[190,592] resided before 1956 in Ohio,[190] resided formerly in Washington, DC,[1625] education Antioch College at Yellow Springs OH.[190] He married Dec-24-1941 in Indianapolis, Marion Co, IN,[1216] **Virginia Craig**, also known as Virginia Craig Supniewski,[1216] b. 1923.

      Children:

      i.   LIVING. She married Living.

      ii.   LIVING. He married (1) Living. He married (2) Living.

      iii.   LIVING.

      iv.   LIVING.

996. Margaret Morrison (570.Tensie[8], 298.Mary[7], 143.William[6], 72.John[5], 21.John[4], 6.Hugh[3], 3.John[2], 1.Jean[1]), b. 1923. She married **Franklin William Kern**.

      Children:

      i.   LIVING. She married Living.

      ii.   LIVING. He married Living.

      iii.   LIVING. She married Living.

997. Milton Householder (572.Nancy[8], 300.Martha[7], 147.James[6], 74.John[5], 22.William[4], 6.Hugh[3], 3.John[2], 1.Jean[1]). He married **Maude Maupin**.

      Children:

i.   MADGE HOUSEHOLDER. She married E. F. Ketter.

998. **James Ernest Gaston** (575.Ernest[8], 302.James[7], 147.James[6], 74.John[5], 22.William[4], 6.Hugh[3], 3.John[2], 1.Jean[1]), b. Jun- 2-1890 in Iowa,[592,12] d. Apr- -1966,[592] resided in Fairhope, Baldwin Co, AL,[592,334] occupation 1930 automobile agent.[334] He married **Olive C. ___**, b. ca 1895 in Iowa,[334] census 1930 in Fairhope, Baldwin Co, AL.
Children:
i.   OLIVE JEAN GASTON, also known as Jean Gaston,[190] census name O. Jean Gaston,[334] b. Aug-13-1918 in Alabama,[592,334] d. Jul-24-2008 in Skillman, Somerset Co, NJ,[764,592] resided in Princeton Junction, Mercer Co, NJ,[mcmlxi[1961]] census 1930 in Fairhope, Baldwin Co, AL, occupation Princeton University Store (30 yrs),[190] education Marietta Johnson School of Organic Education, Fairhope AL.[190] She married[191,mcmlxii[1962]] Oakley MacDonald Woodward, Jr., b. Jan-13-1915,[592] d. Apr- 6-1995,[592] resided in Princeton, Mercer Co, NJ,[592] resided formerly in Oklahoma,[838] occupation electrical engineer, David Sarnoff Research Center of RCA.[191]
ii.   JAMES ERNEST GASTON, JR. b. Jun-20-1921 in Alabama,[592,334] d. Oct- 1-2003,[592] resided in Fairhope, Baldwin Co, AL,[1961,334] occupation owner of Gaston Ford Motor Co, Fairhope AL,[190] military combat engineer, World War II,[190] education Auburn University (mechanical engineering).[190] He married[484] Velma E. ___.
iii.   CLARA LOUISE GASTON b. ca 1925 in Alabama,[334] census 1930 in Fairhope, Baldwin Co, AL. She married[1962] ___ Wengert.

999. **Cornelius Alonzo Gaston** (575.Ernest[8], 302.James[7], 147.James[6], 74.John[5], 22.William[4], 6.Hugh[3], 3.John[2], 1.Jean[1]), b. Oct-29-1891 in Iowa,[592,12] d. Apr- -1982,[592] resided in Charlottesville, VA,[1961] census 1930 in Fairhope, Baldwin Co, AL, occupation chiropractor.[334] He married[12] ca 1921,[334] **Margaret Nichols**, b. ca 1900 in Tennessee,[334] census 1930 in Fairhope, Baldwin Co, AL.
Children:
i.   LIVING.

1000.   **Leah Catherine Gaston** (575.Ernest[8], 302.James[7], 147.James[6], 74.John[5], 22.William[4], 6.Hugh[3], 3.John[2], 1.Jean[1]), b. Nov- -1893,[12] d. Jan-14-1954 in Mobile Co, AL.[693] She married[12] **Max Pittinger McGill**, d. Oct- 8-1956 in Mobile Co, AL.[693]
Children:
i.   MARY EDITH MCGILL. She married[1962] ___ Green.
ii.   FRANCES HARRIETTE MCGILL[1962] also known as Harriet Frances McGill,[521] resided 2007 in Mobile, AL.[521] She married[1962,1101] ___ Jernigan.
iii.   MAX PITTINGER MCGILL, JR. b. Jul- 4-1921 in Central City, Merrick Co, NE,[592,190] d. Feb-15-2007,[592] resided since 1923 in Mobile, AL,[190,1961] occupation Parks & Recreation superintendent, horticulturist, fine-arts enthusiast,[190] military aerial photographer, U.S. Navy, World War II,[190] education Auburn University, Alabama Polytechnic Institute.[190] He married[484] Jul- -1964 in Mobile, AL, Priscilla M. Murdoch, resided 2007 in Mobile, AL.[484]

1001.   **Arthur F. Gaston** (575.Ernest[8], 302.James[7], 147.James[6], 74.John[5], 22.William[4], 6.Hugh[3], 3.John[2], 1.Jean[1]), b. Aug-16-1896 in Alabama,[12,592] d. Feb- -1987,[592] resided in Fairhope, Baldwin Co, AL,[1961] occupation linotype operator for newspaper.[334] He married ca 1921,[334] **Mary P. ___**, b. ca 1902 in Illinois,[334] census 1930 in Fairhope, Baldwin Co, AL.
Children:
i.   MARY FRANCES "BUDDY" GASTON[190] b. Jun-26-1921 in Alabama,[592,334] d. Jan- 9-2007 in Daphne, Baldwin Co, AL,[806] buried in Fairhope Colony Cemetery, Baldwin Co, AL,[190] resided in Fairhope, Baldwin Co, AL,[190,1961,334] education Marietta Johnson School of Organic Education, Fairhope AL.[190]

She ran the printing press, along with other responsibilities, at the Fairhope Courier, the Gaston family-owned weekly newspaper, and she worked at the Fairhope Single Tax Colony for a number of years until she retired as secretary of the organization.[190]

She married __ Godard.

  ii. ERNEST B. GASTON b. ca 1925 in Alabama,[334] census 1930 in Fairhope, Baldwin Co, AL.

1002. **Agnes A. Gaston** (578.Cyrus[8], 303.Robert[7], 147.James[6], 74.John[5], 22.William[4], 6.Hugh[3], 3.John[2], 1.Jean[1]), b. Oct- 1-1887 in Kansas,[592,123] d. Aug- -1976,[592] resided in Glen Elder, Mitchell Co, KS,[592] census 1900, 1930 in Mitchell Co, KS, occupation teacher.[1218] She married[1218] ca 1908,[334] **Franklin T. Forster**, b. Nov- 1-1883 in Iowa,[592,334] d. Dec- -1979,[592] resided in Glen Elder, Mitchell Co, KS,[1158] census 1930 in Beloit, Mitchell Co, KS,[334] occupation life insurance salesman.[334]
  Children:
  i. IDA FORSTER[1218] b. ca 1910 in Missouri,[334] census 1930 in Beloit, Mitchell Co, KS.[334]
  ii. KENNETH E. FORSTER, census name Kenath E. Forster,[334] b. Jun-26-1918 in Kansas,[592,334] d. Jun-22-1996,[592] resided in Sun City, Maricopa Co, AZ,[1158] census 1930 in Beloit, Mitchell Co, KS.[334]
  iii. CATHERINE FORSTER b. ca 1921 in Kansas,[334] census 1930 in Beloit, Mitchell Co, KS.[334]
  iv. DOROTHY A. FORSTER b. ca 1926 in Kansas,[334] census 1930 in Beloit, Mitchell Co, KS.[334]

1003. **Ralph Estep Gaston** (578.Cyrus[8], 303.Robert[7], 147.James[6], 74.John[5], 22.William[4], 6.Hugh[3], 3.John[2], 1.Jean[1]), b. Jul-29-1890 in Mitchell Co, KS,[mcmlxiii[1963]] d. Aug-23-1964 in Clayton, St Louis Co, MO,[652] census 1900 in Mitchell Co, KS, occupation physician.[1218]

Graduated from St. Louis University Medical School in 1914, interning at Alexion Bro's Hospital in St. Louis. Entered the Navy in World War I and was stationed at Great Lakes Naval Training Center. He practiced medicine most of his life in Webster Groves, MO. He was active in church, fraternal and civic organizations in Webster Groves, and was a member of the Missouri Historical Society.[652]

He married[1218] **Lelia Sanford Barradell**, b. Oct-13-1881 in Texas,[693,592] [From family Bible, but Lelia herself claimed to have been born in 1889.], d. Jul-10-1983 in Alameda Co, CA.[693,592]
  Children:
  i. RALPH ESTEP GASTON, JR. b. Sep-27-1925 in St. Louis, MO,[1218,592] d. Jul-21-1994 in Livermore, Alameda Co, CA,[mcmlxiv[1964]] resided in Turlock, Stanislaus Co, CA.[592] He married[1218] Margaret __, b. May-27-1923 in Oakland, Alameda Co, CA,[1218,592] d. Aug-20-1996 in Turlock, Stanislaus Co, CA,[1218,592] resided in San Jose, Santa Clara Co, CA.[592]

1004. **Herbert Brownell Gaston**[1218] (578.Cyrus[8], 303.Robert[7], 147.James[6], 74.John[5], 22.William[4], 6.Hugh[3], 3.John[2], 1.Jean[1]), b. Jun-12-1902,[592] d. Apr- -1981,[592] resided in Danville, VA,[592] resided formerly in Michigan.[592] He married[1218] **Katie Dailey**, b. Feb-23-1901,[592] d. Aug- -1995,[592] resided in Danville, VA,[592] resided formerly in Michigan.[683]
  Children:
  i. JEANNE GASTON[1218] residence in Virginia.[1218] She married[1218] __ Fehrenbaker.

1005. **Ernest Leroy Gaston** (579.David[8], 303.Robert[7], 147.James[6], 74.John[5], 22.William[4], 6.Hugh[3], 3.John[2], 1.Jean[1]), b. Sep- 5-1881 in Iowa,[12] d. Nov-27-1958 in Iowa,[12] census 1900 in Mahaska Co, IA. He married[12] **Georgia Waddell**, b. Jun- 8-1885,[12] d. Dec- 1-1956.[12]
  Children:
  i. THELMA GASTON b. Jan-23-1904 in Iowa,[12] d. Nov-11-1962.[12]
  ii. GWENDOLYN GASTON b. Mar- 9-1906 in Iowa.[12]

1006. **David Gaston** (580.Joseph[8], 303.Robert[7], 147.James[6], 74.John[5], 22.William[4], 6.Hugh[3], 3.John[2], 1.Jean[1]), b. Apr-13-1887,[12] d. Nov-11-1962.[12] He married[12] **Grace Belle Sherbondy**, b. Oct- 9-1889,[592,12] d. Nov-12-1963,[12,592] resided in Kansas.[1158]
  Children:

i.   LEO GEORGE GASTON b. Sep- 4-1909,[592] d. Oct-26-2000,[592,191] resided in Sun City, Riverside Co, CA,[592] resided formerly in Kansas.[1158] He married[191,12] Kathryn Loretta Franzmathes, b. Sep- 6-1909 in Smith Center, Smith Co, KS,[190,592] (daughter of Gus Franzmathes and Anna Schaffer), d. Aug- 6-2003,[190,592] buried Riverside Natl Cem,[190] resided in Tustin, Orange Co, CA.[1275]

1007.   **Lewis Burke "Bert" Gaston**, also known as Bert Gaston,[592] (580.Joseph[8], 303.Robert[7], 147.James[6], 74.John[5], 22.William[4], 6.Hugh[3], 3.John[2], 1.Jean[1]), b. Apr-24-1889,[12,592] d. Oct-19-1967,[12,592] resided in Beloit, Mitchell Co, KS.[1158] He married[12] **Lottie Mary Goodshaw**, b. Apr- 8-1895,[592,12] d. Mar-29-1997,[592,12] resided in Beloit, Mitchell Co, KS.[592]
Children:
i.   FRANK L. GASTON b. Dec- 1-1914,[592] d. Apr- -1981,[592] resided in Frankfort, Marshall Co, KS,[592] resided formerly in Colorado.[1219]
ii.   JUNIOR M. GASTON b. Apr-17-1922,[592,12] d. Mar- 3-1991.[1158]
iii.   LILA JUNE GASTON b. 1926.[12]

1008.   **Robert "Bruce" Gaston**, also known as Bruce Gaston,[592] (580.Joseph[8], 303.Robert[7], 147.James[6], 74.John[5], 22.William[4], 6.Hugh[3], 3.John[2], 1.Jean[1]), b. Feb-13-1893,[592,12] d. Sep-18-1980,[12,592] resided in Glen Elder, Mitchell Co, KS.[592] He married[12] **Cora Goodshaw**, b. Jul-26-1893,[592,12] d. Apr- 1-1978,[12,592] resided in Glen Elder, Mitchell Co, KS.[592]
Children:
i.   VERA GASTON b. 1916.[12]
ii.   JOSEPH W. GASTON b. May-24-1921 near Glen Elder, Mitchell Co, KS,[190,592] d. May-15-2006,[190,592] buried Glenwood Cemetery in Glen Elder, Mitchell Co, KS,[190] resided in Glen Elder, Mitchell Co, KS.[190,1158] He married[484] Ruby ___, resided 2006 in Glen Elder, Mitchell Co, KS.[484]

1009.   **Eldridge Gaston** (580.Joseph[8], 303.Robert[7], 147.James[6], 74.John[5], 22.William[4], 6.Hugh[3], 3.John[2], 1.Jean[1]), b. Oct-24-1894,[592,12] d. May-15-1972,[12,592] resided in Newberg, Yamhill Co, OR,[592] resided formerly in Kansas.[1158] He married **Florence May Shull**, b. Jan-23-1897,[592,12] d. May- 6-1989,[12,592] resided in Newberg, Yamhill Co, OR.[mcmlxv[1965]]
Children:
i.   ELDRIDGE GENE GASTON b. 1921.[12]
ii.   LOLA LEE GASTON b. 1924.[12]
iii.   JIMMY DALE GASTON b. Aug- 1-1926,[592] d. Jul-21-1999,[592] resided in Newberg, Yamhill Co, OR.[1965]

1010.   **Archie Franklin Gaston** (581.George[8], 303.Robert[7], 147.James[6], 74.John[5], 22.William[4], 6.Hugh[3], 3.John[2], 1.Jean[1]), b. Aug- -1887 in Kansas,[123] [Age 41 given in 1930 Census would put birth date in about 1889. But 1900 Census states Aug 1887.], census 1930 in Lincoln, Lancaster Co, NE,[334] occupation florist.[334] He married[12] ca 1920,[334] **Elizabeth Alice Pooler**, also known as Alice Pooler,[334] b. Sep-26-1895,[12,334] census 1930 in Lincoln, Lancaster Co, NE.[334]
Children:
i.   RICHARD DUANE GASTON b. 1920.[12]
ii.   HELEN AILEEN GASTON[12] b. ca 1922 in Colorado,[334] census 1930 in Lincoln, Lancaster Co, NE.
iii.   FREDERICK GASTON, census name Fredrecic Gaston,[334] b. ca 1925 in Colorado,[334] census 1930 in Lincoln, Lancaster Co, NE.[334]
iv.   EVELYN GASTON b. ca 1925 in Montana,[334] census 1930 in Lincoln, Lancaster Co, NE.[334]
v.   WILLMA GASTON b. ca 1926 in Nebraska,[334] census 1930 in Lincoln, Lancaster Co, NE.
vi.   LIVING.
vii.   LIVING.

1011.   **Joseph McClure Albright**, census name McClure Albright (583.Dora[8], 303.Robert[7], 147.James[6], 74.John[5], 22.William[4], 6.Hugh[3], 3.John[2], 1.Jean[1]), b. ca 1901 in West Virginia,[1221] census 1930 in

Fayette Co, PA, census 1910, 1920 in Preston Co, WV. He married ca 1927,[334] **Dorothy __**, b. ca 1907,[334] census 1930 in Fayette Co, PA.

Children:

    i.   ARLEEN ALBRIGHT b. ca 1926,[334] census 1930 in Fayette Co, PA.

    ii.   LIVING.

1012.   **James Edward Estep**, census name J. Edward Estep (585.Harrison[8], 304.Sarah[7], 148.Samuel[6], 74.John[5], 22.William[4], 6.Hugh[3], 3.John[2], 1.Jean[1]), b. Feb- -1860 in Pennsylvania,[123] census 1900 in Marion, Grant Co, IN, census 1880 in Pittsburgh, Allegheny Co, PA, census 1860 in Allegheny Co, PA, occupation glass worker.[123] He married ca 1883,[123] **Isabell __**, b. May- -1866 in Pennsylvania,[123] census 1900 in Marion, Grant Co, IN.

Children:

    i.   HARRY A. ESTEP b. Feb- -1884 in Pennsylvania,[123] census 1900 in Marion, Grant Co, IN.

    ii.   WALTER L. ESTEP b. Apr- -1885 in Pennsylvania,[123] census 1900 in Marion, Grant Co, IN.

    iii.   EDNA H. ESTEP b. Feb- -1886 in Pennsylvania,[123] census 1900 in Marion, Grant Co, IN.

    iv.   KAYE ESTEP b. Aug- -1891 in Indiana,[123] census 1900 in Marion, Grant Co, IN.

1013.   **Ward Minear** (593.Jasper[8], 309.Margaret[7], 150.Charles[6], 75.William[5], 22.William[4], 6.Hugh[3], 3.John[2], 1.Jean[1]), b. Jul-21-1884.[286] He married in Hardin, Big Horn Co, MT,[286] **Carrie Blanche Steele**, b. Jan-26-1891,[592] d. Sep- -1967,[592] resided in Hardin, Big Horn Co, MT.[mcmlxvi[1966]]

Children:

    i.   WARREN MINEAR. He married Maria A. __.

1014.   **Stuart McIlvaine Shotwell**[684,mcmlxvii[1967]] census name Stewart M. Shotwell (595.Stuart[8], 313.Nancy[7], 154.James[6], 77.Hugh[5], 23.Joseph[4], 6.Hugh[3], 3.John[2], 1.Jean[1]), b. Apr-16-1893 in St. Paul, Ramsey Co, MN,[684,1967,592,123] d. Aug- -1973 in Hightstown, Mercer Co, NJ,[592] [Name: Stuart Shotwell SSN: 087-10-7095

Last Residence: 08520 Hightstown, Mercer, New Jersey, United States of America

Born: 16 Apr 1893

Died: Aug 1973

State (Year) SSN issued: New York (Before 1951)], resided in Hightstown, Mercer Co, NJ,[1230] resided 1942 in Morris Co, NJ, census 1930 in Maplewood, Essex Co, NJ, census 1920 in Manhattan, NY, resided 1917 in Chicago, IL,[684] census 1900, 1910 in St. Paul, Ramsey Co, MN, occupation investments. He married **Berenice M. __**, b. Jun-14-1894,[592] d. Jan-29-1990,[592] census 1930 in Maplewood, Essex Co, NJ, census 1920 in Manhattan, NY.

1920 Census, New York City, NY (Manhattan), enumerated on Jan 22 1920:
Stuart (corrected from Stewart, or possibly Stewart corrected from Stuart) M Shotwell, 26, b. Ohio, statistician at bank; wife Berenice, 25, b. Illinois.

1930 Census, Essex Co, New Jersey (Maplewood Twp), enumerated on May 8 1930:
Stewart M Shotwell, 37, b. Minnesota, department head at investment bank; wife Berenice M, 35, b. New Jersey; dau Patricia M, 8, b. New York; son Stewart M, 6, b. New York; servant Agnes Davock, 22, b. in Irish Free State, single.

Children:

    i.   PATRICIA M. SHOTWELL b. ca 1922 in New York,[334] resided 1942 in Ithaca, Tompkins Co, NY, census 1930 in Maplewood, Essex Co, NJ, education Columbia H.S. (Maplewood NJ), Cornell University.

    ii.   STUART M. SHOTWELL, census name Stewart M. Shotwell, b. Mar-12-1923 in New York,[924,334] census 1930 in Maplewood, Essex Co, NJ.

1015. **Eliza V. Crawford**[317] (596.Elizabeth[8], 314.Philander[7], 154.James[6], 77.Hugh[5], 23.Joseph[4], 6.Hugh[3], 3.John[2], 1.Jean[1]). She married[317] **Edward F. Smith.**
   Children:
   i. ANN CRAWFORD SMITH[317].

1016. **Mary Janet Crawford**[317] (596.Elizabeth[8], 314.Philander[7], 154.James[6], 77.Hugh[5], 23.Joseph[4], 6.Hugh[3], 3.John[2], 1.Jean[1]). She married[317] **Harry Pepin.**
   Children:
   i. ELIZABETH PEPIN[317]. She married[317] Ed Smith.
   ii. ALLEN PEPIN[317]. He married[317] Mary Zimmerman.

1017. **Jefferson Crawford**[317] (596.Elizabeth[8], 314.Philander[7], 154.James[6], 77.Hugh[5], 23.Joseph[4], 6.Hugh[3], 3.John[2], 1.Jean[1]). He married **Almira Barnett.**
   Children:
   i. LEDA CRAWFORD[317]. She married[317] Charles Neal.
   ii. HARRY CRAWFORD[317]. He married[317] Lulu Dickerson.

1018. **Philander Crawford**[317] (596.Elizabeth[8], 314.Philander[7], 154.James[6], 77.Hugh[5], 23.Joseph[4], 6.Hugh[3], 3.John[2], 1.Jean[1]). He married[317] **Rose Palmer.**
   Children:
   i. VIOLA CRAWFORD[317].
   ii. WALTER CRAWFORD[317]. He married[317] Nellie Daniels.
   iii. LAURA CRAWFORD[317]. She married[317] Clide Mannon.
   iv. RAYMOND CRAWFORD[317]. He married[317] Sarah Lutz.

1019. **Edward Hugh Crawford** (596.Elizabeth[8], 314.Philander[7], 154.James[6], 77.Hugh[5], 23.Joseph[4], 6.Hugh[3], 3.John[2], 1.Jean[1]). He married[317] **Minnie __.**
   Children:
   i. ADA CRAWFORD[317]. She married[317] John Smith.
   ii. SAMUEL CRAWFORD[317]. He married[317] Dorothy Pepin.
   iii. WILLIAM CRAWFORD[317].

1020. **Charles Rowe**[317] (597.Nancy[8], 314.Philander[7], 154.James[6], 77.Hugh[5], 23.Joseph[4], 6.Hugh[3], 3.John[2], 1.Jean[1]). He married[317] **Margaret Hartford.**
   Children:
   i. JULIA ROWE[317].
   ii. WILLIAM ROWE[317].
   iii. MARGARET ROWE[317].

1021. **Laura Rowe**[317] (597.Nancy[8], 314.Philander[7], 154.James[6], 77.Hugh[5], 23.Joseph[4], 6.Hugh[3], 3.John[2], 1.Jean[1]). She married[317] **Norman Ward.**
   Children:
   i. KENNETH WARD[317]. He married[317] Violet Roughtread.
   ii. ALLEN WARD[317].

1022. **Lola Feezel**[317] (598.Martha[8], 314.Philander[7], 154.James[6], 77.Hugh[5], 23.Joseph[4], 6.Hugh[3], 3.John[2], 1.Jean[1]). She married[317] **Joseph Williams.**
   Children:
   i. MARGARET M. WILLIAMS[317] b. Feb-21-1909 in East Liverpool, Columbiana Co, OH,[693] d. May- 2-1993 in Mahoning Co, OH,[mcmlxviii[1968]] occupation secretary.[693] She married[317] Stewart E. Orndorff, b. ca 1907,[693] d. Oct-17-1961 in Canton, Stark Co, OH,[693] resided in Canton, Stark Co, OH.[693]
   ii. LESTER WILLIAMS[317].

1023. **Raymond C. Feezel** (598.Martha[8], 314.Philander[7], 154.James[6], 77.Hugh[5], 23.Joseph[4], 6.Hugh[3], 3.John[2], 1.Jean[1]), b. ca 1890 in Ohio,[211] census 1910 in East Liverpool, Columbiana Co, OH. He married[317] **Loretta Anderson**.

Children:
i. RALPH S. FEEZEL[317].

1024. **Riley L. Feezel**[693,317] (598.Martha[8], 314.Philander[7], 154.James[6], 77.Hugh[5], 23.Joseph[4], 6.Hugh[3], 3.John[2], 1.Jean[1]), b. Aug-27-1893 in Ohio,[592,211] d. Aug- 6-1967 in Akron, Summit Co, OH,[693,592] resided in Cuyahoga Falls, Summit Co, OH,[693,592] census 1910 in East Liverpool, Columbiana Co, OH. He married[317] **Iris M. Tinkham**, b. ca 1903,[693] d. Apr-13-1975 in Cuyahoga Falls, Summit Co, OH,[693] resided in Cuyahoga Falls, Summit Co, OH.[693]

Children:
i. JEAN FEEZEL[317].
ii. JERRY FEEZEL[317].

1025. **Emily N. Gaston**, also known as Emma,[317] (599.John[8], 314.Philander[7], 154.James[6], 77.Hugh[5], 23.Joseph[4], 6.Hugh[3], 3.John[2], 1.Jean[1]), b. Feb- 2-1891 in Ohio,[693,123,592] d. Feb- 9-1985 in Sebring, Mahoning Co, OH,[mcmlxix[1969],12,592] resided in Sebring, Mahoning Co, OH,[592] resided in Columbiana Co, OH,[1011,123,211] census 1930 in Columbiana, Columbiana Co, OH, census 1920 in Columbiana Co, OH.

Emily N. Gaston had one child with each of her two husbands.[12]

She married[12] (1) __ **Davis**. She married[12] (2) **Harry Chandler Warrick**, b. Jul- 8-1884 in Ohio,[684,681] d. Sep- 8-1975 in Salem, OH,[mcmlxx[1970],12] resided in Columbiana, Columbiana Co, OH,[592] census 1930 in Columbiana, Columbiana Co, OH, census 1920 in Columbiana Co, OH, resided 1918 in Clarkson, Columbiana Co, OH,[684] occupation undertaker, funeral director.[681,334]

Children by Harry Chandler Warrick:
i. ELLEN JANE WARRICK b. ca 1918 in Ohio,[681] census 1930 in Columbiana, Columbiana Co, OH, census 1920 in Columbiana Co, OH.

1026. **Henry Lee Gaston**[681,12] census name Lee H. Gaston,[123,334] (599.John[8], 314.Philander[7], 154.James[6], 77.Hugh[5], 23.Joseph[4], 6.Hugh[3], 3.John[2], 1.Jean[1]), b. Oct- -1893 in Ohio,[123] d. May-15-1965 in Columbiana Co, OH,[1011] census 1900, 10, 20, 30 in Columbiana Co, OH, occupation farmer.[334] He married[12] Aug-12-1914 in Columbiana Co, OH,[64,334] **Florence Wollem**, b. Mar-16-1895 in Ohio,[592,681] d. Apr- -1985,[592] resided in Columbiana, Columbiana Co, OH,[1010] census 1920, 1930 in Columbiana Co, OH.

Children:
i. THELMA M. GASTON[12] b. ca 1919 in Ohio,[681] census 1920, 1930 in Columbiana Co, OH.
ii. DORIS GASTON b. ca 1926 in Ohio,[334] census 1930 in Columbiana Co, OH.

1027. **Martha Alice Gaston** (600.William[8], 314.Philander[7], 154.James[6], 77.Hugh[5], 23.Joseph[4], 6.Hugh[3], 3.John[2], 1.Jean[1]), b. Feb-27-1904 in Ohio,[693,12,592] d. Apr-13-1990 in Cuyahoga Falls, Summit Co, OH,[mcmlxxi[1971],12,592] resided in Uniontown, Stark Co, OH,[592] occupation teacher.[693] She married[12] Jan-30-1926,[12] **John Carroll Burton Stevenson**,[12] also known as Caroll Stevenson,[592] also known as J. C. Stevenson,[693] also known as Carl,[317] b. May-16-1904,[12,693] d. May-30-1973 in Akron, Summit Co, OH,[mcmlxxii[1972],mcmlxxiii[1973],12] resided in Akron, Summit Co, OH.[1010] Martha Alice Gaston and John Carroll Burton Stevenson had three children.[12]

Children:
i. LOIS STEVENSON.
ii. CARL STEVENSON[317].

1028. **Harry Gaston**[12] (601.James[8], 314.Philander[7], 154.James[6], 77.Hugh[5], 23.Joseph[4], 6.Hugh[3], 3.John[2], 1.Jean[1]).

Children:

    i.   DORIS GASTON[12].

1029. **Walter Gaston**[12] (601.James[8], 314.Philander[7], 154.James[6], 77.Hugh[5], 23.Joseph[4], 6.Hugh[3], 3.John[2], 1.Jean[1]). He married[12] **Bell Smith**.

Children:

    i.   WALTER GASTON[12].

1030. **Howard Gaston**[12] (601.James[8], 314.Philander[7], 154.James[6], 77.Hugh[5], 23.Joseph[4], 6.Hugh[3], 3.John[2], 1.Jean[1]). He married[12] **Thelma Garbon**.

Children:

    i.   EVALYN GASTON[12,12].
    ii.   NORMA GASTON[12].
    iii. HOWARD GASTON[12].

1031. **Glen Gaston**[12] (601.James[8], 314.Philander[7], 154.James[6], 77.Hugh[5], 23.Joseph[4], 6.Hugh[3], 3.John[2], 1.Jean[1]). He married[12] **Zelda Dyke**.

Children:

    i.   WILLIAM GASTON[12].

1032. **Sara Louise "Sally" Gordon** (602.Louis[8], 317.Gilbert[7], 156.Jane[6], 78.James[5], 23.Joseph[4], 6.Hugh[3], 3.John[2], 1.Jean[1]), b. Apr-22-1906 in Allegheny Co, PA, baptized Jun-10-1906 in Sharon Presbyterian Church, d. Jan-22-1983. She married **Robert William Wright, Jr.**, b. May- 3-1906, d. Jul- 3-1990 in Crafton, Allegheny Co, PA.

Children:

    i.   LIVING. He married (1) Living. He married (2) Living.
    ii.   LIVING. She married Living.
    iii. LIVING. She married Living.

1033. **Alice Julia (twin) Gordon** (602.Louis[8], 317.Gilbert[7], 156.Jane[6], 78.James[5], 23.Joseph[4], 6.Hugh[3], 3.John[2], 1.Jean[1]), b. Sep- 9-1912 in McKees Rocks, Allegheny Co, PA.[161] She married Nov-25-1936 in Gary, Lake Co, IN,[161] **Glenn Peregrine Carson, Jr.**, b. Mar- 1-1914,[mcmlxxiv[1974]] (son of Glenn Peregrine Carson and Margaret Jane Walker), d. Oct- 7-1992 in Bradenton, Manatee Co, FL,[161,592] resided in Bradenton, Manatee Co, FL,[592] resided formerly in Indiana,[1680] occupation mechanical engineer, U.S. Steel.[161]

Children:

    i.   LIVING. She married Living.
    ii.   LIVING. She married Living.
    iii. LIVING. She married Living.

1034. **Gilbert Griffith (twin) Gordon** (602.Louis[8], 317.Gilbert[7], 156.Jane[6], 78.James[5], 23.Joseph[4], 6.Hugh[3], 3.John[2], 1.Jean[1]), b. Sep- 9-1912 in McKees Rocks, Allegheny Co, PA, d. Jul- 5-1990 in Bradenton, Manatee Co, FL, buried in Mansions Memorial Park, Ellenton, FL. He married Sep- 4-1937, **Leona Haynes**, b. Aug-17-1914 in Elkhart, Elkhart Co, IN (daughter of Worthie W. Haynes and Dora Matilada Nallinger).

Children:

    i.   LIVING. He married Living.
    ii.   LIVING.
    iii. LIVING. She married (1) Living. She married (2) Living.

1035. **Dewey George Steele** (604.Margret[8], 319.John[7], 160.Charity[6], 79.Alexander[5], 23.Joseph[4], 6.Hugh[3], 3.John[2], 1.Jean[1]), b. Feb-23-1898 in Quaker City, Guernsey Co, OH,[164,592] d. Apr-21-1985 in Dallas Co, TX,[420,592] resided in Dallas, TX,[mcmlxxv[1975]] resided 1964 in Lexington, Fayette Co, KY.[164] He married Aug-19-1926,[164] **Lucile Isabelle Norris**, b. Dec- 2-1896,[592] d. Aug-11-1981 in Fayette Co, KY,[mcmlxxvi[1976],592] resided in Lexington, Fayette Co, KY.[592]

Children:
i.   LIVING. She married Living.
ii.   LIVING. She married[164] James Harry Waugh, Jr., also known as Harry Waugh, Jr.,[164] also known as J. Harry Waugh,[592] b. Feb-14-1927,[592] d. Jun- 6-2006,[592] resided in Addison, Dallas Co, TX.[1284]

1036.   **Julia Ann Bryant** (605.Bathanna[8], 322.Hosea[7], 173.Elizabeth[6], 82.Mary[5], 27.Margaret[4], 8.Joseph[3], 3.John[2], 1.Jean[1]), b. ca 1845 in White Co, IL,[64] d. Apr-18-1880 in White Co, IL.[64] She married (1) Apr-24-1865 in White Co, IL,[64] divorced 1876,[64] **William Martin Green**, b. May-14-1841 in Gallatin Co, IL,[64] d. Jun- 8-1897 in Elk Creek, Texas Co, MO,[64] occupation Cumberland Presbyterian minister.[64] She married (2) Mar-18-1880 in White Co, IL,[64] **William Finley Price**, b. Apr-19-1854 in White Co, IL,[64] d. Jan- 1-1937.

Children by William Martin Green:
i.   LAURA BELLE GREEN, also known as Belle Green,[64] b. Jul- 9-1873 in White Co, IL,[64] d. Sep-19-1948 in Searcy, White Co, AR.[64] She married ca 1890 in Fulton Co, AR,[64] James William Crouch, b. May-30-1870 in Fulton Co, AR,[64] d. Nov- 4-1925 in Fulton Co, AR.[64]

James: Middle name is widely reported as William, but the middle initial "P" has also been reported. 1910 Census identifies him as James W. Crouch. Son of William Howard Crouch and Mary Ann Bookout.[64]

1037.   **J. Edward Hedges** (609.Margaret[8], 325.Daniel[7], 175.John[6], 84.William[5], 28.John[4], 8.Joseph[3], 3.John[2], 1.Jean[1]). He married **Amanda Louise Bedell**.

Children:
i.   FRANK LOUIS HEDGES.
ii.   CAROLINE BEDELL HEDGES.

1038.   **Frederick Keiley Gaston** (610.William[8], 325.Daniel[7], 175.John[6], 84.William[5], 28.John[4], 8.Joseph[3], 3.John[2], 1.Jean[1]), b. Jan- 6-1868 in Elizabeth, Union Co, NJ,[669] d. Feb- 8-1931.[mcmlxxvii[1977]] He married Apr-19-1892,[27] **Charlotte M. King**.

Children:
i.   CHARLOTTE KING GASTON b. Nov-28-1895.[27]
ii.   FREDERICK KEILEY GASTON, JR. b. Oct- 6-1897,[592] d. Jun- 6-1966,[592] resided in Millbrook, Dutchess Co, NY.[1157] He married[1977] Madeline Sloan.
iii.   ELIZABETH H. GASTON b. Jul-26-1899.

1039.   **Ida V. Gaston** (610.William[8], 325.Daniel[7], 175.John[6], 84.William[5], 28.John[4], 8.Joseph[3], 3.John[2], 1.Jean[1]), b. Jun- 2-1871.[27] She married (1) Jan-10-1893,[27] **Edgar J. Runyon**, d. Nov-15-1900.[27] She married (2) Aug-19-1905, **Arthur Dracas**.

Children by Edgar J. Runyon:
i.   MARGARET G. RUNYON b. Nov-23-1893.[27]
Children by Arthur Dracas:
ii.   MARY ELIZABETH DRACAS b. Feb- 4-1907.[27]

1040.   **Margaret H. Gaston** (610.William[8], 325.Daniel[7], 175.John[6], 84.William[5], 28.John[4], 8.Joseph[3], 3.John[2], 1.Jean[1]), b. Dec-27-1879. She married Jan-23-1904,[27] **Kenneth Miller**.

Children:
i.   MARGARET K. MILLER b. Jun- 2-1906.[27]

1041.   **John G. Dumont** (614.Naomi[8], 328.John[7], 175.John[6], 84.William[5], 28.John[4], 8.Joseph[3], 3.John[2], 1.Jean[1]), b. ca 1869,[209] census 1920 in Hunterdon Co, NJ, census 1910 in Piscataway, Middlesex Co,

NJ, census 1870, 1880 in Branchburg, Somerset Co, NJ. He married Sep- 1-1897, **Margaret Vail**, b. ca 1874 in New Jersey,[211] census 1920 in Hunterdon Co, NJ, census 1910 in Piscataway, Middlesex Co, NJ. 1910 Census, Middlesex Co, NJ (Piscataway Twp), enumerated on Apr 26 1910 at Dewey Park: John G. Dumont, 40, gardner, married 12 yrs; wife Margaret B. Dumont, 36, mother of 2 children (both still living); son LeRoy Dumont, 12; dau Mable M. Dumont, 8. All born in New Jersey.

1920 Census, Hunterdon Co, NJ (North Readington Twp), enumerated in Jan 1920 on Kinney Saw Mill Road:
John G. DuMont, 50, farmer; wife Margaret E. DuMont; son LeRoy DuMont, 21, machine shop worker; dau Mable N. DuMont, 18. All born in New Jersey.

Children:
i. LEROY DUMONT b. ca 1898 in New Jersey,[211] census 1920 in Hunterdon Co, NJ, census 1910 in Piscataway, Middlesex Co, NJ.
ii. MABLE NAOMI DUMONT b. ca 1902 in New Jersey,[211] census 1920 in Hunterdon Co, NJ, census 1910 in Piscataway, Middlesex Co, NJ.

1042.   **Cora Dumont** (614.Naomi[8], 328.John[7], 175.John[6], 84.William[5], 28.John[4], 8.Joseph[3], 3.John[2], 1.Jean[1]), b. ca 1872 in New Jersey,[210] census 1880 in Branchburg, Somerset Co, NJ. She married Mar-14-1887, **Alvah Haver**.
Children:
i. CLARA MATILDA HAVER. She married William Smalley.
ii. FLORENCE EARLE HAVER.
iii. RUTH HAVER.
iv. RUSSELL HAVER.
v. ELSIE HAVER.

1043.   **Oliver Pillsbury Dumont**, census name Alva Dumont,[211] (614.Naomi[8], 328.John[7], 175.John[6], 84.William[5], 28.John[4], 8.Joseph[3], 3.John[2], 1.Jean[1]), b. Jan- -1880 in New Jersey,[210] census 1930 in Hunterdon Co, NJ, census 1910 in Dunellen, Middlesex Co, NJ. He married Dec- 3-1902, **Carrie Wyhusky**, b. ca 1884 in New Jersey,[211] (daughter of Charles Wyhusky and Anna __), census 1930 in Somerset Co, NJ, census 1920 in Plainfield, Union Co, NJ, census 1910 in Dunellen, Middlesex Co, NJ.

1910 Census, Middlesex Co, NJ (borough of Dunellen), enumerated on Apr 20 1910 on Front Street:
Charles Wyhusky, 50, b. NJ, parents b. Germany, foreman at ironworks, married 26 yrs; wife Anna Wyhusky, 40, mother of 2 children (both still living), son Earl Syhusky, 22, carpenter, married 1 yr; dau-in-law Elizabeth Wyhusky, 22, mother of one child (still living); granddau Elizabeth M. Wyhusky, 11 months; boarder Alva Dumont, 30, trolley car conductor, married 7 yrs; dau Carrie Dumont, 26, mother of one child (still living); grandson Harold E. Dumont, 4. All born in New Jersey.

1920 Census, Union Co, NJ (town of Plainfield), enumerated on Jan 16 1920:
Harry S. Radin, 37, single, retail grocery salesman; father James Radin, 69, widowed; servant Carrie Dumont, 34, married, housekeeper; lodger Naomi Dumont, 8; lodger Evelyn Dumont, 5. All born in New Jersey.

1930 Census, Somerset Co, NJ (borough of North Plainfield), enumerated on Apr 4 1930 at 184 Somerset Street:
Carrie DuMont, head of household, 45, married, age 17 at first marriage; dau Evelyn DuMont, 16; boarder Harry Radin, 47, single, grocery store manager; boarder George Yonick, 19, single.

1930 Census, Hunterdon Co, NJ (borough of High Bridge), enumerated on Apr 19 1930:
Willard Alpaugh, 65, no occupation, married, age 23 at first marriage; wife Emma Alpaugh, 67, age 25 at first marriage; boarder Oliver P. DuMont, 50, oiler at steel plant, married, age 23 at first marriage. All born in New Jersey.

438

Children:

i.   HAROLD E. DUMONT b. ca 1906,[211] census 1910 in Dunellen, Middlesex Co, NJ.

ii. NAOMI ALBERTA DUMONT b. ca 1912 in New Jersey,[681] census 1920 in Plainfield, Union Co, NJ.

iii. EVELYN DUMONT b. ca 1915,[681] census 1930 in Somerset Co, NJ, census 1920 in Plainfield, Union Co, NJ.

1044.   **William Ira Gaston** (615.William[8], 328.John[7], 175.John[6], 84.William[5], 28.John[4], 8.Joseph[3], 3.John[2], 1.Jean[1]), b. Jan- 2-1875,[673] d. Dec-13-1908.[673] He married Jun-20-1900,[1229] **Bertha Adelle Philpott**.

Children:

i.   CLARENCE WARNER GASTON.

ii. ARTHUR HERBERT GASTON.

1045.   **James Herbert Gaston** (615.William[8], 328.John[7], 175.John[6], 84.William[5], 28.John[4], 8.Joseph[3], 3.John[2], 1.Jean[1]). He married Nov-17-1904, **Louisa Rockafellow**.

Children:

i.   EDYTHE LOUISE GASTON.

ii. RUTH TILTON GASTON.

iii. WILLIAM ELLSWORTH GASTON.

1046.   **Ethel Rebecca Gaston** (616.Hugh[8], 328.John[7], 175.John[6], 84.William[5], 28.John[4], 8.Joseph[3], 3.John[2], 1.Jean[1]). She married Dec-15-1908,[1229] **Fred Clinton Kellem**.

Children:

i.   DOROTHY CHARLOTTE KELLEM.

ii. ALICE RAY KELLEM.

1047.   **Cassie Van Nest Smock** (617.Jane[8], 329.Oliver[7], 175.John[6], 84.William[5], 28.John[4], 8.Joseph[3], 3.John[2], 1.Jean[1]). She married Aug-18-1904 in Jamesburg, Middlesex Co, NJ, **Robert Ayres Graff**, b. ca 1870.

Robert: Last name may be Groff.

Children:

i.   JANE GASTON GRAFF b. Oct- 9-1905.

1048.   **George Willets Smock** (617.Jane[8], 329.Oliver[7], 175.John[6], 84.William[5], 28.John[4], 8.Joseph[3], 3.John[2], 1.Jean[1]), b. ca 1887. He married Apr- 5-1907, **Belle Brown**, b. ca 1889.

Children:

i.   HOMER BROWN SMOCK.

1049.   **Augustus Hobart Smock** (618.Catherine[8], 329.Oliver[7], 175.John[6], 84.William[5], 28.John[4], 8.Joseph[3], 3.John[2], 1.Jean[1]). He married (1) Nov-29-1892, **Anna Grace Crook**. He married (2) **Nancy Burgess**.

Children by Anna Grace Crook:

i.   HELEN MARIE SMOCK b. 1893, d. 1893.

1050.   **Ethel L. Smock** (618.Catherine[8], 329.Oliver[7], 175.John[6], 84.William[5], 28.John[4], 8.Joseph[3], 3.John[2], 1.Jean[1]). She married Dec-22-1902, **Henry C. Duden** (son of Frank Duden and Phebe Wright).

Children:

i.   DOROTHY DUDEN.

ii. EULA DUDEN.

1051.   **Charles C. Willits** (619.Sylvia[8], 329.Oliver[7], 175.John[6], 84.William[5], 28.John[4], 8.Joseph[3], 3.John[2], 1.Jean[1]), b. ca 1879 in New Jersey,[681] census 1820 in Cheltenham, Montgomery Co, PA. He married

Oct- -1902,[15] **Ethel Dumont**, b. ca 1880 in New Jersey,[681] census 1920 in Cheltenham, Montgomery Co, PA.

Children:

i. CHARLES WILLITS b. Nov-26-1914 in Pennsylvania,[681] d. Aug-26-1993 in Hudson, Summit Co, OH,[1011,592] resided in Hudson, Summit Co, OH,[948] census 1920 in Cheltenham, Montgomery Co, PA, occupation architect.[1011]

Middle initial given as J in 1920 Census, but D in Ohio Death Index.

1052.   **Grace G. Willits** (619.Sylvia[8], 329.Oliver[7], 175.John[6], 84.William[5], 28.John[4], 8.Joseph[3], 3.John[2], 1.Jean[1]), b. Oct- -1882 in Pennsylvania,[123] census 1900, 1910 in Philadelphia, PA. She married Jan-19-1912,[15] **Henry W. Von Bremen**.

Children:

i. BEREND H. VON BREMEN b. Nov-28-1913,[592] d. Jan-29-1998,[mcmlxxviii[1978]] resided in Wilmington, New Castle Co, DE,[592] resided formerly in Washington, DC.[1625]

1053.   **Carolyn Gaston Williams** (620.Lizzie[8], 329.Oliver[7], 175.John[6], 84.William[5], 28.John[4], 8.Joseph[3], 3.John[2], 1.Jean[1]), b. Sep- 5-1889 in New York,[592,211] d. Jan-15-1977 in Lawrence, Essex Co, MA,[mcmlxxix[1979],592] census 1910 in Elizabeth, Union Co, NJ, resided in Lawrence, Essex Co, MA.[592] She married Apr-22-1910, **Charles Stuart Donovan**, resided in Texas, occupation Captain in U.S. Army.

Children:

i. ELIZABETH STUART DONOVAN.

1054.   **Jane Quick** (621.Catherine[8], 331.Hugh[7], 175.John[6], 84.William[5], 28.John[4], 8.Joseph[3], 3.John[2], 1.Jean[1]). She married **Archibald Derby**.

Children:

i. CATHERINE DERBY.

1055.   **George A. Gaston** (624.John[8], 331.Hugh[7], 175.John[6], 84.William[5], 28.John[4], 8.Joseph[3], 3.John[2], 1.Jean[1]), b. ca 1888 in New Jersey,[681] census 1920, 1930 in Somerville, Somerset Co, NJ, occupation 1930 broker, occupation 1920 manager, dry goods store.[681] He married ca 1912,[334] **Mae E. Brown**, b. ca 1891 in New York,[334] census 1920, 1930 in Somerville, Somerset Co, NJ.

Children:

i. JOHN GARRETSON GASTON b. Nov-23-1915 in New Jersey,[592,681] d. Apr-19-2005,[592] resided in Far Hills, Somerset Co, NJ,[592] resided formerly in New York,[1157] census 1920, 1930 in Somerville, Somerset Co, NJ.

1056.   **George Brown Zahniser** (626.Elizabeth[8], 334.Sarah[7], 177.John[6], 85.Joseph[5], 28.John[4], 8.Joseph[3], 3.John[2], 1.Jean[1]). He married 1902, **Ruth Agnew**.

Children:

i. ELIZABETH ZAHNISER.
ii. GEORGE BROWN ZAHNISER, JR..

1057.   **Albert Wright Zahniser** (626.Elizabeth[8], 334.Sarah[7], 177.John[6], 85.Joseph[5], 28.John[4], 8.Joseph[3], 3.John[2], 1.Jean[1]). He married 1905, **Hannah Oliver Barton**, b. in Philadelphia, PA.

Children:

i. ALBERT WRIGHT ZAHNISER, JR..
ii. GEORGE WRIGHT ZAHNISER.

1058.   **Rezean Blanchard Brown** (628.John[8], 335.Joanna[7], 177.John[6], 85.Joseph[5], 28.John[4], 8.Joseph[3], 3.John[2], 1.Jean[1]). He married **Eliza Schmelzel**.

Children:

i. DOROTHY HATTON BROWN.
ii. LOUISE ELIZABETH BROWN.

iii.   MARJORIE BROWN.

1059.   **George Houston Brown** (628.John[8], 335.Joanna[7], 177.John[6], 85.Joseph[5], 28.John[4], 8.Joseph[3], 3.John[2], 1.Jean[1]). He married **Anna Ethey Dorland**.
Children:
i.   GEORGE HOUSTON BROWN, JR..

1060.   **Morris Houston Brown** (629.George[8], 335.Joanna[7], 177.John[6], 85.Joseph[5], 28.John[4], 8.Joseph[3], 3.John[2], 1.Jean[1]), b. 1880 in New York,[1231] d. Dec-16-1925 in Los Angeles, CA.[1231] He married Nov-21-1914,[1231] **Gertrude Mason**, b. Aug-20-1880 in Milwaukee, WI,[mcmlxxx[1980]] (daughter of Frederick Mason and Isabella Arland), d. May-16-1967 in Salem, Marion Co, OR,[mcmlxxxi[1981],592] buried in Resthaven Cemetery, Eugene, Lane Co, OR, resided in Salem, Marion Co, OR.[mcmlxxxii[1982]]
Children:
i.   GEORGE HOUSTON BROWN b. Dec-27-1915 in Cowlitz Co, WA,[mcmlxxxiii[1983],592] d. Jan-22-2001,[592] resided in Florence, Lane Co, OR.[1965]
ii.   ARLAND MASON "JERRY" BROWN[1231] also known as Jerry Brown,[592,693] b. Sep- 5-1918 in California, d. Feb- 4-1981 in Lane Co, OR,[592,mcmlxxxiv[1984]] resided in Junction City, Lane Co, OR.[1965] He married[228] Jo __.

1061.   **Joan Churchill Brown** (629.George[8], 335.Joanna[7], 177.John[6], 85.Joseph[5], 28.John[4], 8.Joseph[3], 3.John[2], 1.Jean[1]), b. Sep-13-1885.[1231] She married Jun-20-1914,[1231] **William Stockton Cranmer**, also known as Stockton Cranmer, b. Oct-22-1887,[1231] (son of William Stockton Cranmer).
Children:
i.   WINIFRED STOCKTON CRANMER[1231].
ii.   WILLIAM STOCKTON CRANMER[1231].

1062.   **Henry Carmer Brown** (629.George[8], 335.Joanna[7], 177.John[6], 85.Joseph[5], 28.John[4], 8.Joseph[3], 3.John[2], 1.Jean[1]), b. Jan-29-1887.[1231] He married 1913, **Dora Brown**.
Children:
i.   MARJORIE BROWN.
ii.   GEORGIA CHURCHILL BROWN.

1063.   **Sarah Marshall Gilman** (634.Mary[8], 337.Aletta[7], 177.John[6], 85.Joseph[5], 28.John[4], 8.Joseph[3], 3.John[2], 1.Jean[1]). She married **William Jordan**.
Children:
i.   MARY LEIGHTON JORDAN.
ii.   KATHERINE GILMAN JORDAN.
iii.   MARJORIE STEWART JORDAN.

1064.   **William Stewart Gilman** (634.Mary[8], 337.Aletta[7], 177.John[6], 85.Joseph[5], 28.John[4], 8.Joseph[3], 3.John[2], 1.Jean[1]). He married **Florence King**.
Children:
i.   FLORENCE KING GILMAN.
ii.   DANIEL TRIMBLE GILMAN.
iii.   HENRY KING GILMAN.

1065.   **Paul K. Gaston** (639.Eugene[8], 339.Alexander[7], 178.William[6], 85.Joseph[5], 28.John[4], 8.Joseph[3], 3.John[2], 1.Jean[1]), b. Jan- -1873 in Illinois,[123] census 1910, 1920, 1930 in Pratt, Pratt Co, KS, census 1900 in Battle Creek, Calhoun Co, MI. He married ca 1896,[123] **Emma F. __**, b. Jan-21-1875 in Kansas,[592,123] d. Aug- -1969,[592] resided in South Haven, VanBuren Co, MI,[592] census 1920, 1930 in Pratt, Pratt Co, KS, census 1900 in Battle Creek, Calhoun Co, MI.

1900 Census, Calhoun Co, Michigan (city of Battle Creek), enumerated on Jun 11 1900:
Hall K Gaston, 27, b. Jan 1873 in Illinois, student, married 4 yrs; wife Emma, 25, b. Jan 1875 in Kansas, mother of one child (still living); son Harold, 1, b. Aug 1898 in Kansas; father Eugene A, 52, b.

Sep 1847 in Pennsylvania, physician, married 29 yrs; mother Helen E, 29, b. Apr 1851 in Illinois, mother of 2 children (both still living); brother Eugene A, 17, b. Aug 1882 in Kansas.

1910 Census, Pratt Co, Kansas (city of Pratt), enumerated on May 6 1910:
Helen Gaston, 60, b. Illinois, widowed, mother of 2 children (both still living); son Paul, 37, b. Illinois, physician, divorced.

1920 Census, Pratt Co, Kansas (city of Pratt), enumerated on Jun 17 1920:
Paul K. Gaston, 47, b. Illinois, physician; wife Emma F, 45, b. Kansas; son Harold, 21, b. Kansas, single; mother Helen E, 70, b. Virginia, widowed.

1930 Census, Pratt Co, Kansas (city of Pratt), enumerated on Apr 5 1930:
Dr. P. K. Gaston, 57, b. Illinois, (father b. Pennsylvania, mother b. Maryland), medical doctor, age 23 at time of first marriage; wife Emma, 55, b. Kansas, age 21 at first marriage; son Harold P, 32, specialist at S College Michigan, single; mother Helen, 80, b. Maryland, age 21 at first marriage, married.

Children:
  i.   HAROLD P. GASTON b. Aug-22-1898 in Kansas,[592,123] d. Jun-21-1988 in South Haven, VanBuren Co, MI,[682,592] resided in South Haven, VanBuren Co, MI,[683] census 1920, 1930 in Pratt, Pratt Co, KS, census 1900 in Battle Creek, Calhoun Co, MI.

1066.   **Eugene A. Gaston** (639.Eugene[8], 339.Alexander[7], 178.William[6], 85.Joseph[5], 28.John[4], 8.Joseph[3], 3.John[2], 1.Jean[1]), b. Aug- -1882 in Kansas,[123] census 1920, 1930 in Concordia, Cloud Co, KS, census 1910 in Princeton, Bureau Co, IL, census 1900 in Battle Creek, Calhoun Co, MI, occupation jeweler,[211,681,334.] He married 1904,[334] **Fay E. __**, b. Aug-14-1883 in Kansas,[592,211] d. Aug-30-1973 in Framingham, Middlesex Co, MA,[1979,592] resided in Framingham, Middlesex Co, MA,[592] census 1920, 1930 in Concordia, Cloud Co, KS, census 1910 in Princeton, Bureau Co, IL.

1910 Census, Bureau Co, Illinois (city of Princeton), enumerated on Apr 18 1910:
Eugene A. Gaston, 27, b. Kansas, both parents b. Pa, jeweler in jewelry store, married 4 yrs; wife Fan E, 26, b. Kansas, both parents b. Kansas, mother of 1 child (still living); son Clovis E, 2, b. Illinois; boarder Ellen Soderberg, 31, b. Sweden, immigrated 1882, nurse, single; boarder Hulda Alm, 27, b. Sweden, immigrated 1888, nurse, single.

1920 Census, Cloud Co, Kansas (city of Concordia), enumerated on Jan 5 1920 at 446 West Sixth Street:
Eugene A. Gaston, 37, b. Kansas, father b. Pa, mother b. Illinois, retail jewelry merchant; wife Fay E, 35, b. Kansas, both parents b. Kansas; son Eugene A, 12, b. Illinois.

1930 Census, Cloud Co, Kansas (city of Concordia), enumerated on Apr 2 1930 at 446 West Sixth Street:
Eugene A. Gaston, 46, b. Kansas, father b. Pa, mother b. Illinois, retail jewelry merchant, age 21 at time of first marriage; wife Fay E, 42, b. Kansas, both parents b. Kansas, age 18 at first marriage; son Eugene A Jr, 22, b. Illinois, single.

Children:
  i.   EUGENE A. GASTON, census name Clovis E. Gaston, b. Aug-21-1907 in Peoria, Peoria Co, IL,[190,592] d. Jun- 8-1986 in Framingham, Middlesex Co, MA,[806,592] occupation colorectal surgeon,[190] education University of Kansas, Harvard Medical School (1931).[190]

        Dr. Eugene A. Gaston, 78, of Framingham, a staff surgeon at Framingham-Union Hospital for 49 years, died of cancer Sunday, June 8, 1986, in that hospital. A former associate clinical professor of surgery at Boston University School of Medicine, and a former vice president of both the Boston Surgical Society and the American Society of Colon and Rectal Surgeons, Dr. Gaston

442

taught hundreds of surgeons at Framingham-Union and at the Boston University School of Medicine. Widely known for his writings on diseases of the colon and rectum, he was author of 63 scientific articles, and had written or rewritten approximately 1500 abstracts as associate editor of Diseases of the Colon and Rectum. An associate editor of the Scientific Journal, he also was a fellow of the American College of Surgery, the American Medical Association, the Massachusetts Medical Society and the Middlesex West District Medical Society. At the reception at Framingham Union Hospital on his retirement in 1985, Dr. Gaston was honored by proclamations from the Framingham Board of Selectman and from Gov. Dukakis. After earning his medical degree at Harvard Medical School in 1931, he undertook postgraduate internship training at Boston City Hospital and at the Cleveland Clinic. Born in Peoria, Ill., he was raised in Kansas and attended the University of Kansas for three years before entering Harvard Medical School.[190]

He married[484] Helena M. Hotchkiss, b. Sep-17-1909 in Kansas,[1979] d. Feb-29-2000 in Framingham, Middlesex Co, MA,[1979] resided in Needham, Norfolk Co, MA,[592] resided 1986 in Framingham, Middlesex Co, MA.[484]

1067. **Gordon Brooks Gaston** (647.Alonzo[8], 360.Alexander[7], 201.George[6], 100.Alexander[5], 37.Alexander[4], 10.Alexander[3], 3.John[2], 1.Jean[1]), b. May- 6-1913 in Everett, Snohomish Co, WA,[36,592] d. Jan-11-1989 in Everett, Snohomish Co, WA,[36,592] census 1920, 1930 in Everett, Snohomish Co, WA. He married[317] **Anna Refsnes**, b. Feb-28-1914 in Everett, Snohomish Co, WA,[317,592] d. Aug-18-1996.[592]
    Children:
    i.   LIVING.

1068. **Leonard Harry Gaston** (649.Harold[8], 362.Burton[7], 206.James[6], 101.Heman[5], 37.Alexander[4], 10.Alexander[3], 3.John[2], 1.Jean[1]), b. Nov-29-1930,[592] d. Jun- 4-2007,[592] resided in Lynwood, Los Angeles Co, CA.[1152]
    Children:
    i.   ___ GASTON. She married[313] ___ Rodriguez.

1069. **Hubert Arthur Haseltine**, also known as Arthur Hazeltine,[317] (650.Myrla[8], 366.Eunice[7], 207.Edmund[6], 102.Ebenezer[5], 38.David[4], 10.Alexander[3], 3.John[2], 1.Jean[1]), b. Jun-22-1892 in Pennsylvania,[317,211] d. Dec- -1985 in Colorado,[317] resided in Littleton, Arapahoe Co, CO,[708] census 1930 in Asheville, Buncombe Co, NC, resided 1920, 1925 in Tampa, Hillsborough Co, FL,[681,765] census 1910 in Cochranton, Crawford Co, PA, occupation teacher.[681,334]

Both Hubert Haseltine and his wife were teachers. The 1932 City Directory shows Mr. Haseltine teaching at Asheville High School. They started a small family school, the Haseltine School, on Liberty Street. When the fire department condemned the building, the school was merged with Asheville Country Day in 1950. Asheville Country Day School was started because two of the student's mothers wanted a Protestant, non-sectarian school. The merged schools retained the Asheville Country Day name, with Mr. Haseltine being headmaster, or principal. Space was rented in the Grace Presbyterian Church [1951: Asheville Country Day School, 789 Merrimon Ave.] This building was a former home of Asheville-Biltmore College [1942-1949] and was previously built by the Junior League as a baby home [Buncombe County Children's Home].
< http://toto.lib.unca.edu/findingaids/oralhistory/VOA/I_M/McCabe_E.html >

He married[317] **Adaline K.** ___, b. Jan- 8-1894 in Pennsylvania,[592,334] d. Mar-22-1986,[592] resided in Littleton, Arapahoe Co, CO,[592] census 1930 in Asheville, Buncombe Co, NC, census 1920 in Tampa, Hillsborough Co, FL.
    Children:
    i.   JANE HASELTINE b. Jan- 3-1917 in Florida,[592,334] d. Mar-20-2007,[592] resided in Louisville, Boulder Co, CO,[708] census 1930 in Asheville, Buncombe Co, NC, census 1920 in Tampa, Hillsborough Co, FL. She married Dennis Barr.
    ii. ARTHUR BURTON HASELTINE b. Dec-30-1918 in Alturas, Polk Co, FL,[190,592,1123] d. Mar-10-1995 in Gainesville, Alachua Co, FL,[700,1123,592] resided in Gainesville, Alachua Co, FL,[708,190]

census 1930 in Asheville, Buncombe Co, NC, census 1920 in Tampa, Hillsborough Co, FL, military pilot, U.S. Navy (retired),[190] occupation mechanical engineer, educator with state Dept of Education.[190] He married (2) Living.

1070. **Chester Kirk Whittaker** (651.Phylinda[8], 366.Eunice[7], 207.Edmund[6], 102.Ebenezer[5], 38.David[4], 10.Alexander[3], 3.John[2], 1.Jean[1]), b. Nov-28-1889 in Springfield, Greene Co, MO,[684,1237,123] d. Jan-24-1958 in San Diego Co, CA,[1237] census 1930 in Pelham, Westchester Co, NY, census 1920 in Kansas City, Jackson Co, MO, resided 1917 in San Francisco, CA,[684] census 1910 in Cochranton, Crawford Co, PA, census 1900 in Raton, Colfax Co, NM, occupation 1930 manager, automobiles,[334] occupation 1917, 1920 manager, tire & rubber company.[684,681] He married **Lillian I. __**, b. Mar-26-1894 in Pennsylvania,[1237] d. Apr- 3-1975 in San Diego Co, CA,[1237] census 1930 in Pelham, Westchester Co, NY, census 1920 in Kansas City, Jackson Co, MO.
> Children:
> i.   BETTY JANE WHITTAKER b. ca 1921 in Oklahoma,[334] census 1930 in Pelham, Westchester Co, NY.

1071. **Arthur Edmon Brown** (652.Frank[8], 366.Eunice[7], 207.Edmund[6], 102.Ebenezer[5], 38.David[4], 10.Alexander[3], 3.John[2], 1.Jean[1]), b. Sep-15-1896 in Cochranton, Crawford Co, PA,[123,317] d. Apr- -1974 in Washington, DC,[317] census 1920 in Erie, Erie Co, PA, census 1900 in Cochranton, Crawford Co, PA, military U.S. Air Force dentist (retired 1953). He married Dec-24-1921 in Baltimore, MD, **Grace Elsie May Montgomery**, also known as Elsie Montgomery, b. Feb-16-1900 in Washington, DC (daughter of Charles H. A. Montgomery and Dora Ann Virginia Beavers), d. Jul- -2000 in Washington, DC.
> Children:
> i.   LIVING. She married Living.
> ii. LIVING. He married Living.

1072. **Linnie Winsome Brown**, census name Winsome Brown, census name Linnie W. Brown (652.Frank[8], 366.Eunice[7], 207.Edmund[6], 102.Ebenezer[5], 38.David[4], 10.Alexander[3], 3.John[2], 1.Jean[1]), b. Jun- 2-1898 in Pennsylvania,[592,123] [Age 27 in 1930 Census would put birth in about 1903, but age 21 in 1920 Census puts it in about 1899.], d. May- -1980,[592] resided in Saegertown, Crawford Co, PA,[948] census 1920, 1930 in Erie, Erie Co, PA, census 1900 in Cochranton, Crawford Co, PA. She married ca 1926,[334] **James V. Derby**, b. ca 1903 in Pennsylvania,[334] census 1910, 1920, 1930 in Erie, Erie Co, PA.
> Children:
> i.   LIVING.

1073. **Eleanor Rose Brown** (653.Arthur[8], 366.Eunice[7], 207.Edmund[6], 102.Ebenezer[5], 38.David[4], 10.Alexander[3], 3.John[2], 1.Jean[1]). She married 1924,[317] **Gordon Webb**.
> Children:
> i.   MIRIAM OLIVE WEBB b. 1926.[317]

1074. **Doris Rowena Brown** (654.Harry[8], 366.Eunice[7], 207.Edmund[6], 102.Ebenezer[5], 38.David[4], 10.Alexander[3], 3.John[2], 1.Jean[1]), b. Dec- 4-1914 in Cochranton, Crawford Co, PA,[317] d. Jul-31-2007 in North Carolina,[317] resided in Franklin, Macon Co, NC.[317] She married **Edwin Emanuel Phillips**, b. Dec-31-1912 in Shaw, Bolivar Co, MS,[317] d. Dec- 4-1992 in Franklin, Macon Co, NC.[317]
> Children:
> i.   LIVING. He married Living.

1075. **Living** (656.Audley[8], 367.Frank[7], 207.Edmund[6], 102.Ebenezer[5], 38.David[4], 10.Alexander[3], 3.John[2], 1.Jean[1]). She married **Living**.
> Children:
> i.   LIVING. She married Living.
> ii.   LIVING. He married Living.
> iii. LIVING. She married Living.

iv.   LIVING. She married (1) Living. She married (2) Living.

1076.   **Living** (656.Audley[8], 367.Frank[7], 207.Edmund[6], 102.Ebenezer[5], 38.David[4], 10.Alexander[3], 3.John[2], 1.Jean[1]). He married **Living**.
        Children:
    i.   LIVING.

FOOTNOTES

[1] Albert F. Koehler, *The Huguenots, or The Early French in New Jersey* , original publication 1955 by Clearfield Co, republished 1992-2003 by Genealogical Publishing Co, Baltimore, MD, The Gaston entry in its entirety: "The Gaston family was originally from Foix, Southern France. The earliest certain ancestor of the New Jersey Gastons was John Gaston, a Huguenot, born about 1600 in France. The family fled to Scotland where John married and among other children had three sons, John, William and Alexander, who later emigrated to County Antrim, Ireland, about 1660-1680. Joseph Gaston, son of John of Ireland, was born about 1700 in Ireland and came to New Jersey with his brothers Hugh, John and Alexander. It is presumed that their arrival was through the port of Perth Amboy about 1720. Joseph Gaston lived in Bernards Twp, Somerset County, where he died in 1777, leaving his wife Margaret. The widow, Margaret, moved to Hardwick Twp, Sussex County, with her son Joseph, where she died on August 31, 1795, aged 90 years.", pp. 21-22.

[2] Charles A. Hanna, *Ohio Valley Genealogies* , Genealogical Publishing Co, Baltimore MD, 1989 (orig. pub. 1900), Hanna was not definitive regarding Jean Gaston's birthplace, stating that he was born "about 1600, in Scotland (or France), of Huguenot descent." Although he does not provide a date or identify Jean's wife by name, he does specify that Jean married in Scotland. p. 40.

[3] Charles A. Hanna, *Ohio Valley Genealogies* , Genealogical Publishing Co, Baltimore MD, 1989 (orig. pub. 1900), p. 40.

[4] Albert F. Koehler, *The Huguenots, or The Early French in New Jersey* , original publication 1955 by Clearfield Co, republished 1992-2003 by Genealogical Publishing Co, Baltimore, MD, pp. 21-22.

[5] George F. Black, *The Surnames of Scotland: Their Origin, Meaning and History* , The New York Public Library (1946, 1996), The entry for Gaston, in its entirety: "GASTON. An old Roxburghshire surname. David Gastoun in the toun of Lessudden, 1562 (Lauder). Hendrie Gastoun, tenant on lands of the Abbey of Kelso, 1567 (Kelso, p. 527). David Gaustone or Gaustoune in Lessuddane, 1608, and Thomas Gaston or Gastoune there in 1652 (RRM, I, p. 65, 72). Agnes Gastoun in Melrose was accused of witchcraft in 1650 (ibid, I, p. 220). A form of Gascon, 'a native of Gascony,' and Bardsley mentions a person in the reign of Henry III who is referred to as de Gasconia and de Gaston." (Note: RRM refers to "Selections from the records of the regality of Melrose and from the manuscripts of the Earl of Haddington, Edinburgh, 1914-17, 3 v."), p. 291.

[6] Edward H. Couey, Scotts Mills, OR 97375.

[7] *American Ancestry, Vol. V* (originally published 1890 by Joel Munsell's Sons; republished 1968 by Genealogical Publishing Co, Baltimore), p. 104.

[8] Charles A. Hanna, *Ohio Valley Genealogies* , Genealogical Publishing Co, Baltimore MD, 1989 (orig. pub. 1900).

[9] Jane Farrell Burgess, 11700 Dinwiddie Dr, Rockville, MD 20852, *The Gaston Genealogy* (1989), Also, Ireland birth/marriage/christening records on file at Mormon FHC's show

the birth of a William Gaston to a John Gaston (wife not named) in County Antrim in 1680. (Page 10,323), p. 77.

x[10] Mary Gaston Gee (1899-1987), The Ancestry and Descendants of Amzi Williford Gaston II (1841-1911) of Spartanburg County, South Carolina (Charlottesville, VA, 1944), p. 9.

xi[11] Arthur P. Dodge, The Bay State Monthly, A Massachusetts Magazine, Vol II, No. 5, Feb 1885 (www.gutenberg.org).

xii[12] Bill Gaston, Austin TX <bgaston2@mindspring.com>, *Descendants: The Huguenot John Jean Gaston b: About 1600, France* (http://home.mindspring.com/~bgaston2/).

xiii[13] Heritage History of Chester County, South Carolina , 1982, p. 195.

xiv[14] Charles A. Hanna, *Ohio Valley Genealogies* , Genealogical Publishing Co, Baltimore MD, 1989 (orig. pub. 1900), p. 42.

xv[15] Anna Reger Gaston, Gaston Family Lines of Somerset, "Somerset County Historical Quarterly," Somerville, NJ, Vol. 5 (1916) (http://homepages.rootsweb.com/~windmill/html/somersev.html).

xvi[16] Anna Reger Gaston, Gaston Family Lines of Somerset, "Somerset County Historical Quarterly," Somerville, NJ, Vol. 5 (1916) (http://homepages.rootsweb.com/~windmill/html/somersev.html), p. 35.

xvii[17] Headstone.

xviii[18] Headstone, With death given as Aug 1 1777, inscription states she was in the "eightyeth year of her age." Name appears on headstone as "Jennet Gaston.".

xix[19] Charles A. Hanna, *Ohio Valley Genealogies* , Genealogical Publishing Co, Baltimore MD, 1989 (orig. pub. 1900), p. 45.

xx[20] New Jersey marriage record.

xxi[21] Proceedings of the New Jersey Historical Society, p. 57.

xxii[22] Charles A. Hanna, *Ohio Valley Genealogies* , Genealogical Publishing Co, Baltimore MD, 1989 (orig. pub. 1900), p. 46.

xxiii[23] Marcia De Sarro Witt, W. Palm Beach, FL.

xxiv[24] John Littell, Family Records or Genealogies of the First Settlers of the Passaic Valley (1851) (http://www.archive.org/details/familyrecordsorg00litt).

xxv[25] John Littell, *Family Records or Genealogies of the First Settlers of the Passaic Valley (1851)* (http://www.archive.org/details/familyrecordsorg00litt), p. 68.

xxvi[26] Jane Farrell Burgess, 11700 Dinwiddie Dr, Rockville, MD 20852, *The Gaston Genealogy* (1989).

xxvii[27] Max Perry, American Descendants of William Gaston and Mary Olivet Lemon (Midland, TX, 1989).

xxviii[28] Charles A. Hanna, *Ohio Valley Genealogies* , Genealogical Publishing Co, Baltimore MD, 1989 (orig. pub. 1900), p. 47.

xxix[29] *Colonial Families of the United States, 1912* (republished 1966 by Genealogical Publishing Co, Baltimore, MD), Vol III, p. 175.

xxx[30] Charles A. Hanna, *Ohio Valley Genealogies* , Genealogical Publishing Co, Baltimore MD, 1989 (orig. pub. 1900), Other sources state birth of this Alexander Gaston was between 1707 & 1714. "Colonial Families of U.S." (Vol III, p 175) states 1707 in Ballymena. p. 48.

xxxi[31] Jane Farrell Burgess, 11700 Dinwiddie Dr, Rockville, MD 20852, *The Gaston Genealogy* (1989), p. 41.

xxxii[32] Bob Gaston, 139 Victoria St, Longview, WA 98632, <bgaston@tdn.com>, in "Gaston Crier Newsletter," Vol 1, No 2, Nov 1997, at http://mvn.net/genealogy Jane Farrell Burgess, p. 41, identifies it as "Southwest Cemetery, Cone Hill".

xxxiii[33] Charles A. Hanna, *Ohio Valley Genealogies* , Genealogical Publishing Co, Baltimore MD, 1989 (orig. pub. 1900), p. 48.

xxxiv[34] Audley DeForest Gaston & Judy Gaston Woodard, Austin, TX.

xxxv[35] Charles A. Hanna, *Ohio Valley Genealogies* , Genealogical Publishing Co, Baltimore MD, 1989 (orig. pub. 1900), But researcher Audley D. Gaston reports birth in 1714, with last name as Wilkinson or Willson. p. 48.

xxxvi[36] Robert B. "Bob" Gaston, Longview, WA 98632 <bgaston@tdn.com>.

xxxvii[37] Robert B. "Bob" Gaston, Longview, WA 98632 <bgaston@tdn.com>, citing Nola McIntyre.

xxxviii[38] Jane Farrell Burgess, 11700 Dinwiddie Dr, Rockville, MD 20852, *The Gaston Genealogy* (1989), Identified in Richmond, MA death records as Lt. William Gaston, age 43, parents not given. p. 46.

xxxix[39] Son Joseph's Family Bible, per Edward Couey.

xl[40] Jane Farrell Burgess, 11700 Dinwiddie Dr, Rockville, MD 20852, *The Gaston Genealogy* (1989), p. 86.

xli[41] Chalmers Gaston Davidson, *Gaston of Chester* , Davidson Printing Co, Davidson NC (1956), Based chiefly on notes and records preserved by Judge Arthur Lee Gaston, and privately printed according to his will. p. xi.

xlii[42] Jane Farrell Burgess, 11700 Dinwiddie Dr, Rockville, MD 20852, *The Gaston Genealogy* (1989), p. 78.

xliii[43] Jane Farrell Burgess, 11700 Dinwiddie Dr, Rockville, MD 20852, *The Gaston Genealogy* (1989), p. 83.

xliv[44] Charles A. Hanna, *Ohio Valley Genealogies* , Genealogical Publishing Co, Baltimore MD, 1989 (orig. pub. 1900), p. 41.

xlv[45] Heritage History of Chester County, South Carolina , 1982, p. 196.

xlvi[46] Headstone (year only).

xlvii[47] Ireland birth/marriage/christening records, Max Perry reports her birth as 1712, which corresponds to her headstone. DAR Lineage Book (p. 103) states it as 1725.

xlviii[48] Ireland birth/marriage/christening records, Parents listed as William Gaston and Olivet Lemon. Page 10,322.

xlix[49] Mary Gaston Gee (1899-1987), The Ancestry and Descendants of Amzi Williford Gaston II (1841-1911) of Spartanburg County, South Carolina (Charlottesville, VA, 1944), p. 12.

l[50] Jane Farrell Burgess, 11700 Dinwiddie Dr, Rockville, MD 20852, *The Gaston Genealogy* (1989), p. 87.

li[51] Mary Gaston Gee (1899-1987), *The Ancestry and Descendants of Amzi Williford Gaston II (1841-1911) of Spartanburg County, South Carolina* (Charlottesville, VA, 1944), Thomas Pinckney Gaston left notes stating that his grandfather Thomas Gaston (1759-1832) had a brother Joseph who died in Tennessee. p. 13.

lii[52] Bill Gaston, Austin TX <bgaston2@mindspring.com>, *Descendants: The Huguenot John Jean Gaston b: About 1600, France* (http://home.mindspring.com/~bgaston2/), http://wc.rootsweb.com/cgi-bin/igm.cgi?op=GET&db=ancientage&id=I08564.

liii[53] Larry Charles Slaughter, Amarillo, TX, citing Mary Gaston Gee's "The Ancestry & Descendants of Amzi Williford Gaston II (1841-1911) of Spartanburg Co, SC" and other sources. Questionable.

liv[54] J. Herman Schauinger, *William Gaston: Carolinian* , Bruce Publishing Company, 1949.

lv[55] Mary Gaston Gee (1899-1987), The Ancestry and Descendants of Amzi Williford Gaston II (1841-1911) of Spartanburg County, South Carolina (Charlottesville, VA, 1944), p. 10.

lvi[56] J. Herman Schauinger, *William Gaston: Carolinian* , Bruce Publishing Company, 1949, p. 3.

lvii[57] Dorothy Perry Brawley, The Bolling-Gay-Gaston-Brawley Paper Trail with Allied Families and Friends (1995), p. 109.

lviii[58] J. Herman Schauinger, *William Gaston: Carolinian* , Bruce Publishing Company, 1949, p. 201.

lix[59] Birthplace according to Max Perry.

lx[60] Daughters of the American Revolution Lineage Book, p. 322.

lxi[61] Anna Reger Gaston, Gaston Family Lines of Somerset, "Somerset County Historical Quarterly," Somerville, NJ, Vol. 5 (1916) (http://homepages.rootsweb.com/~windmill/html/somersev.html), p. 36.

447

lxii[62] Anna Reger Gaston, *Gaston Family Lines of Somerset, "Somerset County Historical Quarterly," Somerville, NJ, Vol. 5 (1916)* (http://homepages.rootsweb.com/~windmill/html/somersev.html), Ref: NJ Archives, Vol III, pp 89, 99.

lxiii[63] Jane Farrell Burgess, 11700 Dinwiddie Dr, Rockville, MD 20852, *The Gaston Genealogy* (1989), p. 54.

lxiv[64] *One World Tree* (www.ancestry.com).

lxv[65] Rev. Frank R. Symmes, History of the Old Tennent Church, 2nd Edition (1904), p. 211.

lxvi[66] Charles A. Hanna, *Ohio Valley Genealogies* , Genealogical Publishing Co, Baltimore MD, 1989 (orig. pub. 1900), p. 43.

lxvii[67] Peter J. Topoly & Jane Carson Topoly, Fort Washington, MD 20744-2535 (http://topolyp.com/JanesNames/).

lxviii[68] Charles A. Hanna, *Ohio Valley Genealogies* , Genealogical Publishing Co, Baltimore MD, 1989 (orig. pub. 1900), pp. 43-44.

lxix[69] Charles A. Hanna, *Ohio Valley Genealogies* , Genealogical Publishing Co, Baltimore MD, 1989 (orig. pub. 1900), p. 44.

lxx[70] Headstone, Inscription reads "Sacred to the memory of Hugh Gaston who departed this life on the 25th of June 1808 in the 75th year of his age".

lxxi[71] Anna Reger Gaston, Gaston Family Lines of Somerset, "Somerset County Historical Quarterly," Somerville, NJ, Vol. 5 (1916) (http://homepages.rootsweb.com/~windmill/html/somersev.html), p. 37.

lxxii[72] Headstone - Date calculated from age at death, Inscription reads "In Memory of MARY the Wife of HUGH GASTON, Daughter of William and Mary Sloan, who departed this life August the 14th 1766 in the 25th year of her age".

lxxiii[73] John Littell, *Family Records or Genealogies of the First Settlers of the Passaic Valley (1851)* (http://www.archive.org/details/familyrecordsorg00litt), p. 198.

lxxiv[74] Headstone - Date calculated from age at death.

lxxv[75] Headstone, Age at death given as 8m 13d.

lxxvi[76] Headstone, Age at death given as 11y 7m 27d.

lxxvii[77] Birth record - On file at Mormon Family History Center, Kensington, MD.

lxxviii[78] Headstone - Age at death given as 3y 7m 13d, which varies by nine days from the birth/death dates.

lxxix[79] John Littell, *Family Records or Genealogies of the First Settlers of the Passaic Valley (1851)* (http://www.archive.org/details/familyrecordsorg00litt), p. 202.

lxxx[80] John Littell, *Family Records or Genealogies of the First Settlers of the Passaic Valley (1851)* (http://www.archive.org/details/familyrecordsorg00litt), p. 203.

lxxxi[81] John Littell, *Family Records or Genealogies of the First Settlers of the Passaic Valley (1851)* (http://www.archive.org/details/familyrecordsorg00litt), p. 69.

lxxxii[82] Jane Farrell Burgess, 11700 Dinwiddie Dr, Rockville, MD 20852, *The Gaston Genealogy* (1989), p. 52.

lxxxiii[83] Rev. Frank R. Symmes, History of the Old Tennent Church, 2nd Edition (1904), p. 390.

lxxxiv[84] Charles A. Hanna, *Ohio Valley Genealogies* , Genealogical Publishing Co, Baltimore MD, 1989 (orig. pub. 1900), p. 113.

lxxxv[85] Max Perry, *American Descendants of William Gaston and Mary Olivet Lemon* (Midland, TX, 1989), Other sources give circa 1803.

lxxxvi[86] Max Perry provided birth/death dates, as well as first name of Margaret. Other sources give only the last name, which was Linn. In the marriage records in Monmouth Co, N.J. her last name was Lines.

lxxxvii[87] Max Perry, *American Descendants of William Gaston and Mary Olivet Lemon* (Midland, TX, 1989), Date of birth reported as 1762, which cannot be right. The father was born ca 1758 and the mother ca 1766. The date 1792 could have been intended.

lxxxviii[88] Jane Farrell Burgess, 11700 Dinwiddie Dr, Rockville, MD 20852, *The Gaston Genealogy* (1989), p. 40.

lxxxix[89] Jane Farrell Burgess, 11700 Dinwiddie Dr, Rockville, MD 20852, *The Gaston Genealogy* (1989), p. 44.

xc[90] Jane Farrell Burgess, 11700 Dinwiddie Dr, Rockville, MD 20852, *The Gaston Genealogy* (1989), p. 43.

xci[91] George M. Kasson, *Genealogy of a Part of the Kasson Family in the United States and Ireland (1882)* (Brigham Young University Family History Archives, http://www.lib.byu.edu/fhc/).

xcii[92] George M. Kasson, *Genealogy of a Part of the Kasson Family in the United States and Ireland (1882)* (Brigham Young University Family History Archives, http://www.lib.byu.edu/fhc/), p. 8.

xciii[93] Jane Farrell Burgess, 11700 Dinwiddie Dr, Rockville, MD 20852, *The Gaston Genealogy* (1989), p. 46.

xciv[94] Bob Gaston, 139 Victoria St, Longview, WA 98632, <bgaston@tdn.com>, in "Gaston Crier Newsletter," Vol 1, No 2, Nov 1997, at http://mvn.net/genealogy "First Families of America," p. 135, gives marriage in 1786.

xcv[95] Bob Gaston, 139 Victoria St, Longview, WA 98632, <bgaston@tdn.com>, in "Gaston Crier Newsletter," Vol 1, No 2, Nov 1997, at http://mvn.net/genealogy "First Families of America," p. 135, cites same year.

xcvi[96] Jane Farrell Burgess, 11700 Dinwiddie Dr, Rockville, MD 20852, *The Gaston Genealogy* (1989), p. 45.

xcvii[97] Jane Farrell Burgess, 11700 Dinwiddie Dr, Rockville, MD 20852, *The Gaston Genealogy* (1989), His name appears in Richmond, MA marriage records as Henry Gasten. Parents not listed. p. 45.

xcviii[98] *Vital Records of Richmond, Massachusetts, to the Year 1850* (New England Historical Genealogical Society), p. 63.

xcix[99] Audley DeForest Gaston & Judy Gaston Woodard, Austin, TX.

c[100] His family bible, per Edward H. Couey, Scotts Mills, OR. Other sources have given only 1740 for his birth.

ci[101] Death date provided by the Judge, with age at death indicated as 84.

cii[102] *Reid Family Genealogy* (on file at Daughters of the American Revolution Library, Washington, DC).

ciii[103] Marilyn Merritt, Blowing Rock, NC <marilynmerritt@charter.net> (a Gaston descendant).

civ[104] *Reid Family Genealogy* (on file at Daughters of the American Revolution Library, Washington, DC), Birthplace has also been reported at Rowan, NC. [Ancestry World Tree Project g765, posted at http://awt.ancestry.com by <briar@worldnet.att.net>].

cv[105] Birth year provided by a Judge in the family line who had determined that the year 1739 appearing elsewhere (Ohio Valley Genealogies, p. 40) was incorrect.

cvi[106] The Judge.

cvii[107] Rob Salzman, Beaverton, OR, *e-familytree.net* (http://www.e-familytree.net/surnames.htm).

cviii[108] Joyce Gaston Reece <bjreece@bellsouth.net>.

cix[109] Joyce Gaston Reece <bjreece@bellsouth.net>, Birthplace: Chester District, SC.

cx[110] Bill Gaston, Austin TX <bgaston2@mindspring.com>, *Descendants: The Huguenot John Jean Gaston b: About 1600, France* (http://home.mindspring.com/~bgaston2/), http://wc.rootsweb.com/cgi-bin/igm.cgi?op=GET&db=rscrain&id=I03207 http://www.familysearch.org/Eng/Search/AF/family_group_record.asp?familyid=5784929.

cxi[111] Bill Gaston, Austin TX <bgaston2@mindspring.com>, *Descendants: The Huguenot John Jean Gaston b: About 1600, France* (http://home.mindspring.com/~bgaston2/), http://www.meetmyrelatives.com/familytree1/gp583.htm.

cxii[112] Jane Farrell Burgess, 11700 Dinwiddie Dr, Rockville, MD 20852, *The Gaston Genealogy* (1989), p. 85.

cxiii[113] *Daughters of the American Revolution Lineage Book*, Vol 159, p. 287, lineage of Jane Gaston Ketchen, DAR No. 158967.

cxiv[114] Daughters of the American Revolution Lineage Book, p. 103.

cxv[115] Jane Farrell Burgess, 11700 Dinwiddie Dr, Rockville, MD 20852, *The Gaston Genealogy* (1989), p. 84.

cxvi[116] *Daughters of the American Revolution Lineage Book*, Vol 29, p. 103, lineage of Janie Gaston Gage, DAR No. 28278.

cxvii[117] *Heritage History of Chester County, South Carolina* , 1982, Birth date given by Burgess, "The Gaston Genealogies," as 4/10/1767, based on cemetery information. Hanna, "Ohio Valley Genealogies," p 41, gives only 1768. p. 196.

cxviii[118] The Judge, Some sources (e.g., Ohio Valley Genealogies) have birth date as Dec 4 1796, but Judge Gaston determined it to be 1795.

cxix[119] The Judge, Some sources (e.g. Ohio Valley Genealogies, p. 41) have birthdate as 1798, but Judge Gaston determined it to be 1797.

cxx[120] Lineage Book, National Society of the Daughters of the American Revolution.

cxxi[121] Lineage Book, National Society of the Daughters of the American Revolution, p. 103.

cxxii[122] Dorothy Perry Brawley, The Bolling-Gay-Gaston-Brawley Paper Trail with Allied Families and Friends (1995), p. 111.

cxxiii[123] 1900 Census.

cxxiv[124] Mary Gaston Gee (1899-1987), The Ancestry and Descendants of Amzi Williford Gaston II (1841-1911) of Spartanburg County, South Carolina (Charlottesville, VA, 1944), p. 13.

cxxv[125] Jane Farrell Burgess, 11700 Dinwiddie Dr, Rockville, MD 20852, *The Gaston Genealogy* (1989), p. 88 & 96.

cxxvi[126] Nancy A. Sicotte, Palo Alto, CA <NanSicotte@aol.com>.

cxxvii[127] Lineage Book, National Society of the Daughters of the American Revolution, p. 136, which omits the woman's first name. Name Mary provided by direct descendant Frank Reich, Wentzville, MO.

cxxviii[128] Jane Farrell Burgess, 11700 Dinwiddie Dr, Rockville, MD 20852, *The Gaston Genealogy* (1989), p. 88.

cxxix[129] Mary Gaston Gee (1899-1987), The Ancestry and Descendants of Amzi Williford Gaston II (1841-1911) of Spartanburg County, South Carolina (Charlottesville, VA, 1944), p. 14.

cxxx[130] Larry Charles Slaughter, Amarillo, TX, citing Mary Gaston Gee's "The Ancestry & Descendants of Amzi Williford Gaston II (1841-1911) of Spartanburg Co, SC" and other sources.

cxxxi[131] Mary Gaston Gee (1899-1987), The Ancestry and Descendants of Amzi Williford Gaston II (1841-1911) of Spartanburg County, South Carolina (Charlottesville, VA, 1944), p. 18.

cxxxii[132] Mary Gaston Gee (1899-1987), The Ancestry and Descendants of Amzi Williford Gaston II (1841-1911) of Spartanburg County, South Carolina (Charlottesville, VA, 1944), p. 16.

cxxxiii[133] Mary Gaston Gee (1899-1987), The Ancestry and Descendants of Amzi Williford Gaston II (1841-1911) of Spartanburg County, South Carolina (Charlottesville, VA, 1944), p. 15.

cxxxiv[134] Findagrave.com (http://www.findagrave.com).

cxxxv[135] Bill Gaston, Austin TX <bgaston2@mindspring.com>, *Descendants: The Huguenot John Jean Gaston b: About 1600, France* (http://home.mindspring.com/~bgaston2/), http://wc.rootsweb.com/cgi-bin/igm.cgi?op=GET&db=loisbranch&id=I44843.

cxxxvi[136] Bill Gaston, Austin TX <bgaston2@mindspring.com>, *Descendants: The Huguenot John Jean Gaston b: About 1600, France* (http://home.mindspring.com/~bgaston2/), http://www.familysearch.org/Eng/Search/AF/individual_record.asp?recid=21736460 &l.

cxxxvii[137] Bill Gaston, Austin TX <bgaston2@mindspring.com>, *Descendants: The Huguenot John Jean Gaston b: About 1600, France* (http://home.mindspring.com/~bgaston2/), http://www.familysearch.org/Eng/Search/AF/family_group_record.asp?familyid=6802956

http://www.jenforum.com/whitney/messages/897.html.

cxxxviii[138] Bill Gaston, Austin TX <bgaston2@mindspring.com>, *Descendants: The Huguenot John Jean Gaston b: About 1600, France* (http://home.mindspring.com/~bgaston2/), http://awtc.ancestry.com/cgibin/igm.cgi?op=GET&db=*v23t0337&id=I0381.

cxxxix[139] Bill Gaston, Austin TX <bgaston2@mindspring.com>, *Descendants: The Huguenot John Jean Gaston b: About 1600, France* (http://home.mindspring.com/~bgaston2/), http://wc.rootsweb.com/cgi-bin/igm.cgi?op=GET&db=loisbranch&id=I44844.

cxl[140] Bill Gaston, Austin TX <bgaston2@mindspring.com>, *Descendants: The Huguenot John Jean Gaston b: About 1600, France* (http://home.mindspring.com/~bgaston2/), http://www.familysearch.org/Eng/Search/IGI/family_group_record.asp?familyid=345970715&indi_id
=100384983813&lds=1&region=11&frompage=99.

cxli[141] Bill Gaston, Austin TX <bgaston2@mindspring.com>, *Descendants: The Huguenot John Jean Gaston b: About 1600, France* (http://home.mindspring.com/~bgaston2/), http://wc.rootsweb.com/cgi-bin/igm.cgi?op=GET&db=wroll&id=I49581

http://www.familysearch.org/Eng/Search/IGI/family_group_record.asp?familyid=286487807&indi_id
=100242365249&lds=1&region=11&frompage=99.

cxlii[142] J. Herman Schauinger, *William Gaston: Carolinian* , Bruce Publishing Company, 1949, p. 2.

cxliii[143] J. Herman Schauinger, *William Gaston: Carolinian* , Bruce Publishing Company, 1949, p. 224.

cxliv[144] Mary Gaston Gee (1899-1987), The Ancestry and Descendants of Amzi Williford Gaston II (1841-1911) of Spartanburg County, South Carolina (Charlottesville, VA, 1944), p. 11.

cxlv[145] *Colonial Families of the United States, 1912* (republished 1966 by Genealogical Publishing Co, Baltimore, MD), Vol II, p. 316.

cxlvi[146] 1850 Census.

cxlvii[147] J. Herman Schauinger, *William Gaston: Carolinian* , Bruce Publishing Company, 1949, p. 4.

cxlviii[148] Wikipedia.org (http://www.wikipedia.org).

cxlix[149] J. Herman Schauinger, *William Gaston: Carolinian* , Bruce Publishing Company, 1949, p. 216.

cl[150] James Davis, Atlanta, GA <caroljim@mindspring.com>, a direct descendant (Gaston, Knox, Moss, Bonine, Davis).

cli[151] Lineage Book, National Society of the Daughters of the American Revolution, p. 322.

clii[152] Rev. Frank R. Symmes, History of the Old Tennent Church, 2nd Edition (1904), p. 230.

cliii[153] Headstone, Inscription reads: John Gaston, Sen., died Apr 6 1829, aged 76y 6m 20d.

cliv[154] Death Record - Birth date calculated from age at death.

clv[155] G. J. Whittaker, a Gaston descendant and researcher.

clvi[156] Harrison County Death Records, Clarksburg, WV, Identified as Anna Gaston, born in New Jersey, dau of Andrew & Sarah Davison (spelled this way in original handwritten record, but Dawson in a handwritten transcribed copy), wife of John Gaston, died Aug 8 1854, age 89y 5m 19d. (Age is at variance with headstone inscription, which states death date Aug 8 1854, age 89y 5m 17d.) Informant: William Gaston, son.

clvii[157] *Daughters of the American Revolution Lineage Book*, Vol 114, p. 231, lineage of Charlotte Gaston Pence, DAR No. 113695.

clviii[158] Charles A. Hanna, *Ohio Valley Genealogies* , Genealogical Publishing Co, Baltimore MD, 1989 (orig. pub. 1900), pp. 42, 43.

clix[159] Rev. Frank R. Symmes, History of the Old Tennent Church, 2nd Edition (1904), p. 210.

clx[160] Headstone, - Inscription reads "In Memory of Charety Gaston, Consort of John Gaston, Who departed this life February 15th A.D. 1821, aged 86 years & 11 months and 2 days." Spelling "Charety" conflicts with the more conventional "Charity" provided by Hanna.

clxi[161] Jane Carson Topoly, Fort Washington, MD 20744 (http://www.reocities.com/heartland/8904/).

clxii[162] Peter J. Topoly & Jane Carson Topoly, 10015 Mike Road, Fort Washington, MD, give birth as 1769 in Northampton Co, PA, but 1767 date in Somerset Co, NJ, cited by Anna Reger Gaston, appears more likely.

clxiii[163] Peter J. Topoly & Jane Carson Topoly, 10015 Mike Road, Fort Washington, MD 20744-2535, citing highly reliable original sources. But "History of the Upper Ohio Valley," p. 635, gives birthplace as Washington Co, PA.

clxiv[164] Sons of the American Revolution Membership Applications, 1889-1970 , Ancestry.com, SAR Membership No. 90621.

clxv[165] J. A. Caldwell, History of Belmont & Jefferson Counties, Ohio (1880), p. 373.

clxvi[166] History of the Upper Ohio Valley (Brant & Feller - 1890), p. 635.

clxvii[167] Birthplace per Peter J. Topoly & Jane Carson Topoly, concurring on birthdate.

clxviii[168] Birthplace per Peter J. Topoly & Jane Carson Topoly, date given as Sep 6 1811.

clxix[169] Daughters of the American Revolution Lineage Book, Vol. 99, p. 175, lineage of Mrs. Cordelia Gaston Christy, DAR ID No. 98560.

clxx[170] John Littell, Family Records or Genealogies of the First Settlers of the Passaic Valley (1851) (http://www.archive.org/details/familyrecordsorg00litt), p. 204.

clxxi[171] One World Tree (www.ancestry.com), Orange County, North Carolina land and deed records show that a Mary Gomer bought land in Orange County in 1794.

clxxii[172] Rev. Frank R. Symmes, History of the Old Tennent Church, 2nd Edition (1904), Citing research of Prof. Harold W. Johnston, Indiana University. p. 419.

clxxiii[173] Charles A. Hanna, Ohio Valley Genealogies , Genealogical Publishing Co, Baltimore MD, 1989 (orig. pub. 1900), Jane Farrell Burgess, in "The Gaston Genealogy," p. 44, shows in a list of births in Berkshire Co, MA, a Wm Gaston born on 9/4/1772, son of Wm & Naomi Gaston. This cannot be the same family. p. 46.

clxxiv[174] Headstone, Inscription reads: "SACRED in the memory of MARGARET GASTON, widow of the late John M. McCowen, who died Nov 3rd 1827, aged 38 years & 4 days.".

clxxv[175] Headstone, http://ftp.rootsweb.com/pub/usgenweb/pa/northumberland/cemeteries/warrior.txt.

clxxvi[176] Grave marker.

clxxvii[177] Max Perry, American Descendants of William Gaston and Mary Olivet Lemon (Midland, TX, 1989), p. 145.

clxxviii[178] Headstone (year only), Hanna's "Ohio Valley Genealogies," p. 47, reports birth/death dates as Sep 22 1792 - Aug 13 1824. But headstone dates are 1789 - 1824. http://ftp.rootsweb.com/pub/usgenweb/pa/northumberland/cemeteries/warrior.txt.

clxxix[179] Freehold, New Jersey Historical Society.

clxxx[180] American Ancestry, Vol. V (originally published 1890 by Joel Munsell's Sons; republished 1968 by Genealogical Publishing Co, Baltimore), For month and year only. Max Perry reports date as the 10th. p. 104.

clxxxi[181] American Ancestry, Vol. V (originally published 1890 by Joel Munsell's Sons; republished 1968 by Genealogical Publishing Co, Baltimore), Vol V, p. 104.

clxxxii[182] Colonial Families of the United States, 1912 (republished 1966 by Genealogical Publishing Co, Baltimore, MD), Vol III, p. 176.

clxxxiii[183] Obituary, Mortuary Notice, July 15, 1824, The Times (newspaper), Connecticut, "Died - At Plainfield on the 29th May last, Mr. John Gaston, Son of Capt. Alexander Gaston of Killingley, age 17.".

clxxxiv[184] Gene & Norma Harrington Maas, *Maas Family Roots & Branches - Gaston Roots* (http://www.genemaas.net/Gaston_roots.htm).

clxxxv[185] George M. Kasson, *Genealogy of a Part of the Kasson Family in the United States and Ireland (1882)* (Brigham Young University Family History Archives, http://www.lib.byu.edu/fhc/), p. 15.

clxxxvi[186] George M. Kasson, *Genealogy of a Part of the Kasson Family in the United States and Ireland (1882)* (Brigham Young University Family History Archives, http://www.lib.byu.edu/fhc/), p. 16.

clxxxvii[187] George M. Kasson, *Genealogy of a Part of the Kasson Family in the United States and Ireland (1882)* (Brigham Young University Family History Archives, http://www.lib.byu.edu/fhc/), On page 8 of the Kasson genealogy, a birth date of Apr 30 1792 is cited for this Alexander Kasson, but on page 16 it is shown as Apr 3 1792.

clxxxviii[188] George M. Kasson, *Genealogy of a Part of the Kasson Family in the United States and Ireland (1882)* (Brigham Young University Family History Archives, http://www.lib.byu.edu/fhc/), p. 17.

clxxxix[189] Robert B. "Bob" Gaston, Longview, WA 98632 <bgaston@tdn.com>, citing letters of Elvira Gaston Platt and church records from Danby, NY and Oberlin, OH.

cxc[190] Obituary.

cxci[191] Obituary of wife.

cxcii[192] George M. Kasson, *Genealogy of a Part of the Kasson Family in the United States and Ireland (1882)* (Brigham Young University Family History Archives, http://www.lib.byu.edu/fhc/), p. 42.

cxciii[193] First Families of America, p. 135.

cxciv[194] Jane Farrell Burgess, 11700 Dinwiddie Dr, Rockville, MD 20852, *The Gaston Genealogy* (1989), Age given in Richmond, MA death record as 4 years. p. 46.

cxcv[195] Jane Farrell Burgess, 11700 Dinwiddie Dr, Rockville, MD 20852, *The Gaston Genealogy* (1989), Age given in Richmond, MA death record as 4 1/2 months at time of death on Dec 5 1816. But Kasson Genealogy reports death date as Dec 9 1816. p. 46.

cxcvi[196] *Vital Records of Richmond, Massachusetts, to the Year 1850* (New England Historical Genealogical Society), p. 24.

cxcvii[197] Jane Farrell Burgess, 11700 Dinwiddie Dr, Rockville, MD 20852, *The Gaston Genealogy* (1989), Age given in Richmond, MA death record as 18 years at time of death on Jan 13 1838. But Kasson Genealogy reports death date as Jan 17 1838. p. 46.

cxcviii[198] George M. Kasson, *Genealogy of a Part of the Kasson Family in the United States and Ireland (1882)* (Brigham Young University Family History Archives, http://www.lib.byu.edu/fhc/), p. 43.

cxcix[199] Connie Chaffee Leaman <R.leaman@comcast.net>, 4th g-granddaughter of Esther Jane Gaston and Ebenezer Elliott.

cc[200] Connie Chaffee Leaman <R.leaman@comcast.net>, 4th g-granddaughter of Esther Jane Gaston and Ebenezer Elliott, Marriage date thought to be Sep 25 1794.

cci[201] Bill Couch, *The Original Arkansas Genealogy Project, Reid Family* (http://www.couchgenweb.com/family/reid.htm).

ccii[202] Elizabeth Weir McPherson, *Reid, Gaston and Simonton, Related Families* , [per Missy McPherson, gomissymc@aol.com].

cciii[203] <briar@worldnet.att.net>, *Ancestry World Tree Project g765* (posted at http://awt.ancestry.com, citing Broderbund WFT Vol 2, Ed 1, Tree #1670).

cciv[204] Joyce Gaston Reece <bjreece@bellsouth.net>, Birthplace: Richland, Chester District, SC.

ccv[205] Joyce Gaston Reece <bjreece@bellsouth.net>, Place of death reported as either Logan Co, KY, or Marion Co, IL.

ccvi[206] Bill Gaston, Austin TX <bgaston2@mindspring.com>, *Descendants: The Huguenot John Jean Gaston b: About 1600, France* (http://home.mindspring.com/~bgaston2/), http://www.familysearch.org/Eng/Search/AF/family_group_record.asp?familyid=6802 903.

ccvii[207] Chalmers Gaston Davidson, *Gaston of Chester* , Davidson Printing Co, Davidson NC (1956), Based chiefly on notes and records preserved by Judge Arthur Lee Gaston, and privately printed according to his will. p. xiii.

ccviii[208] Daughters of the American Revolution Lineage Book, Vol XLIX, 1904, p. 134.

ccix[209] 1870 Census.

ccx[210] 1880 Census.

ccxi[211] 1910 Census.

ccxii[212] Frank Reich, 2824 S. Pointe Prairie Rd, Wentzville, MO 63385, *Gaston Crier, Newsletter Vol 1, No 2, Nov 1997* (www.mvn.net/genealogy).

ccxiii[213] Mary Gaston Gee (1899-1987), The Ancestry and Descendants of Amzi Williford Gaston II (1841-1911) of Spartanburg County, South Carolina (Charlottesville, VA, 1944), p. 19.

ccxiv[214] Mary Gaston Gee (1899-1987), The Ancestry and Descendants of Amzi Williford Gaston II (1841-1911) of Spartanburg County, South Carolina (Charlottesville, VA, 1944), p. 21.

ccxv[215] Mary Gaston Gee (1899-1987), The Ancestry and Descendants of Amzi Williford Gaston II (1841-1911) of Spartanburg County, South Carolina (Charlottesville, VA, 1944), Notes.

ccxvi[216] Dorothy Perry Brawley, *The Bolling-Gay-Gaston-Brawley Paper Trail with Allied Families and Friends* (1995), citing Jean Bradley Anderson in "The Kirklands of Ayr Mount" (UNC Press, Chapel Hill, NC, 1991), p. 163. p. 111.

ccxvii[217] J. Herman Schauinger, *William Gaston: Carolinian* , Bruce Publishing Company, 1949, p. 97.

ccxviii[218] J. Herman Schauinger, *William Gaston: Carolinian* , Bruce Publishing Company, 1949, p. 96.

ccxix[219] Headstone. Age at death given as 76y 11m 28d.

ccxx[220] Rev. Frank R. Symmes, History of the Old Tennent Church, 2nd Edition (1904), p. 294.

ccxxi[221] D. V. Perrine, Freehold, NJ, *History of the Old Tennent Church* (as copied from a Bible record in possession of Miss B. F. Rightmire).

ccxxii[222] Rev. Frank R. Symmes, History of the Old Tennent Church, 2nd Edition (1904), p. 449.

ccxxiii[223] Headstone, Inscription reads, in part, "In memory of Catharine [sic], wife of William Gaston.".

ccxxiv[224] Rev. Frank R. Symmes, History of the Old Tennent Church, 2nd Edition (1904), p. 283.

ccxxv[225] 1850 Census, Harrison County, (W)VA.

ccxxvi[226] Harrison County Marriage Records, Clarksburg, WV, Marriages 1784-1850.

ccxxvii[227] *Harrison County WV Marriages 1785-1894* , Wes Cochran, 2515 10th Ave, Parkersburg, WV 26101 (1985).

ccxxviii[228] Death record of husband.

ccxxix[229] William F. Donnelly, *The Wests of Duck Creek, Harrison County, Virginia (now West Virginia)* , Gateway Press, Baltimore MD, 1997, p. 411.

ccxxx[230] *Cemeteries of Grant District, Harrison County, WV* , Harrison County Genealogical Society, Clarksburg, WV.

ccxxxi[231] William F. Donnelly, *The Wests of Duck Creek, Harrison County, Virginia (now West Virginia)* , Gateway Press, Baltimore MD, 1997, p. 507.

ccxxxii[232] William F. Donnelly, *The Wests of Duck Creek, Harrison County, Virginia (now West Virginia)* , Gateway Press, Baltimore MD, 1997, p. 198.

ccxxxiii[233] Headstone, - Age at death given as 72y 7m 15d. Name on headstone is Sarah West.

ccxxxiv[234] E. Murray Taylor, Jr., 106 Carli Ct, Lake Mary FL 32746, *Ancestral Record of John Gaston and Anna Davison* (http://www3.sympatico.ca/bkinnon/taylor.htm).

ccxxxv[235] William F. Donnelly, *The Wests of Duck Creek, Harrison County, Virginia (now West Virginia)*, Gateway Press, Baltimore MD, 1997, Birthplace given as either Harrison Co, (W)VA, or Ohio,citing "W. Guy Tetrick Collection" (roll 183), in custody of Historical Collection, Colson Hall, West Virginia University, Morgantown, WV. p. 411.

ccxxxvi[236] Lewis County Death Records, Weston, WV.

ccxxxvii[237] Lewis County Death Records, Weston, WV, Identified as Hugh Gaston, age 100y 1m 21d, died Jul 26 1888. Cause of death: Old age. Parents: (blank). Place of birth: New Jersey. Occupation: Farmer. Marital Status: Widower. Informant & relationship: (blank), step-daughter. DR Bk 1, p. 165.

ccxxxviii[238] Harrison County Marriage Records, Clarksburg, WV, MR Years 1784-1850.

ccxxxix[239] 1830 Census, Harrison County, (W)VA.

ccxl[240] W. Guy Tetrick files.

ccxli[241] Lewis County Marriage Records, Weston, WV, The handwritten record is actually a list of four marriages performed by a particular minister between Aug 1847 and Oct 1848. It reads, in part, "I hereby certify that I joined together ... Mr. Hugh Gaston and Miss Elizabeth Washburn on the first day of June 1848 ... agreeably to a license issued from the clerk's office of Lewis county court. Given under my hand this 29th day of May 1849. Carr Bailey, Minister of the Baptist Church." Just below that entry is a handwritten statement reading "The above certificate of marriages was presented in the clerk's office of Lewis county court on the 11th day of June 1849. Testa John Morrow, Clerk", MR Bk 3, p. 4.

ccxlii[242] *Lewis County WV Marriages 1817-1880*, Wes Cochran, 2515 10th Ave, Parkersburg, WV 26101.

ccxliii[243] Lewis County Death Records, Weston, WV, The 1870 Census of Lewis County (Willey Township), WV, p. 89, reports her birth place as Virginia. But this is contradicted by her death record and other sources stating that she was born in Kentucky.

ccxliv[244] Lewis County Death Records, Weston, WV, Identified as Elizabeth Gaston, age 83, died Sep 16 1885. Cause of death: Old age. Name of parents: Unknown. Place of birth: Kentucky. Spouse: Hugh Gaston. Informant & relationship: Marion Gaston, son. DR Bk 1, p. 151.

ccxlv[245] 1860 Census, Lewis County, (W)VA.

ccxlvi[246] 1870 Census, Lewis County, WV (Willey Township).

ccxlvii[247] 1880 Census, Lewis County, WV.

ccxlviii[248] *W. Guy Tetrick files*, Identified by grand-nephew Ira Dow Gaston as one of his grandfather's brothers, born the same day as another brother, John.

ccxlix[249] Doddridge County Court House, West Union, WV, DR 1-56, 78-6-27.

ccl[250] *W. Guy Tetrick files*, Identified by grand-nephew Ira Dow Gaston as one of his grandfather's brothers.

ccli[251] W. N. Hurley, Jr., *Maddox: A Southern Maryland Family*, Heritage Books, Bowie, MD, ISBN 0-788-0123-8, 1994, p. 105.

cclii[252] Harrison County Marriage Records, Clarksburg, WV, Donnelly, in "Wests of Duck Creek, p. 457, reports marriage date as Dec 23 1811.

ccliii[253] W. N. Hurley, Jr., *Maddox: A Southern Maryland Family*, Heritage Books, Bowie, MD, ISBN 0-788-0123-8, 1994.

ccliv[254] Raymond A. Mann <dermann@earthlink.net>.

cclv[255] Susie Davis Nicholson, *Davis - The Settlers of Salem, West Virginia*, Gordon Printing Co, Strasburg OH, 1979 (Revised & Enlarged), p. 18.

cclvi[256] Headstone, Age at death given as 88y 4m 10d.

cclvii[257] Headstone. Age given as 88Y 4M 10D.

cclviii[258] 1850 Census, Harrison County, (W)VA, 94.

cclix[259] Lewis County Marriage Records, Weston, WV, MR Bk 5, p. 12.

cclx[260] Lewis County Court House, Weston, WV, She was identified as age 24, born & residing in Lewis Co, the daughter of Lewis D. and Margaret Swisher. He was identified as age 23, born & residing in Harrison Co, the son of John and Elizabeth Gaston. MR Bk 5, p. 12.

cclxi[261] *Lewis County WV Marriages 1817-1880* , Wes Cochran, 2515 10th Ave, Parkersburg, WV 26101, Identified as Andrew A. [sic] Gaston & Sarah A. Swisher. Married Feb 5 1859.

cclxii[262] Lewis County Court House, Weston, WV, MR Bk 5, p. 12.

cclxiii[263] Taylor County Death Records, Grafton, WV, Identified as Deborah Taylor, dau of John & Anna Gaston, wife of Joseph Taylor, d. Nov 10 1885 in Taylor Co, WV, at age 87y 3m 1d. Informant: W. D. Taylor, son. DR Bk 2, p. 34.

cclxiv[264] William F. Donnelly, *The Wests of Duck Creek, Harrison County, Virginia (now West Virginia)* , Gateway Press, Baltimore MD, 1997, p. 457 & 557.

cclxv[265] Harrison County Marriage Records, Clarksburg, WV, A marriage bond was executed on Feb 11 1822 between Joseph Taylor and John Gaston for the marriage of Joseph Taylor and Deborah Gaston. Although there is no indication as to when the wedding ceremony took place, the Feb 11 1822 date is used here for that purpose. Marriage Bonds Bk 3, p. 430.

cclxvi[266] Headstone, Inscription does not give a birthdate, but reads that he died on Sep 2 1868 "In His 75 Year of his Age." This would put his birth in about 1793.

cclxvii[267] 1820 Census, Harrison County, (W)VA , Age given as 27.

cclxviii[268] Jeffrey Wood <woodfam@ccia.com> <wood1478@hotmail.com> (Ancestry World Tree, http://awt.ancestry.com).

cclxix[269] Lewis County Court House, Weston, WV, His name appears in the marriage record as Isaac Switzen. MR Bk 1, p. 56.

cclxx[270] 1870 Census, Lewis County, WV (Lincoln Township).

cclxxi[271] 1860 Census, Harrison County, (W)VA.

cclxxii[272] Lewis County Marriage Records, Weston, WV, Her name appears in the marriage record as Charlotte Switzen. MR Bk 1/1829, p. 51.

cclxxiii[273] Headstone, age at death as 68y 2m 2d.

cclxxiv[274] Minnie Kendall Lowther, *History of Ritchie County* (1911, reprinted 1999, McClain Printing Co, Parsons WV, http://McClainPrinting.com).

cclxxv[275] Headstone - Date calculated from age at death, (5y 7m 8d), although other sources (e.g., E. Murray Taylor, Jr. [1I-3]) cite April 3 1834.

cclxxvi[276] Harrison County Death Records, Clarksburg, WV.

cclxxvii[277] Place of birth given as Lewis County, Virginia, in "Early Settlers of Upper Monongahela Valley" by Butcher, p. 869. Other sources (e.g., Murray Taylor) cite Harrison County.

cclxxviii[278] Lauri Buell Boaz, 819 Spruce Drive, Carmel, IN 46033, based on notes of grandmother Frances Virginia Helmick.

cclxxix[279] Katie Dailey Gaston, a Gaston family historian, in a letter to Jacquie Gaston Blevins dated March 19 1968. But DAR Lineage Book, p. 357, in showing lineage for Beulah Standord Gaston (#9971), gives Mary Estep's death as 1851.

cclxxx[280] 1860 Census.

cclxxxi[281] Headstone, - Inscription reads "Samuel Gaston Sen., died Feb 21 1853 in the 81 year of his age.".

cclxxxii[282] *Daughters of the American Revolution Lineage Book*, Vol 163, p. 77, lineage of Mildred Gaston Hibbs, DAR No. 162224.

cclxxxiii[283] Headstone, - Inscription reads "Margaret, wife of Saml Gaston, died Aug 14 1841, aged 65 yrs.".

cclxxxiv[284] Headstone, - Inscription reads "Tephanes, wife of Samuel Gaston, died Dec 24 1883 in her 88th year".

cclxxxv[285] Gordon E. Tye, Jr.

cclxxxvi[286] Maria A. Minear, Box 283, Hardin, MT 59034 <mminear11@mcn.net>.

cclxxxvii[287] U.S. Federal Census Mortality Schedule.

cclxxxviii[288] Iowa State Census, 1856.

cclxxxix[289] Family Bible.

ccxc[290] *History of the Upper Ohio Valley* (Brant & Feller - 1890), p. 146.

ccxci[291] Douglas J. Bower <dwsjdb@rtcol.com> (posted at http://awt.ancestry.com).

ccxcii[292] J. A. Caldwell, History of Belmont & Jefferson Counties, Ohio (1880), p. 278.

ccxciii[293] 1860 Census, Belmont County, OH (Union Twp).

ccxciv[294] J. A. Caldwell, History of Belmont & Jefferson Counties, Ohio (1880), p. 183.

ccxcv[295] Ohio Marriages, 1803-1900 (online database) , Ancestry.com.

ccxcvi[296] John Littell, *Family Records or Genealogies of the First Settlers of the Passaic Valley (1851)* (http://www.archive.org/details/familyrecordsorg00litt), p. 402.

ccxcvii[297] U.S. and International Marriage Records, 1560-1900 , Ancestry.com.

ccxcviii[298] Charles A. Hanna, *Ohio Valley Genealogies* , Genealogical Publishing Co, Baltimore MD, 1989 (orig. pub. 1900), Max Perry gives marriage date as October 17, 1809, but Hanna shows it as 1805. p. 46.

ccxcix[299] Max Perry, American Descendants of William Gaston and Mary Olivet Lemon (Midland, TX, 1989), 148.

ccc[300] Headstone (no dates given).

ccci[301] *Autobiography of Andrew Dickson White (1905)* , http://www.archive.org/details/autobiographyan07whitgoog, p. 5.

cccii[302] Wikipedia.org (http://www.wikipedia.org), http://en.wikipedia.org/wiki/Andrew_Dickson_White.

ccciii[303] *Autobiography of Andrew Dickson White (1905)* , http://www.archive.org/details/autobiographyan07whitgoog.

ccciv[304] *Colonial Families of the United States, 1912* (republished 1966 by Genealogical Publishing Co, Baltimore, MD), p. 176.

cccv[305] George M. Kasson, *Genealogy of a Part of the Kasson Family in the United States and Ireland (1882)* (Brigham Young University Family History Archives, http://www.lib.byu.edu/fhc/), p. 25.

cccvi[306] George M. Kasson, *Genealogy of a Part of the Kasson Family in the United States and Ireland (1882)* (Brigham Young University Family History Archives, http://www.lib.byu.edu/fhc/), p. 24.

cccvii[307] George M. Kasson, *Genealogy of a Part of the Kasson Family in the United States and Ireland (1882)* (Brigham Young University Family History Archives, http://www.lib.byu.edu/fhc/), Altho birthdate stated in Kasson genealogy was May 12 1804, sequence in family was shown as between Margaret (1808) and Ephraim (1810). pp. 15, 25.

cccviii[308] George M. Kasson, *Genealogy of a Part of the Kasson Family in the United States and Ireland (1882)* (Brigham Young University Family History Archives, http://www.lib.byu.edu/fhc/), p. 26.

cccix[309] George M. Kasson, *Genealogy of a Part of the Kasson Family in the United States and Ireland (1882)* (Brigham Young University Family History Archives, http://www.lib.byu.edu/fhc/), p. 20.

cccx[310] George M. Kasson, *Genealogy of a Part of the Kasson Family in the United States and Ireland (1882)* (Brigham Young University Family History Archives, http://www.lib.byu.edu/fhc/), p. 21.

cccxi[311] Sidney Newlon, *Thanks, Tabor, for the Memories* , Midwest Printing Co, Council Bluffs, IA 51503 (1990), Additional information available online at http://www.webroots.org/library/usahist/esagowi0.html and http://freepages.books.rootsweb.com/~cooverfamily/index.html.

cccxii[312] George M. Kasson, *Genealogy of a Part of the Kasson Family in the United States and Ireland (1882)* (Brigham Young University Family History Archives, http://www.lib.byu.edu/fhc/), p. 45.

cccxiii[313] Hal Hatcher <halhai@radiks.net> (posted at http://awt.ancestry.com).

cccxiv[314] *First Families of America* , Kasson Genealogy reports marriage date as Nov 17 1857. p. 135.

cccxv[315] Hal Hatcher <halhai@radiks.net> (posted at http://awt.ancestry.com), Citing obituary in Tabor Beacon of Aug 24 1906.

cccxvi[316] Audley DeForest "Sandy" Gaston, Austin, TX 78731 <adgaston@earthlink.net >, *Family of David Gaston 1757-1830* , http://www.genealogy.com/users/g/a/s/Audley-D-Gaston/TREE/, http://www.familyoldphotos.com/pa/crawford/coll/gaston_and_related_family_photos .

cccxvii[317] Audley DeForest "Sandy" Gaston, Austin, TX 78731 <adgaston@earthlink.net >, *Family of David Gaston 1757-1830* , http://www.genealogy.com/users/g/a/s/Audley-D-Gaston/TREE/.

cccxviii[318] Dallin S. Nielsen, Jr., PO Box 775, Fillmore, UT 84631 (http://mvn.net/genealogy/gv1n2q8.htm).

cccxix[319] Bill Couch, *The Original Arkansas Genealogy Project, Reid Family* (http://www.couchgenweb.com/family/reid.htm), Birth date reported as ca 1799 in "Reid, Gaston and Simonton, Related Families" by Elizabeth Weir McPherson.

cccxx[320] Bill Couch, *The Original Arkansas Genealogy Project, Reid Family* (http://www.couchgenweb.com/family/reid.htm), Birth date reported as ca 1801in "Reid, Gaston and Simonton, Related Families" by Elizabeth Weir McPherson.

cccxxi[321] Lineage Book, National Society of the Daughters of the American Revolution, p. 136.

cccxxii[322] Bill Gaston, Austin TX <bgaston2@mindspring.com>, *Descendants: The Huguenot John Jean Gaston b: About 1600, France* (http://home.mindspring.com/~bgaston2/), http://www.familysearch.org/Eng/Search/AF/family_group_record.asp?familyid=6802 813.

cccxxiii[323] Bill Gaston, Austin TX <bgaston2@mindspring.com>, *Descendants: The Huguenot John Jean Gaston b: About 1600, France* (http://home.mindspring.com/~bgaston2/), http://www.familysearch.org/Eng/Search/AF/family_group_record.asp?familyid=6802 9.

cccxxiv[324] *James McFadden Gaston Papers, 1852-1946* (Southern Historical Collection, Wilson Library, University of North Carolina at Chapel Hill), http://www.lib.unc.edu/mss/inv/htm/01470.html.

cccxxv[325] Cecil Lee Jones Jr., 94 Deerwood Park, Centralia IL 62801 <leemary@miswest.net>, *Gaston Crier* (May 1997).

cccxxvi[326] Daughters of the American Revolution Lineage Book, Vol. 57, p. 56.

cccxxvii[327] *Daughters of the American Revolution Lineage Book*, Vol 57, p. 56, lineage of Eloise Gaston Gay, DAR No. 56161.

cccxxviii[328] Lineage Book, National Society of the Daughters of the American Revolution, p. 102.

cccxxix[329] *Daughters of the American Revolution Lineage Book*, Vol 23, p. 46, lineage of Josepha Bell Gaston, DAR No. 22424.

cccxxx[330] Lineage Book, National Society of the Daughters of the American Revolution, Vol XLIX, 1904, republished 1919. p. 445.

cccxxxi[331] *Daughters of the American Revolution Lineage Book*, Vol 49, p. 445, lineage of Mary Gaston Moise, DAR No. 48975.

cccxxxii[332] Lineage Book, National Society of the Daughters of the American Revolution, Vol XLIX, 1904, republished 1919. p. 134.

cccxxxiii[333] Mary Gaston Gee (1899-1987), The Ancestry and Descendants of Amzi Williford Gaston II (1841-1911) of Spartanburg County, South Carolina (Charlottesville, VA, 1944), p. 36.

cccxxxiv[334] 1930 Census.

cccxxxv[335] Mary Gaston Gee (1899-1987), The Ancestry and Descendants of Amzi Williford Gaston II (1841-1911) of Spartanburg County, South Carolina (Charlottesville, VA, 1944), p. 20.

cccxxxvi[336] Mary Gaston Gee (1899-1987), *The Ancestry and Descendants of Amzi Williford Gaston II (1841-1911) of Spartanburg County, South Carolina* (Charlottesville, VA, 1944), Death reported as age 22, after the Civil War. Date not specified. p. 19.

cccxxxvii[337] *Texas Death Index, 1903-2000 (online)* , Ancestry.com and Texas Dept of Health, Vital Statistics Unit, Certificate No. 11968. Name listed in death index as L. G. Gaston.

cccxxxviii[338] Death Record - Online, Certificate No. 4890. Named listed in death index as E. F. Gaston.

cccxxxix[339] Bruce Price Reynolds, Travelers Rest SC <bpr@blazesite.com>, *Descendants of Amzi Williford Gaston and Jane A. Peden* (self-published, 2009).

cccxl[340] Mary Gaston Gee (1899-1987), The Ancestry and Descendants of Amzi Williford Gaston II (1841-1911) of Spartanburg County, South Carolina (Charlottesville, VA, 1944), p. 22.

cccxli[341] Lineage Book, National Society of the Daughters of the American Revolution, p. 323.

cccxlii[342] Harrison County Death Records, Clarksburg, WV, Identified as Sarah A. Perine, married, 38, b. Ohio, d. Mar 30 1889 at Kincheloe. Cause of death: puerperal peritonitis. Burial at Old Bethel. A resident of West Virginia for 35 years.

cccxliii[343] *Harrison County WV Marriages 1785-1894* , Wes Cochran, 2515 10th Ave, Parkersburg, WV 26101 (1985), Identified as William L. Perine, 20, of Harrison Co, son of Isaac & Nancy; and Sarah A. Jones, 21, of Harrison Co, dau of Benjamin & Anna. Married Nov 16 1871.

cccxliv[344] John Mark Perine, PO Box 2145, Parkersburg WV 26102 <jmperine@verizon.net>, *Perine Family of North Central WV* (http://familytreemaker.genealogy.com/users/p/e/r/John-M-Perine/).

cccxlv[345] Death record of daughter.

cccxlvi[346] Georgia Hileman Halloran, Berkley, MI 48072 <gshalloran@wowway.com>, citing Elissa A. Powell <espowell@juno.com>. No entry found in Doddridge County death records.

cccxlvii[347] Georgia Hileman Halloran, Berkley, MI 48072 <gshalloran@wowway.com>.

cccxlviii[348] Harrison County Marriage Records, Clarksburg, WV, MR Bk 6, p. 216, shows that on Aug 17 1840, Richard Perine and Andrew Gaston signed a marriage bond in the amount of $150 for David Prine [sic] and Matilda Gaston. But MR Bk 3, p. 148, shows that when the minister returned the certificate for the Aug 27 1840 ceremony, the groom's first name was erroneously entered as Daniel. It is clear, however, that it was David Perine who married Matilda Gaston. MR Bk 3, p. 148; MR Bk 6, p. 216.

cccxlix[349] Georgia Hileman Halloran, Berkley, MI 48072 <gshalloran@wowway.com>, citing Paul Skinner <pdskinner@pol.net> at rootsweb.com and <marebarron@neo.rr.com> at ancestry.com.

cccl[350] Paul Douglas Skinner <pdskinner@pol.net> (posted at http://awt.ancestry.com).

cccli[351] Doddridge County Marriage Records, West Union, WV, Groom identified as Robert Willis, age 79, son of William & Annie Willis. Bride identified as Matilda Perine, age 63, dau of Andrew & Dorcas Gaston. It is noted that Matilda's father, Andrew Gaston, married Sarah Romine in 1806, then remarried Dorcas Stephens in 1821, while Matilda was born ca 1818. Dorcas would thus have been Matilda's stepmother. Ceremony held Oct 3 1879. MR Bk 1-A, p. 236.

ccclii[352] *Doddridge County WV Marriages 1845-1937* , Wes Cochran, 2515 10th Ave, Parkersburg, WV 26101 (Jan 1993), Participants identified as Robert Willis, widowed, age 79, b. Harrison Co, resident of Doddridge Co, son of William & Annie Willis; and Matilda Perine, widowed, age 63, b. Harrison Co, resident of Doddridge Co, dau of Andrew & Dorcas Gaston. It is noted that Matilda's father, Andrew Gaston, married Sarah Romine in 1806, then remarried Dorcas Stephens in 1821, while Matilda was born ca 1818. Dorcas would thus have been Matilda's stepmother. Ceremony held Oct 3 1879.

ccclii[353] Minnie Kendall Lowther, *History of Ritchie County* (1911, reprinted 1999, McClain Printing Co, Parsons WV, http://McClainPrinting.com), p. 236.

cccliv[354] *Doddridge County WV Marriages 1845-1937* , Wes Cochran, 2515 10th Ave, Parkersburg, WV 26101 (Jan 1993).

ccclv[355] Doddridge County Death Records, West Union, WV, Identified as Robert Willis, age 87y4m+, died Feb 29 1888. A second entry, DR Bk 1 p. 8, shows his death as occurring on Mar 1 1888 at age 87. DR Bk 1, p. 3.

ccclvi[356] *Doddridge County WV Deaths 1853-1969* , Wes Cochran, 2515 10th Ave, Parkersburg, WV 26101.

ccclvii[357] Doddridge County Death Records, West Union, WV.

ccclviii[358] Minnie Kendall Lowther, *History of Ritchie County* (1911, reprinted 1999, McClain Printing Co, Parsons WV, http://McClainPrinting.com), p. 596.

ccclix[359] Doddridge County Death Records, West Union, WV, DR Bk 4, p. 151.

ccclx[360] Doddridge County Death Records, West Union, WV, Identified as Julia A. Nicholson [sic], a widow, b. Jun 24 1842 in Harrison Co, d. Dec 8 1931 at West Union, dau of David Perine (b. Harrison Co) and Matilda Gaston (b. Harrison Co). Informant: Richard Perine (relationship not specified). Previous information had reported her marriage in 1860 to Cain Nicholas. It is unclear whether Julia remarried a Nicholson, or whether Cain Nicholas was actually Cain Nicholson, or whether the death record was in error and her name was actually Nicholas. The latter is considered more likely. DR Bk 4, p. 151.

ccclxi[361] *Harrison County WV Marriages 1785-1894* , Wes Cochran, 2515 10th Ave, Parkersburg, WV 26101 (1985), Identified as Cain Nicholas, 24, b. Pendleton Co, res. Doddridge Co, son of Francis & Barbara; and Julia A. Perine, 17, of Harrison Co, dau of David & Matilda. Married Nov 18 1860.

ccclxii[362] William F. Donnelly, *The Wests of Duck Creek, Harrison County, Virginia (now West Virginia)* , Gateway Press, Baltimore MD, 1997, p. 412.

ccclxiii[363] Headstone - Birth date not specified, but calculated from stated age at death.

ccclxiv[364] Headstone, Age at death given as 71y 1m 16d. Some sources have given a death date of Nov 11 1854 or Aug 2 1854, and a printed list of Sinclair Cem graves compiled by W. Va. Writers Project gives his death date as November 11, 1851.

ccclxv[365] Sam D. Lawson, Columbus, IN <lawson@hsonline.net>.

ccclxvi[366] Headstone, Inscription does not give a birthdate, but reads that she died on Dec 4 1800 "Aged 84 Yrs 1 Mo 12 Ds." This would put her birth at Oct 22 1806. This is at variance with birthdate of Oct 18 1806 reported by Jeff Whittaker.

ccclxvii[367] Per Smith Family notes by Arlie Smith, per G. Jeff Whittaker.

ccclxviii[368] Place of birth per Jeff Whittaker. Birth date of 9/2/1814 given by Comstock and Butcher, but father's Bible on display at Watters Smith State Park states 9/2/1804. The latter date is also confirmed by death date and age on headstone.

ccclxix[369] Headstone, Inscription does not give a birthdate, but reads that he died on Feb 19 1880 "Aged 75 yrs 5 mos 18 dys." This would put his birth at Sep 2 1804.

ccclxx[370] G. J. Whittaker, a Gaston descendant and researcher, Citing Smith Family notes by Arlie Smith.

ccclxxi[371] Headstone, Birthdate sometimes reported as May 9 1829, but headstone reads "Born May 19 1829, Died May 29 1889, Aged 60 Ys 10 Ds".

ccclxxii[372] William F. Donnelly, *The Wests of Duck Creek, Harrison County, Virginia (now West Virginia)* , Gateway Press, Baltimore MD, 1997, p. 413.

ccclxxiii[373] Marilynn Davis Jones, Fairmont, WV 26554.

ccclxxiv[374] Marriage record of daughter.

ccclxxv[375] Headstone, Name appears as "Belindy, wife of Eli R. West".

ccclxxvi[376] Headstone, Date of birth not specified and is calculated from age at death, 10y7m18d, stated in inscription.

ccclxxvii[377] William F. Donnelly, *The Wests of Duck Creek, Harrison County, Virginia (now West Virginia)* , Gateway Press, Baltimore MD, 1997, p. 414.

ccclxxviii[378] 1850 Census, Age given as 37 as of the data collection date of July 24 1850, making him born in late 1812 or early 1813.

ccclxxix[379] *1880 Census* , The 1880 Census listed him as 68, putting his birth in 1811 or 1812.

ccclxxx[380] *W. Guy Tetrick files* , Family information survey completed by grand-nephew Ira Dow Gaston stated his birth as July 17 1812 in Harrison Co.

ccclxxxi[381] Presumed.

ccclxxxii[382] 1870 Census, Doddridge County, WV (South West Twp).

ccclxxxiii[383] Minnie Kendall Lowther, *History of Ritchie County* (1911, reprinted 1999, McClain Printing Co, Parsons WV, http://McClainPrinting.com), p. 421.

ccclxxxiv[384] *Ritchie County Marriages 1843-1853* , Entry shows a John H. Gaston, b. 1813 in Virginia, and a Jane "Richards" marrying on Feb 2 1847. Despite the name variance, this is considered to be the same couple. Mary Jane Pritchard did go by her middle name. But Wes Cochran's "Ritchie County WV Marriages 1843-1915" shows the same couple with a marriage date of Feb 2 1848. The later date is considered more likely.

ccclxxxv[385] 1900 Census, Doddridge County, WV (Southwest District).

ccclxxxvi[386] Doddridge County Death Records, West Union, WV, Identified as Anna Gaston, age 9 months, dau of John & Jane Gaston, b. at Hughes River, died Nov 17 1854 at Hughes River, cause of death scarlet fever. Informant: John H. Gaston, father. DR Bk 3, p. 2.

ccclxxxvii[387] Harrison County Marriage Records, Clarksburg, WV, Ceremony performed by Elias Bruen. MR yrs 1784-1850.

ccclxxxviii[388] Doddridge County Death Records, West Union, WV, DR Bk 1, p. 45.

ccclxxxix[389] 1850 Census, Doddridge County, (W)VA.

cccxc[390] Doddridge County Birth Records, West Union, WV, BR Bk 1, p. 15.

cccxci[391] Doddridge County Death Records, West Union, WV, The death record actually reflects the name of Sarah A. Gaston, Hannah's older sister, with age as 12 days. But this is clearly incorrect, as Sarah is known to have married six years later. No subsequent record of Hannah exists. DR Bk 3, p. 5.

cccxcii[392] Rev. I. A. Barnes, *The Methodist Protestant Church in West Virginia* , The Stockton Press, Baltimore, MD, 1926.

cccxciii[393] Doddridge County Marriage Records, West Union, WV, The entire handwritten marriage record reads: "This is to certify that the following persons were lawfully married by me. Eli M. Gaston to Rulina Lowther on the 29th day of November 1846. Given under my hand this 16th day of July 1847. Isaac Holland.", MR Bk 1, p. 4.

cccxciv[394] *Doddridge County WV Marriages 1845-1937* , Wes Cochran, 2515 10th Ave, Parkersburg, WV 26101 (Jan 1993), Identified as Eli M. Gaston and Relina [sic] Lowther. Married Nov 29 1846.

cccxcv[395] Obituary of son.

cccxcvi[396] Death record of son.

cccxcvii[397] Doddridge County Death Records, West Union, WV, Identified as Rulina Gaston, widow, died Sep 30 1911 at Oxford, age 86y1m18d. Cause: "Heart disease incident to old age." Parents or maiden name not indicated. DR Bk 2, p. 55.

cccxcviii[398] WV State Dept of Health, Div of Vital Statistics, *Death Certificate* (http://www.wvculture.org/vrr/va_dcsearch.aspx).

cccxcix[399] WV State Dept of Health, Div of Vital Statistics, *Death Certificate* (http://www.wvculture.org/vrr/va_dcsearch.aspx), Identified as Annie M. Gaston, b. Oct 31 1847 in Doddridge Co, d. Feb 26 1924 at Summers, Doddridge Co, dau of Eli M. Gaston & (first name left blank) Lowther. Occupation: farmer's daughter. Informant: B. C. Hickman (this would be Burleigh C. Hickman, husband of her niece Sarah Rulina Gaston).

cd[400] Doddridge County Death Records, West Union, WV, DR Bk 2, p. 56.

cdi[401] Doddridge County Death Records, West Union, WV, Identified as Susannah Gaston, age 5, dau of Eli & Rulinda (sic), died Sep 7 1854 at Hughes River. Cause of death listed as "sore throat." Place of birth given as Harrison County, part of which is now Doddridge County. DR Bk 3, p. 2.

cdii[402] 1880 Census, Doddridge County, WV (Southwest District).

cdiii[403] Doddridge County Death Records, West Union, WV, Identified as Daniel H. Gaskins (sic), 28, farmer, b. Doddridge Co, son of Ely & Rulany Gaskins (sic), d. Jun 20 1880 in Doddridge Co, cause of death illegible (surrg fever ?). Informant: Ely Gaskins, father. DR p. 34.

cdiv[404] Doddridge County Death Records, West Union, WV, Identified as Nancy J. Gaston, age 10y 6m 24d, dau of Eli M. & Rulina, died Oct 4 1866, cause of death diphtheria. Informant: Rulina Gaston, mother. DR Bk 1, p. 12.

cdv[405] Birth record of son.

cdvi[406] Headstone for date. Gilmer County West Virginia History 1845-1989 has birth date of Dec 29 1839, in Lewis Co, (W)VA. [p. 54].

cdvii[407] *Gilmer County West Virginia History 1845-1989* , Gilmer County Historical Society, 1994, p. 54.

cdviii[408] 1900 Census, Lewis County, WV.

cdix[409] *Lewis County WV Marriages 1817-1880* , Wes Cochran, 2515 10th Ave, Parkersburg, WV 26101, Identified as John Butcher and Cordelia Gaston. Married Apr 22 1855.

cdx[410] *Lewis County WV Marriages 1881-1937* , Wes Cochran, 2515 10th Ave, Parkersburg, WV 26101 (Sep 1994).

cdxi[411] Lewis County Birth Records, Weston, WV, BR Bk 1.

cdxii[412] Obituary of sister.

cdxiii[413] *Gilmer County West Virginia History 1845-1989* , Gilmer County Historical Society, 1994.

cdxiv[414] WV State Dept of Health, Div of Vital Statistics, *Death Certificate* (http://www.wvculture.org/vrr/va_dcsearch.aspx), Identified as George D. Butcher, married, age 65y 11m 5, b. Jan 1 1861, d. Dec 6 1926 at Alton, Upshur Co; son of John S. Butcher & Credelia [sic] Gaston. Occupation: head sawyer. Burial: Polk Creek Cemetery. Informant: Mrs. Alda Evans, Weston. (This would be his sister. The Jan 1861 birthdate stated here is inconsistent with the 1863 on his headstone and would also conflict with the Oct 1860 birthdate of his next older brother.).

cdxv[415] *Lewis County WV Marriages 1881-1937* , Wes Cochran, 2515 10th Ave, Parkersburg, WV 26101 (Sep 1994), Identified as George Davis Butcher, 20, of Lewis Co, son of J. S. & D. [sic]; and Mary Agness Turner, 18, of Lewis Co, dau of M. Married Apr 27 1882.

cdxvi[416] Betty Mayfield (compiler) & Matha Byrd (editor), *Obituaries, Marriage & Births from Weston Independent and/or Weston Democrat, 1939-1940* (Hackers Creek Pioneer Descendants, Jane Lew, WV, April 1996), p. 7.

cdxvii[417] 1880 Census, Lewis County, WV, Year only.

cdxviii[418] 1920 Census, Harrison County, WV.

cdxix[419] Harrison County Marriage Records, Clarksburg, WV.

cdxx[420] *Texas Death Index, 1903-2000 (online)* , Ancestry.com and Texas Dept of Health, Vital Statistics Unit.

cdxxi[421] Obituary of niece.

cdxxii[422] Death record of brother.

cdxxiii[423] Harrison County Marriage Records, Clarksburg, WV, MR p. 241.

cdxxiv[424] Obituary of wife's sister.

cdxxv[425] Harrison County Marriage Records, Clarksburg, WV, Identified as John Wesley Evans, 60, widowed, b. Randolph Co, Alabama, resident of Bandera, Texas, son of Joshua R. & Martha E. Evans; and Alda Butcher, 41, single, b. Lewis Co, resident of Harrison Co, dau of John & Cordelia Butcher. Married Oct 26 1920 "at the home of the Bride in Clarksburg.", MR p. 241.

cdxxvi[426] 1850 Census, Lewis County, (W)VA.

cdxxvii[427] 1870 Census, Lewis County, WV (Willey Township), 113.

cdxxviii[428] *Gilmer County West Virginia History 1845-1989* , Gilmer County Historical Society, 1994, p. 208.

cdxxix[429] Lewis County Marriage Records, Weston, WV, Identified as Henry Lee Gaston, 24, farmer, b. & res. in Lewis Co, son of Hugh & Elizabeth Gaston; and Mary Jane Turner [sic], 20, b. & res. in Lewis Co, dau of Jackson & Margarett Turner [sic]. Married May 29 1866. Ceremony by Henry Langfora. MR Bk 5, p. 32.

cdxxx[430] Headstone. Age at death given as 6y 6m 4d, which varies from the listed dates of birth and death.

cdxxxi[431] 1900 Census, Gilmer County, WV (Center District).

cdxxxii[432] Gilmer County Death Records, Glenville, WV.

cdxxxiii[433] *West Virginia Marriage Records, 1863-1900*
(http://www.ancestry.com/search/rectype/inddbs/4484.htm).

cdxxxiv[434] *Gilmer County WV Marriages 1845-1933* , Wes Cochran, 2515 10th Ave, Parkersburg WV 26101 (Jan 1989).

cdxxxv[435] *Gilmer County WV Marriages 1845-1933* , Wes Cochran, 2515 10th Ave, Parkersburg WV 26101 (Jan 1989), Identified as Robert Carpenter, age 30, b. Webster Co, res. Gilmer Co; and Estella Gaston, age 26, of Gilmer Co. Married Nov 23 1913.

cdxxxvi[436] Death record of wife.

cdxxxvii[437] WV State Dept of Health, Div of Vital Statistics, *Death Certificate* (http://www.wvculture.org/vrr/va_dcsearch.aspx), Identified as Marion Gaston, b. Jun 7 1852 in Lewis Co, son of Hugh Gaston & Amanda Washburn. Birthplace of both parents stated as Lewis Co, but Hugh was actually born in New Jersey, and Amanda probably in Ohio. Widowed by wife Adeline Keller Gaston [sic]. Occupation retired farmer. Buried at Sassafras Cemetery in Camden, WV. Informant: Mrs. Myrtle Ellis, Weston, WV.

cdxxxviii[438] Lewis County Death Records, Weston, WV, Identified as Marion Gaston, age 96y 5m 28d, died Dec 2 1948. Cause of death: Strangulated hernia. Marital status: Widowed. Parents: Hugh Gaston & Amanda Washburn. DR Bk 6, p. 131.

cdxxxix[439] Joy Gregoire Gilchrist Stalnaker, *Squires Genealogy* , Hackers Creek Pioneers Descendants, Jane Lew, WV (www.hackerscreek.com).

cdxl[440] Joy Gregoire Gilchrist Stalnaker, *Squires Genealogy* , Hackers Creek Pioneers Descendants, Jane Lew, WV (www.hackerscreek.com), quoting Bill Adler, a Lewis County historian.

cdxli[441] Gilmer County Marriage Records, Glenville, WV, Identified as Marion Gaston, 23, b. & res. in Lewis Co; and Angeline Keller, 19, b. & res. in Gilmer Co. Married Jan 5 1876. MR p. 22.

cdxlii[442] Lewis County Death Records, Weston, WV, Identified as Angeline M. Gaston, died Nov 7 1926 at Weston. Cause of death: Vulvular heart lesion. Entries for age, occupation and spouse were all left blank. DR Bk 4, p. 69.

cdxliii[443] WV State Dept of Health, Div of Vital Statistics, *Death Certificate* (http://www.wvculture.org/vrr/va_dcsearch.aspx), Identified as Angeline M. Gaston, b. Dec 17 1856 in Gilmer Co, dau of Frank Kellar & Margaret Hiney, survived by husband Marion Gaston, died Nov 7 1926 in Weston, buried at Waldeck Cemetery.

cdxliv[444] Lewis County Death Records, Weston, WV, DR Bk 8, p. 138.

cdxlv[445] William F. Donnelly, *The Wests of Duck Creek, Harrison County, Virginia (now West Virginia)* , Gateway Press, Baltimore MD, 1997, p. 555.

cdxlvi[446] Marriage record of son.

cdxlvii[447] Jackson County Death Records, Ripley, WV.

cdxlviii[448] Patti Ashcraft Hickman, The Ward Family of Harrison County.

cdxlix[449] 1880 Census, Jackson County, WV.

cdl[450] Jackson County Marriage Records, Ripley, WV.

cdli[451] Jackson County Marriage Records, Ripley, WV, Identified as Wm D. Maddox, 61, b. Harrison Co Va., res. Jackson Co W. Va. (Kenna P.O.); and Mrs. Rebecca Hickman, 51,

b. Barbour Co, res. Jackson Co. Married Aug 24 1884 "at the residence of the Bride.", MR p. 275.

cdlii[452] Harrison County Death Records, Clarksburg, WV, DR p. 18.

cdliii[453] Raymond A. Mann <dermann@earthlink.net>, citing Census data.

cdliv[454] 1880 Census, Harrison County, WV.

cdlv[455] W. N. Hurley, Jr., *Maddox: A Southern Maryland Family* , Heritage Books, Bowie, MD, ISBN 0-788-0123-8, 1994, p. 106.

cdlvi[456] William F. Donnelly, *The Wests of Duck Creek, Harrison County, Virginia (now West Virginia)* , Gateway Press, Baltimore MD, 1997, p. 553.

cdlvii[457] William F. Donnelly, *The Wests of Duck Creek, Harrison County, Virginia (now West Virginia)* , Gateway Press, Baltimore MD, 1997, p. 465.

cdlviii[458] 1910 Census, Harrison County, WV.

cdlix[459] WV State Dept of Health, Div of Vital Statistics, *Death Certificate* (http://www.wvculture.org/vrr/va_dcsearch.aspx), "The Wests of Duck Creek," p. 466, reports birth date as Sep 13 1855, but death certificate states Aug 13 1855.

cdlx[460] 1900 Census, Marshall County, WV.

cdlxi[461] William F. Donnelly, *The Wests of Duck Creek, Harrison County, Virginia (now West Virginia)* , Gateway Press, Baltimore MD, 1997, p. 466.

cdlxii[462] *Cemeteries of Clark District, Harrison County, WV* , Harrison County Genealogical Society, Clarksburg, WV.

cdlxiii[463] Marshall County Marriage Records , Moundsville, WV.

cdlxiv[464] William F. Donnelly, *The Wests of Duck Creek, Harrison County, Virginia (now West Virginia)* , Gateway Press, Baltimore MD, 1997, p. 554.

cdlxv[465] Harrison County Marriage Records, Clarksburg, WV, Identified as James Warner Kerby, 26, b. Harrison Co Ohio, res. Harrison Co WVa, son of James F. & Jeannie Kerby; and Emma Francis West, 31, b. & res. in Harrison Co WVa, dau of Jefferson & Ruhama West. Married Sep 1 1901 in West Milford. Informants for the marriage license: James W. Kerby & Jed West. MR p. 209.

cdlxvi[466] WV State Dept of Health, Div of Vital Statistics, *Death Certificate* (http://www.wvculture.org/vrr/va_dcsearch.aspx), "The Wests of Duck Creek," p. 466, reports birth date as Jul 3 1872, but death record states Jul 3 1873, and 1900 Census also shows it as Jul 1873.

cdlxvii[467] 1900 Census, Harrison County, WV.

cdlxviii[468] Minnie Kendall Lowther, *Ritchie County in History and Romance* (McClain Publishing Co, Parsons, WV, 1990), p. 315.

cdlxix[469] Ritchie County Historical Society (David M. Scott, Editor), *Ritchie County, West Virginia Cemeteries through 1993* , McClain Printing Co, Parsons, WV, 1995.

cdlxx[470] Minnie Kendall Lowther, *Ritchie County in History and Romance* (McClain Publishing Co, Parsons, WV, 1990), p. 316.

cdlxxi[471] Minnie Kendall Lowther, *Ritchie County in History and Romance* (McClain Publishing Co, Parsons, WV, 1990), pp. 315-316.

cdlxxii[472] Susie Davis Nicholson, *Davis - The Settlers of Salem, West Virginia* , Gordon Printing Co, Strasburg OH, 1979 (Revised & Enlarged), p. 124.

cdlxxiii[473] *Ritchie County WV Marriages 1843-1915* , Wes Cochran, 2515 10th Ave, Parkersburg WV 26101 (July 1985).

cdlxxiv[474] *Ritchie County WV Deaths 1941-1955* , Wes Cochran, 2515 10th Ave, Parkersburg, WV 26101 (Dec 1998).

cdlxxv[475] WV State Dept of Health, Div of Vital Statistics, *Death Certificate* (http://www.wvculture.org/vrr/va_dcsearch.aspx), "Ritchie County Cemeteries Through 1993" incorrectly reports death date as May 1 1956. Middle initial provided by Minnie Kendall Lowther as W, but marriage record, death record and headstone have it as M.

cdlxxvi[476] *Ritchie County WV Marriages 1843-1915* , Wes Cochran, 2515 10th Ave, Parkersburg WV 26101 (July 1985), Identified as Albert M. Ward, age 28, of Ritchie Co; and Flora B. Wade, age 18, of Ritchie Co. Married Apr 18 1895.

cdlxxvii[477] *Ritchie County WV Deaths 1956-1970* , Wes Cochran, 2515 10th Ave, Parkersburg, WV 26101 (Jan 1999).

cdlxxviii[478] James Lock <statework@aol.com>, *The Locke Family* (Ancestry World Tree Project, posted at http://awt.ancestry.com).

cdlxxix[479] *Ritchie County WV Deaths 1956-1970* , Wes Cochran, 2515 10th Ave, Parkersburg, WV 26101 (Jan 1999), Identified as Flora B. Ward, b. in Berea, WV, dau of Andrew & Sally (Bee) Wade, d. Dec 26 1960, age 83. "Ritchie County WV Cemeteries," p. 496, incorrectly reports death date on headstone as Dec 26 1860.

cdlxxx[480] *Goldenseal Magazine* , West Virginia Cultural Center, www.wvlc.wvnet.edu/culture/goldensl.html, Fall 1996.

cdlxxxi[481] *Doddridge County WV Deaths 1853-1969* , Wes Cochran, 2515 10th Ave, Parkersburg, WV 26101, Entry states Apr 27 1911, at variance from other sources.

cdlxxxii[482] Headstone, - Inscribed on the marker are the names of himself and his two wives, along with all of their birth and death dates. His wife Elizabeth also has a separate marker nearby of her own.

cdlxxxiii[483] Obituary, - Pallbearers identified as six of his grandsons: Howard, Earnest & Albert [Bert] Jones, Blair [Josiah Blaine] Nutter, C. W. [Charles Wesley] Britton, and Z. W. [Jebidee or Zebidee Warner] Britton.

cdlxxxiv[484] Obituary of husband.

cdlxxxv[485] Headstone, - Age at death given as 56y 10m 10d. This is on a headstone devoted only to Elizabeth. Her name & dates are also on a headstone with those of husband Samuel and his second wife, Rebecca.

cdlxxxvi[486] Harrison County Marriage Records, Clarksburg, WV, Identified as Samuel M. Gaston, widowed, age 58, b. Harrison Co, res. Doddridge Co, son of John & Elizabeth; and Rebecca J. Furner, 43, b. Loudoun Co VA, res. Harrison Co, dau of John & Sarah. Married Nov 6 1883 in Clarksburg. MR p. 165.

cdlxxxvii[487] WV State Dept of Health, Div of Vital Statistics, *Death Certificate* (http://www.wvculture.org/vrr/va_dcsearch.aspx), Death record states birthplace as Harrison Co, while obituary specifies that she moved to Harrison Co from Loudon Co, VA at age six months.

cdlxxxviii[488] Headstone - Birth date not specified, but calculated from stated age at death, - Marker inscribed "Mary A. - Dau of S. M. & E. Gaston - Died Mch 22 1855 - Aged 7 Ys 4 Mo 16 Ds" Birth date of Nov 6 1847 calculated from this information. Other sources have given birth only as being in 1848 or on Nov 16 or 11 1847.

cdlxxxix[489] Doddridge County Death Records, West Union, WV, Entry states she died at age 8 of scarlet fever. DR Bk 3.

cdxc[490] Headstone, - Marker has no death information. It reads "Rebecca - Infant dau of S. M. & E. Gaston - Born April 29 1849".

cdxci[491] Doddridge County Birth Records, West Union, WV, BR Bk 1, p 24.

cdxcii[492] Headstone, - Marker inscribed "Martha (middle initial illegible) - Dau of S. M. & E. Gaston - Died Feb 6 1871 - Aged 5 Ys 11 Mo 9 Ds" This conforms to the birth date of Feb 28 1865 found in Doddridge County birth records. No death record in Doddridge Co. Death has been reported by others as 1874 at age 9, but this is incorrect based on the headstone.

cdxciii[493] Minnie Kendall Lowther, *History of Ritchie County* (1911, reprinted 1999, McClain Printing Co, Parsons WV, http://McClainPrinting.com), p. 264.

cdxciv[494] Susie Davis Nicholson, *Davis - The Settlers of Salem, West Virginia* , Gordon Printing Co, Strasburg OH, 1979 (Revised & Enlarged), p. 381.

cdxcv[495] *Ritchie County WV Marriages 1843-1915* , Wes Cochran, 2515 10th Ave, Parkersburg WV 26101 (July 1985), Identified as Phineas W. Bartlett, widowed, 64, b.

Harrison Co, res. Barbour Co; and Deborah Law, widowed, 55, b. Harrison Co, res. Ritchie Co. Married Jan 28 1883.

cdxcvi[496] *The Barrett-Law and Related Families of West Virginia* (http://familytreemaker.genealogy.com/users/b/a/r/Michael-Barrett/index.html).

cdxcvii[497] Minnie Kendall Lowther, *Ritchie County in History and Romance* (McClain Publishing Co, Parsons, WV, 1990), p. 309.

cdxcviii[498] 1860 Census, Ritchie County, (W)VA.

cdxcix[499] *Harrison County WV Marriages 1785-1894* , Wes Cochran, 2515 10th Ave, Parkersburg, WV 26101 (1985), Identified as James A. L. Day, 25, of Harrison Co, son of Joseph T. & Ingaby; and Mary E. Sommerville, 24, b. Ritchie Co, res. Harrison Co, dau of Martin & Susan. Married Nov 25 1880.

d[500] *Ritchie County WV Marriages 1843-1915* , Wes Cochran, 2515 10th Ave, Parkersburg WV 26101 (July 1985), Identified as John F. Kelly (sic), 20, b. Doddridge Co, res. Ritchie Co, son of Ezekiel & Estella A.; and Sarah O. Sommerville, 18, of Ritchie Co, dau of Martin S. & Susan. Married Mar 29 1877.

di[501] 1880 Census, Ritchie County, WV.

dii[502] Obituary of daughter.

diii[503] Minnie Kendall Lowther, *History of Ritchie County* (1911, reprinted 1999, McClain Printing Co, Parsons WV, http://McClainPrinting.com), p. 335.

div[504] Headstone, - Marker gives only date of death, Nov 12 1893, and age at death as 62y 11m.

dv[505] Lorna Reese Overberg, *The History of Ritchie County, West Virginia to 1980* (Ritchie County Historical Society, Taylor Publishing Co, 1980), p. 123, in entry by Vonda Gaston Hatfield.

dvi[506] Amy Gaston Smith, *Those Days of Long Ago* (Sep 15 1984, reprinted Jun 1999 by Michael Ruppert Jr., Los Angeles CA, with help of Mike Ruppert Sr., Grove WV and Lou.

dvii[507] *Doddridge County WV Marriages 1845-1937* , Wes Cochran, 2515 10th Ave, Parkersburg, WV 26101 (Jan 1993), Identified as John S. Gaston, age 23, b. Harrison Co, res. Doddridge Co, son of John; and (name blank), age 19, b. Harrison Co, res. Doddridge Co, dau of James T. Richards. Married Jun 15 1854.

dviii[508] *Ritchie County WV Marriages 1843-1915* , Wes Cochran, 2515 10th Ave, Parkersburg WV 26101 (July 1985), Identified as John S. Gaston, widowed, 34, b. Harrison Co, res. Doddridge Co, son of John & Elizabeth; and Catharine Legget [sic], 21, b. Marion Co, res. Ritchie Co, dau of Enoch B. & Sarah. Married May 24 1865. Her stated age is two years older than what appears on her headstone.

dix[509] 1910 Census, Doddridge County, WV (Southwest District).

dx[510] Doddridge County Death Records, West Union, WV, DR Bk 2, p. 55.

dxi[511] Lorna Reese Overberg, *The History of Ritchie County, West Virginia to 1980* (Ritchie County Historical Society, Taylor Publishing Co, 1980), Entry submitted by Vonda Gaston Hatfield. p. 123.

dxii[512] Doddridge County Marriage Records, West Union, WV, MR Bk 7, Page 193.

dxiii[513] *Doddridge County WV Marriages 1845-1937* , Wes Cochran, 2515 10th Ave, Parkersburg, WV 26101 (Jan 1993), Identified as John G. Woofter, 56, b. Lewis Co, res. Doddridge Co; and E. Jane Gaston, 48, of Doddridge Co. Married Aug 13 1904.

dxiv[514] Headstone, - Marker has only the death date of Apr 19 1859, with age as 2 months, 16 days.

dxv[515] Doddridge County Death Records, West Union, WV, Cause of death listed as croup. DR Bk 3, p. 5.

dxvi[516] Headstone. Age at death given as 16y 5m 11d.

dxvii[517] Headstone, - Inscription not entirely legible. Middle initial could be taken for a D, but is a T. Likewise the year, which could be taken for 1861, but is definitely 1864. The marker, which is small and has no death information, reads "Henry T., son of J. S. & E. Gaston, born July 16 1864." The implication is that the child died very young.

dxviii[518] Doddridge County Marriage Records, West Union, WV, MR Bk 4, p. 332.

dxix[519] Olin Joseph Hartman <wegotrocks@sbccom.com>
(http://members.iolinc.net/wegotrocks).

dxx[520] Obituary of half-sister.

dxxi[521] Obituary of brother.

dxxii[522] Doddridge County Marriage Records, West Union, WV, MR Bk 7, p. 27.

dxxiii[523] Doddridge County Birth Records, West Union, WV, Identified as Ida M. Gaston, born March 1878 (date not specified), dau of John S. & Catherine Gaston. Informant: Father. (Note: Age 2y 2m 21d at death shown on her headstone would put birth date at May 17 1878. Since the birth record is a typed transcription of the original entry, it is presumed that a clerical error was made.), BR p. 94.

dxxiv[524] *Cemeteries of Union District, Harrison County, WV* , Harrison County Genealogical Society, Clarksburg, WV (1990).

dxxv[525] WV State Dept of Health, Div of Vital Statistics, *Death Certificate* (http://www.wvculture.org/vrr/va_dcsearch.aspx), Informant for death record: Carl D. Sommerville, Clarksburg.

dxxvi[526] Record of husband's remarriage.

dxxvii[527] 1870 Census, Harrison County, WV.

dxxviii[528] *Harrison County WV Marriages 1785-1894* , Wes Cochran, 2515 10th Ave, Parkersburg, WV 26101 (1985), Identified as Isaac Rinehart Smith, 27, b. Lewis Co, res. Harrison Co, son of John & Mary; and Sarah Gaston, 19, of Harrison Co, dau of John & Charlotte. Married Sep 20 1855. Identification of her parents as John & Charlotte, rather than James & Elizabeth, is considered to be a transcription error. The adjoining entry is for the marriage of George Washington Dayton and Mary Catherine Gaston, also erroneously identified as dau of John & Charlotte rather than James & Charlotte.

dxxix[529] WV State Dept of Health, Div of Vital Statistics, *Death Certificate* (http://www.wvculture.org/vrr/va_dcsearch.aspx), Cause of death: influenza.

dxxx[530] Harrison County Marriage Records, Clarksburg, WV, Exact location not clear, as ceremony is recorded as having occurred in Dayton. But no town of that name can be found in Harrison County. There is a Dayton in Preston County. MR p. 84.

dxxxi[531] Harrison County Marriage Records, Clarksburg, WV, MR p. 158.

dxxxii[532] Harrison County Birth Records, Clarksburg, WV, Identified as Ethel Gaston, b. Oct 24 1882, dau of Enoch & Flora Gaston. Linder, in "Gibson and Related Families," p. 107, erroneously cites her birthdate as Oct 27 1882. BR Bk 2, p. 98.

dxxxiii[533] Headstone, Name inscribed as Ethel Gaston Woofter. Birthdate appears to be Oct 24 1882.

dxxxiv[534] Harrison County Death Records, Clarksburg, WV, Informant: Mrs. S. F. Henderson, Buffalo, NY.

dxxxv[535] *Harrison County WV Marriages 1895-1912* , Wes Cochran, 2515 10th Ave, Parkersburg, WV 26101 (Feb 2001), Identified as Darwin Maxson Davis, 31, b. Doddridge Co, res. Harrison Co, son of Charles G. & Elizabeth; and Gertrude Elma Gaston, 31, of Harrison Co, dau of James W. & Sarah A. Married Sep 16 1908.

dxxxvi[536] Susie Davis Nicholson, *Davis - The Settlers of Salem, West Virginia* , Gordon Printing Co, Strasburg OH, 1979 (Revised & Enlarged), p. 48.

dxxxvii[537] *Harrison County WV Marriages 1895-1912* , Wes Cochran, 2515 10th Ave, Parkersburg, WV 26101 (Feb 2001).

dxxxviii[538] WV State Dept of Health, Div of Vital Statistics, *Death Certificate* (http://www.wvculture.org/vrr/va_dcsearch.aspx), Cause of death stated as acute coronary heart attack; he died in his car while driving alone on Route 50 three miles east of Salem.

dxxxix[539] William F. Donnelly, *The Wests of Duck Creek, Harrison County, Virginia (now West Virginia)* , Gateway Press, Baltimore MD, 1997, p. 294.

dxl[540] Minnie Kendall Lowther, *History of Ritchie County* (1911, reprinted 1999, McClain Printing Co, Parsons WV, http://McClainPrinting.com), www.rootsweb.com.

dxli[541] Headstone, Year only. Name spelled "Theodore".

dxlii[542] Harrison County Death Records, Clarksburg, WV, Identified as F. M. Brooks, farmer, age 57y 4m 4d, born in Hampshire Co, son of (father's name blank) & Mary Brooks; died May 12 1883 in Tenmile District, cause of death heart disease. Informant: Sarah Brooks, wife.

dxliii[543] WV State Dept of Health, Div of Vital Statistics, *Death Certificate* (http://www.wvculture.org/vrr/va_dcsearch.aspx), Death record states birth date as Mar 29 1873 and death date as Dec 29 1924. But it also specifies age as 51y 9m 26y, which would put birth date at Mar 3 1873. A birth date of Mar 3 1872 has also been reported by some researchers, although one, direct descendent Dennis Newell, advises that a birth date of Mar 29 1872 is also a possibility. This would be supported by the fact that her age was given as 8 in the 1880 Census, and as 28 in the 1900 Census, with birth date listed as March 1872. It would thus appear that her actual date of birth was Mar 29 1872.

dxliv[544] *1900 Census, Taylor County, WV* , Age given as 28, with date of birth March 1872.

dxlv[545] 1880 Census, Harrison County, WV (Coal District) , Age given as eight.

dxlvi[546] Dennis D. Newell, 691 Pennsdale Dr, Yardley, PA 19067.

dxlvii[547] *Lewis County WV Marriages 1817-1880* , Wes Cochran, 2515 10th Ave, Parkersburg, WV 26101, The records contain two entries for the marriage of Peter G. Swisher & Margaret Hinzman, one showing a marriage date of Dec 9 1850, and the other showing a date of Dec 12 1850.

dxlviii[548] Penny & O.D. Linder, http://home.comcast.net/~jmlinder609, *The Gibson and Related Families* , McClain Printing Co, Parsons WV, 1991, p. 522.

dxlix[549] Lewis County Birth Records, Weston, WV, Name appears in birth record as Carrieth Jane Swisher. BR Bk 1.

dl[550] Lewis County Court House, Weston, WV, BR Bk 1.

dli[551] *Lewis County WV Marriages 1881-1937* , Wes Cochran, 2515 10th Ave, Parkersburg, WV 26101 (Sep 1994), Identified as Charles William Taylor, widowed, age 29, of Lewis Co, son of Sandy H. Sr. & Augusta; and Iza Swisher, age 29, of Lewis Co, dau of Peter & Margaret. Married Apr 11 1900.

dlii[552] Lewis County Birth Records, Weston, WV, BR Bk 1, p. 174.

dliii[553] *Lewis County WV Marriages 1817-1880* , Wes Cochran, 2515 10th Ave, Parkersburg, WV 26101, There are two entries for the marriage of James L. Swisher and Mary Hinzman. One is for a marriage date of Feb 21 1855 and the other for Feb 25 1855. Though not stated as such, the first is probably the date of the marriage bond, and the second of the wedding itself.

dliv[554] Penny & O.D. Linder, http://home.comcast.net/~jmlinder609, *The Gibson and Related Families* , McClain Printing Co, Parsons WV, 1991, p. 525.

dlv[555] *Lewis County WV Marriages 1881-1937* , Wes Cochran, 2515 10th Ave, Parkersburg, WV 26101 (Sep 1994), Identified as William Henry Swisher, 32, of Lewis Co; and May Cookman, 26, of Lewis Co. Married May 26 1892.

dlvi[556] Tina J. Kutschbach, Chillicothe, OH <tinak@adelphia.net>, *Kutschbach Family Tree* (Ancestry World Tree Project at http://awt.ancestry.com).

dlvii[557] *Lewis County WV Marriages 1881-1937* , Wes Cochran, 2515 10th Ave, Parkersburg, WV 26101 (Sep 1994), Identified as Alfred Washington Swisher, age 22, of Lewis Co, son of James L. & Mary; and Eliza Irena Allman, age 22, of Lewis Co, dau of William & Kitura. Married Mar 25 1886.

dlviii[558] *Lewis County WV Marriages 1881-1937* , Wes Cochran, 2515 10th Ave, Parkersburg, WV 26101 (Sep 1994), Identified as John Emory Swisher, age 23, of Lewis Co, son of James L. & Mary; and Minnie McKinney, age 20, b. Harrison Co, res. Lewis Co, dau of Jasper N. & Lydia. Married Jun 24 1896.

dlix[559] Wood County Death Records, Parkersburg, WV.

dlx[560] 1880 Census, Harrison County, WV (Elk District).

dlxi[561] Lewis County Death Records, Weston, WV, Identified as Sarah Jane Hinzman, sex F, color M, age 77, marital status widow, died Jan 2 1913 at Berlin, cause of death senility. DR p. 368.

dlxii[562] Lewis County Court House, Weston, WV, Wes Cochran's "Lewis County WV Marriages 1817-1880" reports two conflicting entries for this couple: (1) Perry G. Hinzman & Sarah J. Swisher, married Nov 25 1850; and (2) Berry H. Hinzman & Sarah J. Swisher, married Dec 9 1850. But according to Lewis County Marriage Record Book 3, page 28, the marriage occurred on Nov 28 1850. MR Bk 3, p. 28.

dlxiii[563] Lewis County Birth Records, Weston, WV, Handwritten entry had middle initial as either an "I" or a "J". BR Bk 1.

dlxiv[564] *Lewis County WV Marriages 1881-1937* , Wes Cochran, 2515 10th Ave, Parkersburg, WV 26101 (Sep 1994), Identified as David Thomas Allman, widowed, age 50, of Lewis Co, son of William & Kitturah; and Sophia Hinzman, age 43, of Lewis Co, dau of Perry G. & Sarah J. Married Jul 4 1915.

dlxv[565] Penny & O.D. Linder, http://home.comcast.net/~jmlinder609, *The Gibson and Related Families* , McClain Printing Co, Parsons WV, 1991, p. 321.

dlxvi[566] Lewis County Death Records, Weston, WV, Age at death appeared to be 56y 4m 13d (putting birth at Dec 23 1818, nearly impossible), but 36y 4m 13 is more likely, making birth Dec 23 1838. Identified as son of I. Swisher & husband of Eda Swisher. Researcher Jeffrey Wood reports birth as 1840 in Berlin, Lewis Co. DR Bk 1, p. 91.

dlxvii[567] Lewis County Death Records, Weston, WV, DR Bk 1, p. 91.

dlxviii[568] Lewis County Court House, Weston, WV, DR Bk 1, p. 91.

dlxix[569] Lewis County Death Records, Weston, WV, Identified as the son of Isaac R. and Eda Swisher, born in Lewis Co. Birth date not stated, but age at death given as 1y 1m 17d, which would correspond to a birth date of Jun 20 1870. DR Bk 1, p. 69.

dlxx[570] Minnie Kendall Lowther, *Ritchie County in History and Romance* (McClain Publishing Co, Parsons, WV, 1990), p. 317.

dlxxi[571] Harrison County Marriage Records, Clarksburg, WV, MR Bk 7, p. 278.

dlxxii[572] Minnie Kendall Lowther, *Ritchie County in History and Romance* (McClain Publishing Co, Parsons, WV, 1990), Marriage appears elsewhere as 1846. p. 317.

dlxxiii[573] Minnie Kendall Lowther, *Ritchie County in History and Romance* (McClain Publishing Co, Parsons, WV, 1990), Birthdate Oct 6 1825 appears elsewhere. p. 317.

dlxxiv[574] Minnie Kendall Lowther, *Ritchie County in History and Romance* (McClain Publishing Co, Parsons, WV, 1990), pp. 316-317.

dlxxv[575] Susie Davis Nicholson, *Davis - The Settlers of Salem, West Virginia* , Gordon Printing Co, Strasburg OH, 1979 (Revised & Enlarged), p. 116.

dlxxvi[576] *Harrison County WV Marriages 1785-1894* , Wes Cochran, 2515 10th Ave, Parkersburg, WV 26101 (1985), Identified as George Washington Dayton, 23, b. Frederick Co MD, res. Harrison Co, son of Nicholas & Martin [sic]; and Mary Catherine Gaston, 23, of Harrison Co, dau of John [sic] & Charlotte. Married Aug 14 1855. Identification of her parents as John & Charlotte, rather than James & Charlotte, is considered to be a transcription error. The adjoining entry is for the marriage of Isaac Rinehart Smith and Sarah Gaston, also erroneously identified as dau of John & Charlotte rather than John & Elizabeth.

dlxxvii[577] 1880 Census, Harrison County, WV (Grant District).

dlxxviii[578] Newspaper extract (Democrat), But researcher Lauri Buell Boaz, based on notes of grandmother Frances Virginia Helmick, reports his death date as March 3 1914. Issue 3/20/1914.

dlxxix[579] Newspaper extract (Democrat), Age at death given as 73, which is likely to have been in error. Also conflicting with the headstone dates is a source putting her date of death at Oct 10 1917. Issue 10/20/1911.

dlxxx[580] Headstone - Age at death given as 1y 5m 28d.

dlxxxi[581] Headstone, Age at death shown as 3 years. Cemetery directory giving age as 13y 6m appears to be in error.

dlxxxii[582] Headstone - Age at death given as 19y 7d.

dlxxxiii[583] Newspaper extracts (Rep., issue of 6/18/1887) (Ind., 7/2/1887).

dlxxxiv[584] Headstone, Cemetery directory giving age at death as 19y 17d is incorrect. Headstone reads 19y 7.

dlxxxv[585] *West Virginia Marriage Records, 1863-1900* (http://www.ancestry.com/search/rectype/inddbs/4484.htm), One source puts marriage at unspecified date in 1859. Another (Lauri Buell Boaz, based on notes of Frances Virginia Helmick) cites Jan 27 or 28 1864.

dlxxxvi[586] Marion County Marriage Records, Fairmont, WV, Identified as John S. Peirpoint, widowed, 52, b. Ritchie Co, res. Marion Co; and Miss Lucy Helmick, 30, b. & res. in Marion Co. Married May 17 1899 in Fairmont. MR p. 455.

dlxxxvii[587] 1880 Census, Ritchie County, WV (Union District).

dlxxxviii[588] Ritchie County Marriage Records, Harrisville, WV.

dlxxxix[589] Marion County Marriage Records, Fairmont, WV.

dxc[590] *Harrison County WV Marriages 1785-1894* , Wes Cochran, 2515 10th Ave, Parkersburg, WV 26101 (1985), Identified as John Stewart, 25, b. Louisa Co VA, res. Upshur Co, son of Robert & Eliza; and Rebecca A. Gaston, 18, of Harrison Co, dau of James & Charlotte. Married Dec 7 1859.

dxci[591] Headstone, Age at death given as 11m 23d.

dxcii[592] Social Security Death Index.

dxciii[593] *Social Security Death Index* , Social Security card issued in West Virginia in 1973. Name listed in SSDI as Eliza Salzer.

dxciv[594] *Lewis County WV Marriages 1881-1937* , Wes Cochran, 2515 10th Ave, Parkersburg, WV 26101 (Sep 1994), Identified as Alois J. Salzer, widowed, 47, b. Cuyahoga Co OH, res. Lewis Co, son of A. F. & Sadie M.; and Mary Eliza Stewart, 38, of Lewis Co, dau of John & Rebecca A. Married Nov 22 1921.

dxcv[595] *Marion County WV Marriages 1842-1899* , Wes Cochran, 2515 10th Ave, Parkersburg, WV 26101.

dxcvi[596] Marion County Court House, Fairmont, WV, MR C-35.

dxcvii[597] *Marion County WV Marriages 1842-1899* , Wes Cochran, 2515 10th Ave, Parkersburg, WV 26101, But daughter Lelia's death record states her mother's birthplace as Marion County.

dxcviii[598] Marion County Court House, Fairmont, WV, MR 9-4.

dxcix[599] Marion County Court House, Fairmont, WV, DR Bk 14, p. 642.

dc[600] WV State Dept of Health, Div of Vital Statistics, *Death Certificate* (http://www.wvculture.org/vrr/va_dcsearch.aspx), Identified as Olive Jane Chidester, b. Jan 12 1845 in Harrison Co, d. Oct 2 1930 in Weston, dau of James Gaston & Charlotte Swisher, widow of William H. Morris.

dci[601] *Lewis County WV Marriages 1817-1880* , Wes Cochran, 2515 10th Ave, Parkersburg, WV 26101, Identified as Wellington Vincent Chidester, widowed, age 71, of Lewis Co, son of Phineas W. & Susannah; and Olive J. Morris, widowed, b. Harrison Co, res. Lewis Co, dau of James & Charlotte Gaston. Married Apr 6 1897.

dcii[602] Wood County Marriage Records, Parkersburg, WV.

dciii[603] Paula Jones <paulaj@crcom.net> (posted at http://awt.ancestry.com, citing McLinn.FTW).

dciv[604] *Social Security Death Index* , Social Security card issued in West Virginia before 1951.

dcv[605] Lewis County Death Records, Weston, WV, Age at death given as 79y 2m 9d. DR Bk 4, p. 69 : http://www.wvculture.org/vrr/va_view.aspx?Id=4935072&Type=Death.

dcvi[606] Newspaper extract (Independent), Issue 6/18/1918.

dcvii[607] 1870 Census, Lewis County, WV (Lincoln Township), 104.

dcviii[608] Jim Comstock, *West Virginia Heritage Encyclopedia* (Hardesty Books).

dcix[609] Headstone, Name inscribed as "Loman B. Gaston".

dcx[610] *Lewis County WV Marriages 1881-1937* , Wes Cochran, 2515 10th Ave, Parkersburg, WV 26101 (Sep 1994), Identified as Loman Benjamin Gaston, age 38, of Lewis Co, son of Abram & Sarah A.; and Retta Norris, age 32, of Lewis Co, dau of J. W. & Jane. Married Aug 14 1904.

dcxi[611] Lewis County Death Records, Weston, WV, Birth date calculated from age at death given as 67y 1m 24d. Name appears in death record as Maretta. DR Bk 5, p. 65.

dcxii[612] Lewis County Death Records, Weston, WV, DR Bk 5, p. 65.

dcxiii[613] Headstone, Name inscribed as "Retta Gaston".

dcxiv[614] Lewis County Death Records, Weston, WV, DR Bk 1, p. 79.

dcxv[615] Headstone, Name on headstone: Simeon F. Gaston.

dcxvi[616] Newspaper extract (Independent), Issue 2/12/1901.

dcxvii[617] 1870 Census, Lewis County, WV (Lincoln Township), 103.

dcxviii[618] Penny & O.D. Linder, http://home.comcast.net/~jmlinder609, *The Gibson and Related Families* , McClain Printing Co, Parsons WV, 1991, p. 46.

dcxix[619] Newspaper extract (Democrat), Issue 2/19/1909.

dcxx[620] Penny & O.D. Linder, http://home.comcast.net/~jmlinder609, *The Gibson and Related Families* , McClain Printing Co, Parsons WV, 1991, p. 109.

dcxxi[621] Lewis County Marriage Records, Weston, WV.

dcxxii[622] WV State Dept of Health, Div of Vital Statistics, *Death Certificate* (http://www.wvculture.org/vrr/va_dcsearch.aspx), "Cemeteries of Union District, Harrison County WV" reports the following two headstones at Good Hope Masonic Cemetery:

Emma Thrash, b. Nov 14 1864, d. (blank).

Emma Strader, b. (blank), d. Dec 12 1955.

dcxxiii[623] *Lewis County WV Marriages 1881-1937* , Wes Cochran, 2515 10th Ave, Parkersburg, WV 26101 (Sep 1994), Identified as Frank Harrison Rymer, 26, of Lewis Co, son of Silas & Sarah; and Emma Gaston, 22, of Lewis Co, dau of George & Martha. Married Sep 25 1887. (Note: Frank Harrison Rymer does not appear with the Silas Rymer family in the 1870 or 1880 Census. No death record has been found for him.).

dcxxiv[624] Lewis County Marriage Records, Weston, WV, Identified as John Marshall Thrash, 57, b. Hampshire Co, res. Frontier Co Nebraska; and Mrs. Emma Rymer, b. & res. in Lewis Co. Married Sep 3 1893 "at J. S. Law's on Two Lick, Harrison Co, W. Va.", MR p. 174.

dcxxv[625] Harrison County Marriage Records, Clarksburg, WV, Identified as Newton Jefferson Strader, divorced, 58, b. Lewis Co, res. Clarksburg WV, son of Valentine & Mary Strader; and Mrs. Emma Thrash, widowed, 52, b. Lewis Co, res. Harrison Co, dau of George & Martha Gaston. Married Jun 29 1916 "at the home of the bride.", MR p. 323.

dcxxvi[626] Newspaper extract (Democrat), Issue 3/27/1914.

dcxxvii[627] *Cemeteries of Union District, Harrison County, WV* , Harrison County Genealogical Society, Clarksburg, WV (1990), Birth date incorrectly reported as 1863. p. 17.

dcxxviii[628] Penny & O.D. Linder, http://home.comcast.net/~jmlinder609, *The Gibson and Related Families* , McClain Printing Co, Parsons WV, 1991, p. 111.

dcxxix[629] *Harrison County WV Marriages 1785-1894* , Wes Cochran, 2515 10th Ave, Parkersburg, WV 26101 (1985), Identified as John W. Gaston, 21, of Harrison Co, son of William & Mary; and Maria Burnside, 19, of Harrison Co, dau of James & Rebecca. Married Dec 29 1859.

dcxxx[630] *Harrison County WV Marriages 1785-1894* , Wes Cochran, 2515 10th Ave, Parkersburg, WV 26101 (1985), Identified as George A. Davis, 24, of Harrison Co, son of George A. & Sarah; and Leonne Gaston, 23, of Harrison Co, dau of John W. & Mariah. Married Jan 31 1884.

dcxxxi[631] Harrison County Birth Records, Clarksburg, WV, Name listed only as "May Gaston," daughter of John W. & Maria (sic) Gaston. BR Bk 2, p. 54.

dcxxxii[632] Penny & O.D. Linder, http://home.comcast.net/~jmlinder609, *The Gibson and Related Families* , McClain Printing Co, Parsons WV, 1991, p. 107.

dcxxxiii[633] *Harrison County WV Marriages 1785-1894* , Wes Cochran, 2515 10th Ave, Parkersburg, WV 26101 (1985), Identified as Enoch Gaston, 24, of Harrison Co, son of William & Mary; and Laura T. Sheets, 19, of Harrison Co, dau of George H. & Mary J. Married Nov 9 1865.

dcxxxiv[634] Headstone, Age at death: 30y 5m 21d.

dcxxxv[635] *Harrison County WV Marriages 1785-1894* , Wes Cochran, 2515 10th Ave, Parkersburg, WV 26101 (1985), Identified as Enoch Gaston, widowed, age 40, of Harrison Co, son of William & Mary; and Flora Bond, 22, of Harrison Co, dau of Abel P. & Adaline. Married oct 20 1881.

dcxxxvi[636] Penny & O.D. Linder, http://home.comcast.net/~jmlinder609, *The Gibson and Related Families* , McClain Printing Co, Parsons WV, 1991, p. 105.

dcxxxvii[637] Harrison County Birth Records, Clarksburg, WV, Identified as Wade Gaston, born March 7 1868 to Enoch Gaston and Laura T. Gaston. The 1880 Harrison Co Census shows Wade Gaston (age 12) living at his grandparents William (74) & Mary (70) with widowed father Enoch. BR Bk 1, p. 132.

dcxxxviii[638] Harrison County Death Records, Clarksburg, WV, The entry shows Wade Gaston, son of Enoch Gaston and Laura Sheets, died a widower on Feb 17 1943 at the age of 74y 11m 10d. The person providing info identified as Charlie Gaston, presumably Wade's half-brother. DR Bk 13, p. 91A.

dcxxxix[639] Harrison County Death Records, Clarksburg, WV, DR Bk 13, p. 91A.

dcxl[640] Harrison County Marriage Records, Clarksburg, WV, Identified as Jesse A. Woofter, widowed, age 48, b. Lewis Co, son of Alfred & Mary Woofter; and Ethel Gaston, widowed, age 38, b. Harrison Co, dau of Enoch & Flora Gaston. Married Sep 4 1921 at Lost Creek by Rev C. D. Tharp. MR p. 395.

dcxli[641] Harrison County Birth Records, Clarksburg, WV, BR Bk 1, p. 7.

dcxlii[642] William F. Donnelly, *The Wests of Duck Creek, Harrison County, Virginia (now West Virginia)* , Gateway Press, Baltimore MD, 1997, p. 416.

dcxliii[643] *Harrison County WV Marriages 1895-1912* , Wes Cochran, 2515 10th Ave, Parkersburg, WV 26101 (Feb 2001), Identified as Lawrence Golding Kincheloe, 28, of Wood Co, son of J. T. & Florence; and Clara Smith, 26, of Harrison Co, dau of E. N. & Byrd. Married Sep 16 1908.

dcxliv[644] Headstone, But birth given as 7/18/1886 by G. Jeff Whittaker, Upper Marlboro, MD.

dcxlv[645] G. J. Whittaker, a Gaston descendant and researcher, Name sometimes appears as Alice, which is incorrect.

dcxlvi[646] *Daughters of the American Revolution Lineage Book*, Vol 148, p. 255, lineage of Beulah Stanford Gaston, DAR No. 147806.

dcxlvii[647] Charles A. Hanna, *Ohio Valley Genealogies* , Genealogical Publishing Co, Baltimore MD, 1989 (orig. pub. 1900), Death reported as 1888-89 in Des Moines, Iowa. p. 43.

dcxlviii[648] Paul M. Gaston, Man and Mission: E. B. Gaston and the Origins of the Fairhope Single Tax Colony , Black Belt Press, Montgomery, AL (1993), p. 18.

dcxlix[649] Paul M. Gaston, Man and Mission: E. B. Gaston and the Origins of the Fairhope Single Tax Colony , Black Belt Press, Montgomery, AL (1993), p. 17.

dcl[650] Katie Dailey Gaston, a Gaston family historian, in a letter to Jacquie Gaston Blevins dated March 19 1968, pointing out that the actual location was probably in the Finleyville-Gastonville area.

dcli[651] Katie Dailey Gaston, a Gaston family historian, in a letter to Jacquie Gaston Blevins dated March 19 1968, stating that he was visiting a daughter in Cranesville at the time of his death.

dclii[652] Katie Dailey Gaston (1901-1995), a Gaston family historian, in a letter to Jacquie Gaston Blevins dated March 19 1968.

dcliii[653] Headstone, - Inscription reads "Susan C. A., Child & Dau of Wm. & Eliza Gaston, died July 22 1856, aged 20 yrs." Parts of the inscription were barely legible, and there may be another word preceding "Child," possibly "Only.".

dcliv[654] 1850 Census, Washington County, PA (Union Twp).

dclv[655] Headstone, - Inscription reads "In Memory of Hugh Morgan, Son of Samuel & Eliza Morgan, Who departed this life May 2nd A.D. 1833 in the 5th year of his age.".

dclvi[656] Headstone, - Inscription reads "Matilda, daughter of S. & E. Morgan, died Sept 11 1841 in the 12 year of her age.".

dclvii[657] Headstone, Hanna, in "Ohio Valley Genealogies," p. 43, incorrectly reports death date as 1870. Headstone clearly shows it as 1879.

dclviii[658] Peter J. Topoly & Jane Carson Topoly, 10015 Mike Road, Fort Washington, MD 20744-2535, citing highly reliable original sources. But Hanna, "Ohio Valley Genealogies," p. 43, gives death as 1870.

dclix[659] Headstone, - Inscription reads "Jane, wife of Joseph S. Gaston, died Aug 5 1871 in the 63 year of her age.".

dclx[660] Peter J. Topoly & Jane Carson Topoly, 10015 Mike Road, Fort Washington, MD 20744-2535, citing highly reliable original sources. But Hanna, "Ohio Valley Genealogies," p. 43, gives death as 1879.

dclxi[661] Headstone, - Inscription reads "William R., son of Joseph S. & Jane Gaston, died Oct 10 1868 in the 23 year of his age.".

dclxii[662] Peter J. Topoly & Jane Carson Topoly, 10015 Mike Road, Fort Washington, MD 20744-2535, citing highly reliable original sources. Hanna, "Ohio Valley Genealogies," p. 113, gives marriage only as occurring in 1851.

dclxiii[663] Death Record - Online, Death date reported as Aug 14 1922 by researcher Bill Gaston.

dclxiv[664] *History of the Upper Ohio Valley* (Brant & Feller - 1890), Member of the United Presbyterian Church of Toronto, Jefferson Co, OH. p. 146.

dclxv[665] *History of the Upper Ohio Valley* (Brant & Feller - 1890), pp. 635, 636.

dclxvi[666] Peter J. Topoly & Jane Carson Topoly, 10015 Mike Road, Fort Washington, MD 20744-2535, citing highly reliable original sources. But "History of the Upper Ohio Valley," p. 636, gives marriage date as July 9 1857.

dclxvii[667] *History of the Upper Ohio Valley* (Brant & Feller - 1890), p. 636.

dclxviii[668] Max Perry, "American Descendants of William Gaston and Mary Olivet Lemon," gives first name as David. But Cecil Lee Jones, Jr., in "Gaston Crier," May 1997, and "American Ancestry," Vol V, p. 86, give first name as Daniel.

dclxix[669] *American Ancestry, Vol. V* (originally published 1890 by Joel Munsell's Sons; republished 1968 by Genealogical Publishing Co, Baltimore), 86.

dclxx[670] Headstone has Feb- 4-1853 11y 9m 9d [Max Perry], 148.

dclxxi[671] Headstone - Age at death given as 11y 9m 9d.

dclxxii[672] Max Perry, American Descendants of William Gaston and Mary Olivet Lemon (Midland, TX, 1989), p. 148.

dclxxiii[673] Max Perry, American Descendants of William Gaston and Mary Olivet Lemon (Midland, TX, 1989), 149.

dclxxiv[674] Max Perry, American Descendants of William Gaston and Mary Olivet Lemon (Midland, TX, 1989), 150.

dclxxv[675] Cheryl Levine <cdlevine@aol.com>, *James McLene Descendants* (Ancestry World Tree Project, posted at http://awt.ancestry.com).

dclxxvi[676] *Daughters of the American Revolution Lineage Book*, Vol. 32, p. 318, lineage of Ida E. Gaston, DAR ID No. 31862.

dclxxvii[677] *Daughters of the American Revolution Lineage Book*, Vol. 32, p. 318, lineage of Elizabeth Denny Gaston, DAR ID No. 31860.

dclxxviii[678] *Daughters of the American Revolution Lineage Book*, Vol. 37, p. 308, lineage of Emma Gaston Evans, DAR No. 37875.

dclxxix[679] *Daughters of the American Revolution Lineage Book*, Vol. 32, p. 318, lineage of Elizabeth Blanch Gaston, DAR ID No. 31861.

dclxxx[680] Parents' headstone.

dclxxxi[681] 1920 Census.

dclxxxii[682] Michigan Deaths, 1971-1996 (online), Ancestry.com and Michigan Dept of Vital & Health Records.

dclxxxiii[683] *Social Security Death Index* , Social Security card issued in Michigan before 1951.

dclxxxiv[684] National Archives and Records Administration, *World War I Draft Registration Cards, 1917-1918* (Ancestry.com online database).

dclxxxv[685] *Social Security Death Index* , Social Security card issued in Connecticut before 1951.

dclxxxvi[686] U.S. Passport Applications, 1795-1925 (online database) , Ancestry.com.

dclxxxvii[687] George M. Kasson, *Genealogy of a Part of the Kasson Family in the United States and Ireland (1882)* (Brigham Young University Family History Archives, http://www.lib.byu.edu/fhc/), p. 48.

dclxxxviii[688] George M. Kasson, *Genealogy of a Part of the Kasson Family in the United States and Ireland (1882)* (Brigham Young University Family History Archives, http://www.lib.byu.edu/fhc/), p. 27.

dclxxxix[689] George M. Kasson, *Genealogy of a Part of the Kasson Family in the United States and Ireland (1882)* (Brigham Young University Family History Archives, http://www.lib.byu.edu/fhc/), p. 47.

dcxc[690] Sylvia E. "Loy" Wortman Kralik <sylvia@cottagesoft.com> (http://members.aol.com/krhhhh).

dcxci[691] *Social Security Death Index* , Social Security card issued in Nebraska before 1951.

dcxcii[692] Hal Hatcher <halhai@radiks.net> (posted at http://awt.ancestry.com), Citing obituary in Tabor Beacon of Nov 12 1909.

dcxciii[693] Death Record - Online.

dcxciv[694] Bill Gaston, Austin TX <bgaston2@mindspring.com>, *Descendants: The Huguenot John Jean Gaston b: About 1600, France* (http://home.mindspring.com/~bgaston2/), http://wc.rootsweb.com/cgi-bin/igm.cgi?op=GET&db=ebernabe&id=I4002.

dcxcv[695] Lineage Book, National Society of the Daughters of the American Revolution, Vol XLIX, 1904, republished 1919. p. 449.

dcxcvi[696] Headstone, Name on headstone: C. Samuel Gaston.

dcxcvii[697] *North Carolina Death Certificates, 1909-1975 (online)* , Ancestry.com and North Carolina State Archives.

dcxcviii[698] Mary Gaston Gee (1899-1987), The Ancestry and Descendants of Amzi Williford Gaston II (1841-1911) of Spartanburg County, South Carolina (Charlottesville, VA, 1944), p. 37.

dcxcix[699] *Social Security Death Index* , Social Security card issued in South Carolina before 1951.

dcc[700] Obituary - At home.

dcci[701] Mary Gaston Gee (1899-1987), The Ancestry and Descendants of Amzi Williford Gaston II (1841-1911) of Spartanburg County, South Carolina (Charlottesville, VA, 1944), p. 25.

dccii[702] Mary Gaston Gee (1899-1987), The Ancestry and Descendants of Amzi Williford Gaston II (1841-1911) of Spartanburg County, South Carolina (Charlottesville, VA, 1944), p. 28.

dcciii[703] Mary Gaston Gee (1899-1987), The Ancestry and Descendants of Amzi Williford Gaston II (1841-1911) of Spartanburg County, South Carolina (Charlottesville, VA, 1944), p. 43.

dcciv[704] Mary Gaston Gee (1899-1987), The Ancestry and Descendants of Amzi Williford Gaston II (1841-1911) of Spartanburg County, South Carolina (Charlottesville, VA, 1944), p. 44.

dccv[705] *South Carolina Death Records, 1821-1955 (online)* , Ancestry.com and SC Dept of Archives & History.

dccvi[706] Larry Charles "Chuck" Slaughter, Amarillo, TX <LCharlesS@aol.com.

dccvii[707] Larry Charles "Chuck" Slaughter, Amarillo, TX <LCharlesS@aol.com. Citing obituary.

dccviii[708] *Social Security Death Index* , Social Security card issued in North Carolina before 1951.

dccix[709] Doddridge County Marriage Records, West Union, WV, Identified as William H. Elliott, 22, occupation shoe maker, b. & res. in Ritchie Co, son of Jacob & Barbara S. Elliott; and Rosetta Perine, 20, b. & res. in Doddridge Co, dau of David & Matilda Perine. Married Oct 23 1865 in Doddridge County. MR Bk 1-A, p. 252.

dccx[710] Doddridge County Marriage Records, West Union, WV, MR Bk 1-A, p. 252.

dccxi[711] Doddridge County Marriage Records, West Union, WV.

dccxii[712] Doddridge County Birth Records, West Union, WV, Identified as "W. F. Elliott," a child of William & Rosetta Elliott. Geogia Hileman Halloran concurs, citing census records. But death record shows name as Waitman T. Elliott, b. June 1870, source David Elliott. BR Bk 1, p. 48.

dccxiii[713] Doddridge County Birth Records, West Union, WV.

dccxiv[714] Doddridge County Birth Records, West Union, WV, Name recorded as "Eddy Elliott." Georgia Hileman Halloran reports birth exactly one month later, on Jul 10 1881. The 1900 Census puts birth date in Jun 1883. BR Bk 1, p. 114.

dccxv[715] Doddridge County Birth Records, West Union, WV, Identified only as a male child, no first name recorded. The record reports the birth as being on Apr 4 1889, the seventh child of this mother. The Birth Record Index lists birthdate as Apr 3, presumably a clerical error. BR Bk 2, p. 95.

dccxvi[716] Doddridge County Death Records, West Union, WV, Identified as James Elliott, white male, born at Arnolds Creek; died Sep 23 1889 at Arnolds Creek, age 5 mo 20 da, cause of death "enlargement of head," burial at Ruley's. DR p. 23.

dccxvii[717] Doddridge County Court House, West Union, WV, Will Book 3-468, App F15-70. Will probated May 23 1935. Heirs were listed as follows: Daughters: Dona Britton, Lelia Rollins and Lula Sullivan, all of West Union, and Ada Netzer of Charleston, WV; Son: W. T. Perine, Harmony, PA. Administrator of the estate was his daughter Lula Sullivan. No death record for this Richard Perine was found in Doddridge County.

dccxviii[718] Doddridge County Marriage Records, West Union, WV, Identified as Richie Perine, age 24, b. Harrison Co, son of David & Matilda; and Mary J. Fleming, age 17, b. Doddridge Co, dau of Eli & Elmina. MR Bk 1-A, p. 188.

dccxix[719] Doddridge County Birth Records, West Union, WV, Identified as Jane Fleming, b. Mar 25 1857 at Arnolds Creek, dau of E. B. and Emura [sic] Fleming. BR Bk 1, p. 9.

dccxx[720] Headstone, - Name appears on headstone as "Charles Prine.".

dccxxi[721] *West Union WV Cemeteries (Doddridge County)* , Wes Cochran, 2515 10th Ave, Parkersburg, WV 26101 (July 1990).

dccxxii[722] *Doddridge County WV Marriages 1845-1937* , Wes Cochran, 2515 10th Ave, Parkersburg, WV 26101 (Jan 1993), Identified as Edward P. Southworth, 22, b. Harrison Co, res. Doddridge Co; and Sarah A. Prine [sic], b. Harrison Co, res. Doddridge Co. Married Jul 2 1874.

dccxxiii[723] *West Virginia Marriage Records, 1863-1900* (http://www.ancestry.com/search/rectype/inddbs/4484.htm), Identified as John M. Harkins and Viola Southworth. Married in Taylor Co on Sep 12 1900.

dccxxiv[724] Taylor County Marriage Records, Grafton, WV.

dccxxv[725] Doddridge County Death Records, West Union, WV, DR Bk 4, p. 164.

dccxxvi[726] Doddridge County Marriage Records, West Union, WV, MR Bk 1-A, p. 194.

dccxxvii[727] *Doddridge County WV Marriages 1845-1937* , Wes Cochran, 2515 10th Ave, Parkersburg, WV 26101 (Jan 1993), Identified as Columbus D. Perine, 21, b. Harrison

Co, res. Doddridge Co, son of David & Matilda; and Alcinda I Cain, 15, of Doddridge Co, dau of Walter & Lydia. Married Apr 6 1873.

dccxxviii[728] Headstone. Birthplace from Apr 1873 marriage record, which gives age as 15. Headstone reads: "C. D. Perine & Alcindia Perine (his wife)." Her name is clearly spelled "Alcindia." No birth record found in Doddridge Co.

dccxxix[729] Doddridge County Birth Records, West Union, WV, BR Del 1, p. 134-B.

dccxxx[730] Headstone. A single headstone is shared by Beulah H. Perine (1888-1968), her daughter Edith L. [sic] Perine (1910-1963), and her sister-in-law Mary R. [sic] Perine (1882-1969).

dccxxxi[731] Doddridge County Birth Records, West Union, WV, BR Bk 2, p. 262.

dccxxxii[732] William F. Donnelly, *The Wests of Duck Creek, Harrison County, Virginia (now West Virginia)* , Gateway Press, Baltimore MD, 1997, p. 417.

dccxxxiii[733] William F. Donnelly, *The Wests of Duck Creek, Harrison County, Virginia (now West Virginia)* , Gateway Press, Baltimore MD, 1997, p. 207.

dccxxxiv[734] William F. Donnelly, *The Wests of Duck Creek, Harrison County, Virginia (now West Virginia)* , Gateway Press, Baltimore MD, 1997, Citing headstone inscription. p. 417.

dccxxxv[735] William F. Donnelly, *The Wests of Duck Creek, Harrison County, Virginia (now West Virginia)* , Gateway Press, Baltimore MD, 1997, p. 209.

dccxxxvi[736] Harrison County Marriage Records, Clarksburg, WV, Identified as Olandus West, 34, b. Harrison Co, res. Clarksburg, son of William M. & Hannah West; and Alma McWhorter, 27, b. & res. in Harrison Co, dau of John M. & Mary McWhorter. Married Nov 29 1906 "at the Brides's Home." (Note: Other researchers, e.g. William F. Donnelly citing Minnie McWhorter, incorrectly report marriage date one day earlier, on Nov 28 1906.), MR p. 148.

dccxxxvii[737] William F. Donnelly, *The Wests of Duck Creek, Harrison County, Virginia (now West Virginia)* , Gateway Press, Baltimore MD, 1997, p. 210.

dccxxxviii[738] Headstone, Name appears on headstone as "Elizabeth Edmonds".

dccxxxix[739] William F. Donnelly, *The Wests of Duck Creek, Harrison County, Virginia (now West Virginia)* , Gateway Press, Baltimore MD, 1997, Enumerated as a widow with two children. p. 414.

dccxl[740] William F. Donnelly, *The Wests of Duck Creek, Harrison County, Virginia (now West Virginia)* , Gateway Press, Baltimore MD, 1997, p. 415.

dccxli[741] Linn Baiker, Virginia Beach, VA <lb0530@cox.net>.

dccxlii[742] Brandie Coberly-Via <flowerutopia@yahoo.com> (posted at http://awt.ancestry.com, citing <cblyles@aol.com>).

dccxliii[743] *Doddridge County WV Deaths 1853-1969* , Wes Cochran, 2515 10th Ave, Parkersburg, WV 26101, Identified as J. J. West, male, died Jan 24 1906.

dccxliv[744] Harrison County Marriage Records, Clarksburg, WV, Identified as John J. West, farmer, 21, b. Harrison Co, res. Harrison Co, son of Eli R. & Belinda West; and Mary E. Cozad, 19, b. Lewis Co, res. Harrison Co, dau of Jacob J. & Sarah H. Cozad. Married Oct 30 1859. MR p. 13.

dccxlv[745] *Harrison County WV Marriages 1785-1894* , Wes Cochran, 2515 10th Ave, Parkersburg, WV 26101 (1985), Identified as John J. West, 21, of Harrison Co, son of Eli R. & Belinda; and Mary E. Cozad, 19, b. Lewis Co, res. Harrison Co, dau of Jacob J. & Sarah. Married Oct 25 1859. Harrison County marriage records have two entries for this marriage. One is dated Oct 26 1859 and appears to be an administrative document showing referring to witnesses and certificate. The other is a detailed description of the parties to the marriage, which took place on Oct 30 1859.

dccxlvi[746] WV State Dept of Health, Div of Vital Statistics, *Death Certificate* (http://www.wvculture.org/vrr/va_dcsearch.aspx), Identified as Mary E. West, dau of Jacob Cozad & Sarrah Henry, died Feb 11 1922 at Big Isaac at age 81y 10m 13d. Birth date given as Mar 29 1841, but age at death would put birth date at Mar 29 1840, the date provided to researcher William Donnelly by her grandson Russell G. West.

dccxlvii[747] William F. Donnelly, *The Wests of Duck Creek, Harrison County, Virginia (now West Virginia)* , Gateway Press, Baltimore MD, 1997, p. 418.

dccxlviii[748] Death record of father.

dccxlix[749] William F. Donnelly, *The Wests of Duck Creek, Harrison County, Virginia (now West Virginia)* , Gateway Press, Baltimore MD, 1997, p. 419.

dccl[750] 1920 Census, Doddridge County, WV (Greenbrier District).

dccli[751] *Doddridge County WV Marriages 1845-1937* , Wes Cochran, 2515 10th Ave, Parkersburg, WV 26101 (Jan 1993), Identified as George A. Hinkle, 46, b. Harrison Co, res. Doddridge Co; and L. Ellen McIntire, 44, b. Harrison Co, res. Doddridge Co. Married Mar 2 1914.

dcclii[752] William F. Donnelly, *The Wests of Duck Creek, Harrison County, Virginia (now West Virginia)* , Gateway Press, Baltimore MD, 1997, p. 424.

dccliii[753] *Harrison County WV Marriages 1895-1912* , Wes Cochran, 2515 10th Ave, Parkersburg, WV 26101 (Feb 2001), Identified as Wade H. Gulley, 24, of Doddridge Co, son of Joseph & Sarah; and Flora McIntire, 24, of Harrison Co, dau of J. F. & Sarah A. Married Sep 20 1900. Donnelly's "Wests of Duck Creek" (p. 419) reports marriage date as Sep 1 1900, citing D. R. Davisson papers.

dccliv[754] William F. Donnelly, *The Wests of Duck Creek, Harrison County, Virginia (now West Virginia)* , Gateway Press, Baltimore MD, 1997, p. 420.

dcclv[755] Doddridge County Death Records, West Union, WV, Identified as Mary Martha Haught, widow, died at Oxford on Aug 9 1932, age 82y8m20d. Dau of John Gaston & Jane Pritchard. Cause of death listed as myaconditis. Burial at Oxford Cemetery. DR Bk 4, p. 82.

dcclvi[756] Doddridge County Marriage Records, West Union, WV, Identified as Marvel L. Haught, 21, b. Greene Co PA, son of Peter B. & Bashaba Haught; and Mary A. Gaston, 18, b. Doddridge Co, dau of John M. & Jane Gaston. Married Mar 27 1868. Ceremony performed by Eli M. Gaston, uncle of the bride. MR Bk 1-A, p. 154.

dcclvii[757] Doddridge County Death Records, West Union, WV, Two conflicting death record entries have Marvel L. Haught, age 75, dying on Nov 28 1924 at Oxford of old age; and Marville L. Haught, age 78y 7m 18d, dying Dec 28 1924 at Summers of old age. The latter appears to be the more accurate and is the basis for his birthdate of May 10 1846. The Dec 28 1924 date is also given for his death in the obituary of his wife. His headstone gives only the years 1846 and 1924. Birthplace given in death record as Greene Co, PA. DR 4-81 & 2-64A.

dcclviii[758] Headstone, - Military marker gives unit as Co C, 6th Regiment, W.Va. Infantry. Name appears as Marville L. Haught, with birth/death dates of 1846-1924.

dcclix[759] Bradford Spiker (compiled by Barr Wilson), *The Good-Will Community: A History of Holbrook, W. Va., 1814-1945* , http://files.usgwarchives.net/wv/ritchie/history/goodwill.txt.

dcclx[760] Doddridge County Birth Records, West Union, WV, BR Bk 1, p. 49.

dcclxi[761] Doddridge County Birth Records, West Union, WV, Identified as "Columbia J. Hant," born May 16 1873, dau of "Mavel L. & Mary Martha." But headstone had birth date as May 22 1873. BR Bk 1, p. 61.

dcclxii[762] Doddridge County Court House, West Union, WV, BR Bk 1, p. 146.

dcclxiii[763] Doddridge County Birth Records, West Union, WV, Birth record information based on entry in family Bible. Spelling "Lindsey" of middle name is as it appears in the birth record and may be in error. BR Bk 2, p. 140.

dcclxiv[764] Obituary - Nursing home.

dcclxv[765] Obituary of father.

dcclxvi[766] Headstone, - Headstone reads "Dovener I. Haught, 1893-1927, son of M. L. & Mary Gaston Haught".

dcclxvii[767] 1900 Census, Doddridge County, WV (West Union District).

dcclxviii[768] Doddridge County Death Records, West Union, WV, Cause of death listed as lagrippe and typhoid fever. DR Bk 2, p. 146.

dcclxix[769] Doddridge County Marriage Records, West Union, WV, Ceremony performed by Eli M. Gaston. MR Bk 1-A, p. 156.

dcclxx[770] Doddridge County Death Records, West Union, WV, DR Bk 4, p. 188.

dcclxxi[771] Virginia Dunn Smith, Lake Suzy, FL 34266 <zvillesuzy@yahoo.com>.

dcclxxii[772] Doddridge County Birth Records, West Union, WV, BR Bk 1, p. 58.

dcclxxiii[773] Doddridge County Death Records, West Union, WV, DR Bk 3, p. 20.

dcclxxiv[774] Doddridge County Court House, West Union, WV, BR Bk 1, p. 81.

dcclxxv[775] 1920 Census, Doddridge County, WV (West Union District).

dcclxxvi[776] Doddridge County Marriage Records, West Union, WV, MR Bk 9, p. 10.

dcclxxvii[777] Doddridge County Marriage Records, West Union, WV, MR Bk 5, p. 264.

dcclxxviii[778] Death record of mother.

dcclxxix[779] Doddridge County Court House, West Union, WV, BR Bk 1, p. 97.

dcclxxx[780] Doddridge County Birth Records, West Union, WV, Identified only as an unnamed female Smith, born Sep 20 1882. Headstone has birth date as Sep 19 1882. BR Bk 1, p. 123.

dcclxxxi[781] Doddridge County Death Records, West Union, WV, DR Bk 3, p. 58: http://www.wvculture.org/vrr/va_view.aspx?Id=5047862&Type=Death.

dcclxxxii[782] Doddridge County Birth Records, West Union, WV, The birth record entry states birth date as Sep-16-1891. But headstone shows it as Dec-16-1891, which is confirmed by age at death, 1m24d, given in death record. BR Bk 2, p. 310.

dcclxxxiii[783] Doddridge County Death Records, West Union, WV, Age at death on Feb 10 1892 given as 1m 24d. Cause of death: La Grippe. There is another death record for Gracie Smith, dau of Harvey & Ivy Smith, who reportedly died Feb 10 1891 at age 5m 22d, putting her birth at Aug 19 1890. Nothing in the second entry corresponds with other data on this person. DR Bk 3, p. 20.

dcclxxxiv[784] Birth date calculated from age at death on death record.

dcclxxxv[785] Doddridge County Death Records, West Union, WV, Identified as Mary J. Britton, widow, died Dec 15 1915 at Summers, age 72y 3m 6d. Cause of death listed as pneumonia. DR Bk 2, p. 7.

dcclxxxvi[786] Doddridge County Marriage Records, West Union, WV, Identified as Joseph S. Britton, 24, b. in Monongalia Co, son of George W. & Mary Britton; and Mary Jane Gaston, 21, b. in Harrison Co, dau of Daniel & Nancy Gaston. Ceremony held Nov 30 1865, performed by Eli M. Gaston. MR Bk 1-A, p. 252.

dcclxxxvii[787] Doddridge County Death Records, West Union, WV, Identified as Joseph S. Britton, married, farmer, died Jun 25 1915 at Summers, age 73y 5m 24d. Cause of death listed as paralysis. DR Bk 2, p. 7.

dcclxxxviii[788] Doddridge County Death Records, West Union, WV, DR Bk 2, p. 7.

dcclxxxix[789] Doddridge County Death Records, West Union, WV, Identified as Martha A. Britton, single, died Sep 2 1901, age 32, of typhoid fever. DR Bk 1, p. 139.

dccxc[790] Headstone, Month & day barely legible and may be wrong. Middle initial may be "W".

dccxci[791] Headstone, Brothers Charles and Alexander Britton share the same headstone, which is barely legible.

dccxcii[792] Doddridge County Birth Records, West Union, WV, But headstone states both born and died on June 24, 1875. BR Bk 1, p. 71.

dccxciii[793] Doddridge County Birth Records, West Union, WV, BR Bk 1, p. 84.

dccxciv[794] *Doddridge County WV Marriages 1845-1937* , Wes Cochran, 2515 10th Ave, Parkersburg, WV 26101 (Jan 1993), Identified as Arthur A. Valentine, 22, of Gilmer Co; and Nancy Britton, 32, of Doddridge Co. Married Apr 24 1910.

dccxcv[795] Doddridge County Birth Records, West Union, WV, Identified as Mary Britton, b. Apr 12 1881, dau of J. S. & Mary J. Britton. This confirms that the Apr 12 1880 date shown on the headstone is incorrect. BR Bk 1, p. 113.

dccxcvi[796] Doddridge County Death Records, West Union, WV, Identified as Mary J. Britton, single, died Sep 2 1901at Summers. Cause of death given as typhoid fever and hemorrhage of the bowels. Age at death given as 20, which would be incorrect by one year based on the Apr 12 1880 birthdate on headstone. But birth record shows birthdate to have been one year later, on Apr 12 1881. DR Bk 1, p. 139.

dccxcvii[797] Headstone, - Marker is shared with her older sister Martha, with the same death date for both. Nothing further is known on that matter.

dccxcviii[798] Doddridge County Birth Records, West Union, WV, Identified as "F. C. Britton." But middle initial on badly worn headstone appears to be an "E." Name reported by researcher Richard Lyle "Dickie" Britton as "Frances E. Britton.".

dccxcix[799] Headstone, Inscription barely legible; death date was either June 8 or 3, 1886 or January 8 or 3, 1886.

dccc[800] Headstone - Doddridge County death records incorrectly show Sarah Ann Gaston, daughter of Daniel & N. Gaston, dying on July 6, 1859 at age 12 days. The name of the decedent should have been that of her sister, Hannah E. Gaston. DR Bk 3, p. 5.

dccci[801] Doddridge County Marriage Records, West Union, WV, Bride identified as Sarah Ann Gaston, age 19, born in Harrison Co, VA, dau of Daniel and Nancy Gaston. Ceremony performed by Eli M. Gaston. MR Bk 1-A, p. 250.

dcccii[802] Doddridge County Court House, West Union, WV, BR Bk 1, p. 30.

dccciii[803] Doddridge County Birth Records, West Union, WV, BR Bk 1, p. 39.

dccciv[804] Doddridge County Death Records, West Union, WV, Place of death listed as Britton's Rest Home, with cause being heart disease, and age 99 (but erroneously giving birthdate as May 14 1858). Identified as a widower and the son of Daniel (should be David) Richards and Sarah Gaston. DR Bk 5, p. 144-D.

dcccv[805] Doddridge County Court House, West Union, WV, DR Bk 5, p. 144-D.

dcccvi[806] Obituary - Hospital.

dcccvii[807] Doddridge County Birth Records, West Union, WV, BR Bk 1, p. 68.

dcccviii[808] Doddridge County Birth Records, West Union, WV, Identified as Louiza Richards, b. May 28 1874, dau of David & Sarah A. Richards. Hand-carved headstone reads Elizo O. Richards, with birth date May 29 1874. BR Bk 1, p. 68.

dcccix[809] 1900 Census, Ritchie County, WV (Union District).

dcccx[810] Doddridge County Birth Records, West Union, WV, The entry identifies child as S. A. Richards, female, b. Sep 19 1877, daughter of David & S. A. Richards. This is a typed ledger entry, undoubtedly transcribed from the original handwritten records. The middle initial "A" would seem to be a transcription error from the original "R" as found in the 1880 Census, where this child is clearly identifed as Sarah R. Richards. But the 1900 Census identifies her as Lina Richards (b. Sep 1877), the obituary of brother Daniel in 1968 lists a surviving sister Lina Watson of Parkersburg, the marriage record of Lina Richards in Dec 1902 give her age as 25 (i.e., born ca 1877), and the SSDI shows Lina Watson, b. 18 [sic] Sep 1877, a resident of Parkersburg. Thus, it would appear that at some point in her youth, Sarah R. Richards started going exclusively by the name Lina Richards. BR Bk 1, p. 89.

dcccxi[811] Doddridge County Marriage Records, West Union, WV, MR Bk 1-A, p. 212.

dcccxii[812] Doddridge County Death Records, West Union, WV, DR Bk 1, p. 161.

dcccxiii[813] Doddridge County Death Records, West Union, WV, Identified as Rulina A. Richards, age 54, d. Nov 17 1905 at Summers, buried at Summers. DR Bk 1, p. 161.

dcccxiv[814] Doddridge County Marriage Records, West Union, WV, Age of groom given as 38, bride as 24. MR Bk 1-A, p. 212.

dcccxv[815] Doddridge County Death Records, West Union, WV, DR Bk 2, p. 135.

dcccxvi[816] Doddridge County Death Records, West Union, WV, Identified as Samuel Richards, widower, d. Oct 22 1909 at Oxford, age 71y 9m 20d. DR Bk 2, p. 135.

dcccxvii[817] *Cemeteries of Tenmile District, Harrison County, WV* , Harrison County Genealogical Society, Clarksburg, WV (1989, revised 1995).

dcccxviii[818] Doddridge County Birth Records, West Union, WV, Her name appears as "Eliza L. Gasnins" with parents Daniel & Nancy Gaston. BR Bk 1, p. 1.

dcccxix[819] Doddridge County Marriage Records, West Union, WV, Marriage date of Dec 18 1875 reported by other researchers (e.g., Joy Gilchrist) is incorrect. MR Bk 1-A, p. 198.

dcccxx[820] *Doddridge County WV Marriages 1845-1937* , Wes Cochran, 2515 10th Ave, Parkersburg, WV 26101 (Jan 1993), Identified as Virgil B. Squires, 21, b. Barbour Co, res. Doddridge Co; and Eliza L. Gaston, 20, of Doddridge Co. Married Dec 18 1873.

dcccxxi[821] The History of Doddridge County, West Virginia , Taylor Publishing Co, 1979, p. 249.

dcccxxii[822] Doddridge County Court House, West Union, WV, BR Bk 2, p. 326.

dcccxxiii[823] Doddridge County Court House, West Union, WV, DR Bk 1, p. 89.

dcccxxiv[824] Doddridge County Marriage Records, West Union, WV, MR Bk 2, p. 252.

dcccxxv[825] Doddridge County Death Records, West Union, WV, Cause of death given as "Blood Poison", DR Bk 3, p. 51.

dcccxxvi[826] Doddridge County Marriage Records, West Union, WV, He is identified as Hughy J. Pierce, age 27 as of May 29 1883, b. Doddridge Co; and she as Nancy M. Gaston, age 27 as of Jul 22 1883, b. Doddridge Co. Ceremony conducted by Eli M. Gaston at "My Residence Doddridge Co West Va.", MR Bk 2, p. 252.

dcccxxvii[827] Doddridge County Death Records, West Union, WV, Identified as Hughly [sic] James Pierce, d. Dec 13 1938 at Oxford, age 82y 8m 14d, son of J. H. Pierce & Christena [sic] Wilson, burial at South Fork East Cem. Informant identified as Hettie Pierce, Oxford. It is noted that his obituary states that he "died at his home near Oxford, Ritchie County.", DR Bk 5, p. 133.

dcccxxviii[828] Doddridge County Death Records, West Union, WV, DR Bk 5, p. 133.

dcccxxix[829] Preston County Marriage Records, Kingwood, WV.

dcccxxx[830] Doddridge County Birth Records, West Union, WV, BR Bk 2, p. 256.

dcccxxxi[831] Doddridge County Death Records, West Union, WV, Identified as Hettie Jane Pierce, dau of Hughey James Pierce & Mariah Gaston, died Jan 30 1955 at Oxford, buried South Fork Baptist Cemetery, informant James V. Pierce (her half-brother). Birth date given as Apr 27 1889, in Doddridge Co, but this is incorrect. Her birth record shows her birth as Apr 27 1887, and her sister Laura was born in Jan 1889. DR Bk 5, p. 134-D.

dcccxxxii[832] Doddridge County Death Records, West Union, WV, DR Bk 5, p. 134-D.

dcccxxxiii[833] Doddridge County Birth Records, West Union, WV, Identified as Dora E. Pearce [sic], b. Jul 14 1891, dau of Hughey [sic] and Nancy, informant being the father. Another birth record, BR 2-264, is for Dora E. M. Pierce, b. Jul 23 1891 in Grove, dau of James Pierce, age 34, and Marie Gaston, age 36, filed Aug 20 1891, informant being Dr. G. F. Perry. This is either an invalid entry for the same child or is for another person, given the father's age and the fact that Nancy Maria Gaston Pierce died 3 days before the child's reported birth. We believe it is an invalid entry for the same child. BR Bk 2, p. 263.

dcccxxxiv[834] Doddridge County Death Records, West Union, WV, DR Bk 3, p. 57.

dcccxxxv[835] Doddridge County Death Records, West Union, WV, Identified as Dora E. M. Pierce, b. Jul 14 1891, dau of H. J. & Nancy M., d. Jun 24 1898, age 6y11m10d, cause of death given as jaundice. DR Bk 3, p. 57.

dcccxxxvi[836] Dolores Leeson "Dee" Dawson, Circleville, OH <ddawson@bright.net>.

dcccxxxvii[837] Doddridge County Court House, West Union, WV, DR Bk 2, p. 55.

dcccxxxviii[838] *Social Security Death Index* , Social Security card issued in Oklahoma before 1951.

dcccxxxix[839] Headstone, Name on headstone: Danial W. Gaston.

dcccxl[840] Doddridge County Court House, West Union, WV, Resident of Newkirk, Kay Co, Oklahoma, as of October 1922, when the original Daniel Gaston's (b. 1816) Harmony property was conveyed to Nancy Gaston Hart by her three siblings. [Doddridge Co Deed Book 79, p. 10] He was also a resident of Oklahoma at the time of Nancy Gaston Hart's death in 1932, per her obituary.

dcccxli[841] Doddridge Co Deed Book 79, p. 10, dated Oct-10-1922, conveying the original Daniel Gaston's property at Harmony from Eliza E. Gaston, D. W. Gaston, and Stella G. Cumberledge to Nancy C. Hart.

dcccxlii[842] Doddridge County Birth Records, West Union, WV, Name appears in birth record as John M. Gasmins with parents Eli M. Gaston & Julina Gaston, BR Bk 1, p. 1.

dcccxliii[843] Harrison County Death Records, Clarksburg, WV, Identified as John Morris Gaston, widowed, b. Sep 4 1853, son of Eli M. Gaston & Pauline Lowther, d. Nov 11 1927 at 201 Weekley St in Clarksburg, age 74y 2m 7d, cause of death pulmonary tuberculosis & influenza, certifying physician W. Gaston, buried at Gaston Cemetery on Nov 14 1927. Informant: J. S. Gaston. Date filed: Nov 28 1927. DR Bk 8, p. 83.

dcccxliv[844] Doddridge County Marriage Records, West Union, WV, Identified as John M. Gaston, 22, b. & res. in Doddridge Co, son of Eli M. & Rulina Gaston; and Elizabeth Hart, 17, b. & res. in Doddridge Co, dau of John G. & Melinda A. Hart. Married Aug 16 1876. Ceremony performed by A. Thomas. (Note: Wife's obituary states marriage date as being one day later, on Aug 17 1876, as does the couple's family Bible and a W. Guy Tetrick family information survey completed by son Ira Dow Gaston in 1931.), MR Bk 1-A, p. 212.

dcccxlv[845] Doddridge County Birth Records, West Union, WV, But Gaston Family Bible says August 25, 1858, and 1900 Census states Aug 1855. BR Bk 1, p. 10.

dcccxlvi[846] Obituary - At home, Obituary initially misidentifies her as Elizabeth Hart Maxwell, then later correctly refers to her as Mrs. Gaston.

dcccxlvii[847] Obituary - United Hospital Center.

dcccxlviii[848] Headstone, Lot 89,Sect 8,Grv7.

dcccxlix[849] City Directory, Clarksburg, Harrison Co, WV, 1957-58 (R. L. Polk & Co, Pittsburgh, PA).

dcccl[850] Headstone, Lot 89,Sect 8,Grv8.

dcccli[851] Doddridge County Birth Records, West Union, WV, BR Bk 2, p. 131.

dccclii[852] Doddridge County Birth Records, West Union, WV, BR Bk 3, p. 79.

dcccliii[853] Doddridge County Birth Records, West Union, WV, BR Bk 1, p. 10.

dcccliv[854] Upshur County Court House, Buckhannon, WV, DR p. 83.

dccclv[855] Newspaper article.

dccclvi[856] Obituary of mother.

dccclvii[857] Doddridge County Marriage Records, West Union, WV, Ceremony performed by M. Ireland. MR Bk 1-A, p. 232.

dccclviii[858] Upshur County Court House, Buckhannon, WV, MR Bk 5, p. 67.

dccclix[859] Upshur County Death Records, Buckhannon, WV, Cause of death given as "Poison in Blood", DR p. 1.

dccclx[860] Doddridge County Birth Records, West Union, WV, BR Bk 1, p. 121.

dccclxi[861] Ritchie County Death Records, Harrisville, WV, Identified as Minnie A. Gaston, white female, died July 29 1893 near Auburn, age 11y 4m 7d, cause of death diphtheria, burial at Gaston Cemetery on July 30 1893. Undertaker: J. Smith Gaston, Grove W.Va. DR Bk 1, p. 26.

dccclxii[862] Ritchie County Death Records, Harrisville, WV.

dccclxiii[863] Doddridge County Birth Records, West Union, WV, BR Bk 1, p. 146.

dccclxiv[864] Doddridge County Death Records, West Union, WV, DR Bk 3, p. 47.

dccclxv[865] Doddridge County Marriage Records, West Union, WV, Identified as Charles Leeson, 49, b. & res. in Doddridge Co; and Minnie J. Gaston, age 21 as of Oct 24 1915, b. Ritchie Co, res. Doddridge Co. Married Nov 1 1915 "at the residence of the Bride" by John M. Gaston, a Minister of the Gospel. MR Bk 9, p. 445.

dccclxvi[866] Upshur County Birth Records, Buckhannon, WV, BR Bk 4, p. 61.

dccclxvii[867] *Social Security Death Index* , Social Security card issued in California in 1952.

dccclxviii[868] Doddridge County Death Records, West Union, WV, Identified as Jessie [sic] Smith Gaston, b. Summers, Doddridge Co, WV, son of Eli M. Gaston & (mother blank),

d. May 4 1943 at West Union, age 82y 11m 22d, burial at Gaston Cemetery. DR Bk 5, p. 64.

dccclxix[869] Doddridge County Marriage Records, West Union, WV, Groom identified as Jesse S. Gaston, age 27, b. Doddridge Co, resident of Doddridge Co. Bride identified as Lucy M. Swiger, age 19, b. Harrison Co, resident of Doddridge Co. Married Aug 11 1887 "at the bride's father's, Doddridge Co, W. Va." Informants for the marriage license: Jesse S. Gaston & G. W. Swiger. MR Bk 3, p. 204.

dccclxx[870] Lewis County Death Records, Weston, WV, Identified as Hannah Strother, 28, b. Doddridge Co, dau of Eli Gaston, wife of J. E. Strother; died Apr 10 1893 in Lewis Co, cause of death "child bearing." Informant: D. F. Strother, brother-in-law. (Note: Law suit filed in Doddridge County Circuit Court in Nov 1911 identifies Hannah Strother as "a daughter of said Eli M. Gaston and who departed this life before the death of her said father" who died either Jan 27 or 28, 1909.), DR p. 201.

dccclxxi[871] Doddridge County Marriage Records, West Union, WV, Ages at time of marriage on May 20 1881 given as 26 for him and 18 for her. His birthplace given as Harrison County. Susie Davis Nicholson (p. 69) gives his middle name as Edmond, with marriage on May 29 1881 in Spencer, Roane County. Wes Cochran's "Doddridge County WV Marriages" also gives the May 29 1881 date. MR Bk 2, p. 29.

dccclxxii[872] Harrison County Birth Records, Clarksburg, WV, BR Bk 1, p. 16.

dccclxxiii[873] Doddridge County Death Records, West Union, WV, Name listed as "Ed Strouther," marital status "married." Age at death, 52y 4m 16d, would put birth on May 2 1855, at variance with Apr 1854 date shown in birth record. DR Bk 2, p. 146.

dccclxxiv[874] Doddridge County Birth Records, West Union, WV, Name given as "Ruben Strawther" and parents as "James & Hannah Strawther," but this is certainly incorrect. Headstone gives full correct name, Granville Reuben Strother, son of J.E. & H.R. Strother, with birth & death on same date, June (illegible, but possibly 23), 1882. BR Bk 1, p. 123.

dccclxxv[875] Law suit, Jesse S. Gaston, et al, vs. John M. Gaston, et al, filed in Nov 1911 in the Doddridge Co Circuit Court, listed Blanche Richards, nee Blanche Strother, as a surviving child of the late Hannah Strother.

dccclxxvi[876] Doddridge County Marriage Records, West Union, WV, Addison F. Richards listed as 29, born in Ritchie Co. Blanche M. Strother listed as 24, born in Doddridge Co. MR Bk 8, p. 171.

dccclxxvii[877] William Bernard Wilson, *Wilson-Pepper Genealogy 1595-1989* (Gateway Press, Baltimore, MD, 1990), p. 44.

dccclxxviii[878] Doddridge County Birth Records, West Union, WV, BR Bk 1, p. 149.

dccclxxix[879] Doddridge County Birth Records, West Union, WV, Unknown if "Clarl" was intended to be Clark, Carl, Charles or some other variation. BR Bk 2, p. 306.

dccclxxx[880] Doddridge County Birth Records, West Union, WV, He is incorrectly identified in the birth record as David S. Gaston, but his parents are correctly identified. BR Bk 1, p. 24.

dccclxxxi[881] Doddridge County Death Records, West Union, WV, DR Bk 5, p. 64-A.

dccclxxxii[882] Doddridge County Marriage Records, West Union, WV, Family Bible gives location as "Eli Gaston's Residence on Upper Run, Southwest Dist, Hallbrook [sic], W.Va." Witnesses: "Eli Hart and others." Ceremony performed by Rev. James Arnold [sp?]. MR Bk 3, p. 213.

dccclxxxiii[883] Doddridge County Birth Records, West Union, WV, A second birth record entry (BR Bk 1, p. 55) gives a birth date of May 8 1872, but this is believed to have been a clerical error. Her own family Bible states May 8 1871. BR Bk 1, p. 49.

dccclxxxiv[884] Doddridge County Death Records, West Union, WV, DR Bk 4, p. 71.

dccclxxxv[885] Elizabeth Witter Clarke Lerman, Dayton, OH 45406 <Lermanwmi@aol.com>.

dccclxxxvi[886] Family Bible, No record of this child found in Doddridge County birth or death records.

dccclxxxvii[887] *Gilmer County West Virginia History 1845-1989* , Gilmer County Historical Society, 1994, p 54.

dccclxxxviii[888] 1920 Census, Lewis County, WV.

dccclxxxix[889] 1910 Census, Lewis County, WV.

dcccxc[890] Wood County Death Records, Parkersburg, WV, DR Bk 11, p. 93.

dcccxci[891] *Harrison County WV Marriages 1895-1912* , Wes Cochran, 2515 10th Ave, Parkersburg, WV 26101 (Feb 2001), Identified as James Lloyd Gaston, 35, b. Lewis Co, res. Marion Co, son of Henry L. & Mary J.; and Wella Lohan, 26, b. Lewis Co, res. Harrison Co, dau of Michael (last name not stated), mother not identified. Married Jun 4 1906.

dcccxcii[892] Kanawha County Death Records, Charleston, WV.

dcccxciii[893] Kanawha County Death Records, Charleston, WV, Identified as Wella L. Gaston, father: Michael Lohan, mother: unknown.

dcccxciv[894] Kanawha County Death Records, Charleston, WV, Identified as James Kendall Gaston, son of James L. Gaston & Wella Lohan, b. Jan 18 1907 in Parkersburg, died May 13 1937 in Charleston, age 30y 4m 5d. Cause of death: tuberculous peritonitis.

dcccxcv[895] *Gilmer County West Virginia History 1845-1989* , Gilmer County Historical Society, 1994, p. 92.

dcccxcvi[896] *Gilmer County West Virginia History 1845-1989* , Gilmer County Historical Society, 1994, Citing Wayne K. Davis, son of Cecil G. Davis. p. 92.

dcccxcvii[897] *Gilmer County West Virginia History 1845-1989* , Gilmer County Historical Society, 1994, Citing Wayne K. Davis, son of Cecil G. Davis. p. 92.

dcccxcviii[898] *Gilmer County West Virginia History 1845-1989* , Gilmer County Historical Society, 1994, Citing Wayne K. Davis, son of Cecil G. Davis.

dcccxcix[899] *Gilmer County West Virginia History 1845-1989* , Gilmer County Historical Society, 1994, p 92.

cm[900] Headstone, Her age of 30 given at time of marriage in 1912 would put her birth in 1882, but headstone reads May 29 1884.

cmi[901] Doddridge County Marriage Records, West Union, WV, Her age given as 30, birthplace Gilmer County. MR Bk 9, p. 105.

cmii[902] 1930 Census, Doddridge County, WV (Greenbrier District).

cmiii[903] Doddridge County Marriage Records, West Union, WV, Marriage is recorded in Doddridge Co even though it took place in Harrison Co. Both parties were listed as being residents of Doddridge Co. MR Bk 9, p. 105.

cmiv[904] Obituary, At his Nov 1912 marriage to Eva Dell Gaston, Henry Orrahood gave his age as 58, thus putting his birth at ca 1854. But his obit in the Feb 2 1939 issue of the West Union Herald gave his birthdate as Mar 12 1848, the same as his headstone. Birthplace obtained from marriage record.

cmv[905] Obituary of half-brother.

cmvi[906] 1930 Census, Gilmer County, WV.

cmvii[907] Pearl Turner Gaston, Normantown, WV 25267.

cmviii[908] Roane County Marriage Records , Spencer, WV.

cmix[909] National Cemetery Administration. Nationwide Gravesite Locator, *U.S. Veterans Gravesites* (www.ancestry.com).

cmx[910] Obituary of husband's brother.

cmxi[911] Obituary - Veterans Administration Hospital.

cmxii[912] Lewis County Court House, Weston, WV, DR Bk 10, p 101.

cmxiii[913] Lewis County Court House, Weston, WV, DR Bk 8, p 110.

cmxiv[914] Lewis County Court House, Weston, WV, DR Bk 12, p 102.

cmxv[915] Lewis County Court House, Weston, WV, MR Bk 21, p 113.

cmxvi[916] Obituary - Weston Independent.

cmxvii[917] Upshur County Death Records, Buckhannon, WV.

cmxviii[918] Lewis County Marriage Records, Weston, WV, Identified as John Marion Gaston, single, farmer, 24, b. & res. in Lewis Co, son of Marion Gaston & Ellen Riffle; and Carry

Pearl Posey, single, 18, b. & res. in Lewis Co, dau of Isaac Posey & Emma Jane Posey. Married Oct 17 1919 in Orlando WVa. Informants for the marriage license: John M. Gaston & B. H. Riffle, guardian of Carry Posey, giving his written consent. MR p. 290 : http://www.wvculture.org/vrr/va_view.aspx?Id=10289889&Type=Marriage.

cmxix[919] Upshur County Death Records, Buckhannon, WV, Identified as Carrie Pearl Gaston, white female, married, born in Braxton Co, dau of Isaac Posey & Emma Jane Brake (sic); died Oct 6 1929, age 27y 6m 2d, cause of death chronic nephritis, burial at Blake Cemetery.
http://www.wvculture.org/vrr/va_view.aspx?Id=5954882&Type=Death.

cmxx[920] Birth record of daughter.

cmxxi[921] Upshur County Marriage Records, Buckhannon, WV.

cmxxii[922] 1930 Census, Upshur County, WV.

cmxxiii[923] Upshur County Death Records, Buckhannon, WV, Identified as John Franklin Gaston, white male, coal miner, married, 44, born Aug 6 1920, son of John M. Gaston & Carrie Posey; died Jan 31 1965 at St. Joseph Hospital in Buckhannon, cause of death acute myocardial infarction, burial at Big Bend Cemetery.
http://www.wvculture.org/vrr/va_view.aspx?Id=5957410&Type=Death.

cmxxiv[924] U.S. Public Records Index, Vol 1 , Ancestry.com.

cmxxv[925] 1910 Census, Kanawha County, WV.

cmxxvi[926] Lewis County Marriage Records, Weston, WV, Identified as Arkimidas Adolphus Maddox, 21, farmer, b. Harrison Co, res. Lewis Co, son of John & Eliza Maddox; and Flavilla Catharine Jewell, 19, b. & res. in Lewis Co, dau of Abert (?) & Catharine H. Jewell. Married Sep 15 1869. A notation reads: "Mother of female consenting through her son-in-law V. B. Flesher.", MR p. 47.

cmxxvii[927] *Ritchie County WV Marriages 1843-1915* , Wes Cochran, 2515 10th Ave, Parkersburg WV 26101 (July 1985), Identified as Franklin P. Ward, age 21, b. Harrison Co, res. Gilmer Co, son of G. W. & Margaret; and Mary J. Holbert, age 19, b. Gilmer Co, res. Ritchie Co, dau of R. E. & Cyndrilla. Married Mar 12 1874.

cmxxviii[928] 1900 Census, Jackson County, WV.

cmxxix[929] 1910 Census, Jackson County, WV.

cmxxx[930] Jackson County Marriage Records, Ripley, WV, Identified as A. S. Wolfe, 43, b. Jackson Co, res. Kenna; and Ora Bradley, 30, b. Jackon Co, res. Kenna. Married Dec 24 1918 at the residence of the minister, C. J. Allender. MR p. 98.

cmxxxi[931] 1920 Census, Jackson County, WV.

cmxxxii[932] Death record of wife's mother.

cmxxxiii[933] Kanawha County Marriage Records, Charleston, WV.

cmxxxiv[934] Mrs. A. T. Maddox (Alice J. Corbin) in a report to A. M. Prichard and recorded in Allied Families of Read Corbin Luttrell Bywaters on page 168, as reported online at http://awt.ancestry.com by L. P. Kasper <lpkasperjr@hotmail.com>

.

cmxxxv[935] Mercer County Death Records, Princeton, WV.

cmxxxvi[936] *Social Security Death Index* , Social Security card issued in Illinois before 1951.

cmxxxvii[937] 1930 Census, Jackson County, WV.

cmxxxviii[938] Monongalia County Marriage Records, Morgantown, WV.

cmxxxix[939] William F. Donnelly, *The Wests of Duck Creek, Harrison County, Virginia (now West Virginia)* , Gateway Press, Baltimore MD, 1997, p. 468.

cmxl[940] William F. Donnelly, *The Wests of Duck Creek, Harrison County, Virginia (now West Virginia)* , Gateway Press, Baltimore MD, 1997, p. 469.

cmxli[941] Obituary of wife's father.

cmxlii[942] 1910 Census, Marion County, WV.

cmxliii[943] 1920 Census, Marion County, WV.

cmxliv[944] *Harrison County WV Marriages 1895-1912* , Wes Cochran, 2515 10th Ave, Parkersburg, WV 26101 (Feb 2001), Identified as Hiram T. West, 29, b. & res. in Harrison Co, son of Jefferson B. & Ruhama West; and Allie Belle Davis, 20, b. & res. in

Harrison Co, dau of Wm. & Mary Davis. Married Jul 28 1895 in West Milford. MR p. 87.

cmxlv[945] William F. Donnelly, *The Wests of Duck Creek, Harrison County, Virginia (now West Virginia)* , Gateway Press, Baltimore MD, 1997, p. 470.

cmxlvi[946] William F. Donnelly, *The Wests of Duck Creek, Harrison County, Virginia (now West Virginia)* , Gateway Press, Baltimore MD, 1997, p. 425.

cmxlvii[947] William F. Donnelly, *The Wests of Duck Creek, Harrison County, Virginia (now West Virginia)* , Gateway Press, Baltimore MD, 1997, p. 471.

cmxlviii[948] *Social Security Death Index* , Social Security card issued in Pennsylvania before 1951.

cmxlix[949] Randolph County Marriage Records, Elkins, WV.

cml[950] Randolph County Marriage Records, Elkins, WV, Identified as Guy Calvin Bartlett, 27, b. Wood Co, res. West Milford; and Nora Compton, 22, b. Randolph Co, res. Montrose. Married Oct 23 1926 in Elkins. (Note: "The Wests of Duck Creek," p. 471, incorrectly reports marriage date as Oct 22 1926.), MR p. 111.

cmli[951] Randolph County Death Records, Elkins, WV.

cmlii[952] Harrison County Birth Records, Clarksburg, WV, Identified as (first name blank) Bartlett, white male, born May 17 1902 in West Milford, this being the second child born to this mother. Father: George L. Bartlett, 33, farmer. Mother: Ida M. (West) Bartlett, 27, res. West Milford. (Note: Although the child's first name is omitted here, this is the same birth date, location and parents given in the marriage record of Allison Clyde Bartlett. "The Wests of Duck Creek," p. 471, incorrectly reports birth date as May 17 1903.), BR p. 217.

cmliii[953] *Ritchie County WV Deaths 1918-1940* , Wes Cochran, 2515 10th Ave, Parkersburg, WV 26101 (Nov 1998), Identified as Anna Ward Zinn, dau of Martin & Betty Gaston Ward, born in Doddridge Co, died Feb 27 1934 at age 88y2m25d.

cmliv[954] *Ritchie County WV Marriages 1843-1915* , Wes Cochran, 2515 10th Ave, Parkersburg WV 26101 (July 1985), Identified as William B. Zinn, age 23, b. Lewis Co, res. Ritchie Co, son of John W. & Eliza; and Ann M. Ward, age 20, of Ritchie Co, dau of Martin C. & Mary J. Married Jul 27 1865.

cmlv[955] *Ritchie County WV Deaths 1918-1940* , Wes Cochran, 2515 10th Ave, Parkersburg, WV 26101 (Nov 1998).

cmlvi[956] Headstone, Inscription reads "Luetta, dau of W. B. & A. M. Zinn, born Nov 7 1868, died Mar 26 1886.".

cmlvii[957] Ritchie County Historical Society (David M. Scott, Editor), *Ritchie County, West Virginia Cemeteries through 1993* , McClain Printing Co, Parsons, WV, 1995, Goldenseal Magazine, Fall 1996, reports his death date as 1910.

cmlviii[958] WV State Dept of Health, Div of Vital Statistics, *Death Certificate* (http://www.wvculture.org/vrr/va_dcsearch.aspx), Identified as Ledrue K. Ward, son of Thomas Floyd Ward & Frances Virginia Frymier, husband of Essie Hardesty Ward (deceased). Cause of death: aortic insufficiency, probably due to syphillis. Informant: Lorraine Wilson, Baltimore, MD.

cmlix[959] WV State Dept of Health, Div of Vital Statistics, *Death Certificate* (http://www.wvculture.org/vrr/va_dcsearch.aspx), "Ritchie County WV Cemeteries Through 1993," p. 496, reports death date on headstone as Jan 20 1931.

cmlx[960] *Ritchie County WV Marriages 1843-1915* , Wes Cochran, 2515 10th Ave, Parkersburg WV 26101 (July 1985), Identified as James E. Amos, 26, of Ritchie Co; and Eliza J. Ward, 28, of Ritchie Co. Married Sep 1 1885. (NOTE: Minnie Kendall Lowther, RCHR p. 316, reports marriage date for Eliza J. Ward as Sep 1 1865, clearly a typographical error intended to be Sep 1 1885, as shown here.).

cmlxi[961] Susie Davis Nicholson, *Davis - The Settlers of Salem, West Virginia* , Gordon Printing Co, Strasburg OH, 1979 (Revised & Enlarged), p. 385.

cmlxii[962] Susie Davis Nicholson, *Davis - The Settlers of Salem, West Virginia* , Gordon Printing Co, Strasburg OH, 1979 (Revised & Enlarged).

cmlxiii[963] Doddridge County Birth Records, West Union, WV,
http://files.usgwarchives.net/wv/doddridge/vitals/birth.txt.

cmlxiv[964] 1900 Census, Gilmer County, WV (Troy District).

cmlxv[965] Family Bible, of Josiah & Elizabeth Gaston Nutter. Ceremony performed Jan 30
1868 at the S. M. Gaston home by Eli M. Gaston, witnessed by T. E. Nutter & A. M.
Gaston. [per grandson Lane Bush Nutter].

cmlxvi[966] Robert Junior & Laurel Nutter Britton, RR 1, Box 144, West Union, WV 26456.

cmlxvii[967] 1860 Census, Doddridge County, (W)VA.

cmlxviii[968] Don Norman, 41991 Emerson Court, Elyria, OH 44035, *The Descendants of Josiah
Hart* , http://www.rootsweb.ancestry.com/~hcpd/norman/HART/.

cmlxix[969] Ota Reed Fraker (1882-1970) in her 15-page genealogy of the descendants of her
maternal grandparents, Samuel Morris & Elizabeth Law Gaston, misleadingly entitled
"Genealogy or Family Tree of John Gaston, Sr.".

cmlxx[970] *Gilmer County WV Deaths 1881-1903* , Wes Cochran, 2515 10th Ave, Parkersburg
WV 26101 (Nov 2001).

cmlxxi[971] Gilmer County Death Records, Glenville, WV, Identified as Bertie F. Nutter, female,
b. Gilmer Co, d. Jun 11 1884 at Horn Creek, age 8 months. Cause of death whooping
cough. Parents: Josiah & Elizabeth Nutter. Informant: mother. Horn Creek, in Ritchie
Co, is near the Gilmer County line.

cmlxxii[972] Doddridge County Birth Records, West Union, WV, Name appears as Sarah I.
Gasmins, an apparent transcription error from the handwritten original. S. J. (female,
age 7) and Sarah J. (female age 17) are in the 1860 & 1870 censuses with the S. M.
Gaston family, BR Bk 1, p. 1.

cmlxxiii[973] *Doddridge County WV Marriages 1845-1937* , Wes Cochran, 2515 10th Ave,
Parkersburg, WV 26101 (Jan 1993), Identified as Allen Reed, 21, b. Doddridge Co, res.
Ritchie Co; and Sarah J. Gaston, 21, of Doddridge Co. Married Oct 15 1874.

cmlxxiv[974] Ota Reed Fraker. But Marilynn Davis Jones gives birth date as Sep 21 1876.

cmlxxv[975] Doddridge County Marriage Records, West Union, WV, MR Bk 2, p. 208.

cmlxxvi[976] Headstone, - Marker inscribed to read "Susan - Wife of D. Jones - Died Dec 3 1890
- Aged 34 Ys 10 Ms 27 Ds.".

cmlxxvii[977] Doddridge County Marriage Records, West Union, WV, Ceremony performed by Eli
M. Gaston. MR Bk 1-A, p. 218.

cmlxxviii[978] *Doddridge County WV Marriages 1845-1937* , Wes Cochran, 2515 10th Ave,
Parkersburg, WV 26101 (Jan 1993), Identified as Asberry S. Britton, age 26, b.
Monongalia Co, res. Doddridge Co, son of Horation & Elizabeth; and Hannah E.
Gaston, age 18, of Doddridge Co, dau of Samuel M. & Elizabeth. Married Apr 14 1877.

cmlxxix[979] Obituary, Place of death given as "at his home near Revel, W. Va," which is
presumed to be near Auburn, since "funeral service was conducted by Rev. J. E. Burns
of Auburn, in the Church at Revel.".

cmlxxx[980] WV State Dept of Health, Div of Vital Statistics, *Death Certificate*
(http://www.wvculture.org/vrr/va_dcsearch.aspx), Ota Reed Fraker (1882-1970)
reports birthdate exactly one year earlier, on Dec 11 1879.

cmlxxxi[981] Susie Davis Nicholson, *Davis - The Settlers of Salem, West Virginia* , Gordon
Printing Co, Strasburg OH, 1979 (Revised & Enlarged), p. 382.

cmlxxxii[982] Eleanor R. Goodwin, granddaughter of Floyd W. & Columbia Gaston Chapman.

cmlxxxiii[983] Doddridge County Marriage Records, West Union, WV, MR Bk 2, p. 156.

cmlxxxiv[984] *Social Security Death Index* , Social Security card issued in California before 1951.
Name listed in SSDI as Helen G. Chapman.

cmlxxxv[985] Doddridge County Death Records, West Union, WV, DR Bk 5, p. 64-B.

cmlxxxvi[986] Doddridge County Death Records, West Union, WV, Identified as Morris Samuel
Gaston, married, farmer, b. Feb 9 1863, son of Samuel Gaston & Elizabeth Law, d. Jul
31 1951 at Oxford, buried South Fork Cemetery. DR Bk 5, p. 64-B.

cmlxxxvii[987] Doddridge County Marriage Records, West Union, WV, Groom identified as M. S.
Gaston, age 32, b. Doddridge Co, and bride as Hattie I. Adams, age 18, b. Doddridge.

Ceremony held Sep 18 1895 "at the bride's parents." Informants listed as S. Gaston and J. Adams. MR Bk 5, p. 92.

cmlxxxviii[988] Doddridge County Birth Records, West Union, WV, Identified as Hattie I. Adams, b. Jul 25 1877, dau of Joshna [sic] & Sarah E. Adams. BR Bk 1, p. 84.

cmlxxxix[989] Funeral card.

cmxc[990] Ritchie County Marriage Records, Harrisville, WV, Identified as John W. Law, 22, b. Harrison Co, res. Ritchie Co, son of Asby P. & Deborah; and Mary C. Lough, 18, b. & res. in Ritchie Co, dau of Nimrod & Elizabeth. Married Oct 17 1868 in Ritchie County; ceremony performed by S. E. Steele, Minister. MR p. 19.

cmxci[991] Obituary, Ritchie Gazette, 7/28/1916.

cmxcii[992] Amos Beaty Sharps, *The Samuel Barr Family: A Genealogy List of the Various Descendants of This Family* (on file at West Virginia University Library; ca 1961).

cmxciii[993] *Ritchie County WV Marriages 1843-1915* , Wes Cochran, 2515 10th Ave, Parkersburg WV 26101 (July 1985), Identified as Francis M. Law, 21, of Ritchie Co, son of Asby P & Deborah; and Phebe R. Mitchell, 20, of Ritchie Co, dau of Daniel & Nancy. Married Sep 13 1869. But husband's obituary gives marriage date as Sep 19 1869.

cmxciv[994] *Ritchie County WV Marriages 1843-1915* , Wes Cochran, 2515 10th Ave, Parkersburg WV 26101 (July 1985), Identified as Francis Marion Law, widowed, 52, or Ritchie Co; and Etta Sharps, divorced, 40, of Ritchie Co. Married Mar 31 1901.

cmxcv[995] Amos Beaty Sharps, *The Samuel Barr Family: A Genealogy List of the Various Descendants of This Family* (on file at West Virginia University Library; ca 1961), Husband's obituary states marriage date as Mar 30 1901.

cmxcvi[996] *Ritchie County WV Marriages 1916-1945* , Wes Cochran, 2515 10th Ave, Parkersburg WV 26101 (Sep 1998).

cmxcvii[997] Alfred Ray Sharps (1927-2007), Virginia Beach, VA.

cmxcviii[998] Alfred Ray Sharps (1927-2007), Virginia Beach, VA, DR Bk 6, p. 298.

cmxcix[999] Minnie Kendall Lowther, *Ritchie County in History and Romance* (McClain Publishing Co, Parsons, WV, 1990), p. 236.

m[1000] *Ritchie County WV Marriages 1843-1915* , Wes Cochran, 2515 10th Ave, Parkersburg WV 26101 (July 1985), Identified as Ulysses Grant Bonnett, widowed, 46, b. Lewis Co, res. Ritchie Co; and Rose Luella Law, 40, of Ritchie Co. Married Oct 22 1911.

mi[1001] *Gilmer County WV Cemeteries, Vol. I* , Wes Cochran, 2515 10th Ave, Parkersburg WV 26101 (Mar 1992).

mii[1002] 1920 Census, Ritchie County, WV (Murphy District).

miii[1003] 1930 Census, Ritchie County, WV (Murphy District).

miv[1004] Gilmer County Marriage Records, Glenville, WV, Identified as Howard G. Law, 30, b. & res. in Ritchie Co; and Lillie G. Reynolds, 26, b. & res. in Gilmer Co. Married Mar 18 1911. MR p. 89.

mv[1005] Harrison County Marriage Records, Clarksburg, WV, Identified as Howard Gaston Law, widowed, 65, b. Aug 30 1880 in Auburn, Ritchie Co WV, res. Burnt House, Ritchie Co, son of Francis Marion Law & Phoebe Rebecca Mitchell; and Lillie Gertrude Ellyson, divorced, 51, b. Jun 8 1894 in Tanner, Gilmer Co WV, res. Clarksburg, dau of Joab Crites & Eunice Hinkle. Married Apr 11 1946 in Clarksburg. MR p. 110.

mvi[1006] Gilmer County Marriage Records, Glenville, WV.

mvii[1007] Ritchie County Birth Records, Harrisville, WV.

mviii[1008] Obituary, Ritchie Gazette, 6/23/1916.

mix[1009] Harrison County Death Records, Clarksburg, WV, DR, p. 66-A.

mx[1010] *Social Security Death Index* , Social Security card issued in Ohio before 1951.

mxi[1011] Ohio Deaths, 1908-1932, 1938-1944, and 1958-2007 (online) , Ancestry.com and Ohio Department of Health.

mxii[1012] Ritchie County Birth Records, Harrisville, WV, Identified as Ocean Wave Law, white female, born Jun 17 1902 at Lawford, dau of D. G. (farmer, res. Lawford) & Celia Law. Informant: D. G. Law, father. BR p. 102.

mxiii[1013] Ritchie County Death Records, Harrisville, WV, Identified as Wave Law, white female, age one year, died Nov (day blank) 1904, cause of death measles. Informant: D. G. Law. DR p. 113.

mxiv[1014] 1900 Census, Gilmer County, WV (DeKalb District).

mxv[1015] 1910 Census, Ritchie County, WV (Union District).

mxvi[1016] *Ritchie County WV Deaths 1956-1970* , Wes Cochran, 2515 10th Ave, Parkersburg, WV 26101 (Jan 1999), Identified as Iris C. Law, age 98, dau of Jackson & Louisa (Ellyson) Woodford, d. Jan 16 1964.

mxvii[1017] 1900 Census, Ritchie County, WV (Grant District).

mxviii[1018] 1920 Census, Ritchie County, WV (Grant District).

mxix[1019] 1910 Census, Ritchie County, WV (Grant District).

mxx[1020] 1930 Census, Ritchie County, WV (Union District).

mxxi[1021] *Ritchie County WV Deaths 1918-1940* , Wes Cochran, 2515 10th Ave, Parkersburg, WV 26101 (Nov 1998), Identified as Willy Law, son of Asbery & Delora (Gaston) Law, d. Jan 13 1932, age 67y3m27d.

mxxii[1022] Barbour County Marriage Records, Philippi, WV.

mxxiii[1023] Monongalia County Death Records, Morgantown, WV, Identified as Alta Morrison Linger, 75, dau of Willie Law & Ida May Goff, died July 21 1967, cause of death acute myocardial infarction. (Note: "Ritchie County Cemeteries through 1993," p. 541, reports death date on headstone as June 21 1967. But death record shows it as July 21 1967.).

mxxiv[1024] Monongalia County Death Records, Morgantown, WV.

mxxv[1025] Ritchie County Birth Records, Harrisville, WV, Identified as (first name blank) Law, white female, born May 31 1893 at Lawford, length of pregnancy about 8 months, dau of Willy Law (farmer, age 28) & Ida M. (Goff) Law (age 24), this being the mother's third child. BR p. 83.

mxxvi[1026] 1920 Census, Ritchie County, WV (Union District).

mxxvii[1027] Gilmer County Marriage Records, Glenville, WV, Identified as John A. Summerville [sic], 21, b. & res. in Ritchie Co; and Martha F. Brannon, 20, b. & res. in Gilmer Co. Married Sep 19 1872 in Gilmer County. Ceremony perfomed by Samuel Brannon. MR p. 18.

mxxviii[1028] *Ritchie County WV Marriages 1843-1915* , Wes Cochran, 2515 10th Ave, Parkersburg WV 26101 (July 1985), Identified as Robert O. Sommerville, 25, of Ritchie Co, son of Martin S. & Susan; and Rosanna Bee, 21, b. Doddridge Co, res. Ritchie Co, dau of Benjamin W. & Priscilla. Married Nov 22 1877.

mxxix[1029] Susie Davis Nicholson, *Davis - The Settlers of Salem, West Virginia* , Gordon Printing Co, Strasburg OH, 1979 (Revised & Enlarged), p. 84.

mxxx[1030] *Doddridge County WV Marriages 1845-1937* , Wes Cochran, 2515 10th Ave, Parkersburg, WV 26101 (Jan 1993), Identified as Alexander Adams, 20, of Doddridge Co; and Bell Gaston, 17, of Doddridge Co. Married Nov 26 1874.

mxxxi[1031] Doddridge County Marriage Records, West Union, WV, MR Bk 8, p. 321.

mxxxii[1032] Doddridge County Marriage Records, West Union, WV, Groom identified as Marshall F. Gray, age 33, b. Doddridge Co. Bride identified as Miss Eliza A. Adams, age 34, b. Doddridge Co. Ceremony held Jun 8 1910 "at the residence of Alexand Adams.", MR Bk 8, p. 321.

mxxxiii[1033] Doddridge County Birth Records, West Union, WV, Identified as M. F. Gray, b. Sep 28 1877, son of John M. Gray & Dora. BR Bk 1, p. 86.

mxxxiv[1034] Doddridge County Death Records, West Union, WV, Identified as Marshall Franklin Gray, farmer, d. Aug 16 1918 at Oxford of consumption, age 40y 10m 18d. DR Bk 2, p. 55.

mxxxv[1035] West Union Herald.

mxxxvi[1036] *Doddridge County WV Marriages 1845-1937* , Wes Cochran, 2515 10th Ave, Parkersburg, WV 26101 (Jan 1993), Identified as John I. Gaston, 22, of Doddridge Co; and Alice V. Chapman, 19, of Doddridge Co. Married Nov 30 1882.

mxxxvii[1037] Doddridge County Death Records, West Union, WV, Identified as Ida B. Gaston, d. Nov 30 1887 in Doddridge Co, age 10m 6d, cause of death hives, dau of John I. & Alice V., born in Doddridge Co. Informant: John I., father. DR p. 47.

mxxxviii[1038] 1900 Census, Doddridge County, WV (Greenbrier District).

mxxxix[1039] *Social Security Death Index* , Social Securtiy card issued in Ohio in 1952-54. Name listed in SSDI as Itha Allen.

mxl[1040] Obituary of wife's mother.

mxli[1041] Elizabeth Y. Burdette, 1753 Hampton Rd, Akron OH 44305, *Sotha Hickman and Some of His Descendants* (1975).

mxlii[1042] *Social Security Death Index* , Name listed in SSDI as "Tidal Gaston.".

mxliii[1043] Marilyn A. Russell, Junction City, OH 43743.

mxliv[1044] Doddridge County Court House, West Union, WV.

mxlv[1045] Doddridge County Birth Records, West Union, WV, BR Bk 3, p. 86.

mxlvi[1046] *West Union Herald-Record*, Aug 1 1978, p. 7.

mxlvii[1047] Doddridge County Birth Records, West Union, WV, BR Bk 1, p. 53.

mxlviii[1048] Doddridge County Birth Records, West Union, WV, Identified as Lievetta Adams, b. Feb 1 1872, dau of Joshna [sic] & Sarah Elizabeth Adams. Informant: Joshna Adams. She seems to have adopted the name "Luella" early, as no other reference to her by the name Lievetta has been found. BR Bk 1, p. 53.

mxlix[1049] Lewis County Death Records, Weston, WV, DR Bk 7, p. 132.

ml[1050] Doddridge County Marriage Records, West Union, WV, MR Bk 15, p. 4.

mli[1051] Lorna Reese Overberg, *The History of Ritchie County, West Virginia to 1980* (Ritchie County Historical Society, Taylor Publishing Co, 1980), p. 123.

mlii[1052] Doddridge County Death Records, West Union, WV, Age at death: 6 months 20 days. DR Bk 1, p. 88.

mliii[1053] 1930 Census, Doddridge County, WV.

mliv[1054] *Social Security Death Index* , Social Security card issued in Ohio in 1971.

mlv[1055] Doddridge County Court House, West Union, WV, Obituary of Marion Homer Wilson gives marriage date of Sep 24 1896. MR Bk 5, Page 230.

mlvi[1056] Obituary - Camden-Clark Memorial Hospital.

mlvii[1057] *The History of Doddridge County, West Virginia* , Taylor Publishing Co, 1979, p. 290.

mlviii[1058] William Bernard Wilson, *Wilson-Pepper Genealogy 1595-1989* (Gateway Press, Baltimore, MD, 1990), p. 40.

mlix[1059] Janice Zinn Ball.

mlx[1060] *Harrison County WV Marriages 1785-1894* , Wes Cochran, 2515 10th Ave, Parkersburg, WV 26101 (1985), Identified as William S. Burnside, 26, of Harrison Co, son of I. W. & Mary A; and Flora M. Sommerville, 17, of Harrison Co, dau of J. H. & E. C. Married Nov 3 1892.

mlxi[1061] *Harrison County WV Marriages 1785-1894* , Wes Cochran, 2515 10th Ave, Parkersburg, WV 26101 (1985), Identified as James W. Sommerville, 22, of Harrison Co, son of Jacob & Elizabeth; and Lellie M. Burnsides, 16, of Harrison Co, dau of Isaac M. & Mary A. Married Feb 19 1880.

mlxii[1062] Headstone, Age at death given as 16y 9m 9d.

mlxiii[1063] *Harrison County WV Marriages 1785-1894* , Wes Cochran, 2515 10th Ave, Parkersburg, WV 26101 (1985), Identified as James W. Sommerville, widowed, 25, of Harrison Co, son of Jacob & Elizabeth; and Frances E. McConkey, 18, b. Lewis Co, res. Harrison Co, dau of Jacob & Mary J. Married Dec 24 1882.

mlxiv[1064] *Harrison County WV Marriages 1895-1912* , Wes Cochran, 2515 10th Ave, Parkersburg, WV 26101 (Feb 2001), Identified as J. Wesley Sommerville, 41, of Harrison Co, son of Jacob & Elizabeth; and Cora Burnside, 29, of Harrison Co, dau of William & Ruhama. Married Dec 25 1898.

mlxv[1065] Headstone, Age at death 1y 1d.

mlxvi[1066] *Harrison County WV Marriages 1785-1894* , Wes Cochran, 2515 10th Ave, Parkersburg, WV 26101 (1985), Identified as Lewis A. Law, 18, of Harrison Co, son of

James S. & Susanna; and Sarah A. Sommerville, 18, of Harrison Co, dau of Jacob & Elizabeth. Married Nov 6 1879.

mlxvii[1067] Gilmer County Marriage Records, Glenville, WV, Identified as William Ivan Rymer, 25, b. & res. in Gilmer Co; and Ivy Gae Law, 23, b. & res. in Gilmer Co. Married Jul 12 1911.

mlxviii[1068] Harrison County Birth Records, Clarksburg, WV.

mlxix[1069] WV State Dept of Health, Div of Vital Statistics, *Death Certificate* (http://www.wvculture.org/vrr/va_dcsearch.aspx), An incorrect date of death was entered on the death record. The physician's medical certification stated that he had attended the deceased from Nov 25 1942 to Apr 17 1948, that he had last seen him alive on Mar 27 1928, and that the date of death was Feb 17 1948. The certification was dated Apr 17 1948, and date of burial was stated as Apr 19 1948. The date of death was clearly intended to be Apr 17 1948, the same date inscribed on the headstone. The birth date and age at death recorded on the death record also calculate to the same Apr 17 1948 death date. The handwritten entries made on this form were the basis for the typed entries subsequently made for the death record on file at Harrison County, which reflects the same conflicting information and incorrect death date.

mlxx[1070] Headstone, Name appears as "Claude".

mlxxi[1071] Wood County Death Records, Parkersburg, WV, DR Bk 14, p. 403.

mlxxii[1072] Marion County Court House, Fairmont, WV, MR 24-124.

mlxxiii[1073] Wood County Death Records, Parkersburg, WV, DR Bk 16, p.539.

mlxxiv[1074] Harrison County Marriage Records, Clarksburg, WV, Although ceremony was held in Grafton, in Taylor County, the marriage was recorded in Harrison County. In the three sections of the marriage record requiring a date, Jun 11 1936 was entered in the first and third sections, while Jul 11 1936 was entered in the second section. The correct date appears to be Jun 11 1936. MR p. 481.

mlxxv[1075] Headstone, Inscription reads: "Mother, Fannie M. Carr, 1851-1899".

mlxxvi[1076] *Cemeteries of Simpson District, Harrison County, WV* , Harrison County Genealogical Society, Clarksburg, WV.

mlxxvii[1077] *Social Security Death Index* , Social Security card issued in Rhode Island in 1962.

mlxxviii[1078] WV State Dept of Health, Div of Vital Statistics, *Death Certificate* (http://www.wvculture.org/vrr/va_dcsearch.aspx), Birth date may be Dec 4 1873, per direct descendant Dennis D. Newell.

mlxxix[1079] E. Murray Taylor, Jr., 106 Carli Ct, Lake Mary, FL 32746, citing Ann Robinson Thompson, Pittsburgh, PA.

mlxxx[1080] *Social Security Death Index* , Social Security card issued in West Virginia in 1956.

mlxxxi[1081] Lewis County Birth Records, Weston, WV, Parents listed as "Peter G. & Jane Swisher." It is unknown whether Jane was Margaret's middle name that she went by, or whether, thru misunderstanding, Peter's mother's name was given instead of the child's. BR Bk 1.

mlxxxii[1082] WV State Dept of Health, Div of Vital Statistics, *Death Certificate* (http://www.wvculture.org/vrr/va_dcsearch.aspx), Middle name given as Edward, at variance with both of his marriage records, which identify him as James Edwin Swisher.

mlxxxiii[1083] *Lewis County WV Marriages 1881-1937* , Wes Cochran, 2515 10th Ave, Parkersburg, WV 26101 (Sep 1994), Identified as James Edwin Swisher, 26, of Lewis Co, son of Peter G. & Margaret; and Annie Gertrude Reger, 20, of Lewis Co, dau of William & Mary E. Married Oct 15 1891.

mlxxxiv[1084] *Lewis County WV Marriages 1881-1937* , Wes Cochran, 2515 10th Ave, Parkersburg, WV 26101 (Sep 1994), Identified as James Edwin Swisher, widowed, 48, of Lewis Co, son of Peter G. & Margaret; and Eva Elizabeth Boram, 39, of Lewis Co, dau of Francis M. & Annie R. Married Oct 25 1913.

mlxxxv[1085] Penny & O.D. Linder, http://home.comcast.net/~jmlinder609, *The Gibson and Related Families* , McClain Printing Co, Parsons WV, 1991, p. 331.

mlxxxvi[1086] *Social Security Death Index* , Social Security card issued in Maryland before 1951.

mlxxxvii[1087] *Social Security Death Index* , Social Security card issued in Maryland in 1951 and 1952. Name listed in SSDI as Idella G. Swisher.

mlxxxviii[1088] *Social Security Death Index* , Social Security card issued in West Virginia in 1960.

mlxxxix[1089] Lewis County Birth Records, Weston, WV, Handwritten entry appears to have first name as "Allin," rather than the actual "Alvin." Father's middle initial in handwritten entry was difficult to make out, but parents nonetheless identified as "James & Mary Swisher.", BR Bk 1.

mxc[1090] *Lewis County WV Marriages 1881-1937* , Wes Cochran, 2515 10th Ave, Parkersburg, WV 26101 (Sep 1994), Identified as James Blaine Swisher, 29, of Lewis Co, son of I. C. & Mary; and Rosa Mildred Kemper, 24, of Lewis Co, dau of John W. & Addie. Married Nov 16 1913.

mxci[1091] WV State Dept of Health, Div of Vital Statistics, *Death Certificate* (http://www.wvculture.org/vrr/va_dcsearch.aspx), Identified as James Goodloe Swisher, age 78y 4m 7d, widowed, retired farmer, residing on farm in rural Weston, b. Feb 20 1879 in Lewis Co, d. Jun 27 1957 at Weston City Hospital, cause of death cerebral hemorrhage, son of James L. Swisher & Mary Hinzman, buried at Fairview IOOF Cemetery in Lewis County. Informant: Miss Marjorie Swisher, rural Weston.

mxcii[1092] Newspaper wedding announcement of son.

mxciii[1093] 1930 Census, Lewis County, WV.

mxciv[1094] *Harrison County WV Marriages 1895-1912* , Wes Cochran, 2515 10th Ave, Parkersburg, WV 26101 (Feb 2001), Identified as James Goodloe Swisher, 23, of Lewis Co, son of James L. & Mary; and Stella Post, 24, of Harrison Co, dau of Hiram & Statira C. Married Oct 31 1901.

mxcv[1095] Newspaper wedding announcement, Weston Independent, 29 May 1940.

mxcvi[1096] Upshur County Marriage Records, Buckhannon, WV, Identified as James L. Hinzman, single, 29, b. Lewis Co; and Alice B. Flint, single, 24, b. Upshur Co. Married Jan 20 1881. MR p. 46.

mxcvii[1097] *Roane County Marriage Records* , Spencer, WV, Identified as James L. Hinzman, 58, b. Lewis Co, res. Ripley WV; and Miss Margaret C. Morrison, 46, b. Lewis Co, res. Spencer WV. Married Jan 17 1910 "at Abe Hinzman's.", MR p. 158.

mxcviii[1098] Lewis County Death Records, Weston, WV, There are two entries for this death, with conflicting death dates. (1) DR p. 246: Identified as Sarah A. Allman, married, age 44y 10m, died Aug 1 1911 at R 4 Weston, cause of death tuberculosis. (2) DR p. 308: Identified as Sarah Ann Allman, married, age 43y 9m 25d, died Aug 1 1912 at Laurel Lick, cause of death tuberculosis. The 1912 death date more closely conforms to the 1868 birth year inicated in her marriage record and census records, although the exact age at death computes to a birth date of Oct 7 1868 rather than the Sep 1868 given in the 1900 Census. Laurel Lick does correspond to the rural Weston location given in the other entry.

mxcix[1099] *Lewis County WV Marriages 1881-1937* , Wes Cochran, 2515 10th Ave, Parkersburg, WV 26101 (Sep 1994), Identified as David Thomas Hinzman, age 29, of Lewis Co; and Ann Hinzman, age 27, of Lewis Co. Married Oct 25 1894.

mc[1100] 1930 Census, Marion County, WV.

mci[1101] Obituary of wife's brother.

mcii[1102] William F. Donnelly, *The Wests of Duck Creek, Harrison County, Virginia (now West Virginia)* , Gateway Press, Baltimore MD, 1997, p. 423.

mciii[1103] *Ritchie County WV Marriages 1843-1915* , Wes Cochran, 2515 10th Ave, Parkersburg WV 26101 (July 1985), Identified as Eric B. Hoff, 21, b. Harrison Co, res. Ritchie Co, son of John & Elizabeth; and Melinda Ann Hoit (?), 19, b. Virginia, res. Ritchie Co, dau of William C. & Sarah. Married Aug 27 1871.

mciv[1104] 1870 Census, Ritchie County, WV (Union Twp).

mcv[1105] 1900 Census, Wirt County, WV.

mcvi[1106] *Social Security Death Index* , Social Security card issued in Ohio before 1951. Name listed in SSDI as "Espie Wade," although the spelling Espy has also been seen.

mcvii[1107] 1900 Census, Ritchie County, WV (Murphy District).

mcviii[1108] 1880 Census, Webster County, WV.

mcix[1109] 1900 Census, Webster County, WV.

mcx[1110] Braxton County Death Records, Sutton, WV.

mcxi[1111] Webster County Marriage Records, Webster Springs, WV.

mcxii[1112] Braxton County Marriage Records, Sutton, WV.

mcxiii[1113] 1910 Census, Webster County, WV.

mcxiv[1114] Webster County Death Records, Webster Springs, WV.

mcxv[1115] Barbour County Death Records, Philippi, WV.

mcxvi[1116] Record of wife's remarriage.

mcxvii[1117] Mark Kozu <lmk@mochamail.com> (posted at http://awt.ancestry.com).

mcxviii[1118] WV State Dept of Health, Div of Vital Statistics, *Death Certificate* (http://www.wvculture.org/vrr/va_dcsearch.aspx), Minnie Kendall Lowther, in "Ritchie County in History and Romance," p. 317, incorrectly gives death date as 1933.

mcxix[1119] *Ritchie County WV Marriages 1843-1915* , Wes Cochran, 2515 10th Ave, Parkersburg WV 26101 (July 1985), Participants identified as Eusebius L. Bee, widowed, age 34, b. Doddridge Co, residing Ritchie Co; and Rebecca J. Butcher, divorced, age 25, b. Ritchie Co. Ceremony held Dec 7 1884 in Ritchie Co. ... Minnie Kendall Lowther, in "Ritchie County in History and Romance," p. 317, gives marriage date as Jan 2 1883. But this is contradicted by marriage record.

mcxx[1120] *West Virginia Marriage Records, 1863-1900* (http://www.ancestry.com/search/rectype/inddbs/4484.htm), Participants identified as Eusebius L. Bee and Rebecca J. Butcher. Ceremony held Dec 7 1884 in Ritchie Co.

mcxxi[1121] *Ritchie County WV Marriages 1843-1915* , Wes Cochran, 2515 10th Ave, Parkersburg WV 26101 (July 1985), p. 60.

mcxxii[1122] Obituary, Appearing as a news item in the sports section of the U.S. Armed Forces newspaper "Stars & Stripes" edition of April 17 1951, the obituary's dateline was Philadelphia, April 16 1951. The article in its entirety: "Mrs. Genevieve Horner Neale, 57, wife of Earle (Greasy) Neale, former head coach of the Philadelphia Eagles, died in her sleep yesterday of coronary occlusion. The couple had been married 36 years. They had no children.".

mcxxiii[1123] *Florida Death Index, 1877-1998 (online)* , Ancestry.com and Florida Dept of Health, Office of Vital Records.

mcxxiv[1124] 1920 Census, Wetzel County, WV.

mcxxv[1125] Wetzel County Marriage Records, New Martinsville Co, WV.

mcxxvi[1126] 1930 Census, Ohio County, WV.

mcxxvii[1127] Ohio County Marriage Records, Wheeling, WV.

mcxxviii[1128] Ohio County Marriage Records, Wheeling, WV, Identified as George Dayton, 21, b. New Martinsville WV, res. Wheeling; and Alice Mowen, 20, b. Martins Ferry OH, res. Wheeling. Married Dec 1 1928 in Wheeling. MR p. 153.

mcxxix[1129] Ohio County Marriage Records, Wheeling, WV, Identified as George W. Dayton, divorced, 25, b. New Martinsville WV, res. Wheeling; and Anna Viderman, widowed, 24, b. Maynard OH, res. Bridgeport OH. Married Jun 9 1934 in Wheeling. MR p. 120.

mcxxx[1130] Brooke County Marriage Records, Wellsburg, WV.

mcxxxi[1131] City Directory, Clarksburg, WV, 1923.

mcxxxii[1132] 1930 Census, Kanawha County, WV.

mcxxxiii[1133] 1900 Census, Marion County, WV.

mcxxxiv[1134] Marion County Birth Records, Fairmont, WV.

mcxxxv[1135] Lewis County Court House, Weston, WV, DR Bk 6, p. 129.

mcxxxvi[1136] *Lewis County WV Marriages 1881-1937* , Wes Cochran, 2515 10th Ave, Parkersburg, WV 26101 (Sep 1994), Identified as Thomas Charles Gaston, 21, b. Harrison Co, res. Lewis Co, son of I. M. & C. M.; and Nina (or Nona) Myrtle Nicoles, of Lewis Co, dau of W. J. & J. Married Sep 16 1884.

mcxxxvii[1137] Lewis County Death Records, Weston, WV, DR Bk 7, p. 131.

mcxxxviii[1138] Lewis County Birth Records, Weston, WV, BR Bk 2, p. 71.

mcxxxix[1139] Lewis County Death Records, Weston, WV, Age at death given as 2y 9m 8d.

mcxl[1140] Lewis County Birth Records, Weston, WV, BR Bk 1, p. 159.

mcxli[1141] Harrison County Marriage Records, Clarksburg, WV, Identified as Harley Roach Gaston, 35, b. Lewis Co, resident of Weston, son of Isaac M. & Caroline M. Gaston; and Icie Virginia Norman, 31, b. Harrison Co, res. Harrison Co, dau of C. L. & Elizabeth Norman. Married Nov 15 1910 "at the Bride's Home, Harrison Co," performed by Joseph I. Vincent, Minister of the Gospel. MR Bk 20, p. 301.

mcxlii[1142] Harrison County Marriage Records, Clarksburg, WV, MR Bk 20, p. 301.

mcxliii[1143] *Lewis County WV Marriages 1881-1937* , Wes Cochran, 2515 10th Ave, Parkersburg, WV 26101 (Sep 1994), Identified as Hiter Stewart, age 25, of Lewis Co, son of John & Rebecca A.; and Mary Charlotte Morris, age 22, of Lewis Co, dau of William & Olive J. Married Jul 11 1896.

mcxliv[1144] *1880 Census, Harrison County, WV* , Name listed as Mary C. Morris.

mcxlv[1145] *Social Security Death Index* , Social Security card issued in West Virginia before 1951. Name appears in SSDI as "Marlton Stewart.".

mcxlvi[1146] Lewis County Death Records, Weston, WV, Name listed in death record as Albert E. Gaston. DR Bk 1, p. 287.

mcxlvii[1147] Betty Mayfield (compiler) & Matha Byrd (editor), *Obituaries, Marriage & Births from Weston Independent and/or Weston Democrat, 1939-1940* (Hackers Creek Pioneer Descendants, Jane Lew, WV, April 1996), Committed suicide with a revolver at his home on Rush Run. [Ind., 7/12/1904].

mcxlviii[1148] Harrison County Death Records, Clarksburg, WV, DR p. 92-A.

mcxlix[1149] Lewis County Birth Records, Weston, WV.

mcl[1150] Obituary of mother, Weston Independent, 12/11/1929.

mcli[1151] Marion County Marriage Records, Fairmont, WV, MR Bk 6, p. 300.

mclii[1152] *Social Security Death Index* , Social Security card issued in California before 1951.

mcliii[1153] *Social Security Death Index* , Social Security card issued in the state of Washington before 1951.

mcliv[1154] Lewis County Marriage Records, Weston, WV, Although the ceremony was held in Harrison County, the license was issued and filed in Lewis County, residence of the bride.

mclv[1155] Kerin Smith <kerinsmith2000@yahoo.com>, great-granddaughter of Jefferson Davis Butcher and Etta Maude Morris.

mclvi[1156] *Lewis County WV Marriages 1881-1937* , Wes Cochran, 2515 10th Ave, Parkersburg, WV 26101 (Sep 1994), Identified as Jefferson Davis Butcher, age 28, of Lewis Co, son of Isaac & Christiana; and Ettie Maud Morris, age 18, b. Harrison Co, res. Lewis Co, dau of John Life. Married Sep 6 1887.

mclvii[1157] *Social Security Death Index* , Social Security card issued in New York before 1951.

mclviii[1158] *Social Security Death Index* , Social Security card issued in Kansas before 1951.

mclix[1159] Penny & O.D. Linder, http://home.comcast.net/~jmlinder609, *The Gibson and Related Families* , McClain Printing Co, Parsons WV, 1991, p. 369.

mclx[1160] *Dirigo* , Salem College Yearbook, 1927.

mclxi[1161] Ellen Peterson Douglass, Meadville, PA <ebdoug@zoominternet.net>.

mclxii[1162] Harrison County Death Records, Clarksburg, WV, DR Bk 11, p. 92C.

mclxiii[1163] *Lewis County WV Marriages 1817-1880* , Wes Cochran, 2515 10th Ave, Parkersburg, WV 26101, Identified as Minor J. Hall & Amanda J. Gaston. Married Jan 21 1875.

mclxiv[1164] Penny & O.D. Linder, http://home.comcast.net/~jmlinder609, *The Gibson and Related Families* , McClain Printing Co, Parsons WV, 1991, p. 291.

mclxv[1165] Penny & O.D. Linder, http://home.comcast.net/~jmlinder609, *The Gibson and Related Families* , McClain Printing Co, Parsons WV, 1991, p. 293.

mclxvi[1166] Immediate family.

mclxvii[1167] Lewis County Court House, Weston, WV, MR Bk 5, p. 69.

mclxviii[1168] Lewis County Birth Records, Weston, WV, Name appears in birth record as "Eidey M. Gaston.", BR Bk 1.

mclxix[1169] Lewis County Death Records, Weston, WV, DR Bk 6, p. 127.

mclxx[1170] Lewis County Death Records, Weston, WV, DR Bk 8, p. 154.

mclxxi[1171] Lewis County Death Records, Weston, WV, Identified as Adline B. Mundell, died Mar 22 1896, age 32y 3m 5d. Informant: Lee Mundell, husband. DR Bk 1, p. 219.

mclxxii[1172] *Lewis County WV Marriages 1881-1937* , Wes Cochran, 2515 10th Ave, Parkersburg, WV 26101 (Sep 1994), Identified as Leonidas Mundell, 20, of Lewis Co; and Adaline Bell Gaston, 17, of Lewis Co. Married Apr 10 1881.

mclxxiii[1173] *Lewis County WV Marriages 1881-1937* , Wes Cochran, 2515 10th Ave, Parkersburg, WV 26101 (Sep 1994), Identified as Mifflin Blair Norman, 38, of Harrison Co, res. Lewis Co, son of Columbus L. & Sarah E.; and Nora Mundell, 30, of Lewis Co, dau of Lee & Adaline. Married Oct 16 1919.

mclxxiv[1174] *Social Security Death Index* , Social Security card issued in Ohio before 1951. Name listed in SSDI as "Osa Andrick.".

mclxxv[1175] Lewis County Birth Records, Weston, WV, BR Bk 1, p. 132.

mclxxvi[1176] Upshur County Death Records, Buckhannon, WV, DR Bk 5.

mclxxvii[1177] Upshur County Court House, Buckhannon, WV.

mclxxviii[1178] Lewis County Court House, Weston, WV, BR Bk 2, p. 176.

mclxxix[1179] Upshur County Court House, Buckhannon, WV, DR Bk 5.

mclxxx[1180] WV State Dept of Health, Div of Vital Statistics, *Death Certificate* (http://www.wvculture.org/vrr/va_dcsearch.aspx), There is a conflict between the death record maintained at Mineral County and the death certificate on file at the State of West Virginia. The county death record states that Lloyd H. Gaston, age 45, married, occupation dentist, died of ulcerative endocarditis in Keyser on Aug 4 1918. The state death certificate identifies him as Lloyd H. Gaston, age 45y2m20d, born in Lewis Co on Aug 4 1863, son of Abram Gaston & Sarah Morris, died of ulcerative endocarditis in Keyser on Oct 24 1918, burial Oct 27 1918 in Keyser, informant his wife, certificate signed by medical authority on Oct 31 1918. The conclusion is that his correct dates are Aug 4 1873 to Oct 24 1918, that the county-level record inadvertently entered his birth date instead of his death date, and that the state-level record entered 1863 at his birth year rather than the 1873 which would conform to his age given in both death records and in his marriage record. In any event, other reports of his death occuring on Oct 4 1918 or Oct 31 1918 are incorrect.

mclxxxi[1181] Newspaper extract (Independent), Issue 11/5/1918.

mclxxxii[1182] Mineral County Marriage Records , Keyser, WV.

mclxxxiii[1183] *Mineral County Marriage Records* , Keyser, WV, Identified as Lloyd H. Gaston, 30, b. Lewis Co, res. Keyser, occupation dentist, son of Abram & Sarah Gaston; and Edna M. Davis, 21, b. Mineral Co, res. Keyser, dau of Samuel & Mary F. Davis. Married Jul 11 1904 in Keyser. MR p. 458, Certificate No. 45.

mclxxxiv[1184] *U.S. Biographies Project - West Virginia* , http://www.wileygenealogy.com/~usbios/bios/wv.

mclxxxv[1185] *Harrison County WV Marriages 1785-1894* , Wes Cochran, 2515 10th Ave, Parkersburg, WV 26101 (1985), Identified as Willie Gaston, 25, of Lewis Co, son of George & Martha; and Nellie J. Thrash, 20, b. Barbour Co, res. Harrison Co, dau of Richard & Jane. Married Sep 11 1884.

mclxxxvi[1186] Penny & O.D. Linder, http://home.comcast.net/~jmlinder609, *The Gibson and Related Families* , McClain Printing Co, Parsons WV, 1991, p. 110.

mclxxxvii[1187] Doddridge County Death Records, West Union, WV, DR Outside County Bk 1, p. 663.

mclxxxviii[1188] *Social Security Death Index* , Social Security card issued in Ohio before 1951. Spelling "Howe" is correct.

mclxxxix[1189] Death Record - Online, Certificate 105180.

mcxc[1190] *Social Security Death Index* , Social Security card issued in West Virginia in 1958.

mcxci[1191] Harrison County Death Records, Clarksburg, WV, DR Bk 9, p. 66.

mcxcii[1192] Betty Mayfield (compiler) & Matha Byrd (editor), *Obituaries, Marriage & Births from Weston Independent and/or Weston Democrat, 1939-1940* (Hackers Creek Pioneer Descendants, Jane Lew, WV, April 1996), p. 17.

mcxciii[1193] Lewis County Death Records, Weston, WV, Age at death given as 77y 4mo 24da. DR Bk 5, p. 65.

mcxciv[1194] Penny & O.D. Linder, http://home.comcast.net/~jmlinder609, *The Gibson and Related Families* , McClain Printing Co, Parsons WV, 1991, p. 108.

mcxcv[1195] *Harrison County WV Marriages 1785-1894* , Wes Cochran, 2515 10th Ave, Parkersburg, WV 26101 (1985), Identified as George L. Gaston, 21, of Harrison Co, son of John W. & Mariah; and Rachel Bond, 20, of Harrison Co, dau of A. P. & Addie. Married Oct 25 1883.

mcxcvi[1196] Headstone, Death record states birth date as exactly one year later, Aug 12 1867. But age 67y 9m 18d at time of death on Apr 30 1934 would put birth date at Jul 12 1866. All things considered, the Aug 12 1866 date on the headstone is most likely correct.

mcxcvii[1197] Harrison County Marriage Records, Clarksburg, WV, Identified as Hiram J. Gaston, 20, b. & res. in Harrison Co, son of John W. & Mariah Gaston; and Annie E. Highland, 16, b. & res. in Harrison Co, dau of James I. & Sarah L. Highland. Married June 9 1887. MR p. 195.

mcxcviii[1198] Harrison County Birth Records, Clarksburg, WV, Identified as Edna Gaston, white female, born alive as a single birth on Jan 7 1887. Father: Hiram Gaston. Mother: Lee A. Gaston. Informant: Father. BR p. 167, Upper District.

mcxcix[1199] Records in Harrison Co give Edna's birth date as Jan 7, 1887 and the death date (Book 1, Page 144) as March 16, 1887. Her parents' marriage date is given as Jan 9, 1887. Birth/death dates of 1888 are from her headstone.

mcc[1200] Harrison County Death Records, Clarksburg, WV, Identified as Lilly Gaston, white female, age 6 months, dau of Hiram & Lee A. Gaston; died Mar 10 1887, cause unknown. Informant: Father. DR p. 144.

mcci[1201] Harrison County Death Records, Clarksburg, WV, DR p. 62.

mccii[1202] Harrison County Death Records, Clarksburg, WV, Identified as Dessie Gaston, age 16y 0m 4d, single, died Aug 14 1908. Cause of death: blood poisoning. Occupation: sorter at Hazel-Atlas (a glass manufacturer). DR p. 62.

mcciii[1203] William F. Donnelly, *The Wests of Duck Creek, Harrison County, Virginia (now West Virginia)* , Gateway Press, Baltimore MD, 1997, p. 311.

mcciv[1204] William F. Donnelly, *The Wests of Duck Creek, Harrison County, Virginia (now West Virginia)* , Gateway Press, Baltimore MD, 1997, p. 310.

mccv[1205] Headstone, Shared stone with James B. Gaston.

mccvi[1206] Obituary, Died of a heart attack while at work at Laidley & Selby's Store. Dominion News, Fairmont WV, 8/18/1966.

mccvii[1207] Monongalia County Death Records, Morgantown, WV, Identified as James Harry Gaston, 55, son of James B. Gaston & Addie M. Moffett, died Aug 12 1966, cause of death coronary occlusion. Exact place of death is not given, but obituary indicated that death occurred in Marion County, which borders Monongalia County. DR p. 26.

mccviii[1208] 1930 Census, Harrison County, WV.

mccix[1209] West Virginia cemeteries listing on microfilm at Mormon genealogy center in Fairmont, WV.

mccx[1210] Harrison County Death Records, Clarksburg, WV, Identified as Mary Catharine Post, died Nov 19 1905 in Clarksburg, age 10m 14d, cause of death accident burns. Informant: Howard Post, father. DR p. 150.

mccxi[1211] Lewis County Death Records, Weston, WV, Identified as Bertha Stalnaker, widowed, age 88, b. Aug 18 1871 in W. Va., dau of Enoch Gaston & (blank) Smith, res. in Salem WV; died Apr 3 1960 in Jane Lew, buried in Masonic Cemetery (location not given). Informant: Willie E. Stalnaker. (NOTE: Bertha Gaston Stalnaker's mother is documented as being Laura T. Sheets, who died when Bertha was age five. Her father then remarried Flora Bond. Basis for Bertha's mother being identified here as Smith is not known. Informant Willie E. Stalnaker is Bertha's son.), DR p. 408.

mccxii[1212] Harrison County Death Records, Clarksburg, WV, DR p. 92-B.

mccxiii[1213] *Lewis County WV Marriages 1881-1937*, Wes Cochran, 2515 10th Ave, Parkersburg, WV 26101 (Sep 1994), Identified as Charley Hornor Gaston, age 29, of Harrison Co, son of Enoch & Flora; and Nora Melvina Hall, age 27, of Lewis Co, dau of Lot & Bird. Married Feb 19 1914. It is noted that Linder (Gibson & Related Families, p. 107) misspells wife's name as Hill and incorrectly reports marriage date as Feb 19 1919.

mccxiv[1214] Harrison County Death Records, Clarksburg, WV, Identified as Laura S. McWhorter, widowed, b. Sep 8 1878 at Duck Creek, dau of Edward N. Smith & Byrd Gaston; died May 3 1960 at Clarksburg, age 81y7m25d, of myocardial infarction; buried at McWhorter Cemetery. Informant: Mrs. Dewey Randolph, Lost Creek, WV. NOTE: Death date has also been erroneously reported as 1916 and, by G. Jeff Whittaker and by Donnely in "Wests of Duck Creek," as Mar 20 1960. DR p. 182A(2).

mccxv[1215] Headstone, Reports of birthdate of Jul 29 1915 are incorrect. Headstone states Jul 28.

mccxvi[1216] William F. Donnelly, *The Wests of Duck Creek, Harrison County, Virginia (now West Virginia)*, Gateway Press, Baltimore MD, 1997, p. 421.

mccxvii[1217] Paul M. Gaston, Man and Mission: E. B. Gaston and the Origins of the Fairhope Single Tax Colony, Black Belt Press, Montgomery, AL (1993), p. 19.

mccxviii[1218] Jacquie Gaston Blevins, San Jose, CA 95139 < blevinsjc1@aol.com>.

mccxix[1219] *Social Security Death Index*, Social Security card issued in Colorado before 1951.

mccxx[1220] 1900 Census, Preston County, WV.

mccxxi[1221] 1910 Census, Preston County, WV.

mccxxii[1222] *1870 Census*, 1870 Census, Hurlbut Twp, Logan Co, Illinois, enumerated on Jun 23 1870:

Christina Peterson, 25, b. Sweden, housekeeper; Christina Peterson, 1, b. Illinois; Solomon Gregory, 30, b. Illinois, farm worker; Marcellus Albright, 28, b. Virginia, farm worker.

mccxxiii[1223] 1890 Veterans Schedule.

mccxxiv[1224] Preston County Death Records, Kingwood, WV.

mccxxv[1225] 1880 Census, Washington County, PA (Union Twp).

mccxxvi[1226] Death Record - Online, Vol 10657, Cert 22975.

mccxxvii[1227] Jane Carson Topoly, Fort Washington, MD 20744 (http://www.reocities.com/heartland/8904/), Cause of death given as varicose veins of the stomach.

mccxxviii[1228] *Social Security Death Index*, Social Security card issued in Pennsylvania in 1959 and 1961. Name listed in SSDI as Ruth M. Gordon.

mccxxix[1229] Max Perry, American Descendants of William Gaston and Mary Olivet Lemon (Midland, TX, 1989), p. 149.

mccxxx[1230] *Social Security Death Index*, Social Security card issued in New Jersey before 1951.

mccxxxi[1231] *Long Island Genealogy* (http://www.longislandgenealogy.com/rensselaer/surnames.htm).

mccxxxii[1232] Name "John Gaston, Jr." per Max Perry's "American Descendants of William Gaston and Mary O. Lemon," p. 155. No explanation is offered why a son with a name different from his father's would be called a Junior.

mccxxxiii[1233] Wikipedia.org (http://www.wikipedia.org), http://en.wikipedia.org/wiki/Helen_Magill_White.

mccxxxiv[1234] Wikipedia.org (http://www.wikipedia.org), http://en.wikipedia.org/wiki/Horace_White.

mccxxxv[1235] *Social Security Death Index* , Social Security card issued in Iowa in 1959 & 1960.

mccxxxvi[1236] *Social Security Death Index* , Social Security card issued in California in 1954.

mccxxxvii[1237] *California Death Index, 1940-1997 (online)* , Ancestry.com and California Dept of Health Svcs, Center for Health Statistics.

mccxxxviii[1238] California Voter Registrations, 1900-1968 , Ancestry.com.

mccxxxix[1239] *North Carolina Death Collection, 1908-2004 (online)* , Ancestry.com and North Carolina Dept of Health.

mccxl[1240] *Social Security Death Index* , Social Security card issued in Arkansas before 1951.

mccxli[1241] *Social Security Death Index* , Social Security card issued in California before 1951. Name listed in SSDI as "C. Reid".

mccxlii[1242] *Social Security Death Index* , Social Security card issued in California before 1951. Name listed in SSDI as Nina W. Reid.

mccxliii[1243] Death Record - Online, Birth date reported at 1916 in "The Original Arkansas Genealogy Project, Reid Family" <www.couchgenweb.com/family/reid.htm>. But SSDI and California death record (online at Ancestry.com) report birth date as Dec 7 1917.

mccxliv[1244] *Social Security Death Index* , Social Security card issued in New Mexico before 1951. Name listed in SSDI as Tracy Slater.

mccxlv[1245] *Social Security Death Index* , Social Security card issued in Oklahoma before 1951. Name listed in SSDI as Syble H. Reid.

mccxlvi[1246] *Social Security Death Index* , Social Security card issued in California before 1951. Name listed in SSDI as Floy M. Reid.

mccxlvii[1247] Death Record - Online, Identified as Julia Isabel Reid. Father's surname listed as Honeycutt, mother's maiden name as Payne.

mccxlviii[1248] *Social Security Death Index* , Social Security card issued in California in 1955.

mccxlix[1249] *Social Security Death Index* , Social Security card issued in California before 1951. Name listed in SSDI as H. McDaniel.

mccl[1250] Death Record - Online, Name listed as Mary Levonia Buie.

mccli[1251] *Social Security Death Index* , Social Security card issued in California in 1967.

mcclii[1252] *Social Security Death Index* , Social Security card issued in Arkansas in 1960. Name listed in SSDI as Nora Nichols.

mccliii[1253] Social Security Death Index, Social Security card issued in Texas before 1951.

mccliv[1254] Death Record - Online, Name listed in California Death Index as Alta Lee Reid. Father's surname Nowland [sic], mother's maiden name Blanton.

mcclv[1255] *Social Security Death Index* , SSDI entry is for Myrtle M. Hayse, b. May 17 1900, d. Oct 15 1972, resident of Woodlawn, Jefferson Co, IL, Social Security card issued in Illinois in 1963.

mcclvi[1256] Bill Gaston, Austin TX <bgaston2@mindspring.com>, *Descendants: The Huguenot John Jean Gaston b: About 1600, France* (http://home.mindspring.com/~bgaston2/), http://wc.rootsweb.com/cgibin/ igm.cgi?op=GET&db=:3253837&id=I1424.

mcclvii[1257] *Social Security Death Index* , SSDI entry is for Anna Kirkpatrick, b. Mar 2 1924, d. Sep 1982, resident of Sun City West, Maricopa Co, AZ, Social Security card issued in Illinois before 1951.

mcclviii[1258] Obituary - Nursing home, Magnolia Manor.

mcclix[1259] *Social Security Death Index* , Social Security card issued in South Carolina before 1951. Name listed in SSDI as Janie W. Gaston.

mcclx[1260] *Social Security Death Index* , Social Security card issued in Arizona in 1955.

mcclxi[1261] Mary Gaston Gee (1899-1987), The Ancestry and Descendants of Amzi Williford Gaston II (1841-1911) of Spartanburg County, South Carolina (Charlottesville, VA, 1944), p. 29.

mcclxii[1262] Mary Gaston Gee (1899-1987), The Ancestry and Descendants of Amzi Williford Gaston II (1841-1911) of Spartanburg County, South Carolina (Charlottesville, VA, 1944), p. 30.

mcclxiii[1263] Mary Gaston Gee (1899-1987), The Ancestry and Descendants of Amzi Williford Gaston II (1841-1911) of Spartanburg County, South Carolina (Charlottesville, VA, 1944).

mcclxiv[1264] Mary Gaston Gee (1899-1987), The Ancestry and Descendants of Amzi Williford Gaston II (1841-1911) of Spartanburg County, South Carolina (Charlottesville, VA, 1944), p. 31.

mcclxv[1265] Obituary of nephew.

mcclxvi[1266] Mary Gaston Gee (1899-1987), The Ancestry and Descendants of Amzi Williford Gaston II (1841-1911) of Spartanburg County, South Carolina (Charlottesville, VA, 1944), p. 32.

mcclxvii[1267] Mary Gaston Gee (1899-1987), The Ancestry and Descendants of Amzi Williford Gaston II (1841-1911) of Spartanburg County, South Carolina (Charlottesville, VA, 1944), p. 33.

mcclxviii[1268] Mary Gaston Gee (1899-1987), The Ancestry and Descendants of Amzi Williford Gaston II (1841-1911) of Spartanburg County, South Carolina (Charlottesville, VA, 1944), p. 34.

mcclxix[1269] Social Security Death Index , Social Security card issued in Washington, DC, before 1951. Name listed in SSDI as O. J. Youmans.

mcclxx[1270] Mary Gaston Gee (1899-1987), The Ancestry and Descendants of Amzi Williford Gaston II (1841-1911) of Spartanburg County, South Carolina (Charlottesville, VA, 1944), p. 35.

mcclxxi[1271] Marriage record.

mcclxxii[1272] Mary Gaston Gee (1899-1987), The Ancestry and Descendants of Amzi Williford Gaston II (1841-1911) of Spartanburg County, South Carolina (Charlottesville, VA, 1944), p. 38.

mcclxxiii[1273] Obituary of brother's wife.

mcclxxiv[1274] Mary Gaston Gee (1899-1987), The Ancestry and Descendants of Amzi Williford Gaston II (1841-1911) of Spartanburg County, South Carolina (Charlottesville, VA, 1944), p. 39.

mcclxxv[1275] Social Security Death Index , Social Security card issued thru Railroad Board before 1951.

mcclxxvi[1276] Social Security Death Index , Social Security card issued in California in 1956-57.

mcclxxvii[1277] Mary Gaston Gee (1899-1987), The Ancestry and Descendants of Amzi Williford Gaston II (1841-1911) of Spartanburg County, South Carolina (Charlottesville, VA, 1944), p. 40.

mcclxxviii[1278] Social Security Death Index , Social Security card issued in California in 1952. Name listed in SSDI as Marion R. Gaston.

mcclxxix[1279] Social Security Death Index , Social Security card issued in South Carolina before 1951. Name listed in SSDI as H. Taylor.

mcclxxx[1280] Mary Gaston Gee (1899-1987), The Ancestry and Descendants of Amzi Williford Gaston II (1841-1911) of Spartanburg County, South Carolina (Charlottesville, VA, 1944), p. 41.

mcclxxxi[1281] Pleasants County Birth Records, St. Marys, WV, Identified as (first name blank) Metz, white male, born July 18 1897 at Plumb Run, this being the mother's first child. Father: J. B. Metz, age 30, b. W.Va, carpenter. Mother: Nella Metz, nee Devaughan, 20, b. North Carolina, res. Plumb Run. (Note: Roy DeVaughan Metz was reported with this birth date in Mary Gaston Gee's genealogy of Amzi W. Gaston. The community of Plum Run is located in Tyler County, just across the border from Hebron (Pleasants County), which Roy Metz gave as his birthplace to customs officials when crossing the Canadian border at Detroit.), BR p. 64.

mcclxxxii[1282] *Georgia Deaths, 1919-98 (online)* , Ancestry.com and Georgia Health Dept, Office of Vital Records.

mcclxxxiii[1283] Mary Gaston Gee (1899-1987), The Ancestry and Descendants of Amzi Williford Gaston II (1841-1911) of Spartanburg County, South Carolina (Charlottesville, VA, 1944), p. 42.

mcclxxxiv[1284] *Social Security Death Index* , Social Security card issued in Louisiana before 1951.

mcclxxxv[1285] *Social Security Death Index* , Social Security card issued in Florida before 1951.

mcclxxxvi[1286] Florida Marriage Collection, 1822-1875 and 1927-2001 (online) , Ancestry.com and Florida Dept of Health.

mcclxxxvii[1287] 1900 Census, Doddridge County, WV (Central District).

mcclxxxviii[1288] Ritchie County Marriage Records, Harrisville, WV, Identified as Samuel Elliott, 23, b. Harrison Co, res. Doddridge Co; and Mary D. Richards, 19, b. (blank), res. Ritchie Co. Married Mar 5 1892 in Doddridge County.

, MR p. 77.

mcclxxxix[1289] 1910 Census, Doddridge County, WV (Central District).

mccxc[1290] 1910 Census, Doddridge County, WV (West Union District).

mccxci[1291] 1930 Census, Doddridge County, WV (West Union District).

mccxcii[1292] Georgia Hileman Halloran, citing census records.

mccxciii[1293] *Doddridge County WV Marriages 1845-1937* , Wes Cochran, 2515 10th Ave, Parkersburg, WV 26101 (Jan 1993), Identified as Clod (Clad?) Adams, 25, b. Harrison Co, res. Ritchie Co; and Dollie Elliott, 21, of Doddridge Co. Married Feb 5 1929.

mccxciv[1294] Georgia Hileman Halloran, citing census records and Margaret Kennedy <Dncrat@aol.com>, a direct descendant.

mccxcv[1295] Doddridge County Marriage Records, West Union, WV, Identified as J. S. Wilson, age 21, b. Ritchie Co; and Mary Bird Elliott, age 21, b. Doddridge Co. Ceremony held July 3 1895 at West Union. Informants: J. S. Wilson & William Elliott. MR Bk 5, p. 67.

mccxcvi[1296] Doddridge County Marriage Records, West Union, WV, MR Bk 5, p. 67.

mccxcvii[1297] Doddridge County Marriage Records, West Union, WV, Groom identified as Daniel B. Richards, age 30, b. Ritchie Co. Bride identified as Mary B. Wilson, age 24, b. Doddridge Co. Ceremony held Aug 22 1899 "at the Bride's Residence at Arnolds Creek.", MR Bk 6, p. 106.

mccxcviii[1298] Doddridge County Marriage Records, West Union, WV, MR Bk 6, p. 106.

mccxcix[1299] Doddridge County Marriage Records, West Union, WV, MR Bk 10, p. 3.

mccc[1300] Doddridge County Marriage Records, West Union, WV, Informants listed as Ellis Thompson and W. C. Bonnell, relationship of the latter not indicated. MR Bk 10, p. 3.

mccci[1301] Doddridge County Birth Records, West Union, WV, BR Bk 3, p. 215.

mcccii[1302] 1910 Census, Doddridge County, WV (Grant District).

mccciii[1303] Harrison County Marriage Records, Clarksburg, WV, Identified as Harry Clifford Skinner, single, 26, b. Mar 7 1902 in Gilmer Co, res, Shinnston WV, son of John W. & Anna D. (Holt) Skinner; and Rosetta May Richards, 22, b. Sep 10 1905 in Harrison Co, res. Shinnston, dau of Dan B. & Mary B. (Elliott) Richards. Married Mar 7 1928 in Shinnston. Informants for the marriage license: Harry C. Skinner & Rosetta M. Richards. MR p. 441.

mccciv[1304] 1930 Census, Doddridge County, WV (Central District).

mcccv[1305] Marriage record of wife's son.

mcccvi[1306] WV State Dept of Health, Div of Vital Statistics, *Death Certificate* (http://www.wvculture.org/vrr/va_dcsearch.aspx), Cause of death: strychnine poisoning (suicide). Marital status: married.

mcccvii[1307] Doddridge County Marriage Records, West Union, WV, MR Bk 13, p. 230.

mcccviii[1308] Newspaper birth announcement of great-great-grandaughter.

mcccix[1309] Doddridge County Birth Records, West Union, WV, BR Bk 4, p. 126.

mcccx[1310] Newspaper birth announcement of grandchild.

mcccxi[1311] 1920 Census, Doddridge County, WV (McClellan District).

mcccxii[1312] Doddridge County Marriage Records, West Union, WV, Ceremony held at home of William Elliott. MR Bk 5, p. 339.

mcccxiii[1313] *Doddridge County WV Marriages 1845-1937* , Wes Cochran, 2515 10th Ave, Parkersburg, WV 26101 (Jan 1993), Identified as Santford [sic] Smith, 22, of Doddridge Co; and Dollie Elliott, 18, of Doddridge Co. Married Aug 8 1897.

mcccxiv[1314] Doddridge County Death Records, West Union, WV, DR Bk 2, p. 147.

mcccxv[1315] Doddridge County Birth Records, West Union, WV, BR Bk 1, p. 69.

mcccxvi[1316] Doddridge County Death Records, West Union, WV, Cause of death tuberculosis. Age given as 31y1m11d, which would put birth at Nov 20 1876, rather than the Nov 20 1874 documented in birth records. Name entered as "Sanford." Marital status listed as widower. DR Bk 2, p. 147.

mcccxvii[1317] Obituary - Camden-Clark Memorial Hospital, Predeceased by three sisters and one brother.

mcccxviii[1318] *Doddridge County WV Marriages 1845-1937* , Wes Cochran, 2515 10th Ave, Parkersburg, WV 26101 (Jan 1993), Identified as J. W. Pritt, age 34, b. Gilmer Co, res. Doddridge Co; and Bessie Smith, age 21, of Doddridge Co. Married Jun 19 1919.

mcccxix[1319] WV State Dept of Health, Div of Vital Statistics, *Death Certificate* (http://www.wvculture.org/vrr/va_dcsearch.aspx), But age 22 given at time of Aug 1921 marriage would put birth in about 1899.

mcccxx[1320] WV State Dept of Health, Div of Vital Statistics, *Death Certificate* (http://www.wvculture.org/vrr/va_dcsearch.aspx), Identified as Edna Mae Bridwell Smith, b. Aug 26 1902 at Summers, Doddridge Co, dau of Sanford Smith & Dolly Elliott, resident of Pennsboro, died Oct 13 1940 at Harrisville, cause of death pulmonary tuberculosis. Buried at West Union Cemetery. Informant: Mr. Charles Leaseburg, Pennsboro.

mcccxxi[1321] *Ritchie County WV Deaths 1918-1940* , Wes Cochran, 2515 10th Ave, Parkersburg, WV 26101 (Nov 1998), Identified as Edna Mae Bridwell Smith, died Oct 13 1940, age 38y 1m 18d, dau of Sanford Smith & Dolly Elliot.

mcccxxii[1322] Pamela Bridwell Hughes, Seminole, FL <phughes4@tampabay.rr.com> (a Gaston and Pritchard descendant).

mcccxxiii[1323] 1900 Census, Nicholas County, WV.

mcccxxiv[1324] Pamela Bridwell Hughes, Seminole, FL <phughes4@tampabay.rr.com> (a Gaston and Pritchard descendant), His burial plot, which was purchased by Donny & Lois Buyers, is in the children's section of the cemetery. Don considered James his adopted father and bought the plot in the children's section because of James' love of children.

mcccxxv[1325] Doddridge County Birth Records, West Union, WV, BR Bk 1, p. 57.

mcccxxvi[1326] Harrison County Death Records, Clarksburg, WV, DR Bk 17, p. 197.

mcccxxvii[1327] Doddridge County Court House, West Union, WV, Will of father.

mcccxxviii[1328] Doddridge County Court House, West Union, WV, BR Bk 2, p. 269.

mcccxxix[1329] Doddridge County Court House, West Union, WV, MR Bk 10, p. 233.

mcccxxx[1330] Doddridge County Birth Records, West Union, WV, BR Bk 3, p. 159.

mcccxxxi[1331] Doddridge County Death Records, West Union, WV, Identified as (first name blank) Perine, 15, died Mar 1 1913, cause of death appendicitis. DR p. 127.

mcccxxxii[1332] Doddridge County Birth Records, West Union, WV, Conflicting birthdates of May 15 1905 and Jun 26 1905 are cited by Georgia Hileman Halloran and John Mark Perine, respectively. BR Bk 3, p. 167.

mcccxxxiii[1333] Doddridge County Birth Records, West Union, WV, Listed as tenth child born to this mother. This is undoubtedly the result of a misunderstanding in completing the delayed entry form, since she was actually the second of ten children. BR Del 1, p. 134-C.

mcccxxxiv[1334] Doddridge County Court House, West Union, WV, BR Bk 4, p. 134.

mcccxxxv[1335] Doddridge County Marriage Records, West Union, WV, Identified as Charles W. Perine, 27, b. Doddridge Co, res. Zelienople, PA; and Miss Juanita Watson, 18, b. & res. in Doddridge Co. Married Mar 13 1938 at Harmony, PA, which is near Zelienople. (Note: Although the ceremony was held in Pennsylvania, the license was issued and marriage recorded in Doddridge County, residence of the bride.), MR Bk 14, p. 101.

mcccxxxvi[1336] Doddridge County Birth Records, West Union, WV, Name listed in birth record as "Willard Perine." Full name of "Waitman T. Willard Perine" provided by Georgia Hileman Halloran. Nickname "Joe" provided by John Mark Perine and Olin Joseph Hartman. BR Bk 4, p. 134.

mcccxxxvii[1337] Doddridge County Birth Records, West Union, WV, Listing is for a female Perine, no first name specified. Full name provided by Georgia Hileman Halloran. BR Bk 4, p. 136.

mcccxxxviii[1338] Doddridge County Birth Records, West Union, WV, Listed as tenth child born to this mother, which seems unlikely. BR Bk Del 1, p. 134-D.

mcccxxxix[1339] Doddridge County Birth Records, West Union, WV, Listing is for a male Perine, no first name specified. Full name provided by researcher Georgia Hileman Halloran, and he is listed with his family as Ross N. Perine in the 1930 Census of Lancaster Twp, Butler County, PA. BR Bk 4, p. 137.

mcccxl[1340] Doddridge County Court House, West Union, WV, BR Bk 4, p. 138.

mcccxli[1341] Death Record - Online, Ohio Deaths, Certificate No. 016086.

mcccxlii[1342] *1930 Census* , Misidentified as Jack A. Perine, a son, age 5, in the household of Waitman T. Perine in the 1930 Census of Lancaster Twp, Butler County, PA.

mcccxliii[1343] Georgia Hileman Halloran, Berkley, MI 48072 <gshalloran@wowway.com>, The "A. C. Perine" in the 1880 Census is considered to be this Alice Dona Perine.

mcccxliv[1344] Doddridge County Birth Records, West Union, WV, Identified as "Alice D. Perine" born Apr 28 1875 to Richard & Mary J. Perine. But a second handwritten entry shows "Doney Perine" born Apr 27 1875, same parents, source Family Bible. Her obituary gives her birth as Apr 27 1875 at Arnolds Creek, Doddridge Co. BR Bk 1, p. 74.

mcccxlv[1345] Headstone, - Name appears on headstone as "Dona A. Britton".

mcccxlvi[1346] Doddridge County Marriage Records, West Union, WV, Groom identified as P. M. Britton, age 22, b. Doddridge Co. Bride identified as Dona Perine, age 22, b. Doddridge. Ceremony held Sep 8 1902 "at the bride's residence of Arnolds Creek." Her stated age of 22 is inconsistent with her documented birth in 1875. MR Bk 6, p. 476.

mcccxlvii[1347] Headstone, - Inscription reads "Ruth, dau of P. M. & A. C. D. Britton, born July 14 1903, died July 15 1903.".

mcccxlviii[1348] Doddridge County Birth Records, West Union, WV, Child identified only by last name Britton, b. Jul 11 1903 at Arnold Creek, dau of Porter Britton (farmer) and Dona Perine. BR Bk 3, p. 21.

mcccxlix[1349] Headstone, - Inscription reads "Ruth, Dau of P. M. & A. C. D. Britton, Born July 14 1903, Died July 15 1903.".

mcccl[1350] 1910 Census, Doddridge County, WV.

mcccli[1351] Doddridge County Birth Records, West Union, WV, Identified as Jessie Marie Britton, b. Dec 21 1904 at Arnolds Creek, dau of P. M. Britton (occup. tool dresser) & A. C. Perine, this being the 2nd child of this mother. Original typed entry had only the child's last name, with the first and middle names later added by hand. BR Bk 3, p. 23.

mccclii[1352] Doddridge County Birth Records, West Union, WV, Identified as Richie Britton, b. Oct 1 1906, son of Porter M. Britton & Dona Perine. BR Bk 4, p. 10.

mcccliii[1353] Grave marker, Name appears as "Richie N. Britton".

mcccliv[1354] Doddridge County Marriage Records, West Union, WV, MR Bk 12, p. 142.

mccclv[1355] Kathy Bee <beekann@comcast.net> (www.genealogy.com/users/b/e/e/Kathy-Bee-/TREE/index.html).

mccclvi[1356] Doddridge County Birth Records, West Union, WV, Identified as Wanda Mae Britton, b. Jan 24 1912 at Arnolds Creek, dau of Porter M. Britton & Dona Perine. Original typed entry had only the child's last name, gender not specified, no middle initial for father, and no maiden name for mother. Handwritten "correction by affidavit of cousin 7/29/65" made changes as reflected above. BR Bk 4, p. 14.

mccclvii[1357] Newspaper wedding announcement.

mccclviii[1358] Doddridge County Court House, West Union, WV, BR Bk 1, p. 96.

mccclix[1359] Doddridge County Birth Records, West Union, WV, Identified as Charlie H. Rollins, white male, born Apr 6 1903 at (blank), son of Alfred K. Rollins & Lelia M. Perine Rollins. Source of information: Family Bible. (Note: Although the birh record gives only the middle initial H, the middle name Hiram is found in the birth record of son Lewis Alfred Rollins. First name appears in nearly all public records as "Charlie," but as "Charles" in obituary of father. He is listed in the SSDI as "C. H. Rollins."), BR Bk 3, p. 179.

mccclx[1360] *Social Security Death Index* , Social Security card issued in Arizona before 1951.

mccclxi[1361] Doddridge County Court House, West Union, WV, BR Bk 1, p. 148.

mccclxii[1362] Doddridge County Court House, West Union, WV, Will of father.

mccclxiii[1363] Doddridge County Court House, West Union, WV, MR Bk 8, p. 99.

mccclxiv[1364] 1900 Census, Doddridge County, WV (New Milton District).

mccclxv[1365] Doddridge County Birth Records, West Union, WV, Name entered as "Lula Bland Perine.", BR Bk 2, p. 259.

mccclxvi[1366] Doddridge County Marriage Records, West Union, WV, MR Bk 9, p. 31.

mccclxvii[1367] Doddridge County Birth Records, West Union, WV, Identified as Christopher C. Sullivan, white male, born June 21 1889 in West Union, son of Smith Sullivan (occupation runabout) & Savilla Ash Sullivan, this being the mother's fifth child. BR p. 298.

mccclxviii[1368] *Social Security Death Index* , Social Security card issued in Utah before 1951. Name listed in SSDI as Ellen S. Hartman.

mccclxix[1369] *Social Security Death Index* , Name listed in SSDI as "John Perine," with only one R.

mccclxx[1370] Obituary, His wife's obituary 10 months later gives his death date as Feb 2, which is incorrect.

mccclxxi[1371] Headstone, - Name appears as "John H. Perrine".

mccclxxii[1372] Doddridge County Marriage Records, West Union, WV, Last name is spelled in marriage record "Perine," with one R. Ceremony held at residence of G. W. Britton, who was also the source of information for the marriage license. Relationship not specified. MR Bk 10, p. 32.

mccclxxiii[1373] Obituary, Identified in obituary as a daughter of George & Cass Britton. Son Al Austin Perrine's obituary identfes her as Olga Hitt, an apparent typographical error.

mccclxxiv[1374] Doddridge County Marriage Records, West Union, WV, MR Bk 10, p. 32.

mccclxxv[1375] *Social Security Death Index* , Name listed in SSDI as "Olga Perine," with just one R.

mccclxxvi[1376] Obituary of grandson.

mccclxxvii[1377] Doddridge County Marriage Records, West Union, WV, MR Bk 13, p. 223.

mccclxxviii[1378] WV State Dept of Health, Div of Vital Statistics, *Death Certificate* (http://www.wvculture.org/vrr/va_dcsearch.aspx), Wes Cochran's "Doddridge County WV Deaths" incorrectly reports death date as Dec 30 1927, rather than 1937.

mccclxxix[1379] Doddridge County Marriage Records, West Union, WV, He is identified as Ed L. Cox, age 50, b. Doddridge Co, and she as (Miss) Grace Perine, age 37, b. Doddridge. MR Bk 13, p. 223.

mccclxxx[1380] 1930 Census, Doddridge County, WV (New Milton District).

mccclxxxi[1381] Doddridge County Birth Records, West Union, WV, BR Bk 1, p. 130.

mccclxxxii[1382] Doddridge County Marriage Records, West Union, WV, MR Bk 8, p. 85.

mccclxxxiii[1383] Doddridge County Birth Records, West Union, WV, Two birth records on file: The first, BR 3-162, shows her born Jun 26 1899, dau of Chapman Perine & Susan Fleming, the third child born to this mother. The original typed entry had "Platha Perine" for the name, but "Platha" was lined out and "Theresa Harriet" was penned in.

No indication as to who made the change or why. The second birth record was a delayed entry, found in BR Del 1-134. It shows Theresa Harriet Perine born Jun 26 1899 at West Union, dau of Chapman J. Perine & Suzanna Fleming. The delayed certificate was filed on May 25 1942 by the mother. The original handwritten entry had the first name as "Therese," but the final "e" was crossed out and changed to an "a" to make the name "Theresa.".

mccclxxxiv[1384] Doddridge County Birth Records, West Union, WV, BR Bk 3, p. 166.

mccclxxxv[1385] Death Record - Online, Ohio, Vol 29779, Certificate 026558.

mccclxxxvi[1386] Death record, Ohio, Vol 29779, Certificate 026558.

mccclxxxvii[1387] Death record, Ohio, Vol 30472, Certificate 094777.

mccclxxxviii[1388] Doddridge County Marriage Records, West Union, WV, MR Bk 15, p. 40.

mccclxxxix[1389] 1930 Census, Doddridge County, WV (Southwest District).

mcccxc[1390] 1920 Census, Doddridge County, WV (Southwest District).

mcccxci[1391] West Union Herald-Record, 3/14/2006.

mcccxcii[1392] Doddridge County Birth Records, West Union, WV, Identified as Rachel Amelia Smith, dau of Harvey & Virginia Smith. BR Bk 4, p. 164.

mcccxciii[1393] *Social Security Death Index* , Social Security card issued in West Virginia in 1968. Name listed in SSDI as Susanna B. Cain.

mcccxciv[1394] 1910 Census, Tyler County, WV.

mcccxcv[1395] Gary Patterson, Tyler County West Virginia Cemeteries (website), http://myplace.frontier.com/~vzexo0wh/cemidx.htm, Death record states burial location as Stringtown, W.Va. There are three communities by that name in West Virginia, one in Marion County (south of Mannington), one in Barbour County (near Belington), and one Roane County west of Looneyville. But a headstone for her is reported at Five Oaks Cemetery, located about 1/3 mile from Alvy Church of Christ in Tyler County.

mcccxcvi[1396] 1900 Census, Tyler County, WV.

mcccxcvii[1397] Tyler County Death Records, Middlebourne, WV.

mcccxcviii[1398] Gary Patterson, Tyler County West Virginia Cemeteries (website), http://myplace.frontier.com/~vzexo0wh/cemidx.htm.

mcccxcix[1399] 1920 Census, Tyler County, WV.

mcd[1400] 1930 Census, Wetzel County, WV.

mcdi[1401] Tyler County Marriage Records, Middlebourne, WV.

mcdii[1402] 1930 Census, Tyler County, WV.

mcdiii[1403] *Tyler County WV Marriages 1891-1932* , Wes Cochran, 2515 10th Ave, Parkersburg WV 26101 (Apr 1995).

mcdiv[1404] *Doddridge County WV Marriages 1845-1937* , Wes Cochran, 2515 10th Ave, Parkersburg, WV 26101 (Jan 1993), Identified as Walter M. Perine, 25; and Mattie J. Fleming, age 33, b. Greene Co PA. Married Dec 10 1902.

mcdv[1405] Doddridge County Marriage Records, West Union, WV, She is identified as Mattie J. Fleming, age 33, born in Greene Co, PA. MR Bk 6, p. 495.

mcdvi[1406] Death Record - Online, Ohio - Vol 17756, Certificate 55527.

mcdvii[1407] *Doddridge County WV Marriages 1845-1937* , Wes Cochran, 2515 10th Ave, Parkersburg, WV 26101 (Jan 1993), Identified as Julius E. Moffatt, 22, of Doddridge Co; and Ocal Perine, 21, of Doddridge Co. Married Aug 23 1932.

mcdviii[1408] Doddridge County Birth Records, West Union, WV, BR Bk 1, p 97.

mcdix[1409] *The History of Doddridge County, West Virginia* , Taylor Publishing Co, 1979, p. 248.

mcdx[1410] Cemetery marker.

mcdxi[1411] Harrison County Marriage Records, Clarksburg, WV, Identified as Ernest Everett Williams, age 22, res. Wallace, b. Feb 16 1908 in Harrison Co, son of Samuel Williams & Tressie Pope; and Pauline Ida Batton, age 22, res. Wallace, b. Nov 24 1908 in Harrison Co, dau of John Batton & Laura Perrine. Married May 6 1930 in Clarksburg.

It is noted that both parties reported themselves as older than they were, the groom by six years and the bride by four. MR, p. 140.

mcdxii[1412] Doddridge County Birth Records, West Union, WV, Identified as Louis Perine. BR Bk 1, p. 117.

mcdxiii[1413] Doddridge County Death Records, West Union, WV, Identified as Lewis Perine, 28, born at Central Station, married, occupation laborer; died Jul 1 1903 at Sugar Camp, cause of death typhoid fever, buried Jul 3 1903 at Sugar Camp. DR p. 147.

mcdxiv[1414] Obituary, SSDI lists his birth date as Oct 25 1884. But headstone says 1886. Researcher Georgia Hileman Halloran reports birth as Oct 12 1884, while John Mark Perine gives it as Oct 25 1884. Age 25 given at July 1911 marriage would put birth in about 1886. Obituary states birth as Oct 25 1886, with age 85 at death on Mar 6 1972. This is considered most reliable.

mcdxv[1415] Headstone, - Name appears as "E. Goff Perine".

mcdxvi[1416] Doddridge County Marriage Records, West Union, WV, Parties providing information: Emery [sic] G. Perine and Jonathan Bonnell. MR Bk 8, p. 444.

mcdxvii[1417] Doddridge County Marriage Records, West Union, WV, MR Bk 13, p. 154.

mcdxviii[1418] Doddridge County Marriage Records, West Union, WV, MR Bk 17, p. 395.

mcdxix[1419] Obituary of stepfather.

mcdxx[1420] Doddridge County Birth Records, West Union, WV, BR Bk 4, p. 72.

mcdxxi[1421] Doddridge County Birth Records, West Union, WV, The birth record shows a birth date of Jul 29 1887. This is at variance with his headstone, which reads 1888-1977, and with his obituary, which gives his birth on Jul 29 1888, with age at death in Sep 1977 as 89. See Note for further clarification. BR Bk 2, p. 256.

mcdxxii[1422] Doddridge County Death Records, West Union, WV, Death date recorded in death record as Sep 5 1977. This agrees with his obituary, with specifies Monday, Sep 5 1977. A death date of Sep 7 1977 reported by other researchers is apparently in error. DR Outside County Bk 1, p. 512.

mcdxxiii[1423] Doddridge County Marriage Records, West Union, WV, Groom identified as Luther Perine, age 26, b. Doddridge Co. Bride identified as Beulah Hess, age 26, b. Doddridge. Ceremony held Dec 24 1914 at West Union. MR Bk 9, p. 356.

mcdxxiv[1424] *Social Security Death Index* , Name listed in SSDI as "Alice O. Ward.".

mcdxxv[1425] Doddridge County Marriage Records, West Union, WV, MR Bk 15, p. 436.

mcdxxvi[1426] Doddridge County marriage record 18-10 gives birth on Jul 5 1920 in Blandville, Doddridge Co. Doddridge Co death record 7-228 gives birth on Jul 5 1920 at Arnolds Creek, Doddridge Co. And Doddridge Co birth record 4-137 gives birth on Jul 3 1920 at Blandville.

mcdxxvii[1427] Doddridge County Court House, West Union, WV, DR Bk 7, p. 228.

mcdxxviii[1428] Newspaper birth announcement of great-grandchild.

mcdxxix[1429] Clarksburg Exponent-Telegram.

mcdxxx[1430] Doddridge County Marriage Records, West Union, WV, He is identified as Paul H. Smith, age 21, b. in Doddridge Co, son of Virginia Smith Allman. Father not listed. MR Bk 15, p. 170.

mcdxxxi[1431] Doddridge County Birth Records, West Union, WV, Recorded as Harry [sic] Paul Smith Jr., son of Harvy [sic] Smith & Virginia Elliott. BR Bk 4, p. 169.

mcdxxxii[1432] Doddridge County Death Records, West Union, WV, Identified as Paul H. Smith, b. Jan 18 1922 in Doddridge Co, son of Harvey Smith & Virginia Elliott. DR Bk 7, p. 172.

mcdxxxiii[1433] *Ritchie County WV Marriages 1945-1970* , Wes Cochran, 2515 10th Ave, Parkersburg WV 26101 (Dec 2003).

mcdxxxiv[1434] Obituary - St. Joseph's Hospital.

mcdxxxv[1435] Doddridge County Marriage Records, West Union, WV, Husband identified as "Columbus Ritchie Perine," born Mar 27 1930 in West Union, son of Luther M. & Beulah Perine. MR Bk 17, p. 23.

mcdxxxvi[1436] Doddridge County Court House, West Union, WV, MR Bk 17, p. 23.

mcdxxxvii[1437] Obituary, Killed in automobile accident along with her sister Bonnie Mae Stickel Ball.

mcdxxxviii[1438] Doddridge County Birth Records, West Union, WV, BR Bk 2, p. 259.

mcdxxxix[1439] Doddridge County Marriage Records, West Union, WV, MR Bk 17, p. 367.

mcdxl[1440] Doddridge County Marriage Records, West Union, WV, Identified as Shirley Oliver Jones, age 30, born (date blank) in Doddridge Co, res. Blandville, son of Creed & Lenora Jones; and Nellie Jane Perine, age 25, b. (date blank) in Doddridge Co, res. Blandville, dau of Ervin & Ila Perine. Married May 16 1946 at West Union. (Ages of both parties at variance with birthdates documented elsewhere.), MR Bk 15, p. 411.

mcdxli[1441] Doddridge County Birth Records, West Union, WV, Identified as Shirley Jones, male (pen & ink correction from original entry indicating female), born Aug 11 1912, son of Creed & Lenora Jones. BR Bk 4, p. 90.

mcdxlii[1442] Headstone, Name on headstone: S. Oliver Jones.

mcdxliii[1443] Susie Davis Nicholson, *Davis - The Settlers of Salem, West Virginia* , Gordon Printing Co, Strasburg OH, 1979 (Revised & Enlarged), p. 229.

mcdxliv[1444] Doddridge County Marriage Records, West Union, WV, MR Bk 17, p. 303.

mcdxlv[1445] West Union Herald-Record, 2/20/2007.

mcdxlvi[1446] Newspaper engagement announcement of grandson.

mcdxlvii[1447] *Social Security Death Index* , Name listed in SSDI as Margaret R. Bonnell.

mcdxlviii[1448] Doddridge County Birth Records, West Union, WV, Identified as Harvey Stickle [sic], b. Mar 9 1891 [sic], son of Rufus & Bettie. Informant: Mother. BR Bk 2, p. 311.

mcdxlix[1449] Doddridge County Birth Records, West Union, WV, BR Bk 4, p. 162.

mcdl[1450] *Doddridge County WV Marriages 1845-1937* , Wes Cochran, 2515 10th Ave, Parkersburg, WV 26101 (Jan 1993), Husband's middle initial reported as S, an apparent typographical error.

mcdli[1451] Doddridge County Court House, West Union, WV, BR Bk 4, p. 162.

mcdlii[1452] Doddridge County Marriage Records, West Union, WV, Groom identified as Harvey Stickel Jr., age 26, b. West Union, son of Harvey Stickel Sr. & (blank). Bride identified as Melva Sutton, age 36, b. Ritchie Co, dau of (blank). Married Jan 3 1951 at Smithburg. Given her age and the omission of parentage information, it is not clear if Sutton is her maiden name or name from a previous marriage. MR Bk 16, p. 300.

mcdliii[1453] Doddridge County Marriage Records, West Union, WV, MR Bk 16, p. 300.

mcdliv[1454] Newspaper wedding announcement of grandson.

mcdlv[1455] Doddridge County Birth Records, West Union, WV, Name entered as "Davie Perine." No other reference to "Davic" has been found. Marriage record of "Don C. Perine" gives age as 21 as of Aug 9 1918. BR Bk 3, p. 159.

mcdlvi[1456] Doddridge County Marriage Records, West Union, WV, Her age given as 23, born in Doddridge Co. MR Bk 10, p. 285.

mcdlvii[1457] Doddridge County Birth Records, West Union, WV, Identified as daughter of Don Columbus Perine and Ethel Maude Robinson. BR Bk Del- 2, p. 68.

mcdlviii[1458] Birth record of son, Child's father's age given as 16, occupation farmer. Child's mother's age given as 18, which conforms to other sources.

mcdlix[1459] Doddridge County Marriage Records, West Union, WV, MR Bk 17, p. 188.

mcdlx[1460] Newspaper announcement.

mcdlxi[1461] Doddridge County Marriage Records, West Union, WV, Daisy P. Perine is described as being age 21 as of Jan 14 1920, putting her date of birth at Jan 14 1899, born in Doddridge County. However, SSDI and the online Ohio death index show her birth as Jan 14 1900, which is considered to be correct. MR Bk 10, p. 441.

mcdlxii[1462] *Social Security Death Index* , Social Security card issued in Ohio in 1966.

mcdlxiii[1463] Doddridge County Marriage Records, West Union, WV, MR Bk 10, p. 441.

mcdlxiv[1464] *Social Security Death Index* , Social Security card issued in Ohio before 1951. Name listed in SSDI as Carl Squires.

mcdlxv[1465] William F. Donnelly, *The Wests of Duck Creek, Harrison County, Virginia (now West Virginia)* , Gateway Press, Baltimore MD, 1997, p. 426.

mcdlxvi[1466] William F. Donnelly, *The Wests of Duck Creek, Harrison County, Virginia (now West Virginia)* , Gateway Press, Baltimore MD, 1997, p. 422.

mcdlxvii[1467] *Social Security Death Index* , Social Security card issued in Maryland before 1951. Name listed in SSDI as "Art B. Coberly.".

mcdlxviii[1468] *Social Security Death Index* , Social Security card issued in Florida in 1973.

mcdlxix[1469] WV State Dept of Health, Div of Vital Statistics, *Death Certificate* (http://www.wvculture.org/vrr/va_dcsearch.aspx), Identified as Eli Jacob West, widower of Verona May Lynch, b. Jul 24 1860 at West Milford, d. Sep 14 1939 at West Milford in an accident when he "was caught in a cave in at his sand bank. Instant death." His parents were identified as John Elisha West & Elizabeth Ann Cozad, both at variance with their names as documented elsewhere, John Jackson West & Mary Elizabeth Cozad. Source of information for the death record identified as Mrs. Homer McKinley of West Milford. This would be Eli's daughter Calla Oscie West McKinley.

mcdlxx[1470] Death record of wife's father.

mcdlxxi[1471] Harrison County Marriage Records, Clarksburg, WV, Identified as George Thomas Humphreys, widowed, 23, b. Marshall Co WV, res. Newburg (Preston Co) WV, son of John & Elizabeth Humphreys; and Lessie Mae West, single, 18, b. Harrison Co, res. Harrison Co, dau of E. J. & Bert West. Married Jul 14 1922 at Salem WV by Bascom T. Trevey, Minister of the Methodist Episcopal Church. A handwritten notation in the top margin of the record states "Do Not Publish.", MR p. 414.

mcdlxxii[1472] William F. Donnelly, *The Wests of Duck Creek, Harrison County, Virginia (now West Virginia)* , Gateway Press, Baltimore MD, 1997, p. 427.

mcdlxxiii[1473] William F. Donnelly, *The Wests of Duck Creek, Harrison County, Virginia (now West Virginia)* , Gateway Press, Baltimore MD, 1997, p. 428.

mcdlxxiv[1474] William F. Donnelly, The Wests of Duck Creek, Harrison County, Virginia (now West Virginia) , Gateway Press, Baltimore MD, 1997.

mcdlxxv[1475] William F. Donnelly, *The Wests of Duck Creek, Harrison County, Virginia (now West Virginia)* , Gateway Press, Baltimore MD, 1997, Citing obituary of her brother Eli. p. 423.

mcdlxxvi[1476] *Doddridge County WV Marriages 1845-1937* , Wes Cochran, 2515 10th Ave, Parkersburg, WV 26101 (Jan 1993), Identified as John P. King, 23, b. Doddridge Co, res. Gilmer Co; and Sarah E. West, 21, b. Harrison Co, res. Doddridge Co. Married Oct 1 1891.

mcdlxxvii[1477] William F. Donnelly, *The Wests of Duck Creek, Harrison County, Virginia (now West Virginia)* , Gateway Press, Baltimore MD, 1997, p. 429.

mcdlxxviii[1478] William F. Donnelly, *The Wests of Duck Creek, Harrison County, Virginia (now West Virginia)* , Gateway Press, Baltimore MD, 1997, p. 430.

mcdlxxix[1479] Newspaper anniversary announcement of daughter.

mcdlxxx[1480] *Dirigo* , Salem College Yearbook, 1950.

mcdlxxxi[1481] William F. Donnelly, *The Wests of Duck Creek, Harrison County, Virginia (now West Virginia)* , Gateway Press, Baltimore MD, 1997, p. 431.

mcdlxxxii[1482] Washington Death Index, 1940-1996 (online), Ancestry.com and Washington State Dept of Health. State Death Records Index.

mcdlxxxiii[1483] Harrison County Marriage Records, Clarksburg, WV, Identified as Raymond Marshall Floyd, 22, single, b. Harrison Co, res. West Milford, son of (illegible) & Mary Floyd; and Willie Beryl Hinkle, 19, single, b. Doddridge Co, res. Harrison Co, daughter of G. A. & Marcota Hinkle. Married Aug 9 1914 in Clarksburg. MR p. 265.

mcdlxxxiv[1484] Harrison County Marriage Records, Clarksburg, WV, Identified as Robert Stuart Windon, single, 48, b. Oct 28 1897 in Clarksburg, son of William & Ingaby Mae (Stuart) Windon; and Beryl Floyd, single, 49, b. March 22 1895 at Big Isaac, daughter of George & Marcoda (McIntyre) Hinkle. Married Sep 2 1944 in Bridgeport. MR p. 429.

mcdlxxxv[1485] Lewis County Marriage Records, Weston, WV, Although married in Harrison County, the license was issued and filed in Lewis County because of the bride's residence there at the time. Identified as Harold Franklin Shaver, 29, b. Feb 22 1921 in

Clarksburg, res. Clarksburg, son of Arthur Shaver & Dessie Wickham; and Gearldine (sic) McIntyre, 31, b. Jul 12 1918 in Lost Creek, res. Deanville Weston, dau of Dolph McIntyre & Jessie Wilson. Married Feb 11 1950 at Clarksburg. No marital status indicated for either party, but a there is a previous marriage record on file for Harold Shaver in Harrison County, in which the parties are identified as Harold Franklin Shaver, single, 21, b. Feb 23 1916 in Harrison Co, res. Clarksburg, son of Arthur Cyrus Shaver & Dessie Wickham; and Mary Smith, single, 21, b. Feb 14 1916 in Ohio, res. Clarksburg, dau of Omar & Bonnie Smith; license issued Apr 19 1937, but no indication that the marriage ever took place.

mcdlxxxvi[1486] Harrison County Marriage Records, Clarksburg, WV, Identified as Harold Franklin Shaver, divorced (two previous marriages), 45, b. Feb 23 1921 at Clarksburg, res. Hepzibah, son of Arthur Shaver & Dessie Wickham; and Geraldine Dyre Shaver, divorced (one previous marriage), 47, b. Jul 12 1918 at Lost Creek, res. Bristol, dau of Dolph McIntyre & Jessie Wilson. Married Apr 28 1966 at Nutter Fort. There is another marriage record on file for this couple, filed in Feb 1957, in which they are identified as Harold Franklin Shaver, divorced, 35, b. Feb 23 1921 in Clarksburg, res. Wolf Summit, son of Arthur Shaver & Dessie Agnes Wickham; and Geraldine Dyer McIntyre Shaver, divorced, 37, b. Jul 12 1919 in Lost Creek, res. Wolf Summit, dau of Dolph McIntyre & Jessie Wilson; license issued Feb 13 1957 but no indication that the marriage ever took place.

mcdlxxxvii[1487] Obituary of husband's sister.

mcdlxxxviii[1488] Doddridge County Birth Records, West Union, WV, Identified as W. C. Haught, male, b. Feb 21 1876, son of M. L. & M. M. Haught. BR Bk 1, p. 79.

mcdlxxxix[1489] Obituary, 1900 Census of Doddridge Co states her birth date as Sep 1874.

mcdxc[1490] Doddridge County Court House, West Union, WV, BR Bk 3, p. 97.

mcdxci[1491] *West Virginia Blue Book* (Vol. 32, 1948), p. 380.

mcdxcii[1492] Doddridge County Death Records, West Union, WV, DR Bk Misc 12, p. 576.

mcdxciii[1493] *Social Security Death Index* , Name listed as "F. G. Haught".

mcdxciv[1494] Doddridge County Death Records, West Union, WV, DR Bk Misc 12, p. 577.

mcdxcv[1495] Obituary of paternal grandmother.

mcdxcvi[1496] W. B. Haught, Genealogy of the Haught Family of America (1948), 167.

mcdxcvii[1497] Doddridge County Birth Records, West Union, WV, BR Bk 4, p. 74.

mcdxcviii[1498] Susie Davis Nicholson, *Davis - The Settlers of Salem, West Virginia* , Gordon Printing Co, Strasburg OH, 1979 (Revised & Enlarged), p. 548.

mcdxcix[1499] Doddridge County Birth Records, West Union, WV, BR Bk 4, p. 77.

md[1500] *West Union Herald*, Issue 3/26/1936.

mdi[1501] Doddridge County Birth Records, West Union, WV, BR Bk 4, p. 79.

mdii[1502] Ritchie County Death Records, Harrisville, WV, DR Bk 6, p. 338.

mdiii[1503] Headstone, Name reads "Love Gaston Maxwell".

mdiv[1504] John Maxwell DeBrular, 14 Grafton St, Washington, WV 26181 <debrular@suddenlink.net>.

mdv[1505] *Doddridge County WV Marriages 1845-1937* , Wes Cochran, 2515 10th Ave, Parkersburg, WV 26101 (Jan 1993), Identified as B. C. Maxwell, 27, of Doddridge Co; and Love Haught, 21, of Doddridge Co. Married Sep 13 1899.

mdvi[1506] Doddridge County Birth Records, West Union, WV, BR Bk 1, p. 50.

mdvii[1507] Doddridge County Court House, West Union, WV, BR Bk 3, p. 135.

mdviii[1508] Doddridge County Court House, West Union, WV, DR Bk 3, p. 135.

mdix[1509] Doddridge County Birth Records, West Union, WV, Identified as (first name blank) Maxwell, female, b. Aug 12 1908 at Oxford, dau of Boyd C. & Love Maxwell. BR p. 108.

mdx[1510] Doddridge County Death Records, West Union, WV, Identified as "--- Maxwell," sex (blank), age 9 months, died May 12 1909 in Southwest District, cause of death meningitis. Informant: A. J. Osborne, undertaker. DR p. 99.

mdxi[1511] *Doddridge County WV Marriages 1845-1937* , Wes Cochran, 2515 10th Ave, Parkersburg, WV 26101 (Jan 1993), Identified as Kenneth DeBrular, 23, of Ritchie Co; and Mary Grace Maxwell, 18, of Doddridge Co. Married Nov 5 1932.

mdxii[1512] W. B. Haught, Genealogy of the Haught Family of America (1948).

mdxiii[1513] 1930 Census, Ritchie County, WV (Clay District).

mdxiv[1514] Doddridge County Marriage Records, West Union, WV, Identified as J. M. Hickman, 24, b. Doddridge Co; and Ivah M. Haught, 20, b. Doddridge. Married Aug 29 1900 at bride's father's home. MR Bk 6, p. 240.

mdxv[1515] Newspaper anniversary announcement, The wedding ceremony was performed by the Rev. Lemuel Zinn in the home of the bride's parents at Harmony, Doddridge County. For the Golden Anniversary, a "buffet dinner was served by the daughter, Mrs. Ortha Jenkins, who resides with the parents. She was assisted by the two visiting daughters Mrs. Marjorie Townsen of Venezuela, S.A., and Miss Rella Hickman of Arlington, Va.".

mdxvi[1516] Doddridge County Marriage Records, West Union, WV, MR Bk 6, p. 240.

mdxvii[1517] Doddridge County Birth Records, West Union, WV, BR Bk 3, p. 96.

mdxviii[1518] Doddridge County Birth Records, West Union, WV, Identified as Rella J. Hickman, white female, b. May 28 1903, dau of J. M. Hickman & Iva May Haught Hickman. Informant: Iva Hickman, mother. (Note: The adjacent entry in the ledger-style birth record is for Ada Hickman, white female, b. May 27 1903 at Summers WVa, dau of J. M. Hickman (farmer) & Ioah (sic) Haught Hickman, this being the mother's second child. Informant: Dr. D. Leeson. No other record of or reference to this child Ada has been found, and the 1910 Census clearly states that Ivah had only the three children listed, namely Ortha, Rella & Grant. Although we cannot explain how it came about, especially in view of the different name and one-day difference, it is considered that the entry of Ada was a clerical error that pertained to the birth of Rella.), BR Bk 3, p. 98.

mdxix[1519] Newspaper anniversary announcement of parents.

mdxx[1520] Death record of sister.

mdxxi[1521] Doddridge County Birth Records, West Union, WV, The birth record lists only an unnamed male born on Jan 25 1906 date to these parents. But death record states birth date as Jan 2 1906. BR Bk 4, p. 74.

mdxxii[1522] *1900 Census*, Doddridge Co, WV.

mdxxiii[1523] Doddridge County Death Records, West Union, WV, DR Bk 2, p. 65.

mdxxiv[1524] Headstone, Name reads "Susie A. Haught," on same headstone with first husband.

mdxxv[1525] *The History of Doddridge County, West Virginia* , Taylor Publishing Co, 1979, p. 216.

mdxxvi[1526] *Spiker Family Gathering Place* , http://www.spikerfamily.com.

mdxxvii[1527] West Union Herald-Record, 5/2/2006.

mdxxviii[1528] Obituary of son, Year only.

mdxxix[1529] Obituary of cousin.

mdxxx[1530] Wood County Marriage Records, Parkersburg, WV, Identified as Floyd H. Adams, 27, b. Apr 10 1922 in Clarksburg WV, res. Parkersburg WV, son of Worthy E. & Mary E. Adams; and Frankie Leone Sears, 20, b. Dec 28 1928 in Diana WV, res. Parkersburg, dau of Herley M. & Alice J. Sears. Married Dec 22 1949 at Bethany Methodist Church, Parkersburg, WV. (Note: Husband's obituary incorrectly states marriage date as Dec 22 1947.), MR p. 498.

mdxxxi[1531] Doddridge County Marriage Records, West Union, WV, Identified as James W. Smith Jr, 20, b. & res. in Doddridge Co; and Gertie Hammond, 16, b. Pleasants Co, res. Doddridge Co. Married Apr 30 1889 "at John W. Hammond's on the wtrs of Arnolds Creek." Informants for the marriage license: James W. Smith Jr. & John W. Hammond. MR p. 372.

mdxxxii[1532] 1900 Census, Doddridge County, WV (McClellan District).

mdxxxiii[1533] Obituary of stepmother.

mdxxxiv[1534] Doddridge County Birth Records, West Union, WV, Identified as Bessie Lillian Shuman, b. Jun 9 1894 at Rock Run, dau of Calvin Shuman (age 24, b. Monongalia Co, occup farmer) & Lydia E. Freeman Shuman (age 30, b. Doddridge Co), this being the second child born to this mother. BR p. 324.

mdxxxv[1535] Doddridge County Birth Records, West Union, WV, There are two entries on file for the birth of Mary Bird Smith. One is for Jul 5 1889 with information provided by father, and the other for Jul 6 1889 based on information provided several weeks later by the doctor. Her obituary states July 6 1889. BR Bk 2, p. 301.

mdxxxvi[1536] Doddridge County Marriage Records, West Union, WV, Identified as Anthony S. Freeman, 23, b. Doddridge Co, res. Doddridge Co; and Mary B. Smith, 23, b. Doddridge Co, res. Doddridge Co. Married Aug 13 1913 in Clarksburg, WV. (Note: Clarksburg is in Harrison County), MR Bk 9, p. 195.

mdxxxvii[1537] Doddridge County Court House, West Union, WV, BR Bk 2, p. 318.

mdxxxviii[1538] Doddridge County Court House, West Union, WV, BR Bk 1, p. 32.

mdxxxix[1539] Descendants of Wilson Britton , Richard Lyle "Dickie" Britton (1941-2000) (self-published, 1992).

mdxl[1540] Doddridge County Marriage Records, West Union, WV, Groom identified as Daniel W. Britton, age 28, born in Doddridge Co. Bride identified as Charlotte Wade, age 23, born in Ritchie Co. Ceremony held Mar 17 1895, performed by Eli M. Gaston. MR Bk 5, p. 42.

mdxli[1541] William Fred Spuhler Jr. (1940-2004), Richfield, MN, a Husk descendant and genealogist.

mdxlii[1542] Doddridge County Marriage Records, West Union, WV, MR Bk 5, p. 42.

mdxliii[1543] Clarksburg Exponent-Telegram, 5/30/2004.

mdxliv[1544] Goldenseal Magazine , West Virginia Cultural Center, www.wvlc.wvnet.edu/culture/goldensl.html, Winter 1999.

mdxlv[1545] West Virginia Blue Book (Vol. 32, 1948), p. 462.

mdxlvi[1546] Doddridge County Birth Records, West Union, WV, BR Bk 1, p. 59.

mdxlvii[1547] Pleasants County Marriage Records, St. Marys, WV.

mdxlviii[1548] 1910 Census, Harrison County, WV, 1930 Kansas census lists her birthplace as South Dakota, which was where she spent much of her childhood.

mdxlix[1549] South Dakota Marriages, 1905-1949 (online database), Ancestry.com and South Dakota Dept of Health.

mdl[1550] Social Security Death Index, Social Security card issued in South Dakota before 1951.

mdli[1551] Susie Davis Nicholson, Davis - The Settlers of Salem, West Virginia , Gordon Printing Co, Strasburg OH, 1979 (Revised & Enlarged), p. 200.

mdlii[1552] Hancock County Marriage Records, New Cumberland, WV.

mdliii[1553] Social Security Death Index , Social Security card issued in West Virginia in 1952.

mdliv[1554] West Union Herald-Record, 5/26/1998, p. 13 - Article by VFW Post 3408.

mdlv[1555] Newspaper memoriam.

mdlvi[1556] Doddridge County WV Deaths 1853-1969 , Wes Cochran, 2515 10th Ave, Parkersburg, WV 26101, Identified as Monnie Husk Parks.

mdlvii[1557] Obituary, Parents incorrectly listed as "Thomas R. and Anna H. Richards".

mdlviii[1558] Doddridge County Death Records, West Union, WV, Occupation listed as carpenter, marital status as divorced, cause of death as apoplexy, and place of death as Britton's Rest Home. Informant: John Richards, Akron, OH. DR Bk 5, p. 144-B.

mdlix[1559] Doddridge County Death Records, West Union, WV, DR Bk 5, p. 70-E.

mdlx[1560] Doddridge County Marriage Records, West Union, WV, Identified as Perry F. Greathouse, 30, b. & res. in Doddridge Co; and Nancy Richards, 24, b. & res. in Doddridge Co. Married Feb 22 1905 "at Samuel Richards in Doddridge County, W. Va." (Note: Obituaries of both husband and wife incorrectly state marriage date as 1901.), MR p. 242.

mdlxi[1561] 1910 Census, Doddridge County, WV (New Milton District).

mdlxii[1562] Harrison County Marriage Records, Clarksburg, WV, Identified as Samuel Matthew Wyckoff, 21, b. Harrison Co, res. Clarksburg, son of E. D. & Laura K.; and Frankie Luzada Greathouse, 18, b. & res. in Harrison Co, dau of P. F. & Nancy. Married Sep 20 1923 in Clarksburg. MR p. 324.

mdlxiii[1563] Harrison County Birth Records, Clarksburg, WV, Identified as Perry L. Greathouse, white male, b. Jun 26 1921 in Clarksburg, son of Perry F. Greathouse & Nancy M. Richards. BR p. 77.

mdlxiv[1564] *Harrison County WV Marriages 1895-1912* , Wes Cochran, 2515 10th Ave, Parkersburg, WV 26101 (Feb 2001), Identified as Robert M. Orr, widowed, 53, b. Doddridge Co, res. Harrison Co, son of John P. & Louisa; and Nannie A. Squires, 28, b. Doddridge Co, res. Harrison Co, dau of Virgil. Married Mar 17 1902.

mdlxv[1565] Harrison County Marriage Records, Clarksburg, WV, MR Bk 12, 40.

mdlxvi[1566] 1920 Census, Doddridge County, WV (New Milton District).

mdlxvii[1567] Doddridge County Marriage Records, West Union, WV, MR Bk 5, p. 465.

mdlxviii[1568] *Doddridge County WV Marriages 1845-1937* , Wes Cochran, 2515 10th Ave, Parkersburg, WV 26101 (Jan 1993), Identified as D. M. Squires, 22, of Doddridge Co; and Emma [sic] L. Dotson, 18, of Doddridge Co. Married Aug 25 1898.

mdlxix[1569] 1880 Census, Doddridge County, WV.

mdlxx[1570] Doddridge County Death Records, West Union, WV, Identified as Erma Lucreta [sic] Squires, age 79, widow, b. Dec 1 1882 in Doddridge Co, d. Jan 7 1962 at Britton Rest Home. Father: Geraldine Dotson. Mother: Unknown. Informant: Mrs. Oma Sherwood, Zanesville, OH. DR Bk 5, p. 158-C.

mdlxxi[1571] Death record of stepmother.

mdlxxii[1572] Doddridge County Court House, West Union, WV, BR Bk 3, p. 197.

mdlxxiii[1573] Susie Davis Nicholson, *Davis - The Settlers of Salem, West Virginia* , Gordon Printing Co, Strasburg OH, 1979 (Revised & Enlarged), p. 188.

mdlxxiv[1574] Doddridge County Court House, West Union, WV, BR Bk 4, p. 157.

mdlxxv[1575] Doddridge County Court House, West Union, WV, BR Bk 4, p. 164.

mdlxxvi[1576] *Doddridge County WV Marriages 1845-1937* , Wes Cochran, 2515 10th Ave, Parkersburg, WV 26101 (Jan 1993), Identified as Gyles Squires, 21, of Doddridge Co; and Hazel Dillon, 21, of Doddridge Co. Married Jun 6 1936.

mdlxxvii[1577] *Social Security Death Index* , Social Security card issued in Ohio in 1964.

mdlxxviii[1578] Harrison County Court House, Clarksburg, WV, DR Bk 6, p. 72.

mdlxxix[1579] Doddridge County Marriage Records, West Union, WV, MR Bk 7, p. 145.

mdlxxx[1580] Harrison County Death Records, Clarksburg, WV, DR Bk 19, p. 102-D.

mdlxxxi[1581] Harrison County Court House, Clarksburg, WV, DR Bk 5, p. 69.

mdlxxxii[1582] Doddridge County Birth Records, West Union, WV, Name listed as "Mary A. Squires," dau of V. B. & E. L. Squires. BR Bk 1, p. 105.

mdlxxxiii[1583] Joy Gregoire Gilchrist Stalnaker, *Squires Genealogy* , Hackers Creek Pioneers Descendants, Jane Lew, WV (www.hackerscreek.com), p. 328.

mdlxxxiv[1584] Doddridge County Marriage Records, West Union, WV, MR Bk 7, p. 43.

mdlxxxv[1585] Doddridge County Birth Records, West Union, WV, BR Bk 1, p. 111.

mdlxxxvi[1586] Doddridge County Birth Records, West Union, WV, BR Bk 3, p. 211.

mdlxxxvii[1587] Doddridge County Birth Records, West Union, WV, BR Bk 4, p. 157, and BR Del 1, p. 156.

mdlxxxviii[1588] Harrison County Court House, Clarksburg, WV, DR Bk 24, p. 247-A.

mdlxxxix[1589] Harrison County Death Records, Clarksburg, WV, DR Bk 24, p. 247-A.

mdxc[1590] Obituary of wife's half-sister.

mdxci[1591] Obituary of wife's half-brother.

mdxcii[1592] Newspaper wedding announcement, West Union Herald, 12/15/1938.

mdxciii[1593] Doddridge County Marriage Records, West Union, WV, Marriage license issued in Doddridge Co, but ceremony performed in Nicholas Co. An announcement of the wedding, appearing in the Dec 15 1938 issue of the West Union Herald, reported the date as Nov 27 1938. Nov 29th that year was on a Tuesday, while the 27th was on a

Sunday; on that basis, the date in the marriage record may be in error. MR Bk 14, p. 160.

mdxciv[1594] Obituary, West Union Herald-Record, 3/9/1999.

mdxcv[1595] Newspaper anniversary announcement.

mdxcvi[1596] Death Record - Online, Place of death given as nursing home.

mdxcvii[1597] *Social Security Death Index* , Social Security card issued in Ohio before 1951. Name listed in SSDI as Opal M. Morgan.

mdxcviii[1598] *Social Security Death Index* , Social Security card issued in Ohio before 1951. Name listed in SSDI as Erma M. Morton.

mdxcix[1599] Doddridge County Court House, West Union, WV, BR Bk 3, p. 191.

mdc[1600] Susie Davis Nicholson, *Davis - The Settlers of Salem, West Virginia* , Gordon Printing Co, Strasburg OH, 1979 (Revised & Enlarged), p. 511.

mdci[1601] Harrison County Court House, Clarksburg, WV, DR Bk 83, p. 432.

mdcii[1602] Doddridge County Birth Records, West Union, WV, Original typed entry had only the child's last name, Pierce, with a different birth date in July 1903. Handwritten corrections adding first and middle names, Nettie Pearl, and making the birthdate Jul 22 1903, were made on Jan 16 1965 by affidavit of brother-in-law, not identified by name. Her mother's birthplace was given as Roberts Fork. BR Bk 3, p. 165.

mdciii[1603] Susie Davis Nicholson, *Davis - The Settlers of Salem, West Virginia* , Gordon Printing Co, Strasburg OH, 1979 (Revised & Enlarged), p. 512.

mdciv[1604] Obituary, Susie Davis Nicholson (p. 512) reports birth date as May 29 1925.

mdcv[1605] Doddridge County Birth Records, West Union, WV, BR Bk 1, p. 141.

mdcvi[1606] Obituary - Nursing home, Identified in obituary as "O. Wayne Pierce, ... a son of the late James and Amariah Gaston Pierce." He was predeceased by two brothers, three sisters, and two grandsons.

mdcvii[1607] Ritchie County Historical Society (David M. Scott, Editor), *Ritchie County, West Virginia Cemeteries through 1993* , McClain Printing Co, Parsons, WV, 1995, Name on headstone: O. Wayne Pierce. p. 555.

mdcviii[1608] Doddridge County Birth Records, West Union, WV, BR Bk 2, p. 260.

mdcix[1609] Doddridge County Death Records, West Union, WV, DR Bk 4, p. 82.

mdcx[1610] Doddridge County Marriage Records, West Union, WV, Ceremony performed by Eli M. Gaston at his home. MR Bk 6, p. 355.

mdcxi[1611] Doddridge County Birth Records, West Union, WV, Parents identified in BR as "Anda N. & Emaline Hart." Middle name from daughter Wilma's BR. BR Bk 1, p. 73.

mdcxii[1612] Doddridge County Birth Records, West Union, WV, Identified only as a Female Hart born on Feb 2 1902 at Summers, the first child of John W. and Nancy C. Gaston Hart; medical attendants J.C. Lawson & Mrs. David Gaston. BR Bk 3, p. 97.

mdcxiii[1613] Doddridge County Birth Records, West Union, WV, Parents identified as "Latherm" and Frances Ingram. BR Bk 1, p. 109.

mdcxiv[1614] Per grandson Gary Kenneth Cox.

mdcxv[1615] Walter Ray "Shiner" Husk (1900-1993).

mdcxvi[1616] Doddridge County Death Records, West Union, WV, DR Outside County Bk 2, p. 829.

mdcxvii[1617] Doddridge County Birth Records, West Union, WV, BR Bk 4, p. 25.

mdcxviii[1618] Doddridge County Birth Records, West Union, WV, Delayed entry Birth Record filed Apr 2 1960 by affidavit of older sister, recorded May 7 1960. Middle name spelled Idaline in obituary. BR Del Bk 2, p. 36.

mdcxix[1619] Doddridge County Birth Records, West Union, WV, BR Bk Del-1, p. 32-N.

mdcxx[1620] Doddridge County Birth Records, West Union, WV, Delayed certificate filed by father Nov 5 1955. BR Bk Del-1, p. 32-N.

mdcxxi[1621] *The History of Doddridge County, West Virginia* , Taylor Publishing Co, 1979, p. 114.

mdcxxii[1622] Obituary, Obituary of wife incorrectly gives his death date as July 5 1982. His own obituary specifies Tuesday, July 6 1982 at 7:05pm. That date was in fact a Tuesday. SSDI states only July 1982.

mdcxxiii[1623] Doddridge County Marriage Records, West Union, WV, MR Bk 15, p. 120.

mdcxxiv[1624] Harrison County Marriage Records, Clarksburg, WV, MR p. 346.

mdcxxv[1625] *Social Security Death Index* , Social Security card issued in Washington, DC, before 1951.

mdcxxvi[1626] Doddridge County Birth Records, West Union, WV, Identified as parents' 12th child, with 11 still living. BR Bk 4, p. 88.

mdcxxvii[1627] Obituary of granddaughter.

mdcxxviii[1628] Doddridge County Court House, West Union, WV, MR Bk 10, p. 73.

mdcxxix[1629] Doddridge County Death Records, West Union, WV, DR Bk 5, p. 2-A.

mdcxxx[1630] William Bernard Wilson, *Wilson-Pepper Genealogy 1595-1989* (Gateway Press, Baltimore, MD, 1990), p. 43.

mdcxxxi[1631] WV State Dept of Health, Div of Vital Statistics, *Death Certificate* (http://www.wvculture.org/vrr/va_dcsearch.aspx), Cause of death listed in death record as "dropsy and complications." Obituary states Bright's disease.

mdcxxxii[1632] Headstone, Lot 30, Section 3.

mdcxxxiii[1633] *Gilmer County WV Marriages 1845-1933* , Wes Cochran, 2515 10th Ave, Parkersburg WV 26101 (Jan 1989), Identified as E. W. Gaston, age 23, of Doddridge Co; and L. C. Bowyer, age 24, of Gilmer Co. Married June 8 1903.

mdcxxxiv[1634] *City Directory, Clarksburg, WV, 1923* , Identified as C. Laura Gaston, widow of Eli W. Gaston, 441 Stealey Ave, Stealey Heights.

mdcxxxv[1635] Harrison County Marriage Records, Clarksburg, WV, MR p. 247.

mdcxxxvi[1636] *City Directory, Clarksburg, WV, 1923* , 441 Stealey Ave, Stealey Heights; occupation student.

mdcxxxvii[1637] Harrison County Marriage Records, Clarksburg, WV, MR p. 21.

mdcxxxviii[1638] Headstone, Obituary incorrectly states burial as Clarksburg, WV.

mdcxxxix[1639] Doddridge County Birth Records, West Union, WV, The original record (BR 1-120) is entered as Lawrence Gaston, female, b. Jan 2 1882, dau of John M. & Elizabeth. But a delayed entry (BR Del 1-64E), filed 3/15/1948 by uncle D. D.Gaston, corrects that to read Lurana Olive Gaston, b. Jan 2 1883, the third child of Elizabeth Hart. BR Bk 1, p. 120; and BR Del Bk 1, p. 64-E.

mdcxl[1640] Doddridge County Court House, West Union, WV, MR Bk 7, p. 234.

mdcxli[1641] Doddridge County Death Records, West Union, WV, DR Bk 7, p. 119.

mdcxlii[1642] Doddridge County Court House, West Union, WV, BR Bk 3, p. 153.

mdcxliii[1643] Doddridge County Death Records, West Union, WV, DR Bk 6, p. 143.

mdcxliv[1644] Doddridge County Marriage Records, West Union, WV, MR Bk 12, p. 459.

mdcxlv[1645] *Doddridge County WV Marriages 1845-1937* , Wes Cochran, 2515 10th Ave, Parkersburg, WV 26101 (Jan 1993), Identified as Charles Floyd Husk, 23, of Doddridge Co; and Wanda Mae Richards, 21, of Doddridge Co. Married Feb 11 1932.

mdcxlvi[1646] Doddridge County Marriage Records, West Union, WV, MR Bk 14, p. 170.

mdcxlvii[1647] *Social Security Death Index* , Name listed in SSDI as Walter Underwood. Although identified in birth record as Jackson Walter Underwood, son of Wetzel Underwood and Minnie Smith, he was always known as Walter J. Underwood.

mdcxlviii[1648] Doddridge County Birth Records, West Union, WV, BR Bk 2, p. 122.

mdcxlix[1649] Obituary of husband's sister-in-law.

mdcl[1650] Immediate family, Marriage ceremony performed by Rev. S. P. Crummitt, witnessed by Howard (Ira's third cousin) and Miriam Jones.

mdcli[1651] Doddridge County Marriage Records, West Union, WV, Identified as Alfred Randolph Gaston, 20, b. Doddridge Co, res. West Union, son of (blank); and Virginia Williams Kidd, 18, b. Braxton Co, res. Doddridge Co, dau of (blank). Married Apr 8 1945 at West Union by D. Fay Zinn, Minister of the Gospel. MR Bk 15, p. 306.

mdclii[1652] Doddridge County Marriage Records, West Union, WV, Identified as Armand Brown, 23, b. West Union, res. Youngstown Ohio, son of A. A. & Babe Brown; and Geneva Gaston, 19, b. & res. in West Union, dau of I. D. & Opal Gaston. Married Aug 4 1946 at the United Brethren Church in West Union by Paul R. Capehart, minister of the Gospel. (MR Bk 15, p. 432), http://www.wvculture.org/vrr/va_view.aspx?Id=11797816&Type=Marriage.

mdcliii[1653] Doddridge County Birth Records, West Union, WV, Spelling of name recorded as "Armond," which is incorrect. Listed as a son of A. A. Brown and Babe Haught Brown. BR Bk 4, p. 21.

mdcliv[1654] Doddridge County Marriage Records, West Union, WV, MR Bk 16, p. 284.

mdclv[1655] Doddridge County Court House, West Union, WV, BR Bk 5, p. 80-A.

mdclvi[1656] Immediate family, Killed instantly in multi-vehicle accident in blinding sandstorm on I-10 near Lordsburg, NM, along with wife Phillis Baird Holtz, also a trucker and who was driving at the time.

mdclvii[1657] *Doddridge County WV Marriages 1845-1937* , Wes Cochran, 2515 10th Ave, Parkersburg, WV 26101 (Jan 1993), Identified as Larmar Collions [sic], 26, b. Tyler Co, res. Doddridge Co; and Rulana M. Gaston, 24, of Doddridge Co. Married Sep 11 1904.

mdclviii[1658] Doddridge County Marriage Records, West Union, WV, MR Bk 7, p. 201.

mdclix[1659] WV State Dept of Health, Div of Vital Statistics, *Death Certificate* (http://www.wvculture.org/vrr/va_dcsearch.aspx), Wife's obituary states husband's death date as May 23 1943, but his death record shows it as May 22 1943, with burial on May 23 1943. His name appears in his death record as "Lima Martin Collins." The spelling Lima is considered a clerical error, since Larmar is found in all other references.

mdclx[1660] Marion County Court House, Fairmont, WV, DR Bk 11, p. 32.

mdclxi[1661] Marion County Death Records, Fairmont, WV, DR Bk 19, p. 109.

mdclxii[1662] Doddridge County Birth Records, West Union, WV, BR Bk 1, p. 132.

mdclxiii[1663] Upshur County Court House, Buckhannon, WV, MR Bk 7, p. 77.

mdclxiv[1664] *Social Security Death Index* , Social Security card issued in Ohio in 1972. Name listed in SSDI as Lillie Gifford.

mdclxv[1665] National Archives and Records Administration, *World War I Draft Registration Cards, 1917-1918* (Ancestry.com online database), Birth data entered as Feb 22 1888 at Oxford, WV, but birth record indicates Feb 21 1888.

mdclxvi[1666] Per his son, Jesse Lawrence Gaston, but Social Security Death Index gives death date as Jan 1974.

mdclxvii[1667] *Braxton County WV Marriages 1876-1932* , Wes Cochran, 2515 10th Ave, Parkersburg WV 26101.

mdclxviii[1668] Braxton County Marriage Records, Sutton, WV, MR 11-70.

mdclxix[1669] Braxton County Court House, Sutton, WV, DR Fid Bk 6-9C.

mdclxx[1670] *Social Security Death Index* , Social Security card issued in Maryland in 1956-57.

mdclxxi[1671] Obituary, The Republican (Oakland, MD), 7/23/2004.

mdclxxii[1672] Death Record - Online, Name listed as Betty Gaston Lewis.

mdclxxiii[1673] *Social Security Death Index* , SSDI lists name as Betty Lewis.

mdclxxiv[1674] Upshur County Marriage Records, Buckhannon, WV, His age given as 27 at time of marriage in 1907. MR Bk 9, p. 15.

mdclxxv[1675] Newspaper article on family reunion.

mdclxxvi[1676] Upshur County Birth Records, Buckhannon, WV, BR Bk 4, p. 11.

mdclxxvii[1677] Upshur County Birth Records, Buckhannon, WV, BR Bk 4, p. 12.

mdclxxviii[1678] Upshur County Birth Records, Buckhannon, WV, BR Bk 5, p. 2.

mdclxxix[1679] Upshur County Birth Records, Buckhannon, WV, BR Bk 5, p. 3.

mdclxxx[1680] *Social Security Death Index* , Social Security card issued in Indiana before 1951.

mdclxxxi[1681] Upshur County Birth Records, Buckhannon, WV, BR Bk 6, p. 2.

mdclxxxii[1682] *Lewis County WV Marriages 1881-1937* , Wes Cochran, 2515 10th Ave, Parkersburg, WV 26101 (Sep 1994), Identified as John E. Fretwell, 36, b. Randolph Co, res. Lewis Co; and Alma May [sic] Gaston, 23, b. Doddridge Co, res. Lewis Co. Married Nov 18 1921.

mdclxxxiii[1683] WV State Dept of Health, Div of Vital Statistics, *Death Certificate* (http://www.wvculture.org/vrr/va_dcsearch.aspx), Cause of death: Diphtheria or croup.

mdclxxxiv[1684] Upshur County Court House, Buckhannon, WV, MR Bk 13, p. 313.

mdclxxxv[1685] Upshur County Marriage Records, Buckhannon, WV, She was identified as Georgie R. Gaston, age 17, and he as Clarence Birton Skinner, age 23, b. Lewis Co, WV. MR Bk 13, p. 313.

mdclxxxvi[1686] Upshur County Marriage Records, Buckhannon, WV, MR Bk 13, p. 313.

mdclxxxvii[1687] U.S. Public Records Index, Vol 2 , Ancestry.com.

mdclxxxviii[1688] Doddridge County Birth Records, West Union, WV, Identified as Rulina C. Gaston, b. Apr 15 1889 at Summers, dau of Jesse Smith Gaston (age 29, b. Summers, occup farmer) & Lucy M. Swiger (age 20, b. Greenbrier Co VA). Informant indicated as Family Bible. BR Bk 2, p. 123.

mdclxxxix[1689] Doddridge County Marriage Records, West Union, WV, MR Bk 8, p. 26.

mdcxc[1690] Doddridge County Death Records, West Union, WV, DR Bk 6, p. 77.

mdcxci[1691] *Hileman Genealogy (1305) 1780-1981* , Pearl Hileman Cooper and Maysel Hileman Pierce (self-published, 1981), p. 38.

mdcxcii[1692] Marion County Court House, Fairmont, WV, DR Bk 17, p.781.

mdcxciii[1693] Newspaper wedding announcement of daughter.

mdcxciv[1694] Doddridge County Marriage Records, West Union, WV, MR Bk 15, p. 158.

mdcxcv[1695] *Ritchie County WV Marriages 1916-1945* , Wes Cochran, 2515 10th Ave, Parkersburg WV 26101 (Sep 1998), Identified as Charles Alfred L. Hileman, 26, of Doddridge Co, son of A. A. & Rulinna C. Hileman; and Lucy Belle Bee, 17, of Ritchie Co, dau of Ezra & Viola Bee. Married Jun 13 1939.

mdcxcvi[1696] Newspaper birth announcement of daughter.

mdcxcvii[1697] Doddridge County Death Records, West Union, WV, DR Bk 2, p. 65-A.

mdcxcviii[1698] *Doddridge County WV Deaths 1853-1969* , Wes Cochran, 2515 10th Ave, Parkersburg, WV 26101, Identified as Maude A. Hileman, died Jan 12 1921.

mdcxcix[1699] Harrison County Death Records, Clarksburg, WV, Identified as Maude Lee Hileman, born & died (stillborn) at Mason Hospital in Clarksburg on Jul 28 1933, dau of Aaron Hileman (b. Ritchie Co) and Rulina C. Gaston (b. Doddridge Co). Buried Jul 29 1933 at Oxford, WV.

mdcc[1700] Law suit, Jesse S. Gaston, et al, vs. John M. Gaston, et al, filed in Nov 1911 in the Doddridge Co Circuit Court, listed Charles Strother, to turn age 21 on Aug 4 1912, as a surviving child of the late Hannah Strother.

mdcci[1701] Death record.

mdccii[1702] Doddridge County Court House, West Union, WV, MR Bk 8, p. 272.

mdcciii[1703] Susie Davis Nicholson, *Davis - The Settlers of Salem, West Virginia* , Gordon Printing Co, Strasburg OH, 1979 (Revised & Enlarged), p. 465.

mdcciv[1704] Doddridge County Marriage Records, West Union, WV, Identified as Gilbert Robert Hickman, 23, b. Doddridge Co, res. West Union; and Mrs. Marguerite Duckworth Lough (or Laugh), 26, b. Tucker Co WV, res. Doddridge Co. Married Jul 30 1933 in Weston WV. (Note: Although the wedding was held in Lewis Co, the marriage is recorded in Doddridge Co, residence of the bride.), MR p. 108.

mdccv[1705] Newspaper wedding announcement, Susie Davis Nicholson, p. 465, reports marriage occuring in 1950, which is incorrect. Wedding announcement does not give the location, but implies that it was overseas, probably in Germany. West Union Herald, July 5 1951.

mdccvi[1706] Obituary, West Union Herald-Record, Feb 20 1996.

mdccvii[1707] David & Susie Nutter Hickman, Baltimore (Middle River), MD 21220.

mdccviii[1708] Elizabeth Witter Clarke Lerman, Dayton, OH 45406 <Lermanwmi@aol.com>, Death certificate gives place of death as Rushcreek Township, Fairfield Co, OH. Cause of death given as "Labor Pneumonia.".

mdccix[1709] Doddridge County Marriage Records, West Union, WV, MR Bk 8, p. 448.

mdccx[1710] *West Union Record*, 6/19/1952.

mdccxi[1711] Elizabeth Witter Clarke Lerman, Dayton OH, citing family Bible.

mdccxii[1712] Elizabeth Witter Clarke Lerman, Dayton, OH 45406 <Lermanwmi@aol.com>, His obituary states birthplace as Bremen, Ohio.

mdccxiii[1713] Doddridge County Birth Records, West Union, WV, Although the birth record entry states Dec 12 1891, this is considered to be a clerical error. A birth date of Dec 21 1891 is recorded in the Gaston Familyl Bible and is found in her obituary, funeral card, and on the family information sheet completed by her father as part of the W. Guy Tetrick survey in 1932. BR Bk 2, p. 128.

mdccxiv[1714] Doddridge County Marriage Records, West Union, WV, Groom identified as L. Brison Bowyer, age 21, born & residing in Gilmer Co. Bride identified as Lovie M. Gaston, age 21, b. Doddridge Co. Ceremony held May 15 1913 "at the home of D. D. Gaston.", MR Bk 9, p. 163.

mdccxv[1715] 1920 Census, Gilmer County, WV.

mdccxvi[1716] Doddridge County Marriage Records, West Union, WV, MR Bk 9, p. 163.

mdccxvii[1717] *West Union WV Cemeteries (Doddridge County)* , Wes Cochran, 2515 10th Ave, Parkersburg, WV 26101 (July 1990), Headstone reads: Brison Bowyer.

mdccxviii[1718] *Social Security Death Index* , Birth date given in marriage record as Dec 24 1912, but SSDI shows it as Dec 24 1914.

mdccxix[1719] 1930 Census, Doddridge County, WV (Grant District).

mdccxx[1720] Gilmer County Marriage Records, Glenville, WV, Although the ceremony was held in Kanawha County, the marriage license was issued and filed in Gilmer County, residence of the bride.

mdccxxi[1721] *Gilmer County West Virginia History 1845-1989* , Gilmer County Historical Society, 1994, p. 219.

mdccxxii[1722] *Social Security Death Index* , Social Security card issued in Ohio in 1952-53.

mdccxxiii[1723] Wood County Death Records, Parkersburg, WV, DR Bk 13, p. 293.

mdccxxiv[1724] *Gilmer County West Virginia History 1845-1989* , Gilmer County Historical Society, 1994, p. 160.

mdccxxv[1725] Wood County Death Records, Parkersburg, WV, DR Bk 14, p. 222.

mdccxxvi[1726] Obituary, Parkersburg News, 1/29/1998.

mdccxxvii[1727] Wood County Death Records, Parkersburg, WV, DR Bk 6, p. 55.

mdccxxviii[1728] Newspaper memoriam, Clarksburg Exponent-Telegram, 2/11/2007.

mdccxxix[1729] 1900 Census, Wayne County, WV.

mdccxxx[1730] *Social Security Death Index* , Social Security card issued in New Jersey in 1953 and 1955.

mdccxxxi[1731] Marion County Death Records, Fairmont, WV.

mdccxxxii[1732] *Social Security Death Index* , Social Security card issued in West Virginia before 1951. Last Social Security benefit: Winter Park, Orange Co, FL. Name listed in SSDI as "W. Maddox".

mdccxxxiii[1733] 1930 Census, Monongalia County, WV.

mdccxxxiv[1734] *Social Security Death Index* , Social Security card issued in NC/WV before 1951. Name listed in SSDI as Theo Maddox.

mdccxxxv[1735] William F. Donnelly, *The Wests of Duck Creek, Harrison County, Virginia (now West Virginia)* , Gateway Press, Baltimore MD, 1997, p. 472.

mdccxxxvi[1736] William F. Donnelly, *The Wests of Duck Creek, Harrison County, Virginia (now West Virginia)* , Gateway Press, Baltimore MD, 1997, p. 435.

mdccxxxvii[1737] William F. Donnelly, *The Wests of Duck Creek, Harrison County, Virginia (now West Virginia)* , Gateway Press, Baltimore MD, 1997, p. 475.

mdccxxxviii[1738] William F. Donnelly, *The Wests of Duck Creek, Harrison County, Virginia (now West Virginia)* , Gateway Press, Baltimore MD, 1997, p. 476.

mdccxxxix[1739] William F. Donnelly, *The Wests of Duck Creek, Harrison County, Virginia (now West Virginia)* , Gateway Press, Baltimore MD, 1997, p. 473.

mdccxl[1740] William F. Donnelly, *The Wests of Duck Creek, Harrison County, Virginia (now West Virginia)* , Gateway Press, Baltimore MD, 1997, p. 477.

mdccxli[1741] 1920 Census, Monongalia County, WV.

mdccxlii[1742] William F. Donnelly, *The Wests of Duck Creek, Harrison County, Virginia (now West Virginia)* , Gateway Press, Baltimore MD, 1997, p. 474.

mdccxliii[1743] William F. Donnelly, *The Wests of Duck Creek, Harrison County, Virginia (now West Virginia)* , Gateway Press, Baltimore MD, 1997, Citing Harrison County Death Recors, Bk 77, p. 520. Cause of death: smoke inhalation. pp. 474, 492.

mdccxliv[1744] William F. Donnelly, *The Wests of Duck Creek, Harrison County, Virginia (now West Virginia)* , Gateway Press, Baltimore MD, 1997, Citing Harrison County Death Records, Bk 77, p. 519. Cause of death: smoke inhalation. pp. 474, 492.

mdccxlv[1745] Obituary of husband's mother.

mdccxlvi[1746] *Social Security Death Index* , Name appears in SSDI as "Snow Bartlett".

mdccxlvii[1747] 1910 Census, Ritchie County, WV (Auburn).

mdccxlviii[1748] *Ritchie County WV Deaths 1941-1955* , Wes Cochran, 2515 10th Ave, Parkersburg, WV 26101 (Dec 1998), Identified as Edna Cooper Nutter, d. May 22 1948, age 74y10m6d, b. Gilmer Co, dau of Charles Cooper & Mary Jane Hall. This information puts her birth date at Jul 16 1873. We originally had birth date as Jul 16 1874, per Marilyn Davis Jones. But obituary in May 1948 gave age as 63, without stating a birth date. If she was 63 when she died, that would put birth in 1884. But then she would have been only 11 when she married in 1895. There is still some uncertainty on this.

mdccxlix[1749] *Ritchie County WV Marriages 1916-1945* , Wes Cochran, 2515 10th Ave, Parkersburg WV 26101 (Sep 1998), Identified as Charles Howard Barnard, 31, of Ritchie Co; and Maple Nutter, 24, of Ritchie Co. Married Aug 2 1931.

mdccl[1750] *Social Security Death Index* , Social Security card issued in Ohio in 1963.

mdccli[1751] Gilmer County Marriage Records, Glenville, WV, Although recorded in Gilmer County, the ceremony was held in West Union, Doddridge County. Wife's obituary states marriage date as Sep 29 1937 (a Wednesday), but marriage record shows it to be Sep 30 1937. MR p. 379.

mdcclii[1752] 1910 Census, Gilmer County, WV.

mdccliii[1753] U.S. World War II Army Enlistment Records, 1938-1946 , Ancestry.com.

mdccliv[1754] Obituary, Rhode Island Avenue Press, Apr 23 1931.

mdcclv[1755] *Social Security Death Index* , Social Security card issued in Washington DC in 1952.

mdcclvi[1756] Lane Bush Nutter, Cox's Mill, Gilmer Co, WV.

mdcclvii[1757] Newspaper anniversary announcement, West Union Herald Record, 6/16/2009.

mdcclviii[1758] Newspaper anniversary announcement, West Union Herald-Record, 6/15/1999.

mdcclix[1759] *Ritchie County WV Marriages 1945-1970* , Wes Cochran, 2515 10th Ave, Parkersburg WV 26101 (Dec 2003), Identified as Robert Junior Britton, b. May 31 1926 in Ritchie Co, res. Oxford WV, son of Robert E. & Mary (Sweeney) Britton; and Laurel Nutter, b. Oct 8 1924 in Gilmer Co, res. Auburn WV, dau of J. B. & Tracy (Bush) Nutter. Married Jun 24 1949. But newspaper announcement of 50th wedding anniversary stated marriage location as Clarksburg, Harrison County.

mdcclx[1760] *Social Security Death Index* , Headstone directory reports birth in 1874, but this is believed to be incorrect. SSDI specifies birth date as Sep 25 1879. Age not given in marriage record.

mdcclxi[1761] *Ritchie County WV Marriages 1916-1945* , Wes Cochran, 2515 10th Ave, Parkersburg WV 26101 (Sep 1998), Identified as Pryor Hartman Ayers, divorced, 33, b.

Ritchie Co, res. Wood Co; and Conzie Pauline Drain, 24, b. Gilmer Co, res. Ritchie Co. Married Jul 31 1927.

mdcclxii[1762] Ota Reed Fraker (1882-1970) gives marriage date as Jun 24 1903, but this is clearly impossible and is more likely the birthdate of the husband.

mdcclxiii[1763] *Social Security Death Index* , Social Security card issued in West Virginia before 1951. Name listed in SSDI as Ivan D. Englehardt [sic].

mdcclxiv[1764] *Pennsboro News*, 9/27/2006.

mdcclxv[1765] *Social Security Death Index* , Social Security card issued in Ohio in 1956 & 1957.

mdcclxvi[1766] Ota Reed Fraker. Birth year may be off by one.

mdcclxvii[1767] Ota Reed Fraker. But Marilynn Davis Jones gives birthplace as Clarksburg, WV.

mdcclxviii[1768] Doddridge County Birth Records, West Union, WV, Child identified as Minnie Eliza Gaston, the fifth child born to her mother. We have found no other evidence of any previous child, and no basis for this child's last name being that of her mother. Her parents had been married for well over a year at the time of her birth. Father: David Hanes [sic] Jones, age 31, b. Marion Co. Mother: Susan Gaston, age 28. Delayed birth record was filed on Jan 22 1945 by M. S. Gaston, relationship given as uncle. This would be Susan's 81-year-old brother Morris Samuel Gaston. It is possible that his recording of the child's last name as Gaston rather than Jones was an error, and that he mistakenly entered "five" as the child's birth order number in confusion with the total number of children that the mother ultimately had. (Her obituary, however, stated that she was predeceased by 5 brothers and 2 sisters, not identified by name.) It is also noted that while Minnie's obituary stated her birthplace as Doddridge County, the community of Holbrook is within Ritchie County on the border with Doddridge County; Ota Reed Fraker, a first cousin, gives Minnie's birthplace as "near Berea," also in Ritchie County. In her marriage record (per Wes Cochran's "Ritchie County Marriages 1843-1915"), Minnie was identified as Minnie E. Jones, age 20, born in Ritchie County. BR Del Bk 1, p. 64-E.

mdcclxix[1769] WV State Dept of Health, Div of Vital Statistics, *Death Certificate* (http://www.wvculture.org/vrr/va_dcsearch.aspx), "Davis - The Settlers of Salem WV," pp. 110 & 175, reports birth date as Aug 16 1869. But death record shows it as Aug 17 1872, 1900 Census has it as Aug 1872, and headstone shows it as 1872. The Davis book also incorrectly reports death date as July 1963, rather than the Jul 27 1953 shown in death record.

mdcclxx[1770] Wayman Eugene Maxson, grandson of David Haynes Jones & Susan Gaston.

mdcclxxi[1771] Marriage record, Per Sarah Shepherd, sshepherd66@yahoo.com, p. 183.

mdcclxxii[1772] Obituary, Location not specified.

mdcclxxiii[1773] Doddridge County Death Records, West Union, WV, DR Bk 5, p. 90-A.

mdcclxxiv[1774] *The History of Doddridge County, West Virginia* , Taylor Publishing Co, 1979, p. 178.

mdcclxxv[1775] Doddridge County Death Records, West Union, WV, Identified as James Morris Jones, b. May 5 1888 in Doddridge Co, son of David Jones & Susan Gaston, d. Apr 20 1954 at Smithburg, age 67, burial at Masonic Cemetery in West Union. Place of birth is considered to be in error, as obituary and other sources state Berea in Ritchie Co, and no birth record for him was found in Doddridge Co. DR Bk 5, p. 90-A.

mdcclxxvi[1776] WV State Dept of Health, Div of Vital Statistics, *Death Certificate* (http://www.wvculture.org/vrr/va_dcsearch.aspx), Cousin Ota Reed Fraker, in her Gaston genealogy, incorrectly reports his death date as Aug 20 1949.

mdcclxxvii[1777] *Social Security Death Index* , Social Security card issued in Massachusetts before 1951.

mdcclxxviii[1778] Monongalia County Marriage Records, Morgantown, WV, Identified as Luther S. Britton, single, student, age 30, b. Doddridge Co, res. Morgantown, son of A. S. & H. E. Britton; and Pearl J. Rogers, single, 20, b. Monongalia Co, res. Morgantown, dau of (blank) & Mary Rogers. Married Aug 18 1908 in Morgantown. MR p. 136 : http://www.wvculture.org/vrr/va_view.aspx?Id=11338324&Type=Marriage.

mdcclxxix[1779] *Ritchie County WV Marriages 1916-1945* , Wes Cochran, 2515 10th Ave, Parkersburg WV 26101 (Sep 1998), Identified as DeWitt Talmage Britton, divorced, 30, b. Gilmer Co, res. Ritchie Co; and Martha Magdalene Riddle, 24, of Ritchie Co. Married Dec 30 1931.

mdcclxxx[1780] Doddridge County Birth Records, West Union, WV, BR Bk 1, p. 138.

mdcclxxxi[1781] *Social Security Death Index* , Name listed in SSDI as Frances G. Logan.

mdcclxxxii[1782] *Social Security Death Index* , Social Security card issued in California before 1951. Name listed in SSDI as Grace Bortz.

mdcclxxxiii[1783] Ritchie County Birth Records, Harrisville, WV, Identified as Asby Steele Law, white male, born Aug 17 1869 in Union Township, son of John W. Law. BR p. 62.

mdcclxxxiv[1784] Obituary - Hospital, Death data of Dec 19 1974 in Doddridge Co, reported by other other researchers, is incorrect.

mdcclxxxv[1785] *1930 Census, Doddridge County, WV (Cove District)* , No other reference to her by this or a similar name has been found. "Davis - The Settlers of Salem WV," p. 381, provides name as Vicky Stansbury, while obituary of daughter Mary gives it as Vicey Stansberry, her marriage record and the obituaries of husband and daughter Hannah give it as Vicy Stansberry, and obituary of half-sister Dona Stansberry Kincaid gives it as Vicie Stansberry Huff. Her own obituary identifies her as Mrs. Vicy S. Huff, daughter of the late Frank and Evelyn Clayton Stansberry. Her mother has elsewhere been incorrectly identified as Louie Daugherty, but her survivors included seven half-siblings, so the confusion stems from the 1890 remarriage by her father.

mdcclxxxvi[1786] Obituary - At home, "Davis - The Settlers of Salem WV," p. 381, provides name as Vicky Stansbury, while obituary of daughter Mary gives it as Vicey Stansberry, her marriage record and the obituaries of husband and daughter Hannah give it as Vicy Stansberry, and obituary of half-sister Dona Stansberry Kincaid gives it as Vicie Stansberry Huff. Her own obituary identifies her as Mrs. Vicy S. Huff, daughter of the late Frank and Evelyn Clayton Stansberry. Her mother has elsewhere been incorrectly identified as Louie Daugherty, but her survivors included seven half-siblings, so the confusion stems from the 1890 remarriage by her father.

mdcclxxxvii[1787] 1930 Census, Doddridge County, WV (Cove District).

mdcclxxxviii[1788] Obituary of aunt.

mdcclxxxix[1789] Gilmer County Marriage Records, Glenville, WV, Although the ceremony took place in Harrisville, Ritchie County, the marriage is recorded in Gilmer County, residence of the bride. MR p. 106.

mdccxc[1790] 1920 Census, Ritchie County, WV (Clay District).

mdccxci[1791] *Ritchie County WV Marriages 1916-1945* , Wes Cochran, 2515 10th Ave, Parkersburg WV 26101 (Sep 1998), Identified as Louie D. Law, divorced, 56, of Ritchie Co, son of David G. & Celia M.; and Myrtle Goff, widowed, 51, of Ritchie Co, dau of Jonathan A. & Frances L. Haddox. Married Jan 31 1940.

mdccxcii[1792] *Social Security Death Index* , Husband's obituary states that they were married for 66 years and that she died in 1977, so one of those numbers must be wrong. Ritchie County marriage records show that they were married on Nov 8 1930, and SSDI shows her death date as Mar 3 1997.

mdccxciii[1793] *Social Security Death Index* , Name appears in SSDI as Hartzell L. Burns. Spelling Harzel found in sister's obituary, but Hartzel in his marriage record and in brother's obituary.

mdccxciv[1794] *Gilmer County WV Marriages 1845-1933* , Wes Cochran, 2515 10th Ave, Parkersburg WV 26101 (Jan 1989), Identified as Carl D. Law, single, 27, b. & res. in Ritchie Co; and Bonnie Bush, single, 21, b. & res. in Gilmer Co. Married Nov 15 1916. MR p. 101.

mdccxcv[1795] WV State Dept of Health, Div of Vital Statistics, *Death Certificate* (http://www.wvculture.org/vrr/va_dcsearch.aspx), "Ritchie County WV Cemeteries through 1993," p. 539, incorrectly reports death date on headstone as 1927.

mdccxcvi[1796] *Pennsboro News*, 6/14/2006, p. 3-B.

mdccxcvii[1797] *Ritchie County WV Marriages 1945-1970* , Wes Cochran, 2515 10th Ave, Parkersburg WV 26101 (Dec 2003), Identified as Albert E. Brissey, widowed, b. Dec 13 1908 in Ritchie Co, res. Cumberland OH, son of Albert & Blanche (Ayers) Brissey; and Theo Mayrie Law, b. Dec 30 1910 in Ritchie Co, res. Burnt House WV, dau of Royston D. & Gertie (Swisher) Law. Married Aug 25 1956.

mdccxcviii[1798] *Social Security Death Index* , Social Security card issued in West Virginia in 1956.

mdccxcix[1799] Amos Beaty Sharps, *The Samuel Barr Family: A Genealogy List of the Various Descendants of This Family* (on file at West Virginia University Library; ca 1961), But SSDI reports an Arden Law, born Dec 17 1926, died Apr 10 1997, resident of Oceana, Wyoming Co, WV. This is likely the same Arden Law, discrepancy in birth year notwithstanding.

mdccc[1800] *Ritchie County WV Marriages 1916-1945* , Wes Cochran, 2515 10th Ave, Parkersburg WV 26101 (Sep 1998), Identified as Layton Brooks Law, 30, b. Gilmer Co, res. Ritchie Co, son of Jennings & Dulcie Law Barnes; and Norene Bee, 36, of Ritchie Co, dau of Zed & Fan. Married Jun 6 1942.

mdccci[1801] Ritchie County Birth Records, Harrisville, WV, Identified as Orpha L. Law, white female, born Jul 12 1888 in Ritchie Co, dau of Willy Law. BR p. 188.

mdcccii[1802] *Ritchie County WV Marriages 1843-1915* , Wes Cochran, 2515 10th Ave, Parkersburg WV 26101 (July 1985), Identified as Roy S. Zinn, 32, of Ritchie Co; and Lona O. Law, 25, of Ritchie Co. Married Jun 18 1913.

mdccciii[1803] 1930 Census, Ritchie County, WV (Grant District).

mdccciv[1804] *Pennsboro News*, 11/1/2006.

mdcccv[1805] Susie Davis Nicholson, *Davis - The Settlers of Salem, West Virginia* , Gordon Printing Co, Strasburg OH, 1979 (Revised & Enlarged), p. 50.

mdcccvi[1806] 1900 Census, Doddridge County, WV (Grant District).

mdcccvii[1807] Susie Davis Nicholson, *Davis - The Settlers of Salem, West Virginia* , Gordon Printing Co, Strasburg OH, 1979 (Revised & Enlarged), p. 130.

mdcccviii[1808] *Doddridge County WV Marriages 1845-1937* , Wes Cochran, 2515 10th Ave, Parkersburg, WV 26101 (Jan 1993), Identified as Elbert E. Moran, 21, of Doddridge Co; and Emma Adams, 18, of Doddridge Co. Married Aug 11 1895.

mdcccix[1809] 1900 Census, Doddridge County, WV (Cove District).

mdcccx[1810] Obituary - At home, Grass Run.

mdcccxi[1811] *Doddridge County WV Marriages 1845-1937* , Wes Cochran, 2515 10th Ave, Parkersburg, WV 26101 (Jan 1993), Identified as Levi Maxwell, 45, of Doddridge Co; and Mrs. Emma F. Moran, 35, of Doddridge Co. Married Jul 27 1913.

mdcccxii[1812] *Doddridge County WV Deaths 1853-1969* , Wes Cochran, 2515 10th Ave, Parkersburg, WV 26101, Identified as Levi Maxwell, son of Abner Maxwell & Lydia Jane Woofter.

mdcccxiii[1813] *Doddridge County WV Marriages 1845-1937* , Wes Cochran, 2515 10th Ave, Parkersburg, WV 26101 (Jan 1993), Identified as Okey Dilley [sic], 24, b. Barbour co, res. Doddridge Co; and Edna Moran, 16, of Doddridge Co. Married Dec 4 1912.

mdcccxiv[1814] *Doddridge County WV Marriages 1845-1937* , Wes Cochran, 2515 10th Ave, Parkersburg, WV 26101 (Jan 1993), Identified as Ira Adams, 18, of Doddridge Co; and Lona Mason, 21, of Doddridge Co. Married Apr 28 1906.

mdcccxv[1815] Harrison County Marriage Records, Clarksburg, WV, Identified as Ira Clinton Adams, widowed, b. Jun 7 1887 in Doddridge Co, res. Quiet Dell WV, son of Alexander & Mary Isabell (Gaston) Adams; and Iona Virginia Whiting, widow, b. Mar 29 1886 in Harrison Co, res. Clarksburg, dau of Worthy T. & Ella (Howell) Bartlett. Married Apr 29 1934.

mdcccxvi[1816] Nicholas County Marriage Records, Summersville, WV.

mdcccxvii[1817] Death Record - Online, Ohio, Vol 19921, Certificate No. 098724.

mdcccxviii[1818] Newspaper wedding announcement, West Union Herald, 11/16/1911.

mdcccxix[1819] Doddridge County Birth Records, West Union, WV, Identified as "Alvin W. Adams," son of Alex Adams and Mary I. Adams. Born Apr 17 1898. BR Bk 3, p. 4.

mdcccxx[1820] Doddridge County Marriage Records, West Union, WV, He was identified as "Alva W. Adams," age 22, b. in Doddridge Co, and she as Maggie Elizabeth Snider, age 18, b. in Doddridge Co. MR Bk 10, p. 342.

mdcccxxi[1821] Obituary of wife's stepfather.

mdcccxxii[1822] *The History of Doddridge County, West Virginia* , Taylor Publishing Co, 1979, p. 243.

mdcccxxiii[1823] *Doddridge County WV Marriages 1845-1937* , Wes Cochran, 2515 10th Ave, Parkersburg, WV 26101 (Jan 1993), Identified as J. Lee Gaston, 22, of Doddridge Co; and Dessie F. Snider, 19, of Doddridge Co. Married Feb 23 1908.

mdcccxxiv[1824] Birthdate may be Dec 8 1890, per Burdette in "Sotha Hickman and Some of His Descendants," who also gives middle name as Mae.

mdcccxxv[1825] Ira Clinton Gaston, Jr. (1924-1998).

mdcccxxvi[1826] *Social Security Death Index* , Social Security card issued in California in 1958.

mdcccxxvii[1827] Doddridge County Marriage Records, West Union, WV, MR Bk 12, p. 83.

mdcccxxviii[1828] Doddridge County Death Records, West Union, WV, DR Outside County Bk 1, p. 91.

mdcccxxix[1829] Doddridge County Birth Records, West Union, WV, Identified as Alpha Lee Gaston, white female, b. Feb 3 1900 in Doddridge Co, dau of Marion & Ella (Adams) Gaston, this being the mother's second child. The original typed entry in the ledger-type birth record had the child's first name as Caddie (or Gaddie), and the father's first name as Martin, but those were lined out and changed by hand to read as above. A handwritten notation reads: "Corrections made on affidavit of Aunt.", BR p. 81.

mdcccxxx[1830] Doddridge County Court House, West Union, WV, Although recorded in Doddridge Co, the ceremony was performed in Harrisville, Ritchie Co, WV. MR Bk 11, p. 354.

mdcccxxxi[1831] *West Union Herald-Record*, Aug 1 1978, p 7.

mdcccxxxii[1832] Doddridge County Court House, West Union, WV, MR Bk 11, p. 354.

mdcccxxxiii[1833] Doddridge County Court House, West Union, WV, MR Bk 11, p. 355.

mdcccxxxiv[1834] Doddridge County Marriage Records, West Union, WV, Although recorded in Doddridge Co, the ceremony took place in Clarksburg, Harrison Co, WV. MR Bk 11, p. 355.

mdcccxxxv[1835] *Social Security Death Index* , Birthplace from obituary. No birth record for her was found in Doddridge Co.

mdcccxxxvi[1836] *Social Security Death Index* , Social Security card issued in West Virginia in 1965 and 1966.

mdcccxxxvii[1837] *West Union Herald*, 3/11/1943.

mdcccxxxviii[1838] Barbour County Death Records, Philippi, WV, DR Bk 6.

mdcccxxxix[1839] *The History of Doddridge County, West Virginia* , Taylor Publishing Co, 1979, p. 152.

mdcccxl[1840] *Social Security Death Index* , Name listed as Vonda Hatfield.

mdcccxli[1841] Doddridge County Court House, West Union, WV, MR Bk 12, p. 97.

mdcccxlii[1842] Lorna Reese Overberg, *The History of Ritchie County, West Virginia to 1980* (Ritchie County Historical Society, Taylor Publishing Co, 1980), Identified as his parents' third son. p. 124.

mdcccxliii[1843] Lorna Reese Overberg, *The History of Ritchie County, West Virginia to 1980* (Ritchie County Historical Society, Taylor Publishing Co, 1980), p. 124.

mdcccxliv[1844] 1930 Census, Wood County, WV.

mdcccxlv[1845] William Bernard Wilson, *Wilson-Pepper Genealogy 1595-1989* (Gateway Press, Baltimore, MD, 1990).

mdcccxlvi[1846] Newspaper engagement announcement of granddaughter.

mdcccxlvii[1847] Nelson Earl Zinn.

mdcccxlviii[1848] 1910 Census, Barbour County, WV.

mdcccxlix[1849] Headstone, Inscription reads: "NEELY, Grace Carpenter June 6 1877 - Jan 11 1933, George W Nov 6 1875 - July 12 1949, (In Absentia) Their son William Edward, Captain, U.S. Navy".

mdccccl[1850] 1900 Census, Upshur County, WV.

mdcccli[1851] *Social Security Death Index* , Social Security card issued in West Virginia in 1973. Name listed in SSDI as "Grace T. Ballard.".

mdccclii[1852] Newspaper announcement, Clarksburg Exponent-Telegram, Apr 20 2003, p. D-5.

mdcccliii[1853] Harold A. Tichenor, *Tichenor Families in America* , Braun-Brumfield Inc, Ann Arbor, Michigan, 1988, p. 161.

mdcccliv[1854] *Social Security Death Index* , Name listed in SSDI as Madge R. Barbe.

mdccclv[1855] *Social Security Death Index* , Social Security card issued in West Virginia in 1965. Name listed in SSDI as Ruby Janes.

mdccclvi[1856] Russell Lee Davisson, *The Davissons - A History and Genealogy* , McClain Printing Co, Parsons, WV (1993), p. 223.

mdccclvii[1857] Russell Lee Davisson, *The Davissons - A History and Genealogy* , McClain Printing Co, Parsons, WV (1993), pp. 222-223.

mdccclviii[1858] Russell Lee Davisson, *The Davissons - A History and Genealogy* , McClain Printing Co, Parsons, WV (1993).

mdccclix[1859] Russell Lee Davisson, *The Davissons - A History and Genealogy* , McClain Printing Co, Parsons, WV (1993), p. 230.

mdccclx[1860] Newspaper birth announcement of granddaughter.

mdccclxi[1861] Russell Lee Davisson, *The Davissons - A History and Genealogy* , McClain Printing Co, Parsons, WV (1993), p. 223 & 230.

mdccclxii[1862] Russell Lee Davisson, *The Davissons - A History and Genealogy* , McClain Printing Co, Parsons, WV (1993), p. 231.

mdccclxiii[1863] Obituary - Hospice.

mdccclxiv[1864] Obituary, Ashes scattered at Roosevelt Lake.

mdccclxv[1865] Putnam County Marriage Records, Winfield, WV.

mdccclxvi[1866] WV State Dept of Health, Div of Vital Statistics, *Death Certificate* (http://www.wvculture.org/vrr/va_dcsearch.aspx), Handwritten entry looks like Emma Chapel.

mdccclxvii[1867] *Social Security Death Index* , Name appears in SSDI as Nora V. Faber.

mdccclxviii[1868] *Social Security Death Index* , Social Security card issued in Illinois before 1951. Name listed in SSDI as Helen M. Faber.

mdccclxix[1869] *Social Security Death Index* , Social Security card issued in West Virginia in 1952. Her name is listed in SSDI as Leo Casto.

mdccclxx[1870] *Social Security Death Index* , Social Security card issued in New Mexico before 1951.

mdccclxxi[1871] Jack Edward Carr (1920-2001), Fairmont, WV.

mdccclxxii[1872] Jack Edward Carr (1920-2001), Fairmont, WV, Frank Carr and his wife Katherine Levelle Carr were killed in an automobile accident.

mdccclxxiii[1873] Marion County Court House, Fairmont, WV, DR Bk 17, p. 191.

mdccclxxiv[1874] *Social Security Death Index* , Name listed in SSDI as Mary Stilwagner.

mdccclxxv[1875] *Social Security Death Index* , Social Security card issued in West Virginia in 1973.

mdccclxxvi[1876] Taylor County Historical & Genealogical Society, Grafton, WV, *A History of Taylor County West Virginia* , McClain Printing Co, Parsons, WV (1986), pp. 409-410.

mdccclxxvii[1877] 1910 Census, Wetzel County, WV.

mdccclxxviii[1878] *Ritchie County WV Marriages 1843-1915* , Wes Cochran, 2515 10th Ave, Parkersburg WV 26101 (July 1985), Identified as N. C. Hoff, 24, of Ritchie Co; and Ola Bee, 16, of Ritchie Co. Married Jun 13 1907.

mdccclxxix[1879] Clay County Marriage Records, Clay, WV.

mdccclxxx[1880] *Social Security Death Index* , Name listed in SSDI as "B. Miller.".

mdccclxxxi[1881] Harrison County Marriage Records, Clarksburg, WV, MR, p. 248.

mdccclxxxii[1882] *Clarksburg Exponent-Telegram*, 10/31/2004, p. D-3.

mdccclxxxiii[1883] Harrison County Death Records, Clarksburg, WV, The death record on file in Harrison County lists George W. Gaston, son of John L. Gaston and Effie Oliver, as having died on June 4, 1932. (Note different middle initial) But the corresponding death certificate on file at the WV Div of Vital Statistics identifies him as George I. Gaston, and wife Jo Queen's obituary states that her husband George Isaac Gaston died in 1932. DR Bk 9, p. 66.

mdccclxxxiv[1884] City Directory, Clarksburg, WV, 1923 , 647 S. 7th St.

mdccclxxxv[1885] Harrison County Birth Records, Clarksburg, WV, Name on birth record originally entered as George Isaac Gaston, Jr., but corrected to read George Irwin Gaston.

, BR Bk 10, p. 77.

mdccclxxxvi[1886] Harrison County Court House, Clarksburg, WV, MR Bk 62, p. 298.

mdccclxxxvii[1887] Harrison County Birth Records, Clarksburg, WV, BR Bk 11, p. 92.

mdccclxxxviii[1888] Harrison County Marriage Records, Clarksburg, WV, MR Bk 58, p. 120.

mdccclxxxix[1889] Newspaper anniversary announcement, Clarksburg Exponent-Telegram, 3/11/2007.

mdcccxc[1890] Lewis County Birth Records, Weston, WV, BR Bk 2, p. 89.

mdcccxci[1891] Lewis County Birth Records, Weston, WV, BR Bk 2, p. 87.

mdcccxcii[1892] Lewis County Court House, Weston, WV, BR Bk 3, p. 153.

mdcccxciii[1893] Lewis County Court House, Weston, WV, BR Bk 4, p. 299.

mdcccxciv[1894] Kanawha County Death Records, Charleston, WV, DR Bk 57, p. 90.

mdcccxcv[1895] Kanawha County Death Records, Charleston, WV, DR Bk 30, p. 13.

mdcccxcvi[1896] Lewis County Court House, Weston, WV, DR Bk 4, p. 238.

mdcccxcvii[1897] *Lewis County WV Marriages 1881-1937* , Wes Cochran, 2515 10th Ave, Parkersburg, WV 26101 (Sep 1994), Identified as Ralph McWhorter, age 27, b. Harrison Co, res. Lewis Co, son of D. G. & Cora; and Lacy Lucy Gaston, age 25, of Lewis Co, dau of T. C. & Nona. Married Nov 22 1916.

mdcccxcviii[1898] Veterans Administration, *http://gravelocator.cem.va.gov.*

mdcccxcix[1899] 1930 Census, Barbour County, WV.

mcm[1900] Harrison County Marriage Records, Clarksburg, WV, Identified as Charles Nicholes Gaston, divorced, 30, b. Lewis Co, res. Weston, son of Thomas Charles Gaston & Nona Myrtle Nicholes; and Henrietta Mae Beckman, single, 30, b. May 26 1899 in Preston Co, res. Shinnston (Harrison Co), dau of Henry Beckman & Lillian Thompson Beckman. Married Jul 3 1929 in Grafton. (Note: Although the ceremony was held in Grafton, Taylor County, the marriage is recorded in Harrison County, residence of the bride.), MR p. 225.

mcmi[1901] Lewis County Marriage Records, Weston, WV, Identified as Charles Nicoles Gaston, 49, b. Jan 5 1899 in Lewis Co, res. Weston, son of T. Chas Gaston & Nona Myrtle Nicoles Gaston; and Lena Esta Coffman, 47, b. Nov 22 1901 in Taylor Co, res. Lewis Co, dau of Arther Lee Coffman & Emily Susan McDaniel. Married Apr 15 1949 in Clarksburg. (Note: Although the ceremony was held in Harrison County, the marriage is recorded in Lewis County, residence of the bride.), MR p. 33.

mcmii[1902] Lewis County Birth Records, Weston, WV, BR Bk 3, p. 106.

mcmiii[1903] Lewis County Death Records, Weston, WV, DR Bk 6, p. 130.

mcmiv[1904] Lewis County Court House, Weston, WV, DR Bk 5, p. 64.

mcmv[1905] Lewis County Birth Records, Weston, WV, BR Bk 6, p. 110.

mcmvi[1906] Lewis County Death Records, Weston, WV, DR Bk 12, p. 151.

mcmvii[1907] Lauri Buell Boaz, 819 Spruce Drive, Carmel, IN 46033-8677.

mcmviii[1908] *Social Security Death Index* , Social Security card issued in West Virginia before 1951. Name listed in SSDI as Jo Ann S. Barnes.

mcmix[1909] Taylor County Marriage Records, Grafton, WV, Identified as Carl Poe, 23, b. Taylor Co, res. Grafton; and Dona Leigh Morris, 19, b. Lewis Co, res. Grafton. Married Jul 27 1915 in Grafton. MR p. 34.

mcmx[1910] 1930 Census, Taylor County, WV.

mcmxi[1911] Lewis County Birth Records, Weston, WV, In space for father's name, entry reads "Not in matrimony." Person providing information identified as "Abraham Gaston - Grandfather." Birth date of Sep-26-1879 given in "Henry McWhorter Family...", BR p. 194.

mcmxii[1912] Harrison County Death Records, Clarksburg, WV, Mother identified as Mary C. Gaston, father "Unknown." Informant: Mrs. Mae Gaston, McWhorter, WV. DR Bk 23, p. 92B.

mcmxiii[1913] Headstone and death record. Adjacent to the joint headstone for Wade C. and Mae (sic) Gaston, are headstones for sons Robert A. Gaston and George H. Gaston and their wives.

mcmxiv[1914] Harrison County Court House, Clarksburg, WV, DR Bk 23, p. 92B.

mcmxv[1915] Harrison County Marriage Records, Clarksburg, WV, Identified as Wade C. Gaston, 32, son of Mary E. Gaston; and May Gaston, 23, resident of Harrison Co, dau of George & Rachel Gaston. Married Dec 4 1912 at the Monticello Hotel in Weston (Lewis County). Unclear why the marrieage was recorded in Harrison County. MR Bk 23, p. 162.

mcmxvi[1916] Harrison Co BR 2-198 shows Nannie May Gaston born to George & Rachel in March 1889. Doddridge Co BR 2-123 shows N. May Gaston born to George L. & Rachel on Mar-20-1889. Harrison Co DR 76-10 gives her birth on Mar-20-1889 in W. Va. Her obituary states her birth as Mar 20 1889 in Doddridge Co.

mcmxvii[1917] Harrison County Death Records, Clarksburg, WV, Identified as "N. May Gaston," born Mar 20 1889 to George L. Gaston and Rachel Bond. DR Bk 76, p. 10.

mcmxviii[1918] Headstone, - Inscription on headstone (joint with Wade C. Gaston) reads "Mae Gaston 1889-1975." But obituary and death record are clearly 1976.

mcmxix[1919] Harrison County Marriage Records, Clarksburg, WV, Identified as Robert Gaston, 22, b. Dec 4 1912 in Lewis Co, res. Lost Creek in Harrison Co, son of Wade Compton Gaston & May (Gaston) Gaston; and Melba Louise Spicer, 21, b. Sep 8 1913 in Harrison Co, res. Lost Creek, dau of Orville Spicer & Susan (Pratt) Spicer. Married Dec 29 1934 in West Milford. (Ages and birth dates of both parties appear to have been misstated. Headstone & SSDI entry for Robert Gaston show his birth date as Dec 4 1914, and Melba Spicer Gaston's obituary, headstone and SSDI entry all show her birth date as Sep 8 1917.), MR Bk 51, p. 28.

mcmxx[1920] Harrison County Marriage Records, Clarksburg, WV, MR Bk 52, p. 170.

mcmxxi[1921] Harrison County Court House, Clarksburg, WV, MR Bk 52, p. 170.

mcmxxii[1922] Obituary and headstone.

mcmxxiii[1923] Harrison County Death Records, Clarksburg, WV, DR Bk 91, p. 203.

mcmxxiv[1924] Headstone, Death record reports cremation at Omega Crematory, Morgantown, WV.

mcmxxv[1925] Harrison County Birth Records, Clarksburg, WV, Identified as Mary Rachel Gaston, the fourth child of Wade Gaston (farmer, age 51) and May Gaston (age 41). BR Bk 15, p. 82.

mcmxxvi[1926] *Social Security Death Index* , Social Security card issued in Virginia before 1951.

mcmxxvii[1927] *Lewis County WV Marriages 1881-1937* , Wes Cochran, 2515 10th Ave, Parkersburg, WV 26101 (Sep 1994), Identified as Jammes Thaddeum Alfred, 34, of Lewis Co, son of James & Marcelus; and Edna Mundell, 21, of Lewis Co, dau of "Lee & Tweed?" Married May 25 1904.

mcmxxviii[1928] Lewis County Court House, Weston, WV, BR Bk 2, p. 150.

mcmxxix[1929] Upshur County Marriage Records, Buckhannon, WV, MR Bk 12, p. 25.

mcmxxx[1930] Upshur County Birth Records, Buckhannon, WV, BR Bk 4, p. 63.

mcmxxxi[1931] *Lewis County WV Marriages 1881-1937* , Wes Cochran, 2515 10th Ave, Parkersburg, WV 26101 (Sep 1994), Identified as Thomas Knotts Wolfe, age 22, of Summit Co OH, son of T. L. & Oda M.; and Elizabeth Mader Gaston, age 21, b. Upshur Co, res. Lewis Co, dau of A. B. [sic] & Clara. Married May 21 1934.

mcmxxxii[1932] Lewis County Marriage Records, Weston, WV, MR Bk 20, p. 50.

mcmxxxiii[1933] Upshur County Birth Records, Buckhannon, WV, BR Bk 5, p. 75.

mcmxxxiv[1934] Upshur County Marriage Records, Buckhannon, WV, Obituary of wife states marriage date as 1947, but marriage record shows it as Jun 14 1946. MR Bk II 23-109.

mcmxxxv[1935] Lewis County Birth Records, Weston, WV, BR Bk 2, p. 206.

mcmxxxvi[1936] Upshur County Marriage Records, Buckhannon, WV, MR Bk 14, p. 278.

mcmxxxvii[1937] Upshur County Court House, Buckhannon, WV, DR Bk 7, p. 434.

mcmxxxviii[1938] Lewis County Court House, Weston, WV, Misc Records 9-456.

mcmxxxix[1939] Upshur County Court House, Buckhannon, WV, DR Bk 7, p. 339.

mcmxl[1940] Upshur County Court House, Buckhannon, WV, BR Bk 5, p. 68.

mcmxli[1941] Social Security Death Index, Social Security card issued in Delaware before 1951.

mcmxlii[1942] Harrison County Birth Records, Clarksburg, WV, Identified as Osie Gaston, b. Sep 20 1885, dau og G. L. & Rachel Gaston. BR Bk 2, p. 133.

mcmxliii[1943] Harrison County Marriage Records, Clarksburg, WV, Groom identified as William G. Davisson, age 21, b. Harrison Co, resident of Belington, Barbour Co WV, son of C. W. & Mary Davisson. Bride identified as Ocie Gaston, age 18, b. Harrison Co, resident of Harrison Co, dau of George L. & Rachael Gaston. Ceremony held Sep 2 1903 "at the home of the Bride." Informant: George L. Gaston. MR Bk 13, p. 181.

mcmxliv[1944] Harrison County Birth Records, Clarksburg, WV, BR Bk 2, p. 98.

mcmxlv[1945] *Social Security Death Index* , Social Security card issued in Florida in 1963. Name listed in SSDI as "Marie G. Foose.".

mcmxlvi[1946] Doddridge County Birth Records, West Union, WV, Identified as (first name blank) Reed, white male, born Jan 6 1900 in Doddridge County, son of James Reed & Malissa Smith Reed, this being the mother's fourth child. BR p. 176.

mcmxlvii[1947] 1930 Census, Marshall County, WV.

mcmxlviii[1948] Harrison County Birth Records, Clarksburg, WV, There appear to be two entries for this birth. (1) Page 183, entries for Upper District of Harrison County, the child is identified as Alpha Gaston, white female, born alive as a single birth on Jan 3 1889. Father: H. J. Gaston. Mother Anna L. Gaston. Informant: Father. (2) Page 198, entries for Grant District of Harrison County, the child is identified as Alfaretta, white female, born alive as a single birth in January 1889 (date not specified). Father: H. J. Gaston, farmer. Mother: Annie L. Informant: Father. (NOTE: The existence and misinterpretation of these multiple entries has resulted in the one birth being incorrectly reported by genealogists as the birth of twins having similar names. While her name appears in her marriage record as Alpha Louise Gaston, she is identified in her daughter's marriage record as Alpharetta Gaston.).

mcmxlix[1949] Harrison County Marriage Records, Clarksburg, WV, Identified as Peter John Kowalsky, 26, b. in Germany, res. Fairmont, son of Peter & Mary A. Kowalsky; and Alpha Louise Gaston, 23, b. & res. in Harrison Co, dau of Hiram J. & Anna L. Gaston. Married Dec 25 1912 in Clarksburg. MR p. 206.

mcml[1950] Harrison County Marriage Records, Clarksburg, WV, Identified as Charles Wilbur Duty, 21, b. Apr 16 1912 in Harrison Co, res. Mt. Joy Pennsylvania, son of Elery & Zela (Koon) Duty; and Genevieve Kowalsky, 19, b. Jan 6 1914 in Harrison Co, res. Clarksburg, dau of Peter John & Alpha (Gaston) Kowalsky. Married Sep 16 1933 in Clarksburg. (Note: Husband's birth date was misstated in the marriage record; the SSDI shows his birth date as Apr 16 1915.), MR p. 141.

mcmli[1951] Harrison County Marriage Records, Clarksburg, WV, Identified as Melvin Hardman Jr, 22, b. Oct 4 1921 in Clarksburg, res. Clarksburg, son of Melvin & Artie (Fittro) Hardman; and Anna Kowalsky, 21, b. Aug 29 1922 in Clarksburg, res. Clarksburg, dau of Peter John & Alpharetta (Gaston) Kowalsky. Married Dec 23 1943 in Clarksburg. (Note: The bride's name appears twice in the record, once as "Ann" and once as "Anna." Her birth date is reported in "Cemeteries of Clark District," p. 281, as Aug 29 1923.), MR p. 84.

mcmlii[1952] *Cemeteries of Coal District, Harrison County, WV* , Harrison County Genealogical Society, Clarksburg, WV (1990).

mcmliii[1953] Harrison County Marriage Records, Clarksburg, WV, Identified as Charles Gray, 21, b. Ritchie Co, res. Harrison Co, son of Riley & Eliza; and Garnet Hornor Gaston, 17, of Harrison Co, dau of Hiram J. & Annie L. Married Sep 27 1908 in Clarksburg. MR p. 123.

mcmliv[1954] Harrison County Marriage Records, Clarksburg, WV, MR p. 238.

mcmlv[1955] *City Directory, Clarksburg, WV, 1923* , 1638 Gould Ave, North View.

mcmlvi[1956] Harrison County Death Records, Clarksburg, WV, Cause of death listed as homicide resulting from "gunshot wound in left breast.", DR Bk 13, p. 91A.

mcmlvii[1957] Oregon Death Index, 1903-1998 (online), Ancestry.com.

mcmlviii[1958] Young American Patriots: The Youth of West Virginia in World War II (National Publishing Co, Richmond, VA, 1946), p. 238.

mcmlix[1959] Harrison County Court House, Clarksburg, WV, BR.

mcmlx[1960] Newspaper anniversary announcement, Clarksburg Exponent-Telegram.

mcmlxi[1961] *Social Security Death Index* , Social Security card issued in Arkansas before 1951.

mcmlxii[1962] Paul M. Gaston, Man and Mission: E. B. Gaston and the Origins of the Fairhope Single Tax Colony , Black Belt Press, Montgomery, AL (1993).

mcmlxiii[1963] Katie Dailey Gaston, a Gaston family historian, in a letter dated March 19, 1968, to Jacquie Gaston Blevins, who advises that Ralph Estep Gaston's funeral book listed his birth as July 29 1889.

mcmlxiv[1964] Jacquie Gaston Blevins, San Jose, CA 95139 < blevinsjc1@aol.com>, SSDI reports death date as Jul 15 1994.

mcmlxv[1965] *Social Security Death Index* , Social Security card issued in Oregon before 1951.

mcmlxvi[1966] *Social Security Death Index* , Social Security card issued in Montana before 1951.

mcmlxvii[1967] National Archives and Records Administration, *World War II Draft Registration Cards, 1942* (Ancestry.com online database).

mcmlxviii[1968] Death Record - Online, Identified as Margaret W. Orndorff, father's surname Williams, mother's surname Feezel.

mcmlxix[1969] Death Record - Online, Ohio Certificate 014071.

mcmlxx[1970] Death Record - Online, Ohio Certificate 070285.

mcmlxxi[1971] Death Record - Online, Ohio, Certificate 032256.

mcmlxxii[1972] Death Record - Online, Identified as J. C. Stevenson, married white male, res. Akron OH, b. ca 1904, d. May 30 1973 in Akron.

mcmlxxiii[1973] *Social Security Death Index* , Identified as Caroll Stevenson, b. May 16 1904, d. May 1973, resident of Akron OH, Social Security card issued in Ohio before 1951.

mcmlxxiv[1974] Jane Carson Topoly, Fort Washington, MD 20744 (http://www.reocities.com/heartland/8904/), SSDI reports birth date as Mar 2 1914, but daughter Jane Carson Topoly states Mar 1 1914.

mcmlxxv[1975] *Social Security Death Index* , Social Security card issued in Kentucky before 1951.

mcmlxxvi[1976] Kentucky Death Index, 1911-2000 (on-line), Ancestry.com and Kentucky Health Data Branch.

mcmlxxvii[1977] Frederick K. Gaston IV, Wilton, CT <fgaston@gastonassoc.com>.

mcmlxxviii[1978] *Social Security Death Index* , Name listed in SSDI as Berend H. Vonbremen.

mcmlxxix[1979] *Massachusetts Death Index, 1970-2003 (online)* , Ancestry.com and Massachusetts Dept of Health Svcs.

mcmlxxx[1980] *Social Security Death Index* , Reports elsewhere of birth date of Aug 20 1886 are in error. SSDI shows birth date as Aug 20 1880.

mcmlxxxi[1981] Death Record - Online, Oregon Certificate No. 7000.

mcmlxxxii[1982] *Social Security Death Index* , Social Security card issued in Oregon in 1965.

mcmlxxxiii[1983] Birth record - Online.

mcmlxxxiv[1984] Death Record - Online, Identified as Jerry Mas Brown, age 62, b. Sep 5 1918, d. Feb 4 1981 in Lane County, spouse: Jo. Certificate: 81-02664.

www.doddridgecountyroots.com

A

ADAMS
Agnes, 32
Alexander, 222
Alva Wilmer, 223, 394
Anna Belle, 394
Arah Launa, 351
Arlton Glendale, 351
Beryl Vita, 392
Cosby Margarite, 351
Deacon Samuel H., 110
Dennis D., 393
Dennis Wayne, 351
Edith, 393
Edward Nelson, 325
Eliza Alice, 222
Emma Frances, 222, 391
Etta O'Dell, 223, 393
Ettia O'Dell, 393
Eugene Alexander, 324
Ferdinand, 269
Ferdinand Gaston, 269
Flora, 269
Floyd Haught, 325
Frances Eliza, 50
Francis B., 393
Garlton Gay, 351
Gaston Gale, 351
Harvey L., 393
Hattie I., 380
Hattie Idell, 216
Ira Clinton, 222, 392, 393
James Arnold, 351
John, 32
Johnson Carlton, 351
Joshua A., 224
June, 393
Launa, 351
Lawrence Alfred, 402
Lena Veryl, 392
Lenora Bird, 222, 336, 392
Lievetta, 223
Loraine, 393
Luella, 223
Mabel I., 394
Margorie Catherine, 269
Mary, 32
Mary Agnes, 325
Mary Isabelle Gaston, 337
Mary J., 191
Mary Margaret, 394
Meryl, 392
Nellie Frances, 269
Patricia Joan, 402
Pearl, 392

President John Quincy, 28
Sarah B., 204
Worthy Bernard, 324
Worthy Eugene, 223, 324, 393
ADAMSON
George, 362
ADKINS
Geneva Faye, 373
Walter, 373
AGNEW
George Brown, 440
Ruth, 440
AIKEN
Virginia, 178
AISTROPE
Mary Jane, 175
AKIN
Easter, 43
ALBRIGHT
Ada V., 257
Alice M., 257
Archie F., 257
Arleen, 433
Henry, 256
Josep McClure, 432
Joseph McClure, 257
Lloyd Linley, 257
Marcellus, 256
Susan C., 257
ALFRED
Duane, 423
Edna Maxine, 423
Imogene, 423
James, 423
James Thaddeus, 423
Olga, 423
ALKIRE
Anita Mae, 420
Layman O., 420
Virginia, 376
ALLEN
Aaron, 86
James, 75
John, 71, 75
ALLENDER
Mary, 184
ALLMAN
Amrose Kittorah, 236
Clarence Dalton, 235
Darrel, 235
David Thomas, 145, 235
Deskey V., 220
Eliza Irene, 145
Ernest, 191
James Madison, 220
Marjorie, 401

Mary Catherine, 233
Nellie F., 235
Peter Elihu, 144
Peter T., 144
Russell, 401
William, 145, 233, 236
ALVERSON
Green, 180
Rebecca, 180
AMBROSE
Sarah Catherine, 371
AMOS
Alazan Huldah, 236
Esta E., 212
Henry H., 212
James Emory, 212
ANDERSON
Anna Lloyd, 64
Hannah, 64
James, 64
James Milligan, 181
Janette Minerva, 119
John Wesley, 238
Kenneth, 64
Lewis, 63, 64
Loretta, 435
Newton Pierce, 181
Sarah, 265
Thomas, 64
William, 64
ANGEL
Eileen, 404
ANNIN
Catherine, 104
ARCHER
Iris V., 395
John, 395
John Russell, 395
Mary Naomi, 395
ARMERMUN
Mary Elizabeth, 268
ARMSTRONG
Narcissa, 114
ARNOLD
A. Damon, 402
Aaron, 71
George Exel, 401
James, 113
Kezia, 71, 72
Mary Augusta, 170
Thomas, 71
William, 71
ARTHUR
President Chester A., 2

ASHER
Flora, 326
ASHFORD
Madalena C., 211
ATKINSON
Catherine Estep, 154
Ruth, 207
AUSTIN
Caroline, 113
AYERS
Pryor Hartman, 371

B
BACON
John, Jr., 6
BAILEY
_, 36
Hattie, 406
BAIRD
Capt. David, 62
BAKER
Loraine, 220
Mary Ellen, 392
BALL
David Dale, 399
BALLARD
Wilbur Eugene, 402
William Clarence, 401
William Leo, 402
BALLENTINE
John T., 232
Wilma Dondia, 232
BALLOU
Josephine, 111
BARBE
Weaver S., 402
BARBER
Charles E., 169
BARCLAY
Hugh, 34
BARKER
Kathleen, 201
BARLETT
Daisy Alma, 367
Herschel Earle, 409
Reva Pearl, 366
BARNARD
Charles Howard, 368
BARNETT
Almira, 434
BARR
Alfred, 217
Hannah Etta, 217, 356
Jeannie, 360
BARRACKMAN

Spencer E., 138
BARRADELL
Lelia Sanford, 431
BARTLETT
Allison Clyde, 211
Bertha C., 381
Celia M., 218
Claude V., 367
George Lemuel, 210
Guy Calvin, 210, 211
Hollis, 409
Iona Virginia, 392
James F., 218
John Calvin, 210
Lair Dee, 367
Larry, 211
Lida Viola, 383
Loran, 367
Lydia Ellen, 414
Maria N., 143
Nancy, 143
Phineas W., 137
Reva Pearl, 211
Roseborough, 401
Samuel, 143
BARTLEY
Hugh, 34
BARTON
Hannah Oliver, 440
BATES
Richard William, 364
BATTON
Beulah M., 305
Everett Allen, 305
Frank Carliss, 305
Harvey Scott, 306
John Wesley, 305
Lona Belle, 305
Pauline Ida, 305
Warder Brenton, 305
BAYLAN
Samuel, 69
BEASLEY
Martha Ellen, 201
BEAUFORT
Priscilla, 62
BEAVERS
John W., 176
BECKMAN
Henrietta Mae, 418
Henry, 419
BECKNER
Minnie, 369
BEDELL
Amanda Louise, 437
Deborah Melissa, 100

BEE
Azariah, 367
Benjamin Wilson, 222
Bessie Pearl, 384
Blake, 367
E. L., 238
Emmaretta, 414
Ethelyn Mae, 415
Eusebius L., 238
Guy, 415
Harold Lee, 416
Hazel C., 239, 416
Heartha E., 239
Irene, 416
James Lawrence, 415
Julia Ann, 222
Kenneth Ray, 416
Kester O., 415
Lucille Rebecca, 416
Lucy Belle, 353
Norene, 389
Olas, 415
Olena Mae, 238
Olive Lorina, 414
Orazs Creed, 239, 415
Owen Ulysses, 238, 415
Paul, 415
Priscilla Clarissa, 221
Robert Lewis, 416
Rosa Dale, 238
Rosanna N., 222
Roy A., 367
Sally Catherine, 135, 236
Velt, 367
Walter Ezra, 353
BEEBE
Rhoda, 159
BEECHER
Laban Smith, 108
Louisa Augusta, 108
BEEGHLEY
Mary Adeline, 402
BEERS
Julia Ann, 160
BELCHER
Joda, 237
Joseph, 237
Lydia, 73
BELL
Alton B., 312
Colvis, 140
Earl Basil, 312
Herman A., 312
Icie B., 312
John, 9
John P., 116

Josepha "Josie", 116
Lewis, 312
Malvonia A., 140
Marion, 211
Ollie D., 312
Roxie Zona, 211
Virginia, 202
William W., 312
BENNETT
Ashmore, 120
Audra Sue, 360
Brady, 360
Eunice, 72
Evelyn, 425
Harold Theodore, 365
John, 120
Lester H., 363
Lucretia, 120
Mary Alice, 360
Stephen Ernest, 363, 365
BENSON
Ida M., 228
BENTON
Margaret, 40
BERGER
Jessie Elizabeth, 363
Joseph, 363
BESON
Jessie, 268
BIGHAM
Isabella, 82
James, 82
BINKLEY
Chloe, 356
BIRD
Robert Lee, 407
Robert Lee, Jr., 407
BISHOP
Lucy Grant, 119
BISSELL
Louisa, 74
BLACK
George F., 2
BLACKWELL
John Gaston, 163
Margaret, 163
Sarah G., 163
Thomas, 163
BLAGG
Esther C., 237
BLAIR
Mary, 40
BOARD
Mary Louise, 362
BODE
Dora M., 222

BOGGESS
Fannie Gay, 353
Harold Guy, 230
BOGGS
Hampton, 119
BOICE
Clementine, 198
BOLES
Susy, 42
BOND
Abel P., 152
Bettye Hogue, 17, 19, 20
Flora, 141, 152
Martha A., 134
Rachel, 250
Richard E., 134
BONNELL
Edith Gay, 310
Forest Olin, 310
Jonathan Paige, 310
Maggie Lee, 306
Oscar Blaine, 310
Paul, 310
Violet Faye, 310
BONNETT
Fred C., 358
Jane, 235
Martha Jane, 199
Thomas, 358
Ulysses Grant, 217
BOOKER
Alberta, 255
BOOTH
Boyd Odell, 352
BORAM
Francis Marion, 232
Harriet Melissa, 146
John "Jack", 146
Nathan Goff, 232
William, 146
BORLEIN
Luise J., 355
BORTZ
Alice Ann, 379
Lewis Arthur, 379
BOURN
Joyce E., 413
Judith A., 413
Ormand Jerome, 413
Rella M., 413
Richard L., 413
Robert Jerome, 413
BOVARD
Ethel Lucinda, 263
BOVEE
Hannah, 59

John, 59
BOWEN
John, 177
BOWER
Margretta, 162
BOWMAN
Charles H., 30
Frank, 234
Susannah, 153
Virgil Francis, 234
BOWSER
Bruce E., 410
George Daniel, 410
BOWYER
Carl Adron, 358
Eldon Clair, 358
George Allen, 358
L. Brison, 358
Launa Capitola, 344
Zella Lucille, 358
BOYCE
James, 75
Robert, 75
BOYD
Catherine, 35
David, 44
James Clinton, 357
Margaret, 35
Rev. John, 35
Sarah, 80
Shirley Lorraine, 357
William, 35
BOYLE
Alice, 269
BOYTER
Thomas, 119
BRADEN
Jane C., 176
BRADLEY
Charles, 205
Charles Edgar, 205, 206
Chester C., 206
James Christopher, 205, 206
James Russell, 362
Jennings C., 362
Norma M., 205
Ora Belle, 205
Warren L., 362
Wilbur O., 205, 361
BRADY
Thomas Glen, 414
BRAND
Elizabeth "Rosa", 90

BRANNON
Herman, 372

Martha F., 221
Oadney, 201
Robert Herman, 372
Sara Jane, 372
Thornton, 201
BREVARD
Mary Martha Isabella, 115
BRICE
Amanda, 50
Anna, 50
Anna M., 237
Calvin, 53
Charles Strong, 51
Christopher Simonton, 51
Dr. Walter, 51, 52
Etta, 127
Frances Emeline, 54
Infant, 54
James, 47, 49, 50, 51
James A., 53
James Moffatt, 50
James Simonton, 51
Jane, 50, 116
Jane W., 53
Jane Wilson, 51
John A., 50
John Alexander, 51
John Pressly, 53
L. S., 47
Lois Rebecca, 47
Margaret, 53
Margaret Simonton, 50
Margaret Strong, 51
Martha, 51
Martha Simonton, 53
Mary, 50
Mary E., 53
Mary Elizabeth, 51
Nancy, 47
Rev. Robert Wilson, 51
Robert, 49, 50
Robert R., 53
Sallie Agnes, 53
Sarah Amanda, 51
T. S., 50
Thomas, 50
Thomas Scott, 50, 51
Walter, 50
Walter Henry, 53
William, 51, 53
William W., 53
Winifred, 244
BRIDGES
Milda, 254
Ruth, 374
BRIDWELL

Lucy C., 116
BRIGGS
Susan, 72
BRINKLEY
Fleming, 243
Olive Bird, 242
BRISTOL
Phylinda, 112
BRITTON
Alexander W., 192
Alva Alice, 378
Anna Louise, 378
Arlington Gale, 330
Asberoy Stephen, 215
Aubrey Glenn, 330
Ava Alice, 378
Belva D., 329
Cecil Orr, 329
Charles Edward, 377
Charles L., 192
Charles Wesley, 215, 377
Daniel Webster, 192, 328
Dewitt Talmadge, 215
DeWitt Talmadge, 378
Eliza Ellen, 192, 330
Eva Maude, 215, 378
Florence, 330
Francis C., 192
Frankie Pauline, 330
Gaston Bill, 330
George Wade, 192
George Washington, 377
Gordon Y., 330
Harold Rogers, 377
Horace Audubon, 329
Horatio, 215
Howard J., 377
Jean, 32
John Frank, 192
John Franklin, 329
Joseph Stephen, 192
Lena Mabel, 329
Lenna Ruth, 330
Leota Fay, 329
Lora Virginia, 329
Luther, 377
Luther Sherman, 215, 377
Marian Elizabeth, 378
Martha A., 192
Mary Jane, 192
Mary Margaret, 330
Minnie Alice, 215
Mona V., 330
Morris Harding, 377
Nancy O., 192
Otha Ryland, 329

Robert, 370
Robert Elsworth, 370
Warner Max, 378
Wilbur Laughton, 329
Winnie Oda, 215
Winnie Pearl, 377
Zebidee Warner, 215, 377
BROCKWAY
Albert, 160
Aure V., 160
BROHERD
Christopher, 87
BROKAW
John B., 265
Margaretta G., 265
BROME
Clinton, 269
BROOKS
Birdsell, 230
Birdsell Lynn, 231
Charles E., 144
Della Mae, 241
Francis Marion, 143
Francis Newton, 144, 230
Frank M., 231
Helen, 231
Ida May, 143
Lena A., 231, 412
Mary Doris, 425
Robert B., 144
William Brown, 241
William E., 231
William Taylor, 144, 231
BROOME
Anne, 51
BROWER
Henrietta, 80
BROWN
Albert Carl, 390
Anna Ethey, 441
Arland Mason, 441
Arthur Athelston, 175
Arthur Edmon, 444
Belle, 439
Caroline Virginia, 191
Charles Lester, 402
Churchill Houston, 166
Deacon, 36
Doris Rowena, 444
Dorothy Hatton, 440
Edna Ruth, 391
Elias, 69
Elinor Garretson, 268
Eva Maude, 378
Frank Edmund, 175
Geneva Gaston, 2

George Houston, 166, 268, 441
George Houston, Jr., 268
Gordon Glenwood, 417
Harry Gaston, 175
Harry Whitman, 391
Henry Carmer, 269
Henry S., 175
Ida Augusta, 167, 269
Isaac Henry, 166
Isaac V., 166
James, 75
Jane, 45
Janet, 15
Joan Churchill, 269, 441
John Gaston, 268
Julia Pauline, 391
Linnie Winsome, 444
Louise Elizabeth, 440
Mae E., 440
Margaret, 45
Marjorie, 441
Mary Elizabeth, 177
Mary Houston, 166
Mary Loonis, 269
Morris Houston, 269, 441
Myrla Shirley, 175
Pheriba Jane, 114
Phylinda Gaston, 175
R. L., 2
Rezean Blanchard, 268, 440
Thomas C., 57
Walter, 45
William Gordon, 417
William Rezean, 166
William Stewart, 166
Wilma Lee, 379
Wilson, 81

BRUMBY
Richard Trapier, 115
Susan Greening, 115

BRYAN
Ellsworth Victor, 244

BRYANT
Jennie B., 268
Julia Ann, 264, 437
William, 264

BRYNER
Harry Lee, 360
Harry S., 360

BUELL
Harold Hobart, 419
Robert Goode, 419

BUFORD
Priscilla, 62

BULL
Michael Lee, 351

BULLOCK
Sarah, 85

BUMP
George W., 155
Maletus N., 155

BURDICK
Ann, 173

BURGESS
Jane Farrell, 36, 55
Nancy, 439

BURKE
George E., 245

BURNET
Mary E., 167

BURNS
Hartzel, 385
Retha Leona, 388

BURNSIDE
Cora, 225
Isaac N., 225
James, 152
Lillie M., 225
Mariah, 152
Mary Jane, 140
Nancy, 246
William Sherman, 225

BURROWS
Betty Nell, 411
Mary, 358
Willis A., 411

BURT
Wealthy, 72

BUSH
Bonnie Nell, 385
Carl D., 385
Celia Catherine, 385
Cinderella, 204
Elaine, 385
Iza, 233
Laban, 135
Rosemary Nell, 385
Thomas Hughes, 370
Tracy Ruhana, 370
Vinnie, 234

BUTCHER
Alda M., 127
Alexis, 359
Allen W., 200
Alma E., 237
Alpha, 245
Andrew, 359
Anna M., 237
Burke, 199, 358
Carl E., 200
Carrel E., 244
Catherine, 359

Delpha Blanch, 237
Donna, 128
Elizabeth, 359
Exel Jefferson, 211
Flora A., 127
George Davis, 127
George W., 237
Hazel, 199
Hugh D., 127, 199
Iva Sufronia, 349
James A., 359
James Alvin, 127, 199
Jefferson Davis, 243
Jennie, 244
John Henry, 127
John Hoff, 237
John R., 199
John S., 87
John Sherman, 127
Judson E., 199
Lewis W., 238
Louise, 358
Lula May, 244
Luther Sherman, 377
Mabel, 358
Mary B., 199
Mary Caroline, 237
Mary Hazel, 359
Matthew, 359
Maude, 244
Myra A., 237
Nora A., 237
Olive Blanche, 127
Paul Trellan, 243
Pearl, 200
Preston Randolph, 237
Reva Gladys, 245
Rita M., 200
Robert Jackson, 358
Robert R., 200
Roland, 359
Ruel V., 244
Teresa, 359
Vera Joy, 245
William J., 237

BUTE
Drusilla, 99

C

CAILOR
Ray, 195

CAIN
Alcindia G., 185
Walker, 185

CALDWELL
Isabella Hemphill, 116
Margaret, 58
CAMMANN
Sue D., 169
CAMP
Rosanna, 106
CAMPBELL
Alexander, 154
Besie Iona, 373
Mary Elizabeth, 375
Mary Lillian, 227
CANTWELL
Betty V., 374
William Wallace, 374
CAPAK
Robert, 352
CAPRON
Sarah, 109
CARDER
C. Albert, 211
Catherine Ciscelia, 189
Louia Mae, 420
Mary Etta, 316
Myrtle Lucille, 374
Velma Burl, 211
CAREZ
Harry Lee, 360
CARLE
Sarah, 104
CARMER
Gertrude Campbell, 269
CARMICHAEL
Mary Louise, 378
CARPENTER
M. Grace, 400
Robert, 129
CARPER
Mary Ageline, 357
CARR
Allen T., 142
Andrew S., 142
Bertha, 229, 409
Captain, 11
Charles Harry, 229, 408
Charles William, 408
Doris Lee, 408
Elom S., 142
Frank, 229, 408
Fred, Jr., 409
Frederick, 229
George, 408
Harry, 408
Jack Edward, 408
Lucy, 229
Margaret, 229

Martha Olive "Ollie", 142, 229
Mary Jane, 408
Robert James, 408
Rosalea, 408
Theodore L., 142
William Columbus "Lum", 142, 228
CARRICO
Druza Dell, 363
CARRQ
Margaret, 408
CARSON
Andrew, 58
Ann, 58
Elizabeth, 58
CARTER
Ralph Aubrey, 208
CASEY
Cynthia E., 115
Zadok, 11
CASSADAY
Felix, 121
Susanna, 121
CASTLE
Emily, 24
CASTLEBERRY
Winny, 113
CASTLEMAN
John Rutland, 176
Rebecca Irene, 176
CASTNER
David, 103
Margaret, 68
Sarah, 103
CASTO
Cecil C., 210
J. Mance, 203
Mary Louise, 205
Rosetta, 204
William, 210
CAUGHRAN
Robert, 46
CAULDWELL
James, 5
John, 33
William, 5, 33
CAWTHORN
Lorena Edna, 419
CHAMBERLAIN
Jacob, 37
CHAMBERS
David, 35
John, 35
Joseph, 35
William, 35
CHANCE
Donald R., 57

Dorothy Wakefield, 16, 46
CHANDLER
Mrs. Genevieve W., 53
Nellie Bly, 407
William S., 164
CHAPMAN
Alice Virginia, 223
Bruce Gaston, 215
David Maxwell, 215, 223
Emma Grace, 216, 379
Faye Marie, 216
Floyd Wirt, 215
Harley Hall, 216, 379
Jean Lois, 400
Joseph Floyd, 379
Laura Elizabeth, 215, 378
Leona Mae, 215
Lester Maxwell, 216
Majel Ellen, 216, 380
Palbie Gale, 216, 379
Robert Marshall, 379
CHATMAN
Sarah, 6
CHEESMAN
Charity, 64
Joseph, 64
CHESTNUT
Wm., 79
CHIDESTER
Phineas W., 149
Wellington Vincent, 149
CHILDERS
Elizabeth, 138, 192
CHILDRESS
Jeanette, 378
Joseph Britton, 378
Theodore Jackson, 378
CHILDS
Jennie, 174
CHRISTIE
Frank Burton, 383
CHRISTMAN
George Washington, 208
Harry F., 208
Infant, 208
Myrtle, 208
CHRISTY
John, 100
CHURCH
Andrew, 107
Clara, 107
Diodata, 71
Gaston, 71
Horace, 107
John, 71
Nelson, 71

Uriah, 71, 107
Vesta, 71
William, 35
CLARK
Elender, 59
Eugenia Lee, 408
Margaret, 59
Nora, 179
CLARKE
Emma J., 146
Frank M., 357
Ronald Frank, 357
Sarah Ann, 106
CLARKSON
Paul Stephen, 364
CLAYTON
Anna, 90, 133
Bernice, 90
Deborah, 90, 134
Elizabeth, 90
Ellen, 90
Florence Irene, 134
Infant, 90
John, 90, 134
John C., 134
Mary E., 134
Maxson, 90
Patricia Ann, 409
Pauline, 90
Robert Lewis, 409
Sarah C., 134
Sarah Jane, 90
Serusia, 220
Thomas, 90
Thomas A., 134
William Henry, 134
CLEMENS
Abigail, 141
CLINE
Sarah E., 134
CLYBURN
Earl, 208
COBERLY
Adelaide Beatrice, 313
Alfa Retta, 314
Alta Edith, 314
Araminta Bell, 313
Arnetta Bertha, 313
Art Bernard, 313
Artho Buhl, 314
Champ Clark, 314
Daniel Luther, 187, 313
Daniel M., 122
Isom Oppolance, 314
James, 88, 122
Mary Ann, 123

Nathan Granville, 123, 187
Vera Blanch, 313
COBURN
Dora, 419
COFFEY
Evelyn Grace, 406
COFFMAN
Arthur Lee, 419
Lena Esta, 419
COLLINS
Larmar Martin, 348
Lawrence R., 220
Mary, 166
Oval Edison, 349
Roy, 359
Susie Pearl, 388
Warder P., 359
COLLYER
John, 69
COMPTON
John G., 211
Nora, 211
CONGELGON
Oma, 373
CONKLE
Elizabeth, 96
Lucretia (Lucinda), 159
Rebecca, 98
CONKLIN
Anna E., 169
CONLEY
Heta A., 189
CONNELLY
Creed, 352
Rachel M., 265
CONNER
Sarah, 59
CONNOR
R. D. W., 30
CONOVER
Garrett, 69
CONVERSELY
Mary M., 190
COOKMAN
May, 145
Statira, 234
COOPER
Charles S., 368
Dorothy, 208
Edna Cecil, 368
Henry, Jr., 67
Nancy T., 67
Rosanna, 34, 65
CORBIN
Alice Jane, 205, 206
Catherine, 227, 403

Gustavius Adolphus, 142, 227
Ivan Bush, 403
Ivan Shockey, 228, 403
John Byron, 228
John Eldon, 228, 403
Joseph Taylor, 142, 228
Lorenzo Dow, 142
Martha Columbia, 142, 206, 228
Mary Virginia, 142, 228
Nora Pearl, 228, 404
Oliver Gene, 403
Oliver Gustavius, 228, 403
Oliver Perry, 142, 206
Rebecca Ann, 142, 228
Son, 228
CORDELL
Clark, 1
CORDER
Bessie A., 320
CORIELL
Anne, 67
Elias, 67
CORNELL
Edith, 340
Fred E., 340
Hazel, 340
James, 340
Mabel, 340
Mamie E., 339
Mary Belle, 340
William G., 339
CORNWELL
Marguerite, 404
CORRELL
Adam M., 115
COSTILOW
Ellen, 215, 223
COTTRELL
Ruth, 377
COTTRILL
Alda V., 190
Arden B., 190
Birdie Arizona, 345
Earl W., 190
Etta N., 190
Henry B., 190, 210
Lulu S., 190
Minnie Otto, 190, 210, 320
COUEY
Edward H., 6, 40
COUNTS
Norma, 370
COVENHOVEN
Capt. John, 63

COWAN
Andrew, 84
COZAD
Jacob, 188
Mary Elizabeth, 188
CRABB
Amanda J., 257
Jacob, 257
CRAGO
Thelma Freda, 361
CRAIG
David Kline, 268
Elizabeth, 44
Elizabeth Sutphen, 268
Reva Lucille, 428
Virginia, 429
CRAIN
John, 44
CRAMER
Esther M., 410
Euphenia, 165
CRANE
Margaret, 83
CRANMER
William Stockton, 441
Winifred Stockton, 441
CRAWFORD
Ada, 434
Edward Hugh, 262, 434
Eliza V., 262, 434
Gertie, 262
James, 79
Jefferson, 262, 434
Laura, 434
Mary Janet, 262, 434
Philander, 262, 434
Raymond, 434
Samuel, 434
Viola, 434
Walter, 434
William, 434
William H., 262
CREIGHTON
Catherine, 58
CRESSMAN
Doris Marie, 357
Luther, 357
CRITES
Joab, 217
L. Gertrude, 217
CROOK
Anna Grace, 439
CROPP
Cora M., 229
John, 410
John R., 229

CROWELL
Adelaide Gaston, 183
George Henry, 183
Mary Elizabeth, 183
CULBERSON
Edith, 263
CULP
John, 79
CUMBERLEDGE
Daniel G., 343
Jacob A., 343
James Andrew, 342
James Lester, 343
Ruby I., 343
CUMMINGS
Maria, 110
Oregin, 112
Sarah Jane, 112
CUMOR
Marie, 363
CUNNINGHAM
Daniel Martin, 416
Julia M., 98
M. Gordon, 391
Matthew, 58
Samuel, 98
Willis Martin, 416
CURRY
Ella Gladys, 410
CZIGANS
Jessie, 367
Lawrence, 367

D
DAGON
Elizabeth, 371
DAILEY
Katie, 431
DALHOFF
Elsie M, 239
DANIEL
Sarah Elizabeth, 407
DARNALL
E. Dare, 233
R. L., 233
DARNOLD
Bessie, 211
DAUDET
Alphonse, 1
DAVIDSON
Isabella, 80
Mary, 82
DAVIS
Agnes, 402
Allie Belle, 209, 365

Allison Bell George, 399
Barbara Kay, 399
Beverly Sue, 399
Cecil, Jr., 201
Cecil G., 201
Claudius Brooks, 331
Darwin Maxson, 141
Darwin Maxwell, 141
Earl, 263
Edna M., 248
Edwin Gyle, 331
Emaline, 134
Erma Viola, 417
Estella Ann, 138
Freda Alice, 331
George A., 152
Hannah Almeda, 121, 185
Hezekiah Stephen, 331
Isaac, 121
James, 91, 201
Janet, 43
John B., 79
Lance O., 416
Lillian Virginia, 411
Lucinda, 198
Marilyn Jean, 376
Marion Taylor, 175
Mary Edith, 175
Nellie Margaret, 399
Orval, 331
Owen, 121
Owen T., 390
Owen Vanburen, 121
Robert, 417
Ruth, 201
Sarah, 46, 60
Teresa, 201
Veda Irene, 390
Wayne K., 201
William, 209
William Hedges, 402
Wilma Viva, 331
DAVISON
Andrew, 121
Elizabeth, 122
Jane, 160
DAVISSON
Andrew, 63
Ann, 63
Anna, 62
Daniel, 90
Elizabeth, 62
DAVVISON
Anna, 151
Austin Homer, 404
Corbin Late, 404

Ella, 416
Ellen Mae, 404
Evelyn, 426
Helen Joan, 404
Late Bruce, 404
Laura Druzilla, 227
Mary M., 185
Nancy, 124
William G., 425
DAWSON
Charles P., 250
Dora A., 151
Edith M., 151
Edward, 187
Eula, 250
Franklin E., 250
Grace, 250
Homer E., 151, 250
Infant, 250
Isabelle, 187
James R., 250
John, 151
Lewis D., 151, 250
Marguerite, 404
Martha A., 250
Mary E., 151
Oakey C., 151
Ockman T., 152
Roscoe, 250
William E., 151, 250
William J., 250
DAY
Bessie J., 366
James A. L., 138
Joseph T., 138
DAYO
Frank F., 134
DAYTON
Albert C., 147
George Burke, 147
George Waldo, 240
George Washington, 147
Helen L., 240
Hoy, 147
Louella D., 147, 239
William Rush, 147, 239
DEAN
Emma Amanda, 127
DEARING
Edward Newton, 416
Mabel Pauline, 416
DECKER
Martha G., 105
DEMUN
Martha, 104

DENNIS
Thomas S., 82
DENNY
David, 168
Elizabeth Henderson, 168
Emily, 120
Mary, 120
Walter, 120
DERBY
Archibald, 440
James V., 444
DEVEGA
Abram H., 116
Jessie A., 116, 178
DICKSON
Alexander, 35
Andrew, 71, 107
Clara, 107, 171
James, 35, 107
John, 35
Joseph, 35
Nancy, 35
Phebe, 35, 71, 107
DIVERS
Emma May, 200
DONAL
Hezekiah, 79
DONALDSON
Nellie Frances, 352
Robert, 61, 94, 95
DONNELLY
Elizabeth, 100
William F., 121
DONOVAN
Charles Stuart, 440
Elizabeth Stuart, 440
DOOLEN
Prudence, 85
DORAN
Ella, 156
DORSEY
Alpheus C., 251
Ethel Delia, 251
DOTSON
Erma Lucretia, 334
DOUGLAS
Albertie, 237
Ebenezer Elliott, 80
DOUGLASS
Alexander, 47, 48
Alexander S., 48
Jane G., 49
John A., 47, 48
Margaret S., 49
Martha S., 48
Mary Emerline, 49

Mrs. Jane, 48
Nancy Ann, 121
Paulie Carrie, 403
Robert, 75
Samuel Grover, 403
Sarah E., 49
DOYLE
Celia Lois, 420
DRACAS
Arthur, 437
Mary Elizabeth, 437
DRAIN
Connie Pauline, 370
Hayward H., 371
Hunter Holmes, 371
Oma Maxine, 371
William Lewis, 370
Wilma Sarah, 371
DRUMMOND
Ada Nell, 222
DUCKWORTH
Marguerite, 355
Richard, 361
William, 361
William Thomas, 361
DUDEN
Dorothy, 439
Eula, 439
Henry C., 439
DUDLEY
Ota Blanche, 243
DUMONT
Arthur, 268
Cora, 266, 438
Cornelia, 268
Emma Jane, 268
Ethel, 440
Evelyn, 439
Harold, 268
Harold E., 439
Hugh Gaston, 268
Irene, 268
Isaac Newton, 165
John G., 266, 437
Leroy, 438
Lillian, 268
Mable Naomi, 438
Mary, 268
Naomi Alberta, 439
Oliver Pillsbury, 266, 438
Peter, 265, 266
DUNHAM
Polly, 109
DUNLAP
Joshua, 71
Olive, 71

DUNN
Earnest R., 211
Frances Elizabeth, 18, 22
DURHAM
James, 70
Oscar, 267
DYE
Abbie, 182
Alexander Isaac, 24
Lydia Adeline, 395
DYKE
Zelda, 436

E
EAKIN
Edna, 234
EAKLE
Viola May, 416
EARLENBAUGH
Lawrence, 255
EARNEST
Elisha, 81
EASTMAN
Anne Louise, 172
ECKMAN
Leroy G., 374
EDMONDS
Dora E., 186, 312
Hiram Everett, 313
Hiram T., 186, 313
Ruanna B., 186
EDWARDS
Louisa, 130
Sarah, 115
EGBERT
Elizabeth, 254
William P., 254
EHRET
John, 218
Moode, 213
ELBON
Christopher Wayne, 351
ELLIOTT
Benjamin, 76
Cora Lee, 183
Daniel, 76, 77
Daniel, Sr., 77
Dollie B., 183
Ebenezer, 75, 76, 80
Ebenezer Newton, 80
Edward, 183
Edwin Ebenezer, 77, 78
Elizabeth Ferguson, 77
Hugh, 80
Isaiah, 80

Jacob, 183
James, 76, 80, 184
Jane, 76
Janet, 80
Jasper David, 183
John, 80
Joseph Gaston, 80
Joseph T., 80
Margaret, 76
Mary Bird, 183
Samuel N., 183
Vevia, 403
Virginia, 191
Waitman T., 183
William, 76, 80
William Henry, 183
ELLIS
Archie Lawson, 202
John W., 30
Tyree M., 202
William Bentley, 202
EMERSON
Joseph, 416
Mary, 130
Nora Mae, 416
EMLEY
Ann, 93
ENGELHARDT
Ivan D., 371
ENGLAND
Bishop John, 61
Susannah, 203
ENGLISH
Catharine, 86
James, 86
ENLOE
Major A. B., 50
ENSELL
Matilda, 259
ERNEST
Mary, 188
ERWIN
Marie, 379
ESTEP
Amanda, 258
Annie, 257
Bessie, 259
Caroline, 156
Catherine C., 154
Charles, 257
Charles F., 258
Dorcas, 93
Edna H., 433
Harrison, 156, 258
Harry A., 433
Harry C., 258

Henry, 258
Herbert, 258
James, 156, 258
James Edward, 258, 433
Jennie, 257
Josiah, 257, 258
Josiah Morgan, 156, 257
Junious, 257
Kaye, 433
Mabel, 258
Marian, 258
Mary, 93
Olive, 258
Rachel, 156
Robert, 93
Roxanna, 156
Walter, 258
Walter L., 433
William, 257
EVANS
John Wesley, 128
Joshua R., 128
Myrtle, 407
EVERETT
Elijah, 71
Joseph G., 71
Margaret G., 71
Samuel, 71
EVERITT
Dr. Elijah, 35
Elisha, 65
EWING
Mary E., 256
EZZARD
John L., 113
Nancy Ward, 113

F
FABER
Brooks Haden, 406
Charles Lee, 404
Corbett Lee, 228, 407
Darrell Draper, 406
Dennis B., 228
Dovener, 228, 407
Edith Dale, 404
Edward Evans, 407
Eliza Virginia, 405
Elizabeth Mae, 405
Elsie Lea, 406
Forris Ernest, 404
Frank Glen, 404
George Bennet, 228, 406
George Edwin, 406
Hauntie Haden, 228, 407

Hauntie Mae, 406
Hedgeman Taylor, 228, 406
Henry Mason, 405
Hiram Oliver, 405
Hirman Oliver, 228
Hubert C., 405
Hurbert C., 228
Janes Dovener, 407
Jean Elizabeth, 406
John Hamilton, 404
John Henry, 228, 407
John Smith, 405
Juanita May, 406
Lillie Mae, 404
Linnie Erie, 228, 407
Myron Hubert, 406
Olive Florence, 407
Oliver Karr, 405
Ona Belle, 228, 406
Proctor Leander, 406
Raymond Rockford, 405
Robert Harlan, 228, 404
Robert Hoyt, 404
Roy Warren, 404
Sara June, 407
Shelly Oshel, 228, 406
Vaughn Henry, 405
Velva, 228, 407
Zorah Virginia, 406
FAIRFAX
Rena T., 239
FALLS
Sarah Helen, 379
FARLEY
Margaret, 164
FARNSWORTH
Hattie, 224
FAST
Chester LeRoy, 376
Ruby Jones, 376
FAULKNER
Ronnie W., 30
FEASTER
Mary Elizabeth, 201
FEEMSTER
James, 42
FEEZEL
Charles, 262
Ethel A., 262
Jean, 435
Jerry, 435
Lola, 262, 434
Nilla A., 262
Ralph S., 435
Raymond C., 262, 435
Riley L., 262, 435

FELTON
Cornelius Conway, 172
FERGUSON
Henry, 36
Jeremiah, 36
Jonathan, 44
Katherine, 47
FERRELL
Celia I., 187
FETTER
Mary Augusta, 174
FIGLEY
David, 94
FINDLEY
Francis, 91
FISHER
Barbara Elizabeth, 203
Belle, 161
Dorothy Mevina, 405
Elbie, 405
Ercell Lea, 406
Ida L., 405
John O., 161
Mary, 161
Miriam, 205
Rev. C. F., 74
FLEMING
James, 133
Margaret, 133, 211
Mary, 133, 143, 210
Mary Frances, 375
Mary Jane, 184
Nancy Ann, 191
Sarah, 133
FLESHER
Lincoln Brooks, 373
Nay Ercil, 419
Patty Jo, 419
FLETCHER
Alma, 366
Ralph R., 402
FLINT
Alice B., 235
Laura, 232
FLOYD
Samuel S., 251
Willa G., 251
FOLEY
James, 382
FONTENOT
Frances, 198
Frances Irene, 197
FORK
Gladys, 146
FORMAN
Col. Samuel, 63

FORSBACH
William Henry, 407
FORSTER
Catherine, 431
Dorothy A., 431
Franklin T., 431
Ida, 431
Kenneth E., 431
FORZANO
Edna Mae, 358
FOSTER
Lawrence, 172
FOULKE
Sara, 176
FOURNIER
Mickey, 43
FOWLER
Nancy, 67
FOX
Jasper L., 146
FRAKER
John Reed, 372
Joseph, Jr., 372
Joseph E., 372
Ota Reed, 375
William L., 372
FREDERICK
Gordon William, 407
Margaret Sofie, 357
FREEMAN
Anthony Smith, 327
Hester Oleta, 328
Lucy Alexander, 226
Neva Lucille, 328
Ruth, 399
FRETWELL
John E., 351
John Richard, 352
Laura Rose, 352
Stacie Mae, 352
Virginia Bell, 352
FRYE
Sarah A., 260
FRYMIER
Frances Virginia, 212
John, 212
FULKS
Nola Gladys, 405
FULLERTON
David, 23, 24
FURBEE
Edna P., 428
Vance Orlet, 428
FURGUSON
L. Pleasant, 79

FURNER
John, 136
Mary Jane, 128
Rebecca Jane, 136

G

GADDIS
Homer, 404
GAGE
George W., 116
GALBRAITH
Isabel Simonton, 32
GALL
Charles Musser, 144, 231
Lafayette Erastus, 144
Robert Burl, 231
GALLOWAY
Margaret, 47
GAMBLE
Grace, 251
Samuel, 44
GARBON
Thelma, 436
GARDNER
Clarrisa, 161
GARNER
Hallie C., 339
Sallie, 81
GARNES
Mary Jane, 203
GARRETSON
Jane Van Deveer, 164
Magdolena, 265
Peter, 164
GARRISON
Robert H., 245
GASTON
Aaron, 70, 106
Abalena, 80
Abbie Marie, 174
Abraham, 68, 92, 150
Abram Lawson, 248
Ada Vonda, 224, 398
Adaline Bell, 150, 247
Addison T., 150
Agnes, 82, 169
Agnes A., 255, 431
Albert, 37, 265
Albert Dalton, 149, 242, 243
Albert Nelson, 37
Albram Lawson, 425
Alda May, 152
Alecia, 27
Aletta Swan, 104, 167
Alexander, 1, 2, 3, 4, 5, 6, 7, 12, 28,

32, 35, 37, 38, 40, 41, 60, 65, 66,
67, 71, 73, 78, 81
Alexander Cummings, 111, 174
Alexander F., 61, 85
Alexander Kirkpatrick, 104, 167
Alfred, 345
Alfred Randolph, 347
Alice Elizabeth, 170
Alma Gay, 197, 351
Alonzo, 74
Alonzo Alexander, 174
Alonzo Marcellus, 111
Alpha Lee, 224, 396
Alpha Louise, 251, 426
Alva Hirman, 428
Alvin S., 151
Amanda Jane, 150, 231, 246
Amos, 37
Amy Mae, 224, 396
Amzi Cason "Case", 179, 181
Amzi Cecil, 180
Amzi Williford, 84, 118, 119, 181
Anderson Lewers, 119, 182
Andrew, 63, 73, 86
Andrew A., 111
Andrew Davisson, 90
Ann, 5, 35, 42, 43, 44, 58, 93, 113,
176
Ann Eliza, 75
Anna, 87, 88, 120, 158, 182
Anna E., 118, 169
Anna Elizabeth, 197, 349
Anna M., 89, 124, 126
Anna Rebecca, 266
Anna Reger, 1, 32, 164
Anna Rosa, 106
Anna S., 166
Anne, 35, 43, 70
Annie, 105
Anold Marsh, 349
Anzi Williford, 22
Archie Franklin, 256, 432
Arnold Marsh, 19
Arthur, 166
Arthur B., 112
Arthur F., 170, 254, 430
Arthur Herbert, 439
Arthur Lee, 116, 178
Arthur Sutphen, 165
Athelston, 112
Audley DeForest, 176
Augusta, 105
Augustus L., 69
Auldra Ashton, 344
Azalea, 148
Azeltha Arabelle, 112

Bayard Lamar, 181
Benjamin H., 255
Bennett J., 170
Berle, 180
Bernice Helena, 396
Bertha, 152, 252
Bertha Amelia, 100
Bertha Virginia, 120
Bessie, 182
Bessie Mae, 197, 350
Betty Carolyn, 396
Betty Jane, 428
Beulah Stanford, 254
Beverly Hull, 74
Bonnie Meredith, 344
Brady Summers, 243, 420
Bryan W., 255
Burton Cummings, 112
C. Anna, 124
Calvin H., 160
Caroline, 114, 177
Caroline Cutbert, 166
Caroline S., 74
Carrie, 169
Catharine, 31
Catherine, 34, 104, 165, 267, 268
Catherine "Caty", 37
Catherine Harriet, 178
Catherine Jane (Kate), 61
Catherine R., 159
Catherine Van Nest, 164, 266
Cecile, 255
Celia H., 74, 111
Charity, 67, 94, 99
Charles D., 223
Charles Delbert, 179
Charles Henry, 104, 170
Charles Hornor, 153, 252
Charles Kasson, 174
Charles Lee, 429
Charles Nicoles, 241, 418
Charles Robert, 170
Charles W., 65, 95
Charlotte, 70, 163, 253
Charlotte A., 106
Charlotte King, 437
Clara, 153
Clara Louise, 430
Clarence Warner, 439
Clark, 106, 151
Claudius, 152, 252
Claudius J., 226
Cledith, 203
Clifford George, 250
Clinton Dewitt, 255
Clyde, 149

Columbia, 136, 215
Cora, 152, 252, 418
Cora Ellen, 174
Cordelia, 89, 100, 127
Cornelia, 165
Cornelia Jane, 163
Cornelius Alonzo, 254, 430
Corrie, 182
Credilla, 88
Currell Samuel, 179
Cyrus, 156, 254, 255
Dainty Evelene, 182
Daisy Dean, 150, 246
Dan Wellington, 195
Daniel, 31, 34, 62, 70, 88, 89, 125, 135
Daniel Castner, 103, 162
Daniel H., 89, 124, 126
Daniel Oliver, 97
David, 6, 12, 37, 39, 82, 112, 114, 156, 177, 255, 431
David Aiken, 178
David Dow, 126, 199
David Down, 126
David Holder, 181
David Lawrence, 198
David Wilson, 224
Deborah, 63, 90, 91, 136
Dessie Blanche, 247
Dessie W., 251
Dollie May, 180
Dora, 156, 256
Dora E., 158
Dorcas, 94
Dorcas L., 155
Doris, 435, 436
Dorothy Ruth, 243
Dr. Alexander, 112
Druzella, 100
Earnest A., 241
Earnest Ray, 201
Ebenezer, 12, 37, 44, 66, 75, 112
Edgar, 224
Edgar Hamilton, 346
Edgar Kasson, 75
Edgel Thourl, 360
Edith Gae, 350
Edmund Waite, 75, 112
Edna Grace, 176
Edna Lillie, 251
Edward, 169, 259, 264
Edward Baxter, 119, 182
Edward P. Bradstreet, 74
Edward Ullmont, 346
Edward Wesley, 179
Edwin, 151, 249

Edythe Louise, 439
Elbert A., 182
Elcy (Elsie), 37
Eldin Lee, 202
Eldridge, 255, 432
Eleanor, 66, 100
Eleanor Jane, 65, 97
Elenor Lee, 351
Elfa, 224
Eli, 88, 135
Eli Clark, 126, 196, 197
Eli Morris, 89, 124, 125
Eli Willis, 196, 344
Elias Hedges, 70, 105
Elihu, 59
Elijah L., 36, 72
Eliza, 45, 93, 95, 105, 156
Eliza Ann, 61
Eliza Eillene, 195
Eliza W., 85
Elizabeth, 4, 23, 27, 30, 31, 32, 33, 34, 42, 43, 44, 58, 59, 64, 65, 66, 69, 82, 84, 90, 93, 96, 97, 98, 105, 118, 140, 151, 158, 159, 162, 169, 262
Elizabeth A., 181
Elizabeth Ann, 92, 146, 196
Elizabeth Blanch, 168
Elizabeth Catherine, 139, 224
Elizabeth H., 437
Elizabeth Jane, 139, 199, 356
Elizabeth Laverna, 124, 194
Elizabeth Louise, 120, 183
Elizabeth Lucinda, 136, 213
Elizabeth Mader, 423
Ella, 155
Ella May, 223, 395
Ellen, 62
Ellen Frances, 75
Elliott T., 118
Ellner Lee, 352
Eloise, 115
Elsie A., 255
Elvira, 73
Elwood Forrest, 118
Emala Fairchild, 74, 111
Emeretta, 128
Emily, 84, 119, 155
Emily Caroline, 75
Emily Cornelia, 112
Emily N., 263, 435
Emma, 151
Emma Louise, 163
Emma Louise Adele, 168
Enoch, 93, 141, 152, 226
Enoch Arlando, 150

Ephraim, 66, 67, 99
Ephraim Hammond, 112
Ernest B., 431
Ernest Berry, 155, 254
Ernest Dale, 202
Ernest Herman, 174
Ernest Leroy, 255, 431
Ernest Ray, 129
Estella B., 128
Esther, 9, 15, 42, 44, 45, 71, 77, 78, 82
Esther Jane, 15, 40, 75
Esther Waugh, 44, 82
Ethel, 141, 152
Ethel Gertrude, 176
Ethel Rebecca, 266, 439
Etta, 110, 256
Etta Mary, 174
Eugene A., 168, 442
Eunice, 38
Eunice Lucinda, 112, 175
Euphelia Minerva, 111
Eva Dell, 128, 201
Eva Irene, 226
Evalena C., 200, 359
Evalyn, 436
Evelina Belmont Linn, 104
Evelyn, 169
Fannie, 168
Fay, 425
Fitzie Hampton, 181
Flora Jane, 227
Florence, 263, 265
Floyd Simeon, 150
Frances, 62, 86, 169
Frances Irene, 197
Frances Lilly, 254
Francis Enoch, 139, 224
Frank C., 251, 427
Frank Carlton, 428
Frank DeForest, 55, 113, 175
Frank L., 432
Fred, 265
Frederick, 104, 168, 200
Frederick Keiley, 265, 437
Fremont, 104
Gail Adams, 396, 397
Garland, 182
Garner Hornor, 251
Garnet Hornor, 427
General De Foix De Nemours, 1
Geneva Pauline, 347
George, 92, 149, 151
George A., 268, 440
George B., 74, 174
George Belcher, 73, 110

George Elbert, 248, 423
George Harold, 422
George Houston, 167
George Irwin, 417
George Isaac, 241, 417
George L., 152, 250
George M., 170
George Norman, 419
George Rodney, 74
George Rutherford, 112, 175
George Tiffany, 105, 170
George W., 158
George Washington, 35, 156, 256
Georgia Anna, 179
Georgia Leona, 180
Georgia Rachael, 197, 352
Georgiana Anna, 117
Geraldine, 248, 425
Geraldne, 248
Gertrude, 86
Gertrude Elma, 141
Gilbert Eugene, 348
Ging, 6
Gladys Bond, 174
Glen, 263, 436
Glenn A., 395
Golden, 241, 417
Gordon Brooks, 443
Grace, 34, 65, 70, 75, 97
Grace Eileen, 401
Granville, 89
Guy Edmond, 346
Gwendolyn, 431
H. Julia, 105
Hamer E., 105
Hamilton, 96, 158
Hamilton D., 98, 160
Hamilton Rosborough, 117
Hamilton Rosborougj, 84
Hanna, 42
Hanna & Anna Reger, 34
Hannah, 60
Hannah E., 86, 124
Hannah Elizabeth, 136, 215
Hannah Margaret, 61, 85
Hannah R., 126, 198
Harley L., 241
Harley Roach, 148, 241
Harold, 128
Harold Burton, 174
Harold Dean, 202
Harold P., 442
Harold Randall, 428
Harriet B., 259
Harriet J., 170
Harriet Kesiah, 85

Harriet Prevast, 169
Harry, 149, 243, 263, 436
Harry Lee, 435
Harvey, 84, 119, 148, 248
Harvey Junior, 424
Harvey L., 129, 202
Helen, 169, 265
Heman, 37
Henrietta, 67, 100, 162
Henrietta M., 118
Henry, 37
Henry Alexander, 74, 111
Henry H., 88
Henry Lee, 89, 128, 263
Henry T., 139
Henson Davisson, 141, 152
Herbert Brownell, 255, 431
Herbert Louis, 243
Herbert M., 179
Herman, 74
Hiram J., 152, 250
Homer Warren, 170
Hope, 172
Howard, 263, 436
Howard Loman, 248
Howe Russell, 248, 249
Hubert William, 179
Hudson, 80, 113
Hugh, 3, 4, 12, 24, 25, 28, 31, 32, 44,
    58, 59, 62, 63, 65, 66, 68, 84, 87,
    89, 96, 97, 103, 124, 158, 164, 165,
    266
Hugh, Jr., 32
Hugh F., 97
Hugh Joseph, 85
Hugh Kirkpatrick, 169
Hugh M., 104, 169
Hughy, 87
Ida Ann, 164
Ida B., 223
Ida E., 168
Ida Elmira, 167, 269
Ida Mae, 140
Ida Marie, 104
Ida May, 150, 247, 259
Ida V., 166, 265, 437
Infant, 182
Ira, 37
Ira Clinton, 223, 395
Ira Clinton, Jr., 395
Ira Dow, 88, 196, 346
Irl R., 255
Irma Eleanor, 203
Irvin A., 256
Isaac, 34, 67, 69, 103, 165, 167
Isaac E., 166

Isaac Hazlett, 161
Isaac M., 92, 147
Isaac Van Arsdale, 69
Isabella, 66
Ivah Jane, 124, 191
Ivan Valentine, 151
J. Avon, 114
J. Simpson, 129
J. Wayne, 255
Jack Oral, 360
Jacob, 96
Jame Bullock, 120
James, 4, 9, 12, 23, 27, 31, 32, 37,
    42, 43, 44, 58, 62, 63, 65, 66, 67,
    68, 82, 89, 91, 92, 93, 96, 103, 104,
    114, 157, 164
James A. H., 45, 84
James Albert, 179
James Andrew, 119
James Beryl, 360
James Blaine, 196
James Brady, 420
James Bullock, 85
James Burnside, 152, 251
James Cyrus, 59
James Ernest, 254, 430
James Estep, 94, 154, 156, 254
James Eustace, 200, 360
James Gordon, 181
James Harry, 251
James Hedges, 265
James Henderson, 25
James Henry, 115, 177
James Herbert, 266, 439
James Kasson, 75, 111
James Kendall, 201
James Lee, 223, 395
James Lloyd (Huston), 128, 200
James M., 156, 159, 259, 263
James McFadden, 82, 115
James McFadden, Jr., 115
James Monroe, 120, 183
James Morgan, 348
James Newton, 119
James R., 181
James Taylor, 177
James W., 66, 97, 98
James William, 66, 91, 96, 140, 152
Jane, 6, 31, 40, 42, 45, 56, 57, 61, 62,
    63, 66, 67, 81, 98, 119, 165
Jane Catherine, 59
Jane Maria, 164, 266
Janet, 4, 16, 21
Janet A. "Jennie", 6, 36
Janie, 116

Jarvis Frank, 183
Jean, 45
Jean (John), 1
Jeanette Alice, 119
Jeanne, 431
Jeb Stuart, 181
Jennet, 11, 32
Jennie, 36
Jesse, 126
Jesse Lawrence, 350
Jesse Morris, 196, 346
Jesse Smith, 126
Jessie C., 197
Jinny, 16
Joanna, 104, 166
Joanna Brown, 167, 269
Joel R. P., 118
John, 1, 2, 3, 4, 5, 6, 7, 9, 10, 11, 23, 32, 33, 34, 35, 36, 38, 39, 40, 41, 44, 59, 62, 63, 64, 66, 71, 80, 81, 87, 90, 93, 95, 97, 104, 147, 155, 158, 163, 169, 172, 231, 259
John (Jean), 38
John, Jr., 9, 10, 31, 62, 63, 64, 151
John, Sr., 31, 39
John August, 179
John Baird, 86
John Brown, 45, 82
John Brown, Jr., 82, 116
John C., 159, 262
John D., 114, 162, 265
John E., 125, 128
John Franklin, 203
John Frederick, 167
John Garner, 81
John Garretson, 165, 268, 440
John II., 124, 157, 260
John Henry, 180
John Hugh, 89, 123, 124, 135
John I., 69, 104
John Irvin, 139, 223
John "Jean", 40
John Leolin, 148, 240
John M., 92
John M. "Lank", 149
John Marion, 129, 203
John Morris, 126, 195
John Ogden, 170
John Oliver, 241
John Perry, 67
John R., 58
John Sheridan, 196, 345
John Smith, 90, 135, 138
John W., 68, 103, 106, 158
John Walter, 166
John William, 93, 116, 152, 179, 180

John Williford, 181
John Wortman, 164
Johnnie Matthew, 81, 114
Joseph, 3, 5, 6, 9, 11, 15, 23, 32, 33, 34, 35, 38, 45, 58, 64, 66, 67, 68, 70, 77, 78, 79, 93, 96, 103, 104, 156, 163, 164, 168, 255
Joseph A., 168
Joseph Alexander, 80
Joseph Annin, 104, 166
Joseph C., 127
Joseph Clark, 196
Joseph H., 94
Joseph James, 84, 155, 254
Joseph Lucius, 82, 116
Joseph Lucius, Jr., 116
Joseph S., 157
Joseph S., Jr., 261
Joseph Smith, 95, 157
Joseph W., 114, 432
Josephine, 182
Josiah, 156
Josiah Perry, 85
Judge William, 30
Julia, 69
Julia Arabella, 115
Julius, 255
Junior Dale, 346
Junior M., 432
Justice John, 7, 8, 77
Kate Zahniser, 167
Katherine Craig, 268
Kesiah, 42, 43
Laura, 149, 151
Laura Adeline, 119
Lawrence, 119, 182
Lawrence T., 72
Leah Catherine, 254, 430
Lee Maxfield, 395
Lela, 180
Lelia, 149, 243
Lemon Olivet, 58
Lena May, 265
Lenora Squires, 216, 336, 380
Leo George, 432
Leonard, 174
Leonard Harry, 443
Leonard Origen, 112
Leonne Biona, 152
Leonora E., 118
Leroy, 62
Letitia J., 86
Lewis Burke, 255, 432
Lila June, 432
Lillian, 169, 347
Lillie J., 112

Lina, 119
Lizzie, 163, 164, 267
Lloyd Henry, 150, 248, 425
Loman Benjamin, 150
Louellen, 180
Louis Prevast, 169
Louisa Beecher, 45
Louise, 248, 425
Lovie Elizabeth, 350
Lovie Mae, 199, 358
Lucetta, 73
Lucinda, 93
Lucy Belle, 128
Lucy Lacy, 241, 418
Lucy Mariah, 73, 110
Lucy May, 112, 175
Lucy P., 148
Luella, 177
Lula Geneva, 117
Lula Loreen, 424
Lula Loren, 248
Lulu I., 159
Lurana Olive, 196, 344
Luther Goodlett, 118
Luther S., 75
Lydia, 37, 69, 93, 199
Lydia Tapscott, 86
Lyle B., 202
Lyndon Smith, 224
Male, 28
Malissa A., 118
Margaret, 5, 6, 11, 23, 33, 34, 35, 38, 40, 41, 42, 44, 45, 58, 63, 64, 65, 68, 70, 82, 85, 90, 93, 95, 96, 103, 107, 120, 157, 158, 162, 163, 165, 170, 260, 265
Margaret Ann, 41, 57
Margaret B., 69
Margaret Drusilla, 92, 148
Margaret Gene, 424
Margaret H., 265, 437
Margaret Helen, 243, 420
Margaret Jane, 115
Margaret L., 396, 397
Margaret Logan, 58
Margaret Lucile, 180
Margaret M., 105
Margarett, 37
Maria, 37, 73, 94, 111
Marie, 1
Marie Eleanor, 176
Marietta, 75, 104, 165, 267
Marion, 89, 129
Marion A., 199
Marion H., 88
Marion Oscar, 139, 223

Marlin O., 344
Marshall, 6
Martha, 4, 5, 11, 22, 24, 27, 35, 38, 39, 40, 41, 42, 43, 44, 59, 71, 77, 78, 94, 98, 105, 115, 153, 165
Martha A., 159, 262
Martha Alice, 263, 435
Martha E., 157
Martha Emaline, 136
Martha J., 105
Martin, 96, 158
Mary, 3, 4, 5, 6, 15, 27, 28, 31, 34, 44, 65, 66, 67, 70, 93, 97, 98, 116, 120, 154, 155, 162, 165, 168, 169, 182, 254, 259, 264
Mary Amanda, 74
Mary Ann, 58, 114, 136
Mary Ann P., 86
Mary B., 159, 265
Mary Beatrice, 170
Mary Bird, 93, 153
Mary C., 179, 241
Mary Catherine, 92, 147
Mary E., 63, 105, 150, 158, 185, 190, 246
Mary E. "Polly", 87
Mary Effie, 152, 251
Mary Elizabeth, 81, 114, 119, 181, 182, 268
Mary Ellen, 190
Mary Frances, 430
Mary Isabel, 139, 222, 350
Mary Itha, 223
Mary J., 100
Mary Jane, 84, 90, 124, 134, 157, 192
Mary Jo, 417
Mary L., 160
Mary Lou, 180
Mary Louisa, 7
Mary Martha, 124, 190
Mary Maxine, 252
Mary "Minnie", 166
Mary P., 259
Mary "Polly", 96
Mary Rachel, 422
Matilda, 87
Matilda B., 169
Matilda "Tille", 120
Matta Ann, 93
Matthew, 6, 38, 40, 65, 66, 67, 81, 99, 100, 114
Matthew, Jr., 40
Matthew Alexander, 114, 177
May, 182
Melintha E., 115

Mildred, 261, 346
Mildred Elizabeth, 226
Milton C., 419
Minerva, 69
Minnie A., 223, 394
Minnie Alice, 197, 350
Minnie Iris, 150, 245
Minnie Jane, 197
Monna Marie, 250, 426
Morris, 265
Morris Samuel, 136, 216, 380
Myron Clinton, 174
Myrtle, 129, 202
Myrtle Geneva, 180
Nancy, 37, 74, 93, 95, 97, 159, 262
Nancy Clare, 195, 340
Nancy J., 126
Nancy Maria, 124, 194
Nannie May, 250, 421, 426
Naomi, 103, 164, 265
Narcissa, 45, 83, 97, 160
Nellie, 256
Nellie C., 111
Nellie Jane, 179
Nelson, 75
Netta Gay, 128, 201
Nettie, 182
Newton, 182
Norma, 436
Norman Oscar, 178
Norton Reid, 181
Ocie Ota, 250, 425
Ogden, 69, 104
Okey M., 223
Oliva B., 164
Olive Jane, 92, 149, 151
Olive Jean, 430
Oliver, 265
Oliver, Jr., 265
Oliver B., 68, 103, 163, 164
Oliver Berton, 103, 164
Oliver Lawrence, 119
Oma Olena, 395
Opal O., 241
Orley Carson, 224, 396, 397
Orra Maria, 105
Ozro Clair, 174
Palmer Dewitte, 181
Parley Clenney, 85, 120
Parley Ford, 226
Paul Brinkley, 243
Paul K., 441
Pearl, 180
Percy, 265
Phebe, 6
Philander, 97, 159

Phylinda Elise, 176
Pleasant L., 178
Priscilla, 5
Prucilla, 5
Rachel, 94, 154, 155, 180
Ralph Estep, 255, 431
Ralph Leon, 175
Rayburn J., 255
Raymond, 174
Rebecca, 4, 93, 136
Rebecca Alcinda, 92, 148
Rebecca Ann, 90
Rebecca Virginia, 150, 247
Rebecca W., 164
Rhoda Racheal, 350
Robert, 4, 5, 6, 12, 22, 23, 34, 36, 38, 39, 40, 42, 44, 45, 58, 59, 65, 66, 67, 70, 80, 84, 85, 94, 96, 103, 105, 155, 164
Robert Abram, 421
Robert Bruce, 255, 432
Robert Dudley, 243
Robert Lee, 428
Robert Rutledge, 59
Robert Vance, 429
Robert W., 114, 156
Robert White, 181
Roberta Josephine, 174
Rosa, 84
Rosa Bird, 139
Rosalie Cottrill, 346
Rosanna, 70
Rosealtha, 156, 256
Roy, 182
Rulina A., 124, 193
Rulina Belle, 196, 343
Rulina Clemma, 198, 352
Rulina Melinda, 197, 348
Rulina O., 139
Russell Oliver, 170
Ruth, 172
Ruth Tilton, 439
Sallie Lee, 182
Samuel, 39, 58, 64, 82, 84, 93, 94, 96, 116, 119, 153, 157, 259
Samuel, Jr., 95
Samuel Brant, 103, 162, 163
Samuel David, 2
Samuel Eli, 125, 195
Samuel J., 115, 139
Samuel Kirkpatrick, 33, 67
Samuel Morris, 90, 135, 140, 371
Samuel Norton, 37
Samuel Swan, 104, 167
Samuel W., 99, 161
Sarah, 37, 63, 69, 89, 91, 106, 140,

157, 163, 165, 260, 267
Sarah Adeline, 84, 119
Sarah Ann, 106, 124, 192
Sarah Anna, 139
Sarah B., 115
Sarah E., 69
Sarah Eliza, 167
Sarah Elizabeth, 104, 166
Sarah Helen, 243
Sarah Howard, 108
Sarah J., 346
Sarah Jane, 61, 81, 95, 114, 136, 156, 163, 214
Sarah Kirk, 155
Sarah McClure, 58
Sarah Palestine, 92
Sarah Rulina, 199, 355
Sarah "Sallie", 84
Sary, 62
Schuyler Moses, 75
Seldon Obra, 344
Solomon P., 105
Spencer Bryan, 251, 428
Srah, 260
Stella Gay, 195, 342
Stephen, 22, 24, 34, 44, 62, 69, 82, 105
Stephen Harvey, 82, 114, 115
Stobo Rosborough, 180
Stokes K., 241
Stokes Norman, 241, 419
Susan, 60, 85, 90, 136, 137, 214
Susan C., 156
Susan Elizabeth, 177
Susan Laura, 115
Susanna, 42, 75
Susannah, 43, 88, 124, 126
Sylvia Beavers, 164, 266
T. Chalmers, 83, 116
Thelma, 431
Thelma M., 435
Thelma Mae, 174
Thelma Marjorie, 395
Theodore Beecher, 108
Theodore William, 104, 170
Thomas, 6, 22, 23, 27, 58, 60, 179
Thomas Charles, 148, 241
Thomas Craig, 181
Thomas Creighton, 59
Thomas Kirk, 155
Thomas Lawrence, 120
Thomas Logan, 58, 85
Thomas M., 92, 149
Thomas Pinkney, 84, 119
Thomas Reid, 396
Thomas Rosborough, 117, 180

Tidal Wave, 223
Tom, 182
Tom Larkin, 84
Tressa, 255
Vance Orlet, 251
Velma, 203, 224
Vera, 432
Vernon King, 174
Vernon Lincoln, 112, 174
Virgil R., 182
Virgina May, 425
Virginia Dare, 180
Virginia May, 248
Virginia Washburn, 88
Wade, 152
Wade Compton, 246, 421
Walter, 68, 162, 263, 264, 436
Walter Andrew, 179
Walter John, 182
Walter S., 118
Watson, 96
West F., 260
White Oneal, 180
Wilhamena, 260
Willard Edgar, 112, 174
William, 1, 2, 3, 4, 6, 11, 16, 23, 27, 30, 31, 32, 33, 34, 37, 41, 42, 43, 44, 55, 56, 57, 58, 61, 62, 64, 65, 66, 67, 68, 72, 82, 86, 89, 93, 95, 96, 98, 99, 100, 104, 107, 114, 156, 157, 158, 162, 169, 172, 182, 263, 264, 265, 347, 436
William A., 114
William Alexander, 108, 171
William B., 69, 104, 163, 265
William Bell, 178
William Belton, 117, 180
William C., 86
William Crawford, 180
William Davidson, 82, 114
William Denny, 119, 181
William Edgar, 265
William Ellsworth, 439
William F., 85, 168
William Frederick, 169
William G., 63, 92
William Garretson, 165, 268
William Granville, 92
William Grover, 112
William Harvey, 150, 248
William Henry, 154, 155, 167, 253
William Ira, 266, 439
William J., 28, 118, 151, 248
William Joseph, 28, 30, 60, 61
William Jr., 58, 84
William Ker, 103, 162, 164, 266

William Kilgore, 97, 159, 263
William Lougeay, 259
William Porter, 179
William Powers, 84
William R., 157
William Robert, 128, 200
William Rosborough, 84, 116
William S., 160
William T., 81
William Wheeler, 74
Willie, 111
Wilma Cornelia, 174
GAWTHROP
    Launa, 380
GAY
    Annie Bunn, 115
    Margaret, 243
    Thomas Bolling, 115
GEE
    Mary Gaston, 22, 55, 119
GEETING
    John, 97
GEMMILL
    Albert Victor, Jr., 425
GIBB
    Gary, 40
GIBBS
    Leonard Chester, 406
GIBSON
    Adeline, 152
    Martha Ann, 149, 151, 152
    Smith, 151
GILBERT
    Harry, 74
    Henry, 111
    James W., 111
GILL
    Geo., 79
GILLAGHY
    Helen Elsie, 215
GILLELAND
    Mary, 65
GILLETTE
    Alletta Maria, 269
    Austin, 269
    Charles Austin, 269
    William Stewart, 269
GILMAN
    Daniel T., 269
    Daniel Trimble, 441
    Florence King, 441
    Henry King, 441
    Sarah Marshall, 269, 441
    William Stewart, 269, 441
GITHEUS
    Elizabeth, 266

GLADNEY
Charles, 16, 21
Jane Strong, 17, 21
Jane Wilson, 17, 18, 19
Jannet (Jane Strong), 16
Jenet, 16, 21
Joseph, 18
M. Richard, 18
Nancy, 21
Richard, 16, 17, 19, 20, 21
Richard III, 18, 22
Samuel, 18
Thomas, 18
William, 20, 21
GLENN
Olive G., 202
GLOVER
G.F., 365
Minnie Leola, 412
Sarah Elizabeth, 365
GOFF
Alfieri, 381
Andrwe Jason, 218
Blondena W., 385
Charles, 385
Elijah C., 221
Elmas Trevy, 381
Glen L., 381
Ida Mae, 221
Kendall, 385
Lafayette Syrus, 381
Mildred, 381
Paul, 385
Ruble Doy, 381
Simon D., 385
Virginia, 385
Virginia E., 385
GOLDSMITH
Bert, 352
Brooks Arnold, 352
GOMER
Elizabeth, 67, 103
Henry, 67
GONAN
Myrle, 363
GOODE
Justine Melrose, 414
GOODSHAW
Cora, 432
Lottie Mary, 432
GOODWIN
Betty Lee, 379
Earl Smith, 401
Eleanor Ruth, 378
Frances Lucille, 378
James Chapman, 378

Jane Aldine, 379
Martha Ann, 130
Martin V., 131
Otto D., 378
Walter Bruce, 379
GORDON
Alice Julia, 263
Alta Faye, 387
Dorothy, 264
Emaline, 98
Female, 98, 264
Gilbert Gaston, 98, 160
Gilbert Griffith, 263, 436
Gilbert Montgomery, 161, 263
Louis Clark, 161, 263
Lucinda, 98
Male, 98
Maria L., 98
Nathaniel P., 98
Oda C., 387
Robert Gaston, 264
Ruth M., 264
Sara Louise, 263, 436
William, 98
William F., 160, 264
Winona Mildred, 387
GOULD
Arley Kyle, 233
Gilbert, 203
Lois Lucindia, 203
Warren G., 233
GRAFF
Jane Gaston, 439
Robert Ayres, 439
GRAHAM
George W., 61
John, 61
Martha, 97
GRAPES
Alice, 371
GRASON
Margaret, 177
GRAVES
Will, 56
GRAY
Arthur, 427
Carl Lonie, 427
Charles Leonard, 427
Charles Leonard, Jr., 427
James, 427
Jane, 109
John Ferrell, 224
John M., 222
Marshall Franklin, 222
GREATHOUSE
Agnes, 333

Frankie Luzada, 333
Goldie Genevieve, 335
Iva Jewel, 335
Male, 335
Nellie Francis, 333
Perry F., 333
Perry Leon, 333
W. Jason, 335
William, 335
William H., 194
William Henry, 335
GREAVER
Bertha Drucilla, 366
GREEN
Laura Belle, 437
William Martin, 437
GREENAWALT
Rebecca, 412
GREENBANK
Agnes, 168
Elna, 174
GRIBBLE
Howard Hull, 373
Mabel Irene, 373
GRIFFIN
Amelia Virginia, 225
GRIMM
Dora, 197
Herbert, 371
GROSE
Clarence G., 213
GULICK
Andrew J., 69
Anna V., 69
Eliza C., 69
GULL
Mary Ann, 194
GULLEY
Joseph, 189
Wade H., 189
GUTHERIE
Jame Spicer, Jr., 407
GWATKIN
Idella Ford, 233
GWYNN
Hazel Marie, 410

H

HABERMEYER
George C., 177
HACKATHORN
Ella V., 374
HACKLEMAN
Mattie, 182

HADDOX
Etta Larue, 402
Myrtle, 384
HAINES
Mary Whetstone, 103
HALL
Blonda Scott, 246, 422
Catherine Olive, 213
Charles Abraham, 247
Charles Abram, 422
Claude M., 247
David L., 141
Doyle A., 423
Elisha M., 135
Enoch Minor, 246
Freda Mae, 423
Geneva Powers, 423
Harley Hall, 379
Harvey Addison, 246, 422
Hattie E., 141
Inez Merl, 391, 423
James Clark, 246
James Hamlin, 422
James Monroe, 246
John Harvey, 423
John Hobert, 247
John Townsend, 134
Larry, 246
Lawson, 213
Loman Earl, 246
Lot, 252
Mabel Jane, 422
Majorie Ann, 422
Malinda, 151
Marguerite, 353
Martha, 207
Mary, 151
Mary Jane, 368
Minor James, 231, 246
Nora Melvina, 252
Richard Harvey, 247
Roberta Jean, 422
Ruth, 107
Sarah Dell, 231
Sarah Della, 246, 422
Simeon A., Jr., 423
Simeon Asbury, 247, 422
Simeon N., 264
Susan, 61
Tensie Myrtle, 231, 246, 422
Thomas H., 30
William E., 353
William Henry, 246, 390
HALTERMAN
Sarah C., 151
HAMILTON

Ethel Blanche, 203
Mariah L., 96
HAMMER
Alice Victoria, 234
Grover Cleveland, 234
HAMMOND
Gertrude, 325
Hannah, 75
Josephine, 174
Thankful C., 112
HAMPTON
Col. Henry, 23
HANDLIN
Walter F., 184
HANNA
Naoma, 371
HANSEL
Rose, 369
HARBISON
James, 31
Janet, 31
Jas., 79
HARDESTY
Essie Mona, 212
James H., 212
HARDIN
Rebeckah, 40
HARDMAN
Anne Isabelle, 364
Blanche, 210
Fred C., 364
French, 367
Lucy G., 367
Ove, 358
HARKINS
John M., 184
HARMON
Dorothy J., 362
HARPER
Norman L., 237
HARR
Hal, 179
Nadine, 179
HARRIS
Goldie, 371
Margaret, 359
HARRISON
Henry Spain, 407
HART
Anna Dell, 152
Bernice Eliza, 342
Cassa Ann, 196
Dolores Gay, 342
Edmund B., 152
Elizabeth, 196
Ellen, 341

Hannah Belle, 199
Irene Virginia, 341
John G., 196, 199
John W., 342
John Washington, 340
Macel Claire, 341
Malinda Ann, 236
Mary, 213
Oren Victor, 341
Phame, 342
Ronnie Boswell, 340
Ruby Alma, 340
Samuel James, 341
Simeon, 65
William C., 236
Wilma Idolene, 341
HARTFORD
Margaret, 434
HARVEY
Margaret, 12, 44
Margaret J., 115
Mary Jane, 178
HASELTINE
Hubert Arthur, 443
HASKIN
Lavinia, 169
HASKINS
Ruby, 378
HATCHER
Hal, 174
HATFIELD
Clyde Otis, 398
Delma Jean, 398
Mary Lucille, 398
HAUGHT
Amos Peter, 190, 323
Columbia J., 190
Dovener I., 191
Edward Marshall, 324
Harry William, 321
Hayward E., 321
Ivah May, 190, 322
John W., 190
Love, 190
Lovett, 322
Martha, 190
Marvel L., 190
Marvel Lindsey, 190
Marville Lindsay, 190
Mary A., 190
Mary Ellen, 191, 324
Peter B., 190
Ralph Marvel, 321
Wallace Brady, 320
William C., 190, 320

HAVER
Alvah, 438
Clara Matilda, 438
Elsie, 438
Florence Earle, 438
Russell, 438
Ruth, 438
HAWKINS
Bud, 119
Charles E., 408
Docia, 119, 183
Elizabeth Ann, 134
Georgie, 119
Jane, 119
John, 119
Rose Bertha Mae, 408
HAY
John, 60
Susan, 60
HAYDEN
William, 93
HAYHURST
Ethan, 359
Marlene Madge, 359
HAYNES
Nova Jean, 407
HAYS
Prudence, 98
HAZARD
Sally, 109
HAZLETT
Margaret F., 161
HEARN
Sarah, 80
HEDGES
Anna, 69
Caroline Bedell, 437
Edward, 265
Elias, 34
Frank Louis, 437
J. Edward, 437
James English, 265
HELLINGER
Mrs. Claude Crosby, 351
HELMICK
Bess, 242
Carl, 148
Carroll, 148, 242
Ernest, 148, 241
Frances Virginia, 241, 419
Frederick, 148, 241
Harriet Wright, 242, 420
Jane, 242
John Pierpoint, 242, 420
Loma Ethel, 358
Louis Gaston, 148, 242

Louis Gaston, Jr., 420
Lucy, 148
Mary Mason, 242
Nathaniel David, 148
Robert J., 241, 419
Susan, 242
HEMPHILL
David, 116
Margaret, 116
Mary, 54
HENRY
Clara Leona, 176
James, 165
Nancy, 75
Samuel, 176
Sarah, 188
HENSON
Nellie Lucinda, 116
HERNDON
Joel, 207
Sarah Catherine, 207
HERSMAN
John F., 144
HESS
Anthony, 186
Beulah, 307
Ila, 308
Jacob, 186
Olis Clark, 220
HIBBS
Elliott L., 261
HICKMAN
Burleigh C., 355, 357
David Thomas, 355
Esther, 262
Gilbert Robert, 355
James Marshall, 322
Loren Grant, 323
Milton Camdon, 191
Ortha Mabel, 323
Patricia B., 123
Rebecca, 131
Rella J., 323
Sarah Gaston, 357
Susie Nutter, 355
Thomas, 191
HICKOK
Fred, 110
Lucy Gaston, 110
Stephen Camp, 110
HIGGINS
Eaner Peter, 356
Peter Gunnar, 356
HIGHLAND
Anna Lee, 250
Atha Ula, 363

James I., 250, 363
HILEMAN
Aaron Lawson, 353
Anda Aaron, 353
Calvin David, 354
Charles Alfred Lewis, 353
Flod Isaac, 353
Henry Carl, 354
Howard Andrew Taft, 353
Juliet Luanna, 353
Maude Arlene Ruth, 353
Maude Lee, 354
Nancy Catherine, 213
Samuel, 198
Samuel Jacob, 353, 354
HILL
Daniel Frank, 203
Delliah Belle, 206
Elizabeth, 130
Flora Ann, 131
Flora May, 203
John Abraham, 375
Mariam, 375
Miriam, 375
Samuel T., 203
Summers R., 246
William B., 246
HINDMAN
Jane, 157
John, 157
HINES
Myrtle I., 353
HINKLE
Abraham, 189
Charles P., 186
Darius, 186
Dorsey Doyle, 318
Ella Gay, 318, 363, 365
Ethel Julia, 318
Eunice, 217
Eva, 186
George A., 189
George Allen, 189, 318
Henrietta Jane, 315
Henry C., 186
Icy M., 186
John Earl, 189
Margie Virginia, 351
Opal Marie, 319
Sarah, 186
Walter Guy, 319
Willie Beryl, 319
HINRICKSEN
Eugenia, 264
HINZMAN
Abraham, 144, 145, 232

Abram, 145
Eathen Egbert, 414
Effie D., 235
Elizabeth Ann, 146
Florence Almeda, 199
Florence May, 145, 235
Isaac Newton, 145
James Lewis, 145, 234
John William, 145, 232, 235
Laco Raymond, 232, 235
Margaret Mary, 144
Mary, 145
Mary Catherine, 145
Perry Green, 145
Robert R., 199
Sarah Ann, 145, 235
Sophia L., 145
Wanita Lee, 414
William B., 145
HITT
Ruth, 401
HOFF
Adrian C., 414
Alice A., 236, 414
Amos Lewis, 237
Catheline, 414
Charlotte Columbia, 146, 237
Clelland, 414
Edna A., 237
Elizabeth, 414
Elosia M., 236
Emma, 147
Eri Benson, 146, 236
Frank, 237
George S., 146, 236
Hiram J., 146
John, 146, 237
Lela Pearl, 236, 414
Lewis R., 147
Loyd L., 147
Lyda C., 237
Martha N., 147
Mary C., 146
Minnie Maud, 236, 413
Neff Corliss, 236, 414
Rebecca Jane, 146
Rebeccca Jane, 238
Robert, 414
Rosa Byrd, 147
Samuel, 146
Silas Marion, 147
Vera M., 236
Virgil, 414
Virgil R., 236
W. A. L., 146
HOFFMAN

Martha Anderson, 230
William Edwin, 244
HOGUE
Esther, 253
HOLBERT
Carroll Nixon, 403
Edith Elizabeth, 403
Hayward Janes, 403
Irene Margaret, 403
Mary J., 204
Nellie Mildred, 403
Reuben Elijah, 204
Robert Trasin, 403
Samuel Ray, 403
HOLCOMB
Brent H., 40
HOLDER
John Anthony, 181
Margaret, 179, 181
Nancy, 207
HOLLIDAY
Margaret F., 193
Myrtle, 306
HOLMES
Hattie Susan, 364
John M., 364
Kennethe., 378
HORNER
William S., 63
HORNOR
Genevieve, 239
Thomas M., 239
William F., 239
HORTON
Alice, 256
Edna L., 256
Francis A., 256
Georgia D., 256
Hershell, 256
Irene J., 256
Lory, 256
Marshall, 256
Millie M., 256
Omer C., 256
Timothy M., 256
HOSKINS
Elizabeth, 211
Margret, 43
HOTCHKISS
Helena M., 442
HOUSEHOLDER
Daniel, 254
Mardge, 430
Milton, 254, 429
HOUSER
Phillip, 131

HOUSTON
Mary, 166
HOWARD
Frances, 87
HOWELL
Chester Orval, 373
David Lenzie, 416
Wilson Victoria, 416
HOWSER
Phillip, 131
HUCK
Captain, 16
HUDDLESTON
Thomas, 90
HUDGINS
Charles, 408
HUFF
Cecil Alexander, 218
Dorsey Elden, 218, 382, 383
Fern, 382
Hannah E., 382
Jennie Myrtle, 218
John Wesley, 383
Juanita, 382
Mary M., 383
Rachel, 114
William J., 217
HUGHES
Priscilla, 222
HUGO
Anna Flora, 166
HULL
Linda, 48, 76
Margaret, 266
HULLINGER
Lawrence W., 351
HUME
Julius W., 111
Loren, 74, 110
Loren Clark, 111
HUNNINGTON
Eleanor E., 254
HUNT
Rhoda, 71
HURD
Maria, 100
HURLBURT
Robert W., 112
HUSK
Elizabeth, 215
Ida Opal, 347
Mary J., 192
Nancy, 197
HUSTEAD
Magdaline, 229

HUTTO
Martha, 93

I

INGRAM
Nola, 409
IREDELL
James, Jr., 30
IRELAND
Albert Law, 368
Franklin Greydon, 368

J

JACKSON
John, 178
Mary, 151
Norma Lea, 232
P. E., 232
Richard G., 378
Ruth E., 412
Sara Ida, 178
JACQUES
Edwin Denton, 244
JAMES
Edith, 359
Hannah, 121
JAMISON
Norma, 232
JANES
Carline Meredith, 403
Howard Martin, 228, 403
Louis Taylor, 228
Rebecca Louise, 403
Robert L., 228
Zana B., 228, 403
JARRETT
Calvin, 30
JARVIS
G. Jennings, 359
Love Cinderella, 203
Price, 359
Samuel, 203
JEFFREY
Tacy Jane, 135
JEFFREYS
Cora A., 147
JENNINGS
Mary Caroline, 200
JESSUPS
Sellers E., 214
JETT
Letitia, 88, 122
Susan, 88
JEWELL
Albert, 203

Flavilla Catharine, 203
JIVIDEN
Charles A., 130
JOHNSON
Abner, 33
Carolyn Carter, 43
Catharine, 86
Clare Dean, 420
Samuel, 33
Sylvia, 180
Timothy R., 19, 20
Wilda, 405
William, 31
JOHNSTON
Andrew, 68
Ann Wyatt, 264
Caroline, 68
Daniel, 68
DeWitt Clinton, 103
Dewitt Clinton, 103
DeWitt Clinton, 103, 162
Edward Scott, 264
Elizabeth, 68
Eugene Hinricksen, 264
Harold Bauer, 264
Harold Whetstone, 162, 264
James Bower, 162
James Thompson, 68, 103
Jane, 68
John, 31
John Herring, 103
Katherine, 264
Lavinia, 68
Louise, 264
Mary, 264
Sarah Ann, 68
William, 68
William Wirt, 103, 162
JONES
Angeline, 255
Benjamin, 120
Bert David, 215, 376
Boyd Haines, 375
Dale Wren, 376
David Haynes, 214
Elias, 214
Eliza W., 85
Ernest Elias, 215, 374
Flossie, 393
Frances Marie, 375
George Herman, 393, 394
Gerald Nolan, 394
Haynes O., 374
Hayward Denver, 374
Horace King, 183
Howard Harrison, 215, 375

Howard Hill, 376
Hugh, 85
James Morris, 215, 374
Janet Winoadene, 394
Lloyd James, 375
Loanna, 394
Marilyn Davis, 131, 142
Martha, 85
Marvin, 183
Mary Frances, 174
Mary Virginia, 394
Minnie Elizabeth, 215, 373
Pauline Ethel, 394
Roxana, 374
Ruby Fern, 376
Sarah, 264
Sarah A., 120
JORDAN
Katherine Gilman, 441
Madeline, 201
Marjorie Stewart, 441
Mary Leighton, 441
JUSTIS
Marcie, 372

K

KASSON
Achash A., 109, 173
Albert H., 108
Alexander, 36, 109
Alexander J., 72
Alvin, 72
Amasa C., 72, 109
Andrew Eugene, 100
Anna, 36
Annette S., 110
Archibald, 72, 108, 109, 173
Austin, 72
Bernard R., 108
Burrell W., 108
Charles B., 72, 108
Chauncey C., 72, 109
Clara E., 109
Cordelia R., 108
Day H., 108
Dexter N., 109
Doney, 72
Dorsey, 390
Earle C., 109, 173
Edgar A., 109
Edward, 173
Elias, 101
Eliza, 173
Elizabeth, 72
Ellen C., 108

Emily Jane, 173
Emma Jane, 108, 109
Ephraim, 72, 109
Florence, 110
Frank, 109
Frank V., 173
George B., 72, 109
George H., 109
George Washington, 36
Gibson, 109
Harriet, 109
Harry, 173
Harvey, 36, 72
Harvey A., 109
Harvey Z., 72
Hattie, 173
Helen J., 109
Herbert Mason, 173
Hiram, 72
James, 72, 108, 109
James S., 109
James W., 108
Jane, 108
Jane M., 73
Jeremiah William, 109, 173
Joseph, 72, 73
Julius, 109
Kate, 173
Lewis H., 109
Lois Cornelia, 109
Lovina, 72
Lucy S., 108, 173
Lura M., 110
Lydia, 72
Margaret, 72
Martin, 109
Marvin, 73, 110
Mary, 108, 172
Mary F., 173
Mary Marilla, 108
Mason G., 72, 108
Mason T., 108
Melvina, 73
Mortimer, 109
Mortimer Bricknal, 108
Nancy, 72
Nathan B., 72
Nellie, 172
Nelson, 72, 109
Nettie Ann, 173
Olive, 36, 74
Olive M., 109
Ophelia, 108
Orange H., 108
Orrin N., 109
Orson V., 109, 173

Phebe, 36
Polly, 36
Robert, 36, 108
Robert, Jr., 72
Robert N., 108
Sally Ann, 72
Samantha M., 73
Samuel H., 173
Sarah A., 109, 173
Sarah Antonette, 109
Sarah Luella, 109
Smira, 72
Sophronia, 108
Stealla Louisa, 173
Susan E., 110
Susan N., 73
Thompson, 72, 108
Watson, 73
William, 36, 72
William A., 173
William Alexander, 108, 172
William Earle, 108
KAYSER
James H., 228
Lillian E., 224
Scott, 224
KEE
Sallig, 44
KEEN
Nora Vella, 406
KEENER
Lertie T., 359
Marian, 412
Mildred Kathleen, 359
KEILEY
Margaret Ann, 265
Matthew, 265
KELL
Jane, 57
Janet, 41
Thomas, 41, 57
KELLEM
Alice Ray, 439
Dorothy Charlotte, 439
Fred Clinton, 439
KELLER
Angeline M., 129
KELLEY
Ellen, 129
Ezekiel, 138
Ila, 201
John Fillmore, 138
Mary E., 221
KELLISON
Clara, 371
KELLY C.

Jane Louise, 419
KEMPER
John W., 233
Lucinda F., 187
Rosa Mildred, 233
KENNEDY
Dorsey, 390
Dorsey C., 366, 390
Harry W., 390
Jack W., 366
John Loman, 366, 390
Mattie E., 390
KER
Catherine, 34
Elizabeth, 34
William, 34
KERBY
James F., 133
James Warner, 133
KERN
Franklin William, 429
KERNS
Catherine, 131
Laura, 211
KERR
John, 93
KESTER
Dortha Lee, 410
KEY
Eleanor, 55
KIBLER
Carole, 420
Charles H., 420
KIDD
Mary, 113
KIGER
Burl Hartzel, 364
KILGORE
Elizabeth, 96
KINCHELOE
Lawrence Golding, 153
KINDLE
Eddith M., 369
Harmon, 369
KING
Belinda, 123, 185
Carl Brooks, 316
Charles P., 174
Charlotte M., 437
Cornelious, 123
David, 101
Elijah VanBuren, 123
Elizabeth, 88, 103
Enoch, 94, 154
Florence, 441
George Jackson, 316

Ira Arden, 316
James, 101
James Edward, 316
Jane Elizabeth, 101
Janie Iantha, 253
John, 101
John Presley, 316
John Pressly, 236
Lillie Mabel, 236, 316
Martha A., 154
Mary Anne, 101
Mary Gleason, 174
Mary Janeq, 154
Mary Louise, 316
Meta Gay, 316
Nancy Jane, 254
KING HENRY IV, 1
KING LOUIS XIV, 1
KIRACOFE
Larry Hamilton, 380
Otis Ray, 380
KIRBY
Geneva Powers, 406
KIRK
Caleb Lewis, 155
Sarah, 154
KIRKLAND
Samuel Simpson, 85
KIRKPATRICK
Abby, 101
Alexander, 33, 104
Amanda Bausin, 100
Andrew, 33
Ann, 67, 102
Anna, 101
Anne, 34
Anne Amelia, 101
Anne Eliza, 100
David, 33
Elias, 67, 101
Elizabeth, 34, 67, 101, 104
Ellen, 47
Emily, 101
Frederick, 101
Hannah, 34
Hugh, 67, 101, 103
Jacob Hurd, 100
James, 67, 101
James Harris, 101
Jane, 67, 102
Janet, 33
Jennet, 4, 33
John, 33, 67
John Franklin, 103
Josiah Layton, 101
Lydia, 67, 101

Manning Rutan, 100
Margaret, 34
Martha, 35
Mary, 34, 44, 67, 102
Mary "Polly", 33
Sarah, 34, 67, 68, 100
Thomas, 33, 67, 100
Walter, 101
William, 101
KLINE
Anne Eliza, 102
David, 102
Ellen Taylor, 102
Franklin Miller, 102
Joh Cassedy, 102
Mary Malvina, 102
Peter R. Fisher, 102
Phoebe, 102
William H., 102
KNIGHT
Edward J., 231
Esther, 35
Ida, 189
Minnie Myrtle, 313
Ollie Blanche, 231
KNISH
Alex, 356
KNOX
Anna Mary, 181
Hugh, 31, 62
James, 30, 61
James, Sr., 44
Jane, 61
Jannett, 44
Jeanette, 11
John, 30, 31
Nancy Gaston, 62, 85
Sarah, 31
William, 30
KOWALSKY
Anna, 427
Edward, 427
Frances, 426
Genevieve, 426
Helen, 427
Peter John, 426
KRENN
Mary, 370
KROUTH
Jessie E., 213
KUHL
Phillip Aaron, 360
Ruby Chloe, 360
KUHY
Frances C., 134

L
LACY
Col. Edward, 56
LAMAR
Caleb H., 174
LAMBRIGHT
Virgil, 404
LANDRUM
Betty, 411
LANE
Job, 103
Martha Jane, 103
LANHAM
Mary Elizabeth, 404
LANTZ
Arthur William, 203
George Washington, 203
Robert Lester, 374
LARUE
Jane B., 164
LATIMER
Stephen, 59
LATTA
Mary, 80
LAW
Alta C., 221
Alva A., 217, 381
Anna, 217
Arden Lester, 220, 388
Arden Ray, 388
Argil G., 226
Asby S., 90
Asby Steele, 216, 380
Aubrey Elwin, 226
Audley Pall, 217
Audrey Mae, 219
Boneva, 387
Burleigh Aubrey, 219, 388
Byrl L., 387
Carl D., 218, 385
Carl D., Jr., 385
Caroline, 90
Celia Catherine, 385
Clyde O., 219
Daltie L., 221
Darrell G., 387
Darwin, 384
David Gutherie, 218
David Guthrie, 137
David Kyle, 383
Della, 220
Denver Gene, 386
Edith Daire, 384
Elaine, 385
Eldridge Dile, 383

Elizabeth, 135, 136, 137, 218
Elizabeth A., 218
Elizabeth R., 386
Ermine D., 218
Eva Lora, 218, 385
Excel L., 221
Ford D., 384
Francis Marion, 137, 217
Glenn C., 221
Glenn Gale, 219
Hannah, 137, 217
Harlan M., 387
Helen Louise, 386
Herman, 387
Holmes G., 382
Howard Gaston, 217
Icen Dennis, 220
Ila Pearl, 218
Irene, 387
Iva V., 219
Ivy Gae, 226
Jackson Woodford, 219, 387
James David, 386
James Phillips, 399
James S., 226
James Wesley, 226, 399
Jennings Virgil, 220, 389
John, 384
John W., 90
John William, 137, 216
Layton Brooks, 389
Letha Lora, 221
Levi Morris, 137, 219
Lewis A., 226
Lona Orpha, 389
Louie Dow, 218, 384
Lucy Gay, 402
Mabel, 388
Martin Luther, 137, 218
Mary Catherine, 373
Mary M., 386
Mary Mildred, 383
Melva Gay, 387
Melva Roxanna, 220
Merle E., 221
Mona V., 383
Newton, 137, 220
Nora I., 226
Ocean Wave, 218
Olive B., 217, 381
Oma Zella, 218
Ona Orpha, 221
Ora Alice, 217, 381
Ora Lester, 226
Orla F., 226
Orman D., 219

Orphra, 221
Osa E., 226
Owen B., 220
Paul Winfield, 400
Raymond Doyle, 389
Raymond G., 381
Richie D., 218, 383, 384
Rosalie Iris, 388
Rosalie Marie, 381
Rose Luella, 217
Rosemary Nell, 385
Royston D., 219, 386
Russell, 219
Ruth Claire, 384
Sarah Melvian, 367
Starling Dale, 384
Stella M., 220
Sylvia Mida, 218, 386
Thelma V., 384
Theo Mayrie, 387
Thomas Sherman, 137
Tossie Darlie, 220
Tracy Forest, 219, 388
Troy G., 382
Velma M., 219
Vener Vadis, 219, 386
Verl, 387
Verner Vadis, 386
Vernon Swisher, 387
William, 135, 136
William F. E., 137, 221
William Jesse, 226
Zora L., 219, 387
LAWSON
Ailsey, 252
Arnett, 411
Charles Edward, 411
Cornelius, 144
Cornelius Conway, 232
Eda A., 146
Henry C., 145
Ida May, 248
John Columbus, 145
Joseph S., 145
Leroy Mifflin, 246
Mary Ernestine, 246
Molly, 405
Olive Melissa, 232, 235
Rebecca E., 233
Sam D., 121
Theophilus Bailey, 145
William, 146, 169
William T., 144
LAYTON
James Finley, 100
John, 100

Josiah, 100
Mary Anne, 100
Thomas, 100
LEARY
Evelyn, 269
George, 269
George Daniel, 269
Lewis Gaston, 269
Russell Woodward, 269
LEASE
Rosa, 361
LEE
Adelaide, 116
Charles H., 207
Florence Lillie, 209
Ida Alice, 207
J. N., 176
James F., 209
LEESON
Charles L., 197
Eli B., 195
Ida Ellen, 195
John P., 197
LEFEVRE
Laura Hasbrouk, 269
LEGGETT
Alpha Mary, 355
Catherine, 139
Columbus Newman, 354
Martha Ellen, 224
Mina Jane, 367
Zura E., 354
LEIBOLD
Robert Gene, 397
LEMASTERS
Columbus David, 304
LEMASTERS
Donald Daniel, 353
LEMASTERS
Francis Marion, 303
LEMASTERS
Mitchell J., 353
LEMASTERS
Nellie M., 304
Nettie, 304
Ruby Jane, 303
Rufus, 303
Ruth M., 303
Stella, 304
LEMELY
Edis, 425
LEMMON
Mary, 3
LEMON
Olivet, 3, 82

LEONARD
Elizabeth, 181
Kathleen, 417
LEVELLE
Katherine M., 408

LEW
Jane, 151, 401
LEWIS
James, 42
Margaret Eliza, 83, 116
Nancy, 120
Samuel, 83
Sarah Elizabeth, 241
LIEBER
Lottie Laurentine, 195
LIEVING
George Washington, 403
LIFE
B. J., 187
Eliza, 145
Laura Beulah, 187
Noah, 145
LIMAR
Mary, 209
LINDSEY
Mary, 142
LINES
Frances Amelia, 108
LINGER
Charles Bee, 221
Madge Jane, 203
Nicholas Fairburn, 221
LININGER
Lura Alma, 219
LINN
Andrew, 133
Diana, 133
Joseph, 35
Margaret, 35
Mary, 231
LINSEY
Mary, 206
LIPPINCOTT
Albert, 99
Chester, 161
George, 161
John, 99
John Woodrow, 99, 161
Margaret, 99
Margret Orr, 161, 264
Martha, 161
Mary, 161
Wilson, 99
Woodrow, 161
LIPPS

Willa Jane, 234
LOCKWOOD
Hamilton Davidson, 172
May Davidson, 172
LOGAN
Capt. William, 5
Margaret, 22, 41
Roy Emery, 378
William, 4
LOHAN
Michael, 201
Wella, 201
LONG
Ethel Wyn, 175
Frederick Theodore, 175
Frederick W., 175
George L., 175
Mayfred, 175
Ronald, 175
LOOMIS
Eunice, 37
LOUGH
Albert J., 234
Mary Caroline, 216
Ralph Jerome, 234
LOUTHERS
Rulina, 125
LOVE
Jenet, 42
John Boyd, 42
Richard, 43
LOVETT
Laura Lillian, 249
Nelle Lovett, 249
LOWELL
_, 108
LOWRY
John B., 134
Samuel, 15
LOWTHER
Barbara Susana, 183
James Samson, 193
Mary Elizabeth, 193
Minnie Kendall, 121, 211
Rulina A., 125
LQ
Howard W., 221
LUPARDUS
Maysel Lucille, 406
LYLE
Elizabeth, 65
Robert, 65
LYNCH
George M., 140
Isaac, 140
Jesse John, 409

Martha Alice, 409
Mary Jane, 409
Mona Louise, 409
Sara Eliza, 250
Sarah Eliza, 363
Verona May, 314
LYONS
Harry, 262
Joseph, 97
Louisa, 189

M
MAAS
Gene & Norma, 32
MACE
Oliver Francis, 353
Virginia Murl, 353
MACON
Nathaniel, 30
MADDOX
Albert M., 131
Alice, 204
Alonzo T., 131, 205, 206
Anna, 89, 132
Archimedes Adolphus, 203
Arnold M., 89, 131
Ashford Dale, 207
Bess, 204
Brady Craig, 205, 361
Charles Green, 131, 206
Charles Hess, 207
Chester Boyd, 206
Columbia A., 130
Dorcas, 89
Dorcas Ann, 208
Earnest Ray, 204
Edith Jeanette, 208
Effie Ruhamah, 207
Elizabeth Jean, 361
Ellie, 132
Fannie V., 132, 208
Flavius Clinton, 206, 362
Flora Belle, 207
Flourney Matthew, 130, 204
Francis, 362
Freddie, 204
George G., 130, 204
Granville Loebe, 207
Harley, 204
Harry Rector, 207
Henry T., 132
Herman Bruce, 207
Hiram, 130
Hoadley F., 206
Horace M., 131

Ida May, 208
Infant, 361
Irving Thomas, 131, 207
James Bradford, 207
James Gaston, 89, 131
James Lewis, 131, 207, 208
James Oren, 361
James Roy, 207
James S., 363
Jane, 130
Janet Sue, 361
John G., 89, 130
Junius, 204
Kenna, 204
Larry Donovan, 361
Laverna J., 130
Leon, 204
Lloyd Arnold, 207
Lloyd Herbert, 206
Lona Lee, 207
Lory Dove, 206, 362
Lucy J., 132
Lycurgus, 131, 207
M. M., 204
Madeline, 373
Mae, 362
Mansfield, 89, 131
Margaret, 89, 130
Marley M., 204
Martha Elizabeth, 132
Mary E., 130
Mary Elizabeth, 203
Mary L., 131
Matthew, 89, 130
Matthew Arnold, 131
Max E., 363
Maxwell, 362
Mindia A., 206, 362
Montgomery H., 131
Myrtle Ina, 206
Nancy Bell, 132
Nathan King, 362
Ofa O., 204
Okey V., 206
Oley E., 204
Oliver, 89
Ona A., 207
Oren Clair, 205, 361
Orlando Roscoe, 207
Orville B., 206, 362
Otto Oly, 206, 362
Pearly Mae, 206
Raleigh F., 205
Rebecca, 130
Rennea, 204
Robert C., 362, 363

Robert Dale, 361
Robert Matthew, 208
Robert West, 363
Rome Boyd, 206
Roy Leon, 361
Ruby Olive, 208
Ruhama, 89, 132
Sarah C., 130, 131
Sarah Victoria, 131
Susan Adaline, 131, 205, 206
Thomas, 89, 130
Thomas B., 130
Vera Gray, 207
Wade L., 207
Warren Hayden, 207, 363
West Mansfield, 208, 363
Willia, 205, 206
William, 89
William D., 89
William D., Jr., 130
William Hill, 131, 206, 228
William Jeptha, 132
William Rufus, 130, 204
William U., 131
MADDUX
  William Wesley, 82
MADER
  Clara Margaret, 423
MADERA
  Clark, 184
  Marion C., 184
MADSON
  Margaret, 410
MAHAN
  Laura Myrtle, 404
MANFULL
  Berthinda, 154, 155
  Dorcas, 154
  Jane, 154
  Rebecca, 154
  Salina, 154
  William S., 154, 155
MANLEY
  Claudia, 401
  Harrison Jefferson, 209, 365
  Harrison Manley, 209
  James M., 401
  Madison, 132
  Madison West, 209, 365
  Richard T., 209
MANLY
  Charles, 30
  Hannah, 85
  Jane, 85
  Mathias Evans, 85
MANN

Mary, 390
Raymond A., 207
Robert, 425
MANNING
  Raymond A., 132
MANUEL
  William, 29
MARPLE
  Mildred Elizabeth, 226
  Theodore William, 226
MARSH
  Annis Rebecca, 232
  Lucinda, 221
  Ruby, 201
MARSHALL
  Captain, 56, 57
  Faye Mildred, 379
  Harry Richard, 362
  John, 29
  Mathe Eugenia, 362
  Naomi Grey, 362
  Paul, 362
  Ralph L., 362
MARTIN
  Abraham Irving, 164
  Agnes, 18
  Captain Edward, 19
  Charles Leander, 172
  Edward, 15, 172
  Edward William, 172
  Flora Frances, 229
  Frederick H. A., 172
  George B. McClellan, 172
  James Allen, 172
  Robert, 75
MASON
  Edna, 242
  Gertrude, 441
  Jacob A., 224
  Jane, 98
  Lona, 392
  Mary Virginia, 224
MASSEY
  John Murray, 59
MATCHIN
  Lydia, 105
MATHENY
  Maude, 416
MATHIS
  S., 23
MATTHEWS
  Frank Benjamin, 148
  Philena Bird, 148
  William J., 148
MAXEY
  Edward, 11

MAXSON
Carlton Hershel, 373
Elisha John, 373
Elva, 373
Hannah Pearl, 373
Iris Azalia, 373
John David, 373
Mariam Grace, 374
Marvel, 146
Olive Josetta, 373
Susan Jane Gertrude, 373
Wayman Eugene, 374
Winifred Leigh, 374
MAXWELL
Boyd Curtis, 322
Charles L., 322
Infant Son, 322
Levi, 391
Mabel I., 322
Mary Grace, 322
MAYER
Charles Oscar, 362
James Clifton, 362
MAYO
Nellie Frances, 248
MCALISTER
Mattie E., 182
Nora, 181
MCBRIDE
Levi L., 155
MCCAIN
Daniel, 5
James, 5
Jane, 82
MCCALLA
Carolina, 116, 178
Richard C., 116
MCCALLY
Isa M., 242
MCCARTY
Dorothy Lee, 379
MCCAULEY
Maude, 351
MCCLAIN
Charity, 95
Charles, 95
Georgia Amanda, 403
Samuel, 95
MCCLASKEY
Bessie Alma, 328
MCCLOUD
Helen Annette, 216
MCCLUER
Janet, 43
Jas., 43
MCCLURE

Capt. Hugh, 23
Captain, 11
Captain John, 56, 57
Eliza Jane, 83, 116
Hannah, 46, 60, 61, 83
Hannah Martha, 12, 44
Hugh, 46, 83
James, 15, 44
John, 15, 45, 46, 55
Martha, 15, 46, 67, 168
Martha A., 259
Mary, 15, 55
Mary Gaston, 15
Matthew, 15
Samuel, 55
William, 15, 46, 60
MCCONKEY
Frances E., 225
Susanna, 226
MCCONNELL
Ezekiel, 93
Jane, 119
Lucinda Ada, 120
Margaret "Peggy", 115
MCCONNUHHAY
Amanda Catherine, 179
MCCOWEN
John Mehelm, 68
William, 68
MCCRARY
John, 43
Margaret, 9
Samuel, 9
MCCREARY
James, 11, 23, 41
Jno. M., 79
John, 23, 41
Margaret, 57
Samuel, 41
William, 79
Wm., 75
MCCUMBERS
Albert, 202
Jewel Lockie, 202
MCDANIEL
Emily Susan, 419
MCDILL
David, 75
Mary, 47
MCDONALD
Harriett M., 227
Mary Elizabeth, 189
Sabra Ellen, 228
MCDONALD
Sarah, 231
MCDOWELL

Elizabeth Arlene, 378
MCELRATH
_, 119
Mrs. Hugh Gaston, 84
MCEOWEN
Mary, 33
MCFADDEN
Mary Buford ""Polly", 82
Nancy "Jane", 82
MCGEHEE
Benjamine, 59
Catherine, 155
MCGILL
Charles, 268
Frances Harriette, 430
Mary Edith, 430
Max Pittinger, 430
MCGINNIS
Mabel, 422
MCILVAINE
Belle, 261
Caroline, 261
George W., 261
MCINTIRE
Bertha, 189
Dolph C., 189, 319
Ellen Louise, 189
Estella May, 189
Flora D., 189
James F., 189
John P., 189
Julia West, 123
Lura, 415
Marcoda Melinda, 189, 318
Presley, 189
Samuel, 123
Thomas J., 189
MCINTYRE
Clarinda L., 195
Fred C., 189, 320
Geraldine Dyer, 319
Harold Franklin, 320
Howard Lee, 320
Irene V., 319
James Wilson, 319
Julia Virginia, 320
Maxine June, 320
Mildred Rosalee, 396
Samuel, 189
Sophia, 197
MCKELVEY
John, 42
MCKINLEY
Alrose, 236, 368
Mida, 218
William H., 218

MCKINNEY
Evelyn Clara, 410
Jasper N., 145
Laura Belle, 233
Lowman, 235
Minnie, 145
Ray, 235
William P., 233, 235
MCKOWN
Jno. M., 79
MCLURE
Martha, 44, 46
MCMARTIN
Joseph, 34
MCMASTER
Hannah Jane, 112
MCMILLAN
Clyde S., 415
Jane, 58, 67
Jane "Jennet", 84
John Ira, 415
MCMILLEN
Margaret, 80
MCMULLEN
John, 81
MCNEILL
Minnie Hermine, 368
MCON, 225
MCPHERSON
Elizabeth Weir, 113
L. D., 81
Margaret B., 369
Robert Alexander, 369
Ruth, 67
MCQUAIN
Albert M., 237
Fernie Oleta, 237
MCQUISTON
Andrew, 75
Hugh, 75, 77
Margaret, 47
MCREIGHT
Agnes, 18
MCVICKER
Agnes, 363
MCWHORTER
Albert, 122
Alma, 185
Daniel Grant, 252, 418
Eliza Ann, 312
Frank, 253
Helen Virginia, 253
John M., 185
Mary E., 150
Nathan G., 252
Ralph, 252, 418, 429

Walter, 252
William Clayton, 253
William Henry, 253
MEADOR
Rosella E., 179
MEANS
Ethel, 178
Joseph D., 178
Mary Ann, 145
Rebecca, 144, 145, 232
MEEKER
Charlotte, 105
MEEKS
Brady Jackson, 373
Carl A., 373
MEELER
Catherine, 177
Eliza Ann, 176
MEHARD
Churchill Brown, 269
Samuel Smiley, Jr., 269
MEHELM
Martha, 68
MELICK
Aaron, 70
Catherine, 71
Charlotte, 70
Charlotte M., 106
Daniel, 70, 71, 106, 171
David, 71
Elizabeth, 70, 106, 107
Emeline F., 106
John, 70, 106
Joseph G., 106
Margaret, 70
Mary, 70
Nicholas A., 106
Rosanna, 70, 106
William, 71, 106, 171
William H., 106
MELTON
Elaine, 405
Harold C., 405
MERCER
Iva, 177
Silas, 177
MEREDITY
Ruby V., 403
MERRITT
Martha J., 361
Martin, 361
MERSHON
Clara L., 254
METCALF
Nettie, 112
MEYERS

Frank, 372
MICK
Mathias J., 208
Sarah Louise, 208
MILLER
Alexander, 35
Barbara, 388
Ben F., 414
Bernard Lindsey, 405
Catherine, 70
George, 356
Glada, 249
Henrietta, 412
Hunter, 414
Kenneth, 437
Lois Ellen, 356
Margaret K., 437
Opal Faye, 404
Ruth, 35
Vera Mabel, 414
MINEAR
Jasper, 158, 261
Moses, 158
Ward, 433
Warren, 433
MINNIE
Jane, 359
MINTER
Jane, 150
MITCHELL
Daniel, 217
Emma, 372
Iva Gay, 415
Margaret, 75
Phebe Rebecca, 217
Viola Jane, 353
MOELICH
Aaron, 70
MOFFAT
Thomas, 4
MOFFATT
Israel, 50
J. R., 16, 49
MOFFETT
Addie Beatrice, 251
George Washington, 251
Ross, 188
MOISE
T. Sidney, 116
MONTGOMERY
Grace Elsie May, 444
MOODY
Mary, 123
MOORE
Annie, 180
Charity, 159

Margaret Adelaide, 120
Sarah Jane, 97
Sarah Melissa, 261
William, 98
MORAN
Edna Lora, 391
Elbert Ervin, 391
Ocie Virl, 392
Opal, 391
MORGAN
Ann E., 157
Anna Virginia, 353
Francis, 157
Hugh, 157
Mary N., 157
Matilda, 157
Patience A., 157
Samuel, 156, 157
Tephanes, 157
MORRIS
Alta Estel, 338
Benjamin, 150
Dona Leigh, 245, 420
Edwin, 338
Elizabeth, 90
Ellsworth, 231
Erma Marie, 338
Etta Maude, 149, 243
Eva, 230
James Benjamin, 149, 245
Laverna Opal, 338
Lillian L., 245
Lucy Pauline, 149
Mary Charlotte, 149, 242, 245
Mary Margaret, 150
Pauline E., 229
Rosanna, 70
Samuel, 90
Sarah Ann, 150
Thomas Ervin, 149, 151
Thomas S., 150
William Henry, 149, 151
MORRISON
Alice Virqinia, 233
Charles A., 221
Charlotte, 364
John Jay, 221
Luella Jane, 207
Margaret, 253, 429
Margaret Columbia, 235
Marshal Jackson, 253
Marshal Paul, 253
Monroe, 235
Nancy C., 365
O. J., 207
Patience, 95

Susan (Eliza), 156
MORROW
Hallie Louise, 229, 409
Mildred, 229
Othor Jesse, 229
Pauline E., 409
MOSES
George Willard, 411
MOSS
Alma R., 362
Charles W., 362
Elizabeth A., 86
Ephraim, 85, 86
James, 86
John G., 362
Marjorie Catherine, 401
Mary, 86
Thomas Riley, 401
William, 86
William Neely, 401
Wilma Ruth, 401
MOUNT
Catherine, 64
Charles, 93
Elizabeth T., 93
Ezekiel L., 63
James, 63, 93
John Gaston, 63, 93
Margaret, 64
Rebecca, 64
Sexto, 64
Sexton Emley, 93
MOWEN
Alice, 240
MUNDELL
Dale, 247
Edna E., 247, 423
Ernest G., 247
Grace, 247
Leonidas, 247
Nora O., 247
Osa D., 247
MURPHY
Bernard G., 207
Louvena, 211
Sarah Lauretta, 85
MUSGRAVE
Bashaba, 190
Herbert D., 364
Mary Alice, 364
MYERS
Mary E., 251
Rodney Lee, 366

N
NANGLE
Bonnie Faye, 235
J. M., 235
NEALE
Alfred Earle, 239
William Henry, 239
NEALY
James, 10
NEELY
Arnett R., 400
Bertie, 187
Donald R., 400
Edwin R., 400
Emily Gwendolyn, 401
Ethel, 227, 401
George W., 227, 400
Guinn, 227, 400
John Howard, 227, 401
Joseph M., 401
Lee Roy, 401
Lucy Virginia, 400
William Edward, 400
William R., 227, 400
NEILSEN
Dallin S., 80
NELSON
Margaret, 32
NESBIT
Jane, 62
NETZER
Mattie Jane, 304
NEVIRES
Susanna, 103
NEVIUS
Ann, 106
NEWBERGER
Caroline, 235
NEWELL
Carl David, 412
Charles E., 412
Charles Edward, 412
NEWLON
Zelda, 218
NICHOLAS
Cain, 121
Francis, 121
NICHOLES
Alma, 361
NICHOLS
Margaret, 430
NICHOLSON
Bertie, 393
Susie Davis, 90, 198

NICKELS
James, 58
Sarah, 58, 179
NICKLIN
John G., 425
NICOLES
Nona Myrtle, 241
William J., 241
NIEMEIER
Willa A., 244
NIX
Frances Ann, 81
NOOMAN
Maria, 109
NORMAN
Bonnie Beatrice, 412
Charles, 114
Charles Stephen, 177
Columbus L., 241
David D., 128
Icie Virginia, 241
Robert A., 412
Robert Lafayette, 114, 177
NORRIS
J. Wilmer, 150
Lucile Isabelle, 437
Maretta D., 150
Sarah Savannah, 229
NORTHRUP
Miriam, 36
NORTON
Huldah, 37
NUQ
Charles, 188
NUTTER
Alma Fern, 369
Anthony Raymond, 386
Bertie Ford, 214
Brenton Wellington, 369
Constance Elma, 369
Eli Marshall, 355
Elijah, 189
Elijah E., 188
Elizabeth, 370
Eugene Carlton, 369
Florence Cora, 214
Forest Glenn, 369
Harley W., 214
Ira Benton, 214
Ira Brenton, 369
John B., 213
Josiah Blaine, 214, 370
Josiah Porter, 213
Lane Bush, 213, 370
Laurel, 370
Lowell Dean, 369

Maple, 368
Marshal, 369
Marshall Field, 214, 368
Mary Elizabeth, 214, 370
Melinda Ann, 196, 199
Myrl, 368
Myrtle, 368
Nora, 189
Paul Strader, 368
Porter Gaston, 214, 368
Ruth, 368
Sarah, 236
Stella Pearl, 375
Susie Alethea, 355
Thomas Boyd, 375
William Morris, 370

O
OCHILTREE
Jas., 75
OGDEN
Sarah, 34
Stephen, 34
OLDAKER
Alton B., 236
Harrison, 236
OLIVER
Effie Pogue, 240
George P., 240
OLSON
Morgan T., 214
O'NEAL
Nancy, 162
ORR
Robert Meredith, 333
ORRAHOOD
Alexander III, 201
Fred Gaston, 201
Henry, 201
Pauline Olive, 201, 361
Robert Earl, 201
OSBORNE
Elizabeth C., 225
Joseph, 225
OSBURN
Mary L., 396, 397
OTISTO
Louisa M. French, 173
OURS
Richard, 408
OWENS
Clara Virginia, 243

P
PACE

Judge Joel, 11
PAGE
McHenry, 378
PALMER
Eva, 188
Rose, 434
PARENT
Lydia, 64
PARKER
Elmer O., 40
PARKS
Arley Curtis, 332
Ira Thomas, 332
Raymond Richards, 332
PARSONS
Emma, 207
James, 371
Nancy Belle, 131
PATRICK
Paul Elbert, 368
PATTEN
Sarah, 157
PATTERSON
J. L., 362
John, 75
PATTON
Annie Ocie Elzona, 189
Arlington A., 189
Charles C., 188, 317, 365
Daniel Starr, 371
Helen Virginia, 188
James Beryl, 189, 318
James David, 318
John G., 371
Mary Frances, 318
Mary M., 189
Melinda C., 189
Norval Gusman, 188
Phoebe J., 226
Roscoe, 318, 365
Wesley Germannis, 189
Wesley Gusman, 189
William N., 188
Zachariah D., 188
PEARCE
Bathanna, 162, 264
Hosea, 103, 162
James, 103
PEARSE
Harriet, 73
PEARSON
Bessie Mae, 180
William, 84
PEDEN
Andrew, 118
Jane A., 118

INDEX

PELL
Lillie May, 229
PENCE
William D., 253
PENNY
John, 260
Margaret, 94
Mary J., 260
Ruth C., 260
William James, 260
William S., 260
PEPIN
Allen, 434
Elizabeth, 434
Harry, 434
PEPPARD
William, 95
PEREAU
Luella, 170
PERINE
Ada May, 184
Agnes Laura, 302
Alcindia A., 302
Alice J., 185, 310
Alice Opal, 307
Benjamin H., 302
Bert B., 309
Cecil Don, 311
Chapman J., 185
Charles, 184
Charley Luther, 307
Clyde Blaine, 311
Columbus David, 121, 184
Daisy P., 312
David L., 120, 121
Don Columbus, 185, 311
Dona Alice, 184
Edith Pearl, 307
Edna Katherine, 309
Emery Goff, 185, 306
Ernest Carl, 309
Everett Lee, 307
Flossie Lee, 304
Gladys Roberta, 307
Grace Virginia, 302
Harry Goff, 306
Helen Pearl, 308
Howard McKinley, 304
Irvin, Jr., 309
Irvin Scott, 185, 308
Isaac, Jr., 120
John C., 185
Julia A., 121
Lacy Vaude, 304
Laura, 185, 305
Lelia Myrtle, 184

Lewis G., 306
Lillian Mary, 306
Lillie May, 185, 303
Louis, 185, 306
Lula Branch, 184
Luther Martin, 185, 307
Marie Ocal, 311
Martha Jane, 307
Mary Armathea, 185
Mary Magdalene, 311
Matilida, 185
Mattie Ocal, 304
Maude Gay, 185, 310
Nellie Jane, 309
Richard, 120, 121, 184
Richie Columbus, 308
Rosetta, 121, 183
Samuel N., 121
Samuel R., 302
Sarah Ann, 121, 184
Susanna Blanche, 303
Theresa Harriet, 302
Vonda Lenora, 306
Waitman T., 184
Walter Monroe, 185, 304
William L., 120
PERRENS
Artimissa M., 59
PERRINE
John, Jr., 86
Peter, Jr., 64
PERRY
John, 67
Max, 40
Rachel, 67
Thomas Jefferson Rice, 95
PETERS
Stacie Flo, 203
PETERSON
Gertrude, 246
Howard Gaston, 246, 421
Jasper, 245
John Pence, 245
Julia M., 241
Merceline, 232
PETTIGREW
Albert J., 189
PETTIT
Gertrude Maude, 382
PHENIX
Moses, 32
PHILIP
John R., 166
PHILLIP OF NAVARRE, 2
PHILLIPPI
Eva F., 406

PHILLIPS
Edwin Emanuel, 444
Edwin McKinley, 424
Garland F., 366
Garland Vernon, 366
Gertrude J., 264
Jerry, 366
Jessie Lasure, 366
Jo Ann, 366
John William, 219
Maymie Gay, 399
Rhoda Gay, 202
PHILPOTT
Bertha Adelle, 439
PICKENS
Flora May, 404
PIERCE
Dolliver Wendell, 339
Dora Edna M., 194
Hettie Jane, 194
Hughy James, 194
Jacob I., 416
Laura Maud, 194, 339
Lewis Earl, 416
Nettie Pearl, 338
Obidiah Wayne, 194
PIERPOINT
Hermione, 242
John Scott, 148, 242
Zackquill, 148
PIERSON
Alvin Carlos, 208
PILLARS
John H., 44
PITSENBARGER
Sherlie M., 406
PLATT
Elvira Gaston, 74
Lester Ward, 73, 74
PLUMMER
Eli, 162
Frederick, 162
Ralph, 162
POE
Carl W., Jr., 421
Carl Wayne, 421
Charles, 421
Geraldine L., 421
James E., 421
POHL
Emma M., 147
POLK
Samuel, 62
POOLE
Albert Ray, 404
Asby Poole, 136

POOLER
Elizabeth Alice, 432
Evelyn, 432
Frederick, 432
Helen Aileen, 432
Richard Duane, 432
Willma, 432
PORTER
Ann, 11, 42
Anne, 80
Janet, 54
Mary, 46, 55
Rev. A., 75
Rev. Alexander, 75
POSEY
Carrie Pearl, 203
Isaac, 203
POST
Bernard Gaston, 252
Dulcie, 389
Harold, 252
Hiram, 234
Howard, 252
Howard B., 252
Ida Bird, 151
Mary, 92
Mary Catherine, 252
Rachel, 252
Stella, 234
William, 151
POTTER
Emma Jane, 164
Samuel, 164
William K., 71
POWERS
Mary, 84
PREISLER
Anna, 261
PREVAST
Frances Mallet, 169
Louis, 169
PRICE
Sibyl Evelyn Schutte, 410
William Finley, 437
PRIDE
Ava Zetta, 374
PRINCE
Martha E., 176
Rutha Ann, 176
PRINE
Charles, 184
PRITCHARD
Eva Jane, 398
Mary J., 218
Mary Jane, 123
Thomas, 123

William, 124
PROCTOR
Victoria, 20
PRUNTY
Emma Gertrude, 336

Q
QUAST
Arthur Otto, 356
QUEEN
Albert, 359
Brooks Jennings, 234
Eliza, 208
Harley John, 360
Harvey, 360
Ira, 234
John Edward, 359
Lenora E., 359
Lola Josephine, 417
Lydia J., 145
Nina Lennie, 360
Theresa, 360
Verna Inez, 360
QUICK
Andrew, 267
Jane, 267, 440

R
RADABAUGH
Edna Hazel, 408
RAINEY
Ann, 57
Ann Gaston, 55
Matthew, 55, 57, 58
RAMAGE
Ann M., 239
RAMSBURG
Arville O., 419
Dorothea Jean, 419
RAMSEY
Ella R., 165
H. Kline, 166
Harry K., 166
Hugh, 75
John, 75
Joseph, 165
William, Jr., 75
Wm., Sr., 75
RAMSTEAD
Marie, 418
RANDOLPH
Alva Fitz, 146
Asa Fitz, 146
RANKIN
Grace, 405

Maude A., 400
Sarah, 55
RAWSON
Alice C., 173
REAM
Harriet Adelle, 357
Warren B., 357
REED
Alice, 372
Arthur, 229
Arthur Harris, 229, 410
Asbury Harper, 227
Bertie, 227, 402
Boyd Allen, 371
Cecil Alexander, 214, 372
Charles E., 426
Conza Pauline, 370
David Allen, 214
Dorothy Virginia, 372
Ethel Jane, 214
F. M., 219
Fred, 404
Harvey Allen, 214, 372, 373
Helen Christine, 371
Henry G., 214, 372
Herschel Lowe, 229, 409
James H., 426
James Leeman, 426
James Leslie, 371
Julia Frances, 372
Keith, 410
Lucy Elizabeth, 214, 370
Madge, 227, 402
Marian, 187
Mary Melvina, 153
Melinda, 188
Nelson, 227
Nola Mary, 229, 409
Ota Lee, 214, 372
Paul Grapes, 371
Samuel Boyd, 214
Samuel Boyd`, 371
Susan Belle, 214
Thomas Hughes, 229, 410
Walter Scott, 229, 409
Winna Fern, 214, 372
REEDER
Anna May Delores, 424
Clarence H., 351
Russell Frank, 424
Ruth Loreen, 424
William Clarence, 351
REESE
Sara, 404

REEVES
Melva D., 376
REFSNES
Anna, 443
REGER
Anna, 164
Annie Gertrude, 232
Augustun, 164
Carle, 219
James Marion, 413
Loy R., 413
REID
Adaline Anna, 113
Ader Evelyn, 177
Alan Justis, 372
America Pembrook, 176
Andrew Nathan, 177
Ann, 81
Ardela Tennessee, 176
Asa, 81, 113
Asa A., 176
Asa Barton, 113
Asa M., 113
Asa Ulysses Sidney Levi, 176
Catherine "Katie", 81
Charles Jackson, 177
Charles O., 113
David, 113
David Gordon, 176
David Settle, 30
Elizabeth, 113
Ezra Fizer, 177
Francis M., 113
George II, 81
George W., 81, 113, 114, 177
Georgiana, 113
Henry, 113, 176
Homer, 177
Infant, 177
Isaac S., 113
Jack, 81
James, 114
James Henry, 177
James M., 176
Jane, 81, 113
Jane "Jennie", 114
John Altus, 177
John L., 113
John M., 114
John S., 81
John William, 177
Joseph, 81
Joseph Alex, 177
M. Lenora, 113
Margaret A., 114
Margaret Ann, 81

Mariland, 177
Martha, 113
Martha A., 113
Martha Ellen, 176
Martha M., 113
Mary Alice, 177
Mary Ann, 113
Mary E., 114
Mary Jane, 176
Mary Parlee, 176
Mary Priscilla Elizabeth Jane, 176
Mary S., 113
Mathew Franklin, 177
Matthew Gaston, 81, 113, 176
Nancy J., 114
Nancy R., 113
Rachel, 114
Rheca Thomas, 176
Rhesa, 81, 113, 176
Robert A., 113
Robert Alexander, 81
Robert C., 114
Robert Stephenson, 176
Sarah, 113, 176
Sarah Jane, 176
Sarah O., 113
Thomas, 114
Thomas Henry, 81, 114
Wesley H., 113
William Cary, 176
William Jefferson, 176
William R., 114
RENNER
Jason Bernard, 401
Kenzy Bernard, 401
REX
Malinda, 212
REYNOLDS
Anna Elsie, 360
John, 104
Lillie G., 217
Stpehen W., 217
RHOADES
Ella Jane, 313
RHODES
Edna Winfield, 386
Elizabeth R., 386
Mary M., 386
Royston D., 386
RICE
Thomas, 57
RICHARD
Lillian, 262
RICHARDS
Addison Franklin, 198
Alpheus Seymour, 343

Anna Eliza, 193, 331
Arley, 344
Austin D., 193
Carson Lawson, 332
Clair, 333
Clarlton, 332
Daniel, 192
Daniel J., 193
Daniel Tolbert, 193, 332
Darlie Florence, 332
David, 192
Edghar Hamilton, 344
Edna, 343
Eliza, 138, 139
Eliza O., 193
Elvin, 343
Evelyn, 370
Francis Jane, 333
George Clifford, 332
Glen, 343
Henry Clive, 332
Ica Gay, 332
Icy M., 193, 331
Ira Burwell, 332
James Tolbert, 138, 192
John Samuel, 332
Mamie Virginia, 345
Mary J., 193
Nancy E., 193
Nancy M., 193, 333
Perry Gaylord, 332
Perry Samuel, 193
Sally, 72
Samuel, 193
Sarah R. "Lina", 193
Wanda Mae, 345
RICHMOND
Maxine, 404
RICKER
Rufus, 57
RIDDLE
Grace E., 364
Martha Gay, 368
Martha M., 378
Martha Magdalene, 378
Mattie G., 368
RIEBER
Sarah Catherine, 363
RIFFLE
Emma Jane, 203
RIGGS
Mary Ann, 377
Thelma Louella, 420
RIGHTER
Sarah, 209

560

RILEY
Caroline, 185
Catharine, 207
RINEHART
Caroline, 261
Emma C., 147
Oric Earl, 409
Susannah, 91
ROBBINS
Jane Hannah, 31
Joseph H., 112
ROBERTSON
Elizabeth Avaline, 80
Erma Leota, 410
ROBINSON
Anthony Asbury, 144
Anthony Hall, 231, 412
Charles Theodore, 231, 412
Curtis Newton, 144, 231
Elmer Truman, 412
Ethel Maude, 311
Gary Truman, 412
James Alvis, 142
John, 142
Minor Hollis, 231, 412
Robert, 79
Truman Guy, 237
Wilma Louise, 231
ROCHELLE
Lavadia Odell, 374
ROCKAFELLOW
Louisa, 439
ROE
Eunice, 370
John Charles, 370
Mary, 400
ROGAN
Female, 59
ROGERS
Jo Lea, 405
Pearl J., 377
ROHRBOUGH
Sarah Columbia, 202
ROLLINS
Wilma Frances, 424
ROLLYSON
E. G., 382
ROMAN
Susan, 364
ROMINE
Annie Lucy, 364
Jacob, 364
Samuel, 87
Sarah, 87
ROSBOROUGH
Alexander, 22

Alexander II, 54
Alexander J., 83
Alexander M., 54, 83
David D., 54, 83
Edward E., 83, 116
Ellen N., 83
Fanny J., 83
Female, 22
John, 22, 55
Joseph, 22, 54
Joseph Brown, 54
Joseph J., 84
Maclin, 55
Margaret, 22
Mary Martha, 54
William, 55
William Andrew, 54
William Gaston, 22
ROSEBOROUGH
Alexander, 79
P. J., 79
ROSS
Daniell Wesley, 216
Elizabeth, 47
Esther, 32
Hugh Gaston, 59
James, 59
James Howard, 403
Mary, 46
Rebecca, 59
Stella, 359
ROSSITER
Ed, 74, 111
Samuel, 111
ROUSCH
Earl, 407
ROUSE
Nellie M., 427
ROWE
Bazil, 262
Charles, 262, 434
Julia, 434
Laura, 262, 434
Margaret, 434
Mary, 262
Sally, 182
Walter, 262
William, 434
ROWLEY
Capt. Aaron, 37
ROXBOROUGH
George B., 116
RULE
Clarence Sherman, 225
Margaret, 114

RUMBLE
Ruth D., 377
RUNYON
Anna, 101
Edgar J., 437
Margaret G., 437
RUSSELL
Julia, 174
Nathaniel Scott, 351
Nicole Lynn, 351
Orlonzo Babook, 174
RUTAN
Abraham, 33
Hannah, 33
RYAN
Claude, 408
Dennis B., 411
Gladys, 408
RYMER
Frank Harrison, 151
Henry A., 139
Henry Martin, 139
Mollie A., 388
Silas T., 151
William Ivan, 226
William W., 226

S
SADLER
Thelma Rebecca, 354
SALMON
Emeline M., 37
Jane, 37
Luther, 37
SALZER
A. F., 149
Alois J., 149
SAMPLE
George J., 173
James, 173
Margaret M., 173
William, 70
SAMPLES
Myrtle, 377
SANDERS
John L., 30
Patience A., 72
SAPP
Lucy L., 422
SAYRE
Bernice E., 360
SCHLATER
Jean, 201
SCHMEIZEL
Elizabeth, 440

SCHULKE
Dorothy, 208
SCOTT
Bertha Irene, 329
Cyril Alfred, 380
Emma, 259
Frank P., 259
Jacob F., 189
Jesse Wilson, 211
Thomas G., 189
Thornton Allen, 189
Willa Pearl, 144
William Edwin, 211
SCUDDER
Ephraim, 70
Isaac Williamson, 70
John Arnold, 170
Katherine, 170
Mary, 105
Smith, 70
William Mansfield, 70, 105, 170
SECKMAN
Orena, 416
SEIWELL
Charles, 134
Fred R., 134
Mary A., 134
SELBY
Rosa, 188
SEMAN
Elizabeth Lee, 408
SERGEANT
Albert, 166
Dorothy, 268
Elizabeth, 104, 166, 268
William Gaston, 166, 268
SHANNON
Eleanor, 105
Rebecca, 139
SHARP
Henry, 255
Ida Jayne, 255
SHARPE
Margaret, 28
SHARPS
Alfred Ray, 357
Alfred Vance, 356
David Lee, 357
Dorothy Maxine, 357
Elizabeth Jane, 357
Etta Belle, 356
James Earl, 357
Martin Luther, 356
Mary Evelyn, 357
Paul Edwin, 356
Pearl Winona, 356

SHARRER
Cora F., 419
SHATTUCK
DeWitt Clinton, 368
Jessie M., 368
Lois V., 368
SHATZER
John, 358
SHEETS
Alva, 367
Asa James, 367
Denley Udell, 367
Edward, 370
Esta L., 367
George H., 152
Homer R., 370
Jacob, 114
Laura T., 152, 226
Mary, 114
Wendell Ross, 370
SHELHAMMER
Mary E., 133
SHEPARD
Katherine Louise, 373
Katheryn Louise, 373
Orel C., 373
SHERBONDY
Grace Belle, 431
SHERMAN
Sally, 357
SHIELDS
Mary, 32
SHIER
David, 231
SHIPMAN
Archie Oley, 349
Dema Belle, 349
Frederick Burton, 349
Harley Arbendale, 349
Lillie Maude, 349
Zelda May, 349
SHOBE
Sarah, 134
SHOCKEY
Margaret Lincoln, 227
Mary Ellen, 377
SHOTWELL
Margaret M., 261
Martha B., 159
Mary, 159
Patricia M., 433
Stuart Beebe, 159
Stuart Beebe, Jr., 261
Stuart M., 433
Stuart McIlvaine, 262, 433
Walter Gaston, 159, 261

William, 159
William James, 159
SHOW
Jacob, 363
May, 363
SHREVE
Augustus, 376
Florence Ardelia, 376
SHULL
Elridge Gene, 432
Florence May, 432
Jimmy Dale, 432
Lola Lee, 432
SHUMAN
Bessie Lillian, 327
SILLS
Hannah, 135, 136
SIMANTON
Elizabeth, 31
SIMMONS
Thomas W., 130
SIMONTON
Alexander Gaston, 54
Ann, 40, 65
Benjamin, 32
Charles, 50
Charles S., 47
Christopher, 47, 50
Ephraim, 32
Isabel, 32
James, 32, 50
James Strong, 54
Jeanette, 47, 48, 54
John, 18, 46, 47
John, Jr., 47
Major, 46
Margaret, 32, 49, 54
Martha, 54
Mary, 51, 53, 54
Mary E., 47
Peter, 32
Robert, 32, 40, 65
Robert Romaine, Sr., 47
Samuel Robert, 47
Sarah, 47
W. B., 47
William, 47
SIMPSON
Elizabeth Ann, 104
John, 104
Rev. John, 38
Wilma, 362
SINCLAIR
Cary A., 132
Charles Porter, 132
Diora B., 132

Fannie, 132
George R., 132
Hiram Thomas, 132
James A. H., 132
SINGELETON
Asby F., 218
Berlin C., 218
Earlie I., 218
James W., 218
Lovie J., 388
SINGLETON
Lovie J., 388
SINNETT
Sarah, 213
SINNOTT
Mary, 74
SKINNER
Avis Jane, 352
Clarence, 352
Clarence Birton, 352
Kathleen Lillie, 352
Sylvester Arnold, 352
SLAWTER
Henry, 406
Hiram, 406
Leo, 406
SLOAN
Mary, 32, 33
Richard, 75
William, 32
SMALLCHECK
Carl, 364
Susan Elizabeth, 364
SMITH
Alvin, 233
Andrew Jackson, 122, 186
Ann Crawford, 434
Arlie, 153
Arnette, 187
Avery Birchard, 326
Bell, 436
Bertha Mae, 354
Boyd Elston, 153
Caroline V., 140
Cecil Beaumont, 153, 252
Charles A., 140
Charles Lewis, 191
Christian Joy, 253
Clara, 153
Claudius J., 187
Columbia A., 188
Conley, 186
Cora A., 140
Cornelius V. D., 268
Cynthia Ann, 217
Delia Elvira, 150

Della Mae, 405
E. I., 253
Earl B., 403
Earl Dillon, 403
Earnest Watson, 252
Edward, 122, 412
Edward F., 434
Edward Newton, 122, 153, 187
Egbert Bassell, 187
E.I., 429
Electa Luetta, 187
Eliza, 122, 187
Elizabeth, 122, 186
Elizabeth Byrd, 178
Ella, 192
Ella Bergin, 268
Ernest Hoff, 253
Ernest Wellington, 153, 253
Esther Elizabeth, 253
Everett Horner, 153
Floe, 233
Gerald N., 187
Gilbert, 122
Gracie, 192
Harriett Rosendale, 242
Harry A., 253
Harry Monroe, 396
Harvey, 191, 192
Hayden Ray, 230
Hobert Golden, 194
Icy M., 140
Isaac Rinehart, 140
J. H., 25
James, 122
James Boyd, 382
James Wesley, 191, 325
Jeptha, 131
John, 122, 140, 231
John Davidson, 122, 187
John E., 140
L. H., 188
Laura, 153, 253
Lionel Leon, 379
Lydia J., 140
Male Infant, 191
Martha Margaretta, 91
Mary Bird, 192, 327
Mary E., 140
Mary Elizabeth, 122, 186
Mary Mildred, 131
Mary Patricia, 417
Miner Francis, 192, 327
Myrtle Rose, 326
Nancy Jane, 191
Neal Austin, 327
Paul Hugh, 253, 429

Porter W., 187
Rebecca, 90
Robert S., 418
Roxie Elizabeth, 412
Ruby, 327
Ruth G., 252
Samuel, 191
Samuel Earl, 242
Sanford, 191, 327
Sarah, 63
Sarah Ann, 122
Sarah Palestine, 367
Susan V., 409
Tensie, 153, 253
Thomas, 122
Velma, 418, 419
Virginia, 122, 362
Watters, 62
Watters, Jr., 121, 122
Wellington, 122
William, 122, 186
William Columbus, 192
William Columbus "Lum", 328
William Wirt, 187
SMOCK
Augustus Hobart, 266, 439
Cassie Van Nest, 266, 439
Clarence McKay, 266
Edna C., 266
Ethel L., 266, 439
Freddie G., 266
George Henry, 266
George Willets, 266, 439
Helen Marie, 439
Homer Brown, 439
Jennie Alma, 266
John Henry, 266
SMYTH
Florence, 244
SNEDDON
James Edmund, 207
Kathryn, 207
SNEDEGAR
Alice, 246
SNIDER
Coral Edward, 336
Delmis C., 331
Dessie F., 395
Elvin Squires, 335
Fairfield E., 335
Harmon W., 331
Margaret E., 394
Rosco Paul, 336
SNYDER
Grace, 189
Jennings Dallas, 386

Jennings Snyder, 386
Ora Lucrecia, 358
SOMMERVILLE
Alenna, 366
Allena, 222, 390
Caroline V., 138
Charles I., 138
Charles W., 222
Clarence Doyle, 225
Elizabeth, 137, 138
Ella J., 140, 226
Etta B., 140
Flora May, 225
Floyd E., 138, 222
Gertie, 222
Hall Evert, 414
Icie Gay, 225
Ionia, 250
Isa M., 222, 390
Jacob, 140
James Brennie, 225
James Wesley, 140
John Alvin, 221
John Alvin T., 138
John H., 140, 225
Laura A., 140
Martha J., 138
Martin S., 137
Mary E., 138
Orla Robert, 414
Quedar Lynn, 222
Robert, 137
Robert A., 414
Robert O., 138, 222
Sarah Adda, 140, 225
Sarah Olive, 138
Susan M., 138
Virginia W., 415
William Oscar, 140
Zeta Gay, 222, 390
SOULE
Jeann Louise, 372
Lydia, 155
SOUTHWORTH
Blanche "Doc", 184
Cora Randolph, 184
Edna Zana, 184
Edward Pritchard, 184
Jessie Chloe, 184
Mary A., 184
Olive "Ocie", 184
Virginia Viola, 184
SPEAKE
Daniel Webster, 178
Elizabeth, 178
SPELSBERG

Charles A., 417
SPENCER
Mary Kathryn, 358
SPIEGEL
Frances Julia, 241
SPINNING
Martha, 70
SPRIGGS
Luella V., 183
SPRINGSTON
Jefferson, 143
Jefferson Davis, 143
SPURGEON
Clarence A., 396
Hayward Cline, 396
Ira McKinley, 391
Marion Ray, 396, 397
SQUIER
Jane, 101
Ludlow, 101
SQUIRES
Andrew Mead, 194, 336
Annie, 312
Carl Jackson, 312
Daniel Monroe, 194, 334
Edward Gale, 312
Edward Goff, 338
Eliza Kathleen, 338
Forest Boon, 194
Forest Leamon, 334
Freeman Goff, 194
Harry Goff, 312
Helen, 312
Hobert Golden, 338
Hobert Jackson, 339
Ida Oma, 194, 338
Ilda Leon, 336
James Monroe, 194
Jewell L., 337
Leland Gyles, 334
Leonora Bird Adams, 216
Mary Artie, 194, 335
Nancy Ann, 194, 333
Oma May, 334
Richard Franklin, 339
Rosa Jane, 194, 335
Samuel Jackson, 194, 337
Virgil B., 194
Warder Denzil, 334
William Carl, 312
Winifred, 337
STAATS
Theo Carson, 363
STALEY
Nancy, 205
STALNAKER

Bessie J., 364
Charles A., 429
Charles L., 203
Edie, 203
Emily, 130, 131
Frances Eileen, 202
Gerald, 413
Lloyd M., 252
Oda, 203
Samuel Edwin "Ned", 203
Samuel Marion, 252
Thaddeus Sobisca, 243
Vesta Phyllis, 243
W. Beach, 203
Willis E., 252, 429
STANFORD
Martha Jane, 254
STANSBERRY
Amy, 237
Francis, 404
Vicy L., 382
Vista, 404
STARCHER
Alvin S., 236, 368
Bret, 233
Letha Lane, 368
Mantie May, 236
William S., 233
STARR
Eva G., 371
STATTS
Wilma Eileen, 407
STAZEL
Mary A., 212
STEEL
Captain, 11, 56
Catherine, 25
Janet, 25
Joseph A., 25
Mary, 25
William, 25
STEELE
Carrie Blanche, 433
Dewey George, 264, 436
Harrison, 401
Isaac Perego, 264
William Thomas, 401
STEPHENS
Annie, 164
Augustis, 164
Dorcas, 87
George, 164
Isaac Farley, 164
Joseph, 164
STERLING
Harry C., 363

Mattie Virginia, 363
STERN
Jacob, 144
John, 144
STEVENSON
Carl, 435
John Carroll Burton, 435
Lois, 435
STEWART
Aletta, 269
Aletta Young, 167
Arthur D., 148
Charles L., 148, 242
Dent, 149
Edwin, 242
Ethel, 149
Evelina Reynolds, 167, 269
Flora Jane, 410
Franklin, 148
George Brown, 167
Hiter, 148, 242
Ida Maria, 167
James T., 148
John, 148
John C., 148
Josephus, 149
Kelly C., 242
Malitas, 148
Marlton, 242
Mary, 167, 269
Mary Eliza, 149
Morris, 242
Robert, 148
Robert Annin, 167, 269
Susan M., 139
Wanda Marie, 242
William, 148, 167
William Gaston, 167
STICKLE
Fern, 311
Harvey Filmore, 311
Howard Columbus, 311
STILWAGNER
Mary, 409
STINSON
D. G., 45
Daniel G., 45
STOKES
Elizabeth, 97
STONE
Marian, 110
STONEKING
John, 188
STOUT
Icie Elizabeth, 373
Mary, 101

Matilda Jennie, 255
STRADER
Newton Jefferson, 151
Valentine, 151
STRALEY
Ernest Ralph, 373
Joseph F., 373
Mary, 187
Nancy Ann, 123
STRANGE
Robert, 30
STRATTON
Amanda E., 74
STRONG
Charles, 16, 17, 21, 46
Christopher, 18, 22
Elizabeth, 18
James, 18, 22
Jane/Jennet, 18
Janet, 18, 22
Jannet, 20
Jennet Gaston, 16, 17
John, Sr., 48
Letitia, 18, 22
Margaret, 18, 22, 46, 47
William, 18, 22
STROTHER
Aaron Arden, 198
Blanche M., 198
Charles R., 199, 354
Elbert B., 198
Eli Clarl, 199
Garland Blair, 354
Granville Reuben, 198
James Edmund, 198
STRYKER
Margaret, 68
STUART
Charles Francis, 418
STUCKEY
Nelle, 362
STURGIS
James M., 404
STUTLER
Benjamin L., 366
Kenneth Aubrey, 366
Richard A., 366
SUMMERS
Alp, 149
Elijah W., 191
Helen, 149
Lucy Mae, 320
Lydia, 237
Maude, 191
Sarah Ann, 215

SUMNER
David E., 61
SUMPTER
Mary, 418
SUMTER
General, 11
General Thomas, 56
SUNDERLAND
Sarah, 108
SUTPHEN
Catharine Cornelia, 165
Catherine E., 165
Peter, 70
SUTTON
Ollie Gay, 357
SUYDAM
Maria, 106
SWAIN
David Lowry, 30
SWECKER
Archie David, 420
David Gaston, 420
Jo Ann, 420
SWEENEY
Mary Jane, 370
SWIGER
Lucy May, 198
Zachous, 198
SWISHER
Ada Bird, 145
Alfred Washington, 145
Alice Rebecca, 144
Alvin, 145
Amanda Elizabeth, 144
Anna Mariah, 92, 145
Ardelia Maud, 233
Beatrice, 234, 413
Bonnie Irene, 234
Carl Brent, 233
Charles, 145, 234
Charlotte, 92
Dale, 233
Dora Ethel, 233
Ednah Beeghley, 402
Eugenia, 236
Flora Lee, 144
Flossie, 232
George Washington, 144, 232
Gertie G., 386
Grace Leslie, 232
Harland Allman, 236
Harriet Jane, 144
Hazel Ray, 231
Ira Ervin, 146, 236
Isaac Columbus "Lum", 145, 233
Isaac H., 146

Isaac R., 91
Isaac Rinehart, 92, 146
Iza Florence, 144
James Blaine, 233
James Edwin, 144, 232
James Goodloe, 145, 234
James H., 234
James Lee, 92, 145
James Wilbur, 234
John Alden, 144, 233
John Emory, 145
Laco, 232
Lenna M., 234
Lewis D., 91
Margaret Elizabeth, 233
Mary, 144, 233, 413
Mary Ann, 232, 235
Mary Marcella, 144
Mildred May, 234
Odbert, 236
Peter Gaston, 92, 144
Peter S. III, 91
Rella May, 233
Robert Ervin, 145, 233
Robert Ervin, Jr., 234
Robert G., 234
Ruby J., 234
Sarah Ann, 91, 144
Sarah Jane, 92, 145
Virginia, 234
William Henry, 145
William Oscar, 144, 232, 235
William Vaughn, 234
Wirt, 402

SYDENHAM
H. G., 169

SYMMES
Benjamin R., 93
Daniel, 93

T

TALBOTT
Addie May, 245

TALLMAN
Ina, 161
Kirk Casto, 227
O. Roy, 227

TAPSCOTT
Lydia, 62
Mary Lydia, 62

TATE
William, 90

TAYLOR
Adda Wilmona, 143
Albert A., 235

Alma R., 143
Andrew Allen, 91
Arthur Kelso, 230, 411
Attorney Gen. James F., 61
Bartley Norris, 229, 410
Bertie Ivy, 227
Bettie Marshall, 230, 411
Betty Jean, 410
Bonnie Marie, 230, 411
Charles R., 143
Charles William, 144
Clara, 143
Clara Cornelia, 229
Colonel Harvey, 143, 229
Delores Elaine, 402
Earl Grayson, 230, 410
Eddy, 143
Edna, 143
Edward Murray, 143, 230
Edward Murray, Jr., 411
Edward Oliver, 233
Elizabeth, 97
Elizabeth Jane, 91, 142
Ella Nora, 142, 227
Emma T., 143
Estella, 143
Female, 61
Frances Gertrude, 143, 230
Francis Edwin, 233
Gay, 143
Geoge L., 143
Grace Irene, 227, 401
Harley Grant, 227, 402
Hattie Nevada, 143, 230
Helen May, 142
Henrietta, 91, 144
James Gaston, 91, 142
James Robert, 411
Jeanette Louise, 402
Jessie L., 143, 229
John, 91, 141
John Floyd, 143, 229
John Louis, 61
Joseph, 91
Josiah, 91
Lucy E., 142, 227
Lula Jessie, 227, 401
Margaret, 91, 142
Martha, 143
Martha Ellen, 143
Mary, 91
Mary Margaret, 411
Nancy Ann, 91, 142, 206
Nancy Burdell, 232, 235
Opal Merl, 227
Prudie, 143

Rufus Davvison, 227, 402
Sallie Bell, 143
Sandy H., 144
Sarah, 91
Virgil Claudius, 410
Virginia Lee, 410
William, 61
William Davidson, 91, 143
William Donley, 229, 410
William Grant, 142, 227
William Marion, 410

TEASLEY
Elizabeth, 181
John Wiley, 181

TEEPLE
John, 68
Naomi, 68

TELFORD
James, 57
Samuel, 57

TEMPLE
Hazel B., 369

TENEICK
John S., 266
Rachel A., 266

TENEYCK
Judith Tunison, 268

TENNEY
Methany Jane, 227

TENNY
Samuel B., 237

TERHUNE
Anna, 169

TETER
Sarah Jane, 113

TETRICK
A. W. Guy, 88
Harlan Marshall, 371

TETTEMER
Grace, 357

THATCHER
Nancy, 71

THOMAS
Grace, 372
Lilly Delle, 135
Nancy, 149
Rosetta, 226

THOMPSON
Adele Eugenia, 7
Bertha Talita, 318
Clement A., 79
Dennis, 86
Elisha W., 86
Elizabeth, 33
Ellen, 174
Leach, 79

Lillian, 419
Mary, 103
Rachael, 67
Victorene, 255
THOMSON
Alexander, 5
James, 27
Janet, 5
Mary, 5, 27
THRASH
John Marshall, 151
Nellie J., 248
TILDEN
Naomi, 6
Rozanna (Rhoda), 36
TINGLER
Julia Ann, 120
TINKHAM
Iris M., 435
TIPPING
Andrew, 46
TODD
David M., 106
Rev. John, 110
William H., 106
William J., 106
TOPOLY
Jane, 65
Peter, 65
TORR
Doris Marie, 357
TORRANCE
Sarah, 116
TOWNSEND
Beulah, 395
Gladys Augusta, 332
Hannah, 112
Leaven A., 395
TRACY
Andrew, 67
TRAVIS
Donald G., 357
Robert Levi, 357
TREADWAY
Jane, 59
Mary Ann, 59
TRIMBLE
Hoffman, 234
Vivian Daisy, 234
TRIPPETT
William, 409
TRYTKO
Anna Virginia, 240
TUNISON
Abraham, 162
Aletta Margaret, 162

TURNER
Floyd Evert, 202
Mary Jane, 128
Pearl, 202

U
UTT
Rebecca, 376

V
VA
Elizabeth, 102
VAIL
Margaret, 438
VALENTINE
Arthur A., 192
Louise A., 419
Nathan L., 419
VAN ARSDALE
Abraham, 69
Aletta, 101
Eliza, 266
Ida, 68
Jane, 69
John, 102
Peter, 102
Philip, 68, 101, 102
Philip H., 69
Sarah, 162
VAN DERVEER
Jane Maria, 162
Tunis, 162
VAN DUYON
Dennis, 70
VAN DYKE
Catherine, 162
VAN NEST
Anna Maria, 102
Catherine, 164
John, 102
Mary Jane, 102
Phebe Ellen, 102
Sarah Elizabeth, 102
Tunis, 102
William C. A., 102
VAN NORSTRAM
Elizabeth, 109
VAN VEGHTEN
Elizabeth, 104
VANCE
Agnes, 99
VANDERVORT
Martha, 148
VANHORN
Mary, 121

VENORT
Mary, 121
VERNOU
Mary, 169
VICKERS
Charles Warren, 407
Geraldine Lenore, 407
John Faber, 407
Mary Alice, 407
Randall & Patricia, 30
William Henry, 407
VINSON
John, 53
VIRTS
Garnie Craven, 208
VISNES
Anna Melinda Knutsooter, 356
VITZ
Alda, 90
VLIET
Ida Ann, 162
William, 162
VON BREMEN
Berend H., 440
Henry W., 440
VOORHEES
Ella Ramsey, 267
Hugh, 267
Lena May, 267
William, 267
VORHEES
Ira, 165
John S., 165
VOSSELLE
Sarah, 165
VOSSELLER
Margaret, 164
VREELAND
Gertrude, 264

W
WAAGE
Andora, 97
WADDELL
Georgia, 431
WADE
Andrew Montgomery, 135, 236
Charlotte, 328
Espie Augustus, 236
Flora Bell, 135
WADSWORTH
Frances C., 353
WAGGONER
Alonzo, 187

Elijah, 187
George B., 187
George S., 187
Harvey Wellington, 187
Martha O., 245
WAKEFIELD
Ann, 84
Jesse, 58
Sarah, 84
WAKENIGHT
James Thomas, 411
WALDECK
Early Forrest, 234
Madge Elvira, 234
WALDO
Rev. John, 87
WALKER
Alexander, 15, 40, 45, 80
Jane Gaston, 38, 178
John Gaston, 45, 82
Margaret E., 85
Thomas, 15, 40, 45
William, 82, 115
WALLEN
F. A., 143
WANSTREET
Bessie Anna, 416
WARD
Albert M., 135
Allen, 434
Amanda Victoria, 134
Anna M., 134, 211
Barbara E., 217
Calvin Ray, 213
Caroline E., 186
Charles Alvin, 212, 213
Clovis L., 212
Eliza J., 135, 212
Franklin P., 130, 204
George Washington, 130
Goldie, 213
Harry Hazal, 213
Hazel, 367
Henry M., 200
June A., 212
Kenneth, 434
Kenneth Boyd, 212, 367
Ledrue, 212
Ledrue K., 212
Lena M., 213
Lewis M., 134
Lillie M., 364
Marg F., 130
Margaret, 113
Martin Carr, 134
Mary, 137

Mattie, 213, 367
Nellie Snow, 212, 367
Norma, 213
Norman, 434
Ruth M., 213, 368
Sarah, 213
Sarah A., 141, 152
Sarah Elizabeth, 134
Solomon P., 141
Tensy, 213
Theo May, 212, 367
Theodosia, 204
Thomas Floyd, 134, 212
William, 134
William W., 134
Willie J., 200
WARE
Mary, 177
WARNER
Mary, 108
WARNOCK
James, 96
John, 96
William Gaston, 96
WARREN
Mary Beatrice "Minnie", 170
Rev. Square, 170
WARRICK
Harry Chandler, 435
WARRICK,, 435
WASHBURN
Amanda, 88, 89, 129
Elizabeth, 89, 129
Isaac, 88, 129
Marilla, 370
Virginia, 88
WASHBURNE
Mary, 172
WASHINGTON
General, 55
WASSOM
Sharon, 31
WATKINS
E. F., 149
Fay Osborne, 149
James A. H., 149
Mary Elizabeth, 149
Minnie, 408
WATSON
Ezra C., 193
Inis M., 252
Opal Catherine, 226
WATTON
Ellen, 188
WAUGH
Emma, 205

Esther, 7, 38, 77
James Harry, Jr., 437
WAY
Amanda M., 259
WEIR
Charles, 44
Ebenezer, 45
Hugh Gaston, 45
Margaret, 45
Martha, 45
WENGER
James Edward, 420
WEST
Alice Bessie, 210, 366
Allie May, 186
Alta Beryl, 210
Amanda, 141
Ambrose Jefferson, 133, 208, 209
Anna Verle, 317
Aramita L., 185
Arthur Ernest, 133
Belinda Roana, 188
Bell Jane, 133
Calla Oscie, 314
Calvin B., 213
Caroline M., 147
Clarence Dovener, 315
Dale Jennings, 209
Deborah, 87
Deward Corwin, 317
Dorus Jackson, 317
Elbert Boyd, 315
Eli Jacob, 188, 314
Eli R., 87, 123, 185
Eliza Jane, 189, 210
Elizabeth, 87, 122
Emma Frances, 133
Esta Pearl, 315
Fidelia Arrillla, 188
Floyd Albion, 123
Frances, 87, 121
Franklin Earl, 363
Frederick Brook, 208, 363
Gaile, 314
Gladys Leola, 210
Grace, 210, 366
Guira Ciscelia, 315
Harold B., 317
Hattie Odessa, 133
Hattie Vione, 317
Hazel, 210
Hiram Thomas, 133, 209
Hoy D., 314
Hubert Orion, 364
Icy Gay, 188
Ida Mae, 133, 210

James Madison, 133
Jefferson Bowell, 132
Jessie M., 210
Job, 87, 185
John, 87, 141
John J., 315
John Jackson, 123, 188
John Waldo, 87
Judson Lee, 133, 210
Julia Amanda, 189
Laura Alice, 133, 209
Laura V., 210
Leslie Brook, 363
Lessie Mae, 314
Lester H., 364
Leva Wilma, 364
Lilly Belle, 210
Lyle Cecil, 209
Mabel Ann, 312
Mary Frances, 185
Mary Louise, 123, 188
Mary R., 210
Mary Virginia, 133, 210
Maxine, 365
Olandus, 185
Ora Jefferson, 208, 364
Owen A., 188
Owen Aldo, 185, 312
Paul Eldred, 364
Pauline M., 209
Pearl M., 210, 365
Phoebe, 87
Phyllis Glenn, 202
Porter, 202
Robert, 364
Robert E., 315
Ruanna, 87, 121, 122
Rupert W., 317
Russell Goff, 315
Sarah, 87
Sarah Ann, 123, 189
Sarah Elizabeth, 188, 236, 315
Sarah Louise, 251, 364
Thelma Louise, 364
Thomas, 365
Thomas Floyd, 188, 315
Thomas Jefferson, 123
Thomas Woodrow, 210, 366
Urzelda, 186
Velma V., 353
Virginia Dare, 123
Virginia Dorr, 123
William Burr, 188, 316
William Holmes, 364
William Jackson, 133
William Kenna, 208, 364

William Marshall, 123, 185, 187
William Raymond, 209
William Stanley, 317
William West, 208
Winifred Jean, 365
Zachariah R., 353
WESTFALL
Orville, 352
WHEELER
Elizur, 74
Mary, 74
WHERRY
Andrew, 79
WHETHERHOLT
Bessie Ellen, 405
Coda Marie, 406
WHITAKER
Elizabeth, 34
WHITE
Andrew Dickson, 107, 171
Conley Glenn, Jr., 406
Georgia Estella, 422
Horace, 107, 171
Horace K., 171
Hugh, 58
Lucinda, 114
Mary, 86, 120
Nelle, 247
Paul R., 76
Prudence, 150
Robert, 86
WHITENOCK
Margaret Ellen, 167
WHITESEL
Dove Margaret, 150
James Pope, 150
WHITNEY
Elizabeth, 59
WHITTAKER
Betty Jane, 444
Chester Kirk, 444
G. C., 429
WHITTINGTON
Ben, 205
WIANT
Iva Lou, 412
WIGGINTON
Isaac, 81
WILLEY
Charles, 178
Wm., 10
WILLIAM
Charles Howard, 133
Jane Gaston, 115
John Jasper, 134

WILLIAMS
Andrew Johnson, 230
Belle M., 260
Betty June, 358
Caroly Gaston, 440
Carolyn Gaston, 267
Carsie Delman, 358
Charles G., 260
Clarence Edward, 230
Daniel, 57
Emma O., 173
Florence, 230
Florence L., 173
George Mung, 267
Harriet A., 173
Harvey H., 260
Jane M., 260
Joseph, 434
Lena Pearl, 230, 411
Lorania O., 173
Mabel Roxie, 230
Madge Buena, 230
Margaret L., 260
Nancy Genevieve, 230
Nathaniel, 173
Ralph Schuyler, 267
Ralston, 260
Roger, 71
Rosalea, 383
Sarah, 260
William Stephen, 230
WILLIAMSON
Sarah Elizabeth, 346
WILLIS
Ann J., 80
Robert, 121
William Thomas, 121
WILLITS
Albert, 267
Alford, 267
Charles, 440
Charles C., 267
George Sidney, 266
George Sidney, Jr., 266
Grace G., 267, 440
Jessie A., 267
Oliver G., 267
WILLLIAMS
Lester, 434
Margaret M., 434
WILSON
Anna Belle, 215
Avis Mildred, 225
Beatrice, 411
Catherine, 164
Ebenezer, 93

Eula Edith, 225, 399
Frank Marcell, 398
Hugh, 240
Jane, 47, 49, 51, 224
Larry Eugene, 398
Louie Enid, 225, 398
Marion Homer, 224
Mary, 99
Mary "Molly", 6, 36
Max Welty, 409
Minnie C., 147
Nancy, 59
Rebecca, 319
Robert, 50
Rosetta, 201
Virgina Louisa, 220
Wheeler Shirley, 225, 398
WINN
Amanda, 182
WINTERS
Joanna, 95
WISE
Jennie L., 98
Leroy, 98
WISEMAN
Harlan Z., 232
WITTER
Payne Jeffery, 357
Sylvanus Payne, 357
WOLFE
Abraham, 205
Albert Slatton, 205
Archie A., 229
Celia, 187
Goldie Fleming, 328
Marian, 229
Susan, 248
WOLLEM
Florence, 435
WOLVERTON
John Mason, 227
WOOD
Alma, 182
Caddie, 182
Columbus, 228
Harriett, 120
James, 120
Jeff, 182
John, 120
Lillian, 183
Lorraine, 183
Lucinda, 173
Nan, 120
Raymond, 182
Ruel, 182
Sarah Jane, 119

Tom, 119
Virginia Maxine, 396, 397
William, 119
WOODFORD
Iris Columbia, 219
WOODWARD
Benjamin Franklin, 101
John, 101
Phebe Anne, 101
Stephen, 101
William, 101
WOOFTER
Alfred, 153
Elizabeth, 224
Elizabeth J., 136
Elsie Bird, 252
James, 139
Jesse A., 153
John Granviel, 139
WORSTELL
Denton Carl, 388
WORTHINGTON
Charles, 61
Eliza Ann, 61
WORTMAN
John Dwyen, 164
Rebecca Ann, 163
Sarah Alette, 164
WRIGHT
Clemma, 337
Hannah, 69
Reba, 383
Robert William, Jr., 436
WYCKOFF
Clarence, 268
WYHUSKY
Carrie, 438
WYLIE
Elizabeth, 80

Y
YATES
Mary Jane, 142
YEATER
Hazel May, 196
YOAK
Monnie Elizabeth, 411
YOHO
Martha, 209
YOST
Henrietta Maxine, 407
Robert Milton, 408
Thomas Frank, 407

Z
ZAHNISER
Albert Wright, 268, 440
Elizabeth, 440
George Brown, 268, 440
George Wright, 104, 268, 440
Katherine Gaston, 268
ZEIGLER
Benjamin F., 413
Earl E., 413
Helen May, 413
ZELLER
Gordon A., 418
ZIMMERMAN
Mary Ann, 181
ZINN
Dale Wendell, 399
Evelyn L., 389
Everett Clayton, 227
Henry Clay, 222
Ida Mae, 389
John Wesley, 211
Luetta, 212
M. B., 211
Nelson Earl, 399
Overy Earl, 398
Raymond Drummond, 389
Royden Scott, 389
William Buckner, 211
Winifred A., 222
ZOBRIST
Betty Louise, 418
Jean Gaston, 418
Paul Sumpter, 418
Samuel, 418
Thomas Charles, 418

Addendum

Vestle C. Gaston, born June 15, 1913 in Trinity Co., Tx.; died September 09, 1996 in Harris Co.,Tx.. He was the son of Clyde C. Gaston and Rhoda Levara Hutson. He married (1) Ida Bee Huff November 30, 1940 in Trinity Co., Tx.. She was the daughter of Hines Dolphus Huff and Naomi Ruth Tarpley.

This genealogy was presented to me with the latest generation listed first versus the oldest generation first. If you want to trace the ancestry from John Jean Gaston, you will have to go to page 600 and read backwards.

Vestle C. Gaston is a descendant of John Gaston, born 1645 in Scotland; died in Mageragall, Northern Ireland. This John Gaston was the son of Count Jean Gaston de Foix. He had at least two brothers, William and Alexander Gaston, perhaps more. He fled to Ireland in 1668 and lived at Caranlaigh Cloughwater, Ballymena.

John Jean Gaston, born 1600 in France, married Agnes of Navarre. She was the daughter of King Phillip III of Navarre. John "Jean" Gaston, the Huguenot, was banished from France by the Catholics for religious persecution. He fled, with two of his brothers to Calvinist Scotland about 1668. His property was confiscated but his relatives who remained Catholics in France sent means to Scotland for his living. He married in Scotland and had, among other sons, three: John, William, and Alexander. These three sons emigrated to County Antrim, Ireland about 1660 to 1680.

John Gaston , born, 1645 in Scotland, died in Mageragall, Northern Ireland ,was the son of John Jean Gaston and Agnes of Navarre. He married Esther Naugh, born before 1710.

Generation No. 1

I. Vestle C. Gaston, born June 15, 1913 in Trinity Co., Tx.; died September 09, 1996 in Harris Co., Tx.. He was the son of 2. Clyde C. Gaston and 3. Rhoda Levara Hutson. He married (1) Ida Bee Huff November 30, 1940 in Trinity Co., Tx.. She was the daughter of Hines Dolphus Huff and Naomi Ruth Tarpley.

Notes for Vestle C. Gaston:
Following is a letter from the War Department, signed by Brig. Gen. John Magruder, regarding Vestle C. Gaston's participation and service in World War II, as a member of the 101st., followed by the Unit Citation, which was signed by Dwight D. Eisenhower, Chief of Staff.

WAR DEPARTMENT
Office of The Assistant Secretary of War
STRATEGIC SERVICES UNIT
25th & E Streets, N.W.
Washington 25, D.C.

   Date: 11 February 1946

SUBJECT: Award of Distinguished Unit Citation

TO: Officers and Men of Detachment 101

1. On behalf of General Donovan I take great pride in fowarding to you the official War Department order awarding the Distinguished Unit Citation to Detachment 101. While I am doing this on behalf of General Donovan, who was Director of OSS for the period of this citation, I feel that I, too, have a special interest in the award. At that time I was Deputy Director- Intelligence Services and in a position to be very much aware of the fine work of OSS personnel in the difficult Burma campaign.

2. From early 1943 when your operations as American-Kach in Rangers led General Wingate's forces into Burma, through the days when you guided General Merrill's Marauders to the Myitkyina air strip and went ahead of General Willey's forces which drove the Japanese from North Burma, until the last days of the war in Burma when your efforts alone cleared the enemy from a 10,000 square mile area, the story of Detachment 101 stands out as a consistently brilliant one.

3. The Unit Citation, as official recognition from the War Department of the success of the Detachment's operations and of the outstanding heroism of its personnel, should afford to each of you a sense of deep satisfaction and pride of accomplishment. That the Citation does not cover the whole of the Detachment's operations, from its activation to the close of the war in Burma, is regrettable, but as acknowledgement of your greatest single achievement it should be considered an even higher testimony to the worth of the whole.

4. May I add my personal congratulations and those of the many former OSS personnel now with me in SSU and thank you for your part in bringing so high an honor to OSS, an honor which we of SSU fall proud heirs.

(signed)
JOHN MAGRUDER
Brig. Gen., USA
Director

(The Unit Citation accompanying Brig. Gen. John Magruder's letter follows):

GENERAL ORDERS - No. 7
WAR DEPARTMENT, WASHINGTON 25, D.C. 17 January 1946

V. BATTLE HONORS -As authorized by Executive Order 9396 (sec. I, WD But. 22, 1943), Superseding Executive Order 9075 (sec Ill, WD Bu 1. 11, 1942), citation of the following unit in the general orders indicated is confirmed under the provisions of section IV, WD Circular 333, 1943, in the name of the President of the United States as public evidence of deserved honor and distinction. The citation reads as follows:

Service Unit Detachment No. 101, Office of Strategic Services, is cited for outstanding performance of duty from 8 May to 15 June 1945 in capturing the strategic enemy strong points of Lawksawk, Pangtara, and Loilem in the Central Shan States, Burma. This unit, composed of approximately 300 American officers and men, volunteered to clear the enemy from an area of 10,000 square miles. Its subsequent activities deprived the Japanese 15th Army of the only East escape route and secured the Stilwell Road against enemy counterattack. Although Detachment 101 had been engaged primarily in intelligence and guerrilla activities, it set about the infantry mission of ousting a determined enemy from a sector long fortified and strategically prepared. These American officers and men recruited, organized, and trained 3,200 Burmese natives entirely within enemy territory. They then undertook and concluded successfully a coordinated 4-battalion offensive against important strategic objectives through an area containing approximately 10,000 battle-seasoned Japanese troops. Locally known as the "Kachin Rangers", Detachment 101 and its Kachin troops became a ruthless striking force, continually on the offensive against the veterans of the Japanese 18th and 56th Divisions. Throughout the campaign, the Kachin Rangers were equipped with nothing heavier than mortars and had to rely entirely upon air-dropped suppllies. Besides a numerical superiority of three to one, the enemy had the advantage of adequate supplies, artillery tankettes, carefully prepared positions, and motor transportation. Alternating frontal attacks with guerilla tactics, the Kachin Rangers remained in constant contact with the enemy during the entire period and persistently cut him down and demoralized him. During the vicious struggle for Lawksawk, 400 Rangers met 700 Japanese veterans supported by artillery and, in a 12-hour battle, killed 281 of the enemy while suffering only 7 casualties. They took Loilem, central junction of vital roads, despite its protecting system of bunkers and pillboxes after 10 days of unremitting assaults. Under the most hazardous jungle conditions, Americans of Detachment 101 displayed extraordinary heroism in leading their coordinated battalions of 3,200 natives to complete victory against an overwhelmingly superior force. They met and routed 10,000 Japanese throughout an area of 10,000 square miles, killed 1,247 while sustaining losses of 37, demolished or captured 4 large dumps, destroyed th enemy motor transport, and inflicted extensive damage on communications and installations. The courage and fighting spirit displayed by the officers and men of Service Unit Detachment No. 101, Office of Strategic Services, in this successful offensive action against overwhelming enemy strength, reflect the highest traditions of the armed forces of the United States. (General Orders 278, Headquarters United States Army Forces, 16 November 1945, as approved by the Commanding General, India-Burma Theater).
(signed)
DWIGHT D. EISENHOWER
Chief of Staff
and
EDWARD F. WITSELL
Major General
Acting The Adjutant General

Notes for Ida Bee Huff:

The story was repeated many times to all the family- about how Jim & Mae Money would pass a small house off to the side of the road going to Sylvester. There, playing alone and looking as wild as any little Indian, was a tiny little girl, seemingly unsupervised and free as the wind. Again and again, they passed this house and never a soul was seen -except for this tiny little girl, with raven black hair and dark skin. They worried about her and wondered, 'where on earth was her mother?'

They finally began asking questions of people in Sylvester and were told that it was the Huff place and that Mrs. Huff had died and two of the children had already been sent to relatives or adopted out to distant family. Mr. Huff was nearing 70 and in poor health, it was probably only a matter of time until he would seek a home for this little girl.

Mr. Huffs \Vife had been bedridden during most of her last pregnancy. She died when the last baby was just 4 months old and he had adopted the baby out when it was 8 months old. Jim & Mae knew- that meant this little 4 year old child had been on her own, to entertain herself, for well over a year. No wonder she appeared as wild as any little Indian. The wheels began to turn and they let it be known that they would love to take this little girl - this little raven haired beauty, as their own. Before long, word came that Mr. Huff was seeking someone to love and care for this child.

Within hours, they arrived back home with their new daughter and set about cleaning her up - as it appeared a bath was long overdue. You can imagine their surprise, after weeks of thinking of this little dark haired, dark skinned girl, when, out of the bath water came a tow-headed blonde with fair skin. It seems she had been playing in the soot piles and the bum piles and with no mother to put her in the tub on a regular basis, all of that had ground into the skin and changed her color. No matter, she was theirs and they loved her with all their hearts and provided her a wonderful Christian home.

As Bee's daughter, I have heard that story a hundred times and I'm sure that background had a lot to do with her personality and traits later in life. She was always clean, well-dressed, with her hair done. Her house was spotless and she was one of the most organized people I have ever known. She never minded hard work and could get more done in a short time than most people could do all day. She was also fiercely independent - no one has to wonder why.

NOTE: Bee was around 70 years old when she was found by her birth family. Two cousins, Bryant Huff (retired judge in Atlanta, Georgia) and J. Arnold Huff were co-authoring a book on 'John Huff of Gwinnett Co., Georgia'. Bee and her family were some of the last relatives to be included in that book. What a time she had reading about the relatives she had never known.

The authors of this book have given me permission to enter Bee's line, as well as anything else, on this program. Bryant says, "the book was written to be shared", and wishes other Huff researchers to have the information. However, I have entered only Bee's direct line with some information on siblings of each generation.

Children of Vestle Gaston and Ida Huff

      i.   Judith Ann Gaston, born September 23, 1941 in Apple Springs, Trinity County, Texas; married Joe Howard Hathcock June 30, 1961 in Dallas County, Texas.

      ii.   Nelda Lynn Gaston, born June 26, 1944 in Washington D. C.; married James Edward Hale April 06, 1966 in Dallas County, Texas.

Generation No. 2

2. Clyde C. Gaston, born March 20, 1885 in Trinity County, Texas; died August 12, 1954 in Harris County, Texas. He was the son of 4. John Anderson Gaston and S. Bennetta A. Castleberry. He married 3.Rhoda Levara Hutson December 25, 1910 in Trinity County, Texas.
3. Rhoda Levara Hutson, born April 19, 1890 in North Cedar Creek, Trinity County, Texas; died September 1971 in Harris County, Texas. She was the daughter of 6. Abram Preston Hutson and 7. Eliza Ann McClain.

Children of Clyde Gaston and Rhoda Hutson are:

1

      i.   Vestle C. Gaston, born June 15, 1913 in Trinity Co., Tx.; died September 09, 1996 in Harris Co., Tx.; married Ida Bee Huff November 30, 1940 in Trinity Co., Tx..

      ii.   Eathel Gaston, born December 07, 1915 in Trinity County, Texas; died December 03, 1996 in Harris County, Texas; married Donald P. McConnell in Trinity County, Texas.

      iii.   Merion H. Gaston, born July 01, 1921 in Trinity Co., Tx.; died July 1971 in Harris Co., Tx.; married Katherine?.

Notes for Merion H. Gaston:
Obituary:
FUNERAL SERVICES HELD SUNDAY FOR MERLON H. GASTON
Services for Merion H. Gaston, 50, were held Sunday in the Oakley-Metcalf Chapel with Bro. Oliver Murray oficiating. Burial was in the Bennett Cemetery.
Mr. Gaston, 2213 10th St., Galena Park, died in a Houston hospital Friday. He was born July 1, 1921, in Trinity County and had lived in Houston since 1945. He was a member of the Church of Christ and was a veteran of World War II and the Korean Conflict.

Survivors: mother, Rhoda of Galena Park; daughters, Mrs. Jackquelyn Slaton and Mrs. Zelda Jacobs, both of Mesquite; son, Edward of Mesquite; brother, Vestle of Houston; sisters, Mrs. Eathel McConnell of Galena Park and Mrs. Maxine Edingburg of Bellaire; two grandchildren.

Pallbearers: John Jacobs, Gary Slaton, W. C. Hutson, Michael Cloyd, Larry Cloyd and Donald Austin.

Oakley-Metcalf, directors.

IV.   Maxine Gaston, married Pat Edinburgh.

Generation No. 3

4. John Anderson Gaston, born January 01, 1848 in Houston Co., Tx.; died March 02, 1922 in Gause, Milam Co., Tx.. He was the son of 8. Gibson Gaston and 9. Jane Killion. He married 5. Bennetta A. Castleberry July 22, 1875 in Trinity County, Texas.
5. Bennetta A. Castleberry, born September 25, 1858; died January 15, 1925 in Milam County, Texas. She was the daughter of 10. Jacob Ferdinand Castleberry and 11. Nancy M. Higdon.

Notes for John Anderson Gaston:
Served as Justice of the Peace, Trinity County, 1894-1896.

Gaston School existed from 1884 to 1931, known as Gaston Church White School District 6 Number 5, Gaston Church Community School 21, and Gaston District 21. John Anderson Gaston served as Trustee, as did three of his sons at later dates: Clyde C. Gaston, John Alva Gaston and Jacob Gibson Gaston.

Children of John Gaston and Bennetta Castleberry are:

1.   Jacob Gibson Gaston, born August 13, 1876 in Dallas County, Texas; died May 1933 in Dallas County, Texas; married Lillias King October 26, 1902.
2.   Bennetta Ola Gaston, born December 15, 1877 in Trinity County, Texas; died December 21, 1962 in Gause, Milam County, Texas; married Thomas Clyde Wilson March 22, 1909 in Milam Co., Tx..
3.   John Alva Gaston, born March 27, 1879 in Trinity County, Texas; died February 26, 1925 in Apple Springs, Trinity County, Texas; married Della Deaton January 06, 1909 in Trinity Co Tx..
4.   William Robert Gaston, born April 03, 1880 in Trinity County, Texas; died December 25, 1908; married Annie Eleanor Dominy April 03, 1904.
5.   James Jerome Gaston, born January 04, 1882 in Apple Springs, Trinity Co., Tx.; died August 15, 1961 in Gause, Milam Co., Tx.; married Martha Burke September 25, 1904.
6.   Tudor N. Gaston, born May 10, 1883 in Trinity County, Texas; died October 22, 1884 in Apple Springs, Trinity County, Texas.
7.   Clyde C. Gaston, born March 20, 1885 in Trinity County, Texas; died August 12, 1954 in Harris County, Texas; married Rhoda Levara Hutson December 25, 1910 in Trinity County, Texas.
8.   Oran Oshen Gaston, born December 28, 1886 in Trinity County, Texas; died November 04, 1924 in Gause, Milam County, Texas.
9.   Bertha Oma Gaston, born March 28, 1888 in Trinity County, Texas; died May 17, 1956 in Jacksonville, Texas; married Robert Ed McNally December 29, 1907.
10.   Budd B. Gaston, born November 17, 1889 in Trinity County, Texas; died

576

November 08, 1968 in Gause, Milam County, Texas; married Mary Carr July 08, 1931.

- xl. Higdon H. Gaston, born November 03, 1891 in Trinity County, Texas; died December 23, 1960 in Gause, Milam County, Texas; married Elizabeth Arledge May 20, 1927.
- xtt. Blanch Ora Gaston, born November 09, 1893 in Trinity County, Texas; died November 09, 1974 in Gause, Milam County, Texas; married Henry Lee April 16, 1916.

- XIII. Buena Ora Gaston, born August 26, 1896 in Trinity County, Texas; died March 28, 1984 in Ft. Worth, Tarrant County, Texas; married (1) Ray Gallager; married (2) Benjamin Theodore Christian August 30, 1914.
- xiv. Lena Wilmoth Gaston, born April 29, 1902 in Trinity County, Texas; died July 15, 1977; married Vance E. Stallings December 22, 1923.
- xv. Madge Gaston, born October 31, 1903 in Trinity County, Texas; died September 18, 1985 in Illinois; married Willie Canady July 21, 1925.

6. Abram Preston Hutson, born December 24, 1862 in Simpson County, Mississippi; died January 09, 1909 in North Cedar Creek, Trinity County, Texas. He was the son of 12. William H. Hutson and 13. Nancy Elizabeth Womack. He married 7. Eliza Ann McClain January 10, 1883.
7. Eliza Ann McClain, born December 23, 1863 in Centralia, Texas; died January 09, 1955 in Lufkin, Texas. She was the daughter of 14. William Zedekiah McClain and 15. Rhoda Deborah Watson.

Notes for Abram Preston Hutson:
Joicy Hutson McMullen, granddaughter of Abram Preston Hutson made notes about him for inclusion in the book Trinity County Beginnings. Following are some modified excerpts:
Abram Preston Hutson was only four years old when the journey was made from Mississippi to Texas in 1866. The family settled at North Cedar Creek. When Abram was sixteen years old, the family bought a farm in Centralia and moved there.

Abram Preston and Eliza Ann McClain were married in 1884, and bought 200 acres of land at North Cedar Creek, where they farmed the land and raised their family. Abram feared that something would happen to him and Eliza would be left at North Cedar Creek with small children; so they decided to move to Centralia. The deal was made for the farm and Abram took pneumonia. He signed the final papers while he was on his deathbed. He died before the move was made, at the age of 46.

Children of Abram Hutson and Eliza McClain are:

- t. Hernon Hutson, married (2) Ona Maness.
- II. Grover Cleveland Hutson, born October 21, 1884 in Trinity County, Texas; died March 23, 1964 in Trinity County, Texas; married Antionette Valeria Standley October 31, 1909 in Helmic, Texas.
- III. William Zid Hutson, born 1886 in Trinity County, Texas; died 1918 in France; married Ola Maness.
  Notes for William Zid Hutson:
  Zid was drafted into the service in 1917 and sent to France in 1918. He was killed a short time later.

- IV. Rhoda Levara Hutson, born April 19, 1890 in North Cedar Creek, Trinity County, Texas; died September 1971 in Harris County, Texas; married

Clyde C. Gaston December 25, 1910 in Trinity County, Texas.

- v.   Nannie May Hutson, born May 01, 1892 in Centralia, Texas; died 1983; married Marshall Bedford Deaton December 25, 1912.
- vt. Burta Rebecca Hutson, born Abt. 1894; married Richard Milligan.
- vii. Jay Hutson, born April 14, 1896 in Trinity County, Texas; died March 14, 1947; married Yerta Womack June 09, 1918 in Apple Springs, Trinity County, Texas.

- viii. Rosa Lee Hutson, born March 24, 1898 in Centralia, Trinity County, Texas; married Edgar Clifton Dominy August 24, 1918 in Groveton, Texas.
- ix. Ethel Ann Hutson, born Abt. 1900 in Trinity County, Texas; married (1) Espie Hollis; married (2) Earl Trueblood.
- x.   Marvin Preston Hutson, born Abt. 1903 in Trinity County, Texas; died 1976 in Trinity County, Texas; married Alta Milligan.

Generation No. -1

8. Gibson Gaston, born November 23, 1810 in Knox Co., Ky.; died December 17, 1865 in Trinity Co., Tx.. He was the son of 16. Hugh Gaston and 17. Jane?. He married 9. Jane Killion August 05, 1841 in Houston Co., Tx..

9. Jane Killion, born April 17, 1825 in Blount Co., Al.; died June 29, 1915 in Gause, Milam Co., Tx.. She was the daughter of 18. John Anderson Killion and 19. Nancy Jane Moore.
Notes for Gibson Gaston:
Gibson Gaston was born Nov. 23, 1810 in Kentucky. As a youth he lived in Indiana but in 1830 moved to Illinois. On 6/21/ 1830 Gibson bought 40 acres of land in Douglas Co., Illinois, Section 23 Township 16N. On the same day, his twin brother Joseph Gaston also bought 40 acres in the same county, section and township.

He served with the [J)inois Mounted Volunteers in the Black Hawk War in 1832. He volunteered and served three months on an expedition against the Sac and Fox Indians. He was discharged Aug. 15, 1832.

On 7117/1833, Gibson Gaston purchased 40 acres of land in Coles Co_, Illinois, Section 20, Township 13N

In Houston County, Texas, he joined a company of Mounted Rangers on Mar. 26, 1839, and was duly elected as Sergeant, serving under Captain Box. He was discharged Oct. 18, 1839.

He settled at Fort Houston in May, 1841, and on August 4, 1841, married Jane Killian, daughter of John Anderson Killian and Nancy (Moore) Killian.

On Nov. 30, 1841, Gibson filed for 320 acres of land in Rusk County near Henderson. In 1853, the Gaston's moved to Trinity county on land situated near Sumpter. Gibson received a land Script Certificate for 160 acres of land located 12-1/2 miles north of Sumpter in Trinity County, issued Nov. 18, 1857.

(Note on Trinity County: Trinity County was in the original municipality of Nacogdoches and was granted to Joseph Vehlins by the Mexican Government in 1827. Houston County was created from

578

Vehlins' grant by an act of the Republic of Texas, June 12, 1837. This newly formed county included within its bounds all the territory now within the Bounds of Trinity County. Source: "A History of Trinity County, by Flora G. Bowles).

Texas Census lists Gibson Gaston in Houston Co., Tx., in 1840, 1850, & 1860.

Gibson Gaston's last will and testament is found in Book M, page 448, Trinity County courthouse.

Notes for Jane Killion:
Jane Killian was born April 17, 1825 in Blount County, Alabama and came to Texas in 1832 with her parents and grandparents settling near Fort Duty in Anderson County.

Children of Gibson Gaston and Jane Killion are:

i.   Amanda Caroline Gaston, born June 19, 1843 in Houston Co., Tx.; died August 05, 1926 in Anderson Co., Tx.; married George W. Crawford August 22, 1861.
ii.   Mary Isabella Gaston, born September 11, 1845 in Houston County, Tx.; died June 29, 1937 in Trinity County, Tx.; married David Henry Hamilton October 08, 1867 in Trinity Co., Tx..
Notes for David Henry Hamilton:
David Henry Hamilton: In his book, "History of Company M First Texas Volunteer Infantry" (1924), he gives a good description of his activities and experiences in the Civil War. Without a single injury, he returned to Sumpter on May 25, 1865. (Source: Trinity County Beginnings, pg. 411)

A quote from his book:
From this county (Trinity Co., Tx.) with a population of about 3,000 people, there were organized three large companies of soldiers who went to fight for the Confederate States. Besides those enlisting in these three companies, many enlisted in organizations in other sections of the state. The three companies raised in the county were known as Tullos Company, Kirksey Company, and Company M. It is of interest to know that more men enlisted from Trinity County than there were voters within the county. Almost all the men and boys above eighteen years of age and under sixty were in the service. No record of these companies can now be found except that of company M. This company served in Hood's Brigade. Company M. was organized at Sumpter, the county seat of Trinity County, in the year 1862. It was composed of 120 men, about half of whom were between seventeen and twenty one years of age. This company was drilled in the maneuvers of warfare on the court house square at Sumpter in day time and spent the evenings attending balls and entertainments given by the citizens for their pleasure. On the night of May 4, 1862, the citizens gave the Company a grand ball at which the boys danced all night and pledged themselves never to dance again until the Southern Confederacy was established; and the following afternoon at 2:30 o'clock, to the music of the violin and with great joy, the march was begun toward the front.

Company M, which went out from Sumpter, Trinity County, May 5, 1862, with such enthusiasm, received its baptism of fire in all the bloody conflicts in which Hood's Brigade participated. Out of the 120 men and boys that enlisted, only six were present at the surrender at Appomattox. These were Sam Watson, Willoughby Tullos, Sam Stubblefield, John Wilson, Epriam Dial, and David H. Hamilton. Not an officer of the company survived. Captain Ballinger had become disabled by disease and had been discharged. He returned home and died at Waco, Texas. Thomas Sandford, first lieutenant, was killed at Sharpsburg, Dr. William Cecil, second lieutenant., was killed at Knoxville, Tenn. George Wagnon died of measles at Jackson, Mississippi.

A small number of the company returned home maimed for life from the battle front, while some were in Federal prisons. The rest of Company M slept in soldier's graves. The other two companies organized in the county did not suffer such a great mortality as did Company M, but gave a good account of themselves.

Source: A History of Trinity County, Texas, 1827- 1928, by Flora G. Bowles
(Not published until 1966)
pg. 31,32

In the same book, A History of Trinity County, Texas, Mrs. Bowles quotes from a newspaper article by D. H. Hamilton as follows:

The Honorable David H. Hamilton, a respected citizen of Trinity County since 1853, says in the Trinity County News of October 7, 1927, speaking of the wild life of the county at that early day: "It is probably not safe to enter upon a discussion of the hunting and fishing possibilities of that early day. The Nimrod and angler of this day would be apt to think a description of the paradise that existed at this early time merely the result of an over worked imagination, if not downright prevarication. The forests were literally filled with all kinds of game, deer, bear, panthers, wolves, bob-cats - in fact every thing that one would care to hunt for either pelt, fur or food. The streams were filled with fish the mere mention of which makes one long for the good old days again." Then he facetiously says: "If one were to attempt to describe the large catches of fish from the streams of that day it would tax the credulity of the modem mind: In fact it would take two or three able bodied men to believe these fish stories. It has always been dangerous to any man's reputation for veracity to indulge himself in fish stories. So it seems needful to make a period here."

Source: A History of Trinity County, Texas 1827 - 1928, by Flora G. Bowles
pg. 12

111. John Anderson Gaston, born January 01, 1848 in Houston Co., Tx.; died March 02, 1922 in Gause, Milam Co., Tx.; married Bennetta A. Castleberry July 22, 1875 in Trinity County, Texas.

lv. William Riley Gaston, born December 29, 1849 in Trinity Co, Tx.; died February 26, 1879; married Mary Francis Henderson February 1871.

v.   James Moore Gaston, born September 10, 1852 in Trinity Co, Tx.; died October 14, 1881 in Anderson County, Texas; married Mary E. Shaver September 30, 1875.

vi.   Robert Henderson Gaston, born November 20, 1854 in Trinity County, Texas.

vii.   Martha Jane Gaston, born January 22, 1857 in Trinity County, Texas; died November 18, 1900 in Buffalo, Freestone County, Texas; married Charles Wesley Castleberry February 1873 in Pennington, Trinity Co., Tx.

10. Jacob Ferdinand Castleberry, born March 01, 1817 in Georgia; died March 03, 1874 in Trinity County, Texas. He was the son of 20. Robert Castleberry and 21. Mary Forrester. He married 11. Nancy M. Higdon November 04, 1837 in Pike County, Alabama.

11. Nancy M. Higdon, born May 02, 1823; died January 02, 1903. She was the daughter of 22. Robert Higdon and 23. Elizabeth Green.

Notes for Jacob Ferdinand Castleberry:

Jacob Castleberry served in Captain Wiley White's Alabama Militia from Pike Co., Alabama, in the Creek Florida War of 1836.

He married Nancy M. Higdon in 1837, in Pike County, Alabama, then in 1840 moved to Copiah County, Mississippi, with the Higdons and Jacob's father, Robert Castleberry. By 1850, they were living in Bradley County, Arkansas, where they stayed for a short time. Their next move was to Trinity County, Texas, about 1852. They settled near Pennington, Texas.

Children of Jacob Castleberry and Nancy Higdon are:

2
i.   Bennetta A. Castleberry, born September 25, 1858; died January 15, 1925 in Milam County, Texas; married John Anderson Gaston July 22, 1875 in Trinity County, Texas.

ii.   Mary E. Castleberry.

iii.   Robert W. Castleberry.

iv.   Susan Castleberry, married ? Slater.

v.   Charles Wesley Castleberry, born October 29, 1850 in Bradley County, Arkansas; died October 19, 1892 in Fairfield, Freestone County, Texas; married Martha Jane Gaston February 1873 in Pennington, Trinity Co., Tx..

vl.   Mandy (Nancy) Castleberry.

vit.   William Castleberry.

viii.   Fannie Castleberry, married Boggan Boyd.

ix.   Martha (Mattie) Castleberry.

12. William H. Hutson, born March 01, 1835 in Simpson County, Mississippi; died March 29, 1922 in Trinity County, Texas. He was the son of 24. William Thomas Hutson and 25. Rebecca Magee. He married 13. Nancy Elizabeth Womack December 20, 1855 in Simpson County, Mississippi.

13. Nancy Elizabeth Womack, born December 30, 1837 in Rankin County, Mississippi; died April 23, 1906 in Trinity County, Texas. She was the daughter of 26. William B. Womack and 27. Nancy Elizabeth Franklin.

Notes for William H. Hutson:

William Hutson served in the Confederate Army during the Civil War, was captured twice and paroled once. He was captured the second time in Tennessee in the last year of the War and sent to the prisoner of war prison at Camp Douglas, Chicago, Illinois, where he remained until the war was over.

In the spring of 1866, William Hutson and his brother Aaron Hutson, along with their sisters, Ruth Hutson (who married Frank Lee) and Mary Louisia Hutson (who married John Lee), migrated from Mississippi to Texas.

William Hutson lived with his family on North Cedar Creek, later moving to Centralia, where he operated a general store and served as postmaster until his wife, Nancy Elizabeth, died in 1906. After her death, he moved to Apple Springs, living with his son Richmond Lee Hutson and his family until his death in 1922.

William and his wife, Nancy Elizabeth Womack, were the progenitors of most of the Hutson families in Trinity County who descended from their five sons: William Thomas Hutson, Albert Jackson (Jay) Hutson, Abram Preston Hutson, Richmond Lee Hutson, and Womack Hutson.

Children of William Hutson and Nancy Womack are:

       I.   William Thomas Hutson, born 1856; died 1879; married Molly Magee.

      II.   Albert Jackson Hutson, born 1859 in Mississippi; died 1954; married Rebecca Ann McClain.

     III.   Aley Jane Hutson, born 1861 in Mississippi; died 1884; married John Ingram.

     IV.   Abram Preston Hutson, bom December 24, 1862 in Simpson County, Mississippi; died January 09, 1909 in North Cedar Creek, Trinity County, Texas; married Eliza Ann McClain January 10, 1883.

      V.   Mary Etta Hutson, born 1864 in Trinity County, Texas; died 1949; married Henry Largent.

     VI.   Richmond Lee Hutson, born 1866-1868 in Trinity County, Texas; died 1952; married Rosada Susan Burke August 02, 1894.

     VII.   Nancy Rebecca Hutson, born Abt. 1871 in Trinity County, Texas; married James B. Allen.

     VIII. Womack Hutson, born February 01, 1874 in Centralia, Trinity County, Texas; died 1964 in Trinity County, Texas; married (1) Evelyn Ratcliff 1903 in Lufkin, Texas; married (2) Fannie Inez Gann August 20, 1907 in Rusk, Texas.

           Notes for Womack Hutson:
           Womack Hutson was born with an underdeveloped right arm which in no way hindered him as he went about his pursuits. Once when his children were young, a son was having trouble lifting a wheelbarrow. Womack said, 'you had better let me do that.' He looped a rope over his left shoulder, then stood slightly bent between the handles of the wheelbarrow and tied the rope under the right handle. When he straightened up and grasped the left handle, he lifted the wheelbarrow. His young son asked, 'Did you ever miss having two hands?' and Womach replied, 'Did you ever miss having three hands?' while chuckling.
           Source: Trinity County Beginnings, Vol. 1, story by Charles P. Hutson

     Ix.   Lula Pernecia Hutson, born 1877 in Trinity County, Texas; died 1955; married Hardy Standley.

x.   Alice M. Hutson, born December 30, 1857; died December 20, 1909; married (1) L. J. McClain; married (2) Louis Jefferson McClain January 12, 1882.

14. William Zedekiah McClain, born October 19, 1812 in Tennessee; died July 14, 1899 in Trinity Co., Tx.. He was the son of 28. Daniel McClain and 29. Mariah ?. He married 15. Rhoda Deborah Watson April 11, 1844 in Houston Co., Tx..

15. Rhoda Deborah Watson, born May 07, 1825 in Baton Rouge, La.; died April 30, 1913 in Centralia, Trinity Co., Tx.. She was the daughter of 30. William Samuel Watson and 31. Cecelia Ann Watson.

Notes for William Zedekiah McClain:
These McClain's came from Tennessee to Texas in the early 1820's and were granted land from Mexico.

William Zedekiah (Zid) McClain enlisted in the service in the spring of 1862, Captain Ballinger's Company M, Hood's Brigade, I st Texas Regiment, and was discharged in the spring of 1865. (Source: Trinity County Beginnings, p 569)

Zedekiah McClain was a member of the first grand jury that met in Crockett. Since no building was provided for court sessions, the jury met under a large tree near the present site of the Davy Crockett Spring and fountain. During the session, Indians attacked a family on the present Hall's Bluff Road but escaped across the Trinity River.

The Civil War was growing with intensity, and volunteers were needed. On May 4, 1862, Zedekiah and his eldest son, Rufus, enlisted for military service at Sumpter, in Trinity County. He was 50 years of age, and Rufus was 17. They were in Gen. John Bell Hood's Texas Brigade, I st Texas Regiment, Company M, under Capt. Ballinger. They were seperated and did not meet again until both returned from the War.

Children of William McClain and Rhoda Watson are:

i.   William Rufus McClain, born January 28, 1845 in Hagerville, Houston Co., Tx.; died September 23, 1927 in Hagerville, Houston Co., Tx.; married Margaret Texana Hager January 19, 1871.

Notes for William Rufus McClain:
William Rufus McClain, son of William Zedekiah and Rhoda Deborah Watson McClain, was born Jan. 28, 1845 at Hagerville, Houston Co., Tx. He was the eldest of twelve children, two of whom died in infancy.

Rufus attended the Scissil School in Trinity County. The building was made of logs with only one room and a large fireplace. The seats were split logs and desks were planks. The children wrote on slates with slate pencils. In some cases, an entire family of children used the same slate. They studied the "Blue Back" Spelling Book by Noah Webster. Besides reading, spelling and writing, they also studied catechism. By the time "Rufe" was twelve or fourteen years of age, he dropped out of school and worked with his father, helping to provide a livelihood for the large

583

family.

The Civil War brought changes in many early Texas families, and the Zedekiah McClain family was no exception. Rufe and his father enlisted on May 4, 1862 when Rufe was 17 years of age, and his father was 50. They left Sumpter in Trinity County, were assigned to Gen. John Bell Hood's Texas Brigade, 1st Texas Regiment, Company M., under Captain Ballinger, and were sent to Richmond, Virginia for training. However, they were separated and did not meet again until the War was over. Rufe developed serious lung and liver diseases, and was hospitalized until October 1862 when he was discharged due to his health condition, and "being only 17 years of age" (quote from his medical discharge). He returned to his home, but later re-enlisted and served in the Texas Brigade under General Parson. On April 9, 1865 when General Robert E. Lee surrendered, Rufe was fighting with the 12th Regiment, Company B

Rufe married Miss Margaret Texana Hager on Jan. 19, 1871. They made their home in Hagerville where their six children were born. Two of the children died in infancy. Texana died Dec. 30, 1883, when the eldest child was only six years of age.

Source: Story written by Myrtle Petty Beadle in History of Houston County

11. James Artemas McClain, born April 28, 1846; married Harriet Watson.
III. Julius Manson McClain, born October 19, 1847 in Hagerville, Houston Co., Tx.; died 1938 in Trinity Co., Tx.; married Carolyne Chapman.
IV. Sam Houston McClain, born July 02, 1849 in Hagerville, Houston Co., Tx.; died January 10, 1936; married Mary Eddie Hager.
V. William Monroe McClain, born January 29, 1852 in Hagerville, Houston Co., Tx.; married Rebecca Hutson Abt. 1869.
vi. Louis Jefferson McClain, born January 29, 1855 in Hagerville, Houston Co., Tx.; died November 22, 1936; married Alice M. Hutson January 12, 1882.
VII. Benjamin Franklin McClain, born August 12, 1856 in Hagerville, Houston Co., Tx.; married N. E. Gresham.
VIII. Wyatt Beasley McClain, born August 04, 1858 in Hagerville, Houston Co., Tx.; married Alice Grimes.
IX. Rebecca Ann McClain, born June !5, 1861 in Hagerville, Houston Co., Tx.; died January 19, 1951; married Albert Jackson Hutson.
X. Eliza Ann McClain, born December 23, 1863 in Centralia, Texas; died January 09, 1955 in Lufkin, Texas; married Abram Preston Hutson January 10, 1883.

2

Generation No. 5

16. Hugh Gaston, born 1776 in possibly North Carolina; died 1830 in Green Co., Indiana. He was the son of 32. Robert Gaston and 33. Margaret Logan. He married 17. Jane ? Bef. 1798.
17. Jane ?.
Notes for Hugh Gaston:
Hugh Gaston is mentioned as one of the old pioneer settlers of Beech Creek Township, Greene

county, Indiana, in "The Early History of Greene Co., Indiana" by Uncle Jack Baber (printed 1875), as follows:

"Hugh Gaston was born in North Carolina and came to Greene County in the year 1822 and settled on the place and made a farm, and set out the old apple orchard where Mr. Keyes now lives. Mr. Gaston and wife raised eight children, the two youngest being twins. All of them lived to be men and women." pg 42

Hugh Gaston died in 1830. His wife evidently moved back to Coles Co., Ill. where her will was probated later. Little is known regarding Hugh's death or where he is buried. Notes from one researcher says: "He died on a flat boat on the Mississippi River". I have found no proof of this yet. However, in the Early History of Green Co., Ind., page 50, there is a paragraph regarding Eel River Township which states:

"The first flat-boat ever sent to New Orleans from any place in Greene county, was built at Point Commerce, by the Craigs', and was loaded with slaves and hoop-poles. Afterwards, several boats were sent down the river, loaded with corn and pork; and we have a sad history of the fate of four of the neighbor boys or young men - Caleb Jessup's two sons, and James Smith's two sons- who were coming up the river on the streamer 'Car of Commerce'. The boiler exploded and many passengers were scalded to death."

It is possible since Hugh Gaston was not from Eel River Township (he was from Beech Creek Township) that his name was not mentioned as a casualty in this paragraph. Some of the 'many passengers' who were scalded to death were probably from areas other than Eel River.

Notes for Jane?:
Jane_____Gaston's will was probated in Coles Co., Ill. 4/711831.

Children of Hugh Gaston and Jane ? are:

i. Isabelle Gaston, born 1798 in Tennessee; died November 05, 1852 in Green Co., Ind.; married William Chestnut March 04, 1817 in Knox Co., Ky..
ii. Robert Gaston, born Abt. 1799; married Sally Bullock March 1820 in Knox Co., Ky..
iii. Henrietta Gaston, born 1800; married Terrel Reeves Abt. September 20, 1827 in Greene Co., Indiana.
iv. Margaret Gaston, born March 04, 1800 in Knox Co., Ky.; married John Johnson March 04, 1817 in Knox Co., Ky..
v. Elizabeth Gaston, born Abt. 1802 in Indiana; married John Bullock December 1819 in Knox Co., Ky..
vi. James Morrow Gaston, born June 10, 1804 in Knox Co., Ky.; died March 07, 1889 in Green Co., Indiana; married Mary P. Bryan Abt. October 05, 1826 in Greene Co., Indiana.
Notes for James Morrow Gaston:
James Gaston is mentioned in "The Early History of Greene County, Indiana, by Uncle Jack Baber, (printed 1875) as follows:

"Old Uncle James Gaston came to Greene County, more than fifty years ago, and shortly afterwards he was married to Miss Mary Polly Bryan, and settled on his excellent farm, and has lived there until he has seen all his neighbors settle in around him, and yet he can see to read without glasses. Mr. Gaston is seventy years old, and his wife has eleven children - four boys and seven girls." page 42-43

Among the first weddings (in Beech Creek Township, Greene Co.) were John Kellum and Elizabeth Bryan; Wyatt Miller and Polly Bland; JAMES GASTON
and MARY P. BRYAN ... page 43

Among the early school teachers was James Gaston. page 43
[n 1835, James M. Gaston served as Commissioner. page 23

vii.   Gibson Gaston. born November 23, 1810 in Knox Co., Ky.; died December 17, 1865 in Trinity Co., Tx.; married Jane Killion August 05, 1841 in Houston Co., Tx..

viii. Joseph Gaston, born November 23, 1810 in Knox Co., Ky.; died Abt. 1839 in Green Co., Indiana; married Elenor Cessua Abt. April 03, 1828 in Greene Co., Indiana.

18. John Anderson Killion, born March 07, 1806 in White Co., Tenn.; died October 16, 1895 in Anderson Co., Tx. He was the son of 36. Goodwin Killion and 37. Nancy Jane Sharp. He married 19. Nancy Jane Moore May 06, 1824 in Blount County, Alabama.

19. Nancy Jane Moore, born May 31, 1803 in White Co., Tenn.; died May 28, 1881 in Anderson Co., Tx.

Notes for John Anderson Killion:
The Killians, German by origin, had arrived in America in the early 1730's and helped to tame and settle Lincoln County, North Carolina. The Killians of Texas, descendants of the North Carolinians, also were pioneers and were early settlers of Anderson County. They came by wagon from Alabama in 1836 to Texas and settled up and down the old Rusk Road and on Snake Creek, 8-1/2 miles on the old Alder Branch and Palentiue Road.

Children of John Killion and Nancy Moore are:

i.   Jane Killion, born April 17, 1825 in Blount Co., Al.; died June 29, 1915 in Gause, Milam Co., Tx.; married Gibson Gaston August 05, 1841 in Houston Co., Tx..

ii.   John Nelson Killion, born January 01, 1831 in Blount Co., Ala.; died June 02, 1892; married Elizabeth Squyres February 01, 1855 in Anderson Co., Tx.

iii. James M. Killion, born April 13, 1829 in Blount Co., Ala.; died August 02, 1915 in Stephenville, Erath Co.. Tx.; married (1) Elizabeth Palmer October 08, 1847 in Anderson Co., Tx; married (2) Eliza Lucinda Mills 1865 in Woods Co., Tx..

iv.   Francis Caroline Killion, born July 15, 1833 in Blount Co., Ala.; died November 19, 1920 in Anderson Co., Tx; married John Patrick Huddleston November 16, 851.

v.   William Killion.

20. Robert Castleberry. He was the son of 40. Jacob Castleberry. He married 21. Mary Forrester.
21. Mary Forrester.

Child of Robert Castleberry and Mary Forrester is:

    IQ   I.   Jacob Ferdinand Castleberry, born March 01, 1817 in Georgia; died March 03, 1874 in Trinity County, Texas; married Nancy M. Higdon November 04, 1837 in Pike County, Alabama.

22. Robert Higdon. He married 23. Elizabeth Green.
23. Elizabeth Green.

Child of Robert Higdon and Elizabeth Green is:

    11   i.   Nancy M. Higdon, born May 02, 1823; died January 02, 1903; married Jacob Ferdinand Castleberry November 04, 1837 in Pike County, Alabama.

24. William Thomas Hutson, born 1798-1805 in Hutsonville, Illinois; died 1868-1870 in Illinois or Mississippi. He was the son of 48. Thomas Hutson and 49. Esther Maine. He married 25. Rebecca Magee 1824 in Simpson County, Mississippi.

25. Rebecca Magee, born 1803 in Mississippi; died in Illinois. She was the daughter of 50. Jonathan Magee, Sr. and 51. Rebecca James.

Children of William Hutson and Rebecca Magee are:

          I.   Aaron Hutson, born February 01, 1825; died Abt. 1885; married Mary Frances Clark October 01, 1846.
          II.   Thomas E. Hutson, born December 19, 1826; died October 18, 1865.
          III.   Melissa Hutson, born October 17, 1828; died September 05, 1849; married James Tullos.
          IV.   Lorahan Jane Hutson, born November 25, 1830; died Bef. 1886; married John May.
          v.   John Hutson, born December 1832; died June 11, 1833.
    12.   vi.   William H. Hutson, born March 01, 1835 in Simpson County, Mississippi; died March 29, 1922 in Trinity County, Texas; married Nancy Elizabeth Womack December 20, 1855 in Simpson County, Mississippi.
          VII.   Abram Hutson, born January 12, 1837; died June 11, 1922; married (1) Dicey Brown; married (2) Elizabeth Gardner September 1860.
               Notes for Abram Hutson:
               Abram 'Doon' Hutson and his brothers, William Hutson and Aaron Hutson, moved their families from Mississippi, to Trinity Co., Texas in 1867.
               In later years, Abram Hutson moved to Eudora, Arkansas.
          VIII.   Rutha Hutson, born March 10, 1839; died September 10, 1877.
          IX.   Rebecca Hutson, born July 1842; died February 17, 1943; married Lee.
          x.   Winey Hutson, born March 1844; died 1845.
          xI.   Mary Louisa Hutson, born March 01, 1846; died 1878.

xii.   Zeolodia Hutson, born Abt. 1850.

26. William B. Womack, born April 18, 1816 in St Helen Parish, Louisiana; died October 20, 1888 in Trinity County, Texas. He was the son of 52. David Womack, Jr. and 53. Sarah Ann Norris. He married 27. Nancy Elizabeth Franklin December 05, 1835 in Franklin County, Mississippi.
27. Nancy Elizabeth Franklin, born April 20, 1818 in Louisiana; died January 04, 1889. She was the daughter of 54. W. M. Franklin.

Notes for William B. Womack:
William B. Womack left Simpson County, Mississippi, in 1853 with his family, three brothers and a group of other families. They came to Texas and pre-empted a section of land from the state, one section per family, on Cedar Creek, four miles north of Apple Springs.

Children of William Womack and Nancy Franklin are:

       i.   Sarah Womack, born Abt. 1836 in Rankin County, Mississippi.

11   ii.   Nancy Elizabeth Womack, born December 30, 1837 in Rankin County, Mississippi; died April 23, 1906 in Trinity County, Texas; married William H. Hutson December 20, 1855 in Simpson County, Mississippi.

       iii.   Samantha Womack, born 1840 in Rankin County, Mississippi.

       iv.   Caroline Womack, born 1842 in Rankin County, Mississippi.

       v.   William Henry Womack, born December 27, 1845 in Rankin County, Mississippi; died May 27, 1926; married Eliza Ann Magee 1866 in Trinity County, Texas.

Notes for William Henry Womack:
William Henry Womack b. 1845 in Miss., was the son of William B. Womack b. 1816. His ancestors came from England to Henderson County, Virginia, in 1655.

In 1861, the Civil War broke out and William Henry Womack went from Texas back to Mississippi where he enlisted in the spring of 1863 and served two years in Company D, 4th Mississippi Calvary. The records show lhat W. H. Womack, private, Company D, 4th Mississippi Calvary, Confederate States Army, enlisted 8/28/1863; that he was sun·endered May 4, 1865, at Citronelle, Alabama, and was paroled May 12, 1865, at Gainesville, Alabama.

After the war ended, he returned to Texas to his father's farm, which he and his two brothers later inherited. He married Eliza Ann Magee. They bought a two story house in Centralia and eight acres of land that fronted on what was originally planned for a town square. The house was built to be a boarding house. William Henry lived in Centralia, but maintained the farm until near eighty years old. He fanned, raised cattle and hogs and operated a cotton gin while his boys were still at home to help. During World War I, he and his son Naith, sold two thousand hogs to the army.

The Centralia community had four Civil War veterans, William Henry Womack, Red Henry Womack, William (Bill) Hutson and Dr. Evander Gandy. Source: History of Trinity County, pg. 803 (story by Winford Womack) vt.   Celia A. Womack, born 1846 in Rankin County, Mississippi.

vu.   Abraham Richmond Womack, hom 1850 in Rankin County, Mississippi; married Betty Hood.

viii.   Albert J. Womack, born 1853 in Rankin County, Mississippi; married (1) Sarah Jane Womack; married (2) Mattie N. Rhoads January 02, 1887.

28.Daniel McClain, born in Tennessee. He was the son of 56. Thomas William McClain and 57. Rebecca Warren. He married 29. Mariah?.

29. Mariah?.

Children of Daniel McClain and Mariah ? are:

     i.   William Zedekiah McClain, born October 19, 1812 in Tennessee; died July 14, 1899 in Trinity Co., Tx.; married Rhoda Deborah Watson April 11, 1844 in Houston Co., Tx..

     ii.   Eliza Ann McClain. born 1815; married Bryd Ferrell Kerr.

30. William Samuel Watson. He married 31.Cecelia Ann Watson July 17, 1821 in St. Helena, La..

31. Cecelia Ann Watson, born in Georgia.

Notes for William Samuel Watson:
The Watson family came from Baton Rouge, La. to Texas.

Children of William Watson and Cecelia Watson are:

     i.   Rhoda Deborah Watson, born May 07, 1825 in Baton Rouge, La.; died April30, 1913 in Centralia, Trinity Co., Tx.; married William Zedekiah McClain April 11, 1844 in Houston Co., Tx..

     ii.   Sarah Bell Watson, born in St. Helena, La.; married Abner John Womack 1857 in Trinity County, Texas.
          Notes for Sarah Bell Watson:
          Sarah Watson Womack, widowed at age 28, never remarried, and lived to the age of 86, dying in 1917.
          Source: History of Trinity County, pg. 803 (story by Robert D. Womack)
          Notes for Abner John Womack:
          A. J. Womack served in the Civil War from 1861 to 1864 as a private in Co. A of Gould's Battalion, Randal's Brigade, Walker's Division, Captain P. J. Holly's Company. He died on Christmas Day in 1869, at the age of 34. Source: History of Trinity County, pg. 803 (story by Robert D. Womack)

     iii.   John Watson.

Generation No. 6

32. Robert Gaston, born 1722 in Caranliegh Cloughwater, County Antrim, Ireland; died May 09, 1787 in Lynches Creek, Lancaster Co., S.C.. He was the son of 64. William Gaston and 65. Mary Olivet Lemon. He married 33. Margaret Logan August 24, 1756 in Lancaster Co., Pa..

33. Margaret Logan, died 1848 in Lancaster Co., S. C..
Notes for Robert Gaston:
From the book Ancestors of Anzi Williford Gaston, Book II, p. 12-13
Robert Gaston emigrated to Lancaster Co., Penn. before 711 0/1757.
In 1767, he moved to Lynches Creek, 28 miles north of Camden and 2 miles east of Hanging Rock, in Lancaster Co., S.C.

Robert Gaston was a Patriot in the American Revolution. He rendered substantial services as shown by documents on file among records of the Historical Commission of S.C. in Columbia. One of these documents is a certificate dated 4/4/1782, made by Capt. Hugh McClure, to the effect that Mr. Robert Gaston furnished during the Revolution, "one horse for 70 days in Col. Henry Hampton's Light Dragoons. Certified by me, Hugh McClure, Capt." The other document on record is a similar receipt from S. Mathis of the State Commissary for 280 lbs. of beef furnished during the Revolution and certification for the payment of same under date of 8/11/1785.

Robert Gaston's home was destroyed in the war.

There have been at least 2 entries into the Daughters of the American Revolution on the records of this Robert Gaston. One of these is to be found in DAR Lineage Book, Vol. 144, p. 224, Record #143,726. The citation with regard to the Revolution records of Robert Gaston is given as follows: "Robert Gaston was a patriat of S. C., who rendered material aid. He was born in Ireland. Died at Lynches Creek. S. C.

Children of Robert Gaston and Margaret Logan are:

    i.   John Gaston, died 1836 in Shelby Co., Ill..
    ii.   Stephen Gaston.
    iii.   William Gaston, born July 23, 1755 in Lancaster Co., Pa.; died January 14, 1838 in Illinois; married Mary McClure 1781 in Lancaster Co., SC.
        Notes for William Gaston:
        William Gaston (son of Robert Gaston and Margaret Logan Gaston) served in the Rev. War under and with General Washington. He moved from South Carolina to Kentucky, date unknown. After the death of his wife, he emigrated to Illinois with the family of Matthew Rainey in 1829.

        His religion was that of Reformed Presbyterian. Politically he was an Old Line Whig. He was a very quiet unassuming, unpretentious kind of man, a man of integrity, firm in his opinions, uncompromising when he was contending for the right.
        (Source for above: taken from a record written in Aug. 1877).

        William Gaston married Mary McClure, his first cousin. He served in the following battles in the Rev. War.: Rocky Mountain, King's Mountain, Houck's Defeat, and Hanging Rock. All of these battles were fought with the South Carolina troops.

        In 1829, he came to Illinois with his son-in-law, Matthew Rainey and his daughter, Ann Gaston Rainey.
        He died in 1838 and is bnried in the old Covenanter Cemetery near

Walnut Hill, Illinois, in Marion County.

    IV.   Thomas Gaston, born July 18, 1759 in Lancaster Co., Pa.; died April 23, 1832 in Spartanburg Co., S. C.; married Sarah Nichols Abt. 1786.

    V.   James Gaston, born July 24, 1761 in Lancaster Co., Pa.; died March 07, 1840 in Wayne Co., Ill.; married Catherine Creighton March 20, 1783 in Lancaster Co., S.C..

.IQ   VI.   Hugh Gaston, born 1776 in possibly North Carolina; died 1830 in Green Co., Indiana; married Jane ? Bef. 1798.

    VII.   Joseph Gaston, died September 14, 1839 in Green Co., Tenn..

    VIII.   Margaret Gaston, born 1764; died March 06, 1816 in Chester Co., S. C.; married John McCreary.

    IX.   Elizabeth Gaston, died 1810 in St. Clair Co., [Ill.; married David Fulletton 1796 in Chester Co., S.C..

Notes for David Fullerton:
David and Elizabeth Gaston Fullerton moved from SC to Davidson Co., Tenn., then to Rutherford Co., Tenn., then to Illinois where they remained until Elizabeth's death. David then moved to Lincoln Co., Tenn. where he remained until his death in 1835.

    X.   Martha Gaston, died in Pulaski Co., Ky.; married Isaac Dye.

36. Goodwin Killion, born February 09, 1790 in South Carolina; died January 1860. He married 37. Nancy Jane Sharp August 09, 1808 in Lincoln Co., N. C..

37. Nancy Jane Sharp, died March 03, 1843.

Notes for Goodwin Killion:
Goodwin Killian and Nancy Jane Sharp lived for a time in White County, Tenn. before moving to Blount County, Ala. in 1821. Goodwin professed religion and joined the Methodist Episcopal Church and in 1825 was licensed to exhort in Blount Circuit, Alabama, Conference of the Methodist Church. In 1836, they moved to Texas.

When Goodwin Killian came to Texas, his sons, Daniel, John Anderson, William and Perry T. with their families all came with him. Also traveling with the Killians were their neighbors from Blount County; the Newton Huddlestons, Grandpa Ferguson and family, the Dave Hulets, the large Morton family that consisted of William, Jesse, John, Mary Carolina and Margaret. The wagons had first stopped at San Augustine, then Nacogdoches and on into Houston County to what is now Anderson County. The Indians were so hostile in 1836 that the families could not get out to kill game or farm so they moved to what is now Rusk County and then moved back after a year to Snake Creek. Two other families settled near then, the Richard Duty family and the X. V. Anglin family. Richard Duty, along with the Killians and their relatives built a large two-story log house for protection against the Indians. It was known as Fort Duty and was located on the Duty league, 10 miles on Hwy. 22 on the right beyond the Hammond Branch.

Goodwin Killian was shot by two Indians, 5-1/2 miles from Palestine on the Rusk Road. Supposing him mortally wounded, the Indians pursued his horse and he crawled into the high grass and hid. When his horse reached the Fort, a party came out in search of him. He was found and carried back to the Fort where he was given medical aid and eventually recovered.

John Anderson, son of Goodwin, with others ran the Indians out of their village on Snake Creek and settled on the spot because of a fresh water spring located there.

An early camp meeting area was the Snake Creek Camp Meeting Grounds which was located on the headright of Perry T. Killian, Goodwin's son. Killion's Chapel was 6 miles up Snake Creek and on John Anderson Killian's farm and was the only church in that part of the county. Goodwin Killian preached there many times.
(Source: History of Houston County)

In 1831, Goodwin Killian had a land patent, in Alabama, listed in TIO RIE Sec. 28. Neighbors in the same section were Sam') Cargo, Richard Golden, A. & F. Yielding, and Thos. C. Wells. This location works out to about 2/3 of the way from Blountsville northward along US Hwy 231 toward US Hwy 278.
(Source: Killion Newsletter, Issue 4, Mar., 1998)

Goodwin Killion purchased land in Blount Co., Alabama, from the government as follows:
Date Range Twnship Section Part acres
7/30/1833 IE lOS 28 Wl/2SW 80.28
10116/1835 IE lOS 33 NENW 40.52
9110/1838 IE lOS 33 NWNE 40.62
(Source: Killion Newsletter, Issue 4, Mar., 1998)

Listed in the book "1840 Citizens of Texas, Volume 1 Land Grants" by Gifford White, Austin, Tx 1983, on page 140 is the following information: Killion, Goodwin, 1 Dec. 1837, Class: 3, acres 640, Conditional, Where: San Augustine, Cerficicate When: 12 Dec. 1839, Unconditional, Where: San Augustine Unconditional, When: 21 Sep. 1841. Also listed are Killion; John A. Killion, Perry Killion, and William Killion.
(Source: Killion Newsletter, Issue 4, Mar., 1998)

"1840 Citizens of Texas, Volume I, Land Grants", by Gifford White, Austin, Tx 1983. Goodwin KilliAn arrived 1 Dec. 1837, 640 acres, San Augustine Co.
John A. Killion arrived before 1 Oct. 1837, 1280 acres, San Augustine Co.
Perry Killion arrived 1 Jan. 1838, 320 acres, San Augustine Co.
William Killion (married) 28 Sep. 1837, 1280 acres, San Augustine, Co.
(Source: Killion Newsletter, Issue 4, Mar., 1988)

Children of Goodwin Killion and Nancy Sharp are:

18_   I.   .John Anderson Killion, born March 07, 1806 in White Co., Tenn.; died October 16, 1895 in Anderson Co., Tx; married Nancy Jane Moore May 06, 1824 in Blount County, Alabama.
          11.   William Killion, born 1810; married Delila Morton.
          III.   Malinda Killion, married Uriah Nesmith.
          IV.   Thomas Killion, married Charlotte Burns.
          v.   Priscilla Killion, married Jesse Morton.
          vi.   Perry T. Killion, married (I) Martha Minchew; married (2) Rebecca Yates.
          VII.   Nancy Killion, married Benjamin Easley.
          VIII.   Daniel Killion, married (I) Sarah Elizabeth Nesbitt; married (2) Elizabeth Nesbet.

592

40. Jacob Castleberry, born in Warren Co., Georgia.

Child of Jacob Castleberry is:

      1.   Robert Castleberry, married Mary Forrester.

48. Thomas Hutson, born January 09, 1749/50. He was the son of 96. William Hutson and 97. Mary Woodward. He married 49. Esther Maine.

49. Esther Maine, born Abt. 1752. She was the daughter of 98. William Maine and 99. Judith Gignilliat.

Child of Thomas Hutson and Esther Maine is:

      1.   William Thomas Hutson, born 1798-1805 in Hutsonville, Illinois; died 1868-1870 in Illinois or Mississippi; married Rebecca Magee 1824 in Simpson County, Mississippi.

50. Jonathan Magee, Sr., born 1769 in South Carolina; died October 22, 1841 in Simpson Co., Miss.. He married 51. Rebecca James 1787 in Georgia (by contract).

51. Rebecca James, born in South Carolina.

Children of Jonathan Magee and Rebecca James are:

      i.   Jonathan Magee, Jr., married Priscilla James.
      ii.   Holden Magee, born 1796 in Georgia; married Sarah Howell.
      iii. Ruth Magee, born 1805 in Georgia; died 1862; married Lewis Howell 1824.
      iv. Rebecca Magee, born 1803 in Mississippi; died in Illinois; married William Thomas Hutson 1824 in Simpson County, Mississippi.
      v.   Elizabeth Magee, married Simon Short.
      vi. Evan Magee, married Naomi Short.
      vii. Joseph Magee, died in Newton Co., Tx.; married Elizabeth Ford.
      viii. Jemina Magee, married William H. Purvis.

25

52. David Womack, Jr., born March 27, 1785 in Caswell Co.,North Carolina; died March 01, 1856 in Simpson County, Mississippi. He was the son of 104. David Womack, Sr. and 105. Mildred Pryor. He married 53. Sarah Ann Norris February 04, 1807 in Pendleton District, South Carolina. 53. Sarah Ann Norris, born January 01, 1789 in S.C.; died December 12, 1858.

Notes for David Womack, Jr.:
When David Womack II's father (David Womack I) came home to South Carolina after the war, he wanted to move south intending to settle in Mississippi. However, David Womack II had met his Sarah at a social event and he would not leave without her. David II put his things together and took off after Sarah and as soon as he got to her, they were married. Then, on horseback, traveling through Indian country, they caught up with David's family.
David II and Sarah's first nine children were born in St Helena Parish, La. The last three were born after they had moved to Simpson County, Mississippi.

Notes for Sarah Ann Norris:
After David Womack's death, Sarah Ann Norris Womack moved her family from Mississippi to Texas, where she died in Trinity Co., before the Civil War.
(Source: Some Descendants of William Womack, the Immigrant)

There is a gravestone in Mt. Zion Cemetery, Trinity County, Texas, for Sarah Womack. It reads:
"Sarah Womack, wife of David Womack, born January 1, 1789, died December 12, 1858, mother of 12 children all raised to be grown consistent
members of the church for 40 years."

She came to the east side of the Neches River with five covered wagons around 1856. She was one of the ones walking. Three of the wagons belonged to her sons, two belonged to her husband's nephews.

The wagons stayed camped on the east side of the river. The men would go across the river every day to search for land to settle on. After two weeks, they found what they wanted and finally brought their families across into Trinity County.
(Source: History of Trinity County, pg. 811, story by Madie M. Murphy Womack)

Children of David Womack and Sarah Norris are:

    i.   Elizabeth Womack, born 1808 in St Helen Parish, Louisiana; died Aft. 1877; married John Mcilhenny January 03, 1822.

    II.   Mildred Womack, born 1810 in St Helen Parish, Louisiana; married David Womack.

    III.   Nancy Matilda Womack, born February 16, 1812 in St Helen Parish, Louisiana; died June 29, 1892 in Mississippi; married Rhesa Kennedy 1832 in Simpson Co., Miss..

    IV.   Vashti Womack, born 1814 in St Helen Parish, Louisiana; died in Trinity County, Texas; married Richard Swor.

    V.   William B. Womack, born April 18, 1816 in St Helen Parish, Louisiana; died October 20, 1888 in Trinity County, Texas; married Nancy Elizabeth Franklin December 05, 1835 in Franklin County, Mississippi.

    VI.   Abram B. Womack, born April 29, 1818 in St Helen Parish, Louisiana; died May 14, 1902 in Trinity County, Texas; married Lucy Campbell.

    vii.   David Womack III, born 1820 in St Helen Parish, Louisiana; died Abt. 1892 in Trinity County, Texas; married (1) Jane Franklin February 28, 1841; married (2) Mary Margaret Minerva Singletary Abt. 1865.

    VIII.   Richmond Womack, born February 16, 1825 in St Helen Parish, Louisiana; died June 08, 1863 in Vicksburg, Mississippi; married Arcadia Powell December 22, 1842 in Simpson Co., Miss..

    tx.   Henry Young Womack, born October 21, 1825 in St Helen Parish, Louisiana; died February 23, 1902 in Trinity County, Texas; married (1) Laura Virginia Newton Clutts; married (2) Sarah Jane Gibson January 14, 1853 in Rankin Co., Mississippi.

    x.   Sarah Ann Womack, born 1827 in Simpson County, Mississippi; married

26

Preston Campbell.

xt. Mary Jane Womack, born **1830** in Simpson County, Mississippi; died 1918; married John Magee.

xll. Abner John Womack, born 1835 in Simpson County, Mississippi; died December 25, 1869 in Apple Springs, Trinity Co., Tx.; married Sarah Bell Watson **1857** in Trinity County, Texas.

Notes for Abner John Womack:

A.J. Womack served in the Civil War from 1861 to **1864** as a private in Co. A of Gould's Battalion, Randal's Brigade, Walker's Division, Captain P. J. Holly's Company. He died on Christmas Day in 1869, at the age of 34. Source: History of Trinity County, pg. 803 (story by Robert D. Womack)

Notes for Sarah Bell Watson:

Sarah Watson Womack, widowed at age 28, never remarried, and lived to the age of 86, dying in 1917.

Source: History of Trinity County, pg. 803 (story by Robert D. Womack)

54. W. M. Franklin. He was the son of 108. Thomas Franklin.

Child of W. M. Franklin is:

i. Nancy Elizabeth Franklin, born April 20, **1818** in Louisiana; died January 04, \889; married William B. Womack December 05, 1835 in Franklin County, Mississippi.

56. Thomas William McClain, born 1776 in Virginia. He married 57. Rebecca Warren Bef. 1797 in Franklin Co., Tenn..

57. Rebecca Warren, born **1774** in North Carolina.

Children of Thomas McClain and Rebecca Warren are:

t. Daniel McClain, born in Tennessee; married Mariah ?.
11. Sarah McClain, born **1797** in Georgia; died in Kosse, Tx.; married Edmund Hodges.

Generation No. 7

64. William Gaston, born 1685 in Ballymena, County Antrim, Ireland; died Bef. 1755 in Ireland. He was the son of 128. John Gaston and 129. Esther Naugh. He married 65. Mary Olivet Lemon in Ireland.
65. Mary Olivet Lemon, born in Ireland; died in Ireland.

Notes for William Gaston:

William Gaston and Mary Olivet Lemon Gaston remained in Ireland, but all of their sons and daughters came to America.

Children of William Gaston and Mary Lemon are:

i. Alexander Gaston, born in Ireland; died August 20, 1781 in Newbern, Perquiman Co., N.C. married Margaret Sharp 1775.

595

Notes for Alexander Gaston:
Alexander Gaston was murdered by Tories on 8/20/1781.

11. Hugh Gaston, born in Ireland; died October 20, 1766 in South Carolina; married Mary Thomson.
Notes for Hugh Gaston:
Hugh Gaston came to America in 1766. He died 10/2011766 at the home of his brother, Justice John Gaston

111. Justice John Gaston, born April 04, 1703 in Ballymore, County Antrim, Ireland; died 1782 in Fishing Creek, Chester Co., S. C.; married Esther Waugh 1730 in Ireland.

IV. Mary Gaston, born 1712 in Ireland; died 1802; married James McClure in Ireland.

32   V. Robert Gaston, born 1722 in Caranliegh Cloughwater, County Antrim, Ireland; died May 09, 1787 in Lynches Creek, Lancaster Co., S.C.; married Margaret Logan August 24, 1756 in Lancaster Co., Pa..

VI. Janet Gaston, born 1726 in Ireland; died April 1801; married Charles Strong.

VII. Elizabeth Gaston, born 1727 in Ireland; married John Knox.

VII\. William Gaston, born 1735 in Ireland; died 1790 in Chester Co., S. C.; married Jane Harbison 1775.
Notes for William Gaston:
William Gaston drowned at Kell's Ford, Chester Co., SC about 1790.

IX. Martha Gaston, born 1741 in Ireland; died 1804; married Alexander Rosborough in Ireland.
Notes for Martha Gaston:
Alexander Rosborough and Martha Gaston Rosborough were members of the Associated Reform Presbyterian Church in Richburg, Chester Co., S. C. They furnished supplies for the Colonial Army, Revolutionary War (Claim No. 6599- Archives).
Notes for Alexander Rosborough:
Alexander Rosborough and his wife Martha Gaston Rosborough sailed for America on 10/8/1768 with two children, William Gaston Rosborough and Margaret Rosborough. A new baby named Alexander was born at sea on 10/1211768. They arrived in Charleston, S.C. on 2/24/1769, and settled near Richburg, Chester Co., S.C.

They were members of the Associated Reform Presbyterian Church in Richburg, Chester Co., S. C. They furnished supplies for the Colonial Army, Revolutionary War. (Claim No. 6599- Archives).

96. William Hutson, born August 14, 1720 in England; died April 11, 1761 in Charleston, SC. He was the son of **192. Thomas Hutson** and **193. Esther?.** He married 97. **Mary Woodward** 1743.

97. Mary Woodward, born December 06, 1717; died November 21, 1757. She was the daughter of **194. Richard Woodward** and **195. Sarah Stanyarne.**

Children of William Hutson and Mary Woodward are:

      I.   Mary Hutson, born 1744; married Arthur Peronneau April 1762.

      II.   Elizabeth Hutson, born January 11, 1745/46 in McPhersonville, SC; died August 1780 in Jacksonborough, SC; married Isaac Hayne July 18, 1765 in Charleston, SC.

      III.   Richard Hutson, born July 09, 1748; died April 12, 1795.

48   IV.   Thomas Hutson, born January 09, 1749/50; married Esther Maine.

      V.   Esther Hutson, born 1753; married William Hazzard Wigg.

      VI.   Anne Hutson, born 1755; died 1817; married John Barnwell May 08, 1777

98. William Maine. He married 99. Judith Gignilliat.

99. Judith Gignilliat.

Child of William Maine and Judith Gignilliat is:

      I.   Esther Maine, born Abt. 1752; married Thomas Hutson.

104. David Womack, Sr., born Abt. 1747 in Henrico Co., Va.; died Abt. 1805 in Beaufort Dist., S. C.. He was the son of 208. Richard Womack.III and 209. Ann Nancy Childers. He married 105. Mildred Pryor Abt. 1761 in Orange Co., North Carolina.

105. Mildred Pryor, born Abt. 1747 in Orange Co., N.C.; died 1804. She was the daughter of 210. John Henry Pryor and 211. Margaret Gaines.
Notes for David Womack, Sr.:
David Womack, I- is recognized by the DAR as a Patriot, having provided supplies to the revolutionary cause. (David was a Rev. War soldier - NC Rev. Army Accts. Vol. XI, p. 19, folio 2. Soldier, pvt. Raleigh NC ..from Orange and Caswell Counties).

By I 761, David Womack Sr. had left Henrico, VA and went to that part of Orange County NC that became Caswell County, NC in 1777. He was in the Nash Dist., which became Person Co. in 1791. He sold out, and in 1794 went to Northwest SC. (Source: Information given to the Womack Family Assoc. by Mrs. Asa M. Cox d/o William Washington Womack, b. Simpson Co., Ms.)

Children of David Womack and Mildred Pryor are:

      i.   Robert Womack, born 1775 in Orange Co., North Carolina; married (I) Nancy Knight March 09, 1814 in St. Helena Par., La.; married (2) Charlotte Corder November 16, 1817 in St. Helena Par., La.; married (3) Bailis Corder May 10, 1818 in St. Helena Par., La..

      n.   Richard Womack, born 1771 in Orange Co., North Carolina; died Abt. 1825 in Georgia.; married Martha ?.
          Notes for Richard Womack:
          Richard Womack moved to Louisiana from Georgia in the early days of the state (became a state in 1812), buying land in the St. Helena Parish in 1809, joining his brother Col. Abner Womack.

      III.   John Womack, born 1768 in North Carolina; died WFT Est. 1785-1858; married Mary Fletcher.

      iv.   Dorothy Pryor Womack, born Abt. 1784 in North Carolina; died August 24, 1847; married David Mitchell May 10, 1806 in Jackson Co., Ga..

v. David Womack, Jr., born March 27, 1785 in Caswell Co., North Carolina; died March 01, 1856 in Simpson County, Mississippi; married Sarah Ann Norris February 04, 1807 in Pendleton District, South Carolina.

vi. William Womack, born 1773 in Orange Co., North Carolina; married Charity?.

vii. Abner J. Womack, born 1778 in Caswell Co., North Carolina; died February 12, 1844 in St. Helena Par., La.; married Celia Herrin.

Notes for Abner J. Womack:

Abner J. Womack (Sr. designation for convenience since his brother's son was also Abner J. Womack- and designated as Jr.), homesteaded 640-1000 acres in Texas and was followed by his kin from Mississippi. In 1856, the property tax rolls reflect that Abram B., Abner P., David III, and Elbert W. Womack had also migrated from Mississippi to Texas. These were part of an extended family that had lived and farmed in Mississippi from circa 1830-1857, in St. Helena, La. from circa 1815-1830, and in Orange County, N.C. before that.

Several are indicated as owning slaves over this period. A. J. Sr. for example, was listed in the 1860 census as owning $42,000 in personal property, which would indicate 30-40 slaves. (Source: History of Trinity County, pg. 803, story by Robert D. Womack)

vul. Jacob Green Womack, hom October 05, 1780 in Caswell Co., N. C.; died January 27, 1865; married (1) Nancy Jane Walker; married (2) Elizabeth Hopkins August 29, 1806 in Jackson Co., Ga..

1x. Abraham Womack, born April 12, 1782 in North Carolina; died April 26, 1860 in St. Helen Parish, La.; married Elizabeth Burton 1800 in S.C. or La

108. Thomas Franklin.

Child of Thomas Franklin is:

i. W. M. Franklin.

Generation No. 8

128. John Gaston, born 1645 in Scotland; died in Mageragall, N. Ireland. He was the son of 256. John Jean Gaston and 257. Agnes of Navarre. He married 129. Esther Naugh .
129. Esther Naugh.

Notes for John Gaston:
John Gaston is the son of Count Jean Gaston de Foix. He had at least two brothers, William and Alexander Gaston, maybe more. He fled to Ireland in 1668 and lived at Caranlaigh Cloughwater, Ballymena.

Children of John Gaston and Esther Naugh are:

i. William Gaston, born 1685 in Ballymena, County Antrim, Ireland; died Bef. 1755 in Ireland; married Mary Olivet Lemon in Ireland.

ii.   Hugh Gaston, born 1687 in Ballymena, County Antrim, Ireland; died December 22, 1772 in Lamington, Somerset Co., N.J.; married Jennett ? 1718 in Ireland.

iii.   Male Gaston, born in Ballymean, County Antrim, Ireland.

iv.   Joseph Gaston, born 1700 in Ireland; died April 1777 in Bernards Twp., Somerset Co. • N.J.; married Margaret? 1725.

v.   John Gaston, Jr., born 1703 in Ballymena, County Antrim, Ireland; died March 29, 1789 in Voluntown, Conn.; married Janet Thompson.

vt.   Alexander Gaston, born 1707 in Ballymena, County Antrim, Ireland; died August 24, 1783 in Richmond, Massachusetts; married Mary Wilson.

192. Thomas Hutson, born Bef. 1710. He married 193. Esther?.

193. Esther?, born Bef. 1710.

Child of Thomas Hutson and Esther ? is:

i.   William Hutson, born August 14, 1720 in England; died April 11, 1761 in Charleston, SC; married Mary Woodward 1743.

194. Richard Woodward, born July 09, 1683; died 1725. He was the son of 388. Henry Woodward and 389. Mary Godfrey. He married 195. Sarah Stanyarne.

195. Sarah Stanyarne, born Abt. 1685. She was the daughter of 390. James Stanyarne and 391. Mary?.

Child of Richard Woodward and Sarah Stanyarne is:

97   i.   Mary Woodward, born December 06, 1717; died November 21, 1757; married (1) Isaac Chardon November 06, 1735; married (2) William Hutson 1743.

208. Richard Womack III, born December 07, 1710 in Henrico County, Virginia; died July 27, 1785 in Hancock Co., Georgia. He was the son of 416. Richard Womack II and 417. Elizabeth Ann Puckett. He married 209. Ann Nancy Childers in Virginia.

209. Ann Nancy Childers, born 1714 in Henrico County, Virginia; died in Georgia. She was the daughter of 418. Henry Childers and 419. Lucretia Jones.

Notes for Richard Womack III:
Richard Womack III first lived in Henrico Co, VA. By 1739, he was buying land in Amelia Co., VA. By 1765, he was in Burke Co., N.C.

Children of Richard Womack and Ann Childers are:

i.   Richard Womack IV, died 1754; married Margaret?.

ii.   Jesse Womack, born 1739 in Virginia; died 1815 in Madison Co., Ga.; married (1) Dorothy Pryor; married (2) Phoebe?.
Notes for Jesse Womack:
Jesse Womack, b. 1739 VA, served in the Revolutionary War as Lieut. under Brig. Gen. John Twiggs in the Continental Army 10th Co. and

participated **in** the Battles of King's Mountain and Guilford Court House. He received a land grant of287 1/2 acres in Washington Co., Ga. 3/2111787.
(Source: Some Descendants of William Womack, the Immigrant, pg. R-4aa).

    III.   Jacob Womack, born Abt. 1740 in Virginia.
            Notes for Jacob Womack:
            Jacob Womack, b. c1740 was in Orange Co., NC 1764. One of 13 commissioners for Watauga Settlement 1772. Was Major in militia in East Tenn.

    IV.   Abraham Womack, born April 22, 1742 in Henrico Co., Va.; died June 02, 1797 in Hancock Co., Georgia; married (1) Martha Mitchell; married (2) Martha Watkins.

    V.   Sally Patsy Womack, born Abt. 1743 in Virginia; died in Georgia; married Jonathan Kemp 1773 in St. George Parish, Ga..
    VI.   Abner Womack, born Abt. 1744.

I 04   VtL   David Womack, Sr., born Abt. 1747 in Henrico Co., Va.; died Abt. 1805 in Beauford Dist., S. C.; married Mildred Pryor Abt. 1761 in Orange Co., North Carolina.

    VIII.   John Womack, born Abt. 1748 in Henrico Co., Va.; died I 827 in Person Co., N.C.; married Lucy Pryor Abt. September 28, 1771 in Orange Co., North Carolina.

210. John Henry Pryor. He was the son of **420. Robert Pryor** and **421. Betty Virginia Green.** He married **211. Margaret Gaines.**

211. Margaret Gaines, born Abt. 1710. She was the daughter of **422. George Gaines** and **423. Eleanor?.**

Children of John Pryor and Margaret Gaines are:

    I.   Lucy Pryor, married (1)? Tapley; married (2) John Womack Abt. September 28, 1771 in Orange Co., North Carolina.
    II.   Mildred Pryor, born Abt. 1747 in Orange Co., N.C.; died 1804; married David Womack, Sr. Abt. 1761 **in** Orange Co., North Carolina.

Generation No. 9

256. John Jean Gaston, born 1600 in France. He married **257. Agnes of Navarre.**

257. Agnes of Navarre. She was the daughter of **514. King Phillip III of Navarre.**

Notes for John Jean Gaston:
John "Jean" Gaston, the Huguenot, was banished from France by the Catholics (religious persecution) and fled, with two of his brothers to Calvinist Scotland about 1668. His property was confiscated but his relatives who remained Catholics in France, sent means to Scotland for his living.

He married in Scotland and had, among other sons, three: John, William and Alexander. These three sons emigrated to County AJ.ltrim, Ireland about 1660 to 1680.

Children of John Gaston and Agnes Navarre are:

> t. William Gaston, born 1642 in Scotland; died in Ireland.
> n. John Gaston, born 1645 in Scotland; died in Mageragall, N. Ireland; married Esther Naugh.
> 111. Alexander Gaston, born Abt. 1648 in Scotland; died in Ireland.

388. Henry Woodward. He married 389. Mary Godfrey.

389. Mary Godfrey.

Child of Henry Woodward and Mary Godfrey is:

> i. Richard Woodward, born July 09, 1683; died 1725; married Sarah Stanyarne.

390. James Stanyarne, born Bef. 1670. He married 391. Mary ?.

391. Mary?, born Bef. 1670.

Child of James Stanyarne and Mary ? is:

> 1. Sarah Stanyarne, born Abt. 1685; married Richard Woodward.

416. Richard Womack II, born Abt. 1676 in Henrico County, Virginia; died April 1723 in Henrico County, Virginia. He was the son of 832. Richard Womack I and 833. Mary Puckett. He married 417. Elizabeth Ann Puckett in Henrico Co., Va..

417. Elizabeth Ann Puckett, born Abt. 1680 in Henrico County, Virginia. She was the daughter of 834. Thomas Puckett and 835. Frances ?.

Children of Richard Womack and Elizabeth Puckett are:

> t. Richard Womack III, born December 07, 1710 in Henrico County, Virginia: died July 27, 1785 in Hancock Co., Georgia; married Ann Nancy Childers in Virginia.
> 11. Alexander Womack, born Abt. 1708 in Henrico Co., Va.; died in Campbell Co., Va.; married Martha ? Bef. December 13, 1742 in Henrico Co., Va..

418. Henry Childers, born in Henrico Co., Va.; died 1727 in Henrico Co., Va.. He was the son of 836. Abraham Childers, Jr. and 837. Ann Pew. He married 419. Lucretia Jones.

419. Lucretia Jones. She was the daughter of 838. Thomas Jones and 839. Martha Tanner.

Child of Henry Childers and Lucretia Jones is:

> 1. Ann Nancy Childers, born 1714 in Henrico County, Virginia; died in

Georgia; married Richard Womack III in Virginia.

420. Robert Pryor. He married 421. Betty Virginia Green in Gloucester County, Virginia.

421. Betty Virginia Green.

Child of Robert Pryor and Betty Green is:

        1.   John Henry Pryor, married Margaret Gaines.

422. George Gaines, born WFT Est. 1659-1688; died WFT Est. 1713-1773. He was the son of 844. Bernard Gaines and 845. Martha Taylor. He married 423. Eleanor?.
423. Eleanor ?.

Child of George Gaines and Eleanor? is:

211   1.   Margaret Gaines, born Abt. 1710; married John Henry Pryor.

I've included a listing for Gaston's in the Old Covenanter Cemetery Listing in Illinois.
Old Covenanter Cemetery Listing for Gaston's

Submitted by Roy and Deloris Mount

http://marion.ilgenweb.net/coven .html

8 Gaston Charles C. 1867 1939

8 Gaston Ellis 1-10-1872 1-10-1872 Infant-Son ofTK & MA

8 Gaston Edgar N/a 6-23-1872 Infant-Son of TK & MA

8 Gaston Margaret A. 12-16-1842 1-20-1908

8 Gaston Thomas K. 3-9-1833 2-14-1914 Veteran-Co C. 22nd Ill Yol-Civil War

9 Gaston William N/a 9-21-1869 83Y 8M 200

9 Gaston Elizabeth N/a 1-29-1860 Wife of William

9 Gaston Newton A. N/a N/a Veteran- Pvt Co A- 2nd Ill lnf-Mexican War

9 Gaston Laura N/a 11-26-1854 lnfant-9M 70-0au of JM B & MM

9 Gaston E1dorsa N/a 6-30-1850 Infant- 7MDau of JMB & MM

9 Gaston Charley S. N/a 7-28-1866 Infant 1M 140-Son of JMB & MM

9 Gaston Mary M. N/a 9-28-1866 36Y 8M 200- Wife ofJMB

www.ingramcontent.com/pod-product-compliance
Lightning Source LLC
Chambersburg PA
CBHW052128020426

42334CB00023B/2643